THE ROUGH GUIDE TO

Canada

There are more than two hundred Rough Guide titles
covering destinations from Alaska to Zimbabwe
and subjects from Acoustic Guitar to Travel Health

Forthcoming travel guides include
The Algarve • The Bahamas • Bolivia • Cambodia
Caribbean Islands • Costa Brava • Zanzibar

Forthcoming reference guides include
Chronicles series: China, England, France & India
Cult TV • Elvis

Rough Guides Online
www.roughguides.com

ROUGH GUIDE CREDITS

Text editors: Don Bapst, Stephen Timblin and Yuki Takagaki
Series editor: Mark Ellingham

Production: Michelle Draycott, Mike Hancock
Cartography: Maxine Repath
Picture research: Louise Boulton, Sharon Martins

....

ACKNOWLEDGEMENTS

Tim: Geoff Bacall at Bacall Associates, James and Vicky Ballantyne, Tim Burford, Fairmont Hotels, Charlotte Fraser, Air Canada, Ruth Roberts at Tourism British Columbia (London), Amanda Newby at Travel Alberta (in the UK) and Greyhound (UK).

Phil: My thanks to the tourist departments of PEI, Nova Scotia, New Brunswick and Ontario, whose assistance was invaluable. Special thanks also to Valerie Kidney, Sandra Bradt, Chantal Beauchamp, Christine Bates of the Delta Chelsea, Julie MacEachern, Carol Horne and Randy Brooks, as well as Helen and John for all their help and conversation in Toronto and Thunder Bay. Finally, a special word for Diane Helinski of Ontario Tourism who was – there's no other word for it – just great!

Tania: I'd like to thank Tourism BC, Tourism Saskatchewan, Travel Manitoba, Andrew Rosenberg, Don Bapst, Yuki Takagaki, Sara Sol, Karim and Saba Sams.

John W: Roselyne Hébert and the staff at Tourisme Québec, Richard Séguin, Carole Turmel and François Leduc at Greater Québec Area Tourism and Convention Bureau, Marie-Claude Privé at ATR Saguenay–Lac-St-Jean, Dave Prévéreault at ATR Manicouagan, Daphnée Bernier and Aurélie Couffy at ATR Duplessis, and Robert Stewart. Special thanks to Arabella Bowen, Pierre-Yves Legault for 2500km of good company, Steph, Angela

and Darren for making Montréal feel like home again, and Mom and Dad for their love and support.

Arabella: Roselyne Hébert and the staff at Tourisme Québec, Jean-François Perrier at Tourisme Montréal, Pauline-Gervaise Grégoire at ATR Îles de la Madeleine, Any Fortin and Marie-Ève Thérien at ATR Outaouais, and Odette Chaput from the Fédération des Agricotours du Québec. Special thanks to the Rough Guide team, particularly Don Bapst and Yuki Takagaki for their support and quick response time, and to John Watson.

Claus and John Z: Sincere thanks to Lorraine McGrath, Anne St. Croix and all the employees of the Avalon Convention and Visitors Bureau, for helping to make our stay in Newfoundland and Labrador a memorable experience. Thanks also to Noreen Martin and Marine Atlantic for arranging transport to Newfoundland.

The **editors** would like to thank all those who contributed to this edition, especially Donald Young for his editing assistance and Jonathan Cook for indexing, Julia Bovis, Mike Hancock and Michelle Draycott for smooth production, Russell Walton for proofreading, Sharon Martins for photo work, Maxine Repath and Melissa Flack for maps, Narrell Leffman and Amy Brown for extra Basics research, and Andrew Rosenberg for overall guidance.

....

PUBLISHING INFORMATION

This fourth edition published June 2001 by
  Rough Guides Ltd, 62–70 Shorts Gardens,
  London WC2H 9AH. Reprinted April 2002.
Distributed by the Penguin Group:
  Penguin Books Ltd, 80 Strand, London WC2R ORL
Penguin Putnam, Inc. 375 Hudson Street, NY 10014, USA
Penguin Books Australia Ltd, 487 Maroondah Highway,
  PO Box 257, Ringwood, Victoria 3134, Australia
Penguin Books Canada Ltd, 10 Alcorn Avenue, Toronto,
  Ontario, Canada M4V 1E4
Penguin Books (NZ) Ltd, 182–190 Wairau Road,
  Auckland 10, New Zealand
Typeset in Linotron Univers and Century Old Style to an
  original design by Andrew Oliver.
Printed in England by Clays Ltd, St Ives PLC
Illustrations in Part One and Part Three by Edward Briant.

THE ROUGH GUIDE TO

Canada

written and researched by

Tim Jepson, Phil Lee and Tania Smith

With additional contributions by

Arabella Bowen, John Shandy Watson,

Claus Vogel and John Zahara

**ROUGH
GUIDES**

We set out to do something different when the first Rough Guide was published in 1982. Mark Ellingham, just out of university, was travelling in Greece. He brought along the popular guides of the day, but found they were all lacking in some way. They were either strong on ruins and museums but went on for pages without mentioning a beach or taverna. Or they were so conscious of the need to save money that they lost sight of Greece's cultural and historical significance. Also, none of the books told him anything about Greece's contemporary life – its politics, its culture, its people, and how they lived.

So with no job in prospect, Mark decided to write his own guidebook, one which aimed to provide practical information that was second to none, detailing the best beaches and the hottest clubs and restaurants, while also giving hard-hitting accounts of every sight, both famous and obscure, and providing up-to-the-minute information on contemporary culture. It was a guide that encouraged independent travellers to find the best of Greece, and was a great success, getting shortlisted for the Thomas Cook travel guide award,

and encouraging Mark, along with three friends, to expand the series.

The Rough Guide list grew rapidly and the letters flooded in, indicating a much broader readership than had been anticipated, but one which uniformly appreciated the Rough Guide mix of practical detail and humour, irreverence and enthusiasm. Things haven't changed. The same four friends who began the series are still the caretakers of the Rough Guide mission today: to provide the most reliable, up-to-date and entertaining information to independent-minded travellers of all ages, on all budgets.

We now publish more than 150 titles and have offices in London and New York. The travel guides are written and researched by a dedicated team of more than 100 authors, based in Britain, Europe, the USA and Australia. We have also created a unique series of phrasebooks to accompany the travel series, along with an acclaimed series of music guides, and a best-selling pocket guide to the Internet and World Wide Web. We also publish comprehensive travel information on our Web site:

www.roughguides.com

HELP US UPDATE

We've gone to a lot of effort to ensure that the fourth edition of *The Rough Guide to Canada* is accurate and up-to-date. However, things change — places get "discovered", opening hours are notoriously fickle, restaurants and rooms raise prices or lower standards. If you feel we've got it wrong or left something out, we'd like to know, and if you can remember the address, the price, the time, the phone number, so much the better.

We'll credit all contributions, and send a copy of the next edition (or any other Rough Guide if you prefer) for the best letters. Please mark letters: "Rough Guide Canada Update" and send to:
Rough Guides, 62–70 Shorts Gardens, London WC2H 9AH, or Rough Guides, 4th Floor, 345 Hudson St, New York, NY 10014.
Or send email to: mail@roughguides.co.uk
Online updates about this book can be found on Rough Guides' Web site at **www.roughguides.com**

THE AUTHORS

Phil Lee first experienced Canada as a bartender in an Ontario waterski resort. Subsequent contacts have been less chaotic and have given him an abiding interest in the country. Phil has worked as a freelance author with the Rough Guides for the last ten years. His other titles include guides to *Toronto, Norway, Belgium & Luxembourg, The Pacific Northwest,* and both *Mallorca* and *Menorca.* He lives in Nottingham, where he was born and raised.

Tania Smith joined the Rough Guides' squad shortly after returning from a trip to watch the World Cup in Italy, then missed a season after giving birth to a daughter. She returned to the team for this edition of the Canada guide, and took the opportunity to introduce young Saba to the delights of Québec and Ontario. She lives in Brighton, but is a Liverpool supporter.

Tim Jepson's post-university career began with street busking and work in a slaughterhouse. Having acquired fluent Italian, he went on to better things as a Rome-based journalist and a leader of walking tours in Umbria. He is also author of Rough Guides to *Tuscany & Umbria* and *Vancouver.*

READERS' LETTERS

Many thanks go to the readers who have taken the time to contact us with comments and suggestions. Apologies to any who have either been misspelled or left off the list.

Rachel Allen, Brenda Bickerton, Rob Borthwick and Janet Cunningham, Joyce Bourgeois, Kathy Boyden, Tom Brownlee, Angela Bryant, Lucia Calland, Lizelle Cline, Armando Combati, Adam Cornish, Steve Criddle, Marcus Dale, Bethan Davies, Irene Dawling, Richard and Charlotte Dawson, Lino N. Dee, Anna Douglas, Jim Dress, Tony Duarte, Nicole Durepos, David Lee Ellwood, Jamie Fitzmaurice, Chris Frost, Andrew Gambier, Ann Gamble, Larry Gellar, Monica Germana, Matthew Gorman, Denise Grant, Alan Green, T M Grubis, Jenny & Malcolm Gunter, Janne Hansen, Nicola Harris, Ian & Carole Harrison, Nicholas Hunt, Jamie from Ballinastoe, Co. Wicklow, Mike Johnson, Marissa Koster, Jennifer LaRoche, Bill Littlewood, Edgar Locke, M Long, Eugene McConville, K Macdonald, Ian Mckie, Michael Milnes, Deirdre Mulroe & Chris Bedle, S B Morris, Jacqueline de Nooy, Martin O'Connell, Hazel Orchard, Carol Pardy, Charles Paxton, Diane Penttila, Ilene Polansky, Stephen and Kathi Quinn, Louise Reynolds, Dorota Rygiel, Terence Sakamoto, Tia and Stephen Sedley, Rachel Shephard, Stephanie Short, Peter Skeggs, Ann-Marie Smith, Steve Smith, Roger Stein, Ian and Jo Stoter, Sarah Thompson Anton Visser, Dawn Walker, Susan Wassermann, Jeff Wilson, Mark Winkler, Robert Young and any who forgot to sign their emails.

CONTENTS

Introduction xii

• CHAPTER 3: THE MARITIME PROVINCES 329–409

• CHAPTER 4: NEWFOUNDLAND AND LABRADOR 410–458

• CHAPTER 5: MANITOBA AND SASKATCHEWAN 459–548

• CHAPTER 6: ALBERTA AND THE ROCKIES 549–686

• CHAPTER 7: SOUTHERN BRITISH COLUMBIA 687–847

● CHAPTER 8: THE NORTH 848–917

PART THREE CONTEXTS   919

BACKGROUND BOXES

LIST OF MAPS

MAP SYMBOLS

Canadian autoroute		Post office	
Trans-Canada Highway		Subway station	
Yellowhead Highway		Parking	
U.S. Interstate		Ski resort	
U.S. Highway		Golf course	
State Highway		Mountain range	
Tunnel		Mountain peak	
Pedestrianized road		Cliffs	
Steps		Viewpoint	
Path		Glacier	
Railway		River	
Ferry route		Waterfall	
International boundary		Lighthouse	
State boundary		General point of interest	
Chapter-division boundary		Wall	
Airport		Gate	
Hospital		Building of interest	
Accommodation		Church	
Restaurant		Cemetery	
Campsite		Park	
Picnic area		National Park	
Tourist office		Beach	

INTRODUCTION

Canada is almost unimaginably vast. It stretches from the Atlantic to the Pacific and from the latitude of Rome to beyond the Magnetic North Pole. Its archetypal landscapes are the Rocky Mountain lakes and peaks, the endless forests and the prairie wheatfields, but Canada holds landscapes that defy expectations: rainforest and desert lie close together in the southwest corner of the country, while in the east a short drive can take you from fjords to lush orchards. What's more, great tracts of Canada are completely unspoiled – ninety percent of the country's 28.5 million population lives within 100 miles of the US border.

Like its neighbour to the south, Canada is a spectrum of cultures, a hotchpotch of immigrant groups who supplanted the continent's many native peoples. There's a crucial difference, though. Whereas citizens of the United States are encouraged to perceive themselves as Americans above all else, Canada's concertedly multicultural approach has done more to acknowledge the origins of its people, creating an ethnic mosaic as opposed to America's "melting-pot". Alongside the French and British majorities live a host of communities who maintain the traditions of their homelands – Chinese, Ukrainians, Portuguese, Indians, Dutch, Polish, Greek and Spanish, to name just the most numerous. For the visitor, the mix that results from the country's exemplary tolerance is an exhilarating experience, offering such widely differing environments as Vancouver's huge Chinatown and the austere religious enclaves of Manitoba. Canadians themselves, however, are often troubled by the lack of a clear self-image, tending to emphasize the ways in which they are different from the US as a means of self-description. The question "What is a Canadian?" has acquired a new immediacy with the interminable and acrimonious debate over Québec and its possible secession, but ultimately there can be no simple characterization of a people whose country is not so much a single nation as a committee on a continental scale. Pierre Berton, one of Canada's finest writers, wisely ducked the issue; Canadians, he quipped, are "people who know how to make love in a canoe".

The typical Canadian might be an elusive concept, but you'll find there's a distinctive feel to the country. Some towns might seem a touch too well-regulated and unspontaneous, but against this there's the overwhelming sense of Canadian pride in their history and pleasure in the beauty of their land. Canada embraces its own clichés with an energy that's irresistible, promoting everything from the Calgary Stampede to maple-syrup festivals and lumberjacking contests with an extraordinary zeal and openness. As John Buchan, writer and Governor-General of Canada, said, "You have to know a man awfully well in Canada to know his surname."

Where to go

The time and expense involved in covering Canada's immense distances means that most visitors confine their explorations to the area around one of the main cities – usually Toronto, Montréal, Vancouver or Calgary for arrivals by air. The attractions of these centres vary widely, but they have one thing in common with each other and all other Canadian towns – they are within easy reach of the great outdoors.

Canada's most southerly region, south **Ontario**, contains not only the manufacturing heart of the country and its largest city, **Toronto**, but also **Niagara Falls**, Canada's premier tourist sight. North of Toronto there's the far less packaged scenic attraction of **Georgian Bay**, a beautiful waterscape of pine-studded islets set against crystal-blue waters. Like the forested Algonquin park, the bay is also accessible from the capital city of **Ottawa**, not as dynamic a place as Toronto, but still well worth a stay for its art galleries and museums.

Québec, set apart from the rest of the continent by the profundity of its French tradition, focuses on its biggest city, **Montréal**, which is for many people the most vibrant place in the country, a fascinating mix of old-world style and commercial dynamism. The pace of life is more relaxed in the historic provincial capital, **Québec City**, and more easy-going still in the villages dotted along the St Lawrence lowlands, where glittering spires attest to the enduring influence of the Catholic Church. For something more bracing, you could continue north to **Tadoussac**, where whales can be seen near the mouth of the splendid **Saguenay** fjord – and if you're really prepared for the wilds, forge on through to **Labrador**, as inhospitable a zone as you'll find in the east.

Across the mouth of the St Lawrence, the pastoral **Gaspé** peninsula – the easternmost part of Québec – borders **New Brunswick**, a mild-mannered introduction to the three **Maritime Provinces**, whose people have long been dependent on timber and the sea for their livelihood. Here, the tapering **Bay of Fundy** boasts amazing tides – rising and falling by nine metres, sometimes more – whilst the tiny fishing villages characteristic of the region are at their most beguiling near **Halifax**, the bustling capital of **Nova Scotia**. Perhaps even prettier, and certainly more austere, are the land and seascapes of **Cape Breton Island**, whose rugged topography anticipates that of the island of **Newfoundland** to the north. Newfoundland's isolation has spawned a distinctive culture that's at its most lively in the capital, **St John's**, where the local folk-music scene is the country's best. The island also boasts some of the Atlantic seaboard's finest landscapes, particularly the flat-topped peaks and glacier-gouged lakes of **Gros Morne National Park**.

Back on the mainland, separating Ontario from Alberta and the Rockies, the so-called prairie provinces of **Manitoba** and **Saskatchewan** have a reputation for dullness that's somewhat unfair: even in the flat southern parts there's the diversion of **Winnipeg**, whose traces of its early days make it a good place to break a trans-Canadian journey. To the north, the myriad lakes and gigantic forests of the provinces' wilderness regions offer magnificent canoeing and hiking, especially within **Prince Albert National Park**. Up in the far north, beside Hudson Bay, the settlement of **Churchill** – remote but accessible by train – is famous for its polar bears, who gather near town from the end of June waiting to move out over the ice as soon as the bay freezes.

Moving west, **Alberta's** wheatfields ripple into ranching country on the approach to the **Canadian Rockies**, whose international reputation is more than borne out by the reality. The provincial capital, **Edmonton**, is overshadowed by **Calgary**, a brash place grown fat on the region's oil and gas fields, and the most useful springboard for a venture into the mountains. **British Columbia** embodies the popular picture of Canada to perfection: a land of snowcapped summits, rivers and forests, pioneer villages, gold-rush ghost towns, and some of the greatest hiking, skiing, fishing and canoeing opportunities in the world. Its urban focus, **Vancouver**, is the country's third city, known for its spectacular natural setting and a laid-back West Coast hedonism. Off the coast lies **Vancouver Island**, a microcosm of the province's immense natural riches, and home to **Victoria**, a devotedly anglophile little city.

North of British Columbia, wedged alongside Alaska, is the **Yukon Territory**, half grandiose mountains, half subarctic tundra, and full of evocative echoes of the Klondike gold rush. **Whitehorse**, its capital, and **Dawson City**, a gold-rush relic, are virtually the only towns here, each accessed by dramatic frontier highways. The **Northwest Territories** and **Nunavut**, arching over the provinces of Alberta, Saskatchewan and

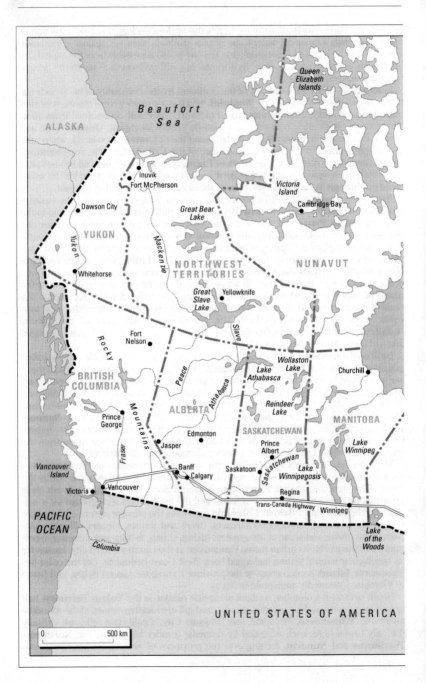

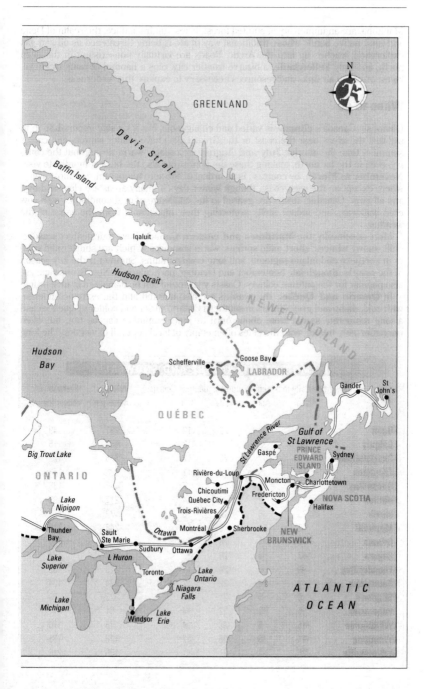

Manitoba, are an immensity of stunted forest, lakes, tundra and ice, the realm of Dene and Inuit native bands whose traditional way of life is being threatened as oil and gas exploration reaches up into the Arctic. Roads are virtually non-existent in the deep north, and only **Yellowknife**, a bizarre frontier city, plus a handful of ramshackle villages, offer the air links and resources necessary to explore this wilderness.

When to go

Obviously Canada's **climate** is varied and changeable, but it's a safe generalization to say that the areas near the coast or the Great Lakes have milder winters and cooler summers than the interior. **July and August** are reliably warm throughout the country, even in the far north, making these the hottest but also the busiest months to visit. **November to March**, by contrast, is an ordeal of sub-zero temperatures almost everywhere except on the west coast, though winter days in many areas are clear and dry, and all large Canadian towns are geared to the challenge of cold conditions, with covered walkways and indoor malls protecting their inhabitants from the worst of the weather.

More specifically, the **Maritimes and eastern Canada** have four distinct seasons: chill, snowy winters; short, mild springs; warm summers (which are shorter and colder in northern and inland regions); and long crisp autumns. Summer is the key season in the resorts, though late September and October, particularly in New Brunswick, are also popular for the autumn colours. Coasts year-round can be blanketed in mist or fog.

In **Ontario and Québec** the seasons are also marked and the extremes intense, with cold, damp and grey winters in southern Ontario (drier and colder in Québec) and a long temperate spring from about April to June. Summers can be hot, but often uncomfortably humid, with the cities often empty of locals but full of visitors. The long

CLIMATE: TEMPERATURE AND SNOWFALL						
	Average daily max. temperatures in degrees Celsius				Annual	Duration of
	Jan	April	July	Oct	snowfall (cm)	cover (days)
Banff	-7	8	22	10	251	149
Calgary	-6	9	23	12	153	116
Charlottetown	-3	7	23	12	275	122
Edmonton	-17	9	22	11	136	133
Goose Bay	-12	3	21	7	445	188
Halifax	-1	9	23	14	217	99
Inuvik	-25	-8	19	-5	177	232
Montréal	-6	11	26	13	243	116
Ottawa	-6	11	26	13	206	121
Regina	-13	9	26	12	87	134
Thunder Bay	-9	8	24	11	213	132
Saint John	-3	8	22	12	224	104
St John's	0	5	21	11	322	109
Vancouver	5	13	22	14	51	11
Whitehorse	-16	6	20	4	78	170
Winnipeg	-14	9	26	12	126	135
Yellowknife	-25	-1	21	1	135	210

autumn can be the best time to visit, with equable temperatures and few crowds.

The **central provinces** of Manitoba, Saskatchewan and Alberta experience the country's wildest climatic extremes, suffering the longest, harshest winters, but also some of the finest, clearest summers, punctuated by fierce thunderstorms. Winter skiing brings a lot of people to the **Rockies**, but summer is still the busiest time, especially in the mountains, where July and August offer the best walking weather and the least chance of rain, though this often falls in heavy downpours, the mirror of winter's raging blizzards.

The **southwestern parts of British Columbia** enjoy some of Canada's best weather: the extremes are less marked and the overall temperatures generally milder than elsewhere. Much of the province, though, bears the brunt of Pacific depressions, so this is one of the country's damper regions – visiting between late spring and early autumn offers the best chance of missing the rain.

Across the **Yukon, the Northwest Territories** and **Nunavut** winters are bitterly cold, with temperatures rarely above freezing for months on end, though precipitation year-round is among the country's lowest. Summers, by contrast, are short but surprisingly warm, and spring – though late – can produce outstanding displays of wild flowers across the tundra.

PART ONE

THE

BASICS

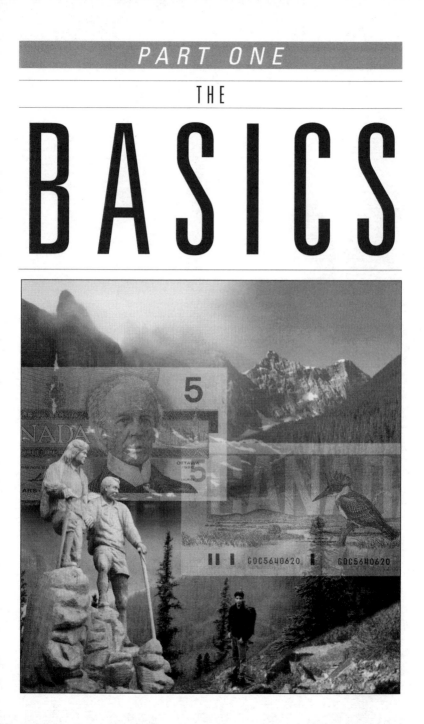

GETTING THERE FROM BRITAIN

The only economical way to get to Canada from Britain is to fly. The main gateways into the country are Montréal and Toronto, but there are also scheduled nonstop flights from Britain to Calgary, Edmonton, Halifax, Ottawa, St John's, Winnipeg and Vancouver, and connecting services to a number of other destinations. You can fly nonstop to Canada from Heathrow, Gatwick, Stansted, Birmingham, Newcastle, Manchester, Edinburgh and Glasgow.

Though competition between Canada's two big carriers once kept scheduled rates reasonable, Air Canada bought Canadian Air in 1999 to form one major **airline**; it remains to be seen how fares will be affected as the companies were still operating under separate licensing agreements at publication. Otherwise, there are a number of **charter flights** to the more popular destinations, especially Toronto and Montréal. Canada 3000, for example, is an international carrier with return flights from London and Manchester to Toronto from £199 and can be booked only via Canadian Affair, Bluebird, First Choice and Pioneer (see "Flight agents" box on p.5). It may also be worth considering a cheap flight **to the US**, as the greater competition between airlines on the US routes can produce fares to New York for as little as £180 return in low season; from the US it's easy to get into Canada cheaply by bus or train (see "Getting there from the US," on p.9).

For a precise picture of all the available options at any given time, contact an **agent** specializing in low-cost flights (see box on p.5) which may – especially if you are under 26 or a student – be able to undercut the regular Apex fares. These agents also offer cut-price seats on charter flights, though these tend to be of limited availability during the summer. Package operators can also be a source of cheap one-off flights, as they sell off any unsold seats at the last moment. Finally, be sure to check the travel ads in the Sunday papers, and, in London, in *Time Out* and the *Evening Standard*.

FARES AND ROUTES

The best-value airfares are the **Apex** (advance purchase) fares; however, there are a variety of restrictions on these tickets to be aware of. The cheapest from Air Canada has to be booked 21 days in advance with a minimum stay of 7 nights and a maximum of one month. Alternatively you can book 14 days in advance with a maximum stay of three months or 7 days in advance with a maximum stay of six months; both have a minimum stay of seven nights. British Airways has 7-, 14- and 21-day advance booking with minimum stays of 7 nights, and maximum of 6 months', 3 months' and 1 month's stay respectively. **Seat-sale** fares, which cost about the same as 21-day Apex deals, are available on Air Canada and must be completely paid for within 7 days of booking. Generally these require a minimum stay of a week and a maximum of 30 days.

Most airlines also offer **"open-jaw"** deals that enable you to fly into one Canadian city and back from another – a useful idea if you want to make your way across the country; fares are calculated by halving the return fares to each destination and adding the two figures together.

Typical **midweek Apex return fares** (low season/high season) from London are as follows:	
Toronto, Montréal, St John's or Halifax	£285/555
Calgary, Edmonton, Vancouver or Winnipeg	£400/665
Seat-sale fares, where available, are usually slightly cheaper than this; standard returns, with fewer restrictions, are considerably more expensive.	

AIRLINES

Air Canada, 7–8 Conduit St, London W1R 9TG (☎0990/247226, *www.aircanada.ca*) and 3rd Floor, Gresham Chambers, 45 West Nile St, Glasgow (☎0990/247226).Nonstop services from London, Heathrow, to Calgary (daily), Halifax (daily, with touchdown in Calgary), Montréal (daily), Ottawa (5 weekly), St John's (5 weekly), Toronto (2–3 daily) and Vancouver (daily). Connections are available to Campbell River, Charlottetown, Cranbrook, Deer Lake, Edmonton, Fredericton, Gander, Goose Bay, Kamloops, Kelowna, Lethbridge, London (Ontario), Moncton, Nanaimo, North Bay, Québec, Quesnal, Regina, Saint John, Sarnia, Saskatoon, Sault Ste Marie, Sudbury, Thunder Bay, Timmins, Victoria, Williams Lake, Windsor and Winnipeg. Nonstop, too, from Manchester to Toronto (daily) with connections to Calgary, Edmonton, Montréal, Ottawa, Québec, Thunder Bay, Vancouver and Winnipeg. From Glasgow, nonstop flights to Toronto (daily), with connections to Calgary, Edmonton, Montréal, Ottawa, Thunder Bay, Vancouver and Winnipeg.

Air India, 55 Berkeley Square, London W1X 5DB (☎020/8560 9996, *www.airindia.com*). Twice weekly non-stop to Toronto from Heathrow.

American Airlines, 45–46 Picadilly, London W1 V9AJ (☎0845/778 9789, *www.aa.com*).Daily flights to Toronto via Chicago or New York from Heathrow; Toronto via Dallas or Chicago from Gatwick; Calgary via Chicago from Heathrow, or via Dallas or Chicago from Gatwick; Halifax via Boston from Heathrow; Montréal via New York or Chicago from Heathrow; Ottawa via Boston or Chicago from Heathrow; and Vancouver via New York from Heathrow, or via Dallas from Gatwick.

British Airways, 156 Regent St, London W1R 5TA (☎0845/722 2111, *www.british-airways.com*). Daily nonstop flights from Heathrow to Toronto, Montréal and Vancouver; also, via London, daily flights from Birmingham, Edinburgh, Glasgow, Manchester and Newcastle to Toronto, Montréal and Vancouver. There's also a daily service from Birmingham to Toronto via New York.

Canada 3000, no telephone or address but available through Canadian Affair, Bluebird Holidays, First Choice and Ilkeston Co-op Travel flight agents.

Icelandair, 172 Tottenham Court Rd, London W1P 0LY (☎020/7874 1000, *www.icelandair.co.uk*).Twice-weekly service to Halifax via Reykjavik from Heathrow and Glasgow.

KLM, Plesman House, 2a Cains Lane, Bedfont, Middlesex TW14 9RL (☎0870/575 0900, *www.en.nederland.klm.com*). Flights to Halifax, Ottawa, Montréal, Calgary and Vancouver via Amsterdam from Heathrow, Manchester, Birmingham, Cardiff, Bristol and Southampton and numerous other UK airports, via connecting flights on KLM's partner, Air UK.

Northwest Airlines, Northwest House, Tinsley Lane, Crawley, West Sussex RH10 2TP (☎01293/561000, *www.nwa.com*). Flights to Toronto, Montréal, Calgary, Vancouver, Saskatoon, Ottawa, Halifax and Winnipeg via Minneapolis and/or Detroit, Edmonton via Minneapolis, Detroit or Seattle from Gatwick.

United Airlines 7–8 Conduit St, London W1R 9TG (☎0845/844 4777, *www.ual.com*). Flights to Toronto via Chicago or Washington, Calgary via Chicago or Denver and Vancouver via San Francisco or Chicago from Heathrow.

Generally, **high season** (and thus the most expensive time to fly) is between early July and mid-September and around Christmas. Mid-May to early July and mid-September to mid-October – the "shoulder" seasons – are slightly less pricey, leaving the rest of the year as low season. Make sure of the exact season dates observed by your operator or airline, as you might be able to make major savings by shifting your departure by as little as a day. Whatever time of year you fly, **mid-week flights** tend to cost around £15 less than weekend ones, and airport taxes of around £32 are usually added to the quoted price. Return **flights from regional airports** cost around £100

more than flights from London, though some shuttles are free.

Courier flights can be a good option for those on a tight budget, but you'll be given strict restrictions on dates and can be limited to hand luggage only. Furthermore, few companies operate a courier service to Canada – it's actually far easier to reach the US on a courier flight. Try Bridges Worldwide (☎01895/465465) or check the *Yellow Pages*.

PACKAGE HOLIDAYS

Package holidays – whether fly-drive, flight-accommodation, flight-guided tours or a combination of all three – can work out cheaper than

FLIGHT AGENTS

Airtours, Wavell House, Holcombe Rd, Helmshore, Rossendale, Lancashire BB4 4NB (☎01708/260000, *www.airtours.co.uk*).

Bluebird Holidays, Vanguard House, 277 London Rd, Burgess Hill, West Sussex RH15 9QU (☎0870/700 0300, *www.bluebirdholidays.com*).

Bridge the World, 1–2 Ferdinand St, London NW1 8AN (☎020/7916 0990, *www.b-t-w.co.uk*).

Campus Travel, 52 Grosvenor Gardens, London SW1W 0AG (☎020/7730 2101); 541 Bristol Rd, Selly Oak, Birmingham (☎0121/414 1848); 39 Queen's Rd, Clifton, Bristol B58 1QE (☎0117/929 2494); 5 Emmanuel St, Cambridge CB1 1NE (☎01223/324283); 53 Forest Rd, Edinburgh EH1 2QP (☎0131/668 3303); 166 Deansgate, Manchester M3 3NW (☎0161/833 2046); 105/105 St Aldates, Oxford OX1 1DD (☎01865/242067); 3 Market Place, Reading RG1 2EG (☎0118/956 7356); Nelson Mandela Building, Pond St, Sheffield S1 2BW (☎0114/275 8366); 14 High St, Southampton SO14 2DF (☎023/8023 6868); Wulfruna St, Wolverhampton WV1 1LY (☎01902/311069). *www.usitcampus.co.uk*.

Canadian Affair, Hillgate House, 13 Hillgate St, London W8 7SP (☎020/7616 9999, fax 7243 2828, *www.canadian-affair.com*). They have cheap charter flights' fares.

Council Travel, 28a Poland St, London W1V 3DB (☎020/7437 7767).

CTS Travel, 220 Kensington High St, London W88 7RG (☎020/7937 3388).

Destination Group, 41–45 Goswell Rd, London EC1V 7EH (☎020/7253 9000).

First Choice Holidays and Flights Ltd, First Choice House, London Rd, Crawley, West Sussex RH10 2GX (☎0161/745 7000, *www.first-choice.com*).

Flightbookers, 177/178 Tottenham Court Road, London W1P 0LX (☎020/7757 2000, fax 7757 2200, *www.flightbookers.com*).

Globeair Travel, 93 Piccadilly, London W1V 94B (☎020/7493 4343).

Globespan (☎0990/561522, *www.globespan.com*).

Ilkeston Co-op Travel, 12 South St, Ilkeston, Derbyshire DE7 5SG (☎0115/932 3546). Biggest in East Midlands/South Yorkshire.

Jetsave, Sussex House, London Rd, East Grinstead, West Sussex RH19 1LD (☎01342/327711, fax 317250, *www.crystalholidays.co.uk*).

Jetset, Amadeus House, 52 George St, Manchester M1 4HF (☎0870/700 5000, fax 236 6693, *www.jetsetworldwide.com*).

Pioneer Tours, The Market Place, Ilkeston, Derbyshire DE7 5BG (☎0115/944 4400, fax 932 4882).

STA Travel, 6 Wrights Lane, London W8 6TA (☎020/7361 6262); University of West England, Coldharbour Lane, Bristol B58 1QE (☎0117/929-4399; 38 Sidney St, Cambridge CB2 3HX (☎01223/366966); 75 Deansgate, Manchester M3 2BW (☎0161/834 0668); 36 George St, Oxford OX1 2OJ (☎01865/792800); and personal callers at 117 Euston Rd, London NW1 25X; 88 Vicar Lane, Leeds LS1 7JH; 9 St Mary's Place, Newcastle-upon-Tyne NE1 85B; and offices at the universities of Birmingham, Kent, Strathclyde, Durham, Sheffield, Nottingham, Warwick, Coventry and Loughborough and at King's College, Imperial College, LSE, Queen Mary's and Westfield College in London. *www.statravel.co.uk*.

Trailfinders, 42–50 Earl's Court Rd, London W8 6EJ (☎020/7938 3366, *www.trailfinders.com*). Branches nationwide.

Travel Bug, 597 Cheetham Hill Rd, Manchester M8 5EJ (☎0161/721 4000, *www.travel-bug.co.uk*).

Travelpack, Clarendon House, Clarendon Rd, Eccles, Manchester M30 9TR (☎0870/5747101, fax 127 2010, *www.travelpack.co.uk*).

Vacation Canada, Cambridge House, 8 Cambridge Rd, Glasgow G2 3DZ (☎0870/707 0444, fax 353 0135, *www.vacationcanada@btinternet.com*).

---

arranging the same trip yourself, though they do have drawbacks: chiefly loss of flexibility and the fact that you'll probably have to stay in nondescript – and sometimes relatively expensive – chain hotels.

Short-stay **city packages** start from around £440 per person for a transatlantic return flight and accommodation in a downtown Montréal or Toronto hotel for four nights – seven nights for more like £600. **Fly-drive** deals, which give cut-price car rental when buying a transatlantic ticket from an airline or tour operator, are always cheaper than renting on the spot and give great value if you intend to do a lot of

TOUR OPERATORS

Air Canada Vacations, 525 High Rd, Wembley, London HA0 2DH (☎0870/574 7101). Canada-wide packages and tours at reasonable rates.

All Canada Travel & Holidays, Sunway House, Raglan Rd, Lowestoft, Suffolk NR32 2LW (☎01502/585825, fax 500681, *www.all-canada.com*). Holidays in all provinces.

British Airways Holidays, Astral Towers, Betts Way, London Rd, Crawley, West Sussex RH10 2XA (☎0870/242 4243, fax 01293/772640, *www.baholidays.co.uk*). Bargain packages and tours of most descriptions. Primarily Québec, Ontario, Alberta and BC.

Canada West Holidays, The Long Barn, Walkmills, Church Stretton, Shropshire SY3 6AY (☎01694/751726). Holidays in Alberta and BC.

Canada's Best, 170 Fulford Rd, York YO10 4DA (☎01904/625114, fax 634598, *www.best-in-travel.com*). All types of holidays Canada-wide.

Canadian Connections, 10 York Way, Lancaster Rd, High Wycombe, Bucks HP12 3PY (☎01494/473173, fax 473588). Canada-wide.

Canadian Travel Service, 16 Bathurst Rd, Folkestone, Kent CT20 2NT (☎01303/249000, fax 240490).

Contiki Holidays, Wells House, 15 Elmfield Rd, Bromley, Kent BR1 1LS (☎020/8290 6422). Holidays to western Canada.

Experience Canada, 14 Terminus Rd, Eastbourne, East Sussex BN21 3LP (☎01323/416699, fax 410864, *www.experience-holidays.co.uk*). Tours and tailor-made holidays in all the provinces except Saskatchewan.

Kuoni Travel Ltd, Kuoni House, Deepdene Ave, Dorking, Surrey RH5 4AZ (☎01306/742888, fax 740328, *www.kuoni.co.uk*). Tailor-made and guided tours to Québec, Ontario, Yukon, Alberta and BC, and city breaks.

Travelbag, 12 High St, Alton, Hampshire GU34 1BN (☎01420/88380 or 020/7287 5559, fax 01420/82133). Tailor-made trips, car hire, flights and itineraries to suit all budgets.

Vacation Canada, Cambridge House, 8 Cambridge Rd, Glasgow G2 3DZ (☎0870/707 0444, fax 0141/353 0135, *www.vacationcanada@btinternet.com*). Skiing, city tours, guided coach tours, rail journeys, etc across Canada.

Virgin Holidays, The Galleria, Station Rd, Crawley, West Sussex RH10 1WW (☎01293/617181, *www.virginholidays.co.uk*). Bargain packages and tours with the emphasis on Québec, Alberta and BC.

travelling: a return flight to Vancouver and a fortnight's car rental might cost as little as £600 per person.

A typical **flight-guided tour** might comprise a fourteen-day trans-Canadian holiday taking in Toronto, Niagara Falls, Ottawa, Montréal,

ADVENTURE AND SPECIAL-INTEREST HOLIDAYS

Agricultural Travel Bureau, 14 Chain Lane, Newark, Notts NG24 1AU (☎01636/705612, fax 707600, *www.agritravel@farmline.com*).

AmeriCan Adventures, 64 Mount Pleasant Ave, Tunbridge Wells, Kent TN1 1QY (☎01892/512700, fax 511896, *www.americanadventures.com*). Adventure camping and hostelling treks which include canoeing, mountain biking, rafting, horse riding and bungee jumping.

Go Fishing Canada, 2 Oxford House, 24 Oxford Rd North, London W4 4DH (☎020/8742 1556, fax 747 4331, *www.go-fishing-worldwide.com*).

Great Rail Journeys, Saviour House, 9 St Saviourgate, York YO1 8NL (☎01904/521915, fax 521905, *www.greatrail.com*).

Ramblers Holidays Ltd, PO Box 43, Welwyn Garden City, Herts AL8 6PQ (☎01707/331133, fax 333276, *www.ramblersholidays.co.uk*).

Sports Travel Tours, PO Box 1369, Aldridge, Walsall, West Midlands WS9 9YF (☎01543/375932, fax 453944).

Wildlife Worldwide, 170 Selsdon Rd, South Croydon, Surrey CR2 6PJ (☎020/8667 9158, fax 7667 1960, *www.wildlifeworldwide.com*).

Window on the Wild, 2 Oxford House, 24 Oxford Rd North, London W4 4DH (☎020/8742 1556, fax 7747 4331, *www.windows-on-the-wild.com*).

SKI HOLIDAYS

Crystal Holidays Ltd, Crystal House, Arlington Rd, Surbiton, Surrey KT6 6BW (☎020/8399 5144, fax 390 6378, *www.Crystalholidays.co.uk*).

First Choice Ski, Olivier House, 18 Marine Parade, Brighton BN2 1TL (☎0870/754 3477, fax 333 0329, *www.first-choice.com*).

Frontier Ski, 6 Sydenham Ave, London SE26 6UH (☎020/8776 8709, fax 7778 0149, *www.frontier-ski.co.uk*).

Inghams, 10–18 Putney Hill, London SW15 6AX (☎020/8780 4444, fax 7780 4450, *www.inghams.co.uk*).

James Orr Heli-Ski, Studio One, The Village, 7 Chalcot Rd, London NW1 8LH (☎020/8483 0300).

Momentum Travel, The Studio, 179c New Kings Rd, London SW6 4SW (☎020/7371 9111, fax 7610 6287, *www.momentum.uk.com*).

Neilson Ski Holidays, 29–31 Elmfield Rd, Bromley BR1 1UT (☎0990/141414, fax 0113/215 1693, *www.neilson.co.uk*).

Powder Skiing in North America, 61 Doneraile St, London SW6 6EW (☎020/7736 8191, fax 7384 2582, *www.cmhski.com*).

Simply Ski, Chiswick Gate, 598–608 Chiswick High Rd, Chiswick, London W4 5RT (☎020/8541 2209, fax 8995 5346, *www.simply-travel.com*).

Ski Activity, Lawmuir House, Methven, Perthshire PH1 3SZ (☎01738/840888, fax 840079, *www.skiactivity.com*).

Ski Independence, Broughton Market, Edinburgh EH3 6NU (☎0845/601 0703, fax 0870/550 2020, *www.ski-independence.co.uk*).

Ski Safari, 41 Canada Wharf, Rotherhithe St, London SE16 1ES (☎020/7740 1221, fax 7740 1223, *www.skisafari.com*).

Ski The American Dream, 1–7 Station Chambers, High St North, London E6 1JE (☎020/8552 1201, fax 552 7726, *www.skidream.com*).

Ski Total, 3 The Square, Richmond, Surrey TW9 1DY (☎020/8948 3535, fax 7352 1268, *www.skitotal.com*).

SkiSar US, Fairhand Holidays, Suite 5, 216 Main Rd, Biggin Hill, Kent TN16 3BD (☎01959/575727, fax 540797, *www.skiarus.com*).

Skiworld, 39A-41 North End Rd, London W14 8SZ (☎020/7602 7444, fax 7371 1463, *www.skiworld.ltd.uk*).

Calgary, the Rockies and Vancouver, including an outbound flight to Toronto, a domestic flight, coach trips, middle-range hotel accommodation and some sightseeing tours, at a cost of around £1700.

To see a chunk of Canada's great outdoors without being hassled by too many practical considerations, you could take a specialist **touring** or **adventure package**, which usually includes transport in Canada, accommodation, food and a guide – but not flights. Some of the more adventurous carry small groups around on minibuses and use a combination of budget hotels and camping, providing all equipment. These deals are not cheap, however – a typical package of thirteen-days' hiking and camping in the Rockies will cost from £513 plus flights and prices are far higher in areas that require detailed planning and outfitting. Operators offering a range of Canadian adventure holidays are listed in the box opposite; local companies specializing in the more extreme locations – for example, Labrador – are given in the appropriate sections of the *Guide*.

GETTING THERE FROM IRELAND

There are no nonstop direct flights from Ireland to Canada, though British Airways and Air Canada will quote you through-fares from Dublin to most major Canadian destina-tions, including the gateway cities of Toronto and Montréal. Surprisingly, Aer Lingus does not fly to Canada.

All flights **from Dublin** to Canada are via London. Air Canada offers flights to Toronto via London, and their fourteen-day Apex return fare costs from IR£618, or from IR£711 if you're head-ing to Vancouver. **From Belfast** with Air Canada a 21-day Apex to Toronto via London costs from £497 return; to Vancouver, £506 return.

Students and under-26s should consult usit, which can usually offer the best deals – their return fares from Dublin or Belfast to Toronto are priced from IR£350 and from IR£488 to Vancouver.

It's often possible to save money by **flying inde-pendently** from Dublin to London on a domestic carrier – British Midland, for example, runs seven flights daily from Dublin to Heathrow with a Super Saver return at IR£66, and an Apex return at IR£125 – to link into the Heathrow network.

AIRLINES

Air Canada, no offices in Northern Ireland or the Republic (reservations ☎08705/247226; www.aircanada.ca).

British Airways, 1 Fountain Centre, Fountain St, Belfast BT1 6ET (reservations ☎0845/773 3377 or ☎0845/60747, www.britishairways.com).

BA doesn't have a Dublin office but Aer Lingus acts as their agents (reservations ☎0845/973 7747, www.aerlingus.ie).

British Midland, Northern Ireland (☎0870/607 0555, www.britishmidland.com); Republic, Nutley, Merrion Rd, Dublin 4 (☎01/283 8833).

FLIGHT AGENTS

American Holidays, Lombard House, Lombard St, Belfast BT1 1BH (☎028/9023 8762) and Pearse St, Dublin 2 (☎01/679 8800 or 679 6611).

Apex Travel, 59 Dame St, Dublin 2 (☎01/671 5933, www.apextravelltd.com).

Budget Travel, 134 Lower Baggot St, Dublin (☎01/661 3122).

Crystal Holidays, 38 Dawson St, Dublin 2 (☎01/670 8444, www.crystalholidays.co.uk).

Thomas Cook, 118 Grafton St, Dublin 2 (☎01/677 1721, www.thomascook.com).

usit, 19 Aston Quay, O'Connell Bridge, Dublin 2 (☎01/602 1600); Fountain Centre, College St, Belfast BT1 6ET (☎028/9032 4073); 66 Oliver Plunkett St, Cork (☎021/270900); 33 Shipquay St, Derry (☎028/7137 1888); Victoria Place, Eyre Square, Galway (☎091/565177); Central Buildings, O'Connell St, Limerick (☎061/415064); 36–37 George's St, Waterford (☎051/872601). www.usitnow.ie.

GETTING THERE FROM THE US

Crossing the longest undefended border in the world is straightforward. Many visitors from the northern US just drive, as the major Canadian cities – Montréal and Toronto in the east, Winnipeg and Calgary in the middle and Vancouver in the west – are all within an hour's drive of the border. However, if you're coming from Florida or southern California, or want to go from New York to British Columbia, flying is obviously a lot quicker. Travelling by train is another alternative, at least if you're not in a hurry and want to see something of the landscapes along the way, and there are a few bus and ferry options too.

CAR

The US highway system leads into Canada at thirteen points along the border. The busiest corridors are Blaine, WA–White Rock, British Columbia; Detroit–Windsor, Ontario; Buffalo–Fort Erie, Ontario; and Niagara Falls. You may encounter traffic jams at the border and long lines, particularly at the weekends, in the summer months and on US or Canadian holidays. From New York to Montréal (383 miles), count on eight hours' driving; from San Francisco to Vancouver (954 miles), around nineteen hours. For route advice in the US, call the AAA (1-800/877-TRIPTIK, *www.aaa.com*). They have offices in most major cities, but you probably won't find them much help unless you're a member. For more detailed route enquiries within Canada, call the Canadian Automobile Association (see "Getting around", p.30).

At customs you will probably be asked to declare your citizenship, place of residence and proposed length of stay. Vehicle insurance, with minimum liability coverage of US$200,000, is compulsory and it is also advisable to obtain a yellow Non-Resident Inter-Province Motor Vehicle Liability Card from your insurance company before you go. Make sure you have your driver's licence, documents establishing proof of insurance and proof of vehicle ownership with you at all times while driving in Canada. If you are renting a car in the US you should mention that you intend to travel to Canada, though this is rarely a problem. Fill the car with gas before going, as US prices are still less than those over the border.

BY BUS

The **Greyhound** (☎1-800/231-2222, *www.grey-hound.com*) bus network extends into Canada from three points on the East Coast and one each from the West and middle America; prices below are approximate. The buses run from New York to Montréal (7 daily; 7hr–8hr 30min; US$71 one-way or US$141 return); Buffalo to Toronto (approximately 8 daily; 2hr 30min–3hr; US$16 one-way or US$32 return); Burlington (Vermont) to Montréal (5 daily; 2hr 30min–3hr; US$19 one-way or $36 return); Seattle to Vancouver (6 daily; 3hr 30min–4hr 30min; US$21 one-way or US$38 return); and Fargo (North Dakota) to Winnipeg (1 daily; 6hr 10min; US$43 one-way or US$83 return). Be sure to arrive at the terminal one hour before departure.

The alternative to long-distance bus hell, **Green Tortoise** (494 Broadway, San Francisco, CA 94133; ☎1-800/227-4766; *www.greentortoise.com*), with its foam cushions, bunks, fridges and rock music, no longer runs a regular service into Canada, but it does still offer a 28–30-day trip from San Francisco north to Alaska, which includes a ferry ride along the Inside Passage and side-trips into the Canadian Rockies (US$1500, plus US$250 for food).

BY AIR

There are plenty of nonstop **flights** on the national carrier, Air Canada, which bought Canadian Airlines, and most US airlines offer

FLIGHT TIMES

Flying north/south between the US and Canada is reasonably quick: from New York to Montréal takes around 1hr 15min; New York to Toronto 1hr 30min; New York to Halifax 1hr 50min; Chicago to Winnipeg 2hr 10min; LA to Vancouver 2hr 45min; LA to Calgary 3hr. **Flying east/west** is fairly painless, too (New York–LA or Montréal–Vancouver takes around 5hr). However, flying east/west between countries usually involves a stopover or onward connection, so New York–Vancouver can take 7–8hr.

regular flights between the US and Canada: Montréal, Toronto and Vancouver are the most popular destinations, but there are also services to Halifax, Calgary, Winnipeg and many others. Connecting flights within Canada serve some 75 additional places.

Flying to Canada from major cities in the US is similar to flying from Boston to New York or from

San Francisco to LA: flights run on a business schedule or are more expensive during the weekdays, with special fares – usually available at the last minute – to capture the "weekend getaway" crowd. Fares of all kinds are available, as are the types of planes – from little commuter planes to charters – and there are frequent specials. Sometimes, businesses buy up blocks of tickets they don't use, so occasionally you can fly standby. Sample budget **return** fares quoted by the major airlines are: New York to Toronto US$195; New York to Montréal US$225; New York to Halifax US$275; Chicago to Winnipeg US$310; LA to Calgary US$260; LA to Vancouver US$220. If you only plan a long-weekend trip, there are often special NY–Toronto fares for US$120 or Chicago–Winnipeg for US$190.

Even more so than with other international connections, you really need to **shop around** to get the very best deals on the busy US–Canada routes. In addition to fares with the usual Apex restrictions (21-day advance booking, Sat night

AIRLINES

Air Canada from US call ☎1-800/776-3000; from Canada call ☎1-800/555-1212 for various local toll-free numbers, *www.aircanada.ca.*

American Airlines (☎1-800/433-7300, *www.americanairlines.com*).

British Airways from US call ☎1-800/247-9297; from Canada call ☎1-800/426-7000, *www.britishairways..com.*

Continental Airlines (☎1-800/231-0856, *www.continental.com*).

Delta Air Lines from US call ☎1-800/241-4141; from Canada call ☎1-800/221-1212, *www.delta.com.*

Northwest Airlines (☎1-800/447-4747, *www.nwa.com*).

Trans World Airlines (☎1-800/892-4141, *www.twa.com*).

United Airlines (☎1-800/241-6522, *www.united.com*).

US Airways (☎1-800/428-4322, *www.usairways.com*).

DISCOUNT FLIGHT AGENTS, TRAVEL CLUBS AND CONSOLIDATORS

Council Travel, Head office: 205 E 42nd St, New York, NY 10017 (☎1-800/226-8624, 1-888 COUNCIL or 212/822-2700). Other offices at: 530 Bush St, Suite 700, San Francisco, CA 94108 (☎415/421-3473); 931 Westwood Blvd, Westwood, CA 90024 (☎310/208-3551); 1138 13th St, Boulder, CO 80302 (☎303/447-8101); 3301 M St NW, 2nd Floor, Washington, DC 20007 (☎202/337-6464); 1160 N, State St, Chicago, IL 60610 (☎312/951-0585); 273 Newbury St, Boston, MA 02116 (☎617/266-1926). Nationwide US organization with information available online

at *www.counciltravel.com*. Mostly, but by no means exclusively, specializes in student travel.

Educational Travel Center, 438 N Frances St, Madison, WI 53703 (☎1-800/747-5551, *www.edtrav.com*). Student/youth discount agent.

Encore Travel Club, 4501 Forbes Blvd, Lanham, MD 20706 (☎1-800/444-9800, *www.preferredtraveller.com*). Discount travel club.

Last Minute Travel Club, 100 Sylvan Rd, Suite 600, Woburn, MA 01801 (☎1-800/LAST-MIN). Travel club specializing in standby deals.

stay, midweek travel, etc), you might find special offers which require you to book before a particular date, limit your stay, fly at a certain time of day, or, perversely, allow you more flexibility than on a higher fare. Your best bet is to first try a **discount agent** like Council or STA, who may be able to dig up scheduled return fares for as little as US$90 (New York–Toronto), US$155 (New York–Montréal) or US$199 (LA–Vancouver); always be sceptical of any alleged rock-bottom fares quoted by telephone booking agents for the major carriers.

Domestic flights wholly within the US or Canada generally cost somewhat less than flights between the two countries, so you may make savings by crossing the border before or after your flight. If you're willing to sacrifice convenience for economy it might be worth your while flying from New York to Buffalo and taking the bus across the border and on up to Toronto, for instance, rather than flying New York to Toronto direct. This is especially true of long-haul flights: a transconti-

nental flight from New York to Seattle can be considerably cheaper than a similar flight to Vancouver, only a hundred miles north. Sample budget return fares within Canada are Toronto to Montréal, C$235; Montréal to Vancouver, C$379; Vancouver to Winnipeg, C$350 and Winnipeg to Toronto, C$279. If your main destination is somewhere upcountry you can often save money by buying a separate, domestic flight from the nearest major Canadian destination, rather than treating that leg of the journey as part of an international itinerary.

BY TRAIN

Three Amtrak routes from the northeastern US have direct connections with **VIA Rail**, Canada's national rail company: the Maple Leaf from New York to Toronto via Buffalo and Niagara Falls (1 daily; 12hr; US$65 in low season/US$99 in high season, one-way); the Adirondack from New York to Montréal via Albany and Plattsburgh (1 daily;

New Frontiers/Nouvelles Frontières, Head offices: 12 E 33rd St, New York, NY 10016 (☎1-800/366-6387, *www.newfrontiers.com*); 1001 Sherbrook E, Suite 720, Montréal H2L 1L3 (☎514/526-8444). French discount travel firm. Other branches in LA, San Francisco and Québec City.

Now Voyager, 74 Varick St, Suite 307, New York, NY 10013 (☎212/431-1616, *www.nowvoyagertravel.com*). Courier flight broker.

STA Travel, ☎1-800/777-0112, *www.statravel.com*. Offices at: 297 Newbury St, Boston, MA 02115 (☎617/266-6014); 429 S Dearborn St, Chicago, IL 60605 (☎312/786-9050); 7202 Melrose Ave, Los Angeles, CA 90046 (☎323/934-8722); 317 14th Ave SE, Minneapolis, MN 55414 (☎612/615-1800); 10 Downing St, New York, NY 10014 (☎212/627-3111); 1905 Walnut St, Philadelphia, PA 19103 (☎215/382-2928); 36 Geary St, San Francisco, CA 94108 (☎415/391-8407). Worldwide specialist in independent travel.

TFI Tours International, 34 W 32nd St, New York, NY 10001 (☎1-800/745-8000 or 212/736-1160, *www.tfitoursinternational.com*). Consolidator; other offices in Las Vegas, San Francisco, Los Angeles and Miami.

Travel Avenue, 10 S Riverside, Suite 1404, Chicago, IL 60606 (☎1-800/333-3335, *www.travelavenue.com*). Discount travel agent.

Travelers Advantage, 3033 S Parker Rd, Suite 900, Aurora, CO 80014 (☎1-800/548-1116, *www.travelersadvantage.com*). Discount travel club.

Worldtek Travel, 111 Water St, New Haven, CT 06511 (☎1-800/243-1723, *www.worldtek.com*). Discount travel agency.

Worldwide Discount Travel Club, 11601 Biscayne Blvd, Suite 310, North Miami, FL 33181 (☎305/895-2082). Discount travel club.

ONLINE TICKET AGENCIES

Expedia *www.expedia.com* The biggest entry in the field, as one would expect from a Microsoft product. Competitive fares, though.

Last Minute Travel *www.lastminutetravel.com* You probably won't want to wait until the last

minute, but if you're flexible, you can take advantage of cheap deals with major airlines here.

Travelocity *www.travelocity.com* One of Expedia's main competitors, and a good, easy-to-use option.

9hr 30min; US$53/66 one-way) and the International from Chicago to Toronto (1 daily; 14hr; US$98 one-way). Sleeping cars have recently been discontinued on these trains, but they may well be reintroduced sometime in the future. In the northwest, the Mount Baker International runs from Seattle to Vancouver (1 daily; 4hr; US$21/33 one-way). All the above snow low and high season fares for travel in economy (the cheapest) class, where pillows are provided for overnight journeys.

For specific journeys, the train is usually more expensive than the bus (and often the plane), though special deals, especially in off-peak periods, can bring the round-trip cost down considerably. There are discounts available on trains for "Student Advantage" pass-holders, senior citizens and travellers with disabilities. Children from 2 to 15 who are accompanied by an adult go for half-fare; children under 2 travel free.

You should always reserve as far as possible in advance, as it is compulsory to have a seat and some of the eastern-seaboard trains in particular get booked up solid. Amtrak information and reservations are available on ☎1-800/USA-RAIL or online at *www.amtrak.com*.

BY FERRY

There are five US–Canada **ferry services**: three on the West Coast and two on the East. Quite apart from the enjoyment of the ferry ride, the services can save you hours of driving on some cross-country routes.

WEST COAST FERRIES

On the West Coast, the *Victoria Clipper* catamaran for foot passengers runs between Seattle and Victoria on Vancouver Island, three times daily from mid-May to mid-September and once daily in spring and fall (2hr 30min; US$54/58 one-way; reservations ☎206/448-5000 or 1-800/888-2535, *www.victoriaclipper.com*).

Further north, Alaska Marine Highway ferries link several Alaskan towns with Prince Rupert. The Juneau service, for instance, operates on alternate days from May to late September (24hr; US$122 one-way, cars US$283; reservations in US ☎1-800/526-6731, in Yukon and BC ☎1-800/478-2268, *www.akferry.com*).

However, the most useful West Coast ferry is the Washington State Ferries service from Anacortes on the Washington mainland to Sidney, on Vancouver Island. The ferry travels twice daily in summer, once in winter via Washington's beautiful San Juan archipelago (average-sized vehicle with driver $25.75 each way, extra adult passengers $9 each; 3hr; reservations essential, ☎1-206/464-6400 or 1-800/84-FERRY Washington State only, *www.wsdot.wa.gov*). Disabled travellers and senior citizens can get discounts of around fifty percent; children from 5 to 11 can get discounts of around seventy percent; under-5s travel free. There are no student discounts.

EAST COAST FERRIES

In the east, from early May to mid-October a car ferry, the *Scotia Prince*, runs almost nightly from Portland, Maine to Yarmouth, Nova Scotia. The travel time is approximately eleven hours. The price varies seasonally: US$60/80 per person one-way; cars US$80/98; cabins US$20–60/32–95. Five- to 14-year-olds pay half one-way fare and under-5s travel free. Also worth looking into are the return discount packages for two adults and car: the Spring Supersaver, the Summer Getaway and the Indian Summer (reservations ☎1-800/482-0955 in Maine, ☎1-800/341-7540 elsewhere, *www.princeoffundy.com*).

In addition, *The Cat* ferry runs from Bar Harbor in Maine to Yarmouth, Nova Scotia daily from May to October. Travel time is roughly four hours. Prices vary seasonally: US$45/55 one-way; cars US$70/80; senior citizens US$40/50; children from 5 to 12 US$20/25; children under 5 travel free (reservations ☎1-888/249-7245, *www.catferry.com*). Advance reservations are strongly recommended on both the East Coast services.

PACKAGES

US **tour operators** offer a variety of options from all-inclusive packages (combining plane tickets, bus or train travel, hotel accommodation, meals, transfers and sightseeing tours to land-only deals based around a single specialized activity (bird-watching, for instance).

These kind of holidays may not sound too appealing to an independent traveller, but one reason why a package could be your best bet – unless you're an expert survivalist – is if you're travelling into the wilderness for backcountry

TOUR OPERATORS

Adventure Center, 1311 63rd St, Suite 200, Emeryville, CA 94608 (☎1-800/228-8747). Adventure and hiking holidays. Their 8-day "Newfoundland, Naturally" package runs from $1575 (land only). The 15-day "Rocky Mountains and the Pacific" starts at $990 (land only).

American Airlines Vacations, 9933 E 16th St, Tulsa, OK 74128 (☎1-800/321-2121, *www.aavacations.com*). City breaks and more extensive packages. Five nights in Québec City, with 3-star hotel accommodation, car rental and return flight out of New York would cost from around $800.

Backroads, 801 Cedar St, Berkeley, CA 94710 (☎1-800/462-2848, *www.backroads.com*). Camping/cycling holidays from $998 (6 days; land only) and hotel/cycling holidays from $1698 (6 days; land only).

Contiki Holidays, 2300 E Katella Ave, Suite 450, Anaheim, CA 92806 (☎1-800/CONTIKI, *www.contiki.com*). Travel specialists for 18–35s.

Different Strokes Tours, 1841 Broadway, Suite 607, New York, NY 10023 (☎1-800/668 3301). Customized tours for gay/lesbian travellers.

Globus and Cosmos, 5301 S Federal Circle, Littleton, CO 80123 (☎1-800/556-5454, *www.globustours.com*). Two weeks or more motor-coach sightseeing tours.

Holidaze Ski Tours, 810 Belmar Plaza, Belmar, NJ 07719 (☎1-800/526-2827, *www.holidaze.com*). Ski holidays at Lake Louise from $282 (4 nights).

Kemwel's Premiere Selections, 106 Calvert St, Harrison, NY 10528 (☎1-800/234-4000). Ten-day transcontinental rail excursion from $2300 (most meals and train/hotel accommodation included).

Maupintour, 1515 St Andrews Drive, Lawrence, KS 66046 (☎1-800/255-4266, *www.maupintour*

.com). Fully escorted group tours (land only): 7-day "Rocky Mountain Escape" from $1750; 12-day "Trans Canada by Train" from $3585.

Questers Worldwide Nature Tours, 381 Park Ave S, New York, NY 10016 (☎1-800/468-8668, *www.questers.com*). Nature tours to Newfoundland and the Yukon.

Rod and Reel Adventures, 3507 Tully Rd, Suite B6, Modesto, CA 95356 (☎1-800/356-6982, *www.rodreeladventures.com*). Fishing holidays.

Saga Holidays, 222 Berkeley St, Boston, MA 02116 (☎1-877/265-6862, *www.sagaholidays.com*). Specialists in group travel for seniors, with a variety of Canada tours.

Suntrek, 77 W 3rd St, Santa Rosa, CA 95401 (☎1-800/292-9696, *www.suntrek.com*). Hiking and walking tours from $795 (2 weeks, May to Oct).

Trek America, PO Box 189, Rockaway, NJ 07866 (☎1-800/221-0596, *www.trekamerica.com*). Camping, hiking, canoeing, horseback riding, white-water rafting, etc. Their 21-day "Frontier Canada" trip, which departs from Seattle or New York and spans the continent, costs around $1239.

United Vacations Ski, PO Box 1460, Milwaukee, WI 53201(☎1-800/328-6877, *www.unitedvacations.com*). Ski trips to Whistler or Banff from $888 (return flights from New York, 3 nights 2-star accommodation, transfers).

Worldwide Quest International, 1170 Sheppard Ave W, Suite 45, Toronto, Ontario M3K 2A3 (☎1-800/387-1483 or 416/633-5666, *www.worldwidequest.com*). A wide range of exotic all-inclusive nature tours: "Hiking in the Canadian Rockies" ($895, 7 days); "Kayaking in Québec" ($795, 8 days).

adventure. Local guides and training (for example, in white-water canoeing) are commonly available as well as the normal flights/lodgings, etc. If you live on the West Coast, one of the cheapest options is to take a Green Tortoise bus to Canada, with included excursions around the Canadian Rockies (see p.9).

ENTRY, ID AND CUSTOMS

If you're a United States citizen, you don't need a visa to enter Canada as a tourist. All you need

is one **ID card** with your photo, plus proof of US citizenship. This can be a valid US passport, an original US birth certificate, certified copy thereof, or original US naturalization papers. Note that a US driver's licence alone is insufficient proof of citizenship. Visitors with **children** must show identification for each child similar to that required by adults and a letter of permission from the parents of any children for whom they don't have legal custody. Divorced parents with shared custody rights should carry legal documents that establish their status. Unaccompanied children should have a letter of permission from their parents or a legal guardian.

Contrary to expectations, since the signing of the North American Free Trade Agreement (NAFTA), entering and exiting Canada has become a particularly sensitive issue – on both sides of the border. You would be well advised, where documentation is involved, to always err on the side of caution.

All US citizens wishing to **work** in Canada, including those exempted from the validation process by the terms of NAFTA, must have employment authorization from a Canadian embassy or consulate before entering the country. **Students** who are US citizens, permanent residents of the US, or Green Card holders, who have already been accepted by a school in Canada and have sufficient funds to cover all expenses, must apply for student authorization at a port of entry or a Canadian consulate four months before entering the country.

Bear in mind that if you cross the border in your car, trunks and passenger compartments are subject to spot searches by the **customs** personnel of both the US and Canada. Officers at the more obscure entry points on the border can be real sticklers, so expect to be delayed. Americans who visit Canada for at least 48 hours and haven't made an international trip in thirty days can bring back goods to the value of US$400. Non-residents of Canada are also entitled to a tax refund on goods worth more than C$50 purchased at one establishment at one time and totally more than $200. The refund is given at the border when exiting the country, provided you are able to supply original itemized receipts; ask the customs official for information before entering Canada or peruse *www.ccra-adrc.gc.ca* before leaving.

Gifts valued at less than C$60 that do not contain tobacco or alcohol can be brought into Canada; those valued at more than C$60 are subject to regular import duty on the excess amount. The US Customs Service (☎202/927-6724) can help with any queries.

GETTING THERE FROM AUSTRALIA AND NEW ZEALAND

Travelling from Australia and New Zealand, there are daily direct flights to Vancouver, Canada's western point of entry, as well as plenty of flights that involve stopovers along the way, likely somewhere such as Honolulu, or perhaps on America's west coast. The direct options on Qantas and Air New Zealand run A$1863/NZ$1899 low season, with other onward destinations from New Zealand being well served by Air Canada (Canadian Airlines shared flights with Qantas until it merged with Air Canada.) You can expect to pay around A/NZ$500 on top of your main ticket to the eastern cities of Toronto and Montréal and around A$300/NZ$350 to Edmonton and Calgary. However, if you intend to do a fair amount of flying around, you'd be better off taking advantage of some of the coupon deals that can be bought with your main ticket and cost US$100–300 each depending on the distance involved. A number of flights stop off in Honolulu, Hawaii, where you can usually stay over for as long as you like for no extra charge. Alternatively, if you don't mind going via Asia, JAL and Korean Airlines fares to Vancouver include a night's accommodation in their home cities and start from around A$1500/NZ$1850 low season. However, if you don't want to spend the night, Cathay Pacific and Singapore Airlines can

AIRLINES

☎800 and ☎300 numbers are toll-free, but only apply if dialled outside the city in the address. ☎13 numbers are charged at the local rate nationwide.

Air Canada, www.aircanada.ca Australia ☎1-300/656 232 or 02/9232 5222; New Zealand ☎09/379 3371. Coupons for extended travel in Canada and the US.

Air New Zealand, www.airnz.com Australia ☎13 2476; New Zealand ☎09/357 3000. Daily flights to Vancouver and Toronto from major Australasian cities via Auckland and either Honolulu or LA; with onward connections to other cities with Air Canada.

Cathay Pacific, www.cathaypacific.com Australia ☎13 17 47 or 02/9931 5500; New Zealand ☎09/379 0861. Several times a week to Vancouver and LA from major Australasian cities via a transfer or stopover in Hong Kong.

JAL Japan Airlines, www.japanair.com Australia ☎02/9272 1111; New Zealand ☎09/379 9906. Several flights a week to Vancouver with either a transfer or an overnight stopover in Tokyo.

Korean Airlines, www.koreanair.com Australia ☎02/9262 6000; New Zealand ☎09/307 3687.

Several flights a week from Sydney and Brisbane to Vancouver via an overnight stopover in Seoul.

Qantas, www.qantas.com.au Australia ☎13 13 13; New Zealand ☎09/357 8900 or 0-800/808 767. Daily to Vancouver from major Australasian cities either direct or via Honolulu, with onward connection to other destinations; however, no longer with Canadian Airlines.

Singapore Airlines, www.singaporeair.com Australia ☎13 10 11; New Zealand ☎09/350 0262; New Zealand ☎09/303 2129 or 0-800/808 909. Three flights a week from major Australian cities to Vancouver via Singapore, and once a week from Auckland; several times a week from major Australian cities to LA via Singapore.

United Airlines, www.ual.com Australia ☎13 1777; New Zealand ☎09/379 3800. Daily to Vancouver, Edmonton, Calgary, Montréal and Toronto from Sydney, Melbourne and Auckland via a transfer in LA.

DISCOUNT TRAVEL AGENTS

All the agents listed below offer competitive discounts on airfares as well as a good selection of packaged holidays and tours, and can also arrange car rental and bus and rail passes.

Anywhere Travel, anywhere@ozemail.com.au 345 Anzac Parade, Kingsford, Sydney (☎02/9663 0411).

Budget Travel, www.budgettravel.co.nz 16 Fort St, Auckland, plus branches around the city (☎09/366 0061 or 0-800/808 040).

Destinations Unlimited, 220 Queen St, Auckland (☎09/373 4033).

Flight Centres, www.flightcentre.com Australia: 82 Elizabeth St, Sydney (☎02/9235 3522), plus branches nationwide (for the nearest branch call ☎13 16 00). New Zealand: 350 Queen St, Auckland (☎09/358 4310 or 0-800/354 448), plus branches nationwide.

Northern Gateway, oztravel@norgate.com.au 22 Cavenagh St, Darwin (☎08/8941 1394).

STA Travel, www.statravel.com Australia, 855 George St, Sydney; 256 Flinders St, Melbourne; other offices in state capitals and major universities (for nearest branch call ☎13 17 76); telesales (☎1-300/360 960). New Zealand: 10 High St, Auckland (☎09/309 0458); other offices in major cities and university campuses (for nearest branch call ☎0-800/874 773); telesales (☎09/366

6673). Fare discounts for students and those under 26, as well as visas, student cards and travel insurance.

Student Uni Travel, 92 Pitt St, Sydney (☎02/9232 8444, sydney@backpackers.net); plus branches in Brisbane, Cairns, Darwin, Melbourne and Perth. Student/youth discounts and travel advice.

Thomas Cook, www.thomascook.com.au Australia: 175 Pitt St, Sydney (☎02/9231 2877); 257 Collins St, Melbourne (☎03/9282 0222); plus branches in other state capitals (for nearest branch call ☎13 17 71); telesales (☎1-800/801 002). New Zealand: 191 Queen St, Auckland (☎09/379 3920).

Trailfinders, www.travel.com.au 8 Spring St, Sydney (☎02/9247 7666); 91 Elizabeth St, Brisbane (☎07/3229 0887); Hides Corner, Shield St, Cairns (☎07/4041 1199). City accommodation and Alamo car rentals.

usit Beyond, www.usitbeyond.co.nz cnr Shortland St and Jean Batten Place, Auckland (☎09/379 4224 or 0-800/788 336); plus branches in major cities. Student/youth travel specialists.

get you there from A$1799/NZ$2099 with a transfer in their home cities.

Seat availability on most international flights out of Australia and New Zealand is often limited, so it's best to book at least three weeks ahead. Tickets purchased direct from the airlines tend to be expensive and you'll get much better deals on fares from your local travel agent, as well as the latest information on limited specials, fly-drive, accommodation packages, stopovers en route and round-the-world fares. The best discounts are through **Flight Centres** and **STA** (for students and under-26s), who can also advise on visa regulations. You might also want to have a look on the Internet; *www.travel.com.au* offers discounted fares, as does *www.sydneytravel.com*.

Airfares are seasonally adjusted: low season from mid-January to end February, and October to November; high season from mid/end May to August, December and January; and shoulder seasons the rest of the year. Seasons vary slightly depending on the airline.

FROM AUSTRALIA

Fares from eastern Australian capitals are generally the same (airlines offer a free connecting service between these cities), whereas fares from Perth and Darwin are about A$400 less via Asia and more via the US.

United Airlines has services to Calgary and Edmonton from Sydney via LA for around A$1949/2299 (low season/high season) and to Toronto and Montréal for A$2100/2499. Air New Zealand and Air Canada offer the lowest: A$1699/2199 to Vancouver and A$2099/2699 to Toronto via Auckland and Honolulu. Qantas no longer code-shares (shares the same flight) with Canadian Airlines. To Vancouver, Qantas and

SPECIALIST AGENTS AND OPERATORS

Adventure Specialists, 69 Liverpool St, Sydney (☎02/9261 2927). Overland and adventure tour agent offering a variety of trips throughout Canada.

The Adventure Travel Company, 164 Parnell Rd, Parnell, Auckland (☎09/379 9755, *advakl@hot.co.nz*). NZ agent for Peregrine (see below).

Adventure World, 73 Walker St, North Sydney (☎02/9956 7766 or 1-300/363 055), plus branches in Adelaide, Brisbane, Melbourne and Perth; 101 Great South Rd, Remuera, Auckland (☎09/524 5118, *www.adventureworld.com.au*). Agents for a vast array of international adventure travel companies that operate a variety of trips in Canada.

American Express Travel, 344 Queen St, Brisbane (☎07/3220 0878). US and Canadian travel arrangements.

Canada and America Travel Specialists, 343 Pacific Hwy, Crows Nest, Sydney (☎02/9922 4600). Wholesalers of Greyhound Ameripasses plus flights and accommodation in North America.

IT Adventures, Level 4, 46–48 York St, Sydney (☎1-800/804 277). Extended small group camping trips through Canada.

Peregrine Adventures, 258 Lonsdale St, Melbourne (☎03/9663 8611), plus offices in Brisbane, Sydney, Adelaide and Perth. Offer a variety of active holidays, from short camping, walking and sea-kayaking trips in British Columbia to longer overland adventures.

Snow Bookings Only International, 1141 Toorak Rd, Camberwell, Melbourne (☎03/9809 2699 or 1-800/623 266, *www.peregrine.net.au*). Agents for a host of ski and snowboarding holidays in British Columbia and Alberta, including Summit Ski's fifteen nights of fully guided ski and snowboard tours.

The Ski & Snowboard Travel Company, 343 Pacific Highway, Crows Nest, Sydney ☎02/9955 3759 or 1-800/251 934, *skitrav@ozemail.com.au*. Individual, group and family ski holidays in British Columbia, Alberta and northwest US.

Sydney International Travel, 75 King St, Sydney (☎02/9299 8000, *www.sydneytravel .com.au*). Extensive range of Canadian tours and accommodation, including short city-stays, ski packages, bus and rail tours. Agent for Swingaway Holidays, which books only through travel agents.

Travel Plan, 118 Edinburgh Rd, Castlecrag, Sydney (☎02/9958 1888 or 1-300/130 754). Heli-skiing and ski holiday packages in British Columbia and Alberta.

Wiltrans/Maupintour, 10/189 Kent St, Sydney (☎02/9255 0899). Fully escorted five- and six-star all-inclusive tours staying in famous hotels through Canada.

United Airlines start at A$1699. A slightly cheaper option is via Asia with either JAL or Korean Airlines, (both A$1559/1899), and often includes a night's stopover accommodation in their respective cities of Tokyo and Seoul.

FROM NEW ZEALAND

Air Canada–Air New Zealand, via Honolulu, and United Airlines, via LA, provide daily connections to Vancouver (NZ$1899 in low season and NZ$2499 in high season), Edmonton and Calgary (NZ$2299/2699) and Toronto and Montréal (NZ$2399/2799) as well as other major cities in Canada. Qantas can get you to Vancouver via Sydney for around NZ$1999/2499, but the best deals are out of Auckland with JAL, with either a transfer or stopover in Tokyo for NZ$1850/2299. Add about NZ$100 for Christchurch and Wellington departures.

If you're interested in skiing, cruises or adventure holidays and prefer to have all the arrangements made for you before you leave, then the specialist agents opposite can help you plan your trip. Unfortunately there are few pre-packaged tours that include airfares from Australasia, however, most specialist agents will also be able to assist with flight arrangements. In turn many of the tours in the box on p.16 can also be arranged through your local travel agent.

ROUND-THE-WORLD AND CIRCLE FARES

If you intend to take in Canada as part of a world trip, then **round-the-world** tickets and **circle** fares offer the best value for money, often working out just a little more than an all-in ticket. There are numerous airline combinations to choose from; for example, a composite ticket from Sydney or Auckland to Honolulu, then Vancouver, Montréal, London, Paris, Bangkok, Singapore and back to your starting point, starts at A$2099/NZ$2399. However, more comprehensive and flexible routes are offered by "One World" and "Star Alliance" allowing you to take in destinations in the US and Canada, Europe, Asia as well as South America and Africa; prices are mileage-based from A$/NZ$2700, for a maximum of 29,000 miles up to A$/NZ$3700 for 39,000 miles. Another option that enables you to visit some of the Pacific Islands on your way to and from Vancouver is Air New Zealand's "Circle Pacific Fare" starting at A$1899/NZ$2299 low season, which allows stopovers in Auckland, Apia, Nadi, Rarotonga, Honolulu, Papeete and LA.

RED TAPE AND VISAS

Citizens of the EU, Scandinavia and most Commonwealth countries travelling to Canada do not need an entry visa: all that is required is a valid passport. United States citizens simply need some form of identification; see p.13 for more details.

All visitors to Canada have to complete a **customs declaration form**, which you'll be given on the plane or at the US–Canada border. On the form you'll have to give details of where you intend to stay during your trip. If you don't know, write "touring", but be prepared to give an idea of your schedule and destinations to the immigration officer.

At the point of entry, the Canadian **immigration** officer decides the length of stay permitted up to a **maximum of six months**, but not usually more than three. The officers rarely refuse entry, but they may ask you to show them how much **money** you have: a credit card or $300 cash per week of the proposed visit is usually considered sufficient. They may also ask to see a return

CANADIAN HIGH COMMISSIONS, CONSULATES AND EMBASSIES ABROAD

AUSTRALIA AND NEW ZEALAND

Auckland 9th Floor, Jetset Centre, 44–48 Emily Place, Auckland 1 (☎09/309 8516, *www.dfait=maeci.gc.ca/newzealand*).

Canberra Commonwealth Ave, Canberra, ACT 2600 (☎02/6270 4000, *www.dfait=maeci.gc.ca/australia*).

Sydney Level 5, Quay West Building, 111 Harrington St, Sydney, NSW 2000 (☎02/9364 3000. 24-hour visa information and application ☎02/9364 3050).

EUROPE

Germany 6th Floor, Internationales Handelszentrum, Friedrichstrasse 95, 10117 Berlin (☎030/203120).

Ireland 65 St Stephen's Green, Dublin 2 (☎01/478 1988).

Norway Wergeslandsveien 7, 0244 Oslo (☎022/995300).

Sweden Tegelbacken 4, 7th Floor, Stockholm (☎08/453 3000).

United Kingdom Macdonald House, 1 Grosvenor Square, London W1X 0AB (☎020/7258 6600).

UNITED STATES

Chicago Suite 2400, 2 Prudential Plaza, 180 N Stetson Ave, Suite 2400, Chicago, IL 60601 (☎312/616 1860, *www.canadachicago.net*).

Los Angeles 9th Floor, 550 S Hope St, Los Angeles, CA 90071-2627 (☎213/346-2700, *www.cdnconsultat-la.com*).

New York 1251 Avenue of the Americas, New York, NY 10020-1175 (☎212/596-1628, *www.canada-ny.org*).

Washington 501 Pennsylvania Ave NW, Washington, DC 20001 (☎202/682-1740, *www.canadianembassy.org*).

There are also consulates in **Atlanta, Boston, Buffalo, Dallas, Detroit, Miami, Minneapolis** and **Seattle**. Check the phone book for details.

or onward ticket. If they ask where you're staying and you give the name and address of friends, don't be surprised if they check.

For visa and immigration enquiries, visits of more than six months, study trips and stints of temporary employment, contact the nearest Canadian embassy, consulate or high commission for authorization prior to departure (see box, above). Inside

Canada, if an extension of stay is desired, written application must be made to the nearest **Canada Immigration Centre** well before the expiry of the authorized visit.

The **duty-free** allowance if you're over 19 (18 in Alberta, Manitoba and Québec) is 200 cigarettes and 50 cigars, plus 1.4 litres of liquor or 24 355ml-sized bottles of beer.

INFORMATION, WEB SITES AND MAPS

Few countries on earth can match the sheer volume of tourist information as that handed out by the Canadians. The most useful sources of information before you go are the various provincial tourist offices in Canada. The box overleaf provides their addresses; if you contact them well in advance of your departure, and are as specific as possible about your intentions, they'll be able to provide you with everything you need to know.

Outside Canada, the consulates, embassies and high commissions (see box opposite) usually have tourist departments, though these cannot match the specific detailed advice dispensed in Canada. One or two Canadian provinces maintain offices or brochure-line numbers in London (see box, overleaf), though these serve mainly as clearing houses for free publicity material. Most of Canada's provinces have at least one **toll-free visitor information number** for use within mainland North America. The toll-free numbers are staffed by tourist office employees trained to answer all manner of queries and to advise on room reservations.

LOCAL INFORMATION

In Canada, there are often seasonal **provincial tourist information centres** along the main highways, especially at provincial boundaries and along the US border. The usual **opening hours** for the seasonal centres are daily 9am–9pm in

July and August and weekdays 9am–5 or 6pm in May, June, September and October. These dispense all sorts of glossy material and, most usefully, have details of local provincial and national parks. The parks themselves (see "Outdoor pursuits", p.54) have offices that sell fishing and backcountry permits and give help on the specifics of hiking, canoeing, wildlife watching and so forth. At the country's **airports** general information is harder to come by, though there's usually a city tourist desk or a free phone which will help arrange accommodation.

All of Canada's large cities have their own **tourist bureaux**, with the services of the main branch complemented by summertime booths, kiosks and offices. Smaller towns nearly always have a seasonal **tourist office, infocentre** or **visitors' centre**, frequently operated by the municipal chamber of commerce, holding local maps and information. The usual opening hours in summer are daily 9am–6pm; in winter, tourist information is often dispensed from the city hall or chamber of commerce (Mon–Fri 9am–5pm). Many larger towns have a **free newspaper** or broadsheet, carrying local reviews and entertainment listings.

WEB SITES

Another excellent source for every conceivable manner of information is, of course, **the Web**; outside of checking Rough Guides own site (*www.roughguides.com*) for our Canada coverage and any other travel needs, we've listed a few of the most useful or just fun sites from which to get ready for your trip (see box, p.21). Plenty of other Web sites are listed for businesses, hotels and sights throughout this Basics section and the rest of the *Guide*.

MAPS

The **free maps** issued by each province, and available at all the tourist offices listed overleaf, are excellent for general driving and route planning, especially as they provide the broad details of ferry connections. The best of the commercially produced maps are those published by Rand McNally, also available bound together in their *Rand McNally Road Atlas of North America*.

PROVINCIAL TOURIST OFFICES IN CANADA

Alberta, Travel Alberta, Visitor Sales and Service, 3rd Floor, 101–102nd St Edmonton, AB T5J 4G8 (☎780/427-4321). Toll-free within Canada and mainland USA ☎1-800/661-8888.

British Columbia, Tourism British Columbia, Box 9830, Parliament Buildings, Victoria, BC V8W 9W5 (☎250/356-6363). Toll-free within Canada and mainland USA ☎1-800/663-6000.

Manitoba, Travel Manitoba, 7th Floor, 155 Carlton St, Winnipeg, MB R3C 3H8 (☎204/945-3777). Toll-free within Canada and mainland USA ☎1-800/665-0040.

New Brunswick, New Brunswick Department of Tourism, PO Box 12345, Campbellton, NB E3N 3T6 (☎506/789-2050, *www.tourismnbcanada .com*).Toll-free within Canada and mainland USA ☎1-800/561-0123, Dept. 057.

Newfoundland and Labrador, Newfoundland and Labrador Department of Tourism, Culture and Recreation, PO Box 8730, St John's, NF A1B 4K2 (☎709/729-2830). Toll free: within Canada and mainland USA ☎1-800/563-6353.

Northwest Territories, NWT Arctic Tourism, PO Box 610, Yellowknife, NWT X1A 2N5 (☎403/873-7200, *www.nwttravel.nt.ca*).Toll-free within Canada and mainland USA ☎1-800/661-0788.

Nova Scotia, Nova Scotia Department of Tourism and Culture, PO Box 456, Halifax, NS

B3J 2R5 (☎902/424-5000, *www.explorens.com*).Toll-free: within Canada and mainland USA ☎1-800/565-0000.

Nunavut, Nunavut Tourism, PO Box 1450, Iqaluit, NU X0A 0H0 (☎867/979-6551, *www.nunatour.nt.ca*).Toll-free within Canada and mainland USA ☎1-800/491-7910.

Ontario, Ontario Travel, Eaton Centre, Level 1, 220 Yonge St, PO Box 104, Toronto, ON M5B 2H1 (☎416/314-0944, *www.ontariotravel.net*). Toll-free within Canada and mainland USA ☎1-800/668-2746.

Prince Edward Island, Tourism PEI, West Royalty Industrial Park, Charlottetown, PEI (☎902/368-5540, *www.gov.pe.ca* or *www.peiplay.com*).Toll-free within Canada and mainland USA ☎1-800/463-4734.

Québec, Tourisme Québec, 1010 St Catherine St W, Montréal, PQ H3B 1G2 (☎514/873-2015, *www.bonjour-quebec.com*). Toll-free within Canada and mainland USA ☎1-877/266 5687.

Saskatchewan, Tourism Saskatchewan, 1922 Park St, Regina, SK S4P 3V7 (☎306/787-2300, *www.sasktourism.com*). Toll-free within Canada and mainland USA ☎1-877/237-2273.

Yukon, NWT Arctic Tourism, PO Box 610, Yellowknife, NWT X1A 2N5 (☎867/667-5340).

TOURIST OFFICES

Australia
Tourist offices are usually sections of a consulate or embassy, so refer to these for further information.

New Zealand
There's no longer a listing for the Canadian Tourist Office. Contact the consulates or embassy in Australia.

UK
Québec Brochure line only: ☎0990/561705.
Visit Canada Centre, 62–65 Trafalgar Square London WC2N 5DY. (☎020/7258 6600).

US
Tourist offices are usually sections of a consulate or embassy, so refer to these for further information.

In the case of **hiking** and **canoe** routes, all the national and most of the provincial parks have visitors' centres, which provide free parkland maps indicating hiking and canoe trails. Many of them also sell proper local survey maps, as do lots of outfitters and some of the provincial parks' departments, whose details are given in the *Guide* or can be obtained through the toll-free numbers.

If you want to be absolutely sure of getting the maps you need for independent wilderness travel, contact the **Canada Map Office**, 130 Bentley Ave, Nepean, Ontario K1A 0E9 (☎613/952-7000 or 1-800/465-6277). It supplies map indexes, which will identify the map you need; it also produces a useful brochure entitled *Topographic Basics* and publishes two main series of maps, 1:250 000 and 1:50 000.

CANADA ON THE INTERNET

Air Canada
www.aircanada.ca/home.html
Details of flight times, fares and reservations.

Assembly of First Nations
www.afn.ca
Lobbying organization of Canada's native peoples, with plenty to get you briefed on the latest circumstances.

Canada Eh? Net Directory
www.canadianeh.com
Impressive array of links to every conceivable Canada-related site.

Canadian Hockey Association
www.canadianhockey.ca
The official site of the amateur governing body for the national obsession.

Canadian Parks
parkscanada.pch.gc.ca/parks/main_e.htm
A good site by Canadian Heritage detailing opening times, camping facilities and how to get there, to all major Canadian parks.

Gateway to the Arts
Artscanadian.com

The Globe and Mail
www.theglobeandmail.com
Canada's premier paper online.

Government of Canada
www.canada.gc.ca/main_e.html
Catalogs official sites of provincial governments and various Canadian businesses.

Infospace
in-101.infospace.com/info/cansvcs.htm
Exhaustive *Yellow Pages*-like listings. If you want to find a vet in Labrador or a body piercer in Prince Albert, this will have it.

MacLean's
www.macleans.ca

Top stories and the editor's pick from past issues of Canada's premier news magazine.

National Atlas of Canada Online
www.atlas.gc.ca/english
Maps, stats and plenty of details on Canada's geographic features.

The Native Trail
www.Nativetrail.com
Insight into the First Nations and Quebec's Inuit peoples.

Northern Stars
www.northernstars.com
They track the progress of all Canada's film stars, with short bios and lists of credits.

Slam! Sport
www.canoe.ca/Slam
A very thorough Canadian site on all matters sporting.

Statistics Canada
www.statcan.ca
A national agency that gives you all the numerical data and analysis on population, economic trends, etc.

Tickets
www.ticketmaster.ca
Ticket booking service for shows, gigs and sporting events across Canada.

Trains
www.viarail.ca
VIA Rail's page with times and tickets for Canada's train services.

Yahoo!: Canada
www.yahoo.ca
The canuck section of the useful Web directory provides good avenues of investigation.

MAP OUTLETS IN BRITAIN

London
National Map Centre, 22–24 Caxton St, SW1H
0QU (☎020/7222 4966, *www.mapsworld.com*).

Stanfords, 12–14 Long Acre, Covent Garden,
WC2E 9LP (☎020/7836 1321,
www.stanfords.co.uk).

Glasgow
John Smith and Son, 26 Colquhoun Ave,
Hillington, G52 4PY (☎0141/570 5400,
www.johnsmith.co.uk).

Maps by **mail or phone order** are available
from Stanfords (☎020/7836 1321).

MAP OUTLETS IN NORTH AMERICA

Chicago
Rand McNally, 444 N Michigan Ave, IL 60611
(☎312/321-1751).

Montréal
Ulysses Travel Guides, 4176 St-Denis, PQ H2W
2M5 (☎514/843-9447, *www
.ulyssesguides.com*).

New York
The Complete Traveller Bookstore, 199 Madison
Ave, NY 10016 (☎212/685-9007).

Rand McNally, 150 E 52nd St, NY 10022
(☎212/758-7488, *www.randmcnally.com*).

San Francisco
The Complete Traveler Bookstore, 3207 Fillmore
St, CA 92123 (☎415/923-1511).

Rand McNally, 595 Market St, CA 94105
(☎415/777-3131, *www.randmcnally.com*).

Santa Barbara
Map Link, Inc, Unit 5, 30 S La Patera Lane, CA
93117 (☎805/692-6777, *www.maplink.com*).

Seattle
Elliott Bay Book Company, 101 S Main St, WA
98104 (☎206/624-6600,
www.elliottbaybook.com).

Toronto
Open Air Books and Maps, 25 Toronto St, ON
M5C 2R1 (☎416/363-0719).

Vancouver
International Travel Maps and Books, 552
Seymour St ☎604/687-3320, *www.itmb.com*).

World Wide Books and Maps, 1247 Granville St,
BC V6Z IG3 (☎604/687-3320).

Virginia
Rand McNally, 7988 Tysons Corner Center,
McLean, VA 22102 (☎ 703/556-8688,
www.randmcnally.com)

MAP OUTLETS IN AUSTRALIA AND NEW ZEALAND

Adelaide The Map Shop, 6–10 Peel St
(☎08/8231 2033).

Auckland Specialty Maps, 46 Albert St
(☎09/307 2217).

Brisbane Worldwide Maps and Guides, 187
George St (☎07/3221 4330, *www.world-
widemaps.com.au*).

Christchurch Mapworld, 173 Gloucester St
(☎03/374 5399, *www.mapworld.co.nz*).

Melbourne Mapland, 372 Little Bourke St
(☎03/9670 4383, *www.mapland.com.au*).

Perth Perth Map Centre, 1st Floor, Shafto Lane,
884 Hay St (☎08/9322 5733,
www.perthmap.com.au).

Sydney Travel Bookshop, Shop 3, 175 Liverpool
St (☎02/9261 8200).

TRAVELLERS WITH DISABILITIES

Canada is one of the best places in the world to travel if you have mobility problems or other physical disabilities. All public buildings are required to be wheelchair-accessible and provide suitable toilet facilities, almost all street corners have dropped **kerbs, and public telephones are specially equipped for hearing-aid users. Though wheelchair users may encounter problems when travelling on city public transport, main population centres are gradually introducing suitable buses.**

CONTACTS FOR TRAVELLERS WITH DISABILITIES

Australia and New Zealand

ACROD (Australian Council for Rehabilitation of the Disabled) PO Box 60, Curtin, ACT 2605 (☎02/6282 4333); 24 Cabarita Rd, Cabarita, NSW 2137 (☎02/9743 2699).
Provides lists of travel agencies and tour operators for people with disabilities.

Disabled Persons Assembly, 4/173–175 Victoria St, Wellington. New Zealand (☎04/801 9100).
Resource centre with lists of travel agencies and tour operators for people with disabilities.

UK

Can Be Done Ltd, 7-11 Kensington High St, London W8 5NP (☎020/8907 2400, fax 020/8909 1854, *www.canbedone.co.uk*). Offers tours to Canada for people with disabilities.

Heathrow Travelcare (☎020/8745 7495, fax 020/8745 4161). Assistance for disabled travellers at Heathrow Airport.

Holiday Care Service, 2nd Floor, Imperial Buildings, Victoria Rd, Horley, Surrey RH6 7PZ (☎01293/774535, fax 784647).
Information on all aspects of travel.

RADAR, Unit 12, City Forum, 250 City Rd, London EC1U 8AF (☎020/7250 3222).
A good source of advice on holidays and travel abroad.

Tripscope, The Courtyard, Evelyn Rd, London W4 5JH (☎020/8994 9294 or 0845/758 5641, fax 020/8994 3618 or 0117/939 7736).
Offers advice and information on travel for sick, elderly and disabled people.

Canada

BC Coalition of People with Disabilities, 204–456 W Broadway, Vancouver, BC V5Y IR3 (☎604/875-0188). Offers advice and assistance for travellers in BC.

Canadian Paraplegic Association. Their main office is at Suite 320, 1101 Prince of Wales Drive, Ottawa, ON K2C 3W7 (☎613/723-1033, fax 723-1060, and there are offices in every province: 520 Sutherland Drive, Toronto ON M4G 3V9 (☎416/422-5644); 780 SW Marine Drive, Vancouver, BC V6P 5YT (☎604/342-3611); 825 Sherbrook St, Winnipeg, MB (☎204/786-4753); Kéroul, 4545 Pierre-de-Courbetin, CP 1000, Montréal HIV 3R2 (☎514/252-3104).

VIA Rail information and reservations for the speech- and/or hearing-impaired are available on ☎416/368-6406 from Toronto, ☎1-800/268-9503 from elsewhere.

Western Institute for the Deaf, 2125 W 7th Ave, Vancouver, BC V6K 1X9 (☎604/736-7391 or 736-2527). Gives advice for the hearing-impaired.

US

Directions Unlimited, 720 N Bedford Rd, Bedford Hills, NY 10507 (☎1-800/533-5343). Tour operator specializing in custom tours for people with disabilities, including travellers who are blind.

Mobility International USA, Box 10767, Eugene, OR 97440 (voice and TDD ☎541/343-1284, *www.miusa.org*).
Information, access guides, tours and exchange programmes. Annual membership $35 (includes quarterly newsletter).

Society for the Advancement of Travel for the Handicapped (SATH), 347 5th Ave, New York, NY 10016 (☎212/447-7284, *www.sath.org*). Information on suitable tour operators and travel agents.

Travel Information Service, Moss Rehabilitation Hospital, 1200 W Tabor Rd, Philadelphia, PA 19141 (☎215/456-9603). Telephone information service and referral.

INFORMATION

The Canadian Paraplegic Association (CPA) can provide a wealth of **information** on travelling in specific provinces, and most of its regional offices produce a free guide on the most easily accessed sights. Provincial tourist offices are also excellent sources of information on accessible hotels, motels and sights. You may also want to get in touch with Kéroul in Montréal, an organization that specializes in travel for mobility-impaired people, and publishes the bilingual guide *Accès Tourisme* (C$15 plus $3 postage). Twin Peaks Press, PO Box 129, Vancouver, Washington (☎1-800/637-2256 or 360/694-2462) also publishes useful guides: the *Directory of Travel Agencies for the Disabled* (US$19.95), which lists more than 370 agencies worldwide, *Travel for the Disabled* (US$19.95) and *Wheelchair Vagabond* (US$14.95), as well as directories for accessible-van rental companies and cruise, ferry, river and canal-barge guides for the physically handicapped.

TRANSPORT AND FACILITIES

Most **airlines**, both transatlantic and internal, will do whatever they can to ease your journey, and will usually allow attendants of more seriously disabled people to accompany them at no extra charge – Air Canada is the best-equipped carrier.

The larger **car-rental** companies, like Hertz and Avis, can provide cars with hand controls at no extra charge, though these are only available on their most expensive models; book one as far in advance as you can – Hertz insists on the request being made five days before the car is needed and supplies are limited. A wheelchair-accessible **coach** with hydraulic lift and on-board accessible toilet can be rented from National Motor Coach Systems, Box 3220, Station B, Calgary, AB T2M 4L7 (☎403/240-1992). In order to obtain a **parking privilege permit**, disabled drivers must complete the appropriate form from the province in question. Contact addresses and organizations

vary from province to province, though the permit, once obtained from one province, is valid across Canada. Contact provincial tourist offices for details. In British Columbia you should contact the Social Planning and Research Council of British Columbia, 106-2182 W 12th Ave, Vancouver, BC V6K 2N4 (☎604/736-8118, fax 736-8697). Their conditions are typical: enclose a letter with name, address, phone number and date of birth; the medical name of the disabling condition; a letter from a doctor with original signature (*not* a photocopy) stating the disability that makes it difficult for a person to walk more than 100m and whether the prognosis is temporary or permanent. You should also include date of arrival and departure in Canada (BC), a contact address if known, a mailing address for the permit to be sent to, date and signature, and a cheque or money order for $15 to cover processing.

All VIA Rail **trains** can accommodate wheelchairs that are no larger than 81cm by 182cm and weigh no more than 114kg, though 24 hours notice is required for the Québec–Windsor corridor and 48 hours on other routes. They offer an excellent service, including served meals, roomettes at no extra charge for blind people travelling with a guide dog, as well as help with boarding and disembarking. Those who need attendants can apply for a two-for-one fare certificate under the "**Helping Hand**" scheme; it's available from the Canadian Rehabilitation Council for the Disabled, if you submit a medical certificate and an application signed by a doctor.

Although **buses** are obliged to carry disabled passengers if their wheelchairs fit in the luggage compartment, access is often difficult. However, nearly all bus companies accept the two-for-one "Helping Hand" certificates, and drivers are usually extremely helpful.

Larger **hotels** like *Holiday Inn* often have specially designed suites for disabled guests, and major motel chains like *Best Western* and *Journey's End* have full access – but it is always worth checking with the tourist offices (and the particular hotel) to confirm facilities.

INSURANCE, CRIME AND PERSONAL SAFETY

A typical travel insurance policy usually provides cover for the loss of baggage, tickets and – up to a certain limit – cash or cheques, as well as cancellation or curtailment of your journey. Most of them exclude so-called dangerous sports unless an extra premium is paid: in Canada this can mean white-water rafting and mountain climbing, though probably not kayaking. Read the small print and benefits tables of prospective policies carefully; coverage can vary wildly for roughly similar premiums. Many policies can be chopped and changed to exclude coverage you don't need – for example, sickness and accident benefits can often be excluded or included at will. If you do take medical coverage, ascertain whether bene-

fits will be paid as treatment proceeds or only after return home, and whether there is a 24-hour medical emergency number. When securing baggage cover, make sure that the per-article limit – typically under £500 equivalent – will cover your most valuable possession. If you need to make a claim, you should keep receipts for medicines and medical treatment, and in the event you have anything stolen, you must obtain an official statement from the police. Bank and credit cards often have certain levels of medical or other insurance included and you may automatically get travel insurance if you use a major credit card to pay for your trip.

Travel agents and tour operators are likely to require some sort of insurance when you book a package holiday, though according to UK law they can't make you buy their own (other than a £1 premium for "schedule airline failure"). If you have a good all-risks home insurance policy it may cover your possessions against loss or theft even when overseas. Many private medical schemes such as BUPA or PPP also offer coverage plans for abroad, including baggage loss, cancellation or curtailment and cash replacement as well as sickness or accident.

Americans and Canadians should also check that they're not already covered. Holders of official student/teacher/youth cards are entitled to meagre accident coverage and hospital inpatient benefits. Students will often find that their stu-

ROUGH GUIDES TRAVEL INSURANCE

Rough Guides now offer their own travel insurance, customized for our readers by a leading UK broker and backed by a Lloyds underwriter. It's available for anyone, of any nationality, travelling anywhere in the world, and we are convinced that this is the best-value scheme you'll find.

There are two main Rough Guide insurance plans: Essential, for effective, no-frills cover, starting at £11.75 for 2 weeks; and Premier – more expensive but with more generous and extensive benefits. Each offer European or Worldwide cover, and can be supplemented with a "Hazardous Activities Premium" if you plan to

indulge in sports considered dangerous, such as skiing, scubadiving or trekking. Unlike many policies, the Rough Guides schemes are calculated by the day, so if you're travelling for 27 days rather than a month, that's all you pay for. You can alternatively take out annual multi-trip insurance, which covers you for all your travel throughout the year (with a maximum of 60 days for any one trip).

For a policy quote, call the Rough Guides Insurance Line on UK freephone ☎0800/015 0906, or, if you're calling from outside Britain on (+44)1243/621046. Alternatively, get an online quote at *www.roughguides.com/insurance*.

dent health coverage extends during the vacations and for one term beyond the date of last enrollment. Homeowners' or renters' insurance often covers theft or loss of documents, money and valuables while overseas, though conditions and maximum amounts vary from company to company.

POLICE AND TROUBLE

There's little reason why you should ever come into contact with the **Royal Canadian Mounted Police** (RCMP), who patrol Canada in the form of provincial and metropolitan forces. In contrast to the US, there's very little street crime and even in Toronto, Vancouver and Montréal you shouldn't have any problems in terms of **personal safety** if you stick to the main parts of town, though it's obviously advisable to be cautious late at night. However, if you're drinking in one of the country's many rough-and-ready bars, don't be too surprised if there's a fight, though the males (very rarely females) involved will almost always be too busy thumping people they know to bother with a stranger – and hitting a woman (in this context) is almost unheard of. **Theft** is also uncommon, though it's obviously a good idea to be on your guard against petty thieves: always keep an eye on your luggage at bus and train stations, secure your things in a locker when staying in hostel accommodation, and avoid leaving valuables on a beach or in a tent or car.

Canadian officials are notorious for coming down hard if you're found with **drugs** – especially on non-Canadians. Stiff penalties are imposed,

even when only traces of any drug are found, so don't even think about it.

If you are unlucky enough to be attacked or have something stolen, phone the police on ☎911. If you're going to make an **insurance claim** or **travellers' cheque refund application**, ensure the crime is recorded by the police and make a note of their crime report number.

Should you lose your **passport**, contact the nearest consulate (see box below) and get them to issue a **temporary passport**, which is basically a sheet of paper saying you've reported the loss. This will get you home, but if you were planning to travel on from Canada, you'll need a new passport – a time-consuming and expensive process.

Another possible problem is **lost airline tickets**. On scheduled and most charter flights, the airline company will honour their commitment on the lost ticket (especially if they can contact the issuing agent), but you may have to pay for a new ticket and wait a period (often as long as six months) for reimbursement once the airline is satisfied the ticket has not been used. Whatever happens, it's bound to involve hassle at the airport and afterwards. With some bargain-basement tickets, airlines will also make you pay again unless you can produce the lost ticket's number. Similarly, if you lose your travel insurance policy document, you won't be able to make a claim unless you quote its number. To avert both calamities, keep a copy of the numbers or documents at home. For **lost travellers' cheques**, if you've followed the issuer's suggestion and kept a record of the cheque numbers separate from the

---

CONSULATES AND EMBASSIES

UK

Dartmouth, 1 Canal St (☎902/461-1381).

Montréal, Suite 4200, 1000 de la Gauchetière St W (☎514/866-5863).

Ottawa, 80 Elgin St (☎613/237-1530).

Québec City, Le Complexe St-Amable, 700-1150 Claire-Fontaine (☎418/521-3000).

St John's, PO Box 452, Station C (☎709/579-2002).

Toronto, Suite 2800, 777 Bay St (☎416/593-1290).

Vancouver, Suite 800, 1111 Melville St (☎604/683-4421).

Winnipeg, 229 Athlone Drive (☎204/896-1380).

US

Calgary, 615 MacLeod Trail SE (☎403/266-8962).

Halifax, Suite 910, Cogswell Tower, 2000 Barrington St (☎902/429-2485).

Montréal, 1155 St Alexander St (☎514/398-9695).

Ottawa, 490 Sussex Drive (☎613/238-5335).

Québec City, 2 Place Terrasse Dufferin, CP 939 (☎418/692-2095).

Toronto, 360 University Ave (☎416/595-1700).

Vancouver, 1095 W Pender St (☎604/685-4311).

actual cheques, all you have to do is ring the issuing company on their given toll-free number to report the loss. They'll ask you for the cheque numbers, the place you bought them, when and how you lost them and whether it's been reported to the police. All being well, the missing cheques should be reissued within a couple of days – and you may get an emergency advance to tide you over.

COSTS, MONEY AND BANKS

Most basic items cost less than in Britain and a bit more than they do in the US; more specific details are given below and throughout the *Guide*. Generally, if you're sticking to a very tight budget – camping and buying food from shops – you could squeeze through on £15–20/US$25–30 a day. You're not going to last long living like this, though, and a more comfortable average daily budget, covering a motel room, bus travel, a museum or two and a restaurant meal would work out at around £40–45/US$65–75. Naturally, once you upgrade your accommodation, eat out two or three times a day, and take in the city nightlife, this figure can easily double. Remember, too, that recently the Canadian dollar has been fairly weak, so if you're coming from abroad your money may stretch further than you thought – though of course there are no guarantees there.

CURRENCY

Canadian **currency** is the dollar ($), made up of 100 cents (¢) to the dollar. Coins are issued in 5¢ (nickel), 10¢ (dime), 25¢ (quarter), $1 and $2 denominations: the $1 coin is known as a "loonie" after the bird on one face; no one's come up with a suitable name for the newer $2 coin – "twoonie" has been tried but hasn't really caught on. Paper currency comes in $2, $5, $10, $50, $100, $500 and $1000 denominations. Although US dollars are widely accepted, it's often on a one-for-one basis, and as the US dollar is usually worth slightly more than its Canadian counterpart, it makes sense to exchange US currency. There's no limit to the amount of money you can take into or out of Canada.

CREDIT CARDS, ATMs, CHEQUES AND BANKS

One of the quickest and easiest ways of obtaining money in Canada is through an **ATM**, particularly if your home bank ATM card is on the Cirrus or Delta networks. It's also virtually essential to have at least one **credit card** to reserve and pre-pay for hotels or car rental, where otherwise you're likely to be asked for a big cash deposit: Visa, MasterCard, American Express and Diners are widely accepted. Credit cards can also be used to obtain **cash advances** over the counter in most banks but there will invariably be a minimum amount you can draw and you'll pay credit-card rates of interest on the cash from the date of withdrawal. If you have a PIN you can also obtain cash from ATMs with your credit card. With other

CURRENT EXCHANGE RATE

£1 = C$2.2

C$1 = £0.45

US$1 = C$1.54

C$1 = US$0.65

A$1 = C$0.84

C$1 = A$1.19

credit cards, state bank cards and ATM cards, you should check with your bank before leaving home.

While it's a good idea to have some Canadian cash from the outset, a good way to carry the bulk of funds is in **travellers' cheques**, available from banks and building societies, usually with a one percent commission on the amount ordered. (Exchange costs are usually waived if you have a bank-issued travel insurance policy.) Buy **cheques in Canadian dollars** and try to take American Express or Visa cheques, which are accepted as cash in virtually every shop, garage, restaurant and bar throughout Canada. Using travellers' cheques in this way is a better option than trying to cash them in a bank – a surprising number of major banks in Canada will not change travellers' cheques, and when they do you'll usually have to pay a commission.

If you run out of money abroad, or there is some kind of emergency, the quickest way to get **money sent out** is to contact your bank at home and have them wire the cash to the nearest bank. You can do the same thing through Thomas Cook or American Express (free to card holders) if there is a branch nearby, and can also have cash sent out through Western Union (☎1-800/235-0000 in Canada; ☎0800/833833 in UK; ☎1-800/325-6000 in US) to a bank, post office or local agent – a process that takes just minutes but will be expensive.

Banking hours are Monday to Thursday 10am to 3pm, and until 6pm on Fridays; the trend is increasingly to longer hours and Saturday morning opening. But don't rely on finding a bank open outside these core weekday hours. The main nationwide banks include the Toronto Dominion, the Royal Bank of Canada, the National Bank of Canada, the Bank of Montréal and the Canadian Western Bank.

AVERAGE COSTS

Canada is generally good value, a fact which becomes evident from the minute you wake up: cheap Canadian breakfasts are the stuff of legend, dishing up coffee, bacon, eggs and toast for around $8 or less, while healthier snacks like soups and salads cost from about $5.

Bus fares are reasonable, the twelve-hour journey from Vancouver to Calgary, for instance, costing about $115 one-way. **Trains** cost a good deal more – around $200 for the 24-hour trip from Vancouver to Edmonton – but usually much less than internal flights, though charter companies

like Canada 3000 are bringing prices of these flights down: Vancouver to Calgary, an hour's flight, will cost around $120 excluding tax on an early-morning or late-evening charter.

Room rates start at around $15 for a hostel dorm, and about $35 for a double in the grottier hotels. In most parts of the country, you should find perfectly good motel rooms from around $45. Basic town **campgrounds** are never expensive, and provincial and national sites start from as little as $10; in fully serviced commercial places it's rare to pay more than $25. Accommodation prices are higher from June to early September, and throughout the more remote areas of the north, particularly the Yukon and NWT.

TIPS AND TAXES

There are several hidden costs to take into account when travelling round Canada. **Tips and service** are generally not added to restaurant bills; it's usual to leave fifteen percent, even after the cheapest meals. More importantly, though, virtually all prices in Canada for everything from bubblegum to hotel rooms are quoted **without tax**. This means the price you see quoted is rarely the price you pay, and round-figures prices of things costing, say, $5 or $55, end up being ludicrous sums like $5.63 or $59.94.

There are both national and provincial taxes. The dreaded **Goods and Services Tax** (GST) – the equivalent of VAT in Europe – is a nationwide seven-percent charge levied on most goods and services, including hotel and restaurant bills. All provinces except Alberta, the Yukon and NWT levy a **Provincial Sales Tax** (PST) of five to ten percent on most goods and services, including hotel accommodation; only visitors to Québec (where it's called TVQ), Manitoba, Nova Scotia and Newfoundland can currently apply for a rebate – claim forms are supplied by tourist offices (the rebate situation changes from time to time, and some other provinces may start to offer rebates to keep their visitors sweet). A so-called **Harmonized Sales Tax** (HST), a fifteen-percent

---

Unless stated otherwise, all **accommodation prices** in this book are for high-season doubles, not including taxes; the majority of **entry charges** are the full adult ticket price – the majority of museums and similar attractions give at least fifty percent **discounts** for children and seniors, as well as **student reductions**.

combination of GST and PST, applies in Nova Scotia, New Brunswick, Labrador and Newfoundland. Most provinces also have a **hotel rooms' tax** of up to ten percent. The net result is that you can end up paying something like seventeen percent over the listed price for hotel rooms in some parts of the country.

As a small mercy, visitors can claim a **rebate** of GST on certain goods over the value of $3.50 if they're for use outside Canada and removed from the country within sixty days. More significantly, a GST rebate is available for **accommodation expenditure** over $100 during a maximum period of one month. Claim forms are available at many hotels, shops and airports or from any Canadian embassy. Return them, with **all original receipts**, to the address given on the form. People leaving by land to the US can claim their rebate at selected border duty-free shops. The amounts can add up, so it's worth thinking about. For more information call ☎902/432-5608 (outside Canada) or ☎1-800/668-4748 (within Canada).

HEALTH

It is vital to have travel insurance (see "Insurance, crime and personal safety" on p.25) against potential medical expenses. Canada has an excellent health service, but it costs nonresidents anything between $50 and $1000 a day to use. There is no free treatment to nonresidents, and in some provinces doctors and hospitals add a surcharge to treatment meted out to foreigners. If you have an accident, medical services will get to you quickly and charge you later.

Doctors can be found listed in the *Yellow Pages*, and ambulance services are usually displayed on the inside cover. In emergencies call ☎911. If you are bringing medicine prescribed by your doctor, bring a copy of the **prescription**; first, to avoid problems at customs and immigration and, second, for renewing medication with Canadian doctors. **Pharmacies** are often well equipped to advise on minor ailments and to distinguish between unfamiliar brand names. Most larger towns and cities should have one open 24 hours, and many chemists stay open late as a matter of course.

SPECIFIC HEALTH PROBLEMS

Canada requires no specific vaccinations, but problems can start when you're walking or camping in the backcountry. Tap water is generally safe to drink, though at campgrounds water is sometimes good for washing only – ask if in doubt. You should always boil **backcountry water** for at least ten minutes to protect against the **Giardia** parasite (or "beaver fever"), which thrives in warm water, so be careful about swimming in **hot springs** – if possible, keep nose, eyes and mouth above water. Symptoms are intestinal cramps, flatulence, fatigue, weight loss and vomiting, all of which can appear up to a week after infection. If left untreated, more unpleasant complications can arise, so see a doctor.

Blackfly and mosquitoes are notorious for the problems they cause walkers and campers, and are especially bad in areas near water and throughout most of northern Canada. Horseflies are another pest. April to June is the blackfly season, and the mosquito season is from July until about October. Before you go, take three times the recommended daily dosage of Vitamin B complex for two weeks, and take the recommended dosage while you're in Canada – this cuts down bites by up to 75 percent. Once you're there, repellent creams and sprays may help: the best repellents are those containing **DEET** – the ointment version of Deep-Woods Off is the best brand, with 95 percent DEET. If you're camping or picnicking you'll find that burning coils or candles containing allethrin or citronella can help (but watch those smells – they'll attract the bears; see pp.642–643). If you're walking in an area that's rife with pests, it's well worth taking a gauze mask to protect your head and neck; wearing white clothes and no perfumed products also makes you less attractive. Once bitten, an **antihistamine** cream like phenergan is the best antidote. On no account go anywhere near an area marked as a blackfly mating ground – people have died from bites sustained when the monsters are on heat.

The **nationwide emergency number** for police, fire or ambulance is ☎911, but in some remoter areas you will still have to call ☎0 for the operator.

If you develop a large rash and flu-like symptoms, you may have been bitten by a tick carrying **lyme borreliosis** (or "lyme tick disease"). This is easily curable, but if left can lead to nasty complications, so see a doctor as soon as possible. It's spreading in Canada, especially in the more southerly and wooded parts of the country. Check on its prevalence with the local tourist authority – it may be advisable to buy a strong tick repellent and to wear long socks, trousers and sleeved shirts when walking. Whether ticks give you anything or not, they're nasty on their own, burying into your skin, often after spending time moving surreptitiously over your body to find a nice warm soft spot.

In backcountry areas look out for **poison ivy**, which grows in most places, but particularly in a belt across southern Ontario and Québec, where poison-ivy ointment is widely available. If you're likely to be walking in affected areas, ask at tourist offices for tips on where it is and how to recognize the plant. It causes itchy open blisters and lumpy sores up to ten days after contact. Wash body and clothes as soon as possible after contact, smother yourself in calamine lotion and try not to scratch. In serious cases, hospital emergency rooms can give antihistamine or adrenalin jabs. Also keep an eye open for **snakes** in certain western areas; pharmacists and wilderness outfitters can advise on snakebite kits, and park wardens can give useful preventive advice. Should you get bitten without an antidote on you, get a good look at the culprit so that the doctor can identify the species and administer the right medicine.

If walking or climbing, go properly equipped and be prepared for sudden changes of weather. Watch out for signs of **exposure** – mild delirium, exhaustion, inability to get warm – and on snow or in high country during summer take a good **sun block**. Finally, of course, take the same precautions against **HIV** infection as you would back home – use a condom and don't share needles.

GETTING AROUND

It's essential to plan carefully how you'll get around. With VIA Rail services becoming more skeletal each year, provincewide bus companies provide the main surface links between major cities, though in isolated areas you may be thrown back on more sporadic local services. Flying is of course more expensive, but competition in the skies can lead to some decent bargains.

On most forms of public transport there are **discounted fares** for children under 12, for youths between 13 and 21, and over-60s. It has to be said, however, that things are always easier if you have a **car**: even if a bus can take you to the general vicinity of a provincial park, for example, it can prove impossible to explore the interior without your own vehicle.

BY BUS

If you're travelling on your own, **buses** are by far the cheapest way to get around. Greyhound Canada runs most of the long-distance buses west of Toronto, including a service along the Trans-Canada Highway from Toronto to Vancouver. The major centres in the east of the country are served by a network of smaller lines and by a wide range of different companies. **Long-distance buses** run to a fairly full timetable (at least during the day), stopping only for meal breaks and driver changeovers. Nearly all are nonsmoking, have toilets and coffee-making facilities and are less uncomfortable than you might expect – it's feasible to save on a night's accommodation by sleeping on the bus, though you may not feel up to much the next day.

Any sizeable community will have a main bus station, but in smaller places a gas station or restaurant will double as the bus stop and ticket office – though often they are inconveniently situated on the edge of town. Seats can be reserved but this is rarely necessary: only those services between nearby cities like Montréal and Québec are likely to get booked out, and even then you'll have to wait only an hour or so for the next departure. Out in the less populated areas, buses are fairly scarce, sometimes only appearing once or twice a week, and here you'll need to plot your route with care.

Fares are pretty standard from company to company: as an example, Toronto to Winnipeg, a distance of 2100km, costs $167 one-way. The free *Official Canadian Bus Guide*, containing all Canadian (and northern US) bus **timetables**, is produced bimonthly but is not made readily available to travellers. Consequently you'll need to rely on free individual timetables from the major bus stations or local tourist offices. Always double-check routes and times by phoning the local terminal (we've included telephone numbers for most cities), or the companies (see box, overleaf). For Greyhound Canada, reservations are not necessary; if a bus is full, another is automatically laid on. However, an increasing number of services can make "seat selection" for a small fee which guarantees a specific seat on the first bus out (useful for window-seat sightseeing).

PASSES

Travellers intending to explore Canada by bus can save a lot of money by purchasing one of two **passes** before leaving home. The **Canada Coach Pass** allows unlimited travel within a fixed time limit on all Greyhound Canada lines operating between Vancouver and Montréal and includes routes to New York, Seattle and Detroit; seven days travel within ten days $249; fifteen days travel in twenty days $379; thirty days travel in forty days $499; sixty days travel in eighty days $599.

The **Canada Coach Pass Plus** covers the same routes as well as service in Québec, Nova Scotia, New Brunswick and PEI for fifteen days travel in twenty days $425, thirty days travel in forty days $529, and sixty days travel in eighty days $685. Both passes are also valid for travel on VIA rail trains between Toronto–Ottawa–Montréal.

Go Canada Budget Travel Pass offers seven, fifteen, or thirty nights in seventy hostels across Canada over a seven-, fifteen-, thirty- or sixty-day period, and includes Canada Coach Pass or Canada Coach Pass Plus. The Go Canada Budget Travel Pass with Greyhound Canada Pass for seven consecutive nights is $456; seven nights in fifteen days $590, in thirty days $656, in sixty $790; fifteen consecutive nights $790; fifteen nights in thirty days $857, in sixty days $999; thirty consecutive nights $1168, thirty nights in sixty days $1310. The Go Canada Budget Travel Pass with Canada Pass Plus for seven nights in fifteen days $612, in thirty days $723, in sixty days $879; fifteen consecutive nights $821; fifteen nights in thirty days $932, in sixty days $1079; thirty consecutive nights $1244; thirty nights in sixty days $1391.

In the UK the passes are no longer available from Greyhound – although they can still give timetable info on ☎0870/888-0225 or *www.greyhound-uk.co.uk* – but can be puchased from STA Travel, usit, Trailfinders and other travel agents. Holders of ISIC and Euro under 26 cards and members of the YHA are entitled to a ten-percent discount on the purchase of the Canada Coach Pass and Coach Pass Plus.

If you are coming in from the **US**, note that **Greyhound**'s West Coast Pass is not valid for travel in Canada except for the Seattle to Vancouver route; while the Northeast Passes include travel to Toronto and Montréal.

The **Moose Travel Network** (☎1-888/816-6673, *www.moosenetwork.com*) runs a jump-on, jump-off mini-coach service around western and eastern Canada from May to October. The coaches stop at least three times a week at various locations and you can take as long as you want to complete your trip, the network also includes a hostel to hostel service. The West Pass costs $379 and makes a loop from Vancouver to Whistler, Kamloops, Valemount, Jasper, Lake Louise, Banff, Calgary, Vernon, Kelowna, Penticton, and back to Vancouver. In the East, the Loonie Pass ($219) travels from Montréal to Trois Rivieres, Québec City, Baie St Paul, Tadoussac, and Stoneham as well as into the Laurentians (Val David and Mont Tremblant); the Beaver Pass ($299) covers Montréal, Val David, Mont Tremblant, Ottawa, Wakefield, Fort Coulonge, Maynooth, Algonquin Park, Lake Simcoe, Toronto, Niagara, Sandbanks and Kingston. The East Pass combines the Beaver and Loonie and costs $379, while the Canada Pass, which covers all destinations, costs $700.

CANADA'S PRINCIPAL BUS COMPANIES

A J Bus Lines Ltd, Box 579, Elliot Lake, Ontario (☎705/838-3013). Service around Elliot Lake in northern Ontario.

Acadian Lines, 100 Midland Drive, Dieppe, New Brunswick (☎1-800/567-5151, fax 506/859-5111, *www.smtbus.com*). Nova Scotia and New Brunswick services.

Alaska Direct Busline, PO Box 501, Anchorage, Alaska (☎1-800/770-6652, fax 907/338-1951). Services from Whitehorse in the Yukon to Alaska.

Can-Ar Coach Service, 221 Caldan Rd, Concord, Ontario (☎905/738-2290, *www.can-arcoach.com*). Services around Toronto and southern Ontario.

Canadian Trailways, 877 Greyhound Way SW, Calgary, Alberta (☎403/265-9111). Montréal and Toronto to New York and Vancouver to Seattle services.

Cherrey Bus Lines, PO Box 83, Drayton, Ontario (☎519/658-3882). Services in southern Ontario.

Dewdney Coach Lines, 1355 Bay Ave, Trail, BC (☎250/368-8117). Small carrier in BC interior.

Farr's Coach Lines, RR8, Dunnville, Ontario (☎1-800/263-2106). Runs from Hamilton to Dunnville in Ontario.

Frontier Coachlines, 16 102nd St, Hay River, NWT (☎867/874-2566). Links Hay River to Yellowknife.

GO Transit, 20 Bay St, Toronto, Ontario (☎416/869-3200, *www.gotransit.com*). Toronto suburban service.

Grey Goose Bus Lines, 301 Burnell St, Winnipeg, Manitoba (☎204/784-4500). Routes around Manitoba from Winnipeg.

Greyhound Canada, 877 Greyhound Way SW, Calgary, Alberta (☎403/260-0877 or 1-800/661-8747 in Canada, ☎1-800/231-2222 in the US, or ☎0870/888 0225 in the UK, *www.greyhound.ca*). Long-distance buses in Ontario and western Canada.

Laidlaw, 700 Douglas St, Victoria, British Columbia (☎250/388-5248 or 1-800/318-0818, fax 250/388-9461, *www.victoriatours.com*). Services on Vancouver Island.

Laidlaw Canadian Rockies,141 Eagle Crescent, Banff, Alberta (☎1-800/661-4946, *www.laidlaw.ca*). Lake Louise to Banff.

McCoy Coach Lines, 1890 Hwy 5 W, Troy, Ontario (☎519/647-3444). Runs from Hamilton to Simcoe and Brantford in Ontario.

North Country Travel Lines, 815 Fort William Rd, Thunder Bay, Ontario (☎807/345-2194). Thunder Bay to Sioux Lookout in northern Ontario.

Northland Bus Lines, 700 Douglas St, Victoria, BC (☎604/388-5248). Fort St James to Prince George in BC.

Ontario Northland, 555 Oak St E, North Bay, Ontario (☎705/472-4500). Serves northern Ontario.

Orleans Express, 420 McGill St, Montréal, Québec (☎514/395-4000, *www.orleansexpress.com*). Québec services.

Penetang-Midland Coach Lines, 475 Bay St, Midland, Ontario (☎705/526-0161, *www.pmcl.on.ca*). Local Ontario service around Toronto and Georgian Bay.

Quick Shuttle, 2020 6 Rd, Unit B, Richmond, BC (☎604/244-3744, fax 244-3745, *www.quickcoach.com*). Vancouver to Seattle shuttle.

Red Arrow, 101 205 9th Ave SE, Calgary, Alberta (☎403/531-0350, *www.redarrow.pwt.ca*). Edmonton to Fort McMurray and Calgary in Alberta.

Saskatchewan Transportation, 2041 Hamilton St, Regina, Saskatchewan (☎306/787-3340, *www.sfn.saskatoon.sk.ca*). Services across Saskatchewan.

SMT (Eastern) Ltd, 100 Midland Drive, Dieppe, New Brunswick (☎506/859-5100, fax 859-5111, *www.smtbus.com*). Buses within New Brunswick, plus services from New Brunswick to New York and Charlottetown, PEI.

Southwestern Bus Line, 528 Ducker St, Boissevain, Manitoba (☎204/534-7111). Brandon to Boissevain service in Manitoba.

Trentway-Wagar, 791 Webber Ave, Peterborough, Ontario (☎705/748-6411 or 1-800/461-7661, fax 705/748-5314, *www.trentway.com*). Wide range of services within southern Ontario, plus routes into the US and Québec.

Voyageur-Colonial, 265 Catherine St, Ottawa, Ontario (☎613/238-5900, fax 238-6964, *voyageur.com/info.html*). Québec and Ontario routes.

Western Trailways of Canada, 7783 Progress Way, Delta, BC (☎604/940-5561, fax 940-5532). Vancouver to Seattle bus.

BY TRAIN

The railway may have created modern Canada but passenger trains are now few and far between – at the beginning of 1990 more than half the **VIA Rail** services were eliminated at a stroke and fares were increased dramatically. Services are notoriously slow and delays common as passenger trains give way to freight, though the city links between Montréal and Toronto are still speedy and efficient. However, rail travel can still be a very rewarding experience, especially on trains with special "dome cars" that allow an uninterrupted rooftop view of the countryside.

One of the saddest losses of the VIA cutbacks was the legendary Canadian train which followed the old Canadian Pacific lines daily from Montréal to Vancouver. Today's Canadian departs three times a week from Toronto and uses the more northerly old Canadian National lines, through the monotonous muskeg of northern Ontario, stopping at Winnipeg, Saskatoon and Edmonton before hitting Jasper. However, the scenery between there and Kamloops, the last big station before Vancouver, is some of the Rockies' best. The trip is scheduled to take three nights but usually runs late; it costs a minimum of $418 per person one-way in low season, $615 in high.

The other major VIA trains still running are the **Western Canada** services from Winnipeg to Churchill, Jasper to Prince Rupert, and Victoria to Courtenay; **Ontario** has services linking Toronto with Windsor, Ottawa and Niagara Falls; **Québec** has trains between Montréal and Québec City – as well as Ottawa; and the **Eastern Canada** network runs between Montréal, Halifax and the Gaspé.

FARES AND PASSES

One-way fares from Toronto to Winnipeg give an idea of the cost of rail travel. **Economy** class, the Canadian equivalent of second class, with reclining seats, costs $227 in low season, $303 in high (prices given respectively below), while **sleeper** class comes in three categories: **double berths**, with large seats that become curtained bunks at night, costing $850/1370 for two – and you can, of course, share with a stranger; **roomettes**, private single rooms with a toilet and a bed that folds out from the wall, costing $570/918; and **bedrooms**, which are spacious cabins with two armchairs, large windows, a table, toilet, wardrobe and bunk bed, costing $1138/1836, again for two. Meals are included in the price of all three sleeper-class categories.

Ten percent **reductions** are available for the over-60s, 2- to 15-year-olds pay half-fare, and students with an ISIC card can save up to 40 percent. In the Windsor/Québec City and Montréal/Halifax corridors, **off-peak fares** – on every day except Friday, Sunday and holidays – are often forty percent less than the standard rate, though discounted seats are limited and seven-day advance purchase is obligatory. Between the Maritimes and

---

VIA RAIL AGENTS

Australia
Canada and America Travel Specialists, ☎02/9922 4600. Wholesalers of Greyhound Ameripasses.

Rail Plus, ☎1300/555 003 or 03/9642 8644, *info@railplus.com.au*. Amtrak passes.

New Zealand
Rail Plus, ☎09/303 2484. Amtrak passes.
Walshes World, ☎09/379 3708. Greyhound passes.

UK
Leisurail, PO Box 5, 12 Connigsby Rd, Peterborough PE3 8HY (brochures ☎0870/750 0246, reservations ☎0870/750 0222, fax 0870/750 0111).

VIA RAIL TOLL-FREE INFORMATION

☎1-800/561-3926 in Newfoundland.
☎1-800/561-3952 in Prince Edward Island, Nova Scotia and New Brunswick.
☎1-800/361-5390 in Québec.

☎1-800/361-1235 (in area codes 519, 613, 705, 905) or ☎1-800/561-8630 (area code 807) in Ontario.
☎1-800/561-8630 from Manitoba, Saskatchewan, Alberta, British Columbia, Yukon and NWT.

Ontario or Québec, the standard rate is reduced by forty percent on economy travel all year except from mid-June to early September and from mid-December to early January, with the requirement of seven-days' advance purchase. In western Canada, a 25 percent (and sometimes even forty percent) reduction applies on Economy travel from November to mid-December and early January to late April; again a week's advance purchase is necessary.

Non-North American visitors can cut fares greatly by buying a **CANRAILPASS** (Jan–May and mid-Oct to mid-Dec $427; June to mid-Oct $684; additional days of travel $33/52; children, students, seniors $355/$545), which allows unlimited Economy class travel for twelve days within a thirty-day period. For further details, VIA can be reached on the Internet (*www.viarail.ca*) and they also have an international network of ticket agents. The passes can be purchased in Canada or abroad; when purchased in advance, travellers can earn up to three extra days of travel.

The **North America Rail Pass** (Jan–May and mid-Oct to Dec $465, June to mid-Oct $1050) allows unlimited travel on VIA trains in Canada and Amtrak trains in the US. Similarly the **Northeastern North America Pass** (Jan–June and Sept–Dec 15-day $288, 30-day $350, July–Aug 15-day $288, 30-day $372) is a pass for VIA and Amtrak trains in eastern Canada and US.

Moose Travel Network sells a **Canada Pass Link** ($345; ☎1-888/816-6673, *www.moosenetwork.com*) to complement their mini-coach service (see p.31); the pass allows three full days of train travel between Toronto and Vancouver by train.

PRIVATE RAIL LINES

Other than VIA Rail, various private companies operate passenger trains that travel through otherwise inaccessible wilderness. Most spectacular is the **Rocky Mountaineer** from Vancouver to Banff and then on to Calgary, or to Jasper, both with an overnight stop in Kamloops, which is best experienced through a package from Rocky Mountaineer Railtours (☎1-800/665-7245) or Leisurail (see box, overleaf). These tours, which are swiftly booked out, run from May to mid-October and cost $640 ($100 less in the shoulder season) one-way to Jasper or Banff, plus a supplement of $70 per person for one-way travel between Banff and Calgary. Rates do not include tax but do include light meals, and a night's hotel accommodation in Kamloops. Another west Canada option is **BC Rail** (☎604/986-2012, fax 984-5428, *www.bcrail.com*). They operate the steam train, the *Royal Hudson*, between Vancouver and Squamish (June–Sept Wed–Sun), the *Cariboo Prospector* between North Vancouver, Whistler and Lillooet and to points further north on to Prince George (thrice weekly), the *Whistler Explorer* from Whistler to Kelly Lake (May–Sept Mon–Fri) and the *Pacific Starlight Dinner Train*, an evening excursion on vintage 40s and dome cars (June–Sept).

In Ontario, trips can be made on Ontario Northland's **Polar Bear Express** (☎416/314-3750, fax 314-3729, *www.ontc.on.ca*), from Cochrane to Moosonee (Sat–Thurs late-June to Aug, see p.176–177); the **Little Bear Train** (thrice weekly), which operates on the same route as the Polar Bear but stops anywhere en route to drop off and pick up passengers; the **Northlander** (Sun–Fri), with service between Toronto and Cochrane; the **Algoma Central Railway** (June to mid-Oct daily ☎705/946-7300, fax 541-2989), through Agawa Canyon; the **Snow Train** (late Dec to early March Sat & Sun), which does the same route as the Algoma but in winter; and **regular passenger services** to Hearst from Sault Ste Marie.

Elsewhere, the **Québec North Shore and Labrador Railway** (2–3 weekly; ☎418/946-7803 or 709/944-8205/8401) operates between Sept-Îles and Schefferville with a stop at Labrador City. The **White Pass & Yukon Railway** (☎907/983-2217, fax 983-2734, *www.whitepassrailroad.com*) runs a coach service from Whitehorse that links up with the train route from Fraser to Skagway (mid-May to mid-Sept daily).

BY AIR

The complexity of Canada's **internal flight network** is immense, and throughout this guide we have given indications of which services are most useful. Now that Air Canada has bought Canadian Airlines, it has the most prolific domestic service, with planes serving more than 125 destinations, linking up with numerous minor lines – like Labrador Airways in Labrador – to reach the farthest-flung recesses of Canada. One company to look out for is Canada 3000, an economical, international carrier that also serves Canada's big cities and links Whitehorse with Vancouver. However, no one could pretend that flying around Canada is, in general terms at least, a low-budget

Air Canada *www.aircanada.ca*
British Columbia ☎1-800/661-3936.
Manitoba ☎1-800/542-8940.
New Brunswick and Nova Scotia ☎1-800/565-3940.
Newfoundland ☎1-800/563-5151.
Northwest Territories ☎1-800/663-9100.
Ontario ☎1-800/268-7240.
Prince Edward Island ☎1-800/776-3000.
Québec ☎1-800/361-8620.
Saskatchewan ☎1-800/665-0520.

Canada 3000 *www.canada3000.ca*
Calgary ☎403/221-1870.
Edmonton ☎403/890-4590.
Halifax ☎902/873-3030.
Montréal ☎514/476-9500.
St John's ☎709/576-0555.
Toronto ☎416/674-0257.
Vancouver ☎604/273-4883.
Winnipeg ☎204/784-0500.

option. For special bargains, look in the travel sections of local newspapers, especially on Sundays, or splash out on one of the many varieties of airpass (see below), each of which brings hefty discounts. If you're set on exploring the deep north, there is no alternative to air transport, as these zones are unpenetrated by rail line or road, with a few rare exceptions, such as Churchill in Manitoba.

PASSES

A multitude of **airpasses** provide internal air travel at special rates. The passes have to be bought before taking a transatlantic (or transpacific) flight, and are available in the UK from Air Canada, British Airways, Canadian Regional Airlines and Horizon Air. All are also available from travel agents.

All airpass deals are broadly similar, involving the purchase of at least three coupons for around £200 (with a maximum purchase of eight) extra coupons costing around £30 each. Every coupon is valid for a flight of any duration within the continent. Air Canada, with the strongest domestic connections, has a good variety of passes; study the possibilities carefully before committing yourself.

BY CAR

Travelling by **car** is the best way to see Canada, even though a vehicle can be a bit of a liability in the big cities, with their stringent parking areas and rush-hour tailbacks. Any US and UK national over 21 with a full driving licence is allowed to drive in Canada, though rental companies may refuse to rent to a driver who has held a full licence for less than one year, and under-25s will

probably get lumbered with a higher insurance premium. Car-rental companies will also expect you to have a credit card; if you don't have one they may let you leave a hefty deposit (at least $300) but don't count on it.

Most of Canada's vehicles – and almost every rental car – run on unleaded fuel, which is sold by the litre; prices vary, but are generally around 70–80¢ per litre. **Fuel** is readily available – there are literally hundreds of gas stations, though they thin out markedly in the more remote regions, where you should exercise some caution by checking locally about the distance to the next one.

CAR RENTAL

Often the least expensive way to **rent a car** is either to take a fly-drive package (see p.5–6) or book in advance with a major rental company like Avis, Budget, Hertz, Thrifty or Tilden (a Canadian outfit). Specialist agents can also offer economical deals – in the UK, Holiday Autos (☎0990/300400) are particularly good. Bear in mind also that at the height of the season in popular tourist areas it's a good idea to book ahead. Amongst the big car-rental companies competition is fierce and, as you might expect, special deals are more commonplace in the shoulder and low seasons when there are scores of vehicles lying idle. It's always worth ringing round to check rates – Budget and Thrifty usually have competitive tariffs. Finally, if you take a transatlantic flight, check to see if your airline offers discounted car rental for its passengers.

In Canada itself, expect to pay from around $250 a week for a two-door economy saloon in low season to $400 for a four-door medium car in high season, though throughout the year special promotions are offered by the major companies, which can get rates down to as low as $175 per week. Provincial **taxes** and GST or HST (see p.28) are not included in the rates, but the biggest **hidden surcharge** is often the **drop-off charge**, levied when you intend to leave your car in a different place from where you picked it up. This is usually equivalent to a full week's or more rental, and can go as high as $400. Also be sure to check if **unlimited mileage** is offered; an important consideration in a country where towns are so widely dispersed: the usual free quota is 150–200km per day – woefully inadequate if you're contemplating some serious touring – after which an extra charge of around 20¢ per kilometre is standard.

You should also check the policy for the excess applied to claims and ensure that, in general terms, it provides adequate levels of financial cover. Additionally, the **Loss Damage Waiver** (LDW), a form of insurance that isn't included in the initial rental charge, is well worth the expense. At around $14 a day, it can add substantially to the total cost, but without it you're liable for every scratch to the car – even if it wasn't your fault.

For **breakdown** problems, there'll be an emergency number attached to the dashboard or stored in the glove compartment. If you're stranded on a major highway, you could do as well to sit tight and wait for the **RCMP** (the police) who cruise by fairly regularly. An extra safety option is to rent a **mobile telephone** from the car-rental agency – you often only have to pay a nominal amount unless you actually use it. Having a mobile can be reassuring at least, and a potential life-saver for trips into the northern wilderness.

If you take a rental car **across the US–Canada border**, be sure to keep a copy of the contract with you. It should bear an endorsement stating that the vehicle is permitted entry into the US.

DRIVEAWAYS

A variation on car rental is a **driveaway**, whereby you drive a car from one place to another on behalf of the owner. The same rules as for renting apply, but you should look the car over before taking it as you'll be lumbered with any repair costs and a large fuel bill if the vehicle's a gas guzzler.

Most driveaway companies will want you to give a personal reference as well as a deposit in the $200–400 region. The most common routes are along the Trans-Canada Highway and between Toronto or Montréal and Florida in the autumn and winter, although there's a fair chance you'll find something that needs shifting more or less to where you want to go. You needn't drive flat out, although not a lot of leeway is given – around eight days is the time allowed for driving from Toronto to Vancouver. Driveaway companies are included in some city listings, or check under "Automobile driveaways" in the telephone directory.

RENTING AN RV

Recreational vehicles (RVs) can be rented through most travel agents specializing in Canadian holidays. It's best to arrange rental before getting to Canada, as RV-rental outlets are not too common there, and travel agents here will often give cheap rates if you book a flight through them as well. You can rent a huge variety of RVs right up to giant mobile homes with two bedrooms, showers and fully fitted kitchens. A price of around $1300 in low and $2100 in high season for a five-berth van for one week is fairly typical, and on top of that you have to take into account the cost of fuel (some RVs do less than 25km to the litre), drop-off charges, and the cost of spending the night at designated trailer parks, which is what you're expected to do. Canada also has strict regulations on the size of vehicle allowed; in Ontario, for example, the maximum length for a trailer is 48 feet, 75 feet for trailer plus car – so if you are coming in from the US check that your RV isn't over the limit. The best UK-based rental company is Hemmingways Ltd, 56 Middle St, Brockham, Surrey RH3 7HW (☎01737/842735, *www.hemmingways.uninet.co.uk*), with various packages and pick-up points throughout Canada or try Motorhome Direct, 6 Coney Hall Parade, Kingsway, West Wickham, Kent BR4 9JB (☎0870/511-0022).

ROADS, RULES AND REGULATIONS

The best **roads** for covering long distances quickly are the straight and fast multilane highways that radiate for some distance from major population centres. These have a maximum of six

MAJOR CAR-RENTAL COMPANIES

Australia

Avis ☎13 6333, *www.avis.com*
Budget ☎1-300/362 848, *www.budget.ca*
Hertz ☎1-800/555 067, *www.hertz.com*

Canada

Avis ☎1-800/387-7600 from Ontario and Québec; ☎1-800/268-2310 from elsewhere, *www.avis.com*
Budget ☎1-800/268-8970 from Québec; ☎1-800/268-8900 from elsewhere, *www .budget.ca*
Dollar ☎1-800/421-6868, *www.dollarcar.com*
Hertz ☎1-800/620-9620 from Toronto; ☎1-800/263-0600 from elsewhere, *www.hertz.com*
Rent-a-Wreck ☎1-800/327-0116, *www.rent-a -wreck.com*
Thrifty ☎1-800/367-2277, *www.thrifty.com*
Tilden ☎1-800/361-5334

New Zealand

Avis ☎0-800/655 111, *www.avis.com*
Budget ☎0-800/652 227, *www.budget.ca*
Hertz ☎0-800/655 955, *www.hertz.com*

UK

Alamo ☎0870/600 0008, *www.goalamo.com*
Avis ☎0870/590 0500, *www.avis.com*
Budget ☎0800/181181, *www.gobudget.co.uk*
Dollar (Europcar) ☎0845/722 2525, *www .europcar.com*
Hertz ☎0990/906090, *www.hertz.com*
Holiday Autos ☎0870/400 0000,*www .holidayautos.co.uk*
Pelican ☎01625/586666, *www.pelicancarhire.com*
Suncars ☎0990/005566, *www.suncars.com*
Sunstyle ☎01932/225544, *www.bargain-car -rental.co.uk*
Thrifty ☎0990/168238, *www.thrifty.com*

US

Alamo ☎1-800/327-9633, *www.goalamo.com*
Avis ☎1-800/831-2847, *www.avis.com*
Budget ☎1-800/527-0700, *www.budget.com*
Dollar ☎1-800/800-4000, *www.dollar.com*
Hertz ☎1-800/654-3131, *www.hertz.com*
National ☎1-800/227-7368, *www.nationalcar.com*
Rent-a-Wreck ☎1-800/944-7501, *www.rent-a -wreck.com*
Thrifty ☎1-800/367-2277, *www.thrifty.com*

lanes divided by a central causeway and are marked on maps with thick lines and shields that contain the highway number. Outside populated areas, highways go down to one lane each way and, though paved, the hard shoulder consists of gravel – which you must on all accounts avoid hitting at speed as this will throw you into a spin, a potentially lethal experience. Up in the north and off the beaten track, highways may be entirely of gravel – broken windscreens are an occupational hazard on some stretches of the Alaska Highway, for example. Note also that after rain gravel and dirt roads are especially treacherous and indeed if you're planning a lot of dirt-road driving, you'd be well advised to rent a four-wheel-drive. The Trans-Canada Highway (TCH) travels from coast to coast and is marked by maple-leaf signs at regular intervals along its length. Different sections of the TCH do, however, carry different highway numbers and in some places the TCH forks to offer more than one possible routing. Lesser roads go by a variety of names – county roads, provincial routes, rural roads or forest roads. Out in the wilds rural and forest roads are rarely paved.

Canadians drive on the **right-hand** side of the road. In most **urban areas** streets are arranged on a grid system, with traffic lights at most intersections; at junctions without lights there will be either yellow triangular "Yield" signs or red octagonal "Stop" signs ("Arrêt" in Québec) at all four corners. In the latter case, **priority** is given to the first car to arrive, and to the car on the right if two or more cars arrive at the same time. Except in Québec, you can turn right on a red light if there is no traffic approaching from the left. Traffic in both directions must stop if a yellow school bus is stationary with its flashing lights on, as this means children are getting on or off. Roundabouts or rotaries are almost unknown.

Exits on multilane highways are numbered by the kilometre distance from the beginning of the highway, as opposed to sequentially – thus exit 55 is 10km after exit 45. This system works fine, but gets a little confusing when junctions are close together and carry the same number supplemented by "A", "B", etc. Rural **road hazards** include bears, moose and other large animals trundling into the road – particularly in the summer, and at dawn and dusk, when the beasts crash through the undergrowth onto the highway to escape the flies, and in spring, when they are attracted to the salt on the roads. Warning signs are posted in the more hazardous areas. Headlights can dazzle wild animals and render them temporarily immobile.

Driving laws are made at provincial level, but the uniform **maximum speed limit** is 100kph on major highways, 80kph on rural highways and 50 kph or less in built-up areas – though there has been some provincial tinkering with the maximum limit on the highways, experiments which may result in permanent change. Canadians have a justifiable paranoia about speed traps and the traffic-control planes that hover over major highways to catch offenders – if you see one, slow down. On-the-spot fines are standard for speeding violations, for failing to carry your **licence** with you, and for having anyone on board who isn't wearing a **seat belt**.

Canadian law also requires that any alcohol be carried unopened in the boot of the car, and it can't be stressed enough that **drunk driving** is a very serious offence. Bars in some provinces now have **designated driver schemes** whereby the driver of a group gives the keys to the head barperson and is then given free soft drinks all night; if the driver is spotted taking a sip of alcohol, he or she must pay for all the soft drinks consumed and leave their keys in the bar until the following morning. On the road, spot checks are frequently carried out, particularly at the entrances and exits to towns, and the police do not need an excuse to stop you. If you are over the limit your keys and licence will be taken away, and you may end up in jail for a few days.

In cities **parking meters** are commonplace, charging 25¢–$1 or more per hour. Car parks charge up to $30 a day. If you park in the wrong place (such as within 5m of a fire hydrant) your car will be towed away – if this happens, the police will tell you where your car is impounded and then charge you upwards of $150 to hand it back. A minor parking offence will set you back around $25; clamps are also routinely used in major cities, with a fine of between $100 and $150. Also, when parking, ensure you park in the same direction as the traffic flows.

If you're using your own vehicle – or borrowing a friend's – get the appropriate insurance and make sure you're covered for free **breakdown service**. Your home motoring organization will issue an appropriate insurance and breakdown policy with all the appropriate documentation. The Canadian Automobile Association, Suite 200, 1145 Hunt Club Rd, Ottawa, ON K1V 0Y3 (☎613/820-1890), is the biggest recovery and repair company in Canada, and has offices in most major cities.

RIDE-SHARING

Ride-sharing is an established means of travel within the more heavily populated parts of Canada. Organizations coordinating ride-share travel come and go – local tourist offices will have the latest details – but Allo-Stop, with main offices in Montréal and Toronto, is well established. With them, all you pay is a nominal registration fee and a share of the fuel costs – Toronto to Ottawa will set you back about $30, less if you are with other people. Rides are also routinely advertised on university and youth-hostel notice boards.

BY BIKE

Cyclists are reasonably well catered for in environment-friendly Canada: most cities have cycling lanes and produce special maps for cyclists, and long-distance buses and trains will allow you to transport your bike, perhaps for a small fee. The Canadian Cycling Association (CCA), 1600 James Naismith Drive, Gloucester, ON K1B 5N4 (☎613/748-5629, *www.canadiancycling.com*), can offer information on cycling throughout the country and publishes several books, including the invaluable *Complete Guide to Cycling in Canada* ($24 including postage and packing). Standard **bike-rental** costs are around $15 per day, plus a sizeable cash sum or a credit card as deposit; outlets are listed throughout the *Guide*.

DRIVING DISTANCES IN KILOMETRES

The figures shown on this chart represent the total distances in kilometres between selected cities in the Canada and the US. They are calculated on the shortest available route by road, rather than straight lines drawn on a map. One kilometre equals five-eighths of a mile.

	Calgary	Chicago	Edmonton	Halifax	Montréal	New York	Ottawa	Regina	St John's	Seattle	Toronto	Vancouver	Whitehorse	Winnipeg	Yellowknife
Calgary	–														
Chicago	2760	–													
Edmonton	299	2750	–												
Halifax	4973	2603	5013	–											
Montréal	3743	1362	3764	1249	–										
New York	4294	1280	4315	1270	610	–									
Ottawa	3553	1220	3574	1439	190	772	–								
Regina	764	2000	785	4225	2979	3534	2789	–							
St John's	6334	3950	6767	1503	2602	2619	2792	5581	–						
Seattle	1204	3200	1352	5828	4585	4478	4334	1963	7200	–					
Toronto	3434	825	3455	1788	539	880	399	2670	3141	4050	–				
Vancouver	977	3808	1164	5970	4921	5382	4531	1742	7323	230	4412	–			
Whitehorse	2385	4854	2086	7099	5850	5660	5382	2871	8452	2796	5528	2697	–		
Winnipeg	1336	1432	1357	3456	2408	2966	2218	571	5010	2548	2099	2152	3524	–	
Yellowknife	1828	4240	1524	6537	5268	5800	5098	2309	7891	2500	4979	2620	1927	2681	–

ACCOMMODATION

Accommodation isn't hugely expensive in Canada, but is still likely to take a good portion of your budget. The least expensive options are camping and dormitory beds in hostels, where prices start at around $15 but be aware that campgrounds and hostels in cities are heavily used. In hotels and motels, double rooms start at around $60; less in rural areas away from the big sights. People on their own pay relatively more, but for travellers in pairs or groups motels and hotels can work out costing little more than hostels.

Canada is big and empty. If you're heading into remote parts of the country, always check the availability of accommodation before setting off. Places that look large on the map often have few facilities at all, and US visitors will find motels far scarcer than in similar regions back home. Wherever you intend to stay, it's best to try to **book a room** well before you arrive, particularly in summer and especially in big national parks like Banff and popular major cities such as Montréal, Québec, Toronto and Vancouver. Also look out for local events and festivals such as the Calgary Stampede, when accommodation is always at a premium. If you're arriving late, stress the fact, as **reservations** are generally held only until 6pm, or even 4pm in major resorts. Reservations can be made over the phone by credit card. Wherever possible take advantage of **toll-free numbers**, but note that some are accessible only in restricted areas, typically a single province, or in Canada or North America only. It can also be worth confirming check-in/check-out times, particularly in busy areas, where your room may not be available until late afternoon. Check-out times are generally between 11am and

1pm. Be certain to **cancel** any bookings you can't make, otherwise the hotel or motel is within its right to deduct a night's fee using your credit card details. Most places have a 24-hour-notice cancellation policy, but in places like Banff it can be as much as three days.

Also be prepared to pay for at least the first night in advance, and be ready for a fifteen percent **surcharge** to a room's advertised price, the result of provincial sales and federal taxes. **Costs** can be kept down if you're in a group – most places will set up a third bed in a double room for around $15 – though single travellers have a hard time of it, for single rooms are usually double rooms let out at only marginally reduced rates. **Costs** also come down outside high season, typically mid-May to early September (Labour Day) when the country's smartest hotels often offer especially large discounts. Also be on the lookout for weekend rates, or last-minute deals offered by hotels trying to fill empty rooms.

Local tourist information offices can often help out with accommodation if you get stuck: most offer free advice and will book a place free of charge, but few are willing to commit themselves to specific recommendations. Some large resorts, like Banff and Jasper in the Rockies, have a privately run central reservations agency that will find rooms for a small fee. Before going to Canada it's worth picking up the full accommodation and camping listings put out by the provinces (see p.20 for office addresses); they all give details of prices, size and facilities.

HOTELS

It is consistently easy to find a plain room in all but Canada's more remote backwoods. Drivers approaching any significant town or city are confronted by ranks of motels on prominent highways, neon signs advertising their presence, room rates and room availability. In-town **hotels** tend to fall into one of two categories: high-class five-star establishments or grim downtown places, often above a bar. Middle-ground spots are thin on the ground, their role often being filled by motels, which are basically out-of-town hotels by another name.

Top-of-the-range hotels can be very grand indeed, for instance particularly those run by

Canadian Pacific in busy tourist spots like Québec City, Banff and Lake Louise. In the cities, the emphasis is on the business traveller rather more than the tourist. Top-notch hotels charge anywhere between $150 and $500, though $250 would get you a fairly luxurious double in most places. It's always worth enquiring about mid-week reductions and out-of-season discounts, as these can reduce rates to as low as $100 a night. If you are going to treat yourself, think whether you want the sort of old-style comfort and building offered by traditional hotels or the high-tech polish provided by the new breed of luxury hotel: most cities and some resorts have both types.

Mid-price hotels are often part of a chain, such as *Holiday Inn* or *Best Western*, and usually offer a touch more comfort than middling motels. You should be able to find a high-season double in such places from around $90; more if you're in a well-known resort or the downtown area of a major city.

Bottom-bracket hotels – those costing anything from $25 to $45 – are mostly hangovers from the days when liquor laws made it difficult to run a bar without an adjoining restaurant or hotel. Found in most medium- and small-sized towns, they usually have the advantage of being extremely central – often they've been there since the town first sprang to life – but the disadvantage is that the money-generating bars usually come first, with the rooms mostly an afterthought. Many have strip joints or live music likely to pound until the small hours, and few pay much attention to their guests, many of whom are long-stay clients as seedy as the hotel itself. Rooms are mostly battered but clean, but probably won't have much in the way of facilities beyond a washbasin and TV. Basic meals are often on hand in the bar, though you'd usually do better to eat in a nearby café or restaurant.

MOTELS

Motels may be called inns, lodges, resorts or motor hotels, but they all amount to much the same thing: driver-friendly, reasonably priced and reliable places on the main highways almost always on the edge of town. The simplest rooms start at around $45, with the **average** price nearer $60 – though in resorts and more remote areas it's not unusual to find well over $100 being charged for what are fairly basic rooms. As a rule of thumb, prices drop in the larger centres the further you move from downtown. Many offer **off-season rates**, usually between October and April, some have triple- or quadruple-bedded rooms, and most are fairly relaxed about introducing an extra bed into "doubles" for a nominal charge. Many also offer a **Family Plan**, whereby youngsters sharing their parents' room stay free. You may also be able to negotiate cheaper deals if you're staying more than one night, and especially if you're staying a week – many places advertise weekly rates.

In all but the most basic motels you can expect a remarkably good standard: a good-sized double bed, a private bathroom, TV and phone, while in smarter places there may be frills like free coffee and the use of saunas, jacuzzis, sun beds and swimming pools. Often there's not much to be gained in paying extra for motels: you don't get a much better deal or better facilities by paying, say, $75 instead of $50. Some places, though, have rooms with **kitchenettes** for self-catering, or basic cooking facilities, either included in the room price or available for a few dollars more. More ritzy spots may also have a small restaurant, but generally you can expect nothing in the way of **food and drink** except for a soft-drinks machine and coffee-maker in the room. What they all have is good parking, often right in front of the door to your room.

BED AND BREAKFAST

In recent years there has been a dramatic increase in the number of **B&Bs/Gîtes du Passant** both in the big cities and in the towns and villages of the more popular resort areas. Standards in B&B homes or guesthouses are generally very high, and prices are around $50 and upwards per couple including breakfast. There are no real savings over cheaper hotels and motels. This said, you may wind up with a wonderful – if often over-homely – room in a heritage building in a great location, with the chance to meet Canadians on closer terms. There are, however, things to watch out for and ask about when making a booking. There's an increasing tendency to provide a light continental breakfast rather than a cooked meal with all the trimmings that'll set you up for the day. Establishments are often keen to indicate whether they have a private guest entrance, useful if you're likely to be staggering in late or simply don't particularly want to mix with your hosts. Another trend is for smaller hotels to advertise themselves as a "Bed and Breakfast Inn", or something similar, meaning simply that they're privately owned rather than in the hands of a chain. These are usually intimate but rather expensive places and not B&Bs in the accepted sense. B&B establishments have a quite rapid turnover, so to find one it's often best to visit tourist offices, many of which have bulging catalogues and photographs of what's available, or in the big cities contact one of the many private agencies who can line you up with something suitable. Take careful note of an establishment's location: in cities and larger towns they're often out in the suburbs and inconvenient for transport and downtown sights, though some hosts will pick you up from the airport or bus station on your arrival.

HOSTELS

Canada has about eighty **Hostelling International** (HI) hostels affiliated to what was formerly known as the International Youth Hostels Federation (IYHF), and many more nonaffiliated mini-hostels (also known as Homes or Backpackers' Hostels), which may or may not figure in HI literature. Reports suggest certain nonaffiliated hostels are slipping in standard as their cheap beds are appropriated by long-stay clients rather than by genuine visitors on a budget. Some are downright unsafe. These sorts of places are also often shoestring operations and may close at short notice. Similarly, new ones appear each year. Try to check local reputations at tourist offices or by word of mouth.

HI hostels are graded in four categories (basic, simple, standard and superior), and accommodation is mostly in single-sex dorms, which cost $10–25 for members, depending on category and location, though family and private double rooms are becoming more prevalent. In theory you're supposed to be an HI member to use hostels; in practice you can usually join the HI on the spot, or rely on most hostels making a higher charge for nonmembers ($12–28). However, most hostels will generally give preference to members, which is an important consideration in some of the more popular locations. Most hostels offer communal recreation areas and all have cooking facilities, plus pillows and blankets, though you're expected to provide, or rent, your own sheet sleeping bag and towels; normal sleeping bags are generally not allowed.

Many hostels have improved beyond recognition in the past few years: premises have been renovated, hostels are open longer and later, cafeterias have been introduced, and the booking system has been partly computerized. You can now book up to six months in advance at the bigger, or gateway, hostels; notably those in the Rockies, where hostels at Banff and Calgary act as central booking agents for a number of smaller hostels around the region. Most major hostels now accept credit-card bookings, with **reservations** strongly recommended in summer for city hostels and most of the Rockies' hostels (toll-free across North America ☎1-800/444-6111). Most HI offices around the world stock the comprehensive Hostelling North America handbook, as do many of Canada's larger hostels.

Mini-hostels tend to be private homes or tiny commercial hotels with breakfast included. Prices

---

ACCOMMODATION PRICE CODES

Throughout this book, accommodation prices have been graded with the symbols below, according to the cost of the least expensive double room in high season.

However, with the exception of the budget motels and lowliest hotels, there's rarely such a thing as a set rate for a room. A basic motel in a seaside or mountain resort may double its prices according to the season, while a big-city hotel in Québec or Vancouver that charges $200 per room during the week will often slash its tariff at the weekend when all the business visitors have gone home. The high and low seasons for tourists vary widely across the country, but as a general rule **high season** refers to July and August, **shoulder season** is May, June, September and October, and **low season** refers to the rest of the year.

Local and federal taxes will also add around fifteen percent to rates. Only where we explicitly say so do the room rates we've indicated include local taxes.

① up to $40	④ $80–100	⑦ $175–240
② $40–60	⑤ $100–125	⑧ $240+
③ $60–80	⑥ $125–175	

YOUTH HOSTEL INFORMATION

Australia
Australian Youth Hostels Association, 1422 Kent St, Sydney (☎02/9261 1111).

Canada
Hostelling International (HI), Room 400, 205 Catherine St, Ottawa, ON K2P 1C3 (☎613/237-7884 or 1-800/444-6111 in Canada).

England and Wales
Youth Hostel Association (YHA), Trevelyan House, 8 St Stephen's Hill, St Albans, Hertfordshire AL1 2DY (☎01727/855215). London information office: 14 Noel St, London W1V 3PD (☎020/7734 1618).

Ireland
An Oige, 39 Mountjoy Square, Dublin 1 (☎01/363111).

New Zealand
Youth Hostels Association of New Zealand, 173 Gloucester St, Christchurch 1 (☎03/379 9970).

Northern Ireland
Youth Hostel Association of Northern Ireland, 56 Bradbury Place, Belfast BT7 1RU (☎028/9032 4733).

Scotland
Scottish Youth Hostel Association, 7 Glebe Crescent, Stirling FK8 2JA (☎01786/891400, *www.syha.org.uk*). There's also an outlet at 161 Warrender Park Rd, Edinburgh EH9 1EQ (☎0131/229 8660, fax 229 2456).

USA
Hostelling International – American Youth Hostels (HI-AYH), 733 15th St NW, Suite 840, PO Box 37613, Washington, DC 20005 (☎202/783-6161, *www.iynf.org*).

are about $10–20, with a surcharge for nonmembers, and you must have your own sheet sleeping bag. A full current list is available from most larger youth hostels.

YS AND STUDENT ACCOMMODATION

Both the **YMCA** and **YWCA** – often known as "Ys" – have establishments in most Canadian cities. In many cases the quality of accommodation is excellent, matching that of the cheaper hotels, and invariably exceeding that of most other hostel-type lodgings. Often the premises have cheap **cafeterias** open to all, and sports facilities, gymnasium and swimming pools for the use of guests. **Prices**, however, reflect the comforts, and though you can usually find bunks in shared dorms from about $15, the trend is increasingly for single, double and family units (with or without private bathrooms), ranging between $30 and $100 depending on private or shared bathroom. This still reflects excellent value, especially in cities, where Ys are usually in central downtown locations. As Ys become more like hotels, so you need to treat them as such, with credit-card **reservations** in advance virtually essential to secure private singles and doubles

in high summer. Most places keep a number of rooms and dorm bunks available each day for walk-in customers, though in places like Banff it's not unknown for queues for these to develop around the block first thing in the morning. The old demarcation of the sexes is also breaking down, though many YWCAs will only accept men if they're in a mixed-sex couple. Some YWCAs accept women with children, others only in emergencies.

In Canada's university cities it's possible to stay in **student accommodation** during vacations. Anyone can use the facilities, though priority is usually given to other students. Often the accommodation is adequate and functional, if soulless, and you'll have access to the campus's sports facilities; on the downside, most places are a good distance from city centres. Prices for single and double rooms start from about $35. Most campuses have a special office to handle such accommodation, and it's a good idea to call well ahead to be sure of a room.

FARM VACATIONS

Farm vacations, on which you spend time as a paying guest on a working farm, give you the chance to eat well, sleep cheaply – and even work (if you want) – as well as mingle with your hosts. There are often a wide range of outdoor activities on tap. Most places offer daily or weekly accommodation, either on rough campsites from as little as $5 per day, bed and breakfast from $20, or room and full board from $35 daily. Most provinces now have farm vacation associations to prepare lists of farms and inspect facilities. For further details, consult tourist offices or provincial accommodation guides or call Farm Tours (☎01509/618810) Devonshire House, Devonshire Lane, Loughborough, Leic's, LE11 0BL or Bay Farm Tours (☎01524/423444), 35 Euston Rd, Morecomber, Lancs LA4 5DF.

CAMPING

Few countries offer as much scope for **camping** as Canada. Many urban areas have a campsite; all national parks and the large proportion of provincial parks have outstanding government-run sites, and in most wilderness areas and in the vast domain of Canada's federally owned Crown Lands you can camp rough more or less where you please, though you should ask permission where possible and – for your own safety and the sake of the environment – adhere strictly to all rules and recommendations that apply to camping in the backcountry. If you're travelling with a tent, check a campsite's small print for the number of **unserviced** (tent) sites, as many places cater chiefly for **recreational vehicles** (RVs), providing them with **full or partial hook-ups** for water and electricity (or "serviced sites"). Anywhere described as an "RV Park" ought to be avoided completely (unless, of course, you have an RV).

During July and August campsites can become as busy as all other types of accommodation in cities, and particularly near mountain, lake or river resorts. Either aim to arrive early in the morning or book ahead – we've given phone numbers wherever this is possible. Generally reservations can only be made at private campsites, not – crucially – at national park or provincial park campsites, where access is mostly on a first-come, first-served basis. This state of affairs is, however, slowly changing, with places at a selection of provincial and national park campsites now reservable through a reservation phone number. Finally, check that your chosen site is open – many campsites only open seasonally, usually from May to October.

CAMPSITE TYPES

At the bottom of the pile are **municipal campsites**, usually basic affairs with few facilities, which are either free or cost only a few dollars – typically $5 per tent, $10 per RV, though many often have tent places only. **Private campsites** run the gamut: some are as basic as their municipal cousins, others are like huge outdoor pleasure domes with shops, restaurants, laundries, swimming pools, tennis courts, even saunas and Jacuzzis. As for **price**, private campsites have several ways of charging. Some charge by the vehicle; others per couple; comparatively few on a tent or per-person basis. Two people sharing a tent might pay anything between $2.50 and $25 each, though an average price would be nearer $15. You can book places in private campsites but there's often no need outside busy areas as most are obliged to keep a certain number of pitches available on a first-come, first-served basis.

Campsites in **national and provincial parks** are run by Parks Canada and individual provincial governments respectively. All are immaculately turned out and most, in theory, are **open** only between May and September. In practice most are available all year round, though key facilities are offered and fees collected only in the advertised period: off season you may be expected to leave fees in an "honesty box". You'll usually find at least one site serviced for **winter camping** in the bigger national parks, particularly in the Rockies. **Prices** vary from about $8.50 to $20 per tent depending on location, services and the time of year – prices may be higher during July and August. See "Outdoor pursuits", p.54, for more details.

Sites in the **major national parks**, especially close to towns, usually offer a full range of amenities for both tents and RVs, and often have separate sites for each. As a rule, though, provincial sites and more remote national park campsites tend to favour tents and offer only water, stores of firewood and pit toilets. Hot showers, in particular, are rare. But both national park and provincial sites, of course, invariably score highly on their scenic locations. Both types of park campsite fill most of their pitches on a **first-come, first-served** basis, but a growing number of parks are setting up reservation services.

PRIMITIVE CAMPING

Camping rough – or **primitive camping** (or backcountry camping) as it's known in Canada –

has certain rules that must be followed. Check that fires are permitted before you start one – in large parts of Canada they aren't allowed in summer because of the risk of **forest fire**. If they are permitted, use a fire pit (if provided), or a stove in preference to local materials. In wilderness areas, try to camp on previously used sites.

Be especially aware of the precautions needed when in bear country (see p.642–643). Where there are no toilets, bury human waste at least 10cm into the ground and 30m from the nearest water supply and campsite. Canadian parks ask for all rubbish to be carried away; elsewhere burn rubbish, and what you can't burn, carry away.

Never drink from rivers and streams, however clear and inviting they may look. If you have to drink **water** that isn't from taps, you should boil it for at least ten minutes, or cleanse it with an iodine-based purifier (such as Potable Aqua) or a Giardia-rated filter, available from camping or sports shops.

EATING AND DRINKING

Canada's sheer number of restaurants, bars, cafés and fast-food joints is staggering, but at first sight there's little to distinguish Canada's mainstream urban cuisine from that of any American metropolis: the shopping malls, main streets and highways are lined with pan-American food chains, trying to outdo each other with their bargains and special offers.

However, it's easy to leave the chain restaurants behind for more interesting options – increasingly so, as the general standard of Canadian cooking has improved dramatically in the last few years. In the big cities there's a plethora of ethnic and speciality restaurants, on either seaboard the availability of fresh fish and shellfish enlivens many menus, and even out in the country – once the domain of unappetizing diners – there's a liberal supply of first-rate, family-run cafés and restaurants, especially in the more touristy areas. Non-smokers may also be relieved to know that almost every café and restaurant has a nonsmoking area and increasing numbers don't allow smoking at all.

BREAKFAST

Breakfast is taken very seriously all over Canada, and with prices averaging between $5 and $12 it's often the best-value and most filling meal of the day. Whether you go to a café, coffee shop or hotel snack bar, the breakfast menu, on offer until around 11am, is a fairly standard fry-up – eggs in various guises, ham or bacon, streaky and fried to a crisp, or skinless and bland sausages (except for Nova Scotia's famous Lunenburg sausage, a hot spicy version pioneered by settlers from Europe). Whatever you order, you nearly always receive a dollop of fried potatoes (called hash browns or sometimes home fries). Other favourite breakfast options include English muffins or, in posher places, bran muffins, a glutinous fruitcake made with bran and sugar, and **waffles** or **pancakes**, swamped in butter with lashings of maple syrup. Also, because the breakfast/lunch division is never hard and fast, mountainous meaty **sandwiches** are common too.

Whatever you eat, you can wash it down with as much **coffee** as you can stomach: for the price of the first cup, the waiters/waitresses will – in most places – keep providing free refills until you beg them to stop. The coffee is either **regular** or **decaf** and is nearly always freshly ground and very tasty, though lots of the cheaper places dilute it until it tastes like dishwater. In the big cities, look out also for specialist coffee shops, where the range of offerings verges on the bewildering. As a matter of course, coffee comes with cream or **half-and-half** (half-cream, half-milk) – if you ask for skimmed milk, you're often met with looks of disbelief. **Tea**, with either lemon or milk, is also drunk at breakfast, and the swisher places emphasize the English connection by using imported brands – or at least brands that sound English.

LUNCH AND SNACKS

Between 11.30am and 2.30pm many big-city restaurants offer special **set menus** that are generally excellent value. In Chinese and Vietnamese establishments, for example, you'll frequently find rice and noodles, or dim sum feasts for $7 to $10, and many **Japanese** restaurants give you a chance to eat sushi very reasonably for under $15. **Pizza** is also widely available, from larger chains like *Pizza Hut* to family-owned restaurants and pavement stalls. Favourites with white-collar workers are **café-restaurants** featuring wholefoods and vegetarian fare, though few are nutritionally dogmatic, serving traditional meat dishes and sandwiches too; most have an excellent selection of daily lunch specials for around $9.

For quick **snacks**, many **delis** do ready-cooked food, including a staggering range of sandwiches and filled bagels. Alternatively, shopping malls sometimes have **ethnic fast-food stalls**, a healthier option (just about) than the inevitable burger chains, whose homogenized products have colonized every main street in the land. Regional snacks include **fish and chips**, especially in Newfoundland; Québec's traditional thick, yellow pea soup, smoked meat sandwiches and **poutine**, fries covered in melted mozzarella cheese or cheese curds and gravy; and the Maritimes' ubiquitous **clam chowder**, a creamy shellfish and potato soup.

Some city **bars** are used as much by diners as drinkers, who turn up in droves to gorge themselves on the free **hors d'oeuvres** laid out between 5pm and 7pm from Monday to Friday in an attempt to grab commuters. For the price of a drink you can stuff yourself with pasta and chilli. **Brunch** is another deal worth looking out for; a cross between breakfast and lunch served up in bars at the weekend from around 11am to 2pm. For a set price ($10 and up) you get a light meal and a variety of complimentary cocktails or wine.

MAIN MEALS

Largely swamped by the more fashionable regional-European and ethnic cuisines, traditional **Canadian cooking** relies mainly on local game and fish, with less emphasis on vegetables and salads. In terms of price, meals for two without wine average between $25 and $50.

Newfoundland's staple food is the cod, usually in the form of fish and chips, supplemented by salmon, halibut and hake and more bizarre dishes like cod tongues and cheeks, scruncheons (fried cubes of pork fat), smoked or pickled caplin and seal flipper pie. The island's restaurants are not usually permitted to sell moose or seal meat, but many islanders join in the annual licensed shoot and, if you befriend a hunter, you may end up across the table from a hunk of either animal.

In the **Maritimes**, lobster is popular everywhere, whether it's boiled or broiled, chopped up or whole, as are oysters, clams, scallops and herrings either on their own or in a fish stew or clam chowder. **Nova Scotia** is famous for its blueberries, Solomon Gundy (marinated herring), Annapolis Valley apple pie, fat archies (a Cape Breton molasses cookie) and rappie pie (an Acadian dish of meat or fish and potatoes). **New Brunswick** is known for its fiddleheads (fern shoots) and dulse (edible seaweed). Fish are **Ontario**'s most distinctive offering – though the pollution of the Great Lakes has badly affected the freshwater catch. Try the whitefish, lake trout, pike and smelt, but bear in mind that these are easier to come by in the north of the province than in the south. Pork forms a major part of the **Québec** diet, both as a spicy pork pâté known as creton, and in tourtière, a minced pork pie. There are also splendid thick pea and cabbage soups, beef pies (cipâte), and all sorts of ways to soak up maple syrup – trempette is bread drenched with it and topped with fresh cream. And, of course, Québec is renowned for its outstanding French-style food.

Northern **Saskatchewan and Manitoba** are the places to try fish like the goldeye, the pickerel and Arctic char, as well as pemmican (a mixture of dried meat, berries and fat) and fruit pies containing the Saskatoon berry. The **Arctic** regions feature caribou steak, and Alberta is also noted for its beef steaks. Finally, **British Columbia** cuisine features Pacific fish and shellfish of many different types, from cod, haddock and salmon to king crab, oysters and shrimp. Here and there, there's also the odd native people's restaurant, most conspicuously

TIPPING

Almost everywhere you eat or drink, the service will be fast and friendly – thanks to the institution of **tipping**. Waiters and bartenders depend on tips for the bulk of their earnings and, unless the service is dreadful, you should top up your bill by fifteen percent or more. A refusal to tip is considered rude and mean in equal measure. If you're paying by credit card, there's a space on the payment slip where you can add the appropriate tip. If you don't know how much to tip, a good bet is to double the tax.

at the **Wanuskewin Heritage Park** in Saskatoon, Saskatchewan, where the restaurant serves venison, buffalo and black-husked wild rice.

Although there are exceptions, like the Ukrainian establishments spread across central Manitoba, the bulk of Canada's **ethnic restaurants** are confined to the cities. Here, amongst dozens of others, Japanese restaurants are fashionable and fairly expensive; Italian food is popular and generally cheap, providing you stick to pizzas and basic pasta dishes; and there's the occasional Indian restaurant, mostly catering for the inexpensive end of the market. East European food is a good, filling standby, especially in central Canada, and cheap Chinese restaurants are common throughout the country. French food, of course, is widely available – though, except in Québec, it's nearly always expensive.

DRINKING

Canadian bars, like their American equivalents, are mostly long and dimly lit counters with a few customers perched on stools gawping at the bartender, and the rest of the clientele occupying the surrounding tables and booths. Yet, despite the similarity of layout, bars vary enormously, from the male-dominated, rough-edged drinking holes concentrated in the blue-collar parts of the cities and the resource towns (dealing in mining and oil) of the north, to more fashionable city establishments that provide food, live entertainment and an inspiring range of cocktails. Indeed, it's often impossible to separate restaurants from bars – drinking and eating are no longer the separate activities they mostly were up until the 1960s.

The **legal drinking age** is 18 in Alberta, Manitoba, Québec, Northwest Territories, Saskatchewan and the Yukon and 19 in the rest of the country, though it's rare for anyone to have to

show ID, except at the government-run liquor stores (closed Sun), which exercise a virtual monopoly on the sale of alcoholic beverages of all kinds direct to the public; the main exception is Québec, where beer and wine are sold at retail grocery stores.

BEER

By and large, Canadian beers are unremarkable, designed to quench your thirst rather than satisfy your palate. Everywhere they're served ice-cold, and light, fizzy beers rule the roost. The two largest Canadian brewers, **Molson** and **Labatts**, market a remarkably similar brew under all sorts of names – Molson Canadian, Molson Export, Labatts Ice, Labatts Blue – that inspire, for reasons that elude most foreigners, intense loyalty. The tastier **Great Western Beer** is made by the country's third largest brewer, based in Saskatoon, Saskatchewan, while the heavily marketed **Moosehead** beer, despite its Arctic image, is produced in Saint John, New Brunswick. There's also a niche market for foreign beers, although **Heineken**, the most popular, is made under licence in Canada; American beers like **Budweiser** and **Coors** are common, too. A welcome trend is the proliferation of independent small breweries, or microbreweries, whose products are sold in a pub on the premises, but as yet these remain pretty much confined to the bigger cities.

Drinking bottled beer in a bar works out a good deal more expensive than the draught, which is usually served by the 170ml glass; even cheaper is a pitcher, which contains six or seven glasses.

WINE AND SPIRITS

Once something of a joke, **Canadian wines** are fast developing an excellent reputation, particularly those from Ontario's Niagara-on-the-Lake region, which are subject to the stringent quality control of the Vintners Quality Alliance, or the VQA (see p.115). However, if you don't want to experiment, **imported wines** from a wide range of countries are readily available and not too pricey.

Copying its giant neighbour, Canada excels with its **spirits**. Even in run-of-the-mill bars there are startling arrays of gins and vodkas, and usually a good selection of rums. In the more traditional places, the most popular liquor is **whiskey** – either Scottish and Irish imports or the domestically made Canadian Club and VO rye whiskey. In the smarter places, you can experiment with all sorts of **cocktails**, costing anywhere between $4 and $10.

COMMUNICATIONS, POST, PHONES AND THE MEDIA

POSTAL SERVICES

Post office opening hours are Monday to Friday 8.30am to 5.30pm, though a few places open on Saturday between 9am and noon. Offices are sometimes found inside larger stores, so look out for Canada Post signs, or Postes Canada in Québec. **Stamps** can also be bought from automatic vending machines, the lobbies of larger hotels, airports, train stations, bus terminals and many retail outlets and newsstands. Within Canada, letters and postcards up to 30g cost 46¢, to the US 55¢ for under 30g, and international mail up to 20g is 95¢. If you're posting letters to Canadian addresses, always include the postcode or your mail may never get there.

USEFUL TELEPHONE NUMBERS AND CODES

DIRECTORY ENQUIRIES

For directory assistance call ☎411 unless you need a number in another province, in which case dial ☎1, then the area code (see below) + 555-1212. The operator's number is ☎0.

EMERGENCY

☎911; ask for the appropriate emergency service: fire, police or ambulance. In smaller towns and rural areas, you may need to dial 0 for an operator, who will connect you to the proper emergency service.

PROVINCE CODES

Alberta ☎403 (Southern Alberta including Banff and Calgary); ☎780 (North of Red Deer, including Edmonton)

British Columbia ☎604 (Vancouver); ☎250 (rest of BC)

Manitoba ☎204

New Brunswick ☎506

Northwest Territories ☎867

Nova Scotia ☎902

Newfoundland and Labrador ☎709

Nunavut ☎867

Ontario ☎416 and ☎647, after 2001 when all local Toronto numbers will become 10-digit (Toronto region); ☎705 (central and northeast); ☎519 (southwest peninsula); ☎613 (Ottawa region); ☎807 (northwest)

Prince Edward Island ☎902

Québec ☎514 (Island of Montréal and surrounding islands); ☎450 (Greater Montréal region, including Laurentians and Eastern Townships); ☎819 (north); ☎418 (east)

Saskatchewan ☎306

Yukon ☎867

INTERNATIONAL CODES

For direct international calls from Canada, dial ☎011, then the country code (see below), the area code minus its first 0, and then the subscriber's number.

Australia ☎61

Belgium ☎32

Denmark ☎45

Germany ☎49

Ireland ☎353

Italy ☎39

Netherlands ☎31

New Zealand ☎64

Spain ☎34

Sweden ☎46

Switzerland ☎41

UK ☎44

SWIFTCALL NUMBERS

London ☎020/7488 0800 or ☎0800/769 8000, or ☎1488 from a British Telecom residential phone. UK (outside London) ☎0800/769 8000 or ☎1488 from a BT residential phone.

Ireland ☎1-800/929800 or ☎131277 from a residential phone or ☎1-800/929111 from a pay- or mobile phone.

CALLING CANADA FROM ABROAD

From the UK, dial 001 + province code + subscriber number.

From the US, dial 1 + province code + subscriber number.

From Australia, dial 0011 + country code.

From New Zealand, dial 00 + country code.

Letters can be sent **poste restante** to any Canadian main post office by addressing them c/o General Delivery or c/o Poste Restante in Québec. Make a pick-up date if known, or write "Hold for 15 days", the maximum period mail will usually be held. After that time the post is returned to sender, so it's a good idea to put a return address on any post. Take some ID when collecting. Letters will also be held by hotels; mark such mail "Guest Mail, Hold for Arrival". If you have an American Express card or travellers' cheques, you can have mail marked "Client Mail Service" sent to Amex offices throughout Canada. Others can pick up mail from Amex for a small fee.

TELEPHONES AND TELEGRAMS

Coin-operated telephones are available in most public places. Whenever you are dialling a number outside the telephone region of the call box you are using, you have to prefix the number with 1; this puts you through to the operator, who will tell you how much money you need to get connected. The operator asks for an amount (about $2.50) to cover the initial time period, which even within a province is fairly brief. Thereafter you'll be asked to shovel money in at regular intervals, so unless you're making a reverse-charge/collect call you need a stack of coins – usually quarters (25¢). Some connections within a single telephone code area are charged at the long-distance rate, and thus need the "1" prefix; a recorded message will tell you if this is necessary as soon as you dial the number. Local calls cost 25¢ from a public phone and are dialled direct; private subscribers pay nothing for these, so you'll find that shops often don't mind you

using their phone for local calls. Emergency (☎911) and information (☎411 local, ☎555-1212 long distance) are free from payphones.

Long-distance calls are cheapest from 11pm to 8am daily, and most expensive from 8am to 6pm Monday to Friday. From 6pm to 11pm on Monday to Saturday and from 8am to 11pm on Sunday, charges are more economical. Detailed rates are listed at the front of the **telephone directory**.

Needless to say, using pocketfuls of money is an inconvenient way of making **international calls**. Payphones taking major credit cards, however, are increasingly common, especially in transport and major tourist centres. In some cities there are Bell offices that enable you to make your call and pay afterwards.

Nearly all the provincial and national phone companies produce **local** and **long-distance calling cards**. Cards are sold in various outlets, including petrol stations, pharmacies and post offices, and in various denominations from $5 to $50, with calls being offered at discounted rates. You are given a number to dial and then a PIN number before you dial your destination. AT&T and other companies also produce affinity cards whereby the cost of your call is debited directly from your credit- or debit-card account.

More upmarket hotels and motels have **direct-dial** phones where the call is automatically charged to your bill. Elsewhere, the hotel switchboard operator will place a call for you, or you'll be linked to an operator who will ask for the room number to which to charge the call – but be warned that virtually all hotels will levy a service charge in the region of 65–95 percent.

Many hotels, tourist offices and transport companies have **toll-free numbers** (prefixed by ☎1-800, 1-877 or 1-777). Some of these can only be dialled from phones in the same province, others from anywhere within Canada, a few from anywhere in North America – as a rough guideline, the larger the organization, the wider its toll-free net.

Increasingly popular the world round, cellular **phones** (mobiles) are sold pretty much everywhere and are sometimes available to rent from information centres in major cities. However, the cheapest and most popular phones are only sold to Canadian residents. Pay-as-you-go accounts are generally expensive to use, and limited to the province you're in. Check before leaving home if your existing mobile can have its chip replaced to operate in Canada. Mobile-phone reception in Canada is still quite limited, and may not work out in the wilds.

To send a **telegram** either within Canada or abroad, contact the local AT&T Canada office, listed in the telephone directory. Credit card holders can dictate messages over the phone. At any time, day or night, you can also phone in **Telepost** messages, a guaranteed next-day or sooner service in Canada and the US; billing arrangements are made at the time of giving the message. **Intelpost** is an international fax service available at main post offices, and paid for by cash.

INTERNATIONAL CALLS

In Britain, it's possible to obtain a free **BT chargecard** (☎0800/345144, *www.bt.com*), with which all calls from overseas can be charged to your domestic account, but they are expensive. To use these cards in Canada, call ☎1-800/408-6420 and you will be asked for your account number and PIN.

British visitors who are going to be making a number of calls to Canada, should take advantage of the **Swiftcall** telephone club (touch tone only ☎0800/769 0800, *www.swiftcall.com*); once you've paid, by credit card, for however many units you want, you are given a 7-digit account number and a 4-digit PIN. Any time you want to get an international line, simply dial the numbers in the box (above), punch in your account number and PIN, and then dial as you would were you in Canada, putting a 001 before the area code, followed by the number. Calls to Canada cost about 6p per minute.

In the **US** you can get telephone calling/bank credit cards from the companies listed below, who can also supply long-distance phonecards and "prepaid" debit phonecards: AT&T (☎1-800/CALL-ATT) or Sprint (☎1-800 PIN-DROP).

Australia's Telstra Telecard (application forms available from Telstra offices) and **New Zealand** Telecom's Calling Card (contact ☎04/382 5818) can be used to make calls charged to a domestic account or credit card.

FAX AND EMAIL

Fax machines are found at hotels, city post offices and at photocopy shops, Internet cafés and similar establishments in main city centres. Charges are generally $1 a page.

Most major cities and small towns now have cybercafés, where you can **email**. They tend to charge around $2–5 an hour for use of their computers, and you can generally sup on cappuccinos and snack on sandwiches. You can also access email at most large, corporate hotels, public libraries and potentially a host of other establishments. If you don't already have an account you can access while abroad, just sign on for one of the many free options, like *www.hotmail.com*, *www.juno.com*, and so on; a quick Internet search will reveal many others.

THE MEDIA

Canada has no truly national **newspaper**. The closest thing is the daily *Globe and Mail*, a Toronto broadsheet also published in a western edition and available more or less throughout the country. Most cities have a quality paper, like the *Toronto Star*, *Calgary Herald*, *Ottawa Citizen* or *Vancouver Sun*, which is also available throughout their province. In Quebec, the French-language *La Presse* is the most widely read in the province and there's also the separatist *Le Devoir*. The conservative *Maclean's* and *Time Canada* are the most popular weekly news magazines. The monthly *Canadian Geographic* covers the great outdoors through articles and fantastic photographs.

To low-budget travellers, watching cable **television** in a motel room may well be the commonest form of entertainment. The Canadian Broadcasting Corporation (CBC) with national and regional broadcasts has the largest volume of Canadian programmes. The main commercial station is the Canadian Television Corporation (CTV), a mix of Canadian, American and national output. There are other public-broadcasting channels and private broadcast companies whose output makes Canada's TV very similar to mainstream American TV. Most US stations can also be picked up.

The majority of Canadian **radio** stations, too, stick to a bland commercial format. Most are on the AM band and display little originality – though they can be good sources of local nightlife and entertainment news, and road and weather reports. On FM, on the other hand, the nationally funded CBC channels provide diverse, listenable and well-informed programmes – for example

This Morning (Mon–Fri 9am–noon), a phone-in programme that gives a good grasp of Canadian opinions and happenings. Although some of the large cities boast good specialist music stations, for most of the time you'll probably have to resort to skipping up and down the frequencies. Driving through rural areas can be frustrating, as for hundreds of kilometres you might only be able to receive one or two very dull stations. With this in mind, it's worth asking your car-rental agency if their cars are fitted with cassette players.

OPENING HOURS, TIME ZONES AND HOLIDAYS

Most shops and supermarkets open from about 9am to 5.30pm Monday to Saturday, though in bigger towns and cities supermarkets and malls may open as early as 7.30am and close around 9pm. Enforced Sunday closing of shops, bars and restaurants operates over much of the country, but a growing number of provinces now have limited Sunday hours, usually 9am to 5pm, particularly in touristy areas. As a general rule, **between BC and Québec there are limited Sunday opening hours; and east of Québec shops will be shut on Sunday. Many retail shops open late on Thursday and Friday evenings. In cities you usually find a pharmacist open 24 hours and there's often a convenience store like Mac's or 7-11 that's open around the clock.**

Time of year makes a big difference to opening times of **information centres, museums** and

NATIONAL HOLIDAYS

New Year's Day (Jan 1)
Good Friday
Easter Sunday
Easter Monday
Victoria Day (third Mon in May)
Canada Day (July 1)

Labour Day (first Mon in Sept)
Thanksgiving (second Mon in Oct)
Remembrance Day (Nov 11)
Christmas Day (Dec 25)
Boxing Day (Dec 26)

PROVINCIAL HOLIDAYS

Alberta Alberta Family Day (third Mon in Feb); Heritage Day (first Mon in Aug).

British Columbia British Columbia Day (first Monday in August).

New Brunswick New Brunswick Day (first Mon in Aug).

Newfoundland and Labrador St Patrick's Day (March 17); St George's Day (third Mon in April); Discovery Day (third Mon in June); Memorial Day (first Mon in July); Orangeman's Day (third Mon in July).

Nova Scotia, Manitoba, NWT, Ontario and Saskatchewan Civic Holiday (first Mon in Aug).

Nunavut Nunavut Day (April 1).

Québec Epiphany (Jan 6); Ash Wednesday; Ascension (forty days after Easter); Saint-Jean-Baptiste Day (June 24); All Saint's Day (Nov 1); Immaculate Conception (Dec 8).

Yukon Discovery Day (third Mon in Aug).

FESTIVALS AND EVENTS

For further details of the selected festivals and events listed below, including more precise dates, see the relevant page of the *Guide*, or contact the local authorities direct. The provincial tourist offices listed on p.20 can provide free calendars for each area.

JANUARY

Polar Bear Swim, Vancouver, BC. A New Year's Day swim in the freezing waters of English Bay Beach – said to bring good luck for the year.

Banff/Lake Louise Winter Festival, Banff and Lake Louise, Alberta. Ski races, skating parties and the incredible International Ice Sculpture Competition on the shores of Lake Louise.

FEBRUARY

Winterlude, Ottawa, Ontario. Winter-warming activities like ice sculpting, snowshoe races, ice boating and skating for all on the canal.

Winter Carnival, Québec City, Québec. Eleven-day festival of winter-sports competitions, ice-sculpture contests and parades. Includes the Canadian ski marathon when skiers race between Lachute and Gatineau.

MARCH

Pacific Rim Whale Festival, Vancouver Island, BC. Celebrating the spring migration of grey whales with lots of whale-spotting expeditions as well as music and dance events.

APRIL

TerrifVic Jazz Party, Victoria, BC. Dixieland, and other jazz bands, from around the globe.

Shaw Festival, Niagara-on-the-Lake, Ontario. Highly regarded theatre festival featuring the work of George Bernard Shaw and his contemporaries. Performances from April to late October.

MAY

Apple Blossom Festival, Annapolis Valley, Nova Scotia. Community-oriented festival held in the small towns and villages of the apple-producing Annapolis Valley.

Stratford Festival, Stratford, Ontario. The small town of Stratford is well-known for its first-class Shakespeare Festival. Runs from May to early November.

Canadian Tulip Festival, Ottawa, Ontario. Three million tulips in an orgy of colour all over the city.

JUNE

Jazz City International Festival, Edmonton, Alberta. Ten days of jazz concerts, free outdoor events and workshops.

Banff Festival of the Arts, Banff, Alberta. Young-artist showcase – music, opera, dance, drama, comedy and visual arts.

International Blues Festival, Halifax, Nova Scotia. Big musical event showcasing the best of US and Maritime blues.

Metro International Caravan, Toronto, Ontario. Nine-day multiethnic celebration with some fifty pavilions dotted across the city.

International Jazz Festival, Montréal, Québec. 2000 jazz acts, including the world's top names, and 75 percent of the performances are free.

JULY

Pow-wows. Traditional aboriginal celebrations that take place on reserves across the country in July and August.

Calgary Stampede, Calgary, Alberta. One of the biggest rodeos in the world: all the usual cowboy trappings, plus hot-air-balloon races, chuck-wagon rides, craft exhibitions, native dancing and a host of other happenings. Billed as the "Greatest Outdoor Show on Earth".

other attractions, most of which, particularly in remote areas, have shorter winter hours or close altogether from late September to mid-May. In cities, more upmarket **restaurants** usually open from around noon to 11pm, longer at weekends; many diner-type places, however, close around 8pm, and small-town restaurants tend to close early too. Opening regulations for **bars** – often part of a hotel or restaurant – vary tremendously from province to province; most open daily from 10am to 1am, but in certain areas all bars except a few hotel lounges are shut on Sunday.

TIME ZONES

Canada has six time zones, but only 4.5hrs separate Newfoundland from British Columbia. Newfoundland is on Newfoundland Standard Time (3hr 30min behind GMT); the Maritimes and

Klondike Days, Edmonton, Alberta. Pioneer era in Edmonton revisited with gold panning, raft races, pancake breakfasts and gambling.

Loyalist City Festival, Saint John, New Brunswick. Celebration of the city's loyalist heritage with parades in period costume.

Antigonish Highland Games, Antigonish, Nova Scotia. All sorts of traditional Scottish sports and activities recall the settlement of the area by Highlanders.

Atlantic Jazz Festival, Halifax, Nova Scotia. First-class jazz festival pulling in big names from round the world.

Canada Day, Ottawa, Ontario and throughout Canada. Fireworks, parades and a day off for patriotic shenanigans.

Caribana Festival, Toronto, Ontario. Large-scale West Indian carnival with music, dance and a flamboyant parade.

Festival d'Été, Québec City, Québec. Arts performances, live bands and other shows on and off the sun-filled streets and parks of Québec City.

Juste Pour Rire, Montréal, Québec. The funniest festival in Canada. Internationally acclaimed comic get-together with comedians from around the world performing in theatres and outdoor stages.

AUGUST

Fringe Theatre Festival, Edmonton, Alberta. One of North America's most prestigious alternative-theatre festivals.

Squamish Days Loggers Sports Festival, Squamish, BC. The continent's biggest lumberjacks' convention with impressive logging competitions.

Acadian Festival, Caraquet, New Brunswick. Celebration of Acadian culture in the northeast of New Brunswick.

Miramichi Folk Song Festival, Newcastle, New Brunswick. New Brunswick's prestigious folk festival, featuring many of the finest fiddlers in the Maritimes.

Nova Scotia Gaelic Mod, South Gut, St Ann's, Nova Scotia. Seven-day Scottish heritage knees-up with all traditional sports, crafts and contests featured. One of the biggest and best of many similar events in Nova Scotia.

World Film Festival, Montréal, Québec. Eclipsed by Toronto's new film festival, but still a good showcase for new movies.

SEPTEMBER

Toronto International Film Festival, Toronto, Ontario. Internationally acclaimed film festival spread over ten days, inundated with Hollywood stars.

OCTOBER

Vancouver International Film Festival, Vancouver, BC. Another of Canada's highly rated film fests.

Okanagan Wine Festival, Okanagan, BC. One of the many wine events in this vine-growing region.

Oktoberfest, Kitchener-Waterloo, Ontario. Alcohol and cultural events in honour of the twin towns' roots.

NOVEMBER

Canadian Finals Rodeo, Edmonton, Alberta. Pure Canuck rodeo.

Royal Agricultural Winter Fair, Toronto, Ontario. The world's largest agricultural indoor fair, apparently.

DECEMBER

Coral Ships, Vancouver, BC. When carol singers sail around Vancouver harbour in sparkly boats.

New Year's Eve, throughout Canada, but celebrated in style in St John's, Newfoundland, where everyone heads from the pub to the waterfront for a raucous midnight party.

Labrador are on Atlantic Standard Time (4hr behind GMT); Québec and most of Ontario are on Eastern Standard Time (5hr behind GMT); Manitoba, the northwest corner of Ontario and eastern Saskatchewan are on Central Standard Time (6hr behind GMT); west Saskatchewan, Alberta, the Northwest Territories and a slice of northeast British Columbia are on Mountain Standard Time (7hr behind GMT), and the Yukon and the bulk of British Columbia are on Pacific Standard Time (8hr behind GMT). Nunavut runs from Mountain Standard Time to Atlantic Standard Time. Daylight saving – when the clocks are put forward one hour – is in effect in all regions except Saskatchewan and northeast British Columbia from the first Sunday in April to the last Saturday in October.

Train, bus and plane **timetables** are always given in local time; something it's worth bearing in mind if you're making long journeys across several zones. Most timetables use the 24-hour clock; those that do not, notably Greyhound bus schedules, use light type for am, bold for pm.

Daylight saving time takes effect in Canada in all regions except Saskatchewan and the northeast corner of British Columbia. Clocks go forward one hour on the first Sunday of April, and back one hour on the last Sunday in October.

HOLIDAYS

Banks, schools and government buildings all over the country close on Canada's **national** **holidays**, and within specific regions on the **provincial holidays** that fall on certain – often moveable – days throughout the year. Many shops, restaurants, museums and sights remain open, however. Campsites, smaller information centres, B&Bs and many resort hotels often use Victoria Day and Labour Day or Thanksgiving as markers for their open and closed seasons. University students have their holidays from May to early September (plus a one- or two-week break in March), while schoolchildren take theirs from the end of June to Labour Day.

OUTDOOR PURSUITS

Canada's mountains, lakes, rivers and forests offer the opportunity to indulge in a vast range of outdoor pursuits. We've concentrated on hiking, skiing and canoeing – three of Canada's most popular activities – and on the national parks, which have been established to preserve and make accessible the best of the Canadian landscape.

Other popular activities such as whale-watching, horse riding, fishing and rafting are covered in some detail in the main text, but whatever activity interests you, be certain to send off to the provincial tourist offices for information before you go. Once in Canada you can rely on finding outfitters, equipment rental, charters, tours and guides to help you in most areas; tourist offices invariably carry full details or contact numbers. Also make a point of visiting Canadian bookshops – most have a separate outdoor pursuits section with a wide variety of specialist guides.

THE NATIONAL PARKS

Canada's thirty or so **national parks** are administered by Parks Canada, a federal body, with information provided locally by **park information centres** (though the terminology may vary from park to park). Visit these to pick up special **permits** if you intend to fish or camp in the backcountry, and for information and audiovisual dis-

plays on flora, fauna and outdoor activities. Many offer talks and nature walks presented by park naturalists, as well as reports on snow, weather and recent bear sightings. **Regulations** common to all national parks include a total ban on firearms, hunting, snowmobiles or off-road vehicles, the feeding of wildlife, and the removal or damaging of any natural objects or features.

Note that most national park regulations relating to the care of the environment and campsite behaviour are usually applicable to **provincial parks**. Entry to these parks is free but you'll have to pay for fishing and hunting permits – though specifics vary from province to province. Where provincial parks provide facilities or contain a specific attraction, you can also expect to pay a modest admission fee and, naturally, you have to pay to use provincial park campsites.

PERMITS

At national parks all motor vehicles, including motorbikes, require a **park permit** before entering, usually from a roadside booth at the point where the road crosses the park boundary. In the past people entering on foot, bicycle, boat or horseback have been exempt, as have vehicles passing straight through certain parks without stopping overnight. This is no longer the case and a permit based on a per-person usage of the park is now required. This costs around \$5 to \$10 per person per day with the customary concessions for the young and old. If you intend to visit a number of national parks, it's worth investing in either a regional or national pass – details from any park information centre. As an illustration, an annual pass providing admission to the dozen or so western parks costs around $35. For more on passes in the Rockies and surrounding parks, see p.607. Additional permits are also required to **fish** in national parks (over and above any provincial permits; see "Fishing", p.57). These are available from park centres, wardens or park administration buildings, and cost around $13 annually, $6 weekly or $5 daily. There may well be quotas on the types and numbers of fish you can catch, which you can find out when you buy a permit; in all parks there's an extra surcharge to fish for salmon.

CAMPING IN THE PARKS

Most parks have large, well-run campsites close to the park's main settlement; some for tents or RVs only, others mixed. Fees depend on facilities, and currently run from $8.50 per tent or per vehicle for semi-primitive sites (with wood, water and pit toilets) up to about $20 for those with electricity, sewage, water and showers. Park permits do not cover campsite fees. Some park campsites have also introduced another fee (around $3) for use of firewood.

Most parks also have **primitive campsites**, which are basic backcountry sites providing, as a rule, just fire pits and firewood. Regulations for **rough camping** vary enormously. Some parks, like Jasper in the Rockies, allow backcountry camping only in tightly defined sites; others, like Banff, have a special **primitive wildland** zone where you can pitch a tent within a designated distance of the nearest road or trailhead. Simply ask at park centres or tourist offices for latest details. Whether you want to use a primitive campsite or camp rough in parks, however, the one thing you must do is obtain an **overnight permit** from the park centre (either free or just a few dollars), which enables the authorities to keep a check on people's whereabouts and regulate numbers in the backcountry.

HIKING

Canada boasts some of North America's finest **hiking**, and whatever your abilities or ambitions you'll find a walk to suit you almost anywhere in the country. All the national and many of the provincial parks have well-marked and -maintained trails, and a visit to any park centre or local tourist office will furnish you with adequate **maps** of local paths. Park trails are usually sufficiently well marked not to need more detailed maps for short walks and day-hikes. This applies to virtually all the hikes described in features in this guide. If you're venturing into backcountry, though, try to obtain the appropriate 1:50 000 (or 1:250 000) sheet from the Canadian Topographical Series. For key hiking areas we've given a brief summary of the best trails in the appropriate parts of the *Guide*, though with over 1500km of paths in Banff National Park alone, recommendations can only scratch the surface of what's on offer. Park staff can advise on other good walks, and **trail guides** are widely available for most of the country's prime walking regions.

It's essential, of course, to be **properly equipped** if you're walking in high or rough country: good boots, waterproof jacket and spare warm clothing. Be prepared for sudden changes of weather and the sort of health problems associated with the Canadian backcountry (see "Health", p.29). Outdoor clothing can be bought easily in most towns, and in walking areas there's a good chance of being able to **rent** tents, specialized cold-weather gear and all manner of other minor outdoor gear.

MAIN HIKING AREAS

In picking out the country's prime walking areas we've usually chosen the parks that are accessible by road, where maps are available and the trail system developed, and where you can turn up without too much planning or special wilderness training.

Best known and most developed of these are the **Rockies national parks** of Alberta and British Columbia. Thousands of kilometres of well-kept and well-tramped paths crisscross the "big four parks" – Banff, Jasper, Yoho and Kootenay – as well as the smaller enclaves of Glacier, Revelstoke and Waterton lakes. Scope for hiking of all descriptions is almost limitless.

More modest areas dotted all over British Columbia boast walking possibilities out of all proportion to their size: we pay less attention to these, but by most relative standards hiking here is still among the best in North America. All the following provincial parks offer a variety of day-hikes, short strolls and longer trails that could keep you happy for a week or more: **Wells Gray**, north of Kamloops; **Kokanee Glacier**, near Nelson; **Manning**, east of Vancouver; **Garibaldi**, north of Vancouver; and **Strathcona**, on Vancouver Island. Walking guides are available for all these regions in local bookstores: tourist offices, as ever, will also offer guidance.

In Manitoba, the **Riding Mountain National Park** offers about thirty hiking trails, but though there's plenty of upland walking to be had in the so-called prairie provinces, you have to move east to Québec's **Mauricie**, **Forillon** and **Gatineau** parks for a taste of mountains comparable to the western provinces. In Ontario, **Lake Superior Provincial Park** and the **Algonquin Park** are the most challenging terrains. New Brunswick's **Fundy National Park** offers coastal walks, while Newfoundland's hiking centres on its two national parks: **Terra Nova** on the east coast, and the high plateau and fjords of the west coast's **Gros Morne**. For the truly bold, however, nothing can match the Arctic extremes of **Baffin Island**, whose principal trail lies over an icecap that never melts.

LONG-DISTANCE FOOTPATHS

In areas with highly developed trail networks, seasoned backpackers can blaze their own **long-distance footpaths** by stringing together several longer trails. Recognized long-haul paths, however, are relatively rare, though more are being designated yearly. One of the best is the Chilkoot Trail from Dyea in Alaska to Bennett in British Columbia, a 53-kilometre hike that closely follows the path of prospectors en route to the Yukon during the 1898 gold rush (see pp.876–877). The most popular is probably Vancouver Island's demanding West Coast Trail, which runs for 80km along the edge of the Pacific Rim National Park (see pp.778).

More far-reaching walks include the **Rideau Trail**, which follows paths and minor roads for 386km from Kingston to Ottawa; the 690-kilometre **Bruce Trail** from Queenston, on the Niagara River to Tobermory on the Bruce Peninsula; and the **Voyageur Trail** along the north shores of lakes Superior and Huron, which is the longest and most rugged route in the province.

Before you set out on any long-distance trail, however, it is vital to seek local advice from either the nearest tourist or park office, or from a local adventure-tour operator.

SKIING

Wherever there's hiking in Canada, there's also usually **skiing**. The increasingly popular resorts of the Rockies and British Columbia are the main areas, followed by Québec, but there's also skiing in Newfoundland and the Maritimes, and even a few runs in Manitoba and Saskatchewan. We've provided special features on the country's leading resorts at Whistler, Banff, Lake Louise and Jasper. Most **cities** are close to excellent downhill and cross-country runs: Vancouver is a ninety-minute drive from Whistler, one of the world's top three resorts; Calgary is the same distance from the Rockies' six big centres; Ottawa lies just half an hour from Camp Fortune and Mont Cascade; and Montréal is around an hour from three hundred runs in the Laurentians and one hundred-plus slopes in L'Estrie (the Eastern Townships).

Canadian **ski packages** are available from most UK and US travel agents, but it's perfectly feasible to organize your own trips, as long as you book well ahead if you're hoping to stay in some of the better-known resorts. **Costs** for food, accommodation and **ski passes** are still fairly modest by US and European standards – a day's pass in one of the Rockies' resorts, for example, costs around $40. Tourist offices in skiing areas are open in winter to help with practicalities, and many nearby towns have ski shops to buy or rent equipment. Companies and hotels in some cities even organize their own mini-packages to nearby resorts. Skiing provinces publish regional ski and winter-sports directories, all available in the UK and US from state or provincial tourist offices.

FISHING

Canada is fishing nirvana. While each region has its specialities, from the Arctic char of the Northwest Territories to the Pacific salmon of British Columbia, excellent fishing can be found in most of the country's superabundant lakes, rivers and coastal waters. Most towns have a fishing shop for equipment, and any spot with fishing possibilities is likely to have companies running boats and charters. As with every other major type of outdoor activity, most provinces publish detailed booklets on everything that swims within the area of their jurisdiction.

Fishing is governed by a range of **regulations** that vary from province to province. These are baffling at first glance, but usually boil down to the need for a **nonresident permit** for freshwater fishing, and another for saltwater fishing. These are obtainable from most local fishing or sports shops for about $30 and are valid for a year. Short-term (one- or six-day) licences are also available in some provinces. In a few places you may have to pay for extra licences to go after particular fish, and in national parks you need a special additional permit (see p.55). There may also be quotas or a closed season on certain fish. Shops and tourist offices always have the most current regulations.

CANOEING

Opportunities for **canoeing** are limited only by problems of access and expertise – some of the rapids and portages on the country's more challenging routes are for real pros only. The most straightforward regions to canoe are in **Ontario**, with its estimated 250,000 lakes and 35,000km of waterways, some 25,000km of which have been documented as practical canoe routes. The key areas are the Algonquin, Killarney and Quetico provincial parks, though the single most popular run is the 190-kilometre **Rideau Canal**, a tame run from Kingston to Ottawa.

The rivers of **British Columbia** offer generally more demanding white-water routes, though the lake canoeing – in the Wells Gray Provincial Park, for example – is among the country's most beautiful. One of the province's other recognized classics is the 120-kilometre trip near Barkerville on the Cariboo River and the lakes of the Bowron Lakes Provincial Park. More challenging still are the immense backcountry lakes and rivers of the **Mackenzie** system and the barren lands of the Northwest Territories, where you can find one of the continent's ultimate river challenges – the 300-kilometre stretch of the **South Nahanni River** near Fort Simpson. Growing in popularity, partly because of improved road access, are trips on and around the **Yukon River system**, particularly the South Macmillan River east of Pelly Crossing. Other areas that will test the resources of any canoeist are to be found in Manitoba and Labrador – all detailed in the *Guide*.

Once you've decided on an area, provincial tourist offices can send you full lists of outfitters and rental agencies whose brochures provide a good idea of what you can expect in their various regions. When you arrive, **outfitters** are available in most centres to rent equipment, organize boat and plane drop-offs, and arrange provisions for longer trips. Typical **costs** are in the region of $80 for weekly canoe rental, $25 daily for a wet suit. Most also supply **maps**, but for longer trips you should contact the Canada Map Office, 130 Bentley Ave, Nepean, ON K1A 0E9 (☎613/952-7000 or 1-800/465-6277) for the map distributor nearest you. Specialist canoe **guides** are also widely available in Canadian bookshops, many giving extremely detailed accounts of particular river systems or regions.

SPECTATOR SPORTS

Canadians are sports-mad – ice hockey, baseball and Canadian football matches are all extremely popular, both the professional games, and the intercollegiate competitions, the intensity of whose rivalries are notorious. Interestingly, lacrosse is the "official" national sport but, unsurprisingly, the unofficial one is ice hockey.

ICE HOCKEY

The sport that really ignites the passions of all Canadians is **ice hockey**. With players hurtling around at nearly 50kph and the puck clocking speeds of over 160kph, this would be a high-adrenaline sport even without its relaxed attitude to combat on the rink – as an old Canadian adage has it, "I went to see a fight and an ice-hockey game broke out". Players, especially in the minor leagues, are as adept at a right hook as they are at skating, and a few years ago the national team waged such a battle against the Soviet Union that the fight only stopped when officials turned all the lights off.

The North American **National Hockey League (NHL)** consists of thirty teams, of which six are from Canada: the Montréal Canadiens, Ottawa Senators, Toronto Maple Leafs, Vancouver Canucks, Calgary Flames and the Edmonton Oilers. There are two conferences – **Western** and **Eastern** – both divided into two divisions. The Canadiens, Maple Leafs and the Senators meet teams from Buffalo and Boston in the Northeast division of the Eastern conference and the Flames, Oilers and Canucks face Colorado and Minnesota in the Northwest division of the Western conference.

Teams have six players and perpetual substitutions are allowed during the game – some players rarely spend more than a few minutes on the ice at one time. There are three twenty-minute periods in a match, but the clock is frequently stopped for a variety of reasons so play usually goes on for three hours. Each team plays over eighty games a **season**, which lasts from October to May, and on alternate weeks will play two and then three games. At the end of the season the top four teams in each division go on into the play-offs for the **Stanley Cup**, ice hockey's most prestigious title. The two most successful teams are the Montréal Canadiens, who have won the Stanley Cup 23 times, and the Toronto Maple Leafs, who have eleven victories under their belt.

Ticket prices range from around $15 for ordinary games to hundreds of dollars for a Stanley Cup final – indeed, you can forget about getting into this event unless you have high-level political

---

NHL TEAMS AND VENUES (*WWW.NHL.COM*)

EASTERN CONFERENCE

Northeast Division

Montréal Canadiens, Le Centre Molson, 1260 de la Gauchitiere, Montréal (☎514/790-1245 or 932-2582, *www.canadiens.com*).

Ottawa Senators, Corel Centre, 1000 Palladium Drive, Kanata (☎1-800/444-SENS, *www.ottawasenators.com*).

Toronto Maple Leafs, Air Canada Centre, 40 Bay St, Toronto (☎416/815-5700, *www.torontomapleleafs.com*).

WESTERN CONFERENCE

Northwest Division

Calgary Flames, Canadian Airlines Saddledome, Calgary (☎403/777-0000, *www.calgaryflames.com*).

Edmonton Oilers, Skyreach Centre, 7424 118th Ave, Edmonton (☎403/471-4000, *www.edmontonoilers.com*).

Vancouver Canucks, General Motors Place, 800 Griffiths Way, Vancouver (☎604/280-4400 or 899-GOAL, *www.orcabay.com/canucks/*).

CFL TEAMS (WWW.CFL.CA)

WEST DIVISION

BC Lions, BC Place Stadium, 777 Pacific Blvd S, Vancouver (☎604/589-ROAR, *www.bclions.com*).

Calgary Stampeders, McMahon Stadium, 1817 Crowchild Trail NW, Calgary (☎403/289-0258, *www.stampeders.com*).

Edmonton Eskimos, Commonwealth Stadium, 11000 Stadium Rd, Edmonton (☎403/448-ESKS, *www.esks.com*).

Saskatchewan Roughriders, Taylor Field, 2940 10th Ave, Regina (☎1-888/4-RIDERS or 306/525-2181, *www.riders.com*).

EAST DIVISION

Hamilton Tiger-Cats, Ivor Wynne Stadium, 75 Balsam Ave N, Hamilton (☎905/547-CATS or 1-800/714-ROAR, *www.tigercats.on.ca*).

Montréal Alouettes, McGill Percival Molson Memorial Stadium, McGill University, 475 Av Des Pins Ouest, Montréal (☎514/871-2266, *www.alouettes.net*).

Toronto Argonauts, SkyDome, 1 Blue Jays Way, Toronto (☎416/341-5151, *www.argonauts.on.ca*).

Winnipeg Blue Bombers, Winnipeg Stadium, 1465 Maroons Rd, Winnipeg (☎204/784-2583, *www.bluebombers.com*).

or sporting contacts. For nearly all matches you have to buy a ticket in advance.

Other than the NHL there are also numerous **minor league** clubs composed of **farm teams**, so called because they supply the top clubs with talent. Ontario and Québec both have their own minor leagues; the rest of the country plays in the Western League, all with play-offs for a variety of awards. For **college hockey**, the University of Toronto and York in Toronto, Concordia in Montréal, St Mary's in Halifax and the University of Alberta in Edmonton all have good teams.

CANADIAN FOOTBALL

Professional **Canadian football**, played under the aegis of the **Canadian Football League (CFL)**, is largely overshadowed by the National Football League in the US, chiefly because the best home-grown talent moves south in search of better money while NFL castoffs move north to fill the ranks. The two countries' football games vary slightly, but what differences do exist tend to make the Canadian version more exciting. In Canada the playing field is larger and there are twelve rather than eleven players on each **team**. There is also one fewer **down** in a game – ie after kickoff the attacking team has three, rather than four, chances to move the ball forward ten yards and score a first down en route to a **touchdown**. Different rules about the movement of players, and the limited time allowed between plays, results in a faster-paced and higher-scoring

sport, in which ties are often decided in overtime or in a dramatic final-minute surge.

Despite the sport's potential, the CFL has suffered a blight of media and fan indifference, which has caused immense financial problems, though recently the crisis seems to be easing, with high-profile celebrity investment. The CFL has tried to expand into the US over the past decade, but all the expansion teams folded at the end of the 1995/96 season. The **season**, played by two divisions of eight teams, lasts from June to November, each team playing a match a week – 72 matches in all. At the end of the season are the play-offs, which culminate with the hotly contested Grey Cup – which the Toronto Argonauts have won twenty-one times, most recently in 1997. Tickets are fairly easy to come by, except for important games, and vary in cost from $20 to a Grey Cup final price of over $150.

BASEBALL

Baseball, with its relaxed summertime pace and byzantine rules, is generally considered an exclusively American sport – despite the first recorded game taking place in Beachville, Ontario. The **Montréal Expos** and the **Toronto Blue Jays** perform in the US's two major baseball leagues, the National and the American respectively. In 1992 and 1993, the Toronto Blue Jays became national heroes when they won the World Series twice in a row, beating America at their own game. Historically a lowlier bunch, the Expos are

BASEBALL TEAMS

MAJOR LEAGUE

AMERICAN LEAGUE

Toronto Blue Jays, SkyDome, 277 Front St W, Toronto (☎416/341-1234 or 1-888/OK-GO-JAY outside Toronto, *www.bluejays.ca*).

NATIONAL LEAGUE

Montréal Expos, Olympic Stadium, Av Pierre-de-Coubertin, Montréal (☎514/790-1245 or 1-800/361-4595 outside Montréal, 1-800/678-5440 from USA, *www.montrealexpos.com*).

MINOR LEAGUE

PACIFIC COAST LEAGUE

Calgary Cannons, Burns Stadium, 1817 Crowchild Trail NW, Calgary (☎403/284-1111, *www.calgarycannons.com*).

Edmonton Trappers, John Ducey Park, 10233 96th Ave, Edmonton (☎780/414-4450, *www.trappersbaseball.com*).

INTERNATIONAL LEAGUE

Ottawa Lynx, JetForm Park, 300 Coventry Rd, Ottawa (☎613/749-9947 or 1-800/663-0985, *www.ottawalynx.com*).

now awaiting the completion of a new $200 million downtown stadium to boost ticket sales – due to open for the 2002 season. However, it was they who became the first non-US team to play in a US league in 1968, eight years before the Blue Jays.

Even if you don't understand what's going on, a game can be a pleasant day out, drinking beer and eating burgers and popcorn in the sun, with friendly family-oriented crowds. Moreover, the home ground of each team is a vast, wondrous modern stadium – the Skydome in Toronto and, for the moment at least, the Olympic Stadium in Montréal. With six teams in each division, there are 81 home games each season, played from April to late September, with play-offs continuing through October; there is no set match day and games are either played in the afternoon or evening. Lasting for anything from two to three hours, baseball games never end in a tie: if the scores are level after nine innings, extra innings are played until one side wins.

Tickets for the Blue Jays are hard to come by and it's easier to get in for games in Montréal. Nothing can match the glitz of the big two, but there are other minor league **farm teams**, including the Edmonton Trappers, Calgary Cannons and Vancouver Canadians.

BASKETBALL

Basketball was invented by a Canadian, Dr James A. Naismith, in 1891. What began with a bunch of his students and a peach basket suspended in the air has become a fast-paced exciting sport with the world's tallest athletes. After a 48-year absence two Canadian teams finally joined the now misnamed National Basketball Association in 1995, the Toronto Raptors and the Vancouver Grizzlies, who did about as well as could be expected in their first season, though the Raptors, with huge star Vince Carter, look like the team more on the upswing.

The NBA consists of 29 teams divided into two conferences, Eastern and Western, which are further divided into two divisions. The Toronto Raptors play in the Central division of the Eastern conference and the Vancouver Grizzlies compete in the Midwest division of the Western conference. Teams play an 82-game season with 41 home games in a season that lasts from November to April – tickets cost from $10 to $130.

BASKETBALL TEAMS

Toronto Raptors, Air Canada Centre, 40 Bay St, Toronto (☎416/366-DUNK, *www.nba.com/raptors*).

Vancouver Grizzlies, General Motors Place, 800 Griffiths Way, Vancouver (☎604/899-4667, *www.nba.com/grizzlies*).

DIRECTORY

ADDRESSES Generally speaking, roads in built-up areas in Canada are laid out on a grid system, creating "blocks" of buildings. The first one or two digits of a specific address refer to the block, which will be numbered in sequence from a central point, usually downtown. For example, 620 S Cedar Ave will be six blocks south of downtown. It is crucial, therefore, to take note of components such as "NW" or "SE" in addresses; 3620 SW King St will be a very long way indeed from 3620 NE King St. Where a number is prefixed to the street number, this indicates an apartment or suite number in a block at the same street address.

BEARS Be aware of the dangers posed by bears. Most people blow a whistle while walking in bear country to warn them off. If confronted don't run, make loud noises or sudden movements, all of which are likely to provoke an attack. Leave the animal an escape route and back off slowly. If you have a pack, leave it as a distraction. If attacked, climbing a tree or playing dead may save you from a grizzly, but not from black bears. Fighting back only increases the ferocity of an attack. For more on bears, see pp.642–643.

ELECTRIC CURRENT Electricity in Canada is supplied at an alternating current of 110 volts and at a frequency of 60Hz, the same as in the US. Visitors from the UK will need transformers for appliances like shavers and hair dryers, and a plug converter for Canada's two-pin sockets.

FLOORS The *first* floor in Canada is what would be the ground floor in Britain; the *second* floor would be the first floor, and so on.

ID Should be carried at all times. Two pieces should suffice, one of which should have a photo; a passport and credit card are your best bet.

MEASUREMENTS Canada officially uses the metric system, though many people still use the imperial system. Distances are in kilometres, temperatures in degrees Celsius, and foodstuffs, petrol and drink are sold in grams, kilograms or litres.

PUBLIC TOILETS Rare even in cities, but bars, fast-food chains, museums and other public buildings invariably have excellent facilities.

SENIOR TRAVELLERS For many senior citizens, retirement brings the opportunity to explore the

METRIC CONVERSIONS	
1 CENTIMETRE (CM) = 0.394IN	1 acre = 0.4 hectares
1 inch (*in*) = 2.54cm	1 litre = 0.22 UK gal
1 foot (*ft*) = 30.48cm	1 UK gallon (*gal*) = 4.55 litres
1 metre (*m*) = 100cm	1 litre = 0.26 US gal
1 metre = 39.37in	1 US gallon (*gal*) = 5.46 litres
1 yard (*yd*) = 0.91m	1 gram (*g*) = 0.035oz
1 kilometre (*km*) = 1000m	1 ounce (*oz*) = 28.57g
1 kilometre = 0.621 miles	1 kilogram (*kg*) = 1000g
1 mile = 1.61km	1 kilogram = 2.2lb
1 hectare = 10,000 square metres	1 pound (*lb*) = 0.454kg
1 hectare = 2.471 acres	

world in a style and at a pace that is the envy of younger travellers. As well as the advantages of being free to travel during the quieter, less expensive seasons, and for longer periods, anyone over the age of 65, often 60, can enjoy the tremendous variety of discounts on offer to those who can produce suitable ID. VIA Rail and Greyhound, for example, offer (smallish) percentage reductions on fares to older passengers; while the majority of museums and similar attractions give at least fifty percent discounts for seniors.

VIDEOS If you purchase a prerecorded video in Canada, make sure it's been recorded on the PAL system, or else it will be useless back in Europe. Blank videos can be used in either continent without any problem.

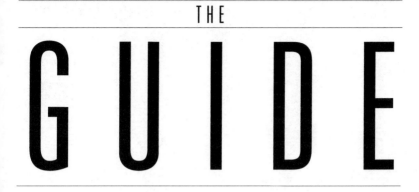

PART TWO

THE GUIDE

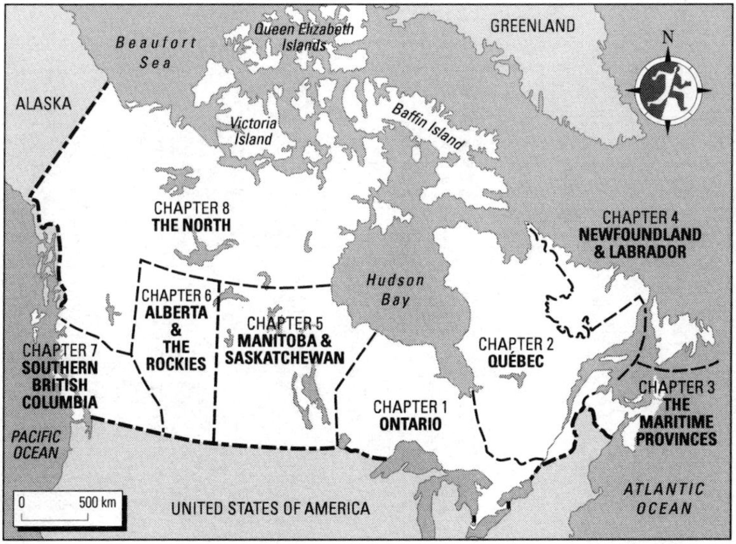

Beaufort Sea
Queen Elizabeth Islands
GREENLAND
N
ALASKA
Victoria Island
Baffin Island
CHAPTER 8
THE NORTH
CHAPTER 4
NEWFOUNDLAND & LABRADOR
Hudson Bay
CHAPTER 6
ALBERTA & THE ROCKIES
CHAPTER 5
MANITOBA & SASKATCHEWAN
CHAPTER 2
QUÉBEC
CHAPTER 7
SOUTHERN BRITISH COLUMBIA
CHAPTER 3
THE MARITIME PROVINCES
CHAPTER 1
ONTARIO
PACIFIC OCEAN
ATLANTIC OCEAN
0 500 km
UNITED STATES OF AMERICA

CHAPTER ONE

ONTARIO

T he one million square kilometres of **Ontario**, Canada's second-largest province, stretch all the way from the St Lawrence River and the Great Lakes to the frozen shores of Hudson Bay. Some two-thirds of this territory – all of the north and most of the centre – is occupied by the forests and rocky outcrops of the Canadian Shield, whose ancient, Precambrian rocks were brought to the surface by the glaciers that gouged the continent during the last ice age. The glaciers produced a flattened landscape studded with thousands of lakes and it was the local Iroquois who first coined the name "Ontario", literally "glittering waters". The **Iroquois** – as well as their **Algonquin** neighbours to the north – hunted and fished the Canadian Shield, but their agricultural activities were confined to the more fertile and hospitable parts of southern Ontario, in which the vast majority of the province's ten million people are now concentrated.

The first **Europeans** to make regular contact with these aboriginal peoples were the **French explorers** of the seventeenth and eighteenth centuries, most famously the intrepid Étienne Brûlé and Samuel de Champlain. However, these early visitors were preoccupied with the fur trade, and it wasn't until the end of the American War of Independence and the immigration of the **United Empire Loyalists** (see p.382) that mass settlement really began. Between 1820 and 1850 a further wave of migrants, mostly English, Irish and Scots, made Upper Canada, as Ontario was known until Confederation, the most populous and prosperous Canadian region. This pre-eminence was reinforced towards the end of the nineteenth century by the industrialization of the region's larger towns, a process that was underpinned by the discovery of some of the world's richest mineral deposits: in the space of twenty years, nickel was found near Sudbury, silver at Cobalt, gold in Red Lake and iron ore at Wawa.

Nowadays, a highly mechanized timber industry, mineral mines, massive hydroelectric schemes and thousands of factories – making more than half the country's manufactured goods – keep Ontario at the top of the economic ladder. However, this industrial success has created massive **environmental problems**, most noticeable in the wounded landscapes around Sudbury and the polluted waters of lakes Erie and Ontario. Furthermore, the province remains firmly in the political hands of the Progressive Conservative Party, whose flinty right-wing agenda owes much to the UK's Mrs Thatcher. As a consequence, privatization and tax cuts are in vogue, along with endless moaning about welfare scroungers, whilst environmental issues take a back (or nonexistent) seat.

With more than four million inhabitants, **Toronto** is Canada's biggest city, a financial and industrial behemoth that boasts a hatful of sights – the pick of which are its art galleries – a great restaurant scene and a vibrant nightlife. To the east and west of the city, along the north shore of **Lake Ontario**, is the so-called "Golden Horseshoe" – named for its economic clout rather than its looks and comprising sprawling suburbs and ugly industrial townships. Highlights here are few and far between, but the steel city of **Hamilton**, at the western end of the lake, does have one or two interesting historic sights and is also near Canada's premier tourist spot, **Niagara Falls** – best visited on a day-trip from Toronto or from colonial **Niagara-on-the-Lake**. Most of the rest of **southwest Ontario**, sandwiched between lakes Huron and Erie, is farming terrain

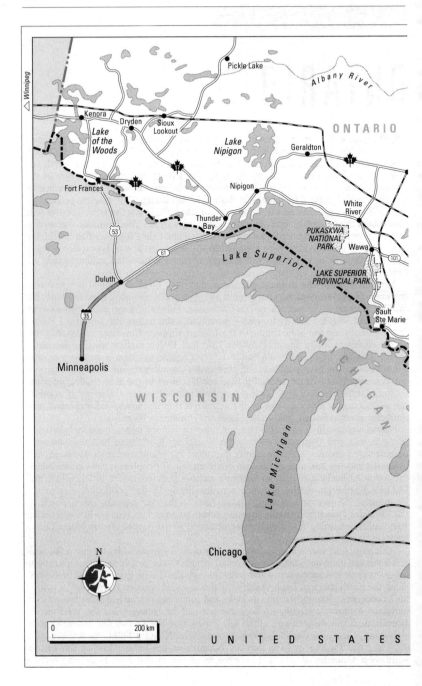

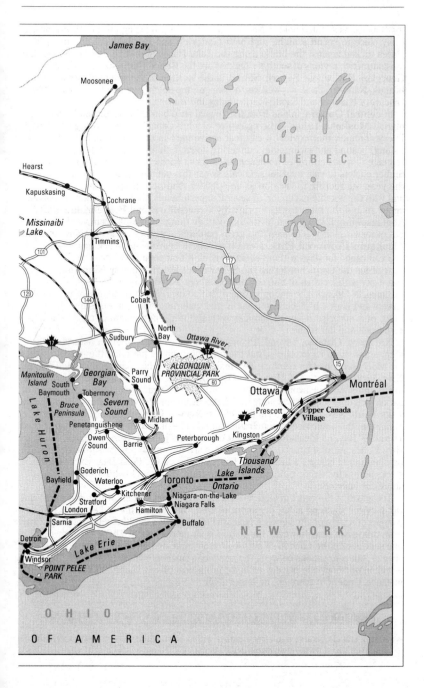

that's as flat as a Dutch polder. Nevertheless, the car-producing town of **Windsor** is a lively place to spend a night, and both **Goderich** and **Bayfield** are charming little places tucked against the bluffs along the Lake Huron shoreline. For landscape, the most attractive regions of southern Ontario are the **Bruce Peninsula** and the adjacent **Georgian Bay**, whose **Severn Sound** is the location of the beautiful Georgian Bay Islands National Park as well as a pair of top-notch historical reconstructions, Discovery Harbour and Sainte-Marie among the Hurons.

In **central Ontario**, inland from the coastal strip bordering Georgian Bay, are the myriad **Muskoka Lakes** – the epicentre of what Canadians call **cottage country**. Every summer, the province's city folk arrive here in their thousands for a spot of fishing, boating and swimming, hunkering down in their lakeside cottages – though "cottages" is something of a misnomer as these second homes range from humble timber chalets to vast mansions. Locals swear this summer jaunt is the best time of the year, but touring the region as an outsider is mostly disappointing. For a start, and with the notable exception of several superb hotels, there is nowhere in particular to go and the main towns – primarily **Gravenhurst** and **Bracebridge** – are far from inspiring. If you get an invite to a cottage things may well seem very different, but otherwise – if you're after the great outdoors – it's best to keep going north to **Algonquin Provincial Park**, a vast tract where beavers and black bears roam and you can canoe for days without seeing a soul. If that sounds too daunting, head east instead for the towns bordering the St Lawrence River, primarily **Kingston**, a handsome city with a clutch of fine colonial buildings. North of here, within easy striking distance, is **Ottawa**, the nation's capital, but a surprisingly small city of impeccable streets and parks, high-class museums and galleries, plus – and this may be something of a surprise if you're familiar with the city's bureaucratic image – a lively restaurant and bar scene.

Northern Ontario, beyond Algonquin Provincial Park, offers a natural environment stunning in its extremes, but the travelling can be hard and the specific sights too widely separated for comfort. Two main roads cross this sparsely inhabited region, **Hwy 11** in the north and **Hwy 17** to the south. The former links a series of mining towns and should be avoided, while the latter passes near or cuts through a string of parks, including the extravagantly wild **Lake Superior Provincial Park**. Hwy 17 also visits **Sault Ste Marie** – terminus of the **Agawa Canyon** train, which affords a glimpse of the otherwise impenetrable hinterland – as well as the gritty grain port of **Thunder Bay**, an ideal stopping point on the long journey west (or east). North of Hwy 11 lies a brutal country where hunters are the only regular visitors, though the passing tourist can get a taste of the terrain on board the Polar Bear Express, which tracks across the Arctic tundra to link **Cochrane**, on Hwy-11, with **Moosonee** on the shores of James Bay.

Toronto is at the heart of Ontario's **public transport** system, with regular bus and rail services shuttling along the shore of Lake Ontario and the St Lawrence River to connect every major city between Niagara Falls, Ottawa and ultimately Montréal. Away from this urban core, however, the picture is far more sketchy. There are fairly regular bus services on the London–Windsor–Detroit route and along the Trans-Canada and Hwy 17, but connections between the province's smaller towns are few and far between – reckon on about one per day even for prominent places, though in some cases (for instance, Goderich) there are no buses at all.

TOLL-FREE INFORMATION NUMBER AND WEB SITE

Ontario Travel operates a toll-free number within North America – ☎1-800/ONTARIO. Their Web site is *www.ontariotravel.net*.

TORONTO

The economic and cultural focus of English-speaking Canada, **Toronto** is the country's largest metropolis. It sprawls along the northern shore of Lake Ontario, its vibrant, appealing centre encased by a jangle of satellite townships and industrial zones that cover – as "Greater Toronto" – no less than 100 square kilometres. For decades, Toronto was saddled with unflattering sobriquets – "Toronto the Good", "Hogtown" – that reflected a perhaps deserved reputation for complacent mediocrity and greed. Spurred into years of image-building, the city's postwar administrations have lavished millions of dollars on glitzy architecture, slick museums, an excellent public-transport system, and the reclamation and development of the lakefront. As a result, Toronto has become one of North America's most likeable cities, an eminently liveable place whose citizens keep a wary eye on both their politicians and the developers.

Huge new shopping malls and skyrise office blocks reflect the economic successes of the last two or three decades, a boom that has attracted immigrants from all over the world, transforming an overwhelmingly anglophone city into a cosmopolitan one of some sixty significant minorities. Furthermore, the city's multiculturalism goes far deeper than an extravagant diversity of restaurants and sporadic pockets of multilingual street signs. Toronto's schools, for example, have extensive "Heritage Language Programmes", which encourage the maintenance of the immigrants' first cultures.

Getting the feel of Toronto's diversity is one of the city's great pleasures, but there are attention-grabbing sights here as well. Most are conveniently clustered in the city centre, and the most celebrated of them all is the **CN Tower**, the world's tallest free-standing structure. Next door lies the modern hump of the **SkyDome** sports stadium. The city's other prestige attractions are led by the **Art Gallery of Ontario**, which possesses a first-rate selection of Canadian painting, and the **Royal Ontario Museum**, where pride of place goes to the Chinese collection. But it's the pick of Toronto's smaller, less-visited galleries and period homes that really add to the city's charm. There are superb Canadian paintings at the **Thomson Gallery** and a fascinating range of footwear at the **Bata Shoe Museum**. The Toronto Dominion Bank boasts the eclectic **Gallery of Inuit Art**, and the mock-Gothic extravagances of **Casa Loma**, the Victorian gentility of **Spadina House** and the replica of **Fort York**, the colonial settlement where Toronto began, all vie for the visitor's attention.

Toronto's sights illustrate different facets of the city, but in no way do they crystallize its identity. The city remains opaque, too big and diverse to allow for a defining personality. This, however, adds an air of excitement and unpredictability to the place. Toronto caters to everything, and the city surges with Canada's most vibrant restaurant, performing-arts and nightlife scenes.

A brief history of Toronto

Situated on the slab of land separating Lake Ontario and Georgian Bay, **Toronto** was on one of the three early portage routes to the northwest, its name taken from the Huron for "place of meeting". The first European to visit the district was the French explorer Étienne Brûlé in 1615, but it wasn't until the middle of the eighteenth century that the French made a serious effort to control the area with the development of a simple settlement and stockade, **Fort Rouillé**. The British pushed the French from the northern shore of Lake Ontario in 1759, but then chose to ignore the site for almost forty years until the arrival of hundreds of Loyalist settlers in the aftermath of the American Revolution.

In 1791 the British divided their remaining American territories into two, Upper and Lower Canada, each with its own legislative councils. The first capital of Upper Canada was Niagara-on-the-Lake, but this was too near the American border for comfort and

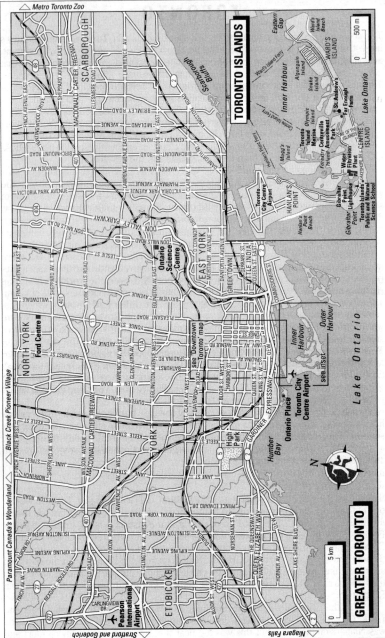

△ Metro Toronto Zoo

TORONTO ISLANDS

GREATER TORONTO

0   5 km

N

the province's new lieutenant-governor, **John Graves Simcoe**, moved his administration to the relative safety of Toronto in 1793, calling the new settlement **York**. Simcoe had grand classical visions of colonial settlement, but even he was exasperated by the conditions of frontier life – "the city's site was better calculated for a frog pond . . . than for the residence of human beings". Soon nicknamed "Muddy York", the capital was little more than a village when, in 1812, the Americans attacked and burnt the main buildings.

In the early nineteenth century, effective economic and political power lay in the hands of an anglophilic oligarchy christened the **Family Compact** by the radical polemicists of the day. Their most vociferous opponent was a radical Scot, **William Lyon Mackenzie**, who promulgated his views both in his newspaper, the *Colonial Advocate*, and as a member of the Legislative Assembly. Mackenzie became the first mayor of Toronto, as the town was renamed in 1834, but the radicals were defeated in the elections two years later and a frustrated Mackenzie drifted towards the idea of armed revolt. In 1837, he staged the **Upper Canadian insurrection**, a badly organized uprising of a few hundred farmers, who marched down Yonge Street, fought a couple of half-hearted skirmishes and then melted away. Mackenzie fled across the border and two of the other ringleaders were executed, but the British parliament, mindful of their earlier experiences in New England, moved to liberalize Upper Canada's administration instead of taking reprisals. In 1841, they granted Canada **responsible government**, reuniting the two provinces in a loose confederation, prefiguring the final union of 1867 when Upper Canada was redesignated Ontario. Even Mackenzie was pardoned and allowed to return, arguably giving the lie to his portrayal of the oligarchs as hard-faced reactionaries; indeed, this same privileged group had even pushed progressive antislavery bills through the legislature as early as the 1830s.

By the end of the nineteenth century Toronto had become a major manufacturing centre dominated by a conservative mercantile elite who were exceedingly loyal to British interests and maintained a strong Protestant tradition. This elite was sustained by the working-class **Orange Lodges**, whose reactionary influence was a key feature of municipal politics – no wonder Charles Dickens had been offended by the city's "rabid Toryism". That said, these same Protestants were enthusiastic about public education, just like the Methodist-leaning middle classes, who also spearheaded social reform movements, principally Suffrage and Temperance. The trappings, however, remained far from alluring – well into the twentieth century Sunday was preserved as a "day of rest" and Eaton's store even drew its curtains to prevent Sabbath window-shopping. Indeed, for all its capital status, the city was strikingly provincial by comparison with Montréal until the 1950s, when the opening of the **St Lawrence Seaway** in 1959 gave the place a jolt and the first wave of non-white immigrants began to transform its complexion. More recently, Toronto was an indirect beneficiary of the assertion of francophone identity in Québec, as many of Montréal's anglophone-dominated financial institutions and big businesses transferred their operations here. The boom that ensued launched downtown property values into the stratosphere – but then came the crash of 1988, which spread near panic amongst developers. Since then, the economy has been more sedate, though many blame Governor Harris and his conservative

TORONTO TELEPHONE NUMBERS

Toronto now has two **area codes**, ☎416 and ☎647, the latter reserved for phone numbers created after March 1, 2001. Since the area code split is not based on distinct city areas, all local telephone calls now require that you dial a ten-digit number. Most of the Toronto phone numbers in the *Guide* use the ☎416 code.

ACCOMMODATION PRICE CODES

All the accommodation prices in this book have been coded using the symbols below, corresponding to Canadian dollar rates. Prices are for the least expensive double room in each establishment in high season, excluding special offers. For a full explanation, see p.42 in Basics.

① up to $40
② $40–60
③ $60–80
④ $80–100
⑤ $100–125
⑥ $125–175
⑦ $175–240
⑧ $240+

cronies for the increase (and increasingly obvious) degree of poverty afflicting the city: since 1980, the number of Toronto families living below the poverty line has quadrupled.

Arrival, information and getting around

Arriving by **air**, you'll almost certainly land at Toronto's main airport, **Lester B. Pearson International**, about 25km northwest of the city centre. There are three terminals – terminals 2 and 3 are where most international flights arrive, and terminal 1 handles the majority of domestic flights. Each of the terminals has a full range of facilities, including money-exchange offices, ATMs and free hotel hotlines. The **Airport Express bus** service (daily: one every twenty minutes 6am–1am, every thirty minutes 1am–5.30am; ☎905/564-6333) picks up passengers outside the terminals and takes between forty and sixty minutes to reach downtown, though heavy traffic can make the journey considerably longer. The bus drops passengers at the bus station (see below for details) and several of Toronto's major hotels, with connecting minibuses taking passengers to most of the other downtown hotels. Tickets for the airport bus can be purchased either at the kiosks next to the bus stop outside the terminal buildings or from the driver. A one-way fare is $13.75, round-trip $23.65; the minibus service costs an extra $3 (round-trip $5). Round-trip tickets are valid for one year. Alternatively, there's an airport **limo** service (a shared-taxi system) next to each terminal's bus platform; limos cost about $30 per person for the journey from the airport to the city centre; they only leave when they're full. Individual **taxis** charge approximately $40 from the airport to downtown Toronto. Lastly, a subsidiary of Air Canada, Air Ontario (☎1-888/247-2262, within Toronto ☎416/925-2311) operates flights from Montréal, Ottawa and London, Ontario, into the much smaller **Toronto City Centre Airport**, which is on Hanlan's Point in Toronto's harbour, close to downtown. From the airport, there's a free minibus service to the *Royal York Hotel* downtown. The minibus uses the car ferry that connects the airport to the mainland from the foot of Bathurst Street.

Well connected to most of the major towns of eastern Canada, Toronto's **bus station** is conveniently located downtown on Edward Street at Bay Street, metres from Dundas Street West. The nearest subway station is a five-minute walk east at Yonge and Dundas. If you're arriving at night, note that the bus station's immediate environs are unsavoury, but it only takes a couple of minutes to reach more reassuring parts of downtown. Nonetheless, if you're travelling alone or late at night, it's probably best to take a taxi.

Union Railway Station is also in the downtown core, at the junction of Bay Street and Front Street West, and has regular services from the larger cities of Ontario and Québec, supplemented by more occasional trains from the Maritime Provinces, the Prairies and Vancouver. In addition, the station is the hub of Toronto's public transport system. The station complex includes a subway station and holds the main terminal for the GO trains and buses that service the city's suburbs. Details of GO services are available at their ticket offices here, or call toll-free ☎1-888/438 6646, within Toronto ☎416/869-3200. Note also that Ontario Northland, who operate trains north to Cochrane and the Polar Bear Express to Moosonee (see p.176) have an information desk in the main hall.

Arriving by **car** from Niagara Falls and points along Lake Ontario, traffic approaches the city along the **QEW** (Queen Elizabeth Way), which funnels into the **Gardiner Expressway**, an elevated motorway that cuts across the southern side of downtown, just south of Front Street. From the east and west, the quickest approach is on **Hwy 401**, which sweeps through the city's suburbs north of the downtown core. Driving in from the north, take **Hwy 400**, which intersects with Hwy 401 northwest of the centre, or **Hwy 404**, which meets Hwy 401 northeast of the centre. Note that on all routes you can expect delays during rush hours (roughly 7.30–9.30am and 4.30–6.30pm). To relieve congestion on Hwy 401, an alternative motorway, **Hwy 407ETR**, has been built further north on the city's edge. It was North America's first all-electronic toll highway: instead of toll booths, vehicles are identified either by an electronic tag or a license plate photo, and the invoice is posted later. Toll charges vary according to the time of day, the day of the week and the distance travelled. During peak periods (Mon–Fri 5.30–9.30am and 4–7pm), the charge is 10¢ per kilometre, daytime off-peak costs 8¢, night time 4¢. If you rent a car, be aware that rental companies slap on an extra administration charge (of around $10) if you take their vehicles on this road.

Information

The excellent **Ontario Tourism Travel Information Centre** (Mon–Fri 10am–9pm, Sat 9.30am–7pm & Sun noon–5pm; ☎1-800/ONTARIO, within Toronto ☎416/314-0944, *www.ontariotravel.net*), on Level 1 of the Eaton shopping centre at Yonge and Dundas, stocks a comprehensive range of information on all the major attractions in Toronto and throughout Ontario. Of particular interest are the free city maps, the *Ride Guide* to the city's transport system, and accommodation and entertainment details in the monthly magazine *Where*. They will also book hotel accommodation on your behalf both in Toronto and across all of Ontario.

Alternatively, the **Info T.O.** visitor information centre (daily: May–Sept 8am–8pm, Oct–April 9am–5pm) is located in the city's Convention Centre at 255 Front St W, a couple of minutes' walk west from Union Station. Privately run, they are more geared up for selling tour tickets than providing information, though they do have a reasonable supply of free literature on the city and its environs. They are not, however, nearly as well organized as the Ontario Tourism Centre. Finally, **Tourism Toronto**, the city's official visitor and convention bureau, operates a telephone information line that can handle most city queries and will make hotel reservations. Phone hours are Mon–Fri 8.30am–5pm, Sat 9am–5pm, Sun 10am–5pm; ☎416/203-2500 or 1-800/363-1990.

Orientation

Toronto's downtown core is sandwiched between Front Street to the south, Bloor to the north, Spadina to the west and Jarvis to the east. **Yonge Street** is the main north–south artery: principal street numbers start and names change from "West" to "East" from here. Note, therefore, that 1000 Queen Street W is a long way from 1000 Queen Street E. To appreciate the transition between the different downtown neighbourhoods, it's best to **walk** around the centre – Front to Bloor is about 2km, Spadina to Jarvis 1km. In an attempt to protect shoppers from Ontario's climate, there's also an enormous sequence of pedestrianized shopping arcades called the **PATH Walkway**, which begins beneath Union Station, twisting up to the Eaton Centre shopping mall and beyond. Both visitor centres issue free PATH maps.

City transport

Fast, frequent, safe and efficient, the city's **public transport** is overseen by the Toronto Transit Commission (TTC); for all TTC inquiries, call the customer information line on ☎416/393-4636, or, for the hearing impaired, ☎416/481-2523 (both phone lines operate daily 8am–5pm). The TTC's integrated network of subways, buses and streetcars serves every corner of the city. With the exception of downtown, where all the major sights are within easy walking distance of each other, your best option is to use public transport to hop between attractions – especially in the cold of winter or the sultry summertime.

The core of the city's public transport, Toronto's **subway** pivots on a simple, two-line system. The Bloor–Danforth line cuts east to west along Bloor, and the Yonge–University-Spadina line forms a loop heading north from Union Station along University Avenue and Yonge. Transferring between the two lines is possible at three stations only: Spadina, St George and Bloor–Yonge. The subway operates Mon–Sat 6am–1am, Sun 9am–1am. A single journey costs $2 (local students and seniors $1.40, and children under two travel free), and **tickets** are available at all subway stations. Metallic **tokens** can also be used, but are impossibly small and difficult to keep track of. More economically, a batch of five tickets or tokens can be bought for $8.50, $17 for ten, at any station and at most convenience stores and newsstands. Each ticket or token entitles passengers to one complete journey of any length on the TTC system. If this involves more than one type of transport, it is necessary to get a paper **transfer** at your point of entry (there are automatic machines that provide transfers at all subway stations). A **day-pass** costs $7, and provides one adult with unlimited TTC travel all day on Saturdays and after 9.30am on weekdays. On Sundays, the same pass becomes a terrific deal for families: it covers up to six people – only two of which can be adults.

Supplementing the subway are the TTC's **buses** and **streetcars**. The system couldn't be simpler, as a bus and/or streetcar station adjoins every major subway stop. Prices are the same as for the subway, and each ticket or token entitles passengers to one complete journey of any length on the TTC system. Transfers to the subway from buses and streetcars are available from the driver.

> The TTC has a **Request Stop Program**, which allows women travelling alone and late at night to get off buses whenever they want, and not necessarily at regular TTC stops.

Accommodation

As Toronto's popularity as a tourist destination has increased, so the availability of **hotel** accommodation, especially in the mid-price range, has shrunk. Indeed, during peak season (late June–Aug), and especially around summer events like Caribana (see p.101), it is essential to book well in advance. Most of the city's hotels occupy modern skyscrapers and although the degree of luxury does vary there is much stylistic uniformity in the standardized chain-hotel fittings and furnishings. Prices reflect floor space and tend to fluctuate depending on when and for how long you stay, but, in general, a clean, centrally located hotel room starts at $80–100.

Bed-and-breakfast accommodation tends to be slightly cheaper – even with breakfast thrown in. While most of these establishments are not as central as the city's hotels, they do take you off the beaten path and into Toronto's quainter neighbourhoods. Budget-conscious travellers might also want to consider Toronto's dreary **hostels**, but at this end of the market the best deal in town is the **summer residences** at local universities. You'll get bare essentials here, but the rooms are much cheerier than the hostels; prices start at about $40.

The Ontario Tourism Travel Information Centre (see p.73), in the Eaton Centre shopping mall, will help in **finding a hotel room**, or you can telephone Tourism Toronto, who operate a telephone hotel reservation line. Phone hours are Mon–Fri 8.30am–5pm, Sat 9am–5pm, Sun 10am–5pm; ☎416/203-2500 or 1-800/363-1990. In addition, Ontario Tourism will issue you with an *Annual Visitor's Guide* that contains a comprehensive list of the city's accommodation.

Hotels

Bond Place Hotel, 65 Dundas St E (☎416/362-6061 or 1-800/268-9390, fax 416/360-6406). Popular with package-tour operators and ideally located, just a couple of minutes' walk from the Eaton Centre; simple, unassuming doubles; some weekend reductions. Dundas subway. ③.

Clarion Essex Park Hotel, 300 Jarvis St (☎416/977-4823 or 1-800/CLARION, fax 416/977-4830). Comfortable, convenient high-rise hotel in busy Jarvis St. Good facilities – indoor swimming pool, sauna, etc. Five-minutes' walk east of Yonge along Gerrard St. College subway. ⑥.

Days Inn Toronto Downtown, 30 Carlton St (☎416/977-6655 or 1-800/DAYS-INN, fax 416/977-0502). Routine modern hotel with competitively priced rooms. Occupies a chunky tower block metres from College subway. ⑤.

Delta Chelsea, 33 Gerrard St W (☎416/595-1975, fax 416/585-4366, *www.deltachelsea.com*). Near the Eaton Centre, this is the biggest hotel in town with excellent leisure facilities, including swimming pool, gym, sauna and childcare. The comfortable, attractively furnished rooms are a comparative bargain, with substantial weekend discounts. Dundas subway. ⑥.

Four Seasons Hotel, 21 Avenue Rd (☎416/964-0411 or 1-800/332-3442, fax 416/964-2301). Luxurious modern hotel in the wealthy and fashionable district of Yorkville. A particularly pleasant place to stay with all mod cons – but it's pricey. Just off Bloor St and a 5min walk north of Museum subway. ⑧.

Howard Johnson Inn Toronto-Yorkville, 89 Avenue Rd (☎416/964-1220 or 1-877/551-4656, fax 416/964-8692). An excellent bargain, this hotel is tucked into a busy section of Avenue Rd, only blocks from the expensive *Four Seasons Hotel* (see above). The large rooms are both tidy and comfortable. Bay subway. ④.

Novotel Toronto Centre, 45 The Esplanade (☎416/367-8900 or 1-800/NOVOTEL, fax 416/360-8285). Located in a splendidly converted old building, with an elegant arcaded facade and other Art Deco flourishes, this polished hotel has all the conveniences. Stands next door to one of the city's most striking skyscrapers – a bright-white triangle of glass and stone. Metres east of Union Station. ⑥.

Royal York Hotel, 100 Front St W (☎416/368-2511 or 1-800/441-1414, fax 416/368-2884). On completion in 1927, the *Royal York* was the largest hotel in the British Empire and retains much of its original grandeur. Rooms aren't as pricey as you might expect, particularly at weekends. Union subway. ⑥.

Strathcona Hotel, 60 York St (☎416/363-3321 or 1-800/268-8304, fax 416/363-4679). This is about as cheap as a downtown hotel can get without becoming irredeemably sleazy. Something of a borderline case, this one is nevertheless clean and undeniably central: about half a block from Union Station, and five minutes from the SkyDome and the CN Tower. Subway: Union Station. ③.

Town Inn Suites, 620 Church St at Charles St E (☎416/964-3311 or 1-800/387-2755, fax 416/924-9466). One of the best bargains in the city, this centrally located hotel offers budget suites equipped with kitchens, and is an excellent option for longer stays, as weekly and monthly rates are available. Very popular with savvy travellers, so book early for the summer months. ④. Subway: Yonge-Bloor or Wellesley.

Hotel Victoria, 56 Yonge St (☎416/363-1666 or 1-800/363-8228, fax 416/324-5920). This charming hotel occupies a dignified old building in the heart of downtown. The 50 rooms are clean and crisply furnished, but a tad cramped. Subway: Union Station. ⑤.

Westin Harbour Castle, 1 Harbour Square (☎416/869-1600 or 1-800/228-3000, fax 416/869-0573). A massive hotel of nearly 1000 rooms, this is a terrific base for forays to the Toronto Islands – ferries dock at the plaza out in front. The *Westin Harbour* makes up for its lack of intimate charm by

BED AND BREAKFAST INFORMATION

Almost all the recommendable B&Bs in Ontario are members of the **Federation of Ontario Bed and Breakfast Accommodation** (☎416/515-1293, *www.fobba.com*). Members details are listed on their Web site and – at least for now – in the association's free handbook, available at most member B&Bs.

catering to its guests every whim, and by the fact that many of the nicely-furnished rooms come with splendid views of either Lake Ontario or downtown's skyscrapers. York Quay stop on tram #510 from Union Station. ⑦.

Windsor Arms, 18 St Thomas St (☎416/971-9666 or 1-877/999-2767). One of the city's most distinctive hotels, the *Windsor* occupies an immaculate brick-and-stone-trimmed building with neo-Gothic flourishes dating from the end of the nineteenth century. Open fires, columns, stained-glass windows and Georgian-style furniture characterize the interior. Off Bloor St W; Bay subway. Recommended – but very expensive: the cheapest rooms are $425. ⑧.

Bed and breakfasts

Beverley Place B&B, 235 Beverley St (☎416/977-0077, fax 599-2242). Appealing and attractively restored three-storey Victorian house, kitted out with antique furnishings. Of the six rooms available, three have private bathrooms and four have fireplaces. A 10min walk west of Queen's Park subway along College St. ③.

Casa Loma Inn, 21 Walmer Rd (☎416/924-4540, fax 259-7017). Located in a leafy residential area, this huge Victorian guesthouse has 23 nicely decorated rooms. Close to Casa Loma and Spadina House (see p.91). Nonsmokers only. ③.

High Park, 4 High Park Blvd (☎416/531-7963, fax 531-0060). This ample home has three rooms, two of which share a bath. The largest room has its own balcony, which overlooks the leafy confines of the surrounding Victorian neighbourhood. The breakfasts here are wonderful, and the host most friendly. A fifteen-minute walk or short bus ride south of Dundas West subway station along Roncesvalles Ave. ③.

Mulberry Tree, 122 Isabella St (☎416/960-5249, fax 960-3853, *emultree@istar.ca*). This delightful B&B, one of Toronto's most agreeable, occupies a stylishly decorated heritage home close to the city centre. Each of the guestrooms is comfortable and relaxing – indeed the whole atmosphere of the place is just right, combining efficiency and friendliness. Highly recommended. Subway: Sherbourne. ④.

Palmerston Inn, 322 Palmerston Blvd (☎416/920-7842, fax 960-9529). This palatial, oak-panelled mansion is situated on one of Toronto's most desirable residential streets. The eight rooms are decked out with varying degrees of luxury, such as fireplaces, fresh flowers and bathrobes. Just off College, two blocks west of Bathurst. College streetcar. ④.

Terrace House, 52 Austin Terrace (☎416/535-1493, fax 535-9616). This pre-World War I, mock-Tudor house is perched high on a hill overlooking the city. The neighbourhood includes noteworthy piles like Casa Loma and Spadina House (see p.91), and is close to some of the most exclusive residential neighbourhoods in the city. There are three rooms (two with fireplaces, one with a private bath), all decked out with antiques and North African rugs. It's only a five-minute walk from the Dupont subway station, but it's all uphill. Subway: Dupont. ④.

University residences

Toronto has two large downtown **universities**: The University of Toronto and Ryerson Polytechnic University. From the second week in May to the end of August there is an abundance of student residences available to budget-wise tourists of all ages on a daily, weekly or monthly basis. Most residences require a night's or week's deposit, depending on the length of your stay.

Ryerson Neill-Wycik College, 96 Gerrard St E (☎416/977-2320, fax 977-2809). All available accommodations (singles, doubles and quads) are apartment suites with shared kitchens. There are telephones in all rooms, laundry facilities and limited on-site parking. The campus itself is scenic and quiet, but the youth-magnet intersection of Yonge and Dundas is only a short walk away – which could be good or bad depending on how you like your Saturday nights. Daily, weekly and monthly rates available on all units. Subway: Dundas. ①/②.

University of Toronto, Innis College, 111 St George St (☎416/978-2553, fax 971-2464). This recently built residence has air conditioning and a daily maid service. Daily and weekly rentals, however, are restricted to the single rooms. Doubles are only available for long-term stays. Subway: St George. ①.

University of Toronto, Loretto College, 70 St Mary's St (☎416/925-2833, fax 925-4058). Singles and doubles are available here, and some of the singles have private baths. Daily rates include breakfast, and weekly rates include three meals a day. Subway: Wellesley. ①/②.

University of Toronto, Massey College, 4 Devonshire Place (☎416/978-2892, fax 978-1759). In addition to being the one-time stomping grounds of author Robertson Davies, this beautiful college reportedly boasts the presence of at least one ghost. Singles and doubles are available with breakfast included on weekdays May–July; rates are lower in August, when breakfast is no longer served. Subway: St George. ①.

University of Toronto, Victoria College, 140 Charles St W (☎416/585-4524, fax 585-4530). This huge campus site includes accommodation in Annesley Hall, Burwash Hall, Law House and Margaret Addison Hall. The daily rates for doubles and singles include a full breakfast. Subway: Museum. ①.

Hostels

Global Village Backpackers Hostel, 460 King St W (☎416/703-8540 or 1-888/844-7875, fax 416/703-3887, *www.globalbackpackers.com*). Basic hostel offering dormitory accommodation for around $20 per person. Central location and 200 beds.

Hostelling International Toronto, 76 Church St (☎416/971-4440 or 1-800/668-4487, fax 416/971-4088, *thostel@hostellingintl-gl.on.ca*). In the heart of the city, one block east of Yonge along Adelaide St. The 180 beds are mostly in air-conditioned dorm rooms; it has a laundry, kitchen and Internet access. Book ahead in summer or all year for groups of six or more. Members $18, non-members a few dollars more. King subway.

YWCA Woodlawn Residence, 80 Woodlawn Ave E (☎416/923-8454, fax 923-1950, *lawn@ywcator .org*). Tucked away in a cul-de-sac in the pretty Summerhill neighbourhood, this women-only residence offers single ($47–52) and double ($62–65) rooms with a continental breakfast. Discounted monthly rates are available too. There are laundry facilities and vending machines on site, and a good selection of cafés and restaurants close by. Subway: Summerhill.

Downtown Toronto

Toronto evolved from a lakeside settlement, but its growth was sporadic and often unplanned, resulting in a cityscape that can strike the visitor as a random mix of the run-down and the new. This apparent disarray, combined with the city's muggy summers, means that, rather than walking the streets, most newcomers to Toronto spend their time hopping from sight to sight on the efficient public transport system. Indeed, there's no doubt that if you've only got a day or two to spare this is the way to get a grip on the city.

On the other hand, if you've the time to get below the surface, the best thing to do is stroll through **Downtown Toronto**, and the logical place to start is the CN Tower, from where you can take in the lie of the land for kilometres around. Nearby Union Station, hub of the city's public transport system, lies on the edge of the business district, whose striking skyscrapers march up Yonge as far as Queen Street, where they give way to the main shopping area, revolving around the enormous Eaton Centre. To the west of this commercial zone lie Chinatown and the Art Gallery of Ontario, while to the northwest, along University Avenue is the most obviously English-influenced area

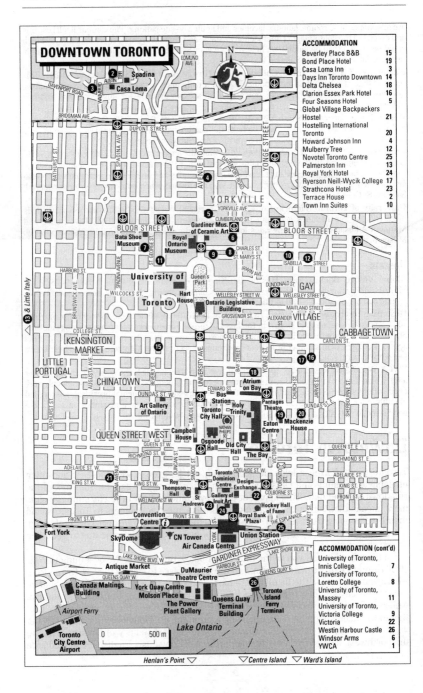

DOWNTOWN TORONTO

ACCOMMODATION

Beverley Place B&B	15
Bond Place Hotel	19
Casa Loma Inn	3
Days Inn Toronto Downtown	14
Delta Chelsea	18
Clarion Essex Park Hotel	16
Four Seasons Hotel	5
Global Village Backpackers Hostel	21
Hostelling International Toronto	20
Howard Johnson Inn	4
Mulberry Tree	12
Novotel Toronto Centre	25
Palmerston Inn	13
Royal York Hotel	24
Ryerson Neill-Wycik College	17
Strathcona Hotel	23
Terrace House	2
Town Inn Suites	10

ACCOMMODATION (cont'd)

University of Toronto, Innis College	7
University of Toronto, Loretto College	8
University of Toronto, Massey	11
University of Toronto, Victoria College	9
Victoria	22
Westin Harbour Castle	26
Windsor Arms	6
YWCA	1

TORONTO'S NEIGHBOURHOODS

One of Toronto's most striking features is its division into distinct **neighbourhoods**, many of them based on ethnic origin, others defined by sexual preference or income. Bilingual street signs identify some of these neighbourhoods, but architecturally they are often indistinguishable from their surroundings. The following rundown will help you get the most from the city's demographic mosaic, whether you want to shop, eat or just take in the atmosphere. But bear in mind that there is a certain artificiality in the nomenclature – Chinatown, for instance, has hundreds of Vietnamese residents, Little Italy many Portuguese.

The Beaches, lying south of Queen Street East between Woodbine and Victoria Park Avenue, is a prosperous and particularly appealing district with chic boutiques, leafy streets and a sandy beach trimmed by a popular boardwalk. Glenn Gould (see p.83) was born here.

Cabbagetown, east of Jarvis and roughly bounded by Gerrard Street East on its south side, Wellesley to the north and the Don River to the east, is renowned for its Victorian housing. Its name comes from the district's nineteenth-century immigrants, whose tiny front gardens were filled with cabbages.

Chinatown is concentrated along Dundas between Bay and Spadina. This is one of Toronto's most distinctive neighbourhoods, with busy restaurants and stores selling anything from porcelain and jade to herbs and pickled seaweed.

The Gay and Lesbian Village, with its plethora of bars, restaurants and bookshops, is centred around Church and Wellesley.

Greektown, a burgeoning neighbourhood along Danforth Avenue, is located between Pape and Woodbine. With scores of authentic restaurants, this is the place to go for Greek food.

Kensington Market, just north of Dundas between Spadina and Augusta, is the most ethnically diverse part of town, combining Portuguese, West Indian and Jewish Canadians, who pack the streets with a plethora of tiny shops and open-air stalls.

Little India is along Gerrard Street East, running one block west from Coxwell Avenue. Visually, it's not too appealing, but the area does have a number of fine restaurants.

Little Italy – the so-called Corso Italia – runs along College between Bathurst and Clinton, and is one of Toronto's liveliest neighbourhoods.

Little Portugal, a crowded, vital area packed with shops and neighbourhood food joints, is focused on Dundas, west of Bathurst as far as Dovercourt.

Queen Street West, between University and Spadina, has one of the highest retail rents in the city and is home to all things trendy and expensive. The students and punks who once hung around here have moved on to what is known as Queen West West, between Spadina and Bathurst.

Yorkville, just above Bloor between Yonge and Avenue Road, was "alternative" in the 1960s, with appearances by figureheads of the counterculture like Gordon Lightfoot and Joni Mitchell. Today, the alternative jive of the place is long gone, and the district holds some of Toronto's most expensive clothing shops and art galleries, as well as several good bars and restaurants.

of town around Queen's Park, incorporating the Ontario Parliament building, the University of Toronto and the Royal Ontario Museum. Moving on to the northern periphery of central Toronto, the key attractions are the intriguing Bata Shoe Museum and a pair of contrasting Victorian mansions – grandiose Casa Loma and genteel Spadina House. Spare time also for Old Fort York to the west of downtown and the redeveloped Harbourfront south of Union Station, which offers flashy shops, the Power Plant Gallery of modern art, and the jetty from where ferries make the short hop over to the Toronto Islands.

The CN Tower, SkyDome and St Andrew's Presbyterian Church

The obligatory start to a Toronto visit is to take your place in the queue at the foot of the minaret-thin **CN Tower** (daily: Jan–April 9am–10pm; May–Dec daily 8am–11pm; $16; *www.cntower.ca*), which tapers to a point 553.33m above the waterfront just off Front Street West. Tourists are whisked up its outside in leg-liquefying glass-fronted elevators and the first port of call is the indoor and outdoor viewing platforms of the 346m **Lookout Level**. From here, it's another 100m to the cramped **Sky Pod** (an extra $5.50) and views as far as Niagara Falls and Buffalo. Dispiritingly, the tower has been equipped with a string of tacky attractions, the worst being the "Daredevil Thrills" simulated rides, the most enjoyable the **glass floor** on the Lookout Level.

Next door to the CN Tower is the **SkyDome**, home to two major Toronto sports teams – the Blue Jays baseball team and the Argonauts of Canadian Football fame. The stadium seats 53,000 and is also used for special events and concerts. Opened in 1989, it was the first stadium in the world to have a fully retractable roof – it only takes twenty minutes to cover the stadium's eight acres of turf and terrace. It was an extraordinary feat of engineering (four gigantic roof panels mounted on rail tracks), and one that was much touted by the city, but unfortunately, the end result is pretty ugly – when the roof is closed it looks like a giant armadillo. **Guided tours** (telephone for schedule ☎416/341-2770; $10.50), worth it only if you're sticking around for a sporting event, last an hour and begin with a fifteen-minute film about the stadium's construction. The ensuing walking tour takes in the media centre, a dressing room and a stroll on the field.

In contrast, **St Andrew's Presbyterian Church** (daily 9am–4pm; free), nearby at Simcoe and King, is a reminder of an older Toronto, its Romanesque Revival towers, gables and galleries given a vaguely Norman appearance by the rose window and triple-arched entrance. Built in 1876 for a predominantly Scottish congregation, the church has a delightful interior, its cherrywood pews and balcony sloping down towards the chancel. More importantly, St Andrew's has an admirable history of social action: the city's churches have played a leading role campaigning against poverty and homelessness since the very earliest days of settlement, and they continue to do so today.

The banking district

To the east of the CN Tower, the beaux-arts subtleties of **Union Railway Station** – and the matching **Royal York Hotel** opposite – mark the boundary of the banking district, whose bizarre juxtapositions of old, low buildings and high-rises evidence one of Toronto's stranger ordinances. The city's buildings have a notional maximum altitude and although owners of older properties are not allowed to extend their buildings, they are permitted to sell the empty space between their roofs and this notional maximum. Thus, the builders of new structures can purchase this space and add it to their own maximum, thereby creating the skyscrapers that the ordinance would seem to forbid. The arrangement enhances neither the old nor the new, but some of the high-rises are undeniably impressive, such as the colossal twin towers of the **Royal Bank Plaza**, at Bay and Front, and the four reflective-black blocks of the **Toronto Dominion Centre**, along Wellington Street West between Bay and York. Just one of these four blocks is on the south side of Wellington and here you'll find the **Gallery of Inuit Art** (Mon–Fri 8am–6pm, Sat & Sun 10am–4pm; free), which boasts an exquisite collection of Inuit sculpture. The exhibits are owned by the Dominion Bank, who commissioned a panel of experts to collect the best of postwar Inuit art in 1965. Exhibited on two levels, their haul features some simple and forceful stone carvings by Johnny Inukpuk, whose impressionistic style contrasts with the precision of the *Migration* by Joe Talirunli, in which the rowers crane forward in eagerness and anxiety. Even more detailed is the incised caribou antler from Cape Dorset, on which natural dyes pick out a cartoon strip of Inuit life.

Around the corner at 234 Bay St, the old **Toronto Stock Exchange** has been mutilated by its incorporation within a skyrise that imitates – but doesn't match – the sober black blocks of the adjacent Toronto Dominion Centre. Nevertheless, the facade has survived, its stone lintel decorated with muscular carvings of men at work, a frieze given a political twist by the top-hatted figure – the capitalist – who dips his hand into a worker's pocket, a subversive subtext by an unknown stonemason. The interior of the Stock Exchange now accommodates the temporary exhibitions of the **Design Exchange** (Tues–Fri 10am–6pm, Sat & Sun noon–5pm; free except during some exhibitions), the DX, whose purpose is to foster innovative design.

From the DX, it's a short stroll to the old Bank of Montréal building, a solid Neoclassical edifice of 1885 that now houses the **Hockey Hall of Fame**, 30 Yonge St at Front Street West (mid-June to Aug Mon–Sat 9.30am–6pm, Sun 10am–6pm; Sept to mid-June Mon–Fri 10am–5pm, Sat 9.30am–6pm, Sun 10.30am–5pm; $12). The place is stuffed with ice-hockey memorabilia, has a replica of the Montréal Canadiens' dressing room and proudly exhibits the sport's most important trophy, the Stanley Cup.

City Hall and around

Nathan Phillips Square, one of the most distinctive of Toronto's landmarks, lies on Queen Street, just north of the banking district. Laid out by the Finnish architect Viljo Revell, the square is framed by an elevated walkway and focuses on a reflecting pool, which becomes a skating rink in winter. The square is overlooked by Toronto's **City Hall**, whose curved glass-and-concrete towers are fronted by *The Archer*, a Henry Moore sculpture that resembles a giant propeller. Revell won all sorts of awards for this project, which was the last word in dynamism in the 1960s, but has since become a rather jaded symbol of urban planning. On a positive note, it is at least associated with political change – its sponsor, Nathan Phillips, was Toronto's first Jewish mayor. Had Revell's grand scheme been carried out fully, the city would have bulldozed the **Old City Hall**, a flamboyant pseudo-Romanesque building on the east side of the square. Completed in 1899, it was designed by Edward J. Lennox, who developed a fractious relationship with his paymasters on the city council. They had a point: the original cost of the building had been estimated at $1.77 million, but Lennox spent an extra $750,000 and took all of eight years to finish the project. Nevertheless, Lennox had the last laugh, carving gargoyle-like representations of the city's fathers on the arches at the top of the front steps and placing his name on each side of the building – something the city council had expressly forbidden him to do.

Immediately to the west of Nathan Phillips Square, along Queen Street, stands **Osgoode Hall**, a Neoclassical pile built for the Law Society of Upper Canada early in the nineteenth century. Looking like a cross between a Greek temple and an English country house, it's protected by a wrought-iron fence designed to keep cows and horses off the lawn. The elegant Georgian mansion on the opposite side of University Avenue is **Campbell House** (Mon–Fri 9.30am–4.30pm, Sat & Sun late May to early Oct noon–4.30pm; $3.50), built on Adelaide Street for Sir William Campbell, Chief Justice and Speaker of the Legislative Assembly – it was transported here in 1972. There are regular guided tours of the period interior and these provide a well-researched overview of early nineteenth-century Toronto. At the time, Campbell was a leading figure, and a progressive one too, eschewing the death penalty whenever feasible and even awarding the radical William MacKenzie damages when his printing press was wrecked by a mob of Tories in 1826.

The Elgin Theatre and Winter Garden

Doubling back along Queen Street, it's a brief stroll to one of the city's most unusual attractions, the **Elgin Theatre and Winter Garden**, across from the Eaton Centre at 189 Yonge St (guided tours only, Thurs 5pm & Sat 11am; 90min; $7; ☎416/597-0965). The first part of the guided tour covers the Elgin, an old vaudeville theatre which has been restored after years of neglect and is now equipped with ornate furnishings and fittings, columns, engravings and gilt mirrors. The Elgin was turned into a cinema in the 1930s and, remarkably enough, its accompaniment, the top-floor **Winter Garden**, also a vaudeville theatre, was sealed off. Such double-decker theatres were introduced in the late nineteenth century in New York and soon became popular along the east coast, but only a handful have survived. Even better, when this one was unsealed, its original decor was found to be intact, the ceiling hung with thousands of preserved and painted beech leaves illuminated by coloured lanterns. In the event, much of the decor had to be replaced, but the restoration work was painstakingly thorough and the end result is delightful.

The Eaton Centre and the church of the Holy Trinity

Across from the Elgin Theatre is the **Eaton Centre**, a mainly three-storey assortment of shops and restaurants spread out underneath a glass-and-steel arched roof. By shopping mall standards, the design is appealing and the flock of fibreglass Canada geese suspended from the ceiling adds a touch of flair. Maps of the shopping mall are displayed on every floor, but the general rule is the higher the floor, the more expensive the shop. The centre takes its name from Timothy Eaton, an Ulster immigrant who opened his first store here in 1869. His cash-only, fixed-price, money-back-guarantee trading revolutionized the Canadian market and made him a fortune. Soon a Canadian institution, Eaton kept a grip on the pioneer settlements in the west through his mail-order catalogue, known as the "homesteader's bible" – or the "wish book" among aboriginal peoples – whilst Eaton department stores sprang up in all of Canada's big cities. In recent years, however, the company has struggled to maintain its profitability and this branch is now run by Sears.

About two-thirds of the way along the Eaton Centre from Queen, a side exit leads straight to the **church of the Holy Trinity**, an appealing nineteenth-century structure whose yellow brickwork is surmounted by a pair of sturdy turrets and matching chimneys. It was here, with the church set against the skyscrapers that crowd in on it, that Canadian movie director David Cronenberg filmed the last scene of *Dead Ringers*. The dubious moral content of the film – the unscrupulous exploits of twin rogue gynaecologists, both played by Jeremy Irons – prompted Cronenberg to defend his subject matter thus: "I don't have a moral plan. I'm a Canadian."

The Thomson Gallery

A second-floor walkway crosses Queen Street to connect the south end of the Eaton Centre with The Bay department store, where, on the ninth floor, the **Thomson Gallery** (Mon–Sat 11am–5pm; $2.50) offers an outstanding introduction to many of Canada's finest artists, especially the Group of Seven (see box, p.86). Highlights include an impressive selection of paintings by Lawren Harris, notably his surreal *Lake Superior*, and a small selection, by J.E.H. MacDonald, whose *Rowan Berries* of 1922 is simply stunning. Tom Thomson, the main inspiration of the Seven, is represented by the vivid *Maple Springs* and his heated *Autumn's Garland,* blotchy contrasts with A.Y. Jackson's smooth-flowing *Road to Chicoutimi* and the wriggling spirals of his *Yellowknife Country,* in which the trees swirl above a heaving, purplish earth. Franklin

GLENN GOULD

In the 1970s, anyone passing the Eaton's department store around 9pm on any day of the year might have seen the door unlocked for a distracted-looking figure swaddled in overcoat, scarves, gloves and hat. This character, making his way to a recording studio set up for his exclusive use inside the shop, was perhaps the most famous citizen of Toronto and the most charismatic pianist in the world – **Glenn Gould**.

Not the least remarkable thing about Gould was that very few people outside the CBS recording crew would ever hear him play live. In 1964, aged just 32, he retired from the concert platform, partly out of a distaste for the accidental qualities of any live performance, partly out of hatred for the cult of the virtuoso. Yet no pianist ever provided more material for the mythologizers. He possessed a memory so prodigious that none of his acquaintances was ever able to find a piece of music he could not instantly play perfectly, but he loathed much of the standard piano repertoire, dismissing romantic composers such as Chopin, Liszt and Rachmaninoff as little more than showmen. Dauntingly cerebral in his tastes and playing style, he was nonetheless an ardent fan of Barbra Streisand – an esteem that was fully reciprocated – and once wrote an essay titled "In Search of Petula Clark". He lived at night and kept in touch by phoning his friends in the small hours of the morning, talking for so long that his monthly phone bill ran into thousands of dollars. Detesting all blood sports (a category in which he placed concert performances), he would terrorize anglers on Lake Simcoe by buzzing them in his motorboat. He travelled everywhere with bags full of medicines and would never allow anyone to shake his hand, yet soaked his arms in almost scalding water before playing in order to get his circulation going. At the keyboard he sang loudly to himself, swaying back and forth on a creaky little chair made for him by his father – all other pianists sat too high, he insisted. And even in a heatwave he was always dressed as if a blizzard were imminent. To many of his colleagues, Gould's eccentricities were maddening, but what mattered was that nobody could play like Glenn Gould. As one exasperated conductor put it, "the nut's a genius".

Gould's first recording, Bach's *Goldberg Variations*, was released in 1956, and became the best-selling classical record of that year. Soon after, he became the first Western musician to play in the Soviet Union, where his reputation spread so quickly that for his final recital more than a thousand people were allowed to stand in the aisles of the Leningrad hall. On his debut in Berlin, the leading German critic described him as "a young man in a strange sort of trance," whose "technical ability borders on the fabulous". The technique always dazzled, but Gould's fiercely wayward intelligence made his interpretations controversial, as can be gauged from the fact that Leonard Bernstein, conducting Gould on one occasion, felt obliged to inform the audience that what they were about to hear was the pianist's responsibility, not his. Most notoriously of all, he had a very low opinion of Mozart's abilities – and went so far as to record the Mozart sonatas in order to demonstrate that Wolfgang Amadeus died too late rather than too soon. Gould himself died suddenly in 1982 at the age of 50 – the age at which he had said he would give up playing the piano entirely.

Gould's legacy of recordings is not confined to music. He made a trilogy of radio documentaries on the theme of solitude: *The Quiet in the Land*, about Canada's Mennonites; *The Latecomers*, about the inhabitants of Newfoundland; and *The Idea of North*, for which he taped interviews with people who, like himself, spent much of their time amid Canada's harshest landscapes. Just as Gould's Beethoven, Bach and Mozart sounded like nobody else's, these were documentaries like no others, each a complex weave of voices spliced and overlaid in compositions that are overtly musical in construction. However, Gould's eighty-odd piano recordings are the basis of his enduring popularity, and nearly all of them have been reissued on CD, spanning Western keyboard music from Orlando Gibbons to Arnold Schoenberg. One of the most poignant is his second version of the *Goldberg*, the last record to be issued before his death.

Carmichael, the youngest original member of the Group, also developed a flowing, harmonious technique, a beautiful example being his *Cranberry Lake* of 1931. Finally, a contemporary of the Group of Seven, Emily Carr, was famous for her paintings of west-coast Indian villages and the totemic figures she developed as a symbol of native culture. *Thunderbird* and *Thunderbird, Campbell River BC* are good examples of her later style, a marked progression from the fastidiousness of the early *Gitwangak, Queen Charlotte Islands*.

The gallery's assortment of early and mid-nineteenth-century Canadian and Canada-based artists is less distinguished, but there are some fine canvases, such as the curiously unflattering *Portrait of Joseph Brant* by William Berczy and the winter scenes typical of the work of Cornelius Krieghoff (see p.163). Interesting in a different way is the series by the artist-explorer **Paul Kane**, whose paintings show a conflict of subject and style that highlights the stylistic achievements of the Group of Seven: Kane's *Landscape in the Foothills with Buffalo Resting*, for example, looks more like a placid German valley than the prairies. Born in Ireland in 1810, Kane first emigrated to Toronto in the early 1820s, but returned to Europe at the age of 30, where, ironically enough, he was so impressed by an exhibition of paintings on the American Indian that he promptly decided to move back to Canada. In 1846, he finally wangled himself a place on a westward-bound fur-trading expedition and started an epic journey – travelling from Thunder Bay to Edmonton by canoe, crossing the Rockies by horse, and finally returning to Toronto two years after setting out. During his travels, Kane made some seven hundred sketches, which he then proceeded to paint onto canvas, paper and cardboard, and in 1859 published *Wanderings of an Artist among the Indian Tribes of North America*, the story of his journey. It includes this account of Christmas dinner at Fort Edmonton: "At the head, before Mr Harriett, was a large dish of boiled buffalo hump; at the foot smoked a boiled buffalo calf . . . one of the most esteemed dishes among the epicures of the interior. My pleasing duty was to help a dish of mouffle, or dried moose nose [while] the worthy priest helped the buffalo tongue and Mr Randall cut up the beaver's tails. The centre of the table was graced with piles of potatoes, turnips and bread conveniently placed, so that each could help himself without interrupting the labours of his companions. Such was our jolly Christmas dinner at Edmonton." Quite.

The Art Gallery of Ontario

Situated just west of University Avenue along Dundas Street West, the **Art Gallery of Ontario** (AGO; Tues, Thurs & Fri 11am–6pm, Wed 11am–8.30pm, Sat & Sun 10am–5.30pm; recommended donation $6 plus fixed charges for temporary exhibitions; *www.ago.on.ca*) is renowned both for its wide-ranging collection of foreign and domestic art and for its excellent temporary exhibitions. The gallery, however, is housed in an oddly discordant and rather confusing building, the result of several different phases of construction, and neither is there enough room to exhibit all of the permanent collection at any one time, which means that the exhibits are rotated. The exterior is a stern, modern facade decorated by a scaffold-like tower and a matching pair of Henry Moore sculptures, large and chunky bronzes uninspiringly called *Large Two Forms*. Inside, the AGO's **Street Level** focuses on Walker Court, which boasts European works, and there is an excellent art shop and café here too. The **Upper Level** holds contemporary art, a superb sample of Canadian paintings and an extensive collection of Henry Moore sculptures. Museum maps are issued free at reception.

Walker Court and the European collection

Just beyond the main entrance, turn right and stroll down a long corridor (S2) lined with marvellous samples of European applied art, all on permanent loan from Ken Thomson's private collection – the same tycoon who funds the Thomson Gallery (see p.82). At the end of the corridor, the central **Walker Court** is surrounded on three sides by the European art galleries (S3–S9), which cover the Italian Renaissance through to French Impressionism. **French** painters are much in evidence too, from the seventeenth century onwards; look out in particular for *St Anne with the Christ Child* by Georges de la Tour, and Poussin's *Venus Presenting Arms to Aeneas*. **Impressionist** works here include Degas's archetypal *Woman in the Bath*, Renoir's screaming-pink *Concert*, and Monet's wonderful *Vétheuil in Summer*, with its hundreds of tiny jabs of colour.

The fourth side of Walker Court (S10) is bordered by the Twentieth Century European Art gallery, where pride of place goes to Picasso's classically Cubist *Seated Woman*; Marc Chagall's *Over Vitebsk*, a whimsical celebration of his Russian birthplace; and Paul Gauguin's evocative *Hina and Fatu*, a wooden stump carved with Polynesian figures. Also exhibited here are Magritte's unnerving *The Birthday*, Barbara Hepworth's *Two Figures*, and Modigliani's *Portrait of Mrs Hastings*, in which you have to assume the subject wasn't seeking flattery.

The Canadian collection

The Upper Level of the AGO holds the outstanding **Canadian Art to 1960** section (U9–U20), where the emphasis is on the work of the **Group of Seven** (see box overleaf) and their contemporaries. One of the most distinctive artists of the Group of Seven was **Lawren Harris**, whose *Above Lake Superior* of 1922 is a pivotal work – its clarity of conception, with its bare birch stumps framing a dark mountain beneath Art Deco clouds, is quite exceptional. The adjacent *West Wind* by **Tom Thomson** is another seminal work, an iconic rendering of the northern wilderness that is perhaps the most famous of all Canadian paintings. Thomson was the first to approach wilderness landscapes with the determination of an explorer and the sense that they could encapsulate a specifically Canadian identity. Several of his less-familiar (but no less powerful) works are here as well, including the moody *A Northern Lake* and the Cubist-influenced preparatory painting, *Autumn Foliage 1915*.

J.E.H. MacDonald, also one of the Group of Seven, was fond of dynamic, sweeping effects, and his panoramic *Falls, Montreal River* sets turbulent rapids beside hot-coloured hillsides. His friend **Fred Varley** dabbled in portraiture and chose soft images and subtle colours for his landscapes as exemplified by the sticky-looking brushstrokes he used for *Moonlight after Rain*. A sample of **A.Y. Jackson**'s work includes the characteristically carpet-like surface of *Algoma Rocks, Autumn*, painted in 1923, while **A.J. Casson**'s bright and rather formal *Old Store at Salem* offers a break from the scenic preoccupations of the rest of the Seven. **Emily Carr**, represented by several works here, was a great admirer of the Seven, but she was never accepted as a member despite her obvious abilities – the deep-green foliage of her *Indian Church* and *Western Forest*, both painted in 1929, are good illustrations.

The Canadian Art section also features the work of earlier leading artists – most notably Paul Kane (see p.163) and Cornelius Krieghoff (see p.163) – and nearby, beside and above the spiral staircase, there are two small galleries of **Inuit art** (U8). Here, look out for examples of the work of Pauta Saila – *Dancing Bear* – and John Tiktak (1916–81), generally regarded as one of the most talented Inuit sculptors of his generation. The death of Tiktak's mother in 1962 had a profound effect on him and his *Mother and Child* forcefully expresses this close connection, with the figure of the child carved into the larger figure of the mother.

Contemporary art and the Henry Moore Sculpture Gallery

Most of the rest of the Upper Level (U3–U7) is given over to the AGO's collection of **contemporary art**, showcasing works by European, British and American artists.

Works are regularly rotated, but watch out for Warhol's *Elvis I* and *II*, Mark Rothko's strident *No.1 White and Red* and Claes Oldenburg's quirky if somewhat frayed *Giant Hamburger*.

The contemporary art exhibits culminate in the **Henry Moore Sculpture Gallery** (U1), the world's largest collection of pieces by Moore, with the emphasis firmly on his plaster casts alongside a selection of his bronzes. Given a whole gallery, Moore's exhibit space is enormous, but it was something of an accident that his work ended up here at all. In the 1960s, Moore had reason to believe that London's Tate Gallery was going to build a special wing for him. When the Tate declined, Moore chose the AGO instead, persuaded to do so by the AGO's British representative, Anthony Blunt, the art expert who was famously uncovered as a Soviet spy in 1979.

The Grange

Attached to the back of the AGO is **The Grange** (May–Oct Tues & Thurs–Sun noon–4pm, Wed noon–9pm, Oct–May Wed noon–9pm & Thurs–Sun noon–4pm; no extra charge), an early nineteenth-century brick mansion with Neoclassical trimmings that was bequeathed to the fledgling Art Museum of Toronto, the predecessor of the AGO, in 1910. The Grange remains part of the AGO and it has been restored to its mid-nineteenth-century appearance. Guides dressed in period costume show you around, enthusiastically explaining the ins and outs of life in nineteenth-century Toronto. Several of the original paintings have survived alongside the antique furnishings and fittings, but it's the beautiful wooden staircase that really catches the eye.

THE GROUP OF SEVEN

In the autumn of 1912, a commercial artist by the name of **Tom Thomson** returned from an extended trip to the Mississauga country, north of Georgian Bay, with a bag full of sketches that were to add a new momentum to Canadian art. His friends, many of them fellow employees of the art firm of Grip Ltd in Toronto, saw Thomson's naturalistic approach to indigenous subject matter as a pointer away from the influence of Europe, declaring the "northland" as the true Canadian "painter's country". World War I and the death of Thomson – who drowned in 1917 – delayed these artists' ambitions, but in 1920 they formed the **Group of Seven**: Franklin H. Carmichael, Lawren Harris, A.Y. Jackson, Arthur Lismer, J.E.H. MacDonald, F.H. Varley and Frank Johnston (later joined by A.J. Casson, L.L. Fitzgerald and Edwin Holgate). Working under the unofficial leadership of Harris, they explored the wilds of Algoma in the late 1910s, travelling around in a converted freight car, and later foraged even further afield, from Newfoundland and Baffin Island to BC.

They were immediately successful, staging forty shows in eleven years, a triumph due in large part to Harris's many influential contacts. However, there was also a genuine popular response to the intrepid frontiersman element of their aesthetics. Art was a matter of "taking to the road" and "risking all for the glory of a great adventure", as they wrote in 1922, whilst "nature was the measure of a man's stature" according to Lismer. Symbolic of struggle against the elements, the Group's favourite symbol was the lone pine set against the sky, an image whose authenticity was confirmed by reference to the "manly" poetry of Walt Whitman.

The legacy of the Group of Seven is double-edged. On the one hand, they rediscovered the Canadian wilderness and established the autonomy of Canadian art. On the other, their contribution was soon institutionalized, and well into the 1950s it was difficult for Canadian painters to establish an identity that didn't conform to the Group's precepts. Among many practising artists the Group is unpopular, but the Ontario artist Graham Coughtry is generous: "They're the closest we've ever come to having some kind of romantic heroes in Canadian painting."

Chinatown and Kensington Market

The Art Gallery of Ontario is hemmed in by **Chinatown**, a bustling and immensely appealing neighbourhood cluttered with shops, restaurants and street stalls selling every and any type of Asian delicacy. The boundaries of Chinatown are somewhat blurred, but its focus has been Dundas Street West between Bay and Spadina ever since the Sixties, when the original Chinatown was demolished to make way for the new City Hall. The first Chinese to migrate to Canada arrived in the mid-nineteenth century to work in British Columbia's gold fields. Subsequently, a portion of this population migrated east, and a sizeable Chinese community sprung up in Toronto in the early twentieth century. Several more waves of migration – the last influx following the handing over of Hong Kong to mainland China by the British in 1997 – have greatly increased the number of Toronto's Chinese in recent years, bringing the population to approximately 250,000 (about eight percent of the city's total).

Next door to Chinatown, just north of Dundas between Spadina and Augusta, lies Toronto's most ethnically diverse neighbourhood, pocket-sized **Kensington Market**. It was here, at the beginning of the twentieth century, that Eastern European immigrants squeezed into a patchwork of modest little brick and timber houses that survive to this day. On Kensington Avenue they established the **open-air street market** that has been the main feature of the neighbourhood ever since, a lively, entertaining bazaar whose stall owners stem from many different ethnic backgrounds. The lower half of the market, just off Dundas Street, concentrates on secondhand clothes, while the upper half is crowded with fresh-food stalls.

The Ontario Legislative Assembly Building and Toronto University

University Avenue cuts north from Dundas to College, lined by gleaming tower blocks and overlooked by the pink-sandstone mass of the **Ontario Legislative Assembly Building** (late May to Aug Mon–Fri 8.30am–6.30pm & Sat–Sun 9am–4.30pm; Sept to late May Mon–Fri 8.30am–6.30pm; free; frequent & free 30min guided tours from Mon–Fri 10am–4pm, plus Sat & Sun 10am–4pm from late May to Aug), which was completed in 1892. No one could say this Romanesque Revival edifice was elegant, but its ponderous symmetries speak volumes of the bourgeois assertiveness that drove the provincial economy. Inside, the foyer leads to the wide and thickly carpeted grand staircase, whose massive timbers are supported by gilded iron pillars. Beyond, among the long corridors and arcaded galleries, is the **Legislative Chamber**, where the formal mahogany and sycamore panels are offset by a series of whimsical little carvings: look for the owl overlooking the doings of the government and the eagle overseeing the opposition benches. Under the Speaker's gallery, righteous inscriptions have been carved into the pillars – which is a bit of a hoot considering the behaviour of the building's architect, Richard Waite. Waite was chairman of the committee responsible for selecting an architect. And as chairman, he selected himself.

Behind the Legislative Building stands a heavyweight equestrian statue of King Edward VII in full-dress uniform, an imperial leftover that was originally plonked down in Delhi – and you can't help but feel the Indians must have been pleased to offload it. A couple of hundred metres to the west are the various faculties of the **University of Toronto**, opened in 1843 and the province's most prestigious academic institution. Its older buildings, with their quadrangles, ivy-covered walls and Gothic interiors, deliberately evoke Oxbridge: **Hart House**, at the end of Wellesley Street, is the best example, attached to the **Soldier's Tower**, a neo-Gothic memorial to those students who died in both world wars. The arcaded gallery abutting the tower lists the dead of World War I and is inscribed with the Canadian John McCrae's *In Flanders Fields*, arguably the war's best-known Canadian poem.

The Royal Ontario Museum

From the Legislative Building, it's a brief walk north along Queen's Park Boulevard to the **Royal Ontario Museum** (Mon–Thurs & Sat 10am–6pm, Fri 10am–9.30pm, Sun 11am–6pm; $15, free after 4.30pm on Fri). Known locally as the ROM, this is Canada's largest and most diverse museum, with ambitious collections of fine and applied art from all over the world as well as a first-rate programme of temporary exhibitions. With over forty different galleries and six million objects and artefacts, the ROM can be overwhelming, and there's precious little point in trying to see everything – at least not on one visit. In addition, some departments, notably the Chinese collections, have first-rate displays of international significance; others, like the Greco-Roman and Medieval European galleries, merely give representation to their subject areas and shouldn't be ranked too high on a must-see list. In this account we have stuck to the highlights. Museum plans are available for free at the entrance.

The ROM makes a cheerful start with a domed and vaulted **entrance hall** whose ceiling is decorated with a brilliant mosaic of imported Venetian glass. Just beyond, bolted into the stairwells, are four colossal aboriginal Haida and Nisga'a **crest poles** (also known as totem poles). Amazing elemental objects (the tallest is 24.5 metres high) and dating from the 1880s, they're decorated with stylized carvings representing the supernatural animals and birds, origins and rights that were associated with particular clans.

Chinese Art

On the museum's street level and straight back from the main entrance is the **Bishop White Gallery of Chinese Temple Art**, one of the ROM's most significant collections. It features three Daoist and Buddhist wall paintings dating from around 1300 AD, including a matching pair of Yuan Dynasty murals depicting the lords of the Northern and Southern Dipper, each of whom leads an astrological procession of star spirits. The murals are complemented by an exquisite sample of Buddhist sculpture, temple figures dating from the twelfth to the fourteenth centuries.

Close by, the **T.T. Tsui Galleries of Chinese Art** contain artefacts spanning six millennia, from 4500 BC to 1900 AD. Among the most important pieces is a remarkable collection of toy-sized tomb figurines – a couple of hundred ceramic pieces representing funerary processions of soldiers, musicians, carts and attendants. Dating from the early sixth to the late seventh century, they re-create the habits of early China – how people dressed, how horses were groomed and shod, changes in armoury, and so forth. There is also a fabulous collection of snuff bottles, some carved from glass and rock crystal, others from more exotic materials – amber, ivory, bamboo and even tangerine skin. Europeans introduced tobacco to China in the late sixteenth century and although smoking did not become popular in China until recent times, snuff went down a storm and anyone who was anybody at court was

THE DISCOVERY CENTRES

On Floor 2, the ROM's **Discovery Gallery** is one of the best education facilities in Toronto, giving children the opportunity to handle and study museum artefacts. Over a dozen workstations are set up with slides and microscopes, or identification drawers containing butterflies, insects, minerals and prehistoric pottery. Kids try on virtual-reality headsets or seventeenth-century helmets, can handle the leg bone of a Stegosaurus dinosaur, and learn how to write in hieroglyphics. The Centre keeps the same hours as the main museum (see above) but is often closed 10am–noon during school terms. Children under ten must be accompanied by an adult.

snorting the stuff by the middle of the seventeenth century. Perhaps the most popular component of the Chinese galleries, however, is the **Ming Tomb**, just beyond the T.T. Tsui Galleries. The aristocracy of the Ming Dynasty (1368–1644 AD) evolved an elaborate style of monumental funerary sculpture and architecture, and this is the only example outside of China – though it is actually a composite tomb drawn from several sources rather than an homogeneous whole. Central to the Ming conception was a Spirit Way, a central avenue to either side of which were large-scale carved figures of guards, attendants and animals. At the end of the alley was the tumulus, or burial mound – in this case the tomb-house of a seventeenth-century Chinese general by the name of Zu Dashou.

Life Sciences

The focal point of the second-floor Life Science exhibits is the **Dinosaur Gallery**. Dioramas and simulations have made this one of the most informative parts of the museum and also one of the most visited. Among the assorted fossil-skeletons, the most dramatic are those retrieved from the Alberta Badlands, the richest source of dinosaur fossils in the world. Millions of years ago, the Badlands were lush lowlands attractive to many types of dinosaur and their remains accumulated in the region's sediments, which were then, over hundreds of thousands of years, turned to stone. The gallery has a superb collection of these fossils, including the aptly named Albertosaurus, but it is the rampant herd of Allosaurus that commands your attention – a Jurassic carnivore of large proportions and ferocious appearance. Other popular sections on this floor are the replica **bat cave** and a large display on the country's **insects** – and a fearsome-looking bunch they are too.

The Gardiner Museum of Ceramic Art

Named after its wealthy patron, the **George R. Gardiner Museum of Ceramic Art** (Mon, Wed, Thurs & Fri 10am–6pm, Tues 10am–8pm, Sat 10am–5pm, Sun 11am–5pm; $5, free the first Tues of every month), just across the street from the ROM, holds a superb connoisseur's collection of ceramics. Spread over two small floors, the museum's exhibits are beautifully presented. Downstairs, the **Pre-Columbian** section is especially fine, composed of over three hundred pieces from regions stretching from Mexico to Peru, providing an intriguing insight into the lifestyles and beliefs of the Mayan, Incan and Aztec peoples. Also downstairs is an exquisite sample of fifteenth- and sixteenth-century tin-glazed **Italian majolica**, mostly dishes, plates and jars depicting classical and biblical themes designed by Renaissance artists. The early pieces are comparatively plain, limited to green and purple, but the later examples are brightly coloured for in the second half of the fifteenth century Italian potters learnt how to glaze blue and yellow – and ochre was added later. The most superb pieces are perhaps those from the city of Urbino, including two wonderful plates portraying the fall of Jericho and the exploits of Hannibal.

Upstairs is devoted to eighteenth-century **European porcelain**, with fine examples of hard-paste wares (fired at very high temperatures) from Meissen, Germany, and an interesting sample of Chinese-style blue-and-white porcelain, long the mainstay of the European ceramic industry. An unusual collection of English ware features both well-known and lesser-known manufacturers. On this floor also is a charming collection of Italian *commedia dell'arte* figurines, doll-sized representations of theatrical characters popular across Europe from the middle of the sixteenth to the late eighteenth century. The predecessor of pantomime, the *commedia dell'arte* featured stock characters – Harlequin, Scaramouche, Columbine and so forth – in improvised settings, but with a consistent theme of seduction, age and beauty: the centrepiece was always an elderly, rich merchant and his beautiful young wife.

Bata Shoe Museum

Within easy walking distance of the ROM, the **Bata Shoe Museum**, at 327 Bloor St W and St George (Tues, Wed, Fri, Sat 10am–5pm, Thurs 10am–8pm, Sun noon–5pm; $6) was built for Sonja Bata, of the Bata shoe manufacturing family, to house the extraordinary assortment of footwear she has spent a lifetime collecting. A leaflet issued at reception steers visitors around the museum, starting with an introductory section entitled "All About Shoes" on Level B1, which presents an overview on the evolution of footwear. Among the more interesting exhibits in this section are pointed shoes from medieval Europe, where different social classes were allowed different lengths of toe, and Chinese silk shoes used for binding women's feet. A small adjoining section is devoted to specialist footwear, including French chestnut-crushing clogs from the nineteenth century, inlaid Ottoman platforms, designed to keep aristocratic feet well away from the mud, and a pair of US army boots from the Vietnam War with the sole shaped to imitate the sandal prints of the Vietcong.

Moving on, Level G holds a glass cabinet of celebrity footwear. The exhibits are regularly rotated, but look out for Buddy Holly's loafers, David Bowie's signed trainers, Elvis's blue-and-white patent-leather loafers, Princess Diana's red court shoes and Elton John's ridiculous platforms. Levels 2 and 3 are used for temporary exhibitions – some of which are very good indeed – and there's also a small section explaining the museum's role in restoring and repairing old footwear.

Casa Loma

From Dupont subway station, it's just a couple of minutes' walk north up Spadina Avenue to the flight of steps that leads to Toronto's most bizarre attraction, **Casa Loma**, 1 Austin Terrace (daily 9.30am–5pm; $9), an enormous towered and turreted mansion built to the instructions of Sir Henry Pellatt between 1911 and 1914. Every inch the self-made man, Pellatt made a fortune by pioneering the use of hydroelectricity, harnessing the power of Niagara Falls to light Ontario's expanding cities. Determined to construct a house no one could ignore, Sir Henry gathered furnishings from all over the world and even imported Scottish stonemasons to build the wall around his six-acre property. He spent more than $3 million fulfilling his dream, but business misfortunes and the rising cost of servants forced him to move out in 1923, earning him the nickname of "Pellatt the Plunger". His legacy is a strange mixture of medieval fantasy and early twentieth-century technology: secret passageways and an elevator, claustrophobic wood-panelled rooms baffled by gargantuan pipes and plumbing.

A free diagram of the layout of the house is available at the reception, as are audio-cassette tours. The clearly numbered route begins on the first floor in the **Great Hall**, a pseudo-Gothic extravaganza with an eighteen-metre-high cross-beamed ceiling, a Wurlitzer organ (of all things) and enough floor space to accommodate several hundred guests. Pushing on, the **Library** and then the walnut-panelled **Dining Room** lead to the **Conservatory**, an elegant and spacious room with a marble floor and side-panels set beneath a handsome Tiffany glass ceiling. Well lit, this is the perhaps the mansion's most appealing room and its worm-like network of steam pipes are original, installed by Pellatt to keep his flowerbeds warm in winter. On the second floor, **Sir Henry's Suite** has oodles of walnut and mahogany panelling, which is in odd contrast to the 1910s white-marble, high-tech bathroom, featuring an elaborate multi-nozzle shower. Lady Pellatt wasn't left behind in the ablutions department either – her bathroom had a bidet, a real novelty in George V's Canada. Of interest on the third floor is the **Windsor Room**, named after – and built for – the Royal Family in the rather forlorn hope that they would come and stay here. Of course they never did – Pellatt was much too parvenu for their tastes.

When you've finished exploring the house, you can wander down the long tunnel that leads to the stables and the carriage room. Spare time also for the terraced **gardens** (May–Oct daily 9.30am–4pm; no extra charge), which tumble down the hill behind the house. They are parcelled up into several different sections including a water garden, a rhododendron dell and a meadow garden flanked by cool, green cedars.

Spadina Historic House & Gardens

Quite what the occupants of **Spadina House** (guided tours only, April–Sept Tues–Sun noon–5pm; $5) must have thought when Casa Loma went up next door can only be imagined, but there must have been an awful lot of curtain-twitching. The two houses are a study in contrasts: Casa Loma a pompous pile, Spadina an elegant Victorian property of genteel appearance dating from 1866. Spadina was built by James Austin (1813–97), an Irish banker whose descendants lived here until 1983 when the house was bequeathed to the city. The Austins' long and uninterrupted occupation means that the house's furnishings are nearly all genuine family artefacts, and they provide an intriguing insight into their changing tastes and interests.

Narrated by enthusiastic volunteers, the **guided tour** is a delight. Particular highlights include the conservatory trap door that allowed the gardeners to come and go unseen by their employers; an assortment of period chairs designed to accommodate the largest of bustles; a couple of canvases by Cornelius Krieghoff (see p.163); and the original gas chandeliers. Pride of place, however, is the Billiard Room, where an inventive Art Nouveau decorative frieze, dating from 1898, is complemented by several fine pieces of furniture, including a sturdy oak desk, bentwood chairs and a swivel armchair in the style of Englishman William Morris.

The waterfront and the Toronto Islands

Toronto's docks once disfigured the shoreline on the edge of the city centre, a swath of warehouses and factories that was unattractive and smelly in equal measure. Today it's another story: the port and its facilities have been concentrated further east, beyond the foot of Parliament Street, while the **waterfront** west of Yonge has been redeveloped in grand style, sprouting luxury condominium blocks, jogging and cycling trails, offices, shops and marinas. The focus of all this activity is the **Harbourfront Centre**, between York and Simcoe, whose various facilities include an open-air performance area and the **Power Plant Contemporary Art Gallery** (Tues & Thurs–Sun noon–6pm, Wed noon–8pm; $4, but free on Wed after 5pm), housed in an imaginatively converted 1920s power station. The gallery presents about a dozen exhibitions of contemporary art every year and often features emerging Canadian artists. It is mostly cutting-edge stuff, indecipherable to some, exciting to others. The gallery shares the power station with the du Maurier Theatre Centre (see p.99). Close by, just to the west, another former warehouse has been turned into the **York Quay Centre** with performance areas, meeting spaces and craft galleries. The south entrance of the Centre lets out to a shallow pond that converts into a skating rink during the winter. To the west is **Molson Place**, an outdoor stage with a graceful fan-like roof designed to suggest a ship's deck. To reach the Harbourfront Centre by public transport, take the #509 or #510 streetcar from Union Station and get off at the third stop – Queens Quay Terminal.

The Toronto Islands

Originally a peninsula, the **Toronto Islands**, the low-lying, crescent-shaped sandbanks that protect the city's harbour, were cut adrift from the mainland by a violent storm in

1858. First used as a summer retreat by the Mississauga Indians, the islands became popular in the late nineteenth century with day-tripping Torontonians, who rowed across to enjoy the cool lake breezes and sample a range of attractions – including J.W. Gorman's "diving horses", who would jump into the lake from a high-diving board. The islands also held the baseball stadium where slugger Babe Ruth hit his first professional home run and once served as a World War II training base for the Norwegian Air Force. Today, the archipelago, roughly 6km long and totalling around 800 acres, is maintained by the Toronto Parks Department, who keep the islands spotless, in part by not allowing visitors to bring their cars. The city side of the archipelago is broken into a dozen tiny islets dotted with cottages, neat gardens and clumps of wild woodland. By comparison, the other (more appealing) side of the archipelago is a tad wilder and more windswept, consisting of one, long finger of land that is somewhat arbitrarily divided into three "islands". From the east, these begin with **Ward's Island**, a quiet residential area with parkland and wilderness. Next up is **Centre Island**, the busiest and most developed of the three and home to **Centreville** (late May to Aug daily plus Sept weekends 10.30am–7pm), a children's amusement park with charmingly old-fashioned rides, from paddle boats shaped as swans to a carousel, a Ferris wheel and the *Lake Monster* roller coaster. Finally, **Hanlan's Point** island, edging Toronto's tiny City Centre Airport, has the best sandy beach – though Lake Ontario is too polluted for swimming. One way to enjoy the islands is to cycle or walk along the archipelago's south (lake) side – there is a combined footpath and cycle track between all three ferry docks. This route is also taken by a free but irregular trackless **train**. Bikes can be rented on the islands – there are several outlets – or you can bring your own over on the ferry, though restrictions may apply on busy weekends.

Three separate **ferries** depart for the Toronto Islands from the mainland ferry terminal, which is located behind the conspicuous *Westin Harbour Castle Hotel*, at the foot of Yonge and Bay streets. To get to the ferry terminal from Union Station, take streetcar #509 or #510 and get off at the first stop – Queens Quay (Ferry Dock). The Ward's Island and Hanlan's Point services run year-round, while the ferry running to Centre Island operates only from spring to early fall. During peak season (May to early Sept), all the ferry lines depart every twenty minutes; at other times of the year they operate at regular intervals, either every half-hour, forty-five minutes or hour. Ferries begin between 6.30am and 9am and end between 9pm and 11.30pm, depending on the service and the season. For schedule details, telephone ☎416/392-8193. Regardless of the time of year, a return **fare** for adults is $5, $3 for seniors and students; the ferry ride takes ten minutes – and provides great views of the downtown skyline.

West of the Waterfront: Fort York

Modern Toronto improbably traces its origins to the ill-starred **Fort York** (late May to Aug daily 10am–5pm; Sept to late May Mon–Fri 10am–4pm, Sat & Sun 10am–5pm; $5), built to reinforce British control of Lake Ontario in 1793. It was, however, never properly fortified, partly through lack of funds and partly because it was too remote to command much attention, and within ten years the stockade was in a state of disrepair, even though the township of York had, in the meantime, become the capital of Upper Canada. In 1811 the deterioration in Anglo-American relations prompted a refortification, but its main military achievement was entirely accidental. Forced to evacuate the fort in 1813, the British blew up the gunpowder magazine, but underestimated the force of the explosion. They killed ten of their own number and 250 of the advancing enemy, including the splendidly named American general, Zebulon Pike. After the war, Fort York was refurbished and its garrison – the largest local consumer of supplies – made a considerable contribution to the development of Toronto, as York was renamed in 1834.

Fort York is situated in the shadow of the Gardiner Expressway, a fifteen-minute walk west from Union Station: follow Front Street West to the end, turn left down Bathurst and, after crossing the railway bridge, take the signposted footpath on the right that leads to the fort's rear entrance. The front entrance is at the end of Garrison Road, a ten-minute walk from Fleet Street – and the route of streetcar #511. The site was opened as a museum in 1934, and is now staffed by guides who provide informative and free tours that take about an hour, or you can wander around under your own steam. The meticulously restored ramparts enclose a sequence of log, stone and brick buildings, notably the attractive **Officers' Quarters** and a stone **powder magazine**, built with two-metre-thick walls and sparkproof copper and brass fixtures. In addition, the **Blue Barracks**, or junior officers' quarters, have an absorbing exhibition on the various military crises that afflicted nineteenth-century Canada, including the War of 1812 and the curious affair of the Fenian raids launched from the US in the 1860s. During the American Civil War, the British had continued to trade with the Confederacy, much to the chagrin of the North. After the war, many believed that the US was itching for the opportunity to seize Canada, no one more so than the **Fenian Brotherhood**, formed by Irish exiles in New York in 1857. Their tactics were simple: believing that an unofficial international incident would push Washington into action, they organized a series of cross-border raids, the most serious of which, in 1866, involved 1000 men. In the event, British regulars drove the Fenians out and Congress didn't take the bait.

Greater Toronto

The satellite suburbs and industrial areas that make up most of the **Greater Toronto Area** – the GTA – are of little appeal, a string of formless settlements sprawling over a largely flat and dreary landscape that extends from Scarborough in the east to Mississauga in the west and north beyond Steeles Avenue. That said, the region is home to several prestige attractions, notably the **Ontario Science Centre**, which comes complete with dozens of interactive science displays, the **Toronto Zoo**, the **McMichael Canadian Art Collection** of the Group of Seven's paintings, and the garish extravagance of **Paramount Canada's Wonderland**.

Ontario Science Centre
Opened in 1969, the **Ontario Science Centre**, 11km from downtown at 770 Don Mills Rd, North York (daily 10am–5pm; $7.50, but free after 5pm. ☎416/696-1000), bills itself as a "vast playground of science" and draws more than one million visitors a year. The centre traces the development of technology through some eight hundred exhibits, many of which invite participation – staring at strangely coloured Canadian flags until you go dotty, piloting a spacecraft, or having your hair raised by a Van der Graaf generator, and there's a massive Omnimax Theatre too, with a 24-metre dome screen. You could spend a day here on your own, though it's much more enjoyable with kids. To reach the Science Centre by **car** from downtown Toronto, take the Don Valley Parkway and follow the signs from the Don Mills Road North exit. By public transport, take the Yonge Street subway line north to Eglington station and transfer to the Eglington East Bus; get off at Don Mills Road. The trip should take about thirty minutes from downtown's Union Station.

Toronto Zoo
Set on the hilly edge of the Rouge Valley in Scarborough, the **Toronto Zoo** (daily: March–Sept 9am–7.30pm, Oct–Feb 9.30am–5.30pm; $12, children $7; ☎416/392-5900) encompasses a 710-acre site that does its best to place animals in their own environments.

To this end, seven **pavilions** representing different geographic regions are filled with indigenous plants and more than 5000 animals. Hardy species live outside in large paddocks, and an open train, the **Zoomobile** ($3), zips around the vast site for those opposed to hiking between enclosures. In addition to grizzly bears, musk ox, Siberian tigers and camels, a variety of wildlife – raccoons, chipmunks and foxes – drop in from the zoo's wooded surroundings. Some of the most popular attractions include the **Underwater Exhibits**, featuring South African fur seals, beavers and the ever-popular otters; and **Edge of Night**, an extension of the Australasian Pavilion, which simulates night-time in the Australian outback.

Arriving by **car**, take Hwy 401 to Scarborough (exit 389) and drive north on Meadowvale Road, following the signs for the zoo. Via **public transport**, catch the Sheppard East #85B bus from the Sheppard subway station; it takes about fifty minutes to get here from downtown. **Eating** at the zoo is dominated by *McDonald's*, which has a monopoly on the hot food concessions. There are, however, pleasant picnic areas if you bring your own lunch.

The McMichael Canadian Art Collection

The **McMichael Canadian Art Collection** (May–Oct daily 10am–5pm; Nov–April Tues–Sat 10am–4pm, Sun 10am–5pm; $7) is situated in the commuter township of Kleinburg, roughly 40km northwest of downtown, off Hwy 400. The collection, housed in a series of handsome log and stone buildings in the wooded Humber River valley, was put together by Robert and Signe McMichael, devoted followers of the Group of Seven, and given to the province in 1965. On the **Lower Level**, a series of small galleries focuses on various aspects of the Group of Seven's work. Gallery Two, for example, begins with the artistic friends and contemporaries who influenced the Group's early style, while Gallery Three zeroes in on the Group's founder, Tom Thomson, displaying small panels the artist painted on location in preparation for the full-sized canvases he worked on back in his studio. Taken together, the galleries on this level contain one of Canada's finest collections of Group of Seven paintings with J.E.H. MacDonald, Lawren Harris, Edwin Holgate, F.H. Varley and L.L. Fitzgerald all well-represented – as is their talented contemporary Emily Carr. The museum's **Upper Level** is devoted primarily to modern First Nations Art and Inuit soapstone carvings and lithographs. Rotating temporary exhibitions appear on the Upper Level as well, but they are often of dubious quality.

When you've finished with the paintings, allow a little time to stroll the footpaths that lattice the woods surrounding the McMichael. Maps are provided free at reception, and as you wander around you'll bump into various pieces of sculpture as well as Tom Thomson's old wooden shack, moved here from Rosedale in 1962.

From downtown Toronto, it's just about possible to make a day-trip visit to the McMichael by subway and bus, but effectively you need your own transport.

Paramount Canada's Wonderland

Located at Vaughan, 30km from downtown and immediately east of Hwy 400 at the Rutherford Road exit, **Paramount Canada's Wonderland** (May–Aug daily, Sept & Oct 2–4 days weekly; opening and closing times vary – call ☎905/832-8131 for latest details) is Toronto's Disneyworld. A massive theme park, it features roller coasters, a twenty-acre water park with sixteen water slides, souped-up go-karts, mini-golf and roaming cartoon and TV characters – everything from Fred Flintstone to *Star Trek*'s Klingons. The roller-coaster rides are enough to make the strongest stomachs churn, if the kitsch doesn't do it first. A one-day pass covering all rides costs $41, children 3–6 years $20, with parking an extra $6.50. By public transport, catch the Wonderland Express GO bus from Yorkdale or York Mills subway station; buses leave every hour and take forty minutes.

Eating and drinking

To get the best from Toronto's kitchens, head for any one of the city's ethnic neigh-bourhoods, where there's an abundance of good **restaurants**, or go to one of the many downtown **cafés**, **café-bars** or **restaurants** that have carefully nurtured a good reputation. Some of the best of the city's restaurants emphasize their use of Canadian ingredients – fish and wild-animal meat especially – but there's no real distinctive local cuisine: if there is a Toronto dish, it's hamburger, fries and salad. **Prices** range from the deluxe, where a meal will set you back upwards of $60, to the cheap fast-food chains, where a decent-sized snack or sandwich works out at about $9. The majority of Toronto's restaurants fall somewhere in between – a $25 bill per person for a two-course meal, excluding drinks, is a reasonable average. Most of the city's popular restaurants feature bargain daily specials from about $8 upwards and serve food till about 10pm, drinks till 1am.

For **drinking**, many of Toronto's neighbourhood **bars** are rough-and-ready places that look and feel like beer halls. Until fairly recently, it was common for them to have one entrance for men accompanied by women, the other for men only, but although these traditional bars remain popular with many of the city's blue-collar workers, they have largely been supplanted by the café-bar. The development of the latter has made the traditional distinction between eating and drinking places obsolete.

Cafés and café-bars

Café Bernate, 1024 Queen St W (☎416/535-2835). The steam machine is in full swing at this neigh-bourhood spot, and the sunny yellow walls are hung with local artists' work. The menu offers 29 plump sandwiches for all tastes, and those drinking regular coffee get free refills. Streetcar: Queen (#501).

Bonjour Brioche, 812 Queen St E (☎416/406-1250). This patisserie/café draws hoards from all over the city to sample its jewel-like fruit tarts, buttery croissants, puffy brioche and its delectable *pissaladiere*, a variation on the pizza from the Provence region of France. There's always a line for Sunday brunch, and almost everything is eaten by 2pm. Streetcar: Carlton (#506).

Goulash Party Haus, 498 Queen St W (☎416/703-8056). This Hungarian café/bistro serves – what else? – goulash, along with other Eastern European staples such as cabbage rolls and schnitzel. The prices are reasonable and regulars like to bring along newspapers and books for a good, long visit. Streetcar: Queen (#501).

Gypsy Co-op, 817 Queen St W (☎416/703-5069). An eclectic mix of old-time candy store and tradi-tional Muskoka lodge, with a hip dining space downstairs and a space for jukebox, jitterbug dance fiends upstairs. The creative, light-fare menu caters to everyone from rare-steak eaters to vegans, and the atmosphere is agelessly cool and poseur-free. Streetcar: Queen (#501).

Insomnia, 563 Bloor St W (☎416/588-3907). Internet cafés have not sprouted throughout Toronto like they have in other cities. Nonetheless, this one is staking a strong claim. Eight terminals with Net access, a full bar and an international menu which includes pastas, and Asian finger foods keep them coming until the wee hours of the night. Subway: Bathurst.

Jet Fuel Coffee Shop, 519 Parliament St (☎416/968-9982). One of the oldest independent coffee establishments in town, this place is the unofficial hangout of Toronto's bicycle couriers. It only serves beverages that can be made with an espresso machine (tea included), and imports a few baked goods for dunking. An excellent choice for relaxing with a huge, inexpensive latte and a newspaper. Streetcar: Carlton (#506).

Kensington Café, 73 Kensington Ave (☎416/971-5632). The international soup-and-sandwich menu here gives a nod to the Middle East. A small, cosy place to slip into if the hectic pace of Kensington Market (see p.87) gets to be too much. Streetcar: Dundas (#505).

Last Temptation, 12 Kensington Ave (☎416/599-2551). A locals' kind of place where gossip and pool are the main sources of entertainment. The terrace caters to people-watching, and the bistro-style menu features a good selection of appetizers, as well as basic sandwiches, stir fries and pastas; don't miss the on-tap microbrews. Streetcar: Dundas (#505).

Café Nervosa, 75 Yorkville Ave (☎416/961-4642). A delightful Yorkville address perfect for sipping coffee and watching the world pass by. The remodelled decor is broadly Mediterranean, as is the food, whose major emphasis is meal-sized salads, pastas and small pizzas baked in a wood-burning oven. The terrace is the place to be and be seen in summer. Bay subway.

Zelda's, 76 Wellesley St E (☎416/922-2526). An unpretentious neighbourhood joint with a menu that runs the gamut from burgers to Asian-fusion salads. The interior is purposely kitschy and heavily Elvis-inspired. Subway: Wellesley.

Restaurants

With its large immigrant population, Toronto prides itself on the diversity of its cuisine. The city has more than four thousand **restaurants** offering a spectacular range of foods from all over the world and this is one of Canada's few cities where you can eat high-quality food of almost any ethnic origin. One cautionary note is that many restaurants are closed on Sundays and sometimes Mondays too – telephone ahead before you start a major excursion. As a broad guide to **price**, we've coded each of the entries below as either inexpensive (under $15), moderate ($15–25) or expensive ($25–40).

Asian fusion

Mata Hari, 39 Baldwin St (☎416/596-2832). The fusion here is Chinese and Malay (known as *nyonya*). Curry, rice and noodle dishes are the stars, with a tempting range of desserts. Vegetarian dishes available. Expensive. Subway: St Patrick.

Monsoon, 100 Simcoe St (☎416/979-7172). The interior here reflects the Asian influence on the menu. Starters are served on delicate *rakku* dishes, and the light, assured cooking boasts imaginative combinations (seared tofu in green-tea marinade; maple-ginger grouper). An excellent place to mark a special occasion. Expensive. Subway: St Andrews.

Queen Mother Café, 208 Queen St W (☎416/598-4719). Neither the name nor the cosy wood-panelled interior gives a hint about the menu: Asian specialities like Pad Thai, crispy spring rolls, and lots of chicken and shrimp entrees. Vegetarians take heart: the house veggie burger is a local tradition. Moderate. Streetcar: Queen (#506).

Tiger Lily, 257 Queen St W (☎416/977-5499). One of the best bargains on the Queen W strip. There's a wide variety of noodle and soup dishes tailored to suit your tastes, as well as fresh spring rolls, innovative desserts, and a cheerful, attentive staff. Moderate. Subway: Osgoode.

Chinese

Happy Seven, 358 Spadina Ave (☎416/971-9820). Predominantly Cantonese-style cooking with a few spicy Szechuan dishes, tanks of soon-to-be seafood, and large, attractively presented servings. Bright and spotless, this establishment is always filled with satisfied customers. Inexpensive. Streetcar: Dundas (#505).

Kowloon, 5 Baldwin St (☎416/977-3773). A Cantonese menu with a long list of noodle dishes, all beautifully presented in a comfortably appointed dining room. Moderate. Subway: Queen's Park.

Lai Wah Heen, *Metropolitan Hotel*, 108 Chestnut St (☎416/977-9899). The name means "elegant meeting place", which it most certainly is. The complex menu is Hong Kong *moderne*, with dishes like Lustrous Peacock (a salad of barbecued duck, chicken and jellyfish on slivered melons garnished with eggs). Also serves what is arguably the best dim sum in the city. Expensive. Subway: St Patrick.

Lee Garden, 331 Spadina Ave (☎416/593-9524). An oasis of calm greenery on the frenetic Spadina strip. Mostly Cantonese menu with a large selection of daily specials. Moderate. Streetcar: Dundas (#505).

Ethiopian

Ethiopian House, 4 Irwin Ave (☎416/923-5438). Off Yonge north of Wellesley, close to the University of Toronto campus. Inexpensive place, popular with students, where the pulses, spices, vegetables and beef of traditional Ethiopian cooking are put through their paces. Inexpensive.

French and French-Canadian

Arlequin, 134 Avenue Rd (☎416/928-9521). One of the best French restaurants in town, offering imaginative bistro-style cuisine with hints of the Middle East. Reservations advised. Expensive. Subway: Bay.

Le Papillon, 16 Church St (☎416/363-0838). A Gallic-Quebecois hybrid. Best are the establishment's signature sweet or savoury crepes, which are Breton-style but stuffed with Canadian ingredients. Moderate. Subway: Union Station.

Le Select Bistro, 328 Queen St W (☎416/596-6406). Standard French-style menu; slick decor; jazz and classical background music. Moderate. Streetcar: Queen (#506).

Greek

Avli, 401 Danforth Ave (☎416/461-9577). An authentic Greek restaurant with a strong emphasis on fancy starters, a combination of which could easily make a full meal. Classic game dishes, casseroles and baklava all served up with smooth efficiency. Expensive. Subway: Chester.

Pappas Grill, 440 Danforth Ave (☎416/469-9595). All the standard items – souvlaki, mezze appetizers, grilled seafood – served with baskets of pitta and lashings of olive oil. Moderate. Subway: Chester.

Indian

Nataraj, 394 Bloor St W (☎416/928-2925). Delhi-specific dishes with a tandoori twist. Delectable naan bakes within view of diners through a window to the kitchen. Try the spicy stews, creamy-sauced kofta, and sugar-rush desserts. Moderate. Subway: Spadina.

Rashnaa, 307 Wellesley St E (☎416/929-2099). This tiny restaurant, crammed into a small Cabbagetown bungalow, offers intriguing Southern Indian and Sri Lankan dishes. The *dosa* – a Sri Lankan crepe that comes with a variety of fillings – is habit-forming. One of the city's best dining bargains. Inexpensive. Streetcar: Carlton (#506).

Italian

Bar Italia, 584 College St (☎416/535-3621). Antipasti, pizzas, pastas and *panini* are dished up amid the clatter of wine glasses and the whoosh of the espresso machine. A recent renovation significantly expanded the seating capacity of this dependable favourite. Moderate. Streetcar: Carlton (#506).

La Fenice, 319 King St W (☎416/585-2377). Consistently high standards (and prices) are evident at this upscale restaurant, from antipasti to desserts. It takes the better part of an evening to dine properly at *La Fenice* – a commitment serious diners readily make. The downstairs café is a scaled-down version, offering expertly prepared pastas to a more budget-conscious clientele. Expensive. Streetcar: King (#504).

Japanese

Masa, 205 Richmond St W (☎416/348-9720). Mouthwatering Japanese food, with part of the restaurant equipped with mats and partitions. All the old favourites – such as eel, seaweed and teriyaki. Reservations advised at weekends. Expensive. Streetcar: King (#504).

Nami, 55 Adelaide St E (☎416/362-7373). One of the finest Japanese restaurants in Toronto, with sushi a speciality. Reservations advised. Moderate. Subway: Union Station.

Seafood

Joso's, 202 Davenport Ave (☎416/925-1930). This much-loved seafood restaurant, famed for introducing Toronto to squid-inked pasta, was described by Margaret Atwood in her novel *The Robber Bride* as a place "decorated with paintings, paintings that twenty years ago could've got you arrested, because they were all of naked women". The paintings are attractive (there's nothing sleazy about the place), as are the servers. Expensive. Subway: Bay.

La Pecherie Mövenpick, 133 Yorkville Ave (☎416/926-9545). This place offers first-rate selections of seafood, expertly prepared and served by an attentive staff. Expensive. Subway: Bay.

Rodney's Oyster House, 209 Adelaide St E (☎416/363-8105). Toronto's favourite oyster bar serves up oysters, oysters and more oysters with an extraordinary variety of sauces. Expensive. Streetcar: King (#504).

Spanish

Segovia, 5 St Nicholas St (☎416/960-1010). Traditional Spanish restaurant right down to the bull-fighting trinkets. Go for the paella – it's fab. Off Yonge north of Wellesley St W. Moderate. Subway: Wellesley.

Tapas Bar, 226 Carlton St (☎416/323-9651). Delicious tapas washed down by Spanish wine on two floors of an old Cabbagetown house. Inexpensive. Streetcar: Carlton (#506).

Steaks

Barberian's, 7 Elm St (☎416/597-0335). No-nonsense dining geared towards carnivores. The atmosphere is stately: well-padded seats, plush carpets and lots of dark wood. Expensive. Subway: Dundas.

Senator, 253 Victoria St (☎416/364-7517). Superb steaks at arguably the best steakhouse in Toronto. Art Deco decor. Behind Pantages Theatre, just one block east of Yonge at Dundas. Expensive. Subway: Dundas.

Thai

Bangkok Garden, 18 Elm St (☎416/977-6748). Soft lighting and plenty of nooks makes this a good spot for an intimate evening. Specialties include interesting treatments of fresh lake fish, and a nice selection of salads, noodles and curries. Moderate. Subway: Dundas.

Vanipha Fine Cuisine, 193 Augusta St (☎416/340-0491). This trim, walk-down restaurant offers the best and most original examples of Thai cuisine in the city. More vegetarian options than in the average Southeast Asian eatery. Top marks for presentation and service. Moderate. Streetcar: Dundas (#505).

Yonge Thailand, 165 John St (☎416/593-9291). Bright colours, ultrafresh ingredients and nothing is too oily or sugary. Things can be on the spicy side, however, so ask your server to prepare dishes to your taste. Moderate. Subway: Osgoode.

Vegetarian

Bo De Duyen, 254 Spadina Ave (☎416/703-1247). Chinese-Vietnamese cooking for vegetarians. The utter absence of any animal by-products means that even the strictest vegan can eat here with a clear conscience. Pages and pages of selections, including "mock" meat and seafood items, fashioned from gluten or soy. Inexpensive. Streetcar: Dundas (#505).

Juice for Life, 336 Queen St W (☎416/599-4442). This gourmet juice bar/vegan café is appended to a teen-positive clothing store and serves up some of the best bargains on the Queen W strip. Aeons away from the horrid, earnest vegan eateries of yore. One caveat: the loud, thrash music might deter patrons over thirty. Inexpensive. Streetcar: Queen (#501).

Lotus Garden, 393 Dundas St W (☎416/598-1883). Ignore the "mock" beef, pork and seafood dishes and go straight to the soups, noodle dishes or stuffed vegetables. The Vietnamese crepes are particularly tasty. Moderate. Subway: St Patrick.

Nightlife and entertainment

Toronto is the cultural centre of English-speaking Canada and has gone to great expense to maintain a wide-ranging programme of **performing arts**, from theatre and opera to ballet and classical music. Predictably enough, **ticket prices** vary enormously, but T.O. Tix (Tues–Sat noon–7.30pm; ☎416/536-6468), on Level 1 of the Eaton Centre, sells spare dance and theatre tickets at half-price for that day's performances, though note that you have to buy the tickets in person. As for film, Toronto's mainstream **cinemas** show Hollywood releases long before they reach the UK and, as you'd expect from a university city, it has good outlets for art-house stuff. The city of the Cowboy Junkies obviously has some life in its **music** scene, and though many local bands who hit the big time move to the States, the city does have its fair share of venues, especially for **jazz**. Several bars and clubs sponsor a range of modern and traditional jazz, and there are free open-air jazz concerts at various downtown locations throughout the summer.

For listings and reviews check out either of the city's main free newspapers, *eye* and *Now*. In addition, both the Ontario Tourism Travel Information Centre, in the Eaton Centre, and Info T.O., in the city's Convention Centre at 255 Front St W, have two other free publications with listings, an *Annual Visitors' Guide* and *Where*. However, their reviews are bland and uncritical. For happenings in the Gay Village, see *Xtra*, the city's third free newspaper.

Performing arts

Du Maurier Theatre at the Harbourfront Centre, 231 Queens Quay W (☎416/973-4940). Renovated from a 1920s ice house, this new theatre puts on theatrical and musical shows in a lakeshore setting.

Ford Centre for the Performing Arts, 5040 Yonge St (☎416/872-2222). This three-theatre venue stages classical concerts in its acoustically impressive Recital Hall as well as mainstream musicals.

Hummingbird Centre for the Performing Arts, 1 Front St E at Yonge (☎416/393-7469). Home of the Canadian Opera Company and the National Ballet of Canada.

Pantages Theatre, 263 Yonge St (☎416/872-2222). Splendidly restored Victorian auditorium, where *The Phantom of the Opera* has been playing for donkey's years.

Princess of Wales Theatre, 300 King St W (☎416/872-1212). Built especially to stage *Miss Saigon* and opened in early 1994, this multimillion-dollar venue has already recouped its investment. The *Lion King* is on now.

Roy Thomson Hall, 60 Simcoe St at King St W (☎416/872-4255). Base of the highly regarded Toronto Symphony Orchestra.

Royal Alexandra Theatre, 260 King St W (☎416/872-1212). Refurbished nineteenth-century theatre, concentrating on top-drawer transfers from London and Broadway.

St Lawrence Centre for the Performing Arts, 27 Front St E (☎416/366-7723). Home to the Canadian Stage Company, which produces modern Canadian plays and is responsible for a classical-music programme, and Theatre Plus, the city's only resident acting ensemble, whose contemporary international and Canadian season runs from April to September.

Tarragon Theatre, 30 Bridgeman Ave (☎416/531-1827). Specializes in new Canadian plays.

Cinema

Bloor Cinema, 506 Bloor St W (☎416/532-6677). A student favourite, with an excellent programme of international and art-house films; mostly two shows daily.

Carlton Cinema, 20 Carlton St at College subway (☎416/598-2309). Toronto's best mainstream cinema, with ten screens and four shows daily.

Eaton Centre, Dundas St at Yonge (☎416/593-4536). Fifteen mainstream films and frequent showings.

The Revue, 400 Roncesvalles Ave (☎416/531-9959). First-rate selection of art-house and key mainstream films.

Bars, music venues and clubs

Acme Bar & Grill, 86 John St (☎416/340-9700). A cross between a jazz club and a sports bar, with a selection of over eighty different single-malt scotches. A good spot to go after watching the ball-game at the nearby SkyDome.

Betty's, 240 King St E (☎416/368-1300). The threat of a lawsuit forced the owners to abbreviate the name from *The Betty Ford Clinic* to just plain *Betty's*, but regulars remain devoted to this long, thin pub/bistro. It has a tree-canopied patio out back in the summer and in the winter its blond-wood booths and tables are packed for most of the day. Excellent sandwiches, hot snacks and burgers can be washed down with a strong microbrew selection.

The Bovine Sex Club, 542 Queen St W (☎416/504-4239). Despite its comically evocative name, the *Bovine* doesn't have a sign – and it's not actually a sex club, just a weird, eccentrically decorated bar. The front of the building is encrusted with bicycle parts and scrap metal, and offers no glimpse of the playground within: banks of TV monitors play oddball background videos, the ceiling bristles with tree branches speckled in fairy lights, and hundreds of empty Jagermeister bottles give you an idea of the hearty partying that goes on here. There are plenty of pinball machines and pool tables, as well as an eclectic range of DJ music to keep you entertained.

Cameron House, 508 Queen St W (☎416/703-0811). This place is half beer hall, half cocktail lounge and all entertainment. Artists have been rearranging the facade for twenty years now, the only constant being the huge metal ants marching up the side of the building. DJs play the front, and live music goes on in the back on weekends.

C'est What?, 67 Front St E (☎416/867-9499). A gem of a bar featuring 28 microbrews on tap and a variety of ales brewed on the premises, some more experimental than others. Board games, deep couches and live music every night make this a home away from home.

Dennison's Brewing Company, 75 Victoria St (☎416/360-5877). Four establishments grouped under one Romanesque roof: the brewery, which produces German-style lagers; *Conchy Joe's*, a casual oyster bar serving oysters, steamed mussels and fresh fish; *Louis' Brasserie*, which serves pasta, snacks and steaks; and *Growler's Pub* downstairs, with its gleaming brass fittings, dark-wood interior and standard pub grub.

The Docks, 11 Polson St (☎416/461-3625). An enormous waterfront bar on the edge of the Port of Toronto dockyards. Features a wide range of music, from Latino to house, with the occasional live act too. Weekends only.

Element Bar and Lounge, 533 Queen St W (☎416/359-1919). Some patrons on the late end of the Gen X spectrum tried to dismiss *Element* as a tad too "Wallpaper", but it works a sleek retro-mod interior to advantage and attracts a youngish but sophisticated crowd. Excellent DJs on weekends – techno though jungle.

Horseshoe Tavern, 370 Queen St W (☎416/598-4753). Lots of Toronto bands got their start here and it's still a good place to spy up-and-coming talent.

Imperial Pub, 54 Dundas E (☎416/977-4667). A favourite of downtowners and students from the nearby polytechnic, this traditional tap house serves up beer and meaty pub food in two bars (there's also a large rooftop patio during the summer).

Lee's Palace, 529 Bloor St W (☎416/532-7383). Hosts some of the best up-and-coming bands from punk through to folk. Upstairs is the *Dance Cave*, a lively alternative dance bar.

McVeigh's New Windsor Tavern, 124 Church St (☎416/364-9698). A three-decade-old Irish pub, featuring Celtic music and food, and dark, creamy Irish ales. Resolutely unfashionable and authentic to the core. Particularly festive on the afternoon of Christmas Eve, when all the businesses close for the holidays and all the Irish musicians in town come here.

Phoenix Concert Theatre, 410 Sherbourne St (☎416/323-1251). The building is getting a bit shabby, but the booking agents here haven't lost their edge. This is one of the better venues to catch big-name rock acts or to dance to the DJ scene in the *Parlour*, a small disco incorporated into the club.

Plaza Flamingo, 423 College St (☎416/603-8884). Flamenco at the *Flamingo* is a summertime institution. International flamenco contests run all summer long, filling the place night and day. The kitchen serves up Spanish dishes, and an all-you-can-eat weekend brunch satisfies those who get peckish after some serious dancing.

Rex Hotel Jazz Bar and Grill, 194 Queen St W (☎416/598-2475). In fierce arguments about which is the best jazz club in town, this one is consistently near the top of the list. A well-primped crowd lounges in the spiffed-up interior, but any reservations about the room's pretentious flare evaporate once the music – which is always top-notch – begins.

Top O' the Senator, 294 Yonge St (☎416/364-7517). Showcases some of the biggest and best names in jazz and blues.

Clubs

Bamboo, 312 Queen St W (☎416/593-5771). Once a rattan furniture warehouse, this place now boasts a large live-music dance club (mostly reggae and salsa) and Caribbean-Asian fusion food.

The Joker, 318 Richmond St W (☎416/598-1313). Heavy techno features at this large club of multiple piercings and black clothes. Not for the faint-hearted.

Lava Lounge, 507 College St (☎416/966-LAVA). This is a great-looking space of curvy red banquettes and blurping lava lamps. The DJ booth emits lounge, trance and new Latin. Good food too.

Whiskey Saigon, 250 Richmond St W (☎416/593-4646). Big nightspot with three floors and a wide range of music – rock and funk through house and disco.

Festivals

Toronto is strong on **festivals** and here is a selection. In late June, there's the outstanding **Toronto Downtown Jazz Festival** (☎416/928-2033), which usually overlaps with the week-long **Toronto Gay & Lesbian Pride** (☎416/92-PRIDE), culminating in a whopping Pride Day Parade. Late July and early August sees the **Caribana** (☎416/465-4884), a West Indian carnival with a fantastic parade plus music and dance, as well as the **Beaches Jazz Festival** (☎416/698-2152). In early September, the widely acclaimed **Toronto International Film Festival** (☎416/967-7371) is a ten-day showing of new films from around the world. The most sedate annual event is perhaps the **International Festival of Authors**, held at the Harbourfront Centre in mid to late October (☎416/973-3000).

Listings

Airlines Air Canada (☎416/925-2311). Air Ontario (☎416/925-2311) has regular, bargain deals from Toronto City Centre Airport to London, Montréal and Ottawa; it also operates flights to more obscure destinations within Ontario; for flights to the States try American Airlines (☎1-800/433-7300) and USAir (☎1-800/428-4322).

Airport enquiries Pearson International (☎416/247-7678); Toronto City Centre (☎416/203-6942).

Algonquin Park Call of the Wild, 23 Edward St, Markham, ON (☎905/471-9453 or 1-800/776-9453, fax 905/472-9453, *www.callofthewild.ca*) run three-day ($390) and five-day ($580) personalized and relaxed adventure canoe trips in Algonquin. Price includes all meals, permits, equipment and transport from Toronto. It's essential to book in advance.

Bike rental Cyclepath, 2106 Yonge St (☎416/487-1717), and Wheel Excitement Inc, south of the SkyDome at 5 Rees St (☎416/260-9000), who also hire out rollerblades.

Bookshops The World's Biggest Bookshop, 20 Edward St, near Yonge and Dundas (☎416/977-7009), is a huge warehouse-like affair with a vast selection of titles. For travel books, try Open Air Books and Maps, downtown at 25 Toronto St (☎416/363-0719), or Ulysses Travel Bookshop, 101 Yorkville (☎416/323-3609). Indigo have several branches, including one in the Eaton Centre (☎416/591-3622). Also see Maps, overleaf.

Bus information General, automated bus information line (☎416/393-7911). Individual companies: PMCL (☎416/695-1867) for Midland, Penetang and Owen Sound; Trentway-Wagar (☎416/961-9666) for Niagara Falls, Kitchener, US destinations and Montréal; Greyhound (☎416/367-8747, *www.greyhound.ca*) for long-distance buses – Montréal, Ottawa, Sault Ste Marie, Winnipeg and points west. Toronto Transit Commission (daily 8am–5pm; ☎416393-INFO).

Camping equipment Mountain Equipment Co-op, 400 King St W (☎416/340-2667); Trail Head, 61 Front St E (☎416/862-0881).

Car rental Budget, 1319 Bay at Davenport (☎416/961-3932) and at the airport (☎416/676-0522); Discount, 730 Yonge St at Bloor (☎416/921-1212) and 132 Front St E at Jarvis (☎416/864-0550); Hertz, 128 Richmond St E (☎416/363-9022) and at the airport (☎416/674-2020); National, beside Union Station (☎416/364-4191) and at the airport (☎416/905/676-4000).

Consulates Australia, 175 Bloor St E (☎416/323-1155); Belgium, 2 Bloor St W (☎416/944-1422); Netherlands, Suite 2106, 1 Dundas St W (☎416/598-2520); Norway, 175 Bloor St E (☎416/920-5529); Sweden, 2 Bloor St W (☎416/963-8768); UK, 777 Bay St (☎416/593-1267); US, 360 University Ave (☎416/595-1700).

Emergencies Assaulted Women's Helpline and Rape Crisis (☎416/597-8808). Police, ambulance, fire ☎911.

Hospital Toronto Hospital, 200 Elizabeth St (main switchboard ☎416/340-3111; 24hr emergency line ☎416/340-3946).

Internet Libraries provide Internet access and so do most of the better hotels. One good outlet is the *Cyberland Café*, 257 Yonge St, opposite the Eaton Centre (☎416/955-9628, *www.cyberlandcafe.com*; Sun & Mon 10.30am–11pm, Tues–Thurs 10.30am–midnight, Fri–Sat 10.30am–1am).

Laundry Dundas Cleaners & Laundry, 345 Dundas St E (☎416/363-3873). The Lounge Laundry, 531 Yonge St, south of Wellesley (☎416/975-4747).

Lost property GO transit (☎416/869-3200); TTC, Bay subway (☎416/393-4100); VIA Rail (☎416/366-8411).

Maps The Toronto maps we have provided should be all you'll need for central Toronto, but if you need something covering the whole of the city, you'll find other maps at most bookshops and newsstands. MapArt is the best manufacturer: their comprehensive *Toronto Pocket Street Atlas* costs $7.95, and their large-scale general *Toronto* map is $2.95. They also publish an excellent *Ontario Road Atlas* book for $19.95.

Newspapers Toronto has two first-rate newspapers, the *Toronto Star* and the *Globe and Mail*, which is sold all over Canada.

Pharmacies There are Shoppers Drug Marts all over town; for the nearest location and late-night opening, call the company's information line on ☎1-800/363-1020.

Post offices Postal facilities at most Shoppers Drug Marts with downtown locations including 360 Bloor St W at Spadina; 69 Yonge at King; Royal Bank Plaza, 200 Bay at Front.

Rail GO Transit (☎416/869-3200); VIA Rail enquiries (☎416/366-8411); Toronto Transit Commission (daily 8am–5pm; ☎416/393-INFO).

Sports The Toronto Maple Leafs, of the National Hockey League, play home fixtures in the Air Canada Centre, behind Union Station (☎416/872-5000). The Blue Jays, of the American Baseball League, play in the SkyDome (☎416/341-1234); the Argonauts, of the Canadian Football League, also play in the Air Canada Centre (☎416/341–5151).

Taxis cruise the city in abundance and can be hailed from any street corner. **Fares** are generally reasonable based on a fixed tariff of $2.50 for the first .235km and 25¢ for every .235km thereafter. Thus, the fare from the airport to downtown will set you back about $40, and a ride from Union Station to the far side of Cabbagetown should cost around $10. Of the multitude of cab companies to choose from, the most reliable tend to be Co-op Cabs (☎416/504-2667) or Diamond Taxicab (☎416/366-6868).

Weather Local weather hotline ☎416/292-1010, then 3180.

Winter sports Ring Metro Parks (☎416/392-1111) for information on outdoor rinks and cross-country ski routes. Ski hire available at Trail Head, 61 Front St E (☎416/862-0881).

SOUTHWEST ONTARIO

The chain of towns to the east and west of Toronto, stretching 120km along the edge of Lake Ontario from Oshawa to Hamilton, is often called the **Golden Horseshoe**, a misleadingly evocative name that refers solely to their geographic shape and economic success. This is Ontario's manufacturing heartland, a densely populated strip whose principal places of interest are in the steel-making city of **Hamilton**, the home of both the Royal Botanical Gardens and the delightful mansion of Dundurn Castle. Further round the lake are the famous **Niagara Falls**, undoubtedly Canada's most celebrated sight, though the Falls adjoin the uninspiring town of the same name – and it's best to use the charming, colonial village of **Niagara-on-the-Lake** as a base for a visit. At neighbouring Queenston the **Niagara Escarpment** begins its rambling journey across the region to the Bruce Peninsula, the major interruption in a generally flat terrain. To the west of this limestone ridge the main attractions lie on the coast, most notably **Point Pelee National Park**, the vigorous town of **Windsor**, and the small-town pleasures of **Goderich** and leafy **Bayfield**. The **Bruce Peninsula** itself boasts dramatic coastal scenery and incorporates two outstanding national parks, which make for some great walking, climbing and scuba diving. To the east of the Niagara Escarpment, along the southern shore of **Severn Sound**, there's a string of lethargic ports, the most agreeable of which is **Penetanguishene**, located a few kilometres from the sturdy palisades of the replica Jesuit mission of **Sainte-Marie among the Hurons**. The northern shore of the Sound boasts the lion's share of the stunningly beautiful **Georgian Bay Islands National Park**, an elegiac land and waterscape of rocky, pine-dotted islets and crystal-blue lake. The park – and its campsites – are best approached by boat from the tourist resort of **Honey Harbour**, but you can sample the scenery on a variety of summer island cruises from Penetanguishene and **Midland** to the south and the dinky little port of **Parry Sound** further north.

There are fast and frequent **buses** and **trains** between Toronto and Niagara Falls, and a similarly efficient service between the region's other major settlements, like Windsor, London and Kitchener. But if you're visiting the smaller towns things are much more patchy: Hamilton, Penetanguishene and Midland, for instance, have reasonably good bus connections, but you can only reach Niagara-on-the-Lake via Niagara Falls. Worse still, there are no buses along the east shore of Lake Huron (to Goderich and Bayfield) and up the Bruce Peninsula – where Tobermory has a **ferry boat** service to South Baymouth on Manitoulin Island (see p.180), a useful short cut to northern Ontario.

Kitchener, Elora and Stratford

The industrial city of **Kitchener** is southern Ontario at its most mundane, but amid the prevailing architectural gloom it does have a couple of sights that are worth an hour or so. In marked contrast, **Elora**, 30km north of Kitchener, is a pleasant little village of old stone houses and mills on the periphery of the **Elora Gorge**, a narrow limestone ravine that's a popular spot for a day's walk and picnic. Fifty kilometres west of Kitchener, **Stratford** is different again, a modest country town that hosts one of Canada's most prestigious cultural events, the **Stratford Festival**.

Kitchener

Just off Hwy 401 about 100km west of downtown Toronto, **KITCHENER** lies at the centre of an industrial belt whose economy is based on rubber, textiles, leather and furniture. The town was founded as Sand Hills in 1799 by groups of **Mennonites**, a tightly knit Protestant sect who came here from the States, where their pacifist beliefs had incurred the wrath of their neighbours during the Revolution. Soon after, German farmers began to arrive in the area, establishing a generally good-humoured trading relationship with the Mennonites. The new settlers had Sand Hills renamed Berlin in 1826, but during World War I it was thought prudent to change the name yet again and to prove their patriotism they chose "Kitchener" after the British field marshal. Today around sixty percent of Kitchener's inhabitants are descendants of German immigrants, a heritage celebrated every year during **Oktoberfest**, nine days of alcoholic stupefaction when even the most reticent of men can be seen wandering the streets in lederhosen. The Mennonites have drifted out of Kitchener itself, and are concentrated in the villages north and west of Waterloo, Kitchener's glum northerly neighbour.

Kitchener's centre is marked by the **Farmers' Market**, open on Saturdays from 6am to 2pm – be sure to sample the delicious German sausages. The Mennonite traders are unmistakeable, with the men wearing traditional black suits and broad-brimmed hats, or deep-blue shirts and braces, the women ankle-length dresses and matching bonnets. The Ontario Mennonites are, however, far from being an homogeneous sect – over twenty different groups are affiliated to the Mennonite Central Committee (MCC) and although they all share certain religious beliefs reflecting their Anabaptist origins – the sole validity of adult baptism being crucial – precise practices and dress codes vary from group to group. Members of the traditional wing of the Mennonite movement, sometimes called **Amish** or Ammanites after the seventeenth-century elder Jakob Ammann, own property communally and shun all modern machinery, travelling to the market and around the back lanes on spindly horse-drawn buggies. To explain their

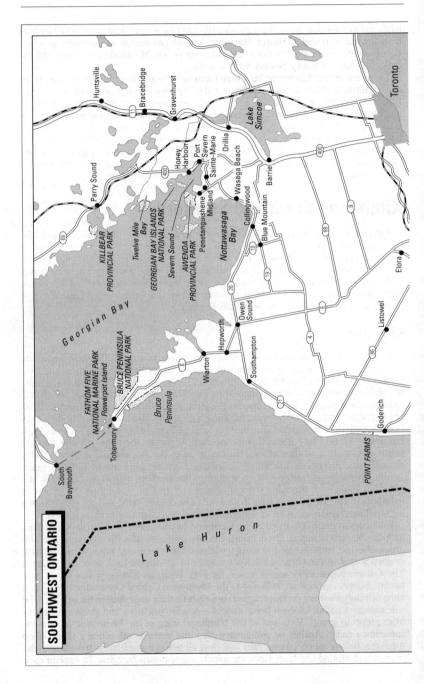

SOUTHWEST ONTARIO

Huntsville
Bracebridge
Gravenhurst
Toronto
Lake Simcoe
Parry Sound
Honey Harbour
Port Severn
Sainte-Marie
Orillia
Wasaga Beach
Barrie
Twelve Mile Bay
KILLBEAR PROVINCIAL PARK
GEORGIAN BAY ISLANDS NATIONAL PARK
Severn Sound
Midland
Penetanguishene
AWENDA PROVINCIAL PARK
Nottawasaga Bay
Collingwood
Blue Mountain
Elora
Georgian Bay
Owen Sound
Listowel
Hepworth
Southampton
FATHOM FIVE NATIONAL MARINE PARK
Flowerpot Island
BRUCE PENINSULA NATIONAL PARK
Wiarton
Bruce Peninsula
Goderich
Tobermory
POINT FARMS
South Baymouth
Lake Huron

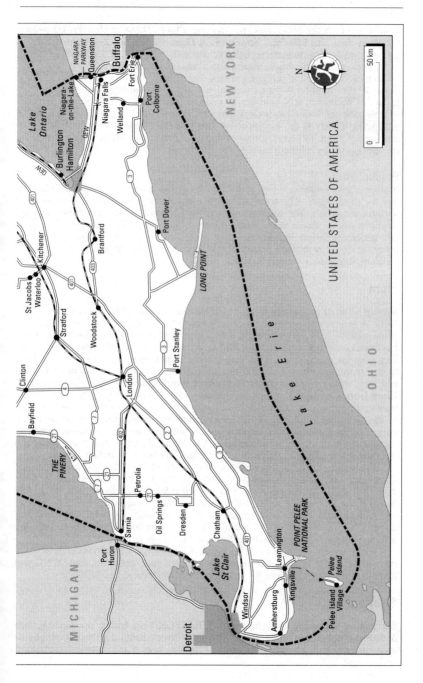

history and faith, the MCC runs **The Meeting Place** (May–Oct Mon–Fri 11am–5pm, Sat 10am–5pm, Sun 1.30–5pm; Nov–April Sat 11am–4.30pm, Sun 2–4.30pm; donation), a small tourist-office-cum-interpretation-centre in the village of **ST JACOBS**, just north of Waterloo on Hwy 86, where there's also a popular Mennonite craft shop.

Back in Kitchener, the only conventional tourist sight of note is **Woodside**, boyhood home of prime minister William Lyon Mackenzie King, about 1km northeast of the centre at 528 Wellington St N (mid-May to mid-Dec daily 10am–5pm; $2.50). Set in a pretty little park, the house has been restored to its late-Victorian appearance and has an interesting display in the basement on King's life and times, though it doesn't give much away about his eccentricities – a dog lover and spiritualist, he amalgamated the two obsessions by believing his pets were mediums.

Practicalities

Kitchener's **bus station** is on Charles Street, one block west of the main street, King, and the town centre. The **train station** is a ten-minute walk north of downtown, at Victoria and Weber. The **Kitchener-Waterloo Tourism Centre**, downtown opposite the library at 80 Queen St N (Mon–Fri 9am–4.30pm; ☎519/745-3536), has free maps and **accommodation** listings, including several B&Bs (①/②); during Oktoberfest many families offer similarly priced rooms. There's a clutch of **motels** north of the centre along Kitchener's Victoria Street.

Elora

Sloping up from the craggy banks of the Grand River, **ELORA** was founded in the 1830s by settlers who harnessed the river's waters to run their mills. Some of their limestone cottages have survived, along with a large grist mill, the main landmark, which has been converted into the *Elora Mill Country Inn*, a clever adaptation of what has long been the most important building in town. Nonetheless, most visitors come here to gaze at the waterfalls beside the inn – even though they're only a few metres high – and then stroll on to viewpoints overlooking the neighbouring three-kilometre-long **Elora Gorge**, a forested ravine with limestone cliffs. To get to the gorge from the inn, walk up Price Street to the top of the hill, turn left on James Street and proceed as far as the park area at the end of Henderson, from where footpaths lead across to the gorge. Elora itself, just ten-minutes' walk from end to end, is most pleasantly approached from the south – along Route 21 – across a narrow bridge that leads into the main street, Metcalfe, which cuts across tiny Mill Street, adjoining the falls.

The **tourist office**, in the library in the centre of the village at 152 Geddes St (June–Aug daily 9am–5pm; Oct–May Mon–Fri 9am–4.30pm, Sat–Sun noon–4.30pm; ☎519/846-9841), has the details of a handful of **B&Bs**. Perhaps the best is *The Old Bissell House*, 84 Mill St E (☎519/846-6695; ③), a smart, modern place with river views and four pleasant guestrooms, two en suite. There's only one hotel, the *Elora Mill Country Inn,* on Mill Street (☎519/846-5356; ⑥), which boasts period bedrooms, log fires and beamed ceilings. The hotel has a first-rate **restaurant**.

If you're keen to see more of the gorge, the **Elora Gorge Conservation Area** (daily dawn–dusk; $3.50) is a popular picnic and camping spot spread out along the Grand River 2km southwest of Elora: it's signposted from the bridge near Metcalfe.

Stratford

Surrounded by flat and fertile farmland, **STRATFORD** is a homely and likeable town of 29,000 people that's brightened by the Avon River trimming the centre and by its grandiose city hall, a brown-brick fiesta of cupolas, towers and limestone trimmings.

More importantly, the town is also the home of the **Stratford Festival** (*www.stratford-festival.on.ca*), which started in 1953 and is now one of the most prestigious theatrical occasions in North America, attracting no fewer than half a million visitors from May to early November. The core performances are Shakespearean, but there's much other drama too, from Racine to O'Casey and Beckett.

The **Festival Box Office** at the Festival Theatre (Jan to late April Mon–Sat 9am–5pm, Sun 9am–2pm; late April to early Nov Mon–Sat 9am–8pm, Sun 9am–2pm; ☎1-800/567-1600 or 519/273-1600) accepts ticket orders by phone or in person; by mail (PO Box 520, Stratford, ON N5A 6V2); by fax (☎519/273-6173); or by email (*orders@stratford-festival.on.ca*). Tickets cost anywhere between $25 and $75 depending on the performance and which seat category you have. Many plays are sold out months in advance, but the box office does set aside a limited number of rush tickets for two of the three main theatres – the Festival and the Avon, but not the Tom Patterson – at about $25. These are for sale from 9am on the day of the performance, but the seats are the worst in the house. The box office also organizes a number of **discount packages** with savings upwards of ten percent for various categories of performance, plus accommodation ranging from hotels down to guesthouses.

Practicalities

From Stratford **bus** and **train stations**, on Shakespeare Street, it's a fifteen-minute stroll north to the town centre on the south bank of the River Avon. There are two **tourist offices**. The first is the main Visitors' Information Centre (early to late May Sun & Mon 9am–3pm, Tues–Sat 9am–5pm; June–Aug Sun & Mon 9am–5pm, Tues–Sat 9am–8pm; Sept to mid-Nov Tues–Sat 9am–5pm, Sun 10am–2pm; ☎519/273-3352), located by the river on York Street, immediately northwest of the town's main intersection, where Erie, Downie and Ontario streets all meet. The second is Tourism Stratford, 88 Wellington St (Mon–Fri 8.30am–5pm; ☎519/271-5140 or 1-800/561-SWAN; *www.city.stratford.on.ca*), which is off Downie Street on the west side of the Market Place.

Stratford has over 250 guesthouses and B&Bs plus around a dozen hotels and motels, but **accommodation** can still be hard to find during the Festival's busiest weekends in July and August. The walls of the Information Centre are plastered with pictures and descriptions of many of these establishments and standards are high. Both tourist offices will help you find somewhere to stay, but one good and convenient recommendation is *Avonview Manor B&B*, 63 Avon St (☎519/273-4603, *www.avonview-manor.on.ca*; ③), which occupies an expansive Edwardian villa overlooking the north bank of the River Avon across from the town centre. The four bedrooms here, all with shared bathrooms, are tastefully decorated and immaculately maintained. Another excellent choice is *Blackwater House*, 122 Douglas St (☎519/273-6490, fax 273-2544; ⑥; May–Oct), in a trim, high-gabled Victorian house in a quiet residential area, ten-minutes' walk from the centre on the north side of the river. The interior, with its antiques and watercolours, has three en-suite guestrooms, and there's a pool in the garden. A third and even more central option is the *Deacon House*, 101 Brunswick St (☎519/273-2052 or 1-877/825-6374, fax 519/273-3784; ⑤), whose six lovely guestrooms – five en suite – occupy a good-looking Edwardian villa with a wide veranda.

Stratford has plenty of excellent **cafés** and **restaurants**, with one of the best being *Fellini's Italian Café & Grill*, 107 Ontario St, which offers a good range of fresh pizzas and pastas at reasonable prices. There are also tasty snacks and light meals at *Let Them Eat Cake*, by the Market Place at 90 Wellington St, and pastries and gourmet coffees at *Balzac's*, 149 Ontario St. *Rundles*, 9 Coburg St (☎519/271-6442; closed in winter), is arguably the classiest restaurant in town, serving up imaginatively prepared French-style cuisine at finger-burning prices.

Hamilton and around

Some 70km from Toronto, **HAMILTON** lies at the extreme western end of Lake Ontario and was the focus of a district first surveyed by George Hamilton, a Niagaran storekeeper-turned-landowner who moved here in 1812 to escape the war between America and Britain. Strategically located, the town was soon established as a trading centre, but its real growth began with the development of the farm-implements industry in the 1850s. By the turn of the last century, Hamilton had become a major steel producer and today its mills churn out sixty percent of the country's output.

The city

For a city of over 300,000 people, Hamilton is not over-endowed with attractions. The finest building in the centre is **Whitehern** (mid-June to Aug Tues–Sun 11am–4pm; Sept to mid-June Tues–Sun 1–4pm; $3.50), a couple of minutes' walk east of the city hall at 41 Jackson St W. A good example of early Victorian architecture, its reworked interior holds an eccentric mix of styles ranging from a splendid mid-nineteenth-century circular stairway to a dingy wood-panelled 1930s basement, the garbled legacy of the McQuestern family who lived here from 1852 until the 1960s. Also in the centre, at 123 King St W, is the **Art Gallery of Hamilton** (Tues & Wed and Fri–Sun 11am–5pm, Thurs 11am–9pm; $4), a brutally modern building whose two floors display a representative sample of Canadian painting drawn from the permanent collection. The gallery has a good selection of works by the Group of Seven (see box, p.86) – Harris, Lismer, J.E.H. MacDonald and Edwin Holgate all make distinctive contributions – and there's a fine painting by Tom Thomson, *The Birch Grove*, dated to 1917. Look out also for Alex Colville's iconic *Horse and Train* of 1954 and for several folksy paintings by Cornelius Krieghoff (see p.163). The gallery also features an imaginative programme of temporary exhibitions with photography a particular favourite.

About twenty-minutes' walk west of the town centre, straight down York Boulevard from James Street, you come to the much more entertaining **Dundurn Castle** (late May to Aug daily 10am–4.30pm; Sept to late May Tues–Sun noon–4pm; $7), a handsome villa built in the 1830s for Sir Allan Napier MacNab, a soldier, lawyer and land speculator who became one of the leading conservative politicians of the day. He was knighted for his loyalty to the Crown during the Upper Canada Rebellion of 1837, when he employed bands of armed Indians to round up supposed rebels and loot their property. Carefully renovated, Dundurn is an impressive broadly Palladian building with an interior that easily divides into "upstairs" and "downstairs": the former filled with fine contemporaneous furnishings, the latter a warren of poorly ventilated rooms for the dozens of servants. Nearby, the gatekeeper's cottage has been turned into a small **military museum** (July–Aug daily 11am–5pm; Sept–June Tues–Sun 1–5pm; free admission with castle), detailing local involvement in the War of 1812 and in the Fenian (Irish–American) cross-border raids of the 1860s (see p.93).

From Dundurn Castle, York Boulevard crosses the four-kilometre-long isthmus that spans the western reaches of Hamilton harbour before heading on into the neighbouring city of Burlington. The **Royal Botanical Gardens** (☎905/527-1158, *www.rbg.ca*) cover some 3000 acres around the northern end of the isthmus, their several sections spread over 15km of wooded shoreline. The flower displays here are simply gorgeous with highlights including the Hendrie Park Rose Garden (best June–Oct) and the neighbouring Laking Garden with its irises and peonies (May & June). These two gardens adjoin the main RBG visitor centre, where there's a shop, café and several inside areas featuring forced bulbs, orchids, cacti and so forth. Wilder parts of the RBG are round to the west with the 800-hectare Cootes Paradise Marsh nature sanctuary latticed with hiking trails. The outdoor garden areas are open daily from 9.30am to dusk and admission costs $7. There are modest additional charges for some of the inside areas, which also close a little earlier – either 4pm or 5pm. As for transport, most Hamilton–Burlington **buses** stop outside the RBG centre and from here a shuttle bus (late April to Aug every 15min; free) visits every section of the gardens. At other times of the year, you'll need a car.

Practicalities

Hamilton **bus station** is at the corner of Hunter and James streets, three blocks south of Main Street – which, together with King Street, one block further to the north, forms the downtown core. The **tourist information office**, 127 King St E at Catherine (Mon–Sat 9am–5pm; ☎905/546-2666 or 1-800/263-8590), can supply you with brochures on the city and its surroundings, plus restaurant and hotel lists. Most of the major **hotel** chains have branches in Hamilton, with rooms starting from around $80; one of the most comfortable is the centrally located *Ramada Plaza Hotel*, 150 King St E (☎905/528-3451; ⑤).

Brantford and the Bell Homestead

The modest manufacturing town of **BRANTFORD**, to the west of Hamilton beside the Grand River, takes its name from Joseph Brant, who led a large group of Loyalist Iroquois here after the American War of Independence, then worked to form a confederation of Iroquois to keep the United States out of Ohio. His dream was undermined by jealousies amongst the Indian nations, whereupon he withdrew to Burlington and lived the life of an English gentleman. The town was later the birthplace of ice-hockey's greatest player, Wayne Gretzky, but no one's built a museum yet.

The most interesting thing to see in the town itself is the **Brant County Museum**, 57 Charlotte St (Wed–Fri 10am–4pm & Sat 1–4pm, plus Sun in summer 1–4pm; $2), where there's a reasonable collection of Iroquois artefacts. However, Brantford's main sight – the **Bell Homestead**, 94 Tutela Heights Rd (Tues–Sun 9.30am–4.30pm; $3.25) – is located about 4km south of the centre, in the low wooded hills overlooking the river. **Alexander Graham Bell** left Edinburgh for Ontario in 1870 at the age of 23, a reluctant immigrant who came only because of fears for his health after the death of two close relatives from tuberculosis. Soon afterwards he took a job as a teacher of the deaf, motivated by his mother's loss of hearing and, in his efforts to discover a way to reproduce sounds visibly, he stumbled across the potential of transmitting sound along an electrified wire. The consequence was the first long-distance call, made in 1876 from Brantford to the neighbouring village of Paris. The Homestead consists of two simple, clapboard buildings. The first, moved here from Brantford in 1969, housed Canada's original Bell company office and features a series of modest displays on the history of the telephone. The second, the cosy family home, fronts a second small exhibition area devoted to Bell's life and research. There's no public transport from Brantford to the homestead.

Niagara Falls and the Niagara River

In 1860 thousands watched as Charles Blondin walked a tightrope across **NIAGARA FALLS** for the third time; at the midway point he cooked an omelette on a portable grill and then had a marksman shoot a hole through his hat from the *Maid of the Mist* tug boat, 50m below. As attested by Blondin and the antics of innumerable lunatics and publicity seekers – not to mention several million waterlogged tourist photos – the Falls simply can't be beat as a theatrical setting. Yet the stupendous first impression of the

Niagara doesn't last long, especially on jaded modern palates. Consequently, to prevent each year's twelve million visitors becoming bored by the sight of a load of water crashing over a 52-metre cliff, the Niagarans have ensured that the Falls can be seen from every angle imaginable – from boats, viewing towers, helicopters, cable cars and even tunnels in the rock face behind the cascade. The **tunnels** and the **boats** are the most exciting, with the entrance to the former right next to the Falls and the latter leaving from the bottom of the cliff at the end of Clifton Hill, 1100m downriver. Both give a real sense of the extraordinary force of the waterfall, a perpetual white-crested thundering pile-up that had Mahler bawling "At last, fortissimo" over the din.

Trains and **buses** from Toronto and many of southern Ontario's larger towns serve the **town of Niagara Falls** (see p.112), 3km to the north of the action; the availability of discount excursion fares makes a day-trip to see the Falls a straightforward proposition, although, if you do decide to spend the night, quaint **Niagara-on-the-Lake**, 26km downstream beside Lake Ontario, is a much better option than the crassly commercialized town of Niagara Falls itself. Niagara-on-the-Lake can be reached from the Falls by shuttle bus (see p.112), but note that accommodation there is extremely tight in high season, when you'd be well advised to book up a couple of days in advance. Both the **Niagara Parkway** road and the **Niagara River Recreation Trail**, a jogging and cycle path, stretch the length of the Niagara River from Fort Erie, 32km upstream from the Falls, to Niagara-on-the-Lake.

The Falls

Though you can hear the roar of the **Falls** miles away, nothing quite prepares you for the spectacle; the fearsome white arc shrouded in clouds of dense spray, with the river boats struggling below, mere specks against the surging cauldron. There are two cataracts, the accelerating water being sliced into two channels by tiny Goat Island: on the far side, across the frontier, the river slips over the precipice of the **American Falls**, 320m wide but still only one-half of the width of the **Horseshoe Falls** on the Canadian side. If anything, it's an even more amazing scene in winter, with snow-covered trees edging a jagged armoury of freezing mist and heaped ice blocks. It looks like a scene of untrammelled nature, but it isn't. Since the 1910s, successive hydroelectric schemes have greatly reduced the water flow, and all sorts of tinkering has spread what's left of the Niagara more evenly over the crest line. As a result, the process of erosion, which has moved the Falls some 11km upstream in 12,000 years, has slowed down from 1m per year to 30cm. This obviously has advantages for the tourist industry, but the environmental consequences of training this deluge for decades on one part of the Niagara riverbed are unclear. At least the cardsharps and charlatans who overran the riverside in Blondin's day are long gone – the Niagara Parks Commission, which controls the area along the river and beside the Falls, ensures that the immaculately tended tree-lined gardens and parkland remain precisely so.

Beside the Horseshoe Falls, **Table Rock House** has a small, free observation platform and elevators which travel to the base of the cliff, where **tunnels**, grandiosely named the "Journey Behind the Falls" (year-round daily from 9am to dusk; $6.50), lead to points behind the waterfall. For a more panoramic view, a pint-sized Incline Railway ($1) takes visitors up the hill behind Table Rock House to the **Minolta Tower**, 6732 Oakes Drive (daily: June–Sept 9am–midnight; Oct–May 9am–11pm; $7), which has observation platforms, though the views are rather better from the Skylon tower (see below).

From Table Rock House, a wide and crowded path leads north along the edge of the river gorge, with the manicured lawns of Queen Victoria Park to the left and views over to the American Falls to the right. After a few minutes, turn left up Murray Street to visit the **Skylon** tower (daily: June–Aug 8am–1am; Sept–May 10am–10pm; $8), on

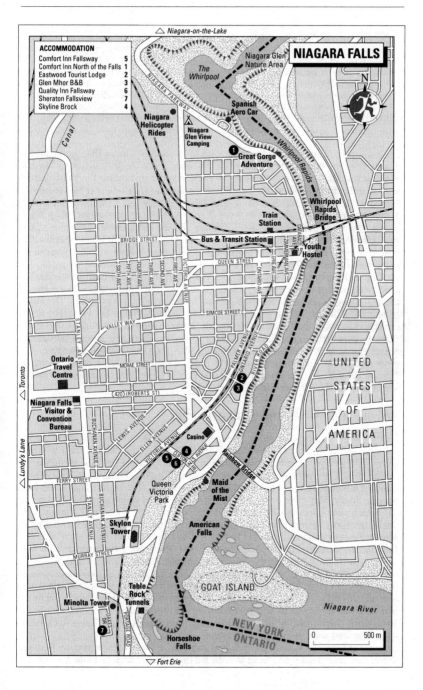

NIAGARA FALLS

ACCOMMODATION

Comfort Inn Fallsway	5
Comfort Inn North of the Falls	1
Eastwood Tourist Lodge	2
Glen Mhor B&B	3
Quality Inn Fallsway	6
Sheraton Fallsview	7
Skyline Brock	4

△ Niagara-on-the-Lake

Niagara Glen
Nature Area

The
Whirlpool

Spanish
Aero Car

Niagara
Helicopter
Rides

Niagara
Glen View
Camping

Great Gorge
Adventure

Whirlpool Rapids

Whirlpool
Rapids
Bridge

Train
Station

Bus & Transit Station

Youth
Hostel

BRIDGE STREET

QUEEN STREET

VICTORIA AVENUE

FIRST AVE.

SECOND AVE.

THIRD AVE.

FOURTH AVE.

FIFTH AVE.

SIXTH AVE.

SIMCOE STREET

VALLEY WAY

MCRAE STREET

STANLEY AVENUE

PALMER AVENUE

ONTARIO AVENUE

RIVER ROAD

ERIE AVE.

ZIMMERMAN AVE.

ONTARIO AVE.

Ontario
Travel
Centre

(420) (ROBERTS ST)

Niagara Falls
Visitor &
Convention
Bureau

BUCHANAN AVENUE

LEWIS AVENUE

ELLEN AVENUE

VICTORIA AVENUE

CLIFTON HILL

Casino

Queen
Victoria
Park

Maid
of the
Mist

Rainbow Bridge

FERRY STREET

BUCHANAN AVENUE

STANLEY AVENUE

American
Falls

Skylon
Tower

MURRAY STREET

Minolta Tower

Table
Rock
Tunnels

OAKES DR.

PORTAGE ROAD

GOAT ISLAND

Niagara River

Horseshoe
Falls

NEW YORK

ONTARIO

UNITED

STATES

OF

AMERICA

Canal

NIAGARA PARKWAY

△ Toronto

△ Lundy's Lane

▽ Fort Erie

0   500 m

The **Explorer's Passport Plus**, a combined ticket covering three of the main attractions – the Journey Behind the Falls (the tunnels at Table Rock), the Great Gorge Adventure and the Butterfly Conservatory – and public transport by People Mover bus between them, is available at each of these sights. It costs $20 for adults, $10 for children (6–12 years old) and is available from mid-May to mid-October. The **Explorer's Passport** is the same deal without the bus – prices $16 ($8 for children). Alternatively, the **Natural Wonder Passport Plus** replaces the Butterfly Conservatory with the Spanish Aero Car and costs $18 ($9 for children 6–12) or $14 ($7) without the bus.

Robinson Street; or continue along the path to the foot of Clifton Hill, the main drag linking the riverside area with Niagara Falls town. From the jetty below Clifton Hill, **Maid of the Mist boats** edge out into the river and push up towards the Falls, an exhilarating and extremely damp trip that no one should miss (April–June & Sept to late Oct Mon–Fri 10am–5pm, Sat & Sun 10am–6pm; July–Aug daily 9am–8pm; boats leave every 15min in high season, otherwise every 30min; $10.65 per person, including waterproofs, $6.55 for children aged 6–12). **Clifton Hill** itself is a tawdry collection of fast-food joints and bizarre attractions, from the innocuous House of Frankenstein to the absurdity of the Believe It or Not Museum, where, amongst other wonders, you can spy a dog with human teeth and a man with double the normal number of eye pupils. Just off Clifton Hill is the area's second-biggest crowd puller, the 24 hr **casino** (☎1-888/946-3255, *www.casinoniagara.com*), a gleamingly modern structure where – to use the old cliché – college kids can watch their parents fritter away their school fees. The casino is near the Rainbow Bridge leading over to the States. If you're keen to avoid all this commercialization, then stick to the **riverside** where the Niagara Parks Commission (*www.niagaraparks.com*) keeps everything in order. There are several outstanding attractions further downstream – beginning with the Great Gorge Adventure, 3km away (see p.114) – and they are all easily reached either by bike or on foot along the Niagara River Recreation Trail, or by car and People Mover bus (as far as Queenston – see below) via the Niagara Parkway road.

Arrival, information and getting around

Unless you're travelling by public transport, you're unlikely to catch sight of the surprisingly low-key centre of **NIAGARA FALLS TOWN**, 3km north of the Falls themselves. It's here you'll find the **train station** directly opposite the **bus terminal**, 420 Bridge St at Erie Avenue. From the bus station, **Niagara Transit** (☎905/356-1179) operates a limited range of town and suburban services. The most useful is the **Falls Shuttle** (daily: May–Sept every 30min; Oct–April hourly; single ticket $2.75, day-pass $5), which runs buses to Clifton Hill and the Skylon Tower. There's also an excellent public transport system along the Niagara River. This is the Niagara Parks' **People Mover System** (daily: April to mid-June & Sept to late Oct 10am–6pm, often later; mid-June to Aug 8.30am–11pm), whose buses travel 30km along the riverbank between Queenston Heights Park, north of the Falls, and the Rapids' View car park just to the south. People Movers appear at twenty-minute intervals and an **all-day pass** costs $5. Note also that People Mover buses have run all year on a trial basis for the last year or two, and this off-season service may be continued in the future. If you're arriving by car, be aware that **parking** can be a real headache. In the summer, try to get here before 10am when there's usually space in the convenient car park beside Table Rock House – any later and you can expect a long queue.

As for **information**, avoid the privately-run tourist offices that spring up here and there, now and again – and head instead for the official **Niagara Falls Visitor and**

Convention Bureau, at 5515 Stanley Ave (June–Aug daily 8am–8pm; Sept–May Mon–Fri 8am–6pm, Sat 10am–6pm & Sun 10am–4pm; ☎905/356-6061 or 1-800/563-2557; *www.niagarafallstourism.com*). They have a full range of information on the town and the Falls and will – if required – help you find a place to stay. They are located about 100m south of Hwy 420, the main road to the Falls from the QEW. Close by, actually on Hwy 420, is the provincial **Ontario Travel Centre** (mid-May to mid-June Mon–Thurs & Sun 8.30am–6pm, Fri & Sat 8am–8pm; mid-June to Aug daily 8am–8pm; Sept to early Oct Mon–Thurs & Sun 8.30am–5pm, Fri & Sat 8.30am–6pm; early Oct to mid-May daily 8.30am–5pm; ☎905/358-3221), where you'll find a wide range of free literature on the whole of Ontario. There are also a number of official tourist kiosks close to the Falls, the most comprehensive being at the Table Rock complex.

Given the excellence of the People Mover System, there's no compelling reason to take a **sightseeing tour**. That said, Double Decker Bus Tours (☎905/374-7423) do leave from beside the ticket office at the bottom of Clifton Hill several times daily from mid-May to mid-October, travelling north as far as Queenston Heights. Passengers can get on and off the bus as and when they wish; the $35 ticket (for Tour Package A) is valid for two days and includes admission to the river's major attractions.

Accommodation

Niagara Falls is billed as the "Honeymoon Capital of the World", which means that many of its **motels** and **hotels** have an odd mix of cheap, basic rooms and gaudy suites with heart-shaped bathtubs, waterbeds and the like. Quite what the connection is between water and nuptial bliss is hard to fathom – but there it is. In summer, hotel and motel rooms fill up fast, so either ring ahead or seek help from the official Niagara Falls Visitor and Convention Bureau, at 5515 Stanley Ave (see above). Out of season it's a buyer's market, which means that haggling can often bring the price way down.

For the most part, the least expensive choices are either out along **Lundy's Lane**, an extremely dispiriting motel strip that extends west of the Falls for several kilometres, or in the uninteresting centre of **Niagara Falls town**. Neither area is much fun (especially Lundy's Lane) and you're much better off spending a little more to stay either in the **Clifton Hill area**, which has – once you've adjusted to it – a certain kitsch charm, or on leafy **River Road** – running north from the foot of Clifton Hill – where there are a couple of good B&Bs and a modern inn. If you want a room with a decent view of the Falls, you'll be paying premium rates. The premier hotels near the **Minolta Tower** on Oakes Drive offer some of the best views but you should always check the room before you shell out: descriptions can be fairly elastic and some rooms claiming to be in sight of the Falls require minor gymnastics for a glimpse.

Hotels

Comfort Inn Fallsway, 4960 Clifton Hill (☎905/358-3293, fax 358-3818, *www.comfortniagara.com*). This spick-and-span modern inn is located just off Clifton Hill. The rooms are kitted out in standard chain style, but they are comfortable enough and the glassed-in patio area has an indoor pool and whirlpool. Reasonably priced. ④.

Comfort Inn North of the Falls, 4009 River Rd (☎905/356-0131, fax 356-1800). Although part of a standard-issue hotel/motel chain, this inn does possess a particularly attractive location, flanked by parkland down on River Rd near the Spanish Aero Car, about 4.5km north of the Falls. ⑤.

Quality Inn Fallsway, 4946 Clifton Hill (☎905/358-3601 or 1-800/263-7137, fax 905/358-3818, *info@ fallsresort.com*). Comfortable, pleasantly furnished motel-style rooms just off Clifton Hill. Indooor and outdoor pools. ⑤.

Sheraton Fallsview Hotel, 6755 Oakes Drive (☎905/374-1077 or 1-800/267-8439, fax 905/374-6224, *sheraton@fallsview.com*). Big, lavish hotel and conference centre overlooking the Falls. Near the Minolta Tower. One of the smartest places in town with two tariffs – one for rooms with views over the Falls (⑦), the others without (⑥).

Skyline Brock Hotel, 5685 Falls Ave (☎905/374-4444 or 1-800/263-7135, fax 905/371-8349, *reserve@vaxxine.com*). Just steps from the foot of Clifton Hill, this is one of Niagara's older hotels, a tidy tower block whose upper storeys (and more expensive rooms) have views over the American Falls. ③–⑧.

Bed and breakfasts, hostels and campground

Eastwood Tourist Lodge, 5359 River Rd (☎905/354-8686). Four commodious, air-conditioned en-suite bedrooms in a rambling old villa with wide balconies and attractive garden. ④.

Glen Mhor B&B, 5381 River Rd (☎905/354-2600). Pleasant, straightforward and well-tended B&B in an older house with five air-conditioned bedrooms. ③.

Niagara Falls Youth Hostel, 4549 Cataract Ave (☎905/357-0770 or 1-888/749-0058, *nfhostel @hostellingintl-gl.on.ca*). HI hostel a 5min walk from the bus and train station in Niagara Falls town. Occupies a two-storey brick building in a dreary location: Cataract Ave is a narrow side street off Bridge St as it approaches the Whirlpool Rapids Bridge over to the States. There are laundry facilities, a kitchen and a lounge. Open all year; 85 beds. Members $18, nonmembers $22.

Niagara Glen View Campground (☎905/358-8689, fax 374-4493, *jja@vaxxine.com*). There are several campsites out along Lundy's Lane, but this site, along the river about 3.5km north of Clifton Hill, occupies a far more agreeable location at the corner of Victoria Ave and the Niagara Parkway. It has nearly three hundred pitches for tents and trailers. Pitches with an electrical hook-up cost $30; $27 without.

Eating

There are literally dozens of cheap chain **restaurants** and fast-food joints along and around Clifton Hill. Most of them are unremarkable, but at least the *Golden Griddle*, in the *Quality Inn Fallsway*, at 4946 Clifton Hill, has a good basic menu with main courses from as little as $9. Other possibilities include Italian pizzas and snacks at both *Mama Mia's*, 5719 Victoria Ave at Clifton Hill (☎905/354-7471), and *Big Anthony's*, nearby at 5677 Victoria Ave (☎905/354-9844). The latter is a family-run place owned by a well-known ex-professional wrestler, pictures of whom decorate the windows. For something more distinctive, take lunch or dinner at the Skylon tower's *Revolving Dining Room* (☎905/356-2651), a smart and fairly formal restaurant with panoramic views over the Falls. At 236m, the restaurant takes an hour to complete one revolution – a gentle, almost imperceptible ride.

Downstream from the Falls

Heading north from Clifton Hill, the **Niagara Parkway** follows the course of the river as does the parallel **Niagara River Recreation Trail**, a combined cycle and walking track. After about 3km, both reach the **Great Gorge Adventure** (May–Oct daily dawn to dusk; $5), where an elevator and then a tunnel lead to a boardwalk beside the Whirlpool Rapids, the point at which the river fizzes violently as it curves round the bend. From here, it's 1.3km more to the brightly painted **Spanish Aero Car** (April–Dec daily from 9am (sometimes 10am) to dusk; $5.50), a cable-car ride across the gorge that's as near as you'll come to emulating Blondin's antics, and another 1.5km to **Niagara Helicopter Rides**, 3731 Victoria Ave (☎905/357-5672), who offer a nine-minute excursion over the Falls for $85 per person – $304 for four. You don't need to book, as the six-seater helicopters whizz in and out with unnerving frequency from 9am until sunset – weather permitting.

Pressing on, next up along the parkway is the **Niagara Glen Nature Area** (daily dawn to dusk; free), where paths lead down from the clifftop to the bottom of the gorge. It's a hot and sticky trek in the height of the summer and strenuous at any time of the year, but rewarding for all that – here at least you get a sense of what the region was like before all the tourist hullabaloo. Nearby, about 800m further along the road is the

Niagara Parks Commission's pride and joy, the immensely popular **Niagara Parks Botanical Gardens** (daily dawn to dusk; free), whose immaculate flower beds are at their best from late May to September. The rhododendrons are, for instance, in full bloom from mid-May to June, while roses are a special highlight from mid-June to September. The gardens also contain a huge, climate-controlled **Butterfly Conservatory** (daily: May–Sept 9am–9pm, Oct–April 9am–6pm; $8) that houses over 2000 exotic butterflies in a tropical rainforest setting.

About 3km further on, **Queenston Heights Park** marks the original location of the Falls, before the force of the water – as it adjusts to the hundred-metre differential between the water levels of lakes Erie and Ontario – eroded the riverbed to its present point, 11km upstream. Soaring above the park, there's a grandiloquent monument to Sir Isaac Brock, the Guernsey-born general who was killed here in the War of 1812, leading a head-on charge against the Americans. From beside the park, the parkway begins a curving descent down to the little village of **QUEENSTON**, whose importance as a transit centre disappeared when the Falls were bypassed by the Welland Canal, running west of the river between lakes Erie and Ontario and completed in 1829. In the village, on Partition Street, the **Laura Secord Homestead** (May–Aug daily 10am–5pm; $1.75) is a reconstruction of the simple timber-frame house of Massachusetts-born Laura Ingersoll Secord (1775–1868). Secord's dedication to the imperial interest was such that she ran 30km through the woods to warn the British army of a surprise attack planned by the Americans in the War of 1812.

ONTARIO'S WINES

Until the 1980s **Canadian wine** was something of a joke. The industry's most popular product was a sticky, fizzy concoction called Baby Duck and other varieties were commonly called block and tackle wines after a widely reported witticism of a member of the Ontario legislature: "If you drink a bottle and walk a block, you can tackle anyone." This state of affairs has, however, been transformed by the **Vintners Quality Alliance**, the VQA, who have, since 1989, come to exercise tight control over wine production in Ontario, which produces eighty percent of Canadian wine. The VQA's appellation system distinguishes between – and supervises the quality control of – two broad types of wine. Those bottles carrying the Provincial Designation on their labels (ie Ontario) must be made from 100 percent Ontario-grown wines from an approved list of European varieties of grape and selected hybrids; those bearing the Geographic Designation (ie Niagara Peninsula, Pelee Island or Lake Erie North Shore), by comparison, can only use *Vitis vinifera*, the classic European grape varieties, such as Riesling, Chardonnay and Cabernet Sauvignon. As you might expect from a developing wine area, the results are rather inconsistent, but the **Rieslings** have a refreshingly crisp, almost tart, flavour with a mellow, warming aftertaste – and are perhaps the best of the present Canadian range, white or red.

Over ten **wineries** are clustered in the vicinity of Niagara-on-the-Lake and most are very willing to show visitors round. Local tourist offices carry a full list with opening times, but one of the most interesting is **Inniskillin**, Line 3 (Service Road 66), just off – and signed from – the Niagara Parkway, about 5km south of Niagara-on-the-Lake (daily: May–Oct 10am–6pm; Nov–April 10am–5pm; ☎905/468-3554, *www.icewine.com*). Here you can follow a twenty-step self-guided tour or take a free guided tour, sip away at the tasting bar and buy at the wine boutique. Inniskillin has produced a clutch of award-winning vintages and have played a leading role in the improvement of the industry. They are also one of the few Canadian wineries to produce **ice wine**, an outstanding sweet dessert wine made from grapes that are left on the vine till December or January, when they are hand-picked at night when frozen. The picking and the crushing of the frozen grapes is a time-consuming business and this is reflected in the price – about $50 per 375ml bottle.

Niagara-on-the-Lake

One of the most charming places in Ontario, **NIAGARA-ON-THE-LAKE**, 26km downstream from the Falls, boasts lines of elegant clapboard houses surrounded by well-kept gardens, all spread along tree-lined streets. The town, much of which dates from the early nineteenth century, was originally known as Newark and became the first capital of Upper Canada in 1792. But four years later it lost this distinction to York (Toronto) because of its proximity to the frontier – a wise decision, for the Americans crossed the river and destroyed Niagara-on-the-Lake in 1813. The town was rebuilt (and renamed) immediately afterwards, and has managed to avoid all but the most sympathetic of modifications ever since. This period charm attracts a few too many day-trippers (and souvenir shops) for the town's own good, but the crowds are rarely oppressive, except on weekends in July and August.

The charm of Niagara-on-the-Lake lies in the whole rather than in any particular sight, but **Queen Street**, the short main drag, does boast a pretty **clock tower** and the old **Apothecary** shop (mid-May to Aug daily noon–6pm; free), worth a peep for its beautifully carved walnut and butternut cabinets, crystal gasoliers and porcelain jars. The town's finest building is, however, the church of **St Andrews**, at Simcoe and Gage streets, a splendid illustration of the Greek Revival style dating to the 1830s. The church has a beautifully proportioned portico and the interior retains the original high pulpit and box pews. Also of some interest is the **Niagara Historical Museum**, 43 Castlereagh St (Jan & Feb Sat & Sun 1–5pm; March, April, Nov & Dec daily 1–5pm; May–Oct daily 10am–5pm; $3), founded in 1895 and the repository for over 20,000 artefacts of local significance, with the Loyalists being particularly well-represented. More importantly, Niagara-on-the-Lake is also home to one of Canada's more acclaimed theatrical seasons, the **Shaw Festival** (April to early Nov), featuring the work of George Bernard Shaw and his contemporaries. There are three main theatres and tickets cost between $34 and $70 – half that for Rush seats which are, when they're on offer, available from 9am on the day of the performance. Contact the **Shaw Festival box office** (☎905/468-2172 or 1-800/511-SHAW, fax 905/468-3804, *www.shawfest.sympatico.ca*) for further details.

Fort George

So close to the border, the British military post of **Fort George** (April–Oct daily 10am–5pm; $6), some 700m southeast of the town centre, was difficult to man. Indeed, so many Redcoats deserted to the US in anticipation of a better life that it eventually had to be garrisoned by the Royal Canadian Rifle Regiment, a force consisting mostly of married men approaching retirement who were unlikely to forfeit their pensions by hightailing it down south. If they did try and were caught, they were branded on the chest with the letter "D" and then either lashed or transported to a penal colony – except in wartime, when they were shot. The fort was one of a line of stockades slung across the waterways of the Great Lakes to protect Canada from the US. The original fort was destroyed during the War of 1812, but the site was thoroughly excavated and the fort rebuilt in the 1930s – and splendidly done it was too. The thick earth-and-stone rampart that encircles the fort is set close to the lie of the land to mitigate against artillery bombardment, while the projecting bastions once enabled the defenders to fire on attackers from a variety of angles. Behind the rampart, in the central **compound**, are a number of replica buildings including barracks, officers' quarters and three pine blockhouses that doubled as soldiers' barracks. The difference between the officers' quarters and the barracks is striking. The former are comparatively spacious and were once – as recorded on shipping lists – furnished with fancy knick-knacks, while the latter housed the men and some of their wives (six wives out of every hundred were allowed to join the garrison) in the meanest of conditions. The only original

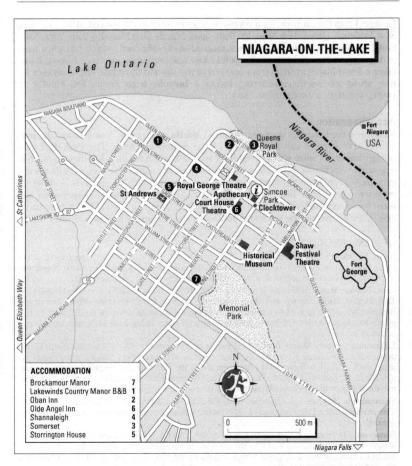

NIAGARA-ON-THE-LAKE

Lake Ontario

Fort
Niagara
USA

Niagara River

Queens
Royal
Park

St Catharines

Queen Elizabeth Way

Royal George Theatre
St Andrews
Apothecary
Court House
Theatre

Simcoe
Park
Clocktower

Shaw
Festival
Theatre

Fort
George

Historical
Museum

Memorial
Park

N

JOHN STREET

ACCOMMODATION	
Brockamour Manor	7
Lakewinds Country Manor B&B	1
Oban Inn	2
Olde Angel Inn	6
Shannaleigh	4
Somerset	3
Storrington House	5

0   500 m

Niagara Falls ▽

building to survive is the powder magazine of 1796, its inside finished in wood and copper to reduce the chances of an accidental explosion – and the soldiers who worked here wore shoes with no metal fastenings.

If all this whets your historical appetite, there are lantern-light **ghost tours** of the fort – good fun with or without an apparition (May & June Sun 8.30pm; July & Aug Mon, Thurs & Sun 8.30pm; $5). Purchase tickets either in advance at the fort or from the guide at the beginning of the tour.

Arrival, information and getting around
The easiest way to reach Niagara-on-the-Lake by public transport is on the **Niagara Shuttle bus** (☎905/358-3232 or 1-800/667-0256) from Niagara Falls. During the summer – from April or May to October – there are three services daily in each direction; the rest of the year there's just one. The return fare is $15. Pick-up points include the Niagara Falls town bus station and several motels in the vicinity of the Minolta Tower and Clifton Hill. In Niagara-on-the-Lake, the Shuttle bus stops either at the car park in the centre on Queen Street, or (when summer traffic restrictions are in effect) at Fort

George. From the car park, it's a couple of minutes' walk to the **tourist office**, 153 King St at Prideaux (Jan & Feb Mon–Fri 9am–5pm; March–Dec Mon–Fri 9am–5pm, Sat & Sun 10am–5pm; ☎905/468-4263, *www.niagara-on-the-lake.com*), which has town maps and operates a free and extremely useful room reservation service (see below). It only takes a few minutes to stroll from one end of the town to the other, but to venture further afield it's worth considering hiring a **bicycle** from Zoom, 280 Hunter Rd (☎905/468-4691, *zoom@niagara.com*).

Accommodation

Niagara-on-the-Lake has over one hundred **B&Bs**, with a few dotted round the leafy streets of the centre and the majority on the outskirts of town. The most distinctive occupy lovely old villas dating from the early nineteenth century, but these tend to be expensive – reckon on $100–150 for a double room per night. The town's B&Bs are also extremely popular, so advance reservations are pretty much essential throughout the summer, when you're likely to need the tourist office's free **room reservation service**. If you arrive after the tourist office has closed, look for a list of last-minute vacancies in their window. The town also possesses several quality **hotels** and **inns**.

BED AND BREAKFASTS

Adam Lockhart's Storrington House, 289 Simcoe St at Gage (☎905/468-8254, fax 468-9023). One of the town's finest B&Bs, this tastefully modernized Georgian villa has three lovely guestrooms with open fireplaces and serves delicious breakfasts. Handy for the town centre. ⑥.

Brockamour Manor, 433 King St at Mary (☎905/468-5527, fax 468-5071, *www.brockamour.com*). This elegant B&B has six en-suite guestrooms ranging from the commodious Sir Brock's Bedchamber ($180) to the two smaller rooms in the old servants' quarters ($120). With its high gables and wide veranda, the house itself is a splendid affair dating from 1812, surrounded by an attractive wooded garden.

Lakewinds Country Manor B&B, 328 Queen St at Dorchester (☎905/468-1888, fax 468-1060, *www.lakewinds.niagara.com*). Expansive Victorian mansion with six air-conditioned guest-rooms and suites, each of which is decorated in a particular style – the Florentine and Singapore rooms for example. The house possesses a handsome veranda and is surrounded by a well-kept garden. Two nights minimum stay on the weekend. Rates vary with the room and the season, beginning at $165. ⑥.

Shannaleigh, 184 Queen St at Simcoe (☎905/468-2630, fax 468-1254, *www.shannaleigh.niagara.com*). This rambling mock-Tudor mansion of 1910 has five spacious, en-suite guestrooms and splendid gardens. ⑥.

Somerset, 111 Front St at Victoria (☎905/468-5565). This flashy brick villa of modern design looks almost shocking when compared with the old wooden houses that characterize the rest of the centre, but it is one of only a couple of places actually on the lake. Great views and very comfortable, air-conditioned guestrooms. ⑦.

INNS

Oban Inn, 160 Front St at Gate (☎905/468-2165 or 1-888/669-5566, fax 905/468-4165). No one could say the owners of the *Oban Inn* lack determination: in 1992 the original Victorian hotel was burnt to the ground, but within a year the new edition, built along similar lines, was open. The end result, with its tartans and dark-wood panelling, looks a little too much like a designer package, but the hotel is comfortable enough and each of the 22 guestrooms – some with lake views – are decorated in a pleasant approximation of Victorian style. ⑦.

Olde Angel Inn, 224 Regent St just off Queen St (☎905/468-3411, fax 468-5451, *angelinn@niagara.com*). Dating from the 1820s, this is the oldest inn in town. Eight simple rooms in the main building and a couple of annexe-cottages too. ③

Eating

By sheer weight of numbers, the day-trippers set the gastronomic tone in Niagara-on-the-Lake, but one or two good **cafés** and **restaurants** have survived the deluge to offer tasty meals and snacks.

Epicurean, 84 Queen St. Inexpensive but good café food with a Mediterranean slant. Vegetarian options offered most days.

Oban Inn, 160 Front St (☎905/468-2165). This hotel restaurant is smart and comparatively formal and the food – steak, salmon and so forth – is reliably good.

Olde Angel Inn, 224 Regent St just off Queen St. With its low-beamed ceilings and flagstone floors, this is the town's most atmospheric pub, serving a first-rate range of draught beers as well as filling bar snacks.

Shaw Café and Wine Bar, 92 Queen St at Victoria. Arguably the best place in town, this café-restaurant caters for theatre-goers (rather than day-trippers). An inventive, wide-ranging menu features everything from pasta dishes through to salmon fillets, all at very reasonable prices. Closes 8pm.

Upstream from the Falls to Fort Erie

Heading upstream from the Falls, the **Old Scow** soon comes into view – it's the rusting barge stuck against the rocks in the middle of the river. In 1918 the barge was being towed across the Niagara River when the lines snapped and the barge – along with the two-man crew – hurtled towards the Falls. There must have been an awful lot of praying going on, because – just 750m from the precipice – the barge caught against the rocks, and it's stayed there ever since.

Pushing on past the Old Scow, both the **Niagara Parkway** road and the **Niagara River Recreation Trail** stay close to the river giving pleasant views over to the US. Nonetheless, this portion of the river is much less appealing than the stretch to the north – especially so beyond dreary Chippawa, where America's Grand Island divides the river into two drowsy channels. Further south, just 32km from the Falls, the Niagara Parkway peters out at **Fort Erie**, a small industrial town that also marks the end of the Queen Elizabeth Way linking Toronto with the American city of Buffalo. The one noteworthy site here is **Historic Fort Erie** (mid-May to Aug daily 10am–6pm; mid-April to mid-May & Sept–Oct daily 10am–4pm; $6), which overlooks Lake Erie from the mouth of the Niagara River just 2km south of town. The Americans razed the original fort in 1814, but it was painstakingly rebuilt in the 1930s as a Depression make-work scheme. The layout is similar to that of Fort George (see p.116) with a dry ditch, earth-and-stone ramparts and protruding bastions encircling a central compound, though here the outer gate is much more imposing, comprising a pair of huge double doors strengthened by iron studs. The central compound holds the usual array of army buildings, including officers' quarters, barracks and a powder magazine, plus a modest museum that explores the fort's bloody history.

London

The citizens of **LONDON**, 125km west of Hamilton, are justifiably proud of their clean streets, efficient transport system and neat suburbs, but to the outsider the main attractions are the leafiness of the centre and the city's two **music festivals** in late June and July – the nine-day Royal Canadian Big Band Festival (☎519/663-9467) and the three-day Home County Folk Music Festival (☎519/432-4310). London owes its existence to the governor of Upper Canada, **John Graves Simcoe**, who arrived in 1792 determined to develop the wilderness north of Lake Ontario. Because of its river connections to the west and south, he chose the site of London as his new colonial capital and promptly renamed its river the Thames. Unluckily, Simcoe's headlong approach to his new job irritated his superior, Governor Dorchester, who vetoed his choice with the wry comment that access to London would have to be by hot-air balloon. When York (present-day Toronto), was chosen as the capital instead, Simcoe's chosen site lay empty until 1826, yet by the 1880s London was firmly established as the economic and administra-

LONDON

ST JAMES STREET
SYDENHAM STREET
OXFORD STREET EAST
PICCADILLY STREET
ANN STREET
MILL STREET
JOHN STREET
PALL MALL STREET
HYMAN STREET
CENTRAL AVENUE
WOLFE ST
Sebastian's Market
Eldon House
Kent Street
St Peter's
City Hall
Dufferin Avenue
St Paul's
QUEENS AVENUE
Art Gallery
DUNDAS STREET
KING STREET
Bus Station
Train Station
YORK STREET
BATHURST STREET
HORTON STREET EAST
SIMCOE STREET
GREY STREET
HILL STREET
SOUTH STREET
NELSON ST
Thames River
GRAND AVENUE

N

ACCOMMODATION

Comfort Hotel – Downtown	3
Delta London Armouries Hotel	4
London's Little Inn B&B	2
Rose House B&B	1

0   500 m

▽ (401) & (402)

tive centre of a prosperous agricultural area. With a population of some 326,000, it remains so today.

The centre

London's **downtown core** is laid out as a grid on either side of its main east–west thoroughfares, Dundas Street and, one block to the north, Queen Avenue. At the west end of Dundas, close to the river, is the chunkily modernist **Art Gallery**, 421 Ridout St N (Tues–Sun noon–5pm; free), designed by Raymond Moriyama of Toronto. A once fashionable architect, Moriyama favoured dramatic concrete buildings characterized by a preference for contorted curves and circles rather than straight lines, but here the end result isn't all that successful. Inside, the gallery's permanent collection features a somewhat indeterminate mix of lesser eighteenth- and nineteenth-century Canadian painters and there's a modest local history section too, but the temporary modern art exhibitions – some of which come here straight from Toronto – are usually excellent.

London's oldest residence, **Eldon House** (Tues–Sun noon–5pm; $3) is a couple of minutes' walk north from the gallery, at 481 Ridout St N. Built in the 1830s by John Harris, a retired Royal Navy captain, the house is a graceful clapboard dwelling, whose interior has been returned to its mid-nineteenth-century appearance. The British influence is also easy to pick out in the nearby **St Paul's Anglican Cathedral** – take Fullarton from the Eldon House as far as Richmond. A simple red-brick structure built in the English Gothic Revival style in 1846, it's in marked contrast to its rival cathedral, **St Peter's Catholic Cathedral**, just to the north at Dufferin and Richmond, a flamboyant, high-towered, pink-stone edifice typical of the French Gothic style that was popular amongst Ontario's Catholics in the late nineteenth century.

The outskirts: Ska-Nah-Doht Iroquoian Village

Though not exactly required viewing, the replica **Ska-Nah-Doht Iroquoian village** (Mon–Fri 9am–4.30pm; donation; ☎519/264-2420), situated 32km southwest of London on Hwy 2, makes for an enjoyable jaunt. Built in 1972, the complex contains a resource centre, where you can gather background information before walking out to the village, which is enclosed by a timber palisade. Inside the palisade are storage areas, drying and stretching racks, a sweat house and three long-houses; outside are a deer run, burial area, a cultivated field and three log cabins dating from the 1850s. The arrangement of the village accurately reflects the archeological evidence unearthed at several prehistoric settlements, one of which was close by. The village also has a lovely rural setting and – if the school groups that come here begin to wear – you can stroll out into the woods.

To get here, head south from London and then go west on Hwy 402. After about 12km, come off Hwy 402 (at Exit 86) and follow Hwy 2 south for about 6km.

Practicalities

London's **train station** is centrally situated at York and Richmond, a couple of minutes' walk east of the **bus depot** at York and Talbot. The most central **tourist office** is in city hall at 300 Dufferin Ave and Wellington (Mon–Fri 8.30am–4.30pm; ☎519/661-5000 or 1-800/265-2602, *www.city.london.on.ca*). As far as accommodation is concerned, the best **hotel** in town is the smart and polished *Delta London Armouries Hotel*, 325 Dundas St and Waterloo (☎519/679-6111 or 1-800/668-9999; ⑤), part of which occupies an old Edwardian drill hall with a robust, crenellated facade. A less expensive but equally convenient option is the *Comfort Hotel – Downtown*, a standard-issue chain hotel at 374 Dundas St and Colborne (☎519/661-0233 or 1-800/228-5150; ④). Incidentally, the cheapest hotels in town are in the vicinity of the bus station, but these are little more than flophouses and are best avoided. London also has around fifteen **B&Bs**, some of which are in fetching Victorian or Edwardian villas. The tourist office has the complete list, but one recommendation is *London's Little Inn B&B*, 321 Dufferin Ave (☎519/642-2323; *vanboxmeer@cheerful.com*, ②), which occupies a cosy, two-storey Victorian home right in the centre at Waterloo Street. Some rooms are en suite, others have shared bathrooms and there's also a pretty garden. A second good choice is the *Rose House B&B*, 526 Dufferin Ave and William Street (☎519/433-9978; ②), in a grand old Edwardian house that has been tastefully decorated in period style. Some rooms are en suite.

In recent years, **eating out** in London has become much more enjoyable, with the opening of a string of café-restaurants along and around Richmond Street, with the majority offering a broadly Mediterranean cuisine at affordable prices. The best deli sandwiches, coffees and cakes in town are sold at *Sebastians*, one of several food stalls in the delightful Sebastians Market, 539 Richmond and Kent. Tempting restaurants include *Bon Appétit*, 476 Richmond at Dufferin Avenue (☎519/439-2560), which serves up Italian meals and has a pleasant patio area, and nearby *Garlics*, 481 Richmond (☎519/432-4092), where the emphasis is also Italian. For something different, *Budapest*, 348 Dundas at Waterloo (☎519/439-3431), is a family-run establishment offering first-rate Hungarian food – the goulash is a treat. London has a music scene too: try the *Old Chicago Speakeasy & Grill* (☎519/434-6600), on Carling, a short side street off Richmond just north of Dundas, where quality R&B, soul and blues bands sometimes perform.

Windsor and around

"I'm going to Detroit, Michigan, to work the Cadillac line" growls the old blues number, but if the singer had crossed the river he'd have been equally at home amongst the car plants of **WINDSOR**, 190km southwest of London. The factories are American subsidiaries built as part of a complex trading agreement which, monitored by the forceful Canadian United Automobile Workers Union, has created thousands of well-paid jobs. Living opposite Detroit makes the "Windsors" feel good in another way too: they read about Detroit's problems – the crime and the crack – and the dire difficulties involved in rejuvenating that city, and shake their heads in disbelief and self-congratulation. A robustly working-class place, Windsor has a clutch of good restaurants, a lively café-bar nightlife, and is also a good base for visiting both the remains of the British **Fort Malden** in Amherstburg, 25km to the south, and **Point Pelee National Park**, some 50km away to the southeast. The main Windsor shindig is the International Freedom Festival with all sorts of folksy events spread over an eighteen-day period in late June and early July.

Windsor

Windsor itself has few specific sights, but **Dieppe Gardens**, stretching along the waterfront from the foot of Ouellette Avenue – and part of a longer riverside park – is a good place to view the audacious Detroit skyline. Close by, just to the east at the bottom of McDougall Street, is the fantastically popular and ultraglitzy **Casino Windsor**, which is open 24hrs a day, 365 days of the year. The casino has played a leading role in the rejuvenation of downtown Windsor, whose formative years are recalled at the **Windsor Community Museum**, one block south of the riverfront at 254 Pitt St W (Tues–Sat 10am–5pm, plus May–Sept Sun 2–5pm; free). The museum occupies a pretty brick house built in 1812 by François Baby (pronounced *Baw-bee*), scion of a powerful French-Canadian clan who proved consistently loyal to the British interest after the fall of New France, an example of the money going with the power.

Back on the riverfront, the **Art Gallery of Windsor**, 401 Riverside Drive West (Tues–Fri 10am–7pm, Sat 10am–5pm, Sun noon–5pm; free; *www.artgalleryofwindsor.com*), has a well-deserved reputation for the excellence of its temporary exhibitions. The permanent collection is first-rate too, its forte being late nineteenth- and early twentieth-century Canadian paintings. In particular, look out for some good examples from the Group of Seven (see p.86) – including Lawren Harris's skeletal *Trees and Snow* and the dramatic perspectives of Arthur Lismer's *Incoming Tide, Cape Breton Island*. Also on display is a splendid sample of Inuit art, with a particular highlight being *Hunters and Polar Bear*, a dark and elemental soapstone carving by Juanasialuk. There's more art at the open-air, open-access **Sculpture Garden**, a whimsical assortment of seventeen modern sculptures dotted along the riverfront lawn between Curry Avenue and the Ambassador Bridge, about 1.2km west of Ouellette Avenue. Lastly, you might venture further afield, some 3km

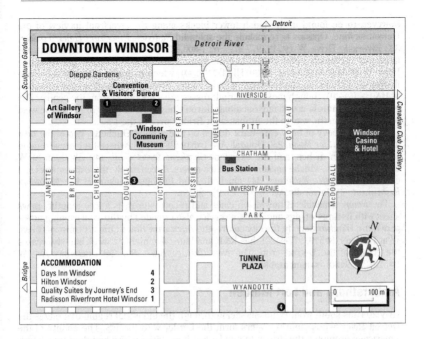

east of the casino, to join a free tour of Hiram Walker & Sons' **Canadian Club Distillery**, 2072 Riverside Drive E at Walker Road (year-round; 1hr; times on ☎519/561-5499), on which guides explain how whiskey is manufactured. Windsor boomed during Prohibition from the proceeds of its liquor industry, with bootleggers smuggling vast quantities of whiskey across the border into the US.

Practicalities

Well connected to London, Toronto and Niagara Falls, Windsor's **bus station** is right in the centre of town on Chatham, just east of the main street, Ouellette Avenue, which runs south from the river. From the bus station, Transit Windsor (☎519/944-4111) runs a shuttle service (1–3 hourly) over to downtown Detroit via a tunnel whose entrance is bang in the middle of town at Goyeau and Park; traffic bypassing Windsor en route to Detroit uses the Ambassador Bridge, on Hwy 3. Windsor **train station** is some 3km east of the city centre, near the waterfront at 298 Walker Rd and Wyandotte; to get into the centre from here, take a taxi ($6). The Windsor **Convention and Visitors' Bureau**, Suite 103, City Centre Mall, 333 Riverside Drive W (Mon–Fri 8.30am–4.30pm; ☎519/255-6530 or 1-800/265-3633, *www.city.windsor.on.ca/cvb*), is located just west of Ouellette and they issue free maps and glossy local brochures. They also run a tourist information kiosk (open daily) in the casino.

The city's **downtown core** is surprisingly compact, with most of the action focused on Ouellette from the river to Wyandotte – merely five-minutes' stroll from top to bottom. If you're staying the night, convenient options near the river include several chain **hotels** like the *Days Inn Windsor*, 675 Goyeau St (☎519/258-8411 or 1-800/DAYSINN, fax 519/258-6771; ④), and *Quality Suites by Journey's End*, 250 Dougall Ave (☎519/977-9707 or 1-800/228-5151, fax 519/977-6404; ④). The best rooms in the city centre are, however, to be found in the plush tower blocks along the riverfront in view of the Detroit skyline. Options here include the splendid *Radisson Riverfront Hotel Windsor*, 333 Riverside Drive W (☎519/977-9777 or 1-800/333-3333; ⑦), where the rooms are large and extremely comfortable; and the comparable *Hilton Windsor*, 277 Riverside Drive W (☎519/973-5555 or 1-800/HILTONS; ⑥), which is graced by some Art Deco flourishes. Otherwise, the Convention and Visitors' Bureau has the details of a handful of **B&Bs** (②–③), though most of their addresses are a good way from the centre. The city's budget **motels** are strung out along Huron Church Road (Hwy 3) just to the west of downtown on the way to the Ambassador Bridge over to the US.

Amongst a bevy of busy **café-bars** dotted on and around Ouellette, two of the best are the chic *Pitt for Pasta*, 250 Dougall Ave (☎519/258-1535), where they serve a good range of Italian dishes, and the excellent *Chatham Street Grill*, 149 Chatham St W (☎519/256-2555), which specializes in grilled meats. Alternatively, there are snacks and cakes at the *Coffee Exchange*, 341 Ouellette, and Ethiopian cuisine at the *Marathon Restaurant*, 60 University Ave W (☎519/253-2215).

The *Room*, available at downtown cafés and record stores, is a free monthly news sheet with **listings** of gigs and clubs, a service also provided by the local evening newspaper, the *Windsor Star*. In the city centre, the *Aar'd'vark Blues Café*, 89 University Ave W at Pelissier (☎519/977-6422), has R&B and blues five nights a week and showcases the cream of the Detroit crop. The *New Chicago Blues Bar*, 98 University Ave W (☎519/252-9480) is comparable.

Amherstburg and Fort Malden

Hwy 20 runs south from Windsor, slicing through the industrial region that edges the Detroit River, whose murky waters form the border with the US. The enmity of the Americans prompted the British to build a fort here, close to the mouth of the Detroit River at **AMHERSTBURG** in 1796, but it proved difficult to supply and they were forced to abandon the stockade during the War of 1812. Reoccupied after the war, the British made half-hearted attempts to improve the fort's defences, but it probably would have been abandoned had it not been for the Upper Canada Rebellion of 1837. In a panic, the colonial powers rebuilt what was now called Fort Malden and garrisoned it with four hundred soldiers, stationed here to counter the efforts of the insurgents and their American sympathizers. The last troops left in 1859 and the fort was handed over to the province, which turned it into a lunatic asylum.

Renovated, the early nineteenth-century ditches and corner bastions of **Fort Malden** (May–Dec daily 10am–5pm; Jan–April call for hours on ☎519/736-5416; $2.75) are now easy to pick out – a sequence of grassy defensive lines surrounding the excavated foundations of several buildings and a single-storey brick **barracks** of 1819. The interior of the barracks, complete with British army uniforms, is deceptively neat and trim for, as the guides explain, conditions were appallingly squalid. Across from the barracks, the asylum's old laundry and bakery has been turned into an **interpretive centre** with intriguing accounts of the various episodes of the fort's history, including the War of 1812 and the Rebellion of 1837. Original artefacts are few and far between, but it's here you'll find the powder horn of the Shawnee chief and staunch British ally, Tecumseh, one of the most formidable and renowned of the region's leaders. Born in what is now Ohio in 1769, Tecumseh spent the better part of his life struggling to keep the American settlers from spreading west into Shawnee territory. To this end he allied himself to the British, who were, he felt, less of a territorial threat, and managed by the sheer force of his personality to hold together an aboriginal army of some size. He was killed in the War of 1812 at Moraviantown and his army promptly collapsed.

Leamington and Pelee Island

About 400km long, the largely flat and often tedious northern shoreline of **Lake Erie** is broken up by a string of provincial parks and a handful of modest port-cum-resorts, such as Port Stanley, whose popularity declined when the more beautiful landscapes around Georgian Bay became accessible. **LEAMINGTON**, 50km southeast of Windsor and with a population of 14,000, is the largest agricultural centre in this highly productive region and the nearest town to the north shore's most distinctive attraction, the elongated peninsula of Point Pelee National Park (see below). Leamington's centre is itself uninspiring, though the **tourist office** (daily: late May–mid-Oct 10am–5pm) always raises a smile: it's sited in a large plastic tomato, a reminder that Leamington is billed as the "tomato capital of Canada" – there's a massive Heinz factory here. Much more enticing is the revamped **dock area** just south of the centre at the foot of Erie Street. It's here you'll find the town's best **restaurant**, the *Leamington Dock Restaurant* (☎519/326-2697), where the seafood is first class, and the best **hotel** – the spick-and-span and modern *Seacliffe Inn*, at 388 Erie St S (☎519/324-9266, *www.seacliffeinn.com*; ⑤). Less expensive accommodation is available back towards the town centre on Erie Street in several chain **motels**: the *Comfort Inn*, at no. 279 (☎519/326-9071; ③) is as good as any. There is a once-daily **bus** service from Toronto to Leamington, but there are no connections on to Point Pelee Park, which begins 8km to the south of town.

From the docks, **ferries** (March–July 2–3 daily; 1hr 30min; one-way: $7.50 per person, bikes $3.75, cars $16.50; ☎519/724-2115) sail out across Lake Erie to **Pelee Island**, whose quiet country roads are flanked by orchards and vineyards. The island possesses a pair of nature reserves – Lighthouse Point and Fish Point – at its northern and southern extremities and one significant settlement, **PELEE ISLAND VILLAGE**, but it's the rural atmosphere that is of most appeal. The best way to explore the island is by **bike** and these can be hired from Comfortech (☎519/724-2828; advance booking required), just behind the *Westview Tavern*, in Pelee Island village. Ferry sailing schedules make it easy to visit the island on a day-trip, but there are several places to stay. The pick is the *Blueberry Hill B&B*, 86 North Shore Rd (☎519/724-1109; ③). Island maps and information are available at the Leamington tourist office.

Point Pelee National Park

Occupying the southernmost tip of Canada's mainland and on the same latitude as Rome and Barcelona, **Point Pelee National Park** (daily: April to mid-Oct 6am–9.30pm; mid-Oct to March 7am–6.30pm; $3.25; no camping) fills the southern half of a twenty-kilometre sandspit. The park boasts a variety of habitats unequalled in Canada, including marshlands and open fields, but most remarkably it is one of the few places where the ancient **deciduous forest** of eastern North America has survived: one-third of its area is covered by jungle-like forest, packed with a staggering variety of trees, from hackberry, red cedar, black walnut and blue ash to vine-covered sassafras. The park's mild climate and its mix of vegetation attract thousands of **birds** on their spring and autumn migrations, and in the latter season – in September – the sandspit

---

PELEE ISLAND FERRY SERVICE

The ferry service from Leamington to Pelee Island only runs from March to July. At other times of the year, the ferry leaves from the neighbouring town of **Kingsville**.

also funnels thousands of southward-moving **monarch butterflies** across the park, their orange and black wings a splash of colour against the greens and browns of the undergrowth.

From the **park entrance**, it's a three-kilometre drive down behind the shore to the start of the Marsh Boardwalk nature trail, where there's a restaurant and also bike and canoe rental during the summer. It's a further 4km to the **visitor centre** (daily 10am–5pm, later in summer; ☎519/322-5700), at the beginning of the Tilden's Wood Trail and the Woodland Trail. From April to October, propane-powered "trains" shuttle the last 3km from the visitor centre to the start of the short footpath leading to the tip of the peninsula. However, the tip itself is merely a slender wedge of coarse brown sand that can't help but seem a tad anticlimactic – unless, that is, a storm has piled the beach with driftwood.

Sarnia and around

The land south and east of **SARNIA**, a border town 100km west of London, was one of the last parts of southern Ontario to be cleared and settled, as its heavy clay soil was difficult to plough and became almost impassable in rain. Established as a lumber port in 1863, Sarnia is a negligible place in itself, but offers the nearest accommodation to a couple of the region's minor sights.

With connecting services to London, Toronto, Port Huron in Michigan, and Chicago, Sarnia's **train station** is on the southern edge of town, at the end of Russell Street, an $8 taxi ride from the workaday gridiron that serves as the town centre. The (moveable) Greyhound **bus depot** is currently located beside the Kwikway supermarket at Exmouth and Capel – but long-distance services are few and far between. The municipal **tourist office** is ten-minutes' walk west from the bus depot at 224 Vidal St N and George (Mon–Fri 9am–5pm; ☎519/336-3232 or 1-800/265-0316), a couple of blocks back from the waterfront. There's also an **Ontario Travel Information Centre** on the northern side of the centre, beside the approach road to the Bluewater Bridge over to the US (mid-May to mid-June Mon–Thurs & Sun 8.30am–6pm, Fri & Sat 8am–8pm; late June to Aug daily 8am–8pm; Sept to mid-May daily 8.30am–5pm; ☎519/344-7403). Both offices have details of local **accommodation**, which includes a reasonable selection of chain motels strung out along London Road, one of the main drags running south of (and parallel to) Hwy 402. There's also a handful of **B&Bs** (from around $40), including *Zoë's B&B*, 286 Vidal St N (☎519/332-0511, fax 332-4318, *zoesbb@tct.net*; ②), which occupies a pleasantly restored old house and has four guestrooms with shared bathroom.

Petrolia and Oil Springs

The grand stone-and-brick buildings of tiny **PETROLIA**, just off Hwy 21 about 35km southeast of Sarnia, speak volumes about the sudden rush of wealth that followed the discovery of oil round here in 1855. This was Canada's first oil town and as the proceeds rolled in so the Victorian mansions and expansive public buildings followed. Several have survived, dotted along and around the main drag, Petrolia Line. Three prime examples are the **Municipal Offices**, at Petrolia and Greenfield, **Nemo Hall**, 419 King at Victoria, an impressive brick building decorated by splendid wrought-iron trimmings, and **St Andrew's Presbyterian church**, close by at Petrolia and Queen, which is awash with neo-Gothic gables and towers. To emphasize the town's origins, its streetlamps are cast in the shape of oil derricks, but really, once you've had a scout round the architecture there's no reason to hang round.

Some 10km to the south along Hwy 21, the hamlet of **OIL SPRINGS** once formed the nucleus of a rough-and-ready frontier district whose flat fields were packed with hundreds of eager fortune-seekers and their hangers-on. The first prospectors were attracted to the area by patches of black and sticky oil that had seeped to the surface through narrow fissures in the rock. These **gum beds** had long been used by local native peoples for medicinal and ritual purposes, but it was not until Charles and Henry Tripp of Woodstock incorporated their oil company in 1854 that serious exploitation began. Four years later, James Miller Williams dug North America's first commercial oil well, and in 1862 a certain Hugh Shaw drilled deeper than anyone else and, at 49m, struck the first gusher. The shock of seeing the oil fly up into the trees prompted Shaw, a religious man, to use the words of his Bible – "And the rock poured me out rivers of oil" (Job 29:6). Shaw became rich, but his luck ran out just one year later when he was suffocated by the gas and sulphur fumes of his own well. At the height of the boom, the oilfields produced about 30,000 barrels of crude a day, most of it destined for Sarnia, transported by stagecoach and wagon along a specially built plank road.

Just 1km south of Oil Springs, signposted off Hwy 21, the **Oil Museum of Canada** (May–Oct daily 10am–5pm; Nov–April Mon–Fri 10am–5pm; $3.50) has been built next to the site of James Williams' original well. Highlights of the open-air display area include a nineteenth-century blacksmith's shop, with some fascinating old sepia photos taken during the oil boom, and an area of gum bed. The inside of the museum has a motley collection of oil-industry artefacts and background geological information. Oil is still produced in the fields around the museum, drawn to the surface and pushed on into an underground system of pipes by some seven hundred low-lying pump jacks.

Uncle Tom's Cabin

Some 25km south of Oil Springs, Hwy 21 slips through the agricultural town of **DRES-DEN**, which is itself just 2km from **Uncle Tom's Cabin Historic Site** (mid-May to June & Sept to mid-Oct Tues–Sat 10am–4pm, Sun noon–4pm; July & Aug Mon–Sat 10am–4pm, Sun noon–4pm; $5), where a handful of old wooden buildings incorporates a simple church and the clapboard house that was once the home of the **Reverend Josiah Henson**, a slave who fled from Maryland to Canada in 1830 by means of the Underground Railroad (see box, below). Henson and a group of abolitionist sympathizers subsequently bought 200 acres of farmland round Dresden and founded a vocational school for runaway slaves known as the "British American Institute". Unable to write, Henson dictated his life experiences and in 1849 these narrations were published as *The Life of Josiah Henson – Formerly a Slave*. It's a powerful tract, unassuming and almost matter-of-fact in the way it describes the routine savagery of slavery – and it was immediately popular. One of its readers was **Harriet Beecher Stowe**, who met

---

THE UNDERGROUND RAILROAD

The **Underground Railroad** – the UGRR – started in the 1820s as a loose and secretive association of abolitionists dedicated to smuggling slaves from the southern states of America to Canada. By the 1840s, the UGRR had become a well-organized network of routes and safe houses, but its real importance lay not so much in the number of slaves rescued – the total was small – but rather in the psychological effect it had on those involved in the smuggling. The movement of a single runaway might involve hundreds of people, if only in the knowledge that a neighbour was breaking the law. To the extent that white Americans could be persuaded to accept even the most minor role in the Railroad, the inclination to compromise with institutional slavery was undermined, though the psychology of racism remained intact: like Beecher Stowe's Uncle Tom, the freed negroes were supposed to be humble and grateful, simulating childlike responses to please their white parent-protectors.

Henson and went on to write the most influential abolitionist text of the day, *Uncle Tom's Cabin* (1852), basing her main character on Henson's accounts. Most of the Dresden refugees returned to the US after the Civil War, but Henson stayed on, accumulating imperial honours that must have surprised him greatly. He was even presented to Queen Victoria and, in commemoration of this royal connection, his tombstone, which stands outside the complex, is surmounted by a crown. He died in 1883.

Henson's book is hard to get hold of, but copies ($6) are sold here at the **interpretive centre**, where there's also a small museum on slavery and the UGRR plus an intriguing video giving more details on Henson's life and times.

Bayfield and Goderich

A popular summer resort area, the southern section of the **Lake Huron shoreline** is trimmed by sandy beaches and a steep bluff that's interrupted by the occasional river valley. The water is much less polluted than Lake Ontario, the sunsets are fabulously beautiful, and in Bayfield and Goderich the lakeshore possesses two of the most appealing places in the whole of the province. Of the two, the more southerly is **BAYFIELD**, a wealthy and good-looking village whose handsome timber villas nestle amongst well-tended gardens beneath a canopy of ancient trees – all about 80km north of London. The villagers have kept modern development at arm's length – there's barely a neon sign in sight, never mind a concrete apartment block – and almost every old house has been beautifully maintained: look out for the scrolled woodwork, the fanlights and the graceful verandas. Historical plaques give the lowdown on the older buildings that line Bayfield's short **Main Street**, and pint-sized **Pioneer Park** on the bluff overlooking the lake at the west end of Main Street is a fine spot to take in the sunset, but it's the general appearance of the place that appeals rather than any particular sight. If you've the time, you should also venture down to the **harbour** on the north side of the village and from there ramble up along the banks of the Bayfield River where, in season, you can pick wild mushrooms and fiddleheads. The Mara Street footpath down to the harbour begins just behind Pioneer Park – it's signed. In winter there's ice fishing and skating to enjoy.

You'll need your own transport to get to Bayfield – there are no **buses** at all. The **tourist office** (May–Sept daily 10am–6pm; ☎519/565-2499), in the booth by Hwy 21 just north of the Bayfield River bridge, has a full list of local **accommodation** and they will help you find a room, though their assistance is only really necessary in July and August when most places – including the B&Bs – are heavily subscribed. At other times of the year, it's easy enough to find a place yourself. The best **hotel** for miles around is the outstanding *Little Inn of Bayfield*, Main Street (☎519/565-2611 or 1-800/565-1832, fax 519/565-5474, *www.littleinn.com*; ⑤), a tastefully modernized early nineteenth-century timber-and-brick building with a handsome second-floor veranda and delightfully furnished rooms, most of which have whirlpool baths. The hotel has an annexe just across the street and, once again, the rooms here are simply splendid. Incidentally, do not confuse this hotel with the *Bayfield Village Inn*, a very different proposition. Other good places to stay include the pleasant *Albion Hotel*, in another old building on Main Street (☎519/565-2641; ②), and several charming **B&Bs**: try beside the village green at either the *Clifton Manor Inn*, 19 The Square (☎519/565-2282; ④; reservations required), or *Clair on the Square*, 12 The Square (☎519/565-2135; ③). There's **camping** at **Pinery Provincial Park** (☎519/243-2220), a popular chunk of forested sand dune beside Lake Huron about 40km south of Bayfield.

Bayfield has several great places to **eat**, but it's hard to beat the smart and chic restaurant of the *Little Inn of Bayfield*, which is the best place to sample fish from Lake Huron – perch, white fish, pickerel or steelhead. Footsteps away, the *Red Pump*

Restaurant (☎519/565-2576) is similarly classy, whilst the *Albion Hotel* has more routine, but appetizing and less costly bar food and meals.

Goderich

Situated just 20km north of Bayfield at the mouth of the Maitland River, **GODERICH** is a delightful country town of eight thousand inhabitants that's saved from postcard prettiness by its working harbour. It began life in 1825, when the British-owned Canada Company bought two and a half million acres of southern Ontario – the **Huron Tract** – from the government at the ridiculously low rate of twelve cents an acre, amid rumours of bribery and corruption. Eager to profit on their investment, the company pushed the **Huron Road** through from Cambridge in the east to Goderich in the west, an extraordinary effort that was witnessed by a certain Mr Moffat – "The trees were so tall, the forest was eternally dark and with the constant rains it was endlessly damp . . . Clearing the centuries of undergrowth and tangled vines was only the beginning, the huge rotted deadfalls of hardwood had to be hauled deeper into the bush, already piled high with broken pine. Since each man was responsible for cooking his own food after a hard day's work, the men sometimes ate the fattest pork practically raw . . . To make up for such fare, a barrel of whiskey with a cup attached always stood at the roadside." Completed in 1828, the road attracted the settlers the company needed. Indeed, within thirty years, the Huron Tract had two flourishing towns, Stratford and Goderich, and was producing large surpluses of grain for export, as it continues to do today.

The Town

The wide tree-lined avenues of the geometrically planned centre of Goderich radiate from a grand octagonal **central circus** dominated by the white-stone courthouse. From here, the four main streets follow the points of the compass with North Street leading in a couple of minutes to the compendious **Huron County Museum** (May–Aug Mon–Sat 10am–4.30pm, Sun 1–4.30pm; Sept–April Mon–Fri 10am–4.30pm, Sun 1–4.30pm; $4, $6.50 with Gaol, see below), which concentrates on the district's pioneers. Highlights include a fantastic array of farm implements, from simple hand tools to gigantic, clumsy machines like the steam-driven thresher. There's also a beautifully restored Canadian Pacific steam engine and intriguing displays on the history of Huron County and the Canada Company, as well as exhibition areas featuring furniture, transportation and military memorabilia, plus a string of period rooms.

A ten-minute walk up to the far end of North Street and right along Gloucester brings you to the high stone walls of the **Huron Historic Gaol** at 181 Victoria St (mid-May to early Sept daily 10am–4.30pm; March to mid-May & early Sept–Oct phone for hours on ☎519/524-6971; $4, $6.50 with Huron County Museum). One of the province's most intriguing attractions, the gaol was constructed as a combined courthouse and jail between 1839 and 1842. Start on the third floor of the main block, whose claustrophobic courtroom and council chamber were originally situated next to a couple of holding cells. The design was most unpopular with local judges, who felt threatened by the proximity of those they were sentencing. The other problem was the smell: several judges refused to conduct proceedings because of the terrible odour emanating from the privies in the exercise yard below. In 1856, the administration gave way and built a new courthouse in the town centre. On the second and first floors, there's the original jailer's apartment and a string of well-preserved prison cells, reflecting various changes in design between 1841 and 1972, when the prison was finally closed. The worst is the leg-iron cell for "troublesome" prisoners, where unfortunates were chained to the wall with neither bed nor blanket. End your tour at the **Governor's House**, with its attractively restored late Victorian interior.

Back in the centre, **West Street** leads the 1km through a cutting in the bluffs to the Lake Huron shoreline at the south end of the harbour and salt works. A footpath leads northeast round the harbour, passing the grain elevators on its way to the **Menesetung Bridge**, the old CPR railway bridge that now serves as a pedestrian walkway across the Maitland River. On the north side of the river, you can pick up the **Maitland Trail** for the brief but enjoyable jaunt along the river's north shore. In the opposite direction – south from the harbour – some 1.5km of shoreline has been tidied up to create a picnic area, but although the sunsets are spectacular the sandy beach, right at the end, is unenticingly scrawny.

Practicalities

There are no **buses** to Goderich, but there is a **tourist office**, beside Hwy 21 at Nelson and Hamilton, a couple of minutes' walk northeast of the central circus (mid-May to Aug Mon–Sat 9am–7pm, Sun 10am–7pm; Sept to early Oct Mon–Fri 9am–4pm; ☎519/524-6600). They have details of the town's twenty-odd **B&Bs**, which average out at about $50 per double per night. One of the more appealing (and expensive) options is the *Colborne B&B*, 72 Colborne St (☎519/524-7400 or 1-800/390-4612, fax 519/524-4943; ③), in a large, plain-brick building dating from the early twentieth century and located just to the west of the central circus; there are four guestrooms here, all en suite. Much better, however, is *Twin Porches B&B*, 55 Nelson St E at Victoria (☎519/524-5505; ②; May–Oct), in a lovely and well-kept Edwardian house of buff-coloured brick embellished with fine gingerbread scrollwork. Also near the central circus – and metres from both the tourist office and a petrol station – this B&B, with its antique furnishings, has three air-conditioned guestrooms with shared bathroom. The **hotel** scene is less varied, but the reasonably priced *Hotel Bedford*, right in the centre at 92 Court House Square (☎519/524-7337; ③), is certainly distinctive. Built in 1896, the *Bedford* has an enormous open stairwell fitted with a grandiose wooden staircase just like a saloon in a John Ford movie – though the modernized rooms beyond are a bit of a disappointment. Much better is the plush *Benmiller Inn* (☎519/524-2191 or 1-800/265-1711, fax 519/524-5150, *www.benmiller.on.ca*; ⑦), which occupies a converted 1830s woollen mill in an attractive wooded dell east of Goderich. To get there, take Hwy 8 out of town and watch for the sign after about 6km. There's **camping** near Goderich, too, just 7km north along the lakeshore at **Point Farms Provincial Park** (mid-May to early Oct; ☎519/524-7124).

For **food**, you're hardly spoiled for choice, but *Big Daddy's Pizza and Grill*, 42 West St (☎519/524-7777), serves up tasty, standard dishes at reasonable prices. The more upscale *Robindale's*, across from the tourist office at 80 Hamilton St (☎519/524-4171), is a comparatively formal restaurant where the pork dishes are delicious. The *Park House*, 168 West St, is the town's liveliest bar and has wide views of Lake Huron.

The Bruce Peninsula

Dividing the main body of Lake Huron from Georgian Bay, the **Bruce Peninsula** holds two of Ontario's national parks. The more distinctive is the **Fathom Five National Marine Park**, at the northern tip of the peninsula, where extraordinary rock formations, plentiful shipwrecks and crystal-clear waters provide wonderful sport for divers. The second is the **Bruce Peninsula National Park**, comprising two slabs of forested wilderness on either side of Hwy 6, its northern portion offering magnificent coastal hiking on a small section of the Bruce Trail. There's camping at both parks and a reasonable choice of hotel and motel accommodation at lively **Tobermory**, an amiable combination of fishing village, port and resort. Spare time also for a quick zip round the interesting old port of **Owen Sound** at the base of the peninsula. The only catch is the lack of public transport – the peninsula has no **bus** services. Note also that Tobermory is where you catch the ferry to Manitoulin Island in Northern Ontario (see p.179).

Owen Sound

Just under 200km northwest from Toronto, **OWEN SOUND** lies in the ravine around the mouth of the Sydenham River, at the foot of the Bruce Peninsula. In its heyday, Owen Sound was a rough and violent port packed with brothels and bars, prompting the Americans to establish a consulate whose main function was to bail out drunk and disorderly sailors. For the majority it was an unpleasant place to live, and the violence spawned an especially active branch of the Women's Christian Temperance Organization, whose success was such that an alcohol ban was imposed in 1906 and only lifted in 1972. The town was in decline long before the return of the bars, its port facilities undercut by the railways from the 1920s, but it's managed to reinvent itself and is now an amiable sort of place, with three central sights of some interest: the **Marine-Rail Museum**, overlooking the harbour in the old railway station at 1165 1st Ave W (June–Sept Tues–Sat 10am–noon & 1–4.30pm, Sun 1–4.30pm; donation), with photos of old sailing ships and their captains; the **Tom Thomson Memorial Art Gallery**, 840 1st Ave W (July & Aug Mon–Sat 10am–5pm, Sun noon–5pm; Sept–June Tues–Sat 10am–5pm, Sun noon–5pm; donation), which has temporary exhibitions by Canadian artists and a clutch of Thomson's less familiar paintings; and the **Billy Bishop Museum**, 948 3rd Ave W (June–Aug daily 1–4pm; $4), concentrating on the military exploits of Canada's Victoria Cross-winning air ace.

Owen Sound **bus station** is on 3rd Avenue East at 10th Street East, ten-minutes' walk from the **tourist office**, which is next door to the Marine-Rail Museum at 1155 1st Ave W (Mon–Fri 9am–4.30pm; June–Aug also Sat & Sun noon–4pm; ☎519/371-9833). They have a list of local accommodation, including details of a dozen **B&Bs** (①–②). One of the handiest is the *Brae Briar*, 980 3rd Ave W (☎519/371-0025; ②), an unassuming two-storey brick house with three guestrooms downtown off 10th Street. The town's **motels** are strung out along highways 6 and 10 (9th Ave E) on the south side of town. Incidentally, **orientation** in Owen Sound is a tad difficult, but the main rules to remember are that *Avenues* run one way, *Streets* the other, while the river, which bisects the compact town centre, separates Avenues and Streets *East* from those marked *West*.

For **food** downtown, try *Jazzmyns*, 261 9th St E, for excellent, inexpensive snacks – anything from tapas to pizzas and burgers – or the very good *Macky's Fish and Chips*, 791 1st Ave E and 8th Street E.

The Bruce Peninsula National Park and Tobermory

Heading north from Owen Sound, Hwy 6 scoots up the middle of the Bruce Peninsula to reach – after about 100km – the turning for the **Bruce Peninsula National Park** at **Cyprus Lake**. The park is a mixture of limestone cliff, rocky beach, wetland and forest that's best visited in June when the wild flowers are in bloom and it's not too crowded. At Cyprus Lake are the park's headquarters and **campsites** (reservations on ☎519/596-2263). Four hiking trails start at the northern edge of Cyprus Lake and three of them connect with one of the most dramatic portions of the **Bruce Trail** (see box, overleaf).

Just 11km beyond the Cyprus Lake turning, Hwy 6 slips into **TOBERMORY**, a bustling fishing village and holiday resort at the northern tip of the peninsula. There are no sights as such, but it's a pleasant spot, its tiny centre focused on a slender inlet, the **Little Tub harbour**. Here, **car ferries** (May to late June & early Sept to mid-Oct 2–3 daily; late June to early Sept 4 daily; $11.20 one-way, cars $24.50; reservations ☎1-800/265-3163) leave for South Baymouth on Manitoulin Island (see p.179) and passenger boats shuttle out to Fathom Five National Marine Park (see overleaf). At the back of the harbour, the **National Park Visitor Centre** (June & Sept Mon–Fri 9am–4.30pm;

THE BRUCE TRAIL

Ontario's oldest and most popular long-distance footpath, the **Bruce Trail** follows the route of the Niagara Escarpment from Queenston to Tobermory. The 782-kilometre-long path is maintained by the **Bruce Trail Association**, PO Box 857, Hamilton, Ontario L8N 3N9 (☎905/529-6821 or 1-800/665-4453, *www.brucetrail.org*), who produce a detailed hiking guide, *The Bruce Trail Reference* ($28) – essential reading if you're planning anything more than a day's walk. The guidebook is available from the Association and at major bookshops across Southern Ontario.

July & Aug daily 9am–9pm; ☎519/596-2233) covers both of the Bruce Peninsula's national parks, issuing maps and free brochures. The Fathom Five National Marine Park is known across Canada for the excellence of its diving; the waters are clear and are dotted with around twenty shipwrecks. Prospective divers must register in person at the harbourfront **Registration Centre** (mid-May to Oct daily 8am–4.30pm; ☎519/596-2503). Diving gear can be hired footsteps away at G&S Watersports (☎519/596-2200, *gswater@kanservu.ca*).

There are a dozen or so **hotels** and **motels** in and around Tobermory, mostly brisk, modern affairs that are comfortable without being especially charming. The pick is the *Grandview Motel* (☎519/596-2220, fax 596-8045, *grandview@log.on.ca*; ③), with eighteen spick-and-span rooms on the east side of the harbour at the junction of Bay and Earl streets. A second good choice, also on the east side of the harbour, is the two-storey, balconied *Blue Bay Motel* (☎519/596-2392 or 1-800/935-4373, fax 519/596-2335, *bluebay@kanservu.ca*; ③). The *Grandview Motel* has the town's best **restaurant** with views out across the harbour and tasty, reasonably priced dishes with seafood a speciality – try the whitefish and ocean perch. There are also several lively **bars** and **cafés** beside the harbour – the *Crow's Nest* is as good as any.

Fathom Five National Marine Park

At **Fathom Five National Marine Park** nineteen uninhabited islands are enclosed within a park boundary that is drawn round the waters at the end of the peninsula, offshore from Tobermory. To protect the natural habitat, only **Flowerpot Island**, 4km from the mainland, has any amenities, with limited space for **camping** – six sites only – and a couple of short hiking trails that explore its eastern reaches. A delightful spot, Flowerpot takes its name from two pink-and-grey rock pillars that have been eroded away from its eastern shore, and are readily seen on the Loop Trail.

Flowerpot Island is easily reached by **boat** from Tobermory. Several operators run regular boats out to the island, either dropping passengers off and then collecting them later or pausing at Flowerpot as part of a longer excursion – just stroll along Little Tub harbour until you find the service that suits. One reliable company is Blue Heron (☎519/596-2999, *www.blueheronco.com*). The return fare from Tobermory to Flowerpot is around $15, a few dollars more for the longer trips. Prospective campers need to make reservations at the National Park Visitor Centre (see above). Both hikers and campers need to pack food and drink.

Nottawasaga Bay: Wasaga Beach and Blue Mountain ski area

East of Owen Sound the southern curve of Georgian Bay forms **Nottawasaga Bay**, one of the province's most popular holiday areas. In summer, the focus of attention is the crowded resort of **Wasaga Beach**, where a seemingly endless string of chalets and cottages fringe the several kilometres of protected sand that make up **Wasaga Beach Provincial Park**. To the west of Wasaga Beach, inland from the gritty town of **Collingwood**, is the **Blue Mountain ski area**, whose slopes utilize the Niagara Escarpment (see below), the limestone ridge that weaves its way from near Niagara Falls to the Bruce Peninsula.

Wasaga Beach

With its amusement parks and fast-food joints, there's nothing subtle about **WASAGA BEACH**, but the beach is of fine golden sand, the swimming excellent and you can rent out all manner of watercraft from jet skis through to canoes. There's also one historical curiosity at the **Nancy Island Historic Site** (mid-May to late June Sat & Sun 10am–6pm; late June to Aug daily 10am–6pm; mid-Sept to mid-Oct Sat–Wed 10am–5pm; free, but parking charge), on the main drag – Mosley Street – behind Beach Area 2. In the War of 1812, the Americans managed to polish off the few British ships stationed in the upper Great Lakes without too much difficulty, and the last Royal Navy vessel, the supply ship *Nancy*, hid out here, just beyond the bay at the mouth of the Nottawasaga River. The Americans tracked down and sunk the *Nancy*, but silt subsequently collected round the sunken hull to create Nancy Island. In 1927, the hull was raised from the silt and today it forms the main exhibit of the island's museum, whose imaginative design resembles the sails of a schooner.

Wasaga Beach makes for a good day's swimming and sunbathing, but if you do decide to stay the night there are lots of reasonably priced **motels** to choose from as well as cottages and campsites – just drive along Mosley Street until someplace takes your fancy. Alternatively, the local Chamber of Commerce's year-round **information centre** at 550 River Rd W, in Beach Area 1 (Mon–Sat 9am–5pm, Sun 10am–4pm; ☎705/429-2247 or 1-866/292-7242), will help you find accommodation.

Collingwood and the Blue Mountain ski area

The small-time port of **COLLINGWOOD**, 20km west along the bayshore from Wasaga Beach, has a clutch of fine early twentieth-century buildings dotted along its main street, **Hurontario** – red-brick facades decorated with geometric designs and roughly dressed sandstone sills. More importantly, the town is also the gateway to the **Blue Mountain**, a segment of the Niagara Escarpment whose steepish slopes are now a major winter sports area, mainly for alpine skiing though several cross-country trails have also been developed. To get there from Collingwood, take the Blue Mountain Road (Route 19) which reaches – after about 10km – the **downhill ski slopes** at the *Blue Mountain Inn* (☎705/445-0231, fax 444-1751, *www.bluemountain.ca*; ④), a large and modern lodge that is the centre of wintertime activity. This is not, however, the best place to stay: instead continue along the Blue Mountain Road for another 400m as far as the *Blue Mountain Auberge* (☎705/445-1497; ③), an informal and attractive lodge, built in Alpine style with a dozen rooms, sauna, kitchen and barbecue area, that's tucked into the wooded slopes of the Blue Mountain. It's a great location and reservations are advised both in the winter and summer, when hikers use the *Auberge* as a jumping-off point for the Bruce Trail (see box, opposite) which passes close by. The *Auberge* doesn't hire out ski gear, but this is readily available from outlets nearby. In total, the Blue Mountain has 39 downhill ski slopes of varying difficulty with a maximum vertical drop of 219m. The prime season is from mid-December to mid-March. A one-day lift pass costs $40 and the lifts rarely get crowded. Operated by PMCL (☎705/737-0330, *www.pmcl.on.ca*), Toronto–Owen Sound **buses** stop in Collingwood and at the *Blue Mountain Inn* at least a couple of times a day, sometimes more.

Severn Sound and around

Severn Sound, the southeastern inlet of Georgian Bay, is one of the most beautiful parts of Ontario. Its sheltered southern shore is lined with tiny ports and its deep-blue waters are studded by the outcrops of the **Georgian Bay Islands National Park**, whose glacier-smoothed rocks and wispy pines were celebrated by the Group of Seven painters. In **Discovery Harbour**, on the edge of **Penetanguishene**, and **Sainte-Marie among the Hurons**, outside **Midland**, Severn Sound also possesses two of the province's finest historical reconstructions – the first a British naval base, the second a Jesuit mission. Leaving Severn Sound, there's more lovely Canadian Shield scenery on the road north to **Parry Sound**, an agreeable little port that also serves as a convenient stopping point on the long road north to Sudbury and Northern Ontario (see p.17). Alternatively, you can head southeast from Severn Sound to **Orillia**, home of the Stephen Leacock Museum – and just 120km from Toronto on highways 11 and 400.

As for public transport, there's a reasonably good network of **bus** services running north from Toronto to – and along – the southern shore of Severn Sound. These services are operated by PMCL (*www.pmcl.on.ca*), who also link Toronto and Orillia. The Toronto–Parry Sound–Sudbury bus route is operated by Greyhound.

Penetanguishene

The most westerly town on Severn Sound, homely **PENETANGUISHENE** – "place of the rolling white sands" in Ojibwa – was the site of one of Ontario's first European settlements, a Jesuit mission founded in 1639, then abandoned in 1649 following the burning of Sainte-Marie (see p.138). Europeans returned some 150 years later to establish a trading station where local Ojibwa exchanged pelts for food and metal tools. However, the settlement remained insignificant until just after the War of 1812, when the British built a naval dockyard that attracted shopkeepers and suppliers from both French and British communities. Today Penetanguishene is one of the few places in southern Ontario that maintains a bilingual tradition.

The town's primary thoroughfare, **Main Street**, is a pleasant place for a stroll, its shops and bars installed behind sturdy red-brick facades. It's the general atmosphere that appeals rather than any particular sight, but the **Centennial Museum**, 13 Burke St (May–Oct Mon–Sat 9.30am–4.30pm; Sun noon–4.30pm; $2.50), a couple of minutes' walk east of Main Street along Beck Boulevard, is worth a quick visit. The museum occupies the old general store and offices of the Beck lumber company, whose yards once stretched right along the town's waterfront. The company was founded in 1865 by Charles Beck, a German immigrant who made himself immensely unpopular by paying his men half their wages in tokens that were only redeemable at his stores. The museum has several displays on the Beck lumber company, including examples of these "Beck dollars", and there's also a fascinating selection of old photographs featuring locals at work and play in the town and its forested surroundings. Doubling back, it's a short walk to the jetty at the north end of Main Street, from where there are enjoyable, three-hour **cruises** of the southern stretches of Georgian Bay and its myriad islands – known collectively as the Thirty Thousand Islands (mid-June to Aug 1–2 cruises daily; May, early June, Sept & early Oct occasional sailings; $15; ☎705/549-7795 or 1-800/363-7447, *www.georgianbaycruises.com*).

Discovery Harbour

Penetanguishene's premier attraction, **Discovery Harbour** (late May to June & early Sept to early Oct Mon–Fri 10am–5pm; July to early Sept daily 10am–5pm; $6; *www.discoveryharbour.on.ca*), situated about 5km north of the town centre, is an ambi-

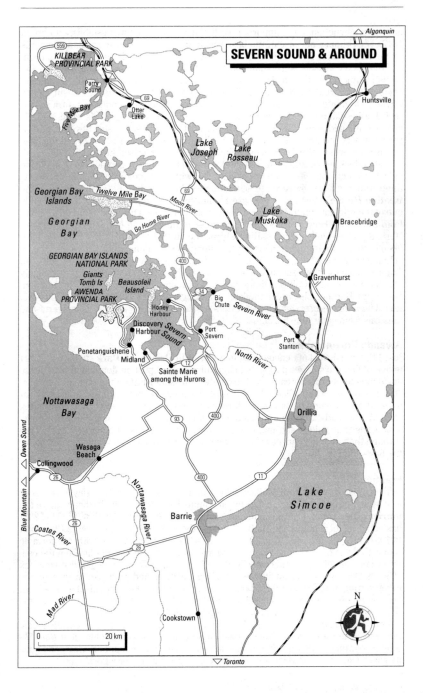

tious reconstruction of the important British naval base that was established here in 1817. The primary purpose of the base was to keep an eye on American movements on the Great Lakes following the War of 1812, and between 1820 and 1834 up to twenty Royal Navy vessels were stationed here. Ships from the base also supplied the British outposts further to the west and, to make navigation safer, the Admiralty decided to chart the Great Lakes. This monumental task fell to Lieutenant Henry Bayfield, who informed his superiors of his determination "to render this work so correct that it shall not be easy to render it more so". He lived up to his word, and his charts remained in use for decades. The naval station was more short-lived. By 1834, relations with the US were sufficiently cordial for the Navy to withdraw, and the base was turned over to the Army, who maintained a small garrison here until 1856.

Staffed by enthusiastic costumed guides, the sprawling site spreads along a hillside above a tranquil inlet, its green slopes scattered with accurate reconstructions of everything from a sailors' barracks to several period houses, the prettiest of which is the **Keating House**, named after the base's longest-serving adjutant, Frank Keating. Only one of the original buildings survives – the dour limestone **Officers' Quarters**, dating from the 1840s. However, pride of place goes to the working harbour-cum-dockyard. Here, a brace of fully rigged **sailing ships**, the HMS *Bee* and HMS *Tecumseth*, have been rebuilt to their original nineteenth-century specifications. Both schooners take on volunteers as members of their crews. Sailing times are only definite in July and August, when the ships set out on 3–4 hour treks three times a week for approximately $22–26 per person. Call for times and reservations (☎705/549-8064). In addition, Discovery Harbour also accommodates the **King's Wharf Theatre** (☎705/549-5555, *www.kingswharftheatre.com*), which offers a season of plays as well as concerts and musicals from early June to August.

Awenda Provincial Park

Just 11km northwest of Penetanguishene, **Awenda Provincial Park** (☎705/549-2231) is one of Ontario's larger parks, its delightful mainland portion dominated by a dense deciduous forest that spreads south from the Nipissing Bluff on the edge of Georgian Bay. The other section, Giants Tomb Island, lies offshore, but you need your own boat to get there. Awenda has a few small rock-and-pebble beaches, four good **campsites** (mid-May to early Oct), and a handful of hiking trails starting near the park office, which has trail guides and maps. A recommended route is to take the Bruce Trail through the forest to connect with the Dune Trail, which leads to a vantage point above the bay – 5km in all.

Practicalities

With regular services from Midland and Toronto, Penetanguishene's tiny **bus depot** is at Main Street and Robert, a five- to ten-minute walk south of the harbour, where the **tourist office** (Mon–Fri 9am–5pm plus summer weekends 9am–5pm; ☎705/549-2232) has details of local hotels and B&Bs. Amongst them, the *Chesham Grove*, 72 Church St (☎705/549-3740, fax 549-5075; ②) is an attractive stone bungalow with comfortable rooms that sits on a wooded ridge with views out across the bay, not far from the centre of Penetanguishene. Alternatively, there is *No.1 Jury Drive*, 1 Jury Drive (☎ & fax 705/549-6851; ③), a pleasant little bed-and-breakfast in a modern house and a leafy suburban setting near Discovery Harbour. If you decide to use Penetanguishene as a base, you can zip off to other local attractions with Union Taxi (☎705/549-7666), who are next door to the bus station. Local buses are run by PMCL (☎705/526-0161).

For **food**, *Memories Roadhouse*, 32 Main St, is a dinky place with an excellent café menu featuring traditional dishes – hamburgers, apple pie and the like, and *Blue Sky Family Restaurant*, 48 Main St, is a most agreeable small-town diner offering good-quality snacks and meals at very affordable prices. A great place for a gossip too.

Midland

MIDLAND, just east along the bay from Penetanguishene, has suffered badly from recurrent recession, losing its engineering plants in the 1930s, its shipyards in 1957 and much of its flour-mill capacity in 1967. But it has bounced back, shrugging off these set-backs with the help of provincial and federal grants, and nowadays the town has a sprightly air, its main drag – **King Street** – an amenable parade of shops and cafés with the occasional mural to brighten up the sturdy brick buildings. Efforts to cash in on the tourist industry have included the construction of a marina and the redevelopment of the harbourfront, where sightseeing **cruises** of the Thirty Thousand Islands that necklace Georgian Bay leave from May to October (1–4 daily; $15; reservations on ☎705/549-3388).

Sooner or later, every schoolkid in Midland gets taken to the **Huronia Museum** and **Huron Indian Village** (May–Dec daily 9am–5/6pm; Jan–April daily 9am–5pm, but phone to confirm times on ☎705/526-2844 or 1-800/263-7745; $6), a twenty-minute walk south of the harbour along King Street. Highlights of the museum include a large number of Huron artefacts and a series of photos tracing the pioneer settlement of Midland. The adjacent Indian Village is a replica of a sixteenth-century Huron settlement, its high palisade encircling storage pits, drying racks, a sweat bath, a medicine man's lodge and two long houses. These characteristic Huron constructions, with their bark-covered walls of cedar poles bent to form a protective arch, contain tiers of rough wooden bunks draped with furs, whilst herbs, fish, skins and tobacco hang from the roof to dry. It's all very interesting and feels surprisingly authentic, but still lags far behind the comparable section of Sainte-Marie among the Hurons up the road.

Practicalities

Midland **bus station** is close to the waterfront on Bay Street, metres from Deluxe Taxi (☎705/526-2217) and a couple of minutes' walk east of the **tourist office**, at the foot of King Street (June–Aug Mon–Fri 8.30am–5pm, Sat & Sun 10am–6pm; Sept–May Mon–Fri 9am–5pm; ☎705/526-7884). They have the details of local and regional **accommodation** – anything from cottage rental through to a handful of downtown **B&Bs** (②). Amongst the latter, two perfectly adequate and fairly central options are *Mark & Margie's B&B*, in a good-looking Victorian house with wrapround veranda at 670 Hugel Ave and 5th Street (☎705/526-4441, fax 526-4426; ②); and the unusual *Little Lake B&B*, 669 Yonge St at 5th Street (☎705/526-2750, fax 526-9005; ③), where the modern front part of the house leads to an older section at the back with high-beamed ceilings and park views. Yonge Street cuts across King about 600m south of the harbourfront. There are also several reasonably priced **motels** in and around town – the *Comfort Inn*, about 2km from the harbour at 980 King St and Hwy 12 (☎705/526-2090; ④), is as good as any.

For **food**, the *Daily Perk*, 292 King St, serves first-class deli-style sandwiches and meals; *Midland Fish & Chips*, 311 King, does what it does rather well; and *Scully's Waterfront Grill*, by the town dock, is a popular, boisterous place with bar food.

Sainte-Marie among the Hurons

One of Ontario's most arresting historical attractions is **Sainte-Marie among the Hurons** (late May to mid-Oct daily 10am–5pm; $9.75), the carefully researched and beautifully maintained site of a crucial episode in Canadian history. It's located 5km east of Midland beside Hwy 12 – and although there are no buses, the taxi fare from Midland is only $6.

In 1608, **Samuel de Champlain** returned to Canada convinced that the only way to make the fur trade profitable was by developing alliances with native hunters. The

Huron were the obvious choice, as they already acted as go-betweens in the exchange of corn, tobacco and hemp from the bands to the south and west of their territory, for the pelts collected to the north. In 1611, having participated in Huron attacks on the Iroqouis, Champlain cemented the alliance by a formal exchange of presents. His decision to champion one tribe against another – and particularly his gifts of firearms to his allies – disrupted the balance of power amongst the native societies of the St Lawrence and Great Lakes area and set the stage for the destruction of Sainte-Marie almost forty years later.

Meanwhile, the **Jesuits**, who established their centre of operations at **Sainte-Marie** in 1639, had begun to undermine social cohesion within the Huron community itself. The priests succeeded in converting a substantial minority of the Huron – by then enfeebled by three European sicknesses, measles, smallpox and influenza – and thus divided them into two camps, Christian and non-Christian. Furthermore, in 1648 the Dutch on the Hudson River began to sell firearms to the Iroquois, who launched a full-scale invasion of Huronia in March 1649, slaughtering their enemies as they moved in on Sainte-Marie. Fearing for their lives, the Jesuits of Sainte-Marie burnt their settlement and fled. Eight thousand Hurons went with them; most starved to death on Christian Island, in Georgian Bay, but a few made it to Québec. During the campaign two Jesuit priests, fathers **Brébeuf and Lalemant**, were captured at the outpost of Saint-Louis, near present-day Victoria Harbour, where they were bound to the stake and tortured, as per standard Iroquois practice: the image of Catholic bravery and Indian cruelty lingered in the minds of French-Canadians long after the sufferings of the Hurons had been forgotten.

A visit to Sainte-Marie starts in the **reception centre** with an audiovisual show that provides some background information before the screen lifts dramatically away to reveal the painstakingly restored mission site. There are 25 wooden buildings here, divided into two sections: the Jesuit area with its watchtowers, chapel, forge, farm buildings complete with pigs, cows and hens, living quarters and well-stocked garden; and the native area, including a hospital and a pair of bark-covered long houses – one for Christian converts, the other for heathens. Fairly spick-and-span today, it takes some imagination to see the long houses as they appeared to Father Lalemant, who saw ". . . a miniature picture of hell . . . on every side naked bodies, black and half-roasted, mingled pell-mell with the dogs . . . you will not reach the end of the cabin before you are completely befouled with soot, filth and dirt". Costumed guides act out the parts of Hurons and Europeans with great gusto, answering questions and demonstrating crafts and skills, though they show a certain reluctance to eat the staple food of the region, sagamite, a porridge of cornmeal seasoned with rotten fish. The grave in the simple wooden **church of St Joseph** between the Christian and native areas is the place where the flesh of Brébeuf and Lalemant was interred after the Jesuits had removed the bones for future use as reliquaries.

A path leads from the site to the excellent **museum**, which traces the story of the early exploration of Canada with maps and displays on such subjects as fishing and the fur trade, seen in the context of contemporary European history. This leads into a section on the history of the missionaries in New France, with particular reference to Sainte-Marie. Information on the archeology of the site follows: its whereabouts was always known as the Jesuits had all the documentation in Rome, even though local settlers helped themselves to almost every chunk of stone – from what was known locally as "the old Catholic fort" – during the nineteenth century. Excavations began on the site in the 1940s and work is still in progress.

The eight Jesuits who were killed in Huronia between 1642 and 1649 are commemorated by the **Martyrs' Shrine** (mid-May to mid-Oct daily 9am–9pm; $2), a twin-spired, 1920s church which overlooks Sainte-Marie from the other side of Hwy 12. Blessed by Pope John Paul II in 1984 – when he bafflingly remarked that it was "a symbol of unity of faith in a diversity of cultures" – the church, along with the assorted shrines and altars in its grounds, is massively popular with pilgrims. Inside, the transepts hold a number of saintly reliquaries, most notably the skull of Brébeuf, and a stack of crutches discarded by healed pilgrims.

Back across Hwy 12 and next door to Sainte-Marie among the Hurons is one last attraction, the **Wye Marsh Wildlife Centre** (daily 10am–4pm, 6pm from late June to Aug; $5), whose footpaths explore a patch of wetland and the surrounding woodland.

Orillia

If you're heading south from Severn Sound towards Toronto, you might consider a brief detour to **ORILLIA**, beside lakes Simcoe and Couchiching – and on Hwy 11, the road to Algonquin Provincial Park (see p.146). The town lies just to the west of the narrow channel that connects the two lakes, a waterway that was once a centre of Huron settlement. When **Samuel de Champlain** arrived here in 1615, he promptly handed out muskets to his Huron allies, encouraging them to attack their Iroquois rivals in order to establish French control of the fur trade – an intervention that was to lead to the destruction of the Jesuit outpost at Sainte-Marie in 1649 (see opposite). Two hundred years later, a second wave of Europeans cleared the district's forests, and today Orillia is a trim little town of 27,000 citizens – part lakeside resort, part farming centre.

Orillia's humdrum **town centre** spreads out on either side of the main drag, Mississaga Street, which runs east from Hwy 11 to Lake Couchiching. At the foot of Mississaga, **Centennial Park** incorporates a marina, a harbour and a boardwalk that runs north to **Couchiching Beach Park**, complete with an Edwardian bandstand and a bronze statue of Champlain. However, the town's principal attraction, the **Stephen Leacock Museum** (mid-June to Aug daily 10am–7pm; Sept to mid-June Mon–Fri 10am–5pm; $7), is located some 3km southeast of the centre along the lakeshore – just follow the signs. Built in 1928 in the colonial style, with symmetrical pitched roofs and an ornate veranda, this was the summer home of the humorist and academic Stephen Leacock until his death in 1944. His most famous book, *Sunshine Sketches of a Little Town*, gently mocks the hypocrisies and vanities of the people of Mariposa, an imaginary town so clearly based on Orillia that it caused great local offence. Some of the rooms contain furnishings and fittings familiar to Leacock, others shed light on his career, interests and attitudes. The books may be engagingly whimsical, but you can't help but wonder about a man who had concealed spyholes in his library so that he could watch his guests and, perhaps worse, carefully positioned his favourite living-room chair so that he could keep an eye on his servants in the pantry via the dining-room mirror. After you've explored the house, take a few minutes for the easy stroll out along the adjacent wooded headland and drop by the giftshop, which sells almost all of his works.

As for practicalities, Orillia's **bus station** occupies the old railway station at the southern end of the town centre off Front Street South, 2km from the Leacock Museum. From here, it's around 800m north along Front Street South to the seasonal **tourist office** (mid-May to early June Mon–Fri 10am–7pm, Sat & Sun 8am–9pm; early June to Aug daily 7am–10pm), right by the harbour; the Chamber of Commerce year-round tourist office is at 150 Front St S (Mon–Fri 9am–5pm; ☎705/326-4424). There's no special reason to hang around after you've done the sights, but if you do decide to stay, both these offices have the details of local **accommodation**.

Port Severn and Honey Harbour

Sitting on the northern shore of Severn Sound at the mouth of the Severn River, tiny **PORT SEVERN** is the gateway to the **Trent–Severn Waterway**, a 400-kilometre canalized route that connects Georgian Bay with Lake Ontario. With a maximum depth of only 2m, it's of little commercial importance today, but until the late nineteenth century this was one of the region's principal cargo routes. It's open from the middle of May to the middle of October and takes about a week to travel from one end to the other. If you've the inclination for a serious boating trip, your first line of enquiry should be to the waterway's free **Cruise Planning Service** (☎1-800/663-2628); for a taster, two-hour **cruises** (June to mid-Oct 1 daily; $14; reservations on ☎705/549-3388) leave from Lock #45 in Port Severn, travelling as far as the **Big Chute Marine Railway**, where boats are lifted over the eighteen-metre drop between the upper and lower levels of the river. Frankly, the Big Chute is something of a yawn, but it certainly attracts its share of visitors, most of whom drive here – just follow the signs off Hwy 400 (Exit 162) north of Port Severn. There are three recommendable **hotels** in Port Severn, beginning with *Rawley Lodge* (☎705/538-2272 or 1-800/263-7358, fax 705/538-0726; ④ including meals), which occupies a rambling, 1920s building with a charming riverside setting. The rooms are modern and a tad spartan – both in the main lodge and the adjacent chalets – but perfectly adequate; they also rent out canoes. The second hotel is the smart and briskly modern *Inn at Christie's Mill* (☎705/538-2354 or 1-800/465-9966, fax 705/538-1836, *www.christiesmill.on.ca*; ⑤), which also has the district's best **restaurant** with views out across the river. Even better, however, is the delightful *Severn Lodge* (☎705/756-2722 or 1-800/461-5817, fax 705/756-8313, *www.severnlodge.on.ca*), which has a wonderful solitary location amongst dense forests overlooking a wide and quiet section of the Trent-Severn Waterway. The lodge has all the facilities of a mini-resort, including canoe and motorboat rental, an artificial beach, a restaurant and an outside swimming pool, and is extremely popular with families. Rooms are available in the main lodge and in the chalets that dot the surrounding woods. Rates vary enormously, and there's usually a minimum stay of two nights, but a lodge room for two nights including meals works out at about $300 per person in summer. To get there, leave Hwy 400 at Exit 162 (also the turning for the Big Chute Marine Railway – see above) and it's 7km along Route 34.

It's 13km northwest from Port Severn across the mouth of the river and down Route 5 to **HONEY HARBOUR**, the nearest port to the Georgian Bay Islands National Park (see below). Little more than a couple of shops, a liquor store and a few self-contained hotel resorts, the village achieved some notoriety in the 1970s when the bar of the *Delawana Inn* was the site of violent confrontations between Toronto's Hell's Angels and local Ojibwa families. The feud ended with the Angels walking home after their bikes had been dynamited. Things are much more civil today, but Honey Harbour is still a lively place in summer, with motorboats whizzing in and out as cottagers drop by to collect supplies. If you decide to stay here – eschewing the offshore campsites of the national park – the best place is the lakeside *Delawana Inn* (☎705/756-2424 or 1-888/DELAWANA, *www.delawana.com*; ⑧ for full board in high season, with discounts on package deals; late June to early Sept), an extensive, resort complex with spacious chalet cabins dotted round its pine-forested grounds. Guests also have use of the resort's canoes, kayaks and windsurfing boards.

In terms of public transport, the Ontario Northland **bus** service(☎1-800/461-8558) from Toronto to Sudbury drops passengers at the petrol station on Hwy 400 on the edge of Port Severn; there are no connections on to Honey Harbour.

The Georgian Bay Islands National Park

A beautiful area to cruise, the **Georgian Bay Islands National Park** consists of a scattering of about sixty islands spread between Honey Harbour and Twelve Mile Bay, about 50km to the north. The park's two distinct landscapes – the glacier-scraped rock of the Canadian Shield and the hardwood forests and thicker soils of the south – meet at the northern end of the largest and most scenic island, **Beausoleil**, a forty-minute boat ride west of Honey Harbour. Beausoleil has eleven short **hiking trails**, including two that start at the **Cedar Spring landing stage**, on the southeastern shore. These are the Treasure Trail, which heads north behind the marshes along the edge of the island, and the Christian Trail, which cuts through beech and maple stands to the balsam and hemlock groves overlooking the rocky beaches of the western shoreline. At the northern end of Beausoleil, within comfortable walking distance of several other **jetties**, there are the Cambrian and Fairy trails, two delightful routes through the harsher Canadian Shield scenery, while, just to the west, the Dossyonshing Trail tracks through a mixed area of wetland, forest and bare granite that covers the transitional zone between the two main landscapes. The **national park office** in Honey Harbour (late June to Aug Mon–Thurs 8am–4.30pm, Fri 8am–8pm, Sat & Sun 8am–4pm; Sept to late June Mon–Fri 8am–4.30pm; ☎705/756-2415) provides a full range of information on walking trails and flora and fauna. In winter, a visit to the park office is essential as the wardens will advise on where it's safe to ski across the ice to the islands; they maintain a marked ski trail out to Beausoleil.

The park has thirteen **campsites**, eleven on Beausoleil and one each on Island 95B and Centennial Island. The charge is $11 a night and all operate on a self-registration, first-come, first-served basis, with the exception of Cedar Spring ($15), where the visitor centre (☎705/756-5909) takes reservations on half the 87 sites for an additional $10 fee. For everywhere else, ask about availability at the park office before you set out – and don't forget the insect repellent. Three Honey Harbour operators run a **water taxi** service over to three of the park's islands – Beausoleil ($30–35 one-way), Centennial Island ($35–40) and Island 95 ($35–40). Honey Harbour Boat Club (☎705/756-2411), about 700m from the park office at the marina at the end of Route 5, is as good as any. Water taxi prices are fixed – the park office has the list – but times are negotiable; be sure to arrange an agreed pick-up time before you get dropped off. If you want to head southwest, a one-way water-taxi trip to Midland costs around $90. In addition – and much more economical – are **day-trips to Beausoleil**, giving four hours on the island, with the park's own Georgian Bay Islands Day Tripper (July to early Sept Thurs to Mon 3 daily; $15 return; reservations on ☎705/756-2415).

Parry Sound

A cheerful little place, **PARRY SOUND**, beside Georgian Bay 85km north of Port Severn, was named after the Arctic explorer Sir William Edward Parry, but it earned the nickname "Parry Hoot" because the log-drivers on the river chose this as the place to get drunk in. Things are more genteel today and the town has become a popular stopover for boats roaming the Thirty Thousand Islands out in the bay. Parry Sound is also the home port of the *Island Queen*, which squeezes through these same islands in

THE MASSASAUGA RATTLESNAKE

The **Massasauga Rattlesnake** is the only venomous snake in eastern Canada and there is a small population of them in and around the Georgian Bay Islands National Park. Tan-coloured with dark brown blotches, an adult specimen is 50 to 70cm long with a heavy body and triangular head. In the unlikely event you stumble across one, give it a wide berth. The snake prefers marsh and mixed forest, so if you are hiking in this kind of habitat, be sure to pick up one of the advisory leaflets at the park office.

a spectacular **cruise** that has become one of the region's most popular attractions (June to mid-Oct daily at 2pm, plus July–Aug daily at 10am; 3hr; $18; ☎705/746-2311 or 1-800/506-2628, *info@island-queen.com*). The jetty for the *Island Queen* is at Government Wharf, just below the centre of town at the end of Bay Street. Otherwise, Parry Sound is short of specific sights, though its pocket-sized harbour is overshadowed by a splendid Edwardian railway **trestle bridge** and the few blocks that make up the commercial centre – along and around **James Street** – are dotted with good-looking old brick and stone buildings. In addition, the town rustles up a well-respected classical music **Festival of the Sound** (details on ☎705/746-2410, *www.festivalofthesound.on.ca*) in the second half of July and early August.

Buses to Parry Sound pull into the depot just off Hwy 69 well to the east of the town centre. To get downtown from here, call Parry Sound Taxi (☎705/746-1221). The **tourist office** is in the former railway station, at 70 Church St (May–Sept Mon–Thurs 8am–4pm, Fri 8am–6pm, Sat 10am–2pm; ☎705/746-4213). From here, it's 800m south along Church Street to the centre and 300m more to Government Wharf. The tourist office has details of local accommodation including several central **B&Bs**. One especially good option is the *Victoria Manor*, in a handsome old house with turrets and with a lovely garden at 43 Church St and Rosetta (☎705/746-5399, *victoria@zeuter.com*; ③). *The Comfort Inn by Journey's End* (☎705/746-6221 or 1-800/228-5150; ③) is east of the centre on the way out to Hwy 69 at 120 Bowes St.

For **food**, head for *Bannerman's*, in the centre at 65 James St (Mon–Fri 7am–5pm & Sat 8am–4pm) – a smashing deli and bakery selling the tastiest of meals and snacks. In the evening, try the *Bay Street Café* (☎705/746-2882), down by Government Wharf at 22 Bay St, where the menu runs from pizza and sandwiches to fish and chips.

Around Parry Sound: Killbear Provincial Park

The wild Georgian Bay shoreline, formed by glaciers that scoured the rock and dumped mighty boulders onto its long beaches, is seen at its finest in **Killbear Provincial Park**, reached by driving 18km north from Parry Sound on Hwy 69 then 20km southwest on Route 559. Along the shore, windswept, crooked cedars and black spruce cling precariously to the Canadian Shield's pink-granite outcrops, whilst the interior of this peninsular park is a forest of maple, beech and yellow birch. The 3.5-kilometre loop of the **Lookout Point Trail**, which starts about 1.5km east of the park office and heads to a lookout across Parry Sound, is the best of the park's three short hiking trails. Killbear has six **campsites**, (mid-May to early Oct; reservations on ☎705/342-5492), some by the water, others in the forest, some with showers, others not, and all costing between $18 and $22.

CENTRAL ONTARIO

Lying between Lake Ontario's northern shore and the Ottawa River Valley, **central Ontario** is largely defined by the Canadian Shield, whose endless forests, myriad lakes and poor soils dip down from the north in a giant wedge. This hostile terrain has kept settlement down to a minimum, though latterly the very wildness of the land has attracted thousands of Canadian holiday-makers, who come here to hunker down in their lakeside cottages. The centre of all this holiday activity is the **Muskoka Lakes**, a skein of narrow lakes and rivers whose main supply towns – **Gravenhurst** and **Bracebridge** – lie on Hwy 11. Staying in a cottage is the one sure-fire way of appreciating the beauty of the area, but passing visitors are better off heading further north to the wondrous expanse of **Algonquin Provincial Park** with its abundant wildlife and extraordinarily large network of canoe routes.

The implacability of the Shield breaks up as it approaches the **St Lawrence River** and it's here that you'll find a string of interesting historic towns. The pick is **Kingston**, founded by United Empire Loyalists (see p.382) and renowned for its fine limestone buildings, not to mention its good restaurants and quality B&Bs. Kingston is also useful as a stepping stone on the road east to either Montréal (see p.201) or **Ottawa**, Canada's engaging capital city, which boasts some of the country's finest museums.

Public transport along the St Lawrence River is excellent by bus and quite good by rail. Things get trickier in the Muskoka Lakes area, but there are buses along Hwy 11 as far as Huntsville.

The Muskoka Lakes

The main route from Toronto to Algonquin Provincial Park passes through the **Muskoka Lakes**, a region of more than 1500 lakes and hundreds of urbanite cottage retreats. Named after an Ojibwa chief, Mesqua-Ukee, who settled here with his people after aiding the British during the War of 1812, the area was opened to tourism in 1860, when two hikers made the two-day trek from Toronto to a small Ojibwa settlement at what is now Gravenhurst. By the 1890s, the lakes had become the haunt of wealthy families from Southern Ontario and although things are more democratic today, this is still primarily the preserve of the well-heeled. The main access towns to the Muskoka Lakes – **Gravenhurst, Bracebridge** and **Huntsville** – are strung out along Hwy 11. None of them have much to offer the passing visitor and neither, for that matter, do the lakes. Just driving round is well-nigh pointless, though there are a couple of splendid hotel-resorts to aim for.

Public transport is limited to Hwy 11 with Ontario Northland **buses** going to all three major Muskoka towns on their way from Toronto to North Bay. Huntsville and Gravenhurst can also be reached by **rail**.

Gravenhurst

The gateway to Muskoka is humdrum **GRAVENHURST**, sited at the southern end of Lake Muskoka, some 170km north of Toronto. Cottagers whizz in and out to collect supplies and arrive in numbers for the **Muskoka Winter Carnival**, in late February, when all manner of events are held from demolition derbies to delicate ice-sculpture competitions. Outside of carnival time, the main attraction is the **Bethune Memorial House**, 235 John St N (mid-May to late Oct daily 10am–noon & 1–5pm; late Oct to mid-May Mon–Fri only; $2.50), the birthplace of Norman Bethune, a doctor who introduced Western medicine to the Chinese in the 1930s and invented mobile blood-transfusion units. The house has been restored to its appearance in 1890 and has displays on Bethune's considerable accomplishments – he was even praised by Chairman Mao – detailed in English, French and Chinese. Afterwards, you could hop aboard RMS *Segwun*, a 105-year-old steamship – the oldest still operating in North America – that cruises up Lake Muskoka from the town wharf (June to mid-Oct daily; $11–70 depending on length of cruise; ☎705/687-6667), giving fine views of the hills and its many mansions.

In the unlikely event you decide to stay, the **tourist office** at 685 Muskoka Rd N (Mon–Fri 8.30am–4.30pm; ☎705/687-4432) has a full list of local **accommodation**. One good spot is the *Pinedale Inn*, 200 Pinedale Lane (☎705/687-2822; ④), a well-maintained motel on the shore of Gull Lake surrounded by pine trees and with rooms that have kitchenettes and bathrooms. For **food**, head for either the pleasant *White Pine Café*, on the main street in a tastefully converted old general store at 195 Muskoka Rd S, or

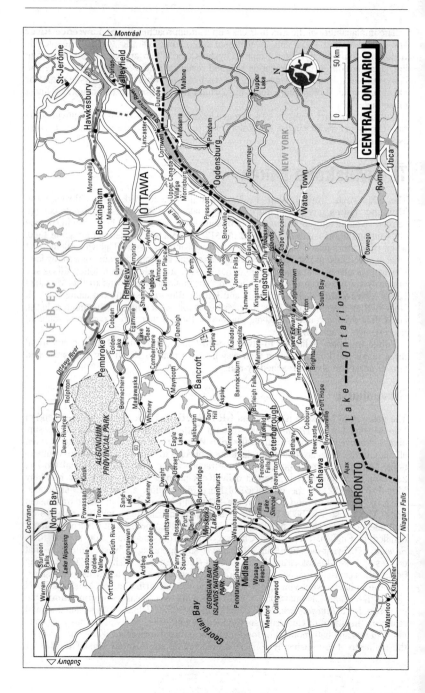

CENTRAL ONTARIO

50 km

△ Montréal

St-Jérôme
Valleyfield
Hawkesbury
Montebello
Buckingham
Masson
HULL
OTTAWA
Renfrew
Arnprior
Pembroke
Bonnechere
Madawaska
Whitney
ALGONQUIN PROVINCIAL PARK
QUÉBEC
Ottawa River
Deux-Rivières
Rolphton
Kiosk
Sand Lake
Dorset
Eagle Lake
Dwight
Kearney
Sprucedale
Magnetawan
Ardbeg
Powassan
Trout Creek
South River
North Bay
Sturgeon Falls
Warren
Lake Nipissing
Golden Valley
Restoule
Port Loring

Doron
Dundee
Malone
Upper Lake
Massena
Potsdam
Cornwall
Lancaster
Ogdensburg
Gouverneur
Water Town
NEW YORK
Morrisburg
Upper Canada Village
Prescott
Brockville
Rideau R.
St. Lawrence Seaway
Oswego
Rome
Utica
N

Aylmer
Ouyon
Shawrock
Carleton Place
Almonte
Calabogie
Golden Lake
Eganville
Cobden
Griffith
Combermere
Clear Lake
Maynooth
Bancroft
Denbigh
Perth
Maberly
Jones Falls
Tamworth
Kingston Hills
Kaladar
Actinolite
Marmora
Bannockburn
Cloyne
Aspley
Burleigh Falls
Lakefield
Peterborough
Kinmount
Haliburton
Tory Hill
Coboconk
Fenelon Falls
Bethany
Beaverton
Port Perry
Oshawa
Ajax
TORONTO
Niagara Falls
Kitchener
Waterloo
Collingwood
Meaford
Wasaga Beach
Midland
Penetanguishene
GEORGIAN BAY ISLANDS NATIONAL PARK
Georgian Bay
Parry Sound
Port Carling
Rosseau
Huntsville
Bracebridge
Gravenhurst
Muskoka Lake
Waubaushene
Orillia
Lake Simcoe
Newcastle
Bowmanville
Port Hope
Cobourg
Trenton
Brighton
Picton
Prince Edward Country
South Bay
Adolphustown
Wolfe Island
Cape Vincent
Gananoque
The Thousand Islands
Kingston
Lake Ontario

△ Cochrane
▽ Sudbury
▽ Niagara Falls

Sloanes, 155 Muskoka Rd S, which has been here as long as Gravenhurst, and serves a divine blueberry pie.

Bracebridge

Situated 25km north of Gravenhurst, **BRACEBRIDGE** prides itself on being "Halfway to the North Pole" – and on that basis is allegedly the summer home of Santa Claus, who hangs out amongst the theme-park rides of **Santa's Village** just south of town (late June to Aug daily 10am–6pm; adults and children over five years $15.95, 2–4s $10.95, under 2s free). If that doesn't appeal, then try the **Maple Orchard Farms Factory Outlet**, in an industrial park at 14 Gray Rd, where they sell everything from Belgian chocolates through to maple syrup. There's not much else, though the short main drag, Manitoba Street, is lined with a pleasant ensemble of Victorian red-bricks, worth at least a few minutes' gander.

The **tourist office**, in the mews by the bridge at the foot of Manitoba Street (May–Aug Mon–Sat 9am–5pm & Sun 10am–4pm; Sept–April Mon–Fri 9am–5pm & Sat 10am–4pm; ☎705/645-8121), has town maps and buckets of local information.

THE BEAVER

The **beaver** is the national animal of Canada – it appeared on the first postage stamp issued by the colony in 1851, and now features on the back of the current 5¢ piece. There was nothing sentimental about this choice – beaver pelts had once kick-started the Canadian economy, but only recently has the beaver been treated with respect and protected from slaughter.

Beavers are actually aquatic rodents, which grow to around 750cm long and weigh about 35kg. Their early importance was due to their thick soft pelts, composed of long guard hairs and a dense undercoat, which was used by the native peoples for clothing long before the arrival of the Europeans. Early fur traders quickly realized the value of beaver-skins, particularly for the manufacture of **felt**, for which there was a huge demand for hat-making. To keep up with demand the beaver was extensively trapped, and the *voyageurs* pushed further and further west along the lake and river systems in pursuit of the animal, thus opening up more and more of present-day Canada. The beaver population was decimated to the point of extinction in some areas of the east, but after beaver hats went out of fashion in the nineteenth century the species rapidly recovered and today they are comparatively common.

Bark (for food) and water (in which to escape from danger) are two vital elements for beavers. They build a **dam** to create a large pond in which to escape from their enemies and to serve as a winter food store. Beavers start their dams, which can be up to 700m wide, by strategically felling one tree across a stream. This catches silt and driftwood and the beaver reinforces it with sticks, stones, grass and mud, which is laboriously smoothed in as a binding element. The **lodge** is constructed simultaneously; sometimes it forms part of the dam and sometimes it is fixed to the shore or an island in the pond. It is about 2m in diameter and has two entrances: one accessible from land and one from underwater. Lodges are topped with grass thatch and a good layer of mud, which freezes in winter, making them virtually impenetrable. During the autumn, the beaver stocks the pond formed by the dam with large numbers of young soft-bark trees and saplings; it drags these below the water line and anchors them to the mud at the bottom. It then retires to the lodge for the winter, only emerging to get food from the store or repair the dam in case of emergency. Beaver lakes are not, however, the tree-fringed paradises portrayed by some nature-film makers; a mud-banked pond, surrounded by untidily felled trees and with a bedraggled-looking domed heap of sticks and sludge somewhere along its banks is often nearer the mark. If you spot an untidy-looking lake anywhere in northwest Ontario, the chances are that a beaver's lodge will be close by, though you're unlikely to see the creature itself.

Huntsville

Workaday **HUNTSVILLE**, 35km beyond Bracebridge on Hwy 11, is as near as the buses and trains get to Algonquin Park. **Buses** pull into the centre at Main and Centre Street, **trains** pause at the station about 600m away. Hammond Transportation runs a reliable if fairly infrequent minibus service on into Algonquin Provincial Park (see below), but if you find yourself stuck here in town, head for the inexpensive chain **motels** lined up along King William Street. Reliable options here include the *Comfort Inn*, at no. 86 (☎705/789-1701 or 1-800/228-5150; ③), and the *King William Inn* at no. 23 (☎705/789-9661; ③).

Algonquin Park

Created in 1893 at the behest of logging companies keen to keep the farmers out, **Algonquin Provincial Park** is Ontario's oldest and largest provincial park and for many is the quintessential Canadian landscape. Located on the southern edge of the Canadian Shield, the park straddles a transitional zone, with the hilly two-thirds to the west covered in a hardwood forest of sugar maple, beech and yellow birch, whilst in the drier eastern part jack pines, white pines and red pines dominate. Throughout the park, the lakes and rocky rounded hills are interspersed with black spruce bogs, a type of vegetation typical of areas far further north. Canoeing is very popular here and with an astounding 2400km of routes there's a good chance of avoiding all contact for days on end.

Wildlife is as varied as the flora – any trip to Algonquin is characterized by the echo of birdsong, from the loons' ghostly call to the screech of ravens. Beavers, moose, black bears and raccoons are all resident, as are white-tailed deer, whose population thrives on the young shoots that replace the trees felled by the park's loggers. Public "howling parties" – which can attract up to 2000 people – set off into the wilderness during August in search of **timber wolves**, or rather their howls: many of the rangers are so good at howling that they can get the animals to reply.

Access to the park is via either the **West Gate**, 45km from Huntsville on Hwy 60, or – if you are arriving from Ottawa and points east – the **East Gate**. A day-pass costs $10 per vehicle. The two gates are linked by the 56-kilometre-long **Parkway Corridor** – also known as the Frank McDougall Parkway – the park's only road. Away from the corridor, walking and canoeing are the only means of transport. The well-signposted main **visitors' centre** is 43km from the West Gate (late April to Oct daily 10am–5pm, July & Aug till 9pm; Nov to late April Sat & Sun 10am–5pm; ☎705/633-5572, *www.algonquinpark.on.ca*), and, besides the usual gift shop, has a series of dioramas explaining the park's general and natural history. The visitors' centre also has a comprehensive range of literature describing every aspect of the park, from maps and detailed hiking trail and canoeing route guides through to booklets on native folklore. The **park offices** at both the West and East gates have trail descriptions and other park information, but there's not so wide a range. Furthermore, individual trail guides (37¢) are available at most trailheads. If you're heading for the backcountry, pick up **food** and water before you get here as outlets in the park are few and far between.

If you're reliant on public transport, the nearest you'll get by **train** or **bus** is Huntsville. However, Hammond Transportation (☎705/645-5431 or 1-800/563-1885, *hammonds@muskoka.com*) operates the Algonquin Park Shuttle from Huntsville to points along the Parkway Corridor in July and August (3 weekly; $18).

The Parkway Corridor

Along the Parkway Corridor, the location of trailheads and campsites (see opposite) is indicated by distances from the West Gate – as in "km 7". Ten **day-hikes** begin beside the road and of these the two-kilometre **Beaver Pond Trail** (km 45) is a rugged but easy trail that takes you past huge beaver dams, while the equally short but steeper **Lookout Trail** (km 39) gives a remarkable view of the park. For a longer trail with greater chances of spotting wildlife, the eleven-kilometre **Mizzy Lake Trail** (km 15) is recommended. Spare time also for the illuminating **Algonquin Logging Museum** (late May to early Oct daily 10am–5pm; free with day-pass), just inside the East Gate at km 54.5. Here, an easy 1.3km loop trail threads past some fascinating old logging leftovers, including a tugboat, a locomotive, sawlog camp and sleighs.

The park interior and backcountry camping

The park interior is best explored by **canoe**, and there are several **outfitters** dotted along the Parkway Corridor. One of the best is the Portage Store at Canoe Lake, km 14 (daily: May, Sept & early Oct 8am–7pm, June–Aug 7am–9pm; in summer ☎705/633-5622, fax 633-5696, in winter 705/789-3645, fax 789-6955, *www.portagestore.com*). **Rates** vary enormously depending on the sort of canoe you hire, but the simplest models cost $20 per day, $17 per day for five days and more. The Portage Store also rents out tents, life vests and all the associated canoeist's tackle and organizes guided canoe trips. Advance reservations are pretty much essential. Note also that given Algonquin's immense popularity, canoeing is best avoided at holiday weekends: horror stories abound of three-hour jams of canoeists waiting their turn to tackle the portages between some of the more accessible lakes. Incidentally, Canoe Lake was where the artist Tom Thomson (see p.86) drowned in 1917 – and there's a monument to him about forty-minutes' canoe paddle from the Portage Store.

If you don't fancy canoeing, the interior can also be experienced on either of two long-distance hiking trails. The **Western Uplands Backpacking Trail** (km 2.5) is composed of a series of loops that allow you to construct a hike of up to 71km, while the equally challenging **Highland Backpacking Trail** (km 29) has loops of up to 35km.

In all cases, **backcountry camping** requires a permit. These are available at both the West and East gates and at the visitor centre ($6.50 per person per night) or from Ontario Parks direct (see below).

CAMPING, YURTS AND CABINS

Strung along the Parkway Corridor are eight park **campsites**. The less popular sites are those that prohibit motorboats – namely Canisbay Lake (km 23; mid-May to early Oct), Coon Lake (km 40; early June to Aug) and Kearney Lake (km 37; early June to Aug). Year-round camping is only available at Mew Lake (km 30). Sites cost $16–20 without showers, $17–22 with showers. **Reservations** are well-nigh essential and cost $9: contact Ontario Parks by phone (☎519/826-5290 or 1-888/ONT-PARK) or book online (*www.ontarioparks.com*). In addition, there are seven **yurts** ($55 per night, $355 per week) at Mew Lake. Each holds up to six people and reservations are essential – again with Ontario Parks. The rangers who roamed the park in its early years built dozens of **log cabins**, some of which have survived and are now rented out for $50–80 for two people per night. Contact Algonquin Provincial Park for further details.

LODGES

Also lining the Parkway Corridor are several privately owned **lodges** and **mini-resorts**, ranging from the simple and unaffected to the comparatively lavish. One of the best is *Killarney Lodge* (☎705/633-5551, *www.killarneylodge.com*; ⑦; mid-May to mid-Oct), whose cosy, prettily painted log cabins dot a spindly promontory that hooks out into the Lake of Two Rivers at km 32. A second good option is *Bartlett Lodge* (☎705/633-5543, fax 633-5746; ⑤), comprising a scattering of older cabins overlooking Cache Lake at km 23. The lodge can only be reached by boat – pick up the marked phone at the jetty and someone will come to pick you up. Both of these lodges provide full meals.

GUIDED TOURS
If you want all the organizing done for you, **Call of the Wild**, 23 Edward St, Markham, Ontario L3P 2NP (☎905/471-9453 or 1-800/776-9453, fax 905/472-9453, *www.callofthewild .ca*) run three-day ($390) and five-day ($580) personalized and relaxed adventure canoe trips in Algonquin. Price includes all meals, permits, equipment and transport from Toronto. It's essential to book in advance.

Kingston

Birthplace of Bryan Adams but prouder of its handsome limestone buildings, the town of **KINGSTON**, a fast 260km east of Toronto along Hwy 401, is the largest and most enticing of the communities along the northern shore of Lake Ontario. It occupies a strategic position where the lake narrows into the St Lawrence River, its potential first recognized by the French who built a fortified fur-trading post here in 1673. It was not a success. The commander, the Comte de Frontenac, managed to argue with just about everybody and his deputy, Denonville, pursued a risky side-line in kidnapping, inviting local Iroquois to the fort and then forcibly shipping them to France as curiosities.

Nevertheless, the fort struggled on until 1758 when it fell to a combined force of British, Americans and Iroquois, a victory soon followed by an influx of United Empire Loyalists, who promptly developed Kingston – as they renamed it – into a major ship-building centre and naval base. The money rolled in and the future looked rosy when the completion of the Rideau Canal (see p.153), linking Kingston with Ottawa in 1832, opened up its hinterland. Indeed, Kingston became the capital of Canada in 1841 and although it lost this distinction just three years later it remained the region's most important town until the end of the nineteenth century. In recent years, Kingston's fortunes have taken a turn for the worse with the decline of the sea trade – and the underuse of the St Lawrence Seaway – hitting it very hard. That said, the local economy does benefit from the presence of **Queen's University**, one of Canada's most prestigious academic institutions, and of the **Royal Military College**, the country's answer to Sandhurst and West Point.

Kingston's attractions include a cluster of especially fine nineteenth-century limestone buildings – most notably **City Hall** and the **Cathedral of St George** – the first-rate **Agnes Etherington Art Centre** gallery and **Bellevue House**, once the home of Prime Minister Sir John A. Macdonald. Add to this several delicious **B&Bs**, a cluster of good **restaurants** and scenic **boat trips** round the Thousand Islands just offshore and you have a town that is well worth a couple of days – maybe more.

Arrival and information

Trains from Toronto, Ottawa and Montréal terminate at the VIA Rail station on Hwy 2, 7km northwest of the city at the junction of Princess and Counter streets; Kingston Transit bus #4 (hourly) goes into downtown. The terminus for Voyageur long-distance **buses** is on the corner of Division and Counter streets about 6km to the north of the city centre; Kingston Transit bus #2 (hourly) goes downtown. Kingston Transit's **local bus** information line is ☎613/546-1181; for a **taxi**, call Amey's Taxi (☎613/546-1111). Maps and information can be picked up at the **tourist office**, 209 Ontario St (June–Aug daily 9am–8pm; May & Sept–April daily 9am–5pm; Oct–April Mon–Fri 9am–5pm, Sat & Sun 10am–1pm; ☎613/548-4415 or 1-888/855-4555, *www.kingstoncanada.com*), right in

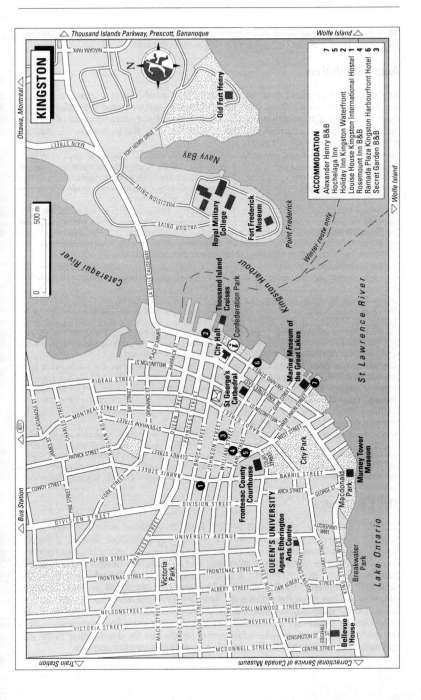

KINGSTON

Thousand Islands Parkway, Prescott, Gananoque

Wolfe Island

Ottawa, Montréal

NIAGARA PARK

MAIN STREET

N

Old Fort Henry

FORT HENRY DRIVE

Navy Bay

PRECISION DRIVE

Cataraqui River

VALDOUR DRIVE

Royal Military College

Fort Frederick Museum

LA SALLE CAUSEWAY

Point Frederick

Winter route only

Kingston Harbour

Wolfe Island

Bus Station

401

CATARAQUI ST

JAMES ST

CHARLES STREET

MONTREAL STREET

RAGLAN ROAD

PATRICK STREET

BAY STREET

SYDENHAM STREET

ORDNANCE ST

PLACE D'ARMES

BARRACK ST

WELLINGTON ST

RIDEAU STREET

QUEEN STREET

BROCK STREET

PRINCESS STREET

CLERGY STREET

JOHNSON STREET

WILLIAM STREET

BAGOT STREET

EARL STREET

WELLINGTON STREET

KING STREET EAST

ONTARIO STREET

LOWER UNION STREET

WEST STREET

St George's Cathedral

City Hall

Thousand Island Cruises

Confederation Park

Marine Museum of the Great Lakes

St Lawrence River

COWDY STREET

PINE STREET

YORK STREET

DIVISION STREET

BARRIE STREET

ARCH STREET

GEORGE ST

City Park

Murney Tower Museum

Macdonald Park

DIVISION STREET

UNIVERSITY AVENUE

QUEEN'S UNIVERSITY

Agnes Etherington Arts Centre

LWR UNIVERSITY

Breakwater Park

Lake Ontario

ALFRED STREET

FRONTENAC STREET

ALBERT STREET

STUART STREET

KING STREET WEST

Victoria Park

NELSON STREET

VICTORIA STREET

MACK STREET

BROCK STREET

JOHNSON STREET

EARL STREET

UNION STREET

COLLINGWOOD STREET

BEVERLEY STREET

LWR ALBERT STREET

QUEEN'S CRESCENT

Bellevue House

EDGEHILL

KENSINGTON ST

MCDONNELL STREET

CENTRE STREET

Frontenac County Courthouse

Train Station

Correctional Service of Canada Museum

ACCOMMODATION

Alexander Henry B&B	7
Hochelaga Inn	5
Holiday Inn Kingston Waterfront	2
Louise House Kingston International Hostel	1
Rosemount Inn B&B	4
Ramada Plaza Kingston Harbourfront Hotel	6
Secret Garden B&B	3

500 m

0

the centre, by the waterfront and opposite City Hall. They will help arrange accommodation and issue free parking passes for downtown car parks.

Accommodation

Kingston has an excellent range of accommodation, much of it in or near the city centre. The best places are those **inns** and **B&Bs** that occupy grand old buildings, but there are less expensive options too, including a **hostel** and – most unusual of the lot – beds/berths in a decommissioned **coastguard ship**. At the top end of the market, advance reservations are advised in July and August.

Alexander Henry Bed and Breakfast, c/o Marine Museum, 55 Ontario St (☎613/542-2261, *www.marmus.ca*). A coastguard ice-breaker moored next to the Marine Museum provides a unique B&B right downtown. Berths vary from a bunk in a tiny cabin ($20) to more comfortable quarters ($70 for a two-person cabin). The ship itself dates from the 1960s and is a sturdy affair with narrow stairways and corridors and the salty taste of the sea. Open late May to early Sept.

Hochelaga Inn, 24 Sydenham St (☎ & fax 613/549-5534 or 1-800/267-0525, *hochelag@kos.net*). This appealing inn occupies a fanciful Victorian mansion – arguably Kingston's finest – with a playful central tower, bay windows and a charming wrapround veranda. There are 23 guestrooms, all en suite, and although the furnishings and fittings are a little over-elaborate, each is very comfortable. In a chichi residential area within easy walking distance of the centre. ⑦.

Holiday Inn Kingston Waterfront, 1 Princess St (☎613/549-8400 or 1-800/HOLIDAY). Not the most distinctive of the city's hotels for sure, but the rooms are comfortable enough and it couldn't be more convenient for the centre. Most rooms have lake views. ⑤.

Louise House Kingston International Hostel, 329 Johnson St at Barrie (☎613/531-8237, fax 531-9763; May to late Aug). This Queen's University residence is used as an HI-affiliated hostel during the summer. Fifty beds in male, female and co-ed sleeping areas, plus laundry facilities and breakfast at $18 per person per night – a few dollars more for non-HI members. Handy for the city centre. From the bus terminal, take bus #2 to Princess St, get off at *Burger King* and walk two blocks south; from the railway station, take bus #1 and follow the same directions.

Rosemount Inn B&B, 46 Sydenham St (☎613/531-8844 or 1-888/871-8444, fax 613/531-9722, *www.rosemountinn.com*). Occupying a handsome, old limestone villa with comely Italianate flourishes, the *Rosemount* has nine guestrooms, all en suite, decorated in period style. The breakfasts are delicious. ⑤.

Ramada Plaza Kingston Harbourfront Hotel, 1 Johnson St (☎613/549-8100 or 1-800/272-6232, fax 613/547-3241). Smart, chain hotel with standard-issue modern furnishings and fittings, but great views out over Lake Ontario and the marina. ⑦.

Secret Garden B&B, 73 Sydenham St (☎613/531-9884, *www.the-secret-garden.com*). One of Kingston's most enjoyable B&Bs, there are four extremely comfortable guestrooms here, all en suite and each decorated in immaculate style. The house itself is a fine Victorian building of timber and stone with verandas and porches, perky dormer windows and a splendid bay-windowed tower. Faces the slender limestone symmetries of Sydenham Street United Church. Recommended. ④.

The City Centre

The obvious place to start a visit is **City Hall** (free guided tours late May to Oct Mon–Fri 10am–4pm, plus Sat & Sun in July & Aug 11am–3pm; 30min), a copper-domed, stone extravagance which, with its imposing Neoclassical columns and portico, dominates the waterfront as was intended. The building was designed in the British Renaissance Tuscan Revival-style; a suitably grand structure for what was to be the Canadian Parliament. By the time the building was completed in 1844, however, Kingston had lost its capital status and – faced with colossal bills – the city council had to make some quick adjustments, filling the empty corridors with shops and stalls and even a saloon. Things are more sedate today, with municipal offices occupying most of the space, but the tour provides a fascinating insight into the development of the city and includes a trip up the **clock tower** via a magnificent circular stairway.

Back outside, the **Market Square**, in the shadow of City Hall, is home to an excellent open-air farmers' market on Tuesdays, Thursdays and Saturdays, while on Sundays the square is given over to craft and antiques stalls. Opposite, the site of the original French outpost is marked by the waterfront **Confederation Park**, whose manicured lawns run behind the harbour with its marina, squat, nineteenth-century Martello tower (see below) and the dock at the foot of Brock Street from where there are **cruises of the Thousand Islands**. These islands litter the St Lawrence River as it leaves Lake Ontario and range from tiny hunks of rock to much larger islands with thick forest and lavish second homes. It's a pretty cruise at any time of the year, but especially so in autumn when the leaves turn – though the cruises from Gananoque (see p.154) do have the scenic edge. Here in Kingston, there are several cruises to choose from, including the *Island Queen*, a replica steamboat (May–Oct 1–4 daily; 2hr; $15), and the *Island Belle* ferry boat (May–Oct, 1–4 daily; 1hr 30min; $14). In addition, the *Island Star* catamaran offers lunch and dinner cruises (May–Oct 1–2 daily; 3hr–3hr 30min; $34/54). The tourist office has the full list of cruises, but for the three mentioned contact Kingston 1000 Islands Cruises, 1 Brock St (☎613/549-5544, fax 549-1608, *www.1000islandscruises.on.ca*).

Back on dry land, it's a couple of minutes' walk from Confederation Park to Kingston's finest limestone building, the **Cathedral of St George** (June–Sept Mon–Thurs 10am–4pm, Fri 10am–7pm & Sat 10am–1pm; Oct–May Fri 4–7pm & Sun noon–1pm; free), at King Street and Johnson. Dating from the 1820s, the graceful lines of the cathedral, with its Neoclassical portico and dainty domes, are deceptively uniform for the church was remodelled on several occasions, notably after severe fire damage in 1899. The interior holds some delightful Tiffany stained-glass windows and a plain **memorial** to Molly Brant, a Mohawk leader and sister of Joseph Brant, whose loyalty to the British interest brought her here after the American War of Independence in 1783.

From the cathedral, it's a brief stroll to the main commercial drag, **Princess Street**, whose assorted shops, offices and cafés stretch up from the lakeshore. Alternatively, it's a short hop back to the waterfront and the **Marine Museum of the Great Lakes** (June–Oct daily 10am–5pm; Nov–May Mon–Fri 10am–4pm; $4.25), a somewhat dowdy accumulation of maritime bygones, where the shipbuilders' gallery is of some mild interest. Moored alongside is the unusual *Alexander Henry Bed and Breakfast* (see opposite).

Murney Tower Museum

From the Marine Museum, a longer stroll of about 800m leads west along the waterfront to the **Murney Tower Museum**, on the corner of Barrie Street and King Street East (mid-May to Aug daily 10am–5pm; $2). The most impressive of four such towers built during the Oregon Crisis of 1846–47 to defend the city's dockyards against an anticipated US attack, this one holds incidental military memorabilia including old weapons, uniforms and re-created nineteenth-century living quarters. The design of the tower, built as a combined barracks, battery and storehouse, was copied from a Corsican tower (at Martello Point) which had proved particularly troublesome to the British navy. A self-contained, semi-self-sufficient defensive structure with thick walls and a protected entrance, the Martello design proved so successful that towers like this were built throughout the empire, only becoming obsolete in the 1870s with advances in artillery technology. Incidentally, on Christmas Day 1885, members of the Royal Canadian Rifles regiment left the tower equipped with their field hockey sticks and a lacrosse ball, skidding round the frozen lake and thereby inventing the sport that has become a national passion.

West of the Centre: the Agnes Etherington Art Centre

Striking inland up Barrie Street, with City Park on the right, it's a ten-minute walk to the top of the park where the **Frontenac County Courthouse** of 1858 is another grand limestone pile whose whopping Neoclassical portico is fronted by a fanciful water fountain and surmounted by a copper dome. Head west from here, along Union Street, and you'll soon be in the midst of the **Queen's University** campus, whose various college buildings fan out in all directions. The place to aim for is the first-rate **Agnes Etherington Art Centre**, on the corner of University Avenue and Queen's Crescent (Tues–Fri 10am–5pm, Sat & Sun 1–5pm; $4). The gallery has an excellent reputation for its temporary exhibitions, so paintings are regularly rotated, but the first room (Room 1) usually kicks off in dramatic style with a vivid selection of Canadian Abstract paintings (1940–60), with French-speakers on one side, English on the other. Beyond, Room 2 is strong on the Group of Seven (see p.86), weighing in with Thomson's painterly *Autumn, Algonquin Park*, a striking *Evening Solitude* by Harris and the carpet-like, rolling fields of Lismer's *Quebec Village*; and Room 3 focuses on European paintings. Other exhibits to look out for are the Inuit prints of Kenojuak and Pitseolak – two of the best-known Inuit artists of modern times – heritage quilts from eastern Ontario, which date back to 1820, and an excellent collection of West African sculpture.

Bellevue House

Born in Glasgow, **Sir John A. Macdonald** (1815–91) emigrated to Canada in his youth, settling in Kingston, where he became a successful corporate lawyer, an MP – representing the town for well-nigh forty years – and ultimately prime minister (1867–73 and 1887–91). A shrewd and forceful man, Macdonald played a leading role in Confederation, arm-twisting here, charming there to ensure the grand plan went through. In the 1840s, Macdonald rented **Bellevue House** (daily: April–May & Sept 10am–5pm; June–Aug 9am–6pm; $3), 35 Centre St, a bizarrely asymmetrical, pagoda-shaped house, in the hope that the country air would improve the health of his wife, Isabella, whose tuberculosis was made worse by the treatment – laudanum. Isabella never returned to good health and died after years as an invalid, leaving Macdonald alone (with the bottle). Both the house and gardens have been restored to the period of the late 1840s when the Macdonalds lived here. Bellevue House is located to the west of the university campus, about 2km from the centre.

East Kingston: Old Fort Henry

The twin headlands to the east of downtown Kingston over the La Salle Bridge have long been used by the military. The first is home to the **Royal Military College**, the training academy for officers of all three services; the second **Old Fort Henry** (late May to late Sept daily 10am–5pm; $9.50; programme details on ☎613/542-7388), a large and imposing fortress with thick stone-and-earth ramparts built to keep the Americans at bay after the War of 1812. As it turned out, it was all a waste of time: Anglo-American relations improved and the fort never saw a shot fired in anger, so when the last garrison upped sticks at the end of the nineteenth century, the fortress fell into disrepair. Restored in 1938, the fort's focus is now the vast parade ground, which comes to life in summer, when students dress up in military gear and fill the fort with the smoke of muskets and cannons and the racket of bugles, drums and fifes. Everything on offer is aimed at families, and there's masses for kids to do, from parading for drill in miniature uniforms and helping with the gun salute, to participating in lessons in a Victorian schoolroom and doing the laundry. If this doesn't appeal you can explore the ramparts, with their vistas of Lake Ontario and the Thousand Islands, as well as the magazines, kitchens and officers' quarters, and the fort's collection of firearms, medals and military equipment. Proto-militarists can also double their fun by visiting the Royal Military College's **Fort Frederick** (late June to Aug daily 10am–5pm; donation), a Martello tower stuffed with the Douglas Arms' Collection.

Eating and drinking

For a city its size, Kingston has a reasonable number of good-quality **restaurants** as well as a healthy supply of inexpensive **cafés**, many of which prosper from the city's large student population. The town also has several lively British-style **pubs** and a modest live music scene: for **listings**, see the monthly *Key to Kingston*, available from major hotels, restaurants and the tourist office.

Cafés and restaurants

Chez Piggy, 68 Princess St at King St E (☎613/549-7673). Kingston's best-known restaurant is housed in restored stables dating from 1810. The patio is packed in summer and the interior has handcrafted pine and limestone walls. The menu has Thai, Vietnamese, South American, African and standard North American influences, with excellent lunch-time specials $7.

Curry Village, 169A Princess St (☎613/542-5010). Popular, reasonably priced Indian restaurant above a shoe shop. Just north of Bagot St. Reservations recommended.

Le Caveau, 354 King St E at Princess (☎613/547-1617). Cosy restaurant specializing in French cuisine. The seafood is especially good and the wine list extensive. Main courses $15–20.

Minos Restaurant, 248 Ontario St at Brock (☎613/548-4654). All the Greek favourites at this long-established downtown restaurant. Main courses $10–20.

Second Cup, 251 Princess St. Downtown branch of this reliable coffee-house chain.

Sleepless Goat, 91 Princess St at Wellington. Laidback bakery-cum-café serving good sandwiches, delicious breads and rolls, and great desserts at affordable prices.

White Mountain Ice-Cream, 176 Ontario St. Seriously rich home-made ice-cream and waffle cones. Try the White Mountain special – vanilla dotted with chocolate, pecan and maple brittle.

Windmills Café, 184 Princess St at Montreal. Amazing cakes and a wide-ranging menu at this agreeable café-restaurant, which serves up everything from tapas and pizzas to salads and noodles. There's a takeout deli round the corner on Montreal too.

Pubs and clubs

Kingston Brewing Company, 34 Clarence St. Arguably the best pub in town, serving natural ales and lagers brewed on the premises, and also bar food. The brewery is open to the public and there is also a beer garden.

KINGSTON TO OTTAWA VIA THE RIDEAU CANAL

Heading on from Kingston to Ottawa, the obvious route is east along Hwy 401 and then north up Hwy 416, a fast journey of around 175km. With more time, however, it's worth considering taking **Hwy 15** (and ultimately Hwy 7) inland from Kingston as this minor road follows much of the route of the **Rideau Canal**. Completed in 1832 after a mere six years' work, the 120-mile canal – and its 27 lock stations – cuts through the chunk of coniferous and deciduous forest, bogs, limestone plains and granite ridges that separate Ottawa and Kingston. It was intended to provide safe inland transport at a time of poor Anglo-American relations, but after the political situation improved it developed as an important route for regional commerce. The canal's construction led to the development of Bytown, renamed Ottawa in 1855, but in the second half of the nineteenth century the railways made it obsolete. Today, it is plied by holiday traffic and motorists visit its **locks**. The two most interesting are **Kingston Mills**, 12km inland from Kingston, and, even better, at **Johnson Falls**, about 50km from Kingston. At the latter, the complex includes four locks, a dam, a former blacksmith's forge and a defensible lockmaster's house.

Royal Oak, 331 King St E. One of Kingston's better English-style pubs, with darts and pool tables. Occasional live music.

Stages, 390 Princess St (☎613/547-3657). Popular nightclub with seven bars on five levels and a huge sunken dance floor. Features laser shows and live entertainment. Open until 3am on Fridays and Saturdays.

Tir Nan Óg, at the *Prince George Hotel*, 200 Ontario St. Opposite the tourist information office, this Irish pub was handcrafted in Ireland and the ceiling was swiped from a century-old Irish nunnery. The Guinness is good and there's live Celtic music a couple of nights a week. Also the starting point for the enjoyable **Haunted Walk of Kingston**, a 90-minute narrated stroll through the older parts of town (early May to Oct 1–2 daily except Wed; $10; ☎613/549-6366).

Toucan, 76 Princess St (☎613/544-1966). Student pub with excellent live music from blues to traditional Irish, and also bar food. Till 2am nightly.

The upper St Lawrence River and the Thousand Islands

To the east of Kingston, Hwy 401 and the prettier Hwy 2 – the Thousand Islands Parkway – strip along the northern shore of the **St Lawrence River**, whose island-studded waters were tricky-going until the 1950s when the US and Canadian governments created the **St Lawrence Seaway**. An extraordinarily ambitious project, the Seaway extends 3790km inland from the Atlantic by means of lakes, rivers and locks to the west end of Lake Superior. Fifteen locks were installed on the St Lawrence, each big enough to handle massive ocean-going freighters, whilst a string of dams harnessed the river's hydroelectric potential. But it all came at a price: the Seaway necessitated the relocation of many riverside towns, a process which one local newspaper bewailed with the headline "once again another patch of Ontario is sickled o'er with the pale cast of progress". There were long-term environmental costs too, with the ships transporting species previously unknown here on their hulls and in their bilge. What's more, the Seaway has been something of a flop, its decline related to the move towards road and air.

As it travels east, Hwy 2 cuts across rolling farmland and offers fleeting views of the region's scenic highlight, the **Thousand Islands**. Local aboriginal peoples called these tiny, lightly forested granite chunks Manitouana – "Garden of the Great Spirit" – in the belief they were created when petals of heavenly flowers were scattered on the river, and more prosaically the islands later gave their name to a salad dressing. Geologically, they form part of the Frontenac axis, a ridge of million-year-old rock that stretches down into New York State. The islands are seen to best advantage on a **cruise** and these are available at most riverside towns, though those from **Gananoque** are often rated the best. However, easily the prettiest town hereabouts is **Brockville**, an unassuming kind of place with several fine old buildings, though it is still very tempting to push on to Ottawa (see p.156), just 175km from Kingston.

With regard to public transport, there are fast and frequent **buses** along Hwy 401 and VIA **trains** shadow the north bank of the river too, on their way from Kingston to Montréal.

Gananoque

Some 30km east of Kingston, workaday **GANANOQUE** offers several types of Thousand Island boat **cruise**. The lead operator is Gananoque Boat Lines (☎613/382-2144, *www.ganboatline.com*), who provide one-hour (May to mid-Oct 3–8 daily; $11) and three-hour excursions (May to mid-Oct 3–8 daily; $17). Highlights of the cruise include a good look at Just Room Enough Island, with its single tiny home, and, at the other extreme, Millionaire's Row on Wellesley Island. The islands have long been a popular retreat for the well-heeled – Irving Berlin and Jack Dempsey, to name but two, were regular visitors – but it was George Boldt, the owner of New York's *Waldorf Astoria*, who distinguished himself by excess. In 1899, he bought one of the islands and reshaped it into a heart as a tribute to his wife – hence the name Heart Island. He then spent $2 million building the huge, turreted **Boldt Castle** (mid-May to mid-Oct daily 10am–5pm; $3.75) with material from around the world, but promptly abandoned it when his wife died, and he took his new salad-dressing recipe back to New York. The castle is open to the public and you can visit it on Gananoque Boat Lines' three-hour cruises, but note that the castle is in American waters, so take your passport if you're not a US citizen.

In the unlikely event you decide to stay in Gananoque, the **tourist office**, at 2 King St E (July & Aug daily 9am–7pm; Sept–June Mon–Fri 9am–5pm; ☎613/382-3250), has a long list of local **accommodation**. Amongst many **motels** and **inns**, two handy places are the *Blinkbonnie Motor Lodge*, 50 Main St (☎613/382-7272 or 1-800/265-7474, fax 613/382-4096; ③), one block from the dock, and the rather more comfortable *Victoria Rose*, on Hwy 2 at 279 King St W (☎613/382-3368, fax 382-8803; ④).

Brockville

Pushing on from Gananoque, it's just 50km east to **BROCKVILLE**, an amiable little town of just 22,000 souls whose pride and joy is its grand main square, which is overlooked by the rambling **County Courthouse** and no less than three Victorian **churches**. Brockville was founded in 1785 by United Empire Loyalists, but takes its name from Isaac Brock, the Canadian general who was killed near Niagara Falls during the War of 1812. The **Brockville Museum**, 5 Henry St (mid-May to mid-Oct Mon–Sat 10am–5pm, Sun 1–5pm; mid-Oct to mid-May Mon–Fri 10am–4.30pm; $1.50), traces the history of the town in entertaining detail. In particular, it features Brockville's role as a holding station for nineteenth-century immigrants who were –temporarily detained in enormous sheds on the waterfront Hospital Island. Other handsome Victorian buildings include **City Hall** and, to the east of the town centre, **Fulford Place**, 287 King St W (Wed, Sat & Sun 1–5pm; $2.50), a vast mansion built for George Taylor Fulford, who made his fortune with a cure-all remedy brilliantly –marketed as "Pink Pills for Pale People". However, most visitors skip the architecture in favour of a Thousand Island **cruise** with Brockville Thousand Islands Seaway Cruises (☎613/345-7333 or 1-800/353-3157, fax 613/345-6454, *www.1000islandscruises.com*). They provide one-hour (May–Oct 1–4 daily; $11) and three-hour excursions (May–June & Sept–Oct 1–2 weekly; July–Aug 2–4 daily; $17), which sail west to cover pretty much the same itinerary as boats departing Gananoque (see opposite).

It's easy enough to complete the cruise and look round Brockville in a long morning or afternoon, but the **tourist office** in City Hall, at 1 King St W (mid-June to Aug daily 8am–8pm; Sept to mid-June Mon–Fri 9am–4.30pm; ☎613/342-8772), does have a complete list of local **accommodation**. Two reliable options are the plush *Royal Brock Hotel*, 100 Stewart Blvd (☎613/345-1400 or 1-800/267-4428, fax 613/345-5402; ⑥), and the *Brockville Super 8 Motel*, 7789 Kent Blvd (☎613/345-3900 or 1-800/800-8000, fax 613/345-3953; ③).

Prescott

Once important as a deep-water port, pocket-sized **PRESCOTT**, 20km east of Brockville, was rendered pretty much obsolete by the St Lawrence Seaway, though it is at least close to the bridge over to Ogdensburg, New York, and this has saved some of its commercial bacon. A General Robert Prescott founded the town in 1810 with land granted to him in thanks for his efforts during the American Revolution, and locals raucously celebrate their Loyalist origins in the third week of July, when the ten-day Loyalist Days Festival includes the largest military pageant in Canada. The pageant takes place at **Fort Wellington National Historic Site**, beside Hwy 2 on the east side of town (mid-May to Sept daily 10am–5pm; ☎613/925-2896; $3). Like Kingston's Fort Henry, this fort guarded the vulnerable St Lawrence frontier and owes its present shape to a hurried refortification commissioned in the tense days following the War of 1812. The Americans never attacked and the fort soon fell into disrepair, though there was another spurt of imperial activity during the rebellion of 1837 when the bloody Battle of the Windmill was fought nearby, and again during the short-lived Irish-American Fenian raids of 1865. Today, the four original 1813 structures are surrounded by artillery-resistant earthworks, while the 1838 stone blockhouse contains a guardroom, armoury, powder magazine and barracks, all refurnished as of the mid-nineteenth century.

Just 5km east of Prescott, there's a choice of routes: Hwy 416 cuts north to Ottawa (see below), while Hwy 401 carries on east to pass the Upper Canada Village en route to Montréal.

Upper Canada Village

In the 1950s, the construction of the St Lawrence Seaway raised the river level, threatening many of the old buildings that dotted the river bank. The pick were painstakingly relocated to a purpose-built complex some 40km east of Prescott and this, the **Upper Canada Village** (mid-May to mid-Oct daily 9.30am–5pm; $12.75), has become one of the region's most popular attractions. Covering a 60-acre site, the village re-creates rural Ontario life as of 1860 and contains a wide range of buildings, from farmhouses and farm outhouses to a bakery, a parsonage, a church, a woollen factory, a saw mill and a blacksmiths. It is all very well done and the staff dress up in period gear to demonstrate traditional skills, producing cheeses, quilts, brooms, bread and cloth in exactly the same way as their pioneer ancestors. Finally, in the adjacent riverside park is the **Battlefield Monument** commemorating the Battle of Crysler Farm in 1813, when a small force of British and Canadian soldiers drove off American invaders; Crysler Farm is itself down below the monument underneath the water.

The village is easily accessible by public transport, as the Colonial Montréal–Toronto **bus** passes by the front gate.

Ottawa

The capital of the second biggest country on the planet, **OTTAWA** struggles with its reputation as a bureaucratic labyrinth of little charm and character. The problem is that many Canadians who aren't federal employees – and even some who are – blame the city for all the country's woes. All too aware of this, the Canadian government have spent lashings of dollars to turn Ottawa into "a city of urban grace in which all Canadians can take pride" – so goes the promotional literature, but predictably this very investment is often resented. Furthermore, the hostility is deeply rooted, dating back as far as 1857 when Queen Victoria, inspired by some genteel watercolours, declared Ottawa the capital, leaving Montréal and Toronto smarting at their rebuff.

In truth, Ottawa is neither grandiose nor tedious, but a lively cosmopolitan city of 330,000 with a clutch of outstanding **national museums**, a pleasant riverside setting and superb cultural facilities like the National Arts Centre, plus acres of parks and gardens and miles of bicycle and jogging paths. It also possesses lots of good **hotels** and **B&Bs** and a busy **café-bar** and **restaurant** scene – enough to keep the most diligent sightseer going for a day or three, maybe more. Here too, for once in English-speaking Ontario, Canada's bilingual laws make sense: Québec's Hull (see p.236) is just across the river and on the streets of Ottawa you'll hear as much French as English.

A brief history of Ottawa

The one-time hunting ground of the Algonkian-speaking Outaouais, **Ottawa** received its first recorded European visitor in 1613 in the shape of Samuel de Champlain. The French explorer pitched up, paused to watch his aboriginal guides make offerings of tobacco to the misty falls which he christened Chaudière (French for "cauldron") and then took off in search of more appealing pastures. Later, the **Ottawa River** became a major transportation route, but the Ottawa area remained no more than a camping spot until 1800, when **Philemon Wright** snowshoed up here along the frozen Ottawa River from Massachusetts. Wright founded a small settlement, which he called Wrightstown and subsequently Hull after his parents' birthplace in England. Aware that the British navy was desperate for timber, Wright then worked out a way of shifting the tall trees that surrounded him by squaring them off, tying them together and floating them as rafts down the river to Montréal. His scheme worked well and Hull was soon flourishing. Meanwhile, nothing much happened on the other side of the river until 1826 when the completion of the **Rideau Canal** (see box, p.153) linked the site of present-day Ottawa to Kingston and the St Lawrence River. The canal builders were commanded by **Lieutenant-Colonel John By** and it was he who gave his name to the new settlement, **Bytown**, which soon became a hard-edged lumber town characterized by drunken brawls and broken bones.

In 1855 Bytown relabelled itself **Ottawa** in a bid to become the capital of the Province of Canada, hoping that a change of name would relieve the town of its sordid reputation. As part of their pitch, the community stressed the town's location on the border of Upper and Lower Canada and its industrial prosperity. In the event, Queen Victoria granted their request, though this had little to do with their efforts and much more to do with her artistic tastes: the Queen had been looking at some romantic landscape paintings of the Ottawa area and decided this was the perfect spot for a new capital. Few approved and Canada's politicians fumed at the inconvenience – Sir Wilfred Laurier, for one, found it "hard to say anything good" about the place. Neither did the politicians enjoy the mockery heaped on them from south of the border with one American newspaper suggesting it would never be attacked as any "invader would inevitably get lost in the woods trying to find it".

Give or take the odd federal building – including the rambling Parliament – Ottawa remained a workaday town until the late 1940s, when the Paris city planner, Jacques Greber, was commissioned to beautify the city with a profusion of parks, wide avenues and tree-lined pathways. The scheme transformed the city and defined much of its current appearance, though nowadays Greber's green and open spaces also serve to confine a city centre packed with modern concrete-and-glass office blocks. Ottawa has municipal ambitions too, encapsulated by the creation of the **Capital Region**, which attempts to bolster its economy and raise its profile by welding together the Québec and Ontario settlements on either side of the Ottawa River.

Arrival, information and city transport

Ottawa's **Macdonald-Cartier International Airport** is located about 15km south of the city. From the airport, a Hotel Shuttle bus runs to various downtown hotels; it leaves every half-hour at a cost of $9 one-way, $14 return. A taxi from the airport to downtown will set you back about $20. Ottawa's **train station** is on the southeastern outskirts at

200 Tremblay Rd, about 5km from the centre. There are direct VIA Rail trains to and from Brockville, Kingston, Montréal and Toronto. Local bus #95 goes downtown from the train station; the same journey by taxi will rush you approximately $15. Long-distance **buses** arrive at and depart from the bus station at 265 Catherine St on the corner of Kent just off the Queensway. Take local bus #4 to get further downtown.

The **Capital Infocentre**, 90 Wellington St (daily: mid-May to Aug 8.30am–9pm; Sept to mid-May 9am–5pm; ☎613/239-5000, *www.capcan.ca*), is handily located right opposite the Parliament Buildings. It's a busy place, but the staff will help you find accommodation and hand you masses of free literature, including city maps, transport maps, a *Where* listings magazine and a useful *Visitor Guide*.

Most of Ottawa's important attractions as well as many of its better restaurants, bars and hotels are clustered in the downtown area within comfortable walking distance of Confederation Square. If you're venturing further afield, however, you may need to use a **bus**. OC Transpo (☎741-4390) provides a comprehensive network of bus services across Ottawa and its suburbs, while STO buses (☎770-3242) cover Hull and the north side of the river. The hub of the OC Transpo system is the **Central Transitway**, which runs from the Mackenzie King Bridge along Albert Street (one-way west) and Slater Street (one-way east). STO buses leave for Hull from outside the Rideau Centre at the west end of Rideau Street, between Nicolas and Sussex. Key buses operate from 5am or 6am to around midnight daily. **Ticket prices** are very reasonable and start at just 80¢, but for many visitors the best deal is a **DayPass** ($5), which allows unlimited travel on the OC Transpo system for one day. Tickets can be bought at corner stores, the tourist office and many hotels, or paid for on the bus itself – exact fare only. The same applies to the DayPass, except you pay a $1 surcharge for buying it on the bus. If you're travelling on an ordinary ticket and need to change buses to complete your journey, ask for a (free) transfer at the point of embarkation. Incidentally, to reach Hull's prime attraction, the Musée Canadien des Civilisations (see p.236), take OC Transpo bus #8 from the Central Transitway.

As regards to **taxis**, these can only be boarded at ranks, which are mostly located outside major hotels and nightspots. **Cycling** is popular in Ottawa too – the city boasts over 100km of cycling trail – and there are several cycle-hire companies, the most central of which is Rent-a-Bike, 1 Rideau St, at the back of the *Château Laurier* hotel (☎241-4140).

> The Ottawa telephone code is ☎613.

Accommodation

As the federal honeypot, Ottawa hosts dozens of business conferences and, although there are hundreds of rooms in the city, things can still get tight – with **hotel** prices rising accordingly. At other times – especially when parliament is in recess and at the weekend – it's much more of a buyer's market and even the poshest hotels offer big discounts. That said, the best bet for a reasonably priced room is in an **inn** or **B&B**, the pick of which offer prime lodgings in old houses of distinction close to the centre. If you stick to the list opposite you should find somewhere, but if not the tourist office (see above) will assist, but note that they won't actually make a booking. Alternatively, you might approach the Ottawa Bed and Breakfast Association, 18 Queen Elizabeth Driveway (☎563-0161 or 1-800/461-7889), who have a reasonable range of properties (from ③) on their books. The cheapest beds in town are at two **hostels**, both of which are open year-round and right downtown, and there are inexpensive **student rooms** too.

Hotels, inns and motels

Albert House Inn, 478 Albert St at Bay (☎236-4479 or 1-800/267-1982, fax 237-9079, *albertinn@ibm.net*). Occupying a good-looking Victorian villa with a sweeping portico, the inn has seventeen en-suite guestrooms, each of which is pleasantly furnished. Full breakfast included. Light sleepers may prefer the rooms at the back, away from busy Albert St. ③.

Capital Hill Hotel and Suites, 88 Albert St (☎235-1413 or 1-800/463-7705, fax 235-6047). This smart, high-rise hotel is furnished in brisk, modern style and all its 150 rooms are spacious and comfortable. Handy downtown location, just off Confederation Square. Very competitive prices. ④.

Château Laurier, 1 Rideau St (☎241-1414 or 1-800/866-5577, fax 562-7030). This superb hotel, Ottawa's finest, has pretty much everything. It was opened in 1912 as a prestige railway hotel for the Grand Trunk Pacific Railway, whose president, Charles Hayes, lavished millions on its construction. A fine example of the French Renaissance – or château – style, the exterior boasts a forest of copper-clad turrets, spires and towers. Inside, the grand public areas boast marble floors, high ceilings, chandeliers and soaring columns, plus extravagantly embossed lifts. The rooms themselves are not quite as grand, but they are thoroughly comfortable and the best offer delightful views over the river. ⑥.

Days Inn Downtown, 319 Rideau St (☎789-5555 or 1-888/789-4949, fax 789-6196). Nothing special perhaps, but this reliable chain motel offers good quality accommodation at reasonable prices in a downtown location. ⑤.

Doral Inn, 486 Albert St at Bay (☎230-8055 or 1-800/263-6725, fax 237-9660, *info@doralottawa.com*). Forty guestrooms and suites with straightforward modern furnishings in this well-maintained Victorian house. Continental breakfast and swimming pool. ④.

Lord Elgin Hotel, 100 Elgin St at Laurier Ave W (☎235-3333 or 1-800/267-4298, fax 235-3223). Occupying a fine château-style-meets-Art-Deco 1940s high-rise close to Confederation Square, this classy hotel has comfortable rooms decked out with crisp, modern furnishings. Reasonable prices and discounts on the weekend. ⑥.

Novotel Ottawa, 33 Nicholas St (☎230-3033, fax 760-4765). This hotel doesn't win any beauty contests – it's overshadowed by a hulking brick high-rise – but the public areas are done out in sharp, modernistic style and the 280 rooms are tastefully and cheerfully decorated; the service is excellent too. Downtown location. ⑥.

Quality Hotel Downtown Ottawa, 290 Rideau St (☎789-7511 or 1-800/544-4444, fax 789-2434). Spick-and-span chain hotel right downtown, with full facilities and comfort. ⑤.

Bed and Breakfasts

Australis Guest House, 35 Marlborough Ave (☎ and fax 235-8461, *waters@intranet.ca*). Straightforward Australian-run B&B with three rooms in an older house about 2km southeast of Parliament Hill. Price includes full delicious breakfast. ③.

Brighton House, 308 1st Ave (☎233-7777, *brighton.bb@sympatico.ca*). In a leafy residential area about 3km south of Parliament Hill, this charming B&B – one of the city's most appealing – offers six, en-suite guestrooms in a 1920s house. Each of the rooms is cozily furnished and the breakfasts are outstanding. Highly recommended. ⑤.

Gasthaus Switzerland Inn, 89 Daly Ave at Cumberland (☎237-0335 or 1-888/663-0000, fax 594-3327, *www.gasthausswitzerlandinn.com*). Twenty-two, en-suite rooms in this unassuming three-storey inn. Central location. ③.

L'Auberge du Marché, 87 Guiges Ave (☎241-6610 or 1-800/465-0079). In the heart of Byward Market, this extremely appealing B&B occupies a modest two-storey nineteenth-century brick house, whose interior has been immaculately renovated in sympathetic style – all pastel colours and wood floors. Often full, and very popular, the B&B has four air-conditioned bedrooms and serves great breakfasts too. ③.

Paterson House, 500 Wilbrod St (☎565-4241 or 1-877/385-5350, fax 565-6546, *www.patersonhouse.com*). Doubling as the Maharishi Vedic Health Centre, this is Ottawa's most luxurious B&B, housed in a handsome stone mansion that was built in a hybrid Neo-Gothic-cum-Renaissance style for a certain Senator Paterson in 1901. Each of the four guestrooms is a model of plush comfort – and this is reflected in the price. In a residential cul-de-sac at the east end of Wilbrod about 3km east of Parliament Hill. ⑥.

Hostels and student rooms

Ottawa Backpackers Inn, 203 York St (☎241-3402 or 1-888/394-0334, *info@ottawahostel.com*). Spartan 35-room hostel in the Byward Market area. Self-catering facilities, Internet access and linen supplied. $17 per night in four- and six-bed dormitories.

Ottawa International Hostel, 75 Nicholas St at Daly (☎235-2595 or 1-800/663-5777, fax 235-9202, *wkirkpatrick@hostellingintl.on.ca*). Stay in cells complete with bars on the windows in Ottawa's nineteenth-century jail now converted into an HI hostel. The solitary confinement area is now a laundry, but Death Row remains the same with its 1m-by-2m cells and gallows. There are a couple of single rooms, but most of the 150 beds are in four-, five-, and six-bed rooms. Members pay $17 per night, nonmembers $21. The hostel is handily located downtown, just south of Rideau St's Rideau Shopping Centre.

University of Ottawa, 100 Université (☎564-5400). From May to August, student rooms in the Stanton Residence, on the University of Ottawa campus off Nicolas St, are rented out to visitors. Double rooms cost $40, singles $35 – $10 or so less for students. The campus has sports and laundry facilities, a pool and café and is located about 1km southeast of Parliament Hill.

The City

Ottawa's major sights are clustered on the steep, south banks of the Ottawa River to either side of the Rideau Canal. It's here you'll find the monumental Victorian architecture of **Parliament Hill**, the outstanding art collection of the **National Gallery**, the military memorabilia of the **Canadian War Museum**, the imposing **Notre Dame Basilica** and **Byward Market**, the hub of the restaurant and bar scene. Many visitors stop there, but there are a clutch of other, lesser attractions too, beginning with the **Laurier House**, packed with the possessions of the former prime minister William Lyon Mackenzie King and located 1km or so east of the centre. Northeast of the centre, on the far side of the Rideau River, is the ritzy suburb of **Rockcliffe**, home to both the governor-general's mansion, **Rideau Hall**, and the **National Aviation Museum**.

Parliament Hill

Perched on the limestone bluff of Parliament Hill, overlooking the Ottawa River, Canada's **Parliament Buildings** have, with their pointed windows and overweening clock tower, a distinctly ecclesiastical air – though that certainly didn't overawe the original workmen, who urinated on the copper roof to speed up the oxidization process. Comprising a trio of sturdy neo-Gothic structures, the complex was begun in 1859 after the land was purchased from the British army, who had plonked a barracks here during the construction of the Rideau Canal. **Centre Block** (guided tours: mid-May to Aug Mon–Fri 9am–7.30pm, Sat & Sun 9am–4.30pm; Sept to mid-May daily 9am–3.30pm; free), home of the Senate and the House of Commons, dominates proceedings, though it is actually a replacement for the original building, which was destroyed by fire in 1916. This second structure was supposed to be the same as its predecessor, but it ended up about twice the size. The **Peace Tower**, rising from the middle of the facade, was added in 1927 as a memorial to Canadians who served in World War I – the floor is paved with stone brought from the battlefields of Europe. Highlights of the guided tour include a quick gambol round the **House of Commons**, where the Speaker's chair is made of English oak from Westminster Hall and from Nelson's ship *Victory*, and the red-carpeted **Senate** with its murals of scenes from World War I surmounted by a beautiful gilded ceiling. At the back of the Centre Block is the **Library**, the only part of the building to have survived the fire; the circular design and the richly carved wooden galleries make this the most charming part of the building. The **debates** in both the House of Commons and the Senate are open to the public, who can observe proceedings from the visitors' galleries – a white light at the top of the Peace Tower indicates when Parliament is in session. Passes are required and are issued by security at the main

Peace Tower entrance. For information about Senate debates, call ☎992-4791. For the House of Commons call ☎992-4793, which is also the number to call for details of Parliament's liveliest debate, held during **Question Period**, when the Opposition interrogates the Prime Minister.

Flanking Centre Block are **West Block** (no public access) and **East Block** (July & Aug daily 10am–5pm; free), where the guided tour pops into four Confederation-era rooms: the original Governor General's office, the offices of Sir John A. Macdonald and Sir George Étienne Cartier, and the Privy Council Chamber. Costumed guides provide the history. The manicured lawns surrounding the Parliament Buildings are dotted with **statues** of the great and the good with two of the more interesting occupying a tiny hillock just to the west of Centre Block. Here, Queen Victoria has been stuck on a plinth guarded by a lion and offered laurels from below, whilst Lester Pearson lounges in an armchair, the epitome of the self-confident statesman. Round the back of Centre Block, there are pleasant views across the Ottawa River to Hull (see p.236) and of the Library's handsome design.

Two events pull the tourist crowds onto Parliament Hill, beginning with the **Changing of the Guard** when the Governor General's Foot Guards and Grenadier Guards march onto the Hill dressed in full ceremonial uniform – bright-red tunics and bearskins (late June to late Aug daily between 9.30am and 10am). The second is a free summer-evening **sound and light show**, illustrating Canada's history (June to early Sept French and English performances nightly; they alternate which goes first). In summer, a white Infotent goes up in front of West Block and has tickets for all the tours and information on what's going on.

Wellington Street and around

Along the river behind West Block are more federal buildings, château-style monoliths with perky dormer windows and green-copper roofs that culminate in the **Supreme Court of Canada building**, a modern edifice built to match its predecessors. From here, turn inland and you'll soon reach Wellington Street and then Sparks Street, where the **Sparks Street Mall** – one of the country's earliest pedestrianized shopping streets – runs from Metcalfe to Lyon. Perhaps inevitably, it looks jaded today, despite some serious money being put in to jazz it up. The main reason to stray into this part of town is to visit the **Currency Museum**, 245 Sparks St (May–Aug Mon–Sat 10.30am–5pm, Sun 1–5pm; Sept–April Tues–Sat 10.30am–5pm, Sun 1–5pm; free), housed in the old HQ of the Bank of Canada. When they expanded their premises, the bank encased the original 1937 stone building within their new offices, which were themselves enclosed by two green-glass towers with an indoor jungle-like garden court. Within the garden, in front of the museum, is a huge Yap stone, a symbol of wealth in the South Pacific; such stones usually remain at the bottom of the sea, their possession simply changing hands among the islanders by agreement. Inside the museum the stress is on Canadian currencies, from the small beads and shells known as wampum through to playing cards, beaver pelts and modern banknotes.

Confederation Square and the Rideau Canal

The eastern end of the Sparks Street Mall empties into the triangular **Confederation Square**, a breezy open space dominated by the magnificent **National War Memorial**, in which a soaring stone arch is surmounted by representations of liberty and peace. Down below, a swirling, finely executed bronze of 1926 depicts returning service men and women passing through the arch – from war to peace – and manages to convey both their exultation and sorrow. On the east side of the square is the complex of low concrete buildings that houses the **National Arts Centre** (see p.169) and this steps down to the **Rideau Canal**, which in winter becomes the world's longest skating rink, with hot chocolate and muffin stands providing sustenance for the skaters. Steps away,

DOWNTOWN OTTAWA

0   250 m

△ Rideau Hall

ACCOMMODATION

Albert House Inn	8
Capital Hill Hotel and Suites	11
Chateau Laurier	3
Days Inn Downtown	5
Doral Inn	9
Gasthaus Switzerland Inn	7
L'Auberge du Marché	1
Lord Elgin Hotel	12
Novotel Ottawa	6
Ottawa Backpackers Inn	2
Ottawa International Hostel	10
Quality Hotel	4
University of Ottawa	13

Musée Canadien
des Civilisations

HULL

Nepean
Point

Royal Mint

War Museum

Ottawa River

National
Gallery

Notre Dame Basilica

Major's
Hill
Park

Bytown
Museum

Locks

Parliament
Buildings

Centre
Block

East
Block

West
Block

Canadian Museum of
Contemporary Photography

Byward
Market

Currency Museum

Conference Centre

National
Arts Centre

Rideau
Centre

Rideau Canal

MACKENZIE KING BRIDGE

ST ANDREW ST
GUIGUES AVE
ST PATRICK STREET
MURRAY STREET
CLARENCE STREET
YORK STREET
GEORGE STREET
RIDEAU STREET

WELLINGTON STREET
SPARKS STREET MALL
QUEEN STREET
ALBERT STREET
SLATER STREET
LAURIER AVENUE
LAURIER AVENUE

Laurier House (2 km)

directly below Parliament Hill, the canal joins the Ottawa River by means of a flight of **locks**, beside which is the **Bytown Museum** (April–Nov Mon & Wed–Sat 10am–4pm, Sun noon–4pm; $5), Ottawa's oldest building, where military supplies were stored during the construction of the canal. Here, a short video display explains the history of the waterway, while the rest of the museum features assorted Ottawan memorabilia, including some of Colonel By's belongings, and temporary exhibitions. During the summer, canal **boat trips** leave from the top of the locks, river trips from the bottom. There are several operators, but Paul's Boat Lines (☎225-6781) is as good as any, charging $12 for an hour-long canal cruise, $14 for the river. There are departures every couple of hours or so.

From the east side of the locks, steps lead up to the **Château Laurier Hotel** (see p.159) and the adjacent **Canadian Museum of Contemporary Photography** (May–Aug Mon, Tues & Fri–Sun 11am–5pm, Wed 4–8pm, Thurs 11am–8pm; Sept–April Wed & Fri–Sun 11am–5pm, Thurs 11am–8pm; donation). The collection numbers around 160,000 photographs, which are used for research as well as being displayed in changing exhibitions. Across the street rise the slender columns of the old railway station, now recycled as a **Conference Centre**.

Sussex Drive and Major's Hill Park

From the *Château Laurier Hotel*, it's a short stroll east to **Sussex Drive**, whose southern section is one of Ottawa's oldest streets: the stone buildings between George and St Patrick hark back to Ottawa's pioneer days and now house expensive shops and galleries. Nearby **Major's Hill Park** was the area chosen by Colonel By as the site of his home so he could overlook the progress of the canal – the extant foundations bear a plaque attesting to its history. The park has a fine setting, its peace disturbed only by the **Noon Day Gun** (except Sun, so as not to disturb churchgoers), a tradition introduced in 1869 to regulate the postal service. Major's Hill Park leads towards **Nepean Point**, an area of land that juts out into the Ottawa River, with excellent views of the Chaudière Falls, Hull and the Laurentian Mountains.

The National Gallery of Canada

In the area between Nepean Point and Sussex Drive rises the magnificent **National Gallery of Canada** (May to mid-Sept daily 10am–6pm, Thurs till 8pm; mid-Sept to April Wed–Sun 10am–5pm, Thurs till 8pm; free), designed by Moshe Safdie to reflect the turrets and pinnacles of the Parliament Library. The collection was founded in 1880 by the Marquis of Lorne, the governor general of the time, who persuaded members of the Royal Canadian Academy to donate a work to the government. Over the next century artworks were gathered from all over the world, resulting in a collection that now contains more than 25,000 pieces exhibited on two levels – Level 1 and Level 2. The gallery also holds world-class temporary exhibitions. Free maps are issued at the reception desk and the gallery shop sells a useful National Gallery Guide for $5.

THE CANADIAN GALLERIES

Predictably, the **Canadian Galleries**, laid out in roughly chronological succession on Level One, are the finest in the building, following the history of Canadian painting from the mid-eighteenth century to the mid-twentieth. They begin with religious art from Québec, including a gilded high altar by Paul Jourdain from Longueuil, followed by a room showing the emergence of secular art in the early nineteenth century, with paintings by immigrant artists trained in Europe. The most notable of these was Joseph Légaré, who was not only a painter but also a politician and nationalist – his *Cholera Plague, Québec*, is a fine example of his fastidiously romantic work. For popularity, though, none could match Cornelius Krieghoff, who could turn his hand to anything requested by his patrons from the emerging middle classes – as illustrated by his *Winter Landscape* and *White Horse Inn by Moonlight*. Next comes the gallery's most intriguing exhibit, the Rideau Street Chapel, rebuilt piece by intricate piece after it was threatened by demolition in 1972. Designed in 1887 by the architect and priest Canon Georges Bouillon for a convent school in Ottawa, it has slender cast-iron columns supporting a fan-vaulted ceiling – one of the few examples of its kind in North America. Contained in the chapel is a collection of silver and wooden church sculptures from Québec.

The growth of the Maritimes and Upper Canada during the nineteenth century is depicted in the room that follows. John Poad Drake's *Port of Halifax* and John O'Brien's dramatic depictions of storm-tossed frigates illustrate the importance of the sea trade in this period, while the native population are shown in the forceful portraits of Paul Kane, Canada's first artist-explorer. Also here is the unique Croscup room from Nova Scotia. Once the living room of a shipping family, it is covered in murals that juxtapose images from mid-nineteenth-century North America and Europe – portraits of Micmac Indians next to bagpipe-playing Scots and so forth.

The construction of the railroads enabled artists to explore the wilder zones of Canada, a development encapsulated in Lucius O'Brien's *Sunrise on the Saguenay*. However, painters of this period were still in thrall to European masters – the Royal

Canadian Academy of Arts sent its students to Paris to complete their training – and the influence of Europe remained unshakeable right into the twentieth century, as shown by the impressionistic work of Cullen and Suzor-Côte, and the sombre rural scenes of George A. Reid and Homer Watson, inspired by the Dutch and Barbizon school.

However, with the **Group of Seven** (see box, p.86) a purely Canadian style emerged, which aimed to capture the spirit of the northern landscape, rather than trying to depict vast vistas in the European style. The Group was inspired by the work of contemporary Scandinavian painters, who were wrestling with similar problems of scale on the other side of the Atlantic. The first room dedicated to their works concentrates on their apprenticeship under Tom Thomson, whose startling *The Jack Pine* could be taken as the Group's clarion call – trees, often windswept or dead, are a constant symbol in the Group's paintings of Canada's *terre sauvage*. Using rapid, brash, often brutal brushstrokes, their works are faithful less to the landscape itself than to the emotions it evoked – Lawren Harris's *North Shore, Lake Superior* and J.E.H. Macdonald's *The Solemn Land* are good awestruck examples.

Following Macdonald's death in 1932, the Group of Seven formed the Canadian Group of Painters, embracing all Canadian artists of the time whatever their style. Initially landscape remained the predominant genre, but the effects of the Depression forced sociopolitical subjects to the fore – *Ontario Farm House* by Carl Schaefer turns a landscape into a social statement, while Jack Humphrey, Miller Brittain and Sam Borenstein depict the harsh reality of urban environments.

A subsequent section focuses on abstract works produced in Montréal from the 1940s to the 1970s. Abstraction was first explored by the Montréal Automatistes, whose emphasis on the expressive qualities of colour was rejected by the Platiciens, with whom geometrical and analytical forms were a preoccupation. Both groups are represented here, as are postwar artists from Vancouver and Toronto – like William Ronald, known for aggressive images such as *The Hero*. The last rooms contain temporary exhibitions of works from the 1950s.

THE CONTEMPORARY ART COLLECTION

The **Contemporary Art Collection**, on Levels 1 and 2, spans the years between 1960 and 1980, and again shows Canadian artists looking for a lead outside their country. The shadow of New York's Abstract Expressionists falls over Charles Gagnon's *Cassation/Open/Ouvert*, while the genealogy of mixed-media pieces like Jeff Wall's *The Destroyed Rooms* becomes clearer when you get to the collection of American contemporary art. Highlights here include Andy Warhol's *Brillo* sculpture, George Segal's life-size assemblage *The Gas Station* and Carl Andre's minimalist *Lever* – a line of firebricks.

THE EUROPEAN GALLERIES

The **European galleries**, situated on Level Two, begin with pieces from the workshops of Duccio in Siena and Giotto in Florence, accompanied by Filippino Lippi's *Triumph of Mordecai* and *Ester at the Palace Gate*, painted for chests that contained a bride's dowry, as well as a fine Bronzino *Portrait of a Man*. Northern European art in the fifteenth and sixteenth centuries is also represented primarily by religious art – note Quentin Matys's abrasive *Crucifixion*, with Jerusalem looking decidedly like a Flemish town circled by ramparts.

The collection of works from seventeenth-century Europe is particularly impressive: apart from Bernini's sculpture of his patron Pope Urban VIII, there's Claude Lorrain's *Landscape with a Temple of Bacchus*, an *Entombment* by Rubens, Rembrandt's sumptuous *Heroine from the Old Testament* and Van Dyck's *Suffer the Little Children to Come Unto Me*, an early, finely observed work that includes portraits thought to be of Rubens and his family. Venetian genre paintings include Canaletto's elegaic *Campo di Rialto* and Guardi's *Santa Maria Della Salute*. From Britain in the eighteenth century there are portraits by Reynolds and Gainsborough, and Romney's *Joseph Brant (Thayendanegea)*, a portrait of a Mohawk chief on a visit to London to discuss the native involvement in the American Revolution with George III. Also here is *The Death of General Wolfe* by Benjamin West, an American who became George III's official painter. West depicts Wolfe in a Christ-like pose, lying wounded and surrounded by his adjutants, and the painting made Wolfe a British hero.

The nineteenth-century selection is basically a show of minor paintings by great artists: Delacroix's romantic *Othello and Desdemona*, Corot's orderly *The Bridge at Narni*, Constable's *Salisbury Cathedral from the Bishop's Grounds* and Turner's *Mercury and Argus*, with a sunset that anticipates his future masterpieces. In stark contrast, the gritty realism of a later generation of European painters is well represented by Courbet's *The Cliffs at Étretat* and Millet's *The Pig Slaughter*, though tranquillity is soon restored by Monet's *Waterloo Bridge: The Sun through the Fog,* beautifying London's notorious fog, and two canvases by Pissarro. Van Gogh's *Iris* and Cézanne's *Forest* are the only worthy Post-Impressionist works.

American art takes over in the following room, residence of Barnet Newman's *Voice of Fire,* the very mention of which causes some Canadians to break out in a cold sweat – not because of its artistic significance but because it cost $1.76 million. The artist intended the 5.5-metre-high piece to give the viewer a "feeling of his own totality, of his own separateness, of his own individuality, and at the same time of his connection to others, who are also separate"; unfortunately the purchase of the painting caused a furore, with one Manitoba Tory MP ranting that it could have been "done in ten minutes with two cans of paint and two rollers". The same room contains minor works by Jackson Pollock and Mark Rothko.

The final galleries have works from twentieth-century Europe, a diverse and high-class assembly that includes the disturbing *Hope I* by Gustav Klimt, Matisse's *Nude on a Yellow Sofa*, Francis Bacon's macabre *Study for Portrait No. 1*, and pieces by Picasso, Léger, Epstein, Mondrian, Dali and Duchamp.

INUIT ART

Level 2 contains three more sections – the Asian Galleries, three rooms devoted to Prints, Drawings and Photographs and one room holding **Inuit art**. The latter includes *The Enchanting Owl* by Kenojuak, whose flamboyant depictions of fantasy birds are the most famous of the Inuit works on display. The **Photograph** section displays a changing selection from the gallery's 17,000 photographs, covering the entire history of photography from its invention in 1835 to today.

The Canadian War Museum, Notre-Dame and the Byward Market

Next door to the gallery, surrounded by tanks and cannons, is the **Canadian War Museum** (May to early Oct daily 9.30am–5pm, Thurs till 8pm; early Oct to April Tues–Sun 9.30am–5pm, Thurs till 8pm; $4, free Thurs 4–8pm), the largest military collection in the country. One of the main exhibits is "Hitler's Limousine" – a Grosser Mercedes Model 770 W 150 Type II Convertible to be precise – which comes complete with bullet holes allegedly the result of Allied strafing. Other exhibits include a mock-up of a World War I trench, a gallery of medals and insignias, an intricate frigate constructed out of matchsticks by a bored sailor, and an arsenal of weapons from Indian clubs to machine guns. Close by, further up Sussex Drive, is the castellated **Royal Canadian Mint** (daily 9am–5pm, with extended hours June–Aug; $2), where you can view different aspects of currency production and design – though the printing and the minting is now done in Winnipeg.

Doubling back down Sussex Drive, opposite the National Gallery is the capital's Catholic cathedral, the plain-looking **Notre Dame Basilica** (daily 7am–6pm; free).

Completed in 1890, it took fifty years to build and is Ottawa's oldest church. Inside, the altar is surrounded by over one hundred wooden sculptures – some with a kitschy marble finish – many of which were created by the sculptors who worked on the Parliament Buildings.

Since the 1840s the **Byward Market**, just east of Sussex and north of Rideau Street, has been a centre for the sale of farm produce, but in the last few years it has become Ottawa's hippest district. The 1927 Byward Market building has been renovated to house the **Ottawa Arts Exchange**, whose arts and crafts merchandise spills out onto the streets to merge with market stalls selling a variety of wares from ethnic gear to fresh fruit and vegetables. Most of Ottawa's best restaurants, cafés and bars are located here and during the day the area is busy with shoppers and buskers; at night it's buzzing until 2am, closing time at the bars.

The Laurier House

About 2km east of Byward Market is the **Laurier House**, 335 Laurier Ave E (April–Sept Tues–Sat 9am–5pm, Sun 2–5pm; Oct–March Tues–Sat 10am–5pm, Sun 2–5pm; $2.50), former home of prime ministers Sir Wilfred Laurier and William Lyon Mackenzie King. Laurier, Canada's first French-speaking prime minister, served from 1896 to 1911, while Mackenzie King, his self-proclaimed "spiritual son", was Canada's longest-serving (1921–30 and 1935–48). Notoriously pragmatic, King enveloped his listeners in a fog of words through which his political intentions were barely discernible. The perfect illustration – and his most famous line – was "Not necessarily conscription, but conscription if necessary", supposedly a clarification of his plans at the onset of World War II. Even more famous than his obfuscating rhetoric was his personal eccentricity. His fear that future generations would view him as the heir of his grandfather William Lyon Mackenzie – who in the 1830s led rebellions in Upper Canada – eventually led him into spiritualism: he held regular seances to tap the advice of great dead Canadians, including Laurier, who allegedly communicated to him through his pet dog.

The house is dominated by King's possessions, including his crystal ball and a portrait of his obsessively adored mother, in front of which he placed a red rose every day. Other mementos include the programme Abraham Lincoln held the night of his assassination, a painting by Rogier van der Weyden and a guest book signed by Churchill, Roosevelt, de Gaulle, Nehru, the Dionne quintuplets (see p.174) and Shirley Temple. The house also contains a reconstruction of a study belonging to prime minister Lester B. Pearson, who was awarded the Nobel peace prize for his role in the 1956 Arab–Israeli dispute. Pearson also had a stab at devising a new flag for his country and although it was rejected the mock-up he commissioned, with blue stripes at either end to symbolize the oceans, is on display.

Laurier Avenue East eventually meets the **Rideau River**, which is escorted by walkways and bicycle paths to the **Rideau Falls**, whose twin cataracts are separated by Green Island – the site of the Ottawa City Hall, an unattractive building built in the 1950s. The Falls themselves were once enveloped in an industrial complex, which has now been cleared away to allow excellent views across the river to Hull.

Rockcliffe

Northeast of the Falls lies **Rockcliffe**, Ottawa's ritziest district, a tranquil haven colonized by parliamentary bigwigs and diplomats – and in the evening by local lovers, who canoodle in the pavilions on the river shore, looking across to the Gatineau Hills. The prime minister resides here too, in a stately stone mansion barely visible through the trees on the lakeshore at 24 Sussex Drive (no public access), while on the opposite side of Sussex is the stately, Neoclassical **Rideau Hall** (free guided tours, call ☎998-7113 for schedule), which has been the home of Canada's governors general since Confederation. The hall's gardens of maples and fountains are usually open from 9am to one hour before sunset – but call ahead if you want to be sure.

At the east end of Rockcliffe, 4km from downtown, is the huge hangar of the **National Aviation Museum** (daily: May–Aug 9am–5pm, Thurs till 9pm; Sept–April 10am–5pm, Thurs till 9pm; $6, free Thurs 5–8pm), served by bus #198. Highlights include a replica of the *Silver Dart*, which made the first powered flight in Canada in 1909; it flew for a full nine minutes, a major achievement for a contraption that seems to be made out of spare parts and old sheets. There are also bombers from both world wars and some excellent videos, including a programme to simulate a helicopter flight and a virtual reality hang-glider.

Eating and drinking

As you might expect of a capital city, Ottawa has a good range of **restaurants**, some geared firmly to the expense account, but the majority informal, reasonably priced affairs – surprisingly so considering the amount of political money floating around. Indeed, a main course and a drink should rarely cost you more than $25. Ethnic restaurants are commonplace – from Italian through Mexican, Chinese and Spanish – and although there is no distinctive Ottawa cuisine as such, the city's chefs borrow strongly from the French-Québecois tradition – Québec is, after all, just across the river. The trendiest joints are in the Byward Market area, but there are also a number of good places in the few blocks to the south of Parliament Hill, and a small Chinatown on Somerset West and Bronson. In addition, Ottawa has sprouted dozens of **café-bars**, some offering little more than glorified bar food, but many dipping into Asian, French and Italian cuisines to provide excellent food at very affordable prices – $10–15 should see you fixed in all but the priciest of places. These café-bars have dented Ottawa's **bar and pub** scene, but there is still a reasonable range of downtown drinking places with a particular concentration in and around the Byward Market, which heaves with revellers on the weekend. Finally, a word about **snack and fast food**. Chip vans are something of an institution here, so be sure to try their mouthwatering *poutine* – fries covered in gravy and cheese curds.

Restaurants

Casablanca Resto, 41 Clarence St (☎789-7855). Wonderful Moroccan cuisine and delicious coffees. Byward Market area.

Chez Jean Pierre, 210 Somerset St W (☎235-9711). The best French restaurant in town, with prices to match. Reservations essential. In the city centre near Elgin St.

Coriander Thai, 282 Kent St (☎233-2828). The best Thai in Ottawa. Amazing satays, rich green and red curries, lemongrass tea and other classic dishes at fair prices. Not far from Parliament Hill.

Courtyard, 21 George St (☎241-1516). In a cobblestone courtyard, this pretty place has a summer terrace and on Sundays brunch is accompanied by live classical music. Advisable to reserve at weekends. Byward Market area.

Empire Street Grill, 47 Clarence St at Parent (☎241-1343). Smart and polished restaurant in the Byward Market area. First-rate steaks and an extensive wine list. Live jazz Thursday through Saturday till 2am.

Good Morning Vietnam, 323 Rideau St (☎789-4080). Lively, nonsmoking Vietnamese place with plain decor and delicious food. Byward Market area.

The Green Door, 198 Main St (☎234-9597). Organic vegetarian buffet that is sold by weight. South of the centre near St Paul University.

Havely, 39 Clarence St at Sussex (☎241-1700). Elegant Indian restaurant of dark wood and brass. The all-you-can-eat lunch buffet is one of the best buys in Ottawa. Good vegetarian food. Byward Market area.

La Pointe, 55 York St (☎241-6221). Superb Byward Market restaurant serving wonderful seafood at reasonable prices in informal, basement premises. Recommended.

Mamma Teresa, 300 Somerset St W at O'Connor (☎236-3023). Home-made pasta, fresh cheeses and olives and real Italian coffee. Very popular, so booking is advisable. Most pasta dishes around $10.

Mekong, 637 Somerset St W (☎237-7717). A wide offering of Vietnamese and Chinese food in the heart of Chinatown.

Saigon, 83 Clarence St (☎789-7934). First-rate and inexpensive Vietnamese cuisine in the Byward Market.

The Siam Kitchen, 1050 Bank St (☎730-3954). Excellent Thai food, especially the noodle and squid dishes. On the southern edge of the centre across from Landsdowne Park.

Silk Roads Café, 47 William St (☎241-4254). Delicious Afghan cuisine with funky art displayed. Byward Market area.

Suisha Gardens, 208 Slater St (☎236-9602). Tasty sushi, tempura, sukiyaki and teriyaki that is cheaper at lunch time. There's also a *tatami* room where you can sit on rush mats and eat Japanese-style. South of Parliament Hill.

Cafés and café-bars

Bagel Bagel, 92 Clarence St. Nine different types of bagel with an assortment of fillings from $2.50. Open late every night. Byward Market area.

Café Crepe de France, 76 Murray St at Parent. Divine crepes from $8 in a distinctive French-style café. Byward Market.

Domus Café, 87 Murray St at Parent. In the Domus houseware store, this is a bright place with excellent cooking that uses produce from the Farmers Market. Good for breakfast and brunch on a Sunday. Byward Market.

Hooker's All Canadian Beavertails, junction of George and William sts in the Byward Market. Fast-food kiosk specializing in the (recently invented) Ottawan snack of "Beavertails" – half-pizza, half-doughnut, fried and covered either in garlic butter and cheese or cinnamon and sugar.

Medithéo, 77 George St. Fashionable Byward Market hangout with stone walls, angular modern furniture and a good menu with a Mediterranean slant.

Nate's, 316 Rideau St at Nelson. At under $5, the cheapest full breakfast in one of the capital's most popular delis.

Pasticceria Gelateria Italiana, 200 Preston St. Pastries, espressos and cappuccinos to die for. Between Gladstone and Somerset.

Tramps Café, 53 William St. Arguably the best café-bar in the Byward Market, with good finger foods; try the deep-fried courgette and chicken wings at weekends.

Café Wim, 537 Sussex Drive at George. Stylish café-bar graced by slick modern furnishings and fittings, plus a good, wide-ranging menu with a Mediterranean slant. Byward Market area.

Zak's Diner, 16 Byward Market. A 1950s-style time warp with chrome decor, rock'n'roll blaring from the jukebox and good all-American food. Open daily until midnight.

Bars and pubs

Blackthorn Café, 15 Clarence St at Sussex. In the Byward Market area, this trendy spot incorporates an English-style pub and has a pleasant outside terrace.

Blue Cactus, 2 Byward Market. Slightly hectic bar with a good line in cocktails and pastel decor.

Heart and Crown, 121 Parent Ave. Popular Irish-style bar with large outside terrace.

Irene's Pub Restaurant, 885 Bank St. Live Celtic and folk music and imported beers.

The Mayflower, 247 Elgin St and 201 Queen St. Two English-style pubs that get jam-packed on the weekend. The one on Queen has the better buzz.

Royal Oak, 779 Bank St, 318 Bank St and 161 Laurier Ave E. Three British-style pubs, all serving draught and bottled beers and inexpensive food, including ploughman's lunch and fish and chips. All branches have rock bands several times a week.

Nightlife and entertainment

Ottawa has several vibrant downtown **nightclubs** and is a major port of call for big-name touring acts, most of whom appear at the Corel Centre, about 15km southwest of downtown (☎755-1166). Otherwise, things aren't too exciting, though **jazz** is extremely popular with regular gigs from leading artists in a variety of informal venues.

For **listings** on events of all sorts, there's the free *Where Ottawa-Hull*, a monthly promotional magazine designed for tourists. On Fridays the *Ottawa Citizen* prints a list of current entertainment, but for gig details as well as other more objective listings and information the weekly *Xpress* newspaper is the capital's trendiest and most comprehensive source.

Venues, music bars and clubs

Atomic, 137 Besserer St (☎241-2411). One of Ottawa's coolest clubs with occasional all-nighters. Most nights are free, but some attract a small admission charge. Techno though to jungle.

Barrymore's Music Hall, 323 Bank St (☎233-0307). Commercial, mainstream and local bands perform live here every night except Sunday. Both U2 and Tina Turner have played in this huge seven-level venue which started out as a Vaudeville theatre.

The Cave, 63 Bank St (☎233-0080). Nightclub with a good reputation for its varied programme with themed evenings (retro, disco and so forth) a special feature.

Market Station Bar-Bistro, 15 George St (☎562-3540). Stylish gay hangout with artworks and funky music. Byward Market.

Mercury Lounge, 56 Byward Ave (☎789-5324). Big loft with great martinis and vinyl couches. Acid-jazz, house and techno with DJs from all over Canada along with weird and wacky live acts.

Rainbow Bistro, 76 Murray St (☎241-5123). Atmospheric blues club with jam sessions on Sunday. Byward Market.

Vineyard's Wine Bar, 54 York St (☎241-4270). Hot jazz spot with a formidable wine cellar. Byward Market.

Zaphod Beeblebrox, 27 York St (☎562-1010). The whole spectrum of live bands from C&W to alternative. Byward Market.

Performing arts and cinema

Ottawa's cultural focus is the National Arts Centre, 53 Elgin St (☎947-7000, *www* *.nac-can.ca*; tickets from Ticketmaster ☎755-1111), which presents plays by the resident **theatre** company as well as touring groups, **concerts** by the resident orchestra, **operas** with simultaneous French and English subtitles, and **dance** from (among others) the National Ballet of Canada and the Royal Winnipeg Ballet. Tickets begin at $12.50 and wherever you sit the acoustics are outstanding.

Quality **theatre** is also presented by The Great Canadian Theatre Company, 910 Gladstone St (☎236-5196), which presents avant-garde Canadian plays with strong social or political overtones; Ottawa Little Theatre, 400 King Edward (☎233-8948), an amateur group who perform a variety of popular plays, usually comedies; and Hull's Théâtre l'Ile, 1 Wellington St (☎819/595-7455), on an island in the Ottawa River.

Ottawa has a good selection of **cinemas**. Options include the Bytowne Cinema, 325 Rideau (☎789-3456), the capital's most popular repertory cinema, and the Canadian Film Institute, 2 Daly Ave (☎232-6727), which shows art-house and mainstream films arranged by theme. Famous Players Inc, in the Rideau Shopping Mall, Rideau Street (☎234-3712), has the latest releases, as does the Mayfair Theatre, 1074 Bank (☎730-3403).

Festivals

Ottawa uses every excuse in the book to put on a **festival**, and its munificence is evident at every jamboree. Public holidays like Canada Day are celebrated here with the sort of spectacle that other cities muster, but with extra dollars to boost the show, while seasonal shindigs like the Winterlude and the Canadian Tulip Festival are as lavish as any in the country. Other than these large bashes, ethnic festivals embracing Canada's diverse population are smaller but equally entertaining and there's a wide variety of musical festivals too. The list below is arranged chronologically.

Winterlude. A ten-day snow-and-ice extravaganza spread over February. Concentrated around the frozen Rideau Canal, it includes ice sculptures at Confederation Park – renamed the Crystal Garden for the duration – and snow sculptures around Dows Lake. Other events include speed skating, bed races and dog-sled races. Further information on ☎239-5000.

Canadian Tulip Festival. Held in mid-May, this is the oldest of Ottawa's festivals – it began in 1945 when the Dutch sent 100,000 tulip bulbs to the capital to thank the Canadian soldiers who helped liberate the Netherlands. More bulbs arrived the following year from Queen Juliana, who had taken refuge in Ottawa when the Netherlands were occupied. The transformation of the city didn't meet with universal approval at first – Mackenzie King thought the planting of tulips around the Parliament Buildings was "undignified", but his staff planted thousands in secret anyway. Nowadays the bulbs are planted around Parliament, along the canal and around Dows Lake, an outbreak of colour that's accompanied by concerts, parades, fireworks and a huge craft show. The major events take place in Major's Hill Park and Dows Lake – but few are free, and the festival now has a reputation for being rather touristy. Further information on ☎567-5757, *www.tulipfestival.ca*.

Franco-Ontarien Festival. Late June. This celebration of French culture has built up a reputation as being the party that brings a bit of wildness to conservative Ottawa. Dalhousie St is closed off to traffic for up to five days, so the bands and street dancers can take over. Further information on ☎741-1225, *www.ffo.ca*.

Canada Day. July 1 The country's national day celebrated in style with parades, processions and much flag waving. Further information on ☎239-5000.

Bluesfest. Early July. Canada's largest festival of blues including international crooners with concerts in various venues and free shows in Confederation Park. Further information on ☎233-8798, *www.ottawa-bluesfest.ca*.

Festival Canada. July. Based around the National Arts Centre, this month-long festival features performances of opera, concerts, choral works, jazz, English and French theatre, cabaret and workshops. Further information on ☎996-5051, *www.nac-can.ca*.

Ottawa International Jazz Festival. Mid-July. One of Ottawa's most popular festivals, showcasing more than 400 musicians. The main stage is in Confederation Park with concerts several times daily. In addition, local bands play around Byward Market and at city clubs. Further information on ☎594-3580, *www.jazz.ottawa.com*.

Ottawa Chamber Music Festival. Late July to early Aug. North America's largest classical music festival, with concerts in venues and churches across the city. Further information on ☎234-8008, *www.chamberfest.com*.

Listings

Airlines Air Canada (Canadian Airlines, Air Alliance, Air Nova and Air Ontario), 275 Slater St (☎247-5000); British Airways (☎1-800/247-9297); Canada 3000 (☎247-1420); Continental (☎1-800/231-0856); Delta (☎1-800/325-1999); Lufthansa (☎1-800/563-5954).

Airport enquiries ☎248-2125.

Bike rental Rent-A-Bike, 1 Rideau St, at the back of the *Château Laurier* hotel (☎241-4140, *rentabike@cyberus.ca*).

Bookshops Chapters, 47 Rideau St (☎241-0073), has a fine selection of Canadian literature and nonfiction. The Book Market, on the corner of Dalhousie and Rideau sts, buys and sells secondhand books (☎241-1753). A World of Map and Travel Books, 1235 Wellington St (☎724-6776), specializes in travel books. Mother Tongue Books, 1067 Bank at Sunnyside (☎730-2346), are feminist, First Nation, gay and countercultural specialists.

Bus information Local: STO (Hull ☎819/770-3242); OC Transpo (Ottawa ☎741-4390). Long-distance: Voyageur Colonial and Greyhound (☎238-5900).

Camping equipment The Expedition Shoppe, 43 York St (☎241-8397).

Car rental Discount, downtown at 421 Gladstone and Kent (☎234-0809); Hertz, Queen at Lyon in the *Crowne Plaza Hotel* (☎230-7607) and at the airport (☎521-3332); National, 226 Queen St (☎232-3536) and at the airport (☎737-7023).

Dental emergencies ☎563-1000.

Embassies Australia, 50 O'Connor St (☎236-0841); Ireland, 130 Albert St (☎233-6281); Netherlands, 350 Albert St (☎237-5030); New Zealand, 99 Bank St (☎238-5991); UK, 80 Elgin St (☎237-1530); US, 490 Sussex Drive (☎238-5335).

Gay Ottawa Gayline Information & Counselling (☎238-1717).

Ice hockey From Sept to April, the Ottawa Senators play NHL games at the new 18,500-capacity Corel Centre, 1000 Palladium Drive, Kanata (☎755-1111), about 15km southwest of downtown. Single game tickets on ☎755-1166.

Internet access Chapters, 47 Rideau St (☎241-0073); *AE Internet Café*, 288 Bank St at Somerset (☎230-9000).

Laundry Rideau Coinwash, 436 Rideau St (daily 8am–10pm; ☎789-4400).

Left luggage There are coin-operated lockers at the train and bus stations.

Pharmacy Rideau Pharmacy, 390 Rideau St (Mon–Fri 9am–9pm, Sat 9am–6pm, Sun noon–6pm).

Post office Postal facilities at Rideau Pharmacy, 390 Rideau St (Mon–Fri 9am–9pm, Sat 9am–6pm, Sun noon–6pm).

Taxis Blue Line ☎238-1111; Capital Taxi ☎746-2233.

Ticket agency Ticketmaster, 112 Kent ☎(755-1111).

Train information VIA rail ☎1-800/361-1235. Local ☎244-8289.

Travel agencies Algonquin Travel, 90 Sparks St (☎237-9200); Club Adventure, 115 Parent Ave (☎789-8000); Thomas Cook, Eatons, Rideau Centre (☎563-3838).

Weather For up-to-date weather details, call ☎998-3439.

Women's Ottawa Rainbow Women's Center, 211 Bronson Ave (☎567-9822), is the place to go for contacts. Useful in emergencies are the Sexual Assault Support Centre (☎234-2266) and the Rape Crisis Centre (☎562-2333).

NORTHERN ONTARIO

Stretching north from the shores of lakes Huron and Superior to the frozen reaches of Hudson Bay, **NORTHERN ONTARIO** is a land of sparse population and colossal distances. Give or take the odd ridge and chasm, the landscape is almost entirely flat, an endless expanse of forest pouring over the mineral-rich rocks of the Canadian Shield and interrupted by thousands of lakes. To the Anglophile elite of the south, the region was (and still is) seen as barbarous and crude. Canadian humorist Stephen Leacock, for instance, dismissed it with "The best that anyone could say of the place was that it was a 'sportsman's paradise', which only means a good place to drink whiskey in". Such disdain always ignored the economic facts. The north once produced the furs that launched the country's economy and its raw materials – gold, silver, nickel, timber and so forth – paid for Toronto's gleaming skyscrapers. The extractive nature of the northern economy and the harshness of the climate have defined the locals' attitude to their surroundings. Hunting and fishing are extremely popular – and most visitors who come here join in – but other types of appreciation have been slow to grow.

Given that the distances are so great, it's important to plan an itinerary carefully. Northern Ontario is traversed by two main highways – Hwy 11 and the much more interesting Hwy 17. **Hwy 11** begins by slicing through workaday **North Bay**, 345km north of Toronto, before pushing on to the hunting and fishing resort of **Temagami**. From here, it's a manageable hop onto **Cochrane**, uninteresting in itself but useful as the starting point for the lonely rail line that strikes north beyond the road network to **Moosonee** on the bleak and barren shores of James Bay. This rail line, plied by Ontario Northland's Polar Bear Express and Little Bear trains, makes for one of the most unusual excursions in the country and is a comfortable way of seeing something of the Arctic north, way beyond the tree line. From Cochrane, Hwy 11 leads west to a series of mining towns, but this part of the highway holds little of interest and is best avoided, even though you have to double back on yourself.

RAILWAY RIDES

Advance booking is recommended for both of Northern Ontario's notable railway rides. The **Cochrane–Moosonee** route is operated by Ontario Northland, 555 Oak St E, North Bay (☎705/472-4500 or 1-800/268-9281, fax 705/495-4745, *www.ontc.on.ca*). The **Algoma Central Railway** is at 129 Bay St, Sault Ste Marie (☎705/946-7300 or 1-800/242-9287, *www.agawacanyontourtrain.com*).

There are two obvious ways to join **Hwy 17**. The faster route comes up from Parry Sound (see p.141) to meet Hwy 17 at the mining town of **Sudbury**, or you can catch the ferry from Tobermory (see p.131) to cross rusticated **Manitoulin Island** on Hwy 6 and join Hwy 17 west of Sudbury. Whichever route you choose (and both have their scenic advantages), your first port of call on Hwy 17 should be **Sault Ste Marie**. In itself, this industrial town is only of middling interest, but it serves as the terminus for a splendid wilderness train trip on the **Algoma Central Railway**. From Sault Ste Marie, Hwy 17 begins its long haul round **Lake Superior** passing by or through a string of parks, notably **Lake Superior Provincial Park** and **Pukaskwa National Park**, both of which have dramatic lakeshore hiking trails and campsites. Beyond lies the inland port of **Thunder Bay**, home to the replica fur trading post of Fort William and the last place of much appeal before Winnipeg (see p.462), a further 680km away to the west.

With regard to public transport, **buses** shuttle between the major towns on both Hwy 17 and Hwy 11, but all the parks and many of the smaller places require private transport. Note also that if you're heading for a particular hotel, motel or campsite, you should check to see how near you'll get by bus – bus stops are often on the edge of towns. In winter, driving on both Hwy 11 and Hwy 17 can be perilous. Remember too

that mosquitoes and blackfly can make life absolutely miserable – take precautions and go hiking either at the start of spring or in the autumn.

North Bay and points north to Moosonee

Highway 11 cuts a 1000km arc through Northern Ontario, eventually meeting up with Hwy 17 as it nears Thunder Bay (see p.188). En route, it links a string of gritty resource towns, who endure a climate which, far from the moderating effects of Lake Superior, is as savage as any in the world. In winter, Hwy 11 is subject to ferocious blizzards, which make it impassable to ordinary vehicles, and at any time of the year there is no point in travelling much of the highway at all. Content yourself with the first stretch, the 400km trip from **North Bay**, a small lakeshore town with hotels and motels, to **Cochrane**, even smaller but the starting point for the region's star turn, the train ride to **Moosonee**, beyond the road network close to the frozen shores of James Bay.

Trains and **buses** connect most of the larger settlements between North Bay and Cochrane, but you really need a car to be sure of getting where you want, when you want – and you don't want to be hanging around too long for a connection. The train from Cochrane to Moosonee is operated by Ontario Northland (see p.176) and should be booked in advance. Note also that food and drink are more expensive in this region than elsewhere in Ontario; on many occasions, your best bet is to eat where you sleep.

North Bay

Once an important stopping point on the canoe route to the west and now a useful place to break your journey on the long drive north, the workaday city of **NORTH BAY**,

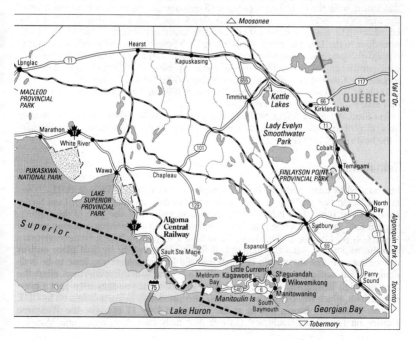

some 160km from Bracebridge (see p.145), is a relative giant hereabouts with a population of 56,000. Glued to the shores of Lake Nipissing, it has one notable attraction, the **Dionne Quints Museum**, by the information centre where Hwy 11 hits the south side of town (daily: late May to June 9am–5pm; July–Aug 9am–7pm; Sept to mid-Oct 9am–4pm; $2.75). The museum is housed in the small log cabin from Corbeil, just west of North Bay, where the Dionne quintuplets were born on May 28, 1934 – to this day the world's only identical quintuplets. Kept alive with drops of whiskey, the quins were considered miracle children by the economically depressed nation, and at the age of three months the government took custody of them, removing them from their parents and five brothers and sisters. Until they were nine years old, the quins were put on display in a glassed-in playground, to the delight of up to 6000 sightseers who turned up each day to watch them and to pay for souvenirs such as "birth-promoting" stones picked up from the North Bay area. The girls were educated in a synthetic "normal school atmosphere" provided by ten classmates, five of whom were English to help the quins with their second language. This bizarre childhood eventually caused a highly publicized estrangement between the quins and their parents, and doubtless contributed to the unhappiness of their later lives, a story dominated by illness, depression and failed marriages. The three surviving quins – Yvonne, Annette and Cécile – now live in Québec and published a biography accusing their father of sexual abuse, their mother of verbal abuse and the Ontario government of exploitation. The small museum contains dresses, toys, photographs, advertising hoardings and souvenirs of the quins' childhood, including the bed they were born in.

Practicalities

Ontario Northland **trains** from Cochrane and Toronto and all long-distance **buses** terminate at the Intermodal station at 100 Station Rd, to the east of the centre. To get downtown, walk through the shopping mall opposite and take a bus from the front of the mall to the local bus terminal on Oak Street, one block from Main Street and the lakeshore. The town's **tourist office** is on the south side of town, beside Hwy 11 and next door to the Dionne Quints Museum at 1375 Seymour St (daily: mid-June to Aug 8.30am–8.30pm; Sept to mid-June 9am–5pm). North Bay's glut of **accommodation** is concentrated on Lakeshore Drive beside Lake Nipissing. Proficient chain **motels** here include the *Comfort Inn*, 676 Lakeshore Drive (☎705/494-9444 or 1-800/221-2222, fax 705/494-8461; ③) and the *Best Western Lakeshore*, 700 Lakeshore Drive (☎705/474-5800 or 1-800/461-6199, fax 705/474-8699; ④).

For **food**, try either *Mike's Seafoods*, 406 Lakeshore Drive, where they serve reasonably priced fish dishes, or *Churchill's*, 631 Lakeshore Drive, which has – so locals claim – the best ribs in Ontario.

Temagami

Surrounded by lakes and forests, the attractive resort village of **TEMAGAMI**, 100km beyond North Bay on Hwy 11, started as a rest stop on the long portage from Snake Lake to Lake Temagami. It has been attracting tourists since the turn of the century, when it built the region's first grand hotel and introduced a steamship company and rail line to transport holiday-makers here. Nowadays, it serves as a base for extended forays into the wilderness – mostly hunters and fishermen travelling by float plane and/or canoe, but note that the terrain is much too wild for the novice: you have to be well-equipped with outback experience to be safe. To get a view of this wilderness, climb the 30-metre-high **Temagami Tower** just before you hit town; you may even spot a peregrine falcon, which was reintroduced in 1997 after previously being polished off by DDT.

Both **trains** and **buses** pull in at the station on Hwy 11 opposite the **Welcome Centre** on Lakeshore Boulevard (July & Aug daily 8am–8pm; Sept–June Mon–Fri

9am–5pm; ☎705/569-3344 or 1-800/661-7609, *www.twp.temagami.on.ca*). The centre has details on **accommodation**, most of which is in tourist camps that cater for hunters and fishers. There's also the rather more comfortable *Smoothwater Wilderness Lodge* (☎705/569-3539, fax 569-2710, *www.smoothwater.com*), 14km north of town on Hwy 11, and **camping** at **Finlayson Point Provincial Park** (mid-May to late Sept; ☎705/569-3205), 1km south of town. Of the park's hundred or so sites, a third of them have hook-ups. There are good facilities, and sites cost from $15.75 to $20.75 and need to be booked in advance.

For complete **canoe outfitting**, head for Smoothwater Outfitters (☎705/569-3539, fax 569-2710, *www.smoothwater.com*), who can provide everything from first-aid kits to frying pans. You can fly in and canoe out to the giant **Lady Evelyn Smoothwater Provincial Park** to the west of Temagami with Lakeland Airways from $200 (☎705/569-3455); their float planes take off from beside the Welcome Centre.

Cobalt

Local legend has it that the silver boom at **COBALT**, just off Hwy 11 some 50km north of Temagami, started when a blacksmith named Fred La Rose threw a hammer at a fox and hit a rock instead, breaking off a great hunk of silver. Whatever the truth, mining began here in earnest in 1903. Subsequently, in the frantic search for silver, new mine shafts were dropped every few weeks and within a decade the haphazard collection of tents, log cabins and huts had swollen to contain seven thousand people. With output burgeoning, Cobalt merged with nearby Haileybury and New Liskeard to form the "tri-towns": the miners lived in Cobalt, the managers on the Lake Temiskaming waterfront in Haileybury; and the mine owners kept their distance in New Liskeard. Life in Cobalt was perilous: typhoid, smallpox and flu were common and many of the homes were built from wooden dynamite boxes, and so were regularly wrecked by fires. The high times ended with the Great Depression, but Cobalt struggled on until the steep decline in silver prices in the 1980s. The last mine closed in 1990 and Cobalt's future looks decidedly gloomy.

Cobalt today is hardly compulsive viewing, but you might drop by Canada's oldest **Mining Museum** (June–Sept daily 9am–5pm; Oct–May Mon–Fri 1–4pm; $3.25), housed in a converted newspaper office, with a vast collection of ores from the mines, including a collection of luminous stones. Up the street, an old head frame (the top of the mine shaft) protrudes from the roof of what was once the grocery store – the store used the disused shaft as a refrigerator – and opposite a small park has a large painted sign listing the 104 mines operating in 1908.

North to Cochrane and Moosonee

Some 100km north of Cobalt, Hwy 11 passes over the **Arctic Watershed**, or Height of Land, a slight elevation in the Canadian Shield that divides Ontario's water flow. To the north, all water flows to James and Hudson bays, and to the south it flows to the Great Lakes and the St Lawrence.

Beyond, it's a tedious haul up Hwy 11 to **COCHRANE**, 280km from Temagami, a modest little place that grew up as a repair and turntable station for the railroad companies serving the far north. Most of the workshops have closed down, but this is still the departure point for Ontario Northland railway's Little Bear and Polar Bear Express trains (see overleaf), which venture north beyond the road network to Moosonee, on James Bay. The popularity of the express train sustains several modest **motels** in Cochrane: the *Chimo* (☎705/272-6555, fax 272-5666; ②) is as good as any, and there's also the more comfortable *Station Inn*, by the train station at 200 Railway St (☎705/272-3500 or 1-800/265-2356, fax 705/272-5713, *www.ontc.on.ca*; ③). For **food**, *JR Ranch BBQ*, 63 3rd Ave, is good for meaty North American meals.

KIRKLAND LAKE AND SIR HARRY OAKES

The mining community of **KIRKLAND LAKE**, off Hwy 11 between Cobalt and Cochrane, isn't much to look at, but it does have an interesting story. To begin with, the town produces one-fifth of Canada's **gold** and the main street, Government Road, is actually paved with gold – the construction crew used the wrong pile of rocks, gold ore instead of waste rock. The town also featured in one of the most sensational stories of Canada's recent past – the tale that Nic Roeg made into the film *Eureka* with Gene Hackman and Rutger Hauer.

In the summer of 1911, **Sir Harry Oakes** arrived in Swastika, close to Kirkland Lake, with $2.65 in his pocket. He left in 1934 with $20 million, the largest fortune ever gained through mining in Canada. Oakes began his quest for gold in 1898, his search taking him to Alaska, where his vessel was blown into the Bering Strait and then captured by Cossacks. He escaped under rifle fire and continued his explorations in Australia, West Africa, Mexico and California until, fleeing a revolution in South America, he joined the gold rush in northern Canada. In 1912, he founded a mine here in what was later to become Kirkland Lake and this produced $100,000-worth of gold a month. In addition, in 1928 he opened up the Lake Shore mine, the most lucrative ore ever discovered in Canada. Oakes, obsessed with keeping his wealth from the tax man, then emigrated to the tax-free Bahamas and it was here that he came to a sticky end.

Around midnight on July 8, 1943, Oakes was murdered in his bed in Nassau, a crime that momentarily knocked World War II off the front pages of the newspapers. Detectives immediately arrested Alfred de Marigny, a handsome playboy who had eloped with Oakes's daughter, Nancy, two years previously. The case against him was thin, resting on the presence of a single fingerprint in Oakes's bedroom and the motive of money – with Oakes dead his daughter would inherit a fortune. During the trial it became obvious that the detectives had planted the fingerprint and de Marigny was acquitted. The case was never reopened, but the murder of Sir Harry Oakes has prompted a variety of theories. Alfred de Marigny implicated Oakes's debt-ridden friend Harold Christie, who had defrauded Oakes in a property deal that was about to be exposed by the auditors. Rumours of voodoo and Mafia involvement were rife at the time, but more intriguing is a possible cover-up involving Oakes's confidant, the **Duke of Windsor**. Apparently, the Duke and Oakes were involved in a money-laundering operation with a Swedish industrialist and alleged Nazi agent; the suggestion is that the Duke, terrified that the scam would come to light in the course of a prolonged police investigation, might have wanted de Marigny's quick arrest in order to throw people off the scent.

Oakes's 1919 Frank Lloyd Wright-style chateau is now the **Museum of Northern History** (Mon–Sat 10am–4pm, Sun noon–4pm; $3), located near the west end of Kirkland Lake. The museum details his climb from rags to riches and displays antique mining equipment, ores, minerals and stuffed animals. One room also highlights the famous hockey players who have come from the town – it's produced 51 NHL stars!

Cochrane to Moosonee by train

A popular excursion, the summer-only **Polar Bear Express** cuts across 300km of Arctic tundra on its way from Cochrane to Moosonee, on the Moose River as it empties into James Bay. This is as far north as anyone can easily (or reasonably) go in Ontario – but, despite the name of the train, you won't see any polar bears. The train runs from late June to August once daily except on Friday. It departs Cochrane at 8.30am and arrives in Moosonee at 12.50pm, departing Moosonee 6pm and arriving back in Cochrane at 10.05pm. The return fare is just $50 return and the service is operated by Ontario Northland, 555 Oak St E, North Bay (☎705/472-4500 or 1-800/268-9281, fax 705/495-4745, *www.ontc.on.ca*). The same company also runs the year-round **Little Bear train**, one of Canada's last remaining flagstop trains, taking freight and stopping along the way to pick up trappers, fishers, hunters and local Crees. This train departs

Cochrane on Mondays, Wednesdays and Fridays at 11.15am, arriving in Moosonee at 4.15pm. It departs Moosonee on Tuesday, Thursday and Saturday at 9am and gets back to Cochrane at 2.30pm. A return fare costs $85.

The Crees have been hunting and fishing James Bay and the Hudson Bay for about ten thousand years and they make up the majority of the population in **MOOSONEE**, which was founded in 1903 by a French fur-trading company, Révillon Frères – today's Revlon. The **Révillon Frères Museum** (late June to Aug daily 9am–5pm; free), in one of the original company buildings, traces the history of the settlement and its largely unsuccessful attempt to challenge the local monopoly of the **Hudson's Bay Company**. The latter had established the trading post of **MOOSE FACTORY ISLAND**, just off-shore from Moosonee, in 1673, which makes it the oldest English-speaking community in Ontario. **Water taxis** ($6 one-way) zip travellers over from Moosonee to the island,

THE HUDSON'S BAY COMPANY

In 1661 two Frenchmen, **Medard Chouart des Groseilliers** and **Pierre-Esprit Radisson**, reached the southern end of Hudson Bay overland and realized it was the same inland sea described by earlier seafaring explorers. They returned to the St Lawrence laden down with furs, upon which the French governor arrested them for trapping without a licence. Understandably peeved, they turned to England, where Charles II's cousin, Prince Rupert, persuaded the king to finance and equip two ships, the *Eaglet* and the *Nonsuch*. After a mammoth voyage, the *Nonsuch* returned with a fantastic cargo of furs and this led to the incorporation of the **Hudson's Bay Company** by Charles II on May 2, 1670. The Company was granted wide powers, including exclusive trading rights to the entire Hudson Bay watershed – to be called **Rupert's Land**.

The HBC was a joint-stock company, the shareholders annually electing a governor and committee to hire men, order trade goods and arrange for fur auctions and shipping. By 1760, **trading posts** had been built at the mouths of all the major rivers flowing into the bay; these were commanded by **factors**, who took their policy orders from London. The orders were often unrealistic and based on the concept of native trappers bringing furs to the posts – the direct opposite to the Montréal-based North West Company, whose mainly Francophone employees spent months in the wilderness working with the natives. Unsurprisingly, the NWC undercut the Company's trade and there was intense competition between the rival concerns right across the north of the continent, occasionally resulting in violence. In 1821 a compromise was reached and the two companies **merged**. They kept the name Hudson's Bay Company and the British parliament granted the new, larger company a commercial monopoly from Hudson Bay to the Pacific. However, the administrative structure of the Company was changed. A North American chief factor was appointed and his councils dealt increasingly with local trading concerns, though the London governor and committee continued to have the last word.

The extensive monopoly rights ceded to the new company were fiercely resented by local traders, and, in a landmark case of 1849, a local jury found a Metis trader by the name of Sayer guilty of breaking the monopoly, but simultaneously refused to punish him. Thereafter, in practice if not by law, the Company's stranglehold on the fur trade was dead and gone. Furthermore, the HBC's quasi-governmental powers seemed increasingly anachronistic and when a company official, **James Douglas**, became governor of British Columbia in 1858, the British government forced him to resign from the HBC. This marked the beginning of the end of the Company's colonial role.

In 1870 the HBC sold Rupert's Land to Canada. In return it received a cash payment, but, more importantly, retained the title to the lands on which the trading posts had been built and one-twentieth of the fertile land open to settlement. Given that the trading posts often occupied land that was the nucleus of the burgeoning western cities, this was a remarkably bad deal for Canada – and a great one for the HBC. Subsequently, the HBC became a major real-estate developer and retail chain, a position it maintains today.

where the **Moose Factory Centennial Museum Park** (late June to early Sept; free) holds the original blacksmith's shop, graveyard, powder magazine (the island's only stone building), and a tepee where the locals sell bannock (freshly baked bread). South of here, **St Thomas Anglican Church**, built in 1860, has an altar cloth of beaded moose hide, prayer books written in Cree, and removable floor plugs to prevent the church floating away in floods. There are other nautical possibilities from Moosonee too: the Polar Princess **cruise boat** sails down the Moose River to James Bay (late June to early Sept daily except Sat 9am–3pm; $45 including lunch), while large **freighter canoes** visit either Moose Factory Island (late June to early Sept daily 1pm; $6) or Fossil Island (late June to early Sept daily except Fri; $15.50), 10km upriver, where 350-million-year-old fossils have been found.

Clearly, if you want to undertake any of the longer trips, the five hours allowed between the arrival and departure of the Polar Express is not enough – and with the Little Bear train you have to stay the night anyway. Moosonee **accommodation** must be reserved ahead of time and there are three choices: the *Moosonee Lodge* (☎705/336-2351; ③), the *Polar Bear Lodge* (☎705/336-2345; ③) and the *Osprey Country Inn* (☎705/336-2226; ④). In addition, note that Ontario Northland offers three- to five-day packages from Cochrane ($275–579 per person, $209–438 per person for two and $184–385 for three), which include accommodation in Cochrane and Moosonee, the Polar Bear Express, most meals and some tours.

Sudbury

The economic centre of northeastern Ontario, sprawling **SUDBURY**, some 165km north of Parry Sound (see p.141), is parked on the edge of the Sudbury Basin, a pit created either by a volcano or, the preferred theory, by a giant meteor. Whatever did the damage, the effect was to throw one of the world's richest deposits of nickel and copper towards the surface. It was the nickel – used to temper steel – that made Sudbury's fortune, but its by-products caused devastation. Most of the damage was done by a smelting method known as heap roasting, used until the 1920s, which spread clouds of sulphurous fumes over forests already ravaged by lumber firms and mineral prospectors, who often started fires to reveal the traces of metal in the bare rocks. Likened to Hell or Hiroshima, the bleak landscape had only one advantage: in 1968 it enabled Buzz Aldrin and Neil Armstrong to practise their great leap for mankind in a ready-made lunar environment.

Having continued to produce sulphur-laden smoke from the stacks of their nickel smelters, the mining companies were finally forced to take action when a whole community of workers from Happy Valley, just northeast of Sudbury, were evacuated in the 1970s because of the number of sulphur-induced illnesses. Since then, pollutants in the immediate environs have been reduced and the city's ambitious re-greening programme was even lauded at the UN's 1992 Earth Summit in Rio. As a result, thousands of acres have now spluttered back to life and the thirty lakes in the vicinity of Sudbury, including one in the middle of town, are no longer stagnant pools of vinegar.

Sudbury's multinational population of 160,000 – over half of them French-speaking – are fiercely proud of their city, though it can seem that the main effect of the recent redevelopment has been an efflorescence of shopping malls. That said, the city can boast two of north Ontario's most impressive tourist sights, Science North and Big Nickel Mine.

The City

Sudbury's key attractions are located to the south of the downtown core, which is focused on Elm Street between Notre Dame and Lorne Street. Making the most of the city's unusual geology, **Science North** (daily: May to late June & Sept to mid-Oct

9am–5pm; late June to Aug 9am–6pm; mid-Oct to April 10am–4pm; $8.95, children $6.50), a huge snowflake-shaped structure on Ramsey Lake Road, is installed in a cavern blasted into the rock of the Canadian Shield. The hands-on displays enable you to simulate a miniature hurricane, gauge your fitness, lie on a bed of nails, learn to lip-read, call up amateur radio hams worldwide, tune in to weather-tracking stations and try different sensory tests, all under the guidance of students from the city's Laurentian University. The museum also has a collection of insects and animals, most of which can be handled. The flying squirrels give exhibitions of their prowess, sailing effortlessly 25m through the air, and there's a rather smelly and somnolent porcupine of considerable charm called Ralf. There's also an **IMAX Theatre** (daily; adults $8, children $6.50) with its 22-metre-wide screen, and, by the IMAX entrance, the **Virtual Voyage** ($6.50), a virtual-reality roller-coaster journey to Mars.

The town's symbol, a nine-metre-high steel replica of a five-cent piece, known as the Big Nickel, stands by the Trans-Canada on the western approach to town. The nickel marks the entrance to the **Big Nickel Mine** (daily: May to late June & Sept to mid-Oct 9am–5pm; late June to Aug 9am–6pm; $8.50), where you can take a less than enthralling tour of a replica mine and mail a card from the underground postbox to let the folks back home know you've travelled 20m below the earth's surface.

A **Play All Day Passport** covering all these sites costs $24.95, children $15.95.

Practicalities

With services south to Toronto and west to Winnipeg, Sudbury's principal **train** station – Sudbury Junction – is about 10km northeast of the town centre on Lasalle Boulevard. There are no buses into town – you have to take a taxi. Sudbury's second train station is in the town centre at Minto and Elgin streets, but the only service is the thrice weekly flagstop train across the bush to White River (see p.186). The Greyhound **bus** depot is at 854 Notre Dame; some long-distance buses also stop at Science North. Sudbury **tourist office** is on the south side of town beside Hwy 69 (May–Aug daily 8.30am–8.30pm; Sept–April Mon–Wed 9am–6pm, Thurs & Fri 9am–8pm, Sat 10am–6pm; ☎705/673-4161 or 1-800/708-2505).

With regard to **accommodation**, Sudbury has a number of proficient chain motels. Options include the *Travelway Inn*, 1200 Paris St (☎705/522-1122 or 1-800/461-4883; ③), the nearby *Travelodge*, 1401 Paris St (☎705/522-1100 or 1-800/578-7878; ③), and the *Days Inn Sudbury*, 117 Elm St W (☎705/674-7517 or 1-800/325-2525; ③), a three-star place right in the middle of town.

For **food**, *The Red Lobster*, 1600 Lasalle (☎705/560-9825), does a good line in local pickerel and so does the more expensive *Teklenburg's* (☎705/560-2662), just down the street at no.893. Italian food is inexpensive at *Mingle's*, 762 Notre Dame, a studenty pizza and pasta restaurant, whilst comfortable *Pasta e Vino*, 118 Paris St, has delicious home-made pasta.

Manitoulin Island

The Ojibwa believed that when Gitchi Manitou (the Great Spirit) created the world he reserved the best bits for himself and created **MANITOULIN** (God's Island) – the world's largest freshwater island – as his own home. A continuation of the limestone Niagara Escarpment (see p.102), Manitoulin is strikingly different from the harsh grey rocks of the Canadian Shield, its white cliffs, wide lakes, gentle woodland and stretches of open, prairie-like farmland presenting an altogether more welcoming aspect. This rural idyll has long attracted hundreds of summer sailors, who ply the lakes that punctuate the island, and has proved increasingly popular with motorized city folk, who arrive here in numbers on the car ferry from Tobermory (see p.131) in southwest Ontario. Nevertheless, it's easy enough to escape the crowds, either by driving along the north shore, the prettiest part of the island, or by hunkering down in one of Manitoulin's resorts or B&Bs.

About a quarter of the island's 12,000 inhabitants are aboriginals, descendants of groups believed to have arrived here over 10,000 years ago. Archeologists have uncovered evidence of these Paleo-Indians at **Sheguiandah**, on the east coast, and the small display of artefacts at the museum here contains some of the oldest human traces found in Ontario. Much later, in 1836, the island's aboriginal peoples – primarily, Ojibwa and Odawa – reluctantly signed a treaty that turned Manitoulin into a refuge for several Georgian Bay bands who had just been dispossessed by white settlers. Few of them came, which was just as well because the whites soon revised their position and wanted the island for themselves. In 1862, this pressure culminated in a second treaty that gave most of the island to the newcomers. It was all particularly shabby and, to their credit, the Ojibwa band living on the eastern tip of the island at **Wikwemikong** refused to sign. Their descendants still live on this so-called "unceded reserve", and, during the August Civic Weekend, **Wiky**, as it's always known, holds the largest **powwow** in the country.

Manitoulin can be reached either by **road** (and bridge) from Hwy 17 to the north or by **car ferry** from Tobermory in the south (May to late June & early Sept to mid-Oct 2–3 daily; late June to early Sept 4 daily; $11.20 one-way, cars $24.50; reservations on ☎1-800/265-3163). Ferries arrive on the island's south coast at South Baymouth. There are no bus or train services to or around the island.

East Manitoulin: South Baymouth to Little Current

Heading north from the South Baymouth ferry dock, Hwy 6 cuts inland before veering east to reach – after 30km – the lakeshore at the hamlet of **MANITOWANING**, where the treaty of 1836 was signed. There's nothing much to detain you here, though you could drop by the modest **Assiginack Museum** (daily June–Sept 10am–5pm; $1.50), whose pioneer bygones are mostly housed within the sturdy limestone building that once served as the local jail. Near here also is the splendid *Manitowaning Lodge and Resort* (June–Sept; ☎705/859-3136, fax 859-3270, *manilodg@kanservu.ca*), which nestles amongst the woods beside the bay. The timber cabins here are plain, but decorated in the most tasteful of styles and the lodge itself, dating to the 1940s, is graced by unusual sculptures, one of which – a representation of the Great Manitou – drapes over the open fire. The food is simply wonderful too and there is a good range of sporting facilities. Rates, which include breakfast and dinner, range from $135 per person in a one-bedroom cabin per night in the shoulder season, to $165 from late June to Labour Day

From Manitowaning, a side road runs east to the **village of WIKWEMIKONG**, 14km from Hwy 6 on Smith Bay and the focus of the eponymous Indian Reserve. Frankly, it's a dispiriting place badly scarred by poverty, but once every year, on the August Civic Weekend, Wiky is transformed by the country's largest **powwow**, which brings in the best of the continent's performers and is packed with stalls selling native foods and crafts. Amongst the programme of traditional dances and ceremonies, the local theatre group **De-Ba-Jeh-Mu-Jig** (Story Teller) relates native legends and performs contemporary plays by native playwrights – call ☎705/859-2317 for details of other performance dates and locations.

Sheguiandah and Little Current

North from Manitowaning, Hwy 6 cuts a straight line across rolling farmland on its way to **Ten Mile Point Lookout**, which overlooks the waters of Georgian Bay as they funnel into the North Channel on the north side of the island. Shortly afterwards, the highway clips through the bayshore village of **SHEGUIANDAH**, where the homely **Little Current-Howland Museum** (April–Oct daily 10am–4.30pm; $3) is mainly concerned with the pioneer families who first farmed and traded here. Named photographs tell you who was who – and who was related to whom – in what was once an extremely isolated and tightly knit community, whose inhabitants were called "Haweaters" by outsiders after their liking for the scarlet fruit of the hawthorn tree. A ragbag of pioneer knick-knacks further illustrates their life and times – as does an 1870s **log cabin**, barn and sugar shack outside. It was in this wooded bayshore setting that archeologists found the remains of a **Paleo-Indian** settlement around 10,000 years old. A remarkable find, most of the artefacts were carted off to big museums elsewhere, leaving the Little Current-Howland with a display case of crudely fashioned quartzite tools – a weak display for something so important.

From the museum, it's another short hop to **LITTLE CURRENT**, Manitoulin's largest settlement – though that's not exactly a major claim to fame as the population is a mere 1500. It is, however, the site of the island's main **tourist office** (late April to late Oct daily 9am–5pm; ☎705/368-3021, *www.manitoulin.on.ca*), who will help arrange accommodation, an especially useful service in July and August when vacancies can be hard to find. They are located beside the swing bridge just outside town.

From Little Current, Hwy 6 travels north to the mainland over a swing bridge and a series of inter-island causeways. It is 63km to Hwy 17 and a further 75km east to Sudbury (see p.178) or 235km to Sault Ste Marie (see below).

North Manitoulin: Little Current to Meldrum Bay

Highway 540 ducks and weaves its way right along the northern edge of Manitoulin, giving long, lingering views over the North Channel. It also accesses several popular **hiking trails**, notably the six-kilometre **Cup and Saucer Lookout Trail**, which starts near – and is signposted from – the junction of Hwy 540 and Bidwell Road, about 22km west of Little Current. The trail reaches the highest point of the island (460m) and involves climbing ladders through natural rock chimneys.

Pushing on, **KAGAWONG**, about 45km west of Little Current, is arguably the best-looking village on the north shore, its attractive ensemble of old timber houses draped around a wide and gentle bay. It also has **Bridal Veil Falls**, the place for cool dips on hot days, and the falls have given their name to one of Kagawong's finer B&Bs, the *Bridal Veil B&B* (☎705/282-3300; ③), in a century-old home in the centre of the village. A second excellent choice is the equally convenient *Bayview B&B*, also in a Victorian house, with a wrapround veranda and three air-conditioned guestrooms (☎705/282-0741; ③; May–Oct); here, as an added bonus, you get home-made bread for breakfast.

From Kagawong, Hwy 540 continues west through hamlets that you'll miss if you blink until, after 70km, it peters out at **MELDRUM BAY**, a pocket-sized settlement that once flourished as a lumber and fishing port. Twelve kilometres beyond stand the red roofs of the century-old **Mississagi Lighthouse and Keeper's Quarters** (late May to mid-Sept daily 8am–8pm; ☎705/282-7258), now converted into a museum and restaurant with pioneer food, soups, beans and bread.

Sault Ste Marie and the Algoma Central Railway

Strategically situated beside St Mary's River, the tortuous link between lakes Superior and Huron, industrial **SAULT STE MARIE** – more popularly the **SOO** – sits opposite the Michigan town of the same name and sees constant two-way traffic, with two sets of tourists keen to see how the other lot lives. The Soo is northern Ontario's oldest community, originally settled by Ojibwa fishing parties who gathered here beside what was then – before the river was canalized – a set of rapids. The French called these Ojibwa *Saulteux* – "people of the falls" – and the Jesuit missionaries who followed added the Christian sobriquet to give the town its present name. Initially, the Soo flourished as a gateway to the fur-rich regions inland, but it was the construction of a **lock and canal** in the nineteenth century that launched its career as a Great Lakes port and industrial centre, churning out pulp, paper and steel. Actually, the American locks were always bigger and better – and indeed the Canadian locks have only just been reopened after overcoming a catalogue of engineering difficulties.

Too industrial to be pretty, the Soo rustles up a reasonable range of attractions and motels, but its real appeal is as the starting point for a splendid wilderness train ride on the **Algoma Central Railway** (see opposite).

The City

Some two kilometres long and three blocks wide, Soo's **downtown** runs parallel to the waterfront to either side of the main drag, Queen Street East. All the principal sights are here, beginning with the enjoyable **Ermantinger Old Stone House**, right at the east end of the town centre at 831 Queen St E and Pim (mid-April to May Mon–Fri 10am–5pm; June–Sept daily 10am–5pm; Oct & Nov Mon–Fri 1–5pm; $2). Built in 1814, the house was originally home to the fur trader Charles Ermantinger and his Ojibwa wife Manonowe – also known as Charlotte – and their thirteen children. Since then the house has served as an hotel, the sheriff's house, a meeting hall for the YWCA and a social club. Restoration has returned its early nineteenth-century appearance and the period-costumed staff bake tasty cakes in the summer. Across the street, and entirely different, is the special-interest **Canadian Bushplane Heritage Centre** (daily: mid-May to Oct 10am–7pm; Nov to mid-May 10am–4pm; $7.50), whose collection of antique bushplanes is stored within a giant hangar. Bushplanes are of particular use in locating forest fires and there are several sections dealing with this aspect of their work. Models on display include a de Havilland Beaver, a Republic Seabee and a Beech 18 – and there's even a replica fire tower to climb.

The spruced-up section of the Soo's elongated **waterfront** begins just five-minutes' walk away to the west of the Heritage Centre, at the foot of East Street, a block or two from Queen Street East. First up is the **Art Gallery of Algoma**, 10 East St (Mon–Sat 9am–5pm; donation), whose temporary exhibitions usually feature local artists. Moving on, it's a couple of minutes more to the **MS Norgona** (guided tours daily from mid-May to mid-Oct; $2.50), an old Great Lakes' passenger ferry that has ended up moored here, and the **Roberta Bondar Pavilion**, a prominent tent-like permanent structure named after Canada's first astronaut, who came from the Soo. The pavilion is used for concerts and exhibitions and locals are proud of the murals running round its exterior, which show aspects of the area painted inside wigwam shapes; subjects range from shipping and lake scenes to autumn colours and winter landscapes. From May to October on Wednesdays and Saturdays, a Farmers' Market, selling fruit and vegetables, is held here, and cruises of the Soo lock system (see below) begin from the adjacent jetty. Strolling on, you'll soon come to the **Station Mall**, a sprawling shopping centre that has sucked the commercial heart out of downtown Soo, and in front of this is the Algoma Central Railway station (see opposite).

The Sault Ste Marie Canal National Historic Site

A good twenty-minute walk west of the Station Mall, Canal Drive crosses one of the river's narrow channels to reach St Mary's Island, home to the **Sault Ste Marie Canal National Historic Site** (open access). Here, you can stroll along the lock and investigate the old stone buildings that surround it with the help of a series of explanatory plaques. It's all mildly interesting – and if you're nautical interest is stimulated there are two-hour **cruises** through the Soo lock system with Lock Tours Canada (June to mid-Oct 2–4 daily; $19; ☎705/253-9850). Cruises leave from beside the Roberta Bondar Pavilion.

The Algoma Central Railway

The 500-kilometre-long **Algoma Central Railway** (ACR) was constructed in 1901 to link the Soo's timber plants with the forests of the interior. It was first used for recreational purposes by the Group of Seven (see box, p.86), who shunted up and down the track in a converted boxcar, stopping to paint whenever the mood took them. The ACR's timber days are long gone, but today the railway offers one of Ontario's finest excursions, with the train snaking through a wonderfully wild wilderness of deep ravines, secluded lakes and plunging gorges. To see it all, sit on the left-hand side – otherwise you'll end up looking at an awful lot of rock.

There are three tours to choose from and all depart from the Algoma Central Railway Terminal, in downtown Soo, at 129 Bay St and Dennis (☎705/946-7300 or 1-800/242-9287; *www.agawacanyontourtrain.com*). The **Agawa Canyon Tour Train** takes the whole day to cover the first 200km of track and back (June to mid-Oct departs 8am, returns 5pm; June to early Sept $54, early Sept to mid-Oct $66). Advance reservations are strongly advised and are pretty much essential in the autumn, when the leaves turn. A two-hour stop within the canyon's 180-metre-high walls allows for a lunch break and a wander around the well-marked nature trails, which include a lookout post from where the rail line appears as a thin silver thread far below. Unless you are properly equipped don't miss the train back – the canyon gets very cold at night, even during the summer, and the flies are merciless. During the winter when the lakes are frozen and the trees are bent low with ice, the **Snow Train** (Jan to mid-March on Sat, plus Sun in Feb; departs 8am, returns 4.20pm; $54) travels a little further north. It passes right through the canyon to the dramatic exit, where the walls are only 15m apart, before returning to the Soo. The third and longest trip is the **Tour of the Line** (mid-May to mid-Oct Wed & Fri–Sun departs 9.20am, arrives 7pm; mid-Oct to mid-May Fri–Sun departs 9am, arrives 6.40pm; $140 return, excluding accommodation), a return trip that takes two days with an overnight stay in Hearst, the ACR's northern terminus. This is arguably the weakest of the three excursions as the scenery north of the canyon is dreary pine forest and small-town Hearst is hardly riveting. Note also that passengers have to arrange their own accommodation in Hearst – ring the Hearst Chamber of Commerce (☎1-800/655-5769) well ahead of time for details of availability; or contact the *Companion Hotel*, 930 Front St, Hearst (☎705/362-4304 or 1-888/468-9888, fax 705/372-1631; ③), direct.

In addition to these well-publicized tourist jaunts, the ACR runs a regular **passenger train** from the Soo to Hearst every day from mid-May to mid-October – though regular is perhaps stretching the point. Passengers on this train, which is commonly called the "moose meat special" on account of its popularity with hunters and trappers, get off and on at various points along the line and pay 23¢ per kilometre for the distance travelled. This service enables serious hikers to step out into the great unknown comforted that they can always flag down the next train up. Schedule details are available from the ACR, who also have information about renting boxcars and on the several outback lodges that dot the line.

Practicalities

The Soo's Greyhound **bus station** is handily located at 73 Brock St and Bay, in between Queen Street East and the waterfront. Local and provincial information is available at the **Ontario Travel Centre**, 261 Queen St W (daily: mid-May to mid-June & Sept 8am–6pm; mid-June to Aug 8am–8pm; Oct to mid-May 8.30am–5pm; ☎705/945-6941), a ten-minute walk west from the bus station along Queen Street.

Amongst the town's many chain **motels** and **hotels**, two of the most convenient are the *Sleep Inn*, at the east end of downtown, close to the waterfront at 727 Bay St (☎705/253-7533 or 1-800/753-3746, fax 705/253-7667; ④), and the *Days Inn*, plumb in the centre, steps from the ACR station at 320 Bay St and Bruce (☎705/759-8200 or 1-800/329-7466, fax 705/942-9500; ④). More distinctively, one good downtown **B&B** is *Brockwell Chambers*, in a sturdy, two-storey Edwardian house at 183 Brock St and Wellington Street East (☎ & fax 705/949-1076; ③); they have three pleasantly furnished guestrooms, all en suite. The town's cheapest accommodation is in the **youth hostel**, in the former *Algonquin Hotel*, at the east end of the centre at 865 Queen St E and Pim (☎705/253-2311; $30 doubles).

For **food**, *Ernie's Coffee Shop*, 13 Queen St E at Gore (Tues–Sat 7am–7pm), is a popular and inexpensive spot serving breakfast specials for as little as $3.95, and jukeboxes on each table. Also great fun is *Mike's Lunch*, 518 Queen St E at Spring, a classic 1960s diner with high stools, a long counter and old pictures of the Soo plastered on the walls. The best downtown **restaurant** is *A Thymely Manner*, 531 Albert St at Brock (☎705/759-3262; Tues–Sun), which is well known for its lamb from nearby St Joseph's Island and its great Caesar salad; reservations are a must. Otherwise, try well-prepared and well-presented Italian dishes at *Cesira's*, 133 Spring St at Albert (☎705/949-0600).

The north shore of Lake Superior to Sleeping Giant Park

With a surface area of 82,000 square kilometres, **Lake Superior** is the largest freshwater lake in the world, and one of the wildest. Its northern shore between Sault Ste Marie and **Sleeping Giant Provincial Park** is a windswept rugged region formed by volcanoes, earthquakes and glaciers, its steep, forested valleys often overhung by a steely canopy of grey sky. In 1872 Reverend George Grant wrote of Superior: "It breeds storms and rain and fog, like a sea. It is cold . . .wild, masterful and dreaded." The native Ojibwa lived in fear of the storms that would suddenly break on the lake they knew as Gitche Gumee, the Big-Sea-Water, and white sailors were inordinately suspicious of a lake whose icy waters caused its victims to sink like stones: Lake Superior never gives up its dead.

For the most part, **Hwy 17** sticks close to the shore of Lake Superior between Saulte Ste Marie and Sleeping Giant Provincial Park, but a screen of trees almost always keeps the lake out of view. This stretch of road is about 660 kilometres long so, unless you're up for a gruelling thrash or have to reach Thunder Bay (see p.188) or bust, it's much better to dawdle. Along the way are three magnificent parks **Lake Superior Provincial Park**, **Pukaskwa National Park** and Sleeping Giant Provincial Park, where there's camping and hiking – though the insects can be unbearable from May to August, sometimes longer. The small towns dotted along the highway mostly fail to inspire, but low-key **Wawa**, about a third of the way along, has several good places to stay, while dinky **Rossport**, a further 300km west, is easily the prettiest settlement hereabouts.

As for public transport, Greyhound **buses** regularly travel Hwy 17 between Toronto and Winnipeg, but don't expect them to drop you exactly where you want. If you are aiming for a specific motel or campsite check how far you'll have to walk.

Lake Superior Provincial Park

Heading north from Sault Ste Marie on Hwy 17, it's about 120km to the southern perimeter of **Lake Superior Provincial Park** (April–Oct), which offers ready access to Lake Superior's granite shoreline and its immediate hinterland. Autumn is the best time to visit, when the blackflies have abated and the forests of sugar maples and yellow birch are an orgy of colour, but the scenery and wildlife are enthralling throughout the year. Moose, chipmunks and beavers are the commonest mammals, sharing their habitat with more elusive species including white-tailed deer, woodland caribou, coyote, timber wolves and black bears, as well as myriad migratory and resident birds. Hwy 17 cuts through the park for around 100km, passing three campsites, a series of trailheads and, after about 70km, the **Park Office** (May–Oct daily 9am–6pm; ☎705/856-2284), which sells hiking and canoe route maps as well as backcountry camping permits ($6.50). These are compulsory. The office also has information on vacancies at the park's three major **campsites**. These are the basic **Crescent Lake** (late June to late Sept) on the southern boundary, popular **Agawa Bay** (mid-May to late Sept), 8km further north and right on Lake Superior, plus **Rabbit Blanket Lake** (May–Oct) just north of the Park Office and ideal for forays into the interior. The last two campsites have electrical hook-ups, showers and laundry facilities. Prices are $16–23 per pitch; pay at the campsite. Day-use **parking** costs $8.50 per vehicle, overnight $6.50. The rangers will warn you if weather conditions look perilous, but always expect the worst – the park receives more rain and snow than any other area in Ontario. There are no park services of any kind from November to April, when service roads (but not of course Hwy 17) are barred and gated.

Agawa Rock

For thousands of years the Ojibwa used the park area for hunting, a single hunter's territory sometimes extending for as much as 1300 square kilometres. Their sacred rock carvings, created at relatively inaccessible sites in order to heighten their mystery, are best seen on **Agawa Rock**, where the pictures represent a crossing of the lake by Chief Myeegn and his men, during which they were protected by Misshepexhieu, the horned lynx demigod of Lake Superior. To reach Agawa Rock, take the short access road west of Hwy 17 about 16km from the southern border of the park; from here a 400-metre trail leads to a rock ledge from where the pictographs can be viewed.

The Coastal Trail

The finest of the park's trails – the **Coastal Trail** – begins some 140km from Sault Ste Marie at Sinclair Cove and runs north to Chalfant Cove, a challenging route of high cliffs, sand and cobbled beaches, sheltered coves and exposed granite ledges. There are numerous designated backcountry campsites on the trail and the burnt-out fires on the beaches indicate where most people choose to pitch. The entire trek takes about five to seven days but access points enable you to do shorter sections of the trail; the southern part of the trail is not as demanding, with fewer climbs and easier going on sand rather than cobbled beach.

Wawa

The inconsequential iron-mining town of **WAWA**, just 14km north of the park, was named after the Ojibwa word for the cry of the Canadian goose – and to hammer home the point there's a great big steel model of the bird at the entrance to town. The model has helped to make Wawa a busy stopping point on the Trans-Canada Highway (Hwy

17), which was just the idea. In the 1960s, much to the chagrin of local businessfolk, the TCH was routed a couple of kilometres to the west of town – hence the goose to pull passing motorists in.

Modern **motels** line up along Wawa's main drag, Mission Road. Amongst them, two good choices are the well-kept, two-storey *Bristol Motel*, 46 Mission Rd (☎705/856-2385, fax 856-2241, *bristol@onlink.net*; ③), and the comparable *Sportsman's Motel*, with bright-red paint and faux stonework across the street at no. 45 (☎705/856-2272, *sportman@onlink.net*; ③). The latter probably has the edge if for no other reason than the stuffed fish on the foyer walls, including the rare fur-bearing trout (yes, it's a joke). **Eat** at the *Wawa Motor Inn*, at the west end of town at 100 Mission St, where *Reich's Restaurant* features Austrian specialities as well as Lake Superior trout and walleye.

White River

Beyond Wawa, the mixed deciduous–coniferous forest gives way to a boreal forest of balsam fir, white birch, trembling aspen, and white and black spruce – and you have plenty of time to observe it on the 90km haul to the next settlement of any interest, **WHITE RIVER**. There's nothing much to the place, but it does have two claims to fame. First, in 1935, the temperature here dropped to a mind-boggling -72°F, the lowest ever recorded in the whole of Canada – and hence the whopping thermometer hanging by Hwy 17. Second, this was the original home of Winnie the Pooh, a small bear cub named Winnipeg who was exported to London Zoo in 1914. To emphasize the connection, you'll spot a fibreglass Winnie up a tree beside the highway. **Winnie's Hometown Festival** on the third weekend of August is when masses of teddy-bear enthusiasts gather here to get down and groove.

Pukaskwa National Park

Pushing on, Hwy 17 loops inland to skirt an enormous headland that harbours **Pukaskwa National Park**, a chunk of hilly boreal forest interspersed with muskeg and lake that rolls down to a stunningly beautiful coastline. The only access to the park is from the north down the 15km-long Hwy 627, which forks off from Hwy 17 just short of Marathon and 85km west of White River. Hwy 627 goes to **Hattie Cove**, where there is the park's one and only serviced **campsite**, three sandy beaches and a visitor centre (early June to Sept daily 8.30am–6.30pm; ☎807/229-0801), which sells trail guides and backcountry camping permits. From here, the **Coastal Hiking Trail** travels 60km south through the boreal forest and over the ridges and cliffs of the Canadian Shield. It is not an easy hike by any means, but it is simply magnificent and there are regular backcountry campsites on the way. In the summer boats will drop you off at various points along the trail, so you can just hike one-way back to Hattie Cove.

Rossport

Some 130km from the Pukaskwa turning, Hwy 17 passes close to **ROSSPORT**, a picture-perfect village draped around a tiny, sheltered bay. Originally a Hudson's Bay Company trading post, the settlement prospered as a fishing port until the 1960s, when a combination of overfishing and a sea-lamprey attack on the lake trout led to the industry's decline. The railway station was closed down too and today Rossport is the quietest of villages and one that makes for a perfect overnight stay on the long trek north. With more time, Rossport Island Cruises (☎807/767-3006 or 1-800/876-2296) offers splendid **boat trips** out across the steel-grey waters of Lake Superior – anything from a quick zip round the wooded islets of the bay to extended expeditions. Alternatively,

---

AMETHYSTS

Amethyst, a purple-coloured variety of quartz, was first discovered near the shores of Lake Superior between the Ouimet Canyon and Thunder Bay, some 70km to the west, in the middle of the nineteenth century. It is still mined hereabouts and in addition particular deposits have been turned into (well-signposted) tourist attractions – Hwy 17 whizzes past a string of them. One of the best is the **Thunder Bay Agate Mine**, about 4km east of the city – 1km off Hwy 17 along Hwy 527 (mid-May to mid-Oct daily; ☎807/683-3595). Tours of the open-pit mine here are free, but you can pick up a bucket and digging tool to gather as many lumps of rock as you want, and pay for your booty ($1 per lb) on the way out. Amethysts can be polished with baking soda.

Superior Outfitters (☎807/824-3314) rents canoes and kayaks on a daily or weekly basis, and gives tuition.

As for **accommodation**, the tiny *Rossport Inn* (☎807/824-3213, fax 824-3217; rooms ③, cabins ②), whose mock-Tudor flourishes date from the 1880s, occupies a fine lakeside setting. It has seven bedrooms in the main house and ten wooden cabins, with double beds, in the garden. The inn has a good restaurant, but the place to eat is the *Serendipity Café* (☎807/824-2890; closes 7–8pm), a surprisingly sophisticated spot with feta cheese, rocket salad, smoked salmon and the like – all at reasonable prices. Lastly, there are two fine **campsites** in the woods by the lake in Rainbow Falls Provincial Park (☎807/824-2298; $14–18; late May to early Sept), just 7km east of Rossport off Hwy 17.

Ouimet Canyon Provincial Park

From Rossport, it's 80km to **NIPIGON**, where Hwy 11 finishes its mammoth trek across Northern Ontario to merge into Hwy 17. After a further 35km or so, Hwy 17 reaches the 11-kilometre-long turning that leads north away from the lake to one of the region's more spectacular sights in **Ouimet Canyon Provincial Park** (mid-May to early Oct daily; free; day-use only). The canyon was formed during the last ice age, when a sheet of ice 2km thick crept southward, bulldozing a fissure 3km long, 150m wide and 150m deep. Nearly always deserted, the canyon has two lookout points that hang over the terrifyingly sheer sides looking down to the permanently dark base – an anomalous frozen habitat whose perpetual snow supports some very rare arctic plants. The vistas are especially stimulating in the autumn, when the forests flash red, orange and yellow.

West to Sleeping Giant Provincial Park

Pushing on west from Ouimet Canyon, it's around 25km on Hwy 17 to Hwy 587, which branches south to scuttle down the 42-kilometre-long **Sibley Peninsula**. The peninsula's entire area is given over to the dramatically scenic **Sleeping Giant Provincial Park** (open year-round), so named because of the recumbent form of the four mesas that constitute its backbone. Established in 1944 to protect what the logging companies had left of the red and white pines, the park covers 243 square kilometres of high, barren rocks and lowland bogs, crisscrossed with 100km of trails. Acting as a sort of catch net for animals, the peninsula is inhabited by beaver, fox, porcupine, white-tailed deer and moose. There are also wolves in the more remote areas – on a still night you can hear them howling.

Highway 587 enters the park about 6km beyond the village of **Pass Lake**. Admission is $8.50 per vehicle. The visitor centre (May–Aug Mon–Fri 8am–4.30pm; ☎807/977-2526) is situated about 20km from the park entrance at the south end of Lake Marie

TERRY FOX

West of Nipigon, highways 17 and 11 merge to become the **Terry Fox Courage Highway**, named after Terrance Stanley Fox (1958–81), one of modern Canada's most remarkable figures. At the age of 18 Terry developed cancer and had to have his right leg amputated. Determined to advance the search for a cure, he nevertheless planned a money-raising run from coast to coast and on April 12, 1980, he set out from St John's in Newfoundland. For 143 days he ran 26 painful miles a day, covering five provinces by June and raising $34 million. In September, at mile 3339, just outside Thunder Bay, Terry was forced by lung cancer to abandon his run; he returned home to Port Coqitlam in British Columbia, where he died the following summer. More than $85 million has now been raised for cancer research in his name. In his honour, the **Terry Fox Monument**, a finely crafted bronze showing the lad running, has been placed on top of a ridge in a little park above the highway just to the east of Thunder Bay. From the monument, there are panoramic views over Lake Superior and Thunder Bay tourism has its main office here (see p.191).

Louise. Pick up maps and hiking trail details either here or at the park entrance. Also at the south end of Lake Marie Louise is the park's one and only **campsite** with 190 sites ($17–22; late May to early Oct); reservations are advised in high season. Backcountry camping is possible too – pick up a permit ($6) at the visitor centre.

Of the park's hikes, the forty-kilometre **Kaybeyun Trail** is the most spectacular and the hardest. Beginning at the southern end of Hwy 587, it runs around the tip of the peninsula via the rock formation known as the Sealion to the Chimney, at the Sleeping Giant's knees, then on to Nanabijou Lookout at the chest of the Giant, and finally to the Thunder Bay Lookout. You have to be fit – the walk to the Chimney takes about nine hours of hard graft up rugged pathways, where the boulders are the size of cars. Other less ambitious trails include the **Talus** and the **Sawyer** – which leave the Kaybeyun at Sawyer Bay on the southwest side of the peninsula – and easier still are the **Joe Creek Trail** and the **Pinewood Hill Trail**, both of which are situated in the northern end of the park near Hwy 587. The latter leads to a fine viewpoint over Joeboy Lake – a favourite spot for moose escaping the flies. The brief **Sibley Creek Trail**, which passes a number of beaver dams, begins near Lake Louise, so you're likely to share the wilderness with a number of other hikers.

At the southern tip of Hwy 587 is the curious **Silver Islet**, not an island at all, but the ice-blasted remains of a thriving silver town, some fifty houses in all, including a customs house, a log jail, and a weathered general store, plus a population of two. Mining magnate Alexander Sibley founded Silver Islet in 1872 and his ambitious plans involved building a wall from his new town to Burnt Island just offshore to get at a silver deposit – you can still see bits of the wall today. Over the years the town exhausted the local firewood supply and had to rely on coal for fuel – and this was to be its undoing. One winter, the coal boat got stuck in the ice and, rather than freeze to death, the miners were forced to leave; they never came back.

Doubling back to the top of Hwy 587, it's 30km west on Hwy 17 to Thunder Bay.

Thunder Bay

The Great Lakes' port of **THUNDER BAY** is much closer to Winnipeg than to any other city in Ontario, and its population of 117,000 is prone to see themselves as Westerners. Economics as well as geography define this self-image, for this was until recently a booming grain-handling port, and the grain, of course, is harvested in the

Prairies. The grain still arrives here by rail to be stored in gigantic grain elevators and then shipped down the St Lawrence Seaway to the Atlantic, but not in the same quantities as before. In the 1990s, the economics of the grain trade changed in favour of Canada's Pacific ports and Thunder Bay suffered accordingly. Consequently, many of the grain elevators that dominate the harbourfront are literally rotting away, while others are hanging on by the skin of their teeth. This unwarranted reversal of fortunes has encouraged Thunder Bay to reinvent itself by encouraging manufacturing and tourism. To boost the latter, the city council has created a cheerful marina and built a spanking new **casino**, though this proved very controversial. Such was the opposition that the casino was, in a rather bizarre compromise, called the "Charity Casino" to remind the citizenry that the profits be spent on good works.

Thunder Bay was created in 1970 when the two existing towns of Fort William and Port Arthur were brought together under one municipal roof. **Fort William** was the older of the two, established in 1789 as a fur-trading post and subsequently becoming the upcountry headquarters of the North West Company. It lost its pre-eminent position when the North West and Hudson's Bay companies merged, but it remained a fur-trading post until the end of the nineteenth century. Meanwhile, in the middle of the nineteenth century, rumours of a huge silver lode brought prospectors to the Lake Superior shoreline just north of Fort William and here they established **Port Arthur**. But the silver didn't last and the Port Arthur, Duluth and Western railway (PD&W), which had laid the lines to the mines, was soon nicknamed "the Poverty, Distress and Welfare". The Canadian Northern Railway, which took over the abandoned PD&W lines, did much to rescue the local economy, but did not bring Fort William and Port Arthur closer together. Rudyard Kipling noted that "The twin cities hate each other with the pure, passionate, poisonous hatred that makes cities grow. If Providence wiped out one of them, the other would pine away and die." Fortunately, the 1970 amalgamation bypassed Kipling's prediction and nowadays these parochial rivalries have all but vanished.

Scarred by industrial complexes and crisscrossed by rail lines, Thunder Bay is not immediately enticing, but it does have enough of interest to make a pleasant stopover on the long journey to or from Winnipeg. The most agreeable part of town is the few blocks stretching inland from behind the marina in **Thunder Bay North** – north of Central Avenue – and here you'll also find several good cafés and restaurants. **Thunder Bay South** is much grittier, but on its outskirts is the city's star turn, the replica fur-trading post of **Old Fort William**.

The telephone code for Thunder Bay is ☎807.

Arrival and information

Thunder Bay Airport is on the west edge of Thunder Bay South – and 13km from the Pagoda. To get from the airport to the Pagoda, take local bus #3 Airport (every 30–40min) to the Brodie Street **bus terminal** in Thunder Bay South and either change or stay on the bus (depending on the bus number) for onward transportation to Thunder Bay North at the Water Street terminal, by the marina. Local buses are operated by Thunder Bay Transit (☎684-3744). The flat fare is $2; ask for a transfer if you need more than one bus to complete your journey. The long-distance Greyhound **bus station**, at 815 Fort William Rd, is the terminal for buses arriving from Sault Ste Marie, Winnipeg (via Kenora) and Duluth. Transit bus #1, connecting the Brodie Street terminal with the Pagoda, runs past the long-distance terminal.

There are two **tourist offices**. One is downtown in the Pagoda (May–Sept daily 9am–5pm; ☎684-3670), the other is in the Terry Fox Centre by the Terry Fox

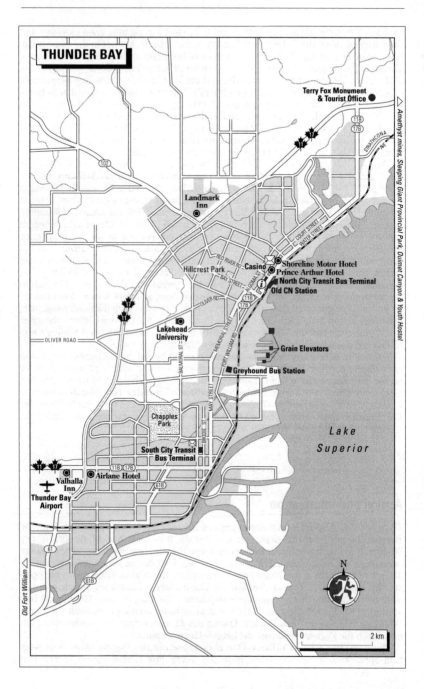

THUNDER BAY

Terry Fox Monument
& Tourist Office

Amethyst mines, Sleeping Giant Provincial Park, Ouimet Canyon & Youth Hostel

102

Landmark
Inn

Casino
Shoreline Motor Hotel
Hillcrest Park
Prince Arthur Hotel
North City Transit Bus Terminal
Old CN Station

Lakehead
University

OLIVER ROAD

Grain Elevators

Greyhound Bus Station

Chapples
Park

Lake
Superior

South City Transit
Bus Terminal

Valhalla
Inn
Airlane Hotel

Thunder Bay
Airport

Old Fort William

N

0   2 km

Monument (daily: mid-May to Aug 8am–8pm; Sept to mid-May 9am–5pm; ☎983-2041 or 1-800/MOST-FUN), on Hwy 17 just outside of town.

Accommodation

Thunder Bay has a healthy supply of reasonably priced **motel** and **hotel** accommodation, as well as lodgings in **student rooms** on Lakehead University's campus and a well-equipped **campsite** on the edge of town. Further out, but reachable on Greyhound buses, is a good **hostel**.

HOTELS, MOTELS AND BED AND BREAKFASTS

Airlane Hotel, 698 West Arthur St and Expressway (☎473-1600 or 1-800/465-5003, fax 475-4852). Within easy reach of Old Fort William and the airport, this bright, modern hotel has all modern conveniences and three restaurants. ⑤.

Prince Arthur Hotel, 17 Cumberland St N at Red River Rd (☎345-5411 or 1-800/267-2675, fax 345-8565). Built by the CNR in 1908, this imposing stone-and-brick block is just up from the Pagoda. Inside, there are flashes of the original Edwardian elegance, but most of the furnishings are modern and the rooms, reached along echoing corridors, are similar, as well as being large and comfortable. ③.

Shoreline Motor Hotel, 61 Cumberland St N at Camelot (☎346-9763). Standard-issue budget motel, but handily located just a couple of blocks from the Pagoda. ③.

Valhalla Inn, 1 Valhalla Inn Rd (☎577-1121 or 1-800/964-1121, fax 475-4723, *www.valhallainn.com*). Perhaps the best-looking of the city's hotels, this brick-and-timber modern hotel offers 267 spacious and well-equipped rooms. ④.

HOSTEL, STUDENT ROOMS AND CAMPSITE

KOA Thunder Bay, Hwy 17 at Spruce River Rd (☎683-6221). The district's largest campsite, 2.5km east of the Terry Fox Lookout on Hwy 17 with a full range of services including a grocery store and laundry. Sites, many amongst the woods, from $15. Mid-April to mid-Oct.

Lakehead University, Lakehead University Campus, off Oliver Rd (☎343-8612). With its manicured lawns and miniature lake – students call it Lake Inferior – the university campus is a pleasant spot. Both single ($22) and double ($34) rooms are available in several student blocks during the summer. Access to the university's sports facilities is included. The campus is located about 4km southwest of the Pagoda; take bus #2 from the Water Street terminal by the marina.

Thunder Bay International Backpackers Hostel (Longhouse Village), 1594 Lakeshore Drive, RR #13 (☎983-2042, fax 983-2914, *www.thunderbayhostel.com*). Run by a knowledgeable husband-and-wife team, who were once missionaries in Borneo, this hostel is the first home of many immigrants and has a friendly commune-like atmosphere, a beautiful setting and no curfew. However, it's 18km northeast of Thunder Bay and not served by city buses. The eastbound Greyhound bus will drop you off at the end of Mackenzie Station Rd on Hwy 17, which is a 20min walk from the hostel. Beds are $20 per person. Camping is also available in the hostel grounds for $18 for two, $11 for one.

Thunder Bay North

Thunder Bay's five-kilometre-long **waterfront** is home to a string of **grain elevators**, whose stirring architecture – all modernist lines and pure functionalism – can't fail to impress. In the middle of the industrial jangle is the **marina** and behind that is the old **CN railway station**, whose distinctive high-pitched gables, turrets and dormer windows were built to resemble a French chateau. The station was erected in 1906 and three years later CN dipped into their pockets again to create the **Pagoda**, a fanciful bandstand just across the street that now houses a tourist office (see p.191). At one time, the local band would strike up a tune or two to welcome any visiting bigwig – which must have been a pleasant way to forget just how long it had taken to actually get here.

Thunder Bay North's most appealing enclave is the Finnish district of **Little Suomi**, focused on the Bay and Algoma streets intersection, about ten-minutes' walk southwest from the Pagoda. There are over forty ethnic groups in Thunder Bay and several of them maintain their own institutions, but no one more so than the Finns – though for most of its history it has been a deeply divided community. Arriving in the 1870s, the first Finns to get here were left-wing refugees escaping the tender mercies of the Tsar, whereas those who arrived after 1917 were right-wing opponents (plus the odd anarchist) of the Bolsheviks. Little Suomi's architecture is resolutely suburban, but the town's most atmospheric restaurants are here (see overleaf).

Keep on going west along Bay Street from Algoma and you'll soon reach **Hillcrest Park**, perched on a low ridge and with flower beds, offering great views out across the lake.

Thunder Bay South: Old Fort William

Thunder Bay's *tour de force* is the reconstructed fur-trading post of **Old Fort William** (mid-May to mid-Oct daily 9am–6pm; $10; ☎473-2344), in a loop of the Kaministiquia River about 15km southwest of the old CN railway station – and 13km upriver from its original site. At the entrance is a **visitors' centre**, where a first-rate film traces the history of the fort and explains its workings. From here, it's a quick stroll or bus ride to the fort, a large palisaded compound which has been restored to its appearance in 1815, when it was the inland headquarters of the North West Company and their major shipment base. Impeccably researched and staffed by students dressed in period gear, the forty-odd buildings that fill out the compound illuminate the fort's original purpose with everything from simple storehouses to the capacious Great Hall. Look out also for the fur warehouse, festooned with the pelts of beaver, lynx and arctic fox, and the canoe workshop, where exquisite birch-bark canoes are made to traditional designs for museums all over Canada. There are demonstrations of contemporary trades and crafts, as well as a working kitchen, kitchen garden and a farm complete with sheep, pigs and cows.

Old Fort William is particularly enjoyable in July, when there is a four-day re-enactment of the **Great Rendezvous**, an annual gathering of the North West Company's employees, fur traders and *voyageurs*.

Eating and drinking

The best places to **eat** are in Little Suomi, at and around Bay and Algoma streets, where you can sample tasty Finnish food in healthy portions (but note that most places here close early). There is a cluster of blue-collar **bars** on Cumberland Street, just up from the Pagoda.

Armando's, 28 Cumberland St N at Red River Rd (☎344-5833). Trim Italian restaurant offering good pizzas, pastas and more. Reasonable prices. Closed Sun.

Hoito Restaurant, 314 Bay St at Algoma. Established in 1918, Thunder Bay's best-known Finnish café-cum-canteen is always full and the specials on the board should not be missed. The salt fish, potatoes and viili (clabbered milk) is delicious and costs just $7. Open Mon–Fri 7am–8pm, Sat & Sun 8am–8pm.

Kangas Sauna, 379 Oliver Rd (☎344-6761). Previously a small counter service for the sauna users, now a larger café-restaurant with delicious home-made soups, omelettes and sweet berry pies. On the edge of Little Suomi. Open daily 7.30am–11pm.

The Office, 16 Cumberland St at Red River. Dark and steamy bar that bills itself as the Home of the Blues. Features frequent live blues bands of variable quality.

Scandinavian Homemade Café, 147 Algoma S at Bay. A friendly, cosy café with full breakfasts for $7 and delicious Finnish pancakes. Open Mon–Sat 7am–4pm.

Listings

Airlines Air Canada, at the airport (☎623-3313).
Bus information Local: City Transit (☎344-9666). Long-distance: Greyhound (☎345-2194).
Camping equipment Gear Up For Outdoors, 894 Alloy Place (☎345-0001, *www.gear-up.com*).
Car rental Avis, at the airport (☎473-8572); Budget, at the airport (☎473-5040); National, at the airport (☎577-1234).
Pharmacy Medical Centre Pharmacy, 63 Algoma St (☎345-1421).
Taxis Diamond (☎622-6001); Roach's (☎344-8481).
Weather For up-to-date bulletins, call ☎345-9111.

West of Thunder Bay

Heading west from Thunder Bay on Hwy 17, it's a long, gruelling drive of almost 500km through the interminable pine forests of the Canadian Shield to the next town of any real interest, **Kenora**, where hundreds of fishermen gather every summer before sidling off into the vast **Lake of the Woods**. The lake straddles the Ontario-Manitoba border and Kenora is itself just 200km from Winnipeg (see p.462). Regular long-distance buses ply Hwy 17 – and remember you save an hour when you cross into Central Standard Time near the start of the journey, about 60km west of Thunder Bay.

Kenora and the Lake of the Woods

KENORA used to be known as Rat Portage until a flour company refused to build a mill here, arguing that the word "rat" on their sacks wouldn't do much for sales. Nowadays the permanent population of 9000 quadruples in the summer, when droves of Americans arrive with their fishing tackle – no wonder the town has a twelve-metre statue of a fish at its entrance. Rod or not, Kenora is a pleasant spot to break the long journey west (or east), especially in summer when there's a really laid-back feel to the place.

From the foot of Main Street, the MS *Kenora* **cruises** the Lake of the Woods' islands and channels for two hours (mid-May to mid-Sept Mon–Sat 4 daily, Sun 1 daily; $15; ☎807/468-9124), offering an opportunity to see **Devil's Gap Rock** at the entrance to the town harbour. In 1884, the rock was painted to resemble a human face and it has been regularly repainted ever since. This is not, however, a gimmicky attraction: Devil's Gap is an Ojibwa spirit rock, to which food and tobacco offerings were once made to propitiate Windigo, the large and threatening personification of winter. Windigo's powers could only be controlled by powerful shamen, and when hunters disappeared in the bush they were thought to have been eaten by him.

As an introduction to the **Lake of the Woods**, the boat trip does just fine, but the sheer vastness of the lake – and its 14,000 islands – is hard to grasp. One way of sampling much more is to hire a **houseboat** with Houseboat Adventures, at the Main Street wharf (☎807/543-2911 or 1-800/253-6672, fax 807/543-3678, *www.houseboatadventures.com*). Their boats have all modern conveniences – from toasters through to freezers – and the onboard fish-cleaning stations reveal the predilections of their customers, but it is still a wonderful way to experience the outback. Prices from $1575 to $3500 per week per boat for up to six people.

Practicalities

Kenora's **bus terminus** is across the bay in neighbouring Keewatin, from where local buses run to Kenora itself. The Lake of the Woods **tourist office** is located on Hwy 17 east of town (mid-May to June daily 9am–5pm; July & Aug daily 9am–8pm; Sept to mid-May Mon–Fri 9am–5pm). First choice for **accommodation** is the eight-storey *Best Western Lakeside Inn & Convention Centre*, 470 1st Ave S (☎807/468-5521 or 1-800/465-1120, fax 807/468-4734; ④), with great views. There's the usual string of **motels** stretching along the highway just outside town, all of which require reservations in the summer: *Lake-Vu Motel*, 740 Lakeview Drive (☎807/468-5501, fax 468-5873; ②), is a moderately priced three-star that is as good as any.

travel details

Trains

Cochrane to: Moosonee (5 weekly in summer, 3 weekly in winter; 5hr 15min).

Kingston to: Toronto (1 daily; 2hr 20min).

Ottawa to: Brockville (3–4 daily; 1hr 15min); Gananoque (1 daily; 1hr 35min); Kingston (3–4 daily; 1hr 45min–2hr 30min); Montréal (2–4 daily; 2hr 20min); Toronto (3–4 daily; 4hr 7min–4hr 12min).

Sudbury to: White River (3 weekly; 8hr 20min).

Toronto to: Buffalo, NY (1 daily; 4hr); Chicago, IL (1 daily; 11hr); Cobalt (6 weekly; 7hr); Cochrane (6 weekly; 10hr); Gravenhurst (6 weekly; 2hr); Huntsville (6 weekly; 2hr 45min); Kingston (7 daily; 2hr); Kitchener (2 daily; 1hr 45min); London (7 daily; 3hr); Montréal (4–6 daily; 4hr 45min; express daily except Sat; 4hr); New York, NY (1 daily; 12hr); Niagara Falls (2 daily; 2hr); North Bay (6 weekly; 4hr 40min); Ottawa (3–4 daily; 4hr); Parry Sound (3 weekly; 4hr 15min); Sarnia (2 daily; 4hr 15min); Stratford (2 daily; 2hr 10min); Sudbury Junction (3 weekly; 7hr 15min); Temagami (6 weekly; 6hr 20min); Windsor (4 daily; 4hr); Winnipeg (3 weekly; 29hr 45min).

Buses

Kenora to: Winnipeg (5 daily; 2hr 30min).

Kingston to: Montréal (2 daily; 3hr 25min); Ottawa (4 daily; 2hr 45min).

London to: Hamilton (2 daily; 2hr); Kitchener (2 daily; 2hr); Niagara Falls (2 daily; 3hr 45min); Owen Sound (1 daily; 3hr 45min); Stratford (2 daily; 1hr); Windsor (1 daily; 3hr).

North Bay to: Cobalt (4 daily; 1hr 50min); Cochrane (5 daily; 6hr 15min–7hr); Haileybury (2 daily; 2hr); Kirkland Lake (7 daily; 3hr 15min–4hr);

New Liskeard (4 daily; 2hr 15min); Sudbury (3 daily; 2hr); Temagami (4 daily; 1hr 10min).

Ottawa to: Brockville (1 daily; 2hr 10min); Cornwall (1 daily; 1hr 20min; summer only 2 daily; 1hr 20min–2hr); Kingston (4 daily; 2hr 45min); Montréal (11 daily; 2hr 20min); North Bay (6 daily; 2hr 30min–4hr 50min); Sudbury (3 daily; 6hr 45min); Toronto (6 daily; 5hr 30min); Upper Canada Village (summer only 1 daily; 1hr 30min).

Sault Ste Marie to: Kenora (1–3 daily; 16hr); Nipigon (1–4 daily; 7hr 40min–8hr 30min); Terrace Bay (1–3 daily; 7hr 30min); Thunder Bay (1–4 daily; 9–10hr); Toronto (3 daily; 10hr 50min); Wawa (1–3 daily; 3hr); White River (1–4 daily; 4hr–5hr 30min); Winnipeg (1–4 daily; 18hr 30min–19hr).

Sudbury to: Montréal (3 daily; 11hr); North Bay (3 daily; 2hr); Ottawa (3 daily; 7hr 30min); Pembroke (3 daily; 5hr); Sault Ste Marie (4 daily; 4–5hr); Toronto (4 daily; 5hr 30min).

Thunder Bay to: Kenora (3 daily; 5hr); Winnipeg (3 daily; 8hr).

Toronto to: Collingwood (4 daily; 2hr 50min); Cornwall (7 daily; 5hr 15min); Espanola (4 daily; 6hr); Gravenhurst (4 daily; 3hr); Hamilton (every 15min–hourly; 1hr); Hunstsville (3 daily; 4hr); Kingston (7 daily; 3hr); Kitchener (8 daily; 1hr 45min); London (8 daily; 2hr 20min–3hr); Midland (3 daily; 2hr 35min); Montréal (10 daily; 7hr); New York, NY (express 7 daily; 12hr); Niagara Falls (hourly; 1hr 30min–2hr); Nipigon (4 daily; 18hr 15min); North Bay (1 daily; 4hr 45min); Ottawa (10 daily; 5–8hr); Owen Sound (3 daily; 3hr 15min); Parry Sound (6 daily; 2hr–4hr 15min); Penetanguishene (3 daily; 2hr 45min); Sault Ste Marie (4 daily; 10hr 50min); Sudbury (4 daily; 5hr); Thunder Bay (4 daily; 21hr 30min); Wasaga Beach (2–3 daily; 2hr 15min); Wawa (4 daily; 13hr

50min); White River (4 daily; 17hr); Windsor (8 daily; 4hr 30min); Winnipeg (3 daily; 30hr 30min).

Flights

Ottawa to: Calgary (5–9 daily; 3hr 40min); Banff (5–9 daily; 3hr 40min); Dartmouth (3–6 daily; 2hr); Halifax (3–6 daily; 2hr); Montréal (7–16 daily; 30min); Québec City (6–18 daily; 1hr); Vancouver (8 daily; 5hr 20min); Winnipeg (6–7 daily; 2hr 20min).

Toronto to: Calgary (5–7 daily; 4hr 15min); Edmonton (5–7 daily; 1hr 40min); Fredericton (5–6 daily; 1hr 45min); Halifax (7–9 daily; 2hr); Moncton (5 daily; 2hr); Montréal (15–26 daily; 1hr 15min); Ottawa (11–22 daily; 1hr); Québec City (8–19 daily; 1hr 45min); Saint John (4–5 daily; 1hr 45min); St John's (6–7 daily; 3hr); Saskatoon (2–3 daily; 3hr 30min); Thunder Bay (2–5 daily; 1hr 30min); Vancouver (6–7 daily; 5hr); Winnipeg (5 daily; 2hr 45min).

CHAPTER TWO

QUÉBEC

As home to the only French-speaking society in North America, **Québec** is totally distinct from the rest of the continent – so distinct, in fact, that its political elite have been obsessed with the politics of secession for the last forty years. The genesis of Québec's potential political separation from its English-speaking neighbours tracks back to France's ceding of the colony to Britain after the Conquest of 1759. At first this transfer saw little change in the life of most Québécois. Permitted to maintain their language and religion, they stayed under the control of the Catholic Church, whose domination of rural society – evident in the huge churches of Québec's tiny villages – resulted in an economically and educationally deprived subclass whose main contribution was huge families. It was these huge families, though, that ensured French-speakers would continue to dominate the province demographically – a political move termed the *revanche du berceau* (revenge of the cradle).

The creation of Lower and Upper Canada in 1791 emphasized the inequalities between anglophones and francophones, as the French-speaking majority in Lower Canada were ruled by the so-called **Château Clique** – an assembly of francophone priests and seigneurs who had to answer to a British governor and council appointed in London. Rebellions against this hierarchy by the French *Patriotes* in 1837 led to an investigation by Lord Durham who concluded that English and French relations were akin to "two nations warring within the bosom of a single state". His prescription for peace was immersing French-Canadians in the English culture of North America, and the subsequent establishment of the Province of Canada in 1840 can be seen as a deliberate attempt to marginalize francophone opinion within an English-speaking state.

French-Canadians remained insulated from the economic mainstream until twentieth-century **industrialization**, financed and run by the better-educated anglophones, led to a mass francophone migration to the cities. Here, a French-speaking middle class soon began to articulate the grievances of the workforce and to criticize the suffocating effect the Church was having on francophone opportunity. The shake-up of Québec society finally came about with the so-called **Quiet Revolution** in the 1960s, spurred by the provincial government under the leadership of Jean Lesage and his Liberal Party of Québec. The provincial government took control of welfare, health and education away from the Church and, under the slogan *"Maîtres chez-nous"* (Masters of our own house), established state-owned industries that reversed anglophone financial domination by encouraging the development of a francophone entrepreneurial and business class.

In order to implement these fiscal policies, Québec needed to administer its own taxes, and the provincial Liberals, despite being staunchly federalist, were constantly at loggerheads with Ottawa. Encouraged and influenced by other nationalist struggles, Québécois' desire for cultural recognition and political power intensified and reached a violent peak in 1970 with the terrorist actions of the largely unpopular **Front de Libération du Québec** (FLQ) in Montréal. The kidnapping of Cabinet Minster Pierre Laporte and British diplomat James Cross, with Laporte winding up dead in the trunk of a car, led then-Prime Minister Pierre Elliott Trudeau to enact the War Measures Act and send Canadian troops into the streets of Montréal. Six years later a massive reaction against the ruling provincial Liberals brought the separatist **Parti Québécois**

(PQ) to power in Montréal. Led by René Lévesque, the Parti Québécois accelerated the process of social change with the *Charte de la langue française*, better known as **Bill 101**, which established French as the province's official language. With French dominant in the workplace and the classroom, Québécois thought they had got as close as possible to cultural and social independence. Still reeling from the terrorist activities of the FLQ and scared that Lévesque's ultimate objective of separatism would leave Québec economically adrift, the 6.5-million population voted 60:40 against sovereignty in a 1980 referendum.

Having made the promise that voting against separation meant voting for a "new Canada", Trudeau set about repatriating the country's **Constitution** in the autumn of 1981. Québec was prepared to contest the agreement with the support of other provincial leaders, but was spectacularly denied the opportunity to do so when Trudeau called a late-night meeting on the issue and did not invite Lévesque to the table. "The night of the long knives", as the event became known, wound up imposing a Constitution on the province that placed its language rights in jeopardy and removed its veto power over constitutional amendments. Accordingly, the provincial government refused to sign it – and hasn't to this day.

The Constitution's failure to include Québec became a lingering source of ire, which the *beau risque* (beautiful risk) equally failed to extinguish. A good-faith alliance between Québécois, the Liberal Party of Québec under Robert Bourassa, and the federal Progressive-Conservatives under Brian Mulroney, the *beau risque* produced the **Meech Lake Accord** in 1990. Inspired by Mulroney's talk of bringing Québec back into the Canadian fold with "honour and enthusiasm", the accord sought to recognize Québec's status as a "distinct society" and give it the power to opt out of federal legislation it didn't like – including the Canadian Charter of Rights and Freedoms, the Canadian equivalent of the American Bill of Rights. The talks collapsed on Québec's national holiday, la Fête St-Jean-Baptiste, and tens of thousands of Québécois took to the streets to demonstrate their frustration. The failure also prompted Lucien Bouchard, one of Mulroney's cabinet ministers and primary promoter of the agreement to English Canada, to resign from the Progressive-Conservative Party and form a new sovereignist federal party, the **Bloc Québécois**. In desperation, the Liberal leader Robert Bourassa hastily threw together a constitutional agreement, the **Charlottetown Accord**, that attempted not only to satisfy Québec, but the rest of Canada, and the aboriginal peoples as well. The accord's scope was so enormous that it failed on all points and was rejected by Québec and several other provinces in a Canada-wide referendum in 1992.

In October 1993, Québec's displeasure with federalism was evident in the election of Lucien Bouchard's Bloc Québécois to the ironic status of Her Majesty's Official Opposition in Ottawa. The cause received added support in 1994 when the Parti Québécois was returned to provincial power after vowing to hold a province-wide referendum on separation from Canada. The **referendum** was held a year later and the vote was so close – the province opted to remain a part of Canada by a margin of under one percent (50.6:49.4) – that calls immediately arose for a third referendum (prompting pundits to refer to the process as the "neverendum").

In 1996, Bouchard left federal politics to take the leadership of the PQ, determined to become the leader of a new country and promising to proceed with the separation process and work on the economy. Another step towards constitutional reform was taken in September 1997, when nine of Canada's ten provincial premiers endorsed the **Calgary Declaration** stating that Québec's unique character should be recognized – a shift from the "distinct society" recognition proposal in the failed Meech Lake and Charlottetown constitutional reform packages. Bouchard, the only premier not in attendance at the meeting, took the new term as "an insult", and the declaration's intentions never really got off the ground. Instead, the federal Liberals enacted the **Clarity**

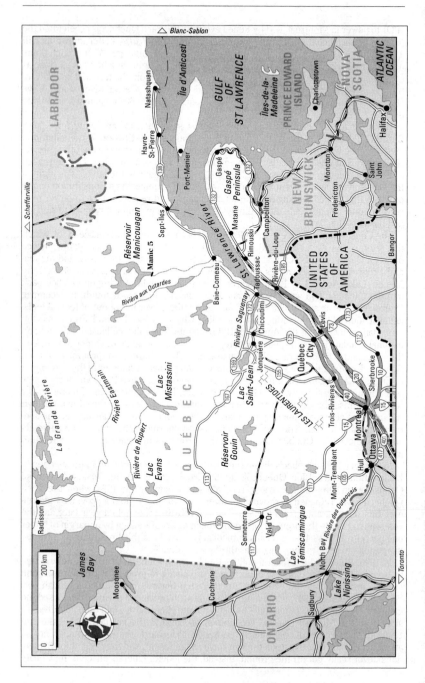

ACCOMMODATION PRICE CODES

All of the accommodation prices in this book have been coded using the symbols below, corresponding to Canadian dollar rates. Prices are for the least expensive double room in each establishment in high season, excluding special offers. For a full explanation, see p.40 in Basics.

① up to $40	④ $80–100	⑦ $175–240
② $40–60	⑤ $100–125	⑧ $240+
③ $60–80	⑥ $125–175	

Act in 1999 – a sharp departure from their previous kowtowing tactics, as the act laid out the requirements Québec needed to meet to secede from Canada. While it infuriated leaders of the sovereignist movement, it also met with sharp criticism from members of the federalist camp who were convinced it would ignite sovereignist fire and result in a definitive Yes vote. Their fears didn't come to pass, however; in a surprising turn of the popular vote, the 2000 federal elections saw the federal Liberals win more in Québec than the Bloc Québécois.

An even greater shock was Bouchard's sudden resignation as Premier of Québec in January 2001, leaving the PQ with no obvious successor that matched his powers of oratory or charisma. Without Bouchard, there is little hope of achieving the dream of a sovereign Québec in the near future – if ever. Whoever the party chooses as his

ABORIGINAL PEOPLES

Francophone–anglophone relations may be the principal concern of most Québécois – eighty percent of them have French as their mother tongue – but the province's population also includes eleven nations of aboriginal peoples, the majority of whom live on reservations "granted" them by the early French settlers. Resentment and racism are as rife here as elsewhere in Canada, but aboriginal grievances are particularly acute in Québec as most of the province's tribes are English-oriented – the Mohawks near Montréal even fought on the side of the British during the conquest. Still, relations are even bad between the authorities and French-speaking groups. The Hurons (see pp.272–273) near Québec City, for example, battled in courts for eight years to retain their hunting rights, while around James Bay the Cree fought and won the right to block the expansion of Québec's hydroelectric network which, had it been completed as planned, would have covered an area the size of Germany. Begun in 1971, the project nonetheless resulted in the displacement of Cree and Inuit, due to flooded lands as well as the pollution of rivers that had not been safely channelled. Aboriginal peoples have categorically voted against separation and have used mostly peaceful methods to register their land claims, which amount to 85 percent of the province's area. There was violence at the Mohawk uprising at Oka near Montréal in 1990 (see p.239), which, though condemned by most Canadians and aboriginals, drew attention to the concerns of aboriginal Canadians. This led to the creation of the Royal Commission on Aboriginal Peoples, a nationwide examination of the issues at stake. In November of 1996, the commission recommended a revamping of the aboriginal welfare system, greater self-government and a settlement of land-claims negotiations. Some of these have been enacted – such as the Nisga'a treaty in British Columbia – but scarcely any movement has been made on other issues. First Nations have also been asserting ownership of natural resources, especially in the eastern provinces where fishing rights are a hotly contested issue, and these have also been upheld by the Supreme Court of Canada. Each decision in favour of aboriginal land claims carries implications for Québec's aboriginal groups who have repeatedly refused to join their territories to a sovereign Québec state in the event of secession.

replacement will have to contend with the current political climate that suggests Québécois are tired of the political wrangling and would rather see a new deal that keeps them in Canada. After suffering through the long recession due, in large part, to the political battles that have dominated Québec for the last two decades, Québécois have a vested interest in maintaining the momentum of economic growth the province is currently experiencing. And, for the time being, they appear more interested in maintaining political peace than encouraging old fights.

The cities and landscapes

Should Québec secede, Canada will lose its largest province – accounting for a sixth of the country's territory; its 1.5 million square kilometres could enclose Portugal, Spain, Germany, France, Belgium and Switzerland. Of this vast expanse, sixty percent is forest land peppered with more than a million lakes and waterways and, though some mining towns dot the interior, the majority of the population is concentrated in the rich **arable lands** along the southern stretches of the mighty St Lawrence.

The Gallic ancestry of most Québécois is clear in their attitude towards hedonistic pleasures – they eat and drink in a style that combines the simplicity of the first settlers with the rich tastes of the French. Nowhere is this more evident than in the island metropolis of **Montréal**, premier port of the province and home to a third of all Québécois. Montréal's skyscrapers and nightlife bear witness to the economic resurgence of French-speaking Canada, whereas in **Québec City** the attraction lies more in the ancient streets and architecture. Beyond these centres, the **Gaspé Peninsula**, poking into the Gulf of St Lawrence, is the most appealing area with its inspiring mountain scenery and rocky coastline. Part of the peninsula, protected as parkland, provides sanctuary for a variety of wildlife, from moose to herons. Here, a score of once-remote fishing villages have become mini-resorts, the most attractive of which is **Percé**. Some 200 miles southeast of the peninsula, in the Gulf of St Lawrence, the **Îlesde la Madeleine**'s windswept archipelagos and beach-trimmed islands are Québec's version of the Caribbean.

Along the north shore of the St Lawrence, the agricultural – and intermittently industrial – settlements that dot the landscape north of Montréal thin out past Québec City, giving way to the bleak desolation of a coastal road that stretches beyond **Havre-St-Pierre**. On the way, you'll pass through the delightful resorts of **Baie-Saint-Paul** and **Tadoussac**; the latter offers magnificent opportunities to go **whale-watching**. The contrasting landscapes of the **Saguenay fjord**, west of Tadoussac, and the northerly **Mingan Archipelago** are among Québec's most dramatic sights. Beyond the regions covered in this guide, Québec's inhospitable and largely roadless **tundra** is inhabited only by pockets of Inuit and other aboriginal peoples; it's a destination only for those travellers who can afford an expensive bushplane and the equipment needed for survival in the wilderness.

Transport

Train services within the province serve Montréal, Gaspé, Québec City and Jonquière, and there are also services to Ontario, New Brunswick and the US – with Montréal very much the pivot. Buses are your best bet for getting around, with the major places connected by Orléans Express and Intercar services, supplemented by a network of smaller local lines. However, distances between communities in the outlying areas can

TOURIST INFORMATION

Tourisme Québec's toll-free information number is ☎1-877/266-5687 and the official Web site is *www.bonjourquebec.com*.

be immense, and in order to reach more remote parks and settlements on secondary roads a car is pretty much essential. Around Montréal and Québec City the shores of the St Lawrence are linked by bridges, and towards the north a network of ferries links the Gaspé with the Côte-Nord. In the far northeast the supply ship *Nordik Express* serves the Île d'Anticosti and the roadless lower north shore as far as the Labrador border – the ultimate journey within Québec.

MONTRÉAL AND AROUND

MONTRÉAL, Canada's second-largest city, is geographically as close to the European coast as to Vancouver, and in look and feel it combines some of the finest aspects of the two continents. Its North American skyline of glass and concrete rises above churches and monuments in a melange of European styles as varied as Montréal's social mix. This is also the second-largest French-speaking metropolis after Paris, but only two-thirds of the city's three and a half million people are of French extraction, the other third being a cosmopolitan mishmash of *les autres* – including British, Eastern Europeans, Chinese, Italians, Greeks, Jews, South Americans and West Indians. The result is a truly multidimensional city, with a global variety of eateries, bars and clubs, matched by a calendar of festivals that makes this the most vibrant place in Canada.

Montréal has always played a major role in advancing Québec **separatism**, as it's here that the two main linguistic groups come into greatest contact with one another. The tension between English and French culminated in the terrorist campaign that the Front de Libération du Québec focused on the city in the late 1960s, and the consequent political changes affected Montréal more than anywhere else in the province. In the wake of the "francization" of Québec, English-Canadians hit Hwy 401 in droves, tipping the nation's economic supremacy from Montréal to Toronto. Though written off by Canada's English-speaking majority, the city did not sink into oblivion. Instead, the city has undergone a resurgence, becoming the driving force behind the high-tech industry that's transforming Canada's economy.

Everywhere you look there are the signs of civic pride and prosperity. In the historic quarter of **Vieux-Montréal**, on the banks of the St Lawrence River, the streets and squares are flanked by well-tended buildings, from the mammoth **Basilique de Notre-Dame** and steepled **Chapelle de Notre-Dame-de-Bonsecours**, to sleek and stately commercial buildings. Old houses have been converted into lively restaurants and shops, abandoned warehouses into condos and the disused **Vieux-Port** into a summer playground with landscaped parklands facing onto the St Lawrence. Beneath the forested rise of **Mont Royal**, **downtown**'s boulevards and leafy squares are alive from the morning rush hour right through to the wee hours, when revellers return from the clubs that pulsate along **rue Ste-Catherine** and the more intimate bars and lounges of the **Plateau** and **Quartier Latin**. Below ground, the walkways of the **Underground City** and the outstanding **Métro** system link the nodal points of the city, while towards the eastern outskirts, the **Stade Olympique**'s leaning tower overshadows the vast **Jardin Botanique**, second in international status only to London's Kew Gardens.

In addition, the city boasts some excellent museums. The **Centre Canadien d'Architecture** has one of the continent's most impressive specialist collections, the **Musée d'Art Contemporain** is Canada's only museum devoted entirely to contemporary art, and the **Musée des Beaux Arts** is the oldest fine-arts museum in the country. Equally fine are the museums devoted to Montréal and Canadian history; of these, the **Musée McCord** has a mint collection of native artefacts, while the **Musée d'Archéologie et d'Histoire de Montréal** delivers a state-of-the-art presentation of archeological findings at the site of Montréal's founding in 1642.

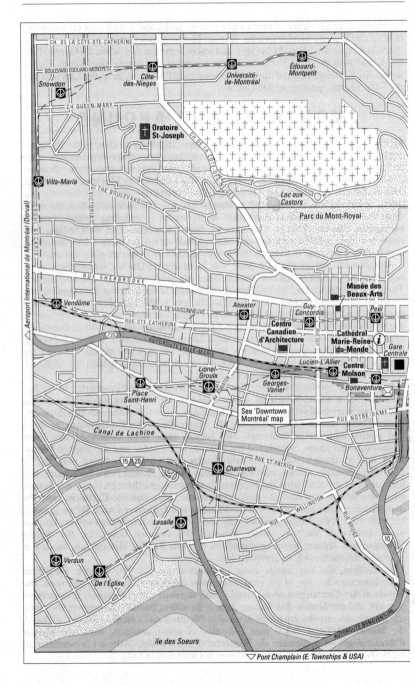

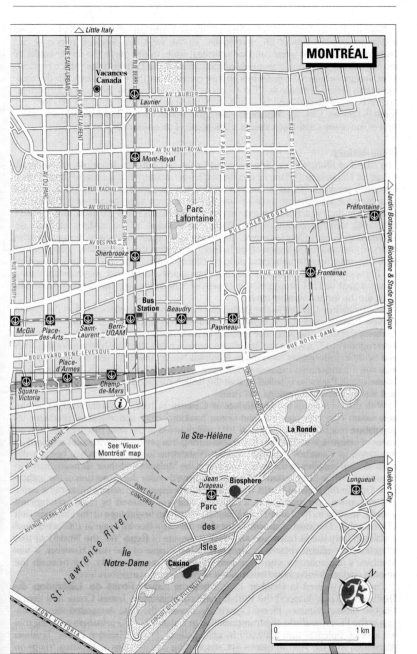

MONTRÉAL

△ Little Italy

Vacances Canada

Laurier

AV LAURIER

BOULEVARD ST-JOSEPH

AV DU MONT-ROYAL

Mont-Royal

RUE RACHEL

AV DULUTH

Parc Lafontaine

△ Jardin Botanique, Biodôme & Stade Olympique

Préfontaine

AV DES PINS

Sherbrooke

RUE SHERBROOKE

RUE ONTARIO Frontenac

Bus Station Beaudry

McGill Place-des-Arts Saint-Laurent Berri-UQAM Papineau

RUE NOTRE-DAME

BOULEVARD RENÉ-LÉVESQUE

Place-d'Armes

Square-Victoria Champ-de-Mars

ⓘ

RUE DE LA COMMUNE

See 'Vieux-Montréal' map

Île Ste-Hélène La Ronde

PONT JACQUES-CARTIER

Jean Drapeau Biosphere

Longueuil

△ Québec City

PONT DE LA CONCORDE

Parc

AVENUE PIERRE-DUPUY

des

St. Lawrence River

Isles

Île Notre-Dame Casino

20

CIRCUIT GILLES-VILLENEUVE

PONT VICTORIA

N

0   1 km

Beyond the city limits, Montréalers are blessed with superb holiday regions, most within an hour or two of the metropolis. To the west, the forested region of the **Outaouais** makes for great outdoor activities, while to the north the fertile banks of the St Lawrence and the lake-sprinkled mountains of the **Laurentians** offer a reprieve from muggy summer temperatures and an escape from the winter blues. To the east, the charm of the **Cantons-de-l'Est** (Eastern Townships) lies in the acres of farmlands, orchards, maple woods and lakeshore hamlets popular among antique collectors. En route to Québec City, the **Mauricie** valley, the province's smallest national park, has a web of waterways and lakes amidst a landscape of mountainous forest.

Some history

The island of Montréal was first occupied by the St Lawrence **Iroquois**, whose small village of Hochelaga ("Place of the Beaver") was situated at the base of Mont Royal. European presence began in October 1535 when Jacques-Cartier was led here while searching for a northwest route to Asia. However, even after the arrival of Samuel de Champlain, the French settlement was little more than a small garrison, and it wasn't until 1642 that the colony of Ville-Marie was founded by the soldiers of **Paul de Chomedey**, Sieur de Maisonneuve. They were on orders from Paris to "bring about the Glory of God and the salvation of the Indians", a mission that predictably enough found little response from the aboriginal peoples. Bloody conflict with the Iroquois, fanned by the European fur-trade alliances with the Algonquins and Hurons, was constant until a treaty signed in 1701 prompted the growth of Ville-Marie into the main embarkation point for the fur and lumber trade.

When Québec City fell to the British in 1759, Montréal briefly served as the capital of New France, until the Marquis de Vaudreuil was forced to surrender to General Amherst the following year. The ensuing **British occupation** suffered a seven-month interruption in 1775, when the Americans took over, but after this hiatus a flood of Irish and Scottish immigrants soon made Montréal North America's second-largest city. It was not a harmonious expansion, however, and in 1837 the French *Patriotes* led by Louis-Joseph Papineau rebelled against the British ruling class. Their insurgency failed and was followed by hangings and exiles.

With the creation of the **Dominion of Canada** in 1867, Montréal emerged as the new nation's premier port, railroad nexus, banking centre and industrial producer. Its population reached half a million in 1911 and doubled in the next two decades with an influx of émigrés from Europe. It was also during this period that Montréal acquired its reputation as Canada's "sin city". During Prohibition in the US, Québec became the main alcohol supplier to the entire continent: the Molsons and their ilk made their fortunes here, while prostitution and gambling thrived under the protection of the authorities. Only in the wake of World War II and the subsequent economic boom did a major anti-corruption operation begin, a campaign that was followed by rapid architectural growth, starting in 1962 with Place Ville Marie and the beginnings of the Underground City complex. The most glamorous episode in the city's face-lift came in 1967,when land reclaimed from the St Lawrence was used as the site of **Expo '67**, the World Fair that attracted fifty million visitors to Montréal in the course of the year. However, it was Montréal's anglophones who were benefiting from the prosperity, and beneath the smooth surface francophone frustrations were reaching dangerous levels.

The crisis peaked in October 1970, when the radical **Front de Libération du Québec** (FLQ) kidnapped the British trade commissioner, James Cross, and then a Québec cabinet minister, Pierre Laporte. As ransom, the FLQ demanded the publication of the FLQ manifesto, the transportation to Cuba of 25 FLQ prisoners awaiting trial for acts of violence, and $500,000 in gold bullion. Prime Minister Pierre Trudeau responded with the War Measures Act, suspending civil liberties and putting troops on the streets of Montréal. The following day, Laporte's body was found in the boot of a car. By December, the so-called **October Crisis** was over, Cross was released, and his captors and Laporte's murderers arrested. But the reverberations shook the nation.

At last recognizing the need to redress the country's social imbalances, the federal government poured money into countrywide schemes to promote French-Canadian culture. Francophone discontent was further alleviated by the provincial election of **René Lévesque** and his Parti Québécois in 1976, the year the Olympic Games were held in Montréal. The consequent language laws (Bill 101) made French a compulsory part of the school curriculum and banned English signs on business premises; only allowing them inside establishments provided the signs were bilingual and the French was printed twice as large as the English. Businesses that fail to comply are at the mercy of the "language police", inspectors of the Office de la Langue Française (OLF) who can go to extraordinary lengths – such as measuring signs and checking Web sites and business cards – to ensure that French is the dominant form of communication. For many anglophones, the threat of sovereignty, combined with language measures they took to be pettily vindictive, prompted an exodus in the tens of thousands from Montréal; plenty of companies left too, moving west to Toronto.

For a while it seemed that Montréal's heyday was over as the changes and political uncertainty that dominated the last two decades of the twentieth century, combined with a Canada-wide economic recession in the mid-1990s, saw Québec lag behind the rest of the country in economic growth. But the turning point came after the 1995 referendum, when a tacit truce was made on the issue of separation. The communal bonds between anglophone and francophone Québécois were further rejuvenated by the **ice storm** of 1998, which plunged pockets of the province into darkness for days after 100mm of icy rain downed power lines, and left 1.4 million people without electricity – some for weeks on end. The ice storm's impact on Montréal's green spaces was enormous, and most pronounced on the mountain, where some 80,000 trees were damaged.

The city's face has changed visibly in other ways recently. The boarded-up shops that lined rue Ste-Catherine in the mid-1990s have reopened and do bustling business nowadays. Derelict pockets on the edges of downtown and Vieux-Montréal have been renovated to house the booming multimedia industry. And with the rising employment and economic prosperity, popular residential areas like the Plateau are being gentrified and apartment developments abound. Even the city's nightlife scene is changing, as full-time workers opt for the *cinq à sept* cocktail hour during the week rather than going out late into the evening. But perhaps the most enduring change is that the gaps left by departing anglophones have been filled by young bilingual francophones who at last feel in charge of their own culture and economy. At the same time, the anglophones that stayed have also become bilingual, and these days it's perfectly normal to hear the two languages intermingling with one another wherever you may be.

Montréal's area code is ☎514

Arrival, information and city transport

The two international **airports** serving Montréal are operated by Aéroports de Montréal (☎394-7377 or 1-800/465-1213, *www.admtl.com*). The main one, **Aéroport de Dorval**, 22km southwest of the city, is the arrival point for international and Canadian flights. Passengers departing from Dorval must pay an Airport Improvement Fee (AIF) of $10, to be handed over in cash to an attendant or by credit card at one of the machines at the entrance to the security checkpoint. The Aérobus airport shuttle service (☎931-9002) runs every 20 minutes from 7am to 1am daily, linking Dorval Airport with the Station Centrale d'Autobus Montréal and the Gare de l'Aéroport, adjacent to the train station (35–45 min; $11 one-way, $19.75 return). Passengers can take the complimentary shuttle service to major downtown hotels from the latter; some hotels also have vans that pick up guests directly from the airport – ask on making a reservation. Several local buses also connect Dorval to downtown but they take ages. A taxi downtown is $28.50, plus tip.

Montréal's second airport, **Aéroport de Mirabel**, 55km northwest of the city, is used solely for charter flights. From Mirabel to the same locations downtown takes just over an hour by bus, although the service is irregular, based on flight arrival times (☎931-9002; $18 one-way, $25 return). The taxi fare is around $72, including tip.

Montréal's main **train station**, Gare Centrale, is below the *Queen Elizabeth Hotel* on the corner of boul René-Lévesque and rue Mansfield, and is entered at 895 rue de la Gauchetière ouest. The station is the major terminus for Canada's VIA Rail trains from Halifax, Toronto, Ottawa, Québec and the Gaspé as well as US Amtrak trains from Washington and New York. The Bonaventure Métro station links it with the rest of the city. An international student card (ISIC) gets 40 percent off regular train fares; but even if you don't have one you can still get a discount by booking six days in advance to get 30 percent off return-trip fares and 20 percent off one-way tickets.

Long-distance **buses** arrive and depart from Station Centrale d'Autobus Montréal at 505 boul de Maisonneuve est. The Berri-UQAM Métro is right below the station. Orléans Express (☎842-2281, *www.orleansexpress.com*) is the province's main coach company. Students and senior citizens receive a 25 percent discount with proper identification.

Information

Montréal's main information centre, **Infotouriste** (daily: June to early Sept 7am–8pm; May & early Sept–Oct 7.30am–6pm; Nov–April 9am–6pm; ☎873-2015 or 1-877/266-5687, *www.bonjourquebec.com*), is at 1001 rue du Square-Dorchester on the corner of rue Metcalfe. The nearest Métro is Peel – go south on rue Peel past rue Ste-Catherine. In addition to masses of useful free information on the province and Montréal, it offers an accommodation service, which will make any number of free calls to find vacancies for you. Otherwise, the **Tourist Information Centre of Old Montréal**, 174 rue Notre-Dame est (mid-April to late June daily 9am–5pm; late June to early Oct daily 9am–7pm; early Oct to mid-April Thurs–Sun 9am–5pm; *www.tourism-montreal.org*) provides information on the city of Montréal only.

Transport

The **public transport** system is one of the city's greatest assets, linking the 65-station Métro to 150 bus routes. The clean, speedy, convenient, reliable and cheap **Métro** system has four colour-coded lines, the major interconnecting stations being Berri-UQAM (which links the orange, green and yellow lines), Lionel-Groulx (green and orange), Snowdon and Jean-Talon (blue and orange). Coloured signs indicate the direction of each line by showing the name of the terminus; maps of the system can be picked up at stations and information centres.

A *correspondance*, available from machines beyond the turnstiles at the Métro stations, allows you to complete your journey by bus at no extra cost, but you must get one at the beginning of your journey, not as you get off the Métro. The transfer system also works in reverse, from buses to Métro – ask the driver for one as you board. Most **buses** stop running at 12.30am, shortly before the Métro, though some run all through the night and cover different routes; they have the same fare system as the Métro, but exact change is required.

One-way fares are a flat $2, and a book of six tickets – a *carnet* – costs $8.25. Better suited to visitors, the STCUM **tourist pass** allows unlimited travel on the Métro and bus routes: it costs $7 a day or $14 for three consecutive days and is available from the information centres, Berri–UQAM Métro station and, from April to October, at all downtown Métro stations.

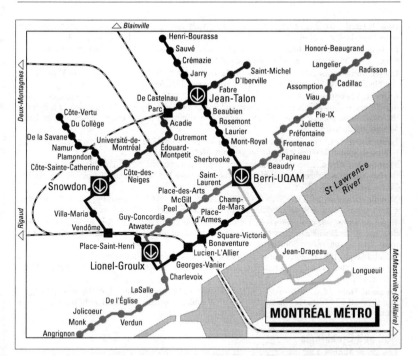

It is rarely necessary to take a **taxi**, and they're not that expensive if you're in a group; they cost $2.80 plus $1.13 per kilometre and an additional ten to fifteen percent tip is normal. Taxis can be boarded at ranks outside hotels and transport terminals, and by simply flagging them down. They can also be ordered by phone: Taxi Diamond (☎ 273-6331) and Taxi Co-op (☎725-9885) are two reliable services.

Accommodation

Much of Montréal's **accommodation** is geared towards expense-account travellers in the downtown hotels. Moderately priced **hotel** rooms are conveniently concentrated around the bus terminal or the livelier St-Denis area, and a growing number of **B&B** places offer budget accommodation in Vieux-Montréal and the Plateau neighbourhood. Rock-bottom prices are charged in the city's **hostels** and **university residences**. For campers the outlook is not good, as the **campsites** are at least twenty-minutes' drive out of town, with no public transport. The peak season is from May to the end of October, with July and August especially busy.

Hotels

Abri du Voyageur, 9 rue Ste-Catherine ouest (☎849-2922, *www.abri-voyageur.ca*). While the location could be better – it is smack in the middle of the city's red-light district – the rooms are clean, several have exposed brick walls, and it is just steps away from Chinatown and Vieux-Montréal. Métro St-Laurent. ②.

L'Appartement-In Montréal, 455 rue Sherbrooke ouest (☎284-3634 or 1-800/363-3010). Apartments with kitchenettes, bathrooms, air conditioning, phones and TVs. Free use of outdoor pool and sauna, though parking is extra; discounts for longer stays. Métro Place-des-Arts. ④.

Bon Accueil, 1601 rue St-Hubert (☎527-9655). Aptly named ("good welcome") central red-brick hotel near the bus station. All rooms have private bathrooms. Métro Berri-UQAM. ③.

Le Breton, 1609 rue St-Hubert (☎524-7273). Near the bus station, this clean and friendly air-conditioned hotel has rooms with TVs; Métro Berri-UQAM. ②.

Castel Saint-Denis, 2099 rue St-Denis (☎842-9719). One of the better small hotels in Montréal, it's right in the trendy St-Denis area, but quiet. Métro Berri-UQAM or Sherbrooke. ③.

Château Versailles, 1659 rue Sherbrooke ouest (☎933-3611 or 1-800/361-3664). A unique, beautifully furnished hotel located in four stone buildings downtown. Book well in advance, as it is one of the city's most popular hotels; family discounts and cheap winter weekend rates also available. Métro Guy-Concordia. ⑥.

Louisbourg, 1649 rue St-Hubert (☎598-8544 or 1-800/466-1949, *www.staymontreal.com*). Cheap hotel with sparse facilities, near the bus station. Métro Berri-UQAM. ①.

Manoir des Alpes, 1245 rue St-André (☎845-9803 or 1-800/465-2929). This Victorian house near the bus station is a three-star hotel with Swiss overtones but rates include breakfast and parking. Métro Berri-UQAM. ③.

Manoir Ambrose, 3422 rue Stanley (☎288-6922). A couple of blocks from the heart of downtown. Cheap rooms, some with air conditioning and private bathrooms. Métro Peel. ②.

Hôtel de Paris, 901 rue Sherbrooke est (☎522-6861 or 1-800/567-7217). An excellent old mansion near rue St-Denis with a balcony café to hang out in. All rooms are en suite with TVs, telephone and most have air-con. Métro Sherbrooke. ③.

Hôtel Pierre, 169 rue Sherbrooke est (☎288-8519). A slightly sketchy nine-bedroom hotel with rooms decorated in vastly different styles ranging from camp to cottage chic. Parking extra. Métro Sherbrooke. ③.

Le Saint-Malo, 1455 rue du Fort (☎931-7366, *www.colba.net/~stmalo*). Near the western edge of downtown; the 14 rooms are clean, if on the small side, and some have quaint architectural features. Métro Guy-Concordia or Atwater. ②.

Bed and Breakfasts

Les Bons Matins, 1393 ave Argyle (☎931-9167 or 1-800/588-5280, *www.bonsmatins.com*). Located on a tree-lined street near downtown and busy rue Crescent, this well-appointed B&B has five large rooms, each with special architectural features (archways, exposed brick, fireplace), large windows, and private bathroom. Métro Guy-Concordia or Atwater. ④.

Au Portes de la Nuit, 3496 ave Laval (☎848-0833, *www.bbcanada.com/767.html*). Well-situated on one of the Plateau's most attractive streets, this Victorian house has five rooms, three of which have private bath. Métro Sherbrooke. ③.

Bienvenue Bed & Breakfast, 3950 ave Laval (☎844-5897 or 1-800/227-5897, *www.bienvenuebb.com*). Offers moderately priced rooms in a Victorian house located on a tree-lined Plateau street steps away from boul St-Laurent and rue St-Denis. Métro Sherbrooke. ②.

BED AND BREAKFAST AGENCIES

These agencies can be big time savers if you're looking to stay at a B&B as each represents several guesthouses across town in a range of prices and offer booking services.

Bed & Breakfast Downtown Network, 3458 ave Laval (☎289-9749 or 1-800/267-5180, *www.bbmontreal.qc.ca*). Almost always has a vacancy in one of their hundred or so homes downtown or in Vieux-Montréal, starting at around $50 and ranging from quaint Victorian homes to modern apartments.

Montréal Downtown Network, 3977 ave Laval (☎287-9635 or 1-800/363-9635, *pages .infinit.net/pearson/B-B/*). A service offering placement in a number of B&Bs situated in downtown or Vieux-Montréal. They also list apartments for longer stays. ②–④.

Montréal Oasis, 3000 rue de Breslay (☎935-2312, *www.bestinns.net/canada/qu /mo.html*). Most B&Bs at this agency are centrally located with the emphasis on gorgeous breakfasts. ②–⑤.

Pierre et Dominique, 271 Square St-Louis (☎286-0307, *www.pierdom.qc.ca*). In a lovely house facing a picturesque square, the three rooms are tastefully decorated, though none has private bathroom. Métro Sherbrooke. ③.

Le Zèbre, 3767 ave Laval (☎844-9868, *www.bbcanada.com/2728.html*). Located in the heart of the Plateau, it has three large rooms and a marvellous sitting room with marble fireplace and bay windows. Shared bathroom. ③. Métro Sherbrooke.

Hostels and student accommodation

Auberge Alternative du Vieux Montréal, 358 rue St-Pierre (☎282-8069,*www.auberge-alternative* *.qc.ca/*). Rooms for six to sixteen people and some doubles. You don't need to be a member to stay here. Métro Place-d'Armes or Champs-de-Mars. ①.

Auberge de Jeunesse Internationale de Montréal, 1030 rue Mackay (☎843-3317 or 1-800/663-3317). Check-in 9.30am–2am. 250 beds, air-con, showers in every room. Single, family or shared rooms. Free parking. Advisable to reserve from June to September. Métro Lucien-L'Allier. ①.

Auberge de Paris, 874 rue Sherbrooke est (☎522-6861 or 1-800/567-7217). A brand-new youth hostel with tiny bunk rooms opposite the *Hôtel de Paris*. Cooking facilities, laundry, café, garden and TV room. ①. The second floor has a few rooms if you fancy more privacy. ③. Check-in after 10pm at *Hôtel de Paris*, 901 rue Sherbrooke est. Métro Sherbrooke.

Downtown YMCA, 1450 rue Stanley (☎849-8393). Expensive, mixed YMCA with a floor for women only, and a swimming pool and cafeteria. Métro Peel. ②.

McGill University Residences, 3935 rue University (summer only: ☎398-6367). Popular residence for visiting anglophones and consequently often full. Good weekly rates. Métro McGill. ①.

Université Concordia, 7141 rue Sherbrooke ouest (summer only; ☎848-4755). Sparse, clean rooms but miles away from the centre of town. ①.

Vacances Canada, 5155 ave de Gaspé (☎270-4459). Two hundred beds available all year, and 550 in July and August in two locations: the Collège Français residence has rooms with one to seven beds that are popular with school groups, so often booked up. Open till 2am. Second location has good deals for longer stays. Métro Laurier. ①.

The Women's Y of Montréal, YWCA, 1355 boul René-Lévesque ouest (☎866-9941). Women only, near the train station and downtown. Laundry facilities as well as swimming pool and cafeteria. Métro Lucien L'Allier. ②.

Camping

Camping Alouette, 3449 rue de l'Industrie, Saint-Mathieu-de-Beloeil (☎450/464-1661 or 1-888/464-7829). Exit 105 off Hwy 20 east. With 300 sites this is the largest of the city's campsites with a store, washing machines, hook-ups and outdoor swimming pool. Sites $19.

Camping St-Claude, 415 Montée St-Claude, Saint-Philippe (☎450/659-3389). Hwy 30 west, exit 104, Hwy 104 east. Big, charmless campsite with hook-ups, playground, showers, washing machines and restaurant. Sites $15.

KOA Montréal Sud, 130 boul Monette, St-Philippe-de-la Prairie (☎450/659-8626 or 1-800/562-8636). About 20km south of downtown; take exit 38 off Hwy 15, turn left, and it's 3km on. Full facilities at well-kept campsite. Sites $20.

The City

Though Montréal island is a large 51km by 16km, the heart of the city is very manageable, and is divided into Vieux-Montréal – along the St Lawrence River – a downtown high-rise business core, on the south side of the hill of Mont Royal, and the lively Plateau and Quartier Latin neighbourhoods to the east. Sherbrooke, de Maisonneuve, Ste-Catherine and René-Lévesque are the main east–west arteries, divided into east (*est*) and west (*ouest*) sections by the north–south boulevard St-Laurent, known locally as "The Main". Street numbers begin from St-Laurent and increase the further east or west you travel: thus 200 rue Sherbrooke ouest is about three blocks west of the Main and 1000 boul René-Lévesque est is about ten blocks east of the Main. North–south street numbers increase north from the St Lawrence River.

You're most likely to start by sampling the old-world charm of **Vieux-Montréal**. The narrow cobblestoned streets, alleys and squares are perfect for strolling, and every corner reveals an architectural gem, from monumental public edifices to the city's first steep-roofed homes. Close by, the **Vieux-Port** holds the new iSci centre and is a departure point for getting out on the water. To the north, in the compact **downtown** area, the glass frontages of the office blocks reflect Victorian terraces and the spires of numerous churches, clustered within the shadow of the city's landmark, **Mont Royal**, which the residents simply call "The Mountain". Meanwhile, the mountain's eastern plateau is the spot where the city's pulse beats fastest as the eateries and bars of **The Main** throng with people day and night. On the city's outskirts the enormous **Stade Olympique** complex and the vast green of the **Jardin Botanique** are the main pull. Beneath street level the passages of the **Underground City** link hotels, shopping centres and offices with the Métro.

Vieux-Montréal

Severed from downtown by the Autoroute Ville-Marie, the gracious district of **Vieux-Montréal** was left to decay until the last couple of decades, when developers stepped in with generally tasteful renovations that brought colour and vitality back to the area. The continent's greatest concentration of seventeenth-, eighteenth- and nineteenth-century buildings has its fair share of tourists, but it's popular with Montréalers, too – formerly as a symbolic place to air francophone grievances; more recently as a spot to while away the hours in a café or restaurant.

Place d'Armes and around

The focal point of Vieux-Montréal is the **Place d'Armes**, its centre occupied by a century-old statue of Maisonneuve, whose missionary zeal raised the wrath of the displaced Iroquois. The mutt among the luminaries represents the animal who warned the French of an impending attack in 1644; legend has it that the ensuing battle ended when the unarmed Maisonneuve killed the Iroquois chief on this very spot.

Despite the addition of an ugly skyscraper on its west side, the square is still dominated by the twin-towered, neo-Gothic **Basilique Notre-Dame**, 110 rue Notre-Dame ouest (daily 7am–8pm; $2), the cathedral of the Catholic faithful since 1829. Its architect, the Protestant Irish-American James O'Donnell, was so inspired by his creation that he converted to Catholicism in order to be buried under the church. The western of the two towers, named Temperance, holds the ten-tonne Jean-Baptiste bell, whose booming can be heard 25km away. The breathtaking gilt and sky-blue interior, flooded with light from three rose windows and flickering with multicoloured votive candles, was designed by Montréal architect Victor Bourgeau. Most notable of the detailed furnishings are Louis-Philippe Hébert's fine wooden carvings of the prophets on the pulpit and the awe-inspiring main altar by French sculptor Bouriché. Imported from Limoges in France, the stained-glass windows depict the founding of Ville-Marie. Behind the main altar is the Chapelle Sacré-Coeur, destroyed by a serious fire in 1978 but rebuilt with an impressive bronze reredos by Charles Daudelin.

Behind the fieldstone walls and wrought-iron gates to the right of Notre-Dame is the low-lying, mock-medieval **Séminaire de St-Sulpice**, saved from blandness by a portal that's topped by North America's oldest public timepiece, which began chiming in 1701. Generally considered Montréal's oldest building, the seminary was founded in 1685 by the Paris-based Sulpicians, who instigated the establishment of Montréal by Maisonneuve as a religious mission. They liked the place so much that they bought the whole island, and until 1854 were in charge of religious and legal affairs in the colony.

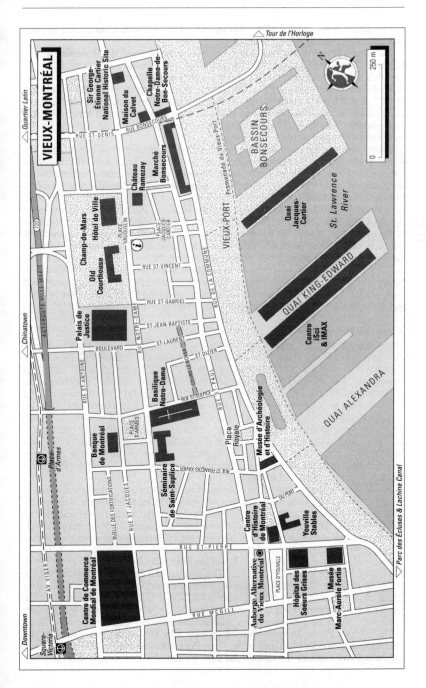

VIEUX-MONTRÉAL

△ Tour de l'Horloge

△ Quartier Latin

△ Chinatown

◁ Downtown

Square-Victoria

N

250 m
0

Sir George-Étienne Cartier National Historic Site
Maison du Calvet
Chapelle Notre-Dame-de-Bon-Secours

RUE ST-DENIS

RUE BONSECOURS

Château Ramezay
Marché Bonsecours

Champ-de-Mars
Hôtel de Ville

Old Courthouse

PLACE VAUQUELIN
PLACE JACQUES-CARTIER

i

RUE ST-VINCENT

Palais de Justice

RUE ST-GABRIEL

ST-JEAN-BAPTISTE

RUE NOTRE-DAME

ST-LAURENT

BOULEVARD

ST-DIZIER

RUE ST-ANTOINE

AUTOROUTE VILLE-MARIE

720

Basilique Notre-Dame

COURS LE ROYER

RUE S. SULPICE

RUE ST-PAUL

Banque de Montréal

PLACE D'ARMES

Place d'Armes

RUELLE DES FORTIFICATIONS

RUE ST-JACQUES

Séminaire de Saint-Sulpice

RUE ST-FRANÇOIS-XAVIER

Place Royale

Musée d'Archéologie et d'Histoire

DU PORT

Centre d'Histoire de Montréal

Youville Stables

RUE ST-PIERRE

PLACE D'YOUVILLE

Auberge Alternative du Vieux Montréal ◉

Hôpital des Soeurs Grises

Musée Marc-Aurèle Fortin

AV. VIGER

RUE MCGILL

Centre de Commerce Mondial de Montréal

RUE DE LA COMMUNE

VIEUX-PORT
Promenade du Vieux-Port

BASSIN BONSECOURS

Quai Jacques-Cartier

St. Lawrence River

QUAI KING-EDWARD

Centre iSci & IMAX

QUAI ALEXANDRA

▷ Parc des Écluses & Lachine Canal

The seminary is still the Canadian headquarters of the Sulpicians, but their duties are now limited to maintaining the basilica.

The domed shrine of Montréal's financial rulers, the **Banque de Montréal**, stands opposite. This grand, classical-revival building still houses the headquarters of Canada's oldest bank, which rose from its foundation by a few Scottish immigrants to serve the entire nation until the creation of the Bank of Canada in the 1930s. Erected in 1837, it was built to resemble the Roman Pantheon. The interior marble counters, black pillars and gleaming brass and bronze fittings ooze wealth and luxury. A small **Numismatic Museum** (Mon–Fri 10am–4pm; free) displays early account books, banknotes, coins and pictures of the bank.

British names once controlled the finances of the continent from the stately limestone, griffin-capped institutions along **rue St-Jacques**, once the Wall Street of Canada, but French businesses now rule the roost. The red-sandstone building on the northeast corner of Place d'Armes and rue St-Jacques was built for the New York Life Insurance Co. in 1888, and at eight stories high, was the city's first skyscraper. Next door at 501 Place-d'Armes, the Aldred Building is among the city's finest examples of the Art Deco style. Both are dwarfed today by the black monolith on the west side of the square that houses the Banque Nationale, built in 1967 as a symbol of newfound francophone business strength. Transformations have also occurred alongside the basilica, in the area around **rue St-Sulpice**, where the warehouses constructed in the Victorian era to cope with the growing trade of Montréal's harbour have been converted into luxurious flats and offices. Many of the continent's first explorers once lived here – including Pierre Gaulthier de Varennes, who charted South Dakota, the Rockies and Wyoming, and Daniel Greysolon du Luth, who roamed over Minnesota.

Along rue Notre-Dame

Ville-Marie's first street, **rue Notre-Dame**, was laid out in 1672 and runs east–west from one end of Vieux-Montréal to the other. Other than the financial buildings of rue St-Jacques, there is little of interest to the west of Place d'Armes; it's more rewarding to head east along Notre-Dame from the top of rue St-Sulpice, past the 1811 **Maison de la Sauvegarde** at no. 160. It stands opposite the imposing **Old Courthouse**, erected by the British to impress upon the French population the importance of abiding by their laws. It went on to become the site of civil trials under the Napoleonic Code after the courts were divided in 1926, and today serves as municipal offices. Criminal trials took place across the street, at no. 100, in the **Édifice Ernest Cormier**, which was built in 1925; step inside to admire the impressive colonnade and unique Art Deco lamps. Both courthouses have been usurped by the shiny black glass of the **Palais de Justice** on the corner of St-Laurent.

Beside the Old Courthouse, **Place Vauquelin**, with its pretty fountain and statue of the naval commander Jean Vauquelin, gives views of the **Champ de Mars** to the north. Excavations to build a car park here hit rock, which turned out to be the original city walls. After a public vote, the car park scheme was abandoned, the walls were excavated and restored, and the area was transformed into a pleasant grassy space that is used as a park, with occasional son et lumière performances.

East of Place Vauquelin, the ornate **Hôtel de Ville** (City Hall) was built in the 1870s and is a typical example of the area's civic buildings of the time when French-speaking architects looked to the mother country for inspiration. On a visit to Expo '67, General de Gaulle chose its second-floor balcony to make his "Vive le Québec Libre" speech that left the city's anglophones reeling at the thought that Québec was on its way to independent status and infused francophones with a political fervour that ended in the October Crisis.

The cobbled **Place Jacques-Cartier** opposite City Hall slopes down towards the river and offers spectacular views of the Vieux-Port, but is overrun with buskers, street artists and hair-braiders throughout the summer months. Restaurants and cafés surrounding the square hustle for business, while the narrow **rue St-Amable** to the west is choked with struggling artists selling quaint pastels of Montréal scenery alongside garish caricatures of stars like Burt Reynolds and Madonna.

A few buildings on the square – Maison Vandelac, Maison del Vecchio and the Maison Cartier – show the architectural features typical of Montréal architecture in the 1800s, with pitched roofs designed to shed heavy snowfall and small dormer windows to defend against the cold. At the top of the square itself, the controversial **Monument to Nelson** stands above the flower stalls that serve as the only reminders that this was once Montréal's main marketplace. The city's oldest monument – the column is a third the height of its more famous London counterpart, but predates it by a few years – was funded by anglophone Montréalers delighted with Nelson's defeat of the French at Trafalgar in 1805. Québec separatists adopted it as a rallying point in the 1970s. Ironically, the anglophones never liked the monument much either, because it faced away from the water.

East of the square, the long and low fieldstone manor of the **Château Ramezay** (June–Sept daily 10am–6pm; Oct–May Tues–Sun 10am–4.30pm; *www.chateau-ramezay.qc.ca*; $6) looks much as it did in 1756, the only addition being an incongruous tower, which hoisted the building into "château" status in the 1800s. One of the oldest buildings in North America, Château Ramezay was built by the Compagnie des Indes as offices and storage space and then became a residence for the French governors, before passing into the hands of the British. During the fleeting American invasion Benjamin Franklin stayed here in an attempt to persuade Montréalers to join the United States, but he lost public and church support by not promising the supremacy of the French language in what would have been the fourteenth state. Nowadays, after a variety of other uses, it is an historical **museum**; despite some poor translations on the explanatory panels, the collection of oil paintings, domestic artefacts, tools, costumes and furniture from the eighteenth and nineteenth centuries is thorough and informative. The most impressive room is a reconstruction of the *Grande Salle* of the Compagnie des Indes, complete with mahogany walls and woodwork imported from Nantes, France. Other rooms are furnished in the bourgeois style of New France, while in the deep stone vaults below, educators teach about the life of the aboriginal peoples before European settlement.

At the intersection of Notre-Dame and Berri, the **Lieu historique national de Sir-George-Étienne-Cartier** (May–Sept daily 10am–6pm; Oct–April Wed–Sun 10am–5pm; $3.25; *www.parcscanada.gc.ca/parks/quebec/cartier/*) comprises two adjoining houses that were inhabited by the Cartier family from 1848 to 1871. The cocky Sir George-Étienne Cartier was one of the fathers of Confederation, persuading the French-Canadians to join the Dominion of Canada by declaring: "We are of different races, not for strife but to work together for the common welfare." Today, leaders of French-Canadian nationalism decry Cartier as a collaborator, and the displays in the east house diplomatically skirt over the issue of whether he was right or wrong and emphasize instead his role in the construction of Canada's railways. This collection is decidedly bizarre however, with Muppet-like figures representing the founding fathers on the main floor, while eight white-painted papier-mâché models of Cartier himself sit around a glass-domed, round table upstairs. The rooms in the west house are more interesting, furnished with more than a thousand original artefacts to evoke the period when Sir George lived here. Strangely, part of the display is concentrated around a dinner theme, and recordings of conversations between fictitious house staff automatically start playing once the infrared sensor catches movement in the room.

Rue St-Paul

A block south of rue Notre-Dame, **rue St-Paul**, one of Montréal's most attractive thoroughfares, is lined with nineteenth-century commercial buildings and Victorian lamp-posts, the buildings little changed from when Charles Dickens stayed here, although they now house restaurants and specialist shops selling everything from Inuit crafts to kites.

Mark Twain noted that in Montréal, "you couldn't throw a brick without hitting a church", and near rue St-Paul's eastern end is Montréal's favourite: the delicate and profusely steepled **Chapelle de Notre-Dame-de-Bonsecours** (daily: May–Oct 9am–5pm; Nov–April 10am–3pm), or the Sailors' Church. The outstretched arms of the Virgin on the tower became a landmark for ships on the St Lawrence and, once safely landed, the mariners would endow the chapel with wooden votive lamps in the shape of ships, many of which are still here. The chapel dates back to the earliest days of the colony, when Maisonneuve helped cut the wood for what was Ville-Marie's first church, under the instigation of Marguerite Bourgeoys, who had been summoned to Ville-Marie to teach the settlement's children. The devout Bourgeoys also founded the nation's first religious order and was in charge of the *filles du Roi* – orphaned French girls sent to marry bachelor settlers and multiply the colony's population. She was canonized in 1982, becoming Canada's first saint. Today's chapel, postdating Bourgeoys by some seventy years, contains a small **museum** devoted to her life (May–Oct Tues–Sun 10am–5pm; Nov to mid-Jan & mid-March to April 11am–3.30pm; $5). Be sure to climb the narrow stairs leading to the summit of the tower above the apse, known as **Le Monument**, for excellent views.

Opposite the chapel is the three-storey, high-chimneyed **Maison du Calvet**, built in 1725 and one of Montréal's best examples of French domestic architecture. Photographed, painted and admired more than any other house in the district, it was the home of a Huguenot draper and justice of the peace called Pierre Calvet, a notorious turncoat who changed his allegiances from the French to the British and then to the Americans. It houses a café today.

Rue Bonsecours, which links rue St-Paul to Notre-Dame, is another typical Vieux-Montréal street. The **Maison Papineau** at no. 440 was home to four generations of the Papineau family, including Louis-Joseph who, as Speaker of the Assembly, championed the *habitants* of the St Lawrence farmlands against the senior Catholic clergy, the British government and Montréal's business class. Calling for democratic election of the executive officers of church and government, he fuelled the rage of the *Patriotes* – the leaders of Lower Canada reform – but deserted the scene as the 1837 rebellion reached a bloody climax (see p.238). The house remains a private residence, but renovations have significantly altered its exterior facade from the days when the Papineaus lived here.

The silver-domed **Marché Bonsecours**, with its long facade of columns, extends beyond the intersection of rue Bonsecours and rue St-Paul. For years this elegant building was used for municipal offices, but for the city's 350th in 1992 it was restored and transformed to house a farmers' market, designer boutiques, expensive artworks and special exhibitions.

Vieux-Port

The south side of the Marché Bonsecours faces onto the **Vieux-Port de Montréal**, once the import and export conduit of the continent. When the main shipyards shifted east in the 1970s they left a vacant lot, which has since been renovated for public use, with biking, cross-country skiing and jogging paths and excellent exhibitions in the quayside hangars.

At the Vieux-Port's easternmost point, the **Tour de l'Horloge** on the Quai de l'Horloge rises 51m above sea level. It was built in 1922 to commemorate the men of the Merchant Fleet who died in World War I; ships were recorded as having entered the harbour as soon as they had passed it. If you can stand the walk up the 192 steps leading to the observatory, you'll be rewarded with excellent views of the harbour, the St Lawrence Seaway, Vieux-Montréal, the Islands and Mont Royal.

Westward, there's a small **information centre** (June to mid-Oct daily 8am–8pm; closed mid-Oct to June) located at the east corner of the **Pavillon Jacques-Cartier**, which is a good place to find out about weekend activities and performances portside. The main events of the Vieux-Port are clustered in and around the next hangar westward, the **Quai King-Edward**. There's an **IMAX** cinema here, with eye-popping films and a seven-storey-high screen (daily: mid-April to early Sept 10.15am–10.15pm; early Sept to mid-April closed on Mon; *www.imaxoldport.com;* $11.95), and the **Centre iSci**, 2 rue de la Commune (daily 10am–9pm; *www.isci.ca;* $9.95), an interactive science and entertainment complex that's heavy on new technology. A joint project between the federal government and private business, the cavernous centre cost $49 million to develop and is divided into three exhibition halls, focusing on themes of life, information and matter. The massive rooms contain little that will keep you occupied, but most kids will enjoy some of the hands-on exhibits, including one that lets you test your sense of smell. At the end of the pier itself there is a **lookout point** up a few flights of stairs, with explanatory panels showcasing a diorama of Vieux-Montréal and the Islands.

The Vieux-Port is the major departure point for various **boat trips**. The best by far is the **Jet Boat** from the Quai de l'Horloge (May–Oct daily 9am–7pm; $45). Scooting through the Lachine Rapids, the boat trip will leave you wet, exhilarated and terrified. Meandering **Bâteau Mouches** tours leave from the Quai Jacques-Quartier (May–Oct 10am, noon, 2pm, 4pm; $20). The glass-topped boats offer lovely views of the surrounding islands and the river. Most tours last around two hours, though there are longer dinner cruises. If you want to take things at a more leisurely pace, there's the **amphibus** (May–Oct daily, times vary; $18) that leaves from in front of the IMAX cinema. In true James Bond style, it sails on water and drives along the streets of Vieux-Montréal.

Place Royale to Place d'Youville

Once the site of duels, whippings and public hangings amidst the pedlars and hawkers who sold wares from the incoming ships, **Place Royale** is dominated by the neat classical facade of the **Old Customs House**. After a nine-day journey from Québec City, Maisonneuve and his posse moored their boats at nearby **Pointe-à-Callière**, now landlocked after the changes in the Vieux-Port. At the extremity of the point stands a monument to **John Young**, who was responsible for enlarging Montréal's port in the seventeenth century, an act that enabled the city to expand as a trading centre.

The **Musée d'Archéologie et d'Histoire de Montréal**, 350 Place Royale (Sept–June Tues–Fri 10am–5pm, Sat & Sun 11am–5pm; July & Aug Tues–Fri 10am–6pm, Sat & Sun 11am–6pm; *www.musee-pointe-a-calliere.qc.ca;* $9.50), occupies a splendid building on the Pointe and spreads underground below the Place Royale as far as the Old Customs House. The $27-million centre focuses on the development of Montréal as a meeting and trading place, as told through the archeological remains excavated here at the oldest part of the city. The high-tech audiovisual presentation is an excellent introduction to the museum, to archeology generally, and to that of Montréal in particular. Early remnants of the city include a cemetery from 1648, eighteenth-century water conduits and sewage systems, and walls dating from different centuries. The underground sections emerge into the Old Customs House, which holds a permanent exhibition on Montréal's history, as well as temporary shows, all with an archeological theme.

Directly behind the archeology museum is **Place d'Youville**, a charming public square that includes the Founder's Obelisk, a monument to, who else, the city founders. At the centre of the square, a red-brick fire station has been converted into the **Centre d'Histoire de Montréal** (mid-May to mid-Sept daily 10am–5pm; mid-Sept to mid-May Tues–Sun 10am–5pm; *www.ville.montreal.qc.ca/chm;* $4.50). Dioramas of the city's history, from its days as an Iroquois settlement to its present expansions under and above ground, aren't terribly interesting, but are fine for a sketchy overview.

If you enjoy kitsch, head up to the second floor, with its focus on the social side of Montréal living, replete with old magazines and department-store boxes. Kids will love the mock tram – enter it and images start running past the windows while a recording of a bus driver calls out stops in French and English. Temporary exhibitions, too, are usually quite stimulating. Ask for an English-language guidebook when you enter the museum.

On the south side of the square, the **Youville Stables**, with its shady courtyard, gardens, restaurants and offices, was one of the first of the area's old buildings to be yuppified. The complex was in fact a warehouse – the stables were next door. Dating from 1825, the courtyard layout is a throwback to a design used by the earliest Montréal inhabitants as a protection against the hostilities of the Iroquois.

From here, turn left onto rue St-Pierre and south past the renovated wing of the Hôpital des Soeurs Grises, where the sick, old and orphaned of Ville-Marie were first cared for. Next door, the **Musée Marc-Aurèle Fortin** at no. 118 (Tues–Sun 11am–5pm; $4) is a small gallery dedicated to a Québécois painter whom the proprietors seem to believe was the greatest artist since the Impressionists. Unfortunately, Fortin's directionless experiments with various styles do nothing to justify the praise. His twee oils of pastoral Laurentian scenes convey no real depth of feeling and, though his paintings were bought by French-Canadians, they were hung in Montréal homes as decoration, not as great statements.

Square Victoria and around

Walking back up towards downtown, take a slight detour to rue St-François-Xavier to find the **Centaur Theatre**. Located at no. 453, and housed in the former Montréal Stock Exchange – Canada's first – it is the main English-language theatre in Montréal today. Back up on rue St-Jacques, going east, you'll pass the sumptuous **Molson** and **Royal banks** at nos. 362 and 360 rue St-Jacques ouest. When it was built in 1866, the 23-storey Royal Bank was the tallest building in the British Empire.

At the northwestern end of Vieux-Montréal, the entire block of rue St-Jacques between rue St-Pierre and Square Victoria is taken up by the **Centre de Commerce Mondial**, an architectural gem and the city's most prominent business address. Inaugurated in 1991 with the hope of reviving the former business district, the structure incorporates the facades of the centuries-old buildings that formerly stood there. Inside, the **ruelle des Fortifications**, so named because it marks the location of the city's stone walls, is a lovely interior arcade adorned with boutiques, restaurants, a soothing fountain and a statue of Amphitrite, Poseidon's wife. At the easternmost end is a chunk of the Berlin wall.

Across the street, there isn't much left of **Square Victoria**, surrounded by Second Empire and neo-Renaissance buildings and bustling with activity from the city's haymarket. The imposing building bracketing the west side of the square used to be the digs of the **Montréal Stock Exchange**, but futures are traded there now instead of shares. Also of note is the **Art Nouveau grill** adorning the Métro station entranceway – which once graced a station on the Paris Métro – donated to the city for Expo '67.

Downtown Montréal

Montréal's **downtown** lies roughly between rue Sherbrooke and rue St-Antoine to the north and south, rue St-Denis to the east and rue Peel to the west, though there's some overlap with the Golden Square Mile, and distinctions are not always clear, to be sure. Of the main streets, **rue Ste-Catherine** offers the most in the way of shopping, dining and entertainment, while **boulevard de Maisonneuve** is more business oriented.

Even if you're not staying in one of the area's hotels, you'll spend at least some time in these parts, as it's here that you'll probably arrive – either at the southerly train station or the easterly bus station. Though the main sights are the high-rises and shopping complexes, the area is also dotted with old churches, museums and public squares filled with activity from buskers, artists and market vendors.

Square Dorchester and around

Formerly a Catholic cemetery, **Square Dorchester** is a leafy spot right in the centre of downtown that is as good a place as any to get your bearings – the Art Deco-inspired Dominion Square Building on the north side of the square is the site of the **Infotouriste** office (daily: June to early Sept 7am–8pm; early Sept to May 9am–6pm) and the starting point for various guided bus tours. The park also hosts occasional lunchtime concerts in summer, and in good weather the office blocks around the square empty their personnel onto the park benches for a snack and a chat. The oldest building here is the Victorian **St George's Anglican Church** (May–Sept Tues–Sun 8.30am–5.30pm), with an impressive tapestry used at the queen's coronation in Westminster Abbey in 1953. The southern half of the square is partitioned off as **Place du Canada**, which commemorates the 1967 centennial.

Dwarfed by its high-rise neighbours, the **Basilique-Cathédrale Marie-Reine-du-Monde** (daily: Mon 7am–8pm, Tues–Fri 7am–7.15pm, Sat 8am–8pm, Sun 9.30am–7.15pm; free) was commissioned by Bishop Ignace Bourget as a reminder that Catholicism still dominated the largest city in the new Dominion of Canada. Impressed by St Peter's while visiting Rome, Bourget created a scaled-down replica of the famous church. While the statues crowning St Peter's facade are of the Apostles, the thirteen statues atop its smaller cousin represent the patron saints of the parishes that donated them. The inside is not as opulent as one might expect, though the high altar of marble, onyx and ivory is surmounted by a gilded copper reproduction of Bernini's baldachin over the altar in St Peter's. To your right on entering is the **Chapelle des Souvenirs**, which contains various relics, including the wax-encased remains of the immensely obscure St Zoticus.

In 1996 the city's ice-hockey team, the Montréal Canadiens, moved into their new home, a 21,000-seat amphitheatre billed as the most modern in North America – **Centre Molson**, at 1260 rue de la Gauchetière ouest. The centre is also the venue for rock concerts, classical-music performances and family entertainment. English guided tours take place daily at 11am and 2pm ($7). If you fancy a puck souvenir or a new T-shirt, check out The Canadiens' Souvenir Boutique (Mon–Wed 9.30am–6pm, Thurs & Fri 9.30am–9pm, Sat 9.30am–5pm) inside.

A few blocks west of the Molson Centre, the **Centre Canadien d'Architecture**, 1920 rue Baile (June–Sept Tues–Wed & Fri–Sun 11am–6pm, Thurs 11am–9pm; Oct–May Wed & Fri 11am–6pm, Thurs 11am–9pm; Sat & Sun 11am–5pm; *www.cca.qc.ca*; $6, free after 5.30pm Thurs) inhabits a wonderfully sleek building with a curiously windowless facade and vast glass doors that open smoothly with the least amount of effort. The Peter Rose design incorporates the beautifully restored Shaughnessy Mansion (the former residence of a president of the Canadian Pacific Railway) and its Art Nouveau conservatory, while the light-filled galleries display the museum's vast collection of prints, drawings and books in exhibitions ranging from individual masters to whole movements from all cultures and periods.

Behind the museum on the south side of boulevard René-Lévesque, on an area known as the Dorchester Plateau, are the whimsical **CCA Sculpture Gardens** (daily: 6am–midnight; free). This whole area, once full of rambling villas like the Shaughnessy Mansion, was ripped apart in 1969 for the construction of the Autoroute Ville-Marie, and the gardens have restored pride in what was until recently a derelict area. Designed by prominent Montréal artist and architect Melvin Charney, the sculptures are a wacky mishmash of architectural references, arranged in a way reminiscent of ancient stone circles.

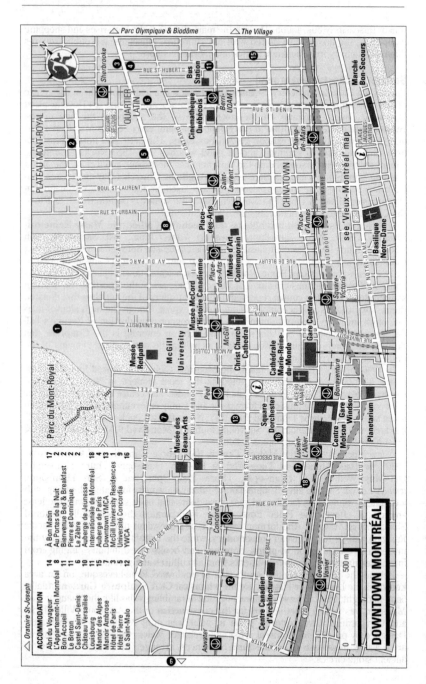

△ Parc Olympique & Biodôme   △ The Village

see 'Vieux-Montréal' map

DOWNTOWN MONTRÉAL

△ Oratoire St-Joseph

ACCOMMODATION

Abri du Voyageur	14	À Bon Matin	17	2
L'Appartement-In Montréal	8	Au Portes de la Nuit		2
Bon Accueil	11	Bienvenue Bed & Breakfast		2
Le Breton	11	Pierre et Dominique		2
Castel Saint-Denis	6	Le Zèbre		2
Château Versailles	10	Auberge de Jeunesse	18	
Louisbourg		Internationale de Montréal	4	
Manoir des Alpes	15	Auberge de Paris	13	
Manoir Ambrose	7	Downtown YMCA	1	
Hôtel de Paris	3	McGill University Residences	9	
Hôtel Pierre	5	Université Concordia	16	
Le Saint-Malo	12	YWCA		

500 m

Centre Canadien
d'Architecture

Ste-Catherine and around

Proceeding north for two short blocks brings you to **rue Ste-Catherine**, the city's main commercial thoroughfare since the early 1900s. The street stretches for 15km across the island of Montréal, with the stretch east of rue Peel serving as the main shopping artery featuring department stores interspersed with exclusive boutiques, souvenir shops and fast-food outlets. For all its consumerist gloss the road still has its seedy bits, with the peepshows and strip clubs enlivening the streetscape. Further along, the street adjoins the Quartier Latin, forms the heart of the gay village, and extends into the working-class neighbourhoods of east Montréal.

From the intersection of Peel and Ste-Catherine (purportedly the busiest in the city) you can see the elegant **Cours Mont-Royal**. Formerly the largest hotel in the British Commonwealth, it now contains four floors of shops (including those of expensive designers), apartments and offices. Peek inside and gawk up at the fourteen-storey-high atria and chandeliers preserved from the hotel. One of these hangs from the coffered ceiling over a permanent catwalk – a testament to the fashion aspirations of the shopping centre.

Montréal's Anglican **Christ Church Cathedral** (daily 8am–6pm; *www.montreal .anglican.org/cathedral*), built in 1859, is five blocks east of Peel, at 635 rue Ste-Catherine ouest, cater-cornered to Square Phillips. By 1927 its slender stone spire was threatening to crash through the wooden roof and was replaced with the peculiar aluminium replica. Inside, the soaring Gothic arches are decorated with heads of saints, gargoyles and angels, but the most poignant feature is the *Coventry Cross*, made from nails salvaged from England's Coventry Cathedral, which was destroyed by bombing during World War II. With the decline in its congregation, the cathedral authorities' desperation for money led them to sell off all the land around and beneath the church. For two and a half years, Christ Church was supported on concrete struts while the developers tunnelled out the glitzy **Promenades de la Cathédrale**, a boutique-lined part of the Underground City. This engineering feat has attracted worldwide interest.

A couple of blocks east of Square Phillips, Ste-Catherine slopes down towards **Place des Arts**, Montréal's leading performing-arts centre and the site of major festivals throughout the summer. The layout tends to throw first-time visitors – the entrances to all the performance halls are via an underground concourse. Atop that is a large plaza, with a series of gardens and fountains. The wide steps create a seating area for use during outdoor concerts, and the walls around the fountains are a popular snoozing spot for nearby office workers during the summer.

THE UNDERGROUND CITY

Place Ville-Marie marks the beginning of Montréal's famous Underground City, planned as a refuge from weather that is outrageously cold in the winter and humid in the summer. The underground network began with the construction of the cruciform Place Ville-Marie in the 1960s. Montréalers flooded into the first climate-controlled shopping arcade, and the Underground City duly spread. Today its 31km of passages provide access to the Métro, major hotels, shopping malls, transport termini, thousands of offices, apartments and restaurants, and a good smattering of cinemas and theatres. Everything underground is well signposted, but you're still likely to get lost on your first visit, unless you pick up a map of the ever-expanding system from a tourist office.

That said, while the tourist office pamphlets make the Underground City sound somewhat exotic, don't plan to make a day out of visiting it – the reality is pretty banal and most Montréalers just consider it as a way to get from place to place, anchored by a number of fairly standard shopping malls. If you want cheap and quick food, though, check out the food courts on the lowest floor of any of the malls en route.

Occupying the west side of the Place des Arts plaza, the **Musée d'Art Contemporain de Montréal** (Tues & Thurs–Sun 11am–6pm, Wed 11am–9pm; $6; *www.macm.org*) is Canada's only museum devoted entirely to contemporary art. The city's foremost showcase for work by Québécois artists, like **Paul-Émile Borduas** and **Jean-Paul Riopelle**, the museum also has works by other Canadian and international artists. One wing is devoted to the permanent collection (rotated two or three times a year); the other stages temporary exhibitions. There's a nice restaurant terrace, often filled with live music, and a small sculpture garden – though difficult to find, it holds a Henry Moore sculpture amidst the greenery.

Rue Sherbrooke and around

Rue Sherbrooke crosses half of Montréal island, but other than the Stade Olympique far out east, its most interesting part is the few blocks from McGill University to rue Guy, an elite stretch of private galleries, exclusive hotels and boutiques for the likes of Yves Saint-Laurent, Ralph Lauren and Armani. At the corner of Drummond is the **Ritz-Carlton Hotel**, Montréal's most ornate hotel – Elizabeth Taylor married Richard Burton here. Inside, the **Claude Lafitte Art Gallery** (Mon–Fri 10am–6pm, Sat 10am–5pm) is a small gallery with works by Picasso, Miro, Chagall and Canadian artists Riopelle, Fortin, Lemieux, Borduas and Pellan. The hotel remains a symbol of what was once known as the **Golden Square Mile**, the area between rue Sherbrooke, Côte des Neiges, the mountain and avenue du Parc. From the late nineteenth century to World War II, about seventy percent of Canada's wealth was owned by a few hundred people who lived here. Known as the Caesars of the Wilderness, the majority were Scottish immigrants who made their fortunes in brewing, fur trading and banking, and who financed the railways and steamships that contributed to Montréal's industrial growth.

Near the Ritz stands Canada's oldest museum, the **Musée des Beaux Arts**, with a pavilion on either side of rue Sherbrooke at nos. 1379 and 1380 (Tues & Thurs–Sun 11am–6pm, Wed 11am–9pm; *www.mmfa.qc.ca*; $15 for special exhibits, permanent collection free). The Canadian art collection is one of the country's most impressive, covering the spectrum from the devotional works of New France, through paintings of the local landscape by, among others, James Wilson Morrice, Maurice Cullen and Clarence Gagnon, to the more radical canvases by the Automatistes – Paul-Émile Borduas and Jean-Paul Riopelle – who transformed Montréal's art scene in the 1940s. Predictably enough, the Group of Seven get a showing too, but the most accomplished paintings are in the European section, where many of the canvases – by such masters as El Greco, Rembrandt and Memling – were donated by merchants during Montréal's heyday. Their contributions are supplemented by equally high-class later acquisitions by Rodin, Picasso, Henry Moore and other twentieth-century luminaries.

Adjoined to the museum, but entered from rue Crescent, a lively street filled with boutiques and bars, the **Musée des Arts Décoratifs**, 2200 rue Crescent (Tues & Thurs–Sun 11am–6pm, Wed 11am–9pm; free permanent exhibit; *www.madm.org*), has a decent display of twentieth century design from the likes of Charles and Ray Eames and Arne Jacobsen in a space designed by architect Frank Gehry. East of the Musée des Beaux-Arts, at the intersection of rue Sherbrooke and Redpath, is another reminder of the Scottish roots of this neighbourhood – the **Church of St Andrew and St Paul**, the regimental church of the Black Watch, the Highland Regiment of Canada. Though the Gothic Revival building is not particularly impressive, Burne-Jones' stained-glass windows are worth a quick peek.

Further east still is the city's most prestigious university, entered through a Neoclassical stone gate at the top of **avenue McGill College**, a principal boulevard with wide pavements adorned with sculptures, most notably Raymond Mason's *Illuminated Crowd*, portraying a mass of larger-than-life people – generally faced by an equally large crowd of tourists. The leafy campus of **McGill University** was founded in 1813 from the bequest of James McGill, a Glaswegian immigrant fur trader, and the university is now world-famous for its medical and engineering schools. The ornate limestone buildings and their modern extensions are perfect for relaxing or for a walk above the street level of downtown. A boulder on the campus near Sherbrooke marks the spot where the original Iroquois village of Hochelaga stood before European penetration.

The university boasts a couple of fine museums. In the middle of the campus is the **Musée Redpath** (Mon–Fri 9am–5pm, Sun 1–5pm; closed Fri late June to early Sept, Sat year-round; free), the first custom-built Canadian museum, with an eclectic anthropological collection that includes a rare fossil collection, crystals, dinosaur bones and two Egyptian mummies. Better known is the **Musée McCord** (Tues–Fri 10am–6pm, Sat–Sun 10am–5pm; $8.50; *www.musee-mccord.qc.ca*;), 690 rue Sherbrooke ouest, an extensive museum of Canadian history housed in the elegant nineteenth-century McGill Union building which underwent a $20 million expansion programme. The main part of the collection was amassed by the rich and worthy Scots-Irish McCord family over an eighty-year period from the mid-nineteenth century and represents a highly personal vision of the development of Canada, which they saw as a fusion of colonial and declining native elements. The first few rooms are devoted to a permanent exhibition on the McCord family, followed by space for changing displays from the huge collections. The museum is particularly strong on native artefacts, textiles, costumes and photographs, and examples of these are found in the themed exhibits. The First Nation gallery is the most interesting, with high-quality examples of furs, ivory carvings and superb beadwork, whose aboriginal name translates as "little shining berries".

The Main and East Montréal

Boulevard St-Laurent – **The Main** – leads all the way up from Vieux-Montréal to the northern extremities of the city. North of rue Sherbrooke is the most absorbing episode along the way, a district where Montréal's cosmopolitan diversity is evident in distinct enclaves of immigrant neighbourhoods. Running parallel to **rue St-Denis**, the heart of the upbeat studenty Quartier Latin, this zone is where the most fun can be had in Montréal, with a huge array of ethnic food outlets and bars spilling out onto the streets. If the party atmosphere is too much, you can head for the landscaped expanse of **Mont Royal** or the overwhelming **Stade Olympique** and the vast **Jardin Botanique** further east.

Boulevard St-Laurent and Plateau Mont-Royal

Traditionally, **boulevard St-Laurent** divided the English in the west from the French in the east of the city. Montréal's immigrants, first Russian Jews, then Greeks, Portuguese, Italians, East Europeans and, more recently, South Americans, settled in the middle and, though many prospered enough to move on, the area around the Main is still a cultural mix where neither of the two official languages dominates. Delis, bars, nightclubs, hardware stores, bookshops and an increasing number of trendy boutiques provide the perfect background to a wonderful jumble of sights, sounds and smells.

Wandering north from downtown will bring you onto one of Montréal's few pedestrianized streets, **rue Prince-Arthur**, thronged with buskers and caricaturists in the summer. Its eastern end leads to the beautiful fountained and statued **Square St-Louis**, the city's finest public square. Designed in 1876, the square was originally the domain of rich corporate Montréalers, but the magnificent houses are now occupied by artists, poets and writers, and plaques identify those of the more illustrious luminaries.

The east side of the square divides the lower and upper areas of **rue St-Denis**. The part of St-Denis leading south from rues Sherbrooke to Ste-Catherine has long had a rather grubby reputation, but has become increasingly colonized by terrace cafés and bars crammed with students from the nearby Université de Québec à Montréal (UQAM) well into the early hours. Further north lies the stamping ground of the francophone intellectual set, where a different yet equally heady atmosphere pervades the sidewalks. Here you'll find some of the city's most upscale boutiques and restaurants.

Mont Royal

Little more than a hill to most tourists but a mountain to Montréalers, **Mont Royal** reaches a less than lofty height of 233m but its two square kilometres of greenery are visible from anywhere in the city. Mont Royal holds a special place in the history of the city – it was here that the Iroquois established their settlement and that Maisonneuve declared the island to be French – but for centuries the mountain was privately owned. Then, during an especially bitter winter, one of the inhabitants cut down his trees for extra firewood. Montréalers were outraged at the desecration and in 1875 the land was bought by the city for the impressive sum of $1 million. Frederick Law Olmsted, designer of New York's Central Park and San Francisco's Golden Gate Park, was hired to landscape the hill, which now provides 56km of jogging paths and 20km of skiing trails to keep city inhabitants happy year-round.

The city has steadfastly refused any commercial developments on this lucrative site, the only construction being **Lac des Castors**, built in the 1930s as a work-creation scheme for the unemployed; it now serves as a skating rink in the winter and paddle boat playground in the summer. In the 1950s, protection of the mountain reached a puritanical extreme when a local journalist revealed that young couples were using the area for amatory pursuits and, even worse, that people were openly drinking alcohol. Consequently all of the underbrush was uprooted, which only succeeded in killing off much of the ash, birch, maple, oak and pine trees. Within five years Mont Royal was dubbed Bald Mountain and a replanting campaign had to be instigated.

There are various access points for a walk up the mountain but the most popular starting point is at the **George-Étienne Cartier monument**, where every Sunday buskers and people of all ages congregate with tam tam drums until the sun goes down in a display out of a Woodstock love-in. From here, several paths lead up to the summit where an illuminated cross marks the spot where Maisonneuve placed his own in 1642. Chemin Olmsted heads on, past the top of rue Peel (the easiest access from downtown), and up to the summit, where a **lookout point** offers fine views of the city. To reach the monument, you can either take the Métro to Mont-Royal station, walk west along avenue du Mont-Royal and turn left on avenue du Parc, or get off the Métro at Place-des-Arts and take the Parc bus (#80).

Oratoire St-Joseph

On the west side of the mountain the awesome **Oratoire St-Joseph** (daily: May–Sept 6.30am–10pm; Oct–April 6.30am–5pm) rises from its green surroundings near Montréal's highest point. If you don't want to walk across the summit, the nearest Métro is Côte-des-Neiges, from where the way to the oratory is signposted.

In 1904, Brother André built a small chapel here to honour St Joseph, Canada's patron saint. Before long, André's ability to heal people had earned him the sobriquet "The Miracle Man of Montréal", and huge numbers of patients took to climbing the outside stairs on their knees to receive his grace. Satisfied clients donated so much money that in 1924 he could afford to begin work on this immense granite edifice, which was completed in 1967, thirty years after Brother André's death. It is topped by a dome second in size only to St Peter's in Rome. The interior of St Jo's – as it's known locally – does not live up to the splendour of the Italianate exterior, though the chapel in the apse is richly decorated with green marble columns and a gold-leaf ceiling. In the adjoining anteroom, thousands of votive candles burn along the walls, and proof of Brother

André's curative powers hang everywhere; crutches, canes and braces are crammed into every available space. The roof terrace, above the portico, has excellent views of the city and the St Lawrence beyond. A small upstairs **museum** displays items relating to Brother André's life, including the room in which he died, which was shifted here from a local hospice. Brother André's heart is enclosed in a glass case; the devout believe it quivers occasionally.

Outside, the **Way of the Cross** has some particularly beautiful sculptures in smooth, white Carrara marble and Indiana buff stone by Montréal artist Louis Parent – a tranquil site used as a setting for the well-known film *Jésus de Montréal*. You can also visit the small building a few metres away from the Oratory that contains the original chapel and Brother André's tiny room.

The Parc Olympique and around

It's best to take the Métro to Viau in order to view Montréal's most infamous architectural construction, the **Parc Olympique**, at 4141 ave Pierre-de-Coubertin. The main attraction, the **Stade Olympique**, is known by Montréalers as the "Big O" for three reasons: its name, its circular shape and the fact that the city owes so much money for its construction. The main facilities for the 1976 Summer Olympics were designed by Roger Taillibert, who was told that money was no object. Mayor Jean Drapeau declared, "It is as unlikely that Montréal will incur a debt as for a man to bear a child." The complex ended up costing $1.4 billion (of which $300 million is *still* outstanding), and was not even completed in time for the games. It's now one of the most heavily used stadiums in the world: in a desperate attempt to pay the debts, the ceaseless schedule features everything from Pink Floyd concerts to baseball games played by the Montréal Expos. Daily **guided tours** are available (12.40pm & 3.40pm; $5.25; *www.rio.gouv.qc.ca*).

The stadium's 168-metre **tower** is a major engineering feat as it's the highest inclined tower in the world. Its main function was to hold a retractable 65-tonne roof. But the 45-minute process never really worked properly, and today sections of the roof are prone to falling in, although the city continues to fork out millions of dollars. The attraction here is the **shuttle ride** that takes you up the tower to an observation deck with eighty-kilometre views and an exhibition of historic photos of Montréal (daily: 10am–5pm, mid-June to early Sept until 9pm; closed early Jan to early Feb; $9).

Close by is the **Biodôme**, at 4777 ave Pierre-de Coubertin (daily: May to mid-Sept 9am–7pm; mid-Sept to April 9am–5pm; $9.50; *www.ville.montreal.qc.ca/biodome*), housed in a bicycle-helmet-shaped building that started life as a venue for cycling events during the Olympics. Now it is a stunning environmental museum comprising four ecosystems: tropical, Laurentian forest, St Lawrence maritime and polar. You can wander freely through the different zones, which are planted with appropriate flourishing vegetation and inhabited by the relevant birds, animals and marine life. Keep an eye out for the sloths in the tropical section; they move so slowly that their fur grows mould, unlike the lively monkeys that swing through the trees. You can look at a beaver dam and a take a televised peek inside its lodge, then move on to an impressive rock pool complete with foaming waves and a multicoloured population of anemones, crabs, lobsters and starfish. Gulls fly overhead and puffins bob and dive, while next door, in the polar zone, temperatures drop so low that penguins can slide down snow-covered slopes into the water. It's all highly educational and good fun, but try to avoid visiting on Sundays, when, it seems, the entire population of Québec and its children head there.

Near the stadium and linked by a free shuttle bus from mid-May to mid-September is the **Jardin Botanique de Montréal**, 4101 Sherbrooke est (daily: mid-June to early Sept 9am–7pm; early Sept to mid-June 9am–5pm; $9.50, Nov–April: $6.75; *www.ville.montreal .qc.ca/jardin*). The grounds contain some thirty types of gardens from medicinal herbs to orchids. Highlights include a Japanese garden designed by the landscape architect Ken Nakajima, its ponds of water lilies bordered by greenish sculptured stone and crossed by delicate bridges. In 1991 the Japanese garden was joined by the Chinese garden, the largest of its kind outside China – more than 1500 tonnes of materials from China were used to reproduce a replica of the Ming Gardens of fifteenth-century Shanghai. Other attractions in the gardens include the **Insectarium** (same hours as the gardens, and the entry is included in the admission fee; *www.ville .montreal.qc.ca/insectarium*), a bug-shaped building containing insects of every shape and size. The museum is mainly geared towards children, but adults will learn a fascinating thing or two – like the fact that the housefly has more than five thousand muscles. If you visit in February, you'll get a chance to eat some of the insects at the Insectarium's annual bug fry.

Near the southwest corner of the gardens, on the junction of Pie-IX and Sherbrooke, is the stately mansion of the **Château Dufresne**, 2929 rue Jeanne-d'Arc (Thurs–Sun 10am–5pm; $5), built in the 1910s for the Dufresne brothers – one an architect, the other an industrialist – who were instrumental in Montréal's expansion. The château's impressive Edwardian interior has been partially restored and includes many of the Dufresne's original nineteenth- and early twentieth-century furnishings.

Montréal's other attractions

The islands of Montréal, Île Ste-Hélène and Île Notre-Dame and their environs, offer various slightly-out-of-the-way sights, all well served by public transport but mostly worth the trip only if you have time to kill. Lying just south of Montréal, the combined 2.7 square kilometres of the **smaller islands** were the main venue for Expo '67 and have been developed as playgrounds for the city's inhabitants, with the **La Ronde** amusement park the main draw. The **Maison St-Gabriel** is included in this section as it is a bit of a hike from central Montréal. The fur-trading centre of **Lachine** is on the western shore of Montréal island, about the same distance from downtown as the art museum in the suburb of **St-Laurent**, while the **Musée Ferroviaire Canadien** (Canadian Railway Museum) is off the island on the south shore of the St Lawrence.

Biosphère, 160 chemin Tour de l'Île (June–Sept daily 10am–6pm; Aug–May Tues–Sat 10am–4pm; $8.50; *www.biosphere.ec.gc.ca*). An interactive museum focusing on the St Lawrence Seaway and the Great Lakes. The exhibits change yearly and there's lots to amuse children, from interactive touch-screens to skill-testing games, movies, user-friendly computers, multimedia displays and educational workshops. On the fourth floor, a gorgeous lookout point takes in the St Lawrence River and the city. Métro Île-Ste-Hélène.

Cosmodôme and Space Camp Canada, 2150 Autoroute des Laurentides, Laval (late June to early Sept daily 10am–6pm; early Sept to late June Tues–Sun 10am–6pm; $9.75). A voyage through the solar system in a moving theatre, where you can walk on the moon, see a real moon rock, take control of the space shuttle *Endeavour* and become a cosmonaut. Buses #60 and #61 from Métro Henri-Bourassa.

Écomusée du Fier Monde, 2050 rue Amherst (Wed 11am–8pm, Thurs–Sun 10.30am–5pm; $5). Housed in a wonderful Art Deco former public bathhouse, this museum focuses on the history of Montréal's industrialization with exceptionally good temporary exhibits. Métro Beaudry.

Leonard & Bina Ellen Art Gallery, 1400 boul de Maisonneuve (Mon–Fri 11am–7pm, Sat 1–5pm; *ellen-gallery.concordia.ca*). Canadian art by both established and emerging artists on the main floor of Concordia University's George-Webster building. Métro Guy-Concordia.

Lieu historique national du Commerce-de-la-Fourrure-à-Lachine, 1255 boul St-Joseph, Lachine (April to mid-Oct Mon 1–6pm, Tues–Sun 10am–12.30pm & 1–6pm; mid-Oct to early Dec Wed–Sun 9am–12.30pm & 1–5pm; $2.50; *www.parcscanada.gc.ca/fourrure*). On the shore of Lac St-Louis, the old Lachine warehouse puts on an exhibition on the fur trade; the staff wear the costumes of natives, *coureurs des bois* and the Scottish merchants who worked here in the eighteenth and early nineteenth centuries. Bus #195 west from Métro Angrignon.

Maison St-Gabriel, 2146 Place Dublin (daily: late June to early Sept guided tours hourly 10am–5pm; mid-April to late June & early Sept to mid-Dec guided tours Tues–Sun 1.30pm, 2.30pm,

3.30pm; $5). Dating from 1698, this stone farmhouse was the home of Marguerite Bourgeoys (see p.214); antique furniture and the restored kitchen are the main attractions. Bus #57 from Métro Charlevoix.

Musée d'Art de St-Laurent, 615 boul Ste-Croix, Ville St-Laurent (Wed–Sun noon–5pm; $3, free Wed). A small museum in the former neo-Gothic chapel of St-Laurent college, featuring early traditional arts and crafts from Québec. Métro Du Collège.

Musée Ferroviaire Canadien, 122a rue St-Pierre, St-Constant (May to early Sept daily 9am–5pm; Sept to late Oct Sat & Sun 9am–5pm; $6). Canada's largest collection of railway, tramway and steam locomotives is hard to reach without a car, though bus #160 near Métro Bonaventure does the (infrequent) journey.

Musée Stewart, Old Fort, Île Ste-Hélène (mid-May to early Sept 10am–6pm; early-Sept to mid-May Wed–Mon 10am–5pm; $6; *www.stewart-museum.org*). In the fortified arsenal commissioned by the Duke of Wellington, the museum contains a collection of weapons and assorted domestic and scientific artefacts. The fort is also the summer venue for the re-enactment of seventeenth- and eighteenth-century military manoeuvres by the Fraser Highlanders and Compagnie Franche de la Marine. Métro Île-Ste-Hélène.

Musée de la ville de Lachine, 110 chemin LaSalle, Lachine (Wed–Sun 11.30am–4.30pm; closed Jan–March; free). This seventeenth-century fur-trading post contains a humdrum collection of contemporaneous artefacts and a display on the history of the Lachine canal. Bus #110 from Métro Angrignon.

Planétarium de Montréal, 1000 rue St-Jacques ouest (several performances daily; ☎872-4530; $6; *www.planetarium.montreal.qc.ca*). Shows include "guided tours" of the solar system and more distant galaxies, while various performances explain eclipses, sunspots and the movement of the planets. Métro Bonaventure.

La Ronde, Île Ste-Hélène (late May to late August 10.30am–10pm; $29, ground admission only $15). Ticket gives unlimited access to every ride in the amusement park and admission to the nearby Aqua Parc, a waterslide park. La Ronde is the venue for various celebrations throughout the year, including the annual Fireworks Competition from June to July. Métro Île-Ste-Hélène.

Eating

Montréalers conduct much of their business and their social lives in the city's **eating places**, and Montréal food is as varied as its population, ranging from the rich meat dishes of typical Québécois cuisine to bagels bursting with cream cheese. Masses of restaurants line the area around rue **Ste-Catherine** downtown, though American fast-food chains seem to be taking over, while **Vieux-Montréal** has an ever-expanding number of places to eat, though here most are touristy and slightly overpriced. The best for food, and upbeat atmosphere, is in the more French area of the metropolis, around the **Plateau** and **Quartier Latin**. Montréal comes a close second to New York as the **bagel** capital of the world, and they are sold everywhere from grimy outlets to stylish cafés – particularly delicious when fresh, warm and crammed with cream cheese and lox (smoked salmon).

For those on a **tight budget** the delis, diners and cafés are perfect, and if you're really broke the so-called pizza war downtown has got slices of pizza down to 99¢. *Apportez votre vin* establishments, of which there are many on rue Prince Arthur and ave Duluth, are the cheaper restaurant alternatives.

Snacks and cafés

Ambiance, 1874 rue Notre Dame ouest. Old French tearoom and antique shop.

Bagel Etc., 4320 boul St-Laurent. Trendy New York-type diner. Excellent bagels from the simple cream cheese to caviar and extravagant breakfasts. Daily 8am–5pm.

Beauty's, 93 ave du Mont-Royal ouest. A brunch institution with wonderful 1950s decor. Be prepared to get up early on the weekend to avoid the lineup.

Ben's Delicatessen, 1475 rue Metcalfe. Lithuanian Ben Kravitz opened his deli in 1908 and his sons and grandsons still run this Montréal institution. Its gaudy 1930s interior still draws a few people in the wee hours for delicious smoked meat and diner fare, but the wall of fame attests to happier days.

La Binerie Mont-Royal, 367 ave du Mont-Royal est. Four tables and a chrome counter seat the hundreds of people who visit this well-known café daily. The menu consists of beans, beans and more beans with ketchup, vinegar or maple syrup. Also served is pork, beef, *tourtière* (a minced porkpie) and *pouding chômeur* – "unemployed pudding" – a variation on bread pudding.

Briskets, 705 rue Ste-Catherine ouest and 1073 Beaver Hall. Plain decor with wooden tables, popular with students. Smoked meat to eat in or take away. Closed Sun.

Café Ciné-Lumière, 5163 boul St-Laurent. Antique Parisian decor, cheap French food and a wide selection of mussels. Black-and-white films are regularly projected onto the back wall.

Café El Dorado, 921 ave du Mont-Royal est. Coffees from all over the world, and fine desserts.

Café Laika, 4040 boul St-Laurent. The sleek interior draws urbane hipsters from the Plateau for daily specials and *cafés au lait*.

Café Santropol, 3990 rue St-Urbain. Mostly vegetarian café on the corner of Duluth. Spectacular during the summer when its flowered and fountained back terrace is a welcome oasis from the busy streets, *Santropol* still retains its charm in winter thanks to its cozy atrium. Huge sandwiches, quiches and salads are offered as well as various herbal teas and coffees.

Fairmount Bagel Bakery, 74 ave Fairmount ouest. Possibly the best bagel outlet in Montréal, offering a huge variety of bagels. There is nowhere to sit, but arm yourself with a bag of bagels, a pot of cream cheese and some smoked salmon (lox), sit on the nearest curb and you'll soon be in bagel heaven. Open daily 24hr.

Faubourg Ste-Catherine, 1616 rue Ste-Catherine ouest. A gigantic restored building on the corner of Guy. Downstairs is a wealth of food stalls from cookies to fresh veg; upstairs a fast-food mall to surpass all others – everything from fresh salmon to crepes and cookies.

Kilo, 5206 boul St-Laurent. Creating the most divine cakes, particularly the cheesecake, this patisserie is expensive but worth every cent. Open late on weekends.

Reuben's Deli, 892 and 1116 rue Ste-Catherine ouest. An excellent deli with great jars of pimentos in the window and a wealth of smoked meats. Frantic atmosphere and friendly service. A favourite with local business types, and thus packed at lunchtime.

Schwartz's Montréal Hebrew Delicatessen, 3895 boul St-Laurent. *Schwartz's* is a Montréal institution: a small, narrow deli serving up colossal smoked-meat sandwiches, with surly service thrown in as part of the package. Line-up out the door on weekends.

Wilensky's Light Lunch, 34 ave Fairmount ouest. Used for countless filmsets because the decor hasn't changed since 1932 and that includes the till, the grill and the drinks machine. The Wilensky Special includes four types of salami and costs around $4. Closed weekends.

Restaurants

Montréal's ethnic diversity is amply displayed by the variety of **cuisines** available and Montréalers try to outdo each other by indulging in exotic fare from Japanese rotis to earthy Portuguese grub. The city has its own **Chinatown** just north of Vieux-Montréal, a **Little Italy** around Jean-Talon Métro, a **Greek** community whose cheaper restaurants are concentrated along Prince Arthur – but for more traditional Greek cuisine head further north along avenue du Parc where a number of Greek-Canadians live. Most prominent of the ethnic eateries are the **Eastern European** establishments dotted around the city. Opened by immigrants who came to work in the garment factories, their speciality is **smoked meat**, which has become a Montréal obsession, served between huge chunks of rye bread with pickles on the side.

Asian

Azuma, 5263 boul St-Laurent (☎271-5263). A popular Japanese restaurant with a reasonable $20 a head menu.

Chu Chai, 4088 rue St-Denis (☎843-4194). Excellent, fresh vegetarian Thai at budget prices.

Katsura, 2170 rue de la Montagne (☎849-1172). Large and popular downtown Japanese restaurant. Fairly reasonable at $20 a meal.

Maison Kam Fung, 1008 rue Clark (☎878-2888). Montréal's vast temple to dim sum, right in the heart of Chinatown. Well-priced menu but not dirt-cheap. There are often long queues so get there early.

Mikado, 368 ave Laurier ouest and 1731 rue St-Denis (☎279-4809 or 844-5705). Excellent sushi in a smashing setting, but it's expensive at around $30.

Nanthas Cuisine, 9 ave Duluth est (☎845-4717). Reasonably priced and delicious Malaysian place with wonderful samosas and noodle dishes in both meat and veggie options.

Pho Bang New York, 970 boul St-Laurent (☎952-2032). The servings of *pho* (tonkinoise) noodle soup are huge and delicious, and extremely affordable.

Red Thai, 3550 boul St-Laurent (☎289-0998). This resto serves up exquisite Thai in a decor straight out of *Anna and the King*.

Soto, 3527 boul St-Laurent and 500 rue McGill (☎842-1150 or 864-5115). Simple yet sleek decor meets excellent sushi and *maki*, though the prices here aren't cheap.

Soy, 3945 rue St-Denis (☎499-9399). Deliciously prepared light dishes from the Orient. *Soy* is especially good for lunch, when a three-course meal costs under $10.

Thai Express, 3710 boul St-Laurent (☎287-9957). The name says it all: speedy Thai at low prices – for under $8, you'll get a seriously hearty serving of rice or noodles with wonderfully aromatic spices.

French

Bonaparte, 443 rue St-François-Xavier (☎844-4368). Moderately priced, well-situated French restaurant in Vieux-Montréal. The fish is good and there are tables on the balconies.

L'Express, 3927 rue St-Denis (☎845-5333). Fashionable Parisian-style bistro, with hectic service. Pretty expensive, and reservations are essential – though you might be able to squeeze in at the bar without one.

Fonduementale, 4325 rue St-Denis (☎499-1446). Set in a historic two-storey house with a warm fireplace in winter and a blooming outdoor terrace in summer. The fondue is divine and the meals are long and languid.

Laloux, 250 ave des Pins est (☎287-9127). This Parisian-style bistro serves pricey – and exquisite – *nouvelle cuisine*.

Au 917, 917 rue Rachel est (☎524-0094). An inexpensive bistro with a reliable menu in a comfortable atmosphere. Bring your own wine.

Au Petit Extra, 1690 rue Ontario est (☎527-5552). Large, lively and affordable bistro with great food and authentic French feel.

Toqué!, 3842 rue St-Denis (☎499-2084). Renowned chef Normand Laprise rules here and the dining experience is ultra chic, high-end and unforgettable – if you can get a seat and afford the price tag. Reservations are essential.

Mediterranean

Amelios, 201 rue Milton (☎845-8396). Basic and hearty pasta and pizza in a tiny half-basement restaurant in the heart of the McGill University student ghetto. The prices are excellent and the service friendly. Bring your own wine.

Arahova Souvlaki, 256 rue St-Viateur ouest (☎274-7828). Superb, yet inexpensive choice for authentic Greek cuisine.

Eduardo, 404 ave Duluth est (☎843-3330). Crowded cheap Italian with huge portions. Bring your own alcohol and expect a queue.

Euro Deli, 3619 boul St-Laurent and 1206 rue Peel (☎843-7853 or 878-3354). Busy deli where you can get stuffed for about $5 on sandwiches, calzone, pasta and veggie food.

La Casa Greque, 200 rue Prince Arthur est (☎842-6098). One of numerous cheap Greek establishments in this area, all of much the same standard.

Maestro SVP, 3615 boul St-Laurent (☎842-6447). When oysters are in season, this is the place to go to get them, served in a myriad of ways.

Milos, 5357 ave du-Parc (☎272-3522). Expensive, but the finest Greek restaurant in the city.

Misto, 929 ave du Mont-Royal est (☎526-5043). Chic design, hip bourgeois francophones, and deliciously creative pasta and thin-crust pizzas. No fettucine alfredo here. Reservations advised.

Modigliani, 1251 rue Gilford (☎522-0422). Lots of plants and a pianist. Reasonable prices for great Italian food.

Pizzédélic, 3509 boul St-Laurent (☎282-6784). Modern decor and experimental pizzas.

Pizzeria Napoletana, 189 rue Dante, Little Italy (☎276-8226). Very cheap; take your own alcohol and expect to queue at the weekend.

North American

L'Anecdote, 801 rue Rachel est (☎526-7967). Small, cosy hamburger and sandwich joint.

Bar-B-Barn, 1201 rue Guy, just off Ste-Catherine (☎931-3811). Brilliant ribs served in Western "Yeee-Ha" decor; a favourite with the local "cowboy" business world – hundreds of business cards are stuck in the log rafters. Always packed to the hilt.

Bio Train, 410 rue St-Jacques (☎842-9184). Self-serve health-food restaurant with tasty soups and hearty sandwiches.

Chez Claudette, 351 ave Laurier est (☎279-5173). Cheap family bistro, great for a big breakfast fry-up.

Chez Delmo, 211 rue Notre-Dame ouest (☎849-4061). Popular with anglophones and workers from the nearby stock exchange in Vieux-Montréal, the food doesn't come cheap. Eat in the first room with its two long oyster bars. Fish and seafood dishes are the speciality, and the chowder is excellent. Closed Sun.

Le Commensal, 1204 ave McGill College and 1720 rue St-Denis (☎871-1480 or 854-2627). Cheap vegetarian with hot or cold buffet paid for by weight. The St-Denis location has the best atmosphere. Open daily until late.

Laurier BBQ, 381 ave Laurier ouest (☎273-3671). Great hunks of Québec-style barbecued chicken and huge salads; a Montréal favourite for half a century.

Moishe's, 3961 boul St-Laurent (☎845-3509). Favourite haunt of Montréal's business community. Excellent (and huge) steaks, but very expensive, with notoriously bad-tempered service. Reservations recommended.

La Paryse, 302 rue Ontario est (☎842-2040). Delicious home-made hamburgers and chips in a 1950s-style diner. Highly recommended.

Patati Patata, 4177 boul St-Laurent (☎844-0216). Small place with excellent and cheap home-made food.

Shed Café, 3515 boul St-Laurent (☎842-0220). Hamburger, salad and sandwich joint where trendy Montréalers come to see and be seen. Avant-garde, wacky interior. Open late Fri & Sat.

Bars and nightlife

Montréal's **nightlife** keeps going into the small hours of the morning, and its bars and clubs cater for everyone – from the students of the Quartier Latin and the punks who hang out on the corner of Ste-Catherine and St-Denis, to the anglophone yuppies of rue Crescent. The places listed here are the best of the bunch and are open until 3am unless stated otherwise. Always tip the bar staff – the perks constitute the main whack of their wages. Many bars have regular music nights, with **jazz** being especially popular. Other than the bars, there are numerous venues in the city, with top-name touring bands playing at the new Centre Molson and the Olympic Stadium.

For up-to-date **information**, the *Mirror* (*www.montrealmirror.com*) and *Hour* (*www.afterhour.com*) are free English weekly newspapers with excellent listings sections. The English-language daily *The Montreal Gazette* also carries comprehensive listings – the Friday weekend guide is particularly good. *Montréal Scope*, available in tourist information offices and the better hotels, is primarily for mainstream tourists.

Bars

Angels, 3604 boul St-Laurent. Young, university hangout, with the atmosphere of the average common room and house music on the weekends.

Bar St-Laurent, 3874 boul St-Laurent. A dark and dank rockabilly bar popular among punks and squeegee kids.

Le Bifteck, 3702 boul St-Laurent. Studenty, cheap beer bar/venue with taped music from grunge to hip-hop.

Bily Kun, 354 ave du Mont-Royal est. Packed brasserie-pub,with stuffed ostrich heads on the walls.

Blizzarts, 3956a boul St-Laurent. Funked-out lounge-bar with retro furnishings, Sputnik-lighting, and a tiny dance floor. Draws a late-twenty-something Plateau crowd.

Le Central, 4479 rue St-Denis. Unpretentious, old jazz bar. Another student hangout, as the drinks are cheap and admission is free.

Le Cheval Blanc, 809 rue Ontario est. Old-style Montréal pub with the same Art Deco decor as when it opened in the 1940s. They brew their own beer, and it's good.

Else's, 156 rue Roy est. A warm and friendly neighbourhood bar-pub with green walls, huge windows onto the street, newspapers and magazines for loan and plants galore.

Futenbulle, 273 ave Bernard ouest. Probably the largest selection of beers in Montréal.

Hurley's Irish Pub, 1225 rue Crescent. Very popular Irish pub with smooth Guinness on tap.

Île Noire, 342 rue Ontario est. Sophisticated Scottish-type bar with warming whiskeys.

Jello Bar, 151 rue Ontario est. Enjoy live jazz and blues at this bar furnished with 1960s and 1970s novelties. Martini cocktails are the house speciality.

Laïka, 4040 boul St-Laurent. Café by day, lounge by night, *Laïka's* got it all: good food, drinks, music and chic decor, though the service can be a bit spotty.

Pub Sir Winston Churchill, 1459 rue Crescent. Known locally as *Winnie's*, this English-style pub attracts an older crowd of local and visiting anglophone professionals. Pool tables and a small dance floor. Prime pick-up joint.

Pub le Vieux-Dublin, 1219 rue University. Irish pub with Celtic music and a massive choice of draught beers. Popular with everyone.

Sainte-Elizabeth, 1412 rue Ste-Elizabeth. Nice outdoor courtyard with ivy-covered walls that give the impression of drinking a quaff with good friends in your very own backyard.

Le St-Sulpice, 1682 rue St-Denis. A well-decorated, fashionable bar on three floors in the heart of Montréal's Quartier Latin. Terrace at the back and front, perfect for people-watching.

Sofa, 451 Rachel est. A cigar-bar lounge with an extensive scotch and porto list, funky furniture to sit in, and groovy music from acid jazz to house, depending on the night. Cover charge usually applies after 10pm.

Le Swimming, 3643 boul St-Laurent. In a bizarre c. 1900 building, this is a massive pool hall and happening bar with occasional live acts on the weekend.

Whisky Café, 3 ave Bernard ouest. Elegantly decorated with a young wealthy clientele. The prices aren't cheap, but then, there are no blended malts on the menu here. What there is in addition, though, is a girl's urinal – the only one in Montréal.

Venues, clubs and discos

L'Air du Temps, 194 rue St-Paul ouest (☎842-2003). The most famous of Montréal's jazz spots. In the heart of Vieux-Montréal with ornate antique interior. Admission $10, but arrive early to get a decent seat. Live acts from 10pm Thurs–Sun, but call ahead to confirm; closed Mon–Wed.

Aux Deux Pierrots, 104 rue St-Paul ouest. Québécois folk singers are the mainstay of this club and everyone sings along. There's usually a good crowded atmosphere but don't expect to understand a word unless your French is excellent. Outside terrace in the summer. Admission from $3.

Le Balattou, 4372 boul St-Laurent. Montréal's only African nightclub. Dark, smoky, crowded, hot, loud and friendly. Live acts every night; entrance $5 on weekdays, $7 at weekends (includes one drink).

Le Belmont, 4483 boul St-Laurent. Yuppie francophone disco dance-bar, cover charge Thurs–Sat. Closed Mon–Wed.

Cabaret, 2111 boul St-Laurent. Probably the best place in town to see a live act – it's an old-school venue with a balcony and chandeliers.

Café Campus, 57 rue Prince-Arthur est. Great place to see live acts, the cover is always reasonable as is the price of beer.

Club 737, 1 Place Ville-Marie. Popular with financial district crowd; the main selling point is the panoramic view of the city, not the meat-market atmosphere.

Club Soda, 1225 boul St-Laurent. One of Montréal's most popular venues. Attracts good acts, especially during the comedy and jazz festivals.

Les Foufounes Électriques, 87 rue Ste-Catherine est. A bizarre name ("The Electric Buttocks") for a bizarre and wonderful bar/club/venue. Known as *Foufs*, it's the best place in Québec for alternative bands, attracting a young crowd from ravers to students. Huge outside terrace perfect for summer evenings. Tickets for bands from $10, otherwise admission is free and pitchers of beer are cheap.

Jailhouse Rock Cafe, 30 rue Mont-Royal ouest. On the corner of St-Laurent with eclectic live bands from punk to ska to spoken-word events.

Le Loft, 1405 boul St-Laurent. With its indigo techno decor and odd arty exhibition, the bar attracts trendy under-25s – but it's a real meat market.

Le Passeport, 4156 rue St-Denis. Small dance-music club with long queues at weekends. Frequented by Québec's rich and famous; drinks are overpriced. Cover charge usually applies.

Sona, 1439 rue de Bleury. Weekend all-nighters (3am–10am) for ecstatic kids. Designed to look like a Japanese airport, it's got lasers, house, techno and drum'n'bass. $25 and expect a long queue.

Stereo, 858 rue Ste-Catherine est. Said to have the best sound system in Montréal. The stereo in question kicks techno, house and drum'n'bass all night long, usually manned by an internationally renowned DJ. Opens at 2am and closes whenever. Fri & Sat only.

The performing arts and cinema

Montréal's most prestigious centre for the **performing arts** is the Place des Arts, 175 rue Ste-Catherine ouest (information ☎285-4200, tickets ☎842-2112, *www.pdarts.com*), a five-hall complex with a comprehensive year-round programme of dance, music and theatre. The Théâtre de Verdure in Parc Lafontaine is an outdoor theatre with a summer-long programme of free plays, ballets and concerts. Another eclectic venue is the Théâtre St-Denis, 1594 St-Denis (☎849-4211), which presents blockbuster musicals and other shows. The Saidye Bronfman Centre, 5170 chemin de la Côte Ste-Catherine (☎739-2301), contains an exhibition centre and a three-hundred-seater venue for English (or Yiddish) music, dance, film and theatre.

The city's foremost French-language **theatre** is the Théâtre du Rideau Vert, 4664 St-Denis (☎845-0267), which gives prominence to Québec playwrights, while the Théâtre du Nouveau Monde, 84 Ste-Catherine est (☎866-8667), presents a mix of contemporary and classic plays in French. Montréal's main English-language theatre is the Centaur Theatre, housed in the former stock exchange at 453 St-François-Xavier (☎288-3161).

Montréal has more than ten excellent **dance** troupes from the internationally acclaimed Les Grandes Ballets Canadiens (☎849-8681) and Ballets Classiques de Montréal to the avant-garde LaLaLa Human Steps and Tangente, who perform at various times at the Place des Arts, Théâtre de Verdue and during the festivals. The continent's premier contemporary dance festival is the **Festival International de Nouvelle Danse**, held at various city locations on odd-numbered years from late September to early October.

There are two well-known **orchestras** based in the city, the Orchestre symphonique de Montréal (☎842-9951) and the Orchestre Métropolitain (☎598-0870), each of whom holds regular concerts at Place des Arts and the Basilique Notre-Dame. The city also has a programme of free summer concerts in various city parks (information ☎842-3402). L'Opéra de Montréal (☎985-2258) produces five bilingually subtitled productions a year at Place des Arts.

Films in English, usually the latest releases from the US, can be caught at most cinemas. Central ones include Centre Eaton, 705 rue Ste-Catherine ouest; the ornate Egyptian, 1455 rue Peel; the subterranean Faubourg, 1616 rue Ste-Catherine ouest; and the wide-screened and armchaired Paramount, 977 rue Ste-Catherine ouest. The city's only English rep cinema is the Cinema du Parc, 3575 ave du Parc (☎281-1900 for listings). For Québécois film-makers, check out the Cinémathèque Québécoise, 335 boul de Maisonneuve est (Tues–Sun 11am–9pm), which has screening and exhibition programmes that bring together the history, events and future of cinema, TV and new media; Ex-Centris, 3536 boul St-Laurent has a penchant for alternative French film. Call ☎849-FILM for films and times or check the weeklies – make sure to verify that the English film you want to see is playing in v.o. (version originale), not v.f. (version français); the latter means it's dubbed.

Festivals and other events

Montréal has a different festival every week throughout the summer months (check *www.festivals.qc.ca* for a comprehensive list). Of these, the **Festival International de Jazz de Montréal** (*www.montrealjazzfest.com*) is North America's largest, with more than 400 shows, most of them free. From late June to early July, more than 2000 internationally-renowned musicians descend on the city; past years have drawn the likes of B.B. King, Etta James, Al Jarreau, Dave Brubeck, Ben E. King and Branford Marsalis. Continuing the superlatives, there's the mid-July **Juste pour Rire** ("Just For Laughs"), which is the world's largest comedy festival, with past headliners including Tim Allen, Rowan Atkinson, Jim Carrey, John Candy, Lily Tomlin and David Hyde Pierce. Theatres host 650 comedians from 14 countries performing in more than 1000 shows (*www.hahaha.com*). Hot on the heels of the Comedy Fest, the **Francofolies** (*www.francofolies.com*) brings French musicians from around the world to various downtown stages.

The most visually spectacular of the city's shindigs is the **International Fireworks Competition**, whose participants are competing to get contracts for the July 4 celebrations in the US. Held from June to July, the music-coordinated pyrotechnics are a breathtaking sight. The action takes place at La Ronde and tickets are around $20, but across the water and on the Jacques-Cartier Bridge the spectacle is free, and the music for the displays is broadcast live on local radio.

There are also a number of food-tasting events and, in some cases, boozy ones, like the June **Beer Mundial** event in the Vieux-Port, which offers the opportunity to get legless on more than 250 brands of beer from around the world. In August, the **Fêtes Gourmandes Internationales** takes over Île Notre-Dame for mouthwatering taste-tests. Come late-January, the islands host ice-sculpting and general carousing with the **Fête des Neiges de Montréal** (*www.pdi-montreal.com*).

Montréal has **film festivals** practically every month, some thematic, some devoted to individuals. The most notable is the **Montréal World Film Festival** in late August, the city's answer to Cannes, Berlin, Venice and Toronto (*www.ffm-montreal.org*), but the **Vues d'Afrique** (*www.vuesdafrique.org*) is gaining prominence for bringing African and Caribbean films to Montréal.

Finally, the **Cirque du Soleil** (☎522-2324, *www.cirquedusoleil.com*) is a fantastic circus company that travels all over the world; every other year it has a big-top season in its home city. Refusing to exploit animals, the circus's acrobats, trapeze artists, clowns, jugglers and contortionists present an incredible show, with original music scores, extravagant costumes and mind-blowing stunts.

Most event **tickets** can be purchased through Admission (☎790-1245 or 1-800/678-5440, *www.admission.com*).

Gay Montréal

Montréal has an excellent **gay** scene, with the action concentrated in the area known as **The Village** – roughly located on rue Ste-Catherine est between rue Amherst and the Papineau Métro station. Two English **information lines** provide up-to-date news on the latest events in the city: Gay-Info (24hr recorded message; ☎252-4429) is bilingual, Gayline (daily 7–11pm; ☎866-5090 or 1-888/505-1010) is in English and doubles as a helpline. Gai-Écoute (☎521-1508) provides a similar service to French-speakers. For contacts, L'Androgyne, 3636 boul St-Laurent, is a gay and lesbian bookshop, and Priape, 1311 rue Ste-Catherine est, is a Village-based sex shop and clothing store that sells tickets to most events. *Fugues* is the city's monthly French gay and lesbian magazine (there's usually a small English section hidden among the ads and pictures). In early August **Divers/Cité**, the gay and lesbian pride parade, is the event of the year.

Cafés and restaurants

Most of the restaurants and hangouts in The Village cater to a lesbian, bisexual and gay crowd, but are more mixed during the day.

L'Amorican, 1550 rue Fullum. Excellent French eatery.

Bato Thai, 1310 rue Ste-Catherine est. An excellent Thai restaurant with slow service – but the boys wearing sarongs make up for it.

La Paryse, 302 rue Ontario est. Extraordinary and exotic range of burger fillings.

Piccolo Diavolo, 1336 rue Ste-Catherine est. Hip place to eat Italian.

Saloon, 1333 rue Ste-Catherine est. Pizzas, burgers, salads and brunch. Mixed crowd of young and old, gay and straight.

Bars, clubs and discos

Aigle Noir, 1315 rue Ste-Catherine est. Trashy leather bar.

Cabaret l'Entre Peau, 1115 rue Ste-Catherine est. The best (and outrageously worst) of Montréal's drag shows, with a mixed fun-loving clientele.

Drugstore, 1360 rue Ste-Catherine est. Multilevel bar complex that's busiest before 11pm. Rooftop terrace.

Sisters, 1333 rue Ste-Catherine est. Upstairs from *Saloon* (see above), this is a swanky joint allowing mainly women, though men accompanied by women are welcome.

Sky, 1474 rue Ste-Catherine est. Two dance floors (one retro, the other more technofied), pool tables and a bar/restaurant on the ground floor, attracting the beautiful-people set. Sunday afternoon happy hour in the pub has two-for-one deals.

La Track, 1584 rue Ste-Catherine est. Men-only gay bar and disco. Cruisey male leather crowd. Very cheap on Wednesdays and Sundays.

Unity, 1400 ave Montcalm. The only real competition *Sky*'s had in years, *Unity* has become extremely popular, with two dance floors (one playing techno, the other retro Eighties hits), a huge rooftop terrace in summer and ground floor bar.

Listings

Airlines Air Canada, Air Alliance, Air Nova and Air Ontario, 2020 boul Université (Canada and US ☎393-3333); Air France, 2000 rue Mansfield (☎847-1106); British Airways, 1501 ave McGill College (☎287-9282); Swissair, 1253 ave McGill College (☎879-9154).

Airport enquiries Dorval ☎394-7377; Mirabel ☎394-7377; both airports ☎1-800/465-1213.

Baseball The Montréal Expos' home ground is the Olympic Stadium, 4141 ave Pierre-de-Coubertin (Métro Pie-IX). Tickets cost $8–36 (☎253-3434 or 1-800/GO-EXPOS, *www.montrealexpos.com*).

Bike rental Bicycletterie JR, 151 rue Rachel est (☎843-6989), rents from $20 per day, with credit card needed as deposit; The Maison des Cyclistes, 1251 rue Rachel (☎521-8356, *www.velo.qc.ca*)

charges $8 per hour, $25 per day and is an excellent resource for cycling information and organized tours. La Cordée, 2159 rue Ste-Catherine est rents bikes from $35 a day (☎524-1106); Vélo Aventure, Quai King Edward, Vieux-Port (☎847-0666) charges bikes out at $20 a day and rollerblades from $8.50 an hour.

Bookshops English books can be bought from most major bookshops. Paragraphe Books and Café, 2220 ave McGill College, is the best independent bookstore in town. Double Hook, 1235a ave Greene, specializes in English-Canadian authors. Chapters, 1171 Ste-Catherine ouest, is huge, as is Indigo, 1500 ave McGill College. Androgyne, 3636 St-Laurent, is Montréal's definitive gay bookstore. Travel books in English and French are available at Ulysses Travel Bookshop, 4176 rue St-Denis, 560 ave du President-Kennedy and 1307 Ste-Catherine ouest.

Bus information Local transportation: ☎288-6287; long-distance travel: Orléans Express ☎842-2281; Adirondack Trailways (to New York) ☎914/339-4230.

Camping equipment You can hire or buy all you need for the outdoors at Altitude, 1472 Peel (☎288-8010).

Canadian football The Montreal Alouettes (☎871-2255, *www.alouettes.net*) represent the city in the Canadian Football League. Home games are at McGill University's Percival-Molson Stadium, and tickets range $15–50.

Car rental Avis, 1225 rue Metcalfe (☎866-7906); Budget, 1240 Guy (☎938-1000); Discount, 607 boul de Maisonneuve ouest (☎286-1554); Hertz Canada, 1073 rue Drummond (☎938-1717); Thrifty, 800 boul de Maisonneuve est (☎845-5954); and Via Route, 1255 rue Mackay (☎871-1166), which charges a bit less than the majors.

Consulates Belgium, 999 boul de Maisonneuve ouest (☎849-7394); Denmark, 1 Place Ville-Marie (☎877-3060); Germany, 1250 boul René-Lévesque ouest (☎931-2277); Greece, 1170 Place du Frère-André (☎875-2119); Italy, 3489 rue Drummond (☎849-8351); Japan, 600 rue de la Gauchetière ouest (☎866-3429); Netherlands, 1002 rue Sherbrooke ouest (☎849-4247); Norway, 1155 boul René-Lévesque ouest (☎874-9087); Spain, 1 Westmount Square (☎935-5235); Sweden, 8400 boul Decarie (☎345-2727); Switzerland, 1572 ave Docteur-Penfield (☎932-7181); UK, 1000 rue de la Gauchetière ouest (☎866-5863); US, 1155 rue St-Alexandre (☎398-9695).

Dental emergencies 24hr dental clinic, 3546 rue Van-Horne (☎342-4444); Walk-in Clinic, Montréal General Hospital, 1650 ave Cedar (☎934-8397; Mon–Fri 8.30am–4.30pm; after-hour emergencies call ☎934-8075).

Exchange Agence Worldwide Maison de Change, 1411 rue Peel; American Express, 1141 boul de Maisonneuve ouest (☎284-3300); Bureau de Change de Vieux-Montréal, 230 rue St-Jacques; Downtown Currency Exchange, 2000 ave McGill College; Thomas Cook, 777 rue de la Gauchetière ouest. You can also withdraw money at ATMs throughout the city, so long as your card is Cirrus or Plus compatible.

Hospital Montréal General Hospital, 1650 ave Cedar (☎937-6011); Royal Victoria Hospital, 687 ave des Pins ouest (☎842-1231).

Ice hockey The Montréal Canadiens play at the Centre Molson, 1250 rue de la Gauchetière ouest (☎989-2841, *www.canadiens.com*). Métro: Lucien L'Allier or Bonaventure.

Internet cafés *Le Café Électronique*, 1425 boul René-Lévesque ouest (☎871-0307), has forty online computers and French food to boot, $5.50/30min; *Cyberground Café Internet*, 3672 boul St-Laurent (☎842-1726) provides access for $8/hr, as does *Network Café*, 5120 Queen Mary (☎344-0959) where you can lunch on bagels, sandwiches and muffins at the same time. Online access also at many photocopy shops.

Laundry Net-Net, 310 ave Duluth, will wash, dry and fold your clothes in neat bags for you within 24 hours for 69¢/pound; doing it yourself works out to $7. Nettoyeur Daoust, 3654 rue St-Denis, does both dry cleaning and washing; $6.50 gets a load washed, dried and folded.

Left luggage There are $2 lockers at the Gare Central and Station Centrale d'Autobus de Montréal.

Métro General information (☎280-5666); timetable information (☎288-6287); lost and found (☎280-4637). If you tire of being on hold, get your info online at *www.stcum.qc.ca*. Commuter rail and off-island bus services are co-ordinated by the Agence métropolitaine de transport (*www.amt.qc.ca*).

Museum passes The Montréal Museums Pass (☎845-6873 or 1-800/363-7777) allows visitors free admission to 20 museums in the city on any two of three consecutive days at a significant discount; $20 at both tourist offices and participating museums. The Get an Eyeful package ($22.50) is valid for 30 days and includes admission to the Olympic Tower, Botanical Garden, Insectarium and Biodôme, none of which are covered by the Museums Pass.

Pharmacy Pharmaprix, 5122 chemin de la Côte des Neiges, open 24hr (☎738-8464). Most downtown outlets are open 8am–midnight.

Post offices The main post office downtown is Station B, 1250 rue Université (Mon–Fri 8am–5.45pm, Sat 8am–noon). The city's poste restante is at Station A, 285 rue St-Antoine ouest (Mon–Fri 8am–5.45pm, Sat 8am–noon).

Ridesharing Allô-Stop, 4317 rue St-Denis (☎985-3032 or 985-3044, *www.allo-stop.com*). A carpool service matching drivers with passengers for destinations within Québec and the Maritime Provinces only. Membership costs $6 per year plus your share of petrol. Drivers pay $7 per year but receive about sixty percent of passenger fees. Typical prices are: Québec $15, Gaspé $42 and Rimouski $30. But plan ahead for Gaspé trips, as they're not common. Most cars stop in Rimouski.

Sexual Assault Centre Bilingual crisis line (☎934-4504) or McGill University's hotline (☎398-2700 day or ☎398-8500 eve).

Taxis Co-op (☎725-9885); Diamond (☎273-6331). $2.80 minimum fare, then 1.13¢ per kilometre.

Telephones Bell-Canada, Bureau Public, 700 rue de la Gauchetière ouest on the corner of Université (Mon–Fri 9am–5pm). 25¢ pays for unlimited local calls at a payphone; dial 411 for information, zero to reach an operator.

Train information Amtrak (☎1-800/835-8725, *www.amtrak.com*); Via Rail (☎989-2626 or 1-888/842-7245, *www.viarail.ca*)

Travel agencies Tourisme Jeunesse Boutique, 4008 St-Denis (☎844-0287) and Tourbec, 595 de Maisonneuve ouest (☎288-4455) are both excellent sources for budget travellers. Voyages Campus, 1455 de Maisonneuve ouest (☎288-1130), 3480 McTavish (☎398-0647), 225 du President Kennedy (☎281-6662) and 1613 St-Denis (☎843-8511) does bookings primarily for students with an International Student Identification Card (ISIC).

Weather and road information ☎283-3010 or 1-900/565-MÉTÉO.

White-water rafting The Rivière Rouge offers the best white-water rafting in the Montréal vicinity. Adventures en Eau Vive, 120 chemin de la Rivière Rouge, Calumet (☎242-6084 or 1-800/567-6881), runs rafting trips for $69/person during the summer, including two meals, taxes and five hours on the river.

Around Montréal

The lake-dotted countryside **around Montréal** offers a range of recuperative pleasures for the city-dweller, starting with the largely wilderness stretch of the **Outaouais** to the west, 135km northwest of Montréal and extending along the north side of the Ottawa River. Once the domain of Algonquin tribes, the region was not developed until the 1800s, when it became an important centre for the lumber industry. While the bulk of the activities in the region are of an outdoorsy nature – hiking, canoeing, snowmobiling, cycling and cross-country skiing – **Montebello** and the lush farmland of the **Cantons-de-l'Est** (Eastern Townships), east towards the US border, are worth visiting for their atmosphere and historical heritage. Even **Hull**, formerly Ottawa's dull cousin, is now a draw thanks to the **Musée Canadien des Civilisations**, Québec's finest museum.

Extending along the north side of the St Lawrence from the Ottawa River to the Saguenay are the **Laurentians** – one of the world's oldest ranges – where five hundred million years of erosion have moulded it into a rippling landscape of undulating hills and valleys. Immediately north of Montréal, the more accessible **Lower Laurentians** are dotted with whitewashed farm cottages and manor houses, but settlement in the **Upper Laurentians** did not begin until the 1830s, when the construction of the P'tit Train du Nord railway tracks let in the mining and lumber industries. When the decline in both industries left the area in a depression, salvation came in the form of the recreational demands of the growing populace of Montréal. The region is now one of North America's largest ski areas, with the number of resorts increasing annually.

The areas to the north, west and east of Montréal are served by the following tourist organizations, each of which can provide a free tourist guide that includes basic maps of the region.

Outaouais: ☎819/778-2222 or 1-800/265-7822, *www.western-quebec-tourism.org*

Laurentides: ☎450/436-8532 or 1-800/561-6673, *www.laurentides.com*

Eastern Townships: ☎819/566-4445 or 1-800/455-5527, *www.tourisme-cantons.qc.ca*

West to Hull: Montebello and Plaisance

The drive from Montréal to Hull on scenic Hwy 148 takes in a few riverside villages that used to be thriving logging towns. The first stop, about 130km west of Montréal, en route is **MONTEBELLO**, a picturesque village named after seigneur and Rebellion leader Louis-Joseph Papineau's estate. Today, the town is the Outaouais's star attraction thanks to a resort-like atmosphere that includes horseback riding, boating, upscale boutiques and the inimitable **Château Montebello**, 392 rue Notre Dame (☎819/423-6341, *www.chateaumontebello.com*; ⑦), the world's largest log building. Built by the Seigneury Club in 1930 in 90 days, the original three buildings are made up of 10,000 red-cedar logs. Today, it's a five-star hotel; even if you can't afford to stay, check out the six-hearthed fireplace and tour the photo gallery.

The *Château* abuts the **Site historique national du Manoir Papineau**, 500 rue Notre Dame (mid-May to early Sept Wed–Sun 10am–noon & 1–5pm; early Sept to early Oct Sat & Sun 10am–noon & 1–5pm; free), Papineau's tranquil estate comprising his spectacular manor house, chapel and granary over a sizeable tract of land. The **house** contains a ground-floor ballroom, a turreted library tower and a gorgeous glass tea-room-cum-gazebo nearby that was formerly a three-storey greenhouse. The **Papineau Memorial Chapel**, a modest stone building (1855) nestled among tall pines and maple, is especially remarkable for being of Anglican, not Catholic, denomination – Papineau's son converted to Anglicanism after his father was refused a Catholic burial. Papineau senior and eleven other family members are buried here, and the Patriotes' flag is on display. Photographs and historical background on the estate and Papineau himself are displayed in the old **Granary** building.

You won't find rock-bottom **accommodation** in Montebello. The most reasonable is *Gîte des 3D Chez Dodo*, an unremarkable **B&B** at 493 rue Notre Dame (☎819/423-5268; ②). If you can go slightly higher, *Le Clos des Cèdres*, 227 rue St-Joseph (☎819/423-1265; *www.bbcanada.com/4148.html*; ②) has more character. Otherwise, try *Motel Bel-Eau*, 600–602 rue Notre Dame (☎819/423-6504 or 1-888/666-0586; ③) or the attractive *Motel l'Anse de la Lanterne*, at 646 rue Notre Dame (☎819/423-5280; ③), which has a good restaurant for dinner. Most **restaurants** are on the main drag; *Le Pot au Feu*, 489 rue Notre Dame, serves Italian and French for under $10; and the equally affordable *Le Zouk*, at no. 530, has a bistro menu. **Information** is available at 502 rue Notre Dame (late June to early Sept daily 10am–6pm; early Sept to late June Tues–Sun 9am–4pm). Voyageur **buses** drop passengers off twice daily down the street at no. 570.

The only other stop of interest between Montréal and Hull is **PLAISANCE**, 15km onwards from Montebello and 30km east of Hull. Once the region's main lumber centre, the main draw today is the **Réserve Faunique de Plaisance** (late April to mid-Oct), a tiny provincial park made up of three *presqu'îles* covering 27 square kilometres replete with hiking trails, picnic areas and footbridges. A dull **interpretive centre** in the old presbytery on Hwy 148 tells the town's history (late June to early Sept daily 10am–6pm; $2.50; ☎819/772-3434). **Camping** is available at the Réserve Faunique (☎819/427-6974 or 427-6900; $14.79 for a two-person site).

Hull

Though recognized as part of Canada's capital region in 1969, **HULL** remains distinctly separate and predominantly francophone. For years, it served mainly as Ottawa's nightlife spot, as its bars closed two hours later than those of its Ontario neighbour – a disparity that has ended with both cities now closing shop at 2am. The shift has resul-ted, unfortunately, in the decline of **Place Aubry** – the pretty pedestrian-only square where the greatest concentration of bars was found. Still, the opening of a **casino** in 1996 has given Ottawa bureaucrats and tourists another late-night playground.

Originally a paper-milling town, Hull was an industrial working-class area removed from the bureaucratic rat-race on the south side of the Ottawa River separating the city from Ottawa. Pressure on the Canadian government to share the wealth – both financially and job-wise – prompted the construction of high-rise administrative buildings and the **Musée Canadien des Civilisations**, the curvy contours of which dominate the waterfront. The city's other main attraction, the sprawling **Gatineau Park**, is a nature-lover's paradise intersected with numerous bike paths, lakes and wildlife, and the site of the **MacKenzie King Estate**, former Prime Minister William Lyon Mackenzie King's summer hideout.

The **Hull-Chelsea-Wakefield Steam Train**, at 165 rue Devault (☎819/778-7246 or 1-800/871-7246; $29 return-trip; reservations recommended) departs daily for Wakefield, 32km north of Hull. Built in 1907, Canada's only still-functioning steam train travels ninety minutes through the lush foliage and cottage country along the Gatineau River, while a musical troupe plays amusing ditties to pass the time.

For more information on Ottawa, across the river from Hull, see p.156.

Musée Canadien des Civilisations

Set by the foot of the Alexander Bridge on the southeast side of town, the **Musée Canadien des Civilisations** (May to June & early Sept to mid-Oct Mon–Wed & Fri–Sun 9am–6pm, Thurs 9am–9pm; July to early Sept Mon–Wed, Sat & Sun 9am–6pm, Thurs & Fri 9am–9pm; mid Oct to April Tues–Wed, Sat & Sun 9am–5pm, Thurs 9am–9pm; $8, family $20, children $4; *www.civilization.ca*) is the one museum in the capital region not to be missed. The building is an amazing sight, undulating over 24 acres. Douglas Cardinal, a Blackfoot from Red Deer, Alberta, designed it to represent the landscape created by the meeting of the rocky Canadian Shield and the snow and ice of the deep north. Fossil sightings are common; the building's Tyndall limestone is a fossilized mud 460 million years old.

Inside is a state-of-the-art presentation of Canada's human history. In the **Grand Hall**, the world's largest indoor collection of totem poles stands outside five houses from Pacific Coast tribes. The interiors have displays of aboriginal ceremonies and their present-day relevance, and excellent videos present a balanced view of the plight of the aboriginal peoples today.

Canada Hall illustrates Canada's history from 1000 AD to the present, utilizing life-size reconstructions of historical environments, beginning with Norsemen disembarking on Newfoundland's shores and moving on to an Acadian settlement from the

French period, farmhouses from eighteenth-century New France, a fur-trading post and Métis camp, a full-scale section of a schooner and an Ontarian main street of 1900.

Elsewhere you'll find exhibitions of Inuit and First Nation art, the **Canadian Postal Museum**, and a **Children's Museum** whose interactive "world tour" takes children through eight countries. Next is **Adventure World** where children can play on the tugboat featured on Canada's old $1 bill. The new **First Peoples Hall** will present the art, crafts, legends, history and way of life of aboriginal Canadians from the East Coast.

The **Cineplus** (adults $8.50, children $6, combined rates of $14 and $9 for both museum and IMAX) is a space-age cinema equipped with an IMAX screen and another that projects films on a two-storey-high, domed screen. At the waterfront facing the museum, Expédition Eau Vive (☎819/827-4467 or 1-888/820-4467; $10; *www.orbit.qc.ca/canoe*) launches one-hour trips on the Ottawa River in Rabaska canoes. However, while the real ones are made of birch bark, these are fibreglass.

Gatineau Park

On the city's western borders, the 356-square-kilometre **Gatineau Park** was founded in 1934 when the government bought the land to stop the destruction caused by the need for cheap firewood during the Depression. Short hikes in the park lead to the geologically rare **Pink Lake** – named for a settler, not the colour of the lake, which is actually green due to its unusual amount of algae mixing with phosphorous leaching from the shores. The **Champlain Lookout** gives a view onto the granite outcroppings of the Canadian Shield and the rich green fields of the St Lawrence lowlands. The belvedere offers arresting views at sunset. For longer hikes, ask for maps and guidance at the **Visitor's Centre**, 33 rue Scott (daily: late June to early Sept 9am–6pm; early Sept to late June 9am–5pm; *www.capcan.ca*); its interpretive centre examines park wildlife.

The park's main attraction is the sumptuous **Mackenzie King Estate** (May–Oct Mon–Fri 11am–5pm; Sat & Sun 10am–6pm; $7/car). Spread over 2.5 square kilometres in the residential area of Kingsmere, the estate was the summer getaway for William Lyon Mackenzie King, prime minister between 1921 and 1948. In a characteristically eccentric manner (he communed with his dead mother via crystal ball), he bestrew the grounds with architectural follies – chunks of the old Parliament Buildings, Corinthian columns and blocks of the British House of Commons retrieved after the Blitz. The two main buildings have been painstakingly restored and the ground floor of the main house, **Moorside**, now a tearoom, offers English tea, cucumber sandwiches and pastries (daily 3–5pm; $10) on the terrace overlooking the gardens.

The park has excellent **campsites**. *Philippe Lake* has 250 wooded sites while *Taylor Lake* has 35 around the lake; both cost $21 per pitch. *La Pêche Lake*, less expensive at $17 per pitch (mid-May to mid-Oct), is ideal for canoe-camping and fishing. Call ☎819/827-2020 or 1-800/465-1867 for more information.

Practicalities

Information is available at Hull's tourist office, 103 rue Laurier (mid-June to early Sept Mon–Fri 8.30am–8pm, Sat & Sun 9am–6pm; early Sept to mid-June Mon–Fri 8.30am–8pm, Sat & Sun 9am–4pm). Free **bike rentals** are available at the Maison du Vélo, 350 rue Laurier (May–Oct Mon–Fri 9am–8pm, Sat & Sun 9am–5pm). The library at the Hôtel de Ville (City Hall) supplies **Internet** access, 25 rue Laurier (hours vary; $2/30min).

For **B&B** accommodation, *À la Maison Ancestrale*, 227 rue Laurier (☎819/771-0770; ②), *Au Pignon sur le Parc*, 63 rue des Ormes (☎819/779-5559; ②), and *Au Versant de la Montagne*, at 19 du Versant (☎819/776-3760; ②), are all good-quality, affordable options. The cheapest motels are *Motel Casino* at 275 rue St-Joseph (☎819/776-8888 or 1-888/652-7466; ③) and *Motel le Chateauguay*, 469 boul Taché (☎819/595-1000 or 1-877/595-5100; ②). For more standard accommodation, the *Auberge de la Gare*, 205 boul St Joseph

(☎819/778-8085 or 1-800 567-1962; ④) provides breakfast near the bus station. The luxurious *Chateau Cartier* in Aylmer, at 1170 chemin Aylmer (☎819/778-1088 or 1-800/807-1088; ⑤), has well appointed rooms, some with fireplaces, and a full spa center.

The city has a number of good **restaurants**. The funky *Le Twist*, at 88 rue Montcalm, is a Fifties restaurant with a huge outdoor terrace in the summer and great hamburgers. Downtown, in Place Aubry, *Piz'za* at 36 rue Laval, has thin-crust pizza and a lively atmosphere, and *Le Troquet*, across the street is an artsy café that turns into an animated bar at night. For upscale dining, head to the elegant *Bistro 1908*, at 70 Promenade du Portage. *Laurier sur Montcalm*, 199 rue Montcalm, in the old train station, serves great French food. The city's best **bars** are in and around Place Aubry. *Café au Quatre Jeudis*, 44 rue Laval, brews its beer; *Le Bistro*, 3 rue Kent, draws an older business crowd; *La Turlotte Boîte à Chanson*, 117 Promenade du Portage, is good for typical Québécois music; and *Le Bop*, 5 rue Aubry, draws mostly a youthful set for Top 40 fare.

The **bus** terminal is near downtown, at 238 St-Joseph. Hull is served by Ottawa's train station and airport, and a cab to Hull costs around $17.

The Lower Laurentians (Les Basses Laurentides)

Once the domain of various aboriginal groups, the **Lower Laurentians** were granted by Ville-Marie's governors to the colony's first seigneurs who, using a modified version of the feudal land system of the motherland, oversaw the development of the land by their tenants, or *habitants*. As the St Lawrence was the lifeline of the colony, these tenant farms were laid out perpendicular to the river in long, narrow rectangular seigneuries evoke life under the long regime.

The first town of note in the region is **ST-EUSTACHE**, about forty-minutes' drive northwest of Montréal by Hwy 13 or 15 then Hwy 640. Alternatively, take bus #46 from Métro Henri-Bourassa in Montréal ($2.55; 1hr). It was here that the frustrations of the *habitants* with the British occupancy met a tragic end in the 1837 Rebellion. About thirty buildings survived the battle that put down the rebellious *Patriotes* led by Louis-Joseph Papineau (see box, below) and these are located along two narrow streets in Vieux St-Eustache. Most are simply marked with heritage signs, and inaccessible to the public, but the **church**, at 123 rue St-Louis, still bears the scars and offers free guided tours (Thurs–Fri 9.30am–4.30pm). The cross street, rue St-Eustache, has two sights worth visiting, the most impressive being the wedding-cake **Manoir Globensky** at no. 235 (Tues–Sun 10am–5pm; $3), which doubles as the **Musée de St-Eustache et des Patriotes** and includes a thorough permanent exhibition on local history. Opposite, the eighteenth-century **Moulin Légaré**, at no. 236 (Mon–Fri 9am–5pm; mid-May to mid-

---

THE REBELLION OF 1837

In the early 1800s, British immigrants to Lower Canada were offered townships (*cantons*) while the francophones were not allowed to expand their holdings, exacerbating the resentment caused by the favouritism extended to English-speaking businesses in Montréal. The situation was worsened by high taxes on British imports and a savage economic depression in 1837. Wearing Canadian-made garments of *étoffe du pays* as a protest against British imports, the leaders of Lower Canada reform – known as the *Patriotes* – rallied francophones to rebel in Montréal. As Louis-Joseph Papineau, the Outaouais region seigneur whose speeches in the Assembly (see p.214) had encouraged the rebellions, fled the city, fearful that his presence would incite more rioting, the government sent military detachments to the countryside, the hotbed of the *Patriotes*. Two hundred *Patriotes* took refuge in Saint-Eustache's church, where eighty of them were killed by British troops, who went on to raze much of the town.

THE OKA MOHAWK STAND-OFF

In the summer of 1990, Oka became the stage for a confrontation between **Mohawk** warriors and the provincial government. The crisis began when Oka's town council decided to expand its golf course onto a sacred burial ground, a provocation to which the Mohawks responded by arming themselves and barricading Kanesatake, a small reserve near Oka. Although the Native Affairs Minister for Québec was close to reaching an agreement with the Mohawks, the mayor of Oka sent in the provincial police to storm the barricades. In the ensuing fracas a policeman was killed – no one knows by whom, but the autopsy established it was not by a police bullet. Hostilities reached a new pitch and the two sides became ever more polarized: as the Mohawks set up barricades across the Mercier Bridge, one of Montréal's main commuter arteries, groups of white Québécois attacked them with stones, while sympathetic groups of aboriginal people showed solidarity throughout Canada and the USA. The federal government offered to buy the land for the natives on the condition that they surrender, but the stand-off continued as negotiators failed to agree on terms. The crisis lasted 78 days, until the core of fifty Mohawks was encircled by 350 Canadian army soldiers and forced to give up. The fate of the disputed land, along with hundreds of other similar claims, is still being negotiated. However, many believe that the natives went too far at Oka, and the existing distrust between aboriginal Canadians and other Canadians seems to have deepened. As George Erasmus, former national chief of the Assembly of First Nations, said: "Our demands are ignored when we kick up a fuss – but they are also ignored if we do not."

Oct also Sat & Sun 11am–5pm; $2), is the oldest water-powered flour mill in operation in Canada. For something different, drop by the slithery **Exotarium**, 846 chemin Fresnière, exit 8 Hwy 640 ouest (Feb–June & Sept–Dec Fri, Sat & Sun noon–5pm; July & Aug daily noon–5pm; $5.75), a breeding farm on the outskirts of town featuring cobras, pythons, crocodiles and lizards.

Oka

Southwest of St-Eustache, on Hwy 344, lies the small lakeside town of **OKA**. Although associated with the armed stand-off between the Mohawks and police (see box, above), there isn't much to see here, though worth a visit is the **Abbaye Cistercienne d'Oka**, 1600 chemin d'Oka (daily: 4am–8pm), one of North America's oldest monasteries. Commanding a spectacular site just outside town, its century-old bell tower rises amidst the hills. The Trappists arrived here from France in 1880, their life in Canada beginning in a miller's house that's now overshadowed by the rest of the complex and the landscaped gardens of the abbey. The monastery shop sells organic Trappist products, from maple syrup and chocolates to variations on the delicious Oka cheese. The nearby **Calvaire d'Oka** with its mid-eighteenth-century chapels is best visited on September 14, when native pilgrims hold the Feast of the Holy Cross along the banks of Lac des Deux Montagnes. The Calvaire is set in the **Parc d'Oka**, a magnificent park with 45km of hiking trails, and reached by a 5.5km trail up the Colline d'Oka, a hill that gives views of the region. There isn't much accommodation except **camping** (☎450/479-6303 or 1-888/727-2652; $21.50; *www.sepaq.com*) in one of the park's 800 campsites, and *La Clos des Lilas*, a **B&B** at 14 rue Ste-Anne (☎450/479-8214, *www.laurentides.com/membres/028f.html*; ②). There is no public transportation to Oka.

The Upper Laurentians (Les Hautes Laurentides)

The slopes of the **Upper Laurentians**, a vast sweep of coniferous forest dotted with hundreds of tranquil lakes and scored with rivers, was once Montréal's "wilderness back yard". Nowadays, winter sports have done away with the region's former tranquillity as thousands of Québécois take to the slopes at more than 25 ski resorts, causing mind-numbing traffic jams. Still, much of the land has remained relatively untouched – like the **Parc du Mont Tremblant** – and the area is a must when autumn colours take over. The Upper Laurentians really cater to families on a week's sporty vacation, and much of the **accommodation** is pricey, as it includes gyms, tennis courts, golf courses and the like. However, a smattering of B&Bs and numerous motels are an alternative to those on a tight budget, as do the youth hostels in Val-David and Mont-Tremblant itself (see opposite). Check out travel agents in Montréal – weekend packages can be a bargain. Use the free telephone accommodation service for the region (☎1-800/561-6673, *www.laurentides.com*), or pick up **information** on the resorts at the regional tourist office in Mirabel, 14142 rue de la Chapelle; take exit 39 off Hwy 15 (daily: late June to early Sept 8.30am–8.30pm; early Sept to late June 9am–5pm). During the ski season, snow-condition information can be found on *www.skinetcanada.com*.

Two **roads** lead from Montréal to this area of the Laurentians: the Autoroute des Laurentides (Hwy 15) and the slower Hwy 117, which is the way to go if you want to go antique hunting as there are a number of large shops around Piedmont. Limocar Laurentides offers regular service from the Station Centrale d'Autobus de Montréal to most of the towns (☎514/842-2281). Except for Tremblant – which costs a small fortune – rates for **ski passes** are around $30 a day in the decent areas, a few dollars more at weekends.

Saint-Sauveur-des-Monts

The ski resorts start 60km from Montréal and can be done easily as day-trips. The first of these is **SAINT-SAUVEUR-DES-MONTS**, with 42 pistes in the immediate vicinity and an ever-increasing number of apartment complexes. Its resident population of seven thousand is boosted to a peak-season maximum of thirty thousand, and the main drag, rue Principale, reflects the influx by boasting every type of restaurant imaginable, designer boutiques and craft shops. Come nightfall, skiers take to the numerous flash clubs and discos.

For those with money, Saint-Sauveur is *the* place to be seen, and **hotel** prices reflect the fact – the excellent and luxurious *Le Relais St-Denis*, 61 St-Denis (☎450/227-4766 or 1-888/997-4766; ⑥), leads the way for class with a pool and beautifully decorated rooms. Cheaper options are the *Auberge de la Vallée*, 520 rue Principale (☎450/227-5998; ③) or the **B&B** *Auberge aux Petits Oiseaux*, at no. 342 (☎819/227-6116 or 1-877/227-6116; ③). Budget travellers will be pretty well limited to the **food** at *Brûlerie des Monts*, 197 rue Principale, *La Cage aux Sports* for burgers and steaks, at 75 rue de la Gare, and *Mexicali Rosa's* average Mexican fare on the same street at no. 61. **Information** on shopping and skiing is available from the Bureau Touristique, 3rd floor, 100 rue Guindon (Mon–Fri 9am–5pm).

Val-David

Further north along Hwy 117, **VAL-DAVID** is the bohemian resort of the Laurentians, favoured by artists and craftspeople: the main street, rue de l'Église, has galleries and shops run by the artisans themselves. The town also has some non-ski-related attractions come summertime, the best of which, **Les Jardins de Rocailles**, 1319 rue Lavoie (mid-June to early Sept daily 10am–5.30pm; autumn and spring weekends only 10am–5.30pm; $4), features more than 450 plant varieties in a secluded rock garden. On a wholly different note, the tackiest attraction in the Laurentians, the **Village du Père Noel**, 987 rue Morin (early June to early Sept daily 10am–6pm; $8.50), is a Santa's village "highlighted" by a Wise Goat – his claim to wisdom stems from being able to climb an obstacle course and feed himself from pails suspended on pulleys. Save your money.

Val-David's excellent **youth hostel**, *Le Chalet Beaumont*, 1451 Beaumont (☎819/322-1972 or 1-800/461-8585; ①), is a massive chalet with roaring fires in the winter, and great views all year. A twenty-minute walk from the bus station, the hostel offers a pick-up service. Other **accommodation** in Val-David is fairly expensive: the most affordable options are **B&Bs** – *Le Temps des Cerises* (☎819/322-1751; ②) at 1347 chemin de la Sapinière, has pleasant rooms and chalet-style decor and *La Chaumière aux Marguerites* (☎819/322-2043; ③), is in a sweet little house at no. 1267. Hotels are costlier – the rooms at *Pause Plein Air*, 1381 rue de la Sapinière (☎819/322-2727 or 1-877/422-6880; May–Oct; ②) are about as cheap as they come. The swishest ski lodge, *La Sapinière*, by Mont Alta at 1244 chemin de la Sapinière (☎819/322-2020 or 1-800/567-6635, *www.sapiniere.com*; ⑧), is built of logs. At the one **campsite** along Hwy 117 – *Camping Laurentien* (☎819/322-2281) pitches start at $18.25. Rue de l'Église has decent, well-priced **restaurants**, including the friendly *Le Grand Pa*, at no. 2481, which serves simple French food; and *L'Express*, a café-bistro at rue de l'Eglise and de la Sapinière. **Information** is available at the tourist office, 2501 de l'Eglise (daily 9.30am–5pm).

Ste-Agathe-des-Monts

Nearby, on the shores of Lac des Sables, is **STE-AGATHE-DES-MONTS**, a luxurious resort since the 1850s and the largest town in the Laurentians. Situated 97km from Montréal and almost entirely quashed by commercialism, it's a good base for exploring the less developed towns and the wildlife reserves further north; there is little to do here.

Ste-Agathe is expensive. The cheapest **accommodation** is the dull *Motel St-Moritz*, 1580 rue Principale (☎819/326-3444 or 1-800/567-6752, *www.polyinter.com/st-moritz*; ②). Of the three **B&Bs**, only *Au Nid d'Hirondelles*, 1235 des Hirondelles (☎819/326-5413 or 1-888/826-5413; *www.nidhirondelles.qc.ca*; ③) verges on affordable, and all rooms come with private bath. The pricier *Auberge de la Tour-du-Lac*, 173 chemin Tour du Lac (☎819/326-4202 or 1-800/622-1735, *www.delatour.qc.ca*; ④), is one of the town's most beautiful historic homes with its pointed roof and wrapround veranda. The nearest **campsite** is *Parc des Campeurs* (☎819/324-0482 or 1-800/561-7360; $24), 15km from town (follow signs for *"Camping Ste Agathe"* and take exit 53 off Hwy 15), an enormous place with a beach on Lac des Sables.

Most of Ste-Agathe's **restaurants and bars** are on the lakefront, the most attractive part of town: *Del Popolo*, at 1 Principale est, serves Italian, and *Chez Girard*, at 18 Principale ouest, has reasonably priced, delicious French cuisine. *Sauvagine*, 1592 Hwy 329 nord (☎1-800/787-7172), is a chapel converted into a French restaurant with **rooms** upstairs (③/④). For **information**, go to 24 rue St-Paul est (late June to early Sept daily 9am–8pm; early Sept to late June 9am–5pm); the bus stops across the street.

Saint-Jovite-Mont-Tremblant

Situated some 130km north of Montréal, **SAINT-JOVITE-MONT-TREMBLANT** is the Laurentians' oldest and most renowned ski area, focused on the range's highest peak, **Mont Tremblant** (960m), so called because the native population believed it was the home of spirits that could move the mountain. In 1997, the company that developed B.C.'s Whistler ski-resort (see p.799) pumped some $50 million into Mont-Tremblant, and the resulting European-style ski village has made it a premier ski destination in Canada. The 92 slopes are for all levels, with a maximum vertical drop of more than 640m and the longest ski run in Québec. One-day **ski passes** cost $49 weekdays and $54 on weekends.

Saint-Jovite is the commercial centre of the area, while Mont-Tremblant (10km north) is a tiny village with only the most basic services. In and around the two are a variety of lodges, including the two most glamorous in the Laurentians: *Club Mont-Tremblant*, by Lac Tremblant at the base of the mountain (☎1-800/467-8341; ⑦), and *Auberge Gray Rocks*, near Saint-Jovite (☎819/425-2771 or 1-800/567-6767; ⑥). Less pricey **rooms** are available at *Hôtel Mont Tremblant*, 1900 rue Principale (☎819/425-3232; ④ including breakfast), and the five-room **B&B** *Le Couvent*, 135B rue du Couvent (☎819/425-8606 or 1-877/425-8606, *www.bbcanada.com/3388html*; ③). For **eating** in Saint-Jovite, there's a cheap pub-style restaurant, *Bagatelle Saloon*, at 852 rue Ouimet, and a bargain café, *Le Brunch Café*, at no. 816, in the same complex as *La Crémerie du Hameau*, a chocolate and sweet-tooth candy store. For dinner, *Chez Roger*, 444 St-Georges, offers rich French cuisine at slightly elevated prices – the three-course table d'hôte costs around $30. **Information** is available from the Saint-Jovite/Mont-Tremblant tourist office, 305 chemin Brébeuf in Saint-Jovite (daily: June–Sept 9am–7pm; Oct–May 9am–5pm).

The **Parc du Mont Tremblant**, a wilderness area of more than one thousand square kilometres spreading northwards from the villages, is a favourite with Québécois. Skiing, snowmobiling and snowshoeing are winter sports; in summer the park attracts campers, canoeists, hunters and hikers – in remote areas you may see bears, deer and moose (see box on pp.642–643). The park's three lakeside **campsites** must be reserved in advance (☎819/688-2281 or 1-877/688-2289; $15–16.50). There's no public transport, but hitching is possible.

The Eastern Townships (Cantons-de-l'Est)

Beginning about 80km southeast of Montréal and extending to the US border, the **Eastern Townships** were once Québec's best-kept secret, but the nineteenth-century villages are fast becoming no more than shopping arcades fringed with apartment complexes for Montréal commuters. A growing ski industry – concentrated around Mont Sutton, just north of the Vermont border – is making its mark on the land too. However, the region's agricultural roots are still evident, especially in spring, when the maple trees are tapped for syrup. At this time of year, remote *cabanes à sucre* offer sleigh rides and Québécois fare such as maple taffy – strips of maple syrup frozen in the snow.

The land, once the domain of scattered groups of aboriginal peoples, was first cultivated by United Empire Loyalists hounded out of the United States after the American Revolution. Their loyalty to the crown resulted in land grants from the British, and townships with very English names like Sherbrooke and Granby were founded. In the mid-nineteenth century the townships opened up to industry, which attracted an influx of French-Canadians seeking work: today, 95 percent of the 400,000 population are francophone. Even so, the attempt to rechristen the area as L'Estrie was abandoned for the name Cantons-de-l'Est, a direct translation of the area's original English name of the Eastern Townships.

You can reach the Cantons-de-l'Est from Montréal by the Autoroute des Cantons-de-l'Est (Hwy 10), which has a useful **information centre** for the whole region at exit 68 (daily: Mon–Fri & Sun 8.30am–5pm, Sat 8.30am–6pm; ☎1-800/263-1068). Hwy 112, which wends through small villages and past forests and lakes, is picturesque but requires more time. Most towns are served by Sherbus **buses** from Montréal (☎514/842-2281) that stop in Granby, Magog and Sherbrooke.

Granby and Bromont

Coming from Montréal, the Cantons-de-l'Est begin at the horrendously unappealing city of **GRANBY**, home of the **Zoo de Granby** (late May to Aug daily 10am–dusk; Sept to early Oct Sat & Sun 10am–dusk; $19.95) – Québec's best-known zoo and a nightmare. The animals are kept in terrible conditions without a blade of grass in sight and most look suicidal. The town redeems itself with the **Centre d'Interpretation de la Nature du Lac Bolvin**, 700 Drummond (daily 8.30am–4.30pm; free) where observation towers allow a terrific vantage point for watching birds peck and preen on the marsh. Granby's **information centre** is at 650 Principale (daily: June to early Sept

8am–6pm; early Sept to May 9am–5pm; ☎450/372-7273 or 1-800/567-7273). There are several **motels** along rue Principale, and two **campsites**, *Bon-Jour*, at no. 1633 (☎450/378-0213 or 1-800/265-0213; $25 for two-person site), and *Plage Tropicana*, at no. 1680 (☎450/378-9410; $22 for four-person site).

Just south of Granby, **BROMONT** is much more pleasant, even though it basically revolves around the 405m ski and snowboarding hill at its centre, **Ski Bromont** (Mon–Thurs 9am–10pm, Fri 9am–10.30pm, Sat & Sun 8.30am–10.30pm, *www.ski-bromont.com*; $36). In summer, the hill metamorphoses into a hiking centre and swimming playground thanks to the **Bromont Aquatic Park** (daily: early to late June 10am–4pm; late June to late Aug 10am–6.30pm; Sept to late Oct weekends only 10am–4pm; $22). Less energetic options include the **Musée du Chocolat**, 679 rue Shefford (Mon–Fri 10am–6pm, Sat & Sun 9am–5.30pm; *www.makisoft.net/confis-eriebromont*), where you can learn about chocolate making while nibbling on some fine specimens from the candy store next door, and the **Flea Market** alongside Hwy 10 – it's the largest one in the Townships (May–Oct Sun 9am–5pm). There are four **B&Bs** in town, the least expensive are *La Maison aux Pignons Verts*, 129 rue Adamsville (☎450/260-1129; ②) and *Tournesol*, 948 rue Shefford (☎450/534-2482; ③). Otherwise, try the *Auberge au Vieux Manoir*, 871 rue Shefford (☎450/534-2502; ③) for more traditional hotel accommodation. *Baffetto de Roma*, 89 boul Bromont, serves up Italian **food** in all price ranges and *Le Madrigal*, at no. 46, has more expensive region-al cuisine.

Magog and around

About 25km southeast of Knowlton, along Hwys 243 and 245 to Bolton Centre, and then just off the road to Austin, is the **Abbaye Saint-Benoît-du-Lac**, its presence signalled by white-granite turrets. Occupied by about sixty Benedictine monks (many of them under a vow of silence) and a small number of nuns, it often serves as a refuge for flus-tered politicians and prominent figures who need time for contemplation. The abbey's doors are open to anyone who wants to stay. Food and **accommodation** are free, though a donation is expected (☎819/843-4080 men or 843-2340 women; appropriate clothing required; *www.st-benoit-du-lac.com*). There is no public transport to the abbey; a taxi costs about $25 from Magog.

The summer resort town of **MAGOG**, forty or so kilometres east of Bromont, gets its name from a corruption of an aboriginal word meaning "great expanse of water" – the expanse of which is one of the township's largest lakes, **Lac Memphrémagog**, which reaches into the town. The lake is unremarkable except for the fact that the actors Sylvester Stallone and Donald Sutherland have homes on its shore and a strange beast known as Memphré supposedly lurks in its waters (the subject of various fishy tales since 1798). A cruise boat plies the lake daily in summer and at weekends in September and October (1hr 45min tour; $12). There's also the option of a day-long ride to Newport in the US (☎1-888/842-8068 to reserve; June–Aug 2–3 weekly; $45 includ-ing meals). One quirky diversion is at the **Labyrinthe Memphrémagog** on the beach fronting the lake – you can navigate a maze on rollerblades or on foot (late June to early Sept daily 10am–9pm; early Sept to late June Sat & Sun 10am–9pm; $6). Explore the area on numerous well-kept bike trails; Ski-Vélo Vincent Renaud, 49 rue Principale, can provide wheels for around $15 a day.

The **bus** stops on rue Sherbrooke, parallel to the main drag, rue Principale. The **information centre**, at 55 rue Cabana, is accessed by Hwy 112 (June to mid-Oct daily 8.30am–8pm; mid-Oct to May Mon–Fri 9am–5pm; ☎1-800/267-2744). There are many places to stay, including a few century-old houses converted into **B&Bs**: *Ô Bois Dormant*, 205 rue Abbot (☎819/843-0450, *www.oboisdormant.qc.ca*; ②) is the least expensive option; it comes with a veranda and pool. *Au Coeur du Magog*, 120 rue Merry Nord (☎819/868-2511, *www.au-coeur-de-magog.qbc.net*; ③), is a fine old house with home-made breakfasts; *La Belle Victorienne*, 142 rue Merry Nord (☎819/847-0476; ③), has beautiful gardens and comfy rooms. **Hotels** are expensive in Magog but if you want to splurge, *Auberge du Grand Lac*, 40 rue Merry Sud (☎819/847-4039 or 1-800/267-4039; *www.grandlac.com*; ⑤ including breakfast), is near the lake with a rooftop terrace for sunsets, full facilities, and a basic breakfast; *Le Manoir St-Christophe*, 2316 Hwy 112 (☎819/843-3355; ④) is a standard hotel with ten rooms. Several **bars and restaurants** are clustered along rue Principale: *Le Panier à Pain*, at no. 382, serves up healthy sandwiches and soups, while *Le Martimbeault*, at no. 341, is a good dinner option specializing in rich French food that will set you back about $30 a meal. Alternatively, get a veggie fix at *Bonjour Santé* at 108 Place du Commerce. Many people hang out at the bistro/bar *La Grosse Pomme* at no. 276 rue Principale in the evening.

Around Magog, a local attraction is the **Parc du Mont-Orford**, 10km north of Magog via Hwy 141. Ski on Mont Orford (859m) in winter (ski passes $36) or hike in the summer – the chair lift operates year-round ($6.50 one-way, $9.50 return). There's not much to see in the town of **ORFORD** itself, but the summertime youth hostel, *Auberge du Centre d'Arts*, 3165 chemin du Parc (Hwy 141) (☎819/843-8595 or 1-800/567-6155; ①; May–Oct), is a great base for exploring the park and neighbouring Magog. You can also **camp** at either of the park's two main sites (☎819/843-9855 or 1-877/843-9855; $16.75). The only other accommodation options are more upscale in price and service: *Le Gîte de la Tour*, 1837 Alfred-Desrochers (☎819/868-0763, *www.auberge-de-la-tour.com*; ④), is a charming country inn while the *Auberge Au Lion d'Or*, 2240 chemin du Parc (☎819/843-6000; ④), has a health spa and a heated outdoor pool. For dining, *Tonnerre de Brest*, 2197 chemin du Parc, serves up crepes, mussels and fries, and *La Mérise*, at no. 2329, has regional cuisine.

Near the northwest corner of the park, a twenty-minute drive from Magog, is the unusual **Mine Crystal Québec**, near the village of **Bonsecours** off Hwy 243 (July & Aug daily 10.30am–5pm; June & Sept Sat & Sun 10.30am–5pm; guided tours at 11am, 1.30pm & 3.30pm – phone ahead to book an English-speaking tour $7; ☎450/535-6550, *www.crystalsanctuary.com*). This small operation is the only quartz-crystal mine in Canada – a peaceful place that just mines enough to sell in the shop. One of the northern hemisphere's largest crystals, a four-foot-long great smoky quartz from Brazil, is here, and regular quartz-crystal-bowl "concerts" produce extraordinary singing harmonies.

North Hatley

The region east of Magog holds its Loyalist connections dear, and this is one of the few areas in Québec where you'll encounter vestiges of the snobbish anglophone attitudes that once pervaded the whole province. **NORTH HATLEY**, a thirty-minute drive east from Magog along Hwy 108, is an anglophone bastion, with boutiques selling Lipton teas, Liberty products, tweeds and Aran jumpers; the resident population steadfastly refuses to change the town's name to "Hatley Nord". Otherwise the village is home to Québec's longest-running English-language theatre, **The Piggery** (☎819/842-2431 for reservations), which puts on several quality productions throughout the summer, and there are several art galleries and antique shops clustered along the waterfront. A few kilometres northeast, you can visit the underground galleries of an old copper mine at the **Mines Capelton**, 800 Hwy 108 (April–Oct; reserve tours on ☎819/346-9545; $14.95).

The village boasts two of Québec's classiest **inns**: the romantic *Manoir Hovey* (☎842-2421 or 1-800/661-2421; ⑥), nestled along the lake with its private beach and boats; and *Auberge Hatley* (☎819/842-2451; ⑥), set on the wooded hillside overlooking the lake and town. Decent **pub food** can be had at either the English-style *Le Pilsen*, 55 rue Principale, with its locally brewed draught and basic meals, or *Café de Lafontaine*, which serves more of the same next door at no. 35. The slightly more expensive but exquisite *Restaurant Café Massawippi*, 3050 chemin Capelton, is open for dinner only.

Sherbrooke

The 100,000-strong university town of **SHERBROOKE**, 147km east of Montréal, revels in the title "Queen of the Eastern Townships", a strange accolade for a town that's no great shakes and has just three minor attractions. The city's two museums are modest in scope, but the **Musée des Beaux Arts de Sherbrooke**, 241 rue Dufferin (late June to early Sept Tues–Sun 11am–5pm, Wed 11am–9pm; early Sept to late June Tues–Sun 1–5pm, Wed 1–9pm; $4; *mba.ville.sherbrooke.qc.ca*), the better of the two, displays local work that includes a fairly impressive collection of naive painters and visiting collections of good quality. The two halls of the **Musée du Séminaire de Sherbrooke**, 222 Frontenac (late June to early Sept daily 10am–5pm; early Sept to late June Tues–Sun 12.30–4.30pm; $4), are unconventional by comparison. The dusty Musée de la Tour, up in the seminary's tower, has rows of glass cases displaying pickled toads, stuffed bison heads, shells, crystals and moccasins, while the other part of the museum, the Centre d'Exposition Léon-Marcotte, has interactive displays on the natural sciences. Otherwise, the **Centre d'interpretation de l'histoire de Sherbrooke**, 275 rue Dufferin (July & Aug Tues–Fri 9am–5pm, Sat & Sun 10am–5pm; Sept–June Tues–Fri 9am–noon & 1–5pm, Sat & Sun 1–5pm; $5), focuses on the history of Sherbooke and the Townships and rents audio tapes for walking or driving tours of the city.

The **bus** station, with connections to and from Montréal, Québec City and various local towns, is at 20 rue King ouest. The **information centre** is on the same street at no. 3010 (daily 9am–5pm; ☎1-800/561-8331). Sherbrooke's **accommodation** lacks charm; the few inexpensive options include the student residence at 2500 boul Université de Sherbrooke (☎819/821-7000; summer only; ②). Otherwise, you could try *Auberge Élite*, at 4206 rue King ouest (☎819/563-4755 or 1-877/563-4755; ②), or one of the numerous modern motels along the same street – the cheapest are the three-star *L'Ermitage* at no. 1888 (☎819/569-5551 or 1-888/569-5551; ②) and *Motel la Réserve* at no. 4235 (☎819/566-6464 or 1-800/265-7119, *www.la-reserve.com*; ②). The Delta, 2685 rue King ouest (☎819/822-1989 or 1-800/268-1133; ⑤), is the plushest hotel in town.

For **restaurants**, *Café Bla-Bla*, 2 Wellington, has a good selection of imported beers in addition to its well-priced bistro fare, and *Au Four à Bois*, 3025 rue King ouest, is a sound pizza joint. *Le Petit Parisien*, 243 rue Alexandre, is a small ambient resto; bring your own wine. *Délia Egg-xtra*, 661 King est, has more than 100 breakfast options. Local specialties are served at *La Falaise St-Michel* at 100 Webster.

Montréal to Québec City

Two **autoroutes** (highways) cover the 270km between Montréal and Québec City, though plenty of VIA Rail **trains** and Voyageur **buses** also trawl the route: the boring Hwy 20 cuts along the south shore of the St Lawrence, and the even more banal Hwy 40 takes to the north side with very few rest-stops en route, so fill up before leaving Montréal. The slower Hwy 138 also meanders along the north shore but gives a closer look at rural Québec and farms left over from the seigneurial regime, like the **Seigneurie de Terrebonne** (late June to Aug Tues–Sun 10am–8pm; free), on the Île des Moulins about thirty minutes northeast of downtown Montréal via Hwy 25 (exit 17 est). A seigneury from 1673 to 1883, the restored nineteenth-century buildings – including the manor house of the area's last seigneur and Canada's first francophone millionaire, Joseph Masson – powerfully evoke life under the old regime.

Trois-Rivières

The major town between Montréal and Québec City is **TROIS-RIVIÈRES**, located midway between the two, at the point where the Rivière St-Maurice splits into three channels – hence the name "Three Rivers" – before meeting the St Lawrence. The

European settlement dates from 1634, when the town established itself as an embarkation point for the French explorers of the continent and as an iron-ore centre. Lumber followed, and today Trois-Rivières is one of the world's largest producers of paper, with the delta chock-full of logs to be pulped. It's often dismissed as an industrial city and little else, but its shady streets of historic buildings – neither as twee as Québec City, nor as monumental as Vieux-Montréal – are well worth a wander, and the town is a good starting point for exploring the Mauricie Valley.

Trois-Rivières' compact downtown core branches off from the small square of **Parc du Champlain** and extends south down to the waterfront. Facing the park to the east, at 363 rue Bonaventure, the **Cathédrale de l'Assomption** (Mon–Sat 7–11.30am & 2–5.30pm, Sun 8.30–11.30am & 2–5pm; free), is notable for its Florentine stained-glass windows and massive Gothic Revival style reminiscent of Westminster Abbey. One of the town's oldest buildings, the pretty **Manoir Boucher-de-Niverville**, is close by at 168 rue Bonaventure, and it contains a small collection of eighteenth-century Québécois furniture dating from 1730, when it was the home of the local seigneur (late June to early Sept 2–8pm; free). Continue south along rue Bonaventure until the water is in sight, and take a left turn to reach the narrow and ancient rue des Ursulines, the city's most attractive thoroughfare. The three-storey **Manoir de Tonnancour** at no. 864 (Tues–Fri 10am–noon & 1.30–5pm, Sat & Sun 1–5pm; free) holds temporary exhibitions on various themes from stamps to sculpture. Local art is on display at the nearby **Maison Hertel-de-la-Fresnière** at no. 802 (late June to early Sept daily 8am–5.30pm; free), while historical exhibits are the norm at the **Musée des Ursulines**, whose slender, silver dome dominates the street. A former convent established by a small group of Ursuline nuns who arrived from Québec City in 1697, it includes a chapel with attractive frescoes and gilt sculptures. The nunnery's treasures are displayed in a little museum in the old hospital quarters (May–Nov Tues–Fri 9am–5pm, Sat & Sun 1.30–5pm; March & April Wed–Sun 2–5pm; Nov–Feb by appointment only; $2.50).

On the nearby, rather characterless waterfront, the **Centre d'Exposition sur l'Industrie des Pâtes et Papiers**, 800 Parc-Portuaire (June to early Sept daily 9am–5pm; Sept Mon–Fri 9am–5pm, Sat & Sun 11am–5pm; $3), has an informative if unthrilling exhibition on the pulp and paper industry that's the backbone of the community. Finally, the ruins of **Les Forges du Saint-Maurice**, 10,000 boul des Forges, (early May to mid-Oct daily 9am–5pm; $4.50) which put the town on the map as a supplier to the farmers and arsenals of Québec and Europe, is now a national historic park, linked to downtown by bus #4 – get on at the bus terminal at the corner of rues Badeaux and St-Antoine.

PRACTICALITIES

The **information centre** at 1457 rue Notre Dame (late June to early Sept daily 9am–5pm; early Sept to late June Mon–Fri 9am–5pm), has pamphlets on all the town's activities, sights and restaurants. For **accommodation**, the cheapest option is the clean and comfortable **youth hostel**, *La Flottille*, in the heart of downtown at 497 rue Radisson (☎819/378-8010 or 1-800/461-8585; ①). Three attractive **B&Bs** are situated in heritage homes in Vieux Trois-Rivières: the ten-roomed *Gîte du Huard*, 42 rue St-Louis (☎819/375-8771; ②–④), has a room with kitchenette; *La Campanule*, 634 rue des Ursulines, offers three rooms and access to a garden with whirlpool tub (☎819/373-1133, kg@infoteck.qc.ca; ②); and *Le Fleurvil*, across the street at no. 635, has three rooms in a low-lying house (☎819/372-5195; ②). Centrally located, modern **hotels** include the high-rise *Delta*, 1620 Notre Dame (☎819/372-5975, www.deltahotels.com; ⑥), and *Hôtel Gouverneur*, 975 Hart (☎819/379-4550 or 1-888/910-1110, www.gouverneur.com; ④).

Most of the city's **restaurants** are located in the downtown core, along rue des Forges. *Le Bolvert Royal*, 1556 rue Royale, is a hearty, affordable breakfast option and

Angeline, 313 rue des Forges, has imaginative pasta and pizza choices for under $10. The nearby *Gaspard* at no. 475 offers steak, fish and chicken, plus some cheap lunch specials. *Le Zenob*, 171 rue Bonaventure, is a **bar** with a small terrace that also sells sandwiches; for coffee and a snack, head to *Café Morgane*, at 100 rue des Forges, a sleek coffee shop with three other outlets around town.

Parc National de la Mauricie

Sixty kilometres north of Trois-Rivières lies the mountainous area of the Saint-Maurice valley – known as the **Mauricie** – where the best of the landscape is demarcated by the **Parc National de la Mauricie** (☎819/533-7272, *www.parkscanada.pch.gc.ca*; May–Nov; $3.75). Situated on the southernmost part of the Canadian Shield, the park contains over 500 square kilometres of soft-contoured hills, lakes and rivers, waterfalls and sheer rock faces. The one drawback is the lack of public transport; to get there, take Hwy 55 north of Trois-Rivières to exit 226 and follow the signs to the St-Jean-des-Piles entrance.

The park offers numerous hiking trails of various lengths and abilities, ranging from the Cache Trail, a mere 1km walk leading to the Lac du Fou where a raised platform has a telescope for marine and wildlife watching, to the Laurentian Trail, a 75km trek which takes five to eight days to complete. Information centres at the park's entrances have excellent maps and booklets about the park's well-maintained trails, canoe routes and bike paths, and also provide canoe rentals (for $17/day). The park has hundreds of **camping** places ($14.50–22.50 a pitch) allocated on a first-come, first-served basis and they're rarely filled to capacity. If you'd rather sleep under a roof, there are also two **lodges** with dormitory-style accommodation open year-round. The *Wabenaki*'s two dormitories sleep up to 26 people each, and *Andrew*'s four rooms each sleep four (☎819/537-4555 for both lodges, *info.nature.mauricie@sh .cgocable.ca*; ② for two nights).

QUÉBEC CITY AND AROUND

Spread over Cap Diamant and the banks of the St Lawrence, **QUÉBEC CITY** is Canada's most beautifully located and most historic city. Vieux-Québec, surrounded by solid fortifications, is the only walled city in North America, a fact that prompted UNESCO to classify it as a World Heritage Site in 1985. In both parts of the Old City – Haute and Basse – the winding cobbled streets are flanked by seventeenth- and eighteenth-century stone houses and churches, graceful parks and squares, and countless monuments. Although some districts have been painstakingly restored to give tourists as seductive an introduction to Québec as possible, this is an authentically and profoundly French city: 95 percent of its 600,000 population are French-speaking, and it is often difficult to remember which continent you are in as you tuck into a croissant and a steaming bowl of coffee in a Parisian-style café. Moreover, despite the fact that the city's symbol is a hotel, the **Château Frontenac**, the government remains the main employee, not tourism, and some of the more impressive buildings are government-run and off-limits.

Arriving from Montréal you're immediately struck by the differences between the province's two main cities. Whilst Montréal is international, dynamic and forward-thinking, Québec City is more than a shade provincial, often seeming too bound up with its religious and military past – a residue of the days when the city was the bastion of the Catholic Church in Canada. On the other hand, the Church can claim much of the credit for the creation and preservation of the finest buildings, from the quaint **Église Notre Dame-des-Victoires** to the **Basilique Notre Dame de Québec** and the vast **Seminary**. In contrast, the austere defensive structures, dominated by the massive

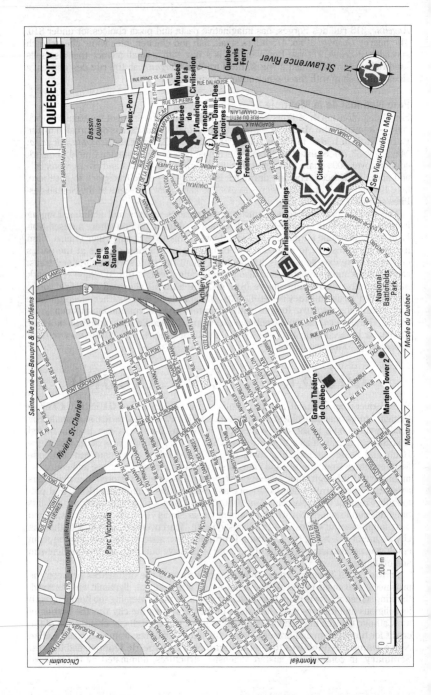

QUÉBEC CITY

Citadelle, reveal the military pedigree of a city dubbed by Churchill as the "Gibraltar of North America", while the battlefield of the **Plains of Abraham** is now a national historic park. Of the city's rash of museums, two are essential visits – the modern **Musée de la Civilisation**, in Vieux-Québec, expertly presenting all aspects of French-Canadian society, and the **Musée du Québec**, in the Haute-Ville, west of Vieux-Québec, which has the finest art collection in the province.

Outside the city limits, the town of **Lévis** and the Huron reservation, **Wendake**, make worthwhile excursions, whilst the churches and farmland of the **Côte-de-Beaupré** and the **Île d'Orléans** hark back to the days of the seigneurs and *habitants*. The gigantic **Basilique de Ste-Anne-de-Beaupré**, attracting millions of pilgrims annually, is one of the most impressive sights in Québec, and for equally absorbing natural sights there are the spectacular waterfalls at **Montmorency** and **Sept-Chutes**, and the wildlife reserve in the **Laurentians**.

Some history

For centuries the clifftop site of what is now Québec City was occupied by the **Iroquois** village of **Stadacona**, and although Cartier visited in the sixteenth century, permanent European settlement did not begin until 1608, when Samuel de Champlain established a fur-trading post here. To protect what was rapidly developing into a major inland trade gateway, the settlement shifted to the clifftop in 1620 when Fort St-Louis was built on the present-day site of the *Château Frontenac*. Québec's steady expansion was noted in London, and in 1629 Champlain was starved out of the fort by the British, an occupation that lasted just three years.

Missionaries began arriving in 1615, and by the time Bishop Laval arrived in 1659 Québec City and the surrounding province were in the grip of Catholicism. In the city's earliest days, however, the merchants of the fur trade wielded the most power and frequently came into conflict with the priests, who wanted a share in the profits in order to spread their message amongst the aboriginal peoples. The wrangles were resolved by **Louis XIV**, who assumed power in France in 1661 and was advised to take more interest in his kingdom's mercantile projects. By 1663, New France had become a royal province, administered by a council appointed directly by the crown and answerable to the king's council in France. Three figures dominated the proceedings: the governor, responsible for defence and external relations; the intendant, administering justice and overseeing the economy; and, inevitably, the bishop.

Before the century was out, the long-brewing European struggles between England and France spilled over into the colony with French attacks on the English in New York and New England in 1689 and a foiled naval attack on the city by Sir William Phipps, governor of Massachusetts, in the following year. It was at this time that the **Comte de Frontenac**, known as the "fighting governor", replaced Champlain's Fort St-Louis with the sturdier Château St-Louis, and began work on the now-famous fortifications that ring Vieux-Québec.

In September 1759, during the Seven Years War, the most significant battle in Canada's history took place here, between the British under general **James Wolfe** and Louis Joseph, **Marquis de Montcalm**. The city had already been under siege from the opposite shore for three months and Montcalm had carefully protected the city from any approach by water. Finally, Wolfe and his four thousand troops heard of an unguarded track, scaled the cliff of Cap Diamant and crept up on the sleeping French regiment from behind. The twenty-minute battle on the Plains of Abraham left both leaders mortally wounded and the city of Québec in the hands of the English, a state of affairs confirmed by the Treaty of Paris in 1763. Madame de Pompadour commented: "It makes little difference; Canada is useful only to provide me with furs".

In 1775 – the year after the Québec Act of 1774 allowed French-Canadians to retain their Catholic religion, language and culture – the town was attacked again, this time by the Americans, who had already captured Montréal. The battle was won by the British and for the next century the city quietly earned its livelihood as the centre of a **timber-trade** and **shipbuilding** industry. By the time it was declared the provincial capital of Lower Canada in 1840, though, the accessible supplies of timber had run out. The final blow came with the appearance of steamships that could travel as far as Montréal, while sailing ships had found it difficult to proceed beyond Québec City. Ceasing to be a busy seaport, the city declined into a centre of small industry and local government, its way of life still largely determined by the Catholic Church.

With the Quiet Revolution in the 1960s and the rise of Québec nationalism, Québec City became a symbol of the glory of the French heritage – for example, the motto *Je me souviens* ("I remember") above the doors of its parliament buildings was transferred to the licence plates of Québec cars, to sweep the message across Canada. Though the city played little active part in the changes, it has grown with the upsurge in the francophone economy, developing a suburbia of shopping malls and convention centres as slick as any in the country.

Arrival, information and city transport

Québec City's **airport**, 20km west of the city, caters almost exclusively for domestic flights, primarily those of Air Canada and its regional carriers: most international flights arrive at Montréal. A shuttle connects the airport with several downtown hotels (8.45am–10.20pm; 7–8 daily; $9 to Vieux-Québec). The twenty-minute trip by taxi is a fixed rate of $24.50.

Trains from Montréal arrive at the central Gare du Palais in Basse-Ville, whereas services from the Atlantic provinces arrive at Charny, across the St Lawrence, from Ste-Foy, in the very early morning; a shuttle is available to Gare du Palais but reservations must be made in advance. The long-distance **bus terminal** is at 320 Abraham-Martin, adjoining the Gare du Palais (see "Listings" on p.271 for bus and train information numbers). **Parking** downtown can be a real pain: it's best to leave your vehicle outside the centre, off Grande-Allée or in the Vieux-Port area (for parking details, see "Listings" on p.271).

Information

For **information** about Québec City's sights and events, as well as an accommodation service, the main information centre is beside the Voltigeurs de Québec armoury, off Place Georges V at 835 ave Wilfrid-Laurier (late June to mid-Oct daily 8.30am–7.30pm; mid-Oct to late June Mon–Thurs & Sat 9am–5pm, Fri 9am–6pm, Sun 10am–4pm; ☎649-2608, *www.quebecregion.com*), in the same building as the Discovery Pavilion of the Plains of Abraham. Information on the whole province (as well as Québec City) is available at the Centre Infotouriste on the other side of Place d'Armes from the *Château Frontenac* at 12 rue Ste-Anne (daily: late June to early Sept 8.30am–7.30pm; early Sept to late June 9am–5pm; ☎1-877/266-5687, *www.bonjourquebec.com*). Both centres provide a free booklet, *Greater Québec Area*, which has a good map.

City transport

Québec City's sights and hotels are packed into a small area, so walking is the best way to get around. Motorcycles are banned from Vieux-Québec. For sights further out, like the Musée du Québec, STCUQ **local buses** are efficient and run from around 6am to 1am (certain routes run until 3am Fri & Sat). Fares are a standard $1.75 per journey by prepaid ticket, available at newsstands, grocery stores and supermarkets across town, as are one-day passes ($4.70); the cash fare per journey is $2.25, exact fare only. If you need more than one bus to complete your journey, pick up a transfer (*une correspondance*) from the driver, which enables you to take the second bus for no extra charge.

The main bus stop in Vieux-Québec is on the west side at Place d'Youville, near Porte St-Jean. The main transfer points for STCUQ buses are here and at Place Jacques-Cartier, reachable by buses #3, #5, #7, #8 and #30. Even if it means a longer walk, the frequency of the STCUQ's Métrobus services (#800, etc) makes them the best option.

Québec City's area code is ☎418

Accommodation

The **accommodation** in Québec City is perfect for budget travellers. In the Vieux-Québec quarter there are two **youth hostels**, and the **budget hotels** are as well located as those at the top end. As the city is one of Canada's most frequented tourist destinations, try to reserve in advance, particularly during the summer months and the Carnaval in February. Even at those times, though, you're not likely to find the city completely full, as the suburbs have masses of motels and B&Bs, all of them just a local bus ride away.

The hotels in Vieux-Québec are usually renovated town houses with the rooms fitted to provide a variety of accommodation. For cheaper rooms in the $40–80 range, head for the area around rues St-Louis and Ste-Ursule, streets lined with budget hotels; the posher places are around the Jardin des Gouverneurs, in the shadow of the prestigious *Château Frontenac*, and in the Quartier Latin. In Basse-Ville, hotel accommodation is surprisingly more expensive and options are limited to a couple of special places mentioned here or a mass of run-of-the-mill motels.

All of Québec City's **campsites** are around 20km outside town, convenient only for those with their own transport; the ones listed below are the closest.

Basse-Ville

Hôtel Dominion 1912, 126 rue St-Pierre (☎692-2224 or 1-888/833-5253, *www.hoteldominion.com*). Fabulous boutique hotel with all the touches – feather pillows and duvets, subdued lighting, stylish modern decor and cool frosted-glass sinks lit from below. Some rooms have river views. ⑦.

Le Priori, 15 rue du Sault-au-Matelot (☎692-3992 or 1-800/351-3992, *www.quebecweb.com/lepriori*). Tastefully renovated old house; an excellent place to stay. ⑥.

Auberge St-Antoine, 10 rue St-Antoine (☎692-2211 or 1-888/692-2211, www.saint-antoine.com). Close to the Musée de la Civilisation. Cosy hotel divided into two buildings. Some rooms have views of the river and all are tastefully decorated. ⑥.

Avenue Ste-Geneviève

Hôtel Cap-Diamant, 39 ave Ste-Geneviève (☎694-0313, *www.hcapdiamant.qc.ca*). Two-star, nine-bedroom guesthouse with Victorian furnishings near the Jardin des Gouverneurs. Rooms all have bathrooms. ③.

Hôtel au Château Fleur de Lys, 15 ave Ste-Geneviève (☎694-1884, *www.quebecweb.com/cfl*). Just off the Jardin, on the corner of rue de la Porte. Air-conditioned rooms. ④.

Le Château de Pierre, 17 ave Ste-Geneviève (☎694-0429). An 1853 mansion with plush rooms also just off the Jardin. ⑤.

Hôtel Maison du Fort, 21 ave Ste-Geneviève (☎692-4375, *www.quebecweb.com/maisondufort*). Another small guesthouse near Jardin des Gouverneurs with a friendly owner and air-conditioned rooms. Two stars. ④.

Au Manoir Ste-Geneviève, 13 ave Ste-Geneviève (☎694-1666 or 1-877/694-1666, *www.qubecweb .com/msg*). This charming two-star hotel dating from 1800 has nine beautiful Victorian rooms. ⑤.

Hôtel Manoir sur le Cap, 9 ave Ste-Geneviève (☎694-1987, *www.manoir-sur-le-cap.com*). Two-star, 14-room hotel overlooking the Jardin des Gouverneurs. All rooms have private bath and TVs. ⑥.

Rue St-Louis

Hôtel Le Clos St-Louis, 69 rue St-Louis (☎694-1311 or 1-800/461-1311, *www.quebecweb.com /clos_saint-louis*). Three-star hotel in an 1854 house with decor to match. ⑤.

Auberge St-Louis, 48 rue St-Louis (☎692-2424 or 1-888/692-4105, *www.quebecweb.com/aubergestlouis*). The cheapest two-star inn in the St-Louis area. Basic furnishings but comfy; excellent location. Cheaper rooms have shared bath. ②.

Jardin des Gouverneurs and around

Hôtel Château Bellevue, 16 rue de la Porte (☎692-2573 or 1-800/463-2617, *www.vieux -quebec.com/bellevue*). Modern hotel in an old building, with views of the Jardin and the *Château Frontenac*. Free parking. ⑥.

Hôtel Château de Léry, 8 rue de la Porte (☎692-2692 or 1-800/363-0036, *www.quebecweb.com /chateaudelery*). Two-star rooms right on the Jardin des Gouverneurs. ⑤.

Le Château Frontenac, 1 rue des Carrières (☎692-3861 or 1-800/441-1414, *www.fairmont.com*). This opulent Victorian "castle", built for William Van Horne, president of CP Railways, opened in 1893, and has accommodated such dignitaries as Churchill, Roosevelt, Madame Chiang Kai-shek and Queen Elizabeth II. It's the most expensive place in town, with splendid rooms, and even offers its own guided tours. ⑧.

Au Jardin du Gouverneur, 16 rue Mont-Carmel (☎692-1704). On the corner of rues Mont-Carmel and Haldimand, next to the *Château Frontenac*. Seventeen rooms all with adjoining bathrooms. ③.

Hôtel Terrasse-Dufferin, 6 place Terrasse-Dufferin (☎694-9472, *www.terrasse-dufferin.com*). The better rooms have the best views in town, overlooking the St Lawrence. ④.

Rue Ste-Ursule

Hôtel l'Ermitage, 60 rue Ste-Ursule (☎694-0968, *www3.sympatico.ca/ermitage*). Quality hotel with ten bedrooms, all of which have bathrooms and air conditioning. ⑥.

Hôtel La Maison Acadienne, 43 rue Ste-Ursule (☎694-0280 or 1-800/463-0280, *www.maison-aca-dienne.com*). Three ancestral dwellings with cosy rooms. Some with shared bathrooms. ③/④.

Hôtel La Maison Demers, 68 rue Ste-Ursule (☎692-2487 or 1-800/692-2487). Parking and break-fast included in the price; the more expensive rooms have bathrooms en suite. ③.

Hôtel La Maison Ste-Ursule, 40 rue Ste-Ursule (☎694-9794). Built in 1759, with green shutters, tiny doors, this is a clean hotel with bare-bones furnishing. There's also a mall courtyard with pic-nic tables. ②.

Maison historique James Thompson, 47 rue Ste-Ursule (☎694-9042, *www.bedandbreakfastque-bec.com*). B&B in historic 1793 house with sleigh beds, antiques throughout and a lovely sitting room. ③.

Hôtel Manoir La Salle, 18 rue Ste-Ursule (☎692-9953). Small century-old red-brick hotel. Only two of the eleven rooms are en suite, one of which has a bathroom. ③.

Au Petit Hôtel, 3 ruelle des Ursulines (☎694-0965, *www3.sympatico.ca/aupetithotel*). Situated in a peaceful cul-de-sac just off rue Ste-Ursule, parallel to St-Louis. ③.

Rue Ste-Anne and rue d'Auteuil

Auberge la Chouette, 71 rue d'Auteuil (☎694-0232). In the road running parallel to Ste-Ursule, in the shadow of the city walls; all rooms have bathrooms. ④.

Hôtel Clarendon, 57 rue Ste-Anne (☎692-2480 or 1-888/554-6001, *www.hotelclarendon.com*). Québec City's oldest hotel, dating from 1870. Renovated in the 1930s, it has a classic Art Deco reception area. ⑥.

Hôtel la Maison Doyon, 109 rue Ste-Anne (☎694-1720, *www.quebecweb.com/doyon*). Well situated near the Quartier Latin. Most rooms have private bath. ③.

Hôtel Manoir d'Auteuil, 49 rue d'Auteuil (☎694-1173, *www.quebecweb.com/dauteuil*). Lavish 1835 town house by the city walls, with three-star Art Deco rooms. ⑥.

Auberge de la Place d'Armes, 24 rue Ste-Anne (☎694-9485). Perfectly situated opposite the Anglican Cathedral, on the pedestrianized part of rue Ste-Anne. Some shared baths. ③.

Auberge du Trésor, 20 rue Ste-Anne (☎694-1876 or 1-800/566-1876, *www.aubergedutresor.com*). Modern rooms with private bathrooms in a house built in 1676. ⑤.

Elsewhere in Vieux-Québec

Hôtel Belley, 249 rue St-Paul (☎692-1694 or 1-888/692-1694, *www.oricom.ca/belley*). Eight-bed-room, slickly designed hotel near the Gare du Palais. Three-star rooms, with off-season price reductions. ③.

Hôtel Manoir des Remparts, 3 1/2 rue des Remparts (☎692-2056). At the north end of Vieux-Québec on the ramparts, near the Quartier Latin, with views of the St Lawrence. Simple hotel with some en-suite rooms and TVs and telephones. ②.

Hôtel Manoir Victoria, 44 côte du Palais (☎692-1030 or 1-800/463-6283, *www.manoir-victoria.com*). A four-star hotel, off rue St-Jean. Rambling manor with pool, sauna, gym and modern rooms. ⑥.

Motels, hostels and student accommodation

Centre International de Séjour de Québec, 19 rue Ste-Ursule (☎694-0755 or 1-800/461-8585, *www.cisq.org*). The official youth hostel, in a former hospice run by nuns, is often full and is very impersonal, though it offers laundry facilities, Internet access ($2 for 20min), luggage lockers and tourist information. No curfew, but need to be buzzed in after 11pm. ①.

Motel Doyon, 1215 chemin Ste-Foy (☎527-4408 or 1-888/433-6966, *www.doyonmotel.com*). One of the cheapest motels around, in the University suburb of Ste-Foy. Basic but clean, with free parking. 10min bus ride to Vieux-Québec. ②.

Auberge de la Paix, 31 rue Couillard (☎694-0735). Situated in the Quartier Latin, this is by far the best hostel in Québec City. Large courtyard to hang out in; rate includes breakfast. ①.

Services des Résidences de l'Université Laval, Pavillon Alphonse-Marie-Parent, Room 1604, Cité Universitaire, Ste-Foy (☎656-5632, *www.ulaval.ca/sres*). Single and double rooms are available in the student residences, a fifteen-minute bus ride from Haute-Ville. Cheap breakfast in cafeteria, but it's best avoided. Early May to mid-Aug. ①.

YWCA, 855 ave Holland (☎683-2155). Men are accepted as well as women here, though there are no double beds. Just off chemin Ste-Foy, about a 15min bus ride from the Old Town. ②.

Campsites

Camping Aéroport, 2050 rte de l'Aéroport (☎871-1574 or 1-800/294-1574, *www.geocities.com /vacance.geo*). Take exit 305 nord off Hwy 440 onto rte de l'Aeroport – the campsite is around 5km north of the airport itself. $19 for a party of four.

Camping de la Base de Plein Air Ste-Foy, rue Laberge, Ste-Foy (☎654-4641). Exit 306 off Hwy 440 leads to this park-set campsite; if travelling eastbound, double back to rue Blaise-Pascal to cross the highway. Reservations recommended. $20 for a party of four.

Camping Municipal de Beauport, 95 rue Sérénité, Beauport, off boul Rochette (☎666-2228, *www.campingquebec.com/beauport*). Take exit 322 off Hwy 40. Bus #800 to Beauport, then #50 or #55. Mid-June to early Sept. $20 for a party of four.

The City

Québec City spreads from its historic heart into a bland suburbia but the highlights lie beside the St Lawrence, with main attractions being evenly distributed between the upper and lower portions of what is known as **Vieux-Québec** (Old Québec). On the Cap Diamant, **Haute-Ville** (Upper Town) continues along the St Lawrence from the old city walls and the furthest you need to wander from here is to the Musée du Québec, set in the extensive parkland of the Plains of Abraham. As the oldest part of the city, this area comprises some of the main sights of interest, including the magnificent Citadelle. The Terrasse Dufferin is also worth a stroll to watch street entertainers, unproductive students or the views over the river, but it gets overcrowded in the evening. The second part of the city, the **Basse-Ville** (or Lower Town) is connected to Haute-Ville by funicular from Terrasse Dufferin or by several windy streets and stairs. One of the main pleasures of the area, besides the wonderful old houses and small museums, is the Musée de la Civilisation.

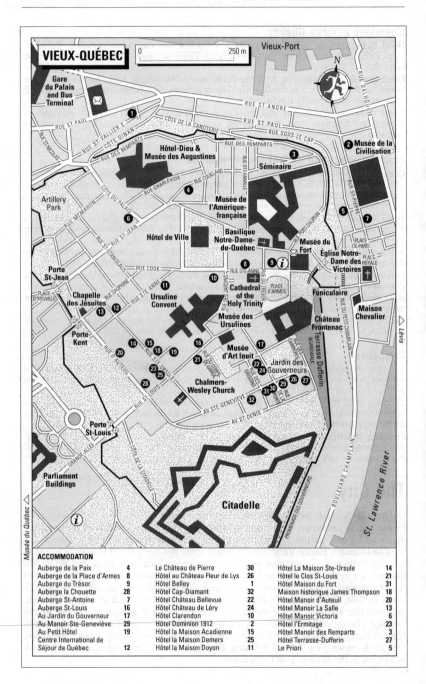

VIEUX-QUÉBEC

0 ———— 250 m

Vieux-Port

Gare du Palais and Bus Terminal

RUE ST-PAUL

RUE ST-VALLIER E.

RUE ST-ANDRE

CÔTE DE LA CANDOTERIE

RUE ST-PAUL

RUE SOUS-LE-CAP

RUE ST-NICOLAS

CÔTE DINAN

RUE DES REMPARTS

CÔTE DU PALAIS

RUE CHARLEVOIX

RUE COUILLARD

RUE DES REMPARTS

Hôtel-Dieu & Musée des Augustines

Séminaire

Musée de la Civilisation

Artillery Park

RUE McMAHON

Musée de l'Amérique-française

Hôtel de Ville

Basilique Notre-Dame-de-Québec

Musée du Fort

Église Notre-Dame des Victoires

Porte St-Jean

RUE COOK

Chapelle des Jésuites

Ursuline Convent

Cathedral of the Holy Trinity

Funiculaire

Maison Chevalier

Porte Kent

Musée des Ursulines

Château Frontenac

Terrasse Dufferin

Musée d'Art Inuit

Jardin des Gouverneurs

Chalmers-Wesley Church

Porte St-Louis

RUE ST-LOUIS

AV STE-GENEVIÈVE

AV. ST-DENIS

Parliament Buildings

Citadelle

BOULEVARD CHAMPLAIN

St. Lawrence River

Musée du Québec

Lévis

ACCOMMODATION

Auberge de la Paix	4	Le Château de Pierre	30	Hôtel La Maison Ste-Ursule	14
Auberge de la Place d'Armes	8	Hôtel au Château Fleur de Lys	26	Hôtel le Clos St-Louis	21
Auberge du Trésor	9	Hôtel Belley	1	Hôtel Maison du Fort	31
Auberge la Chouette	28	Hôtel Cap-Diamant	32	Maison historique James Thompson	18
Auberge St-Antoine	7	Hôtel Château Bellevue	22	Hôtel Manoir d'Auteuil	20
Auberge St-Louis	16	Hôtel Château de Léry	24	Hôtel Manoir La Salle	13
Au Jardin du Gouverneur	17	Hôtel Clarendon	10	Hôtel Manoir Victoria	6
Au Manoir Ste-Geneviève	29	Hôtel Dominion 1912	2	Hôtel l'Ermitage	23
Au Petit Hôtel	19	Hôtel la Maison Acadienne	15	Hôtel Manoir des Remparts	3
Centre International de		Hôtel la Maison Demers	25	Hôtel Terrasse-Dufferin	27
Séjour de Québec	12	Hôtel la Maison Doyon	11	Le Priori	5

This itinerary begins at Vieux-Québec's **Place d'Armes** and then explores the upper part of Vieux-Québec and the rest of Haute-Ville as far west as the Musée du Québec. To finish the tour, you can explore Vieux-Québec's compact Basse-Ville, which can be reached directly from Place d'Armes. Strapped between the cliffs and the St Lawrence, this district is of considerable interest and is a pleasant area to wander around.

Place d'Armes and around

The ten square kilometres of Vieux-Québec's Haute-Ville, encircled by the city walls, form the Québec City of the tourist brochures. Its centre of gravity is the main square, the **Place d'Armes**, with benches around the central fountain serving in the summer as a resting place for weary sightseers. It was here that Champlain established his first fort in 1620, on the site now occupied by the gigantic **Château Frontenac**, probably Canada's most photographed building. New York architect Bruce Price drew upon the French-Canadian style of the surroundings to produce a pseudo-medieval red-brick pile crowned with a copper roof. Although the hotel he designed was inaugurated by the Canadian Pacific Railway in 1893, its distinctive main tower was only added in the early 1920s – during which time the hotel never closed – resulting in an over-the-top design that makes the most of the stupendous location atop Cap Diamant. Numerous celebrities, including Queen Elizabeth II, have stayed here, and the hotel has hosted one pair or more of newlyweds every night since it opened. The hotel has fifty-minute guided tours departing on the hour from the lower level (May to mid-Oct daily 10am–6pm; mid-Oct to April Sat & Sun noon–5pm; $6.50; reservations preferable ☎691-2166).

The cape's clifftop is fringed by the wide boardwalk of the **Terrasse Dufferin**, which runs alongside the château and the Jardin des Gouverneurs (see p.260) to the fortifications of the Citadelle, overlooking the narrowing of the river that was known to the aboriginal peoples as the *kebec* – the source of the province's name. At the beginning of the walkway – which offers charming views of the river – stands a romantic statue of **Champlain** and, beside it, a modern sculpture symbolizing Québec City's status as a UNESCO World Heritage Site. From here steep steps and a funicular descend to Vieux-Québec's Basse-Ville (see p.264).

Beside the *Château Frontenac*, where rue St-Louis enters the square, is the **Maison Maillou**, which houses the Québec chamber of commerce. Dating from 1736, this grey-limestone house, with metal shutters for insulation and a steeply slanting roof, displays the chief elements of the climate-adapted architecture brought over by the Norman settlers. On the west side of the square, on the spot where the Récollet missionaries built their first church and convent, stands the former **Palais de Justice**, a Renaissance-style courthouse designed in 1877 by Eugène-Étienne Taché, architect of the city's Parliament Buildings.

On the northeast corner of Place d'Armes, where rue Ste-Anne intersects with rue du Fort, is the **Musée du Fort** (late Jan to March Thurs–Sun 11am–4pm; April–June & Sept–Oct daily 10am–5pm; July–Aug daily 10am–6pm; $6.75), whose sole exhibit is a 37-square-metre model of Québec City circa 1750. You can only see it as part of the quaint thirty-minute sound and light show, when the city's six major battles, including the battle of the Plains of Abraham and the American invasion of 1775, are re-enacted – a fairly pricey history lesson.

Parallel to rue du Fort is the narrow alley of **rue du Trésor** where French settlers paid their taxes to the Royal Treasury; nowadays it is a touristy artists' market. Visitors who want to take home a portrait rather than a saccharine cityscape should shuffle into the pedestrianized section of Ste-Anne to the west of du Trésor, which is full of portraitists and their subjects. At 22 rue Ste-Anne, in the impressive 1732 Maison Vallée, the **Musée de Cire de Québec** (daily: June–Sept 9am–10pm; Oct–May 10am–5pm;

$3) is populated by unrealistic wax figures of Québécois luminaries from Champlain to Lévesque. Production values are a bit higher at the **Québec Expérience** show back around the corner at 8 rue du Trésor (8 daily; 30min; $6.75). The 3D multimedia show will appeal more to the MTV generation than to history buffs as holographic characters and animatronics give a potted history of Québec.

The Quartier Latin

Québec City's small **Quartier Latin**, in the northeast section of Vieux-Québec, is dominated by the seventeenth-century seminary in whose grounds stands the **Basilique Notre Dame de Québec** (Mon–Fri 9am–2pm, Sat & Sun 9am–5pm and between shows – see below; free). The oldest parish north of Mexico, the church was burnt to the ground in 1922 – one of many fires it has suffered – and was rebuilt to the original plans of 1647. Absolute silence within the cathedral heightens the impressiveness of the Rococo-inspired interior, culminating in a ceiling of blue sky and billowy clouds. The silver chancel lamp, beside the main altar, was a gift from Louis XIV and is one of the few treasures to survive the fire. In the crypt more than nine hundred bodies, including three governors and most of Québec's bishops, are interred. Champlain is also rumoured to be buried here, though archeologists are still trying to work out which body is his.

Access to the cathedral is limited to half an hour at a time in the afternoons unless you pay for the 45-minute *Act of Faith* sound and light show (May to mid-Oct Mon–Fri 4–5 shows daily from 3.30pm, Sat & Sun 2–3 shows daily from 6.30pm; $7.50). Architectural details are illuminated and isolated in the darkness to give you a sense of the volumes that make up the church's interior.

Next door to the cathedral, in the Maison du Coin, is the entrance to – and departure point for one-hour guided tours of – the ever-expanding **Musée de l'Amérique Française**, whose four sections occupy a small part of the old **Séminaire** (June–Sept daily 9.30am–5pm; Oct–May Tues–Sun 10am–5pm, *www.mcq.org*; $4, free on Tues Sept–June). The Séminaire was founded by the aggressive and autocratic **Monseigneur François de Laval-Montmorency** in 1663. In the three decades of his incumbency, Laval secured more power than the governor and intendant put together, and any officer dispatched from France found himself on the next boat home if Laval did not care for him. Laval retired early due to ill health, brought on by a religious fervour that denied him blankets and proper food. Death finally came after his feet froze on the stone floor of the chapel during his morning prayer session.

At its construction, the seminary was the finest collection of buildings the city had seen, leaving Governor Frontenac muttering that the bishop was now housed better than him. Primarily a college for priests, the seminary was also open to young men who wanted to follow other professions, and in 1852 it became Laval University, the country's first francophone Catholic university. Today, only the school of architecture remains; most of the other departments were moved to the western suburb of Ste-Foy.

The Welcome Pavilion in the Maison du Coin has a small exhibition on the early colonists upstairs and adjoins the Roman-style chapel, whose Second Empire interior houses Canada's largest collection of relics – bones, ashes and locks of hair, a few of which are on display. Laval's memorial chapel contains his ornate marble tomb, but not his remains, which were moved to the basilica when the chapel was deconsecrated in 1993. The whole interior is a bit of a sham, though – fed up with rebuilding after the chapel burnt down yet again in 1888, the church authorities decided to construct the pillars and coffered ceilings out of tin and paint over them; the stained-glass windows have been painted on single panes of glass and even the tapestries are the result of some deft brushwork.

The wrought-iron gates between the Welcome Pavilion and the basilica lead into a vast courtyard flanked by austere white buildings with handsome mansard roofs, through which you can pass to visit the rest of the museum. Alternatively, take the underground corridor directly from the chapel; a photo exhibit fills in the history of the Séminaire's buildings. Either way, you end up at the **Pavillon Jérôme-Demers** (same opening hours as the museum), which displays mostly well-presented, historical exhibitions, which are only a tiny sample of the eclectic items gathered by Québec's bishops and academics at Laval: scientific instruments, an Egyptian mummy – with a remarkably well-preserved penis – a diverting collection of European and Canadian paintings assembled by the art historians, as well as silverware and some of Laval's personal belongings.

Parc Montmorency

To the east, between the upper and lower parts of the old city, lies **Parc Montmorency**, its monuments recalling the historic figures of the area. This land was granted by Champlain to Canada's first agricultural settler and seigneur, Louis Hébert, and was later the meeting place of Québec's first legislature in 1694. The park gives wonderful views of Québec's port and its massive grain elevators, as does the flanking rue Port Dauphin, which becomes rue des Remparts, where the cannons that once protected the city still point across to Lévis.

Hôtel-Dieu and Artillery Park

The ten-minute walk along rue des Remparts circles round the north side of the Séminaire to the **Hôtel-Dieu du Précieux Sang**, the oldest hospital north of Mexico. The adjacent stone buildings are still occupied by the Augustinian order of nuns, who founded the hospital in 1639. Turning left up Côte du Palais and first left again leads to the **Musée des Augustines de l'Hôtel-Dieu de Québec**, 32 rue Charlevoix (Tues–Sat 9.30am–noon & 1.30–5pm, Sun 1.30–5pm; donation), where the artworks include some of Québec's oldest paintings, among them the earliest-known portrayal of the city in the background of the portraits of the Duchess of Auguillon and her uncle Cardinal Richelieu, who together funded the hospital. Another notable painting is the *Martyrdom of the Jesuits*, a gruesome tableau showing the torture of Jesuit missionaries in southern Ontario by the Iroquois in 1649. (Only a disappointing black-and-white engraving is on display to the public.) Grateful patients also donated a fine collection of antique furniture, copperware and ornaments. Many of the items are from France, as the first settlers usually found themselves interned in the hospital to recover from the diseases rife on the ocean crossing. A collection of medical instruments from the seventeenth to mid-twentieth century is also on display. On request the Augustines offer free guided tours of the chapel and the seventeenth-century cellars where the nuns sheltered from the British in 1759.

Artillery Park

Backtracking to Côte de Palais and down the hill a few steps, rue McMahon leads to the northwest corner of Vieux-Québec and **Artillery Park**, whose immense defensive structures were raised in the early 1700s by the French, in expectation of a British attack from the St Charles River. After Québec fell the British added to the site, which was used primarily as a barracks for the Royal Artillery Regiment for more than a century. In 1882 it became a munitions factory, and a foundry was added in 1902, later providing the Canadian army with ammunition in both world wars; it finally closed in 1964. The massive Dauphin Redoubt, named after Louis XIV's son, typifies the changes of fortune here: used by the French as the barracks for their garrison, it became the officers' mess under the British and then the residence of the superintendent of the Canadian Arsenal. The jumble of fortifications is well explained at the reception and **interpretive centre** (Feb–March & Nov–Dec Wed–Sun noon–4pm; April to early May Wed–Sun

10am–5pm; early May to Oct daily 10am–5pm, except July & Aug until 6pm; $3.25, guided tours an additional $3.25; *www.parkscanada.gc.ca/artillerie*) in the former foundry beside Porte St-Jean. The centre has displays on the military pedigree of the city, including a vivid model of Québec City in 1808. The nearby Officers' Quarters, where the British officers lived until 1871, is set up as it was circa 1830, with costumed guides relating the everyday lives of the soldiers and officers.

The Faubourg St-Jean-Baptiste

If you want to take a break from the old city, head through the Porte St-Jean and across Place D'Youville to where rue St-Jean picks up again in the former *faubourg* – the name given to the settlements that once stood undefended outside the city walls – of **St-Jean-Baptiste**. The quarter's studenty atmosphere is more laid-back than the rest of Québec, with cheaper restaurants and great nightlife spots.

A five-minute walk will bring you to the **Protestant Burying Ground** (May to mid-Nov daily 7am–11pm), Québec City's first Protestant cemetery and now the oldest one remaining in the province. Many historical figures were buried here between 1772 and 1860, including Lt Col James Turnbull, Queen Victoria's presumed half-brother. Further along on the same side of the street, **Maison Jean-Alfred Moisan** has been in the grocery trade since 1871, making it the oldest grocery store in North America. The tin ceilings and wooden furnishings provide a backdrop for fine foods and baked goods.

The district's namesake, the **Église St-Jean-Baptiste**, 410 rue St-Jean (late June to mid-Sept Mon–Fri & Sun 11am–4pm, Sat 9am–4pm), dominates the faubourg, its spire rising to 73m. When reconstruction began after a fire destroyed the original church in 1881, local architect Joseph Ferdinand Peachy looked to France for inspiration – the facade is a close reproduction of the Église de la Trinité in Paris.

Around the Jardins de l'Hôtel de Ville

Returning to the old city at Porte St-Jean, head south on the steep rue d'Auteuil as it runs alongside the fortifications up to Porte Kent, next to the **Chapelle des Jésuites**, 20 rue Dauphine (Mon–Fri 9am–11.30pm & 1–4.30pm; free). The church's delicately carved altar and ecclesiastical sculptures are by Pierre-Noël Levasseur, one of the most illustrious artists to work on the early Québec parish churches.

Rue Dauphine continues northeast to rue Cook, which leads east to the **Jardins de l'Hôtel de Ville**, scene of numerous live shows in the summer. The park surrounds the Hôtel de Ville (City Hall), which dates from 1883, and is overlooked by the far more impressive Art Deco buildings of the **Hôtel Clarendon** and the **Édifice Price** (the city's first skyscraper), at nos. 57 and 65 Ste-Anne, respectively.

By the corner of rue Ste-Anne and rue des Jardins stands the first Anglican cathedral built outside the British Isles, the **Cathedral of the Holy Trinity** (daily: May & June 10am–6pm; July & Aug 9am–8pm; Sept–Nov 10am–6pm; free guided tours; *www.ogs.net/cathedral*). The king of France gave the site to the Récollet Fathers but their church burnt down in the late eighteenth century. Its replacement, constructed in 1800–04 on orders from George III, followed the lines of London's church of St Martin-in-the-Fields. The simple interior houses the 1845 bishops' throne, reputedly made from the wood of the elm tree under whose branches Samuel de Champlain conferred with the Iroquois. Many of the church's features came from London, including the silverware from George III. The golden bars on the balcony denote the seats for the exclusive use of British sovereigns. In the courtyard are Les Artisans de la Cathédrale, Québec-based artisans whose small crafts and clothes stalls avoid tourist tack.

The Chapelle des Ursulines and around

Heading south along rue des Jardins brings you to the narrow rue Donnacona, where a sculptured hand holding a quill – a monument to the women who, since 1639, have dedicated their lives to teaching young Québécois – rests on a pedestal. It seems to point the way to the **Chapelle des Ursulines**, built by a tiny group of Ursuline nuns who arrived in Québec in 1639 calling themselves "the Amazons of God in Canada". Their task was to bring religion to the natives and later to the daughters of the settlers, a mission carried out in the classrooms of North America's first girls' school – the buildings still house a private school. They also cared for the *filles du roi*, marriageable orphans and peasant girls imported from France to swell the population. These girls were kept in separate rooms in the convent for surveillance by the local bachelors, who were urged to select a wife within fifteen days of the ship's arrival – a fine of three hundred livres was levied on any man who failed to take his pick within the period. Fat girls were the most desirable, as it was believed they were more inclined to stay at home and be better able to resist the winter cold.

The Ursulines' first mother superior, Marie Guyart de l'Incarnation, was widowed at age 19 and left her son with family when she entered the Ursulines de Tours monastery twelve years later. Her letters to him once she finally made it to Québec give some sharp insights into the early days of the city: "It would be hard to live here an hour without having the hands protected and without being well covered. Although the beds are covered well with quilts or blankets, scarcely can one keep warm when lying on them." Her likeness can be seen in a replica of a posthumous portrait by Pommier in the interesting little **museum** (May–Sept Tues–Sat 10am–noon & 1–5pm, Sun 1–5pm; Oct–April Tues–Sun 1–4.30pm; $4), housed in the former home of one of the first nuns. A painting by Frère Luc, though executed in France, pictures a Canadian version of the Holy Family: Joseph is shown presenting a Huron girl to Mary, while through the window one can glimpse Cap Diamant and the St Lawrence flowing past wigwams and campfires. Other paintings, documents and household items testify to the harshness of life in the colony, but lace-work and embroidery are the highlights, particularly the splendid ornamental gowns produced by the Ursulines in 1739.

Marie de l'Incarnation's remains are entombed in the oratory, but public access is limited to the adjoining **chapel** (May–Oct Tues–Sat 10–11.30am & 1.30–4.30pm, Sun 1.30–4.30pm; free), rebuilt in 1902 but retaining the sumptuous early eighteenth-cent-ury interior by sculptor Pierre-Noël Levasseur. A plaque indicates General Montcalm's resting place below the chapel, though only his skull is buried there. The collection of seventeenth and eighteenth-century paintings were acquired from France in the 1820s. Next to the museum the **Centre Marie-de-l'Incarnation** (Feb–Nov same hours as chapel; free) sells religious and historical books, and displays a few of Marie's personal effects.

Maisons Jacquet and Kent

On the corner of rue des Jardins and rue St-Louis – the main restaurant strip in Vieux-Québec – stands **Maison Jacquet**, occupied by the restaurant *Aux Anciens Canadiens*. The name comes from Québec's first novel, whose author, Philippe Aubert de Gaspé, lived here for a while in the middle of the nineteenth century. Dating from 1677, the house is another good example of seventeenth-century New France architecture, as is the blue-and-white **Maison Kent** at no. 25 on the other side of rue St-Louis, which was built in 1649. Once home of Queen Victoria's father, the Duke of Kent, it's best known as the place where the capitulation of Québec was signed in 1759.

Musée d'Art Inuit Brousseau

Between the two historic houses the delightful **Musée d'Art Inuit Brousseau**, 39 rue St-Louis (daily 9.30am–5.30pm; $6), traces the development of Inuit art from the naive works of the mid-twentieth century to the highly narrative and intricately carved sculptures by contemporary artists. The few ancient items include simple ivory works from the nomadic Dorset and Thulé cultures. Stone sculpture really began in the 1940s, replacing the declining fur and hunting industries as a source of income – the Inuit artists used aspects of everyday life such as animals and hunting for inspiration, but would also carve an ashtray if they thought they could sell it to a traveller passing through. One such man, James Houston, became convinced that these sculptures needed a wider audience and organized sales of their work in the south – the nucleus of the Brousseau's collection came from these sales, one sculpture per year. A video shows the surprisingly coarse tools used to make the graceful objects.

Jardin des Gouverneurs and around

Rue Haldimand, around the corner from the Musée d'Art Inuit, leads to the **Jardin des Gouverneurs**, whose wonderful prospect of the St Lawrence was once the exclusive privilege of the colonial governors who inhabited the Château St-Louis. The garden's Wolfe–Montcalm obelisk monument, erected in 1828, is rare in paying tribute to the victor and the vanquished. Converted merchants' houses border this grandiose area, and the nearby streets are some of the most impressive in Vieux-Québec – check out rue de la Porte and the parallel rue des Grisons on the park's west side, which boasts some fine eighteenth-century homes.

To escape the tourist hordes for a bit, follow rue Mont-Carmel, on the northern side of the square, to the almost unnoticed **Parc du Cavalier du Moulin**, a quiet little park that's perfect for a picnic. The remnant of a defensive bastion built atop Mont Carmel hill, this was part of the seventeenth-century French fortifications that protected the city's western side. You can't really see the walls from this angle, but you can see the rear facades of the houses on rue St-Louis.

From the Jardin des Gouverneurs, ave Ste-Geneviève runs west towards Porte St-Louis. En route, turn right onto rue Ste-Ursule for the **Chalmers-Wesley United Church** at no. 78 (July & Aug Mon–Fri 10am–5pm; free), built in 1852 and one of the most beautiful in the city. Its slender, Gothic Revivalist spires are a conspicuous element of the skyline and, inside the stained-glass windows are worth a look. Opposite, the 1910 **Sanctuaire de Notre Dame du Sacré-Coeur** (daily 7am–8pm; free) also has impressive stained-glass windows.

A left turn onto rue St-Louis leads to the Porte St-Louis, one of the four gates in the city wall. It's surrounded by **Parc de l'Esplanade**, the main site for the Carnaval de Québec, and departure point for the city's smart horse-drawn calèches. The park's **Centre d'interprétation des Fortifications-de-Québec**, 100 rue St-Louis (early May to early Oct daily 10am–5pm, except late June to early Sept 9am–5pm; $2.75; *www.parkscanada.gc.ca/fortifications*), includes a powder house constructed in 1815 and a dull exhibition on the fortifications. Most visitors start their 4.5-kilometre stroll around the city wall from here. You can also take a ninety-minute tour with a costumed guide for $10.

The Citadelle

Dominating the southern section of Vieux-Québec, the massive star-shaped **Citadelle** is the tour de force of Québec City's fortifications. Occupying the highest point of Cap Diamant, 100m above the St Lawrence, the site was first built on by the French, but most of the buildings were constructed by the British under orders from the Duke of Wellington, who was anxious about American attack after the War of 1812.

The complex of 25 buildings covers forty acres and is the largest North American fort still occupied by troops – it's home to the Royal 22nd Regiment, Canada's only French-speaking regiment. Around the parade ground are ranged various monuments to the campaigns of the celebrated "Van-Doos" (*vingt-deux*), as well as the summer residence of Canada's governor general and two buildings dating back to the French period: the 1750 powder magazine, now a mundane museum of military artefacts, and the Cap Diamant Redoubt, built in 1693 and thus one of the oldest parts of the Citadelle.

In addition to entertaining hour-long **guided tours** around the Citadelle (daily: April 10am–4pm; May & June 9am–5pm; July & Aug 9am–6pm; Sept 9am–4pm; Oct 10am–3pm; $6; *www.lacitadelle.qc.ca*), other activities include the colourful **Changing of the Guard** (mid-June to early Sept daily 10am) and the **Beating of the Retreat** tattoo (July & Aug Wed–Sat 6pm).

The Parliament Buildings

Sweeping out from Porte St-Louis and flanked by grand Victorian mansions, the tree-lined boulevard of **Grande-Allée** is proclaimed the city's equivalent of the Champs Élysées, with its bustling restaurants, hotels and bars. Adjacent to the *Loews Le Concorde* hotel, Place Montcalm has a monument to Montcalm and a more recent statue of Charles de Gaulle, the French president who declared "Vive le Québec libre" in the 1960s, much to the separatists' delight. This area is now known as Parliament Hill, a new name that caused a lot of controversy, as Canada's Parliament area in Ottawa has the same title and anglophones thought it presumptuous of Québec City to label itself like a capital city. However, there is indeed a hill here, and upon it, at the eastern end of Grande-Allée, stand the stately buildings of the **Hôtel du Parlement** (late June to early Sept Mon–Fri 9am–4.30pm, Sat & Sun 10am–4.30pm; early Sept to late June Mon–Fri 9am–4.30pm; *www.assnat.qc.ca*), designed by Eugène-Étienne Taché in 1877 in the Second Empire style using the Louvre for inspiration. The ornate facade includes niches for twelve bronze statues by Québécois sculptor Louis-Philippe Hébert of Canada's and Québec's major statesmen, while finely chiselled and gilded walnut panels in the entrance hall depict important moments in Québec's history, coats of arms and other heraldic features. From here the corridor of the President's Gallery, lined with portraits of all the Legislative Assembly's speakers and presidents, leads to the Chamber of the National Assembly, where the 125 provincial representatives meet for debate.

National Battlefields Park

Westward of the Citadelle are the rolling grasslands of the **National Battlefields Park**, a sizeable chunk of land stretching along the cliffs above the St Lawrence. The park encompasses the historic **Plains of Abraham**, which were named after Abraham Martin, the first pilot of the St Lawrence River in 1620. The Plains were to become the site on which Canada's history was rewritten. In June 1759 a large British force led by **General Wolfe** sailed up the St Lawrence to besiege **General Montcalm** in Québec City. From the end of July until early September the British forces shuttled up and down the south side of the river, raking the city with cannon fire. Montcalm and the governor, Vaudreuil, became convinced that Wolfe planned a direct assault on the citadel from Anse de Foulon (Wolf's Cove), the only handy break in the cliff face – opinion confirmed when lookouts observed a British detachment surveying Cap Diamant from across the river in Lévis. Montcalm thus strengthened the defences above Anse de Foulon, but made the mistake of withdrawing the regiment stationed on the Plains themselves. The following night the British performed the extraordinary feat, which even Wolfe had considered "a desperate plan", of scaling the cliff below the Plains via Anse de Foulon, and on the morning of September 16 Montcalm awoke to find the British drawn up a couple of kilometres from the city's gate. The hastily assembled French battalions, flanked by aboriginal warriors, were badly organized and rushed headlong at the British, whose volleys of gunfire mortally wounded Montcalm. On his deathbed Montcalm wrote a chivalrous note of congratulations to Wolfe, not knowing that he was dead. Québec City surrendered four days later. The park's **Discovery Pavilion**, below the tourist office at 835 ave Wilfrid-Laurier est (May–Oct daily 11am–5.30pm except Mon Sept–Oct), has maps, information panels and a short film.

The dead of 1759 are commemorated by a statue of Joan of Arc in a beautifully maintained sunken garden just off ave Wilfrid-Laurier at Place Montcalm by the Ministry of Justice. More conspicuous, standing out amid the wooded parklands, scenic drives, jogging paths and landscaped gardens, are two Martello towers, built between 1805 and 1812 for protection against the Americans. Martello Tower 2, on the corner of Wilfrid-Laurier and Taché, is only open to school groups, whilst **Martello Tower 1** (June & Sept to mid-Oct Sat & Sun 10am–5.30pm; late June to early Sept daily 10am–5.30pm; $3.50), further south in the park, has superb views of the St Lawrence from its rooftop lookout. The views are almost as good from the base of the tower, and you don't have to pay for an unmemorable exhibition in order to reach the top; children get to dress up in costumes for the optional tour. Further west, outside the Musée du Québec, there's a monument to General Wolfe, whose body was shipped back to England for burial, pickled in a barrel of rum. Beyond the park's western peripheries, cannons ring the perimeter of a large playing field and there's another lookout point above where Côte Gilmour winds down the cliffs at Anse de Foulon.

The Musée du Québec

Canadian art had its quiet beginnings in Québec City three hundred years ago, and the full panoply of subsequent Québécois art can be found in the 20,000-strong collection of the **Musée du Québec**, whose bright, glassy entrance is at the foot of rue Wolfe-Montcalm, on the western edge of Parc de Champs-de-Batailles (June to early Sept Mon–Tues & Thurs–Sun 10am–6pm, Wed 10am–9pm; early Sept to May Tues & Thurs–Sun 11am–5pm, Wed 11am–9pm; $7, free on Wed Sept–May only; *www.mdq.org*). If you don't fancy walking, bus #11 connects Vieux-Québec to avenue Wolfe-Montcalm along Grande-Allée. As you face the entrance hall, the museum's original Neo classical building, now known as the Gérard-Morisset Pavilion, is to the right; and the recently renovated Victorian prison, renamed the Charles-Baillairgé Pavilion, is to the left.

It's a bit of a shame that the Musée du Québec's impressive permanent collection is no longer on display to the degree that it once was, but the space freed up does allow for touring exhibitions in addition to artist or movement-specific shows using parts of the collection as the nucleus. A good survey of Québécois art up to 1945 can be found in the two galleries on the top level of the **Gérard-Morisset Pavilion**, though. The first of these hosts "Québec, l'art d'une capitale nationale", which covers the period from the beginnings of Québécois art in the early seventeenth century until the end of the nineteenth century. **Religious art** dominates the earliest works, which coincide with Québec City's role as the capital of New France until the British conquest. The influential output of painter **Frère Luc**, a former assistant to Poussin, can be seen in *The Guardian Angel* (1671), depicting the story of Tobias and the archangel Raphael. Sculptures in this period were also heavily influenced by Catholic themes as Québec churches were the primary art commissioners at the time. The most notable contributions to the collection are by two dynasties: the works of brothers **Pierre-Noël** and **François-Noël Levasseur** from the mid-1700s displayed here capped a century of family achievements. Three generations of Baillairgés succeeded them, their copious output including the architecture of churches as well as their interior decoration, evidenced by **François Baillairgé**'s pulpit for the old church in Baie-St-Paul.

Under the British, Québec City's next incarnation as a capital saw a broadening in subject matter with a penchant for portraiture among the middle and upper classes. The bourgeoisie's favourite portrait painter was **Antoine Plamondon**, who trained in Paris under Charles X's court painter Guérin, himself a pupil of the classicist David – a lineage evident in Plamondon's poised *Madame Tourangeau* (1842). **Théophile Hamel**, a pupil of Plamondon, combined what he learned from his tour around Europe in the 1840s – the palette of Rubens and the draughtsmanship of the Flemish masters – in his *Self-portrait in the Studio*, painted soon after his return. The first artist to depict Canadian landscapes was the Québec-born **Joseph Légaré**, whose sympathy with radical French-Canadians led to his imprisonment after the 1837 Rebellion. His *View of the Fire in the Saint-Jean District of Quebec City, Looking West* – depicting the 1845 conflagration that made 10,000 homeless – is the most powerful of his many paintings recording local scenes and events. His contemporary, Amsterdam-born **Cornelius Krieghoff**, became one of the best-known artists of the period for his romanticized landscapes of Québec-area landmarks. Unfortunately, only one is on display – *Indian Encampment at Lac Saint-Charles* – painted in 1854, the year after he arrived in Québec City.

The adjacent gallery, "Tradition et modernité au Québec", covers the **modernist period** of Québécois art, contrasting the changing tastes and styles between the 1860s and 1940s through paintings, prints, drawings, decorative arts and sculpture. In the first part of the exhibition, paintings fight for space on the walls, much as they would have in a late-nineteenth century *salon*. The subsequent decades are a tug-of-war of styles, as European movements had a strong impact on Québécois artists visiting or studying there at the time. Although born in Ontario, **Horatio Walker** moved to Québec in the 1880s and became completely engrossed in the lives of the French-Canadian *habitants*, as shown in his *The Return from the Wedding* (1930). The European influence made itself felt in sculpture throughout this period as well, largely due to Rodin, as evidenced in **Alfred Laliberté**'s bronzes and the plaster works of **Marc-Aurèle de Foy Suzor-Côte**. The latter is perhaps better known for his paintings, which also have a Parisian influence: *Cartier Meets the Indians at Stadacona* (1907) was painted shortly after his return, and the contrast between impressionistic style and traditional subject is emblematic of the entire exhibition.

The works of the Group of Seven (see box, p.86) are more usually associated with the remote wilds of Ontario, but **Arthur Lismer**, one of the Group's founders, visited Charlevoix many times, producing pieces such as *Québec Village, Ste-Hilarion* (1925). Urban life at the time is admirably recorded by **Adrien Hébert**. *Rue St-Denis* (1927) wonderfully captures the spirit of Montréal in the 1920s with the chic cut of a woman's coat contrasting with an ever-omnipresent church in the background. The contemporaneous **Marc-Aurèle Fortin**'s best works were his impressionistic renditions of trees, as seen in *The Elm at Pont-Viau*, where one gigantic tree of numerous intense greens dominates the entire riverscape. The modernism of Matisse and Picasso was introduced to Canada by **Alfred Pellan**, who returned from Paris in 1940 to teach at Montréal's École des Beaux-Arts. Pellan's comparative radicalism is best represented by his *Young Woman with a White Collar* (1934).

The only permanent **contemporary** exhibition is a room devoted to **Jean-Paul Riopelle** on the ground floor of the Gérard-Morisset Pavilion. As you enter, you are immediately confronted by his *Sun Spray* (1954), a large canvas that feels like a stained-glass mosaic and leaves no doubt regarding his abstract leanings. The principal work, and the impetus for devoting the gallery to him, is *L'Hommage à Rosa Luxemburg* (1992), a forty-metre-long triptych, whose thirty segments create a narrative and "a painted metaphor for his life and art". The title of the piece is misleading, though – it was more of a reaction to the death of his companion of 25 years, the American painter Joan Mitchell, and the ghostly spray-painted outlines – made by placing objects both natural and man-made on the canvas – seem to suggest this sudden void. Nearby, what appear at first glance to be map cabinets have pull-out drawers – an ingenious way to put as many etchings and lithographs on display as possible.

In the **Charles-Baillairgé Pavilion**, the red-brick interior walls of the former jail have been spruced up, creating a warm atmosphere in sharp contrast to the sombre grey stonework that prevails outside. Vaillancourt's *Tree on rue Durocher* sweeps up into the atrium, which leads to the temporary galleries and a few of the old prison cells. Look out for the prison's tower, where Montréal sculptor David Moore has created a unique two-storey sculpture of huge wooden torsos and legs that scale the walls and a central figure that dives from the summit. The building also shares space with the Centre d'Interprétation de Champs Batailles ($3.50). Give it a miss – the disjointed narrative and sometimes unclear visuals of the centre's multimedia show don't do a great job of telling the history of the Plains of Abraham. Do have a look to see if the free temporary exhibits by the entrance are worthwhile, though.

Basse-Ville

The birthplace of Québec City, **Basse-Ville** (Lower Town), can be reached from Terrasse Dufferin either by the steep **escalier casse-cou** (Breakneck Stairs) or by the **funicular** alongside (daily 7.30am–11pm, until midnight in summer; $1.25; *www.funiculaire-quebec.com*), which turned out, in October 1996, to be far more dangerous than the stairs when a cable snapped and it plummeted – two people were killed and a dozen others injured. It reopened in 1998 and again ferries tourists between the upper and lower parts of the city. The Basse-Ville station of the funicular is the 1683 **Maison Louis-Jolliet**, 16 Petit-Champlain, built for the retired discoverer of the Mississippi, Louis Jolliet; it now houses a second-rate souvenir shop.

Dating back to 1685, the narrow, cobbled **rue du Petit-Champlain** is the city's oldest street, and the surrounding area – known as **Quartier du Petit-Champlain** – is the oldest shopping area in North America. The boutiques and art shops in the quaint seventeenth- and eighteenth-century houses are not too overpriced and offer an array of excellent crafts, from weird and wonderful ceramics to Inuit carvings. Older artefacts can be seen closer to the river, on the corner of boulevard Champlain and rue du Marché Champlain, where the 1752 **Maison Chevalier** and two adjoining nineteenth-century merchant houses – Maison Chesnay and Maison Fréort – are now used by the Musée de la Civilisation to depict interior scenes comprising period furniture, costumes, toys, folk art and domestic objects (May to late June & early Sept to Oct Tues–Sun 10am–5pm; late June to early Sept daily 9.30am–5pm; Nov–April Sat & Sun 10am–5pm; free).

Place-Royale

From here it's a short walk along rue Notre Dame to **Place-Royale**, where Champlain built New France's first permanent settlement in 1608, to begin trading fur with the aboriginal peoples. The square – known as Place du Marché until the bust of Louis XIV erected here in 1686 – remained the focal point of Canadian commerce until 1759, and after the fall of Québec the British continued using the area as a lumber market, vital for shipbuilding during the Napoleonic Wars. After 1860 Place-Royale was left to fall into disrepair, a situation reversed as recently as the 1970s, when the scruffy area was renovated. Its pristine stone houses, most of which date from around 1685, are undeniably photogenic, with their steep metal roofs, numerous chimneys and pastel-coloured shutters, but it's a Legoland townscape, devoid of the scars of history. Fortunately, the atmosphere is enlivened in summer by entertainment from classical orchestras to jug-gling clowns, and by the Fêtes de la Nouvelle-France, when everyone dresses in period costume and it once again becomes a chaotic marketplace.

In Maison Hazeur, a seventeenth-century merchant's house, the **interpretive centre** at 27 rue Notre Dame (late June to mid-Oct daily 10am–5.30pm; mid-Oct to late June Tues–Sun 10am–5pm; $3), outlines the stormy past of Place-Royale, the mercantile aspects and the changes in the look of the square from the days when it was inhabited by the Iroquois to its recent renovation. Domestic objects and arrowheads are on the upper floors, from where you can see Gille's Girard's *À rebrousse-temps*, an enigmatic three-storey sculpture that plays with the idea of determining an artefact's original pur-pose. The vaulted cellars have modern-looking displays of 1800s domestic scenes; kids can try on period costumes.

The **Église Notre Dame-des-Victoires** (daily 9am–4.30pm), on the west side of the square, nearly always has a wedding in progress during the summer. It was instigated by Laval in 1688 but has been completely restored twice – after being destroyed by shellfire in 1759 and after a fire in 1969. Inside, the fortress-shaped altar alludes to the two French victories over the British navy that gave the church its name: the destruc-tion of Admiral Phipp's fleet by Frontenac in 1690 and the sinking of Sir Hovenden Walker's fleet in 1711. Above the altar, paintings depicting these events hang by copies of religious paintings by Van Dyck, Van Loo and Boyermans, gifts from early settlers to give thanks for a safe passage. The model ship suspended in the nave has a similar ori-gin.

The Musée de la Civilisation

Rue de la Place leads to **Place de Paris**, where a modern sculpture called *Dialogue with History* marks the disembarkation place of the first settlers from France. Close by, the **Batterie Royal**, trimly restored in the 1970s, was used to defend the city during the siege of 1759. The **ferry to Lévis** (6.30am–2.20am; June–Sept $2.25, Oct–May $1.80; see p.277) leaves from one block south, while a walk north along rue Dalhousie brings you to Québec City's most impressive and dynamic museum, the **Musée de la Civilisation**, 85 rue Dalhousie (late June to early Sept daily 10am–7pm; early Sept to late June Tues–Sun 10am–5pm; $7, free on Tues Sept–June; *www.mcq.org*). Designed by Canada's top-rank modern architect, Moshe Safdie, the building reflects the steeply pitched roofs of Québec's earliest architecture and has won numerous awards for the way it blends with the historic surroundings. It actually incorporates three historic structures, including the two-storey merchant's house called the Maison Estèbe, whose vaulted cellars now contain an excellent gift shop.

Concentrating primarily on Canada but also diversifying into a wider perspective, the museum presents various changing exhibitions ranging from soap operas to immigra-tion. Other than the foyer sculpture, Astri Reusch's *La Débâcle*, which symbolizes the break-up of the ice in the spring thaw, there are two permanent exhibitions. "Memories" is a labyrinth that expertly displays life in Québec from the early days of the settlers to the present. "Encounter with the First Nations", set up in consultation with all eleven of the First Nations of Québec, presents the history and culture of these earlier residents using artefacts and videotaped oral histories; the larger items – includ-ing a *rabaska*, a large birchbark canoe used by the Atikamekw – were crafted in recent years.

Vieux-Port and around

To the east and north, near the confluence of the St Charles and the St Lawrence rivers, lies the **Vieux-Port de Québec**, the busiest harbour in the province until its eclipse by Montréal. Much of the harbour has been renovated as a recreational area, with the-atres, yuppie flats, sheltered walkways, restaurants and a marina packed with pleasure boats and yachts. A remodelled cement plant bordering the Bassin Louise at 100 rue St-André now hosts an **interpretive centre** for the Vieux-Port (daily: May to early Sept 10am–5pm; early Sept to mid-Oct 1–5pm; rest of year by reservation: ☎648-3300, *www.parkscanada.gc.ca/vieuxport;* $3), housing a display on the lumber trade and shipbuilding in the nineteenth century. Nearby, along the basin, the **Marché du Vieux-Port** (March–Nov daily from 8am) is a throwback to how the port used to be – its busy market stalls selling cheap, fresh produce from the local area.

Also on the south side of the Bassin Louise, the next street down from St-André is rue St-Paul, heart of Québec's **antiques district**. Numerous cluttered antique shops, art galleries, cafés and restaurants now occupy warehouses and offices abandoned after the demise of the port. From rue St-Paul the steep Côte du Colonel Dambourgès leads to rue des Remparts on the northern borders of the Quartier Latin.

The Cartier-Brébeuf National Historic Site

Northwest of Vieux-Québec, on the banks of the St-Charles River (bus #3 or #4), the **Cartier-Brébeuf National Historic Site**, 175 de l'Espinay (daily: May to early Sept 10am–5pm; early Sept to mid-Oct 1–4pm; $3; *www.parkscanada.gc.ca/brebeuf*) has a double claim to fame. It marks the spot where Jacques Cartier spent the winter of 1535–36 in friendly contact with the people of the surrounding Iroquoian villages – a cordial start to a relationship that Cartier later soured by taking a local chief and nine of his men hostage. It is also where Jean de Brébeuf, with his Jesuit friends, built his first Canadian residence in 1625: Brébeuf is best known for his martyrdom near today's Midland in Ontario (see p.137). The **interpretive centre** features an excellent account of Cartier's voyages and of the hardship he and his crew endured during the winter. The guided tour of the site (included in the entrance fee) leads to a mock-up of an Iroquoian longhouse and sweat lodge set within a palisade, where costumed guides demonstrate daily tasks, mostly to the benefit of the kids. Keep an eye out for the resident muskrat.

Eating

It is when you start **eating** in Québec City that the French ancestry of the Québécois hits all the senses: the eateries of the city present an array of culinary delights adopted from the mother country, from beautifully presented gourmet dishes to humble baguettes.

Whether you are on a tight budget or not, Québec's lively **cafés** are probably where you will want to spend your time, washing down bowls of soup and croutons (toasted baguettes dripping with cheese) with plenty of coffee. Decked out in a variety of decors, traditional to stylish, they are always buzzing with activity, as students and workers drop in throughout the day. As you might expect, Vieux-Québec is home to most of the gourmet **restaurants** and cafés, but other areas – notably along rue St-Jean (quirky and cheaper) and Grande-Allée (generally touristy and expensive), just outside the city walls – have their fair share. Your best bet for good-value mid-price restaurants is to head for avenue Cartier near the Musée du Québec, with its numerous terrace-fronted restaurants.

Snacks and cafés

A.L. Van Houtte, 995 Place D'Youville. Reliable chain with sandwiches and salads until 11pm. Internet access for $6 per hour.

Bistro St-Jean, 481 rue St-Jean. Café/restaurant that serves late breakfasts and decent hamburgers.

Bouche Bée, 383 rue St-Paul. Cheap café in Basse-Ville, serving sandwiches, quiches, soups and the like.

Brûlerie Tatum Café, 1084 rue St-Jean. All-day omelettes and light snacks. Exposed brick walls and roasting coffee beans provide ambience.

Café Buade, 31 rue Buade. In a central location, with good light breakfasts and passable bistro fare throughout the day. It's nicer upstairs. Open from 7am.

Buffet de l'Antiquaire, 95 rue St-Paul. An institution, popular with locals for breakfast and home-cooked comfort food like *poutine* and *pâté chinois* (shepherd's pie).

Chez Temporal, 25 rue Couillard. Bowls of steaming *café au lait*, croissants and *chocolatines* make this Quartier Latin café, a few doors from the *Auberge de la Paix* hostel, a perfect place for breakfast. Soups and sandwiches are also available until 1.30am.

Dazibo Café, 526 rue St-Jean. Full Irish breakfast (11am–3pm). Soda bread and light meals help to soak up the best Guinness in town. Closed Mon.

L'Omelette, 66 rue St-Louis. Reasonable tourist joint with omelette specialities; breakfast from 7am.

Café Retro, 1129 rue St-Jean. Well-priced if touristy café/restaurant; serves everything from sandwiches to T-bone steaks.

Ste-Ursule Smoked Meat, 7 rue Ste-Ursule. Carnivore heaven: stacked slices of smoked meat on rye for $5.

Restaurants

In Québec's finer **restaurants** high-quality French cuisine is easy to come by and, although prices tend to be rather high, even the poshest restaurants have cheaper lunch-time and table d'hôte menus. For a change of taste, the dishes of other countries are also represented, including Italian, Greek, Swiss and Thai – as well as the good old hamburger. Strangely though, typical French-Canadian cooking – game with sweet sauces followed by simple desserts with lashings of maple syrup – is available at very few places in town, although the many *cabanes à sucre* on Île d'Orléans (see p.276) offer typical meals to tourists.

On and around rue St-Jean

Casse-Crêpe Breton, 1136 rue St-Jean (☎692-0438). Diner-style restaurant where crepes are made in front of you with two or three fillings, costing $5. There's often a queue, but it moves quickly.

Le Commensal, 860 rue St-Jean (☎647-3733). Great spot for vegetarians. Buffet where the food is sold by weight.

La Crémaillère, 21 rue St-Stanislas (☎692-2216). Superior European cuisine at reasonable prices; advance booking advised. Recommended.

Les Frères de la Côte, 1190 rue St-Jean (☎692-5445). Very friendly bistro with snails, smoked salmon and great mussels and pizzas on the menu.

Le Hobbit, 700 rue St-Jean (☎647-2677). One of the best bargains around, with great vegetarian food and a good studenty atmosphere; advance booking advised.

La Maison de Serge Bruyère, 1200 rue St-Jean (☎694-0618). Three restaurants under one roof: the *Restaurant la Grande Table* is one of the best in the city, serving fresh produce, beautifully prepared and presented. The eight-course *ménu de dégustation* is $150 per person including wine; reservations are standard. Closed Sun & Mon. *Chez Livernois Bistro*, downstairs, is more affordable.

Au Petit Coin Breton, 1029 rue St-Jean (☎694-0758). A pretty good and reasonably priced specialist creperie, where servers wear traditional Breton costume – it may put you in the mood.

Le Petit Coin Latin, 8.5 rue Ste-Ursule (☎692-2022). Cosy café/bistro with a secluded courtyard.

Piazzetta, 707 rue St-Jean (☎529-7489). Trendy pizzeria with funky furnishings – the pizzas come close to perfection and are dead cheap.

On and around rue St-Louis

L'Apsara, 71 rue d'Auteuil (☎694-0232). Cambodian, Vietnamese and Thai food in Vieux-Québec near Porte St-Louis. Three-course lunch is around $10, dinners in the $30 region.

Aux Anciens Canadiens, 34 rue St-Louis (☎692-1627). This expensive (table d'hôte from $30) and touristy restaurant is in one of the oldest homes in Québec City. It serves typical Québécois food like duck glazed with maple syrup, turkey in hazelnut sauce, and lamb in blueberry-wine sauce. As a side dish, baked beans gain a whole new meaning; for pudding there's blueberry tart or maple-syrup pie.

Le Continental, 26 rue St-Louis (☎694-9995). Old-fashioned place down the street from the *Château Frontenac*. Their three-course table d'hôte is $28–38.

Café de la Paix, 44 rue des Jardins (☎692-1430). The desserts in the front window taste as good as they look – and the rest of the menu is equally delicious. Closed Sun.

Au Parmesan, 38 rue St-Louis (☎693-0341). Bland Italian and French food, but popular with tourists because of its central Haute-Ville location and better prices than some of its neighbours. Accordion players roam the room.

La Primavera, 73 rue St-Louis (☎694-0030). The specialities here include pizzas from a wood-burning oven and mouthwatering mussels.

Le St-Amour, 48 rue Ste-Ursule (☎694-0667). Romantic French restaurant with a glass-roofed courtyard. Excellent food at around $80 for two.

Vieux-Québec's Basse-Ville

Aviatic Club, Gare du Palais (☎522-3555). Surprisingly good international cuisine in the train station. Sushi plates from $20.

Le Cochon Dingue, 46 boul Champlain (☎692-2013). Fun and reasonably priced pasta-and-burger bistro.

Le Délice du Roy, 33 rue St-Pierre (☎694-9161). Around the corner from Place-Royale, this canteen-style place dishes up traditional Québécois food at reasonable prices.

L'Échaudé, 72 rue du Sault-au-Matelot (☎692-1299). Behind rue St-Pierre. Upscale bistro with a relaxed atmosphere and a good selection of wines.

Initiale, 54 rue St-Pierre (☎694-1818). One of Québec City's best restaurants. A chic place with a lighter take on fine French classics.

Le Lapin Sauté, 52 rue du Petit-Champlain (☎692-5325). Very popular, informal restaurant specializing in rabbit.

Laurie Raphael, 117 rue Dalhousie (☎692-4555). Warm and relaxed atmosphere in a restaurant that is very popular and needs reservations. The food is beautifully presented with fish being a speciality.

Le Marie Clarisse, 12 rue du Petit-Champlain (☎692-0857). Fine fish restaurant in Basse-Ville, serving a three-course meal for $40–45; advance booking advised. A good spot for people-watching.

Le Café du Monde, 57 rue Dalhousie (☎692-4455). Fairly pricey and chic bistro.

Poisson d'Avril, 115 quai St-André (☎692-1010). Seafood and grilled steaks near the Vieux-Port.

On and around Place d'Armes

Au Café Suisse, 32 rue Ste-Anne (☎694-1320). Touristy fondue place, which is good for people-watching, as the restaurant spills out onto the pedestrian-only part of Ste-Anne in the heart of Vieux-Québec.

Charles Baillairgé, *Hôtel Clarendon*, 57 rue Ste-Anne (☎692-2480). Opened in 1870, this is supposedly Canada's oldest restaurant and serves classic French cuisine. Expensive, and dress is formal.

Gambrinus, 15 rue du Fort (☎692-5144). Excellent Italian and French food in the shadow of *Château Frontenac*, with seafood specialities; advance booking advised.

Grande-Allée

L'Astral, 1225 Place Montcalm (☎647-2222). Rotating restaurant on the top floor of the *Hôtel Loews le Concorde*. The food is generally expensive but the views can't be beaten. The all-you-can-eat Buffet Royal costs $40.95.

Cosmos Café, 575 Grande-Allée est (☎640-0606). By far the best spot on the Grande-Allée – cool decor, great breakfasts and imaginative menu. Crowded and lively at lunch and for the *cinq à sept* cocktail hour.

VooDoo Grill, 575 Grande-Allée est (☎647-2000). Above *Cosmos*. Mid-priced Southeast Asian dishes and grilled sandwiches for $10. African art creates the mood.

Avenue Cartier

Le Cochon Dingue, 46 boul René-Lévesque ouest (☎523-2013). Close to ave Cartier, sister joint to the branch in Basse-Ville.

Garam Massala, 1114 ave Cartier (☎522-4979). Indian restaurant in a cosy basement. Dinner for two is around $35.

Le Graffiti, 1191 ave Cartier (☎529-4949). Chic French-Italian restaurant that also does a good Sunday brunch.

Café Krieghoff, 1089 ave Cartier (☎522-3711). A typical French bistro *à la Québécois* that's a local favourite. Good spot to sit and read or write in the day, especially on the terrace.

L'Olive Noire, 64 boul René-Lévesque ouest (☎521-5959). On the corner of ave Cartier. Pasta, seafood and meat dishes accompanied by a good selection of ports and scotches.

Pizzadélic, 1145 ave Cartier (☎525-5981). Trendy spot with creative pizzas and pastas and a large, packed terrace.

Bars and nightlife

Nightlife in Québec City is far more relaxed than in Montréal: an evening spent in an intimate bar or a jazz or blues soiree is more popular than a big gig or disco, except among the younger set. Few major bands tour here, except during the Festival d'Été in July, when everyone lets their hair down. Québec City's main bar and nightclub strip is around St-Jean – the stretch outside the city walls in the Faubourg St-Jean-Baptiste has studenty bars and gay nightspots. Places on Grand-Allée tend to cater to tourists, but there are a few decent spots mixed in. For up-to-date **information** on the goings-on, check out the listings section in the French daily newspapers *Le Soleil* and *Journal de Québec* and the free weekly newspaper *Voir*. The quarterly bilingual magazine for tourists *Voilà Québec* also carries information, as does the English *Québec Chronicle Telegraph*, published every Wednesday.

Bars and live music

L'Amour Sorcier, 789 Côte Ste-Geneviève. Popular, intimate lesbian bar with cheap beers, soft music and roof terrace.

Chez Son Père, 24 rue St-Stanislas. Just off St-Jean in Vieux-Québec, above street level. Québécois folk singers create a great thigh-slapping atmosphere. Free admission.

Le Drague, 804 rue St-Augustin. A gay bar, café and nightclub, with cheap imported beers. Sunday night drag shows are great fun.

L'Emprise, *Hôtel Clarendon*, 57 rue Ste-Anne. Art Deco surroundings attract a sophisticated touristy crowd to evenings of smooth jazz and blues.

L'Étrange, 275 rue St-Jean. Relaxed alternative-rock bar with regular two-for-one specials.

Le Fou Bar, 525 rue St-Jean. Trendy, packed student bar.

Fourmi Atomik, 33 rue d'Auteuil. The best alternative bar in Vieux-Québec, with cheap beers, snacks, pool tables and loud music. Lively terrace fills up when the sun's out.

L'Inox, 37 rue St-André. The city's lone brewpub, serving fine cheeses to go with the fine ales.

Jules et Jim, 1060 ave Cartier. Long-time local hangout, it's a small, quiet place amidst all the restaurants on ave Cartier.

Kashmir, 1018 rue St-Jean. Loud and packed full some nights, dead others, depending on the DJ or the band playing.

Lazyboy, 811 rue St-Jean. Low-key gay bar with pool tables above *Le Ballon Rouge*.

Le Mâle, 770 Côte Ste-Catherine. Rough and ready gay bar. Men only.

Le Pape-Georges, 8 rue Cul-de-Sac, near Place Royale. Small wine bar with traditional folk singing.

Pub Java, 1112 ave Cartier. Good selection of imported and draught beers and you can even come back for Sunday brunch.

Le Pub St-Alexandre, 1087 rue St-Jean. More than 200 beers and 40 single malts in this yuppie English-style pub.

Le Rappel, 972 rue St-Jean. Blues bands in an intimate venue between La Capitole and the city walls. Bands play Wed–Sun from 10pm.

Sacrilège, 447 rue St-Jean. Friendly watering hole with a popular terrace in back in the Faubourg St-Jean-Baptiste.

Voyages en Alsace, 63 rue St-Paul. German-Alsatian bar/brasserie with the appropriate cuisine.

Clubs and discos

Absolute, 1170 rue d'Artigny. Dance-music club that's popular with the student crowd.

Le Ballon Rouge, 811 rue St-Jean. Gay male disco, with loud, good music and free entry.

Chez Charlotte, 575 Grande-Allée est. Live music and Latin dancing in a loungey atmosphere.

Chez Dagobert, 600 Grande-Allée est. A huge club in a renovated warehouse, with its dance floor upstairs and a stage for mainly rock bands downstairs, it draws a very young crowd. Free unless a band is playing.

Maurice, 575 Grande-Allée est. Happening club with different DJs each night.

Merlin, 1175 rue Cartier. Young, chic Québécois disco hangout.

Scanner, 291 rue St-Vallier est. Two-floor club with live bands and techno nights, down the hill from the Faubourg St-Jean-Baptiste.

Entertainment and festivals

Québec City is not especially renowned for its high culture, but from May to September there are **dance**, **theatre** and **music** events at various outdoor venues, and throughout the year performances can be caught at the city's theatres. The liveliest periods are in February and July, when the entire city is animated by its two principal **festivals**: the excellent Carnaval and the equally frenzied Festival d'Eté. Tickets for most events can be purchased through the Admission agency (☎1-800/361-4595, *www.admission.com*).

Theatre

Québec City has a fair smattering of **theatres**, all producing plays in French only. The city's main theatre for the performing arts is the Grand Théâtre de Québec, 269 boul René-Lévesque est (☎643-8131), which has a sound programme of drama, as well as opera, dance shows and classical music concerts. Other main theatres include Le Palais Montcalm, 995 Place D'Youville (☎670-9011), and Salle Albert-Rousseau, 2410 chemin Ste-Foy (☎659-6710). For small-scale dramatic productions, check out the Théâtre de la Bordée, 1143 rue St-Jean (☎694-9631), and Théâtre Le Capitole, 972 rue St-Jean (☎694-4444).

Open-air **summer theatres** are particularly popular in Québec. The largest is the Agora, in the Vieux-Port at 120 rue Dalhousie (☎648-4370), a huge amphitheatre used for a range of productions from comedies to classical music. A summer-long programme of activities is also enacted on open stages in the Jardins de l'Hôtel-de-Ville; at the Parc de la Francophonie beside Grande-Allée, just beyond the Parliament Buildings; on the Plains of Abraham near the Citadelle and in the Place D'Youville.

Music

Canada's oldest symphony orchestra, **L'Orchestre Symphonique de Québec**, performs at the Grand Théâtre. Other classical concerts can be caught at the Bibliothèque Gabrielle-Roy, 350 rue St-Joseph est (☎529-0924). In Place d'Youville and Place Royale, there are various free classical music concerts in the summer, and the Agora is used for summer concerts too. Seventeenth- and eighteenth-century music is performed at the chapel in the Séminaire in summer as well.

Lake of Two Rivers, Algonquin Provincial Park, Ontario

Moose statue, Toronto

Beaver

CHRIS COE/AXIOM

Downtown Toronto, Ontario

CHRIS COE/AXIOM

Parliament Buildings, Ottawa, Ontario

CHRIS COE/AXIOM

Niagara Falls and the *Maid of the Mist*, Ontario

Château Frontenac, Québec City, Québec

A harbour in Nova Scotia

Old houses in winter, Montréal, Québec

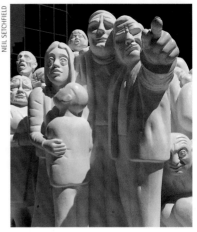

The Illuminated Crowd, Montréal, Québec

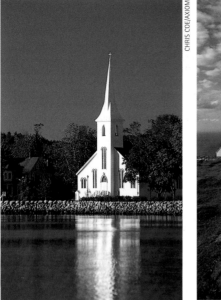
CHRIS COE/AXIOM

JOHN ZAHARA

A church at Mahone Bay, Nova Scotia   Lighthouse at Cape Spear, Newfoundland

B&C ALEXANDER

Fishing boats iced in at Rose Blanche, Newfoundland

Cinema

The city has a smattering of **cinemas**, mostly out in the suburbs – the most convenient are the multiplexes in Ste-Foy, which usually have some undubbed English films when they first come out, as well as Québécois and French movies: Cinéplex Odéon Ste-Foy, 1200 boul Duplessis (☎871-1550) and Star Cité Ste-Foy, 1150 boul Duplessis (☎874-0255). Films are often listed under their English titles, but make sure that it says "v.o.a." (original English version) or "s-t.f." (in the original language but with French subtitles). Cinéma le Clap, also in Ste-Foy at no. 2360 chemin Ste-Foy (☎650-2527, *www.clap.qc.ca* bus; #7), is the city's rep cinema. The Theatre IMAX, 5401 boul des Galeries (☎627-4629; bus #60) shows films that take full advantage of the immense visuals and wraparound sound.

Festivals

Québec City is renowned for two large annual **festivals**. The eleven-day **Carnaval de Québec** (*www.carnaval.qc.ca*) is in freezing early February, when large quantities of the lethal but warming local brew, *caribou*, are consumed amid parades and ice-sculpture competitions, all presided over by the mascot snowman called Bonhomme Carnaval. In early July, the ten-day **Festival d'Été** (*www.infofestival.com*) is an equally cheery affair, especially as the provincial law prohibiting drink on the streets is temporarily revoked. The largest festival of francophone culture in North America attracts hundreds of artists, and everyone is roped into the celebration, with restaurants offering discounts and all of Québec's major performers pitching up to dance, make music and lead the party from massive open-air stages all over town.

Summer's **Fêtes de la Nouvelle France** (*www.nouvellefrance.qc.ca*) returns Basse-Ville to the seventeenth and eighteenth centuries. It's great fun if you're in the mood: thousands of Québécois from around the province dress up in period costume, often ones they've sewn themselves. It is also worth being in the city on **St-Jean Baptiste** Day on June 24, the provincial holiday, when an outpouring of Québécois pride spills onto the streets in a massive celebration, with the entire city decked with thousands of fleur-de-lis flags.

Listings

Airlines Air Canada and Air Alliance, Aéroport de Québec (☎692-0770 or 1-800/630-3299); Canadian Airlines, Aéroport de Québec (☎692-1031 or 1-800/665-1177), Continental Airlines (☎1-800/231-0856).

Banks and exchange American Express, Place Laurier, 2700 boul Laurier, Ste-Foy; Banque Royale, 700 Place d'Youville and 140 Grande-Allée est. Caisse Populaire Desjardins du Vieux-Québec, 19 rue des Jardins (summer daily 9am–6pm; winter Mon, Tues & Fri 9.30am–3pm, Wed & Thurs 9.30am–6pm) has exchange facilities and a cashpoint (ATM) in Vieux-Québec; as does Banque Nationale, 1199 rue St-Jean (summer: Mon–Fri 9am–8pm, Sat & Sun 9.30am–8pm; winter: Mon–Thurs 9am–5pm, Fri 9am–4.30pm).

Bike rental Vélo Passe-Sport Plein Air, 22 Côte du Palais is conveniently situated, but Cyclo Services, 84 rue Dalhousie in the Vieux-Port, is cheaper, rents rollerblades and is close to the start of the bike trail. Information on cycle trails from Promo-Vélo (☎522-0087).

Bookshops English books can be purchased at Librairie Smith, Place Laurier, 2700 boul Laurier in Ste-Foy; La Maison Anglaise, Place de la Cité, 2600 boul Laurier in Ste-Foy; and there's a small selection at Pantoute, 1100 rue St-Jean. For travel books, there's a small shop inside the tourist office at Place d'Armes.

Bus enquiries Long-distance: bus terminal, 320 rue Abraham-Martin (☎525-3000). Local: STCUQ (☎627-2511). Ski shuttle: Hiver Express (☎525-5191; winter only).

Car parks Hôtel-de-Ville, rue Pierre-Olivier Chauveau (near Hôtel-de-Ville), rue Haldimand (near Jardin des Gouverneurs), ave Wilfrid-Laurier near the tourist office outside Porte St-Louis, Place D'Youville (off Dufferin), rue Dalhousie, Vieux-Port. Long-term parking: opposite bus terminal.

Car rental Avis, *Hôtel Hilton*, 900 boul René-Lévesque est (☎523-1075) and at the airport (☎872-2861); Budget, 380 rue Wilfred-Hamel (☎687-4220), 29 Côte du Palais (☎692-3660) and at the airport (☎872-9885); Discount, 12 rue Ste-Anne (☎692-1244); Hertz, airport (☎871-1571), 44 Côte du Palais (☎694-1224), and 580 Grande-Allée est (☎647-4949); Thrifty, *Château Frontenac* (☎877-2870) and near the airport, 6210 boul Wilfred-Hamel (same phone).

Consulate US, 2 Place Terrasse-Dufferin (☎692-2095).

Dentists For dental emergencies, ring ☎653-5412 (Mon–Wed 8am–8pm, Thurs 8am–6pm, Fri 8am–4pm) or ☎656-6060 at the weekend.

Gay and lesbian information Gai Écoute and Gay Line (☎1-888/505-1010).

Hospitals Hôtel-Dieu Hospital, 11 Côte du Palais (☎691-5042); Jeffrey Hale Hospital, 1250 chemin Ste-Foy (☎683-4471, ext 0).

Ice hockey The Rafales, who are not in the NHL, play at 350 boul Wilfred-Hamel (tickets ☎691-7211 or 1-800/900-SHOW; season is mid-Sept to April).

Laundry Lavoir la Lavandière, 625 rue St-Jean; Lavoir Ste-Ursule, 17B ave Ste-Ursule (Mon–Sat 9am–9pm, Sun 9am–6pm).

Left luggage Both the train and bus stations have $2 luggage lockers.

Medical advice 24hr medical service (☎648-2626).

Pharmacy 24hr service: Pharmacie Brunet, Les Galeries Charlesbourg, 4250 ave 1ère, in the northwesterly suburb of Charlesbourg.

Post office 300 rue St-Paul (Mon–Fri 8am–5.45pm); also 5 rue du Fort (same hours).

Rape crisis line Viol Secours (☎522-2120).

Ridesharing Allo-Stop, 665 rue St-Jean (☎522-0056, *www.allostop.com*).

Road conditions For 24hr information, call ☎648-7766 (Nov to mid-April).

Taxis Taxi Coop (☎525-5191); Taxi Québec (☎525-8123).

Train enquiries VIA Rail (☎692-3940 or 1-800/361-5390); Gare du Palais, 450 rue de la Gare-du-Palais; Gare de Ste-Foy, 3255 chemin de la Gare.

Weather information For 24hr bulletins (☎648-7766).

Around Québec City

There are various options for a swift or protracted trip out from the city. In **Wendake**, west of the city, the past and present crafts of Canada's only surviving Huron community can be seen, while to the east the **Côte-de-Beaupré**, though something of a city annexe, boasts the spectacular waterfalls of **Chute Montmorency** and in the **Canyon Ste-Anne**. Just offshore, the **Île d'Orléans** has a tranquil charm, its agricultural landscapes dotted with gîtes and auberges, and the homes of the well-heeled. For those in search of wilderness, the **Réserve Faunique des Laurentides** is within easy reach and there are a number of ski hills in the area. **Lévis**, on the opposite shore of the St Lawrence, is less inundated by visitors than Québec City and has great views of its more illustrious neighbour.

City **buses** and bicycle paths run to Chute Montmorency and Wendake, a few Intercar buses go daily to **Ste-Anne-de-Beaupré**, and a quick **ferry** trip lands you in Lévis. The HiverExpress winter shuttle bus (☎525-5191) connects the ski slopes with downtown hotels for around $25 return. The only places for which your own transport is essential are the wildlife reserve, Île d'Orléans and Canyon Ste-Anne.

Wendake

Just to the northwest of Québec City lies **WENDAKE**, the only **Huron reserve** in Canada. Its name derives from the Hurons' own name for their people – *Wendat*, meaning "people of the island". In 1650, French Jesuit missionaries led three hundred Huron from Ontario's Georgian Bay to the shores of the St Lawrence around today's Vieux-

Québec, thereby saving the smallpox-weakened population from extermination at the hands of the Iroquois. As more French settlers arrived, so the Hurons were successively relocated, ending up here beside the St-Charles River in 1697. Today, with a population of 1600, the central village core of the reserve retains typical Québécois wooden houses with sloping and gabled roofs, but is rather dilapidated – the main activities for visitors are at Onhoüa Chetek8e (see below), though there is a pretty waterfall.

In nice weather, the best way to get here is by bike – a 25km round trip along the bike path (La Route Vert 6) from the Vieux-Port. The STCUQ #801 bus runs from Place D'Youville to its terminus at Charlesbourg, from where the #72 goes to Wendake; get a transfer (*une correspondance*) and the 45-minute or so journey will set you back $2.25. The bus arrives at the church of **Notre Dame-de-Lorette** on boul Bastien, which contains a small museum displaying old manuscripts and religious objects. To visit the church, you must first visit the **Maison Aroüanne** opposite (late June to late Aug daily 9am–4pm; free), an early wooden house displaying a collection of Huron cultural objects, including ceremonial attire beaded with pearls and porcupine quills, drums of moose hide and feathered headdresses used for festive occasions. The waters of the **Chute Kabir-Kouba** tumble into a 42m-deep canyon visible from the bridge just west of the church. For a closer look, take the path, which starts at the end of the car park directly opposite the church and leads to the slippery rocks below.

At Maison Aroüanne ask for a map to the **Onhoüa Chetek8e** site, 575 rue Stanislas Kosca (daily: April–Oct 8.30am–6pm; Nov–March 9am–5pm; $8; *www.huron-wendat.qc.ca*), a thirty-minute walk north. This replica of a seventeenth-century Huron village constructed for the benefit of tourists consists of wooden long houses, Hurons in traditional garb and delicious native foods such as bison, caribou, trout and sunflower soup at the *Nek8arre* restaurant (May–Oct noon–3.30pm). You're greeted by a traditional welcome dance; participatory activities such as shooting arrows cost extra. The few products in the shops not made by Huron artisans come from other First Nations reserves.

The Réserve Faunique des Laurentides

The zone of the Laurentians to the north of Québec City is considerably more wild than the mountains near Montréal, thanks to the creation of the 8000-square-kilometre **Réserve Faunique des Laurentides**. The vast wooded terrain, with summits of more than 1000m towards the east, was once a hunting ground of the Montagnais, until the Hurons, armed by the French, drove the small population further north. The wildlife reserve became a protected area in 1895 to conserve the caribou herds, an intervention that was not a great success – very few exist today. However, though it allows controlled moose-hunting, the reserve's main function is still to preserve native animals such as the beaver, moose, lynx, black bear and deer, all of which you may see in remote areas.

Hwy 175 from Québec City traverses the reserve; halfway through is **L'Étape**, the only spot to fill up your tank or yourself until just before Chicoutimi. Nearby there's **camping** beside Lac Jacques-Cartier at the *La Loutre* campsite (☎846-2201; $18), and chalets are available for $80 for two. About 25km north of **L'Étape**, Hwy 169 branches off to Alma on Lac St-Jean (see p.316), while Hwy 175 continues on to Chicoutimi (see p.311). Intercar (☎525-3000 or 1-888/861-4592) runs a bus service through the park from Québec City's bus station to both Alma (3 daily; 2hr 45min) and Chicoutimi (4–5 daily; 2hr 30min). If you want to stop in the park, the **Camp Mercier** reception centre, near the reserve's southern perimeter, gives out **information** (☎848-2422 or 1-800/665-6527, *www.sepaq.com*). The heavy snowfall makes the park an excellent place for cross-country skiing ($9 per day).

In 1981, the southernmost portion of the reserve was set off as the **Parc de la Jacques-Cartier**; a **visitor centre**, 10km from Hwy 175 (mid-May to late Oct;

☎848-3169), serves as the gateway to the Jacques-Cartier river valley, enclosed by 550m-high forested slopes. Rent canoes, kayaks, inflatable rafts and bicycles from Les Excursions Jacques-Cartier (☎848-7272), who also manage the park's **campsites**. Pitches are available from $16.50, both near the visitor centre and in more peaceful spots further into the park.

The Côte-de-Beaupré

Dubbed the "coast of fine meadows" by Jacques Cartier, the **Côte-de-Beaupré** stretches along the St Lawrence past the **Basilique de Ste-Anne-de-Beaupré**, 40km northeast of Québec City, as far as the migratory bird sanctuary on Cap Tourmente, where you can see the greater snow goose in spring and autumn. There are two roads along the coast: the speedy Autoroute Dufferin-Montmorency (Hwy 440, then Hwy 138) and the slower avenue Royale (Hwy 360), which is served by local buses. The latter gives a far better introduction to the province's rural life, passing through little villages with ancient farmhouses and churches lining the way. Beyond Ste-Anne-de-Beaupré, Hwy 360 leads to one of the best ski resorts in the province – **Mont Ste-Anne** (☎827-5281 or 1-800/463-1568, for snow conditions call ☎1-888/827-4579, *www.mont-sainte-anne.com*), which has everything from golf to canyoning in summer. In winter, lift tickets are $40.85 per day and $18.25 for night skiing (4–10pm).

Chute Montmorency

Nine kilometres northeast of Québec City the waters of the Montmorency River cascade 83m down from the Laurentians into the St Lawrence, which makes the **Chute Montmorency** one and a half times the height of Niagara, though the volume of water is considerably less. The falls, named by Champlain in honour of the governor of New France, were the site of Wolfe's first attempt on the colony. However, Wolfe and his men were driven off by Montcalm's superior forces. In those days – before a hydroelectric dam cut off much of the flow – the falls were far more impressive, but the cascade remains an awesome spectacle, especially in winter, when the water and spray become a gigantic cone of ice, known locally as the "sugar loaf". Inevitably, the falls attract droves of tourists, especially now that the site has been thoroughly developed. From the main car park ($7), a **cable car** (Feb to mid-April Sat & Sun 9am–4pm; mid-April to Oct daily 8.15am–7pm except mid-June to Aug until 9pm; closed Nov–Jan; $5 one-way, $7 return) shoots up to the **interpretive centre** (daily 9am–8pm; June–Aug until 10pm; free; *www.chutemontmorency.qc.ca*), in the Manoir Montmorency, which also has a bar and restaurant with a terrace. From here, a cliffside walkway leads to the bridge over the falls (wooded trails follow the river upstream) and onto the zigzag path down the other side. Local STCUQ bus #53 stops 15 minutes' walk from the bottom of the falls, #50 at the top; both buses leave from Place Jacques-Cartier in Québec and take around fifty minutes, each costing $2.25. You can also cycle here – 25km round-trip from the Vieux-Port, and the path passes the **Domaine Maizerets** park, where you can have a pleasant break.

Ste-Anne-de-Beaupré

Québec's equivalent of Lourdes, the **Basilique de Ste-Anne-de-Beaupré**, 39km northeast of Québec City (25min by Intercar coach from Gare Centrale; 3 daily; $5.50), dominates the immediate area, its twin spires soaring proudly above the St Lawrence shore. The church began in 1658 as a small wooden chapel devoted to St Anne (the Virgin Mary's mother). During its construction a crippled peasant was cured. The legend of St Anne's intercession really got going, though, when some Breton sailors were caught in a storm on the St Lawrence in 1661 and vowed to build a chapel to St Anne if she saved them. The ship capsized at nearby Cap Tourmente but the sailors survived.

Word of this miracle spread, and from then on everyone caught in the St Lawrence's frequent storms prayed to St Anne and donated *ex votos* to the shrine. In 1876, the same year that St Anne was declared patron saint of Québec, the church was distinguished as a basilica (or pilgrimage church), to which the devout came on their knees from the beach or walked shoeless from Québec City; now, one and a half million pilgrims flock to the site every year in comfortable coachloads.

The neo-Romanesque granite cathedral with lofty symmetrical spires is the fifth church to stand here, fires and floods having destroyed the first four. The statue of St Anne between the steeples miraculously survived the 1922 destruction of the fourth church, even though the roof and both steeples fell in the blaze. The basilica seats 1500, though on St Anne's feast day (July 26) up to 5000 pilgrims crowd inside. Most of its decoration – countless stained-glass windows and massive murals – depict the miraculous powers of St Anne, though the wooden pews bear delightful animal carvings. Behind the ornate golden statue of St Anne, depicted holding her daughter Mary, is a chapel said to contain a portion of Anne's forearm, donated by the pope in 1960. Those who have been cured by her intervention have left a vast collection of crutches and wooden limbs hanging on the basilica's pillars near the entrance. The **information centre** in front of the basilica (daily: early May to mid-Sept 8am–5.30pm; mid-Sept to early May 8.30am–4.30pm) runs pious, free, guided tours daily at 1pm from the basilica entrance. The hours of the basilica itself vary, but it is open 8am–4.30pm at a minimum, and 6am–10pm at the height of the mid summer pilgrimage. The church is open to all even during Mass although photos are prohibited at that time. The information centre has a schedule of Masses conducted in English.

Several little chapels cringe in the basilica's shadow. The simple **Chapelle Souvenir** (early May to mid-Sept daily 8am–7pm), across the street behind the basilica, contains some of the stones from the second chapel and was built in the nineteenth century on the foundations of the transept of the third church (1676–1877), hence its north–south orientation. Nearby, the small white chapel of the **Scala Santa** (same times) contains stairs that replicate those climbed by Christ on his meeting with Pontius Pilate. Glass boxes, embedded in each stair, contain lumps of earth from various holy places, and the devout accomplish the ascent on their knees. Another obligatory part of the penitential route is the nearby **Way of the Cross**, which curves steeply up the hillside. There are two daytime processions, and on some summer evenings torchlit processions wend their way through each station. Less athletic visitors can pay their respects to the basilica's collection of *ex votos* and treasures in the **Musée de Ste-Anne** (mid-April to mid-Oct daily 10am–5pm; mid-Oct to mid-April Sat & Sun 10am–5pm; $5), which contains displays on the early churches and some of the surviving furnishings.

The vaguely Middle Eastern building at the other end of the car park contains the **Cyclorama de Jerusalem** (daily: April–June & Sept–Oct 9am–5pm; July–Aug 8am–8pm; $6), an enormous 360-degree painting set at the time of Christ's crucifixion. It has been there longer than the present basilica, though the 3D cut-outs were added in the 1950s in a misguided attempt to make it more realistic.

Canyon Ste-Anne

Just off Hwy 138 some 6km east of Ste-Anne-de-Beaupré, the falls at the **Canyon Ste-Anne** (daily: May to late June & early Sept to Oct 9am–5pm; late June to early Sept 8.30am–5.45pm; $7; *www.canyonste-anne.qc.ca*) can only be reached by car, which takes about thirty minutes from Québec City. Here, the river has carved a gorge where the water tumbles 74m in a waterfall flanked by a chasm fringed with woodlands and short nature trails. A bridge crosses just before the precipice, giving views down the canyon, while in front of the falls a precarious suspension bridge allows for splendid and terrifying views.

Île d'Orléans

From just northeast of Québec City to a short distance beyond Ste-Anne-de-Beaupré, the St Lawrence is bottlenecked by the **Île d'Orléans**, a fertile islet whose bucolic atmosphere and handy location have made it a popular spot for holiday-making Québécois. More than most places on the mainland, Île d'Orléans, with its old stone churches, little cottages and seigneurial manors, has kept a flavour of eighteenth-century French Canada. This is largely because it was cut off from the mainland until 1935, when a suspension bridge was constructed from Hwy 440, about 10km out of the city, connecting it to the west end of the island.

To its first inhabitants, the **Algonquins**, the island was known as Minigo, which means "enchanting place". Jacques Cartier christened it Île de Bacchus because the wild grapes he saw here were "such as we had seen nowhere else in the world". (He was soon to change the name to Île d'Orléans in honour of the king's son). Tourism and agriculture are the mainstays for the population of seven thousand: roadside stalls heave under the weight of fresh fruit and vegetables, jams, dairy products, home-made bread and maple syrup, and the island's restaurants and B&Bs are some of the best in the province, thanks to the supplies from local farms.

Encircling the island, the 67-kilometre **chemin Royal** (Hwy 368, though the name occasionally changes) dips and climbs over gentle slopes and terraces past acres of neat farmland and orchards, passing through the six villages with their churches evenly spaced around the island's periphery. The island's **information office** (☎828-9411, *www.iledorleans.qc.ca*) is on the right at the top of the hill after the bridge at 490 côte du Pont. The place is well set up for finding a B&B – photos and descriptions of the properties have numbers corresponding to roadside plaques that are also indicated on the adequate map in the *l'Île d'Orléans Tourist Guide* ($1), which also lists other stops of interest. The centre also has self-guided driving tours (cassette or CD; English available) for $10.

From here it's best to head west towards Ste-Pétronille in the region known locally as the "end of the island", a district still characterized by the grand homes of the merchants who made their fortunes trading farm produce with Québec City.

Ste-Pétronille

In the eighteenth century rich anglophones spent their leisure time in **STE-PÉTRONILLE**, the island's oldest and most beautifully situated settlement, with the noble rise of Québec City dominating the horizon. Wolfe observed the city from this spot before his bombardment. The white **Maison Gourdeau-de-Beaulieu** at no. 137 chemin Royal was the island's first permanent dwelling, built in 1648 and still the private residence of the Beaulieu family. Some of the best views can be had from rue Horatio Walker, named after the landscape painter **Horatio Walker**, who had his home and studio here. Known unofficially as the grand seigneur of Ste-Pétronille, Walker lived here from 1904 until his death in 1938. He despised his English heritage, continually emphasizing a French branch in his ancestry and refusing to speak English. His subject matter was almost entirely based on the Île d'Orléans, which he viewed as a "sacred temple of the muses and a gift of the gods". Many of his paintings now grace Canada's larger galleries.

Budget **accommodation** in the village is limited to two often booked-out **B&Bs**: the better is the *Gîte le 91 du Bout de l'Île*, 91 chemin du Bout de l'Île (☎828-2678; ②/③), a clean and cosy spot with a view of the Chute Montmorency from the garden. A pricier stay can be had at the delightful *Auberge la Goéliche*, 22 chemin du Quai (☎828-2248; ⑥), a wooden waterside Victorian inn with delicious French/Québécois cuisine (table d'hôte from $25) and great views. For cheaper **food**, *Café d'Art Pingasut Nukariit* opposite rue Horatio Walker makes a great stop for pizzas and snacks, and serves Inuit cuisine at night, including arctic char, caribou and seal.

St-Laurent and St-Jean

The south shore of the island was once the domain of sailors and navigators, with the village of **ST-LAURENT** being the island's supplier of "chaloupes", the long rowing boats that were the islanders' only means of getting to the mainland before the bridge was built. At the Parc maritime de St-Laurent **interpretive centre**, 120 chemin de la Chalouperie (May to mid-June & early Sept to mid-Oct Sat & Sun 10am–5pm; mid-June to early Sept daily 10am–5pm; $2), you can get info on attractions like **La Forge à Pique-Assaut**, 2200 ave Royale (June to mid-Oct daily 9am–5pm; mid-Oct to May Mon–Fri 9am–noon & 1.30–5pm; free), which features a blacksmith's shop and an eighteenth-century bellows.

ST-JEAN, on the east side of the island, was similarly nautical; the cemetery of its red-roofed local church contains gravestones of numerous mariners. In the prettiest village on the island, most of the mid-eighteenth-century mariners' homes have dormer windows and wide porches, with Victorian-inspired filigree. St-Jean's museum of antique furniture and domestic objects, housed in the stately **Manoir Mauvide-Genest**, 1451 Royal (☎829-2630), has been undergoing restoration. At this one-time home of Louis XV's surgeon, the metre-thick walls withstood the impact from Wolfe's bombardment – you can still see dents in the wall. Nearby, up the hill at no. 1477, *La Maison sur la Côte* (☎829-2971; ②) is a friendly **B&B**.

St-François, Ste-Famille and St-Pierre

From St-Jean, the road continues to the island's easterly tip and the village of **ST-FRANÇOIS**, where a precarious observation tower offers a view of both shores of the St Lawrence. The village church was rebuilt in the early 1990s after a suicidal driver wrecked the 1734 church; the wall in front was added to avoid a repeat. If you intend to **camp**, try the lovely and convenient *Camping Orléans*, near the village jetty at 357 chemin Royal (☎829-2953; $23 for two people). The rural *Auberge Chaumont*, 425 chemin Royal (late April to early Nov; ☎829-2735 or 1-800/520-2735, *www.aubergechaumont.specialistes.com*; ④), is a quiet place by the river.

Among the French-Regime stone buildings in **STE-FAMILLE**, the **Maison Canac-Marquis**, 4466 chemin Royal, is a particularly fine example, but only the 1675 **Maison Drouin**, at no. 4700 (late June to mid-Oct daily noon–5pm), with its exhibits on the architecture of these early houses, is open to the public. The richly decorated **church**, built in 1743, has a painting of the Holy Family by Québec's foremost early painter, Frère Luc. The local *boulangerie*, G.H. Blouin, 3967 chemin Royal, is one of the island's oldest and best, with mouthwatering bread and pastries. Next door, *Café de mon Village* (May–Oct) serves cheap snacks and a pricier table d'hôte on a terrace overlooking the river. Nearby, at no. 3879, *Au Toit Bleu* (☎829-1078, *www.bbcanada.com/3116.html*; ②/③) offers **B&B** in three comfortable rooms.

ST-PIERRE, to the west of Ste-Famille, is notable for its **church**, the oldest in rural Québec; constructed in 1718, it has pews with special hot-brick holders for keeping bottoms warm on seats. *Gîte de la Colombe*, 1501 chemin Royal (☎828-2417; ②) is a pleasant four-bedroomed **B&B**. You can also try the *Vieux Presbytère*, 1247 ave Monseigneur D'esgly (☎828-9723 or 1-888/828-9723, *www.presbytere.com*; ③), a charming inn with a good restaurant that serves game dishes and has terrific views of the river; they also rent bicycles ($6 per hour, $25 per day).

Lévis

It's hard to think of any commuters who have as pleasant a morning trip as those who cross the St Lawrence from **LÉVIS** to Québec City. Lévis itself is an attractive Victorian town, but the views of Québec make the visit a treat. The regular ferry leaves day and night (until 2am) from near Québec City's Place Royale, and costs $1.80 ($2.25 June–Sept) for the fifteen-minute crossing – double that if you go back.

Most tourists stay on the ferry for the return trip, but those dauntless enough to scale the staircase to the **Terrasse** on the heights of Lévis are rewarded with an even greater panorama. The Terrasse runs through a landscaped park whose centrepiece is a statue of Father Joseph David Déziel, founder of Lévis. The main street of Lévis, rue Déziel, is a couple of blocks north from the Terrasse and runs parallel to the river. The streets leading off it are as narrow and steep as those in Québec City – on rues Notre Dame, Wolfe and Guenette, look out for examples of elaborate brickwork and ornate roof lines that are as fine as those across the water. The **Maison Alphonse-Desjardins**, 6 Mont-Marie (Mon–Fri 10am–noon & 1–4.30pm; free), is a particular delight with its cake frosting-like facade. Inside, a permanent exhibition explains the evolution of the cooperative credit union in Québec.

Along Hwy 132: towards the Gaspé Peninsula

Heading east from Lévis **towards the Gaspé Peninsula**, the most scenic route is **Hwy 132**, which sticks religiously to the St Lawrence shoreline – as opposed to the Trans-Canada (Hwy 20) that zips along to just past Rivière-du-Loup, effectively the start of the Gaspé Peninsula. Hwy 132 twists across a flat agricultural landscape, whose long, narrow fields are remnants of the old seigneurial system (see box, opposite), and passes through a string of quiet villages overshadowed by their oversized Catholic churches. The three stops worth making on the 180-kilometre trip between Lévis and Rivière-du-Loup are at the woodcarving centre of **St-Jean-Port-Joli**, the seigneurial **St-Roche-des-Aulnaies** and pretty **Kamouraska**, with its quaint architecture.

St-Jean-Port-Joli

The first settlement of any note along Hwy 132, some 80km east of Lévis, is **ST-JEAN-PORT-JOLI**, where the long main street accommodates the galleries of the region's most popular **woodcarvers**. A traditional Québécois folk art, woodcarving flourished in the eighteenth and nineteenth centuries, but had almost expired by the 1930s, when the Bourgault brothers established their workshop here. Initially, religious statuary was their main source of income, but their folksy style and francophone themes were adopted and popularized by the nationalists in the 1960s.

Along the main road, on the west side of the village, the ugly **Musée des Anciens Canadiens**, 332 ave de Gaspé ouest (May–June & Sept–Oct daily 9am–5.30pm; July & Aug 8.30am–9pm; $4), has an interesting collection of woodcarvings cut in white pine and walnut, many of which are the work of the Bourgaults. The most impressive piece is the giant *Les Patriotes*, a tribute to the Québécois rebels of 1837 who, under the leadership of Louis-Joseph Papineau, tried to drive out the British (see p.238). The studied

TOURIST INFORMATION

The regions on the south shore and the offshore islands are divided into the following tourist associations, each providing a free regional guide including basic maps of the region. The telephone code for all of these areas is ☎418.

Chaudière-Appalaches ☎831-4411 or 1-888/831-4411, *www.chaudapp.qc.ca*

Bas Saint-Laurent ☎867-3015 or 1-800/563-5268, *www.tourismebas-st-laurent.com*

Gaspésie ☎775-2223 or 1-800/463-0323, *www.tourisme-gaspesie.com*

Îles-de-la-Madeleine ☎986-2245, *www.ilesdelamadeleine.com*

romance of the woodcarving bears little relation to the actual rebellion, though, which was badly organized and easily suppressed. A few doors down the same road at no. 322, the **Maison Médard-Bourgault** (late June to early Sept 10am–6pm; $2) concentrates on the life and work of Médard Bourgault. He was the most talented of the brothers – he even carved the walls and furniture. The delicate and ornate interior of the village church, **Église St-Jean Baptiste** at no. 2, celebrates the work of an earlier generation of Québécois woodcarvers from the 1770s, the Baillairgé brothers. Any of the dozen or so galleries along the main road sell woodcarvings; the shop adjoining the museum is one of the best. And at nearby no. 377, housed in an octagonal barn, the **Centre d'Art Animalier Faunart** (daily: May & June, Sept & Oct 9am–6pm; July & Aug 9am–9pm; $4) displays artworks inspired by nature and animals – a good intro to Canadian wildlife, though the taxidermy exhibits might make some stomachs churn.

There are some pleasant **B&B**s, of which *La Maison de L'Ermitage*, 56 rue de l'Ermitage (☎598-7553; ③), has a lovely turreted, red-and-white roof – if you're feeling particularly flush you can stay in one of the turrets (④). Two **campsites**, *Au Bonnet Rouge*, 762 Hwy 132 est (☎598-3088; $16.50; May–Oct) and *De La Demi-Lieue*, farther down the road at no. 589 (☎598-6108 or 1-800/463-9558; $15; May–Oct), are cheaper options. **Restaurant**-wise, check out *Café Bistro OK*, 254 rue du Quai for inexpensive burgers, fries, and fine-crust pizza or *Café la Coureuse des Greves*, 300 Hwy 204, for regional gastronomy and good breakfasts served on a lushly flowered outdoor terrace. For more upscale regional dining with views of the river, try the *Auberge du Faubourg*, 280 Hwy 132 ouest.

St-Roch-des-Aulnaies and La Pocatière

Fourteen kilometres east of St-Jean-Port-Joli is the village of **ST-ROCH-DES-AULNAIES**, where a gorgeous water mill and manor house have survived on a nineteenth-century seigneurial estate formerly the home of a rich merchant. Offering a fascinating glimpse into that era, **La Seigneurie des Aulnaies** (mid-June to early Sept daily 9am–6pm; $7), is named after the alder trees that grow along the banks of the Ferrée River. The river powered Québec's largest bucket wheel in the estate's three-storey communal grist mill. Now refurbished and in full working order, the mill has frequent flour-grinding displays and mouthwatering muffins and pancakes in the café. Just

---

THE SEIGNEURIAL SYSTEM

In the seventeenth century, the agricultural settlement of New France – now Québec – was conceived as an extension of European-style feudalism with the granting of **seigneuries** to religious orders, nobleman, merchants and, in a break from tradition, others of humble birth. The average seigneury covered around fifty square kilometres and part of the land was owned by the seigneurs, the rest rented by **habitants**, who were secure in their tenancy (they could sell the land and pass it on to their children) provided they met certain obligations. They had to pay a yearly tithe for the upkeep of the parish church, pay rent in kind (usually grain, as the seigneurs had a monopoly on milling), work on the roads and make themselves available for the militia.

In the early days the waterways provided the easiest form of transportation and so each *habitant's* farm had a riverfrontage of around a couple of hundred metres in length, with the rest of his land extending back in a narrow strip. One result of this was that *habitants* lived near their neighbours and, content with this decentralized way of life, long resisted the development of nuclear settlements. You can still see these ribbon farms and villages, which are very much in evidence along the St Lawrence today.

The seigneurial system was abolished in Ottawa in 1854 by legislation that passed land ownership rights to the *habitants*.

upstream from the mill, the veranda-wrapped manor house has period rooms, guides in costume and diverting interactive displays on the seigneurial system.

A few minutes' drive from St-Roch, agricultural **LA POCATIÈRE** sits on a ridge above the coastal plain, bereft of charm. It's worth stopping if you want information on the Bas Saint-Laurent region that stretches from here to Rimouski. The **information centre** is at exit 439 from Hwy 20 (daily: late June to early Sept 9am–8pm; mid-May to late June & early Sept to mid-Oct 9am–5pm), and signposted from Hwy 132.

Kamouraska

Some 40km further east along Hwy 132 is **KAMOURASKA**, a pretty village where well-heeled citizens of Québec City once congregated to take the air. While they no longer visit to the same degree, it's not for lack of good air, which still has its way with the town's current residents, many of whom live to more than 100 years of age. The village boasts many examples of the Bas-St-Laurent region's most distinctive architectural feature, the Kamouraska roof. Extended to keep the rainwater off the walls, the arched and rounded eaves project from the houses in a design borrowed from the shipyards. One of the best examples is the **Villa St-Louis**, at 125 ave Morel, a private residence that was once the home of Adolphe Basile-Routhier, the man who scripted the words to Canada's national anthem.

You may also spot several nets attached to wooden stakes emerging out of the river – these ensnare eels, traditionally the village's economic mainstay. Learn something about the industry at the slightly bizarre **Site d'interpretation de l'anguille**, 205 ave Morel (June to mid-Oct daily 9am–6pm; $4); aside from a barn filled with nets, there's not much to see here except the taxidermy collection of various non-eel animals ensnared in the nets, which is particularly morbid.

The enormous **Palais de Justice**, at the centre of town, once served as the region's superior court, but today merely displays early registries, maps and various pictures of the village (June–Oct daily 9am–noon & 1–5pm; $3). A better collection of artefacts – crockery, farming tools and the like – is at the **Musée de Kamouraska**, 69 ave Morel (June–Oct daily 9am–5pm; Oct to mid-Dec daily except Mon; $4), housed in a former convent.

Kamouraska has a host of charming **B&Bs**. *Chez Nicole et Jean*, at 81 ave Morel (☎492-2921; ②), is one of the best, with cheerful rooms and a bountiful breakfast of regional and organic food. For views of the river, the *Auberge Foin de Mer*, 85 ave LeBlanc (☎492-7081; ②), and *Auberge des Iles*, 198 ave Morel (☎492-7561; ②), are both good options; the latter also has a very good **restaurant**. A fine **bakery** is at no. 82 ave Morel, and there's a **café** at no. 88. If everything's booked up, try the *Motel au Relais*, 253 ave Morel (☎492-6246; ②), for standard accommodation and food.

THE GASPÉ PENINSULA AND ÎLES-DE-LA-MADELEINE

The scenic **Gaspé Peninsula** has always been sparsely inhabited and poor, its remote communities eking out an existence from the turbulent seas and the rocky soil. Still, it functions as a major summer holiday spot, especially busy during the last two weeks of July for Québec's **construction holiday**; if you travel during this period, book your accommodation and activities well in advance.

The people of the peninsula are predominantly and proudly Québécois, though there are pockets of long-established English-speaking settlements, particularly in and around **Gaspé** town, while **Carleton** and **Bonaventure** are centres of Acadian culture, established in 1755 in the wake of the British deportation of some 10,000 Acadians from around the Bay of Fundy in Nova Scotia (see p.357). Neither of these communities has created visually distinctive villages or towns, however, and the Gaspé looks as French as the heartlands of rural Québec.

Bounded by the Gulf of St Lawrence to the north and west, and by the **Baie des Chaleurs** to the south and east, the peninsula is roughly 550km long, with a chain of mountains and rolling highlands dominating the interior and the northern shore. These provide some wonderful scenery of forested hills cut with deep ravines and vistas of craggy mountains tumbling to the jagged coastline fronted by the St Lawrence. The landscape makes the winding coastal drive along Hwy 132 a delight, although the principal towns strung along this shore – **Rimouski, Matane** and Gaspé – are in themselves less appealing than smaller villages like **Bic, Mont-St-Pierre** and busy **Percé**.

The Gaspé Peninsula also has two outstanding parks: the extravagantly mountainous **Parc de la Gaspésie**, inland from **Ste-Anne-des-Monts**, and the **Parc National de Forillon**, at the tip of the peninsula, with its mountain and coastal hikes and wonderfully rich wildlife. Just to the south of the Forillon park, the village of Percé is famous for the offshore **Rocher Percé**, an extraordinary limestone monolith that has been a magnet for travellers for more than a hundred years. East of here, stuck out in the middle of the Gulf of St Lawrence, the **Îles-de-la-Madeleine** are most easily reached by ferry from Prince Edward Island (see p.396). This windswept archipelago has majestic, treeless landscapes, fringed by fine beaches and crazily eroded sandstone cliffs, and appeals particularly to cyclists, walkers and people who just want to lie on a beach in complete solitude.

The **south coast** of the Gaspé is, for the most part, flatter and duller than the north but the resort of Carleton, where the mountains return to tower over the coast, is an agreeable place to break your journey, especially as it's near the extraordinary fish and plant fossils of the **Parc de Miguasha**, a UNESCO World Heritage Site.

The Gaspé is well served by **bus**, with regular services travelling both the north and south coasts of the peninsula from Rimouski, Rivière-du-Loup and Québec City. The interior and the peninsula's parks are, however, difficult to explore without a car. VIA Rail links Montréal by **train** with Rivière du Loup and Rimouski, then follows the southern coast of the peninsula to Carleton and Percé, terminating in Gaspé town after 17.5 hours – there's no service between Gaspé and Rimouski on the northern coast, though. Be warned: some stations (like Percé) are miles from the towns they serve.

Rivière-du-Loup and Cabano

Whether you come up from the heartlands of Québec or cross over from New Brunswick on the Trans-Canada Highway via Cabano (see p.284), **RIVIÈRE-DU-LOUP** is essentially the beginning of the Gaspé Peninsula. The town is a prosperous-looking place, whose hilly centre, complete with broad streets and handsome Victorian villas, owes its development to the timber industry and the coming of the railway in 1859, which established Rivière-du-Loup as a crossroads for traffic between the Maritimes, the peninsula and the rest of the province. Its significance as an administrative and commercial centre has grown accordingly and today it has a population of around 18,000.

The river that gives the place its name crashes down a thirty-metre drop close to the centre, at the top of rue Frontenac, near **Parc de la Croix Lumineuse**, which offers a panoramic view of the mountains on the north shore. The town's **waterfall** is disappointing, however; although it generates a lot of noise and spray, even the specially built platform that crosses it fails to make the view enthralling. Similarly modest are the town's three museums. The central **Musée du Bas-St-Laurent**, 300 rue St-Pierre (daily: June–Sept 10am–6pm; Oct–May 1–5pm, Mon & Wed also 6–9pm; $5), combines

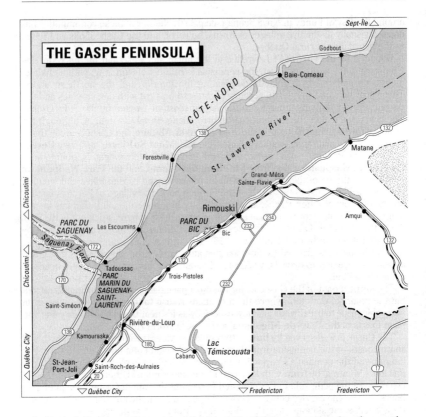

ethnological displays of the region with historical exhibits and works of modern art by local artists. The **Musée des Carillons**, on the eastern edge of town at 393 rue Témiscouata (late June to early Sept daily 9am–8pm; Sept–Oct daily 9am–5pm; $5), is a unique collection of 250 bells of all types from around the world. The **Musée de bateaux miniatures et légendes du Bas-St-Laurent**, 80 boul Cartier (late June to early Sept daily 8.30am–9pm; May–June & early Sept to Oct daily 10am–8.30pm; $3.50), houses an interesting collection of model boats built by local craftspeople.

If you're interested in the architectural heritage pick up the interpretive booklet ($1) from the **tourist office**, at 189 boul de l'Hôtel-de-Ville, and stroll round the centre: although there's nothing special, it's a pleasant way to pass an hour. The most intriguing historical site in town is **Le Manoir Fraser**, 32 rue Fraser (late June to Oct daily 10am–5pm; $3.50), the home of Seigneur Fraser; instead of costumed guides, a computer-animated seigneur introduces you to his life and times. The red-brick manor house also has a fancy tearoom and garden. If you plan to take in the manor house, the miniature boat museum and the bells, pick up a **discounted pass** for $9 at one of the participating museums.

Rivière-du-Loup is a good place for **boat trips** on the St Lawrence River. Beginning at around $40 per person per trip, these excursions are not cheap, but they are well organized and you may see beluga, minke and finback whales throughout the summer. All of the companies are by the marina at 200 rue Hayward – Croisières AML (☎867-

3361 or 1-800/563-4643), specializes in **whale-watching** trips, while Exceptionelle Aventure (☎862-7775), takes in the river's aquatic life in 12-person zodiacs – inflatable raft-type boats that get you very close to the whales. Alternatively, La Société Duvetnor (☎867-1660, *www.duvetnor.com*; June–Oct), has daily cruises to various midstream sea-bird and mammal sanctuaries, with overnight stops offered ($20–185 per person; reservations required). A **car ferry** provides service to St-Siméon, on the north shore (April–Jan 2–5 trips daily; 65min; ☎862-5094, *www.travrdlstsim.com*; passengers $10.40, cars $26.40).

Practicalities

Highway 132 runs through the centre of Rivière-du-Loup. The town's **bus station** is on boul Cartier, beside the junction of Hwys 132 and 20, about ten-minutes' walk northeast of the centre. The **tourist office** at 189 boul de l'Hôtel-de-Ville (daily: late June to early Sept 8.30am–9pm; early Sept to late June Mon–Fri 8.30am–noon & 1.30–5pm), will help you get your bearings and provides accommodation listings.

The **youth hostel** (☎862-7566 or 1-800/461-8585; ①), on the same street at no. 46, occupies an attractive wooden building with ornate banisters and balustrades. A similarly inexpensive and equally convenient option is the *CÉGEP*, 325 rue St-Pierre (☎862-6903 ext 282; ①), a college residence offering 100 spartan rooms throughout the summer. **Motels** and **hotels** include the bargain-basement *Motel au Vieux Piloteux*, 185

Fraser (☎867-2635; ②). More agreeably, the *Auberge de la Pointe*, 10 boul Cartier (☎862-3514 or 1-800/463-1222; ③), has comfortable rooms and its own health spa. Two magnificent **B&Bs** are virtually across from each other on a gorgeous tree-lined stretch of Hwy 132 west of town: *Auberge La Sabline*, 343 rue Fraser (☎867-4890; ③), and the summer residence of Canada's first prime minister, Sir John A. MacDonald, *Les Rochers*, at no. 336 (☎868-1435; ④). The municipal **campsite**, exit 507 from Hwy 20 (☎862-4281; $17 a pitch; mid-May to late Sept), is off Hwy 132, near the harbour.

Pricey **restaurants** abound in the centre of town – *Le St-Patrice*, 169 rue Fraser, being among the best and devoted to serving regional produce. A walk down rue Lafontaine, near the river, reveals less expensive alternatives – the best value is *La Gourmande* at no. 120, where salads and vegetarian meals average about $11, though things get more pricey in the evenings; closer to the pier, *Aux Boucaneux* offers seafood in a funny little restaurant fronted by a teepee and an Indian head. *Les Jardins de Lotus*, no. 334, is your last chance to get Asian food on the peninsula. In the evenings, the bright young things of Rivière-du-Loup gather at *L'Estaminet*, 299 rue Lafontaine, a **bar** with 150 types of beer.

Cabano and Lac Témiscouata

The area southeast of Rivière-du-Loup, along the Trans-Canada Highway towards New Brunswick, is saved from mediocrity by the graceful sweep of **Lac Témiscouata**, where a combination of lake, river, woods and hills is adorned by a dazzling display of wild flowers in spring. The Trans-Canada Highway offers glimpses of the lake, but it's Hwy 232 that tracks along the prettiest stretches, leaving the main road at the sprawling lakeside village of **CABANO**. Aside from **Fort Ingall** (June–Sept daily 9.30am–6pm; $6.50), a restored British fortification dating from 1839, there's little to do here except hang out by the lake. Built during a border dispute with the Americans, the fort was part of a series of schemes that strengthened the land link between the St Lawrence and the Bay of Fundy, protecting the area's timber resources. Abandoned in 1842, having seen no action, Ingall has been painstakingly reconstructed, its high stockade surrounding a squat wooden barracks, blockhouse and officers' quarters. Inside the officers' quarters are enjoyable displays on the background to the fort's construction, contemporaneous army life and local archeological finds. There's also a section on Archie Belaney, aka **Grey Owl**, the British conservationist turned native, who settled in the area in the 1920s (see p.945). From Cabano, Hwy 232 follows the shore of the lake before snaking back to the St Lawrence at Rimouski – or you can take the more direct Hwy 293 from the lake's northern extremity to Trois-Pistoles (see below).

There are several **campsites** along the shores of Lac Témiscouata, the nearest to Cabano being the *Témilac*, 33 rue de la Plage, near the junction of Highway 232 and the TCH (☎854-7660; $14; mid-May to Sept). For more comfortable **accommodation**, the campsite adjoins the unpretentious *Hébergement Témilac* (same number; ④). Alternatively, you could try the *Motel Royal*, 19 rue St-Louis (☎854-2307; ②), a decent and inexpensive place to stay. For **food**, *Le Quai des Brumes*, at 140 rue Commercial, is a cheerful place with a terrace; *Auberge de la Gare*, 5 rue de la Gare, specializes in crepes and pasta and offers **B&B** accommodation upstairs (☎845-9315 or 1-888/463-4273; ②).

Trois-Pistoles

Heading east from Rivière-du-Loup along Hwy 132, with the far bank of the St Lawrence clearly visible, the coastal highway passes through a succession of farming and fishing villages on its way to **TROIS-PISTOLES**, so-named after a silver goblet worth three *pistoles* (gold coins) that a French sailor dropped into the river while trying to fill it with water in 1621. It is now popular among Québécois as the home of scriptwriter and novelist Victor-Lévy Beaulieu, who has created several *téléromans* – a distinctly Québécois genre which is part soap opera, part drama – that are set in the area. His house and studio at 23 rue Petellier (June to mid-Sept daily 9am–5pm; $7) are nothing special unless you're a fan of such hits as *Bouscotte*. The town is dominated by the enormous church of **Notre Dame-des-Neiges-de-Trois-Pistoles** (late June to early Sept daily 9am–4pm), built between 1882 and 1887. From a distance the church looks like something out of Disneyland, as the roof, surmounted by four pinnacles, is painted silver. Inside, the vaulted Italianate ceiling is supported by massive trompe-l'oeil marble columns with ornate gilded capitals, while the walls are dotted with nineteenth-century devotional paintings.

The **Musée St-Laurent**, 552 rue Notre Dame ouest (late June to mid-Sept daily 8.30am–6pm; $3) has a great ensemble of cars, with vehicles from the 1930s to the 1970s and an eclectic collection ranging from old packs of cigarettes to harpoons.

The town's **information centre** is on the highway with a miniature windmill and lighthouse outside (late June to early Sept daily 10am–6pm). A **car ferry** crosses to Les Escoumins (mid-May to mid-Oct 2–3 daily; 1hr 15min; $10.75 single, $27.50 for cars) on the Côte-Nord (see p.31). **Whale-watching** excursions are handled by Les Écumeurs (trip times vary between 2.5 and 5 hours; $35–55). Should you want to break your journey here, try *Motel Trois-Pistoles*, 64 Hwy 132 ouest (☎851-2563; ②), which has 32 comfortable rooms, some with views of the river. There's not much in the way of **B&Bs** in the downtown area, with the exception of *Le Pistolois* at 15 rue Rousseau (☎851-4481; ②). Otherwise, *Aux Terroir des Basques* at 65 rang 2 est (☎851-2001; ②; summer only) is worth a try. *Café l'Essentiel*, opposite the church door, is an inexpensive **restaurant** with a table d'hôte under $10, and *L'Ensoleillé*, at 138 rue Notre Dame ouest, serves up vegetarian and fish dishes on an outdoor terrace.

Bic and Rimouski

Heading east from Trois-Pistoles, Hwy 132 crosses a comparatively tedious landscape of fertile agricultural land, until it reaches the rocky wooded hummocks of the shoreline's **Parc du Bic**. A naturalists' paradise whose headlands push up tight against the river, it's possible to see herds of grey seals, especially at dusk. The park has three short hiking trails, a beach, a visitors' centre (mid-June to Sept daily 10am–5pm; free) and a **campsite**, *Camping Bic* (☎736-4711; $16 a pitch plus $4.35 administration charge; early June to early Sept). From late June to early September, shuttle buses depart regularly from the visitors' centre heading up to the highest peak, Pic Champlain ($5 return trip), and around the park (2hr; $14). You can also view the park from a **sea kayak** from Rivi-Air Aventure (☎736-5252; $30–60 per person).

Just beyond the park along Hwy 132, the elongated village of **BIC**, perched on a low ridge above its snout-shaped harbour, is a handsome medley of old and modern architectures. Samuel de Champlain named the place Pic (for peak), but the "P" morphed into a "B" instead. The *Auberge du Mange Grenouille*, 148 rue Ste-Cécile (☎736-5656; ②; summer only) has a superb **restaurant** (reservations advised) and attractively furnished double **rooms**. *Aux Cormorants* is a **B&B** nestled along Pointe des Anglais facing onto the river (☎736-8113; ②). The **bakery**, *Folles Farines*, at 113 rue St-Jean Baptiste, has a wicked selection of tasty breads, croissants and thin-crust pizzas. Up the hill and facing the handsome church, *Chez Saint-Pierre* is a sunny bistro with an imaginative menu and a terrace overlooking the town's rooftops (open seven days a week in summer; weekends only rest of year).

Rimouski

Some 20km northeast of Bic, **RIMOUSKI**, called Riki by its residents, appears quite unattractive from Hwy 132 thanks to a major fire that destroyed one-third of the buildings from the river to midtown in 1950, forcing the city to rebuild in 1960s strip-mall style. But forge past the highway and into the town, the administrative capital of eastern Québec, and you'll find a number of interesting places. The excellent **Musée régional de Rimouski**, at 35 rue St-Germain (mid June to mid Sept Mon–Tues & Sun 10am–6pm, Wed–Sat 10am–9pm; mid Sept to mid June Wed & Fri–Sun noon–5pm, Thurs noon–9pm; $4), is housed in the oldest **church** in eastern Québec. While the exterior has stayed intact, the inside has been renovated and the three floors now focus on science and technology and contemporary art. An **architectural walking tour** takes you past buildings spared by the fire; pick up a free pamphlet at the tourist office.

Rimouski's **tourist office**, 50 rue St-Germain ouest (mid-June to early Sept daily 9am–8pm; early June & early Sept to early Oct daily 9am–4.30pm; early Oct to mid-June Mon–Fri 9am–4.30pm; ☎723-2322 or 1-800/746-6875) is in the centre of town, on the waterfront. They have **accommodation** listings, including college rooms available during the summer vacation, at *Logis Vacances*, 320 rue St-Louis (☎723-4636 or 1-800/463-0617; ③) and *Les Logements étudiants de l'UQAR*, 329A Allée des Ursulines (☎723-4311; ②). For **B&B** accommodation, *Chez Charles et Marguerite*, 686 boul St-Germain ouest (☎723-3938; ②), has cheery rooms looking out onto fields that lead down to the St Lawrence. The town's cheapest motel is the *Motel St-Laurent*, 740 boul St-Germain ouest (☎723-9217; ①; summer only). For **camping**, *Le Bocage*, 124 Hwy 132 (☎739-3125; $15), is east of Pointe-au-Père, near a lake.

Rimouski has a number of affordable places to **eat**, not the least *Central Café*, 31 rue de l'Évêché ouest with great salads and pizza in a home decorated with birdcages from around the world. The *Maison du Spaghetti* at 35 boul St-Germain est serves up hearty pasta; and if you're into kitsch, *Retro 50 Restaurant*, across the street, is a 1950s diner where the waitresses are dressed accordingly. For onward transport, the Orléans Express **bus** station is at 90 ave Léonidas (☎723-4923), the **train** station at 57 de l'Évêché est (☎722-4737 or 1-800/361-5390), and the rideshare outfit Allô-Stop at 106 rue St-Germain est (☎723-5248, *www.allo-stop.com*). There's also a **car ferry** to Forestville on the Côte-Nord (☎725-2725 or 1-800/973-2725; late April to early Oct: 2-4 trips daily; 55min; $13 single, $32 for cars), which only holds 30 cars so reservations are essential.

Around Rimouski

A few kilometres east from Rimouski along Hwy 132, the small town of **POINTE-AU-PÈRE** holds not much more than the **Maison Lamontagne**, 707 boul du Rivage (mid-May to mid-Oct daily 9am–6pm; $3), the oldest house in eastern Québec; though there's not much inside that's worth your time or money, the gardens are free and quite educational. Further down the road, the **Musée de la Mer** (daily: late June to late Aug 9am–7pm; June & late Aug to mid-Oct 10am–5pm; $8.50) is housed in a modern building that resembles a tilting ship. The exhibit includes a 3D film on the *Empress of Ireland*, a luxury liner that sank offshore here in 1914, a disaster second only to the *Titanic*, with more than a thousand lives lost.

Rimouski to Matane

From Rimouski to Matane a few places are worth a stop. The first is **SAINTE-FLAVIE**, a small coastal town that's home to Gaspesie's **regional tourist office**, 357 rue de la Mer (mid-June to early Sept daily 8am–8pm; early Sept to mid-Oct daily 8am–6pm; (mid-Oct to mid-June Mon–Fri 9am–5pm; ☎1-800/463-0323). Nearby at no. 564, the

Centre d'art Marcel Gagnon offers a unique sight. The artist's outdoor work, *Le Grand Rassemblement* (The Great Gathering), groups more than eighty life-size statues and seven rafts starting on a strip of land and then leading into the water. The works are especially remarkable at high tide, as the statues emerge out of the river, and the rafts seem to float.

MATANE, 56km further east, appears to be dominated by oil refineries and cement works, but in fact fishing and forestry have long been the mainstays of the local economy. The Matane River, which bisects the town, is spanned by a pair of bridges – one beside the harbour (part of Hwy 132), the other a shorter affair a few hundred metres north, next to the fish ladder, which was built to help salmon head upstream to spawn. The **Festival de la Crevette**, during the last week in June, takes its name from the prawn harvest but, in fact, celebrates the entire range of local seafood – all the town's restaurants and bars participate. At the **Barrage Mathieu-D'Amours**, the dam's observation area allows visitors to watch salmon battling to get upstream.

Matane's **tourist office** is beside Hwy 132, just west of the centre, in the lighthouse at 968 ave du Phare ouest (late June to mid-Sept daily 8.30am–8.30pm; mid-Sept to late June Mon–Fri 8.30am–5pm; ☎562-1065). Simple institutional **accommodation** can be rented at *CÉGEP de Matane*, 616 ave St-Rédempteur (☎562-1240; ①), while *Auberge la Seigneurie*, at 621 ave St-Jérôme (☎562-0021 or 1-877/783-4466; ②), and *Gîte du Phare*, 984 ave du Phare ouest (☎562-6606; ②), are both good **B&Bs**. Most of Matane's **hotels** and **motels** are pricey: *Le Beach*, 1441 rue Matane-sur-Mer (☎562-1350; ②), is the least expensive of the lot but it isn't nearly as nice as *Belle Plage* on the same street, at no. 1310 (☎562-2323 or 1-888/244-2323; summer only; ③), which has a good restaurant and is right on the sea. There's a municipal **campsite** south of the centre of town at 150 rte Louis-Félix-Dionne (☎562-3414; $12.16 for two-person site; mid-June to Aug). The *Cafés du Monde*, 338 ave St-Jerome, has a nice atmosphere and serves *panini*. Across the river, the *Bistro de l'Estuaire*, 50 rue d'Amours, is the place to go for mussels, and *Italia Pizzeria*, 101 St-Pierre, serves good pizza.

From Matane, **car ferries** run to Godbout (April–Dec: 1–3 trips daily; Jan–March: Mon–Sat 1 daily; 2hr 10min; $11.85 single, $28.35 for cars); and Baie-Comeau (April–Dec: 1–2 trips daily; Jan–March: 4 per week; 2hr 20min; $11.85 single, cars $28.35) on the Côte-Nord (see p.316). Call ☎562-2500 or 1-877/562-6560 for sailing times.

Sainte-Anne-des-Monts and Parc de la Gaspésie

East of Matane the highway hugs the shoreline, passing through increasingly rugged scenery where the forested hills of the interior push up against the fretted, rocky coast. A string of skimpy fishing villages breaks up this empty landscape – places like Capucins, with its fine headland setting, and **Cap Chat**, whose 76 towering wind turbines are visible for miles around. Of these, the 110m-tall **Éolienne de Cap-Chat** (late June to late Sept daily 8.30am–5pm; $6) is the tallest and most powerful vertical-axis wind tower in the world. Just 16km beyond Cap-Chat, unenticing **SAINTE-ANNE-DES-MONTS** sprawls along the coastline, its untidy appearance only offset by its relaxed atmosphere and its convenience – it's an easy place to break your journey before heading on to the cape, or inland to the Parc de la Gaspésie (see overleaf). The lone sight is the **Explorama** at 1 rue du Quai (early June and mid-Aug to mid-Oct daily 9am–6pm; late June to mid-Aug daily 9am–8pm; mid-Oct to early June Mon–Fri 9am–5pm, Sat & Sun 1–5pm; $8; *www.centre-explorama.com*), a so-called marine and birdlife discovery centre on two floors. If you choose to visit, head straight to the aquarium downstairs where you can pick up living sea creatures such as starfish, sea cucumbers and scallops.

For **accommodation**, the **youth hostel** *Auberge internationale l'Échouerie*, 295 1ère Avenue est (☎763-1555; ①) has great views over the river and the *Motel Manoir sur Mer*, 475 1ère Avenue ouest (☎763-7844; ②), has rooms backing onto the beach. For **B&B** accomodation, try *Chez Marthe-Angéle*, at no. 268 1ère Avenue ouest (☎763-2692; ②), or head for the unassuming *Courant de la Mer*, 3 rue Belvedère in nearby Tourelle (☎763-5440 or 1-800/230-6709; ②).

Parc de la Gaspésie

As you travel south from Ste-Anne-des-Monts on Hwy 299, the snowcapped **Chic-Choc Mountains** – which make up most of the **Parc de la Gaspésie** – can be spotted in the distance, a stark and forbidding backdrop to the coastal plain. The Chic-Chocs are the most northerly protrusions of the Appalachian Ridge, which extends deep into the US, and the serpentine road reveals the full splendour of their alpine interior. The sequence of valleys framed by thickly wooded slopes culminates in the staggering ravine that lies at the foot of the towering **Mont Albert**. In this ravine, 40km from Sainte-Anne-des-Monts, the park's reception and interpretive centre (early June to late Sept daily 8am–8pm; ☎763-3181 or 763-7811, *www.sepaq.com*) rents out hiking equipment and has details and maps of half a dozen well-signposted **hiking trails**; most are about a day's duration though a couple around the base are shorter. Prospective hikers should come equipped with warm clothes, food and water, and log their intended route at the centre. The trails ascend to the summits of the area's three highest mountains – Mont Jacques-Cartier, Mont Richardson and Mont Albert – and are remarkable in that they climb through three distinctive habitats. Herds of **Virginia deer** thrive in the rich vegetation of the lowest zone, while **moose** live in the boreal forest, and **caribou** in the tundra near the peaks. This is the only place in Québec where the three species exist in close proximity.

The park has four **campsites**, one of which, *Camping Mont Albert* (☎763-1333; $22.75), is conveniently situated near the interpretive centre. Close by, too, is the smart and modern *Gîte du Mont-Albert* (☎763-2288 or 1-888/270-4483; ⑤), which offers the only fixed **lodgings** in the park; room prices rocket during the summer and skiing seasons, but you couldn't wish for a handier location. The *Gîte* also controls a number of **chalets** (③) around the park, offering simple but reliable facilities.

Sainte-Anne-des-Monts to Parc National de Forillon

Heading east from Sainte-Anne-des-Monts towards the tip of the Gaspé Peninsula, the road often squeezes between the ocean and the sheer rock faces of the mountains, its twists and turns passing tumbling scree and picturesque coves. If you're hungry by the time you reach **MARSOUI**, a tiny fishing village 34km east of Ste-Anne, try a reasonably priced **restaurant**, *La Vieille Tablé*. One hundred percent French-Canadian, it started life in 1937 as the refectory of the defunct local lumber mill; today the interior remains functional, with simple hard benches beside six long tables. The daily specials are typically Québécois – try the salmon or the meat and vegetable stew (*cipaille*), real bargains at around $10. The village also has a sheltered shingly **beach**.

The view as you approach **MONT-SAINT-PIERRE** is majestic, the curving seashore and the swelling mountains together framing this little community set at the mouth of a wide river valley. Mont-Saint-Pierre is a low-key resort, dedicated to bathing and sea fishing, except during the **hang-gliding festival** at the end of July. During the rest of the summer you can fly in tandem for $100 with Carrefour Aventure (☎797-5033 or 1-800/463-2210, *www.carrefouraventure.com*) or Vol Biplace (☎797-2896). There are several cheap-and-cheerful **motels** along rue Prudent-Cloutier: Try *Chalets Auberge Bernatchez* at no. 12 (☎797-2733; ①), the *Motel Mont-Saint-Pierre* at no. 60 (☎797-2202 or 1-800/797-2202; ②) or the *Motel Restaurant au Délice* at no. 100 (☎797-2850 or 1-888/797-2955; ③). For **camping**, there's *Du Pont* on Hwy 132 (☎797-2951; two-person sites $14.50; June–Sept) and a **municipal campsite** at 103 rue Pierre-Godfroie-Coulombe (☎797-2250; six-person sites $13.04; June–Sept). There are a couple of good places to **eat**: *Le Croissant d'Art*, on the main thoroughfare, is an inexpensive artsy café ideal for light lunches, while *Les Joyeux Naufragés* (the French translation of *Gilligan's Island*), 7 rte Pierre-Mercier, offers more substantial fare at equally affordable prices.

The Parc National de Forillon

Lying at the very tip of the peninsula, the **PARC NATIONAL DE FORILLON** is the scenic culmination of the Gaspé, encompassing some 250 square kilometres of thick forest and mountain, crossed by hiking trails and fringed by stark cliffs along a deeply indented coastline. The splendour of the landscape is complemented by the **wildlife**: black bears, moose, beavers, porcupines and foxes are all common to the area – although to chance sighting them, you're best to arrive early in the morning or at dusk. More than two hundred species of birds have also been seen, ranging from sea birds like gannets, cormorants and guillemots, to songbirds such as the skylark and chaffinch. From the coastal paths around Cap Gaspé itself, **whales and porpoises** can also be spotted between May and October. As Thomas Anburey, a British soldier, observed in the 1770s, "They cause most beautiful fire works in the water: for being in such abundance, and darting with amazing velocity, a continued stream of light glides through the water, and as they cross each other, the appearance is so picturesque that no description can reach it."

Roughly triangular in shape, the park is sandwiched between the Gulf of St Lawrence and the Baie de Gaspé and encircled by Hwys 197 and 132, the former crossing the interior to delineate the park's western limits, the latter mostly keeping to the seashore and threading through Anse-au-Griffon and Cap-des-Rosiers – tiny coastal villages with views onto the river and Forillon's wooded parkland. Make the time to take this route as the views are spectacular. You can also stop for a cup of tea at the **Manoir LeBoutillier**, a restored 1850s house at 578 boul Griffon, in Anse-au-Griffon (June to mid-Oct daily 9am–5pm; $4; guided tours only). Closer to the park, the **lighthouse** at Cap-des-Rosiers is the tallest in Canada (mid-June to mid-Sept 10am–7pm; $2.50; guided tours only, free access to the site). On a clear day, you can see the outlines of Île d'Anticosti (see p.324) from the top.

Parc Forillon has numerous hiking trails, the best of which takes you to the tip of **Cap Gaspé** – otherwise known as "land's end". The ninety-minute return trip starts a few kilometres to the south of the **interpretive centre** (daily: early June 1–4pm; mid-June to early Sept 9am–6pm; early Sept to mid-Oct 9am–4pm; ☎892-5572), close to the lighthouse near the village of Cap-des-Rosiers on the park's north side. Here, you can also get an imaginative overview of the natural and human history of the area and a wealth of suggestions as to how to spend your time.

The trail extends from the end of the paved road beyond Grande-Grave, a restored fishing village founded by immigrants from Jersey – the inhabitants were relocated as recently as 1970 when the park was established. Their historical presence is enshrined in two sites situated along the trail that follows the southern coast of the cape. The first, **Hyman & Son's General Store and Warehouse** (mid-June to mid-Oct 10am–5pm; free with park entry) is a marvellous restoration of a 1920s general store; nearby **Anse-Blanchette** (mid-June to mid-Sept 10am–5pm; free with park entry), a fisherman's house dating from the same era, has also been painstakingly restored and the on-site barn frequently does duty as a stage for storytelling and musical acts. You'll also note unfinished buildings down near the edge of the cliff: these are the remnants of the set for the popular Québec television series *L'Ombre de l'Épervier*. After these, the path rises and falls until it makes the final steep ascent to the **lighthouse**, which is set on a 150-metre cliff with the ocean on three sides. On a clear day, you can see the rock at Percé, 25km to the south. More leisurely pursuits include two-hour **boat trips** along the northern shore to see seals and a bird sanctuary, from the quay near the interpretive centre (mid-June to mid-Sept every 2hr from 9am; 2hr; $20), while **whale-watching** excursions depart from Grande-Grave (June–Oct 10am, 1.30pm & 4.30pm; 2hr 30min; $40).

Park practicalities

The park has two **visitors centres** off Hwy 132 in addition to the interpretive centre. One is at **Anse-au-Griffon** (daily: early June to Aug 8.30am–9.30pm; Sept to mid-Oct 9am–4pm; ☎368-5505 or 1-800/463-6769); the other is on the south coast at **Penouille** (same hours; ☎892-5661). Entrance fees to Parc Forillon range from $3.75 for adults to $2 for students and children between 6 and 16, $3 for senior citizens and $8.75 family rate.

There are half a dozen **campsites** in the park and all of them are pleasantly situated and well maintained; call ☎368-6050 for reservations ($14.35 for six-person site). *Camping Cap Bon-Ami* (early June to early Sept) has a particularly delightful setting just south of the interpretive centre. The visitors centres and interpretive centre have details of all sites and can also arrange accommodation in **chalets** (③) around the park, which are cheaper if booked by the week. Alternatively, the villages edging the park offer a smattering of plain accommodation that includes Anse-au-Griffon's *Motel le Noroît*, 589 boul Griffon (☎892-5531; ②), while Cap-aux-Os has a **youth hostel**, at 2095 boul Grande-Grève (☎892-5153; ①), with a café, laundry facilities and a **mountain-bike rental** shop.

Gaspé

The town of **GASPÉ**, straddling the hilly estuary of the York River, is a disappointment after the scenic drama of the national park, a humdrum settlement of about 17,000 people whose hard-pressed economy is reliant on its deep-water port. This is the spot where the French navigator and explorer **Jacques Cartier** landed in July 1534, on the first of his three trips up the St Lawrence. He stayed here for just eleven days, time enough to erect a wooden cross engraved with the escutcheon of Francis I, staking out the king's – and Christianity's – claim to this new territory. Cartier's first aim was to find a sea route to the Orient, but he also had more extensive ambitions – to acquire land for himself and his men, exploit the Indians as fur gatherers and discover precious metals to rival the loot the Spaniards had taken from the Aztecs. Naturally, Cartier had to disguise his real intentions on the first trip and his initial contacts with the Iroquois were cordial. Then, in the spring of 1536, he betrayed their trust by taking two of the local chief's sons back with him to Francis I. They were never returned, and when Cartier made his third trip in 1541 the Iroquois were so suspicious that he was unable to establish the colony he had been instructed to found. Desperate to salvage his reputation, Cartier sailed back to France with what he thought was a cargo of gold and diamonds. His cargo turned out to be iron pyrite and quartz crystals.

Just to the east of the town centre, at 80 boul Gaspé, the **Jacques Cartier monument** looks out over the bay from the grounds of the town museum. It consists of six striking bronze dolmens carved in relief that record Cartier's visit and treatment of the natives in ambivalent terms, along with anodyne homilies on the nature and unity of humankind.

The **museum** itself, 80 boul Gaspé (late June to early Sept daily 9am–7pm; early Sept to late June Tues–Fri 9am–5pm, Sat & Sun 1–5pm; $4), illuminates the social issues that have confronted the inhabitants of the peninsula to the present – isolation from the centres of power, depopulation and, more recently, unemployment. Temporary displays concentrate mostly on local subjects, like the peninsula's artists and musicians.

A good ten-minutes' walk west, near the top of rue Jacques-Cartier, stands the **Gaspé Cathedral**. Built in 1970, it's the only wooden cathedral in North America and its barn-like exterior has an extraordinarily dour and industrial appearance. The interior is completely different: the nave – all straight lines and symmetrical simplicity – is bathed in warm, softly coloured light that pours in through an enormous stained-glass window in the style of Mondrian.

Just outside town, the white **Sanctuaire Notre Dame-des-Douleurs** is a popular pilgrimage site due to the healing powers it's said to have – and which are supported by the collection of crutches, braces and canes found in the chapel entombing Father Watier, the sanctuary's founder. Up a slight incline behind the church, the replica of the Lourdes Grotto (replete with outdoor altar) and the Garden of Mary's Sorrows are both attractive gardens with remarkable religious sculptures. Next door, the **Site Historique Micmac de Gespeg** (mid-June to mid-Sept daily 9am–5pm; $4; guided tours only), is a replica of the aboriginal village that stood at *Gespeg* ("the end of the land" in the Micmac language) in 1675, when aboriginal trading with Europeans was in full swing. The site offers interesting insight into how to build tepees and animal traps and carve utensils, but the visit is overlong at two hours.

Practicalities

Buses to Gaspé stop on the main street, rue Jacques-Cartier, at the *Motel Adams*. The **tourist office** (mid-June to Aug daily 8am–8pm) is on the far side of the river from the town centre along Hwy 132; it has accommodation listings and maps of the town. **College rooms** are available during the summer at the CÉGEP de la Gaspésie et des Îles at 94 rue Jacques-Cartier (☎368-2749, *www.cgaspesie.qc.ca*; ①). Most of the town's **B&B** accommodation is of high quality, but *Les Petits Matins* at 129 rue de la Reine (☎368-1370; *www.bbcanada.com/petitsmatins;* ②) is definitely the best, located in an old bank building and with excellent breakfasts. Bargain-basement **motel** accommodation is available at *Motel Plante*, 137 rue Jacques-Cartier (☎368-2254 or 1-888/368-2254, *www.motelplante.com;* ②).

Le Bourlingueur, next to the Jacques-Cartier mall opposite the main bridge at 207 de la Reine, is recommended for **breakfast** (around $4), though the Chinese and Canadian dishes on the evening menu are rather pricey, with main courses costing $13. Otherwise, *Brise-Bise*, 2 Côte Carter, is a great café and a swinging bar at night. Nearby *La Fringale*, a bakery at 10 rue Carter, is good for stocking up if you're heading for the parks; a pre-wrapped sandwich and a drink will cost about $4. Healthy treats can be had at *Croque Nature*, 119 rue de la Reine, a natural-foods store. If you can afford to splurge, do it at the *Café des Artistes*, 249 boul Gaspé – it's one of the best restaurants on the peninsula for French cuisine. Even if you can't afford to dine there, the upstairs cigar room nestled under the eaves is worth a visit of its own. The owners also run an excellent **café** at 101 rue de la Reine.

Percé

Once a humble fishing community, **PERCÉ** is a prime holiday spot, thanks to the tourist potential of the gargantuan limestone rock that rears up from the sea here facing the reddish cliffs of the shore. One of Canada's most celebrated natural phenomena, the **Rocher Percé** – so named for the hole at the western end – is nearly 500m long and 90m high, and is an almost surreal sight at dawn, when it appears bathed in an eerie golden iridescence. The town is now replete with tacky gift shops and rather pedestrian restaurants and bars; off-season, when much of the resort closes down, Percé maintains a delightfully relaxed and sleepy feel.

At low tide it's possible, if you hurry, to walk around most of the rock – ideally wearing waterproof shoes with good treads – starting from the lookout beyond the red-roofed houses at the end of rue Mont-Joli. Access to the rock now costs $1 – allegedly for upkeep of the belvedere and stairway leading to the stone beach. One of the most spectacular longer-range views of the monolith is from the top of **Mont Sainte-Anne**, which rises directly behind Percé town; the path is signposted from behind the church on avenue de l'Église, and the walk takes about an hour each way. A separate trail leads to the **Grotto**, a lovely spot with waterfalls and statues of the Virgin Mary nestled into the mountain's crevasses.

Apart from the rock, there's precious little to see in Percé, though the **Centre d'Interprétation du Parc de l'Île-Bonaventure-et-du-Rocher-Percé** (early June to mid-Oct daily 9am–5pm; free), some 2km to the south of the centre (exit Hwy 132 at route des Failles and turn left along route d'Irlande), has some enjoyable displays on the area's flora and fauna. In the middle of town, in the old Charles Robin Company building formerly used for processing and storing fish, the **Musée la Chafaud**, 145 Hwy 132 (daily: 10am–10pm; $5), displays traditional and contemporary art and occasionally gets high-calibre exhibitions. A small room downstairs has some old pictures of Percé. A few kilometres west of Percé, **La Vieille Usine de l'Anse-à-Beaufils** (daily 10am–10pm) showcases a wide range of local art in a renovated fish-packing plant that fronts a decent beach.

Otherwise, Percé makes a useful base for visiting several natural attractions, including the **Grande Crevasse**, a volcanically formed split in a rocky outcrop that's just a few millimetres wide but several hundred metres deep. The clearly marked path takes about an hour to walk in each direction and begins behind the *Auberge de Gargantua*, a first-class restaurant on route des Failles. From the wharf in the centre of Percé, frequent boat trips (1hr 30min to 3hr; $20–30) go around the nearby **Île Bonaventure** bird reserve (daily: June & Sept to mid-Oct 8.15am–4pm; July & Aug 8.15am–5pm), whose precipitous cliffs are favoured by gannets in particular, as well as kittiwakes, razorbills, guillemots, gulls, cormorants and puffins. You can also arrange to disembark at the island's tiny jetty, where all of the lengthy walking trails lead to the clifftops above the gannet colonies, and one includes a visit to **Le Boutillier**, a restored nineteenth-century fisherman's home.

The wharf is also the departure point for **whale-watching** excursions – between May and October the blue and humpback whales are often in the area, and you may also see porpoises, seals and the rarer white-sided dolphins. Zodiacs speed out with Observation Littoral Percé (☎782-5359), but as they fill up quickly, you may have to opt for a larger glassed-in boat with Les Croisières Julien (☎782-2161 or 1-877/782-2161). Trips last from two to three hours and cost around $40 and should be reserved in advance at the various ticket kiosks lining the main drag.

Practicalities

Highway 132 bisects Percé and passes just to the north of the main wharf, close to the **tourist office** (mid-June to Aug daily 8am–8pm), which has a comprehensive list of accommodation, operates a free room-reservation service and keeps a variety of boat and tide timetables. Arriving from Carleton or Gaspé, **buses** drop passengers in the centre of Percé at the Petro-Canada service station, but the VIA Rail **train** station is 10km south of town on Hwy 132.

Most of Percé's accommodation is open during the summer months only, so if you're coming in the off-season, you'll likely have to stay in Gaspé (see p.290). Some of the cheapest **rooms** in town are at the seasonal *Maison Avenue House* guesthouse, 38 ave de l'Église (☎782-2954; ①), and *Chez Despard*, a B&B with smallish rooms about 2km west of Percé (☎782-5446; ②). Alternatively, **motels** dot Hwy 132 and, although there's little to distinguish them, advance bookings are advised in July and August. Some of the less expensive options include *Le Macareux*, no. 262 (☎782-2414; ①); *Bleu Blanc Rouge*, no. 103 (☎782-2142; ②); *Motel Bellevue*, no. 183 (☎782-2182; ③); and at no. 288, *Le Mirage* (☎782-5151 or 1-800/463-9011; ③). Rather more upmarket, the *Hôtel la Normandie*, 221 Hwy 132 ouest (☎782-2112 or 1-800/463-0820, *www.normandieperce.com*; ④), has a clutch of bright, modern bedrooms with superb views along the coast. The are two noteworthy **campsites**, *Camping Tête d'Indien*, on the way into town (☎645-3845 or 1-877/530-8383, *www.campnetamerica.com*; $14), and *Camping Côte Surprise* on Hwy 132 (☎782-5443; four-person sites from $15), with great views of the rock.

La Maison du Pêcheur, just up from the wharf, has fine **seafood** dishes; while *Le Matelot*, 7 rue de l'Église, serves lobster with live entertainment. Substantial **snacks**, coffees and vegetarian dishes are best in the faintly bohemian atmosphere of *Les Fous de Bassan*, also on the main street. For very fine food, dine at *Auberge Gargantua*, 222 rte des Failles (☎782-2852), with gourmet French cuisine and great panoramas over town, or *La Normandia*, 221 Hwy 132 (☎782-2112), for such delights as lobster baked in champagne.

The Baie des Chaleurs

Along the coastal road to the southwest of Percé, the dramatic mountains that dominate the north and east of the peninsula are replaced by a gently undulating landscape of wooded hills and farmland. **Chandler**, the first town of any size on this route, is an ugly lumber port notable solely for the wreck of the Peruvian freighter *Unisol* in the mouth of the harbour. It ran aground in a gale in 1983, allegedly because its captain, unable to negotiate entry into the port for his cement-laden vessel, got drunk and allowed the vessel to run onto the sandbank where it remains today. Beyond Chandler lies the **Baie des Chaleurs**, the long wedge of ocean that separates the heart of the Gaspé from New Brunswick. It was named by Jacques Cartier; as its name implies, this sheltered inlet has relatively warm waters and the bay is dotted with seaside resorts-cum-fishing villages and farming communities connected by the coastal highway.

Bonaventure

The most easterly resort on the bay is **BONAVENTURE**, whose tiny centre, beside Hwy 132, edges the marshy delta and man-made lagoon of the river that sports its name. The town is, uniquely, a centre for the production of fish-leather products such as purses and wallets, but it's usually visited for its salmon fishing and sandy beach. A wildlife observation centre, **Bioparc de la Gaspésie**, 123 rue des Vieux Ponts (early June to early Oct daily 9am–6pm; $10), showcases the region's animals – caribou, lynx, otters and mountain lions included – in their respective ecosystems. But Bonaventure is really known for being a stronghold of **Acadian culture**. Their traditions and heritage are celebrated at the **Musée Acadien du Québec**, 95 ave Port-Royal (late June to early Sept daily 9am–6pm; early Sept to mid-Oct 9am–5pm; mid-Oct to late June Mon–Fri 9am–noon & 1–5pm, Sat & Sun 1–5pm; $5), set in an imposing blue and white wooden building, once the church hall, in the town centre. Highlights of the collection include some delightful handmade furniture dating from the eighteenth century and a whole range of intriguing photographs that encapsulate something of the hardships of Acadian rural life.

Next door, Bonaventure's **tourist office**, 91 ave Port-Royal (mid-June to Aug daily 9am–6pm), has background information on the town and **accommodation** lists. The latter include the *Motel le Bocage*, 173 ave Port-Royal (☎534-3430; ②; summer only); *Motel Grand Pré*, 118 ave Grand-Pré (☎534-2053 or 1-800/463-2053; ③) and the **B&Bs**: *Au Foin Fou*, 204 rte de la Rivière (☎534-4413; ②); and *Auberge du Café Acadien*, 168 ave Beaubassin (☎534-4276; ②), over the excellent *Café Acadien*, which serves imaginative French-Canadian **food**. *Cime Aventure* at 200 chemin A. Arsenault (☎534-2333) has tepees (①) to sleep in alongside the Bonaventure river and runs adventure trips into the local area (3hr to 6 days; prices vary). *Camping Plage Beaubassin*, 154 ave Beaubassin (early June to Aug; ①) is a municipal **campsite** on the spit of land between the lagoon and the bay.

New Richmond

NEW RICHMOND, 30km from Bonaventure, has only one worthy attraction, the **Centre d'Héritage Britannique de la Gaspésie**, beside the bay towards the west end of town, 7km from the highway, at 351 boul Perron ouest (daily: June to early Sept 9am–6pm; Sept to early Oct 9am–4pm; $5). Set in wooded parkland around the old light-house at Duthie's Point, near the mouth of the Rivière Cascapédia, it's a kind of Loyalist theme park-cum-ghost town made up of a collection of wooden buildings assembled from the surrounding region. Although they were all restored to their nineteenth- or early-twentieth-century appearance, many are ill-kept and falling into disrepair today. Even so, the centre is spacious enough for a pleasant stroll along the shore. It even has its own tiny beach.

Carleton and around

Just to the west of New Richmond, Hwy 299 runs north along the banks of the Cascapédia towards the Parc de la Gaspésie (see p.288), while the coastal Hwy 132 continues on to the popular bayside resort of **CARLETON**, where the mountains of the interior return to dominate the landscape. Founded in 1756 by Acadian refugees, Carleton is an unassuming little place that stands back from the sea behind a broad lagoon, linked to the narrow coastal strip by a couple of long causeways. The town has a bird sanctuary – a favourite haunt of wading species like the sandpiper and plover – and several accessible bathing beaches where you can rent kayaks (☎364-7802). But what makes the place special is the contrast between the coastal flatlands and the backdrop of wooded hills that rise up behind the town. At 582m, **Mont Saint-Joseph** is the highest of these and is presided over by the **Oratoire Notre Dame-du-Mont-Saint-Joseph**, a disappointing church that incorporates the walls of a stone chapel built on the site in 1935. A three-kilometre maze of steep footpaths slip past streams and waterfalls before they reach the summit. You can also take the less adventurous option and drive up. You must pay ($4) to see the splendid panoramic views over the bay and across to New Brunswick.

Carleton is a good place to stay overnight and, while you're here, the hilly **Miguasha Peninsula**, some 20km to the west off Hwy 132, makes a pleasant excursion. Famous for its fossils, this tiny peninsula is home to the **Parc de Miguasha**, where the cream of the fossil crop is displayed at the combined **research centre and museum** (daily: June to early Sept 9am–6pm; Sept to mid-Oct 9am–5pm; free). Frequent and free guided tours take in the museum, the research area and a walk along the beach and cliffs. About 800m from the museum is the jetty for the little **car ferry** (late June to early Sept hourly 7.30am–7.30pm; 20min; $12 one-way for driver and car, $1 per additional passenger) that crosses over to Dalhousie in New Brunswick, a short cut that avoids the tip of the Baie des Chaleurs.

Carleton's many **motels** line the main street, boul Perron. The cheaper choices include: *Auberge la Visite Surprise*, no. 527 (☎364-6553 or 1-800/463-7740; ②); *L'Abri*, no. 360 (☎364-7001 or 1-800/827-7001; ③); and *Manoir Belle Plage*, no. 474 (☎364-3388 or 1-800/463-0780; ②). A **B&B**, *Les Leblanc*, is at no. 346 (☎364-7601; ②). The town has a well-situated **campsite**, *Camping Carleton*, on the causeway, Banc de Larocque (☎364-3992; sites from $19; mid-June to Aug).

Le Bleu Marine, 203 rte du Quai, offers affordable lunchtime menus overlooking the beach, while more substantial seafood **meals** are available at *Restaurant le Héron*, at no. 561 (where the **bus** stops), and the expensive but superb *La Maison Monti*, at 840 boul Perron. If you're heading off to the Parc de Miguasha, pack up a picnic lunch at the bakery *La Mie Véritable*, 578 boul Perron.

Pointe-à-la-Croix and around

Some 50km to the west of Carleton, humdrum **Pointe-à-la-Croix** is the site of the interprovincial bridge over to Campbellton, New Brunswick. During the summer, a **tourist booth** in the tiny wooden house by the turn-off for the bridge on Hwy 132 (daily 8am–8pm) offers a full range of information on the Gaspé Peninsula. Just before the bridge, a right turn leads to the little waterside community of **LISTUGUJ** (Restigouche), the heart of a Micmac Indian reservation that functions on New Brunswick time because the children go to school in Campbellton. The village is home to the Micmacs, an Algonquian-speaking people who spread across the Atlantic seaboard from Nova Scotia through to the Gaspé and east Newfoundland. Their history is a familiarly sad one: trading furs for European knives, hatchets and pots, the Micmacs quarrelled with other aboriginal groups over hunting grounds until there was a state of perpetual warfare. In later years, the Micmacs proved loyal allies to the French military cause, but, as with all other aboriginal groups, their numbers were decimated by European diseases and they remain a neglected minority. However, the reserve is self-governing and one of the five richest in Canada (there are 800-odd reserves).

On your right as you enter the reserve, the locals have reconstructed **Fort Listuguj** (June to mid-Oct daily 10am–7pm; $6; *www.johnco.com/~fortlistuguj*), based on a 1760 Acadian fort where the last battle for New France took place. Built entirely of cedar with a tepee circle in the centre, the fort is staffed by costumed guides and the atmosphere is entertaining and laid-back with traditional singing, drumming, storytelling, craftmaking and incredible food – try the local bread (*lusgnign*), baked in the outside ovens, or the Acadian-style smoked fish. It's possible to stay in the tepees on a bed of fir boughs (①) and in the bunks of the soldiers' cabins (①) – warm bedding is provided. Opposite the fort's entrance, the **Listuguj Arts and Cultural Centre** (May–Sept daily 9am–5pm; $5) offers a small display of traditional crafts and buildings from before European contact. The clothing, canoes and porcupine quill boxes are all made locally to rekindle interest in Micmac culture and traditional skills.

A couple of kilometres west of the bridge, back along Hwy 132, **La Bataille-de-la-Restigouche**, a national historic site, commemorates the crucial naval engagement of 1760, which effectively extinguished French hopes of relieving their stronghold in Montréal, the year after the fall of Québec City. The French fleet, which had already taken casualties in evading the blockade of Bordeaux, was forced to take refuge in the mouth of the Rivière Restigouche and then, despite assistance from local Micmacs and Acadians, was overpowered by superior British forces. The site's excellent **interpretive centre** (daily: June to early Oct 9am–5pm; $3.75; *parkscanada.pch.qc.ca*) contains relics of the French fleet, especially the frigate *Le Machault*, which has been partly reconstructed. An audiovisual display provides a graphic account of the battle and of its strategic significance.

You wouldn't want to stay in Pointe-à-la-Croix, but if you're marooned here, try a most unusual **youth hostel**, *Auberge du Château Bahia* (☎788-2048; ①, including breakfast), in Pointe-à-la-Garde, some 6km east of Listuguj and signposted off Hwy 132. It's in an eccentric Renaissance-style wooden castle built by the owner and his father – and the food is excellent.

Matapédia

At the western tip of the Baie des Chaleurs, at the confluence of the Restigouche and Matapédia rivers, the tiny village of **MATAPÉDIA**, a Micmac term meaning "there where the two rivers meet", is surrounded by steep green hills and lies at the centre of an excellent salmon-fishing region. Not a lot else happens here aside from canoe trips down the river, and the **restaurants** leave much to be desired: *La Vieille Gare*, at 50 boul Perron ouest, has somewhat pricey seafood fare, while the more reasonably priced but uninspired *Café Resto-Bar Matapédia*, at 13 rue des Saumons, is on the ground floor of the town's rather dilapidated **youth hostel** (☎865-2444; ①). Close by, the *Motel Restigouche*, at no. 5 (☎865-2155; ③), is the place to **stay** if you're into fishing and hunting, and the **B&B** *Aux Bois d'Avignon*, in nearby Saint-Alexis-de-Matapédia (☎299-2537 or 1-877/767-8027; ②), provides large, attractive rooms and a pool. From Matapédia, Hwy 132 cuts north across the interior of the peninsula through Amqui, a dreary little town that serves as a ski resort in the winter, before heading back up to Ste-Flavie (see p.286).

The Îles-de-la-Madeleine

The archipelago of the **Îles-de-la-Madeleine** (Magdalen Islands), in the middle of the Gulf of St Lawrence some 200km southeast of the Gaspé Peninsula and 100km east of Prince Edward Island, consists of twelve main islands, seven of which are inhabited. Six of these are connected by narrow sand spits and crossed by paved and gravel roads, while the last is only accessible by boat. Together these dozen islands form a crescent-shaped series of dunes, lagoons and low rocky outcrops that measures about 80km from end to end, with the main village and ferry port roughly in the middle at **Cap-aux-Meules**. The islands lie in the Gulf Stream, which makes the winters warmer than those of mainland Québec, but they are subject to almost constant winds, which have eroded the red-sandstone cliffs along parts of the shoreline into an extraordinary array of arches, caves and tunnels. These **rock formations**, the archipelago's most distinctive attraction, are at their best on the central **Île du Cap-aux-Meules** and the adjacent **Île du Havre-aux-Maisons**.

In 1534, **Jacques Cartier** stumbled across the Îles-de-la-Madeleine on his way west to the St Lawrence River. Cartier, always keen to impress his sponsors with the value of his discoveries, wrote with characteristic exaggeration, "The islands are full of beautiful trees, prairies, fields of wild wheat, and flowering pea plants as beautiful as I've ever seen in Brittany." Despite Cartier's eulogy, the islands attracted hardly any settlers until the Deportations of 1755, when a few Acadian families escaped here to establish a mixed farming and fishing community. Remote and isolated, the **Madelinots**, as the islanders came to be known, were unable to control their own economic fortunes, selling their fish at absurdly low prices to a series of powerful merchants who, in turn, sold them tackle and equipment at exorbitant rates. The most notorious of these men was **Isaac Coffin**, who was granted the land in 1798 by the British Crown in return for services rendered during the American Civil War. Coffin developed a classically colonial form of oppression by forcing most of the islanders to pay him rent for their lands. Only in 1895 did a provincial statute allow the Madelinots to buy them back, and the province of Québec purchased the islands outright in 1958.

Today the 15,000 inhabitants are largely dependent on fishing in general and the lobster catch in particular. Herring, mackerel, scallops and halibut are also mainstays, and most people work at local companies that freeze, can, smoke, ship or market the catch. Until recently, when international pressure brought it to an end, the annual seal hunt supported many islanders (in March, the seals can be easily spotted on the ice floes). Other sectors of the fishery are now suffering because of fish-stock depletion, and the community's future livelihood revolves around tourism. Many residents worry about preserving their way of life and the fragile ecology of their beautiful islands. Tourists come to the archipelago for its wide-open landscapes and sense of isolation – it's easy to find a dune-laden beach where you can be alone with the sea. Bear in mind, though, that throughout the islands powerful currents and changeable weather conditions can make sea bathing dangerous, and the waters are occasionally home to stinging jellyfish.

With only fourteen **inns**, **motels** and **hotels** on the Magdalens, it's a good idea to book a bed before you fly or sail here. The tourist office at Cap-aux-Meules also has details on the islands' many B&B addresses, and on cottage and apartment rentals, starting at roughly $250 per week. In addition to the places detailed below, it is possible to **camp** just about anywhere – though make sure you ask permission first.

Île du Cap-aux-Meules

The ferry from Souris, Prince Edward Island (see p.396), docks in the middle of the archipelago, at Île du **Cap-aux-Meules**, which boasts the Magdalen's largest community – **CAP-AUX-MEULES**, on the eastern shore. A useful base for exploring the neighbouring islands, the town is the islands' administrative and business centre and their least attractive enclave. However, just a couple of kilometres west of the village, there are fine views of the entire island chain from the **Butte du Vent**, the area's highest hill. Further west, on the other end of the island near the fishing port of **Étang-du-Nord**, you'll find some extravagant coastal rock formations and a port where kayaking tours take off. In the opposite direction, the main road skirts the southern tip of the islands' longest lagoon before heading on across the Île du Havre-aux-Maisons. Reasonable **accommodation** options include the *Motel Bellevue*, 40 chemin Principal (☎986-4477; ③); and the *Auberge du Village*, 205 chemin Principal (☎986-3312; ③/④). Alternatively, the large *Château Madelinot*, 323 Hwy 199 (☎986-3695 or 1-800/661-4537; ⑤), offers fine sea views, great food and comfortable rooms, whilst *Auberge Chez Sam*, in Étang-du-Nord (☎986-5780; ②), has more modest accommodation in an equally relaxing setting.

Close to the harbour, *La Jetée*, 153 chemin Principale, has pub grub at good prices. For outstanding but pricier **food**, try the seafood at *La Table des Roy*, 1188 Hwy 199 (closed Mon) in La Vernière just west of Cap-aux-Meules; dinner will set you back over $50. The *Petit Café* in the *Château Madelinot*, 323 Hwy 199, is open all year, with a menu that ranges from hamburgers to lobsters; evening specials cost about $25; and *La Factrie* is a fun and inexpensive cafeteria-style lobster restaurant attached to a lobster-processing plant at 521 chemin Gros Cap.

Île du Havre-aux-Maisons

Île du **Havre-aux-Maisons**' smooth green landscapes contrast with the red cliffs of its southern shore. Crisscrossed by narrow country roads and littered with tiny straggling villages, this island is best known for a unique oral tradition. The Acadians that settled here post-deportation were so irate with their treatment they decided never to utter the word "king" ("roi" in French) again; over the years, they wound up dropping the letter "r" altogether from their language.

The weird shapes of the coastal rocks around **Dune-du-Sud** are well worth a visit, as is the **Fumoir d'Antan**, 27 chemin du Quai (daily 9am–5pm; free tour), the last remaining traditional herring smokehouse on the islands. Down by the lagoon, the hodgepodge collection of artefacts at the **Centre d'Interpretation de Havre-aux-Maisons** (June to mid-Sept daily 9am–9pm) is on loan from local families and offers an excellent introduction to the local lore. Next door, **Les Excursions de la Lagune** takes off three times daily for a two-hour tour of the lagoon on a glass-bottom boat

(☎969-4550; $20) that's both highly entertaining and educational. Deserted twin beaches edge the hamlet islet of **Pointe-aux-Loups** north of here, across the sand spit and along Hwy 199.

Should you want to **stay**, the *Auberge la P'tite Baie*, 187 Hwy 199 (☎969-4073, *www3.sympatico.ca/auberge.petitebaie*; ③), with its lovely rooms and sea vistas, is your best bet. For great **seafood**, try the restored convent *Au Vieux Couvent*, 292 Hwy 199, which also has a lively basement **bar** with regular live music acts – even without, the place gets packed every night.

Grosse-Île and Île de la Grande-Entrée

At the far end of the archipelago, the twin islets of anglophone **Grosse-Île** and francophone **Île de la Grande-Entrée** border the wildlife reserve of the **Pointe-de-l'Est**, whose entrance is beside the main road. On its south side, the reserve is edged by the enormous sandy expanse of La Grande Échouerie **beach**, whose southern end is framed by yet more splendid rock formations at Old Harry's Point. This is where Europeans first came to the islands in order to slaughter **walruses** (sea cows), depleting the stock by 1800. Nowadays, the 10km walk down the beach offers a good chance to spot **seals**, and there have been renewed – albeit very rare – walrus sightings. A kilometre past the rustic wharf at **Old Harry**, a pretty white church with beautifully sculptured doors uses the islands as backdrop for biblical tales. A little further, the old red schoolhouse is home to the Council for Anglophone Magdalen Islanders and a **museum** (June–Sept Mon–Sat 9am–4pm, Sun 11am–4pm; free) tells the history of the anglophone population, most of whom are of Scottish descent. To learn more about seals head to the **Centre d'Interpretation du Phoque**, 377 Hwy 199 (daily: mid-June to late Aug 11am–6.30pm; Sept to mid-June 9am–noon & 1–4pm; $5.50, *www.ilesdelamadeleine.com/cip*).

The lobster port of **Grande-Entrée**, the last island to be inhabited, has a couple of **accommodation** options: *Domaine de la Grenouille sur Mer*, 83 chemin des Pealey (☎450/658-1130; ③) and *Club Vacances "Les Îles"*, 377 Hwy 199 (☎985-2833 or 1-888/537-4537, *www.clubiles.qc.ca*; ⑤), which is open all year and has camping space as well as rooms. The food is expensive but you can save money by opting to pay for full board. The club also offers various activities – like trips to the caves on offshore Île Boudreau and seal-spotting excursions in the summer.

Île du Havre-Aubert

To the south of Île du Cap-aux-Meules, **Île du Havre-Aubert** has one significant community, **HAVRE-AUBERT**, that's edged by round sloping hills. It's the most attractive of the islands' communities, and its picturesque location and undoubtable charm attract a lot of visitors. It is situated around **La Grave**, a pebbly beach flanked by a boardwalk and wooden buildings once used by sailors and fishermen and now transformed into bars, cafés, restaurants, souvenir shops and an art gallery for the island's new trade in tourists; for the best spot to buy things from lampshades and fisheads to household decorations made of sand, try Les Artisans du Sable. On the beach the **Aquarium** (early June to mid-Aug daily 10am–6pm; mid-Aug to mid-Oct 10am–5pm; $5.50, *www.ilesdela-madeleine.com/aquarium*) displays fish and crustaceans found in the waters around the island – you can handle the creatures thanks to open-access aquariums on the main floor and there's a small seal tidal pool out back.

Overlooking La Grave, the **Musée de la Mer** (late June to late Aug daily Mon–Fri 9am–6pm, Sat & Sun 10am–6pm; late Aug to late June Mon–Fri 9am–noon & 1–5pm, Sat & Sun 1–5pm; $4) has a series of displays on local fishing techniques and the history of the islands. Especially interesting is the exhibit focused on the more than 400 shipwrecks that have occurred just offshore.

Set apart from Havre-Aubert, in the community of Bassin, the **Site d'Autrefois** (July–Aug Mon–Wed 10am–6pm, Thurs–Sun 10am–11pm; mid–late June & Sept 10am–6pm; $6) is a fanciful spot that tells the story of Madelinot life through life-sized mannequins of fishermen, boats and model houses. La Chevauché des Îles, also in Bassin, offers **horseback riding** tours of the island (☎937-2368 or 937-5453; $25–40) while Centre Nautique de l'Istorlet, 100 chemin de l'Isorlet (☎937-5266) rents out **sea and surf kayaks**, a fun way to explore the cliffs and caves of the coast, and also rents out cheap **rooms** (①).

You can **stay** on La Grave at *Chez Charles Painchaud*, 930 Hwy 199 (☎937-2227; ②), or the seasonal *Le Berceau des Îles*, 701 chemin principal in Havre-Aubert (☎937-5614; ②–⑤). Both are **B&Bs** and can arrange for pick-ups from the airport or ferry as well as organize winter and summer activities – they even rent cars. If you want to be right on the main drag, the forest-green ancestral house *La Maison de Camille*, 946 chemin de la Grave (☎937-2516; ②) is a well-situated and affordable option, while *Auberge Chez Denis à François*, 404 chemin d'en Haut (☎937-2371, *www.ilesdelamadeleine.com/auberge*; ③) offers fine views of the strip.

Restaurants are of good quality in Havre-Aubert: even if you don't stay at *Auberge Chez Denis à François*, you should definitely try the seafood – they even have seal on the menu. *La Saline*, 1009 Hwy 199 in La Grave, is open for delicious evening fare – there's also live music in the adjoining bar. The much more expensive *La Marée Haute*, 25 chemin des Fumoirs, is also only open at night and serves up some of Canada's finest seafood, including sea urchins and smoked seal. For chunky sandwiches and clam chowder served in bread, head for the marvelously atmospheric *Café de la Grave* in the old general store. *Le Petit Mondrain* on chemin de La Grave is popular with locals and possibly has the islands' cheapest seafood.

Île d'Entrée

To the southeast, tiny anglophone **Île d'Entrée** is the only inhabited island not linked by land to the rest of the archipelago. Home to 175 people, this grassy hillock is encircled by footpaths and makes a pleasant day out, providing the sea is calm on the **ferry** trip from Cap-aux-Meules (Mon–Sat 2 daily; $20 return; ☎986-5705). Human-friendly horses and cows roam freely on the slopes of the Îles de la Madeleine's highest point, **Big Hill** (174m), accessible from the port by taking chemin Main and then chemin Post Office, and following the path across the fields to the top for a view of the whole archipelago. On your way towards the path, a tiny **museum** (opening hours vary, call ☎986-6622) displays island artefacts and historical household items. The only official lodging is the basic **B&B** *Chez McLean* (☎986-4541; ②). Otherwise, you'll probably end up in someone's home – call the regional tourist office for more information (☎986-2245). For **food**, there's a bar-restaurant and a grocery store near the port.

The Îles-de-la-Madeleine practicalities

Every month except February and March a daily car **ferry** goes to Cap-aux-Meules from Souris, on Prince Edward Island (Souris ☎902/687-2181 or 1-888/986-3278; Cap-aux-Meules ☎418/986-6600 or 1-888/936-3278); a return trip costs $280 for a car with two passengers, and it's a five-hour trip each way. Reservations are advised in July and August. A cargo and fifteen-passenger **ship**, the CTMA *Voyageur*, leaves Montréal for the islands every Friday and takes 48 hours to sail down the St Lawrence (Montréal ☎514/937-7656; Cap-aux-Meules ☎418/986-6600; $510 one-way including meals, plus $220 if you bring a car). During February and March, there's also service from Matane (☎418/986-5705). Daily scheduled **flights** leave Gaspé town, Québec City, Montréal, and Halifax on Air Nova (bookings via Air Canada; ☎514/393-3333 or 1-800/630-3299). Book a fortnight in advance and include a Saturday overnight stay for discount flights.

The islands' **airport** is inconveniently situated at the north end of Île du Havre-aux-Maisons, some 20km from Cap-aux-Meules. Some flights have connecting buses to Cap-aux-Meules, but otherwise you'll have to take a Lafrance **taxi** (☎986-6649; about $35), or **hire a car** from Tilden (☎969-2590 or 1-888/657-3036) or MCR (☎969-4209 or 986-6057) at the airport; book in advance in the summer. The **ferry terminal** at Cap-aux-Meules is near the **tourist office**, 128 chemin du Débarcadère (late June to early Sept daily 7am–9pm; early Sept to late June Mon–Fri 9am–noon & 1–5pm; ☎986-2245). They have masses of free leaflets and operate a free room-reservation service with a special emphasis on B&Bs.

The best way to tour the principal islands is by a **bike**, which may be rented at Le Pédalier, 365 chemin Principal, Cap-aux-Meules (☎986-2965). **Mopeds** can be rented from Cap-aux-Meules Honda, Hwy 199 at La Vernière, southwest of Cap-aux-Meules (☎986-4085). Departures for **boat** and **fishing trips** are near the ferry terminal throughout the summer (☎986-4745).

There are several **campsites**: try the peaceful *Le Barachois*, chemin du Rivage, Fatima (☎986-6065 or 986-5678; $18 for a two-person site; May–Oct) or *Camping Gros Cap*, 74 chemin du Camping, Étang du Nord (☎986-4505; $14 for a two-person site). You can also camp on Île de la Grande-Entrée at *Club Vacances "Les Îles"* (☎985-2833, *www.clubiles.qc.ca*), where there's also a dorm. They organize excursions and have a great cafeteria.

NORTH OF THE ST LAWRENCE

Québec's true north is a mighty, inhospitable tundra inhabited only by mining communities, groups of Inuits, and the hardy characters who staff the hydroelectric installations with which so many of the rivers are dammed. The only readily accessible region, along the north shore of the St Lawrence and its main tributary, the Saguenay, covers an area that changes from trim farmland to a seemingly never-ending forest bordering the barren seashore of the St Lawrence.

Immediately northeast of Québec City is the beautiful **Charlevoix** region of peaceful villages and towns that bear the marks of Québec's rural beginnings – both in the architecture of the seigneurial regime and in the layout of the land. Often the winding highways and back roads pass through a virtually continuous village, where the only interruptions in the chain of low-slung houses are the tin-roofed churches. The beguiling hills and valleys give way to dramatic ravaged rock just beyond the Charlevoix borders, where the **Saguenay River** crashes into the immense fjord that opens into the St Lawrence at the resort of **Tadoussac**.

TOURIST INFORMATION

The areas to the north and east of Québec City are divided into the following regional tourist associations, who can each provide a free tourist guide, which includes basic maps of the region. The telephone code for all of these areas is ☎418.

Charlevoix: ☎665-4454 or 1-800/667-2276, *www.tourisme-charlevoix.com*

Saguenay–Lac-Saint-Jean: ☎543-9778 or 1-800/463-9651, *www.atrsaglac.d4m.com*

Manicouagan: ☎294-2876 or 1-888/463-5319, *www.tourismecote-nord.com*

Duplessis: ☎962-0808 or 1-888/463-0808 ext 11, *www.tourismecote-nord.com*

Inland, **Lac Saint-Jean** – source of the Saguenay – is an oasis of fertile land in a predominantly rocky region, and its peripheral villages offer glimpses of native as well as Québécois life. Adventurous types following the St Lawrence can head beyond Tadoussac to **Havre-St-Pierre** through a desolate, sparsely populated region where the original livelihoods of fishing and lumber have largely given way to ambitious mining and hydroelectric projects. The remoteness of Gulf of St Lawrence islands such as the Île d'Anticosti and the sculptured terrain of the **Mingan archipelago** – a national park, well served by boats from Havre-St-Pierre – is matched by the isolation of the unmodernized fishing communities along the **Lower North Shore**, where no roads penetrate and visits are possible only by supply ship, plane or snowmobile.

Charlevoix

Stretching along the north shore of the St Lawrence east of Québec City, from the Beaupré coast to the Saguenay Fjord, the area of **Charlevoix**, named after the Jesuit historian Francois Xavier de Charlevoix, is the world's only inhabited UNESCO World Biosphere Reserve. Species like the arctic caribou and great wolf, not usually associated with such southerly latitudes, can be seen in the more remote areas, and because the Ice Age that shaped the rest of eastern Canada missed this breathtaking portion of the Canadian Shield, numerous pre-glacial plants still thrive here. Its 6000 square kilometres consist of gently sloping hills, sheer cliffs and vast valleys veined with rivers, brooks and waterfalls, a landscape that Québec's better known artists – Clarence Gagnon, Marc-Aurèle Fortin and Jean-Paul Lemieux – chose for inspiration. Though Charlevoix has been a tourist destination for years, the land has been carefully preserved, and quaint villages and tin-roofed churches still nestle in an unspoiled countryside. The tourist office produces a brochure, *La Route des Saveurs de Charlevoix*, which is useful on a gastronomic trip – it lists agricultural producers and the restaurants that use local products in regional cuisine.

Highway 138, the main route through Charlevoix, travels 225km from Québec City to Baie-Ste-Catherine on the Saguenay. The main towns along this highway are served by Intercar buses from Québec City, but many of the quintessential Charlevoix villages – in particular those along the coastal Hwy 362 – are not served by public transport. Be prepared to rent a car or bike – the expense is well worth it.

Baie-Saint-Paul

One of Charlevoix's earliest settlements and longtime gathering place for Québec's landscape painters, the picture-perfect **BAIE-SAINT-PAUL** is tucked into the Gouffré valley at the foot of the highest range of the Laurentian mountains. Dominated by the twin spires of the church, the streets wind from the centre of town flanked by houses that are more than two hundred years old – and just wandering around Baie-Saint-Paul is the main attraction. For an overview of the works of art produced in Charlevoix, visit the **Centre d'Art de Baie-Saint-Paul**, behind the church at 4 rue Ambroise-Fafard (daily: late June to early Sept 9am–7pm; early Sept to late June 9am–5pm; free), which has excellent exhibitions of paintings and sculptures mostly inspired by the surrounding countryside; the Centre's boutique also sells local crafts. Opposite, at no. 23, the plush **Centre d'Exposition** (same times; $3) has established an international reputation for the excellence of its temporary exhibitions of Québécois and international art. Also every August to early September, at a symposium, the public can watch young Canadian and European artists at work in the nearby arena.

From beside the church, the rue St-Jean-Baptiste slips through the commercial heart of the town edged by numerous quaint cottages characteristic of Québec's earliest houses, with curving roofs and wide verandas, many converted into commercial galleries. At 58 rue St-Jean-Baptiste, **La Maison de René Richard** (daily 10am–6pm; $2.50) offers an insight into the works of René Richard, an associate of the Group of Seven. The 1852 house has been left exactly the same since Richard died in 1982; bilingual guided tours take you around his studio and living quarters, a rare glimpse at the Charlevoix of the 1940s when some of Québec's finest painters hung out here. At no. 41 on the same street, Randonnées Nature-Charlevoix (☎435-6275) runs excellent bike tours of the environs (2hr; $6; $4 if you rent a bike – $10 per half-day, $15 per day) and tours around the **Charlevoix Crater** – one of the planet's largest craters and made by a meteorite – by bus (late June to early Sept; 1 daily; 2hr; $15).

Some of the province's most dramatic **skiing** and the province's highest vertical (770m) can be found at Le **Massif** (☎632-5876 or 1-877/536-2774, *www.lemassif.com*; $34.75 per day), perched over the St Lawrence to the west of town. Baie-Saint-Paul also makes a good base to explore the **Parc des Grands-Jardins** (daily: late May to mid-June & late Aug to mid-Oct 9am–5pm; mid-June to late Aug 8am–8pm; $5 fee for parking; *www.sepaq.com*), 42km away on Hwy 381 but with no public transport. Within the forests and lakes of the park, the 900-metre Mont du Lac des Cygnes gives the best of all Charlevoix panoramas; it's a four-hour climb there and back from the trailhead just beyond the **Thomas-Fortin reception centre** (same hours as park; ☎457-3945) at the park entrance on Hwy 381. Hwy 381 continues to Chicoutimi on the Rivière Saguenay (see p.311). **Chalets** (④), huts (①) and campsites ($17.60) are available but must be reserved in advance (☎1-800/665-6527). Attracting hikers, mountain bikers and cross-country skiers, the **Traversée de Charlevoix** (☎639-2284, *www.charlevoix.net/traverse*) begins near the park on Hwy 381, traverses 100km of mountainous terrain including the Parc des Hautes-Gorges-de-la-Rivière-Malbaie and ends at Mont Grand-Fonds near La Malbaie. Accommodation in cabins or cottages starts at $122 for the six nights needed to complete the hike.

In the winter months Husky Aventure, 25 Hwy 138 in St-Urbain (☎639-2500, *www.quebecweb.com/dogsled*), organizes dog-sled excursions. They cost $120 per person per day ($160 for a 24-hour trip), including meals, a guide and a lot of fun.

Practicalities

The **information centre** for Baie-Saint-Paul and the whole Charlevoix area is at the Belvédère Baie-Saint-Paul off Hwy 138 before you descend into town from the west (daily: mid-June to early Sept 9am–7pm; early Sept to mid-June 9am–4.30pm; ☎435-4160 or 1-800/667-2276, *www.baiestpaul.com*); there is also a seasonal office in the Centre d'Art, 4 rue Ambroise-Fafard (late June to late Sept daily 10am–7pm; ☎435-5795). The Intercar bus stops at *Restaurant La Grignote*, 2 rte de l'Equerre (☎435-6569), in the shopping centre by Hwy 138.

For a town its size, Baie-Saint-Paul has an excellent variety of **accommodation**, from luxurious historic hotels to an outstanding youth hostel. The best hotels are the 1840 *Auberge la Maison Otis*, 23 rue St-Jean-Baptiste (☎435-2255 or 1-800/267-2254, *www.quebecweb.com/maisonotis*; ⑦), and the *Auberge La Pignoronde*, 750 boul Mgr-de-Laval (☎435-5505 or 1-888/554-6004, *www.quebecweb.com/lapignoronde*; ⑧). Next door to each other on the waterfront, the *Domaine Belle-Plage*, 192 rue Ste-Anne (☎435-3321, *www.cormoranbelleplage.com*; ③), and the *Auberge le Cormoran* at no. 196 (☎435-6030; ④), both have comfortable doubles, while in the centre of town the *Auberge La Muse*, 39 rue St-Jean-Baptiste (☎435-6839, *www.lamuse.com*; ⑥) includes breakfast and dinner in high season (③ in low season, without dinner). The numerous **B&Bs** include the *Gîte la Tourterelle*, further up the street at 77 rue St-Jean-Baptiste (☎435-2441; ①), and the *Gîte Panoramique*, 197 rang St-Antoine nord (☎435-0223; ②), which exits Hwy 138 opposite the tourist office. The town's best bargain is the **hostel/campsite** *Le Balcon Vert* (☎435-5587; mid-May to early Oct) up a gravel road about 3km out on Hwy

362 to Malbaie, with four-berth cabins (①), camping – $16.50 for a four-person site – and a restaurant and bar on site. Summer **camping** is also available at the riverside *Camping du Gouffre*, 439 chemin St-Laurent (☎435-2143; from $18 for a four-person site), or the larger *Camping le Genévrier*, 1175 boul Mgr-de-Laval (☎435-6520 or 1-877/435-6520, *www.genevrier.com*; $21.50 for a two-person site).

Food is plentiful within a block or two of the church: *Café d'Artistes*, 25 rue St-Jean-Baptiste, serves thin-crust pizzas while *Les Deux Soeurs* is an excellent patisserie-café across the street at no. 48. *Le Mouton Noir*, 43 rue Ste-Anne, serves hearty country cooking, like smoked sausages with maple syrup. The restaurant of the *Belle-Plage* also serves traditional Québécois cuisine, with an all-you-can-eat for buffet is around $15. Two good spots combine eating and **drinking**: *Le Saint-Pub*, 2 rue Racine (corner of St-Jean-Baptiste), and *Cuore di Lupo*, 29 rue Ambroise-Fafard – the former is a terrific brewpub with delicious bistro fare, while the latter has a packed-out terrace and reasonably priced pizza and pasta.

Hwy 362 – the coastal route

From Baie-Saint-Paul the main route onwards is Hwy 138, but if you have your own transport you should opt for the coast-hugging detour of **Hwy 362**, which twists and turns through a succession of clifftop villages along the shore of the St Lawrence. Keep an eye out for the poorly marked lookout point two-thirds of the way up the hill from Baie-St-Paul – there's a magnificent view back over the town.

The first settlement on this route is LES ÉBOULEMENTS, which means "landslides" – named after the massive earthquake of 1663, one of many that shaped this region. Just west of the village at no. 157 rue Principale is the eighteenth-century **Moulin Banal** (late June to early Sept daily 10am–5pm; $2), an operating flour mill atop a pretty waterfall on the well-kept grounds of the **Manoir de Sales-Laterrière**. The manor and mill are among the few intact structures left from the seigneurial regime of New France. The manor (a school) is not actually open to the public but a path leads up from the mill, with interpretive panels on the grounds. At the entrance to the grounds is a charming chapel (1840) built of wood and relocated here from St-Nicholas, a village on the St Lawrence. Further down the road, in the village itself, the **Centre d'Interpretation de la Forge Tremblay**, 214 rue Principale (☎635-1401 or 1-888/935-1401; Nov to mid-May; free but reservations required), dating from 1888, is still used by blacksmiths. Seek refreshment in the tearoom in the *Auberge le Surouët* across the street.

From Les Éboulements, a steep secondary road leads to the pretty coastal village of SAINT-JOSEPH-DE-LA-RIVE, once a shipyard; some heritage can be seen in the **Exposition Maritime**, 304 rue Félix-Antoine-Savard (mid-May to late June & early Sept to mid-Oct Mon–Fri 9am–4pm, Sat & Sun 11am–4pm; late June to early Sept daily 9am–5pm; $2), a museum with a few nautical displays, a workshop and boat-building yards. Pop into the local **church** (June–Oct daily 9am–8pm; free) on chemin de l'Église, where anchors prop up the altar and the font is a huge seashell from Florida. *Le Loup-Phoque*, 188 rue Félix-Antoine-Savard, a funky spot good for **food** and views, has occasional live music. A free **car ferry** departs hourly (every half-hour in summer at peak times) for nearby Île aux Coudres.

Île aux Coudres

The sixteen-kilometre-long island of **Île aux Coudres**, fifteen minutes by ferry from Saint-Joseph-de-la-Rive, is said to have been formed when an earthquake shook it from the escarpment at Les Éboulements. Cartier celebrated Canada's first Mass here in 1535 and named the island after its numerous hazelnut trees. Missionaries were the first permanent settlers, arriving in 1748, and the growing population came to depend on shipbuilding and beluga-whale hunting for their livelihoods. Ship- and canoe-building still takes place here, but the main industry of its 1600 inhabitants is harvesting peat moss from the bogs in the centre of the island.

The island's stone manors and cottages nowadays attract huge numbers of visitors, who drive and cycle around the 26-kilometre peripheral road that connects – in a clockwise direction – the three villages of **ST-BERNARD**, **LA BALEINE** and **ST-LOUIS**. Of the incidental attractions along the way, the only real diversions are the restored wind and adjacent water mills – **Les Moulins de l'Isle-aux-Coudres** (mid-May to late June & Sept to mid-Oct daily 10am–5pm; late June to Aug daily 9am–6.45pm; $2.75) – in the southwest corner of the island, both of which are in full working order. There is an **information centre** (mid-June to Aug daily 8.30am–7pm) near the ferry dock in St-Bernard, with maps of the island. **Bikes** can be rented from either Gérard Desgagnés, near the jetty at 34 rue du Port (☎438-2332), or from Vél 'O'-Coudres, 743 chemin des Coudriers in La Baleine, 5km from the dock (☎438-2118; free hourly shuttle). Rent **kayaks** for $39 per day at Kayak de Mer Isle-aux-Coudres, down the road at no. 783 (☎438-4388); they also offer guided trips for $25–70.

Most **hotels** are in La Baleine – the best deals are the *Motel la Baleine*, 138 rue Principale (☎438-2453; ②), and *Motel Écumé*, 808 chemin des Coudriers (☎438-2733; ②), a bizarre place with deliberately tilted windows and mismatched furniture in very basic rooms. The island's best bargain is the *Motel l'Islet*, 10 chemin de l'Islet (☎438-2423, *www.quebecweb.com/lislet*; ②; May to mid-Oct) in an isolated spot near St-Louis, on the west tip of the island. **Campsites** include *Camping Leclerc*, 183 rue Principale, La Baleine (☎438-2240; $18 for a two-person site) and *Camping Sylvie*, 191 rue Royale ouest, St-Bernard (☎438-2420; $12 for a four-person site).

For good local **meals** head to *La Mer Veille*, 160 des Coudriers, in St-Louis; the lunch menu is $10. The island's posh hotel, the *Cap-aux-Pierres* at 246 rue Principale in La Baleine, serves $10 breakfast buffets.

La Malbaie and around

Highways 362 and 138 converge about 50km from Baie-Saint-Paul, at **LA MALBAIE** – "Bad Bay", so called because Champlain ran aground here in 1608. Situated at the mouth of the Malbaie River, the town sprawls along the riverfront with little to detain you, though the **tourist office**, beside the main road at 630 boul de Comporté (daily: mid-June to Sept 9am–9pm; Oct to mid-June 9am–5pm), has a full range of regional tourist info; the bus arrives nearby at Dépanneur Otis, 46 rue Ste-Catherine (☎665-2264). *Motel Murray Bay*, 40 rue Laure-Conan (☎665-2441; ②), is a simple **accommodation** option, although half a dozen of the town's fifteen or so **B&Bs** are in the same price range, including *Gîte E.T. Harvey* (☎665-2779; ②) and *La Maison Dufour-Bouchard* (☎665-4982; ②) on the same street at nos. 19 and 18. If you have the equipment, head for Charlevoix's oldest and most beautifully situated **campsite**, *Camping Chutes Fraser*, 500 chemin de la Vallée (☎665-2151; sites $16 for four persons; mid-May to mid-Oct), by the falls of the same name about 3km north from La Malbaie.

Now a part of La Malbaie – back along Hwy 362 – is the ritzy resort of **POINTE-AU-PIC**, where you'll find the luxurious chateau-like pile that is *Le Manoir Richelieu*, 181 rue Richelieu (☎665-3703 or 1-800/441-1414, *www.fairmont.com*; ⑦). Originally built in 1899 for the Richelieu and Ontario Navigation Company, who ferried tourists here from New York and Montréal, the hotel was rebuilt after a fire in the 1920s, and has been recently renovated. It makes for a delightful overnight **stay** – and you can wager the rest of your travel budget at the *Casino de Charlevoix* next door. Many manor houses in Pointe-au-Pic have been converted into delightful if pricey country inns – the *Auberge des 3 Canards*, 49 Côte Bellevue (☎665-3761 or 1-800/461-3761, *www.aubergedes3canards.com*; ⑥), is an inn with one of the finest restaurants in Québec, and prices to match. **B&Bs** are pricier than average as well, but the Victorian *Gîte Harrop's*, 400 rue Richelieu (☎665-4120, *www.harrops.com*; ③), compensates with gardens overlooking the St Lawrence.

Recently amalgamated with La Malbaie, **Cap-à-l'Aigle**, an agricultural village to the east, has an excellent **B&B** – *Claire Villeneuve*, at 215 rue St-Raphaël (☎665-2288; ②) – that's one of the best examples of Québécois rural architecture.

The Hautes-Gorges

One sight that should not be missed in the Charlevoix region is the **Parc des Hautes-Gorges-de-la-Rivière-Malbaie**, a network of valleys that slice through a maze of lofty peaks 45km west of La Malbaie. To get there take Hwy 138 to **Saint-Aimé-des-Lacs**, a small town 13km northwest of La Malbaie from where the way to the park is well marked. It's a stunning thirty-kilometre drive along an unpaved forest road. The park's **information centre**, Chalet l'Écluse (☎439-1227; June to mid-Oct daily 9am–5pm), is located beside the Malbaie River just off rue Principale. On all sides the cliff faces rise more than 700m, constituting Canada's deepest canyon east of the Rockies, formed by a slip in the earth's crust 800 million years ago. The uniqueness of the park lies not just in this astounding geology but also in the fact that all of Québec's forest species grow in this one comparatively small area. From the Chalet l'Écluse a tiring but rewarding five-kilometre **hike** leads to the canyon's highest point, passing through a Laurentian maple grove on the way to the arctic–alpine tundra of the 800-metre summit. Other shorter trails offer less strenuous alternatives, and from the l'Écluse dam, beside the information centre, leisurely ninety-minute river cruises depart regularly in summer ($20). As well as free maps, the centre has **canoes and kayaks to rent** ($10 an hour, $30–32 a day) for the six-kilometre paddle along the calm "Eaux Mortes" of the river, and mountain bikes ($23 a day). The park has just one **campsite**, *Camping du Pin Blanc* ($20; June–Aug), though rustic camping is available for $10 – reservations for both from the information centre.

Port-au-Persil and Saint-Siméon

Leaving La Malbaie en route to Saint-Siméon, Hwy 138 bypasses the harbour community of **PORT-AU-PERSIL**, a peaceful Québécois village 25km down the road that's worth a stop for its vista of the St Lawrence. Nearby, the hillside village of **SAINT-SIMÉON** marks the junction of Hwy 138 to Tadoussac and the Côte-Nord and Hwy 170 to the awesome Parc du Saguenay and Lac Saint-Jean (see p.313)– public transport serves only the former route. Saint-Siméon also has a **car ferry** service to Rivière du Loup (see p.281) across the St Lawrence (2–5 daily; 1hr 15min; $10.40 single, cars $26.40). Missing the last boat is about the only eventuality that will make you want to **stay**: should it arise, the century-old **B&B** *Gîte Le Dorand*, 375 rue St-Laurent (☎638-5198; ②) is cosy and not too far from the quay.

The Saguenay and Tadoussac

A stupendous expanse of rocky outcrops, sheer cliffs and thick vegetation, the provincial **Parc du Saguenay** perches above both sides of one of the world's longest fjords, which cuts through the Canadian Shield before merging with the St Lawrence. The walls of the fjord extend to a depth of 270 metres in places, almost as much as the height of the cliffs above the waterline. The lower depths consist of icy-cold saltwater from the St Lawrence, while on the surface is the warmer water that drains out of Lac Saint-Jean, via the Rivière Saguenay. The **Parc Marin du Saguenay–St-Laurent**, a federal–provincial marine park wedged between the two halves of the Parc du Saguenay and extending out to the confluence zone where the fjord's freshwater meets the salty St Lawrence – perfect conditions for the krill that form the basis of a whale's diet.

Subsequently, the area has become immensely popular for **whale-watching** (see box on p.308).

The main centre of the region and the "gateway to the Kingdom of the Saguenay", **Tadoussac** lies some 40km north of Saint-Siméon along Hwy 138, at the confluence of the St Lawrence and the Saguenay. Traffic crosses the neck of the fjord by a free **car ferry** from Baie-Ste-Catherine to Tadoussac; you may have to wait as long as an hour or two in mid summer. Supplementing the adventure on the high seas is a bewildering array of interpretive centres, including the excellent **Centre d'Interprétation des Mammifières Marins** in Tadoussac and two centres where you have a decent chance to glimpse whales while leaving them in peace – **Baie Ste-Marguerite** is a popular beluga hangout on the north shore of the Saguenay, while northeast of Tadoussac other species of whales pass by the Cap-de-Bon-Désir off Bergeronnes, a small town 22km further along the Côte-Nord (see p.316).

No bridges cross the fjord for the 126km between Tadoussac and Chicoutimi, and there are spots where you may need to backtrack. For a taste of both the terrestrial and marine parks, drive from Saint-Siméon as far as **Baie-Éternité** on the south side of the fjord, and then double back to Saint-Siméon and continue on to Tadoussac. From Tadoussac, Hwy 172 runs parallel to the north side of the fjord past the turn-offs to Baie Ste-Marguerite and the pretty waterside village of **Ste-Rose-du-Nord** before reaching the bridge to **Chicoutimi**, from where Hwy 175 winds its lonely way through boreal forests to Québec City. If you have the time, continue west past **Jonquière** and make a circuit of the flat farming country of **Lac Saint-Jean**. It's an ideal location to cycle, and the recently completed **Véloroute des Bleuets** allows you to travel the 256km around the lake without trucks forcing you off the road. It's about five hours to Montréal on Hwy 155 (via Trois-Rivières) from the lake's southern shore; from the southeast, you can take the moose-infested Hwy 169 until it joins up with Hwy 175 on its way to Québec City. Of course, you can see it all by travelling up the south side of the fjord, circling Lac Saint-Jean and returning along the Saguenay's north side to Tadoussac, but it does mean passing through Chicoutimi twice.

Parc du Saguenay

Coming from Charlevoix, the best approach – as noted above – to the **Parc du Saguenay** (*www.sepaq.com*) is to drive along the wriggling Hwy 170 from Saint-Siméon, a road that strikes the fjord after about 50km, close to **L'ANSE-ST-JEAN**. The only village on the Saguenay when it was founded in 1838, L'Anse-St-Jean is famous for its Pont du Faubourg, the covered bridge that was featured on the back of the now-retired Canadian $1000 note and which managed to survive the flood of 1996, though the rest of the village was badly affected. The town's other claim to fame is that, on January 21, 1997, it became a monarchy following a local referendum – the new ruler, King Denys I, also known as "l'Illustre Inconnu" (the Illustrious Unknown) hasn't given up his day job as an artist and professor, though. As kingdoms go, this one isn't bad at all – there's a terrific view of the Saguenay fjord and surrounding hills from the marina, and it makes a good base to explore the park (see opposite). The village has a few **B&Bs** – *Le Nid de l'Anse*, the last house on rue St-Jean-Baptiste (☎272-2273; ②; June–Sept), overlooks the fjord and is close to the quay and walking trails. Other options are the clifftop cottages and condos at *Gîtes du Fjord*, 344 rue St-Jean-Baptiste (☎272-3430 or 1-800/561-8060; ④), as well as a couple of **campsites** – *Camping de l'Anse* (☎272-2554; $17 for a four-person site) is in a good position close to the fjord and has excellent facilities. L'Anse-St-Jean also boasts a particularly fine view of the Saguenay from the L'Anse-de-Tabatière lookout – the half-kilometre trail begins at the lookout's car park. Inland from L'Anse-St-Jean, **Mont-Edouard** (☎272-2927), with a 450m vertical, attracts **skiers** in the wintertime.

Continuing along the fjord, **RIVIÈRE-ÉTERNITÉ**, 83km from Saint-Siméon and 61km east of Chicoutimi (see p.311), is the main gateway to the Parc du Saguenay ($3.50). The park's **information centre** (☎272-3008 or 1-877/272-5229; daily: mid-May to mid-Oct 9am–5pm; late June to early Sept 9am–9pm; *www.sepaq.com*), 8km from the village, has maps of hiking trails ($3) and kayak routes ($4), and expert naturalists on hand. A smaller information post is 1.5km from the village, on the park's border. Halfway between the two is the park's main **campsite** – reservations are available from the information centre. A word of warning about the park's only unpleasant feature – be prepared, as blackflies love this place, though the worst is over by late July.

Exploring the park

From the main information centre, a couple of short hikes and a long one are laid out through this sector of the park (there are more than a hundred kilometres of trails in total). The best short hike is the **statue hike**, a four-hour round trip up the massive bluff of Cap Trinité, which flanks the deep-blue water of the Baie Éternité. The summit is topped by a huge statue known as *Our Lady of the Saguenay*, erected in 1881 by Charles-Napoléon Robitaille after he was saved from drowning in the river. The long-distance hike (25km) follows the bay of the Éternité River back to L'Anse-St-Jean via massive plateaus, ravines, waterfalls and stunning views. The hike takes about three days and there are wilderness campsites and a couple of refuges along the way; registration with the information centre is a must. A number of companies offer water-taxi services for backpackers, enabling you to hike as far as Tadoussac (it takes a week) – and you can even have your vehicle sent on to your destination by boat.

The Centre équestre des Plateaux, 31 chemin des Plateaux in L'Anse-St-Jean (☎272-3231) offers three-hour **horseback** trips for $45 as well as multiday excursions. Ninety-minute **cruises** of the Baie Éternité (May–Sept 2–3 daily; $18) leave from near the information centre. Two- and four-hour cruises departing from the quay in L'Anse-St-Jean are also available (June–Sept 2 daily; $25 and up). The best way to see the fjord, though, is by **kayak**. Rentals are available at a number of locations and the park is well set up for multiday kayak trips – rustic campsites only accessible by kayak dot both shores. Maps and information are available at the information centre and reservations are required. Guided trips are available from next to the information centre at *Explo-Fjord* (☎545-3737; 3 daily; 2–3 hours; $25–35), which also runs zodiac cruises (same prices and times). In L'Anse-St-Jean, *Fjord en kayak*, 4 rue du Faubourg (☎272-3024, *www.fjord-en-kayak.qc.ca*), has three-hour trips for $39 and two- to five-day excursions starting at $230.

The Parc Marin du Saguenay–St-Laurent

The **Parc Marin du Saguenay–St-Laurent**, which contains six different ecosystems supporting hundreds of marine species, extends up the Saguenay almost as far as La Baie and along the St Lawrence from south of St-Siméon to Les Escoumins on the Côte-Nord. The geographical centre of the park is Tadoussac, and it's here that most people set off on whale-watching excursions.

The region covered by the park is part of the hydrographic basin of the St Lawrence and the Great Lakes, and the toxic waste tipped into the St Lawrence once made this the most polluted waterway in Canada. Since the creation of the park, government initiatives have succeeded in reducing ninety percent of the pollutants from industrial plants in the immediate vicinity. The damage has already been done, though – pollutants remain in the sediment and the number of **St Lawrence beluga whales** is down from five thousand in the early twentieth century to one thousand, placing them on Canada's list of endangered species. That said, the area continues to attract the whales because the mingling of the cold Labrador sea waters with the highly oxygenated freshwater of the Saguenay produces a uniquely rich crop of krill and other plankton. The

WHALE-WATCHING

Every season more companies offer **whale-watching trips** from Tadoussac and the surrounding communities from mid-May to mid-October. Prices in Tadoussac are around $40 for trips in the larger (not to mention sturdier and more comfortable) boats and $48 in a zodiac – which provide a more thrilling ride – for a trip of up to three hours. The price drops as you go north – similar excursions from Bergeronnes and Les Escoumins cost around $30 for a zodiac for two to two and a half hours. Officially they are not allowed to approach the protected belugas or stray within 400m of these peaceful creatures, but the whales don't know that and often come close to the crafts – a magical sight.

South of Tadoussac: Croisières Famille-Dufour (☎692-0222 or 1-800/463-5250, *www.familledufour.com*) offers a ten-hour trip from **Québec City** for $129 with pickups/drop-offs in **Ste-Anne-de-Beaupré**, **Île aux Coudres** and **Pointe-au-Pic**. A coach trip and cruise package is the other option from Québec City – Croisières AML (☎692-1159 or 1-800/563-4643, *www.croisieresaml.com*) charges $75. They also run a boat from **Rivière-du-Loup** on the south shore of the St Lawrence (☎867-3361; 3 daily; 3hr 30min; $42).

Tadoussac: If you're worried about missing a reservation in Tadoussac because of the ferry queue, it's worth asking if you can board at the quay in **Baie-Ste-Catherine** instead – many of the companies fill up their boats on both sides of the Saguenay's mouth before heading off to see the whales. Some of the firms also run cruises up the Saguenay fjord, and even have combined whale/fjord packages – load up with brochures at the tourist office and compare what's on offer. You'll find that most charge $48 for a zodiac and $40 for the larger boats for three hours. For trips in a cabin-cruiser contact Les Croisières Express, 161 rue des Pionniers (☎235-4770 or 1-888/235-6842); they also have *L'ExploraTHOR Express*, a zodiac-type boat that holds 48. Smaller zodiacs are provided by Compagnie de la Baie de Tadoussac, 145 rue du Bord de l'Eau (☎235-4548) and Otis Excursions, 431 rue Bateau-Passeur (☎235-4197); the former also has a water-taxi service for hikers in the Parc du Saguenay. Croisières AML (☎237-4274 or 1-800/563-4643) gives you the option of a large boat or 24-person zodiac, and the other big outfit, Croisières Famille-Dufour at the *Hôtel Tadoussac*, 165 rue du Bord de l'Eau (☎235-4421 or 1-800/561-0718), offers whale safaris aboard a catamaran, a 48-person zodiac or the more sedate 1922 schooner *Marie Clarisse*.

North of Tadoussac: Although you'll spend less time on the water with the following companies, their points of departure on the Côte-Nord are closer to where the whales are most likely to be, so you get around the same amount of contact time for cheaper – the trips are all around $30. Heading north on Hwy 138, there's a turn-off on the right just after the overpass at **Bergeronnes** where Les Croisières Neptune has a ticket office at 507 rue du Boisé (☎232-6716). The Montagnais company, Croisière Essipit, uses the quay in Bergeronnes as well, though they're based at 32 rue de la Réserve Essipit (☎232-6778, *www.essipit.com*), near **Les Escoumins**; it is the only company north of Tadoussac to offer a catamaran in addition to 12-person zodiacs. Les Pionniers des Baleines, 41 rue des Pilotes (☎233-3274), launches its zodiacs from Les Escoumins, at the northern limit of the marine park.

Other options: There are numerous lookout points along the shore where you may be lucky to see whales – the two best options are beluga-spotting at **Baie-Ste-Marguerite** west of Tadoussac in the Parc du Saguenay and **Cap-de-Bon-Désir** just past Bergeronnes. At the other end of the scale, Aviation du Fjord, 231 rue des Pionniers (☎235-4640), takes you up in a **seaplane** ($55 for twenty minutes), so you can see whales, the fjord and backcountry from the air. Les Ailes du Nord, near the airstrip in Bergeronnes at 482 rue de la Mer (☎232-6764), offer a similar view for $39 and a forty-minute trip for $62.

white St Lawrence beluga lives in the area all year round, and from May to October it is joined by six species of migratory whales including the minke, finback and the blue whale, the largest animal on earth.

Tadoussac

One of Canada's oldest villages, **TADOUSSAC** is beautifully situated beneath the rounded hills that gave the place its name – it comes from the Algonquian word *tatoushak*, meaning "breasts". Basque whalers were the first Europeans to live here and by the time Samuel de Champlain arrived in 1603 Tadoussac was a thriving trading post. The mid-nineteenth century saw Tadoussac evolve into a popular summer resort for the anglophone bourgeoisie: the first hotel opened in 1846 and by the 1860s steamer-loads of rich anglophones were arriving every summer to escape the heat of the city. Nowadays it's the best place in Québec for **whale-watching** (see box, opposite). Pop into *La Croisière*, 231 des Pionniers, who have full information and sell tickets (at the same price as the companies) for all the available trips; you can also compare directly down at the quay. If you can't afford a boat trip take the short hike around the Pointe de l'Islet from the marina, which has lookout points for whale-watching. Late June is a good time to be here, when traditional Québécois folk singers, jazz pianists and rock guitarists all play a part in the popular **Festival de la Chanson**.

The waterfront rue de Bord-de-l'Eau is dominated by the red roof and green lawns of the *Hôtel Tadoussac*, a landmark in Tadoussac since 1864 and the focus of the historic quarter. Across the road is the oldest wooden church in Canada, the tiny **Chapelle de Tadoussac** (late June to early Oct daily 8am–9pm; $2), built in 1747; visits are possible out of season by reservation (☎235-4324). Tucked on the other side of the hotel, the steep-roofed wooden **Poste de Traite Chauvin** (daily: May, June & Oct 9am–noon & 3–6pm; July–Sept 9am–9pm; $2.75) exactly replicates – right down to the handmade nails – the first trading post on the north shore of the St Lawrence as described in Champlain's 1603 diary. It houses a small museum of beaver pelts and bits and pieces pertaining to the fur trade, but a peek in from the doorway will suffice.

Following the waterfront towards the harbour brings you to the modern **Centre d'Interprétation des Mammifères Marins**, 108 rue de la Cale-Sèche (daily: mid-May to mid-June & late Sept to late Oct noon–5pm; mid-June to late Sept 9am–8pm; *www.gremm.org*; $5.50), run by the nonprofit Group for Research and Education on Marine Mammals (GREMM). This is a must if you intend to go whale-watching, as its excellent documentary films and displays explain the life cycles of the whales in the St Lawrence and the efforts being made to save their ever-diminishing numbers. The small, but informative **Musée Maritime de Tadoussac**, back near the ferry terminal at 145 rue du Bateau-Passeur (July–Sept daily 9am–5pm; $2), has exhibits on the history of shipbuilding and navigation in the area.

The Tadoussac sector of the **Parc du Saguenay** offers some easy **hikes** around the village and a 42km trek to Baie-Ste-Marguerite further along the fjord; an **information office** (mid-June to Sept daily 9am–5pm) in the car park just after the ferry terminal supplies maps of the trails. From near the Chapelle there is a two-hour walk along the beach – you should check what time the tide rolls in as you'll have to clamber over rocks at high tide. It ends northeast of Tadoussac at the long terraced **sand dunes** on the Baie du Moulin-Baude, known locally as *le désert*. To reach the 112-metre-high dunes, you can also follow chemin du Moulin-Baude for 5km to the interpretive centre, the Maison des Dunes (mid-June to mid-Oct daily 9am–5pm; free).

Practicalities

The **bus** terminus is at 443 rue du Bâteau-Passeur on Hwy 138 by the campsite (☎235-4653). The excellent **information** centre for the entire Côte-Nord is in the smart red-brick manor at 197 rue des Pionniers (daily: late June to early Sept 8am–9pm; early Sept to late June 9am–5pm; ☎235-4744); they have a load of leaflets, an accommodation service and next door you can watch videos of the area. The pick of Tadoussac's wealth of **accommodation** is the *Hôtel Tadoussac*, 165 rue du Bord de l'Eau (☎235-4421 or

1-800/561-0718, *www.hoteltadoussac.com*; ⑤), with the river-view rooms naturally costing more. Cheaper is the *Motel le Jaseur*, 414 rue du Bateau-Passeur (☎235-4737; ③), or the *Motel de l'Anse-à-l'Eau*, 173 rue des Pionniers (☎235-4313; ④), which does a fine breakfast. A number of the town's **B&Bs** are ranged along rue des Pionniers, including *Maison Clauphi* at no. 188 (☎235-4303; ③/④), a B&B-cum-motel. *Maison Hovington*, no. 285 (☎235-4466; ③; May to mid-Oct), is a century-old B&B with five beautifully decorated rooms – and the bilingual owners will pick you up from the bus station. *La Maison Boularch*, near the harbour at 118 rue de la Cale Sèche (☎235-2000; ②) is another friendly bilingual place, with comfy beds in mostly tiny rooms.

The **youth hostel** *Maison Majorique*, 158 rue du Bateau-Passeur (☎235-4372, *www.fjord-best.com/ajt*; ①), is one of the best in Québec. Canoes, cross-country skis, skidoos and snowshoes are all available for rent; various activities such as guided hikes, snowshoe excursions and dog-sleigh trips are organized in their relative seasons. All-you-can-eat breakfasts for $3.50 are optional, and camping ($6) is available in the hostel grounds. Family-style **camping** away from the hostels is available in summer at *Camping Tadoussac*, 428 rue du Bateau-Passeur (☎235-4501; $19 for two-person site), 2km from the ferry terminal on Hwy 138. Less central but certainly more unique is a stay at the keeper's house at the **lighthouse** on Île Rouge in the middle of the St Lawrence (☎235-1212 or 1-877/335-1212). The rooms are more luxurious than what the keeper would have been used to, and it's reflected in the price – an expensive $349 for two people ($259 if you go solo), that includes transport by zodiac (including an hour whale-watching), breakfast, a five-course dinner and tour of the island. Day-trips (2 daily; 2hr 30min; $23) will suffice for most people.

Eating possibilities include: the *Hôtel Tadoussac*, which has a vast dining room and a reasonably priced set menu; *Chez Georges*, 135 rue du Bateau-Passeur, is in Tadoussac's oldest house with seafood and steaks on the table d'hôte for $21, *La Bolée*, 164 rue Morin, is a pricey place with crepes, salads and a takeaway deli underneath with delicious breads; and *Le Bâteau*, 246 rue des Forgerons, is a popular place that churns out an all-you-can-eat buffet of Québécois food for $17 – but has the atmosphere of a school cafeteria. Cheaper food and great evenings of **drinking** can be had at *Le Gibard*, which stays open until 3am, and at *Café du Fjord*, 154 rue du Bateau-Passeur near the youth hostel, a young hangout with good music – they also have food. The best spot, though, is *Le Père Coquart Café* with its large terrace, around the corner from *Le Gibard* at 115 rue Coupe de L'Islet. They serve light meals until 9pm when the place morphs into an intimate *boite à chanson* – a great place to hear Québécois and other music.

Hwy 172 – along the Saguenay

Running parallel to the Saguenay fjord, Hwy 172 is a dramatic route that gives occasional panoramas over the water and provides access to a couple of pretty towns en route, where cruises are available or kayaks can be rented. The daily (except Sat) Intercar bus from Tadoussac follows the highway, terminating at Chicoutimi.

Baie-Ste-Marguerite

The 42km hiking trail from Tadoussac ends at **Baie-Ste-Marguerite**, where the main interpretive centre (☎236-1162 or 1-877/272-5229; mid-May to mid-Oct daily 9am–5pm; late June to early Sept until 7pm; *www.sepaq.com*) for the northern part of the **Parc du Saguenay** ($3.50) is located. To get here by car, you need to travel three kilometres down a dusty gravel road that exits the highway just after tiny Rivière-Ste-Marguerite, itself worth a quick stop for its covered bridge. The main draw here is **belugas**, and the interpretive centre has displays that cover all facets of the cute white beasts as well as the fjord in general – ask at the desk for an English-language guidebook. An easy three-kilometre trail leads through the woods to an observation platform where the belugas can frequently be spotted. Despite its appearances, the centre's cafeteria serves up good, hearty grub for hungry hikers from 7am in summer.

Ste-Rose-du-Nord

About 80km from Tadoussac is the turn-off for **STE-ROSE-DU-NORD**, a tiny village of white houses crammed beneath the precipitous walls of the fjord, 3km from the main road. The seasonal **tourist office**, 213 rue du Quai (late June to mid-Sept 9.30am–7.30pm) has free maps of **hiking trails**, including the Plate-Forme trail that leads to a fabulous panoramic viewpoint above the town. The **Musée de la Nature**, 199 rue de la Montagne (daily 8.30am–9pm; $4.50), is a small but surprisingly informative museum housing an eclectic range of exhibits from stuffed animals to knotty roots from the local region. The church of **Ste-Rose-de-Lima** (daily 8am–8pm), with its interior of wood, birch bark, branches and roots, is also worth a peek. *Croisière Marjolaine* runs three-hour **cruises** of the fjord's most stunning stretch (☎1-800/363-7248; $30; late June to Aug 10.15am & 1.15pm). The boat then travels on to Chicoutimi from Ste-Rose-du-Nord in the late afternoon (2hr; June–Sept 4.15pm; $15), useful if you intend to visit Lac Saint-Jean. Sometimes there's a boat connection with Tadoussac as well; enquire at the information centre for details.

Should you want to **stay** over, you could try the award-winning *Auberge le Presbytère*, 136 rue du Quai (☎675-2503 or 1-877/676-2503; ③), which has an outstanding restaurant, with full menus at around $21. Rooms are also available above the Musée de la Nature (☎675-2348; ②), while *Camping la Descente des Femmes* (☎675-2500 or 675-2581; June to mid-Oct) has sites from $12 for four persons.

The Upper Saguenay and Lac Saint-Jean

The Saguenay fjord's source – the vast **Lac Saint-Jean** – sits 210km inland, linked by the Rivière Saguenay. Along this stretch, a glut of aluminium and paper plants using the river as a power source has resulted in the growth of characterless industrial towns, the largest of which is **Chicoutimi**. Further west, beyond **Jonquière**, the lake's farmland periphery is still relatively untouched and offers the opportunity to stay on the Montagnais reserve at **Mashteuiatsh** near Roberval, a unique **zoo** at **Saint-Félicien** and the strange sight of **Val-Jalbert**, Québec's most accessible ghost town. A bike route connects the lake's towns and is an increasingly popular option for travellers from Montréal or Québec who pop their bike on the train or bus for a three- to five-day tour of the lake.

In July 1996, the Saguenay–Lac-Saint-Jean region was devastated by one of the biggest catastrophes in Canada's recent past – a major flood that wiped out homes and businesses in several towns. After unusually heavy rainfall, a delay in opening the floodgates caused water to surge downstream, passing two metres over the dam in downtown Chicoutimi. In all, 39 municipalities were affected, with 596 houses destroyed and 1953 damaged. Hardest hit were Chicoutimi, La Baie, L'Anse St-Jean, Jonquière, Ferland-Boileau and Laterrière. La Baie suffered $165 million of damage and Chicoutimi $67 million. As the flood was an "act of God" no one received insurance, but those who lost their homes were helped out by donations from across the country.

Chicoutimi

Since its founding by a Scottish immigrant in 1842, the regional capital of **CHICOUTI-MI** has grown from a small sawmill centre into one of the province's largest towns and as such is not a particularly enticing place. The city's main attraction is **La Pulperie de**

Chicoutimi at 300 Dubuc, five austere brick buildings built along the rapids by the Chicoutimi Pulp Company, which was founded in 1896 and quickly became Canada's largest producer of paper pulp. Left to rot in 1930, these gigantic ghosts of Chicoutimi's industrial past had been restored to prime condition but the flood of 1996 (see overleaf) caused $1 million damage and the site lost its restaurant and summer theatre.

Relocated to the Pulperie site in 1994 is the strange **Maison du Peintre Arthur Villeneuve**. The former home of Naive painter Arthur Villeneuve, the house is in effect one big painting, with murals covering inside and out. The subject matter is somewhat unadventurous, but the artist's work is bright and cheery while scenes of 1950s Chicoutimi – when Villeneuve started his project after retiring as a barber – are intriguing. Tours, in French, are given on the half-hour (summer only). The whole site is undergoing restoration and a final date for work to be completed is uncertain; for the latest on which parts of the site are open, telephone ☎698-3100 or 1-877/998-3100.

Practicalities

Chicoutimi's **bus station** (☎543-1403) is on the corner of Tessier and Racine, right in the centre of town. Buses from Montréal, Québec City, Lac Saint-Jean and Tadoussac all connect here. The CITS local bus (☎545-2487) link with Jonquière's **train station** (arrival point for trains from Montréal) runs at least hourly from 7.15am to 9.45pm. The Allo-Stop **ride-sharing** office is at 355 rue Ste-Anne (☎695-2322, *www.allo-stop.com*). There's a municipal **tourist office** at 295 Racine est (mid-June to early Sept daily 8am–8pm; early Sept to mid-June Mon–Fri 8.30am–noon & 1.30–4.30pm; ☎698-3167 or 1-800/463-6565) and a handy **Internet café**, *Le Cybernaute*, up the road at no. 391.

Accommodation is readily available in Chicoutimi, as the town hosts a variety of business conferences all year round. Budget rooms can be obtained through the college *CÉGEP de Chicoutimi*, 534 rue Jacques-Cartier est (☎549-9520 ext 258 or 257; ①), in the summer. *Auberge Centre-Ville*, 104 rue Jacques-Cartier est (☎543-0253; ②), is a small, central **hotel** with cheap rates for rooms with shared bath, while *Le Montagnais*, 1080 boul Talbot (☎543-1521 or 1-800/463-9160, *www.lemontagnais.qc.ca*; ④), is a modern hotel further out.

There are numerous small **restaurants** on rue Racine, east of the tourist office. Recommended are *La Cuisine Café-Resto* at no. 387, which has French food in the $10–20 range; *Au Café Croissant* at no. 400 is good for light lunches. For a better class of meal, *La Bourgresse*, 260 rue Riverin (☎543-3178), serves French cuisine for $20–40. Most **nightlife** is also located on rue Racine – the **bars** *Pub Avenue* at no. 381 and *L'International Café-Bar* at no. 460 and the **disco** *Le Loft Dansing* also at no. 460 are all young, lively spots.

Croisière Marjolaine (☎543-7630 or 1-800/363-7248) offer summer **cruises** ($34.75) on the Saguenay as far as Cap Trinité, stopping both ways at Ste-Rose-du-Nord (see p.311), where they provide a coach back to Chicoutimi on the morning run (in the afternoon, the first Chicoutimi–Ste-Rose-du-Nord leg is by coach). Finally, the town is host to one of the best of Québec's **festivals**. For the ten-day **Carnaval Souvenir** in mid-February, what seems like the entire population dresses in costumes from circa 1900; lumber camps, can-can clubs, operetta shows and the period-authentic-heavy drinking, augment the pioneer atmosphere.

Jonquière

Fifteen kilometres west of Chicoutimi, **JONQUIÈRE** thrives due to its Alcan aluminium smelter, one of the largest in the world, and its two paper mills. The smelter brought many Eastern European immigrants to the area when it was first opened in 1925, and the industry overtook the Price sons and their wood empire as the largest employer. A modern town with wide avenues, it can make a good stop for budget travellers because of an Allo-Stop office and train connections with Montréal – it also has a better nightlife than Chicoutimi.

Practicalities

The **tourist office**, 2665 boul du Royaume in the Centre des Congrès (mid-June to early Sept daily 8am–8pm; early Sept to mid-June Mon–Fri 8am–noon & 1.30–4.30pm; ☎548-4004 or 1-800/561-9196, *ville.jonquiere.qc.ca*), has information on the town, and in summer there's a smaller office at 3885 boul Harvey (same hours). **Buses** terminate at 2249 rue St-Hubert (☎547-2167) and **trains** arrive at the VIA Rail station (☎1-800/361-5390, *www.viarail.ca*). Allo-Stop's **ride-sharing** office is at 2370 rue St-Dominique (☎695-2322, *www.allo-stop.com*).

If you decide to stay, the *Hôtel Jean Dequen*, 2841 boul du Royaume (☎548-7173; ③), is cheap and reasonable, but all amenities are available at the *Holiday Inn Saguenay* at no. 2675 on the same street (☎548-3124 or 1-800/363-3124; ④). You can also stay at the stately 1911 *Auberge Villa Pachon*, 1904 rue Perron (☎542-3568 or 1-888/922-3568; ⑤), which was the private manor where VIPs from the Price company stayed; its very expensive restaurant has an excellent reputation.

For **eating**, *Le Puzzle*, 2497 St-Dominique, is a fun place with cool decor; *Les Pâtes Amato*, 2655 boul de Royaume, has coffees, pasta and Italian desserts to die for; and, more expensive, *L'Amandier*, 5219 chemin St-Andre (☎542-5395), is out of town but worth the trip for the bizarre dining room of carved plaster and wood. The **bars** along rue St-Dominique – including *Le Puzzle* and *Le Zinc* – are all a good laugh.

Lac Saint-Jean

To the west of Chicoutimi, around **Lac Saint-Jean**, stretches a relatively untouched area whose tranquil lakeshore villages are linked by the circular route of Hwy 169. Named after Father Jean Duquen, the first European to visit the region in 1647, the huge glacial lake is fed by most of the rivers of northeastern Québec and – unusually for an area of the rocky Canadian Shield – is bordered by sandy beaches and a lush, green terrain that has been farmed for over a century. The local cuisine, especially the delicious coarse meat pie called a *tourtière* and the thick blueberry pie, is renowned throughout the province. Further bonuses for budget travellers are the lake's excellent youth hostel and its **public transport**: there's a daily bus service between Chicoutimi and both Alma and Dolbeau, the latter running round the south side of the lake; during the winter and spring a bus runs on Sundays only from Dolbeau to Alma via the villages on the north shore, and on Fridays only there's a service in the opposite direction.

A relatively flat 256km bike route – the **Véloroute des Bleuets** (*www.veloroute-bleuets.qc.ca*) – encircles the whole lake, mostly as a wide paved shoulder, but a total of 60km of the route is completely free of cars. The path passes close to most of the major attractions and through many of the villages around Lac Saint-Jean and there are beaches all along the lakeshore where you can cool off after a hard day's ride. It's well set up for getting there – the train from Montréal to Jonquière stops at Chambord on the south shore near Val-Jalbert and there's a bus from Québec City to Alma. A growing number of **B&Bs** and other services are popping up to serve the two-wheeled visitors, and even the locals are laying out a warm welcome – some have even set up garden chairs to rest on near the bike path.

Val-Jalbert

From Chicoutimi, Hwy 170 runs 50km west to Hwy 169, which continues to one of the main tourist attractions of the region, **VAL-JALBERT** (daily: early May to mid-June & Sept to mid-Oct 9am–5pm; mid-June to Aug 9am–7pm; $12). The 72m-high Ouiatchouan waterfall, which dominates the town, led to the establishment of a pulp mill here at the turn of the last century, and by 1926 the village had around 950 inhabitants. In the following year, though, the introduction of chemical-based pulping made the mill redundant, and the village was closed down. Val-Jalbert was left to rot until 1985, when the government decided to renovate it as a tourist attraction.

From the site entrance a bus (with on-board French commentary) runs around the main sights of the village, ending at the mill at the base of the falls. You can then wander around whatever catches your eye along the way – the abandoned wooden houses, a former convent (now a museum) or the general store (now a souvenir shop). From the mill – itself converted into an excellent crafts market and cafeteria – a cable car leads to the top of the falls, from where there are stunning views of the village and Lac Saint-Jean beyond. It is possible to stay in Val-Jalbert's renovated **hotel** above the general store (☎275-3132 or 1-888/675-3132; ④), in apartments in the converted houses on St George Street ($72–112 for one to six people), or in the **campsite** (same phone; from $19.50 for four-person site) just outside the village. In autumn and winter, when the site is officially closed, you can still gain access for free and it is a beautifully tranquil place to spend some time.

Mashteuiatsh

Ten kilometres west, at Roberval, a turn-off leads to the Montagnais reserve of **MASHTEUIATSH**, also known as **Pointe-Bleue**. Before European contact the Montagnais ("Ilnu" in the local language) were a migratory people who split into small family groups for summer hunting. When the Europeans arrived they found the Montagnais in bitter conflict with the Iroquois, an enmity that Champlain intensified by allying himself with the Montagnais for trade. By the late seventeenth century their population had been greatly weakened by warfare, European diseases, depletion of game and displacement from their lands. This reserve was created in 1856, and today around 1800 of eastern Québec's 14,000 Montagnais live here. Like many Canadian reserves, Mashteuiatsh is dry in an attempt to reduce alcoholism and its attendant problems, yet the Montagnais suffer a great deal of prejudice from the surrounding white communities – so much so that there's no bus service, because Québécois bus drivers refuse to go there.

The village is situated right on the lake, and has an **information centre** on the main street at 1516 Ouiatchouan (mid-June to Sept daily 8am–8pm. At the end of July a **pow-wow** is held on the waterfront by the four concrete tepee sculptures that represent the seasons. Up the hill, at 1787 rue Amishk, is the recently renovated **Musée Amérindien** (☎275-4842 or 1-888/875-4842; mid-May to mid-Oct daily 10am–6pm; mid-Oct to mid-May Mon–Fri 9am–noon 1–4pm; $5.50), where visitors start with a twenty-minute film showing traditional Montagnais life, much of it revolving around hunting and fishing. The permanent exhibition Pekuakami Ilnuatsh, which translates as "the Lac St-Jean Montagnais", continues the theme with artefacts and interpretive panels that also describe domestic life and the impact of European contact; temporary exhibitions highlight the works of aboriginal artists.

There is **camping** as you enter the reserve – *Camping de la Pointe*, 1358 rue Ouiatchouan (☎275-6006 or 275-4212) charges $18 for pitches near the lakeshore.

From August to September, *Aventure Mikuan*, 1562 Ouiatchouan (☎275-2949 or 679-6087 ext 33), organizes **adventure trips** into the bush where you are completely submerged in the traditional way of life, relying on the resources of the surrounding woodlands and rivers to build shelters, make fires and prepare food (from $135 per person per day).

Saint-Félicien and around

In the village of **SAINT-PRIME**, 13km west of Roberval, is a surprising little museum, **La vieille fromagerie Perron**, 148 15e Avenue (June–Sept daily 9am–6pm; $6), where since 1895 four generations of cheese-makers have worked their craft. The one-hour guided tour covers the whole process of producing cheddar – almost all of which was shipped to England (the locals had plenty of fresh milk, so couldn't be bothered with cheese). The unexpected part of the tour is upstairs, where the Perron family residence appears as it would have in 1922 and a very convincing "Marie Perron" tells about her life, how the best piece of furniture was reserved for the priest who visited but once a year, and why kitchen counters used to be so low – so the children could make themselves useful. You also get to try a bit of the cheese produced by the modern cheese factory.

Situated on the western extremity of the lake on the Ashuapmushuan River, **SAINT-FÉLICIEN** is the site of Québec's best zoo, the **Zoo Sauvage de Saint-Félicien** (mid-May to mid-Oct daily 9am–5pm; $17; ☎679-0543 or 1-800/667-5687, *www.zoosauvage .qc.ca*), located on Chamouchouane Island. Don't let the giant car park put you off – the first part of the zoo is in a beautiful riverine setting. The rest mimics a number of ecosystems where around 80, mainly Canadian, species roam free all over the site – the humans are the ones in cages, hauled around on the back of a mini-train (provisions are made for disabled travellers). The Arctic environment for the polar bears allows you to see the magnificent beasts swim underwater – they put on their best show at feeding time. The zoo also has an historical angle, with mock-ups of an Indian village, trading post, loggers' camp and settlers' farm, staffed by costumed guides performing everyday tasks to match the setting. English guidebook available at the entrance. The zoo is open in winter on a limited schedule, so it's best to call ahead.

Saint-Félicien's **information office** is located at 1209 boul Sacré-Coeur (late June to early Sept Mon–Fri 8.30am–8pm, Sat & Sun 9am–8pm; early Sept to late June Mon–Fri 8.30am–noon & 1–4.30pm). For **accommodation**, check out the cheap *Hôtel Bellevue*, 1055 boul Sacré-Coeur (☎679-0162; ①/②), or one of the ten **B&Bs** (all ②) in the town and surrounding farmland.

From here, the highway and bike path separate, rejoining 15km inland at **Normadin**, where **Les Grands Jardins de Normandin**, 1515 ave du Rocher (late June to early Sept daily 9am–6pm; $10; *www.cigp.com/jardin.html*) is an overpriced and over-hyped formal garden. More worthwhile is one of the local **B&Bs** – at *Les Gîtes Makadan*, 3km off the highway at 1728 rue St-Cyrille (☎274-2867 or 1-877/625-2326; ②), the owners serve up huge portions of local country dishes, much of which is fresh produce from their farm down the road; you need to tell them ahead of time that you want dinner ($15).

Dolbeau-Mistassini to Alma

Continuing clockwise around the lake from Normandin brings you to **DOLBEAU-MISTASSINI**, 28km further on. Dolbeau, the western half of the recently amalgamated town, is at its best during mid-July's ten-day **Western Festival**, with rodeos and people wandering around in stetsons and spurs. Mistassini, the region's blueberry capital, outdoes it's neighbour in early August, with the **Festival du Bleuet** – one big blowout on blueberries dipped in chocolate, blueberry pie, blueberry cheesecake and an extremely potent blueberry wine. Over the Mistassini River the **Monastère des Pères Trappistes** sells its own organic produce – a large quantity of the berries are on offer in season. If you get stranded, the *Hôtel du Boulevard*, 1610 boul Wallberg (☎276-8207 or 1-800/268-1061; ③), is passable; the *Auberge La Diligence*, 414 ave de la Friche (☎276-6544 or 1-800/361-6162; ④) is nicer, if pricier. The town's two **B&Bs** are similarly split on price: *Gîte Bonjour, Bienvenue*, 1824 boul Wallberg (☎276-1291; ②) and *Gîte Jardin des Quatre Saisons*, at no. 2562 (☎276-5561; ③).

Another 20km round the shore, just before the village of **Sainte-Monique**, you'll find a **youth hostel** and **campsite**: the *Auberge de l'Île du Repos de Péribonka* (☎347-5649 or 1-800/461-8585; ②, dorms for $18, camping from $15.60). It's useful for an excursion to **Parc de la Pointe-Taillon** (☎347-5371, *www.sepaq.com*; free, but parking is $5), which also has rustic camping available two to four kilometres from the car park ($19 for a six-person site), but they'll give you a lift if you need one. Occupying a finger of land that juts into Lac Saint-Jean, the park is bordered by long and often deserted beaches, and there are 30km of cycle trails, a portion of which coincides with the Véloroute des Bleuets.

From Sainte-Monique, it's 29km to the dull aluminium-producing city of **ALMA**, useful for its **buses** to Chicoutimi and Québec City. If you are cycling around the lake, you can park your car for free at the **information centre**, 140 rue St-Joseph (mid-June to early Sept daily 8.30am–noon & 1.30–4.30pm), which shares the building with the Véloroute's office. There's a free **bicycle ferry** (every 10–15min; early June to early Sept Mon–Fri 10am–7pm, Sat & Sun 10am–8pm; early Sept to early Oct Mon–Fri 1–4pm, Sat & Sun 10am–5pm), which bypasses the heavily used bridge east of here – as well as most of Alma. If you're feeling even lazier, you could take your bike right across the lake to Roberval – the cruise ship *La Tournée* departs from the *Dam-en-Terre* holiday camp (☎668-3016; 2hr 30min; $18.75 with your bike; $15.75 without), but bicycles are only welcome on Sundays, at 8.30am.

Beyond Alma, the cycle path follows along shoreline inaccessible by highway, joining up with Hwy 170 beyond **Saint-Gédéon**, a popular beach town. If you want to treat yourself, the lakefront *Auberge des Îles*, 250 rang des Îles (☎345-2589 or 1-800/680-2589; ④) is a lovely inn just north of St-Gédéon with a four-course menu of game and local flavours for $32.

The Côte-Nord

The **St Lawrence River** was the lifeline of the wilderness beyond Tadoussac (see p.309) until the 1960s, when Hwy 138 was constructed along the **Côte-Nord** to Havre-St-Pierre, 625km away. In 1996, the road was extended to Natashquan, a further 145km. The road sweeps from high vistas down to the rugged shoreline through the vast regions of Manicouagan and Duplessis, the few distractions offered in the villages and towns en route being supplemented by panoramas of spruce-covered mountains, the vast sky and the mighty river. **Bears** and **moose** often lumber out of the stunted forest onto the highway, and in the summer the shiny backs of **whales** are frequently spotted arching out of the water.

Basque whalers were the first Europeans to penetrate this chilly shore in the sixteenth century, but later, when they began to trade fur with the aboriginal Montagnais, Naskapi and Inuit, they were ousted by French merchants. After the British conquest the fur trade continued but fishing remained the main industry until the twentieth century, when mining, lumber and hydroelectric projects led to the growth of a few settlements into fair-sized towns. Despite this, the region has a population density of just five people per square mile, and the distances between communities become longer and longer the further you travel, overwhelming the visitor with the sense of Canada's vastness.

The Québec City to Tadoussac Intercar **bus** serves the Côte-Nord as far as Baie-Comeau, from where another travels to Sept-Îles, where you have no choice but to spend the night before continuing on to Havre-St-Pierre. At the time of publication there is no public transport to Natashquan, but a bus service is expected – ask at tourist information for details. At Natashquan the highway gives out altogether and the only onward transport is by snowmobile, plane or the supply **ship** from Sept-Îles and Havre-St-Pierre, which serves the wildlife haven of Île d'Anticosti and undertakes a breathtaking journey along the inlets of the windswept coastline of the Basse Côte-Nord (Lower North Shore). Ferries link various points to the south shore and the Gaspé, which means you can plot a varied return trip.

Manicouagan

The craggy terrain is the chief attraction of the 200km of highway from Tadoussac to Baie-Comeau, though there are a few interesting stops and cheaper **whale-watching** excursions in Bergeronnes and Les Escoumins (see box on p.308) than those offered from Tadoussac. Along the route, the landscape takes in lakes surrounded by granite outcroppings and boreal forest, interspersed with stretches of sandy beaches and salt marshes. If you want to dawdle, there are lookout points and short trails in many of the villages, as well as interpretive centres for just about everything.

Bergeronnes and Les Escoumins

As accommodation fills up in Tadoussac in high season, you may wind up having to stay in the community of **BERGERONNES**, 22km along the road. The **Centre d'Interprétation et d'Observation de Cap-de-Bon-Désir**, 166 Hwy 138 (mid-June to mid-Oct daily 8am–8pm; $5), built around the Cap de Bon Désir lighthouse, has displays on the whale's life and a lookout post by a popular whale-feeding ground. **Accommodation** is available at *Le Bergeronnette*, 65 rue Principale (☎232-6642 or 1-877/232-6605, *www.bergeronnette.com*; ②; May–Oct) and there's a **campsite**, off the highway east of town, whose beautiful site has views over the St Lawrence: *Camping Bon Désir* (☎232-6297) charges $19 for a pitch with a view, $17 without.

From **LES ESCOUMINS** there's a **ferry** to Trois-Pistoles (see p.284) across the St Lawrence (mid-May to mid-Oct 2–3 daily; 1hr 15min; $10.75 single, $27.50 for cars). In addition to whale-watching trips, the area is popular for **diving**, especially at night when the phosphorescence creates an eerie underwater landscape. **Le Centre des Loisirs Marins**, 41 rue des Pilotes (☎233-2860; interpretive centre: 9.30–11am & 1.30–3.30pm; $5) is only worthwhile if you intend to dive (diving card required) or really fancy people in drysuits. At a dive shop downstairs you can rent a complete set of gear for $55 per day. If you want to **eat**, try the excellent burgers at *Auberge Manoir Bellevue*, 27 rue de l'Eglise, which also does a pricey table d'hôte for dinner and has comfortable rooms (☎233-3325 or 1-888/233-3325; ④). The town's **youth hostel**, *Auberge de la plongée*, 118 rue St-Marcelin (☎233-3289 or 1-800/375-3465, *www.escoumins.com*; ①) is a bit shabby.

Forestville to Baie-Comeau

Another 61km along the coast from Les Escoumins, the town of **FORESTVILLE** is not as dire as it appears from the highway, with some pleasant residential areas along the two kilometres to the quay. The only real reason for stopping, though, is the seasonal **ferry** to Rimouski (☎725-2725 or 1-800/973-2725; late April to early Oct: 2–4 daily; 55min; $13 single, $32 for cars), which only holds 30 cars so reservations are essential. While you are waiting, picnic next to the river; there's a pleasant beach where you can also camp or hang out.

The highway passes next through the reserve of **BETSIAMITES**, 44km to the north, where a week-long series of festivities culminates in the **Montagnais Festival** on August 15, which symbolically marks the departure of the hunters to the backwoods. You can get an appreciation of local culture at other times at the nearby **Centre de Villégiature de Papinachois**, which has a small collection of traditional buildings that don't look like much unless you have a guided tour (call in advance for English tours). You can **stay** overnight in a traditional tent for $20 or in the more comfortable inn (☎567-8863 or 1-888/246-5834; ③), and traditional cuisine such as beaver and game are available in the restaurant. A variety of excursions along the rivers that penetrate the forest are available on request, starting around $60.

As you continue north, you'll notice a white obelisk on a peninsula near **Ragueneau**. Although it doesn't symbolize anything – it was the whim of a local artisan – it does mark a pretty lookout point half a kilometre off the highway, where you can picnic or clamber along the rocks. Across the bay, the **Parc Nature de Pointe-aux-Outardes**, at the end of rue Labrie, 14km off Hwy 138 (June–Sept daily 9am–6pm; $4; *www.virtuel.net/prpao*), is really only worth the admission price when migratory birds flock here around May and mid-September. Still, easy trails take in a variety of ecosystems including salt marshes and sand dunes, and ninety-minute guided tours of the plant- and birdlife are included in midsummer. **Camping** is available for $12 for a two-person site, $18 for four people. If you want to visit the beach (where the water is apparently warm enough to swim after a few hot sunny days), there's access at the quai municipale on rue Labrie.

Baie-Comeau

The road into the western sector of **BAIE-COMEAU** may be a fairly drab landscape of strip malls, but it's nothing compared to the eastern sector, where a monstrous newsprint mill plant churns out poisonous emissions 24 hours a day. It was established in 1936 by Colonel Robert R. McCormick, the publisher of the *Chicago Tribune*, and Baie-Comeau has done nothing but boom ever since – with a population of 26,000, it dwarfs the communities around it. There's no real reason to hang around here, but while waiting for a northward bus or a ferry to Gaspé's Matane you might stroll through the **quartier Sainte-Amélie** in the eastern Marquette sector, where the streets are lined by grand houses dating from the 1930s. The **Église Sainte-Amélie**, 37 ave Marquette (daily: June to mid-Sept 9am–6pm; mid-Sept to May 10am–5pm; free), is worth a quick peek for its frescoes and stained-glass windows, designed by the Italian artist Guido Nincheri.

There's a seasonal **tourist information** office on the western edge of town at 3503 boul Laflèche (June–Aug daily 8am–8pm). **Buses** terminate at 212 boul Lasalle (☎296-6921); the departure point for the **car ferry** to Matane is beyond the eastern end of boul Lasalle on rue Cartier (Jan–March: 4 per week; April–Dec: 1–2 daily; 2hr 20min; $11.85 single, cars $28.35; ☎294-8593 or 1-877/562-6560).

Accommodation is available at the rambling stone hotel *Le Manoir*, 8 Cabot (☎296-3391 or 1-800/463-8567; ④), which overlooks the St Lawrence. Less expensive **motels** are along boul Lasalle; try the modern *Hôtel-Motel La Caravelle*, at no. 202 (☎296-4986 or 1-800/463-4986; ③). The cheapest place in town is *Motel Lasalle*, 196 boul Lasalle (☎296-6601; ②) but for a few dollars more, there are a few **B&Bs**: *Gîte au vieux quartier*, 57 rue Champlain (☎294-2614; ②) is the only one in the older Marquette area. For **camping**, *Camping Manic 2* at km24 on Hwy 389 (☎296-3951 or 2810) has six-person sites for $15. The hotel, *Le Manoir* is pricey but has an excellent reputation. For down-to-earth eats, *Le 3 Barils*, 200 boul Lasalle, is convenient, and *Brasserie Le Boucannier*, in the western sector at 720 boul Laflèche, has surf and turf and pizza. If you're desperate for a **drink**, *Le Blues Bar*, 48 place Lasalle, has a small terrace out back.

The Manic Dams

One of the few roads to penetrate the bleak terrain north of the St Lawrence is the partly paved Hwy 389 (Manic Road), which runs 215km into the forest from the east sector of Baie-Comeau. The road was built as a supply route for the hydroelectric company that built the colossal **dam system** on the Rivière Manicouagan, the only artificial site to rival the landscape in these parts.

The first dam in the system, **Manic 2**, is a half-hour drive from Baie-Comeau, a journey that takes in great views of the rocky Canadian Shield. A free guided tour takes you inside the massive wall (☎294-3923 or 1-800/ENERGIE; late-June to early Sept daily 9am, 11am, 1.30pm & 3.30pm), but an even more stupendous structure awaits two and a half hours' drive further north at the end of the paved stretch of the road – the awesome **Manic 5** or Daniel Johnson dam. Constructed in 1968, it is named after the premier of Québec who died here on the morning of the opening ceremony. With a length of 1314m and a central arch of 214m, the dam is the world's largest multiple-arch structure, and apparently contains enough concrete to build a pavement from pole to pole. Free guided tours (same phone and times as Manic 2) take visitors to the foot of the dam and across the top, giving panoramic views of the Manicouagan valley and the 2000-square-kilometre reservoir. The 90km-wide donut-shaped depression was created by a massive meteor impact more than 200 million years ago, but the water level only became high enough to fill in the entire depression after the dam was constructed. There's **accommodation** two kilometres before Manic 5 at the *Motel de L'Énergie* (☎584-2301 or 1-800/760-2301; ③) and at *Auberge en Bois Rond Manic 5*, eight kilometres to the west (☎648-6040 or 1-800/480-6040; ②; May–Oct).

Beyond Manic 5, it's another 385km along a gravel highway to Labrador City (see p.457), a six-hour journey through the wilderness with very little in the way of services. The Ministère des Transports du Québec in Baie-Comeau (☎295-4500 or 4765) can provide information on road conditions.

Godbout and Pointe-des-Monts

The attractive fishing village of **GODBOUT**, situated on a crescent-shaped bay 54km from Baie-Comeau, is not just the most pleasant place hereabouts – it also has an excellent **Musée Amérindien et Inuit**, 134 rue Pascal-Comeau (late June to Sept daily 9am–10pm; $3). The museum was founded by Claude Grenier, who spent ten years in the frozen north in the 1970s on a government scheme to boost the Inuit economy by promoting aboriginal culture. Consequent commercialism has diluted the output since then, but the private collection of the Greniers features nothing but genuine pieces, from the characteristic soapstone carvings to domestic artefacts. Just down the road, the old general store houses a seasonal **tourist office** (mid-June to early Sept Mon–Fri 8am–6pm, Sat & Sun 9am–6pm) with a few relics from its former life on display. The village is linked to Matane on the south shore by **car ferry** (April–Dec: 1–3 daily; Jan–March: Mon–Sat 1 daily; 2hr 10min; $11.85 single, $28.35 for cars; ☎568-7575 or 1-877/562-6560). For **accommodation**, try one of the **B&Bs** facing the water: the pretty, century-old *La Maison du Vieux Quai*, 142 rue Pascal-Comeau (☎568-7453; ②), the simpler *La Maison de la Plage*, at no. 252A (☎568-7706; ②), or *Aux Berges*, at no. 180 (☎568-7748, *www.maisonnettes-chalets-quebec.com*; ②; mid-April to mid-Oct), which also has chalets for rent. There's **camping** at *Camping l'Estuaire* (☎568-7737) on the highway, with pitches from $15 for four people.

Situated where the St Lawrence River merges into the Gulf of St Lawrence, scenic **POINTE-DES-MONTS**, 28km from Godbout (and a further 11km off the highway), has not changed since the nineteenth century. Mind you, there's not a lot to change – all that stands on this rocky outcrop is Canada's oldest **lighthouse** dating from 1830 and a small missionary **chapel** built in 1898. The lighthouse now contains a small **museum** (late June to mid-Sept daily 9am–7pm; $2.50), whose nautical displays and history of the lighthouse keeper and his family provide adequate distraction as you make your way to the top. The adjacent house contains a fairly expensive seafood **restaurant** and a **B&B**, while nearby chalets handle the overflow of this popular spot (☎939-2332; June–Aug; ②). **Camping** is available at *Domaine de l'Astérie* (☎939-2327; mid-June to Sept; $14), two kilometres before the lighthouse.

Port-Cartier

From Pointe-des-Monts, an uneventful journey of 113km to Sept-Îles passes through Pointe-aux-Anglais with its beaches (you can camp free one kilometre north of town), and, 63km further, the lumber and iron-ore centre of **PORT-CARTIER**. The town is the entrance to the **Réserve Faunique de Port-Cartier-Sept-Îles**, a 2423-square-kilometre wildlife reserve with more than 1000 lakes, popular for its hunting and salmon and trout fishing. Information, permits and reservations are available from the administration offices in Port-Cartier at 24 boul des Îles (☎766-2524 or 1-800/665-6527, *www.sepaq.com*). It's a bumpy 27km drive to the **reception post** (☎766-4743; late May to late Oct 7am–7pm) at the southern tip of Lac Walker, where **campsites** ($18) and **chalets** (②) are available, as well as canoe rentals ($13.75 per day) and hiking trails.

Sept-Îles

The largest ore-exporting port in eastern Canada, **SEPT-ÎLES** is a good base for trips further north, owing to its rail links with Labrador. The town itself has as much character as a pile of iron ore, but it's pleasantly situated on the St Lawrence shore and you could spend an enjoyable day here – especially in August, when one of Québec's foremost native-music festivals is held nearby.

The town is best appreciated along the waterfront – a 27km bike path leads from **Parc Rivière des Rapides**, with a three-kilometre walking trail and ice-fishing in winter, to the beaches east of town. The road down to the third beach, **Plage Routhier**, offers the best view of the seven islands that gave Sept-Îles its name. Along the way, the path passes through the **Jardins de l'Anse** – a good spot for bird-watching – and along the riverfront promenade in the **Parc du Vieux Quai**, where evening concerts of Québécois music are held under the yellow tent (late June to Aug Thurs–Sun; free).

An interesting overview of local history is offered by **Le Vieux-Poste**, on boulevard des Montagnais, west of the centre (late June to mid-Aug daily 9am–5pm; $3.25). Prior to the British conquest, when the Hudson's Bay Company took over the trade here, Sept-Îles was leased by the French crown to merchant traders. Settlements like these opened up Québec for the Europeans but practically destroyed the lives of the native Montagnais. Converted to Christianity and overwhelmed by their desire for and subsequent need of European goods – particularly firearms, which aided them in their battles against the feared Iroquois – the Montagnais were forced by market pressure to hunt more and more fur-bearing animals. The resulting depletion of game was worsened so much by the later lumber and mining industries that the Montagnais were obliged to live on official reserves in order to become eligible for state hand-outs. The reconstructed Vieux-Poste, with its small chapel, store and postmaster's house, presents an absorbing portrayal of the Montagnais culture and is staffed by local Montagnais who produce crafts and food, which are sold at a decently priced handicrafts store.

The excellent **Musée Shaputuan**, 290 boul des Montagnais (late June to early Sept daily 9am–5pm; early Sept to late June Mon–Fri 9am–5pm, Sat 1–5pm; $3) presents the traditional life of the Innu (Montagnais) people as it is shaped by the seasons. Unlike most descriptive museums, the exhibits speak to the viewer – often literally. Trilingual interpretive panels and audio and video recordings continue the tradition of oral history, with the stories of hunting, fishing, food preparation and scapulomancy (predicting the movement of caribou herds by "reading" the scorch marks left on a bone placed in the fire) told by specific individuals. Artefacts on display supplement the histories, and sculptures illustrate the myths and folk tales of the Innu. Temporary exhibitions in summer feature works by aboriginal artists, while in winter they are more educational, focusing on a single aspect of life such as trapping. The round hall is used for symposia, primarily for Innu people who want to learn more about their own culture.

Just offshore, the largest island in the archipelago, **Île Grande Basque**, has 12km of easy walking trails and picnic spots; obtain **camping** permits for $7 at the kiosk in Parc du Vieux Quai. From June to September, the quay is the departure point for regular **passenger ferries** (20 min; $15) and **cruises** offered by Les Excursions La Petite Sirène (☎968-2173; 1–3 daily; 2–4hr), Croisière Petit Pingouin (☎968-9558; 1–3 daily;

2–3hr) and Crosière Archipel des Sept-Îles (late June to early Oct daily; 3hr). Whales and a sea-bird sanctuary are the main attractions, but **fishing trips** are also available if you fancy cod for dinner; you can also catch herring right from the quay in early summer. **Kayak tours** are another possibility – Vêtements des Îles, 637 ave Brochu (☎962-7223 or 1-800/470-7223, *www.vetementsdesiles.com*) offers rentals for $39 per day and two-day guided tours for $150.

The Innu Nikamu Festival

One of the more offbeat Canadian music chart successes of recent years was the local aboriginal group Kashtin, the only nationally known band to perform in a native tongue. Although Claude McKenzie and Florent Vollant have gone on to solo careers, they still appear occasionally at the excellent **Innu Nikamu Festival** of song and music (information ☎927-2985), held in early August, 14km east of Sept-Îles in the Montagnais reserve of Maliotenam. Inspired by Kashtin's success, numerous other groups travel to the four-day festival to produce some of the best of Canada's contemporary and traditional native music. As well as the music, the festival includes native food and craft stalls – despite the reserve's alcohol ban, there is always a good buzz. There is no public transport to the reserve: by car, take Hwy 138 towards Havre-St-Pierre and turn right at the Moisie intersection for the Maliotenam entrance. Tickets cost around $10 and are available by phone or at the gate.

Practicalities

Sept-Îles has a seasonal **tourist office**, 516 rue Arnaud (mid-June to Aug daily 9am–6pm) down by the waterfront in the Parc du Vieux-Quai, and another on the outskirts of town at 1401 boul Laure (mid-June to mid-Sept daily 8.30am–8.30pm; mid-Sept to mid-June Mon–Fri 8.30am–5pm). Rent **bicycles** from Rioux Vélo Plein Air, 391 ave Gamache (☎968-8356).

The *Le Tangon* **youth hostel**, 555 rue Cartier (☎962-8180 or 1-800/461-8585; June–Sept; ①), is a cheap, family-run place with breakfast for $3.50; camping is allowed in the grounds for $8. Alternatively, try the luxurious *Hôtel Gouverneur Sept-Îles*, 666 boul Laure (☎962-7071 or 1-888/910-1111; ④) or the *Hotel Sept-Îles*, 451 ave Arnaud (☎962-2581 or 1-800/463-1753; ③) on the waterfront. For budgets in between, the town's **B&Bs** are more attractive than the motels along the highway – *Gîte Les Tournesols*, 388 rue Évangéline (☎968-1910; ②) is nearest the quay. The area's two **campsites** lie 27km to the east, off Hwy 138 next to the salmon-filled Rivière Moisie: *Camping Laurent-Val* (☎927-2899; $13) and *Camping de la ZEC de la rivière Moisie* (☎927-2021; $10).

For **eating**, Sept-Îles has great seafood restaurants such as the rather expensive *Chez Omer*, 372 ave Brochu. Get cheaper seafood, pizza and pasta (as well as a few rounds of **drinks**) at nearby *Café du Port* at no. 495, while the *Pub St-Marc* further down the road at no. 588 is a surprisingly stylish bar serving microbrews, with a more expensive restaurant upstairs. Montagnais specialties are pricey but well-prepared at *Chez Jonathan*, in the Musée Shaputuan at the west end of town.

The **bus** station, 126 rue Monseigneur-Blanche (☎962-2126), has buses east to Havre-St-Pierre; the QNS&L **train** station, with 2–3 trains a week to Labrador City ($100 return; see p.45) and Schefferville ($137 return), is on rue Retty at the east end of town; information and tickets are available from Vacances Inter (☎962-9411). The *Nordik Express* supply **ship** (see box on p.325) from Rimouski leaves Sept-Îles every Wednesday morning at 6am, arriving at Port-Menier on the Île d'Anticosti ($45.45; $63.12 with meals) that afternoon and Havre-St-Pierre ($63.82; $97.22 with meals) in the evening, before continuing along the Basse Côte-Nord to Blanc-Sablon near the Labrador border. It does not stop in Sept-Îles on the return trip.

The Mingan Coast

There is little of specific interest along the blackfly-ridden (from May to June) stretch of shore known as the Mingan Coast until you reach **Longue-Pointe-de-Mingan**, but the scenery changes constantly with sand dunes followed by granite outcroppings of the Canadian Shield, then eerie landscapes of rounded grey boulders surrounded by scrubby vegetation. Most visitors make the journey for the stunning islands of the **Mingan Archipelago**, a unique environment of sculptured rock formations and profuse wildlife lying off the coast between Longue-Pointe-de-Mingan and **Havre-St-Pierre**, the region's largest town and a good base for visiting the archipelago. As the tourist season is short here, accommodation can be at a premium – it's a good idea to book ahead.

If you want to break up the journey, park your car at the small tourist office 86km east of Sept-Îles (just after the marker for km 61 – distances are measured from the Rivière Moisie) and visit the **Chutes Manitou**. Cross the river via the highway bridge and walk five minutes on the marked trail along the river to a viewing point beside the rocky cascades. A more substantial waterfall is ten minutes further down the trail, with secluded pebble beaches along the way. It's dangerous to swim here, though; a couple of drownings have occurred.

Longue-Pointe-de-Mingan

Although Havre-St-Pierre is the more popular departure point for cruises of the Mingan Archipelago, it is worth stopping in **LONGUE-POINTE-DE-MINGAN** for the **Centre de Recherche et d'Interprétation de la Minganie (CRIM)**, 625 rue du Centre (mid-June to mid-Sept daily 9am–6pm; $4.75), a joint venture between Parks Canada and the Mingan Island Cetacean Study. In addition to the film *The Mingan Islands* and displays on whales and other marine life, the centre provides information on excursions to the islands, issues camping permits and, for the more adventurous, offers a day with one of the **whale researchers** (☎949-2845; June–Oct; $75). The latter are not cruises – you are with a marine biologist in a small boat from dawn until whenever their work is finished – but they are a unique experience.

Less taxing cruises are offered by La Randonnée des Îles, 138 rue de la Mer (☎949-2307), who lead trips to the westernmost islands – an important consideration if you want to see **puffins**, as most of the cruises from Havre-St-Pierre only visit the islands in the centre sector. They offer cruises aboard *Le Paspéyas* (4 daily, $33), as well as on *Le Flo Bleu* (3 daily, $30.50) and *Le Macareux* (2 daily, $56).

These latter cruises depart from the nearby Montagnais village of **Mingan** – tickets are available at the Boutique le Phare on rue du Quai. While in the village, visit the **church**, whose pine interior is decorated with antlers, pelts, stylized tepees and other Montagnais motifs. The stained-glass windows to either side of the entrance depict the wondrous rock monoliths found in the archipelago.

Longue-Pointe-de-Mingan isn't much of a gourmet hot spot, but adequate **seafood** is available at the restaurant of the basic *Hôtel-Motel de la Minganie*, 860 chemin du Roi (☎949-2992; ②). If you go on a research trip, the **B&B** *Gîte La Chicoutée*, 198 rue de la Mer (☎949-2434; ②) will lay out breakfast the night before. Their sister establishment, *Gîte La Bécassine* (same details) offers a rarity among B&Bs – a kitchen you can use to prepare dinner. Both B&Bs are a few steps from the wooden promenade that runs along the sea front.

Havre-St-Pierre

The community of **HAVRE-ST-PIERRE** would have remained a tiny fishing village but for the discovery in the 1940s of a huge deposit of ilmenite, the chief source of titanium. The quarries are 45km north of the town itself, where fishing and tourism provide employment for the non-miners, the latter industry having received a major boost when the forty islands of the **Mingan Archipelago** were made into a national park in 1983. Before setting off to the park, check out the **interpretive centre**, 975 de l'Escale (mid-June to early Sept 10am–5.30pm, evening talks 7–9pm mid-season; free), with the film *The Mingan Islands*, and photographic displays and info on the flora, fauna and geology of the islands. It opens around 8.30am if the weather is too poor for the tour boats to depart. At a smaller kiosk on the wharf, part of a row of kiosks, you can book cruises to the archipelago.

Havre-St-Pierre's **information centre** shares the old general store at 957 rue de la Berge (daily: late June to mid-Aug 10am–10pm; mid-Aug to early Sept 11am–9pm) with a **centre d'interprétation** that depicts the local history (same hours; $2). The *Auberge de la Minganie* **youth hostel** (☎538-3902 ext 08; ①; camping $8; May–Nov) is inconveniently situated 15km west of town, but the bus from the west will let you off early. An old fishing camp with minimum renovations and lots of bugs, the hostel doesn't even have breakfast available. In town, you could try the *Hôtel-Motel du Havre*, 970 rue de l'Escale (☎538-2800; ③), or *Camping Municipal* at the east end of ave Boréal ($17). The tourist office can provide a list of **B&Bs**. For good seafood and smoked-salmon pizza, try the **restaurant** *Chez Julie*, 1023 Dulcinée. *Resto-Bar Les Moutons Blancs*, 1121 ave Boréale, has occasional live music and also serves seafood. The **bus station** is at 843 rue de l'Escale (☎538-2033). The wharf is the departure point for the *Nordik Express* (see box on p.325).

The Mingan Archipelago

Immediately offshore from Havre-St-Pierre, the **Mingan Archipelago National Park Reserve** (*www.parcscanada.gc.ca/parks/quebec/mingan*) offers some of the weirdest and most beautiful landscapes in Québec. Standing on the islands' white-sand shore-lines are innumerable eight-metre-high rocks like ancient totem poles, with bright orange lichen colouring their mottled surfaces and bonsai-sized trees clinging to their crevices. These formations originated as underwater sediment near the equator. The sediment was thrust above sea level more than 250 million years ago and then covered in an icecap several kilometres thick. As the drifting ice melted, the islands emerged again, seven thousand years ago, at their present location. The sea and wind gave the final touch by chipping away at the soft limestone to create the majestic monoliths of today.

Bizarre geology isn't the archipelago's only remarkable feature. The flora constitutes a unique insular garden of 452 arctic and rare alpine species, which survive here at their most southern limit due to the limestone soil, long harsh winters and cold Gulf of Labrador current. As for **wildlife**, other than the Gulf's whale populations, the perma-nent inhabitants of the national park include puffins, who build nests in the scant soil of three of the islands from early May to late August, and 199 other species of birds.

One of the best ways to see the islands is by **sea kayak**. The friendly folks at Expédition Agaguk, 1062 ave Boréale (☎538-1588, *www.expedition-agaguk.com*) organize one- to six-day excursions from May to September for $79 per day, $129 per day if you want them to supply camping equipment and local cuisine. Even if you have your own gear, this is an excellent place for tips on currents and other conditions. On prior request, they will also organize backcountry trips to the lakes and rivers to the north.

From June to September **boat tours** around portions of the archipelago are available from the wharf at Havre-St-Pierre, but they must be booked in advance: *La Relève II* operates from kiosk no. 5 (3 daily; $33; ☎538-2865), while Tournée des Îles, kiosk no. 2 (☎538-2547), runs the *Perroquet de Mer* (3 daily; $33) and Le Calculot (2 daily; $33), a small boat whose captain's unrelenting commentary may spoil your trip. Tours in zodi-acs offered by Pneumatique Transport (☎538-1222) from kiosk no. 4 cover the central area (1–2 daily, $39) and eastern area (2 daily, $51) where **puffins** cavort on Île à Calculot. Cruises to see the puffins in the western sector of the park depart from Longue-Pointe-de-Mingan (see p.322).

Camping is allowed on Île Quarry ($9) and five other islands ($6) but the only transport besides a sea kayak is the *Bateau-Mouche* sea bus (☎538-3427; $17–34 depending on destination). Obtain permits from the interpretive centre in Longue-Pointe or the wharfside kiosk in Havre-St-Pierre.

Information is available from two visitor centres – 625 rue du Centre in Longue-Pointe-de-Mingan and 975 rue de l'Escale in Havre-St-Pierre, where there's also an info kiosk on the wharf at 1010 Promenade des Anciens. Biologists on some islands meet passengers from the cruise boats (mid-June to Aug) to explain aspects of the geology and flora. Parks Canada employees also lead guided excursions (late June to late Aug Tues & Fri; $13.50) to Grosse Île au Marteau from the kiosk on the wharf at Havre-St-Pierre; departures for the four-hour trip are morning or afternoon depending on tide levels.

Île d'Anticosti

In the Gulf of St Lawrence between the Jacques Cartier and Honguedo straits, the remote 220-kilometre-long **Île d'Anticosti** was once known as the "Graveyard of the Gulf", as more than four hundred ships have been wrecked on its shores, including Admiral Phipp's fleet, retreating from Québec City in 1690. The island's 7770-square-kilometre expanse is made up of windswept sea cliffs and forests of twisted pine, criss-crossed by turbulent rivers and sheer ravines.

Known as Notiskuan – "the land where we hunt bears" – by the natives, and a walrus- and whale-fishing ground for the Basques, Île d'Anticosti became the private domain of Henri Menier, a French chocolate millionaire, in 1873. He imported white-tailed Virginia deer, red fox, silver fox, beaver and moose to his domain in order to gun them down at his leisure. Nowadays a less exclusive horde of hunters and fishers comes here to blast the deer from the back of their four-wheel-drives and to hoist the salmon from the rivers, which now fall under the jurisdiction of the province. For other travellers it presents an opportunity to explore an area that's untamed and still practically deserted, with a population of just 340.

Menier established the tiny village of Baie Ste-Claire on the western tip in 1873; less than thirty years later the settlers moved to **PORT-MENIER** on the south side of this tip, and Baie-Ste-Claire's homes were left to the ravages of the salt air. The human population is now concentrated in the blue-roofed houses of Port-Menier, where the *Nordik Express* comes in once a week each from Havre-St-Pierre and from Sept-Îles (see box, opposite).

Port-Menier edges the westerly portion of the **Réserve Faunique de l'Île d'Anticosti** (☎535-0156 or 1-800/463-0863, *www.sepaq.com*) whose protected landscapes are continued further east in the reserve's two other sectors – one deep in the interior, the other covering the island's eastern tip. The twisting gravel road that crosses the island, jokingly called the "Trans-Anticostian", provides access to the central and eastern portions of the reserve. Driving is the only way to get there – a four-wheel-drive is necessary, and it's not uncommon to get a few dents or a flat tyre. You can hire a car in Port-Menier at Location Pelletier (☎535-0204). En route, a rough track leads from the "main" road to Québec's largest cave. Discovered as recently as 1982, the glacial **Caverne de la Rivière à la Patate**, 120km east of Port-Menier, has a modest opening that leads into a cathedral-like chamber and a warren of 500-metre-long passages. Ten kilometres further on you can glimpse the impossible canyon of the **Rivière Observation**, whose bleak walls rise to over 50 metres. The reserve's scenery is equally impressive and a good basis for its attempt to encourage adventure tourism during the summer months. SÉPAQ Anticosti, the government body responsible for the Réserve Faunique, runs a variety of ecologically sound packages which, although pricey (around $500 a week per person, based on two people flying from Sept-Îles), include transport to the island, meals, accommodation and four-wheel-drive vehicles (☎535-0156). Other outfitters offer similar fly-in packages starting around $250 for a 24-hour excursion from Sept-Îles. Safari Anticosti has 24-hour packages starting at $219 from Havre-St-Pierre (☎538-1414, *www.safarianticosti.com*) and $259 from the Îles-de-la-Madeleine.

The *Nordik Express* **supply ship** from Havre-St-Pierre costs $35.58 each way and from Sept-Îles is $45.45 ($63.12 including meals). You can also stop off for two hours en route. There is no boat from Port-Menier to Sept-Îles – it goes straight on to Rimouski instead. A number of local **airlines** serve the island from Gaspé, Baie-Comeau, Sept-Îles and Havre-St-Pierre. **Accommodation** is available in Port-Menier at *Auberge Port-Menier* (☎535-0122; ④) or one of the two **youth hostels**: *Auberge Au Vieux Menier*, 26 chemin de la Faune (☎535-0111; ①; mid-June to mid-Oct), which also has camping for $10. They pick up from airport and wharf and also organize excursions. *Auberge Pointe-Ouest*, 20km west of Port-Menier (☎535-0155; ①) also has camping for $10 per day.

The Basse Côte-Nord

Until 1996, Hwy 138 terminated at Havre-St-Pierre, leaving the dozen or so villages along the rugged **Basse Côte-Nord** cut off from the rest of Québec for centuries – to such an extent that most inhabitants speak only English. Now a new section of Hwy 138 links Havre-St-Pierre with **Natashquan** and three other villages on the 145-kilometre stretch. If you make the lonely journey by car – as yet there is no bus – you will receive a welcome unique to a people that have only recently been connected by road to the rest of Canada.

THE NORDIK EXPRESS

One of the more spectacular ways to see the communities along the Côte-Nord is by the *Nordik Express* supply ship (☎723-8787 or 1-800/463-0680), which runs from April to January. Its weekly journey begins in Rimouski, stopping in Sept-Îles, Port-Menier on Île d'Anticosti, Havre-St-Pierre and Natashquan, before calling in at the roadless communities along the Basse Côte-Nord, reaching Blanc-Sablon near the Labrador border, then following the same route in reverse. It does not, however, stop in Sept-Iles on the way back to Rimouski.

For shorter daytime journeys you can book passage only, otherwise prices include surprisingly good meals and cabin berths. A full return journey from Rimouski to Blanc-Sablon will set you back a whopping $773.99, but a shorter journey such as from Havre-St-Pierre to Port-Menier costs $35.58 each way.

You can also bring your car, although it is inaccessible during the voyage. Fares are based on distance and the weight of the car – if you are intending to continue on to Newfoundland and Labrador, a one-way journey from Natashquan to Blanc-Sablon costs $194.70 per passenger, plus at least $200 for the car.

With careful planning you can arrange to spend a couple of days in one community and catch the boat on the return voyage, or just hop off at each port of call – a bicycle is particularly handy if you want to see much but it adds $18.40 to the fare. Plan ahead, though – although each village receives at least one daytime visit, either the upstream or downstream stop may be in the middle of the night.

The original inhabitants of the area were Montagnais, Naskapi and Inuits, who were invaded by Vikings in the year 1000. Cartier saw the coast in 1534 but did not register it as a discovery because it was already seasonally occupied by Basque, Spanish and Portuguese fishermen, and fishing is still the only industry on this desolate coast. The current 7500 inhabitants are descendants of fishermen from the Channel Islands and Newfoundland.

To Natashquan

The first settlement 65km east of Havre-St-Pierre is the 100-strong village of **BAIE-JOHAN-BEETZ**, named after the painter and sculptor whose extraordinary and enormous house is open to the public (June to mid-Sept daily 9am–6pm; $3; reservations recommended ☎539-0137); you can also sleep in one of its seven historic bedrooms (②). Afterwards you can head straight for the fishing village of Natashquan, passing through **Aguanish** and **Île-à-Michon**, the tiny hamlets en route. At the end of the road, a small church, wooden houses and the old fishing huts are about all there is to see in **NATASHQUAN**, the one-time home of poet Gilles Vigneault. The century-old general store has been reborn as yet another **centre d'interprétation** that focuses on local history (late June to Aug daily 10am–6pm; $3.50). **Accommodation** is available in the ten rooms of *Auberge la Cache*, 183 chemin d'en Haut (☎726-3347 or 1-888/726-3347; ③), whose seafood restaurant is open from June to August. Nearby is the Montagnais reserve of **Pointe-Parent** – the locals run canoeing and snowmobiling expeditions; contact Expédition Grande Natashquan for details (☎726-3417).

Beyond Natashquan

When the road peters out, access further along the coast is by boat, floatplane or, in winter, snowmobile. The trip by the *Nordik Express* **supply ship** (see box, overleaf) affords stunning views of a rocky, subarctic landscape, which is so cold that icebergs float past the ship even in the height of summer. During the day, whales, dolphins and a wealth of sea birds are a common sight, and at night during the autumn and winter the northern lights present an unforgettable display. At each stop the village inhabitants surround the boat, as its twice-weekly arrival is about all that happens here. The Web site for the local residents' group, the Coasters Association – *www.htmlweb.com/LNS* – has a comprehensive listing of what you can do in each village.

Chief stops include the village of **Kegaska**, whose roads are covered with white seashells, and **Harrington Harbour**, a pretty village set on a island whose topography of large rounded rocks made it necessary to make the pavements out of wood. Harrington Harbour is best seen on the upstream journey, when the boat arrives in the daytime rather than at midnight. If you decide to stay, **accommodation** is available at *Amy's Bed & Breakfast* (☎795-3376; ⑤), which includes three meals a day; they also have a shop selling local handicrafts.

To visit the roadless Basse Côte-Nord, the *Nordik Express* leaves Havre-St-Pierre on Wednesday night and arrives in **Blanc-Sablon**, Québec's most easterly village, on Friday evening. The boat then departs at midnight, arriving back in Havre-St-Pierre on Sunday afternoon. The price is pretty hefty but includes meals and a cabin berth: Havre-St-Pierre to Blanc-Sablon is $456.33 return. The nearest **accommodation** is over the border in L'Anse-au-Clair, Labrador, a five-minute drive away.

By car, it's now possible to backtrack westwards for 65km on Hwy 138 as far as **Vieux-Fort**, where you can always see seals sunning themselves on the rocks surrounding the bay. Eastward from Blanc-Sablon you can take a **ferry** across to St Barbe in Newfoundland (May–Dec 1–3 daily; 1hr 30min; ☎461-2889 or 1-800/563-6353, *www.gov.nf.ca/ferryservices*; see p.446) or drive along the coast into Labrador (see p.450).

travel details

Trains

Montréal to: Bonaventure (3 weekly; 13hr 10min); Carleton (3 weekly; 12hr); Cornwall (4–5 daily; 1hr 5min); Gaspé (3 weekly; 17hr 30min); Jonquière (3 weekly; 8hr 55min); Kingston (4–5 daily; 2hr 30min); Matapédia (6 weekly; 10hr 10min); New York, USA (1 daily; 9hr 40min); Ottawa (4–6 daily; 2hr 10min); Percé (3 weekly; 16hr 5min); Québec City (4–5 daily; 3hr); Rimouski (6 weekly; 7hr 40min); Rivière-du-Loup (6 weekly; 5hr 55min); Toronto (4–5 daily; 4hr 30min–5hr 30min; express daily except Sat; 4hr; sleeper daily except Sat; 8hr 50min); Washington, DC, USA (1 daily; 16hr 10min including bus to St Alban's, Vermont).

Sept-Îles to: Labrador City (2–3 weekly; 8hr 30min–10hr 30min); Schefferville (1 weekly; 11hr 15min).

Buses

Baie-Comeau to: Godbout (1 daily; 50min); Port-Cartier (1 daily; 2hr 15min); Sept-Îles (1 daily; 3hr 5min).

Chicoutimi to: Alma (1–2 daily; 1hr 15min); Dolbeau (2 daily; 3hr 55min); Jonquière (3–4 daily; 30min); St-Félicien (2 daily; 2hr 55min); Val-Jalbert (2 daily; 2hr 15min).

Dolbeau to: Alma (1 weekly; 1hr 15min); Péribonka (1 weekly; 30min).

Montréal to: Bromont (2 daily; 2hr); Chicoutimi (4 weekly; 4hr 55min); Chicoutimi via Québec City (3–5 daily; 5hr 45min); Granby (4–8 daily; 1hr 30min); Jonquière (4 weekly; 5hr 25min); Jonquière via Québec City (3–5 daily; 6hr 15min); Kingston (7 daily; 3hr); Magog (7–11 daily; 1hr 30min); Mont-Tremblant (3 daily; 2hr 40min); New York, USA (6 daily; 8hr 30min); North Bay (2 daily; 7hr 40min); Orford (3 daily; 3hr); Ottawa (hourly; 2hr 20min); Québec City (hourly; 3hr); Rimouski (4 daily; 7hr); Rivière-du-Loup (4 daily; 5hr 30min); Ste-Adèle (6 daily; 1hr 25min); Ste-Agathe (6 daily; 1hr 45min); St-Jovite (5 daily; 2hr 15min); St-Sauveur (6 daily; 1hr); Sherbrooke (7–11 daily; 2hr 5min); Toronto (8 daily; 6hr 45min); Trois-Rivières (6–8 daily; 2hr); Val-David (6 daily; 1hr 30min).

Québec City to: Alma (3 daily; 2hr 45min); Baie-Comeau (2 daily; 6hr 5min); Baie St-Catherine (2 daily; 3hr 20min); Baie-St-Paul (3 daily; 1hr 10min); Chicoutimi (3–5 daily; 2hr 30min); Dolbeau (2 daily; 5hr 25min); Forestville (2 daily; 4hr 45min); Jonquière (3–5 daily; 3hr); La Malbaie (3 daily; 1hr 50min); Les Escoumins (2 daily; 4hr 10min); Rimouski (4 daily; 3hr 55min); Rivière-du-Loup (4 daily; 2hr 20min); St-Félicien (2 daily; 4hr 25min); St-Siméon (2 daily; 2hr 20min); Sherbrooke (2 daily; 3hr 30min); Tadoussac (2 daily; 3hr 35min); Val-Jalbert (2 daily; 3hr 45min).

Rimouski to: Bonaventure (2 daily; 6hr); Cap-aux-Os (summer 1 daily; 6hr 50min); Carleton (2 daily; 4hr 15min); Gaspé via Carleton (2 daily; 9hr 10min); Gaspé via Matane (2 daily; 6hr 50min); Matane (2–3 daily; 1hr 30min); Matapédia (2 daily; 2hr 50min); Mont St-Pierre (2 daily; 4hr 20min); New Richmond (2 daily; 5hr 30min); Percé (2 daily; 8hr 20min); Ste-Anne-des-Monts (2–3 daily; 2hr 50min); Ste-Flavie (2–3 daily; 30min).

Rivière-du-Loup to: Edmundston (3 daily; 3hr).

Sept-Îles to: Havre-St-Pierre (5 weekly; 2hr 45min).

Sherbrooke to: Trois-Rivières (4 weekly; 2hr 10min).

Tadoussac to: Chicoutimi (6 weekly; 1hr 40min); Rivière Ste-Marguerite (6 weekly; 30min); Ste-Rose-du-Nord (6 weekly; 55min).

Trois-Rivières to: Grand-Mère (3 daily; 1hr).

Ferries

Baie-Ste-Catherine to: Tadoussac (1–3 hourly; 10min).

Blanc-Sablon to: St Barbe, Newfoundland (May–Dec 1–3 daily; 1hr 30min).

Matane to: Baie-Comeau (4 weekly–2 daily; 2hr 20min); Godbout (1–3 daily; 2hr 10min).

Québec City to: Lévis (1–3 hourly; 15min).

Rimouski to: Forestville (April–Oct 2–4 daily; 55min).

Rivière-du-Loup to: St-Siméon (April–Dec 2–5 daily; 1hr 15min).

St-Joseph-de-la-Rive to: Île-aux-Coudres (8 daily–2 hourly; 15min).

Trois-Pistoles to: Les Escoumins (May–Oct 2–3 daily; 1hr 15min).

Supply Ship

Continuous voyage on the *Nordik Express*. Broken down into segments here for clarity.

Havre-St-Pierre to: Natashquan (1 weekly; 6hr 15min); Kegaska (1 weekly; 11hr 30min); La Romaine (1 weekly; 16hr); Harrington Harbour (1 weekly; 24hr 45min); Tête-à-la-Baleine (1 weekly; 29hr 15min); La Tabatière (1 weekly; 32hr 45min); St-Augustin (1 weekly; 37hr 15min); Blanc-Sablon (1 weekly; 43hr 45min).

Rimouski to: Sept-Îles (downstream only; 1 weekly; 11hr 30min); Blanc-Sablon (1 weekly; 78hr 30min).

Sept-Îles to: Port-Menier (1 weekly; 7hr 45min); Havre St-Pierre (1 weekly; 15hr 15min).

Flights

Montréal to: Bagotville (Chicoutimi) (4–8 daily; 1hr 5min); Baie-Comeau (3–4 daily; 1hr 30min); Bathurst (2–3 daily; 1hr 45min); Calgary (3–4 daily; 4hr 30min); Fredericton (3–4 daily; 1hr 30min); Gaspé (2–3 daily; 2hr 40min); Halifax (10–12 daily; 1hr 25min); Îles-de-la-Madeleine (1–3 daily; 3hr 50min); Moncton (3–4 daily; 1hr 20min); Mont Joli (3–4 daily; 1hr 25min); Ottawa (9–11 daily; 40min); Québec City (13–20 daily; 50min); Saint John, NB (3–5 daily; 1hr 35min); St John's, NF (1–2 daily; 2hr 35min); Sept-Îles (3–6 daily; 2hr 45min); Toronto (19–40 daily; 1hr 15min); Vancouver (4–6 daily; 5hr 20min); Wabush (2 daily; 4hr 5min); Winnipeg (2–3 daily; 2hr 55min).

Québec City to: Baie-Comeau (1–3 daily; 1hr 35min); Gaspé (1–2 daily; 2hr 10min); Halifax (1 daily; 1hr 40min); Îles-de-la-Madeleine (1–2 daily; 3hr 20min); Ottawa (2–7 daily; 1hr 10min); Sept-Îles (2–3 daily; 1hr 30min); Toronto (6 daily; 1hr 30min); Wabush (1–2 daily; 2hr 50min).

CHAPTER THREE

THE MARITIME PROVINCES

The **MARITIME PROVINCES** – Nova Scotia, New Brunswick and Prince Edward Island – are Canada's three smallest provinces, and their combined population of around one-and-three-quarter million has been largely confined to the coasts and river valleys by the thin soils of their forested interiors. Even today, the bulk of the region remains intractable – 84 percent of New Brunswick, for example, is covered by pine, maple and birch forests – and this rough-and-ready wilderness combines with a ruggedly beautiful coastline to form one of Canada's most scenic regions. Of some appeal too are the chunks of fertile land that punctuate the forests, principally in the undulating fields of PEI (Prince Edward Island) and the lowlands around New Brunswick's Grand Falls, both of which produce massive crops of potatoes, and in Nova Scotia's Annapolis Valley, a major fruit-producing area.

Most visitors to the Maritimes come for the coastal scenery and the slow pace of the "unspoilt" fishing villages, but the Maritimes were not always as sleepy as they appear today. When the three provinces joined the Dominion in the middle of the nineteenth century, their economies were prospering from the export of their fish and timber and the success of their shipyards. But, as opponents of the confederation had argued, the Maritimers were unable to prevent the passage of protectionist measures favouring the burgeoning industries of Ontario and Québec. This discrimination, combined with the collapse of the shipbuilding industry as steel steamers replaced wooden ships, precipitated a savage and long-lasting recession that, within the space of thirty years, transformed most of the Maritimes from a prosperous, semi-industrialized region to a pastoral backwater dependent on the sale of its raw materials – chiefly wood and fish. In recent years, tourism has helped to keep the region's economy afloat and the tourist industry hereabouts is extremely well-organized, though out of season – before mid-May and after mid-October – many attractions and B&Bs are closed.

Bypassed economically, many of the region's villages still retain their nineteenth-century appearance, with pastel-shaded clapboard houses set around rocky coves and bays. However, the Maritimes offer much more variety than this bucolic image suggests. In **Nova Scotia**, the southwest coast does indeed have a clutch of quaint fishing ports, but it also harbours the busy provincial capital of **Halifax**, whilst **Annapolis Royal**, with its genteel mansions, is but a few kilometres from **Port Royal** and its reconstruction of the fort Samuel de Champlain built in 1605. Further east, **Cape Breton Island**, connected to the mainland by a causeway, is divided into two by **Bras d'Or Lake**: the forested plateau flanking industrial **Sydney** is unremarkable, but in the west the elegiac hills and lakes framing the resort of **Baddeck** lead into the mountainous splendour of **Cape Breton Highlands National Park** – a rare chunk of mountain in a region that is relatively flat. Moving on, **New Brunswick** has urban pleasures in the shape of its cosy capital **Fredericton** and the gritty, revitalized port of **Saint John**

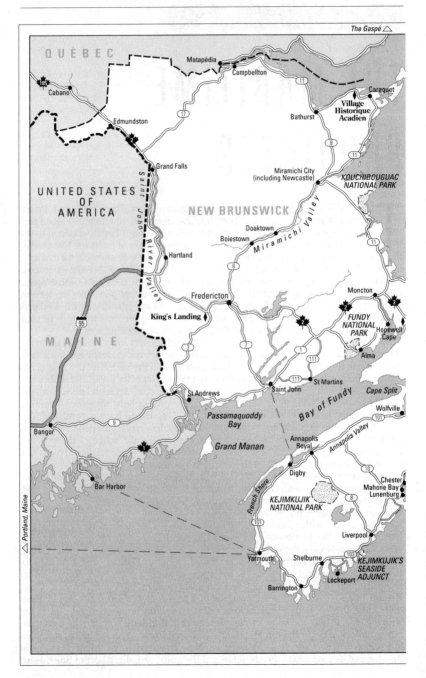

The Gaspé △

QUÉBEC

Matapédia
Campbellton

Cabano

185

Edmundston

17

Grand Falls

UNITED STATES
OF
AMERICA

Saint John River Valley

NEW BRUNSWICK

Caraquet

**Village
Historique
Acadien**

Bathurst

11

8

11

Miramichi City
(including Newcastle)

*KOUCHIBOUGUAC
NATIONAL PARK*

Doaktown
Boiestown

Miramichi Valley

Hartland

8

11

MAINE

95

Fredericton

King's Landing

Moncton

2

*FUNDY
NATIONAL
PARK*

Hopewell
Cape

2

3

7

1

111

Alma

111

St Martins

Cape Split

Saint John

Bay of Fundy

Wolfville

101

St Andrews

*Passamaquoddy
Bay*

Grand Manan

Annapolis
Royal

Annapolis Valley

10

Bangor

9

Digby

Chester
Mahone Bay
Lunenburg

8

French Shore

*KEJIMKUJIK
NATIONAL PARK*

△ Portland, Maine

Bar Harbor

Liverpool

101

103

*KEJIMKUJIK'S
SEASIDE
ADJUNCT*

Yarmouth

Shelburne

Lockeport

Barrington

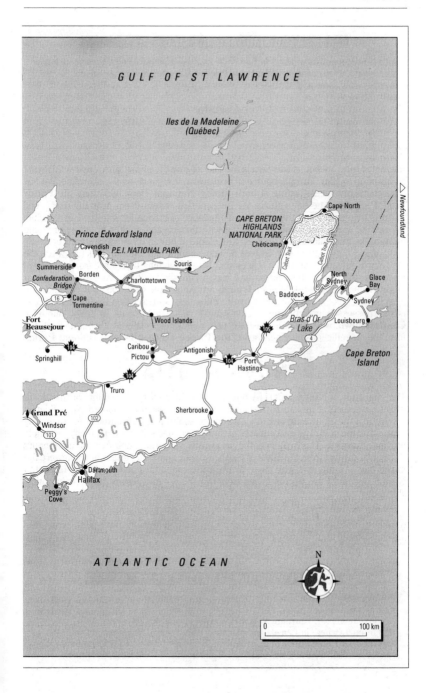

GULF OF ST LAWRENCE

Iles de la Madeleine
(Québec)

△ *Newfoundland*

Cape North

CAPE BRETON
HIGHLANDS
NATIONAL PARK

Chéticamp

Prince Edward Island

Cavendish
P.E.I. NATIONAL PARK

Souris

Summerside
Confederation
Bridge
Borden
16
Cape
Tormentine

Charlottetown

North
Sydney
Glace
Bay

Baddeck
Sydney

Cabot Trail

Cabot Trail

Wood Islands

Bras d'Or
Lake

Louisbourg

Fort
Beausejour

105
4

Caribou

Antigonish

Cape Breton
Island

Springhill

104

Pictou

Port
Hastings

104

104

Truro

Grand Pré

102

Sherbrooke

S C O T I A

Windsor

101

N O V A

Dartmouth
Halifax

Peggy's
Cove

ATLANTIC OCEAN

N

0   100 km

ACCOMMODATION PRICE CODES

All the accommodation prices in this book have been coded using the symbols below, corresponding to Canadian dollar rates. Prices are for the least expensive double room in each establishment in high season, excluding special offers. For a full explanation, see p.40 in Basics.

① up to $40   ④ $80–100   ⑦ $175–240
② $40–60   ⑤ $100–125   ⑧ $240+
③ $60–80   ⑥ $125–175

(never "St John") – but its star turn is the **Bay of Fundy**, whose taper creates tidal variations of up to 12m. This phenomenon is observable right along the shoreline, but has a spectacularly scenic setting at both **Fundy National Park** and along the **Fundy Trail Parkway**. The tides churn the nutrient-rich waters down near the ocean bed towards the surface and this draws an abundance of marine life into the bay – including several species of **whale**, beginning with finback and minkes in late spring, and humpbacks from mid- to late June. By the middle of July all three species are frequently sighted and they usually stay around till late summer and autumn, which is when the rare North Atlantic right whale is seen too. Whale-watching trips leave from a string of Fundy ports in both Nova Scotia and New Brunswick – those from Westport, near **Digby**, Alma and **Grand Manan Island**, are among the best. Last but certainly not least is **PEI**, linked to the mainland by the whopping Confederation Bridge in 1997. The island possesses one of the region's most amenable towns in leafy, laid-back **Charlottetown**, well worth at least a couple of days especially as it's but a short hop from the magnificent sandy beaches of **the Prince Edward Island National Park**.

NOVA SCOTIA

The character of **NOVA SCOTIA** has been conditioned by the whims of the North Atlantic weather, a climate so harsh in wintertime that the seaboard Nova Scotian colonists of the eighteenth century earned the soubriquet **"Bluenoses"** for their ability to stand the cold. The descendants of these hardened sailors do not typify the whole province, however. The farmers of the **Annapolis Valley** and their Acadian neighbours were quite distinct from the mariners of the Atlantic coast, and different again were the mixed bag of emigrants who came to work the coal mines and steel mills of central Nova Scotia and Cape Breton Island from the 1880s – differences that remain noticeable today.

To get the full sense of Nova Scotia you have to do a tour, and the logical place to start is the capital, **Halifax**, which sits beside a splendid harbour on the south coast. With its excellent restaurants, lively nightlife and handful of historic attractions, the city can easily fill a couple of days. To continue the tour, it's best to take in the beguiling

---

TOLL-FREE INFORMATION NUMBERS

The Nova Scotia Department of Tourism operates an information and accommodation reservation service on ☎1-800/565-0000 from anywhere in Canada and the USA, *www.explore.ns.com*. **Tourism New Brunswick** runs a similar service on ☎1-800/561-0123 from anywhere in Canada and mainland USA, *www.tourismnbcanada.com*. And so does the **PEI Department of Tourism**, information ☎1-888/734-7529, accommodation ☎1-888/268-6667 from anywhere in Canada and mainland USA, *www.peiplay.com*.

fishing villages of the southwest shore, amongst which handsome **Lunenburg** and solitary **Lockeport** stand out. Between them is **Liverpool**, where you turn inland for both the remote forests and lakes of **Kejimkujik National Park** and, beyond, on an arm of the Bay of Fundy, the delightful little town of **Annapolis Royal**. Heading east from here along the Annapolis Valley, it's a further 110km to the pleasant college town of **Wolfville** and another 90km back to Halifax.

Nova Scotia's other outstanding circular tourist route is the **Cabot Trail**. Named after the explorer John Cabot, who is supposed to have landed here in 1497, it encircles the northern promontory of **Cape Breton Island**, where the mountainous landscapes of **Cape Breton Highlands National Park** constitute some of eastern Canada's most stunning scenery. Cape Breton Island – and the strip of Nova Scotia coast bordering the Northumberland Strait – attracted thousands of Scottish highlanders at the end of the eighteenth century, mostly tenant farmers who had been evicted by Scotland's landowners when they found sheep-raising more profitable than renting farmland. Many of the region's settlements celebrate their Scots ancestry and Gaelic traditions in one way or another – museums, Highland Games and bagpipe-playing competitions – and in **South Gut St Ann's**, on the Cabot Trail, there's even a Gaelic college. The final attraction of Cape Breton is the reconstructed eighteenth-century French fortress of **Louisbourg**, stuck in splendid isolation on the southeast coast.

Southwest Nova Scotia is reasonably well served by **bus**, with daily connections running between Halifax and Yarmouth via both the south shore and – less frequently – the Annapolis Valley. There are also frequent buses from Halifax to Baddeck, Sydney and Truro, for connections on to New Brunswick and PEI. **VIA Rail** services run between Halifax and Truro, then continue on to New Brunswick and Québec. Elsewhere, however, you'll need a **car**, particularly if you're keen to see anything of the wilder sections of the Cabot Trail. **Car ferries** link Yarmouth with Bar Harbor and Portland in Maine; North Sydney with Newfoundland; Caribou, near Pictou, with PEI; and Digby with Saint John, which often makes a useful short cut.

> The Nova Scotia telephone code is ☎902.

A brief history of Nova Scotia

The original inhabitants of the Maritime Provinces were the **Micmacs** and **Malecites**, Algonquian-speaking peoples who lived a semi-nomadic life based on crop cultivation, fishing and hunting. Never numerous, both groups were ravaged by the diseases they contracted from their initial contacts with Basque and Breton fishermen in the late sixteenth century. Consequently, they were too weak to contest European colonization, although the Micmacs were later employed by the French to put the frighteners on the colonists of northern Maine.

Founded by the French in 1605, **Port Royal**, on the south shore of the Bay of Fundy, was Nova Scotia's first European settlement, but it was razed by Virginian raiders in 1613 and abandoned the following year. In 1621, James I, King of England and Scotland, granted "**Nova Scotia**" – as New Scotland was termed in the inaugural charter – to William Alexander, whose colony near Port Royal lasted just three years. The French returned in the mid-1630s, establishing themselves on the site of today's Annapolis Royal and this time designating the region as the French colony of **Acadie**. These competing claims were partly resolved by the **Treaty of Utrecht** in 1713 – when Britain took control of all the Maritimes except Cape Breton Island and today's PEI – and finally determined after the fall of New France in 1759, a British victory tarnished by the cruel expulsion of the Acadians from their farms along the Bay of Fundy.

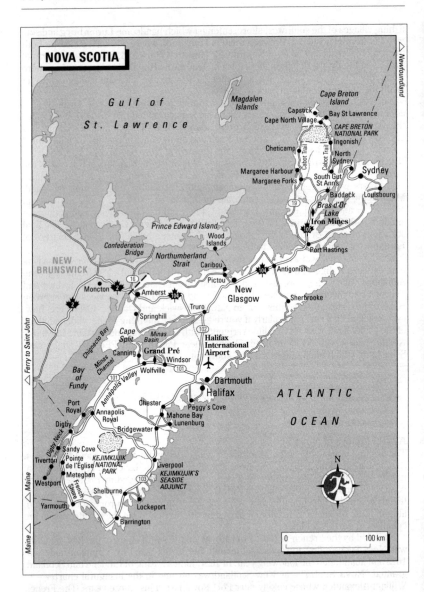

NOVA SCOTIA

Gulf of St. Lawrence

Magdalen Islands

Cape Breton Island

Capstick
Cape North Village
Bay St Lawrence

CAPE BRETON NATIONAL PARK

Cheticamp

Ingonish

Cabot Trail

North Sydney

Sydney

Margaree Harbour
Margaree Forks

South Gut St Ann's

Baddeck

Louisbourg

19

Bras d'Or Lake

Iron Mines

105

Prince Edward Island

Wood Islands

Confederation Bridge

Northumberland Strait

Caribou

Port Hastings

NEW BRUNSWICK

Pictou

Antigonish

104

16

Moncton *2*

Amherst *104*

New Glasgow

Sherbrooke

Springhill

Truro

Cape Split

Minas Basin

Chignecto Bay

Canning

Grand Pré

Windsor

Halifax International Airport

102

Minas Channel

Bay of Fundy

Annapolis Valley

Wolfville

101

Dartmouth

Halifax

Port Royal

Chester

Peggy's Cove

ATLANTIC OCEAN

Annapolis Royal

Mahone Bay

Lunenburg

Digby

Bridgewater

Digby Neck

Sandy Cove

Tiverton

Pointe de l'Eglise

KEJIMKUJIK NATIONAL PARK

Meteghan

Westport

French Shore

Liverpool

KEJIMKUJIK'S SEASIDE ADJUNCT

103

Shelburne

Yarmouth

Lockeport

Barrington

N

0   100 km

△ Newfoundland

△ Ferry to Saint John

△ Maine

△ Maine

With France defeated and the British keen to encourage immigration, there was a rapid influx of settlers from Ireland, England and Scotland as well as United Empire Loyalists escaping New England during and after the American War of Independence. This increase in the population precipitated an administrative reorganization, with the creation of Prince Edward Island in 1769 and New Brunswick in 1784. The new, streamlined Nova Scotia prospered from the development of its agriculture and the expansion

EATING A LOBSTER

Throughout Nova Scotia and PEI, **lobsters** are a favourite dish and they appear, in various guises, on many restaurant menus. For whole lobster, you pay by weight with the smaller lobsters averaging 450g and costing about $20–25. Also, look out for all-you-can-eat lobster suppers, rural community events held in village halls and the like, though these are now something of a rarity. Given that the Maritimers are so familiar with eating lobster, it's particularly embarrassing if you don't know how. There are eight main steps:

1. Twist off the claws.

2. Crack each claw with the nutcracker you receive with the lobster.

3. Separate the tailpiece from the body by arching the back until it breaks.

4. Bend back and break off the flippers from the tailpiece.

5. Insert a fork where the flippers broke off and push.

6. Unhinge the back from the body – the meat in the back, the tomalley, is considered by many to be the choicest part of a lobster.

7. Open the remaining part of the body by cracking apart sideways.

8. Suck out the meat from the small claws.

of its fishing fleet. Further profits were reaped from shipbuilding, British-sanctioned privateering and the growth of Halifax as the Royal Navy's principal North Atlantic base. In 1867 Nova Scotia became part of the Dominion of Canada confident of its economic future. However, the province was too reliant on shipbuilding and, when this industry collapsed, Nova Scotia experienced a dreadful recession, whose effects were only partly mitigated by the mining of the province's coalfields and the industrialization of Cape Breton's **Sydney**, which became a major steel producer. Most of the pits and steel mills were closed in the 1950s, and the province is now largely dependent on farming, logging, fishing and tourism.

Halifax

HALIFAX, set on a steep and spatulate promontory beside one of the world's finest harbours, has become the focal point of the Maritimes, the region's financial, educational and transportation centre, whose metropolitan population of over 500,000 makes it seven times the size of its nearest rival, New Brunswick's Saint John. This pre-eminence has been achieved since World War II, but long before then Halifax was a naval town *par excellence*, its harbour defining the character and economy of a city which rarely seemed to look inland.

The British were the first to develop Halifax, founding a base here in 1749 to counter the French fortress of Louisbourg (see p.368) on Cape Breton Island. When New France was captured shortly afterwards, the town became a heavily fortified guarantor of the Royal Navy's domination of the North Atlantic, a role reinforced when the British lost control of New England. The needs of the garrison called the tune throughout the nineteenth century: the waterfront was lined with brothels; martial law was in force till the 1850s; and most Haligonians, as the local citizenry are known, were at least partly employed in a service capacity.

In the twentieth century Halifax acted as a key supply and convoy harbour in both world wars, but since then its military importance has declined, even though the ships of the Canadian navy still dock here. Disfiguring office blocks reflect the city's new commercial successes, but interrupt the sweep of the town as it tumbles down to the harbour from the Citadel, the old British fortress that is the town's most significant sight. Nevertheless, Halifax retains a compact, bustling centre whose appealing and relaxing air is a far cry from the tense industriousness of many a metropolis.

Arrival, information and city transport

Halifax International Airport is located 35km northeast of the city centre and has its own **tourist information office** (daily 9am–10pm). Airbus runs a **bus shuttle** service from the airport to the classier downtown hotels (daily: every 30min to 1hr from 7.30am to 11pm; 40min–1hr 15min depending on traffic; $12 single, $20 return). If you're not staying at one of these, ask the driver how near to your destination he will let you off; for downtown get off at the *Delta Barrington Hotel*, which is on Barrington Street at Duke, right in the centre. The **taxi** fare from the airport to the centre is around $40. The Acadian Lines bus terminal, 6040 Almon St, about 4km northwest of the centre just off Robie Street, houses the long-distance bus station and also DRL buses (for Yarmouth and the South Shore). Transit bus #7 connects the terminal with downtown. The VIA Rail station, Hollis Street at Cornwallis Park, handles just six **trains** in and out per week, connecting Halifax with Truro, New Brunswick, the Gaspé and Montréal. From the train station it's a fifteen-minute walk into the centre down Barrington Street, or else catch the #7 or #9 bus (every 15min during the week, hourly on the weekend).

Information

Both of Halifax's main **tourist offices** cover the city and province, and are centrally situated. The **International Visitor Information Centre** (June–Aug daily 8.30am–8pm; Sept to mid-Oct & May daily 9am–6pm; mid-Oct to April Mon–Fri 8.30am–4.30pm; ☎490-5946, *www.halifaxinfo.com*) at 1595 Barrington St and Sackville, will gladly fix up accommodation in town and across the whole of Nova Scotia, advise on tours and provide you with armfuls of maps, brochures and leaflets including the comprehensive *Halifax Visitor Guide*. Five-minutes' walk away, just off the waterfront in the area known as the Historic Properties, the **Nova Scotia Visitor Information Centre** (May–Oct daily 9am–7pm; Nov–April Wed–Sun 9am–4.30pm; ☎424-4248) offers a similar service. At both, the room reservation service is free.

City transport

The best way to see **downtown** Halifax is on foot, but for outlying attractions and accommodation **Metro Transit** (☎490-6600) bus services are reliable and efficient, though they are sharply curtailed in the evenings and on weekends. There's a flat fare of $1.65 in the Halifax area – exact fare only. If you need to change buses on the same journey, ask for a free transfer ticket at the outset. The ferries that cross Halifax harbour from the downtown terminal to Dartmouth and Woodside are part of the Transit system and apply the same tariff. Free Metro Transit route maps and schedules are available from the International Visitor Information Centre.

Accommodation

Finding **accommodation** in Halifax is rarely a problem and the International Visitor Information Centre is especially helpful in emergencies. To get a flavour of the city your best bet is to stay in – or at least close to – downtown. Here you'll find a number of modern sky-rise **hotels**, ranging from the comfortable to the luxurious, as well as several more distinctive offerings. These include a couple of stylish hotels with Art Deco flour-

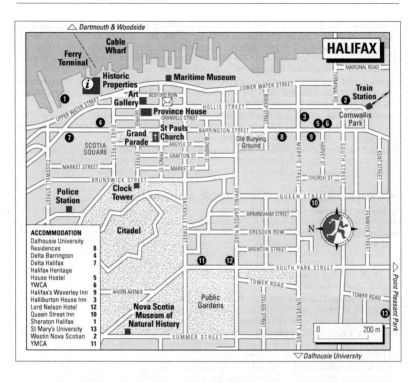

ishes, two **inns** occupying tastefully converted old town houses and the occasional **B&B**, though most of the city's B&Bs are far from downtown. Halifax's **motels** are stuck out on the peripheries of town too, inconveniently concentrated about 10km northwest of the centre along Bedford Highway (Hwy 2), beside Bedford Basin bay. The main budget alternatives are the **student rooms** offered by several city universities between mid-May and mid-August, and the pleasant, centrally located youth hostel. There is no city campsite.

Hotels and inns

Delta Barrington, 1875 Barrington St (☎429-7410 or 1-800/268-1133, *www.deltahotels.com*). Modern luxury, bang in the middle of downtown, with weekend discounts of up to 30 percent. Attached to one of the city's larger shopping malls. ⑥.

Delta Halifax, 1990 Barrington St (☎425-6700 or 1-800/268-1133, *www.deltahotels.com*). Large, modern downtown hotel occupying a concrete-and-glass tower block with attractive, spacious rooms that are discounted at weekends. ⑥.

Halifax's Waverley Inn, 1266 Barrington St (☎423-9346 or 1-800/565-9346, *www.waverleyinn.com*). Elegant Victorian mansion, with thirty rooms, that's been pleasantly refurbished with period furnishings. Oscar Wilde stayed here on a North American lecture tour, apparently turning up in green-velvet pantaloons – outlandish gear which only seems to have added to his notoriety amongst the locals. The inn is situated about a 5min walk from the train station; reservations advised. All rooms are en suite. Rates include breakfast. ④.

Halliburton House Inn, 5184 Morris St (☎420-0658, *www.halliburton.ns.ca*). Near the railway station off Barrington St, this attractively restored Georgian town house with garden offers good value and includes breakfast. Thirty rooms. ⑤.

Lord Nelson Hotel, 1515 South Park St (☎423-6331 or 1-800/565-2020, *www.LordNelsonHotel.com*). Opposite the Public Gardens at the corner of Spring Garden Rd. The lobby of this popular brown-brick hotel is spacious and elegant, with Art Deco details dating from its 1920s construction. The 200-odd rooms do not quite live up to the lobby, but they are comfortable and furnished in smart modern style – and certainly compare well with those of their rivals. ⑤.

Queen Street Inn, 1266 Queen St at Morris (☎422-9828). Southwest of downtown, this pleasantly renovated Victorian villa is decked out with local bygones. There are just six guestrooms with shared baths; breakfast is not included in the rate. ②.

Sheraton Halifax, 1919 Upper Water St (☎421-1700 or 1-800/325-3535, fax 422-5805). One of the city's grandest hotels, built in a broadly retro style to blend in with the adjacent Historic Properties. Overlooks the waterfront and has saunas, swimming pool and whirlpool. ⑨.

Westin Nova Scotian, 1181 Hollis St (☎421-1000 or 1-877/9-WESTIN, *www.westin.com*). Massive, lux-urious hotel in the upgraded premises of the old railway hotel, which – with its Art Deco touches – is next door to the train station. A 15min stroll along Barrington or Hollis sts from the centre. ⑨.

Bed and Breakfasts, hostels and student accommodation

Dalhousie University Conference Services, Room 407, Student Union Building, 6136 University Ave (☎494-8840, *www.dal.ca/confserv*). Halifax's premier academic institution, Dalhousie University is geared up for conferences during the summer recess, and also offers rooms to tourists from early May to late August. There are several locations, beginning at the west end of University Ave – 2km southwest of the centre – with facilities that include swimming pool and sports halls. Also at the uni-versity's DalTech, O'Brien Hall, 5217 Morris St – off Barrington St, a 10min walk south of the cen-tre. Single and double rooms available, usually with shared bathrooms, but breakfast is included. Singles $25, doubles $43.

Halifax Heritage House Hostel, 1253 Barrington St (☎ & fax 422-3863). Only 500m from the train station, this clean and agreeable HI hostel with family rooms (doubles $34) and dorm beds ($18) has a laundry, kitchen, patio and parking.

St Mary's University, 923 Robie St (☎420-5485 or 1-888/347-5555). About 2km southwest of the centre, on the way to Point Pleasant Park; singles and doubles available; shared bathrooms. Open mid-May to mid-August. Singles $23, doubles $33.

Virginia Kinsfolks B&B, 1722 Robie St at Quinpool (☎423-6687 or 1-800/668-7829). Situated beside a busy main road about 1.5km west of downtown – opposite Halifax Infirmary – this well-kept B&B occupies a suburban house with rear sun deck. Four spacious en-suite rooms and gourmet breakfast. Discounts for stays of more than three days. ⑥.

YMCA, 1565 South Park St at Sackville (☎423-9622). Opposite the Public Gardens, this YMCA, for men and women, has fifty single rooms, none of which are en suite but there's a gym. $28.

YWCA, 1239 Barrington St (☎423-6162). Near the train station, this women-only hostel has facilities that include kitchen, gym, laundry and sauna. Twenty-seven rooms, mostly shared bathrooms. Singles $32, doubles $48.

The City

With its shopping malls and brusque tower blocks, the commercial and social heart of modern Halifax clambers up the steep hillside from the harbourfront, its narrow streets dotted with scores of bustling bars and restaurants. The city's main attractions – most notably the **Art Gallery**, with its eclectic collection of modern Canadian paintings, the **Maritime Museum** and the Georgian **Province House** – all huddle close together in the lower part of town beneath Halifax's star turn, the Vaubanesque **Citadel**. On a sunny day, a pleasant diversion is a trip to see a couple of the **outer fortifications** built to defend Halifax harbour, and you can also catch the ferry over to neighbouring **Dartmouth**, home of the old **Quaker House**.

The Citadel

The distinctively bright Georgian **Clock Tower**, a solitary landmark sitting at the top of George Street beside the path up to the Citadel, looks somewhat confused, its dainty balustraded tower set on top of the dreariest of rectangular shacks. Completed in 1803, the tower is a tribute to the architectural tastes of its sponsor, Edward, Duke of Kent and father of Queen Victoria, who was sent here as military commandant in 1794. The Duke insisted on having a clock on each of the tower's four faces so none of the garrison had an excuse for being late, a preoccupation typical of this unforgiving martinet.

Up above the Clock Tower, the present fortifications of the **Citadel National Historic Site** (daily: July–Aug 9am–6pm; Sept–June 9am–5pm; $6 June to mid-Sept, $3.75 in shoulder season, otherwise $1.50) were completed in 1856, the fourth in a series dating from Edward Cornwallis's stockade of 1749. The star-shaped fortress, constructed flush with the crest of the hill to protect it from artillery fire, seems insignificant until you reach the massive double stone and earth walls flanking the deep encircling ditch, a forbidding approach to one of Britain's most important imperial strongholds. Despite their apparent strength, however, the walls, faced with granite and ironstone, were a source of worry to a succession of British engineers. The sunken design simply didn't suit the climate – in winter the water in the mortar and earth froze and the spring melt came with regular collapses.

A slender footbridge spans the ditch and leads into the fort, whose expansive **parade ground** is flanked by stone walls and dominated by the three-storey general **barracks**, whose long, columned galleries now mostly house offices, though one particular barrack room has been returned to its appearance as of 1869. Here also is an **Army Museum** (recommended donation $1), which adopts an earthy soldier's outlook in the labelling of its wide collection of small arms. Ancient and sometimes rare photos track the Canadian army through its various imperial entanglements – from the Boer War onwards – and there's an interesting section tracing Canadian involvement with the Anglo-French attack on Bolshevik Russia after World War I. The walls themselves contain a string of storehouses stuffed with military bric-a-brac. Here you'll find a couple of reconstructed powder magazines, the former garrison school room and several exhibits exploring the Citadel's history, including a small theatre where an hour-long film, *The Tides of History*, details the development of Halifax. Also of interest is the **Communications Exhibit**, which explains the niceties of the Admiralty's signalling system – a complicated affair with, for instance, different flags for different types of ship and whether they had been sighted or had actually arrived.

Free and entertaining half-hour **guided tours** (May to late Oct) of the Citadel depart from the information office in the barracks building every hour or so. Throughout the summer, bagpipe bands and marching "soldiers" perform on the parade ground in period uniform and one of the cannons is ceremoniously fired every day at noon. If militarism leaves you cold, the Citadel is still worth a visit for the grand view from its ramparts over the city and harbour.

Downtown

If you retrace your steps past the Clock Tower and head down George Street, you'll hit the tree-lined, elongated square known as the **Grand Parade**, the social centre of the nineteenth-century town. For the officer corps, this was the place to be seen walking on a Sunday, when, as one obsequious observer wrote, "their society generally [was] sought, frequently courted, and themselves esteemed" – a judgement rather different from that of the radical journalist Joseph Howe, who hated their "habits of idleness, dissipation and expense". The southern edge of the parade borders the handsome **St Paul's Church** (Mon–Fri 9am–4.30pm; free), whose chunky cupola and simple timber frame date from 1750, making it both the oldest building in town and the first Protestant church in Canada. Inside, the church's simple symmetry – with balcony and sturdy pillars – is engaging, an unpretentious garrison church enlisting God to the British interest; look out, too, for the piece of wood embedded in the plaster above the inner entrance doors, a remnant of the 1917 Halifax Explosion (see box, p.342). Following the disaster, the vestry was used as an emergency hospital and the bodies of hundreds of victims were laid in tiers around the walls.

Charles Dickens, visiting in 1842, described the graceful sandstone **Province House**, a couple of minutes' walk from Grand Parade down George Street at Hollis (July & Aug Mon–Fri 9am–5pm, Sat & Sun 10am–4pm; Sept–June Mon–Fri 9am–4pm; free), as "a gem of Georgian architecture" whose proceedings were "like looking at Westminster through the wrong end of a telescope". Highlights of the free guided tour include a peek into the old upper chamber, with its ornate plasterwork and matching portraits of Queen Caroline and her father-in-law, George I. She should have been pictured with her husband, George II, of course, rather than her father-in-law, but no one has ever bothered to rectify this costly decorative error. The present legislature meet in the Assembly Room, a cosy chamber that partly resembles a Georgian bedroom rather than Nova Scotia's seat of government.

Across the road from the Province House, the **Art Gallery of Nova Scotia**, 1741 Hollis St (Tues–Fri 10am–6pm, Sat & Sun noon–5pm, plus July–Aug Mon noon–5pm; $5, free on Tues), occupies two adjacent buildings – one a stern Art Deco structure, the other an embellished Victorian edifice that has previously served as a courthouse, police headquarters and post office. The gallery is attractively laid out and although there is some rotation of the exhibits most of the pieces described here should be on view. Pick up a free gallery plan at the entrance in the more southerly of the two buildings, Gallery South. The Courtyard Level – the ground floor – contains a delightful section devoted to the Nova Scotian artist **Maud Lewis** (1903–70). The daughter of a Yarmouth harness maker, Lewis overcame several disabilities, including rheumatoid arthritis, to become a painter of some regional renown, creating naive, brightly coloured works of local scenes. Lewis's tiny cabin – awash with her bright paintwork – has been moved here intact from the outskirts of Digby.

In Gallery North, the two lower levels – the Lower Lobby and Level 1 – hold temporary exhibitions of modern sculpture and painting and a small but enjoyable selection of the work of modern Canadians drawn from the permanent collection: the egg tempera on masonite *Island in the Ice* by the Nova Scotian artist Tom Forrestall is perhaps the most striking painting here (in Gallery 7), its sharp, deep-hued colours and threatening ice- and seascape enhanced by a tight control of space. Level 2 features local folk art, largely naive and boldly painted woodcarvings and panel paintings comparable to the work of Maud Lewis, as well as a small sample of Inuit work. On Level 3, there's an excellent collection of **Canadian Art**, whose earlier canvases are distinguished by four intriguing views of Halifax in the 1760s produced by Dominique Serres in the minutely observed Dutch land- and seascape tradition (Gallery 15). Surprisingly, Serres never actually visited Canada, but painted Halifax while in Europe, from drawings produced by a camera obscura. In the same gallery, there's Joshua Reynolds' flattering *Portrait of George Montagu Dunk, 2nd Earl of Halifax*. As the man responsible for colonial trade, Dunk permitted his recently acquired title to be used in the naming of "Halifax" – what would have happened but for his timely ennoblement (Dunk Town?) is anyone's guess. On the same floor, Gallery 19 holds several canvases by Cornelius Krieghoff (see p.163) and outstanding contributions by members of the **Group of Seven** (see p.86). In particular, look out for Lawren Harris's haunting *Algoma* landscape and A.Y. Jackson's dinky *Houses of Prospect*, typical of Jackson's later (post-Group) style of softly coloured landscapes. Next door, Gallery 20 is devoted to modern Atlantic Canadian painters. Forrestall makes another appearance here, but it's his mentor, **Alex Colville**, who takes pride of place, with several characteristically disconcerting works, a sort of Magic Realism of passive, precisely juxtaposed figures caught, cinema-like, in mid-shot. Finally, on Level 4 (Room 28), there's a tiny selection of British and European paintings, and – a real surprise – an assortment of ribald Hogarth engravings.

The waterfront

One block south of the east end of George Street stands the **Maritime Museum of the Atlantic**, 1675 Lower Water St (May–Oct Mon & Wed–Sat 9.30am–5.30pm, Tues 9.30am–8pm, Sun 11am–5.30pm; Nov–April Tues 9.30am–8pm, Wed–Sat 9.30am–5pm, Sun 1–5pm; $6), which houses a fascinating exhibition covering all aspects of Nova Scotian seafaring from colonial times to the present day. By the entrance, there's a reconstruction of a nineteenth-century chandlery, stocked with everything from chains, ropes, couplings and barrels of tar through to ships' biscuits and bully beef. Other displays include a collection of small boats and cutaway scale models illustrating the changing technology of shipbuilding, a feature on the history of the schooner *Bluenose* (see below) and a number of gaudy ships' figureheads: look out for the tur-baned Turk once attached to the British barque *Saladin*. In 1844, the *Saladin*'s crew mutinied in mid-Atlantic, killed the captain and ran the boat aground near Halifax, where they were subsequently tried and hanged. There's also a feature on the Halifax Explosion, illustrated by a first-rate video, *One Moment in Time*, and don't miss the section on the *Titanic*, which sank east of Halifax in 1912. Several pieces of fancy wood-work found floating in the ocean after the sinking have ended up in the museum, a pathetic epitaph to the liner's grand Edwardian fittings. Docked outside the museum are an early twentieth-century steamship, the CSS *Acadia*, and a World War II corvette, HMCS *Sackville*. The first is part of the museum, the second is a (free) attraction in its own right; both can only be boarded in the summer.

The much-vaunted **Historic Properties** comprise an area of refurbished wharves, warehouses and merchants' quarters situated below Upper Water Street, 400m north of the Maritime Museum – and just beyond the Dartmouth and Woodside ferry termi-nal. The ensemble has a certain urbane charm – all bars, boutiques and bistros – and the narrow lanes and alleys still maintain the shape of the waterfront during the days of sail, but there's not much to see unless the schooner *Bluenose II* is moored here, as it often is during the summer. The original *Bluenose*, whose picture is on the 10¢ coin, was famed throughout Canada as the fastest vessel of its kind in the 1920s, although she ended her days ingloriously as a freighter, foundering off Haiti in 1946. The repli-ca has spent several years as a floating standard-bearer, representing Nova Scotia at events such as the Montréal Expo, but it's now on its last sea legs and its future is uncertain. Pressure groups are campaigning to have it berthed permanently here at Halifax or at its home port of Lunenburg.

The Old Burying Ground and the Nova Scotia Museum

Mysterious and spooky at dawn and dusk, the **Old Burying Ground**, five-minutes' walk south of Grand Parade at Barrington Street and Spring Garden Road, looks some-thing like the opening shot of David Lean's *Great Expectations* – though the over-blown memorial by the gates in honour of a brace of Canadian officers killed in the Crimean War does somewhat undermine the effect. Many of the tombstones are badly weath-ered, but enough inscriptions survive to give an insight into the lives (and early deaths) of the colonists and their offspring. The oldest tomb is that of a certain John Connor, who ran the first ferry service over to Dartmouth and died in 1754.

Walking west up Spring Garden Road from the Burying Ground, it's about 800m to South Park Street, where a set of handsome iron gates serve as the main entrance into the city's **Public Gardens** (dawn–dusk; free). First planted in the 1870s, the gardens cover sixteen acres of meticulously maintained exotic shrubs, flower beds and trees set around ornamental statues, water fountains, ponds and a brightly painted band-stand. All together, the gardens are a pleasant interlude on the way to the **Nova Scotia Museum of Natural History**, in the rear of the old grassy commonland at the back of the Citadel, at 1747 Summer St (June to mid-Oct Mon–Sat 9.30am–5.30pm, Wed open till 8pm, Sun 1–5.30pm; mid-Oct to May Tues–Sat 9.30am–5pm, Wed till 8pm, Sun

1–5pm; $3). The best of the museum's wide-ranging exhibits are those depicting the region's marine and land-based wildlife, and there's a modest archeological section too.

The outer fortifications

In the eighteenth century the British navy protected the seven-kilometre-long sea passage into **Halifax harbour**, and the Bedford Basin behind it, with coastal batteries strung along the shore between the city and the Atlantic. Two of these are worth a visit, though more for their commanding views than the ragbag of military remains. There's one at Point Pleasant, at the tip of the Halifax peninsula about 3km south of the city, whilst the other is on McNab's Island, sitting in the middle of the main seaway, 4km south of the city.

At the end of South Park Street and its continuation, Young Avenue, **Point Pleasant Park** (bus #9 from Barrington St) incorporates the remains of four gun batteries and the squat **Prince of Wales Martello Tower** (July–Aug daily 10am–6pm; free), which was built at the end of the eighteenth century as a combined barracks, battery and storehouse. One of the first of its type, the design was copied from a Corsican tower (at Martello Point) which had proved particularly troublesome to the British. The self-contained, semi-self-sufficient defensive fortification with its thick walls and protected entrance proved so successful that Martello towers were built throughout the empire, only becoming obsolete in the 1870s with advances in artillery technology. The surrounding park, 200 acres of wooded hills and shoreline, is crisscrossed by paths and trails and remains one of the few places in North America where heather grows, supposedly originating from seeds shaken from the bedding of Scots regiments stationed here.

THE HALIFAX EXPLOSION

Nothing in the history of the Maritimes stands out like the **Halifax Explosion** of 1917, the greatest human-caused cataclysm of the pre-atomic age. It occurred when Halifax was the departure point for convoys transporting troops and armaments to Europe during World War I. Shortly after dawn on December 6, a Norwegian ship called the *Imo*, a vessel carrying relief supplies to Belgium, and a French munitions carrier called the *Mont Blanc* were manoeuvring in Halifax harbour. The Norwegian ship was steaming for the open sea, while the *Mont Blanc*, a small, decrepit vessel, was heading for the harbour stuffed with explosives and ammunition, including half a million pounds of TNT – though it flew no flags to indicate the hazardous nature of the cargo. As the ships approached each other, the *Imo* was forced to steer into the wrong channel by a poorly positioned tugboat. With neither ship clear about the other's intentions and each attempting to take evasive action, they collided, and the resulting sparks caused the ignition of the drums of flammable liquid stored on the *Mont Blanc*'s deck. A fire took hold, and the crew abandoned their vessel, which drifted under the force of the impact towards the Halifax shore.

A large crowd had gathered on the waterfront to witness the spectacle when the TNT exploded. The blast killed 2000 people instantly and flattened over 300 acres of north Halifax, with fire engulfing much of the rest. Windows were broken in Truro over 90km away and the shock-wave was felt in Cape Breton. Nothing remained of the *Mont Blanc*, and part of its anchor, a piece of metal weighing over half a ton, was later found more than 4km away. To make matters worse, a blizzard deposited 40cm of snow on Halifax during the day, hampering rescue attempts. The bodies of many victims were not recovered until the spring.

It's hard to appreciate today the vision of Armageddon that haunted Halifax after the explosion, but haunt the city it did, as the poignant newspaper cuttings in the Maritime Museum show.

McNab's Island, 5km long and 2km wide, contains the remnants of five different fortifications, dating from the middle of the eighteenth century to the establishment of Fort McNab in 1890. The island, half of which is parkland, is laced with hiking trails and dotted with picnic spots, making it a relaxing retreat from the city. The island is accessible by ferry from the Eastern Passage jetty on the east (Dartmouth) side of Halifax harbour – call ☎465-4563 or 1-800/326-4563 for schedule; the round trip costs $8. To reach Eastern Passage jetty from downtown Halifax, take the Dartmouth ferry and then bus #60 (every 30min, hourly on the weekend) from outside the terminal building. Ask the driver to let you off or else you're likely to go whistling past.

Dartmouth

Humdrum **DARTMOUTH**, across the harbour from Halifax, is often ignored by visitors as it lacks the more obvious appeal of its neighbour. Nevertheless, it is the province's second largest town, with 70,000 inhabitants, and although it's primarily an industrial centre the ferry ride over provides wide views of the harbour and downtown Halifax – and there are a couple of minor attractions to further justify a sortie. The Dartmouth **ferry** leaves the Halifax waterfront from beside the Historic Properties at the foot of George Street (Mon–Sat 6.45am–11.30pm; every 15–30min, plus June–Sept Sun noon–5.30pm; $1.65). The journey takes about ten minutes. The twin cities are also connected by two road bridges: the MacDonald, running just to the north of both city centres, and the Mackay, part of the outer ring road. Metro Transit bus #1 uses the MacDonald.

Turn left outside Dartmouth ferry terminal and then take the first right for the five-minute stroll to the **Quaker House**, 57 Ochterloney St (June–Aug only; call for hours ☎464-2253; free), a small, grey-clapboard residence sitting three blocks up the hill from the dock. After the American War of Independence, several Quaker whaling families emigrated from Nantucket Island, off Cape Cod, to Dartmouth, but this is the only one of their houses to survive. The interior has been painstakingly restored to its late eighteenth-century appearance, its spartan fittings reflecting Quaker values. Among the exhibits are a two-hundred-year-old pair of shoes found under the floorboards during renovations in 1991, and the eye of a Greenland whale preserved in formalin – though the staff won't show you this if they think you're squeamish. From here, it's another five-minute walk along – and left at the end of – King Street to a very short stretch of the **Shubenacadie Canal**, which once connected the Bay of Fundy to Dartmouth, a distance of 90km. Begun in 1826, this monumental feat of engineering, linking a dozen existing lakes with new watercourses and locks, was completed in 1860, but the canal only made a profit for ten years before it was superseded by the railways – and then left to rot.

To return to the Dartmouth ferry terminal, double back across the end of King Street and keep straight until you reach the **park** that leads round the harbourfront – in all, a five-minute walk.

Eating and drinking

It's easy to **eat** well and cheaply in Halifax. There's a wide selection of **downtown** cafés, diners, café-bars and restaurants within easy walking distance of Grand Parade with particular concentrations along Spring Garden Road from Queen Street to South Park, Argyle Street, and Granville Street north of Duke. All three of these areas largely cater to locals, whereas the more touristy spots are clustered in the Historic Properties. At the majority of restaurants, a substantial meal will only set you back about $15–20, excluding drinks. Seafood is the leading local speciality, with **lobster** being a particular favourite – expect to pay about $25 for a medium-sized specimen. Bear in mind also that most kitchens start to finish up at around 9.30–10pm and that many restaurants close on Sunday, sometimes Monday too.

They say Halifax has more **bars** per head than anywhere in Canada, except St John's Newfoundland, and although cafés and café-bars have made inroads, there are still several good bars, and most of them offer pub food. Incidentally, bars and restaurants sometimes occupy different floors of the same premises, which can be a little confusing.

Cafés, café-bars, grills and diners

Big Life House, 5220 Blowers St. Lively, informal café with good, wholesome snacks and speciality coffees. New Ageish. Open Mon–Sat 9am–9pm, Sun 11am–3pm.

The Bluenose, 1824 Hollis at Duke St. Something of an institution, this long-established diner serves filling and fairly tasty meals until 10pm. Lobster, in various guises, is the speciality.

Caffe Roma, 1572 Argyle St. Fashionable, pastel-painted coffee house offering tasty salads and doorstep sandwiches, all at inexpensive prices.

Daily Grind Café, 5684 Spring Garden Rd at South Park. Easy-going, amenable coffee house where you can browse a vast selection of newspapers and glossy magazines.

Economy Shoe Shop Café, 1663 Argyle St. Everything here is imaginative – from the name and the decor through to the menu, offering tapas to Italian. One of a cluster of fashionable café-bars on Argyle.

Grabbajabba Fine Coffee, 5475 Spring Garden Rd at Queen. This excellent coffee house sells great coffees and delicious pastries – the cheesecake is especially delicious. Also a branch at 1791 Barrington St.

Mediterraneo, 1571 Barrington St. Inexpensive downtown café serving tasty Lebanese dishes. Popular spot with a youthful clientele. Between Sackville and Blowers.

Midtown Tavern and Grill, at Prince and Grafton. One of the most enjoyable places in town, this blue-collar favourite serves up tasty steaks at amazingly reasonable prices. It's a far cry from the tourist-industry niceties down on the waterfront, and none the worse for it. Closed Sun.

Steve-o-Reno's, Brunswick St, just off Spring Garden Rd. Fashionable café-bar with pastel decor and angular, modern furnishings. Great food – everything from Thai noodles to Italian – and great prices too: many main courses for just \$5.

Restaurants

Dharma Sushi, 1576 Argyle St (☎425-7785). First-rate Japanese restaurant serving all the favourites. Traditional decor; reasonable prices. Main courses from around \$12.

Five Fishermen, 1740 Argyle St at George (☎422-4421). One of Halifax's better restaurants, where the all-you-can-eat mussel bar is a popular (at no extra charge) adjunct to the restaurant, whose speciality is seafood. The cosy interior is decked out in antique nautical style. Fairly expensive with main courses \$15–25, but well worth it. Reservations required. Popular with tourists.

Il Mercato, 5475 Spring Garden Rd at Dresden (☎422-2866). Laid-back, tastefully decorated restaurant featuring well-prepared, very tasty Northern Italian dishes. Main courses for around \$15.

La Cave, 5244 Blowers at Grafton (☎429-3551). Tiny bistro serving French and Italian cuisine and great desserts at affordable prices. Tucked away in a basement.

Salty's, Historic Properties (☎423-6818). On the waterfront, this busy restaurant with its large patio area heaves with tourists, who feast on the lobster – generally thought to be as well prepared as anywhere.

Satisfaction Feast, 1581 Grafton St at Blowers (☎422-3540). Vegetarian restaurant with an imaginative menu. Vegan options available. Main courses around \$10. Open daily 11am–10pm.

Spice Trail, 1580 Argyle St (☎423-0093). Oodles of noodles at bargain-basement prices. Chinese specialities.

Bars

Granite Brewery, 1222 Barrington St at South. In the style of a British pub, this charmingly intimate bar occupies a nineteenth-century stone building not far from the train station. Most of the ale is brewed on the premises – try the "Peculiar", a fair approximation of the sultry grandeur of the legendary British Theakston's.

Peddlers' Pub, Granville St at Duke. Occupying part of an old commercial block at the pedestrianized northern end of Granville St, this pub has a pleasant outside area and a big and breezy bar.

Rogue's Roost Brew Pub, 5435 Spring Garden Rd at Queen. Upstairs brewpub decorated in brisk, modern style. A student favourite.

Split Crow, 1855 Granville St at Duke. Another supposedly English pub. Very central, often featuring live Maritime fiddle music.

Your Father's Moustache, 5686 Spring Garden Rd at South Park. Good range of ales with frequent live acts – blues a speciality. Seasonal rooftop patio.

Nightlife and entertainment

If you want to go out and groove, Halifax has a vibrant **live music scene** with around fifty of its café-bars and bars offering everything from blues and jazz through to indie and techno. Many of these places have live music on just a couple of nights a week, and detailed entertainment listings, along with reviews, are given in a free weekly newssheet, *The Coast*, which is available at record shops, bars and the tourist office. The local newspaper *The Chronicle-Herald* carries reviews and listings on Thursdays, and *Where*, a free magazine supplied by the tourist office, has a section describing the city's most popular bars and giving some opening hours. The venues listed below are places where you can expect to see live music on most nights of the week. The main musical **event** is the eight-day Atlantic Jazz Festival, held in mid-July and featuring many of the biggest international names. Halifax, as the provincial capital, also attracts major live acts in key **classical** and theatrical performances and has a fairly prestigious **theatre** scene.

Folk, jazz and blues

Bearly's House of Blues, 1269 Barrington St (☎423-2526). Near the HI youth hostel, this low-key bar has regular acts with the emphasis – you guessed it – on blues. Thurs–Sun.

Birmingham Bar and Grill, 5657 Spring Garden Rd at South Park St (☎420-9622). Wide range of wine and beers with nightly jazz.

Lower Deck, in the Privateer's Warehouse, one of the Historic Properties down on the waterfront (☎425-1501). Traditional Maritime folk music most nights of the week.

Contemporary

Café Mokka Ultrabar, 1588 Granville St (☎492-4036). Fashionable downtown spot showcasing up-and-coming local bands plus jazz and blues.

JJ Rossy's, 1883 Granville St (☎422-4411). Varied DJ sounds with a dance floor on the main level, big-screen TV action up above. Popular with students.

New Palace, 1721 Brunswick St (☎429-5959). Massive, brash and noisy nightclub where Halifax's young more than get acquainted; open till 3.30am nightly.

Reflections Cabaret, 5184 Sackville St (☎422-2957). Halifax's main gay and lesbian bar and nightclub. House music predominates.

Tickle Trunk, 5680 Spring Garden Rd (☎429-2582). Wide range of music featuring local bands, some of whom just turn up and play.

Cinemas

Empire Bayers Lake, 190 Chain Lake Drive (☎876-4800). Mainstream multiscreen near Hwy 102, about 6km west of downtown.

Park Lane 8, 5657 Spring Garden Rd (☎423-4598). Mainstream cinema in the Park Lane Mall.

Theatre and classical music

Neptune Theatre, 1593 Argyle St (☎429-7300). The doyen of Halifax's live theatres, offering a wide range of mainstream dramatic productions; closes for three months in summer.

Symphony Nova Scotia, box office at the Dalhousie Arts Centre, 6101 University Ave (☎494-3820 or 1-800/874-1669). Professional orchestra that usually performs at the university's Rebecca Cohn

Auditorium – at University Ave and Marchant St. Concert season from September to April. Everything from Piaf to Beethoven.

Listings

Airlines Air Canada (☎429-7111); Air St Pierre (☎873-3566); Canada 3000 (flight information ☎873-3555; tickets from travel agents).

Banks Amongst many downtown branches, there's a Bank of Novia Scotia at Scotia Square, Barrington St and Duke; a CIBC at 1809 Barrington St; and a Royal Bank at the corner of Spring Garden Rd and Queen St.

Bike rental Bike People, 1471 Birmingham St (☎420-0777).

Bookshops There are several good bookshops in the city centre, both new and secondhand. The Book Room, 1546 Barrington at Blowers (☎423-8271; closed Sun), originated in 1839 (Canada's oldest) and has a good selection of new books with its Maritimes section especially noteworthy. JWD Books, 1684 Barrington at Blowers (☎429-1652; closed Sun), specializes in antiquarian and secondhand books. The chain bookshop Smithbooks (☎423-6438), with an outlet at Scotia Square, is more mainstream.

Car rental Budget, 1588 Hollis (☎492-7500) and at the airport (same number); Discount, 1240 Hollis St (☎468-7171); Dollar, 1960 Brunswick inside the *Citadel Inn Hotel* (☎429-1892) and at the airport (☎860-0203).

Consulates Netherlands, 1959 Upper Water St (☎422-1485); Norway, 11 Morris Drive (☎468-1330); USA, Cogswell Tower (☎429-2480).

Email/Internet Ceilidh Connections, 1672 Barrington St at Prince (☎422-9800, *www.ceilidhconnect.ns.ca*; April–Oct Mon–Fri 10am–10pm, Sat & Sun noon–8pm; Nov–March Mon–Wed 10am–6pm, Thurs & Fri 10am–10pm, Sat & Sun noon–8pm).

Emergencies General emergency number ☎911.

Hospital Halifax Infirmary, 1796 Summer St (☎473-2700).

Laundry Bluenose Laundromat, 2198 Windsor at Duncan (daily 7.30am–9pm). Self-service and service washes, with dry-cleaning too.

Post office Central office at 1680 Bedford Row and Prince (Mon–Fri 7.30am–5.15pm).

Taxis Yellow Cab (☎420-0000).

Transport Acadian Bus Lines (☎454-9321, *www.acadianbus.com*); DRL bus (1 daily to south shore and Yarmouth; ☎450-1987 or 1-888/263-1852); Halifax Metro Transit (☎490-6600); VIA Rail (☎1-800/561-3952).

Weather For up-to-date bulletins, call ☎426-9090.

Southwest Nova Scotia

The jagged coastline running southwest of Halifax to **Yarmouth**, a distance of 300km, boasts dozens of tiny fishing villages glued tight against the shore by the vast forest that pours over the interior. Most were founded by Loyalists, whose dedication to the British interest both during and after the American War of Independence obliged them to hotfoot it out of the US, often as penniless refugees. Today, the most beguiling of these villages are **Peggy's Cove**, an incredibly picturesque smattering of higgledy-piggledy clapboard houses dotted along a wild shore, and lesser-known **Lockeport**, with its old-fashioned air and fine sandy beaches. Equally diverting are the towns of **Lunenburg**, with its stunning Victorian architecture, and ritzy, leafy **Chester**, both of which derived their former prosperity, like their coastal neighbours, from the now-defunct shipbuilding business and from privateering.

Travelling the shoreline is the **Lighthouse Route**, a tourist trail that details everything of any possible interest: you're better off sticking to the main road, Hwy 103, and dropping down to the coast for the highlights. At workaday **Liverpool**, there's a choice of routes: you can stick to the coast, passing the seashore section of Kejimkujik

National Park and Lockeport on the way to Yarmouth, where the **Evangeline Route** continues along the **French Shore** to Annapolis Royal (see p.355). Or – and this is probably the better option, unless you've bags of time – you can cut across the peninsula to Annapolis Royal on Hwy 8, past the wilderness splendours of the main portion of **Kejimkujik National Park**.

The area is popular with tourists, but not oppressively so, and almost every settlement has at least a couple of fine old Victorian mansions that have been converted into **inns** or **B&Bs**. These provide first-rate accommodation at reasonable prices and reservations are only essential in the height of the season and on holiday weekends. In terms of **restaurants**, seafood is the big deal around here – usually simply prepared and quite delicious. For **public transport**, DRL bus, based at the Halifax bus station, operates a daily service between Halifax and Yarmouth along the southern shore, and Acadian Bus Lines connect Halifax with Yarmouth four times weekly via the Annapolis Valley, Digby and the French Shore.

Peggy's Cove

Highway 333 leaves Hwy 103 a few kilometres west of Halifax to make its slow progress through the forested hinterland that so successfully confined the region's early settlers to the coast. Once at the shoreline, the road slips through ribbon fishing villages, past glacial boulders and round rocky bays to reach tiny **PEGGY'S COVE**, 45km from Halifax. Founded in 1811, the hamlet, with a resident population of just sixty, surrounds a rocky slit of a harbour, with a spiky timber church, a smattering of clapboard houses and wooden jetties on stilts. It's a beautiful spot, the solitary lighthouse set against the sea-smoothed granite of the shore, and it attracts swarms of tourists; try to visit at sunrise or sunset, when the coach parties leave the village to its inhabitants. Behind the lighthouse, *The Sou'wester* dispenses mundane meals, while the three-roomed *Peggy's Cove B&B*, overlooking the harbour from the end of Church Road (☎823-2265 or 1-800/725-8732; ④), provides simple but perfectly adequate accommodation – advance reservations are advised.

Beyond Peggy's Cove Hwy 333 sticks closely to the coastline, meandering through a magnificently desolate landscape of stunted firs and cumbersome seashore boulders. Pull in at any of several places for a stroll along the shore or press on north through the gentler scenery that leads back to Hwy 103.

Chester

It's a thirty-minute drive north from Peggy's Cove to Hwy 103 and a further 40km west to **CHESTER**, a handsome and prosperous-looking town tumbling over a chubby little peninsula. Founded by New Englanders in 1759, the town, with its fine old trees and elegant frame houses, has long been the favoured resort of yachting enthusiasts whose principal shindig is the Race Week regatta held in mid-August. In July and August, Chester also hosts an excellent summer festival of contemporary music and Canadian-oriented drama at the **Chester Playhouse**, right in the middle of town (information and reservations ☎275-3933 or 1-800/363-7529, *www.ChesterPlayhouse.ns.ca*; tickets around $14). Finally, out in the bay and reached from Chester jetty by **passenger ferry** (Mon–Fri 4 daily, Sat & Sun 2 daily; 45min; $5 return) are two tiny islets, **Big** and **Little Tancook**, whose quiet country roads and benign scenery are popular with walkers, who pop across for a day's ramble. Big Tancook is the prettier of the islets and there's somewhere to eat here too – *Carolyn's Café* (June–Oct), opposite the jetty.

Chester **tourist office** (June & Sept Mon–Sat 10am–5pm, Sun noon–5pm; July & Aug Mon–Sat 9am–7pm, Sun 10am–5pm; ☎275-4616) is located in the old train station on the northern edge of town, beside Hwy 3. The office will have town maps and leaflets for an historic walking tour, and will help arrange **accommodation**, but even so you'll be lucky to find anywhere during the festival. The rest of the year, things are easier – especially on weekdays – and the town has a reasonable range of inns and B&Bs. Best of the lot is the *Captain's House Inn*, a tastefully refurbished nineteenth-century villa at 29 Central St (☎275-3501; ④), followed by the four-roomed *Mecklenburgh Inn*, a B&B in a Victorian house at 78 Queen St (☎275-4638; ③; June–Oct). There's also a B&B on Big Tancook, the *Levy House* (☎228-2120; June–Sept), in an old timber home across from the jetty; they have just two guestrooms with shared bathroom. For delicious **seafood**, head for the *Rope Loft* (☎275-3430; May–Oct) by Chester jetty, or the more informal *Sea Deck* on the floor below.

Mahone Bay

In 1813, the wide waters of **Mahone Bay** witnessed the destruction of the splendidly named American privateer the *Young Teaser*, which had been hounded into the bay by a British frigate. On board was a British deserter who knew what to expect if he was captured, so he blew his own ship up instead – a tribute to the floggers of the Royal Navy. Legend has it that the ghost of the blazing vessel reappears each year and neither is this the only strange story attached to the area. In 1795, three boys discovered the top of an underground shaft on tiny **Oak Island**, a low-lying, offshore islet a few kilometres west of Chester. The shaft, or "Money Pit", soon attracted the attentions of treasure hunters, who were convinced that this was where a vast horde of booty had been interred. At first the betting was on Drake, Kidd or Morgan, but present favourites include the Templars and even the Rosicrucians. No treasure has ever been found, but the diggings became so dangerous that the island's owners have closed it to the public; if you go, you can only get to the chain at the start of the causeway.

Just 25km west of Chester lies the **village of MAHONE BAY**, whose waterfront is dominated by three adjacent church towers, which combine to create one of the region's most famous views. There's not much else to the place, though you could drop by the **Settlers' Museum**, 578 Main St (mid-May to Aug Tues–Fri 10am–5pm, Sat & Sun 1–5pm; free), for a look at its period furniture and early nineteenth-century ceramics. You can also have a bite to eat at the *Market at Mahone Bay*, beside the crossroads marking the centre of the village, which sells fresh local produce and superb sandwiches. Another option is the first-rate *Mimi's Ocean Grill*, a five- to ten-minute walk south at 662 Main St (☎624-1342; May–Oct), where they serve up delicious lunches in attractive waterfront surroundings. Nearby, the four-roomed *Heart's Desire B&B*, 686 Main St (☎624-8470; ③), has bay views and occupies a large and well-tended Victorian shipbuilder's house.

Lunenburg

Comely **LUNENBURG**, 10km south of Mahone Bay village, perches on a narrow bumpy peninsula, its older central streets, sloping steeply down to the southward-facing harbourfront, decorated by brightly painted wooden houses. Dating from the late nineteenth century, the most flamboyant of these mansions display an arresting variety of architectural features varying from Gothic towers and classic pillars to elegant verandas, high gables and peaked windows, all embellished with intricate scrollwork. Amidst the virtuosity, a distinctive municipal style is noticeable in the so-called "Lunenburg Bump", where overhanging window dormers are surmounted by triple-bell cast roofs – giving the town a vaguely European appearance appropriate to its original settlement. Lunenburg was founded in 1753 by German and Swiss Protestants, who of necessity soon learned to mix the farming of their homeland with fishing and shipbuilding. They created a prosperous community with its own fleet of trawlers and scallop-draggers, although nowadays the town earns as much from the tourist industry as from fishing.

Lunenburg's pride and joy is its **Fisheries Museum of the Atlantic** (early May to late Oct daily 9.30am–5.30pm; late Oct to early May Mon–Fri 8.30am–4.30pm; $7), housed in an old fish-processing plant down by the quayside. It has an excellent aquarium, a room devoted to whales and whaling, and displays on fishing and boat-building techniques. Another section features the locally built 1920s schooner *Bluenose* and its replica *Bluenose II* (see p.341), whilst the August Gales display has wondrous tales of mountainous seas and helmsmen tied to the mast to stop being swept overboard. Moored by the jetty, there's a trawler and a scalloper, but the real high spot here is the *Theresa E. Connor*, a saltbank fishing **schooner** launched in 1938. Superbly restored, the schooner was one of the last boats of its type to be built, a two-masted vessel constructed to a design that had changed little since the early eighteenth century: if you read *Treasure Island* as a child and were confused by the layout of the boat, all is revealed. The main change in schooner design came with the installation of engines in the early 1900s: the helmsman no longer needed to keep an eagle-eye on the sails and so he could be moved aft. Further protection was provided by a wheelhouse, though there were teething problems with these and initially an alarming number were lost at sea. With or without engines, fishing schooners worked in the same way: each carried several **dories**, small row boats that were launched at the fishing grounds. The men rowed the dories away from the schooner, fanning out to trail long hand-lines with baited hooks over the ocean – line-fishing. At the end of the day, the catch would be brought back to the schooner. Dory-fishing was a dangerous business – the transfer of the catch was especially risky and there was always the chance of being caught in the dory by a sudden squall. Not surprisingly, therefore, local fishermen did not need much persuading to abandon their schooners and dories for the larger **trawlers** that replaced them in the 1950s. The *Theresa E. Connor* soldiered on, but her last voyage was an ignominious failure: in 1963 she sailed out of Lunenburg bound for Newfoundland to raise the rest of her 25-man crew. No one turned up and the schooner had to return home empty-handed.

There's more of maritime interest down along the harbourfront at the **Dory Shop**, where they make wooden boats in traditional style and hire out sail and row boats. If you haven't the confidence/experience to sail out on your own, regular boat trips leave the jetty near the museum throughout the summer. There are also two- to three-hour **whale-watching** trips operated daily during the summer by Lunenburg Whale Watching Tours (☎527-7175).

Lunenburg practicalities

Lunenburg **tourist office** (May–Oct daily 9am–8pm; ☎634-3656) occupies an imitation lighthouse on Blockhouse Hill Road, above the hilly gridiron that comprises the town centre. It operates a free room-reservation service, has a book with illustrations of local accommodation, and supplies a leaflet detailing the town's architectural highlights – though their $7 guidebook is far more interesting and informative. Many of the town's historic houses have been turned into first-class **inns** and **B&Bs**. Pick of the bunch are the delightful shingle-clad *1826 Maplebird House B&B*, 36 Pelham St (☎634-3863 or 1-888/395-3863; ③), with its outside pool, garden and patio area overlooking the harbour; the beautifully maintained *Hillcroft Guest House*, 53 Montague St (☎634-8031; ③; May–Dec); the grand Victorian *Bluenose Lodge*, a couple of minutes' walk from the central gridiron at Dufferin Street and Falkland Avenue (☎ & fax 634-8851 or 1-800/565-8851; ③); and the salmon-pink *Kaulbach House Inn*, an ornate villa at 75 Pelham St (☎1-800/568-8818, fax 634-8818; ③; mid-March to mid-Dec). The municipal **campsite** (☎634-8100; May–Oct) is next door to the tourist office.

Eating places abound in the centre. The moderately priced *Magnolia's Grill*, just off the waterfront at 128 Montague St, is a small café with a good atmosphere and tasty snacks, while the *Hillcroft Café*, 53 Montague St (April–Nov), offers delicious meals from a wide-ranging and imaginative menu. If you're crying out for lobster or seafood generally, there's no better place than Lunenburg: both the *Grand Banker Seafood Bar & Grill* (☎634-3300; year-round), by the harbour on Montague Street, and the *Old Fish Factory Restaurant* (☎634-3333; May–Oct), next to the museum, serve a splendid range of mouthwatering seafood dishes. The other local culinary delights are the **Lunenburg sausage**, traditionally served at breakfast, which is made of lean pork and beef, flavoured with coriander and allspice, and the **Solomon Gundy**, marinated herring with sour cream or occasionally mustard.

Liverpool

Like its British namesake, **LIVERPOOL**, 140km from Halifax along Hwy 103, skirts the mouth of a Mersey River and has a strong seafaring tradition, but there the similarities end. Nova Scotia's Liverpool was founded by emigrants from Cape Cod in 1759, who established a fearsome reputation for privateering during both the American Revolution and the War of 1812, when their most famous ship, the *Liverpool Packet,* claimed a hundred American prizes. These piratical endeavours were cheekily celebrated in a local broadsheet of the time as upholding "the best tradition of the British Navy". Nowadays, Liverpool is a minor fish-processing and paper-making town, a desultory settlement only cheered by the fine old houses grouped around the eastern end of Main Street. One of these, the **Perkins House** (June to mid-Oct Mon–Sat 9.30am–5.30pm, Sun 1–5.30pm; free), has been restored to its late eighteenth-century condition, when it was the home of Simeon Perkins, who moved here from New England in 1762. A local bigwig, Perkins was a shipowner, a merchant, a colonel in the militia and a justice of the court, but he still had time to keep a detailed diary from 1766 until his death in 1812. The diaries provide an insight into the life and times of colonial Nova Scotia and they show Perkins as a remarkably unflappable man: in 1780 Liverpool was attacked by Americans, who Perkins outwitted and drove off, describing the dangerous emergency as just a "dubious and difficult affair". Copies of the four-volume diary are on display at the house, whilst the adjacent **Queens County Museum** (June to mid-Oct Mon–Fri 9.30am–5.30pm, Sun 1–5.30pm; mid-Oct to May Mon–Sat 9am–5pm; free) sometimes sells excerpts ($2) – and also possesses a diverting collection of early local photographs.

Liverpool has one good **B&B**, the *Taigh Na Mara*, 58 Main St (☎354-7194; ②), in an attractive, creeper-clad building overlooking the bay from near the Perkins House. For simple sustaining meals, try the *Liverpool Pizzeria*, 155 Main St, or *Lane's Privateer Inn* (☎354-3456), just across the bridge from the centre, at 27 Bristol Ave.

Kejimkujik National Park

There's no better way to experience the solitude and scenery of the southwest Nova Scotian hinterland than to head north 70km from Liverpool along Hwy 8 to Maitland Bridge, the entrance to the **Kejimkujik National Park**. This magnificent tract of rolling wilderness has a rich variety of forest habitats – both hardwood and softwood – interrupted by rivers and brooks linking about a dozen lakes. The park is a riot of wild flowers in the spring and autumn and provides cover for an abundance of porcupines, white-tailed deer and beavers, as well as three sorts of turtle – the Painted, the Snapping and, rarest of all, the Blanding's turtle, a green and yellow amphibian that grows to around 25cm.

Hiking trails crisscross Kejimkujik, but the easiest way to explore the park and its flat-water rivers and lakes is by canoe. These can be rented for $24 a day – plus $30 deposit – from **Jakes Landing** (☎682-2196; reservations recommended), roughly

10km by road from the entrance to the park. A couple of clearly defined, day-long **canoe trips** begin here, the delightful paddle amongst the islets of Kejimkujik Lake and an excursion up the Mersey River beneath a canopy of red maples. For overnight trips, the park has around fifty primitive **campsites** dotted along both canoe routes and hiking trails, which are a better bet than the large year-round campsite (reservations ☎1-800/414-6765) at **Jeremys Bay**, also 10km by road from the main entrance. A park entrance fee of $3.25 per adult per day is levied from mid-May to October. For back-country camping, you must register at the **information centre** (mid-June to Aug daily 8.30am–9pm; Sept–May usually 8.30am–4.30pm; ☎682-2772), near the entrance, where you can also pick up detailed maps and trail advice. The best time to visit is in the early spring and autumn, when the insects aren't too troublesome: the blackfly peak between mid-May and late June. The nearest **beds** are at the eight-room, nineteenth-century *Whitman Inn* (☎682-2226 or 1-800/830-3855, *www.whitman.ns.ca*; ②) in **Kempt**, 4km south of Maitland Bridge on Hwy 8; the nearest town is Annapolis Royal (see p.355), 50km to the north.

Kejimkujik's Seaside Adjunct

Back on Hwy 103, about 25km west of Liverpool, is the hard-to-find and poorly signed **Seaside Adjunct of Kejimkujik National Park**, a parcel of pristine coastline that provides an ideal half-day's hike. The Adjunct straddles the tip of a beautiful but inhospitable peninsula where the mixed forests and squelchy bogs of the interior back onto the tidal flats, lagoons, headlands and beaches of the coast. If you're lucky, you'll catch sight of the rare piping plover, which nests here between May and early August. Two wet and rough hiking trails provide the only access into the park. Of the two, the more convenient is the three-kilometre hike down to the shore along an old cart track – now the Harbour Rocks Trail – that begins on the park's west side. There are no signs off Hwy 103 to the park, but turn down **St Catherine's Road**, a six-kilometre-long dirt road that leads off the highway to the combined car park and trailhead.

Lockeport

Well off the beaten track, 65km west of Liverpool, the sleepy fishing village of **LOCK-EPORT** sits on a tiny island that's reached across a 1.5-kilometre-long causeway, fringed by the white sands of **Crescent Beach**. The beach is never crowded, the sea is deep and clear, and the village features a row of five contrasting houses built by the prosperous Locke family over a forty-year period in the nineteenth century. It's a lovely, relaxing spot, where nothing much seems to happen except for the comings and goings of the odd fishing smack. It also boasts one of the most delightful **B&Bs** on the coast in *Seventeen South*, 17 South St (☎656-2512, *shorebb@auracom.com*; ③), a tastefully modernized Cape Cod house with three guestrooms perched on a wooded knoll in sight of the seashore, not far from the harbour. If it's full, the seasonal tourist office (☎656-3123), in the brash building at the end of the causeway, has details of a few other local B&Bs and beachside cottages. Lockeport has a good restaurant too, in *Locke's Island Dining*, 18 North St.

Shelburne

SHELBURNE, 70km southwest of Liverpool, took heart when it was chosen as the backdrop for the 1994 cinematic version of Nathaniel Hawthorne's classic *The Scarlet Letter*, but the film was such a dodo that it did the town no favours. Indeed, despite the well-kept shingle and clapboard houses that string down from Water Street, the main drag, to Dock Street and the waterfront, Shelburne manages a vaguely disconsolate air.

It does, however, boast the third largest harbour in the world, after Halifax and Sydney – easily big enough, so the plan went, to accommodate the British fleet if Hitler managed to launch a successful invasion. The British would have been welcome: Shelburne has been intensely anglophile ever since thousands of Loyalists fled here in the 1780s – including two hundred free blacks, ancestors of the town's present black community.

Shelburne is home to the **Nova Scotia Museum Complex**, centred on Dock Street, which has three distinct elements. The **Shelburne County Museum** (mid-May to mid-Oct daily 9.30am–5.30pm; mid-Oct to mid-May Tues–Sat 2–5pm; $2) provides a broad overview of the town's history and its maritime heritage; the adjacent **Ross-Thomson House** (June to mid-Oct daily 9.30am–5.30pm; $2) is a Loyalist merchant's store and home, pleasingly restored to its appearance circa 1800; and the nearby **Dory Shop** (June–Sept daily 9.30am–5.30pm; $2) comprises a waterfront boat factory/museum. Rarely more than 5m long and built to ride the heaviest of swells, the flat-bottomed **dory** was an integral part of the fishing fleet during the days of sail. Each schooner carried about six of them: manned by a crew of two, they were launched from the deck when the fishing began, fanning out to maximize the catch. The Dory Shop produces three a year, but only for private use for hand-fishing – the few dories used today in the offshore fishery are steel-hulled. Allow about an hour to visit the three sites (combined tickets $4) – and while you're here take a peek at the handful of heavyweight shingle buildings left over from the film set, just off Dock Street.

There's no special reason to stay in Shelburne, but the **tourist office** (summer daily 9am–7pm), at the north end of Dock Street, does operate a free room-reservation service. The most agreeable **hotel** in town is the *Cooper's Inn*, which occupies a lavishly refurbished old shingle house at 36 Dock St (☎875-4656 or 1-800/688-2011; ④; April–Oct). Wooded, lakeside **camping** is available 5km west round the bay at the *Islands Provincial Park* (☎875-4304; $14; mid-May to Aug). There's inexpensive and unpretentious **food** at *Claudia's Diner*, 149 Water St; wholesome meals at *Charlotte Lane Café*, down an alley – Charlotte Lane – off Water Street; and first-rate cuisine at the *Cooper's Inn* restaurant – try the steaks.

Barrington

There's not much to delay you on the 100-kilometre journey west from Shelburne to Yarmouth, but you should make a brief stop at minuscule **BARRINGTON**, where the **Old Meeting House** (June to mid-Sept Mon–Sat 9.30am–5.30pm, Sun 1–5.30pm; donation), with its simple wooden pews and severe pulpit, reflects the intellectual rigour of the Nonconformist settlers who migrated here from New England in the mid-eighteenth century. In its simplicity, it's a beautiful building, which is more than can be said for the adjacent **Lighthouse Museum** (same hours; free), where a smattering of light-keepers' memorabilia is housed in a replica of the lighthouse that once stood on remote Seal Island – though this version stands on a hillside apropos of nothing in particular.

Yarmouth

Arriving by ferry from Maine, many American visitors get their first taste of Canada in **YARMOUTH**, and most of them leave immediately. And indeed it is a mundanely modern place, though gallant efforts have been made to freshen up the waterfront and the town's deep, tidal bay provides a modicum of scenic interest. It's also a good place for tourist information with the **Nova Scotia Visitor Centre**, just uphill from the ferry terminal (daily: May, June, Sept & Oct 9am–5pm; July & Aug 8am–7pm), issuing bucketloads of free leaflets and brochures. If you're stuck here for the night, there's a comfortable B&B right opposite the visitors' centre, the *Murray Manor*, 225 Main St (☎ & fax 742-9625; ②). Alternatively, the *Midtown Motel*, 13 Parade St (☎742-5333 or

1-877/742-5600; ②), offers simple but adequate rooms a ten-minute walk north along Main Street from the ferry terminal.

From Yarmouth, Bay Ferries (☎902/742-6800 or 1-888/249-SAIL, *www.nfl-bay.com*) operate high-speed, car-carrying **catamarans** to Bar Harbor, Maine (June to late Oct 1 daily; 3hr; passengers $60–70, vehicles $90–105), and Scotia Prince (☎1-800/341-7540, *www.princeoffundy.com*) run **car ferries** to Portland, Maine (May to late Oct 1 daily; 11hr; passengers $60–80, cars $80–100, cabins from $20–95; up to forty percent discounts for returns and on some midweek sailings).

The French Shore

North from Yarmouth, Hwy 101 and the far slower Hwy 1 slip across the flat littoral of the 100-kilometre **French Shore**, whose straggling villages house the largest concentration of Acadians in the province. Their gold-starred red, white and blue flags are everywhere, but there's nothing worth stopping for – **METEGHAN**, the main town, is strikingly ugly – until you reach **POINTE DE L'EGLISE** (Church Point). Here, right next to the sea, is the massive church of **St Mary's** (July to mid-Oct daily 9.30am–5pm; free), whose stolid tower and steeple, finished in 1905, reach a giddy 56m. Unfortunately, the fastidiously clean interior holds some of the worst religious paintings imaginable, nineteenth-century dross with none of the medievalism suggested by the reliquaries beside the altar, amongst which are wooden shards purportedly from the Holy Cross. Ten kilometres further north is the church of **St Bernard** (June–Sept daily 9.30am–5pm; free), a cumbersome granite pile that took 32 years to complete (1910–42) – and is, if nothing else, certainly a tribute to the profound Catholicism of local Acadians.

Digby and around

It's around 30km from St Bernard to the fishing port of **DIGBY**, whose workaday centre spreads over a hilly headland that pokes out into the Annapolis Basin. The latter is connected to the Bay of Fundy by a narrow channel known as the Digby Gut, thereby subjecting Digby **harbour** to the swirling effects of the Fundy tides – and it's the pocket-sized harbour, with its rickety wooden piers, which is the most appealing part of town. Otherwise, Digby is notable for two things: its smoked herrings – or "Digby chicks" – chewy, dark and salty delicacies on sale beside the north end of the harbour at the Royal Fundy Seafood Market; and its delicious scallops, which you can sample at the popular *Fundy Restaurant*, 34 Water St (☎245-4950), the pick of several restaurants lining the harbourfront's Water Street and its continuation, Montague Row.

Buses to Digby stop at the Irving petrol station, just off Montague Row at the south end of the waterfront, a couple of minutes' stroll from the **tourist office**, on Water Street (☎245-5714). They operate a room-reservation service and give information on Digby Neck whale-watching trips (see overleaf). Digby has several good **places to stay**, beginning with the agreeable *Thistle Down Inn*, an old two-storey house with a motel-style annexe at 98 Montague Row (☎245-4490 or 1-800/565-8081; ③; May–Oct). There's also the *Bayside Inn*, 115 Montague Row (☎245-2247 or 1-888/754-0555; ②), which occupies an old timber house, has eleven rooms – six en suite – and is equipped with a pleasant patio.

Finally, Digby's ferry port is 5km north of town and from here Bay Ferries (☎1-888/249-7245) runs regular **car ferries** across the Bay of Fundy to Saint John in New Brunswick (see p.380), thereby saving a long drive (Jan to late June & mid-Oct to Dec 1–2 daily; late June to mid-Oct 2–3 daily; 3hr; passengers $25–30 single, cars $55–60, bicycles $15–20). There's a provincial tourist office in between the town and the ferry port.

Around Digby: Digby Neck and whale-watching excursions

Heading west from Digby, the 65km-long **Digby Neck** comprises a narrow finger of land that gingerly nudges out into the Bay of Fundy, sheltering the French Shore from the full effects of the ocean. The Neck's far reaches are broken into two little islands – **Long Island** and, at the tip, **Brier Island** – and a pair of car **ferries** shuttle across the narrow channels between them, running every hour, 24 hours a day and charging $3 each for the return trip. Ferry times are co-ordinated, so it takes about two hours to reach Brier Island from Digby – ferry timetables are available at Digby tourist office. For the most part, the road along the Neck travels inland and is fairly monotonous, but then most people venture down here to join a **whale-watching trip**. The nutrient-rich waters of the Bay of Fundy attract dozens of whales and several companies organize daily excursion trips from June to early October. They are heavily subscribed, so advance reservations are highly recommended and note that, if the weather is poor, it is a good idea to check to see if a sailing has been cancelled before you set out. Trips usually last about three hours and cost in the region of $35. To state the obvious, no one can guarantee you'll spy a whale, but there's every chance, beginning with finback and minkes in late spring, and humpbacks from mid- to late June. By the middle of July all three species are sighted and usually hang around the Bay of Fundy till late summer and autumn, which is when the rare North Atlantic right whale is seen too. (See p.935 in Contexts for information about whales.) Amongst a bevy of Digby Neck whale-watching companies, one of the more proficient is Ocean Explorations Whale Cruises (☎839-2417, *www.oceanexplorations.ns.ca*), who use zodiac boats and are based in tiny **TIVERTON** on Long Island. In addition, there are several whale-watching companies in the forlorn little fishing village of **WESTPORT**, on Brier Island. These include Brier Island Whale & Seabird Cruises (☎839-2995 or 1-800/656-3660) and Mariner Cruises (☎839-2346 or 1-800/239-2189).

From either Digby or (even better) Annapolis Royal (see opposite), it's easy enough to complete the drive along the Neck and the whale-watching excursion in a day, but if you decide to stay the night, there are two good options. The first is in Tiverton, a quiet sprawl of wooden houses dotted round a forested bay, which possesses the appealing *Seacliff B&B* (☎839-2129; ②; mid-June to Sept), in a pretty Victorian house overlooking the harbour and with two guestrooms – and shared bath. The second is the *Olde Village Inn* (☎834-2202 or 1-800/834-2206, *www.oldevillageinn.com*; ③; mid-May to mid-Oct), a cosy nineteenth-century inn set among the densely wooded coastal hills of **SANDY COVE**, a picturesque little place of old white-painted houses about 30km from Digby. The inn has six rooms in the old building and seven more in the annexe.

The Annapolis Valley

The **Annapolis Valley**, stretching 110km northeast from Annapolis Royal to Wolfville, is sheltered from the winds and fog that afflict much of the central part of the province by a narrow band of coastal hills. This factor, combined with the fertility of the soil, makes the valley and the coast as far as Windsor – another 25km to the east – ideal for fruit growing. As a consequence, the brief weeks of apple-blossom time, from late May to early June, are the subject of much sentimental and commercial exploitation – as well as the communal knees-up of the **Apple-Blossom Festival**. The string of little towns that dot the valley were settled by Loyalists from New England after the expulsion of the Acadians, but although several of them are pretty places where old wooden houses are sheltered by mature trees only two stand out. These are delightful **Annapolis Royal**, with its handsome Victorian mansions and proximity to the historic site of **Port Royal**, and **Wolfville**, an amiable university town of some charm. Wolfville is also within easy striking distance of **Grand Pré National Historic Site** and the harsh scenery of **capes Blomidon** and **Split**. Further east, **Windsor** is no great shakes, but it is the site of the Haliburton House Museum, the former home of the nineteenth-century humorist Thomas Haliburton.

Annapolis Royal and Wolfville are both served by Acadian Lines **bus**, who operate a once daily service from Halifax along the Annapolis Valley.

Annapolis Royal

With a population of just seven hundred, the township of **ANNAPOLIS ROYAL**, 40km northeast of Digby and 118km northwest of Liverpool, spreads across a podgy promontory tucked between the Annapolis River and its tributary, the Allain River. The long main drag, St George Street, part of Hwy 8, sweeps through the leafy southern outskirts to reach the end of the promontory, where it turns right to run parallel to the waterfront through the commercial heart of town. Here, restaurants and shops have replaced the merchants and shipwrights of yesteryear and there's a tourist-oriented boardwalk near the jetty, but it's all very low-key and the town maintains a relaxed and retiring air that's hard to resist.

Edging St George Street just before it swings right are the remains of **Fort Anne** (open access), whose grass-covered ramparts surround the old parade ground. A few military remains are encased within the ramparts – namely a couple of powder magazines – but the only significant remaining building is the officers' quarters right in the middle of the compound. These quarters were completed by the British during the Napoleonic Wars and, surmounted by three outsize chimney stacks, they now house a small **museum** (mid-May to mid-Oct daily 9am–6pm; $2.75) comprising a ragbag of military memorabilia, a reconstruction of an Acadian domestic interior and an outline of the fort's development. There's also a contemporaneous copy of the original charter by which James I incorporated "Nova Scotia" in 1621, and a cheerful community tapestry tracing the town's history. The view downriver from Fort Anne is simply delightful and it's a lovely peaceful spot, but it wasn't always so. Both colonial powers, France and England, neglected the fort and its garrison, and when a new military governor arrived at the fort in 1708 he told his superiors in Paris that the officers stationed here were "more in need of a madhouse than a barracks". If you want more of the flavour of early Annapolis Royal, ask at the museum (or your B&B) for details of the candlelight tours of the **old graveyard** (June to mid-Oct 3 weekly) next to the fort – good fun, and a snip at $4.

Five-minutes' walk from the fort – back along St George Street – lie the ten-acre **Historic Gardens** (daily: June–Aug 8am–dusk; late May, Sept & early Oct 9am–5pm; $5), which feature a string of "theme gardens", from the formality of a Victorian garden to an extensive rose collection in which the different varieties are arranged broadly in chronological order. The whole site slopes gently down towards the Allain River, with a dykewalk offering views of mud flats and salt marshes and also twisting through elephant grass, a reed imported by the Acadians to thatch their cottages.

Practicalities

One **bus** a day on the Acadian Lines route between Halifax and Digby stops at the *Royal Annapolis Inn* on Hwy 1 with four weekly pushing on to Yarmouth – and the same vice versa. From the inn, it is 1.3km north to St George Street and the town centre. The **tourist office** is on the other side of town, inside the generating station on the Hwy 1 bridge about 1km north of the centre (daily: late May to June & Sept to mid-Oct 10am–5pm; July & Aug 8am–8pm; ☎532-5454). They can arrange accommodation. Best are the **B&Bs**, several of which are in immaculately maintained heritage properties. The *Hillsdale House Inn*, 519 St George St (☎532-2345 or 1-877/839-2821; ③; May–Oct), and the *Queen Anne Inn*, opposite at no. 494 (☎532-7850, fax 532-2078, *www.queenanneinn.ns.ca*; ④), are the finest choices – the former occupying an elegant villa of 1849, the latter a grand turreted and towered extravagance of the 1860s. Alternatively, try the *Turret*, 372 St George St (☎532-5770; ②; mid-May to Oct), in another old but rather more modest house, or the well-tended *Bread and Roses Inn*, a spiky late Victorian mansion at 82 Victoria St (☎532-5727 or 1-888/899-0551; ④). The *Dunromin* **campsite** (☎532-2808; mid-April to mid-Oct), just beyond the tourist office on the far side of the Annapolis River, occupies a wooded position by the riverside.

Eating well and in style is easy here, and prices are reasonable. *Newman's*, 218 St George St (☎532-5502), has a brisk and pleasant atmosphere and offers delicious meals featuring local ingredients – beef stew, scallops and the like – with main courses averaging $13. Next door, *Leo's Café* (closes 5.30pm) serves first-rate snacks and lighter meals, while the inexpensive *Fort Anne Café*, opposite the entrance to the fort, sells tasty and substantial meals from a traditional Canadian – don't be put off by the downbeat decor.

For **entertainment**, *Ye Olde Towne Pub* at 9 Church St – just down the street from Newman's and across from the boatyard – serves good draught beer, while the King's Theatre, 209 St George St (☎532-5466 or 1-800/818-8587), showcases all sorts of enjoyable acts from folk music through to storytellers, comedians and mime artists. Films are shown here too and there's often live theatre, mostly with a local theme.

Port Royal

Port Royal National Historic Site (mid-May to mid-Oct daily 9am–6pm; $2.75), 12km west of Annapolis Royal on the opposite side of the Annapolis River, was where Samuel de Champlain and Pierre Sieur de Monts first set up camp in 1605 after their dreadful winter on the Île Saint-Croix. Their scurvy-ridden men, scared of English attack, hastily constructed a *habitation* similar in design to the fortified farms of France, where a square of rough-hewn, black-painted timber buildings presented a stern, partly stockaded face to any enemy. The stronghold dominated the estuary from a low bluff, as does today's replica, a painstaking reconstruction relying solely on the building techniques of the early seventeenth century. The *habitation* was captured by roving Virginians in 1613 and passed over to the British, who, led by Sir William Alexander, settled the district in 1629. This venture was enthusiastically supported by King James I, who wished to found a New Scotland – in the Latin of the deeds, "Nova Scotia" – near Port Royal, but after three years of hardship and starvation, the Scots settlers were forced to withdraw, like their French predecessors.

For both French and Scot settlers alike, the problem of survival was compounded by acute boredom during the months of winter isolation. To pass the time Champlain constituted the **Order of Good Cheer**, whose "entertainment's programme" starred the poet Marc Lescarbot – though the role hardly filled him with colonial zeal, to judge from a poem he wrote for a gang of departing buddies:

We among the savages are lost
And dwell bewildered on this clammy coast
Deprived of due content and pleasures bright
Which you at once enjoy when France you sight.

There are **no bus services** from Annapolis Royal to the *habitation*.

Wolfville

The well-heeled university town of **WOLFVILLE**, 110km northeast from Annapolis Royal, was originally called Mud Creek until the daughter of a local dignitary, Justice DeWolf, expressed her embarrassment at the hick-sounding name. He modestly had it

THE ACADIANS

Acadia – *Acadie* in French – has at different times included all or part of Maine, New Brunswick and Nova Scotia. The etymology of the name is as vague as the geographical definition, derived from either the local Micmac word *akade*, meaning "abundance", or a corruption of *Arcadia*, an area of Greece that was a byword for rural simplicity when transient French fishermen arrived here in the early 1500s.

Whatever the truth, the origins of Acadian settlement date to 1604, when a French expedition led by Pierre Sieur de Monts and Samuel de Champlain built a stockade on the islet of **Saint-Croix**, on the west side of the Bay of Fundy. It was a disaster: with the onset of winter, the churning ice floes separated the colonists from the fresh food and water of the mainland, and many died of malnutrition. The following spring the survivors straggled over to the sheltered southern shore of the bay, where they founded **Port Royal**, considered Canada's first successful European settlement.

However, Champlain and Sieur de Monts soon despaired of Port Royal's fur-trading potential and moved to the banks of the St Lawrence, leaving Acadia cut off from the main flow of French colonization. Port Royal was **abandoned** in 1614 and, although it was refounded on the site of present-day Annapolis Royal in 1635, there were few immigrants. Indeed, the bulk of today's Acadians are descendants of just forty French peasant families who arrived in the 1630s. Slowly spreading along the **Annapolis Valley**, the Acadians lived a semi-autonomous existence in which their trade with their English-speaking neighbours was more important than grand notions of loyalty to the French Empire. When the British secured control of Port Royal under the Treaty of Utrecht in 1713, the Acadians made no protest.

But then, in the 1750s, the tense stand-off between the colonial powers highlighted the issue of Acadian loyalty. In 1755, at the start of the Seven Years War, British government officials attempted to make the Acadians swear **an oath of allegiance** to the Crown. They refused, so Governor Lawrence decided – without consultation with London – to **deport** them en masse to other colonies. The process of uprooting and removing a community of around 13,000 was achieved with remarkable ruthlessness. As Lawrence wrote to a subordinate, "You must proceed with the most vigorous measures possible not only in compelling them to embark, but in depriving those who should escape of all means of shelter or support, by burning their houses and destroying everything that may afford them the means of subsistence in the country."

By the end of the year over half the Acadians had arrived on the American east coast, where they faced a cold reception – the Virginians even rerouted their allocation to England. Most of the rest spread out along the North Atlantic seaboard, establishing communities along New Brunswick's Miramichi Valley, on Prince Edward Island and in St-Pierre et Miquelon. Many subsequently returned to the Bay of Fundy in the 1770s and 1780s, but their farms had been given to British and New England colonists and they were forced to settle the less hospitable lands of the **French Shore**, further west. For other deportees, the expulsion was the start of wider wanderings. Some went to Louisiana, where they were joined in 1785 by over 1500 former Acadian refugees who had ended up in France – these were the ancestors of the **Cajuns**, whose name is a corruption of "Acadian".

The Acadian communities of the Maritime Provinces continued to face discrimination from the English-speaking majority and today they remain firmly planted at the bottom of the economic pile. Nevertheless, the Acadians have resisted the pressures of assimilation and have recently begun to assert their cultural independence, most notably in New Brunswick, where Moncton University has become their academic and cultural centre.

renamed after himself, but the mud flats around the dinky little **harbour** – now a park located just off Main Street – remain the town's most distinctive feature. They are the creation of the **Fundy tides**, which rush up the Cornwallis River from the Minas Basin to dump the expanse of silt that's become home to hundreds of herons and waders, with thousands of sandpipers arriving in early August on their annual migration from Arctic breeding grounds. From Wolfville harbour, two short and easy loop walking trails lead out along the causeway that encircles a portion of the wetland and its enclosing dykes. The more westerly route, the Wolfville Dyke Trail – running from the harbour to Cherry Lane – is the one to take as it also provides pleasing views of Wolfville, its skyline punctured by the sedate lines of **Acadia University**, whose three thousand students double the resident population.

Wolfville's other curiosity is the **Robie Tufts Nature Centre**, down Elm Avenue from Main Street, which is best visited an hour before sunset on a summer's evening – usually from the second or third week in May till late August – when there's an amazing performance by an enormous flock of brown-grey **chimney swifts**. After a long day hunting for insects, the birds fly in ever-decreasing circles above the centre, which is no more than a wooden shelter built around an old chimney, then suddenly swoop en masse into the chimney to roost for the night.

Practicalities

Wolfville is on the Acadian Lines **bus** route connecting Halifax and Yarmouth. Buses stop – inconveniently – on the Acadia University campus, a good ten-minute walk west of the tiny town centre, which consists of a few blocks of Main Street and several subsidiary side streets. The **tourist office** is located on the east side of the town centre, just off Main Street on Willow Avenue (daily: May–June & Sept to mid-Oct 9am–5pm; July & Aug 9am–7pm; ☎542-7000). They have information on the whole of the Annapolis Valley as well as local accommodation lists and details of the Cape Split hike (see opposite). The town has several splendid **inns** and **B&Bs**, the pick of the bunch in attractively renovated old mansions. Tempting choices include the *Blomidon Inn*, 127 Main St (☎542-2291 or 1-800/565-2291, *www.blomidon.ns.ca*; ④), an elegant sea captain's mansion with 21 guestrooms and four acres of carefully maintained gardens; the plush and rather formal Victoriana of the balconied and high-gabled *Tattingstone Inn*, just 700m or so west of the centre at 434 Main St (☎542-7696 or 1-800/565-7696, *www.tattingstone.ns.ca*; ④); and the appealing *Seaview House B&B*, in an attractive older house with a balcony and veranda in the centre just off Main Street at 8 Seaview Ave (☎542-1436; ②; May–Sept).

For **food**, there are good snacks and cakes and great coffee at *The Coffee Merchant*, Elm at Main; everything from pizzas through to burgers and sandwiches at inexpensive *Al's* (closes at 6pm), just down the street; and delicious salads and seafood at the smart *Acton's Café*, 268 Main St (☎542-7525). Finally, there's the *Chez la Vigne* restaurant, 17 Front St, which offers exquisite French regional cuisine at surprisingly affordable prices.

Grand Pré

In 1847, Henry Wadsworth Longfellow chose **GRAND PRÉ**, 5km east of Wolfville along Hwy 1, as the setting for his epic poem *Evangeline – A Tale of Acadie*, which dramatized the Acadian deportations through the star-crossed love of Evangeline for her Gabriel. Horribly sentimental and extremely popular, the poem turned the destruction of this particular community into a symbol of Acadian suffering and British callousness. However, the **Grand Pré National Historic Site** (mid-May to Oct daily 9am–6pm; free), located amidst the dykelands of the Minas Basin, is – with its trim lawns, planted trees and statues of Longfellow and Evangeline – a strangely antiseptic tribute. The chapel, which stands on the site of the original church, has a modest Acadian display, but there's nothing very insightful and the Acadian blacksmith's shop and garden at the end of the site seem very much an afterthought.

Capes Blomidon and Split

The rugged, hook-shaped peninsula north of Wolfville encompasses the dramatic scenery of **Cape Split** and of **Cape Blomidon**, which, local legend has it, takes its name from the sailors' phrase "Blow me down". To reach the peninsula from Wolfville, take Hwy 1 west for a couple of kilometres and then turn north at the sign along Hwy 358 for the 10-kilometre drive to **CANNING**, where there's a choice of routes depending on the cape you're aiming for. One road – a 13km-long minor road – leads down to **Blomidon Provincial Park**, a narrow slice of seashore where steep sea cliffs back onto a lush, coastal forest of maple, birch, fir and beech, laced by some 14km of footpath. It is a lovely spot and the park has a popular, shaded **campsite** (☎582-7319; mid-June to mid-Oct) – but Cape Split is much wilder and bleaker. To get there, take Hwy 358 north from Canning. The road climbs steeply for the first 4km until it reaches the highest point of the peninsula, the **Look-off**, where the view over the Annapolis Valley and the Minas Basin is truly spectacular. There's a café here and behind it is the *Look-off Campground* (☎582-3022; mid-May to mid-Oct), one of the best-sited in the province.

From the Look-off, it's a further 17km to the end of the road, where one of the region's most popular and not-too-difficult hiking trails leads the 7km to the tip of **Cape Split**. Reckon on two hours each way and be sure to pick up trail information and maps at Wolfville tourist office before you set out. The trail starts by threading up through thick forest beneath towering cliffs and passes heavily eroded rock formations before emerging onto a small open area, from where there are wondrous views across the Bay of Fundy.

Windsor

Pint-sized **WINDSOR**, sloping along the shore of an inlet of the Minas Basin 25km from Wolfville, was originally settled by Acadians and it was here in 1750 that the British built a fort to overawe them. The stockade was subsequently used to hold Acadians during the deportations, but all that remains today is a sorry-looking timber blockhouse conserved as the **Fort Edward National Historic Site** (mid-June to Aug daily 9am–5pm; free), which, complete with musket loopholes and cannon portholes, perches on a grassy, treeless hill overlooking Hwy 101 and the tidal mud flats that stretch out towards the basin. On the other side of town, set in its own leafy grounds on a hillside 1km west of the centre, is the **Haliburton House Museum** (June to mid-Oct Mon–Sat 9.30am–5.30pm, Sun 1–5.30pm; donation), one-time home of Thomas Chandler Haliburton, a mid-nineteenth-century judge and humorist. The house has been returned to something akin to its appearance when Haliburton lived here, writing the short stories that made him famous – cuttingly sarcastic tales whose protagonist, the itinerant Yankee clock pedlar, **Sam Slick of Slickville**, travels Nova Scotia meanly defrauding its gullible, unenterprising inhabitants. Immensely popular at the time, the stories are interesting as literary history, but leave a nasty High-Tory taste, although it was through Slick that Haliburton coined a bucketload of epigrams that remain in use: "six of one and half a dozen of the other"; "facts are stranger than fiction"; "raining cats and dogs"; "the early bird gets the worm"; and "as quick as a wink" – and many more – all came from his pen. Most of Haliburton's work is out of print, but the museum has a small supply and, if you're keen to sample his stories, begin with *The Clockmaker* ($7.50).

Central Nova Scotia

Most visitors hurry through **central Nova Scotia**, the chunk of forested land north and east of Halifax, on their way to Cape Breton Island, PEI or New Brunswick. By and large they're right to do so, but there is the odd pleasant diversion en route, and a couple of places make for a convenient overnight stay. One place it's difficult to avoid is workaday **Truro**, the region's largest town and major crossroads, situated at the east end of the Minas Basin and so subject to the Bay of Fundy tides. The most appealing parts of the bay are well to the west in New Brunswick (see pp.370–394), but if time is tight you can view the tidal bore here at Truro – the downtown tourist office, at the corner of Prince and Commercial streets (☎893-2922), has tide tables and will provide directions. Heading northwest from Truro, the Trans-Canada Highway heads off to New Brunswick's Fort Beauséjour (see p.390), scooting past the old coal-mining centre of **Springhill**, home to the Anne Murray Centre detailing the life and times of the town's most famous daughter. Near here too – though there's absolutely no need to actually go there – is Spencer's Island, not an island at all, but a former shipbuilding centre and home port of the *Mary Celeste*, which posed one of the greatest mysteries of Victorian times when she was discovered in the mid-Atlantic without a crew – and with the table set for dinner. In the opposite direction, the highway travels just inland from the northeast shore, whose gently rolling countryside was a centre of Scottish settlement from the end of the eighteenth century. The Scots first landed in **Pictou**, and this is the pick of the fishing, lumber and agricultural communities round here – especially as it's both conveniently close to the PEI ferry terminal and midway between Halifax and Cape Breton.

An alternative route between Halifax and Cape Breton is along the **southeast shore**, an isolated region of skinny bays and the tiniest of fishing villages connected by a tortuous 320-kilometre road. The coastal scenery is often quite delightful, but the villages don't deserve their redolent names – Spanish Ship Bay, Ecum Secum, Mushaboom – and the only place worthy of attention is **Sherbrooke**, where around thirty old buildings have been preserved to create an enjoyable village museum. Sherbrooke lies some 200km east of the capital on the coastal road, but is more rapidly reached from the Trans-Canada Highway from outside either New Glasgow or Antigonish.

Acadian Bus Lines operates a four times daily **bus** service from Halifax to Truro, with three buses daily continuing either northeast to New Glasgow and Cape Breton Island, or northwest to New Brunswick's Moncton. **VIA Rail**'s Halifax–Montréal **trains** pass through Truro en route to Moncton. There's no public transport to either Pictou or Sherbrooke.

Springhill

Just off the Trans-Canada, 200km from Halifax and 30km from New Brunswick, **SPRINGHILL** is an Appalachian lookalike, its tangle of modern buildings set amidst a vast forest that rolls over the surrounding hills. A coal mine was first sunk here in 1872 and it was coal that dominated the local economy until the last mine closed in the 1970s, leaving the town's population – which now numbers about 4000 – pretty much high and dry. Of all the coalfields in Canada, Springhill's was the most disaster prone, with three major tragedies grabbing national headlines: 125 miners perished in an underground explosion in 1891, 39 died in a gas explosion in 1956 and in 1958 a tunnel collapse – or "bump" as it is known hereabouts – accounted for 75 more. As if this wasn't enough, in 1957 and 1975 fires wiped out the town's commercial district. A **memorial** in the centre of town – beside the junction of highways 142 and 2 – remembers the dead miners and there are contemporary photographs of the sites of the two later disasters at the **Tour a Mine Springhill Miners' Museum**, on Black River Road, 2.5km south of town just off Hwy 2 (mid-May to mid-Oct daily 9am–5pm; $5.20). The museum's outdoors section contains several wooden shacks looking exactly as they did when the pit closed in the 1970s. One is the lamp room and another the wash house, outside of which is what the miners themselves called the Liars' Bench – after, no doubt, a certain tendency to exaggerate their coal-cutting feats. What you won't see is winding gear:

Springhill's coal seams were fairly near the surface and the miners walked down to the coalface – as visitors can do today in the company of a guide. Coalface or not, it's the **Anne Murray Centre**, 36 Main St (late May to late Oct daily 9am–5pm; $5.50), which pulls the crowds to Springhill – an exercise in organized sycophancy that tracks through the extraordinarily successful career of the Springhill-born balladeer. Murray shot to fame with her sugary song *Snowbird* in 1970 and her latest releases keep up the easy listening. Naturally enough, if you're a fan you'll love it – and you can feel good that all the centre's proceeds go to the local community.

Pictou

Signs proclaim **PICTOU**, 170km from Halifax, as the "Birthplace of New Scotland" on the basis of the arrival in 1773 of the ship *Hector*, loaded with settlers from Rosshire, the advance guard of the subsequent Scots migrations. To maintain the connection, the town has its own middle-of-August **Hector Festival**, a five-day affair featuring Scottish traditional dancing and the playing of the bagpipes – and very good it is too. Pictou has also spent years building itself a replica of the *Hector*, an expensive and time-consuming project because they stuck to the original shipbuilding techniques. The boat was finally launched in September 2000 and now either bobs around the harbour or sallies forth along the Nova Scotian coast. The dock where the boat was built forms part of the **Hector Heritage Quay Interpretative Centre** (May, Sept & Oct Mon–Sat 9am–6pm & Sun noon–6pm; June–Aug Mon–Sat 9am–8pm, Sun 10am–6pm; $4), which gives the historical lowdown on the original voyage – complete with nautical sound effects. It's all excellently done and spruces up Pictou's unassuming centre, where the narrow streets slope up from the harbour dotted with stone buildings of Scottish appearance.

Pictou is a convenient place to spend the night and there are several quality **inns** and **hotels** to choose from. The best is the *Consulate Inn*, 157 Water St (☎485-4554 or 1-800/424-8283; ③), housed in an elegant early nineteenth-century mansion that once served as a US consulate. There's also the modern and comfortable *Braeside Inn*, on a hillside above the harbour at 126 Front St (☎485-5046 or 1-800/613-7701; ③), and the *Auberge Walker Inn*, 34 Coleraine St (☎485-1433 or 1-800/370-5553; ③), a pleasantly renovated Victorian house metres from the Hector Quay. For **food**, the best restaurant in Pictou is at the *Consulate Inn*, where both the seafood and the steaks are delicious. Amongst several rather average town-centre cafés, try the filling snacks of the *Stone House Café*, just up from the Hector Quay at 11 Water St.

Pictou is 8km south of **Caribou**, where there are frequent **car ferries** over to Prince Edward Island most of the year (May to mid-Dec 4–9 daily; 1hr 15min; $11 return, $49 for car and passengers; schedules ☎1-888/249-7245, *www.nfl-bay.com*).

Sherbrooke

Developed as a timber town in the early nineteenth century, **SHERBROOKE** boomed when gold was found near here in 1861, the start of a short-lived gold rush that fizzled out within the space of twenty years, though a handful of mines struggled on until the 1940s. Most of the population checked out after the gold rush, and Sherbrooke returned to the lumber trade but without much success: the decline of the industry gradually whittled the population down to the 400 of today. One result has been the creation of the open-air museum of **Sherbrooke Village** (June to mid-Oct daily 9.30am–5.30pm; $7.25), which encompasses those late nineteenth- and early twentieth-century buildings that are, for the most part, now surplus to requirements. It's a large site, several streets situated beside St Mary's River just beyond the modern part of the village, and costumed "interpreters" preside. Amongst the thirty-odd buildings highlights include the Neoclassical lines of the surprisingly grand 1850s Court House and the Victorian luxury of the high-gabled Greenwood Cottage nearby. Also of special note are the assorted baubles and throne-like chairs of the Masonic Lodge, which still meets on the second floor of the Masonic Hall; the Temperance Hall of 1892; Cummings Bros General Store; and the jail, where jailer and prisoner lived cheek by jowl right up until the 1960s. Finally, a replica nineteenth-century water-powered sawmill has been built about 600m outside the village. Allow two to three hours to do the place justice.

There are three main ways to reach Sherbrooke: from the west along Nova Scotia's southeast shore, and from the north by turning off Hwy 104 (the Trans-Canada) either along Hwy 347 just east of New Glasgow or down Hwy 7 about 50km further east still near Antigonish. The most agreeable of the four **places to stay** in Sherbrooke is *Vi's B&B* (☎522-2042; ②; June–Sept), in the centre of the village. The tiny *Riverside Campground* (☎522-2913; mid-May to Oct) is near the sawmill. There's not much choice about where to eat, but fortunately the central *Bright House* is an excellent **restaurant** – be sure to try the seafood casserole. The *Main Street Café* sells competent snacks and pizzas.

Cape Breton Island

"I have travelled the globe. I have seen the Canadian and American Rockies, the Andes and the Alps and the Highlands of Scotland, but for simple beauty Cape Breton outrivals them all." With these words Alexander Graham Bell summed up a part of Nova Scotia whose scenery continues to attract its share of hyperbole. From the lakes, hills and valleys of the southwest to the ripe, forested mountains of the north, **Cape Breton Island** – or at least its more westerly half – offers the most exquisite of landscapes, reaching its melodramatic conclusion along the fretted, rocky coast of the **Cape Breton Highlands National Park**. Encircling the park and some of the adjacent shore is the **Cabot Trail**, a 300-kilometre loop that is reckoned to be one of the most beguiling drives on the continent and one that is best approached in a clockwise direction.

By contrast, the more easterly half of Cape Breton – east, that is, of **Bras d'Or Lake** and its subsidiary channels – was once a busy coal-mining and steel-milling region, centred on the town of **Sydney**. It was here in the early 1920s that the struggles of the miners against the pit companies grabbed national headlines. The worst of several disputes began when the owners, the British Empire Steel Corporation (BESCO), decided to cut the men's wages by a third. The miners went on strike and the dispute escalated until BESCO persuaded prime minister King to send in the militia – and the colliers were forced back to work. Today the area's industries have largely collapsed and a deindustrialized sprawl blotches the landscape, only relieved by the splendid reconstruction of the French fortress town of **Louisbourg**, stranded out on the east coast.

Yet Cape Breton is not just about scenery and sights: the Scottish Highlanders who settled much of the island in the late eighteenth and early nineteenth centuries brought with them strong cultural traditions and today these are best recalled by the island's **musicians**, especially the **fiddle players**. Names to watch out for include Buddy MacMaster, Ashley MacIsaac, Natalie MacMaster and the Rankin family, not to mention Glenn Graham, Rodney MacDonald and Jackie Dunn – though it's impossible to pick out "the best" as each fiddler has their own particular style. Local tourist offices will gladly advise you on **gigs**, whether it be a ceilidh, concert or square dance, and listings are given in the weekly *Inverness Oran*, a local newspaper available at tourist offices and convenience stores. During the summer there's something happening almost every day, but, that said, the Saturday night Family Square Dance at West Mabou Hall is highly regarded – and takes place all year. The largest festival is the **Celtic Colours** (☎564-6668 or 1-888/355-7744, *www.celtic-colours.com*), with performances all across Cape Breton held over ten days in early October.

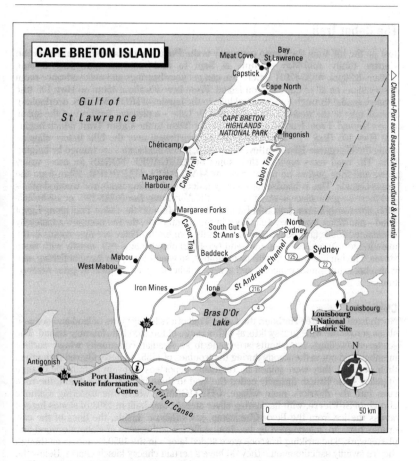

The scenic delights of Cape Breton attract thousands of summer tourists and consequently, although there's a liberal sprinkling of **accommodation** across the island – especially in the west – it's still a good idea to make a reservation a day or two beforehand. Failing that, all the island's tourist offices offer a free room-reservation service. There's no obvious place to aim for on Cape Breton and most visitors stay in the tiny ribbon villages that dot the island, but two of the most enjoyable spots are undoubtedly the busy resort of **Baddeck** and the quieter coastal community of **Chéticamp**.

Without your own transport, getting around much of Cape Breton is a struggle. **Buses** from Halifax and Truro (for Fredericton and Moncton) bomb along Hwy 105 via Baddeck and **North Sydney** – the departure port for **ferries to Newfoundland** – en route to Sydney, still the island's largest town. All traffic has to cross the **Strait of Canso causeway** as this is the only road route onto the island. There are no buses to either Louisbourg or the Cape Breton Highlands National Park, though a local company does run minibus excursions to the park from Baddeck, starting from around $30.

Finally, note that Cape Breton's **weather** is notoriously unpredictable, even in summer, and the Cabot Trail is pretty miserable in mist and rain.

The Cabot Trail

Just up the hill from the Canso causeway is the **Port Hastings Visitor Information Centre** (daily: mid-May to June & Sept to mid-Oct 9am–5pm; July & Aug 8.30am–8.30pm; ☎625-4201), where you can get your bearings and make advance room reservations on all of Cape Breton Island. From here it's about 45km on Hwy 105 (the Trans-Canada) through low, forested hills to the hamlet of **IRON MINES**, overlooking a small inlet at the western limit of Bras d'Or Lake – a pleasant foretaste of the splendours beyond. From Iron Mines, it's a further 30km to the **Cabot Trail**, which begins – at Hwy 105 (Exit 7) – by weaving its way northwest over the hills before slipping along the **Margaree River Valley**, whose soft, green landscapes are framed by bulging hills. The road veers north at the hamlet of **MARGAREE FORKS** for more valley views and then pushes on to the coast at **MARGAREE HARBOUR**, 50km from the Trans-Canada. This is handsome scenery indeed – all rolling fields and wooded hills – and there's a great place to stay here too – the *Normaway Inn* (☎248-2987 or 1-800/565-9463, *normaway@atcon.com*; mid-June to late Oct), 4km off the Cabot Trail along Egypt Road – and 28km from Hwy 105. Deep in the countryside, the inn occupies a tastefully maintained 1920s farmhouse and stands in its own estate. There are nine rooms in the main lodge (④) and nineteen one- and two-bedroomed cabins (⑤), mostly with wood stoves. The inn has contacts with local ghillies, so you can try your hand at fishing, and it also hosts folk-music concerts and serves a delicious evening meal by prior reservation.

Chéticamp

North from Margaree Harbour, the Cabot Trail offers lovely views of land and sea as it slices across the wide grassy littoral with a range of forested hills looming inland. The scattered dwellings hereabouts are home to an Acadian community whose earliest members hid out in the woods during the troubles of 1755. As news filtered through of their survival, they were joined by returning deportees and – in a dramatic change of policy – the British formally ceded the land to them in 1790. After 40km, the road runs into the district's main village, **CHÉTICAMP**, where the towering Catholic church of **St-Pierre**, with its soaring silver steeple, was built in 1893 of stones lugged across the ice from the Île-de-Chéticamp, just offshore. Inside, the lines of the cavernous nave are interrupted by two long galleries and oceans of elaborate wood and plasterwork. The striking frescoes were added later – in the 1950s – and, even though they're awfully sanctimonious, they do have a certain cheery kitsch charm. Below the church – a couple of hundred metres back down the road – is the **Co-operative Artisanale** (early May to Oct daily 8am–9pm; ☎224-3207), where a tiny Musée Acadien features a selection of the crudely patterned hooked rugs that are a characteristic craft of the area. The display is hardly spellbinding, but the co-operative's simple café-style *Restaurant Acadien* is excellent and great value. In particular, the *poulet fricot* (chicken stew) is mouthwatering, and so are the fruit pies and pea soup. There's a much better exhibition of Acadian crafts at the north end of the village in **Les Trois Pignons** (late May to mid-Oct daily 9am–5pm; mid-Oct to late May Mon–Fri 9am–5pm; $3.50), a cultural centre that proudly displays the hooked mats of Elizabeth LeFort, an artist of some local renown. LeFort's hooked mats often depict religious and historical scenes, mostly large-scale, multicoloured affairs that took as long as a year to complete, but her portraits are perhaps more unusual, pushing the limits of mat making with admittedly mixed results – though her *Jackie Onassis* of 1962 is quite delightful.

Chéticamp straggles along the main road for about 5km. In between the church – at the south end of the village – and Les Trois Pignons is a **tourist kiosk** (July–Sept), where they have the latest details on a variety of boat trips, several of which leave from the adjacent jetty. Options include **deep-sea fishing** on board the *Danny Lynn* (July &

Aug 3 daily, June, Sept & Oct 1–3 daily; 3–4hr; $25; ☎224-3606) and **whale-watching** with the highly reputable Whale Cruisers Ltd (May & mid-Sept to mid-Oct 2 daily, June to mid-Sept 3 daily; 3hr; $28; ☎224-3376 or 1-800/813-3376, *www.whalecruises.com*). Indeed, summer whale-watching cruises are big business in these parts and they are available at almost every significant settlement – usually three-hour trips for about $30.

There are around twenty **motels** and **B&Bs** in and around Chéticamp. A good choice is the *Ocean View Motel* (☎224-2313 or 1-877/743-4404; ③; mid-April to mid-Nov), whose well-maintained, shingle-clad chalets sit right by the seashore on the main road opposite Les Trois Pignons. Another option is *L'Auberge Doucet Inn* (☎224-3438 or 1-800/646-8668; ③; May–Oct), above the main road on the south side of the village, which has twelve straightforward, modern rooms. More distinctive is *Chéticamp Outfitters B&B* (☎224-2776; ②; April to mid-Dec), perched on a hilltop just off the main road about 4km south of the village and with splendid views over the surrounding shoreline. The rooms are plain and simple, but the breakfasts are good, the breakfast room has great views and the Acadian family who run the place offer bicycle rental. A third choice, the *Park View Motel* (☎224-3232, *www.seal-trail.com/parkvie*; late May to late Oct; ③), occupies a pair of well-kept but routine motel blocks on the main road about 8km north of Chéticamp – in a pretty wooded dell across the Chéticamp River from the national park.

For **food**, stick to the *Restaurant Acadien* (see opposite); a reserve option is the *L'Auberge Doucet Inn* (also see above), where the crab dinners ($14) have a good reputation.

Cape Breton Highlands National Park

The 950 square kilometres of **Cape Breton Highlands National Park**, beginning just 9km north of Chéticamp, offer some of the most gorgeous scenery anywhere in the Maritimes – a mix of deep wooded valleys, rocky coastal headlands, soft green hills and boggy upland. Although visitors get a sniff of the park travelling by car – 120km of highway trimming all but its southern edge – the essence of the place is only revealed on foot: thirty **hiking trails** are signposted from the road, some of them the easiest of woodland strolls, others striking deep into the interior to the small lakes and wetlands of the central plateau. One of the most popular is the seven-kilometre **Skyline loop trail** which clambers up the coastal mountains north of Corney Brook, a few kilometres up the coast from Chéticamp. Another good trail is the seven-kilometre **Franey loop trail**, a steep walk up through the mountains and lakes north of Ingonish Beach. Most of the wildlife inhabits the inner reaches of the park – garter snakes, red-backed salamanders, snowshoe hares and moose are common; bald eagles, black bear and lynx are rare. The only artificial sight is the **Lone Sheiling**, a somewhat battered replica of the stone shelters once built by Highlanders beside their mountain pastures. The hut is on the northern perimeter of the park in a valley that was settled by Scots in the early 1800s; it is accessible along a short and easy footpath from the road.

The park has two **information kiosks** – one at the west-coast entrance just beyond Chéticamp (daily: mid-May to mid-June & Sept to late Oct 8am–5pm; late June to Aug 8am–8pm; ☎224-2306), the other at the east-coast entrance near Ingonish Beach (same details). There's also a **visitors centre** (same details) at the west-coast entrance with displays on local flora and fauna and a well-stocked bookshop. Both the visitors centre and the east-coast kiosk sell 1:50,000-scale maps, have details of the park's hiking trails, which are in peak condition from July to September, and issue backcountry camping permits ($15). There is a park entrance fee of $3.50 per adult per day. The park has six serviced **campsites** ($15–17), all within easy reach of the road, and one **wilderness campsite** – Fishing Cove – along one of the more arduous trails. Campsite services are only available from late May to early October, but you can camp in the park at any time of the year. Reservations are not required.

Cape North

Beyond the northern perimeter of the national park is **Cape North**, a forested hunk of hill and valley that juts out into the sea where the Gulf of St Lawrence meets the Atlantic Ocean. The Cabot Trail skirts the periphery of the cape, passing through the tiny village of **CAPE NORTH**, no more than a few lonely buildings straggling along the road. There are, however, several **places to stay** round here, beginning with the handy *Macdonald's Motel* (☎383-2054; ②; mid-May to Oct), a straightforward, modern affair at the village crossroads. Much more enticing, however, is *Oakwood Manor B&B* (☎ & fax 383-2317, *oakwood.manor@ns.sympatico.ca*; ③; May–Oct), whose ensuite guestrooms are in a charming 1930s timber farmhouse. The 200-acre farm occupies a gentle valley and is dotted with shingle-clad barns and outbuildings. To get there, take the Bay St Lawrence road north from Cape North village and, after about 1.3km, turn left at the sign, down the 1.2km-long gravel road leading to the farm. The best place to **eat** is *Morrison's Restaurant*, a casual café serving tasty seafood at the village crossroads.

There aren't many reasons to push on up the North Cape, away from the Cabot Trail, but one of them is to join a **whale-watching trip** at tiny **BAY ST LAWRENCE**, 17km from Cape North village. Several operators line up beside the harbour with one of the most dependable being Captain Cox, whose cruises depart from here throughout the summer (June, Sept & Oct 1–3 daily; July & Aug 3 daily; 2–3hr; $25; ☎383-2981 or 1-888/346-5556). Just before you reach Bay St Lawrence, there's a 5km-long turning to the hamlet of **CAPSTICK**, where a string of houses spreads out along a wide bay with wooded hills pressing in from behind. Beyond, at the end of a bumpy, occasionally hairy 8km-long gravel road, lies **MEAT COVE**, which passing sailors once raided for moose and caribou – hence the name. The small **campsite** here (☎383-2379; June–Oct; sites $15) is full of the roar of the ocean.

Ingonish and the Gaelic Coast

Beyond Cape North village, the main road skirts the national park, cutting east across the interior before veering south along the coast to reach the series of roadside resorts that make up **INGONISH**. Amongst several **places to stay** here, the *Glenghorm Beach Resort* (☎285-2049; June–Oct) is as good as any – and better than most – its neat and trim motel rooms (④) and cabins (⑤) spreading out along a pleasant slice of seashore. The attractions of Ingonish do, however, pale in comparison with *Keltic Lodge* (☎285-2880 or 1-800/565-0444, *www.signatureresorts.com*), one of the province's finest hotel complexes, perched high above the cliffs amidst immaculate gardens on a rocky promontory some 40km from Cape North village – and close to the national park's east entrance. The lodge has a comprehensive range of facilities, from beaches, restaurants and tennis courts through to hiking trails that explore the locale's scenic nooks and crannies. You can stay in the main lodge (⑧), a handsome Edwardian mansion with high gables and dinky brick chimneys, or the modern Keltic Inn (⑧), but the cottages (⑧) are perhaps more enjoyable, the best of them prettily located amongst the woods that cover much of the promontory.

Leaving the national park, the Cabot Trail threads down the eighty-kilometre **Gaelic Coast** – named after the Scottish Highlanders who first settled here – passing through **SOUTH GUT ST ANN'S**, the location of the **Gaelic College of Celtic Arts and Crafts**. Standing on its own campus in the hills, the college offers courses in the Gaelic language and all manner of Highland activities – bagpiping, tartan-weaving, dancing and Scots folklore. The main focus of a visit here is the **Great Hall of the Clans** (July to early Oct daily 9am–5pm; $2.50), which provides potted clan descriptions alongside wax models dressed in the appropriate tartan.

From the college, it is a few hundred metres to the Trans-Canada for either Baddeck to the southwest or Sydney (see p.368) to the east.

Baddeck

The amenable resort and yachting town of **BADDECK**, some 90km east of the Canso causeway along Hwy 105, enjoys an attractive lakeside setting on St Patrick's Channel, an inlet of the Bras d'Or Lake. It is also home to the fascinating **Alexander Graham Bell Museum** (daily: June, Sept & early Oct 9am–6pm; July & Aug 8.30am–7.30pm; mid-Oct to May 9am–5pm; $4.25), which overlooks the waterfront from a tiny park and whose excellent exhibits do full justice to the fertility of Bell's mind. The museum is a mine of general biographical information about Bell and gives detailed explanations of all his inventions – both successful and unsuccessful. Most famous for the invention of the telephone, Bell also made extraordinary advances in techniques for teaching hearing-impaired children, a lifelong interest inspired by the deafness of his mother, and undertook pioneering experiments in animal husbandry. He also worked on aircraft and boats, and his nautical adventures culminated in 1919 with the launch of the world's first hydrofoil, the HD-4 (of which there's a full-scale replica in the museum), which reached a speed of 70mph on the lake right in front of town. Bell (1847–1922) spent his last 37 years in Baddeck, working away at **Beinn Bhreagh** (no public access), the family mansion that still stands amongst the trees just across the bay from town. The museum is Baddeck's only significant sight, but the town's waterfront makes for an enjoyable stroll and in July and August the local Lion's Club runs a free shuttle-boat service from the municipal jetty to **Kidston Island**, a couple of hundred metres offshore, where you can take a walk in the woods.

Baddeck is on the main Acadian Lines **bus** route between Halifax and Sydney, with one bus daily in each direction stopping at the Irving petrol station 3.5km west of town on Hwy 105 (Exit 8). The **tourist office** (June–Oct daily 9am–7pm; ☎295-1911) has lots of useful local information and sits by the side of the resort's main intersection – at Shore Road and the top of the short main drag, Chebucto Street. Baddeck is a popular holiday spot, so there's a wide range of **accommodation**, but it fills up fast in the height of the season. Downtown choices include the delightful *Duffus House Inn* (☎295-2172; ④; mid-May to late Oct), which occupies two attractively renovated Victorian town houses by the lake on Water Street, and *Heidi's B&B* (☎295-1301; ②; June–Oct), in a pleasant old timber building with a terrace about 400m from the tourist office at 64 Old Margaree Rd. The former has seven en-suite rooms, the latter two with shared bath. In addition, several smart resort-hotels line up along Shore Road, west of the town centre. These include the *Silver Dart Lodge* (☎295-2340 or 1-888/662-7484; ④; May–Oct), whose spacious chalets spread over a hillside in view of the lake; *Auberge Gisele's Country Inn* (☎295-2849 or 1-800/304-0466; ④; May–Oct), where the sixty commodious bedrooms are decked out in modern style; and, best of the lot, the *Inverary Resort* (☎295-3500 or 1-800/565-5660), an extensive and immaculately maintained complex that spreads from Shore Road down to the bay. The *Inverary* offers rooms in the main lodge (⑤) and in several different types of cottage (from ⑥). If your budget doesn't stretch that far, the *Restawyle B&B* (☎295-3253; ②; mid-May to mid-Oct), also on Shore Road, occupies a good-looking Edwardian house set in its own grounds. This B&B has four comfortable guestrooms, two with shared bath. The nearest **campsite** is the *Bras d'Or Lakes* (☎295-2329; June–Sept), about 6km west on Hwy 105.

With regard to **food**, most visitors eat where they sleep because Baddeck is surprisingly short on cafés and restaurants. The best café in town is the *High Wheeler*, on Chebucto Street, which serves up a reasonable range of wholefood snacks and cakes, whilst the *Bell Buoy* (☎295-2581), further down Chebucto Street, is OK for steaks and seafood.

If you're without your own transport, Bannockburn Tours (☎295-3310 or 1-888/577-4747) run day-long **excursions** along the Cabot Trail through the Cape Breton Highlands National Park during the summer at $55 per person. Bannockburn Tours also operates a shuttle minibus service to Louisbourg costing $40 for the return trip. **Car hire** is available in Baddeck with Macaulay's, 404 Shore Rd (☎295-2500).

Sydney and around

Poor old **SYDNEY**, sprawling along the east bank of the Sydney River 430km from Halifax and 80km from Baddeck, was once the industrial dynamo of eastern Canada. From the late nineteenth century to the 1950s its steel mills processed Newfoundland iron ore with Nova Scotian coke, but as gas and oil came on stream this arrangement became uneconomic and the subsequent decline has been severe and long-lasting: the city has regularly recorded an unemployment rate twice the national average. It's hardly surprising, therefore, that the town lacks charm, though brave efforts have been made to reinvigorate the **North End** waterfront, along and around the **Esplanade**, downtown between Prince and Amelia streets. This is the district to head for and it's here you'll find Sydney's oldest buildings, including the early nineteenth-century **St Patrick's Church**, 87 Esplanade, a broadly Gothic structure that now holds a local history museum (June–Aug Mon–Sat 9.30am–5.30pm, Sun 1–5.30pm; donation). Nearby, the **Cossit House**, 75 Charlotte St (same details), was built for the town's first Anglican minister in 1787.

Arriving from Baddeck and Halifax, long-distance Acadian Lines buses pull in to the **bus station** at 99 Terminal Rd off Prince Street, a good ten- to fifteen-minute walk from the Esplanade. There are several **hotels** along the Esplanade, with two good options being the *Delta Sydney* (☎562-7500 or 1-800/268-1133; ⑤), a large and well-equipped chain hotel at no. 300, and the more basic *Pauls Hotel* (☎562-5747; ②), in an old building on the corner of Pitt Street. The **tourist office** (☎539-9876), on the edge of town beside Hwy 125 (Exit 6), has the list of all the town's accommodation and can also advise on local minibus services to the Cabot Trail. The leading company is Cape Breton Tours, 24 Kings Rd (☎564-6200), who also shuttle visitors out to Louisbourg for $30 return. For **car hire**, contact Avis (☎564-8341), who have a Sydney branch.

Sydney's airport offers the shortest and least expensive (1–3 weekly; $290 return) flights from the mainland to St-Pierre et Miquelon (see p.433): for details, contact Air St-Pierre (☎562-3140) or Air Canada, its international partner. Finally, **NORTH SYDNEY**, 21km west of Sydney along Hwy 125, is the harbour for the **Newfoundland ferry** (☎794-5254, *www.marine-atlantic.ca*; see also p.414). Acadian Lines buses drop passengers near the ferry terminal on their way to and from Sydney and usually run to meet sailing times. Inside the ferry terminal building, there's a **Newfoundland tourist office**, which operates a room-reservation service for that province and has armfuls of free literature. North Sydney is itself unremarkable, but if for some reason you get stuck here there's a comfortable chain hotel, the *Best Western North Star Inn*, on the hill next to the ferry terminal at 39 Forrest St (☎794-8581 or 1-800/561-8585; ④).

Louisbourg

Beginning work in 1719, the French constructed the coastal fortress of **LOUISBOURG**, 37km southeast of Sydney, to guard the Atlantic approaches to New France and salvage their imperial honour after the humiliation of the Treaty of Utrecht. The result was a staggeringly ostentatious stronghold covering a hundred acres and encircled by ten-metre-high stone walls; it took so long to build and was so expensive that Louis XV said he was expecting its towers to rise over the Paris horizon. However, Louisbourg was wildly ill-conceived: the humid weather stopped the mortar from drying, the fort was overlooked by a score of hillocks, and developments in gunnery had already made high stone walls an ineffective means of defence. As Charles Lawrence, the British governor, confirmed, "the general design of the fortifications is exceedingly bad and the workmanship worse executed and so disadvantageously situated that . . .

it will never answer the charge or trouble". And so it proved: Louisbourg was only attacked twice, but it was captured on both occasions, the second time by the celebrated British commander, James Wolfe, on his way to Québec in 1758.

A visit to the **Fortress of Louisbourg National Historic Site** (daily: June & Sept 9.30am–5pm; July & Aug 9am–7pm; $11) begins just 2km beyond the modern village at the Reception Centre, where there's a good account of the fort's history and its reconstruction in the 1960s. From here, a free shuttle bus runs to the fort, whose stone walls rise from the sea to enclose more than four dozen restored buildings, a mid-eighteenth-century fortress town set beneath a soaring church spire. There are powder magazines, forges, guardhouses, warehouses, barracks and, last but not least, the chilly abodes of the soldiers, all accompanied by costumed guides to provide extra atmosphere. It's an extraordinary reconstruction in a lovely coastal setting and particular care has been taken with the **governor's apartments**, which have been splendidly furnished according to the inventory taken after the death of Governor Duquesnel here in 1744. It's amazing the man hadn't died before: already minus a leg from early in his military career, Duquesnel's body was buried under the chapel floor and when it was exhumed in the 1960s the remains showed him to have been suffering from a bewildering variety of ailments from arthritis and arteriosclerosis through to dental abscesses.

Allow at least a couple of hours to look round the fortress and sample the authentic refreshments that are available at the taverns and eating houses; the most sustaining food of all is the soldiers' bread (wheat and rye wholemeal), sold by the loaf at the **King's Bakery**.

Stringing along the seashore down the bay from the fortress, the modern **village of Louisbourg** has a cheerful setting and several good **places to stay**. Choices include the *Stacey House B&B*, 7438 Main St (☎733-2317 or 1-888/924-2242; ②; June–Oct), an attractive, high-gabled old home with just four guestrooms; the fiercely pink *Cranberry Cove Inn*, 12 Wolfe St (☎733-2171 or 1-800/929-0222; ④; June to mid-Oct), a lavishly refurbished old house on the edge of the village on the way to the fort; and the *Manse B&B*, 10 Strathcona St (☎733-3155; ②; April–Oct), which occupies a pleasant Victorian house down an alley just off Main Street, though its waterfront location is spoilt by an abandoned fish factory. There's a no-frills **campsite**, the *Louisbourg Motorhome Park* (☎733-3631; mid-May to Oct), down by the harbour in the centre of the village. The **tourist office**, on Main Street (June & Sept Mon–Fri 9am–5pm; July & Aug daily 8am–8pm), has the complete lodgings list.

Amongst several **cafés** and **restaurants**, the *Grubstake*, 1274 Main St (☎733-2308; June–Oct), is recommended for its fish platters and home-baked pastries. Both the breakfast and dinner at the *Cranberry Cove Inn* are excellent.

From Louisbourg to the Canso causeway via Iona

From Louisbourg, it's a dreary 20-kilometre thrash north then west along highways 22 and 4 back to the Canso causeway. Instead, if you have the time, leave Hwy 4 west of Sydney and take Hwy 216 over the hills and along a slender arm of Bras d'Or Lake to **IONA**, a remote hamlet where many of the inhabitants speak Gaelic. Iona is also home to the **Highland Village** (daily: June to early July & late Aug to mid-Oct 9am–6pm; early July to late Aug 9am–8pm; $4), a modest collection of old pioneer buildings brought here from all over Cape Breton. The views from the museum, over the lake, are, however, quite delightful – as they are from the nearby *Highland Heights Inn* (☎725-2360 or 1-800/660-8122, *www.highlandheightsinn.com*; ④; late May to mid-Oct), a smart modern place with thirty well-appointed, motel-style rooms.

Iona is 13km – and a five-minute ferry ride – from Hwy 105 (Exit 6) between Baddeck and the Canso causeway.

NEW BRUNSWICK

The province of **NEW BRUNSWICK**, roughly 320km long and 260km wide, attracts less tourist attention than its Maritime neighbours, and it's hard to understand quite why. It's true that the forested upland that makes up the bulk of the province is a trifle repetitious, but the long river valleys that furrow the landscape compensate and the funnel-shaped **Bay of Fundy**, with its dramatic tides and delightful coastline, is outstanding. Equally, in **Fredericton**, the capital, the province has one of the regions most appealing towns, a laid-back easy sort of place which, besides offering the bonus of the Beaverbrook Art Gallery, also possesses strings of fine old villas and a good-looking cathedral. Handsome scenery is within easy reach too – it's a short trip south to scenic **Passamaquoddy Bay**, an island-studded inlet of the Bay of Fundy that's home to the likeable resort of **St Andrews**. Southeast of Fredericton, the Saint John River snakes a tortuous route to the Bay of Fundy at the busy port of **Saint John**. Along with most of the settlements of southern New Brunswick, Saint John was founded by United Empire Loyalists, whose descendants, mingled with those of British colonists, account for around sixty percent of the province's 725,000 inhabitants. Some 130,000 people live here in Saint John, making this the province's big city – it's much larger than Fredericton – and although hard times have left the place frayed at the edges the city boasts a splendid sample of Victorian architecture. Also, although industry has scarred the Fundy coast hereabouts, there's still no denying the rugged charms of Saint John's setting, and not far away are the more pristine land- and seascapes of both the coastal **Fundy Trail Parkway** and **Fundy National Park**.

The remaining third of New Brunswick's population are French-speakers, the descendants of those Acadians who settled in the region after the deportations of 1755. To avoid further persecution, these refugees clustered in the remote northern parts of the province, though since the 1960s they have become more assertive – following the example set by their Québecois cousins – and have made **Moncton**, in southeast New Brunswick, the effective capital of modern Acadia, with a French-speaking university as their cultural centre. Moncton is, however, of limited interest to the passing visitor – it's a modern, brassy, breezy sort of place – and is chiefly of use as a stepping stone either west to Fundy National Park or east to the beautifully remote remains of **Fort Beauséjour**. As for the other Acadian districts, they are best visited on the way to Québec. Two main roads link Fredericton with its northern neighbour. The first – which is both more scenically diverting and more direct – slices up the western edge of the province along the Saint John River Valley to French-speaking **Edmundston**, en route to Rivière-du-Loup (see p.281). The second cuts northeast for the long haul up the **Miramichi River Valley** to the cluster of small towns that are known collectively as **Miramichi City**. Near here are the untamed coastal marshes of the **Kouchibouguac National Park** and, in the northeast corner of the province, the **Acadian Peninsula**, whose pride and joy is the re-created **Village Historique Acadien**, near the fishing village of **Caraquet**.

SMT **buses** run a reasonable provincewide network of services, with daily connections along the Saint John River Valley and up the east coast from Moncton to Campbellton. There are also regular buses from Fredericton, Saint John and Moncton over to Charlottetown on PEI, via the Confederation Bridge. The Saint John to Digby **car ferry** is a useful short cut if you're heading down to southwest Nova Scotia.

A brief history of New Brunswick

Administered as part of the British colony of Nova Scotia until 1784, **New Brunswick** was created to cope with the sudden arrival of thousands of Loyalists in the early 1780s. The New Englanders were concentrated in Saint John, which they expected to be the

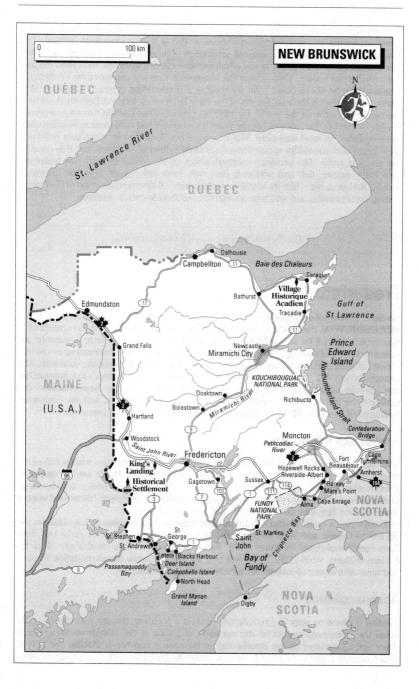

new provincial capital. However, the governor's aristocratic claque outmanoeuvred them, managing to get Fredericton chosen as the seat of government instead. This unpopular decision led to an unusual separation of functions, with Fredericton developing as the province's political and administrative capital, whereas Saint John became the commercial centre. Throughout the nineteenth century conservative Fredericton stagnated whilst liberal Saint John boomed as a shipbuilding centre, its massive shipyards, dependent on the vast forests of the New Brunswick interior, becoming some of the most productive in the world. By 1890 the province was Canada's most prosperous region, but within the space of twenty years its economy had collapsed as wooden ships were replaced by steel steamers. The recession was long-lasting, ultimately reflecting New Brunswick's inability to develop a diversified industrial economy, and this remains the problem today. The province splutters along on the profits from its raw materials, principally timber, fish and potatoes, plus zinc, lead and copper from the northeast around Bathurst, but – like its Maritime neighbours – it exercises no control over price-setting mechanisms, and sharp boom-and-bust economic cycles continue.

The New Brunswick telephone code is ☎506.

Fredericton

Situated 100km inland from the Bay of Fundy on the banks of the Saint John River, **FREDERICTON**, the capital of New Brunswick, has a well-padded air, the streets of its tiny centre graced by well-established elms and genteel villas. There's scarcely any industry here and the population of 46,000 mostly work for the government or the university, at least partly fulfilling the aims of one of the town's aristocratic sponsors, who announced in 1784: "it shall be the most gentlemanlike place on earth". Fredericton has few specific sights, but what there is is good, principally the **Beaverbrook Art Gallery**, the gift of that crusty old reactionary Lord Beaverbrook, and the occasional building left from the **Military Compound** that once housed the garrison.

Arrival and information

The SMT **bus** terminal is at 101 Regent St at King, about five-minutes' walk south of the river and one block south of the main drag, Queen Street. There are no **trains** to Fredericton: the nearest service is to Moncton. Air Canada provides a wide range of domestic and a few international flights into Fredericton **airport**, 16km southeast of town; the taxi fare into the centre will cost you around $20.

Fredericton's main **Visitors Information Centre** is downtown in City Hall on the corner of Queen and York streets (mid-May to mid-June & Sept to early Oct daily 8am–5pm; mid-June to Aug daily 8am–8pm; mid-Oct to mid-May Mon–Fri 8.15am–4.30pm; ☎460-2129). They will ring ahead to reserve accommodation for free and have all manner of leaflets on the city and its surroundings.

Accommodation

Finding a **place to stay** in Fredericton is rarely a problem, though you should try to avoid the humdrum motels on the outskirts in favour of the downtown area, where there are a couple of tip-top **hotels** and an increasing number of **B&Bs**, the best of which occupy grand old timber houses. If you're strapped for cash, the university hires out **student rooms** in the summer and there's a downtown HI **hostel**. Finally, there are several **campsites** out of town along the Saint John River Valley.

Hotels, bed and breakfasts and inns

Carriage House Inn, 230 University Ave at George (☎452-9924 or 1-800/267-6068, fax 458-0799). This ten-room inn, on the east side of the city centre, occupies a grand Victorian house in one of the older residential areas. Comes complete with antique furnishings, ballroom, and capacious veranda. Some rooms with shared bathroom. Rate includes delicious breakfast. ③.

Comfort Inn, 797 Prospect St (☎453-0800). Routine but entirely adequate chain motel south of the town centre – take Exit 289 off the Trans-Canada, Hwy 2. One of several motels on Prospect St. ④.

Elmcroft Place B&B, 9 Elmcroft Place (☎452-1700 or 1-888/354-4588, *stayat@elmcroftplacebb.nb.ca*). Fredericton has several Georgian mansions and one of them has been turned into this B&B, whose two guestrooms are large and comfortable and decorated in appropriate period style. It is situated about 2km east of downtown, in its own grounds and close to the south bank of the river. ④.

Lord Beaverbrook Hotel, 659 Queen St (☎455-3371 or 1-800/561-7666, fax 455-1441). Polished downtown hotel with Art Deco flourishes; overlooks the river. Facilities include an indoor pool. Often has weekend discounts of up to 25 percent. ④.

Sheraton Fredericton Hotel, 225 Woodstock Rd (☎457-7000 or 1-800/325-3535, fax 457-4000). Modern high-rise hotel in an attractive retro style with dormer windows and stone finishings. Luxurious suites and posh doubles with views of the river; located a few blocks west of the centre. ⑤.

The very best, A Victorian B&B, 806 George St at Church (☎451-1499, fax 454-1454). This pleasant B&B, in a rambling old house within easy walking distance of the centre, offers three tastefully renovated, en-suite guestrooms as well as an outside pool and sauna. ④. "The very best" is a common aphorism in Miramichi, which is where one of the owners comes from.

Student room accommodation, hostel and campsite

Fredericton International Hostel, 621 Churchill Row (☎450-4417, fax 462-9692). Friendly, HI hostel in a sparse, but well-kept older building about 500m south of downtown at the corner of Regent St. Kitchen facilities and study areas. Dorm beds for $20 (nonmembers $22). Also doubles ①.

Mactaquac Provincial Park Campground, near Mactaquac (☎363-4747). Large, popular and well-equipped campsite some 20km west of Fredericton, on the north side of the Saint John River off Hwy 105. May–Oct. Sites $23.

UNB Residence Accommodation, Residence Administration Building, University of New Brunswick, 20 Bailey Drive (☎453-4891). Over a thousand single ($28) and double ($40) rooms for rent, on the university campus, at the south end of University Ave just beyond Beaverbrook St, about 2km south of the river. June to mid-Aug.

The City

The **Saint John River**, running from northern Maine to the Bay of Fundy, was for a long time the fastest way to reach **Fredericton**, whose early streets, bounded by Brunswick Street to the south and York Street to the west, were laid out close to a curve of the south bank. Here the provincial administration set up shop and the garrison, stationed to counter the threat of American attack, paraded on the **Officers' Square**, at the foot of Regent Street. Mostly grassed over, the square still has space for the Changing of the Guard, a re-enactment of British drill that takes place during the summer (July & Aug Tues–Sat 11am & 7pm). If you miss it, the sentry changes every hour on the hour, a brief march between the square and City Hall just along the street.

The square forms the eastern perimeter of the **Military Compound**, which once stretched over to York Street between Queen Street and the river. It was a large garrison for such a small place and, once Canada–US relations were on a secure footing, the attitude of the local citizenry towards the antics of the military hardened. They could put up with the grog shops and brothels discreetly located on the other side of the river,

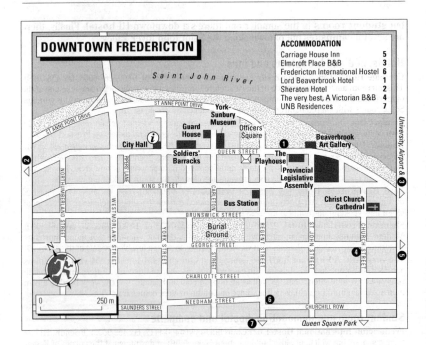

DOWNTOWN FREDERICTON

but they were infuriated by a huge brawl between soldiers and sailors that swept right across town – and when the British regulars finally departed in 1869 many were relieved. One reminder of the British presence is the elegant three-storey **Officers' Quarters**, on the square's west side, whose symmetrical columns and stone arches follow a design much used by the Royal Engineers of the nineteenth century. Inside, the **York-Sunbury Historical Museum** (May & early June Tues–Sat noon–5pm; mid-June to Aug daily 10am–5pm; Sept to mid-Dec Tues–Sat noon–5pm; $2) possesses an intriguing assortment of local bygones, which fills every nook and cranny of this warren-like building. The ground floor kicks off with displays on Fredericton under the British and up above – on the second floor – are military uniforms, armaments and a reconstruction of a World War I trench. Moving on, the third floor holds a couple of Native Canadian rooms, with a ragbag of archeological finds, plus the stuffed remains of the twenty-kilo "Coleman Frog", a giant-sized amphibian of dubious origins. It's not known whether the creature is real or not, but the local innkeeper, who produced it in the 1880s, claimed to have fed it on beer and buttermilk.

A few metres west along Queen, at the foot of Carleton Street, is the **Guard House** (June–Aug daily 10am–6pm; free), where guides in period British uniforms show you round a restored orderly room, a guardroom and detention cells that create a fearsome picture of military life in the middle of the nineteenth century. The guardroom is not, actually, too different from the airless cells where villains were locked up waiting to be flogged, branded or transported. Directly opposite, with its back to Queen Street, is the **Soldiers' Barracks** (same times) a sturdy three-storey block that at one time accommodated more than two hundred squaddies. Most of the building has been turned into offices and its street-level arcades house arts and craft stalls, but one room has been restored to its appearance in the early 1800s.

The Beaverbrook Art Gallery

Lord Beaverbrook (1879–1964), the newspaper tycoon and champion of the British Empire, was raised in New Brunswick's Newcastle, and although he moved to England in 1910 at the age of 31 – becoming a close friend of Churchill and a key member of his war cabinet – he sustained a sentimental attachment to his homeland. In Fredericton his largesse was extended to the university, the Playhouse Theatre, and the **Beaverbrook Art Gallery**, by the river at the foot of St John Street (June–Sept Mon–Fri 9am–6pm, Sat & Sun 10am–5pm; Oct–May Tues–Fri 9am–5pm, Sat 10am–5pm, Sun noon–5pm; $3). It's a first-rate gallery, where an eclectic and regularly rotated collection of mostly British and Canadian art is squeezed into a dozen or so rooms, sharing valuable space with an imaginative programme of temporary exhibitions; free plans are issued at reception. The entrance is dominated by a permanent fixture, Salvador Dali's monumental *Santiago el Grande* depicting St James being borne up towards a vaulted firmament on a white charger. After Dali's blitzkrieg, it takes time to adjust to the subtler works beyond, where the Brits are represented by Hogarth, Reynolds, Gainsborough, Constable, Turner, Landseer, Augustus John, Francis Bacon and Lowry. There's also a small sample of medieval paintings and a haunting *Lady Macbeth Sleep-Walking* by Delacroix.

The fulsome Canadian collection features well-known artists like Paul Kane (see p.84), the Group of Seven (see p.86) and Emily Carr, as well as lesser figures like the early nineteenth-century artist George Chambers, whose *"The Terror" Iced in off Cape Comfort* is a wonderfully melodramatic canvas, the creaking ship crushed by the ice underneath a dark and forbidding sky. Dominique Serres (1722–93), a favourite of George III, never visited Canada, but he saw sketches made by returning naval officers, sufficient for him to produce *The Bishop's House with Ruined Town of Québec* and *The Intendant's Palace, Québec*, townscapes in the soft-hued Italian style. There's also a good selection of the works of the prolific Cornelius Krieghoff (1815–72), who made a living churning out souvenir pictures of Indians and French Canadians from the time of his arrival in Canada in 1840. Krieghoff had a roller-coaster life. Born to a German father and Dutch mother, he emigrated to New York in 1836 and promptly joined the US army, serving in the Second Seminole War down in Florida. Discharged in 1840, Krieghoff immediately re-enlisted, claimed three months' advance pay and deserted, hotfooting it to Montréal with the French-Canadian woman he had met and married in New York. Montréal was a disaster – no one would buy his paintings – but when he moved to Québec City he found a ready market for his work amongst the British officers of the large garrison and their well-heeled friends. This was Krieghoff's most productive period and the finely detailed, carefully composed anecdotal scenes of French-Canadian life he painted during these years are his best – and two of the finest, *Merrymaking* and *Coming Storm at the Portage*, can be seen here amongst no less than 27 of his paintings.

The Legislative Assembly Building and around

The **Legislative Assembly Building** (guided tours June–Aug daily 9am–6pm; Sept–May Mon–Fri 9am–4pm; free), the home of New Brunswick's parliament, stands opposite the art gallery, its robust and imposing exterior topped by a ponderous tower and cupola. The interior holds a sumptuously decorated Assembly Chamber, adorned with portraits of George III and Queen Charlotte by Joshua Reynolds, as well as a splendid oak and cherry spiral staircase leading to the chamber's visitors' gallery. The Reynolds were rescued from the previous parliament building, which burnt down in 1880.

The Legislature occupies the grandest building in Fredericton, but the nearby **Christ Church Cathedral**, King Street and Church (mid-June to Aug Mon–Fri 9am–6pm, Sat 10am–5pm, Sun 1–5pm; Sept to mid-June Mon–Sat 9am–4pm; free guided tours from mid-June to Aug), comes a close second. A mid-Victorian copy of the fifteenth-century parish church of Snettisham, in Norfolk, England, it's distinguished by the elegance of its tapering spire and the intricate grace of its red-pine hammerbeam ceiling. The church also marks the beginning of the smartest part of town, whose leafy streets, lined by handsome Victorian mansions complete with gingerbread scrollwork and expansive verandas, stretch south towards tiny **Queen Square Park**. Near here too – at the east end of Brunswick Street – the old **railway bridge** has been pedestrianized and is easily the nicest way to cross the Saint John River. The bridge is actually part of a system of hiking trails that loops through and around Fredericton focused on the river. There are several jetties dotted along the trails and in the summertime passenger **boats** ($2 per trip, $3 return; ☎447-7494) link them several times daily, except in bad weather. Maps of the hiking trails and boat timetables are available from the tourist office.

Eating and drinking

Downtown Fredericton offers a reasonable range of informal **cafés** and **restaurants** and there are enough **bars** to entertain for a night or two. In the summer there's free outdoor theatre and live music down on Officers' Square. The Playhouse (☎458-8344 or 1-800/442-9779, *www.theplayhouse.nb.ca*), beside the Legislative Assembly Building, puts on a good variety of shows and is home to the province's only professional English-speaking **theatre** company, Theatre New Brunswick (Sept–April season). The tourist office has the details of all up-and-coming events.

Cafés and restaurants

Brewbakers, 546 King St between Regent and Carleton (☎459-0067). Jam packed at the weekend, *Brewbakers* offers first-rate wood-fired pizzas at affordable prices. Lively bar area too.

Bruno's Seafood Café, at the *Sheraton Fredericton Hotel*, 225 Woodstock Rd (☎457-7000). One of the most popular spots in town, this café-restaurant is noted for its lavish help-yourself buffets where the emphasis is on pasta and seafood. Eat either inside the hotel or outside on the large riverside patio and watch the sunset.

Coffee & Co, 415 King St at York. Great coffees – probably the best range in town – plus tasty cakes and sandwiches. Also, White Mountain, a wonderful ice cream from Kingston in Ontario, makes a rare Maritime appearance here – don't miss it. Inexpensive.

Dimitri's, Pipers Lane, 349 King St (☎452-8882). Good, standard-issue Greek restaurant amongst the café-bars crowding Pipers Lane, in between King and Queen sts, just west of York.

The Lobster Hut, in the *City Motel*, 1216 Regent St (☎455-4413). Nautical decor and lobsters galore, kept fresh in a whopping water tank. Prices fluctuate with the season.

M & T Deli, 602 Queen at Regent St. Arguably Fredericton's best deli, specializing in New York-style bagels and Montréal smoked meat. Mon–Fri 7.30am–4pm.

Mei's Chinese Restaurant, 73 Carleton St at Queen (☎454-2177). Justifiably popular, family-run Chinese restaurant featuring Szechuan and Cantonese specialities. Lunches (Tues–Fri only) are especially good value. Closed Mon.

Molly's Coffee Shop, 554 Queen St opposite Officers' Square. Fine coffee and tasty snacks in this little, touch-of-New-Age café.

Bars

Dolan's Pub, Pipers Lane, 349 King St (☎454-7474). Bustling bar with imported and domestic beers on draught. Some live folk music.

Fiddlehead Pub, 66 Regent St at Queen (☎454-9463). Low-key, downtown bar with a good range of local brews.

Lunar Rogue Pub, 625 King St (☎450-2065). Busy bar serving British and Maritime ales as well as filling bar food. Live music on most weekends. Summer patio.

Rockin' Rodeo, 546 King St between Regent and Carleton (☎444-0122). Fredericton's only C&W pub-cum-club, with occasional live acts.

MOVING ON FROM FREDERICTON – AND GAGETOWN

When it comes to **moving on from Fredericton**, you're spoiled for choice: it's north-west up the Saint John River Valley to Edmundston (see p.391) and Québec, northeast along the Miramichi to Newcastle and the Acadian Peninsula (see p.394) and a short trip southwest to Passamaquoddy Bay (see below). A fourth option is to head southeast to Saint John (see p.380), either on the fast and direct Hwy 7 or, more leisurely, along Hwy 102, which weaves its way along the rusticated banks of the Saint John River. If you choose Hwy 102, be sure to spend an hour or two in **GAGETOWN**, a pretty little village whose graceful old houses are sprinkled along the riverside about 60km from Fredericton – and 100km from Saint John. There are several enjoyable craft and pottery shops here, including **Grimross Crafts**, where thirty artists exhibit under one roof, as well as gentle riverside walks, a prim and proper Anglican church, and a grand old courthouse, now home to a modest local museum. *Beamsley's Café* offers tasty snacks and sandwiches and, if you decide to hang around, there are several **places to stay**. Two recommendations are the *Steamers Stop Inn* (☎488-2903 or 1-877/991-9922, fax 488-1116; ③), in a nineteenth-century building down by the river, and the well-kept, if somewhat plainer, 1880s *Step-Aside B&B* (☎488-1808; ②; May–Oct), also down by the river.

Passamaquoddy Bay

In the southwest corner of New Brunswick, abutting the state of Maine, lies **Passamaquoddy Bay**, a deeply indented inlet of the Bay of Fundy whose sparsely populated shoreline is a bony, bumpy affair of forest, rock and swamp. Easily the prettiest of the region's coastal villages is **St Andrews**, a Loyalist settlement turned seaside resort, 135km south of Fredericton. The other main attraction is the **Fundy Islands** archipelago at the mouth of Passamaquoddy Bay. Here, accessible from the US by road and from mainland New Brunswick by ferry (via **Deer Island**), lies **Campobello Island**, the site of Franklin Roosevelt's immaculately maintained country home. Finally, stuck out in the bay two hours by ferry from the Canadian mainland, the far larger **Grand Manan Island** is a much wilder and more remote spot that is noted for its imposing sea cliffs and variety of birdlife.

St Andrews

ST ANDREWS was once a busy fishing port and trading centre but is now a leafy resort with a laid-back, low-key air that makes for a restful place to spend a night. The town is at its prettiest amongst the antique clapboard houses flanking King Street – which leads up the hill from the busy little pier – while Water Street, the main drag, tracks along the waterfront lined with cafés and craft shops. The only sights as such are the **Horticultural Garden** on the crest of King Street and the squat, minuscule **St Andrews blockhouse**, a replica of the original wooden fort built in 1813 to protect the area from the Americans. It's at the west end of Water Street, and at low tide you can scramble around the reefs and rock pools just below. The pier is packed with boat-tour companies. Amongst several, Quoddy Link Marine (☎529-2600 or 1-877/688-2600) operate first-class **whale-watching** cruises (late May to Sept; 3hr; $45), each of which has a naturalist on board; and Seascape runs regular **kayak** trips from $55 per half-day (same months ☎529-4866).

Of particular interest also are the guided tours of **Minister's Island** (June to mid-Oct 1–2 daily; 2hr; $5; ☎529-5081), whose undulating farmland is reached by car along a tidal causeway. The island was once the property of William Van Horne, a Victorian railway baron, who built a grand stone mansion here as well as a clutter of farm buildings. Highlights of the two-hour tour include a romp round the dilapidated mansion and inspection of the windmill, with its kerosene-powered reserve engines. You also get to check out the tidal bathhouse down on the seashore and the magnificent, state-of-the-art livestock barn, where Horne pampered his horses and cattle – treating them, according to local legend, rather better than he did his workforce.

Practicalities

St Andrews is accessible by SMT **bus** from Saint John (1 daily; 1hr 30min) and passengers are dropped on Water Street, a couple of blocks east of the pier. The **tourist office** is on Hwy 127 as you enter the town (May to late Oct daily 9am–8pm; ☎529-3556). They issue free tide tables and town maps, supply information on local bicycle hire, have the schedule for visits to Minister's Island, and will happily help you with accommodation, though advance bookings are a good idea during the height of the season. Most illustrious of all the **hotels** is the *Algonquin* (☎529-8823 or 1-800/441-1414; ④–⑧), a sprawling and well-equipped resort complex whose turrets and gables, dating from 1915, dominate the northwest of town, about 1.5km from the waterfront on Prince of Wales Street. Even more unusual – and almost in the shadow of the *Algonquin* – is the *Pansy Patch B&B*, 59 Carleton St (☎529-3834 or 1-888/726-7972; ⑥/⑦; June–Oct), where nine quaint guestrooms, each with a sea view, occupy a charming country home, built in a variation of the French Normandy style in 1912; the food here is excellent too and the garden is beautiful. Other less expensive **B&Bs** within a few minutes' walk of the pier include the *Hanson House*, in a trim and well-cared-for old house at 62 Edward St (☎529-4947; ②; May–Oct); the *Harris Hatch Inn*, 142 Queen St (☎529-4713; ④; May–Oct), in an elegant, broadly Georgian mansion with shutters, fanlight and Neoclassical columns; and the *Garden Gate*, whose wide verandas and lovely garden are in a quiet part of town at 364 Montague St (☎529-4453; ④; June–Oct). The *St Andrews Motor Inn*, 111 Water St (☎529-4571; ⑤), is a spick-and-span modern motel on the seashore. The popular *Passamaquoddy Park Campground* (☎529-3439; May–Oct) has a great seaside location just over 1km east of the town centre along Water Street.

St Andrews has an excellent range of **cafés** and the occasional good **restaurant**. The *Chef's Café*, 180 Water St, offers reasonably priced fish platters as part of a wide-ranging menu and occupies an old-fashioned diner decked out with all sorts of retro bits and bobs. Nearby, the inexpensive *Gables Restaurant Bar & Patio*, 143 Water St (☎529-3440), is a funky little place, serving tasty food from its bayshore location, while the *Lobster Bay Eatery*, just along the street at no. 113 (☎529-4840), is a family-oriented restaurant offering up delicious lobsters – though many regular visitors swear by the lobsters at the *Algonquin*. For a special meal in fairly formal surroundings, head for *L'Europe Dining Room*, an expensive restaurant at 48 King St (☎529-3818).

Deer Island

Deer Island, a pocket-sized member of the Fundy archipelago, is uninspiring – its handful of ribbon villages straggling amongst low forested hills – but you do have to cross it to reach Campobello Island from the rest of New Brunswick. **Ferries to Deer Island** (summer every 30min 7am–7pm, then hourly till 9pm; less frequent in winter; 25min; free; first-come, first-served) leave from Letete on the southeast shore of Passamaquoddy Bay, 14km south of Hwy 1 (and the village of St George). They dock at the island's northern shore, from where it's 16km south to **Deer Island–Campobello ferry** (late June to mid-Sept 6–7 daily; 35min; car & driver $13, foot passengers $2; ☎747-2159; first-come, first-served). Ferries also sail from this jetty to Maine's Eastport (late June to mid-Sept, hourly 9am–7pm; 20min). Metres from the jetty, at the southern tip of the island, is **Deer Island Point Park**, which overlooks a narrow sound where it's sometimes possible to hear the whirlpool known as the Old Sow. It's caused by the Fundy tides as they sweep round the island and is at its peak three hours before high tide. There's a well-appointed seashore **campsite** in the park (☎747-2423; June–Sept).

Campobello Island

Franklin D. Roosevelt loved **Campobello Island**, 16km long by 5km wide, for its quiet wooded coves, rocky headlands, and excellent fishing. Those sleepy days are long gone, but although the island is now sprinkled with second homes and busy with day-trippers – who come here by ferry from Deer Island (see opposite) or over the bridge from Lubec in Maine – the southern half is protected as the **Roosevelt Campobello International Park**. Here, mixed forests, marshes, tidal flats, beaches and gullies are explored by 24km of gravel road, which gives access to a variety of gentle hiking trails. Several of these – including the enjoyable, 1.5-kilometre-long walk over to Friar's Head – begin beside the island's star turn, the red and green **Roosevelt Cottage** (late May to mid-Oct daily 10am–6pm; free), set amongst the woods by the seashore about 3km south of the ferry dock. One look at the place and you'll see that "cottage" is an understatement – it's a 35-room mansion built in a Dutch colonial style and packed with memorabilia, from the great man's childhood potty to the Christmas list he made when he was knee-high and the megaphone with which the children were summoned to dinner. It was at the cottage in 1921 that Roosevelt contracted polio and, poignantly, the stretcher on display was the one used to carry him off the island.

Campobello is easily seen in a day, but if you decide to stay the night head for *Lupine Lodge* (☎752-2555; ②–⑤; June–Oct), whose delightful log cabins, with their Art Deco lines, occupy a clearing in the woods, in sight of the sea about 500m north of Roosevelt Cottage. The lodge itself dates from 1915 and holds a first-class restaurant.

Grand Manan Island

Poking into the Bay of Fundy, **Grand Manan Island**, 30km from tip to toe, has a scattered population of around 2500, who are largely dependent on fishing and tourism. The ferry arrives at the tiny settlement of **North Head**, from where footpaths lead to the cliffs of the truncated north shore and its brace of lighthouses. The main road begins at North Head too, then slips down the east coast past rocky coves and harbours to reach the main settlement, **Grand Harbour**, where tourist information is available at the museum (mid-June to Sept; ☎662-3442). En route, a rougher road cuts west across the island to the ninety-metre sea cliffs and battered beach of **Dark Harbour**, famous for its dulse (edible seaweed) and periwinkles. Marking the island's southern tip are yet more precipitous sea cliffs and a third lighthouse. Grand Manan has long been noted for its sea birds – the celebrated naturalist and painter, John James Audubon, visited in 1831 – and puffins, gannets, guillemots, stormy petrels and kittiwakes are just some of the three hundred species that gather in their thousands on the coastal cliffs. The best bird-watching times are in the spring migratory period (early April to early June), the summer nesting season and during the autumn migration (late Aug through Sept).

To get to Grand Manan, catch the car **ferry from Blacks Harbour**, 10km from Hwy 1 between St Andrews and Saint John (July & Aug 6–7 daily; Sept–June 3 daily; 1hr 30min–2hr; foot passengers $8.75 return, cars $26.20; ☎662-3724). Spaces are allocated on a first-come, first-served basis and you should be prepared for lengthy delays in July and August. Amongst a number of Grand Manan boat-tour companies, Sea Watch Tours (☎662-8552), based in the south part of the island at Seal Cove, offer bird-watching trips from mid-June to August and whale-watching from mid-July to mid-September – expect to pay $45 per adult per trip. North Head's Adventure High Sea Kayaking (reservations required: ☎662-3563 or 1-800/732-5492) organizes guided excursions and also does **bike rental**.

For **accommodation**, Grand Manan has a handful of inns as well as a wide selection of B&Bs and cottages, but things still get tight in the height of the summer, when advance booking is recommended. In North Head, good choices include the 15-room *Marathon Inn* (☎662-8144; ③; May–Oct), a grand Victorian mansion overlooking the harbour, and the arty *Aristotle's Lantern B&B* (☎662-3788; ②; June–Sept). Another tempting option is *McLaughlin's Wharf Inn* (☎662-8760; ③; June–Sept), which occupies a converted post office at Seal Cove on the southern shore.

Saint John

At first sight **SAINT JOHN** seems a confusing hotchpotch of industrial and residential zones spread over the bluffs, valleys and plateaus where the Saint John River twists and turns its way into the Bay of Fundy, 100km southeast of Fredericton. In fact, the downtown area is squeezed onto a chubby peninsula immediately east of the river mouth – a surprisingly compact centre for a city of 130,000 people with the focus firmly on the short main drag, **King Street**. In 1877 a fire wiped out most of the town, but as a major shipbuilding centre Saint John was sufficiently wealthy to withstand the costs of immediate reconstruction. Consequently, almost all the city's older buildings – at their most resplendent along and around **Prince William Street** – are late Victorian. Most of the shipyards have now gone and the place survives as a modest seaport and manufacturing town – hence the belching chimneys – with a good range of restaurants. Apart from its diverting Victorian architecture, Saint John's leading attractions are the **New Brunswick Museum** and the **Reversing Falls Rapids**; the latter is a good place to see the effects of the Fundy tides. The town's most famous son is Donald Sutherland; its most celebrated product, Moosehead beer.

Arrival, information and city transport

Saint John **bus station**, 300 Union St at Carmarthen, ten-minutes' walk east of Market Slip, is where SMT buses arrive from – and depart to – all of New Brunswick's major settlements. There are no **rail** services to Saint John; the nearest you'll get is Moncton. Saint John's **ferry terminal**, 5km west of the centre across the mouth of the Saint John River, is served by Bay Ferries (☎649-7777 or 1-888/249-7245), who sail across Bay of Fundy to Digby, in Nova Scotia (Jan to late June & mid-Oct to Dec 1–2 daily; late June to mid-Oct 2–3 daily; 3hr; passengers $25–30 single, cars $55–60, bicycles $15–20). There are no buses direct to the centre from the terminal – take a waiting cab or call Saint John Taxi (☎648-8888). **Driving** into downtown Saint John can be a baffling experience; the easiest route is to keep on Hwy 1 and follow the signs from Exit 111. The main **tourist office** is right in the centre of town in the Market Square mall, beside Market Slip at the foot of King Street (daily: early June to Aug 9am–8pm; Sept to early June 9am–6pm; ☎658-2855 or 1-888/364-4444). They will help with accommodation and have a wide range of local and provincial information. This is also the best place to get the latest details of local **boat trips**, the two most appealing being jet-boat rides up the Reversing Falls Rapids (see p.384) and the Bay of Fundy whale-watching excursions. Of particular note, too, are the three excellent and free walking-tour leaflets the tourist office issues – one each for the Loyalist, Victorian merchants' and residential Victorian trails. As for **city transport**, Saint John Transit (☎658-4710) operates a reasonable range of bus services; most start and finish downtown at King's Square. The East–West

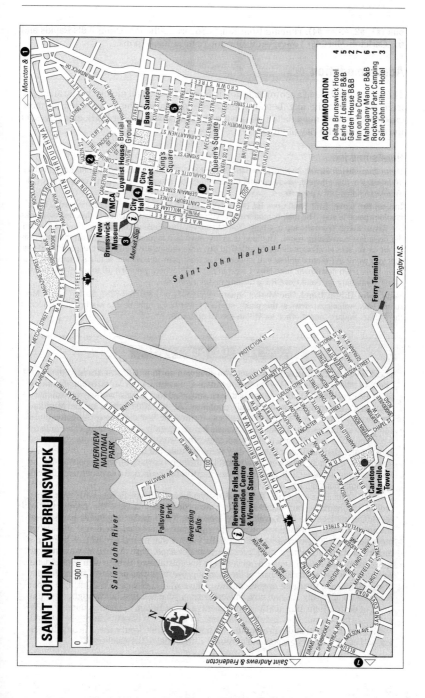

SAINT JOHN, NEW BRUNSWICK

Saint John River

Saint John Harbour

RIVERVIEW NATIONAL PARK

Fallsview Park

Reversing Falls

Fallsview Park

i Reversing Falls Rapids Information Centre & Viewing Station

Carleton Martello Tower

New Brunswick Museum

YMCA

City Hall

Loyalist House

Market Slip

King's Market

King's Square

Queen's Square

Old Loyalist Burial Ground

Bus Station

Ferry Terminal

▷ Moncton & ①

▷ Digby N.S.

▽ Saint Andrews & Fredericton

0   500 m

N

ACCOMMODATION

Delta Brunswick Hotel	4
Earle of Leinster B&B	5
Garden House B&B	2
Inn on the Cove	7
Mahogany Manor B&B	6
Rockwood Park Camping	1
Saint John Hilton Hotel	3

bus (#1, #2, #3 or #4), running from King's Square to the Reversing Falls Rapids and the Carleton Martello Tower, is the one you're most likely to use.

Accommodation

There's no shortage of **accommodation** in Saint John. Budget motels line up along the main routes into the city, but for something more interesting – and often no more expensive – you're much better off staying in a downtown hotel or B&B, or just west of the city, beside the Bay of Fundy.

Hotels and inn

Delta Brunswick Hotel, 39 King St (☎648-1981 or 1-800/268-1133, fax 658-0914). Right in the thick of downtown, this efficient, modern hotel has 250 high-rise rooms decorated in a crisp, chain style. Fitness facilities and a pool. ④.

Inn on the Cove, 1371 Sand Cove Rd (☎672-7799, fax 635-5455, *www.innonthecove.com*). This is a fabulous place to stay. The mainly modern inn, with its five ornately furnished bedrooms, overlooks the Bay of Fundy from the top of a bluff. You can survey the whole of the seashore from the splendid breakfast-cum-dining room. The food is as inventive as it is mouthwatering, with the emphasis on the freshest of local ingredients. Needless to say, reservations are pretty much essential and anyway you won't get dinner unless you've booked at least 24hr in advance. It takes about 10min to drive there from downtown: take Hwy 1 west to exit 107A, where you turn off to travel south along Bleury, watching for Sand Cove Rd, a turning on the right. ④.

Saint John Hilton Hotel, One Market Square (☎693-8484 or 1-800/561-8282, fax 657-6610). Most rooms have waterfront views at this plush, modern tower block right beside Market Slip. Check at the Market Square tourist office for Hilton special offers. ⑥.

THE LOYALISTS

The 40,000 **United Empire Loyalists** who streamed north to British Canada in the aftermath of the American War of Independence accounted for a sizeable chunk of the New England population. Many had been subjected to reprisals by their revolutionary neighbours and most arrived virtually penniless. All but 8000 settled in the Maritime provinces, where they and their descendants formed the kernel of powerful commercial and political cliques. As a result, the Loyalists have frequently – and not altogether unfairly – been pilloried as arch-conservatives, but in fact they were far from docile subjects: indeed shortly after their arrival in Canada they were pressing the British for their own elective assemblies. Crucially, they were also to instil in their new country an abiding dislike for the American version of republican democracy – and this has remained a key sentiment threading through Canadian history.

Before their enforced exile, the Loyalists conducted a fierce debate with their more radical compatriots, but whereas almost everyone today knows the names of the revolutionary leaders, the Loyalists are forgotten. The Loyalist argument had several strands – loyalty to Britain, fear of war, the righteousness of civil obedience and, rather more subliminally, the traditional English Tory belief that men are most free living in a hierarchical society where roles are clearly understood. One of their most articulate spokesmen was Daniel Leonard, who during his epistolary debate with John Adams wrote: "A very considerable part of the men of property in this province, are at this day firmly attached to the cause of government . . . [and will] . . . if they fight at all, fight under the banners of loyalty . . . And now, in God's name, what is it that has brought us to this brink of destruction? Has not the government of Great Britain . . . been a nursing mother to us? Has she not been indulgent almost to a fault?. . . Will not posterity be amazed, when they are told that the present destruction took its rise from a three penny duty on tea, and call it a more unaccountable frenzy . . . than that of the witchcraft?"

Bed and breakfasts

Earle of Leinster B&B, 96 Leinster St at Wentworth (☎652-3275, *leinster@nbnet.nb.ca*). Seven, en-suite guestrooms in a rather solemn Victorian house, in a frayed area, about 15min walk east of the Market Slip. ②.

Garden House B&B, 28 Garden St (☎646-9093, *ghouse@nbnet.nb.ca*). Comfortable, downtown B&B with just four guestrooms occupying a Victorian timber house. To get there, walk east along King, turn left at Charlotte and keep straight on to Coburg, which you follow round; Garden St is on the left. ②.

Mahogany Manor B&B, 220 Germain St at Queen (☎636-8000 or 1-800/796-7755). This is the pick of the town's B&Bs, just five en-suite guestrooms in an elegant Victorian villa with high gables and wraparound veranda. Located in a quiet, leafy part of town about 10min walk southeast of Market Slip. ③.

Campsite

Rockwood Park Campground (☎652-4050). Popular campsite located near the southern entrance of Rockwood Park about 2km east of the city centre. Take Exit 113 off Hwy 1. Late May–Sept. From $15 per-tent site with electricity.

The City

The tiny rectangular harbour at the foot of King Street, known as the **Market Slip**, witnessed one of the more dramatic Loyalist migrations, when three thousand refugees disembarked here in 1783. They were not overly impressed by their new country; one recorded that it was "the roughest land I ever saw . . . such a feeling of loneliness came over me that I sat down on the damp moss with my baby in my lap and cried". The Slip no longer functions as a port, but it's still at the heart of Saint John and is next to its most entertaining "shop" (really a museum), **Barbour's General Store** (mid-May to mid-Oct 9am–6pm), a refurbished emporium stuffed with Victorian paraphernalia from formidable-looking sweets to an old barber's chair. The opposite side of the Slip has been gentrified, the old brick wharf warehouses converted into wine bars, restaurants, and boutiques fronting the modern Market Square shopping mall behind. Inside the mall, the gleaming **New Brunswick Museum** (Mon–Wed & Fri 9am–5pm, Thurs 9am–9pm, Sat & Sun noon–5pm; $6) is devoted to the province's human, natural and artistic life and has a particularly revealing section on the Age of Sail as well as a fine collection of Chinese decorative and applied art. In addition, there's much on the region's marine life, including the skeleton of a rare North Atlantic right whale in the "Hall of Great Whales" and a thirteen-metre-high tidal tube constructed to illustrate the rise and fall of the Bay of Fundy tides.

A five-minute walk east on King Street and left along Germain, the white wooden **Loyalist House**, at 120 Union St (mid-May & June Mon–Fri 10am–5pm; July–Aug Mon–Sat 10am–5pm, Sun 1–5pm; $3), was erected in 1810 for merchant David Merritt, whose descendants lived here for six generations. Inside, the early nineteenth-century furnishings and fittings include a fine, sweeping staircase, cleverly worked curved doors, and hand-carved mouldings; costumed guides give the lowdown on Loyalist life. Just down the hill, back along Germain, is the entrance to the lively **City Market** (Mon–Thurs 7.30am–6pm, Fri 7.30am–7pm, Sat 7.30am–5pm), heaped with the characteristic foods of New Brunswick – fiddleheads, a succulent fern tip that tastes rather like asparagus, and dulse, a dried seaweed that enlivens the chowders hereabouts. Behind the market are the Union Jack paths and fanciful Edwardian bandstand of **King's Square**.

After the fire of 1877, the city's merchant class funded a rebuilding programme that would, they believed, properly reflect Saint John's status as a major seaport and shipbuilding centre. Blissfully unaware of the hard years ahead, they competed with each other in the construction of grand offices and banks, brimmingly self-confident structures that line up along **Prince William Street**, south of the Market Slip. There's an extraordinary attention to detail here, the careful symmetries of each red-brick facade patterned with individualistic designs – everything from angular stone trimmings and dog-tooth window ledges through to hieroglyphic insets and elaborately carved window arches. Amongst the predominate red-brick are the grandiose Neoclassical and Second Empire facades of the Old Post Office at no. 115, the Old City Hall at no. 116, and the Nova Scotia Bank's Palatine Building at no. 124. These finely worked stone extravagances, with their columns, pediments and arcades, were built as institutional confirmation of the city's excellent prospects. To the middle class of the time this was all in good taste, but there were limits. The Chubb building, 111 Prince William St at the corner of Princess, was – and still is – decorated by a singular series of mini-gargoyles: "We trust no more of our buildings will be adorned by such buffoonery," thundered the local newspaper.

The outskirts

Like just about every other place along the shores of the Bay of Fundy, Saint John is proud of its tides. What you have here are the **Reversing Falls Rapids**, created by a sharp bend in the Saint John River about 3km west of the centre. At low tide, the river – still some 60m deep – flows quite normally, but the incoming tide forces it into reverse, causing a brief period of equilibrium when the surface of the water is totally calm, before a churning, often tumultuous, surge upstream. You need to stick around for a couple of hours to see the complete process, and there's a **viewing station** (mid-May to mid-Oct daily 8am–8pm; free) high above the river at the far end of the bridge on Hwy 100. To get there by public transport, take the East–West transit bus (#1, #2, #3 or #4) from King's Square. The attached **information centre** shows a film telescoping a day's tidal flow into fifteen minutes. There are also a couple of mini-parks beneath the bridge where you can view the phenomenon from near the river bank – one upstream in eyeshot of the noxious paper mill, the other downstream and reached via a short, steep path from the car park. Better still, Reversing Falls Jet Boat operates **boat trips** through the Reversing Falls during the summer from their jetty near the bridge (June to mid-Oct; 30min; $28; ☎634-8987 or 1-888/634-8987).

When you've finished with the river, it's another short drive (or ride on the East–West transit bus #1, #2, #3 or #4) west via Hwy 100 to the **Carleton Martello Tower** on Fundy Drive (June to mid-Oct daily 9am–5pm; $2.50): beyond the viewing station, take the first left along Lancaster Avenue and follow the signs. This stone tower was raised as part of a projected series to protect the Fundy coast from American attack, its squat design – and that of several hundred others dotted across the empire – copied from a Corsican tower that had previously proved especially troublesome to the British navy. Completed in 1815, too late to be of much use in the struggle against the States, the tower was soon abandoned, though it was eventually recycled as a detention centre for deserters in World War I. Later still, in World War II, it became the focal point of the coastal defence system protecting Saint John harbour – hence the ungainly concrete structure plonked on top. Inside, there's a reconstruction of a nineteenth-century barrack room and displays on World War II – and splendid views over town and bay.

The tower is perched on the same headland as the ferry port beyond which – just 1km out in the bay – you'll spy **Partridge Island**, the first quarantine station in North America. A lighthouse was built on this 24-acre islet in 1791, but by the middle of the nineteenth century no fewer than thirteen hospitals had been placed here as well, with teams of doctors separating the healthy from the sick. The busiest period was during the Irish famine and a Celtic cross commemorates the many Irish who died on the island. After a hundred years, the station was closed in 1938. The island bristles with World War II ruins and holds six cemeteries, where over one thousand unfortunate would-be immigrants are buried. It's uninhabited now but there are occasional boat trips out to the island – check the tourist office for details.

Eating, drinking and nightlife

Saint John is a boisterous, lively place to **eat and drink**. A good place to start is *Reggie's*, a well-lived-in diner near the city market at 26 Germain St, which serves up superb chowders, all sorts of sandwiches, and whopping breakfasts. Alternatively, inside the market, the *Wild Carrot Café* provides wholesome snacks, and *Billy's Seafood Company* has fine fresh seafood and an oyster bar (☎672-3474). Down by the Market Slip, amongst a string of bars and cafés, the pick is *Grannan's Seafood Restaurant* (☎634-1555), where the catch of the day is a treat. For something a little spicier, try *Taco Pica*, a Mexican-Guatemalan restaurant at 96 Germain St (☎633-8492). Nearby is *Incredible Edibles*, 42 Princess St at Canterbury (☎633-7554), which has a wide-ranging menu specializing in simply prepared and thoughtfully presented seafood and vegetarian dishes. *Vito's Restaurant*, at 1 Hazen Ave at Union (☎634-3900), specializes in Greek and Italian food and *Beatty and the Beastro*, 60 Charlotte St (☎652-3888), is a café/restaurant offering crepes, pasta and seafood through to delicious New Brunswick lamb. Best of the lot, however, is *Il Fornello*, 33 Canterbury St and Church (☎648-2377), where they serve delicious, reasonably priced pizzas and pastas in an imaginatively converted old warehouse with high ceilings and oceans of wood.

After dark, the rollicking *3 Mile Pub,* 1 Golden Grove Rd (☎657-8325), northeast of the centre off Hwy 100 (Rothesay Ave) – exit onto McAllister Drive and it's the first on the left – puts on all sorts of live shows and dances but is best for C&W. More convenient is *O'Leary's*, 46 Princess St, which has draught imported and domestic beers and features live music towards the back end of the week – mostly folk, Irish or Maritime. *Tapps Brewpub*, 7 King St, the city's first microbrew pub, offers several especially tasty light ales, as well as live music Thursday to Saturday. For **performance arts**, the city's leading venue is the Imperial Theatre, a refurbished Edwardian theatre at 24 King's Square (☎674-4100).

The Fundy Coast east of Saint John

About 40km east of Saint John along Hwy 111, one of the most beautiful portions of New Brunswick's coastline has been opened up by the **Fundy Trail Parkway**, a newly created, 13km-long scenic highway that drifts along a dramatic stretch of seashore. It begins at the attractive seaside village of **St Martins**, which boasts no less than two covered bridges and where there are several first-rate places to stay. Even more beautiful and a good deal wilder – but much further east – is **Fundy National Park**, whose rugged sea cliffs, bays and coves are patterned with superb hiking trails. Highway 114 cuts a diagonal through the park, branching off the Trans-Canada about 100km east of Saint John to access its trails and campsites, before finally emerging at the seaside hamlet of **Alma**, the only sizeable settlement hereabouts and a handy spot to break your journey. If you're after visiting both the parkway and the park, allow at least a couple of days especially as the drive between the two is a time-consuming, wearying business – though there are long-term plans to build a coastal road between St Martins and Alma.

East of Alma, a lovely coastal drive passes by turnings for tide-battered **Cape Enrage**, the bird sanctuary of **Mary's Point**, and the curiously shaped **Hopewell**

Rocks on the way to workaday **Moncton**, the province's third city. Beyond Moncton, the isthmus linking New Brunswick with Nova Scotia lies beside Chignecto Bay, at the east end of the Bay of Fundy. Of brief strategic significance after the Treaty of Utrecht, with the British in control of Nova Scotia and the French in Québec, the isthmus and its surrounding shoreline have long been a sleepy backwater of tiny fishing villages and Acadian-style marshland farming, with past imperial disputes recalled by the windswept remains of **Fort Beauséjour**.

The Fundy coast is a popular holiday spot, so it's a good idea to book **accommodation** ahead of time. Also, pick up a tide table at any local tourist office – the tides rise and fall by about 9m, making a spectacular difference to the shoreline – and be prepared for patches of pea-soup fog: the Bay of Fundy is notoriously prone to them. There's **no public transport** to either St Martins or the national park.

St Martins and the Fundy Trail Parkway

The fishing village of **ST MARTINS** drizzles along the Bay of Fundy shoreline to the east of Saint John. To get there from downtown Saint John take Hwy 100 and exit at Loch Lomond Road or (and this is a much longer route) follow Hwy 1 and then Hwy 111. First impressions of the village aren't especially favourable, but things improve when you finally (after 3km) reach the harbour, a dinky affair of lobster pots and skiffs set within a ring of hills. A matching pair of covered bridges flanks the harbour and you drive through one of them for the 8km-journey east to the **Fundy Trail Parkway** ($5 per car), one of the province's most recent tourist initiatives. It works very well. The 13km-drive is a pleasurable jaunt along the seashore, threading past craggy headlands, and the road is shadowed by a multiuse trail that offers fine and comparatively easy hiking as well as access to several beaches. The Parkway ends at the **Salmon River Interpretive Centre** (currently mid-May to mid-Oct daily 8am–8pm; ☎833-2019), whose exhibits provide lots of details about the Parkway and give the historical lowdown on the lumber town of Big Salmon River, whose inhabitants packed up shop in the 1940s; the centre is actually built on the site of an old bunkhouse. From the centre, you can stroll down the hillside to the river below or negotiate the steep ninety-minute hike up into the hills to the hunting and fishing **lodge** built here by the Hearsts – as of newspaper fame – in the 1960s. The Interpretive Centre will advise on routes and conditions.

Exploring the Parkway takes time – a day is about long enough – which means you'll need to overnight in St Martins. **Accommodation** here includes several good options, most notably the first-rate *St Martins Country Inn* (☎833-4534 or 1-800/565-5257; ④; April–Dec), whose high Victorian gables and fancy gingerbread scrollwork overlook Hwy 111 (but not the shore). A good, second best – and it's cheaper – is the *Village B&B*, also in a Victorian house and with three comfortable guestrooms (☎833-1893 or 1-877/833-1893; ②; May–Oct).

The provincial government plans to bulldoze a link along the coast from St Martins to the national park (see below) in the next few years, but in the meantime you're stuck with a long, looping drive inland (along Hwy 111 and Hwy 114).

Fundy National Park

Bisected by Hwy 114, **Fundy National Park** encompasses a short stretch of the Bay of Fundy shoreline, all jagged cliffs and tidal mud flats, and the forested hills, lakes and river valleys of the central plateau behind. This varied scenery is crossed by more than 100km of hiking trails, mostly short and easy walks taking no more than three hours to complete – though the 45-kilometre Fundy Circuit links several of the interior trails and takes between three and five days. The pick of the hiking trails are, however, along the

Fundy shore and it's here you'll find the spectacular Point Wolfe Beach trail, a moderately steep, 300-metre hike down from the wooded headlands above the bay to the beach below. Of equal appeal is the 4.5-kilometre loop of the Coppermine trail, which meanders through the forests with breathtaking views out along the seashore.

All the park's trails are described in a free booklet issued on arrival at either of the two Hwy 114 **entrance kiosks** – one at the west entrance near Lake Wolfe, about 20km south of the Trans-Canada (mid-May to mid-June & early Sept to early Oct daily 10am–5.45pm; mid-June to early Sept Mon–Thurs 10am–5.45pm, Fri–Sun 8am–7.45pm); the other about 20km to the east, on the coast next door to Alma (same details). In addition, there is a **visitors centre** (mid-May to mid-June & early Sept to early Oct Mon–Fri 8am–4.30pm, Sat–Sun 9am–5pm; mid-June to early Sept daily 8am–10pm; ☎887-6000) on Hwy 114 near the east entrance. The visitors centre features displays on local flora and fauna, organizes guided walks, issues backcountry permits and sells hiking maps and trail descriptions. Entrance to the park costs $3.50 per adult from mid-May to early October, but is free the rest of the year. The park is well equipped for **camping**, with two serviced ($19) and two unserviced ($11–13) campsites as well as a string of backcountry sites ($3). The serviced grounds largely operate on a first-come, first-served basis, though reservations are taken for a minority of sites at ☎1-800/414-6765. Backcountry sites require reservations with the visitors centre. You can either take pot luck and register on arrival or ring ahead, which is certainly the better option in July and August. Both serviced campsites – *Chignecto North* (mid-May to early Oct) and *Headquarters* (mid-June to Aug; unserviced rest of year) – plus one of the unserviced campsites, *Chignecto South*, are located near the east entrance (close to Alma) along with most of the park's tourist facilities. For a greater degree of isolation, take the ten-kilometre byroad southwest from the visitors centre to **Point Wolfe**, where a medium-sized, unserviced campsite (late June to Aug) is tucked in amongst the wooded hills above the coast – and near the starting point of the Point Wolfe Beach and Coppermine trails.

If you're after a roof over your head, there are a couple of modern **chalet** complexes just inside the park near the visitors centre. These are *Fundy Park Chalets* (☎887-2808; ②; May–Oct) and the marginally more comfortable – and air conditioned – *Caledonia Highland Inn & Chalets* (☎887-2930; ③; May–Oct). In both, the rooms come with kitchenettes. There's also an extremely basic **youth hostel** (☎887-2216, *fundhost@nbnet.nb.ca*; $10; mid-May to mid-Oct) on Devil's Half Acre Road, some 2km from the Alma information centre. Hidden away amongst the woods, the hostel overlooks the bay and its beds are in simple cabins. Much more enticing accommodation is, however, on offer at Alma.

East of Fundy National Park: Alma and Cape Enrage to the Hopewell Rocks

Across the Salmon River from the east entrance to the national park is **ALMA**, a pleasant little village whose 300 inhabitants make a tidy living from fishing, farming and tourism. All Alma's facilities are clustered on a short stretch of its Main Street including several **motels** and **hotels**. The pick is the trim *Captain's Inn B&B* (☎887-2017, fax 887-2074; ③) with nine cosy and homely rooms. There is also the spick-and-span, bayshore *Alpine Motor Inn* (☎ & fax 887-2052; ②; May–Sept) and the two-storey, motel-like *Parkland Village Inn* (☎887-2313; ③; April–Oct). **Food** is a bit of a problem, but the *Parkland* has a (just about) competent restaurant – stick to the simpler dishes; *Kelly's Bake Shop* is well-known for its sticky buns; enormous, delicious things that look rather like brains.

On the east edge of Alma, Hwy 915 branches off Hwy 114 to stick close to the coast, threading over the hills and along the valley past isolated farmsteads sheltering behind rugged sea-cliffs. Here and there the coast comes into view – wide vistas of beach and cliff – but the most dramatic scenery is at **Cape Enrage**, 6km down a side road off Hwy 915, where the lighthouse is glued to a great shank of rock soaring high above the sea. It's actually quite remarkable that you can drive down to the cape at all. When the light-house was automated in 1988, the keepers moved away, abandoning their old house to the elements. Offended by the neglect, a Moncton schoolteacher – from Harrison Trimble High – initiated an ambitious plan to protect and develop the site with the enthusiastic help of his students. In the last five years, they've transformed the place. There's now a wooden walkway up to the foot of the lighthouse and the old keepers' house has been converted into a pleasant café – try the fish chowder. The students staff the cape in the summer and help run a programme of adventurous pursuits, principally sea-kayaking (May–Oct; 4hr; $50) and rappelling (May–Oct; 2–3hr; $40); bookings on ☎887-2273, *dktate@nbnet.nb.ca*.

Mary's Point bird reserve, Harvey and Riverside-Albert
Doubling back to Hwy 915, it's a short drive east to the two country lanes that lead to **Mary's Point bird reserve** – though only the second turning is currently signposted; the two lanes connect to form a (partly gravel) 6km-long loop off Hwy 915. Mary's Point is the prettiest of headlands, a varied terrain of forest, beach, marsh and mud flat that attracts thousands of migrating shorebirds on their way south from the Arctic in the late summer. The migration begins in July and continues through until early October, depending on the age of the particular bird and the species. Of all the birds, it's the semipalmated sandpiper that attracts most attention, a small grey and white creature with black bill and legs. They appear in late July and peak in the first two weeks of August, tearing round in formation, the greyish white of their undersides flashing in the sun. They can't swim, so the best time to see them – and it is an extraordinary sight – is a couple of hours either side of high tide when they fly closest to the shore. The reserve's **information office** (☎882-2544) will advise on what birds are around and when best to see them. Even if the birds are gone, Mary's Point makes for some delightful walking with a network of footpaths running down from the information office to explore its nooks and crannies.

If you're after **accommodation** hereabouts, the minuscule hamlet of **HARVEY** – at the junction of Hwy 915 and the more easterly lane to Mary's Point – has two good options, beginning with the *Sandpiper's Rest B&B* (☎882-2744, *marshsp@nbnet.nb.ca*; ②; May–Sept), in an appealing nineteenth-century cottage and with three guestrooms – one en suite. The other recommendation is the *Florentine Manor* (☎882-2271 or 1-800/665-2271, *florainn@nbnet.nb.ca*; ③), a large Victorian house set in its own grounds and with period furnishings. The manor has nine guestrooms, all en suite.

Some 3km north of Harvey, Hwy 915 rejoins Hwy 114 and at the crossroads is the local **tourist office** (☎882-2015), distinctively housed in the old bank building, a Victorian extravagance that comes complete with its original vault and wickets. The tourist office marks the start of **RIVERSIDE-ALBERT**, an elongated village that trails along the bayshore for several kilometres. There's a good place to stay here too – the *Cailswick Babbling Brook B&B* (☎882-2079, *cailsbb@nb.sympatico.ca*; ②), in an older house set in its own grounds beside Hwy 114.

The Cape Hopewell Rocks
Beyond Riverside-Albert, Hwy 114 travels east passing through farmland and offering attractive views of headlands and tidal flats on its way to Hopewell Cape, where the Petitcodiac River flows into the bay. The cape is the site of the red-sandstone **Hopewell Rocks** (daily: mid-May to mid-June & mid-Aug to early Oct 9am–5pm; mid-June to mid-Aug 8am–8pm; $4.25), gnarled pinnacles rising up to 15m above the beach and snared within a coastal park – formally an Ocean Tidal Exploration Site – that attracts too many

visitors for its own good. The interpretive centre explains the cape's geological where-withal and the marine complexities of the Bay of Fundy, but you'll soon be wandering down the footpath – past several vantage points – to the rocks. The rocks were pushed away from the cliff face by glacial pressure during the Ice Age, and the Bay of Fundy tides have defined their present, eccentric shape. At high tide they resemble stark lit-tle islands covered in fir trees, but at low tide look like enormous termite hills. Steps lead down to the beach and you can safely walk round the rocks two to three hours either side of low tide, or you can paddle round them at high tide by hiring a kayak for a nominal fee.

From the Hopewell Rocks, it's 50km along the west bank of the Petitcodiac River to Moncton.

Moncton

MONCTON, 90km from Alma, was named after Colonel Robert Monckton [sic], though the Acadians had originally called the place *Le Coude* ("the elbow"), which at least hinted at its setting on a sharp bend of the Petitcodiac River. Indeed, the river pro-vides Moncton with its most singular attraction, the tidal bore, which sweeps up from the Bay of Fundy, 35km downstream. Otherwise, Moncton is a minor commercial cen-tre and major transport junction surrounded by marshy flatlands. This may sound unpromising, but the downtown area has recently been spruced up and there are now enough good restaurants and hotels to make an overnight stay enjoyable, and the town is a convenient stop on the journey between Fundy National Park and PEI's Confederation Bridge. Moncton's rejuvenation partly reflects the increasing confidence of local Acadians: the town hosts the province's only French-speaking university and is proud of its bilingualism – the result of Acadian ex-deportees settling here in the 1790s.

Moncton's **tidal bore** is a wave that varies from a few centimetres to a metre in height, depending on weather conditions and the phase of the moon. At low tide you'll be in no doubt as to why the locals called the Petitcodiac the "chocolate river" – but the mud flats disappear after the bore arrives, when the river level rises by up to 8m. Tiny **Tidal Bore Park**, downtown at Main and King streets, has information plaques on the tide times and a small grandstand so you can watch the phenomenon in comfort. If you are so inclined, you could also visit the **Crystal Palace Amusement Park** (☎859-4386), on Paul Street just east of downtown in the suburb of Dieppe, which features everything from an indoor roller coaster to virtual-reality games.

Practicalities

Moncton's **bus station** is about 1km west of Tidal Bore Park, at 961 Main St. SMT buses arrive here from most major settlements in New Brunswick and they also operate two buses daily to and from PEI's Charlottetown; SMT and Acadian Bus Lines combine to link Moncton with Halifax in Nova Scotia. Moncton's **train station** is near-by – behind the Eaton Centre, a couple of blocks further west along Main Street – with services running to Halifax and Montréal. Moncton's main **tourist office** is in the gleamingly modern City Hall, at 655 Main St (Sept–May Mon–Fri 9am–5pm; June–Aug 8.30am–8pm; ☎853-3590). They'll book accommodation for no charge, provide free city maps and give information on forthcoming events.

Moncton has a good supply of convenient **accommodation**. Amongst several down-town **hotels**, the *Delta Beauséjour*, at 750 Main St (☎854-4344 or 1-800/268-1133; ④), is the most lavish, a big modern high-rise bang in the middle of town, though the motel-style rooms of the much more modest *Rodd Parkhouse Inn*, beside Tidal Bore Park at 434 Main St (☎382-1664 or 1-800/565-7633; ③), are perfectly adequate if rather routine. Alternatively, several pleasant **B&Bs** are dotted amongst the leafy residential avenues to the north of Main Street. The pick of the bunch is the *Bonaccord House*, 250 Bonaccord

St (☎388-1535, fax 853-7191; ②), north of the bus station in an attractive Victorian villa with picket fence and portico. A good reserve is the gracious *Park View,* beside the park to the north of Main Street's Eaton Centre at 254 Cameron St (☎382-4504; ②).

For **food**, *Le Château à Pape*, 2 Steadman St (☎855-7273), serves the finest of Acadian cuisine from its premises in a big old house a couple of minutes' walk west along the river bank from Tidal Bore Park. Less expensive places include *Rye's Deli & Pub*, 785 Main St, where the bagels and the daily specials are excellent, and the *Café Robinson*, off Main Street at 187 Robinson St, for quality snacks and coffee. *Jean's Diner*, 369 St George St, about three blocks north of Main Street, is worth a trip at lunch time for its clams. **Bars** throng the centre – try the popular *Pump House Brewpub*, at 7 Orange Lane, just off Main Street a few metres east of City Hall.

Fort Beauséjour

Stuck on a grassy treeless hill, with the wide sweep of Chignecto Bay and its flattened foreshore in full view, **Fort Beauséjour National Historic Site** (June to mid-Oct daily 9am–5pm; $2.50) lies about 50km south of Moncton, just 2km from the junction of Trans-Canada Hwy 2 – to Nova Scotia – and TCH 16 to PEI. The French built the first fort here in 1750 to inhibit incursions from the south, but after a two-week siege in 1755 it fell into the hands of the British, who refortified the site initially to deter resistance from the local Acadian population, and later – until its abandonment in 1835 – as a defence against the Americans. Flush with the brow of the hill, the remains of the star-shaped fort include much of the original earthwork, the concentric ditches and mounds typical of the period, as well as a sally port and a couple of deeply recessed casements, used for general storage. The site also has a delightful **museum** with excellent displays on the history of the fort and of the Acadian farmers who settled the region in the 1670s – some of the most interesting exhibits, like ancient clogs and farm tools, were recovered when the fort was repaired and restored in the 1960s. The Acadians enclosed and drained the marshes below the fort to produce hay, grain crops and vegetables – and the lines of their dykes and ditches are still visible from the hill.

The Saint John River Valley

The **Saint John River Valley** between Fredericton and **Edmundston**, a distance of 275km, is not consistently beautiful but does have its moments, when it slips through maple and pine forests or, to the north, where its low-lying hills and farmland are finally replaced by more mountainous, heavily forested terrain. The valley towns, dotted along the Trans-Canada, are not especially memorable, but the restored pioneer village of **King's Landing** is first-rate and well worth at least a couple of hours, as is the waterfall at **Grand Falls**.

SMT operates a twice-daily **bus** between Fredericton and Edmundston, with services continuing on to Québec City and Montréal.

King's Landing

Some 25km west of Fredericton on the Trans-Canada lies the **Mactaquac Dam**, part of a hydroelectric project whose reservoir stretches 75km up the valley. **King's Landing Historical Settlement** (June to mid-Oct daily 10am–5pm; $10), 10km west of the dam, exists because of the project. Making a virtue of necessity, several nineteenth-century buildings were carefully relocated to form the nucleus of a fictitious agricultural community as of 1850. Further judicious purchases added to the housing stock and, supplemented by a handful of replicas, there are now no less than thirty buildings spread out amidst the delightful waterside woods and fields. Like similar reconstructions, King's Landing aims to provide a total experience to its visitors, with its "inhabitants" engaged in bread-making, horseshoeing, logging, milling, weaving, cattle-driving, and so on. Perhaps it is a bit daft, but it all works very well and several of the buildings are fascinating in their own right – particularly the Jones House, a stone dwelling built into the hillside in a manner typical of this area; the Ingraham House, once the property of a well-to-do farmer; and the fully operational sawmill.

Hartland and Grand Falls

Surrounded by forest, **HARTLAND**, some 90km from King's Landing, advertises itself exclusively on the size of its **wooden bridge**, which at 391m is by far the longest covered bridge in the world. It was completed in 1901, the idea being to protect the timbers of the bridge from the elements by means of a long shed-like affair built in the manner of a barn. It's not graceful – but it is long.

North of Hartland, the scenery changes as the maples give way to the beginning of a great undulating belt of potato fields. This is really dreary, but a surprise lies in store at **GRAND FALLS**, 105km from Hartland. Here, right in the centre of an otherwise nondescript town, a spectacular weight of water squeezes through hydroelectric barriers to crash down a 23-metre pitch. Even if the diversion of water through nearby turbines has deprived the falls of their earlier vigour, they're still impressive, as is the two-kilometre gorge they've carved downstream, a steep-sided ravine encircling half the town. There are two short walks into the gorge: one leads to near the base of the falls themselves, the other to the bottom of the gorge, where, amid the pounding of the water and the sheer faces of the rock, it's hard to believe you're still in the middle of town.

There's nothing else to see in Grand Falls, and the **visitors centre** on the bridge (☎475-7788) is preoccupied with the river too, though it does have a mildly diverting section outlining the history of the town. If you're marooned, there's straightforward **accommodation** right by the gorge (and its waterfall) at the *Hill Top Motel*, 131 Madawaska Rd (☎473-2684 or 1-800/496-1244; ②).

Edmundston

Lying at the confluence of the Saint John and Madawaska rivers, wood-pulping **EDMUNDSTON** is the largest town in the north of New Brunswick, with a population of nearly twelve thousand. It's a brash, modern place, where a profusion of flashing neon signs proclaim the proximity of the USA, which lies just over the biggest of the town's three bridges. Edmundston is mainly French-speaking and, curiously, regards itself as the capital of the enclave known as the **Republic of Madawaska**, the snout-shaped tract of Canadian territory jutting out into the state of Maine. While the idea of an independent state here is preposterous, the "Republic" is more than a publicity stunt: it signifies the frustration of a people over whom the British and Americans haggled for thirty years until 1842, and who still feel ignored by Fredericton. Yet the town packages the Republic frivolously, with Ruritanian touches such as a coat of arms, a flag, honorary knights and a president (otherwise the mayor).

There's a seasonal **tourist office** (☎737-6766) adjoining the municipal museum just off the Trans-Canada (Exit 18) at the top of Boulevard Hébert, which runs downtown. SMT **buses** pull in at 169 Victoria St, just off Boulevard Hébert before the Fournier Bridge over the Madawaska River into the town centre. For downtown **accommodation**, head for the standard-issue comforts of the *Howard Johnson Hotel*, 100 Rice St (☎739-7321 or 1-800/654-2000; ④). Another, much cheaper option is the simple *Hotel Praga*, near the marina at 127 Victoria St (☎735-5567; ②).

The Miramichi Valley

Running northeast of Fredericton, Hwy 8 traverses the **Miramichi River Valley**, passing endless stands of timber en route to the **City of Miramichi**, an amalgamation of the six tiny logging ports that flank the mouth of the river – and amongst which **Newcastle** is easily the most diverting. The 180-kilometre trip takes three to four hours, longer if you pause at the one sight of any real interest, the Woodmen's Museum in **Boiestown**. The river valley is, however, much more famous for its salmon fishing, which draws anglers from all over the world. The season begins anywhere between April and July, depending on the waters to be fished, and every angler has to buy a licence, with nonresidents charged between $30 and $110. A veritable raft of regulations controls the sport but any local tourist office will have the details. The other big deal hereabouts is the **Miramichi Folksong Festival** (☎622-1780), held over five days in early August in Miramichi City and generally reckoned to be one of the best of its kind, with fiddle music its forte. Look out for two big local names, Ned Landry and Winston Crawford.

SMT **buses** ply Hwy 8 once daily, and at Chatham (part of Miramichi City) there are connecting services north to Montréal and south to Moncton.

Boiestown and Doaktown

Some 70km north of Fredericton, **BOIESTOWN** was once a rowdy loggers' settlement whose drunken "goings-on" inspired the region's balladeers – "If you're longing for fun and enjoyment, or inclined to go out on a spree, come along with me to Boiestown, on the banks of the Miramichi". The **Woodmen's Museum**, beside Hwy 8 (May–Sept daily 9am–5pm; $5), recalls these rougher days beginning with a pair of large huts jam-packed with loggers' artefacts, from all sorts of strange-looking tools to fascinating photographs of the men floating the logs downstream. There are more intimate exhibits too: the loggers collected resin from spruce trees, chewed it until it was smooth and sweet and then placed it in "gumbooks", a couple of which are on display, to give to their kids back home. After the huts, it only takes a few minutes to wander the rest of the site, where there's an incidental assortment of old lumber-industry buildings, including a sawmill, pitsaw, an earthy bunkhouse and cookhouse, and a fire tower. For some obscure reason, an old and well-built fur-trapper's cabin has ended up here as well, and a small train, the *Whooper* ($2), runs round the edge of the museum.

DOAKTOWN, 20km further down the valley, is a favourite spot for fishermen, who congregate here to catch the **Atlantic salmon** as it struggles up the Miramichi, one of its major spawning rivers, on the last leg of its complex life cycle. Early each spring, thousands of tiny Atlantic salmon emerge from pea-sized orange eggs deposited in the riverbed the previous autumn. These young fish – or **fry** – soon acquire dark markings and are then known as **parr**. The parr remain in the river for two to six years (determined by water temperature and the availability of insects and other aquatic food) before a springtime transformation when their internal systems adapt for saltwater life and they turn silver, becoming **smolt**. It seems that the odours of the smolt's native river are imprinted in its memory before it heads out to sea, to be recalled when it returns to spawn. Some fish, the **grilse**, return to spawn after a year, but the majority, the salmon, swim back after two years or more, entering the Miramichi between April and November and weighing anywhere between 4kg and 20kg. Once they're back in the fresh water, the salmon stop feeding and their bodies deteriorate in favour of egg or sperm production, with the male developing a hooked lower jaw or kype. After they spawn in late autumn, the adults (now known as **kelt**, or black salmon) return to the ocean to begin the cycle again – unlike their Pacific cousins, all of whom die after their first and only spawning. Incidentally, the kelt are nowhere near as tasty as the smolt. Doaktown's **Atlantic Salmon Museum** (daily: early June to Sept 9am–5pm; $4; ☎365-7787), beside Hwy 8, illustrates the salmon's arduous life cycle, has a small aquarium, and looks at different fishing techniques – but you're much better off having a go at fishing yourself: there are lots of outfitters and guides in and around town; ask for information at the museum.

Newcastle and around

Now incorporated within the City of Miramichi, the old shipbuilding centre of **NEW-CASTLE** sits on the north bank of the Miramichi River as it nears the sea. Its compact centre is cheered by a pleasant little park at **Ritchie Wharf** and by the trim town square which, with its Italian gazebo and English garden seats, was spruced up at the whim of local-lad-made-good Max Aitken, otherwise Lord Beaverbrook, whose bust sits in the square too. There's nothing much else to the place, but it is a convenient stopping point on the long drive north to Québec's Gaspé Peninsula (see p.280) and there are a handful of reasonable **places to stay**. These include the modern, motel-like *Wharf Inn*, near the bridge at 1 Jane St (☎622-0302 or 1-800/563-2489; ④), and the *Comfort Inn*, 201 Edward St (☎622-1215 or 1-800/228-5150; ③). Alternatively, across the river from Newcastle in **NELSON**, the *Governor's Mansion B&B* (☎622-3036 or 1-877/647-2642, *govnorin@nbnet.nb.ca*; ②) occupies a handsome Victorian villa that was once the Lieutenant-Governors residence. The mansion is graced by antique furnishings and holds eight guestrooms on the two upper floors. The *Wharf Inn*'s **restaurant** offers a reasonable range of seafood and meat dishes. If you're in town for the Miramichi Folksong Festival (see opposite), the **visitors centre**, in the Lighthouse on Ritchie Wharf (mid-May to early Sept daily 9am–6pm; ☎623-2152), has gig details.

Kouchibouguac National Park

From Chatham on the eastern edge of Miramichi City, Hwy 11 slices southeast across the interior for the 50km trip to the coastal forests, bogs, salt marshes, lagoons and sandy beaches of the **Kouchibouguac** ("Koo-she-boo-gwack") **National Park**. Near the park's main entrance (mid-May to early Oct admission $3.50 per person, otherwise free) is the **visitors centre** (daily: June–Aug 8am–8pm; late May & Sept to mid-Oct 9am–5pm; ☎876-2443), where displays explore the area's complex ecology and the habits of some of its rarer inhabitants. From here, it's a few kilometres' drive, past the trailheads of several short woodland walks, to the turning down to the sandy expanse of **Kellys beach** – the park's main attraction. The seawater here is, you're assured, the warmest north of Virginia, with temperatures between 18°C and 24°C. Further on, past the turning, there's a restaurant as well as bike, kayak and canoe rental at seasonal **Ryans Rental Centre** (☎876-3733), on the south bank of the Kouchibouguac River. Just upriver is the trailhead of the longest track, the 13-kilometre **Kouchibouguac River Trail**, which wriggles west along the river bank passing one of the park's few wilderness campsites. Hikers have to use the same trail in both directions and the whole excursion takes at least six hours, but check trail conditions at the visitors centre before you set out – superactive beavers have closed the trail on several recent occasions. Another much shorter option is the 800m Cedar Trail loop, which offers wide views over salt marshes, lagoons and dunes. Hikers should on no account forget the insect repellent.

The park has two serviced and three wilderness **campsites**. One of the wilderness campsites is open all year, the rest are seasonal. Easily the biggest serviced campsite is the *South Kouchibouguac* (mid-May to mid-Oct), near Ryans Rental Centre. The park fills up fast, so either arrive early in the day or take advantage of the reservation system (☎876-1277). If you're not camping, the park is easily visited on a day-trip from Newcastle, or you can stay in one of the settlements nearby. The modern *Habitant Restaurant and Motel,* 213 Main St (☎523-4421 or 1-888/442-7222; ③), is located in **RICHIBUCTO**, a short drive south of the park entrance on Hwy 134 – take Exit 64.

The Acadian Peninsula

The **Acadian Peninsula**, which protrudes some 130km into the Gulf of St Lawrence in the northeast corner of New Brunswick, is promoted as a part of the province where the twentieth century has yet to gain a foothold. For the Acadians who fled here to avoid the deportations, the isolation was a life-saver, and more than anywhere else in the Maritimes this is where they have maintained their traditional way of life, based on fishing and marshland farming – though frankly there's precious little actually to see: the countryside is uniformly dull and the ribbon villages are hardly enticing. The mundane port of **Caraquet**, on the north shore, serves as the peninsula's cultural focus and is the best base for a visit to the replica **Village Historique Acadien**, the one sight of any note.

Caraquet

Heading east from the mining town of Bathurst, Hwy 11 bobs along the Acadian Peninsula's northern shore, trimming the edge of the rolling countryside before reaching, after about 60km, the district's pride and joy, the **Village Historique Acadien** (daily: June to early Sept 10am–6pm; mid-Sept to mid-Oct 10am–5pm; $10). This holds around forty old Acadian buildings relocated from other parts of New Brunswick – only the church was built specifically for the village. Costumed "inhabitants" emphasize the struggles of the early settlers and demonstrate traditional agricultural techniques as well as old methods of spinning, cooking and so on – all in a rustic setting. Another section focuses on the early years of the twentieth century with a hotel and train station amongst a modest assortment of urban buildings. From the historic village, it's a further 11km east on Hwy 11 to **CARAQUET**, a fishing port that was founded by Acadian fugitives in 1758 and now straggles along the seafront for some 13km. It may not be much to look at, but Caraquet does have one or two sights, beginning with the **Musée Acadien de Caraquet**, at 15 Blvd St-Pierre East/Hwy 145 (June–Aug Mon–Sat 10am–8pm, Sun 1–6pm; $3), which chronicles the hardships of those early settlers and has a small gallery devoted to the work of local artists. At the west end of town, there's also the shrine of **Ste-Anne-du-Bocage** built to commemorate the founding families' trials and tribulations. Caraquet is the setting for the region's most important **Acadian Festival** (☎727-6515), a ten-day programme of music and theatre held in early August, which begins with the blessing of the fishing fleet by a local bishop.

Amongst several simple and inexpensive **motels**, **inns** and **B&Bs** in Caraquet, the pick is the *Hotel Paulin,* 143 Blvd St-Pierre West (☎727-9981; ④), a comfortable, quaintly decorated little place that also offers genuine Acadian meals – the pea soup is a treat – on request. A second, less expensive choice is *Le Pignon Rouge,* a B&B at 338 Blvd St-Pierre East (☎727-5983; ②).

PRINCE EDWARD ISLAND

The freckly face and pert pigtails of Anne of Green Gables are emblazoned on much of **PRINCE EDWARD ISLAND**'s publicity material, and her creator, local-born novelist Lucy Maud Montgomery, was the island's most gushing propagandist, depicting the place floating "on the waves of the blue gulf, a green seclusion and haunt of ancient peace . . . invested with a kind of fairy grace and charm". Radical William Cobbett, who soldiered here in the 1780s, was not so dewy-eyed, and saw instead "a rascally heap of sand, rock and swamp . . . a lump of worthlessness [that] bears nothing but potatoes". Each had a point. The economy may not be quite as uniform as Cobbett suggested, but PEI does remain thoroughly agricultural – Million-Acre Farm, as it's sometimes called. On the other hand, the country's smallest province – a crescent-shaped slice of land separated from Nova Scotia and New Brunswick by the Northumberland Strait – can be beguiling. The island's long and complicated shoreline is banded by sandy beaches in the north and serrated by dozens of bays and estuaries, where the ruddy soils and grassy tones of the rolling countryside are set beautifully against the blue of the sea.

Charlottetown, the capital and only significant settlement, sits on the south coast beside one of these inlets, the tree-lined streets of the older part of town occupying a chunky headland that juts out into a wide and sheltered harbour. With its graceful air, wide range of accommodation, and good restaurants, this is easily the best base for exploring the island, especially as almost all of PEI's villages are formless affairs whose dwellings ribbon the island's roads. One exception is **Victoria**, a tiny old seaport southwest of Charlottetown, which makes a peaceful overnight stay. Otherwise, **Orwell Corner Historic Village**, just to the east of the capital, is an agreeable attempt to re-create an island village as of 1890; **Cavendish**, on the north coast, boasts the house that Montgomery used as the setting for her books; and, close by, **Prince Edward Island National Park**, the island's busiest tourist attraction, has kilometres of magnificent sandy beach. Further east is the rough-and-ready township of **Souris**, ferry port for the Îles-de-la-Madeleine (Magdalen Islands, see p.281) and located just down the coast from the beach and fishery museum of **Basin Head**. In the west, the chief interest is social: descendants of PEI's **Acadian** settlers – once the majority of the population – today constitute some fifteen percent of the island's inhabitants and many of them live on the wedge of land that runs down from the village of Wellington to Cap-Egmont.

PEI is a major holiday spot, so there's plenty of **accommodation** to choose from with B&Bs, inns, cottages and campsites liberally sprinkled across the whole of the island – though it's still a good idea to make advance reservations during July and August. Note, also, that although it's easy to reach Charlottetown by bus the rest of PEI has hardly any **public transport**. On a culinary note, PEI has a reputation for the excellence of its **lobsters**, which are trapped on the west side of the island during August and September and in the east from June to July. A number of restaurants specialize in lobster dishes, but keep a look out for local posters advertising lobster suppers, inexpensive buffet meals served in some church and community halls during the summer.

Getting to the island

There are regular domestic **flights** to Charlottetown airport from most cities in eastern Canada, but the majority of visitors arrive via the 13km-long **Confederation Bridge** spanning the Northumberland Strait between New Brunswick's Cape Tormentine and Borden, 60km west of Charlottetown. There's a toll of $36.25 per vehicle for using the bridge and this is collected on the way off the island. Cycling is a popular pastime on PEI, but cyclists still aren't allowed on the bridge; instead, they are transported across in a free shuttle bus within two hours of arrival – advance reservations are not accepted. The bridge is used by the twice-daily SMT **bus** service connecting Fredericton or Saint John in New Brunswick, with Charlottetown via Moncton.

You can also reach the island by **ferry**: Northumberland Ferries take 75 minutes to cross from **Caribou**, Nova Scotia, to **Wood Islands**, 61km east of Charlottetown ($49 return for car and passengers; ☎902/566-3838 or 1-888/249-7245, *www.nfl-bay.com*).

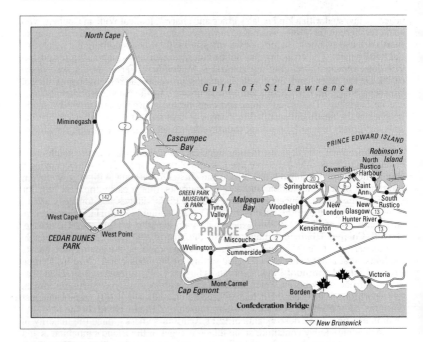

△ New Brunswick

Again, fares are collected when you leave the island, but not when you arrive. Ferries run roughly every one and a half hours from July to September and every three hours in May, June, October, November and early December. There's no ferry from late December to April. Ferries operate on a first-come, first-served basis and queues are common in high season, when you should arrive about an hour and a half before departure to be safe.

A second ferry does the five-hour hop between **Cap-aux-Meules** on the Magdalen Islands (Îles-de-la-Madeleine) and **Souris**, 81km northeast of Charlottetown (Feb & March no ferries; summer & autumn 6–10 weekly; winter 3–5 weekly; $36 single, $68 per car; call ☎902/687-2181 in Souris for schedules; reservations on ☎418/986-3278 or 1-888/986-3278, *www.ilesdelamadeleine.com*).

A brief history of Prince Edward Island

Jacques Cartier claimed Prince Edward Island for France on the first of his voyages across the Atlantic, naming it the **Île-St-Jean** in 1534. However, the French and the Acadian farmers he brought with him from the Bay of Fundy made little impact on the island until they were reinforced in 1720 by three hundred French colonists, who founded a tiny capital at **Port La Joye**, near the site of present-day Charlottetown. In 1754, there were about three thousand settlers, but their numbers doubled the following year with the arrival of refugees from the deportations (see p.357), a sudden influx with which the island was unable to cope. After the capture of Louisbourg in 1758, the British army turned its attention to Île-St-Jean and its starving, dispirited population. Lord Rollo, the local British commander, rounded up and shipped out all but three hundred of the Acadians and the colony was subsequently renamed the Island of St John in 1763, and **Prince Edward Island** in 1799.

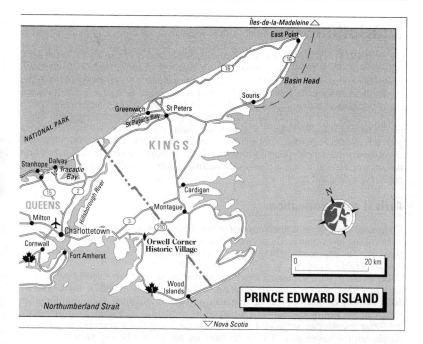

After the expulsion of the Acadians, the island was parcelled out to wealthy Englishmen on condition that they organized settlement, but few did. Consequently, when the island's population climbed from around seven thousand to eighty thousand in the first half of the nineteenth century, the majority of the colonists were tenant farmers or squatters, victims of an absentee landowning system that was patently unjust and inefficient. Although most of these immigrants were drawn from the poor of the Scottish Highlands and Ireland, the new citizens had come here in the hope of owning land. Their ceaseless petitioning eventually resulted in the compulsory **Land Purchase Act** of 1875, and within a decade PEI became a land of freeholders.

With the agricultural, fishing, shipbuilding and logging industries buoyant, the late 1870s marked the high point of the island's fortunes, but this prosperity was short-lived. The Canadian government's protectionist **National Policy** discriminated in favour of the manufactured goods of Ontario and Québec and the result was a long-lasting recession that helped precipitate a large-scale emigration, which left PEI a forgotten backwater, derisively nicknamed **Spud Island**. Depopulation remains a problem to this day, though the successful exploitation of the island's tourist potential has brought much relief, as has the modernization of its agriculture and fishery. Many islanders also argued that the construction of a bridge between PEI and the mainland would provide a further economic boost, whilst their opponents asserted that the island would be swamped by outsiders, its farms bought up as second homes and its closely knit communities overwhelmed. Those in favour of the bridge won the day (if not the argument) and the **Confederation Bridge** was completed in 1997; locals await the long-term consequences with mixed feelings.

The PEI telephone code is ☎902.

Charlottetown

Tiny **CHARLOTTETOWN**, the administrative and business centre of PEI, is the most urbane spot on the island, its comfortable main streets – Grafton and Kent – hemmed in by leafy avenues of clapboard villas, the most opulent of which spread west of the centre towards **Victoria Park**. But although these well-disposed streets give the place a prosperous and sedate appearance, this is not the whole truth: Charlottetown has a relatively high rate of unemployment and you'll glimpse the poverty here and there, particularly in the abject stuff on show in its cheaper department stores – a contrast with the upmarket touristy shops on the snazzily developed harbourfront. That said, Charlottetown is an exceptionally pleasant place to spend a couple of days and it also has, in small-island terms, a reasonable **nightlife**, with a handful of excellent restaurants and a clutch of good bars.

Arrival and information

Connected with all of Canada's major cities, Charlottetown **airport** is located 8km north of the town centre. There's no public transport from here to town, but the **taxi** fare costs just $8. Incoming **buses** all arrive centrally at the SMT depot, 330 University Ave at Gerald – a five-minute walk from the centre.

Inside the airport, a seasonal **tourist information desk** has buckets of information and provides a free room-reservation service – as does PEI's main **Visitor Information Centre**, on the harbourfront, a couple of minutes' walk from the town centre at the foot of Hillsborough Street (daily: Sept–May 9am–5pm; June 8am–8pm; July–Aug 8am–10pm; ☎368-4444). Both have copies of the comprehensive *Visitors' Guide,* but the larger office has much more on the island's B&Bs, national park and farm-holiday spots as well as free Charlottetown maps.

Accommodation

Charlottetown has no shortage of **places to stay** and only in the height of the season (July & Aug) is there any difficulty in finding somewhere reasonably convenient. To get the flavour of the place, you're much better staying in the oldest part of town – between Fitzroy Street and the waterfront. Options here include several reasonably priced **inns** and **B&Bs**, the best of which occupy grand late nineteenth-century houses, as well as a smattering of **hotels**, mostly expensive places that are either smart, modern highrises or well-conceived conversions of some of the town's oldest properties. At the other end of the market are a handful of small **guesthouses** – few of which accept credit cards – and – to the north of town – **student rooms**, available in the summer at the university.

Hotels, inns and bed & breakfasts

Delta Prince Edward Hotel, 18 Queen St (☎566-2222 or 1-800/268-1133, fax 566-2282). Charlottetown's plushest hotel, in a high-rise overlooking the harbour; luxurious rooms with superb facilities including pool and health centre. ⑥.

Dundee Arms Inn and Motel, 200 Pownal St at Fitzroy (☎892-2496 or 1-877/638-6333, fax 368-8532, *www.dundeearms.com*). The inn occupies a flashy, late nineteenth-century timber mansion and has eight guestrooms with period furnishings. The adjacent ten-room, two-storey motel is modern and comparatively mundane, but attractively well maintained. Motel and inn ⑤.

Fitzroy Hall, 45 Fitzroy St at Pownal (☎368-2077, fax 894-5711). This lavishly restored Victorian mansion with pillars, portico, dormer windows and wrought ironwork has six well-appointed, en-suite guestrooms, one of which has a jacuzzi. Excellent place to stay. Breakfast included. ④.

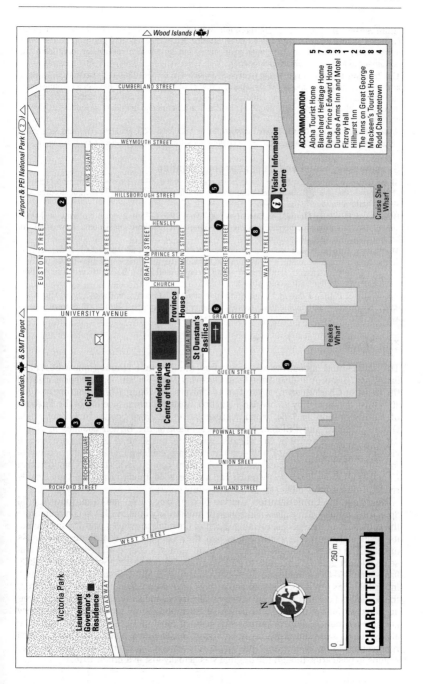

△ Wood Islands (🍁)

Cavendish, 🍁 & SMT Depot △

Airport & PEI National Park (②) △

CUMBERLAND STREET

WEYMOUTH STREET

KING SQUARE

HILLSBOROUGH STREET

HENSLEY

PRINCE ST

CHURCH

UNIVERSITY AVENUE

Province House

VICTORIA ROW

St Dunstan's Basilica

Confederation Centre of the Arts

City Hall

GREAT GEORGE ST

QUEEN STREET

POWNAL STREET

UNION SREET

HAVILAND STREET

ROCHFORD STREET

ROCHFORD SQUARE

WEST STREET

EUSTON STREET

FITZROY STREET

KENT STREET

GRAFTON STREET

RICHMOND STREET

SYDNEY STREET

DORCHESTER STREET

KING STREET

WATER STREET

Visitor Information Centre

Cruise Ship Wharf

Peakes Wharf

Victoria Park

Lieutenant Governor's Residence

PARK ROADWAY

ACCOMMODATION

Aloha Tourist Home — 5
Blanchard Heritage Home — 7
Delta Prince Edward Hotel — 9
Dundee Arms Inn and Motel — 3
Fitzroy Hall — 1
Hillhurst Inn — 2
The Inns on Great George — 6
Mackeen's Tourist Home — 8
Rodd Charlottetown — 4

CHARLOTTETOWN

N

0   250 m

Hillhurst Inn, 181 Fitzroy St at Hillsborough (☎894-8004, *www.hillhurst.com*). Classily renovated Georgian Revival mansion with finely carved interior. Nine large, en-suite guestrooms, each with ornate antique furnishings. It is open year-round, but by advance reservation only from late November to March. Breakfast included. ⑤.

The Inns on Great George, Great George St (☎892-0606 or 1-800/361-1118, fax 628-2079). Bang in the centre of town, opposite St Dunstan's, a row of old timber houses has been carefully renovated to hold this immaculate and atmospheric hotel. All the rooms are comfortable and tastefully decorated – the most appealing overlook the Basilica. Continental breakfast included. Highly recommended. ⑤.

Rodd Charlottetown, Kent at Pownal (☎894-7371 or 1-800/565-7633, fax 368-2178). Imposing 1930s hotel (part of a chain) with appealing Art Deco flourishes, though the rooms lack a certain intimacy. ④.

Guesthouses, hostel and student accommodation

Aloha Tourist Home, 234 Sydney St at Hillsborough (☎892-9944). This well-kept, unpretentious guesthouse occupies a 1930s home in the town centre facing a little park. Three guestrooms with shared bathroom. ②.

Blanchard Heritage Home, 163 Dorchester at Prince (☎894-9756). Modest but quite well-maintained place in an old shingle and clapboard dwelling with just three guestrooms. Downtown. No credit cards. May–Oct. ①.

Mackeen's Tourist Home, 176 King St at Prince (☎892-6296 or 1-800/668-6296). In a quiet residential area a couple of minutes' walk from the town centre, this three-room guesthouse is a neat and trim affair in a pleasantly modernized, pastel green-painted timber house. No credit cards. Bike shed and small garden with picnic table. ②.

University of Prince Edward Island, 550 University Ave (June–Aug ☎566-0442, Sept–May ☎566-0362). Single ($30) and double ($42) rooms on the university campus, 3km north of town. Rooms available May to late Aug. Advance reservations required.

The Town

The island's most famous historical attraction, the **Province House** (June & Sept daily 9am–5pm; July & Aug daily 9am–6pm; Oct–May Mon–Fri 9am–5pm; free) is right in the heart of Charlottetown, at the foot of University Avenue. This squat brownstone structure, dominated by its overlarge portico, hosted the first meeting of the **Fathers of Confederation** in 1864, when representatives of Nova Scotia, New Brunswick, Ontario, Québec and PEI met to discuss a union of the British colonies in North America. Today it's used by the island's legislature, but some of its rooms are open to visitors. On the ground floor, a fifteen-minute film provides a melodramatic account of that original meeting and explains its historical context, whilst the Confederation Chamber up above looks pretty much like it did in 1864, though frankly it's not exactly riveting – just a large table and some heavy-duty chairs.

Next door, the **Confederation Centre of the Arts** (daily 9am–5pm, June–Aug till 8pm; free) is housed in a glass and concrete monstrosity built in 1964 to commemorate the centenary of the epochal meeting. Each of Canada's provinces paid 15¢ for each of its resident to cover its construction and they continue to contribute towards its upkeep. The centre contains the island's main library, a couple of theatres, and a museum and **art gallery** (mid-June to mid-Sept daily 9am–7pm; mid-Sept to mid-Oct daily 9am–5pm; mid-Oct to mid-June Tues–Sat 11am–5pm & Sun 1–5pm; $4), whose changing exhibitions are often first-rate and always have a Canadian emphasis. Items from the permanent collection are also regularly displayed, and although much is fairly average look out for the manuscripts, papers and scrapbooks of Lucy Maud Montgomery and the portraits of Robert Harris, who painted most of PEI's business elite in the 1880s. Harris also painted the iconic *Fathers of Confederation*, a picture of bewhiskered representatives in debate that has been reproduced for everything from postage stamps to postcards, though the original was actually lost in a fire in 1916.

Metres away, fringed by the pretty terraced houses of Great George Street, rise the twin spires and imposing facade of **St Dunstan's Basilica** (daily 8am–5pm; free). Finished in 1897 and ten years in the making, the church has all the neo-Gothic trimmings, from blind arcaded galleries and lancet windows through to heavy-duty columns and a mighty vaulted ceiling. There were, however, some economies – tap the marble inside and you'll find it is mostly wood painted like marble. The basilica marks the centre of the oldest part of Charlottetown and the surrounding side streets are lined with rows of simple wood and brick buildings, mostly dating from the middle of the nineteenth century. Some of the best ensembles are concentrated on and around **King Street** to either side of Great George Street, whilst pedestrianized **Victoria Row**, also near the church, has the city's finest example of commercial architecture, a long and impressive facade that now holds a series of restaurants and bars.

Below Water Street, the sequence of jetties that make up the **harbourfront** has been refurbished with ice-cream parlours and restaurants, a yacht club, the lavish *Prince Edward Hotel* and the souvenir shops of Peake's Wharf. Big cruise liners are often moored here too, disgorging hundreds of day-trippers. From the harbourfront, it's a pleasant ten-minute stroll west to **Victoria Park**, on the edge of which is the grandiose lieutenant-governor's residence. Inside the park are the scant remains of the gun battery built to overlook the harbour in 1805.

Eating, drinking and nightlife

Charlottetown has a reasonable range of **restaurants** – quite enough to keep you going for a day or two – and several are excellent. The best are downtown, with particular concentrations along Victoria Row, beside the Confederation Centre and on Sydney Street at Queen. The best **cafés** and **bars** are here too – nothing amazingly exciting perhaps, but still amenable, easy-going places to enjoy a drink. Note also that in several cases, restaurants share their premises with bars – food below and booze up above.

As for the **performing arts**, the programme of events at the Confederation Centre of the Arts (☎566-4648 or 1-800/565-0278, *www.confederationcentre.com*) encompasses an extensive variety of acts, from rock and jazz through to comedians, magicians, theatre, opera and ballet. The centre is also the home of the main show of the annual **Charlottetown Festival** (June to mid-Oct), which – surprise, surprise – is a musical adaptation of *Anne of Green Gables* (tickets $16–34). The musical has been running for years, though modifications are made every year to freshen it up. During festival time in particular, Charlottetown also offers all sorts of comedy revues and shows both indoors and out. The *Buzz*, a free monthly newssheet available all over town and at the tourist office, carries comprehensive listings and reviews.

Cafés and restaurants

Beanz, 38 University Ave and Grafton. Great coffee and a range of tasty sandwiches and snacks from around $8 at this agreeable little café. Popular at lunch times with the town's office workers.

Cedar's Eatery, 81 University Ave and Kent (☎892-7377). Cosy and intimate café-cum-restaurant serving Lebanese specialities at bargain prices.

Claddagh Room Restaurant, 131 Sydney at Queen (☎892-9661). Pleasant, fairly traditional restaurant offering a good selection of reasonably priced seafood – including lobster – and beef dishes. Closed Mon eve. It's beneath the *Olde Dublin Pub* (see overleaf).

Delta Prince Edward Hotel, 18 Queen St (☎566-2222). Some locals swear by the lobsters here – but the restaurant is much more formal than the rival *Lobster on the Wharf*. A one-pound lobster will rush you about $25. By the harbour.

Lobster on the Wharf, at the foot of Prince St (☎368-2888). This long-established, bayside restaurant specializes in lobster dinners. Expect to pay around $25 per pound. Has a bayside deck.

Meeko's, Victoria Row, 146 Richmond St at Queen (☎892-9800). For something a little different, try this cheerfully decorated Mediterranean café and grill. The moussaka has a good reputation.

Off-Broadway Restaurant, 125 Sydney St at Queen (☎566-4620). Almost certainly the best restaurant in town, *Off-Broadway* features a creative menu of traditional and modern dishes – but not always lobster! The house specialities are exotic crepes and home-made desserts. Prices are reasonable – a salmon main course costs, for instance, $18.

Bars

D'Arcy McGee's, corner Kent St and Prince (☎894-3627). They do serve food here, but it's perhaps as a neighbourhood bar that the place has most appeal. Occupies an old but extensively remodelled clapboard house and has an outside terrace.

42nd Street Lounge, 125 Sydney St at Queen (☎566-4620). Laid-back lounge bar above the *Off-Broadway Restaurant*. Good range of brews.

Myron's, 151 Kent at University (☎892-4375). Popular for yonks, *Myron's* puts on a wide range of live music and club nights.

Olde Dublin Pub, 131 Sydney (☎892-6992). Intimate and justifiably popular spot with imported and domestic ales. Live folk music – mostly Irish – nightly from May to September.

Listings

Airlines Air Canada (☎892-1007) has an office at the airport.

Bike rental MacQueen's, 430 Queen St (☎368-2453); Smooth Cycle, 172 Prince St at Kent (☎566-5530).

Bus companies The Shuttle connects Charlottetown with Cavendish (☎566-3243). SMT, 330 University, provides long-distance services to New Brunswick and Nova Scotia (☎566-9744). PEI Express Shuttle (☎462-8177) operates a minibus service between Charlottetown and Halifax; advance reservations are essential; the one-way fare is $45.

Car rental Avis, at the airport (☎892-3706); Budget, at the airport and 215 University Ave (both ☎566-5525); Hertz, at the airport (☎566-5566); National, downtown at the *Prince Edward Hotel*, 18 Queen St (☎628-8868) and at the airport (☎628-6990); Rent-a-Wreck, 57a St Peter's Rd (☎566-9955). All these companies do good deals on short-term rentals.

Ferry companies Northumberland Ferries, 94 Water St (☎566-3838 or 1-888/249-7245).

Hospital Queen Elizabeth Hospital, Riverside Drive (☎894-2111).

Ice cream Something of an island institution, **Cows** produces delicious ice cream; there are outlets down on the harbourfront and on the corner of Grafton and Queen, opposite the Confederation Centre.

Internet and email access *Café Diem*, 128 Richmond St, opposite the Confederation Centre (daily 9am–9pm; ☎892-0494).

Laundries Midtown Laundromat and Café, 236 University Ave at Bishop (☎628-2329).

Newspapers The main local daily is *The Guardian*, which makes an enjoyable read; its motto is likeable too – "covers PEI like the dew".

Pharmacy Shoppers Drug Mart, 128 Kent St (☎566-1200) and 390 University Ave (☎892-3433).

Police General inquiries (☎566-7112). General emergency number (☎911).

Post office 135 Kent St (Mon–Fri 8am–5.15pm).

Taxis City Cab, 168 Prince St (☎892-6567); Co-op Taxi, 91 Euston St (☎628-8200).

The rest of the island

Prince Edward Island is divided into three counties. In the middle is **Queens County**, which incorporates the province's most popular tourist attractions and has some of its prettiest scenery. It also boasts the island's finest beaches, stretching along the northern shore and protected within the **Prince Edward Island National Park**. To the east of Queens lies **Kings County** comprising two broad geographical areas, with the tree-dotted farmland and estuary townships of the south giving way to wilder scenery further north, and to the west is **Prince County**, which makes up the flattest part of PEI, its broad-brimmed, sparsely populated landscapes curving round a handful of deep bays. The provincial government has worked out three **scenic drives** covering each of the counties: Lady Slipper Drive (287km) to the west, Blue Heron Drive (191km) in the centre, and the Kings Byway Drive (367km) to the east. However, although these drives visit everything of interest, they are frequently dreary, so unless you really love driving it's better to be more selective.

PEI's **public transport** system is rudimentary, but from early June to September there is a **shuttle** (2–4 daily; $16 return; ☎566-3243) linking Charlottetown's visitors centre with Cavendish visitors centre, at the junction of Hwy 6 and Hwy 13. Alternatively, several Charlottetown companies operate **sightseeing tours**, with the busiest being Abegweit, 157 Nassau St (☎894-9966), who offer tours of the southern and northern shores ($60 each) as well as Charlottetown ($9). The island is also good for all manner of outdoor sports, with specialist companies offering everything from diving and deep-sea fishing to canoeing and sailing, and is strong on **cycling**. There are several **cycle-tour operators**, though it's a good deal cheaper (and entirely straightforward) to plan your own route: in Charlottetown, both Smooth Cycle, 172 Prince St at Kent (☎566-5530), and MacQueen's, 430 Queen St (☎368-2453), rent out all the necessary gear and will advise on routes. The most popular is the **Confederation Trail**, a combined hiking and cycling trail that weaves its way right across the island, partly following the route of PEI's old railway, which was closed in the 1980s.

Queens County

Drawing thousands of visitors every summer, **Queens County**'s main attraction is the **Prince Edward Island National Park**, whose gorgeous sandy beaches, extending along the north shore for some 40km, are ideal for swimming and sunbathing. Rarely more than one or two hundred metres wide, the park incorporates both the beaches and the sliver of low red cliff and marram-covered sand dune that runs behind – a barrier which is occasionally interrupted by slender inlets connecting the ocean with a quartet of chubby little bays. A narrow road runs behind the shoreline for most of the length of the park, spanning several of these inlets, but forced into a detour at the widest, the main channel into Rustico Bay, which effectively divides the park into two. The smaller, more westerly portion runs from Cavendish – the site of Green Gables House – to North Rustico Harbour; the other (and much more enjoyable section) from Robinson's Island to Dalvay and Tracadie Bay. In either section, it's easy enough to drive along the shore road behind a goodly proportion of the beach until you find a place to your liking.

There's a seasonal **visitors centre** or **information kiosk** at every entrance to the park and from June to August they levy an entrance fee of $3 per adult per day. On arrival, you're issued with a free and comprehensive guide and out of season this is available at Charlottetown's Visitor Information Centre (see p.398). The park has eight short **hiking trails**, easy strolls that take in different aspects of the coast from its tidal marshes and farmland through to its woodlands. The most strenuous is the five-kilo-metre-long Woodlands Trail, up through a red-pine plantation near Dalvay. It doesn't take long to cycle to the park from Charlottetown, but **bicycle hire** is also available amongst the many tourist facilities on the park's peripheries.

The park has three **campsites**. The largest is the well-equipped Cavendish (mid-May to late Sept), where there's a supervised sandy beach that's great for swimming. The Stanhope (mid-June to late Oct), a short walk from the beach in the eastern section, is similarly well equipped and appointed, while Robinson's Island (late June to

Aug) occupies a quieter location, in a lovely spot amongst the wooded dunes beside Rustico Bay. A few sites are allocated on a first-come, first-served basis, but most can be reserved (☎1-800/414-6765). Sites cost $15–20.

Prince Edward Island National Park – east section

The fastest route from Charlottetown to the eastern section of the park is the half-hour, 22-kilometre thump along Hwy 15, which branches off Hwy 2 on the north side of town. This takes you past long ranks of chalet-style second homes and, as you near the park, the delightful *Dunes Studio Gallery and Café*, located just 600m beyond the Hwy 6 and Hwy 15 junction. The *Dunes* is a combined pottery shop, art gallery and **restaurant** (June–Sept daily 11.30am–9pm; ☎672-2586), which serves mouthwatering and reasonably priced snacks and meals from an imaginative menu of seafood and vegetarian dishes; it's one of the best places to eat on the island. Close by, another 1km or so north on Hwy 15, is the pick of the resorts and cottage complexes hereabouts, the charmingly rustic *Shaw's Hotel and Cottages* (☎672-2022; ⑥ for full board), whose hotel rooms (June–Sept) and all-year chalets and cottages occupy extensive grounds and farmland about ten-minutes' walk from the beach; *Shaw's* also does **bike rental** for guests and non-guests alike.

Inside the park, at the end of Hwy 15, you turn left along the coast for the causeway over to wooded **Robinson's Island** (and its campsite) and right for the 5km trip to **STANHOPE**, the setting for a string of perfectly placed beachside cottage complexes. These include *Del-Mar Cottages* (☎672-2582 or 1-800/699-2582; ③ – for up to 4 people; June–Sept) and *Surf Cottages* (☎651-3300; ③ for up to 6; June to mid-Sept). Just 6km further east, at the end of the beach road, is pocket-sized **DALVAY**, whose most conspicuous asset is the *Dalvay-by-the-Sea Inn* (☎672-2048, *www.aco.ca/dalvay*; ⑦ including breakfast and dinner; early June to early Oct). By any standard, the inn is an especially grand affair, a Victorian mansion that comes complete with high gables, rough-hewn stonework, a magnificent wraparound veranda, a yawning wood-panelled and -balconied foyer, and even a croquet lawn. The inn holds just 26 tastefully decorated rooms and has an ideal location inside the park just a couple of hundred metres from the beach. Advance reservations are pretty much essential.

Along the coast to the east of Dalvay, there are two more segments of the national park, the first being the slender sandspit that shelters much of **Tracadie Bay** from the ocean. There are no roads to this part of the park – just hiking trails – and a similar caution applies to the second segment, the spatulate, partly wooded headland at the mouth of **St Peter's Bay**. In this case, Hwy 313 travels west from Hwy 2 along the north shore of the bay, slipping through **GREENWICH** before grinding to a halt at the car park. From here, hiking trails head across the headland, exploring its beaches, dunes and wetlands.

Cavendish and Prince Edward Island National Park – west section

The forty-kilometre journey from Charlottetown to Cavendish and the western portion of the National Park covers some of PEI's prettiest scenery – take Hwy 2 west from the capital and, after about 23km, turn north along Hwy 13 at Hunter River. This country road wends over hill and dale and then threads through the tiny settlement of **NEW GLASGOW**, whose matching pair of black and white clapboard churches sit on opposite sides of an arm of Rustico Bay. In the centre of the village, the Prince Edward Island Preserve Company (☎964-4301) is a great place to buy local jams, mustards and maple syrups, and the attached **café** serves first-rate breakfasts, lunches and – in the summer – evening meals: try the Atlantic salmon. There are **lobster suppers** available in the village too, at *New Glasgow Lobster Suppers*, on Hwy 258 (June to early Oct daily 4–8.30pm; reservations ☎964-2870), though those at the church of **SAINT ANN**, a neighbouring hamlet about 5km west of New Glasgow along Hwy 224 – follow the signs

– are generally considered better (June–Oct Mon–Sat 4–9pm; reservations ☎621-0635). At both, reckon a 500-gramme (1lb) lobster in its shell will set you back about $25.

Northwest from New Glasgow, clumped around the junction of Hwy 6 and Hwy 13, is **CAVENDISH**, an inconsequential village little more than a stone's throw from the park's long sandy beaches. However, the busloads of visitors who descend on the place are mostly headed for **Green Gables House** (daily: May to late June, Sept & Oct 9am–5pm; late June to Aug 9am–8pm; $5), situated in a dinky dell just 500m west of the crossroads. Part of a tourist complex, with a gift shop and visitors centre, the two-storey timber Green Gables House was once occupied by the cousins of Lucy Maud Montgomery, one of Canada's best-selling authors. In 1876, when Montgomery was just two years old, her mother died and her father migrated to Saskatchewan, leaving her in the care of her grandparents in Cavendish. Here she developed a deep love for her native island and its people and, although she spent the last half of her life in Ontario, PEI remained the main inspiration for her work. Completed in 1905 and published three years later, *Anne of Green Gables* was her most popular book, a tear-jerking tale of a red-haired, pigtailed orphan girl that Mark Twain dubbed "the sweetest creation of child life ever written". As for the house itself, the mildly diverting period bedrooms and living rooms – supposedly the setting for *Anne* – are worth a quick look, though you may think twice when you see the crowded car park. Surprisingly, many of the tourists are Japanese – the book has been on school curricula there since the 1950s and remains extremely popular. If you decide to **stay** in Cavendish, go for *Shining Waters Country Inn & Cottages* (☎963-2251 or 1-877/963-2251; ③; May–Oct), 200m north of the crossroads on the way to the park. They have rooms in the old inn, a pleasant, homely structure with a wide veranda, as well as in a motel-style annexe and a string of modern chalets. The petrol station at the crossroads rents out **bikes**.

The Cavendish crossroads is about 600m from the national park's **Cavendish beach** and **campsite**. From here, the park's coastal byroad travels east, sticking close to the beach and its swelling dunes on the way to the scrawny fishing port of **NORTH RUSTICO**, the home of the *Fisherman's Wharf Restaurant* (☎963-2669; mid-May to mid-Oct), a good place to sample the island's lobsters. Beyond the port, Hwy 6 leaves the park, slipping round the peaceful waters of Rustico Bay on its way to meet – after 15km – Hwy 15 from Charlottetown (see p.398).

West of Cavendish

West of Cavendish, Hwy 6 passes through the most commercialized part of the island, an unappealing tourist strip stretching as far as New London. Here, Hwy 20 branches north along the coast and you'll soon see signs to PEI's most bizarre sight, the large-scale reproductions of famous British buildings that make up **Woodleigh** (daily: June & Sept to mid-Oct 9am–5pm; July & Aug 9am–7pm; $8.50). Built by a certain Colonel Johnston, who developed an obsessional interest in his ancestral home in Scotland, it features models of such edifices as the Tower of London, York Minster and Anne Hathaway's cottage. Some of the structures are even big enough to enter and their interiors have been painstakingly re-created, right down to the Crown Jewels in the Tower.

South Queens County – Victoria and Orwell Corner Historic Village

The southern reaches of Queens County are split into west and east by the deep inlet of Charlottetown harbour. In the west, the **Confederation Bridge** has become a major attraction in its own right and the tourist facilities of the adjoining Gateway Village take a stab at introducing visitors to the island. Elsewhere, **Fort Amherst/Port-La-Joye National Historic Site** (mid-June to Aug daily 9am–5pm; $2.25), perched on an isolated promontory across the bay from Charlottetown, marks the spot where the Acadians established their island headquarters, Port-La-Joye, in 1720. The British subsequently built Fort Amherst here, but all that survives today is a scattering of grass-covered earthworks. Much more diverting is the old seaport of **VICTORIA**, overlooking the Northumberland Strait about 30km west of Charlottetown. There's nothing remarkable among its gridiron of nineteenth-century timber houses, but it's a pretty spot and a relaxing place to while away a couple of hours. Victoria also has an attractive old **hotel**, the *Orient* (☎658-2503 or 1-800/565-6743; ④; June–Sept), and is home to the Victoria Playhouse (☎658-2025 or 1-800/925-2025), where a good range of modern plays and musical evenings are performed during July, August and September. There are several places to **eat**, including the *Hotel Orient's* cosy tea shop and the inexpensive *Actor's Retreat Café*.

Some 30km east of Charlottetown just off the Trans-Canada Highway lies the delightfully rustic **Orwell Corner Historic Village** (mid-May to mid-June & mid-Oct Mon–Fri 10am–3pm; late June to Aug daily 9am–5pm; Sept to early Oct Tues–Sun 9am–5pm; $4), which was settled by Scottish and Irish pioneers in the early nineteenth century. At first, the village prospered as an agricultural centre, but by the 1890s it was undermined by the expansion of Charlottetown and mass emigrations to the mainland. Orwell was finally abandoned in the 1950s, but the historic graveyard and a handful of buildings remained, principally the main farmhouse-cum-post-office-cum-general-store, the schoolhouse and the church. In recent years, these have been restored and supplemented by replicas of some of the early buildings, like the blacksmith's shop, barns and shingle mill. What's more, the interiors give a particularly authentic flavour of Orwell's rusticated past, from the farmhouse's darkened, cluttered living rooms and the austerity of the Presbyterian church to the impudent graffiti carved into the schoolhouse desks. In addition, the gardens are splendidly maintained in period style, farm animals root around, and the village hosts a wide variety of special events – ploughing contests, ceilidhs and so forth.

Close by – just 1.4km further up the same side road as the village – is the **Sir Andrew MacPhail Homestead** (daily: late June & Sept 10am–5pm; July–Aug 10am–9pm; donation). This features MacPhail's farmhouse, a comfortable nineteenth-century building whose period furnishings and fittings have a real sense of Victorian gentility, albeit in what was then the backcountry. It was from here that MacPhail (1864–1938) ran his farm, dabbled in medical research, and wrote as a journalist, banging on about the passing of the hierarchical, rural society he (as a Tory) loved. The veranda accommodates a pleasant **tearoom** (☎651-2789), where they serve dinner in the evenings from June to September, except on Saturdays; advance reservations are recommended. Bordered by the Orwell River, the homestead's woods and meadows offer several nature trails – details at the farmhouse.

Kings County

Just 600m beyond the Orwell/MacPhail turning, Hwy 210 branches off the Trans-Canada to snake its way east across the rich farmland bordering the Montague River on its way to the little town of Montague. From here, Hwy 4 – **Kings County's** principal north–south road – leads the 40km or so to PEI's northeast corner, where **SOURIS**, curving round the shore of Colville Bay, has a busy fishing port and harbour with a regular ferry service to the Magdalens (Îles-de-la-Madeleine; see p.281). The docks are a few hundred metres north of the scrabble of older houses that passes for the centre, and the stretch of shoreline between the two is the most elegant part of town. Here you'll find a sequence of Victorian mansions that includes the excellent *Matthew House Inn B&B*, on Breakwater Street (☎687-3461; ⑥; late June to early Sept), which has six attractive guestrooms. Alternatively, the nearby *Dockside B&B* (☎687-2829; ②; mid-June to mid-Oct) is a more economical option, occupying a 1960s house of expansive, open design with views out across the ferry terminal and ocean; there are four guestrooms here, two en suite.

The **Basin Head Fisheries Museum** (mid- to late June & most of Sept Mon–Fri 10am–3pm; July & Aug daily 10am–6pm; $3.50), a 13km drive up the coast from Souris, has a lovely setting, lodged on a headland overlooking a wedge of sandy beach that's trapped between the sea, the dunes and a narrow stream that drains an elongated lagoon. Too isolated and barren for any settlement, Basin Head was never more than a fishermen's outpost, and the museum details the lives of these men with displays of equipment, photographs of boats and miniature dioramas showing the fishing techniques they employed. Nonetheless, it is the setting that really appeals and several timber huts have been built here to provide shelter, picnic and changing facilities, erected alongside the original timber cannery building.

From here, it's possible to drive right round the island's northeast corner along Hwy 16 but, with the possible exception of the mid-nineteenth-century lighthouse at **East Point**, there's nothing much to see.

Prince County

Some 50km west of Charlottetown, Hwy 2 crosses the **Prince County** boundary, from where it's another 10km to **SUMMERSIDE**, PEI's second largest settlement, a sprawling and uninspiring bayside city of fifteen thousand people that was once the island's main port. If you're in town, pop into the curious **International Fox Museum and Hall of Fame**, a couple of blocks from the harbourfront at 286 Fitzroy St (June–Sept Mon–Sat 9am–6pm; donation). This traces the history of the island's fox-ranching industry from its beginnings in 1894 to its heyday in the 1920s, when fox-fur collars reached the height of their popularity in the cities of Europe and the US. There are potted biographies of the leading fox-ranchers, some of whom grew extremely rich from the furs of the silver fox, a rare variety of the common red fox, whose pelts reached astronomical values – up to $20,000 each. At one time, indeed, fox pelts became PEI's leading export.

Heading west from Summerside, it's a few minutes' drive along Hwy 2 to **MIS-COUCHE**, where the **Acadian Museum** (July–Aug daily 9.30am–7pm; Sept–June Mon–Fri 9.30am–5pm; $3) is devoted to the island's French-speaking community. Miscouche was the site of the second Acadian Convention in 1884, when the assembled representatives boldly chose their own flag – the French tricolour with a gold star, the *Stella Marae* ("Star of Mary"), inserted onto the blue stripe. The museum's exhibits are, however, rather paltry – a series of modest displays outlining Acadian historical development, from pioneer days and deportation through to today – and it's the interesting fifteen-minute video that (partly) saves the day. There are around 17,000 Acadians on PEI, of whom only 7000 speak French as their first language, a state of linguistic affairs that has made community leaders apprehensive of the future. The museum aims to support the Acadian identity and houses an Acadian Research Centre, complete with a library and extensive archives.

Continuing west, the headland south of the village of **WELLINGTON** is a centre of Acadian settlement, but it doesn't look any different from the surrounding districts until you reach **MONT-CARMEL**. This tiny coastal village is dominated by the hulking red-brick mass and mighty spires of the **Église Notre-Dame**, whose fantastically ugly appearance is made bizarre by a series of peculiarly sentimental statues and statuettes dotted around the entrance.

After the church, there's nothing else of any real interest around here, and it's a time-consuming drive north before you leave the flattened farmland of this part of Prince County for the slightly hillier scenery along the west shore of **Malpeque Bay**. The bay's reedy waters were once fringed by tiny shipbuilding yards and the scant remains of one of them have been conserved as part of the **Green Park Shipbuilding Museum** (daily: June–Sept 9am–5pm; $3). The museum also incorporates an interpretive centre, focusing on PEI's shipbuilding industry, and the **James Yeo house**. The most successful of the island's shipbuilders, the Yeos, the descendants of Cornish immigrants, maintained close contacts with their Cornish relatives and the two branches of the family combined to develop a prosperous transatlantic shipping business. Some of the proceeds went on the Yeo House, whose slender gables and mini-tower date from the 1860s. The interior, with its fetching Victorian furnishings and fittings, is a real delight – look out for the beautiful wax fruit in the parlour.

There's no real reason to hang around once you've visited the museum, but there is a bayshore **campsite** in the Green Park Provincial Park next door (☎831-2370; late June to early Sept). Furthermore, the minuscule village of **TYNE VALLEY**, 4km away, is home to the pleasant *Doctor's Inn B&B* (☎831-3057; ③), which occupies a big old house and has just a couple of guestrooms. The owners run the adjoining two-acre organic garden, whose produce is well-known hereabouts, and you can have dinner at the inn providing you make an advance booking.

It's about 70km from Green Park to the southwest corner of the island – follow the signs from Hwy 2 along Hwy 14 – where the remote and windswept **West Point Lighthouse** (daily: early June & mid- to late Sept 8am–8pm; mid-June to early Sept 8am–9.30pm) contains a small collection of photographs and memorabilia portraying the lives of the lighthouse keepers. Next door, the *West Point Lighthouse Inn* (☎859-3605 or 1-800/764-6854; ④; June–Sept), with its nine en-suite guestrooms, makes the most of a great seaside location, overlooking a long sandy beach. The lighthouse and inn are surrounded by the **Cedar Dunes Provincial Park**, which has a **campsite** about 500m down the coast (☎859-8785; late June to mid-Sept).

travel details

Trains

Halifax to: Moncton (1–2 daily except Tues; 4hr 20min); Montréal (1–2 daily except Tues; 19hr); Truro (1–2 daily except Tues; 1hr 30min).

Moncton to: Halifax (1–2 daily except Tues; 4hr 20min); Montréal (1–2 daily except Tues; 14hr).

Buses

(Not necessarily direct; some services may involve changing)

Charlottetown to: Fredericton (2 daily; 6hr); Halifax (2 daily; 7hr); Moncton (2 daily; 3hr); Saint John (2 daily; 5hr 30min); Sydney (1 daily; 13hr).

Edmundston to: Fredericton (2 daily; 3–4hr); Québec City (3 daily; 4hr); Rivière-du-Loup, Québec (3 daily; 1hr).

Fredericton to: Charlottetown (2 daily; 6hr); Edmundston (2 daily; 3hr); Halifax (2 daily; 7hr); Moncton (2 daily; 2hr 30min); Montréal (2 daily; 12hr); Newcastle, Miramichi City (1 daily; 2hr 20min); Saint John (2 daily; 1hr 30min).

Halifax to: Annapolis Royal (1 daily; 3hr 20min); Charlottetown (2 daily; 7hr); Fredericton (2 daily; 7hr); Liverpool (1 daily; 3hr); Lunenburg (1 daily; 1hr 30min); Moncton (3 daily; 3hr 30min–4hr); Montréal (2 daily; 18hr); Sydney (3 daily; 6–7hr); Truro (4 daily; 1hr 30min); Yarmouth, via the Annapolis Valley (4 weekly; 5hr 15min), and via the southwest shore (1 daily; 6hr).

Moncton to: Charlottetown (1–3 daily; 3hr); Chatham, Miramichi City (1 daily; 2hr); Fredericton (2 daily; 2hr 45min); Halifax (3 daily; 4hr); St Andrews (1 daily; 3hr); Saint John (2 daily; 2hr).

Sydney to: Halifax (3 daily; 6–7hr); North Sydney (3 daily; 25min); Truro – for New Brunswick and PEI (3 daily; 5hr).

Yarmouth to: Annapolis Royal (4 weekly; 2hr 30min); Chester (1 daily; 4hr); Halifax, via the Annapolis Valley (4 weekly; 5hr 15min), and via the southwest shore (1 daily; 6hr); Liverpool (1 daily; 3hr).

Ferries

Cap-aux-Meules, Îles-de-la-Madeleine, to: Souris, PEI (April to June & late Sept 1 daily except Mon; July to early Sept 1–2 daily; Oct–Jan 3–5 weekly; no ferries in Feb & March; 5hr).

Caribou, Nova Scotia, to: Wood Islands, PEI (July–Sept every 90min; May, June, Oct, Nov & early Dec every 3hr; no service from late Dec to April; 1hr 15min). Ferries operate on a first-come, first-served basis, and queues are common in high season.

North Sydney, Nova Scotia, to: Argentia, Newfoundland (late June to early Sept 2–3 weekly; mid-Sept to mid-Oct 1 weekly; 14hr); Channel-Port-aux-Basques, Newfoundland (June–Oct 1–2 daily; 6hr).

Saint John, New Brunswick, to: Digby, Nova Scotia (Jan to late June & mid-Oct to Dec 1–2 daily; late June to mid-Oct 2–3 daily; 3hr).

Yarmouth to: Bar Harbour, Maine by high-speed catamaran (June to late Oct 1 daily; 3hr); Portland, Maine (May to late Oct 1 daily; 11hr).

Flights

Charlottetown to: Halifax (8 daily; 35min); Montréal (5 daily; 1hr 40min); St John's, Newfoundland (5 daily; 3hr 30min); Toronto (4 daily; 2hr).

Fredericton to: Halifax (3 daily; 1hr 20min); Montréal (2 daily; 45min); St John's, Newfoundland (3 daily; 3hr 30min); Toronto (4 daily; 2hr).

Halifax to: Charlottetown (8 daily; 35min); Fredericton (3 daily; 1hr 20min); Montréal (3 daily; 1hr 40min); St John's, Newfoundland (5 daily; 2hr); Toronto (7 daily; 2hr 20min).

Sydney to: St Pierre (1–3 weekly; 45min).

CHAPTER FOUR

NEWFOUNDLAND AND LABRADOR

n 1840 an American clergyman named Robert Lowell described Newfoundland as "a monstrous mass of rock and gravel, almost without soil, like a strange thing from the bottom of the deep, lifted up, suddenly, into sunshine and storm", an apt evocation of this fearsome island, which is still referred to – by Newfoundlanders and mainlanders alike – as "The Rock". Its distant position between the Atlantic Ocean and the Gulf of St Lawrence has fostered a distinctive, inward-looking culture that has been unfairly caricatured by many Canadians in the stereotype of the dim "Newfie" – a term coined by servicemen based here in World War II. This ridicule can be traced to the poverty of the islanders, the impenetrability of their dialect – an eclectic and versatile mix of Irish and English – and even to their traditional food. Fish and chips, the favourite dish, is reasonable enough in the eyes of most people, but many stomachs churn at stand-bys such as cods' tongues, fried bread dough with molasses ("toutons") and seal-flipper pie.

Isolated from the rest of the country, Newfoundland is also a place of great isolation within its own boundaries. Only in recent years have many of the **outports** – the ancient **fishing settlements** that were home to the first Europeans – been linked by road to the solitary highway, the Trans-Canada, which sweeps 900km from the southwest corner of the island to the **Avalon Peninsula**, where **St John's**, the capital, sits on the northeast shore. Ferries from Nova Scotia touch the southwest and the Avalon, but most visitors fly straight to St John's, the island's only significant town and the obvious place to start a visit, for its museums, its flourishing **folk music** scene and its easy access to the **Witless Bay** sea-bird reserve. Yet there are more delightful spots than this: tiny **Trinity**, on the **Bonavista Peninsula** north of the Avalon isthmus, is easily the most beguiling of the outports; the French-owned archipelago of **St-Pierre et Miquelon** is noted for its restaurants; **Gros Morne National Park**, in the west, features wondrous mountains and glacier-gouged lakes; and at the far end of the **Northern Peninsula** you'll find the scant but evocative remains of an eleventh-century Norse colony at **L'Anse aux Meadows**, the only such site in North America.

ACCOMMODATION PRICE CODES

All the accommodation prices in this book have been coded using the symbols below, corresponding to Canadian dollar rates. Prices are for the least expensive double room in each establishment in high season, excluding special offers. For a full explanation, see p.40 in Basics.

① up to $40	④ $80–100	⑦ $175–240
② $40–60	⑤ $100–125	⑧ $240+
③ $60–80	⑥ $125–175	

The Newfoundland and Labrador telephone code is ☎709.

The definition and control of Labrador is the subject of a seemingly interminable dispute between Québec and Newfoundland, a row so intense that a Newfoundland senator, Alexander Baird, was once roused to declare, "We Newfoundland-Canadians don't want to fight, but, by jingo, if we have to, then I say we have the ships, the money and the men", to which Québecois senator Maurice Bourget added sneeringly – "and the fish". The major point of contention was the establishment of the massive **Churchill Falls** hydroelectric project, whose completion was a boost to the Newfoundland–Labrador economy, yet despite the last few years of industrial development and the construction of a few incongruous planned towns, Labrador remains a scarcely explored wilderness, boasting some of Canada's highest mountains, wonderful fjords, crashing rivers, a

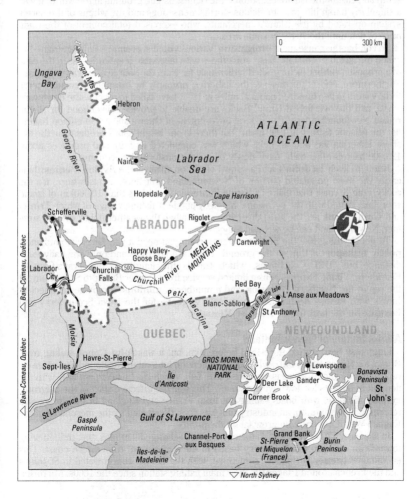

spectacular shoreline with minuscule coastal settlements and a forested hinterland teeming with wildlife. A trip to Labrador is not something to be undertaken lightly, but its intimidating landscapes are the nearest thing eastern Canada can offer to the challenge of the deep north.

NEWFOUNDLAND

The inhospitable interior and the fertile ocean kept the first European settlers on **Newfoundland** – most of English and Irish extraction – glued to the coast when they founded the outposts during the sixteenth and seventeenth centuries. Though they hunted **seals** on the winter pack ice for meat, oil and fur, they were chiefly dependent on the codfish of the **Grand Banks**, whose shallow waters, concentrated to the south and east of the island, constituted the richest fishing grounds in the world. It was a singularly harsh life, prey to vicious storms, dense fogs and the whims of the barter system operated by the island's merchants, who exercised total control of the trade price of fish until the 1940s in some areas.

To combat the consequent **emigration**, various populist premiers have attempted to widen the island's economic base, sometimes with laughable ineptitude – as in the case of a proposed rubber factory, sited ludicrously far from the source of its raw materials. Furthermore, efforts to conserve the fisheries, primarily by extending Canada's territorial waters to two hundred nautical miles in 1977, have failed to reverse the downward spiral, and the overfished Grand Banks are unable to provide a livelihood for all the reliant Newfoundlanders. The federal government in Ottawa spent $39 million bailing out the Atlantic fishery in 1992 alone, but there is one bright spot – profits from the offshore Hibernia gas and oil field, which was completed in 1997 and produces about 125,000 barrels of oil daily, have slowly begun to transform the economy.

Home to lively **St John's** and a sprawl of ribbon villages, the **Avalon Peninsula** is easily the most populated portion of Newfoundland, but here, as elsewhere, it's the rocky, craggy coast that makes a lasting impression – no less than 10,000km of island shoreline, dotted with the occasional higgledy-piggledy fishing village of which **Trinity** and **Grand Bank** are the most diverting, especially if the weather holds: even in summer, Newfoundland can be wet and foggy.

To get anything like the best from this terrain you need a car, for Newfoundland's **public transport** is thin on the ground. There are no trains and only one daily long-distance bus, DRL Coachlines, which travels the length of the Trans-Canada. Elsewhere, Viking Express runs a limited service from Corner Brook to St Anthony, at the top of the Northern Peninsula, and a number of **minibus** companies connect St John's with various destinations, principally Argentia for the Nova Scotia ferry and **Fortune** for the boat to **St-Pierre et Miquelon**.

A brief history of Newfoundland

Vikings may have settled the island before him, but it was **John Cabot**, sailing from Bristol for Henry VII in 1497, who stirred a general interest in Newfoundland when he reported back that "the sea is swarming with fish, which can be taken not only with the net, but in baskets let down with a stone". This was the effective start of the **migratory ship fishery**, with boats sailing out from France and England in the spring and returning in the autumn, an industry that was soon dominated by the merchants of the English West Country, who grew fat on the profits.

In the early 1700s the English fishery began to change its modus operandi, moving towards an offshore **bank fishery** based in the harbours of the eastern coast. This encouraged greater permanent settlement, with the British concentrated in St John's and the French around **Placentia**, their main fishing station since the 1660s. Mirroring

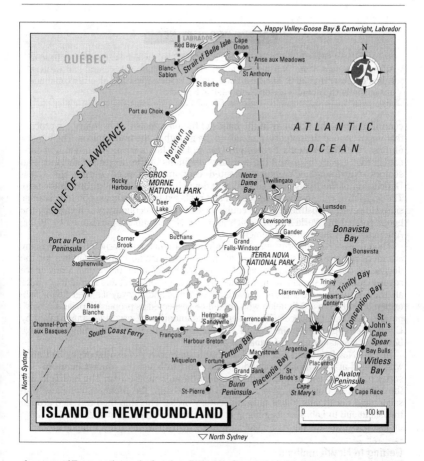

△ Happy Valley-Goose Bay & Cartwright, Labrador

QUÉBEC

LABRADOR
Red Bay
Cape Onion
L'Anse aux Meadows
Blanc-Sablion
Strait of Belle Isle
St Anthony
St Barbe

Port au Choix

ATLANTIC
OCEAN

GULF OF ST LAWRENCE

Northern Peninsula

430

GROS MORNE NATIONAL PARK
Rocky Harbour

Notre Dame Bay
Twillingate

Deer Lake

Lumsden

Lewisporte
Gander

Port au Port Peninsula

Corner Brook
Buchans

Grand Falls-Windsor

Bonavista Bay

Stephenville

TERRA NOVA NATIONAL PARK

Bonavista

360

Trinity
Trinity Bay

Clarenville
Heart's Content

Conception Bay

Rose Blanche

480

Hermitage-Sandyville
Terrenceville

St John's
Cape Spear

Channel-Port aux Basques

Burgeo

South Coast Ferry
François

Harbour Breton

Marystown
Argentia

Bay Bulls

Witless Bay

North Sydney

Miquelon
Fortune

Fortune Bay

Placentia Bay

Placentia

Avalon Peninsula

Cape Race

Grand Bank

St Bride's

St-Pierre
Burin Peninsula

Cape St Mary's

ISLAND OF NEWFOUNDLAND

0   100 km

▽ North Sydney

the wars of Europe, these rival nationalities fought a series of desultory campaigns until the **Treaty of Utrecht** in 1713, when France gave up her claims to the island in return for the right to catch, land and dry fish on the northwest coast, the so-called **French Shore** – an arrangement that lasted until 1904. In 1763 the French also swapped Labrador for St-Pierre et Miquelon.

Meanwhile, in 1729 the British government had introduced a bizarre system, whereby the commanders of the naval convoy accompanying the fishing fleet became the temporary **governors** of Newfoundland, even though they returned home in the autumn. Largely left to their own devices, the English and Irish settlers, who numbered about thirty thousand by 1790, spread out along the coasts, massacring the native Beothuks who, by 1829, had completely died out. A permanent governor was eventually appointed in 1817; the island was recognized as a colony in 1824; and representative, ultimately **responsible government** followed shortly after.

Struggling through a period of sectarian violence, Protestant English against Irish Catholic, Newfoundlanders decided not to join newly formed Canada in the 1860s, opting instead for self-governing **dominion** status. However, by the 1910s class conflict had replaced religious tension as the dominant theme of island life, reflecting the

TIME ZONES

Newfoundland island is on Newfoundland Standard Time, which is 30 minutes ahead of Atlantic Standard Time. Northern (from Cartwright northward), central and western Labrador, observe Atlantic Standard Time, while Paradise River and all other communities in southern Labrador are on Newfoundland Time.

centralization of the economy in the hands of the bourgeoisie of St John's – a process that impoverished the outports and fuelled the growth of the trade unions. The biggest of these, the **Fishermen's Protective Union**, launched a string of hard-fought campaigns that greatly improved the working conditions of the deep-sea fishermen and sealers. Newfoundland's export-oriented economy collapsed during the Great Depression of the 1930s, and the bankrupt dominion turned to Great Britain for help. The legislative chamber was suspended and replaced by a London-appointed commission. However, almost before they could start work, the economy was revived by the boom created by World War II, which also saw Newfoundland garrisoned by 16,000 American and Canadian servicemen.

Though a narrow majority voted for **confederation** in the referendum of 1949, many islanders remain at least suspicious of the rest of Canada, blaming Ottawa for the decline of the fishing industry and the high levels of unemployment. Many more regard Québec's claims to distinct status with a mix of contempt and incredulity – after all, they argue, no one's as distinctive as themselves and anyway it's their fellow fishermen on St-Pierre et Miquelon who should be respected as proper "Parisian French", not the charlatan Québécois. These sentiments underlie the assertive stance taken by **Clyde Wells**, premier from 1989 to 1996, in the constitutional wranglings that have become a constant feature of Canadian politics.

In 1997 Newfoundland celebrated the 500th anniversary of its **discovery** by Cabot, who landed at Cape Bonavista, and – in an effort to boost the **tourist economy** – a series of festivals and special events was held throughout the year. The highlight was the landing, in Bonavista, of a replica of Cabot's ship, the *Matthew*, complete with sailors and deckhands in late fifteenth-century dress. The ship then travelled around the island and to Labrador, beginning at Bonavista and stopping at sixteen other ports on its course, at each place re-enacting Cabot's landing on the "New Founde Lande".

Getting to Newfoundland

There are regular domestic **flights** to St John's from all of Canada's major cities and frequent services onward across the island to several smaller settlements; most usefully Deer Lake, for Gros Morne National Park.

Marine Atlantic operates three **ferries** from North Sydney, on Cape Breton Island in Nova Scotia. Two, including a new high-speed ferry that cuts travel time in half, go to **Channel-Port aux Basques**, 900km west of St John's (early Jan to mid-Jan 1–2 daily except Mon & Tues; mid-Jan to mid-June & mid-Sept to Dec 1–2 daily; mid-June to mid-Sept 3–5 daily; 5–7hr, or 3hr by high-speed ferry; $20 one-way, $62 for cars, cabins $45–90; reservations ☎1-800/341-7981; information ☎695-2124 or 4266, *www.marine -atlantic.ca*), from where a DRL Coachlines **bus** leaves for St John's (1 daily at 8am; 13hr 55min; $90). The other serves **Argentia** (mid-June to Aug 3 weekly; early Sept to mid-Sept 2 weekly; 14hr; $55 one-way, $124 for cars, $125 for cabins; reservations ☎1-800/341-7981, information ☎227-3755 or 227-2431, *www.marine-atlantic.ca*) on the Avalon Peninsula 131km southwest of St John's where Newhook's **minibuses** connect with the capital, a two-hour drive away, for $17. Reservations are essential for both ferries during July and August. On board, you'll find a cafeteria, lounge, gift shop, children's play area, a bar with live entertainment, movies and tourist information.

Labrador Marine operates a ferry connecting Blanc Sablon, Québec, with **St Barbe**, on Newfoundland's Northern Peninsula (mid-June to early Oct 1–3 daily; mid-Oct to Dec 1–2 weekly; May 1–2 weekly; 2hr; $9 one-way, $18.50 for cars, $3.50 for bicycles; information ☎535-6866; reservations ☎1-800/563-6353). Another ferry in the system connects Goose Bay, Labrador, via Cartwright, with **Lewisporte**, 390km northwest of St John's (mid-June to Aug 3–4 weekly; 35hr; $97 one-way, $160 for cars, $37.50–150 for cabins; reservations ☎1-800/563-6353, *www.gov.nf.ca/ferryservices/*).

St John's and around

For centuries, life in **ST JOHN'S** has focused on the harbour. In its heyday it was crammed with ships from a score of nations, but today – although its population is about 105,000 – it's a shadow of its former self, with just the odd oil tanker or trawler creeping through the 200-metre-wide channel of The Narrows into the jaw-shaped inlet. Once a rumbustious port, it's become a far more subdued place, the rough houses of the waterfront mostly replaced by shops and offices, its economy dominated by white-collar workers who are concentrated in a string of downtown skyscrapers and in the Confederation Building, the huge government complex on the western outskirts.

Yet although the city's centre of gravity has begun to move west, the waterfront remains the social centre, home of lively bars that feature the pick of Newfoundland **folk music** – the best single reason for visiting. Almost all of the older buildings were destroyed by fire in the nineteenth century or demolished in the twentieth, so although St John's looks splendid from the water, with tier upon tier of pastel-painted houses rising from the harbour, there are not a lot of major sights, with the notable exception of the grand **basilica**, and the **Newfoundland Museum**, which provides an excellent introduction to the history of the island and its people. Elsewhere, **Signal Hill National Historic Site**, overlooking The Narrows, has great views back over the city and out across the Atlantic, while the drive out to the rugged shoreline of **Cape Spear**, the continent's most easterly point, makes for a pleasant excursion, as does the trip to the **Witless Bay Ecological Reserve**.

Newfoundland Department of Tourism, Culture and Recreation
☎1-800/563-6353, *www.gov.nf.ca/tourism*

Arrival and information

St John's **airport** is about 6km northwest of the city centre and there's a **tourist information desk** inside (open year round; ☎758-8515). There's no public transport from the airport to the centre, so you may well need to get a taxi, which should cost around $14. Oddly enough, for a city of its size, St John's has no **bus station**. Travellers come into the city from towns along the Trans-Canada with DRL Coachlines and are dropped off at either the airport or at Memorial University (see "Listings", p.426). From the university you can take bus #3 to the city centre. To get around the city itself, you'll use the **Metrobus**, run by St John's Transportation Commission (☎722-9400), although schedules can be a bit erratic and intervals between buses are thirty minutes during the day and one hour during the evenings. Buses have a standard single fare of $1.50, with tickets available from the drivers – exact fare only; a Metropass, good for ten rides, costs $12.50. If you're not quite sure where you're going, aim in the direction of the *Hotel Newfoundland*, the city's most prominent and convenient landmark.

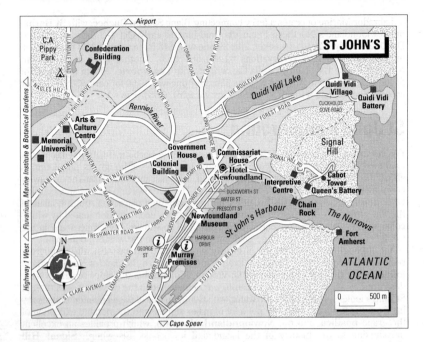

St John's has two downtown **tourist offices**: one in the lower level of the City Hall Annex building, on New Gower Street across from City Hall (Mon–Fri 9am–4.30pm; ☎576-8106, *www.city.st-johns.nf.ca*), the other in the old railcar next to the waterfront, halfway along Harbour Drive at the foot of Ayre's Cove (June to mid-Sept daily 8.30am–5.30pm; ☎576-8514). Both outlets have bucketfuls of free literature, most usefully a *St John's Visitor Guide*, which lists everything from accommodation and events through to church services and radio-station frequencies. They also have free city and provincial maps, the tourism department's comprehensive *Newfoundland and Labrador Travel Guide* and a variety of specialist leaflets detailing local sights, guesthouses and B&Bs.

Accommodation

St John's has a handful of convenient downtown **hotels**, but their charges are fairly high and, with the exception of the *Hotel Newfoundland*, they're of precious little distinction. The town's **motels** also tend to the mundane and most of them are inconveniently located on the main roads into town, with charges that start at about $60 per double. On the other hand, several of the city's **B&Bs – hospitality homes –** are outstanding with the best located in some of the fine nineteenth-century houses that are spread across the centre. Reckon on $60–70 per double, including breakfast. To book a bed and breakfast, check out *www.bbinn-nfld.org* or call Hospitality Newfoundland and Labrador (☎722-2000 or 1-800/563-0700, *www.hnl.nf.net*). Far cheaper, **Memorial University** offers rooms throughout the summer and, although Newfoundland's weather is too wet and windy for most campers, there is a city **campsite**.

SIGHTSEEING TRIPS

Several tour companies operate in the city, but the best land-based sightseeing tours of St John's and its environs are by McCarthy's Party Tours, Topsail, Conception Bay (May to early Sept daily; ☎781-2244, 781-2266 or 1-888/660-6060, *mccarthys.party@nf.sympatico.ca*, *www.newfoundland-tours.com*). They charge $25 for a three-hour trip that includes all the main sights, but it's the historical gossip that makes it worth the money. They also do tours to Cape Spear and Petty Harbour ($25), plus other excursions, including ones to Bay Bulls and Conception Bay ($35–50). There's also one particularly good boat trip organized by Adventure Tours, on the *Scademia* (May–Oct daily 10am, 1pm, 4pm & 7pm; 2hr–2hr 30min; $30; ☎726-5000 or 1-800/77-WHALE, *www.nfld.com/scademia*), a refurbished two-masted schooner that sails to Cape Spear and offers a chance to see some whales and icebergs; it leaves from Harbour Drive, near the railcar tourist information booth. Similar and slightly cheaper sea trips are organized by J&B Schooner Tours, departing from the waterfront at Pier 6 (mid-May to mid-Oct daily 9am, noon, 3pm & 6pm; 2hr; $28.75; 9pm moonlight cruise with live entertainment; 1hr; $15; ☎753-7245, *www.schoonertours.com*). If the above tours are overcrowded, try Dee Jay Charters (mid-May to mid-Oct, 3 tours daily; 2hr 30min; $25 adults, $10 under 16; ☎753-8687 or 726-2141), departing from the railcar tourist information booth, for boat tours around the harbour, or Morrissey's Boat Tours, which offers tours of the harbour or out to Cape Spear, the most eastern point in North America (mid-May to Oct, several tours daily; ☎748-5222 or 579-4195, *www.atyp.com/morrisseys*), from Pier 6, on their 76-foot yacht the *SeaKruz*.

There are also several walking tours that give you a feel for the city's historic past. St John's Historic Walking Tours (May–Oct by appointment; $20; ☎738-3781) organizes a thorough walk around the city, including diversions down lanes and back alleys; departure point is *Le Petit Paris Restaurant*, 73 Duckworth St. Legend Tours (reservations ☎753-1497, information ☎753-1498) does a Signal Hill Walk (daily 2pm; 2hr 30min; $25) and a tour of historic locations in the city centre (daily 9.30am, 1.30pm & 4.30pm; 2hr 30min–3hr; $25). A self-guided Women's History Walking Tour (2hr), beginning at Cavendish Square, covers the homes and workplaces of several eighteenth- to twentieth-century St John's women who have contributed to the history of the city and Newfoundland. There's also a highly recommended Haunted St John's Tour (Aug Tues & Thurs 9.30pm; June, July & Sept Mon & Thurs 9.30pm; $5; ☎685-3444, *www.avint.net/hardticket*) departing from the west entrance of the Anglican cathedral, Cathedral Street; the local historian points out the scenes of murders and ghost sightings, accompanied by dramatic readings and re-enactments.

On Your Own Tours (OYOT), 112 Duckworth St (☎753-5353, *oyot@nfld.com*), designs customized tours – ranging from one-day boat or hiking tours to four-week excursions around the entire province. If your feet are sore, you can take a ride through the city in a horse-drawn coach, driven by a coachman in eighteenth-century dress (daily 10am–midnight; 30min for $30, 1hr for $50; ☎738-6999), departing from beside the *Hotel Newfoundland* or from Kilometre 0 beside City Hall. (Kilometre 0 is where the Trans-Canada begins its long trek across the country.) Double-decker buses also take people around the city centre and to outlying areas such as Quidi Vidi Village (daily 9.30am & 1.30pm; 3hr; $20; ☎738-8687); buses depart from the Newfoundland Museum on Duckworth Street, the *Delta St John's Hotel* on New Gower Street or the *Holiday Inn* on Portugal Cove Road (free pick-up at other hotels and some B&Bs).

Hotels

Delta St John's Hotel and Conference Centre, 120 New Gower St (☎739-6404 or 1-800/268-1133, *www.deltahotels.com/properties/stjohns.html*). Luxurious downtown tower block with over 250 rooms, a swimming pool, whirlpool, saunas and gym. ⑥/⑦.

Hotel Newfoundland, at Cavendish Square near the intersection of King's Bridge and Military rds (☎726-4980 or 1-800/441-1414, *www.cphotels.ca*). Convenient location near the northern end of Water St. Grand and elegant, with most of the three hundred rooms having great views over the harbour and Signal Hill; swimming pool, sauna and whirlpool; two restaurants. Weekend and off-season discounts of up to thirty percent. ⑥–⑧.

Quality Hotel Harbour Front, 2 Hill O'Chips (☎754-7788 or 1-800/228-5151, *www.choicehotels.ca /cn246*). Standard-issue, modern hotel overlooking the waterfront at the north end of Water St. ④/⑤.

Hotel St John's, 102–108 Kenmount Rd (☎722-9330 or 1-800/563-2489, fax ☎722-9231). Large rooms within walking distance of St John's biggest shopping center. ③–⑤.

Motels

Best Western Travellers Inn, 199 Kenmount Rd (☎722-5540 or 1-800/261-5540, *www.bestwestern-natlantic.com*). About 5km southwest of the centre, along the Trans-Canada Hwy. Comfortable singles and doubles; pool, dining room and cocktail lounge. ④.

1st City Motel, 479 Kenmount Rd (☎722-5400 or 1-877/722-5422, fax 722-1030). Reasonably priced motel with about thirty rooms, 6km from the city centre. ②/③.

Holiday Inn – St John's, 180 Portugal Cove Rd, between Kent's Pond and Kenny's Pond (☎722-0506 or 1-800/933-0506, fax 722-9756). Motel with restaurants and amenities, as well as an outdoor pool, fitness center and executive rooms. ④–⑥.

Bed and breakfasts

Bonne Esperance House, 20 Gower St (☎726-3835, fax 739-0496, *bonne@wordplay.com*). Central and attractive Victorian mansion, built by a fishing captain; serves huge breakfasts. ③–⑤.

Compton House, 26 Waterford Bridge Rd (☎739-5789, fax 738-1770, *www3.nf.sympatico.ca/comptonhouse*). About 2km south of the centre, straight along Water St, in a delightful old home surrounded by an English garden. Five doubles, plus six en suites with fireplaces and whirlpools. No smoking. ③–⑤.

Monkstown Manor, 51 Monkstown Rd (☎754-7324 or 1-888/754-7377, fax 722-8557). Two large, attractive rooms filled with photos and memorabilia of musician Rufus Guinchard (see box on p.428) and Newfoundland writer Ted Russell. Jacuzzi, garden and patio; also two housekeeping units next door. ②/③.

O'Briens Topsail Star, 150 Topsail Rd (☎753-4850 or 1-877/639-4253, fax 753-3140). Nicely furnished rooms with shared baths, and each equipped with phone and TV. From the city centre, take bus #5 along Topsail Rd and Craigmiller Ave and then walk down the steep gravel path across from the church. ②.

Oh What a View, 184 Signal Hill Rd (☎576-7063). Four comfortable rooms, en suite and shared-bath, in a modern home, with possibly the best views of the city and harbour. Open mid-May to mid-Oct only. ③.

Prescott Inn, 19 Military Rd (☎753-7733 or 1-888/263-3786, *www.prescottinn.nf.ca*). Friendly and relaxed B&B near the historic St Thomas's Anglican Church offering up comfortable, spacious doubles, with gourmet breakfasts included. ③/④.

The Roses, 9 Military Rd (☎726-3336 or 1-877/767-3722, fax 726-3345, *www.wordplay.com/the_roses*). Another old house converted into a four-bedroom B&B, with a convenient location near downtown. Breakfast served in the balconied rooftop kitchen, which has harbour views. ③.

Winterholme Heritage Inn, 79 Rennie's Mill Rd (☎739-7979 or 1-800/599-7829, fax 753-9411, *winterholme@nf.sympatico.ca, www.winterholme.nf.ca*). Seven en-suite rooms, four with jacuzzis, fireplaces and king-sized beds. In a 1905 Queen Anne mansion, declared a National Historic Site. More like a luxury resort than a B&B. ②/③.

Hostel and student accommodation

The Backpacker, 138 Gower St (☎739-9994, *home.thezone.net/~backpack*). Small four-person rooms, with a bagel and coffee breakfast included in the price. ①.

Catherine Booth House Travellers' Hostel, 18 Springdale St (☎738-2804). On the southern edge of downtown; a Salvation Army hostel, with spartan singles and doubles. ①.

Hostel on the Hill, 65 Long Hill (☎754-7658 or 682-0718, *oboag@yahoo.com*). Clean; inexpensive; nonsmoking; shared and double rooms. ①.

Memorial University of Newfoundland, off Elizabeth Ave (☎737-7657 or 737-4003, *munconf@mun.ca*). Pleasant basic rooms 3km west of the centre. Discount for students; reservations advised. Mid-May to mid-Aug. ①.

Campsite

Pippy Park Trailer Park and Campground, in C.A. Pippy Park (☎737-3669). About 4km west of the city centre, near the Confederation Building; turn off Elizabeth Ave at Allandale Rd, then turn left along Nagle's Place. Clean accessible washrooms. Convenience store. May–Sept daily 7am–10pm. Unserviced sites and tents $16, serviced $20.70–23.

The City

Running the length of the town centre, **Water Street** has long been the commercial hub of St John's, though the jumbled storefronts of the chandlers and tanners, ship suppliers and fish merchants have mostly been replaced by a series of ill-considered redevelopments. In the architectural gloom, look out for the odd elegant stone and brick facade or take a peek at the old **courthouse**, a monumental Romanesque Revival building of 1904 that overlooks the harbour from Water Street at Baird's Cove.

The Newfoundland Museum to Murray Premises

It's the briefest of walks up the hill from the courthouse to the rather small **Newfoundland Museum** (June–Aug Mon–Wed & Fri–Sun 10am–6pm, Thurs 10am–9pm; Sept–May Tues, Wed & Fri 9am–5pm, Thurs 9am–9pm, Sat & Sun 10am–6pm; free), housed in a sturdy stone edifice on Duckworth Street at Cathedral Street. Here, the second floor is devoted to the prehistoric peoples of Newfoundland and Labrador, beginning with a few artefacts that are the sole traces of the Maritime Archaic Indians and their successors, the Dorset Eskimos. This is pretty dull stuff, but there are also an enjoyable series of displays on the **Beothuks**. These Algonquian-speaking people reached Newfoundland in about 200 AD and were semi-nomadic, spending the summer on the coast catching fish, seals and sea birds, and moving inland during the winter to hunt caribou, beaver and otter. They were also the first North American natives to be contacted by British explorers, who came to describe them as **Red Indians** – from their habit of covering themselves with red ochre, perhaps as some sort of fertility ritual or to keep the flies off. (The term then came to apply to all Indian groups.) The initial contacts between the two cultures were quite cordial, but the whites soon began to encroach on the ancient hunting grounds, pushing the natives inland; their tactics were summarized by Joseph Banks, a contemporary observer: "the English fire at the Indians whenever they meet them, and if they happen to find their houses or wigwams, they plunder them immediately". The last of the tribe, a young woman by the name of **Shanawdithit**, died at age 29 of tuberculosis in 1829. She had spent the last years of her life in the protective custody of the attorney general in St John's, and it was here that she built a small model of a Beothuk canoe and made ten simple drawings of her people and their customs. Copies of the drawings are on display in the museum, a modest memorial to a much-abused people.

Below, the first floor accommodates a **Natural History** collection, where there are models of the fauna of Newfoundland and Labrador, including rare and extinct species; there's also a clifftop diorama showing the various sea birds that breed and nest along the shores of the province. The third floor houses displays dealing with the daily life of the **fishermen**, including a reconstruction of a "stage" (a wharf building used for gutting, cleaning and salting cod), and a "store" (a workshop shed where fishermen made boats, furniture and barrels). Another section on this floor shows various **Newfoundland furnishings** and fittings, as part of a display recalling the

---

SEALING

The Newfoundland seal hunt has always been dependent on the **harp seal**, a gregarious animal that spends the summer feeding around the shores of Greenland, Baffin Island and northern Hudson Bay. In the autumn they gather in a gigantic herd that surges south ahead of the arctic ice pack, passing the coast of eastern Labrador before dividing into two – one group pushing down the Strait of Belle Isle into the Gulf of St Lawrence to form the **Gulf herd**, the other continuing south as far as Newfoundland's northeast coast, where they congregate as the **Front herd**. From the end of February to early March, the seals of the Front herd start to breed, littering the ice with thousands of helpless baby seals or **whitecoats**, as they're known. It's just two or three weeks before the pups begin to moult and their coats turn a shabby white and grey.

From early days, the Front herd provided the people of northeast Newfoundland with fresh meat during the winter, but it was the value of the whitecoats' fur that spawned a clutch of hunting centres – such as Bonavista, Trinity and Twillingate – and thousands of jobs: in 1853, the seal fleet consisted of 4000 ships manned by 15,000 sailors, who combined to kill no fewer than 685,000 harps. However, in the 1860s **steamers** made the old sailing ships obsolete and provoked a drastic restructuring of the industry. The new vessels were too expensive for the shipowners of the smaller ports and control of the fleet fell into the hands of the wealthy traders of St John's. By 1870, the bulk of the fleet was based in the capital and hundreds of Newfoundlanders were obliged to travel here for work every winter.

For those "lucky" enough to get a berth, conditions on board were appalling: as a government report noted, a captain could "take as many men as he could squeeze onto his ship... When the seal pelts began to come aboard, the crew had to make way until, by the end of a successful voyage, the men would be sleeping all over the deck, or amongst the skins piled on the deck, even in the most savage weather conditions". All this hardship was endured on a basic diet of "hardtack", hard bread or ship's biscuit, and "switchel", black unsweetened tea, enlivened by the odd plate of "duff", a boiled-up mixture of old flour and water. "Small wonder", as one of the sealers – or **swilers** – recalled, that "most

---

kitchen and parlour of a house in a remote outport village around 1900. Many of the outports remained beyond the cash economy right up until the 1940s, and consequently much of their furniture was made from packing cases and driftwood. The kitchen furniture was painted in bright, primary colours, as seen in the blue balsam–fir sideboard loaded with crockery, but much of the rest was stained dark brown to imitate a decorative graining; this is especially noticeable in the furniture of the rather sombre parlour, whose walls are lined with stitched samplers in frames. Also on the third floor is a small stage where free **performances** of folk and Irish music are held year-round.

As you walk south along Duckworth Street from the museum, the next major building on the left is the imposing 1904 **courthouse**. Duckworth Street veers left down steep McBride's Hill, flanked by murals, and merges with Water Street, where, after a five-minute walk, you'll come to the **Murray Premises**, sandwiched between Water Street and Harbour Drive. The building was formerly an 1840s fish storehouse that luckily survived the fire of 1892 that destroyed much of St John's; in 1979 it was renovated to house restaurants and shops, and bits of the original brick and timber walls have been sensitively incorporated into the reconstruction.

Military Road

Military Road and adjacent **Kings Bridge Road** boast St John's finest old buildings, a handful of elegant structures beginning near the *Hotel Newfoundland* with the clapboard and elongated chimneys of the **Commissariat House** (1818–20) on Kings Bridge Road (mid-June to mid-Oct daily 10am–5.30pm; $2.50; ☎729-6730, *lbabcock@toursism.gov.nf.ca*)

of us learned to eat raw seal meat. The heart, when it was cut out and still warm, was as good as steak to we fellows". There were two compensations: money and status – as it left for the Front the seal fleet was cheered on its way and the men of the first ship back, the **highliner**, dispensed seal flippers, an island delicacy, and got free drinks all round.

In the early 1900s, the wooden-walled steamships were, in their turn, replaced by **steel steamers**. Once again, the traders of St John's invested heavily, but the shrinking seal population reduced their profit margins. Increasingly, they began to cut corners, which threatened the safety of the swilers. The inevitable result was a string of disasters that culminated in 1914 in the loss of the *Southern Cross* with all 173 hands. Shortly afterwards, a further 78 men from the *Newfoundland* died on the ice as a consequence of the reckless greed of one of the captains. These twin catastrophes destroyed the hunt's communal popularity, and a decade later the economics of the industry collapsed during the Great Depression. By 1935 most of the sealing firms of St John's had gone broke.

After World War II sealing was dominated by the ships of Norway and Nova Scotia, with the Newfoundlanders largely confining their activities to an inshore cull of between 20,000 and 40,000 whitecoats per year – enough work for about four thousand people. Thus, sealing remained an important part of the island's bedraggled economy up until the 1960s, when various conservationist groups, spearheaded by **Greenpeace**, started a campaign to have it stopped. Slowly but surely, the pressure built up on the Canadian government until it banned all the larger sealing ships and closely restricted the number of seals the islanders were allowed to kill. This remains the position today.

The **conservationists** have always objected to the cruelty of the cull, and it's certainly true that the killing of a hapless whitecoat is a brutal act. Yet the furore has much to do with the doleful eyes and cuddly body of the baby seal, an anthropomorphism that doesn't wash with an island people whose way of life has been built on the hunting of animals, and who are convinced that the increasing number of seals has damaged the fisheries. Nothing angers many Newfoundlanders more than the very mention of Greenpeace, whose supporters are caricatured as well-heeled, urban outsiders who have no right to meddle in their traditional hunting practices.

whose interior has been restored to its appearance circa 1830. Costumed staff provide entertaining guided tours of the building, which was the home and offices of the assistant commissariat general, in charge of supplying the British military with their nonmilitary goods. The most intriguing room is the clerk's office, into which the soldiers entered by a side door to collect their wages. Upstairs, the small sewing room has two tiny paintings by Turner. A few buildings complete the period look, such as the coach house out back, and the nearby black-and-white-painted clapboard of the **Anglican Church of St Thomas**, 8 Military Rd (mid-June to mid-Aug daily 8.30am–4.30pm; 2hr; free; *st.thomas@nf.sympatico.ca*).

Continuing along Military Road, it's a couple of minutes' walk to the impressively stylish Palladian-influenced **Government House** (1827–31), the governor's residence until 1949 (grounds open only; for tours of the house, call ☎729-4494, *www.mun.ca/govhouse/*). Just across Bannerman Road from Government House, the **Colonial Building** (1846–50), fronted by a large portico of Ionic columns (year-round Mon–Fri 9am–4.15pm; free), once housed the provincial assembly and now contains the island's historical archives. From here, it's a further five minutes along Military Road to the grandest of the town's churches, the mid-nineteenth-century Catholic **Basilica of St John the Baptist** (Mon–Fri 8am–4.30pm, Wed until 8pm, Sat 8am–6.30pm, Sun 8.30am–12.30pm), whose twin-towered limestone and granite mass overlooks the harbour from the crest of a hill. The basilica is fronted by a reasonable attempt to mimic the Romanesque churches of Italy. It's at its best inside, where the coloured stained glass illuminates a delightfully ornate maroon and deep-green ceiling. Guided tours are available from mid-June to August (Mon–Sat 10am–5pm; $15). The **cemetery** alongside the basilica has headstones dating from the eighteenth century, and the grey-stone **museum** to the church's left has a small but splendid collection of sacred objects (June–Sept daily; free).

Down the hill to Water Street, you'll pass the Anglican **Cathedral of St John the Baptist**, designed in Gothic Revival style by the English architect Sir George Gilbert Scott. Begun in 1847, much of it burnt down in 1892 but was rebuilt to his plans by his son. The lofty interior is an impressive sight, with wooden ceilings and an array of stained glass of exceptionally high quality. Tours are given by knowledgeable guides (June–Aug Mon–Wed & Fri 10am–5pm, Thurs & Sat 10.30am–5pm, Sun 12.30–4pm; free; ☎726-5677), and there's a tearoom in the crypt (June–Aug Mon–Fri 2.30–4.30pm). The streets in the vicinity of the two churches constitute the oldest residential part of town, with rows of simple, brightly painted clapboard (or vinyl imitation) houses spilling down steep hills and festooned by a quaint cobweb of power and telephone cables.

Signal Hill

Soaring high above The Narrows, **Signal Hill National Historic Site** (open daily 24hr; free) is a massive, grass-covered chunk of rock with views that are dramatic enough to warrant the strenuous half-hour walk up from the northern end of Duckworth Street – there's no city bus transport up here. Known originally as the Lookout, Signal Hill took its present name in the middle of the eighteenth century, when it became common practice for flags to be hoisted here to notify the merchants of the arrival of a vessel – giving them a couple of hours to prepare docking facilities and supplies. The hill was also an obvious line of defence for the garrison of St John's, and the simple fortifications that were first established during the Napoleonic Wars were restructured every time there was a military emergency, right up until World War II.

Signal Hill is bare and treeless – though speckled with seagull-filled ponds – but there's the odd diversion as you clamber up the approach road. The first is the **Interpretive Centre** (daily: mid-June to Sept 8.30am–8pm; Sept to mid-May 8.30am–4.30pm; $2.50 for exhibit entrance; ☎772-5367), which entertainingly explores the history of the city and the island. **Gibbet Hill**, beside the centre, was where the bodies of hanged criminals, wrapped in chains, were put on public display in the nineteenth century. Close by, the antiquated guns of the **Queen's Battery** peer over the entrance to the harbour directly above **Chain Rock**, which was used to anchor the chain that was dragged across The Narrows in times of danger. Near the battery, a military tattoo (mid-July to mid-Aug Wed, Thurs, Sat & Sun 3pm & 7pm; 45min; $2.50, or presentation of exhibit ticket) is performed by costumed guards, accompanied by their mascot, a large web-footed Newfoundland dog. From the battery you can look directly across The Narrows to the remains of the centuries-old **Fort Amherst**. Right on the top of Signal Hill, the squat and ugly **Cabot Tower** was built between 1897 and 1900 to commemorate both John Cabot's landing of 1497 and Queen Victoria's Diamond Jubilee (daily: early June to Aug 8.30am–9pm; Sept to early June 9am–5pm; free). The tower features a small display on electronic signalling, and outside there's a plaque in honour of Guglielmo Marconi, who confirmed the reception of the first transatlantic radio signal here in December 1901. From the top you can walk down to the rocky headland below, a wild and windswept route on all but the balmiest of days.

Guided **tours** of Signal Hill leave from the Interpretive Centre or from the Cabot Tower car park (daily 2pm; $2.50, or free with Interpretive Centre ticket).

Quidi Vidi Village

Quidi Vidi (pronounced "kiddy-viddy") is one of the province's most photographed locations: several fishing shacks and drying-racks flanked by sharp-edged cliffs, about 3km from the city centre – take Kings Bridge Road and turn first right down Forest

Road, or take #15 bus from downtown. The scenery's great, with cliffs sticking out from the deep-blue waters of a tiny inlet that's connected to the sea by the prettiest of narrow channels. It's also worth the trip out to visit **Mallard Cottage Antiques and Collectibles**, right in the centre of the village (June–Oct daily 10am–6pm; Nov–May daily except Tues noon–6pm; donation), built around 1750 and said to be the oldest existing cottage in North America. You can also visit the **Quidi Vidi Brewery**, in a large green-and-white fish plant on the water's edge (year-round Mon–Sat 10am–4pm; ☎738-4040). Tours and tastings ($2) are given; call for times as they vary from day to day. A short walk round the coast leads to the Quidi Vidi **gun battery**, reconstructed to its original 1812 appearance (mid-June to mid-Oct daily 10am–5.30pm; $2.50). At nearby **Quidi Vidi Lake**, the annual Royal St John's Regatta, the oldest continuous sporting event in North America, featuring fixed-seat rowing races and a huge garden party, is held every August.

Memorial University, C.A. Pippy Park and Rennie's River

Overlooking the city from the heights above Elizabeth Avenue are the scattered buildings of **Memorial University**, of which the modern **Arts and Culture Centre**, on Allandale Road, holds the most interest, though you'd likely only come out here to see a theatrical performance or check out the **Art Gallery of Newfoundland and Labrador** (Tues, Wed & Sun noon–5pm, Thurs–Sat noon–5pm & 7–10pm; free), with its decent collection of works by local artists.

Behind the university is **C.A. Pippy Park**, home to the **Botanical Gardens**, 110 acres of natural habitat and gardens, at Oxen Pond (May, June & Sept–Nov Wed–Sun 10am–5pm; July & Aug daily same hours; $1), but whose major attraction is the **Fluvarium** in the Newfoundland Freshwater Resource Centre (mid-June to Aug daily 9am–6pm; tours hourly 9am–3pm & 5pm; Sept to mid-June tours only at 11am, 1pm & 3pm daily except Wed; $5, tour included in price of ticket; ☎754-3474, *www.fluvarium.nf.net*). From the uppermost level, where the reception is, you descend to level 2, where displays concentrate on freshwater ecosystems and the marine life within them; one intriguing model is of an **iceberg** – similar to the massive chunks of frozen fresh water that break off from glaciers in Greenland and drift south on the Labrador Current in the summer, then float along the Newfoundland coast, often into small bays and coves, where they remain until they melt. Down at level 3, below the level of the brook outside the building, three areas of the brook – a shallow pool, a fast-flowing stream and a deep pool – can be seen through the glass, and eels, brook trout, rainbow trout and salmon swim by. The best time to be here is at **feeding time** at 4pm, when the hungry fish put on a show. Note that the water becomes rather murky after a rain, so plan to visit the Fluvarium only on a fine day. Just north of the Fluvarium, you can continue your aquatic investigations at the **Marine Institute of Memorial University**, 155 Ridge Rd (tours only July & Aug Mon–Fri 1.30pm & 3pm; free), given over more to interactive exhibits including the world's largest flume tank and an aquaculture facility. You can get to the Fluvarium and Marine Institute by bus #10 from Water Street.

From the Fluvarium and the university, you can follow some of the course of **Rennie's River** through the south part of C.A. Pippy Park to Elizabeth Avenue along a partly boardwalked footpath – the most pleasant **walking trail** in St John's. Purple thistles, ferns, wild flowers and partridgeberry bushes grow along the path and on the rocky banks of the river, which drops in a series of cascades.

Eating, drinking and entertainment

In recent times, St John's **restaurant** scene has broken free of its rather humdrum traditions with a rash of bistros featuring good-quality seafood or ethnic cuisines. Slightly cheaper are a number of central **café-restaurants** catering for the city's office workers, while many of the downtown pubs also sell reasonably appetizing **bar food** at lunch time and sometimes at night. There's also a clutch of inexpensive **snack bars**, usually fish-and-chip shops, the best of which serve hearty meals for as little as $5. For **drinking**, St John's has dozens of **bars** – it's said to have more drinking places per square kilometre than any other city in North America – though many of them get rowdy late at night: as a general rule, stick to the pubs where there's **folk music**, which you shouldn't miss in any case. You'll find a number of Newfoundland **beers** worth trying, such as Red Dog and Black Horse, but the best is 1892 Traditional Ale, a dark golden ale with a rich, tart flavour, brewed in Quidi Vidi Village (see overleaf).

There are a decent number of pubs and bars dotted around the centre that regularly showcase island musicians, who vary enormously in quality and the type of music they play, ranging from what sounds like C&W with an eccentric nautical twist, through to traditional unaccompanied ballads. If you're content to take pot luck, follow the crowds along George Street, but otherwise ask for advice at **O'Brien's Music Store**, 278 Water St (☎753-8135), where you can also get a comprehensive list of future gigs. Another good contact is the St John's Folk Arts Council, 155 Water St (☎576-8508), which organizes regular folk-music concerts and a monthly folk dance at various locations where you can learn the dances and join in a "real Newfoundland time". At the end of July, **George Street** comes alive for a few days with a **street festival** featuring lots of good folk music. The best of the island's dozen folk festivals, the **Newfoundland and Labrador Folk Festival**, is held in Bannerman Park in St John's on the first weekend in August.

The Friday and Saturday editions of the local newspaper, the *Evening Telegram*, have arts and entertainment listings. The *Express* publishes comprehensive listings on Wednesdays, and *What's Happening* is a monthly arts and entertainment magazine available at hotels; the latter two are free.

Cafés and restaurants

Bianca's, 171 Water St (☎726-9016). One of St John's most elegant eating places, this attractive bistro specializes in Mediterranean-style cuisine. Reservations recommended. Closed Sun.

Bruno's Fine Foods, 248 Water St (☎579-7662). Small restaurant serving authentic Italian food at reasonable prices; great selection of wines, too. Open daily.

Ches's, 9 Freshwater Rd at LeMarchant Rd, with branches at 655 Topsail Rd and 29–33 Commonwealth Ave (☎722-4083). A 15min walk from the *Hotel Newfoundland, Ches's* is one of the best fish-and-chip shops in town; seafood platters are around $7.49. They also do takeaways.

Chucky's Fish 'n' Ships, 10 King's Rd (☎579-7888). Great place with friendly owner and staff that serves freshly caught snow crab, as well as mussels, scallops and salmon, to a background of piped-in Newfoundland sea shanties. Delicious fish and chips. Be sure to look at the map on the wall pinpointing all the shipwrecks from the 1830s to the present day. Reasonably priced and highly recommended.

Classic Café, 364 Duckworth St (☎579-4444). An atmospheric 24hr place serving traditional Newfoundland main courses and desserts from $6. A bit noisy, and tables are crowded together.

Crooked Crab Café and Savage Lobster Restaurant, 98 Duckworth St (☎738-8900). A small café downstairs (nonsmoking) and more formal restaurant upstairs (smoking), serving excellent food prepared with fresh, wholesome ingredients. Friendly and obliging staff. Not licensed and no BYO.

The Galley Fish and Chips, 288 Water St at George St (☎726-7786). Cod, clams, squid and scallops fried with not a hint of grease.

Heritage Bakeshop & Delicatessen, 320 Duckworth St (☎739-5353). Not much to look at from outside, but this busy snack bar-cum-restaurant serves big juicy sandwiches and tasty salads.

The Hungry Fisherman, the Murray Premises on Water St (☎726-5791). Fresh seafood in an attractive setting with friendly service. The chocolate Screech cake – a chocolate mousse cake on a dark crumble crust filled with rum (Screech) – is a highlight.

Leo's Restaurant and Take-Out, 27 Freshwater Rd (☎726-2658). Good spot to try some of the local specialities like cods' tongues and, in season, seal-flipper pie, as well as superb fish and chips. Closed Sun.

Nautical Nellie's, 201 Water St (☎738-1120). Pasta, pizza and seafood main courses starting from $8. Excellent chowder and salads. Model ships fill the dining area.

Stella's Natural Foods, 106 Water St (☎753-9625). Imaginative and well-conceived menu with a health-food slant; excellent lunches for around $8, main evening courses starting from $12. Short opening hours, but the food's well worth it.

Stone House, 8 Kenna's Hill (☎753-2380). Located near the west end of Quidi Vidi Lake, this expensive place serves traditional Newfoundland game and seafood dinners; reservations advised.

Zachary's Restaurant, 71 Duckworth St (☎579-8050). Close to the *Hotel Newfoundland*, this restaurant serves good Newfoundland seafood dishes, though the main courses are pricey. Ask for their breakfast special.

Music bars, pubs and clubs

Blarney Stone Irish Pub, corner of George and Adelaide sts. Good live folk acts, with rather a boisterous atmosphere after about 10pm. Foot-tapping Newfoundland Irish and traditional music nightly. The place is a bit hard to find: at the street corner, look for the *Holdsworth Court* sign, go to the end of the court and up the steps. $3–5 cover charge Thursday to Saturday.

Corner Stone Video Dance Bar, 16 Queen St. In a historic stone building that was a fisherman's hall and later a Roman Catholic girls' school. Live rock, folk or disco from Thursday to Saturday.

Duke of Duckworth Pub, 325 Duckworth St (down the steps south to Water St). Serves a wide range of traditional Newfoundland ales and lagers and their own brew, plus daily lunch.

The Edge, above the *Rob Roy* pub, 8a George St. Rock and alternative music – absolutely no folk or Celtic. Live bands Wednesday to Saturday. $3 cover charge.

Erin's Pub, 186 Water St. Popular and well-established bar, showcasing the best of folk acts six nights a week. No cover charge.

Fat Cat Blues Bar, 5 George St. Lively venue, playing R&B and jazz through to folk. Live music nightly. Ten draught beers on tap. $5 cover charge.

Jungle Jim's Bar and Eatery, corner of George and Holdsworth sts. The food's nothing to write home about, but this lively bar is always good fun and features some of the best folk acts around. $3 cover charge Friday and Saturday.

Ship Inn, down the steps (Solomon's Lane) south off Duckworth St. Dark, sea captain's pub with pool tables and eclectic live music attracting a mix of grizzled old-timers and arty, black-clad young people.

Sundance Saloon, 33a New Gower St at George St. Thumping music at this crowded disco bar. $4 cover charge Friday and Saturday.

Westminster Pub and Eatery, 210 Water St. An English-style pub and eatery offering daily lunch and dinner specials as well as a selection of classic British pub fare. Twelve draught beers on tap.

Zone 216, 216 Water St. St John's liveliest gay bar. Dark, cramped and sweaty.

Listings

Airlines International and domestic flights: Air Alliance (Québec City to Wabush; ☎1-800/363-7050); Air Canada in the *Hotel Newfoundland*, Cavendish Square, and Scotia Centre, Water St (both ☎726-7880, rest of Canada ☎1-800/4-CANADA, USA ☎1-800/776-3000); Air Labrador (within Newfoundland ☎753-5593 or 1-800/563-3042, outside Newfoundland ☎896-3387); Air Nova (an Air Canada partner) in the *Hotel Newfoundland*, Cavendish Square (☎726-7880 or 1-800/563-5151); Air St-Pierre (in St-Pierre ☎508/414718, in Halifax ☎902/873-3566, in Sydney ☎902/562-3140). Local flights: Air Atlantic (a Canadian Airlines partner), St John's airport (☎576-0274 or 1-800/665-1177); Interprovincial Airlines, St John's Airport (within Newfoundland ☎1-800/563-2800, outside Newfoundland ☎576-1666).

Bike rental Canary Cycles, 294 Water St (☎579-5972), rents bikes for $20 per day.

Bookshops Afterwords, 245 Duckworth St (☎753-4690), has a good secondhand selection; Wordplay, 221 Duckworth St (☎726-9193), has a large range of Newfoundland titles, as well as a coffee bar and art gallery.

Bus companies There are several minibus companies connecting St John's with the towns and villages across the island, but the biggest and most reliable is DRL Coachlines (☎738-8088, *www .drlgroup.com*), which has daily departures from the airport and the Education Building at Memorial University for towns along the Trans-Canada: principal stops are Clarenville ($28), Gander ($42), Grand Falls-Windsor ($52), Deer Lake ($69), Corner Brook ($73), Stephenville ($79) and Channel-Port aux Basques ($90). DRL also goes to the Burin Peninsula, departing daily from St John's and arriving in Grand Bank and Fortune ($20 one-way to both places). For complete details check at their desk at the airport (☎738-8088). Newhook's Transportation, 13 Queen St (☎726-4876), has frequent services to Argentia ($18), connecting with the ferry to Nova Scotia. For services to Trinity and Bonavista villages, call Catalina Taxi (☎682-9977), whose minibuses go to the Lockston intersection, 6km from Trinity, for $20, and to Bonavista for $24. To get to Harbour Grace and the Conception Bay area, take Fleetline Buses (1 Mon–Sat; $10; ☎722-2608) from the *Delta St John's Hotel*, 120 New Gower St. You can also get to the north shore of the Bonavista Peninsula with Bonavista North Transportation, 1 Macklin Place (☎579-3188). Cheeseman's (☎753-7022) goes daily to the Burin Peninsula, picking up door-to-door and charging $20 one-way.

Camping equipment Try Outfitters' Adventure Gear and Apparel, 220 Water St (☎579-4453, *outfitters@nf.aibn.ca*).

Car rental Budget, at St John's Airport, behind the *Hotel Newfoundland* and at 954 Topsail Rd (all ☎747-1234 or 1-800/268-8900, *www.budget.ca*); Discount, 350 Kenmount Rd (☎722-6699 or 1-800/263-2355); Rent-a-Wreck, 43 Pippy Place (☎753-2277 or 1-800/327-0116); Thrifty, 39 Airport Heights Drive (☎576-4351, *www.thrifty.com*) and 278 Kenmount Rd (☎576-4352).

Consulates Netherlands, 55 Kenmount Rd (☎737-5616 or 722-6436); UK, 113 Topsail Rd (☎579-2002 or 579-0475).

Dental emergencies Village Dental Office, Village Shopping Centre, corner of Topsail Rd and Columbus Drive (☎364-2453).

Disabled visitors For information on disabled-accessible facilities and accommodation in St John's, call ☎576-8455; for the rest of the province and Labrador, call ☎1-800/563-5363.

Emergencies ☎911 for police, fire and ambulance.

Hospitals General Hospital, Prince Philip Parkway (☎737-6300, emergency ☎737-6335); Janeway Child Health Centre, Janeway Place (☎778-4222, emergency ☎778-4575, medical advice line ☎722-1126); Grace General Hospital, 241 LeMarchant Rd (☎778-6222, emergency ☎778-6710); St Clare's Mercy Hospital, 154 LeMarchant Rd (☎778-3111, emergency ☎778-3500 and ext 3501, 3502 or 3503).

Laundry Merrymeeting Laundromat, 154 Merrymeeting Rd (Mon–Fri 8.30am–9pm, Sat 8.30am–6pm, Sun 10am–6pm); Mighty White's, 150 Duckworth St, near the *Hotel Newfoundland* (daily 7.30am–9.30pm); Laundromat Twin Cities, 918 Topsail Rd, Mount Pearl (daily 8.15am–10pm).

Lost property (☎722-9400 or 570-2064).

Pharmacy Shopper's Drug Mart, 193 LeMarchant Rd (Mon–Sat 9am–10pm, Sun 10am–10pm).

Police (☎772-4546 or 772-5400).

Post office The main central post office is at the corner of Water and Queen sts (Mon–Fri 8am–5pm).

Rape crisis and information line (☎726-1411).

Shopping The best places to purchase genuine Newfoundland handicrafts, knitwear and jewellery are The Cod Jigger, 245–247 Duckworth St; Devon House Craft Shop and Gallery, 59 Duckworth St; the Newfoundland Heritage Gift Shop, Murray Premises, Harbour Drive and the Avalon Mall; Newfoundland Reflections, 202 Water St; Nonia Handicrafts, 286 Water St; and The Salt Box, 194 Duckworth St.

Swimming Aquarena, Memorial University complex, corner of Prince Philip Drive and Westerland Rd; Olympic-sized pool.

Taxis Bugden's, 266 Blackmarsh Rd (☎726-6565); Co-op, Churchill Park (☎726-6666); Jiffy Cabs, Avalon Mall, Kenmount Rd (☎722-2222); plus ranks outside the *Hotel Newfoundland*.

Travel agencies Harvey's Travel, 92 Elizabeth Ave (☎726-4115 or 726-4715); St-Pierre Tours, 116 Duckworth St (☎722-4103 or 1-888/959-8214); Travel Management, 162 Water St (☎726-9200).

Weather For up-to-date bulletins, call ☎772-5534.

Women's contacts St John's Status of Women Council, 83 Military Rd (☎753-0220).

Around St John's: Cape Spear, Bay Bulls and the eastern shore

It's a twenty-minute drive along Route 11 from St John's – take the signposted turning off Pitts Memorial Drive, the southward continuation of New Gower Street – to the rocky headland that makes up **Cape Spear National Historic Site**, often visited because it's nearer Europe than any other part of mainland North America. To cater for the tourists, the cape is encircled by a winding walkway, from which there are superb views along the coast and of The Narrows, which lead into St John's harbour. In spring and early summer, the waters off the cape are a good place to see both passing whales and the blue-tinged icebergs that have cracked away from the Arctic pack ice and drifted south. In early summer, when the capelin (smelt) roll onto the Avalon Peninsula's sandier coves to spawn, they're often pursued by shoals of whales devouring hundreds of fish at a gulp. It's a remarkable sight, but there's no way of knowing which cove and when; the park rangers may be able to point you in the right direction.

The park walkway connects incidental attractions: a **visitor centre** (daily: mid-May to June & Sept to mid-Oct 10am–6pm; July & Aug 9am–8pm; ☎772-4862); the remains of a World War II gun emplacement where outdoor concerts are held each Tuesday and Thursday between July and September (9pm; 1hr 30min; adults $10, students $5, children under 12 free; *www.voices.nf.ca*); a modern lighthouse; and an **old lighthouse** (late June to mid-Oct daily 10am–6.30pm; $2.50), which has been returned to its 1830s appearance with a keeper's residence inside.

From Cape Spear it's a fifteen-minute drive south to the village of **PETTY HARBOUR**, where a dramatic headland dotted with houses looms over the community. If you have to stay in Petty Harbour, **stay** at the *Orca Inn Hospitality Home* (☎747-9676 or 1-877/747-9676, *orcainn.nf.ca*; ②), in the south part of town, which offers four rooms in an attractive white-clapboard house.

Another enjoyable excursion is to the straggling village of **BAY BULLS**, 30km south of St John's along Route 10, sitting at the head of a deep and pointed bay that witnessed the surrender of one of the last active German U-boats in 1945 – much to the amazement of the local inhabitants, who watched from the shoreline. There's nothing much to the place itself, although the **Catholic church**, on Northside Road, is interesting for its iron gate flanked by statues of saints perched on cannons for pedestals. However, the village is the base for **boat tours out to Witless Bay Ecological Reserve**, four sea-bird-covered islets just south of Bay Bulls: O'Brien's Whale and Bird Tours, beside the waterfront on Southside Road (7 tours daily; 9.30am–7.30pm, call for times; ☎753-4850 or 1-877/639-4253, *www.netfx.ca/obriens*); Mullowney's Puffin and Whale Tours, next to O'Brien's (daily 9.30am, noon, 3pm & 6pm; ☎334-3666, *www3.nf.sympatico.ca /puffins-whales*); Gatheralls Puffin and Whale Watch, on Northside Road (6 tours daily; ☎334-2887 or 1-800/419-4253, *mgwhales@seascape.com*); and Captain Murphy's Seabird and Whale Tours, Witless Bay along the Southern Shore Highway (Route 10), 20 kilometres south of St John's (4 tours daily; 9am–6pm, call for times; ☎334-2002 or 1-888/783-3467, *www.witlessbay.com*). All companies run two-hour sea trips ($30–40) between May and October to the reserve. Reservations are recommended and many operators will also provide transport to and from major hotels in St John's for roughly $20 return. The best time to visit is between mid-June and mid-July, when over five million birds gather here – the reserve has the largest puffin colony in eastern Canada and there are also thousands of storm petrels, kittiwakes, razorbills, guillemots, cormorants and herring gulls. The waters of Bay Bulls and **Witless Bay** are home to the largest population of **humpback whales** in the world, and finback and minke whales are also often spotted in the area between June and August. Icebergs are a common sight in late

June to early July, with as many as 800 of them floating by Newfoundland's coast each year. These magnificent chunks of ice can be spotted from the shore, usually weighing from one to two hundred tonnes and towering fifteen storeys high. Just north of Bay Bulls is **The Spout**, a wave-driven geyser that shoots water at tremendous speed through a tiny opening in the rock; the boat tours will sometimes include it on their itinerary.

For those seeking adventure, **sea kayaking** in the protected harbour of Bay Bulls is an exciting way to explore the coastline and nearby sea caves. Contact Bay Bulls Sea Kayaking Tours (☎ and fax 334-3394, *www.netfx.ca/kayak*) to arrange for tours, which include on-shore instruction followed by a three-hour paddle.

If you find you need to **stay** in Bay Bulls, *Gatherall's Hospitality Home and Restaurant*, Northside Road (☎334-2887 or 1-800/419-4253; ②; mid-May to mid-Oct), has three double rooms and serves good home-cooked meals. There are also several comfortable bed and breakfasts in Witless Bay: *Armstrong's B&B* (☎334-2201, *anita@avalon.nf.ca*; ②); *Elaine's B&B by the Sea* (☎334-2722, *www.netfx.ca/elainesbythesea*; ②/③); *Jean's B&B* (☎334-2075; ②); and *Marie's B&B* (☎334-2245; ②; mid-May to mid-Sept).

Places to **eat**-in are limited: try the *O'Brien's Restaurant* on the main wharf (open until 8pm only) or the *Captains Table Restaurant*, in Witless Bay, known for its good fish and chips at a reasonable price.

It's worth continuing on to **FERRYLAND**, 40km south of Bay Bulls, to see the remains of the "Colony of Avalon" established by George Calvert in 1621 (see opposite) and the first continuous settlement in Canada. Archeologists are still unearthing traces

---

NEWFOUNDLAND FOLK MUSIC

The musical culture of Newfoundland was defined by the early settlers from England and Ireland, whose evenings would typically begin with step dances and square sets performed to the accompaniment of the **fiddle** and the **button accordion**, followed by the unaccompanied **singing** of locally composed and "old country" songs. The music was never written down, so as it passed from one generation to another a distinctive **Newfoundland style** evolved, whose rhymes and rhythms varied from village to village – though its Irish and English roots always remained pronounced.

Newfoundland's musical fabric began to unravel in the 1930s and 1940s with the arrival of thousands of American soldiers during World War II and the advent of radio and television. A multitude of influences became interwoven with the indigenous forms, none more pronounced than C&W, whose introduction has produced a hybrid in which an old story or ballad is given a C&W melody and rhythm, the accordion supported by lead and bass guitar and drum. The unadulterated style of folk music is becoming increasingly hard to find, especially after the deaths in the 1980s of the island's most famous fiddlers, **Rufus Guinchard** and **Émile Benoit**, the latter from the Port au Port Peninsula on the island's west coast. Nevertheless, marginally modified versions of Newfoundland's traditional songs are regularly performed by younger generations of revivalists: singer-songwriters such as Jim Payne and Ron Hynes, musician-producers such as Kelly Russell, and groups such as **Figgy Duff** have all played important roles in this process. Other important musicians include **Dermot O'Reilly**, **Phyllis Morrissey**, **Pamela Morgan**, **Anita Best**, and the groups **Great Big Sea** and the **Irish Descendants**, who are among the most popular on the island today.

More than 350 recordings of the island's music are available at two principal St John's outlets: **O'Brien's Music Store**, 278 Water St, and **Fred's**, 198 Duckworth St. The **Pigeon Inlet Productions** label is the one to look out for: the company is run by Kelly Russell, and you can get a comprehensive brochure or the recordings themselves direct from him at Pigeon Inlet Productions, 51 Monkstown Rd, St John's, NF A1C 3T4 (☎754-7324, fax 722-8557). Pigeon Inlet also organizes **Dance-Up**, where you're given lessons in the various traditional Newfoundland folk dances.

THE IRISH LOOP

The circuit made by routes 10 and 90 around the southeastern shores of the Avalon Peninsula are known, in a bit of tourism-friendly lingo, as the Irish Loop, though to be sure there are definite signs of Newfoundland's Irish heritage in many of the communities and businesses along here. The loop takes in evocative spots like Ferryland, Bay Bulls and **TREPASSEY**, the last of these right nearby the **Mistaken Point Ecological Reserve**, where soft-bodied marine **fossils** that have been found are estimated to be at least 525 million years old – possibly the oldest fossils in the Western Hemisphere. Tours can be begun from the tourist information centre some sixteen kilometres north at tiny **Portugal Cove South** – it's very name proving that there's a bit more of a multicultural story to the area than the designation might suggest.

---

of the short-lived settlement (destroyed by the French in 1696), including several stone buildings, a **cobblestone street** and a stone **privy** (the earliest-known flush toilet in North America, allegedly). A new **Interpretation Centre** (daily: June to Aug 9am–7pm; Sept to mid-Oct 9am–5pm; $5.75 adults; ☎432-3200 or 1-877/326-5669, *www.heritage.nf.ca/avalon*) gives you an insight into the establishment of the colony. Price of admission includes a guided tour of the site, though you can also explore on your own. Much of the **excavations** are carried out around the houses of the local inhabitants, and it's amusing to listen to the banter between archeologists and the townspeople, who keenly observe what's being dug up from their streets and gardens. To get a sense of post-1696 local history, visit the **Historic Ferryland Museum** (Mon–Sat 9am–5pm, Sun 1–5pm; $1), located in a 1916 courthouse, which counts among its displays a fisherman's room, full of nets, hooks and other angler gear, an original jailhouse and traditional tools for fishing and building.

If you need to stay the night, the *Downs Inn B&B* (☎432-2808, *acostello@nf.sympatico.ca*; ②/③), in an old convent next to the historical museum has spacious rooms. Some have superb views of the harbour and coastline. For **food**, the *Irish Loop Drive Restaurant*, on the main road overlooking the village has shrimp or scallops and chips for $4.95.

Much of the length of the peninsula's east coast is made walkable by the **East Coast Trail**, a system of backcountry routes and hunting paths that passes through fishing communities, provincial parks, national historic sites and a couple of ecological reserves. Currently, a two hundred-kilometre section of the trail connects St John's to Cappahayden, and construction is underway to expand the trail to Topsoil, in the north, and Trepassey in the south. For more information on the status of the trail, and for the word on where the best walks are along the way, contact the East Coast Trail Association (☎738-4453, *www.ectna.nf.ca*).

The Avalon Peninsula

St John's lies on the eastern shore of the **Avalon Peninsula**, a jagged, roughly rectangular slab of land that's connected to the rest of Newfoundland by a narrow isthmus only 4km wide. Concentrated around **Conception Bay**, whose eastern shoreline lies 15km west of the capital, the Avalon's settlements stick resolutely to the coast, hiding from a bare and rocky interior that received its inappropriate name when **George Calvert**, later Lord Baltimore, received a royal charter to colonize the region in 1621. Calvert subsequently became the victim of a confidence trick: the settlers he dispatched sent him such wonderful reports that he decided to move there himself. He only lasted one winter, writing to a friend – "I have sent [my family] home after much sufferance in this woful country, where with one intolerable wynter were wee almost undone. It is not to be expressed with my pen what wee have endured".

Harbour Grace and around

Conception Bay's prettiest settlement is **HARBOUR GRACE** on its western shore, tucked in against Route 70, 100km from the capital and reached by Fleetline Buses (see "Listings", p.426). This elongated village – originally called "Havre de Grace" by the French in the sixteenth century – stretches out along another Water Street, which is at its most attractive near the northern end, where a handful of elegant clapboard houses, the handsome silver and green-spired Church of the Immaculate Conception, and the pretty stone St Paul's Anglican church, are set against a slender, rock-encrusted inlet. The old red-brick Customs House, now the Conception Bay Museum, has been turned into a mildly entertaining **museum** (June–Sept Mon–Fri 10am–6pm; free; ☎596-1309), featuring photos of the village and its Victorian inhabitants, and an outdoor plaque commemorating **Peter Easton**, the so-called "Pirate Admiral" who was based here at the beginning of the seventeenth century. Easton's phenomenally successful fleet was run by five thousand islanders, who made their leader rich enough to retire to a life of luxury in the south of France. Next door, the tiny park has a further plaque in honour of the early aviators who flew across the Atlantic from the Harbour Grace area, including **Amelia Earhart** in 1932, the first woman to complete the journey solo.

There's no reason to spend more than a couple of hours here, but if you decide to **stay** there's the *Hotel Harbour Grace* on Water Street (☎596-5156 or 1-877/333-5156; ③), which has an excellent fish restaurant, or *Rothesay House Inn*, 34 Water St (☎596-2268, *www.rothesay.com*; ②/③), a historic Queen Anne Victorian home.

Heart's Content and south

In the middle of the nineteenth century, **HEART'S CONTENT**, 30km northwest of Harbour Grace on the eastern shore of Trinity Bay, was packed with engineers attempting to connect North America with Britain by **telegraph cable**, a project that had begun when the USS *Niagara* hauled the first transatlantic line ashore here in 1858. However, after Queen Victoria and the American president James Buchanan had swapped inaugural jokes, the cable broke and it was eight years before an improved version, running from Valentia in Ireland, could be installed. Heart's Content became an important relay station to New York, a role it performed until technological changes made it obsolete in the 1960s. Squatting by the waterfront, in the centre of the village, the **Cable Station Provincial Historic Site** (mid-June to mid-Oct daily 10am–5.30pm; mid-Oct to mid-June Mon–Fri 9am–4.30pm; free) boasts an intriguing cable operating room in pristine condition, and houses a series of displays on the history of telecommunications, including a replica of the original Victorian cable office and details of the problems encountered during the laying of the first telegraph lines.

Heart's Content is approached from Harbour Grace along Route 74 or from the Trans-Canada Highway, 60km to the south, via Route 80. About 2km from the village is the junction of routes 74 and 80, where *Legge's Motel* (☎583-2929; ②/③) has basic double rooms and its attached restaurant does reasonable fish and chips.

Further up the highway is **HIBBS COVE**, another picturesque fishing village. Visit the **Fisherman's Museum** (late June to early Sept daily 11am–7pm; $2; ☎786-3912 or 786-3900) and the **one-room schoolhouse** (built in 1910) for a fascinating look into the daily life of this community. The schoolhouse is filled with period detail, from the daily readers and notepaper on each desk down to the dunce chair and pointy cap in the corner. Placards with original photos show the area's history. Visitors include many former students and residents who come to relive their earlier years. Just around the corner from the schoolhouse, the *Copper Kettle* serves tea with cakes and biscuits.

WHITBOURNE
Some 45 or so kilometres south on Route 81 from Heart's Content, **WHITBOURNE** holds one of Newfoundland's more intriguing wineries, **Rodrigues Winery** (July–Sept daily 9am–4.30pm; Sept–June Mon–Fri 9am–4.30pm; $1; *www.rodrigueswinery.com*), located in an old hospital. They produce varietals from strange fruit indeed, like partridgeberry, blueberry and bakeapple (an orange-colored fruit that resembles a raspberry but has a unique taste); personalized tours help demonstrate the process.

Castle Hill National Historic Site and Cape St Mary's

The thumb-shaped promontory filling out the southwest corner of the Avalon Peninsula is a foggy wilderness of marsh and rock trimmed by St Mary's and Placentia bays. Its northern section is crossed by **Route 100**, branching off the Trans-Canada Highway at Whitbourne, 80km from St John's, and as this is the main road to the ferry terminal at Argentia most people drive straight past the turning for the tiny **Castle Hill National Historic Site**, just 5km short of the port (daily: mid-June to Aug 8.30am–8pm; Sept to mid-June 8.30am–4.30pm; $2.50; ☎227-5614). This is a pity, because Castle Hill is magnificently located overlooking a watery web of harbour, channel and estuary that combine to connect the fjord-like inlets of the South East Arm and North East rivers with Placentia Bay.

The topography makes **Placentia Harbour** one of Newfoundland's finest anchorages, and its sheltered waters attracted the French, who in 1662 established Plaisance, their regional headquarters, here. Castle Hill was the area's key defensive position and so, as the fortunes of war seesawed, it was successively occupied and refortified by the British and the French. Today, little remains of these works – just a few stone walls and ditches – but make the trip for the views and drop into the **Interpretive Centre** (mid-May to Oct daily 8.30am–8pm) which has excellent displays and artefacts depicting daily life in the late 1600s and early 1700s. Guided tours are available during the summer months. Daily live performances re-enact scenes from 1696 when the French struggled to establish a colony at Plaisance (Wed–Fri 11am & 2pm, Sat & Sun 2pm & 3pm; $5 adults, $2 seniors, $1 students; ☎227-2299).

Seen from the top of Castle Hill, the village of **Placentia**, at the start of the road leading to Cape St Mary's, looks pretty enough, a ribbon of buildings sandwiched between the green of the hills and the blue of the bay. However, on closer inspection, the village has little to offer in terms of particular sights, and you're better off continuing south for the fifty-kilometre drive to the tiny community of **St Bride's**. From here it's a further 20km to the lighthouse and interpretive centre (daily: May 9am–5pm; June–Sept 8am–7pm; Oct 9am–5pm; ☎277-1666 or 682-9024) of **Cape St Mary's Ecological Reserve**. The reserve is best visited between May and early August, when hundreds of thousands of sea birds, principally gannets, kittiwakes, razorbills and murres congregate on the rocky cliffs and stumpy sea stacks along the shore. The best vantage point along the trail, from which you'll get closest to the nesting pairs of gannets covering Bird Rock, is about a half an hour's walk from the lighthouse. A word of caution: it is extremely important to wear good hiking shoes and follow the marked trail as fog can quickly settle in without any notice and portions of the trail follow steep cliffs on which one wrong step can lead to disaster. **St Bride**'s is the nearest village to Cape St Mary's and has three **places to stay**: the dramatically sited *Bird Island Resort* (☎337-2450 or 1-888/337-2450, *cmanning@thezone.ne*t; ③) which has whale- and bird-watching opportunities; the slightly cheaper *Atlantica Inn* (☎337-2860 or 1-888/999-2860; ②), which has a fairly standard restaurant; and the *Cape Way Motel* (☎337-2163 or 337-2028; ②), about midway between the others in comfort and price range.

The Burin Peninsula

The 230-kilometre-long, bony **Burin Peninsula** juts south into the Atlantic between Fortune and Placentia bays from the west side of the isthmus connecting the Avalon Peninsula with the rest of Newfoundland. It's crossed by Route 210, a turning off the Trans-Canada about 160km from St John's, a road that starts promisingly with the melodramatic scenery of the **Piper's Hole River** estuary, where there's excellent salmon fishing and hiking trails in the small park ($2 entry). After that, the journey runs across bog-filled plateau, seemingly impenetrable, and probably not worth the time for most. The main reason for travelling the Burin is to catch the ferry to St-Pierre et Miquelon (see opposite) from **Fortune** (for services to Fortune, see p.435).

Grand Bank

Spreading out beside the sea 200km south of the Trans-Canada, the older streets of **GRAND BANK** incorporate a charming assortment of late nineteenth-century timber houses, a few of which are equipped with the so-called "widow's walks", rooftop galleries where the women watched for their returning menfolk. Some of these houses are splendid, reflecting a time when the village's proximity to the Grand Banks fishing grounds brought tremendous profits to the shipowners, if not to the actual fishermen. Nowadays the fishery is in an acute state of decline, much to the frustration of local people, who apportion blame amongst a number of old enemies: foreigners who overfish, big marketing corporations who are indifferent to local interests, and a government that imposes unrealistic quotas. With many of its fishermen out of work, the future of Grand Bank looks grim, especially as many feel an inflexible affinity to the fishing that it's hard for outsiders to understand: as one of their representatives declared, "Without fish there is no soul, no pride, no nothing."

To see something of this tradition, visit the **Southern Newfoundland Seamen's Museum** (mid-June to Sept 9.30am–4.45pm; $2.50; *www.nfmuseum.com*), situated off Marine Drive on the edge of the village in a modern building shaped like the sails of a schooner. It has all sorts of models, paintings and photographs of different types of fishing boats, and a relief model of Newfoundland and the surrounding ocean that shows where the illustrious "Banks" actually are. There's a self-guided **walking tour** of the scenic architecture of the town, as well as marine and nature walks; pick up descriptive brochures at the Brumac Building, 15 Water St (☎832-1574).

Grand Bank has a **B&B**, the *Thorndyke*, a stately old sea captain's house at 33 Water St (☎832-0820; ②; May–Oct), and a newly renovated **motel**, *Granny's*, on Grandview Boulevard (☎832-2180 or 832-2355; ③). For **food**, the only option is the unexciting *Manuel's Restaurant*, 3 Main St – the service and decor are indifferent, but the seafood platter is a bargain at only $10. Foote's Taxi (☎364-1377 in St John's, ☎832-0491 in Grand Bank) operates a daily service to Grand Bank from St John's ($30), departing at 4pm.

Fortune

FORTUNE, perched on the seashore a couple of kilometres from Grand Bank, is a slightly smaller village, whose 2500 inhabitants are mostly employed in the fish-processing plant and the inshore fishery. A modest and sleepy little place, it has one reasonable motel, the *Fair Isle*, just back down the main road towards Grand Bank (☎832-1010, *fred.nurse@nf.sympatico.ca*; ③); there are no B&Bs in town. The *Fair Isle* serves superb **seafood**, at about $12 for a main course; the only other decent eating place is the *Central Restaurant*, near the ferry terminal at 17 Bayview St, where the usual fried seafood is dished up. For **campers** there's the *Horsebrook Trailer Park* (☎832-2090; May–Sept) on Eldon Street on the outskirts of the village, with unserviced sites for $4. The only **public transport** to the Fortune ferry is provided by a local operator, Oceanview Taxi, in Grand Bank (☎832-2311). St-Pierre Tours, 116 Duckworth St, St John's (☎722-3892, 722-4103 or 1-888/959-8214 in St John's, ☎832-0429 in Fortune), also offers a minibus service from St John's to Fortune on most days throughout July and August, as part of their St-Pierre vacation package; it adds an extra $100 to the cost of the trip. If you're planning to go to St-Pierre et Miquelon – and that's probably the reason why you've come to Fortune anyway – keep in mind that you're not allowed to take your car over; however, you can **park** it in Fortune in a secure, fenced-off and patrolled compound near the ferry terminal ($8 flat fee) and pick it up when you return.

St-Pierre et Miquelon

The tiny archipelago of **St-Pierre et Miquelon**, 25km off the coast of the Burin Peninsula, became a fully fledged *département* of mainland France in 1976 and a *collectivité territoriale* in 1985, giving a legalistic legitimacy to the billing of the islands as "a little bit of France at your doorstep" – a phrase that attracts several thousand visitors each year and manages to gloss over the lack of actual attractions and the wetness of the climate. Yet the islands are still worth a day or two for the francophone atmosphere of the main settlement, **St-Pierre**, whose fine restaurants and simple guesthouses have a genuinely European flavour. All but 700 of the 6500 islanders live in the town of St-Pierre, with the remainder – mainly of Acadian and Basque descent – marooned on **Miquelon** to the north. The third and middle island, **Langlade**, has just a scattering of houses and is inhabited only in summer.

The St-Pierre et Miquelon telephone code is ☎508.

The three islands of St-Pierre et Miquelon were first discovered by the Portuguese in 1520 and claimed for the French king by **Jacques Cartier** in 1536. Subsequently settled by fishermen from the Basque provinces, Normandy and Brittany, they were alternately occupied by Britain and France until the French finally lost their North American colonies in 1763, whereupon they were allowed to keep the islands as a commercial sop. St-Pierre et Miquelon soon became a vital supply base and safe harbour for the French fishing fleet, and provided France with a yearly harvest of salted cod.

After World War I, the French colonial authorities wanted to expand the local fishing industry, but their efforts became irrelevant with **Prohibition** in 1920. Quite suddenly, St-Pierre was transformed from a maritime backwater into a giant transit centre for booze smuggling – even the main fish-processing plant was stacked high with thousands of cases of whisky destined for Boston and Long Island; some of the Prohibition warehouses still line the waterfront. It was an immensely lucrative business, but when Prohibition ended thirteen years later the St-Pierre economy dropped through the floor. Those were desperate days, but more misery followed during World War II, when the islands' governor remained controversially loyal to the collaborationist **Vichy** regime. Both the Canadians and the Americans considered invading, but it was a **Free French** naval squadron that got there first, crossing over from their base in Halifax and occupying the islands in late 1941 without a shot being fired.

There was further trouble in 1965 when a **stevedores' strike** forced the administration to resign. De Gaulle promptly dispatched the Navy, who occupied the islands for no less than nine years. Perhaps surprisingly, the St-Pierrais remained largely loyal to France, and they certainly needed the support of Paris when the Canadians extended the limit of their territorial waters to 200 nautical miles in 1977. The ensuing wrangle between Canada and France over the islands' claim to a similar exclusion zone remains unresolved, although the tightening of controls on foreign vessels has largely ended St-Pierre's role as a supply centre.

St-Pierre

The tidy, narrow streets of the town of **ST-PIERRE** edge back from the harbour fronted by a string of tall, stone buildings of quintessentially French demeanour. However, although the central area makes for an enjoyable stroll, there's nothing particular to aim for, with the possible exception of the early twentieth-century **cathedral**, which does at least attempt to look imposing, although its bell tower, made of grey stone from Alsace, is greatly at odds with the rest of the church's exterior, painted an unappealing yellow. Nearby, on rue Gloanec, a 1906 **fronton** (a court on which the game of *pelote*, or *jai alai*, is played) proclaims the island's predominantly Basque heritage; behind it is a typically French *pétanque* field, frequented mainly by older men. The new **museum**, perched on a slope above the harbour in the west part of town, is a striking building whose upswept roof emulates the curves of a ship's hull; the displays here include just about everything relating to the islands' colourful history. To the rear of the building is the flamboyant Baroque-style **war memorial**, honouring the dead of the two world wars. The airy concrete and glass-walled **Francoforum**, at the foot of the hill where the museum is, is where the purity of the French language is preserved through a wide variety of French-language courses offered to Canadian and American students and businesspeople. From the compact town centre it's easy to walk out into the surrounding countryside, passing bare hillocks and marshy ponds to reach the rugged cliffs of the northern shore, just 8km away.

The tiny **Ile aux Marins**, across the harbour from St-Pierre's quayside, can only really be seen on a tour (see opposite), but it's worth it, and is the most enjoyable excursion to be made while in St-Pierre. The island, originally settled by people from Normandy but totally abandoned by 1964, comprises a collection of weather-beaten buildings, including a lighthouse, town hall, school (incorporating a museum) and washhouse, plus stone Stations of the Cross leading to a small cemetery perched on the windiest of promontories. Across the cove from the cemetery is the rusted hulk of the German ship *Transpacific*, which was wrecked there in 1971. The most fascinating building on the island, however, is the 1874 **church**, its isolation having prevented it from being altered over the years in any way; the late nineteenth-century furnishings, brought from Brittany, remain intact, including a large black-wrapped catafalque, used for carrying coffins.

Miquelon and Langlade

At the north end of the archipelago, the dumpy-looking island of **Miquelon** is comprised of a peat bog, marsh and a couple of isolated hills, sloping west from its only village, which bears the same name. The tiny **tourist office** on rue Antoine Soucy (Mon, Wed, Thurs & Sat 8.30am–noon & 2–5pm; Tues, Fri & Sun 8.30am–noon & 2–7.30pm) can provide you with details of what to see on the island, and you can rent a *rosalie* (bicycle) from them to do some touring of your own (F50 for 1hr). Miquelon's 1865 **church**, on rue Sourdeval (daily 9am–noon & 2–6pm) is a delight, filled with *faux-marbre* columns and containing a good copy of a Murillo *Virgin* (donated by Napoléon III) on the altar. Just down the street from the church, the cramped **museum** (Mon 10–11.30am & 2–4pm, Tues & Fri 10am–noon & 2–5pm, Wed & Sun 10–11.30am, Thurs

10am–noon & 2–4pm; F10) features a collection of artefacts salvaged from the island's shipwrecks, plus a curious reconstruction of a 1913–14 photography laboratory set up by a local doctor.

The island's pride and joy is the **Dune of Langlade**, a sweeping ten-kilometre sandy isthmus that connects with the archipelago's middle island, Langlade. The dune began to appear above the ocean two hundred years ago as a result of sand collecting around shipwrecks, and it has continued to grow to its current width of up to 2500m. Although there's a **road** along the Dune connecting Miquelon and Langlade, in heavy seas parts of the Dune can be engulfed by seawater, so stick to the guided tours (see below), which stop at the **Grand Barachois**, a large saltwater pool at the northern end of the isthmus that's a favourite haunt of breeding seals. You'll also probably see herds of wild ponies running along the Dune.

Langlade itself has a more varied landscape than Miquelon – high hills, deciduous forests and rushing brooks – and is at its liveliest in summer, when the St-Pierrois arrive in droves and open up their summer homes.

Practicalities

The cheapest **flights** to the islands are on Air St-Pierre from St John's (April–Oct 3 weekly; 45min; $97; ☎709/722-4103) and from Sydney, Nova Scotia (April–Oct 1–3 weekly; 45min; $106; ☎902/562-3140), but there are also regular connections on other airlines with Halifax and Montréal. St-Pierre **airport**, with its startlingly pink terminal, is located just south of the town across the harbour, and is connected by taxi to the centre.

Flights here are often delayed by fog and the **ferries** plying between Fortune and the town of St-Pierre are more dependable and far cheaper, though the crossing can get mighty rough. If you come by ferry (May–Sept daily; 2.45pm; 1hr 10min; $37.95 one-way, $59.95 return for a solo traveller; Oct to early Dec Fri & Sat only, same times and fees; reservations/information from Lake's Travel, Fortune ☎709/832-2006 or 1-800/563-2006), you usually have to stay the night. There is no same-day return ferry, except about nine times on designated days during July and August – usually one weekly (departing from Fortune 9am, returning from St-Pierre 4.30pm; $46.95). Ferry services are often subject to change with little advance notice, so it's best to check with Lake's Travel before arriving in Fortune.

To clear St-Pierre et Miquelon's **customs control**, Canadians and citizens of the United States need only present an identity document such as a driver's licence or social-security card; EU visitors need a passport. On the return journey to Newfoundland, Canadian customs officials examine the baggage of about every fourth person, looking for excess purchases of alcohol and foodstuffs. St-Pierre et Miquelon's currency is the French franc, but Canadian dollars are widely accepted; however, you'll usually be given back small change in francs. Also, when you're shopping remember that virtually all shops and public buildings close between noon and 2pm, in keeping with French tradition.

The **Agence Régionale du Tourisme de St-Pierre et Miquelon**, on Place du Général de Gaulle on the waterfront (May–Sept Mon–Sat 8.30am–noon & 1–6pm, Sun 8.30–11.30am & 1–6pm; ☎1-800/565-5118), has the timetables of the **ferries** that run from the town of St-Pierre to the village of Miquelon (mid-April to mid-June Tues, Fri & Sun 1–2 daily; mid-June to Sept same days 2 daily; Oct to mid-April same days 1–2 daily; 1hr 10min; F120 return), plus details of the excellent **day-trips by bus and boat**: the all-day Miquelon trip includes the village of Miquelon and the lagoon of the Grand Barachois (mid-June to Sept Tues, Fri & Sun; 11hr; F195); the bus tour around St-Pierre takes in all the sights of town, as well as the rocky south coast (July–Sept daily 10.30am & 6pm; 2hr; F35); the zodiac tour goes along the coasts of St-Pierre and

Langlade, where you can examine at close range the prolific birdlife, seals and whales (mid-June to mid-Sept daily 9am & 2pm; 3hr; F170); and the tour to Ile aux Marins (mid-June to Sept daily 9.30am & 2.30pm; 3hr; F53).

Accommodation

St-Pierre has a good selection of hotels and pensions, though reservations are strongly recommended from July to early September. The easiest solution is to book on a package: Lake's Travel in Fortune (see p.435) offers overnight excursions from $136 and two-night stays from $209; St-Pierre Tours in St John's (☎709/722-3892, 722-4103 or 1-888/959-8214) has a two-night deal from $248. The town's deluxe **hotels** include the *Hôtel Île de France*, 6 rue Maître Georges-Lèfvre (☎41 28 36 or 41 20 22; ⑤), and the *Hôtel/Motel Robert*, 10–12 rue du 11 novembre (☎41 24 19; ⑤), which was where Al Capone stayed during Prohibition (a small museum off the foyer has one of his straw hats and other memorabilia from that period). For **pensions**, which charge a fixed rate per double including breakfast, try the comfortable *Chez Marcel Hélène*, 15 rue Beaussant (☎41 31 08; ②; April–Dec); *Chez Roland Vigneau*, 12 rue des Basques (☎41 38 67; ②; April–Sept); or *L'Arc-en-Ciel*, 26 rue Jacques-Cartier (☎41 25 69; ②). The village of Miquelon has one hotel, one motel and two pensions: the *Hôtel l'Escale*, 30 rue Victor Briand (☎41 64 56; ③); *Motel de Miquelon*, on the sea at 42 rue Sourdeval (☎41 63 10; ④); *Chez Paulette*, 8 rue Victor-Briand (☎41 62 15; ②); and *Chez Monique*, 3 rue Ernest Petitpas (☎41 61 75; ②; May–Sept).

Eating and drinking

St-Pierre's **restaurants** are splendid, combining the best of French cuisine with local delicacies such as *tiaude*, a highly seasoned cod stew. Prices are quite high – reckon on about F80 for a main dish – but it really is worth splashing out at *La Ciboulette*, 2 rue Marcel-Bonin, for *nouvelle cuisine* at its fanciest; at *Le Caveau*, 2 rue Maître Georges-Lefèvre, for the Basque fish and lamb specialities; at *Chez Dutin*, 20 rue Amiral-Muselier, for the salmon; or at *L'Outre-Mer*, 29 rue Boursaint, for any of their local specialities. If you're on a tight budget, stick to the **snack bars** such as *Le Marine Bar* on Place du Général de Gaulle, or drop into *Le Maringouin'fre*, 16 rue Général-Leclerc, for excellent-quality crepes. On Miquelon, some good traditional food is available at the *Snack Bar-à-Choix*, 2 rue Sourdeval.

The Bonavista Peninsula

The thickly wooded **Bonavista Peninsula**, crossed by Route 230 – which leaves the Trans-Canada 190km west of St John's at Clarenville – is trimmed by lots of little outports that were first settled by the English in the seventeenth century. With Trinity Bay on its south coast and Bonavista Bay on its north, the peninsula juts out into the Atlantic, which pounds its wild and remote shores. Dotted along its rocky headlands are attractive fishing villages such as **Trouty** and **Dunfield**, as well as the historic settlement of **Trinity**.

If you want to find out about the attractions when doing a circuit of the peninsula, call the **Discovery Trail Tourism Association** in Clarenville (☎466-3845, *www.thediscoverytrail.org*) and the staff will help you plan your route. Otherwise, stop in at the **tourist information office** on the Trans-Canada Highway near Clarenville (daily: May to mid-Sept 9am–9pm; mid-Sept to mid-Oct 10am–5pm; ☎466-3100).

Trinity

TRINITY, 70km along the peninsula off the main road on Route 239, is the most enchanting of the peninsula's villages. A gem of a place, whose narrow lanes are lined by delightfully restored white and pastel-coloured clapboard houses that reflect its importance as a commercial fishing centre during the nineteenth century. Sandwiched between a ring of hills and a deep and intricate bay lined with lupins, it also boasts the island's finest wooden church, **St Paul's Anglican Church** (1892), whose graceful and dignified interior has a ceiling built to resemble an upturned boat. There's a modest and overcrowded **Community Museum** (daily: mid-May to mid-June & mid-Sept to mid-May 10am–noon & 1–5pm; mid-June to mid-Sept 10am–7.30pm; $2), in the saltbox house on Church Road near St Paul's, with an eccentric collection of bygones, such as an old shoemaker's kit, an early cooperage and an 1811 fire engine, thought to be the oldest existing one in North America. Nearby, on Ash's Lane, is the green-trimmed **Holy Trinity Catholic Church** (1835) serving a congregation of only three people. The orange and green **Hiscock House** on Dock Lane (June to mid-Oct daily 10am–5.30pm; $2.50) has been returned to its appearance circa 1910 when it served as a widow's mercantile home; as ever, costumed guides give the background. Closer to the harbour, on West Street, is a **Blacksmith's Museum**, in an old forge (same hours and price as the Community Museum), and an **interpretive centre** (mid-June to mid-Oct daily 10am–5.30pm; free) that displays material related to the community's three-hundred-year-old history. Next door to the centre is Trinity's newest historic attraction, the **Lester-Garland Premises** (mid-June to mid-Oct daily 10am–5pm; $2.50), a three-storey brick home that belonged to a prominent family of merchants and politicians, which has been reconstructed to its appearance in the 1830s. An early twentieth-century **general store** and old accounting office next to it completes the ensemble. The most striking building in town, however, is the brown and yellow **Parish Hall**, on Dandy Lane, its elegance accentuated by the roof and cupola.

The **Trinity Pageant**, a combination of live theatre and audience participation, is one of Newfoundland's most famous theatrical events. It's performed on various days throughout June, July and August, when the costumed actors walk you through the town while enacting some of the community's most historic and colourful moments. Tickets are $7, sold at the Trinity box office in the Trinity arts centre on the waterfront; for information about performance dates, call ☎464-3232.

Practicalities

Trinity has half a dozen charming B&Bs, foremost of which is the *Campbell House*, on High Street (mid-May to mid-Oct; ☎464-3377, *www.campbellhouse.nf.ca*; ③/④), a handsome early Victorian house perched on a hill in the west part of town. The owners also have two cottages just down the hill, and they serve excellent breakfasts featuring such local delicacies as partridgeberry crepes. The *Beach B&B*, nearby on Church Road (mid-May to mid-Oct; ☎464-3695, *www.bbcanada.com*; ②/③), is another pleasant, if more modest, spot. The *Village Inn* (☎464-3269, *www.oceancontact.com*; ③) is said to be Trinity's oldest established inn, circa 1910. Sit and enjoy the owner's famous

---

WHALE-WATCHING

Based at the *Village Inn* in Trinity, Ocean Contact (☎464-3269) runs an extensive programme of **whale-watching** excursions, or rather, as they insist, whale "contact" trips designed to encourage close encounters between whales and humans. They can't guarantee contact, of course, but there is an excellent chance of sighting minke, finbacks and humpbacks, particularly between mid-June and early August. Expertly run, these excursions take place daily during the peak whale season, and prices begin at $45 for a half-day trip (departures 10am, 2pm & 6pm; 3hr, preceded by an introductory talk). If the sea is too rough for a boat trip, Ocean Contact provides escorted whale-watching walks along the nearby cliffs at half the price.

Manhattans, and listen to his research on human and whale communication. The best place to **eat** is at the *Heritage Tea Rooms*, in the *Eriksen Premises B&B* on West Street (☎464-3698 or 464-3327, *www.trinityexperience.nf.ca*; ③–⑤; May–Sept), which serves gourmet seafood dinners, or the cheaper *Polly's Pantry*, in the same building, which has chowder, stuffed croissants and thick sandwiches. Afterwards, you can stroll up the hill to *Rocky's Place* for a drink. Good food is also available at the *Dock Marina Restaurant* (☎464-2133) on Dock Lane.

You can **get to** Trinity from St John's with Catalina Taxi (☎682-9977), which, for $20, will take you to the Lockston intersection, a few kilometres away. Alternatively, DRL Coachlines drops passengers at the Irving petrol station on the edge of Clarenville, and the waiting taxis charge about $30 for the onward trip. There are historical tours of Trinity's harbour (May–Sept daily 10am, 1.30pm & 5pm; $16; ☎464-3355 or 464-3400) departing from near the *Dock Marina Restaurant*.

Trinity Bay and Cape Bonavista

Exploring the serrated shoreline of **Trinity Bay** is a fine way to spend a day or two, with Route 239 twisting its way south from Trinity through a string of remote outports. **Dunfield** occupies a dramatic setting, straggling along a jutting promontory, whilst tiny **TROUTY**, just 6km from Trinity, is tucked into the rockiest of coves, whose steep and bare cliffs rise all around. This delightful village, with its tumbling brook and rickety wooden jetties, has a real hideaway, the *Riverside Lodge and Tourist Home* (☎464-3780; ②; April–Oct), an unpretentious hotel-cum-B&B. A few kilometres on, **Old** and **New Bonaventure** circle another rocky bay at the end of the road – on a rainy day it seems like the end of the world. Heading north from Trinity, via Route 230, is the ribbon village of **TRINITY EAST**, home to the reputedly haunted *Peace Cove Inn* (☎464-3738 or 464-3419, 781-2255 in the off-season, *www.atlanticadventure.com*; ②/③; May–Oct), whose owners run excellent coastal excursions – Atlantic Adventures – on a motorsailer (May–Oct daily 10am & 2pm; 2hr 30min; $30; 6.30pm; 1hr 30min; $20; full-day charters $85 per person; ☎464-2133).

Cape Bonavista

Some 55km north of Trinity, the red-and-white-striped lighthouse on **Cape Bonavista** looks out over a violent coastline of dark-grey rock and pounding sea. This beautifully desolate headland, populated by hundreds of puffins, is supposed to be the spot where the English-sponsored Genoese explorer **John Cabot** first clapped eyes on the Americas in 1497. The tourist literature claims he cried out, "O buona vista!" ("O, happy sight") – whatever the truth of the matter, a statue has been built here in his honour.

The **lighthouse** (mid-June to mid-Oct daily 10am–5.30pm; $2.50), now a Provincial Historic Site, has been restored to its appearance in 1870 when it was occupied by an 80-year-old lighthouse keeper, Jeremiah White, and his family; costumed guides give the background. Close to the lighthouse are the **Dungeons**, huge rock caves formed by collapsing sedimentary rock.

The cape is 5km from the expansive fishing village of **BONAVISTA**, which spreads out across the flattish headlands surrounding its double harbour. Here you'll find another historic site, the plain white clapboard **Mockbeggar Property** on Roper Street (same times as lighthouse; $2.50), once the home of F. Gordon Bradley, one of the island's first representatives in the Canadian Senate. Most of the house is 1940s-style, but has the surprising addition of heavily ornate, English-made Victorian and Edwardian furniture, plus a large library and conference room featuring a stained-glass window of Cabot's landing. On Ryan's Hill, at the other end of town, is the **Ryan Premises National Historic Site**, opened in 1997 (mid-June to mid-Oct daily 10am–6pm; $3.25), a group of plain, solid buildings that replicates a nineteenth-century fish-processing factory and retail store and effectively evokes the importance of the fish industry to the local economy. Several imaginatively designed exhibits explain the significance of the North Atlantic fisheries in a surprisingly engaging manner – tanks of live cod and barrels of highly pungent actual salted cod are strategically placed to appeal to the senses. Close by, at the docks, you can board a replica of **Cabot's ship**, the *Matthew* (June to mid-Sept 10am–6pm; $3; ☎468-1493, ☎468-7747 off-season, *www.home.thezone.net/~matthew*) and visit the interpretive centre.

Bonavista has a handful of **B&Bs** perched among the rocks, all charging about the same price and all open year-round. You could try *Butler's by the Sea*, Red Point Road (☎468-2445; ③), or *White's Bed & Breakfast* (☎468-7018; ③), which rents out bikes and is just 2.5km from the lighthouse. There's a meagre assortment of **restaurants**; your best option is to eat at the *Baie-Vista*, on John Cabot Drive, right in the town centre. No bus service runs to Bonavista from St John's, but Catalina Taxi (☎682-9977) has a speedy and efficient **minibus** service that will get you there for $24.

Terra Nova National Park to Corner Brook

The **Trans-Canada Highway** is the only major road running along Newfoundland's central northern shore, slicing through **Terra Nova National Park** (mid-May to mid-Oct $3.25 entry fee; mid-Oct to mid-May admission is free; *parkscanada.pch.gc.ca/parks /Newfoundland/terra_nova*) before connecting the towns of the interior – **Gander**, **Grand Falls-Windsor** and **Deer Lake** – a distance of about 450km. Heading north from Clarenville along the Trans-Canada, it's about 40km to the southern entrance of Terra Nova National Park, whose coniferous forests, ponds and marshes border the indented coastline of southwest Bonavista Bay. The **park administration** is located just off the Trans-Canada Highway at Newman Sound in the principal **campsite**, *Frontcountry Camping* ($12–17; year-round), which also has a convenience store, snack bar, laundromat, gift shop and bike-rental shop. A few kilometres further up the Trans-Canada there's a turn-off onto a gravel road that will take you to the town of Saltons, where you'll find the **Marine Interpretive Centre** (daily May–Oct 9am–9pm, reduced hours in Oct; admission with park entry fee; ☎533-2801), which has aquariums, interactive displays, videos and murals dealing with the mysteries of the sea. The main **Visitor Information Centre** is in the same building (same hours and telephone number as the interpretive centre). Also from the centre, the reputable Ocean Watch (☎533-6024, *www3.nf.sympatico.ca/oceanwatch*) runs daily **boat trips** (mid-June to Sept daily 9am, 1pm, 4pm & 7pm) around the fjord (2hr; $25) and out into the Atlantic (3hr; $30); boats depart from Saltons Wharf. Whales are a common sight, but the best part of the trip is handling such things as jellyfish, plankton and lobster. Terra Nova Adventures (mid-May to Oct; ☎533-9797 or 1-888/533-8687, *www.kayak.nf.ca*) offers sea-kayaking trips around the coastline.

Several excellent **walking trails** thread through the park, most notably the strenuous Outport Trail, an eighteen-kilometre (5hr) walk along the south shore of the fjord to the rugged slopes of Mount Stamford and beyond. On the way there are a couple of primitive **campsites** for $8 per night, plus some semi-serviced ones closer to the Trans-Canada ($14–16) – wilderness camping permits are available from the main information centre. For a less strenuous way to see the countryside, Ocean Watch will drop passengers off near the end of the Outport Trail, and you can either walk back or wait for the boat to collect you. The park also maintains eight backcountry campsites that can be accessed by foot, canoe or sea kayak. Reservations for the interior are recommended for July and August. If you're not content to camp – or the weather turns foul – the village of **CHARLOTTETOWN**, inset into park property 13km south of

Newman Sound along the Trans-Canada, has a **motel**, the *Clode Sound* (☎664-3146, fax 664-4471; ③; May–Oct), with a reasonably priced restaurant known for its apple pies and apple crisps.

If you have the time, a worthwhile detour can be made off the Trans-Canada at the northern edge of the park, 20km along Hwy 310 to the tiny community of **EASTPORT**, hub of a small peninsula known for its artists' colonies and sandy beaches. **Burnside**, 8km north of Eastport, is the departure point for most tours. Close by the site of **Bloody Bay Cove**, one of the principal settlements of the Beothuks; the largest and richest archeological finds from this ill-fated culture have been unearthed here (mid-June to late-Oct daily 10am–8pm; ☎677-2221 or 677-2474). Burnside Archaeological Boat Tours (mid-June to late-Oct; ☎677-2474 or 579-0466, *lmclean@thezone.net*) offers scenic tours to the former settlements that were occupied successively by the Maritime Archaic, Paleo-Eskimo and Beothuk aboriginal peoples over 5000 or so years. Basing yourself in Eastport, you can wend your way through islands and past abandoned outports on a tour with Smokey Hole Wilderness Tours (late May to mid-Oct daily; 2–4hr; $25; ☎677-2036 or 579-7888, *www.chuckys.com*); they'll even pick you up at your hotel or B&B in St John's and take you to Eastport. If you want to **stay** overnight in Eastport, your best bets are *Pinsent's Bed & Breakfast*, 17 Church St (☎677-3021, *walterpinsent@nf.sympatico.ca*; ②), a quaint saltbox house surrounded by rose gardens and lilac bushes; *Laurel Cottage*, 41 Bank Rd (☎ and fax 677-3138 or 1-888/677-3138, *www3.nf.sympatico.ca/laurel*; ③); or the *Doctor's Inn*, 5 Burden Rd (☎ and fax 677-3539 or 1-877/677-3539, off-season ☎489-3273; ③; May–Oct).

Gander

The Trans-Canada Highway leaves Terra Nova National Park – interrupted about halfway at **Gambo**, where the **Smallwood Interpretive Centre** (June–Sept daily 9am–7pm; *www.gambo.net*; $3), has several exhibits and memorabilia commemorating Newfoundland's Father of Confederation, the late premier Joey Smallwood – to sprint 60km to **GANDER**, an inconsequential town built around an airport, whose site was chosen by the British in the 1930s – they considered it ideal because it was far enough inland to escape Newfoundland's coastal fogs and near enough to Europe to facilitate the introduction of regular transatlantic flights. During World War II, the airport was a major staging point for American planes on their way to England and later developed into an important air-traffic control centre for much of the northwest Atlantic. Since the 1960s the airport has been a major stopover destination for incoming flights from Europe. In the 1970s and 1980s several Eastern European airlines used Gander as a refuelling stop on the flight to Cuba, and hundreds of passengers decamped here to ask for political asylum. There's no reason to stop – unless you're tired from the long drive – but in emergencies *Friends Bed and Breakfast*, 66 Bennett Drive (☎ and fax 651-2269; ②/③), situated not far from the **tourist chalet** on the Trans-Canada (June–Sept daily 9am–9pm; ☎256-7110), has pleasant double rooms. For standard **motel** accommodation, the *Comfort Inn*, on the Trans-Canada (☎256-3535 or 1-800/4-CHOICE, *www.comfortinn.com*; ③/④), and the *Country Inn*, 315 Gander Bay Rd (☎256-4005, *countryinn.inc@nf.sympatico.ca*; ②), provide comfortable, no-frills rooms. If you're **hungry**, try *Jungle Jim's* (☎256-3535) on the Trans-Canada at the *Comfort Inn*.

Twillingate and around

The myriad headlands and inlets around the northern outport of **TWILLINGATE**, 100km north of Gander along routes 330, 331 and 340, on an island linked by a bridge to the mainland, ensnare dozens of **icebergs** as they drift down from the Arctic between May and July. Tinted by reflections from the sea and sun, they can be wondrously beautiful and, if you're particularly lucky, you might witness the moment when one of them rolls over and breaks apart, accompanied by a tremendous grating, wheezing explosion. Twillingate Island Boat Tours, South Side, Twillingate, runs excellent two-hour **iceberg-watching tours** from mid-May to September, daily at 9.30am, 1pm and 4pm for $25 per person. You can book at the Iceberg Shop (☎884-2242 or 884-2317, *www.icebergshopboattours.nf.ca*), an arts and crafts shop and interpretive centre in an old barn in Durrell, a couple of kilometres north of Twillingate. Twillingate Adventure Tours (☎884-5999 or 1-888/447-8687) offers similar boat tours. From the mainland, the best vantage point from which to spot icebergs is at the northern end of narrow Main Street, near the Long Point Lighthouse, which is built on a high rocky cliff that juts into the Atlantic Ocean. The breathtaking view may also afford a glimpse of the odd whale, possibly a killer whale, the largest predator of mammals averaging 20 feet long and weighing up to 10,000 pounds. Don't forget to bring your camera and sturdy footwear; the cliffs are rather rocky and slippery. The **Long Point Interpretive Centre** across the street from the lighthouse (daily: July–Sept; ☎884-5755; free) has a tearoom, crafts shop and a small natural-history museum, which runs cultural and natural-history tours of the area. For an evening of old-time music, dance and skits, accompanied by hearty Newfoundland food, visit the All Around the Circle Dinner Theater Company, which has performances every summer in the Crow Head Community Centre (June–Sept Mon–Sat 7pm; ☎884-5423 or 884-2687).

At the end of July Twillingate hosts the four-day **Fish, Fun and Folk Festival** (☎884-2678, fax 884-2836); folk dancers and musicians gather here from all over the province. The best of the accommodation is the *Hillside Bed and Breakfast*, 5 Young's Lane (☎884-5761; ②; June–Sept), and the quaint *Toulinguet Inn Bed & Breakfast*, 56 Main St (☎884-2080 or 1-877/684-2080, *sites.netscape.net/davidthompson2ca*; ③). Other accommodations in the area include *Mariner's Rest B&B*, 63 Toulinguet St (☎884-2677; ②; June–Sept); *R&J Hospitality Home*, 139 Main St (☎884-2212; ②/③; April–Nov); and the *Evening Sun Inn B&B*, 319 Bayview St (☎884-2103 or 628-5247; ②/③). For food, try the simple *R&J Restaurant* located directly across from their bed and breakfast.

To find out more about Newfoundland's extinct native people, it's worth a visit to the **Beothuk Interpretive Centre** at Boyd's Cove (daily: mid-June to mid-Oct 10am–5.30pm; ☎729-0592 or 656-3114; $2.50), 35km south of Twillingate along Hwy 340. In the early 1980s, archeologists discovered an ancient Beothuk village here that provided valuable clues to the Beothuk's lifestyle. View an informative video and exhibits, and take a 1.5-kilometre trail to some of the archeological sites – grass covered mounds that once supported sturdy bark-covered wigwams. Further into the forest is a bronze statue honouring Shanawdithit, the last of the Beothuks.

Lewisporte
LEWISPORTE, west of Gander and just 16km from the Trans-Canada along Route 340, is the terminal for the twice-weekly **ferry** to Goose Bay, in Labrador. DRL Coachlines from St John's drops you at the Irving petrol station, on the Trans-Canada 16km from the dock, and Freake's Taxi Service (☎535-8100) will come and collect you, but the times of the buses don't tally with those of the boats, leaving you with several hours to kill, if you're catching the 10pm boat, or an overnight stay, for the 4pm sailing. For overnight **accommodation**, stick to the *Northgate Bed and Breakfast*, close to the ferry at 106 Main St (☎535-2258, *www.bbcanada.com/3130.html*; ②; May–Oct).

Grand Falls and Windsor
GRAND FALLS, 96km west of Gander, sits in the middle of some of the island's best stands of timber, an expanse of forest that's been intensively exploited ever since Alfred Harmsworth, later Lord Northcliffe, had a paper mill built here in 1905. Harmsworth, the founder of Britain's *Daily Mirror* and the *Daily Mail*, funded the project to secure a reliable supply of newsprint well away from Europe, which he believed was heading towards war. It was an immensely profitable venture, which also established the first

Newfoundland community sited, as one contemporary put it, "out of sight and sound of the sea". For many of the employees, recruited from the outports, it was the first time they had ever received a cash wage, though this particular pleasure was countered by some bitter management–union disputes. The worst was in 1959, when the Mounties broke a well-supported strike with appalling barbarity, at the behest of Newfoundland's premier Joey Smallwood.

Grand Falls remains a company town, a singularly unprepossessing place built up around the hulking mass of the paper mill that towers over the Exploits River. Nevertheless, there is one interesting surprise, the **Mary March Regional Museum** at 22 St Catherine St (daily: May to mid-Oct 9am–4.45pm; $2.50), just to the south of the Trans-Canada where the highway separates Grand Falls from the adjacent drab township of **WINDSOR**. The museum has a good section on the history of the town and an intriguing series of displays on the **Beothuks**, including an explanation about one of the last of the Beothuks, Mary March, or Demasduit, who was captured near here in March 1819. A reconstructed Beothuk **village** (daily: mid-June to early Sept 9am–7pm; $2; ☎489-3559 or 1-888/491-9453, *www.exploitschamber.nf.ca/evta*) stands next to the museum. There's also a **tourist information booth**, on the Trans-Canada just west of the twin towns (daily: June–Aug 8.30am–9pm; Sept–May 9am–5pm; ☎489-6332).

If you're coming by **bus**, DRL Coachlines drops you off at the *Highliner Inn* on the Trans-Canada just west of town. For lower-priced **accommodation**, the *Poplar Inn Bed and Breakfast*, 22 Poplar Rd (☎489-2546 or 489-9184; ②), is a good choice. If that's full, try the slightly more luxurious *Hotel Robin Hood*, 78 Lincoln Rd (☎489-5324, *robin.hood@nf.sympatico.ca*; ③), or the large, comfortable *Mount Peyton Hotel*, just off the Trans-Canada at 214 Lincoln Rd (☎489-2251 or 1-800/563-4894, *www.mountpeyton.com*; ③/④). There are few good **restaurants** in town; the *Peyton Corral Steakhouse*, in the *Mount Peyton Hotel*, is by far the best choice.

Deer Lake

DEER LAKE, 210km west of Grand Falls, lies at the start of Route 430, the only road up to L'Anse aux Meadows, and has the nearest airport to Gros Morne National Park (see opposite), so if you fly in and rent a car at the airport you miss the long trek across the island. There are regular reasonably priced flights in from St John's (from $290 return) and a clutch of **car-rental** offices inside the terminal building: try Budget (☎635-3211), Tilden (☎635-3282) or Avis (☎635-3252). DRL Coachlines' service from St John's stops at the Irving petrol station in Deer Lake daily at 5.12pm. From here you can take the only bus service up the Northern Peninsula, operated by Viking Express (☎634-4710 or 688-2112), running to Rocky Harbour (Mon–Fri 5.40pm; $13) and St Anthony for L'Anse aux Meadows (Mon, Wed & Fri 5pm; $40). If you want more information about Deer Lake and the surrounding area, stop in at the **tourist information booth** on the Trans-Canada, just east of town (daily: June–Aug 8.30am–9pm; Sept & Oct 10am–7pm; ☎635-2202). One of the more popular attractions in Deer Lake is the **Newfoundland Insectarium**, a few minutes north off the Trans-Canada on Hwy 430 (July to early Sept daily 9am–9pm; early Sept to June Tues–Fri 9am–5pm, Sat–Sun 10am–5pm; ☎635-4545, *www.newfoundlandinsectarium.nf.net*; $6), which exhibits insect specimens from Newfoundland and from around the world and features a working beehive which visitors can view from behind glass.

If you get stuck in Deer Lake, there's fairly convenient **accommodation** at the newly renovated *Deer Lake Motel* (☎635-2108 or 1-800/563-2144, *www.deerlakemotel.com*; ③), just 2km from the airport; alternatively, the *Driftwood Inn* (☎635-5115 or 1-888/635-5115; ③), on Nicholsville Road, is a ten-minute drive east of the airport. *Watkins House*, at 17 Phillip Drive (☎635-3723; ②) and the newly opened *Lucas House*, on 22 Old Bonne Bay Rd (☎635-3622, *deandrews@nf.sympatico.ca*; ②) are the only bed and breakfasts in the area. There are no decent **restaurants** in Deer Lake itself, so you'd best stick to the dining rooms of the motels or grab a snack at the convenience places on the Trans-Canada, which cuts through the town.

Corner Brook

CORNER BROOK, 50km south of Deer Lake, is magnificently sited, surrounded by steep wooded hills dropping down to the blue waters of the Humber Arm. However – although it's Newfoundland's second largest city – there's not really a lot to do or see, as it's essentially a **pulp-and-paper** producing town supplying newsprint to much of the world, and a large mill on the waterfront pours out smoke from its stack. DRL Coachlines stops at the Robertson's Irving petrol station near the Trans-Canada, about 3km from the centre. From here, City Cabs (☎634-6565) or Star Taxi (☎634-4343) will take you down into town. The Millbrook Shopping Mall on Herald Avenue stands near the main stop for the Viking Express **bus** up to St Anthony; always call ahead to confirm schedules and connecting services.

To find out what's on in the town and area, visit the **tourist information centre**, on Confederation Drive, just off the Trans-Canada (May–Aug daily 9am–5pm; Sept–April Mon–Fri 9am–5pm; ☎634-5831 or 639-9792). The only attraction that will cause you to linger for a while is the **Captain James Cook Memorial**, in the west part of the city at the end of Hill Road, which honours the British navigator who explored and charted the nearby coastline and inlets of the Bay of Islands in 1767.

If you're stranded in Corner Brook, three good **accommodation** stand-bys are the basic *Hotel Corner Brook*, at 47 Main St (☎634-8211 or 1-800/738-8211; ②/③); *Bell's Bed and Breakfast*, 2 Fords Rd (☎634-5736; ②); and the *Bide-a-Nite Hospitality Home*, centrally located at 11 Wellington St (☎634-7578; ②). The best places to **eat** are *Maggie's Restaurant*, 26 Caribou Rd, specializing in pastries and pies; *Lynn's Café*, 37 Broadway, offering traditional Newfoundland meals; and the *Carriage Room* in the Glynmill Inn on Cobb Lane, where you can enjoy a buffet in a 1920s Tudor-style former hotel.

The Northern Peninsula

Stretching between Deer Lake and the township of St Anthony, a distance of about 450km, the **Northern Peninsula** is a rugged and sparsely populated finger of land whose interior is dominated by the spectacular **Long Range Mountains**, a chain of flat-topped peaks that are some of the oldest on earth, punctuated by the starkest of glacier-gouged gorges above the bluest of lakes – or "ponds" as the locals incongruously call them. Most of the region remains inaccessible to all except the most experienced of mountaineers, but **Route 430** – whose bus services are so poor that it's hard to manage without a car – trails along the length of the western part of the peninsula, connecting the small fishing villages of the narrow coastal plain with the remains of the Norse colony at **L'Anse aux Meadows**.

Gros Morne National Park

The southern section of the Long Range Mountains, beginning about 35km from Deer Lake and bordering the Gulf of St Lawrence, has been set aside as the **GROS MORNE NATIONAL PARK** (mid-May to mid-Oct $5 entry fee; mid-Oct to mid-May free), a UNESCO World Heritage Site, some 1800 square kilometres of the peninsula's finest and most approachable scenery. The bays, scrawny beaches, straggling villages and sea stacks of the littoral are set against bare-topped, fjord-cut mountains, whose forested lower slopes are home to moose, woodland caribou and snowshoe hare.

The best place to start a tour is the **Visitor Information Centre** (daily: mid-June to Aug 9am–10pm; Sept to mid-June 9am–5pm; ☎458-2066 or 458-2417, *www.grosmorne.pch.gc.ca*), situated beside Route 430 as it approaches Rocky Harbour just 70km from Deer Lake. The centre has a series of excellent displays on the geology, botany, biology and human history of the park, and its efficient and helpful staff issue free maps, brochures on Gros Morne's key hiking trails and boat excursions; they also run a programme of guided walks. If you intend to use one of the park's basic **campsites** ($10–15), which are dotted along the longer trails, then you have to register here first.

Rocky Harbour

It's a couple of minutes' drive from the Visitor Centre to **ROCKY HARBOUR**, the park's largest and prettiest village, which curves around a long and sweeping bay with the mountains lurking in the background. Although there's nothing special to do or see here, the long walk round to the **Lobster Cove Head Lighthouse** is a pleasant way to spend an afternoon. Rocky Harbour is also near several of Gros Morne's **hiking trails**, notably the lung-bursting, sixteen-kilometre James Callaghan Trail, curiously named after the former British prime minister. The trail – for experienced hikers only – begins beside Route 430, just 7km east of the village, and climbs to the top of Gros Morne Mountain where, at 806m above sea level, the views are stupendous. If you decide to stay on the mountain overnight, there's a primitive **campsite** on the way down from the summit ($10 per night; July–Oct).

Rocky Harbour is the best place to stay in the park, not least because it's relatively compact and has a reasonable range of tourist facilities. **Accommodation** includes the comfortable *Ocean View Motel*, beside the waterfront (☎458-2730 or 1-800/563-9887, *www.oceanviewmotel.com*; ③); *Bottom Brook Cottages*, on Main Street (☎458-2236; ②/③), consisting of six fully equipped individual housekeeping units; and *Parson's Harbour View Cabins*, also near the waterfront (☎458-2544; ②). In all cases, advance bookings are recommended in July and August. The nearest **campsite** is *Juniper Campground*, on Pond Road in the village (☎458-2917; $11–16; late May to Sept), which also has a six-bed hostel ($12 per person); or try the more attractive sites at *Berry Hill*, 4km north of Rocky Harbour along Route 430 (no phone; $15.25 per night; June to mid-Oct).

For **food**, the restaurant of the *Ocean View Motel* serves excellent seafood dishes for around $12; the nearby *Fisherman's Landing Restaurant* also serves good food.

Bonne Bay, Woody Point and the Tablelands

BONNE BAY, just along the coast from Rocky Harbour, lies at the mouth of a great gash that slices inland from the Gulf of St Lawrence framed by the severest of mountains. Most of the park's villages lie on the shore of the fjord, and it's possible to drive right round, but you have to take a long detour on Route 431, which branches off from Route 430 at Wiltondale, at the park's south entrance. Unfortunately, the ferry, which connected with **Woody Point** across the bay and which shortened the distance considerably, no longer runs. **Minuscule WOODY POINT** has a pleasant guesthouse, the *Victorian Manor* (☎453-2485, *www.grosmorne.com/victorianmanor*; ③–⑤), and the small and basic *Woody Point Youth Hostel* (☎453-7254; ①; May–Oct). If you want to see the mountains from the water, **tours** of Bonne Bay are available with Bontours (mid-June to early Sept daily 10am & 2pm; 2hr; $20; ☎458-2730 or 1-800/563-9887); boats depart from Government Wharf at Norris Point.

The **Lookout Trail** (5km return) begins about 1km from Woody Point and has the best panoramic views in the park. Heading further west from the village along Route 431, it's 3km to the start of the **Tablelands Hiking Trail**, a four-kilometre circular track that cuts across a forbidding area of bare and barren rock. Another 8km along Route 431 leads to the sixteen-kilometre loop of the **Green Gardens Trail**, which twists its way to some secluded coves, caves and sea stacks and is equipped with three primitive campsites (each $10 per night). Continuing down the road, it's a further

4km to **Trout River Pond**, sandwiched by the yellowed bareness of the Tablelands and the massive cliffs bordering the Gregory Plateau – this is one of the places where you really notice the tremendous uplifts of land caused by the collision of the North American and European continents 450 million years ago. The views here are splendid and the best way to see the lake is on the **Tablelands Boat Tour** (daily: mid- to late June & early to mid-Sept 1pm; July & Aug 10am, 1pm & 4pm; 2hr; $25; ☎451-2101). For **accommodation**, there are simple lodgings at *Crocker Cabins* in Trout River (☎451-3236; units ③; mid-May to mid-Sept).

Western Brook Pond and Broom Point

Western Brook Pond, reached by just one access point, 25km north of Rocky Harbour beside Route 430, is one of eastern Canada's finest landscapes, 16km of deep, dark-blue water framed by mighty mountains and huge waterfalls. The whole ensemble is a view rivalling the fjords of Norway. This freshwater fjord is one of the most remote spots in eastern Canada and until the 1970s very few people knew of its existence outside of the hunting and fishing fraternity.

From the access-point car park it's a forty-minute walk on a well-maintained trail through forest and over bog land to the edge of the lake's gorge along the **Western Brook Pond Trail**, which crosses the narrow coastal plain. When you get to the end, don't skimp on the two-hour **boat trip** – weather permitting, they run three times daily (10am, 1pm & 4pm) from mid-June to early September, and once daily (1pm) from early to mid-June and early September to mid-October, with an additional evening tour (6.15pm) from mid-July to mid-August, depending on numbers ($27; ☎458-2730 or 1-800/563-9887). The boat takes you between the cliffs right to the extreme eastern end of the lake, past several huge rockslides, dramatic **hanging valleys** and former sea caves high up in the cliff faces; at one point you are taken virtually underneath a large waterfall. Western Brook Pond also boasts a couple of extremely difficult hiking trails, the 27-kilometre **Snug Harbour–North Rim** route, which branches off from the main path between the road and the pond, and the 35-kilometre **Long Range Mountains** trail at the eastern end of the pond. Both these tracks have rudimentary campsites at $35 per night – obtain advice and permits from the Visitor Centre at Rocky Harbour. If you're without a car, Pittman's Taxis in Norris Point (☎458-2486) will take you from Rocky Harbour to the access point for $35, or Gros Morne Adventure Tours (☎458-2250) will get you there on its shuttle bus for roughly the same price.

At **Broom Point**, 6km north of Western Brook Pond, there's a **fisherman's cabin** and store restored to its appearance in the 1940s, when it was an important station for local fishermen (mid-June to Sept daily 10am–6pm; admission with park pass). It's an evocative place, surrounded by **tuckamores** – clumps of balsam firs and spruce stunted by constant exposure to wind.

Port au Choix

The tiny fishing village of **PORT AU CHOIX**, 160km from Rocky Harbour, sits on a bleak headland beside the **Port au Choix National Historic Site** (daily: June–Aug 9am–8pm; Sept to mid-Oct 9.30am–4.30pm; $2.75), established where a mass of prehistoric bones, tools and weapons were accidentally discovered in the 1960s. The ensuing archeological dig unearthed three ancient cemeteries, confirming the area as a centre of settlement for the **Maritime Archaic People**, hunters and gatherers who lived here around 2000 BC. The nearby **Visitor Reception Centre** (same times) provides the background on this culture and on that of the later **Groswater** and **Dorset Eskimos**, whose scant remains in the area confirm that about two or three thousand years ago Port au Choix was their most southerly settlement. Among the centre's exhibits are an actual excavated Dorset house and a collection of artefacts discovered in the area. From the centre it's a short walk to a **lighthouse**; it is possible to walk on the adjoining beach, which is rich with fossils; fossil hunting is forbidden, however. You can take a short guided walk to nearby **Phillip's Garden** and the remains of a Dorset settlement. Opposite the fish-processing plant you can also see the site of the Maritime Archaic **burial ground** – although it's nothing more than a grassy mound.

The Port au Choix area has a handful of **places to stay**: try the recently renovated *Sea Echo Motel*, right in the centre of town (☎861-3777, or 1-800/861-3777; ③), or better yet try *Jeannie's Sunrise B&B* (☎861-2254, *www.bbcanada.com/3032.html*; ②/③) near the community Heritage Centre. For **food**, the choices are limited: there's the *Anchor Café*, beside the burial ground, where for $12 you'll get a plate heaped with fresh cod, salmon or shrimp, the latter a specialty of the Port au Choix area; or the *Point Riche Room*, in the *Sea Echo Motel*, which offers a variety of fresh seafood dishes.

St Barbe and St Anthony

Pressing on from Port au Choix, it's about 80km to the hamlet of **ST BARBE**, where there's a **car ferry** service on the MS *Apollo* (May–Dec 1–3 daily; 1hr 30min; $9 passengers, $18.50 vehicles; ☎726-0015 or 1-800/563-6353) across the Strait of Belle Isle to **Blanc-Sablon**, on the Québec–Labrador boundary (see p.452); vehicles are taken on a first-served basis. Tickets for the ferry can be purchased at the *Dockside Motel and Cabins* just up the road from the terminal (☎877-2444, *www.docksidemotel.nf.ca*; ②/③). If you're waiting for the ferry, the only place to eat is in the motel dining room.

From St Barbe, Route 430 slips through a handful of fishing villages before cutting east across the peninsula for the fishing and supply centre of **ST ANTHONY**. With a population of about four thousand, this is the region's largest settlement, but it's not much more than a humdrum port stretched out around the wide sweep of its harbour, the main recompense being the remains of the Norse village at L'Anse aux Meadows, 42km north along route 430 (see opposite).

In town, the one worthwhile attraction is the **Grenfell House Museum** (daily: June–Aug 9am–8pm; Sept 9am–1pm & 2–5pm; off-season by appointment), tucked behind the Charles S. Curtis Hospital. The building, a dark-green shingled house in New England cottage style, is the restored home of the pioneering missionary doctor, Sir Wilfred Grenfell, an Englishman who first came here on behalf of the Royal National Mission to Deep Sea Fishermen in 1892. He never moved back home and, during his forty-year stay, he established the region's first proper hospitals, nursing stations, schools and co-operative stores. Behind the house, there's a pleasant woodland path that leads to the top of a hill, where the ashes of Grenfell and his wife are kept. The newly constructed **Grenfell Interpretive Centre** (daily: June–Aug 9am–8pm; Sept–Dec 9am–5pm; ☎454-4010, *www3.nf.sympatico.ca/grenfell*; $5, includes admission to museum), opposite the hospital, has two floors on Grenfell's life and a shop that sells local handicrafts.

Practicalities

There are daily **flights** to St Anthony from most of Newfoundland's larger settlements and from several of eastern Canada's main cities. The **airport** is near Seal Bay, a rather distant 55km west of town on Hwy 430, and onward transport to the centre is by taxi only – reckon on $40. If flying is out of your price range, Viking Express runs a **bus** service to St Anthony from Deer Lake (see p.442). For central **accommodation**, there's *Spruce Inn B&B*, 1 Spruce Lane (☎454-3402 or 1-877/454-3402; ①/②; April–Nov; the *St Anthony Haven Inn*, 24–38 Goose Cove Rd (☎454-9100 or 1-877/428-3646, fax 454-2270; ③); and the *Vinland Motel*, 19 West St (☎454-8843 or 1-800/563-7578, fax 454-8468; ③). Most attractive of the lot is *Lynn's Bed & Breakfast*, 340 West St (☎454-2677, ②), a house surrounded by colourful flowerbeds. You'll find good seafood meals at the *Lightkeeper's*

Café, at Fishing Point at the end of West Street. Next door is *The Great Viking Feast* – dinner theatre performed in a sod-grass hut – which serves up salmon, cod and moose to accompany the Viking-themed live entertainment. Dinners begin most evenings (June–Sept) at 7.30pm. Reservations are required (☎454-4900 or 1-877/454-4900; $32 prix-fixe).

Unfortunately, there are no public transport connections between St Anthony and L'Anse aux Meadows, and the return taxi fare will cost you about $60. Alternatively, Tilden, at Woodward Motors on West Street (☎454-4000) and at the airport (☎454-8522), has reasonably priced, short-term car-rental deals.

L'Anse aux Meadows: the Norse village

L'Anse aux Meadows National Historic Site (daily: mid-June to Aug 9am–8pm; Sept to mid-Oct 9.30am–4.30pm; $5; hourly 45min guided tours), a UNESCO World Heritage Site comprising the scant remains of the earliest verified European settlement in the Americas, is a tribute to the obsessive drive of **Helge Ingstad**, a Norwegian writer and explorer who from 1960 hunted high and low to find Norse settlements on the North Atlantic seaboard. His efforts were inspired by two medieval Icelandic sagas, which detailed the establishment of the colony of **Vinland** somewhere along this coast in about 1000 AD.

At L'Anse aux Meadows, Ingstad was led by a local to a group of grassed-over bumps and ridges beside Epaves Bay. This unremarkable area, next to a peat bog, contained the remnants of the only **Norse village** ever to have been discovered in North America – the foundations of eight turf and timber buildings and a ragbag of archeological finds, including a cloak pin, a stone anvil, nails, pieces of bog iron, an oil lamp and a small spindle whorl. Ingstad concluded that these were left behind by a group of about one hundred sailors, carpenters and blacksmiths who probably remained at the site for only one or two years and used it as a base for further exploration of the area.

The site was thoroughly excavated between 1961 and 1968 and there followed an acrimonious academic debate about whether it was actually "Vinland". The geographical clues provided in the sagas are extremely vague, so the argument is essentially linguistic, hinging on the various possible interpretives of the old Icelandic word "Vinland", with one side insisting that it means "Wine-land" and therefore cannot refer to anywhere in Newfoundland, the other suggesting the word means "fertile land" and therefore it could.

Whatever the truth of the matter, hundreds of tourists come here every summer and begin their tour at the **Visitor Reception Centre** (same hours as site; ☎623-2601 or 623-2608), where the Norse artefacts and changing exhibitions on Viking life and culture are beefed up by an excellent if somewhat melodramatic thirty-minute film entitled *The Vinland Mystery*. From here it's a few minutes' walk to the cluster of gentle mounds that make up what's left of the original village, and another short stroll to a group of full-scale replicas of a **long house**, storage shed, workshop and a *faering*, a small boat used for coastal hunting. A full-scale replica of a square-masted **Viking ship** dominates the village just a few hundred metres away. July 2000 marked the thousandth anniversary of the arrival of the Vikings to the New World.

For those wishing to stay near the site, *Marilyn's Hospitality Home* (☎623-2811 or 1-877/865-3958; ②) and the *Viking Nest B&B* (☎623-2238; ①/②, in neighboring Hay Cove, come highly recommended. Most people use St Anthony as a base for visiting L'Anse aux Meadows, but if you're traveling by car it's also worth considering a **stay** at the *Tickle Inn* (☎452-4321 June–Sept, 739-5503 off-season, reservations essential; *www3.nf .sympatico.ca/adams.tickle*; ②), an attractive late-nineteenth-century house located on the shores of a secluded cove at remote **Cape Onion**. The Cape is approached along Route 437, a 25-kilometre-long paved road that branches off from Route 436, the main-

---

VINLAND AND THE VIKINGS

The first **Viking** voyages, in the eighth century, had no wider purpose than the plunder of their Scandinavian neighbours, but by the start of the ninth century overpopulation at home had pushed them towards migration and colonization. By 870 they had settled on the shores of Iceland, and by the start of the eleventh century there were about three thousand Norse colonists established in Greenland. As good farmland became scarce, so it was inevitable that there would be another push west.

The two **Vinland sagas** – the *Graenlendinga* and *Eirik's Saga* – give us the only extant account of these further explorations, recounting the exploits of Leif Eiriksson the Lucky and Thorfinn Karlsefni, his merchant brother-in-law, who founded a colony they called **Vinland** in North America around 1000 AD. Although eventually forced to abandon Vinland by relentless threats from the local peoples – whom they called skraelings, literally "wretches" – the Norse settlers continued to secure resources from the region for the next few decades, and it seems likely that the site discovered at **L'Anse aux Meadows** is the result of one of these foragings.

The Norse carried on collecting timber from Labrador up until the fourteenth century, when a dramatic deterioration in the climate made the trip from Greenland too dangerous. Attacks from the Inuit and the difficulties of maintaining trading links with Scandinavia then took their toll on the main Greenland colonies. All contact between Greenland and the outside world was lost around 1410 and the last of the half-starved, disease-ridden survivors died out towards the end of the fifteenth century – when Christopher Columbus was eyeing up his "New World".

---

highway between St Anthony and L'Anse aux Meadows. Camping facilities are available at Pistolet Bay Provincial Park (☎454-7570; $11; May–Sept), also on Route 437. Guided natural-history tours to the Burnt Cape Ecological Reserve can be arranged by contacting the park. If the *Tickle Inn* is full, try the closer community of **Gunner's Cove**, 10km from L'Anse aux Meadows on Route 436; it's where the American author E. Annie Proulx stayed when she was researching and writing her best-selling novel, *The Shipping News*.

Channel-Port aux Basques and the south

CHANNEL-PORT AUX BASQUES sits by the ocean right in the southwest corner of Newfoundland, serving as the region's fishing and transportation centre, with regular ferry connections to North Sydney in Nova Scotia (see p.368), and a daily bus service to St John's, about thirteen-hours' drive away. The town is divided into two distinct sections, an older part stuck on a bare and bumpy headland behind the ferry terminal, and a newer section spread out around Grand Bay Road, about 2km to the west.

Apart from the ferries, there's no possible reason to come here, but in emergencies it's useful to know that the place has a clutch of reasonably priced **accommodation**. Walking out of the ferry port, turn left towards the old part of town, along Caribou Street, where you'll find the *Heritage Home*, 11 Caribou St (☎695-3240, *www.bbcanada .com/2665.html*; ②; May–Oct). Alternatively, in the newer part of town, there's the *Caribou Bed and Breakfast*, 30 Grand Bay Rd (☎695-3408, *home.thezone.net/~gibbons*; ②; May–Oct), which is near the *Hotel Port aux Basques* (☎695-2171 or 1-877/695-2171, *www.gatewaytonewfoundland.com*; ③). The *Harbour Restaurant*, on Caribou Road, is the best place in town to **eat**, but for a taste of real home-cooked food in a typical outport community, drive 10km east on Hwy 470 to **Margaree**, where you'll find the reasonably priced and friendly *Seashore Restaurant*.

The only tourist attraction in Channel-Port aux Basques is the **Gulf Museum**, 118 Main St (June–Sept daily 10am–8pm; $2; ☎695-7604), which has a collection of marine artefacts, all of which are rather unexciting, save for an early seventeenth-century astrolabe. The **tourist information chalet**, overlooking the town about 1km north along the Trans-Canada (daily: mid-May to Aug 6am–11pm; Sept & Oct 7am–8pm; ☎695-2262), has a range of literature dealing with the whole of Newfoundland.

The south coast

The submerged rocks and jutting headlands of Newfoundland's **south coast** have witnessed the shipwreck of hundreds of vessels as they attempted to steer round the island into the Gulf of St Lawrence, some running aground in a fog bank, others driven ashore by tremendous gales. Such was the frequency of these disasters that many outports came to rely on washed-up timber for firewood and building materials, a bonus for communities all too dependent on the trade price of fish. The flotsam and jetsam days are long gone, but the south coast remains one of the poorer parts of Newfoundland, an isolated region where most of the tiny villages remain accessible only by sea. If you're after a slice of traditional outport life, then this is the nearest you'll come, though it's difficult to select one place over another. Most of the outports have simple **guesthouses** (usually in price category ②, including all meals), but unfortunately there's no central agency that has lists of which families in which outports take in guests. It's best to check the phone book for each community to see if there's a chamber of commerce – or at least a town office – and give them a call. If you express interest in a particular outport, you won't have any problem finding accommodation there – the townsfolk will be only too pleased that you're coming and, with true Newfoundland hospitality, will set you up for a couple of days or a week.

At one time you could travel the entire length of the south coast by **boat** from Channel-Port aux Basques to Terrenceville, 260km away, but this is no longer possible; visiting the outports now requires more advance planning, with careful attention given to ferry schedules. You have to travel 40km east to Rose Blanche, where the road ends, or take Strickland's Taxi (☎695-3333; $45). From Rose Blanche (the turn-off for the ferry is just a few kilometres west of town) you can get as far as Hermitage-Sandyville, about 180km east, but this involves several changes of ferries and several overnight stays of two or three days, as boats run to very irregular schedules. **ROSE BLANCHE** itself is not to be missed, a picturesque village with the steepest roads and the most brightly coloured houses you'll encounter anywhere in Newfoundland. The Department of Works, Services and Transportation Boat Service (☎635-4100) leaves for Grand Bruit Monday, Wednesday, Friday and Saturday at 3pm (2hr 30min; $3.50), where you have to change for Burgeo (Thurs 9.15am; 3hr; $4.25). In **GRAND BRUIT**, the only approved lodgings are the *Blue Mountain Cabins* (☎492-2753; ②; June–Sept). In **BURGEO**, a much larger community, you can stay either at *Gillett's Motel*, on Inspiration Road (☎886-1284; ②), or the *Haven Bed and Breakfast*, right on the harbour (☎886-2544, *a.parsons@nf.sympatico.ca*; ②), but be sure to book ahead.

Two of the outports on the south coast are **accessible by road** – Burgeo and Harbour Breton. Devin's Bus Line (5 weekly; ☎886-2955 or 886-2576) links Burgeo with Corner Brook along Hwy 480, and Hickey's (3 weekly; ☎885-2523 or 885-2167) connects Harbour Breton with Grand Falls along Hwy 360. Besides private guesthouses, the only place to **stay** in **HARBOUR BRETON** is the *Southern Port Hotel* (☎885-2283 or 885-2505; ②/③), which has only ten rooms. In all cases, reserve and confirm onward transport before you set out.

One of the prettier outports is **RAMEA**, perched on a tiny island stuck out in the ocean near Burgeo, 83 nautical miles from Channel-Port aux Basques. To **get there**, take the ferry from Burgeo (mid-May to mid-Oct Mon & Wed 2 daily, Tues & Thurs 1 daily, Fri & Sun 3 daily; mid-Oct to mid-May Mon, Wed, Sat & Sun 2 daily, Tues & Thurs 1 daily, Fri 3 daily; 1hr 20min; $2.50; *www.gov.nf.ca/ferryservices/schedules/L-ramea.htm*). There's one **B&B**, the *Four Winds Tourist Home* (☎625-2002; ②); for bookings at guesthouses call the Town of Ramea (town office) (☎625-2280). A second attractive spot is **FRANÇOIS**, forty nautical miles further east, an ancient settlement sitting precariously under the steep slopes of "The Friar", a startling rocky outcrop. In this truly isolated community of 175 people, there are no automobiles, no locked doors and no policemen. For **lodgings**, contact the François Tourism and Development Committee (☎842-4112).

LABRADOR

Labrador, 293,347 square kilometres of subarctic wilderness on the northeastern edge of the Canadian Shield, is a place so desolate that it provoked Jacques Cartier to remark "I am rather inclined to believe that this is the land God gave to Cain". It's a land full of soaring mountains, unspoiled wilderness and cool, clean rivers that seem to run forever. The adjacent towns of **Happy Valley-Goose Bay**, located on the westernmost tip of the huge Hamilton Inlet, have an average maximum temperature of −16°C/3°F in January and an annual snowfall of 445cm, much of which remains on the ground for half the year. Further inland and up north the climate is even colder. Just thirty thousand people live in Labrador, concentrated in coastal villages that are linked by a ferry service from early July to mid-October, and inland mining areas that have only received road access in the last ten years – the road from **Labrador City** to Happy Valley-Goose Bay was completed in 1991. Travelling in and around Labrador is extremely costly as tourist facilities are lacking: many communities are accessible only by plane or boat and have very few, if any, places to stay or eat. Most visitors are adventure seekers who come to trek or paddle the coastline. But if you have good camping equipment, an adventurous spirit and a healthy budget, there are few landscapes that match the untouched, rugged beauty of the area.

This barren terrain has long been a bone of contention between Québec and Newfoundland, whose current **common border** was set in the 1920s by the Privy Council when it ordained that Newfoundland had jurisdiction not just over the undisputed northern shore – the traditional domain of Newfoundland fishermen – but also over the central Labrador plateau, from which the north shore's rivers drained. Newfoundland's territory was expanded by some 293,000 square kilometres, more than twice the size of the island itself, whilst Québec was left ranting about anglophone imperialism. The border again became a problem in 1961, when it was decided to develop the hydroelectric potential of Labrador's **Churchill Falls**, a project that required Québec's participation, as Québec would have to buy some of the electricity if it were to be a viable scheme, and the power lines would encroach on its land as well. Eventually a compromise was reached whereby Newfoundland could receive Labrador's power via a toll-free route through Québec, in return for which Québec could tap the headwaters of five rivers in southern Labrador. However, the Québécois remain indignant about their loss of territory and the issue is likely to be debated again as they move towards separation.

The original owners of this land, the Naskapi, Innu and Inuit, who collectively number around five thousand, were more or less left alone until the last few decades, when the economic potential of Labrador was realized. Dams and mines have disrupted the local ecology – the Labrador Trough in western Labrador has the highest concentration of **iron ore** in North America, and in August 1997 Inuit and Innu set up blockades in an attempt to disrupt the construction of a **nickel mine** and mill at Voisey Bay, in northern Labrador. Even more destructive is the use of the area by Dutch, British and German air forces to practise wartime drills and bombing raids. Inuit have been imprisoned for staging sit-ins and chaining themselves to the gates of the Goose Bay air base, which is built on their land, and do not intend to halt the protests until the low-level sorties (up to ten thousand a year) and bombings are halted.

Information and tours

Labrador is one of Canada's most forbidding areas, so any trip needs a fair amount of organization, and a great deal if you are heading for the hinterland. It is perhaps best to opt for one of the various **tours** available (see box on p.454) which, though expensive, make the exploration of Labrador's wilds as trouble-free as possible. Whichever way you go, it's important to take the strongest fly ointment you can find (workers in Labrador carry emergency syringes of the stuff) and heavy winter clothing, as even in the height of summer fierce snowstorms can occur.

Maps, timetables and other **information** are available in advance from the **Department of Tourism, Culture and Recreation**, PO Box 8730, St John's, Newfoundland A1B 4K2 (☎729-2830 or 1-800/563-6353, fax 729-1965). *www.labradorstraits.nf.ca.*

The Newfoundland and Labrador telephone code is ☎709.

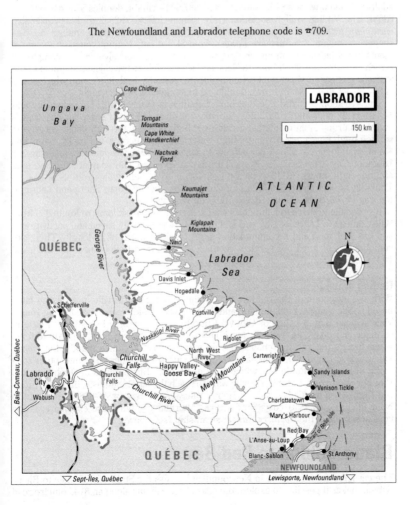

Getting there

Labrador has **airports** at Happy Valley-Goose Bay, Wabush and Churchill Falls, with regular flights by Air Nova (☎726-7880 or 1-800/776-3000) and Air Labrador (☎753-5593 or 1-800/563-3042) from Newfoundland. Expect to pay $610 for a return Québec City–Wabush flight and $690 for a return Montréal-Wabush flight; it's half that for a flight from St John's and Deer Lake in Newfoundland.

Less expensive are the **ferries** from Newfoundland. Labrador Marine runs a service from St Barbe, about 80km north of Port au Choix, across the Strait of Belle Isle to Blanc-Sablon in Québec, on the southern border of Labrador (May–Dec 1–3 daily; 1hr 30min; adult $18 return, car $37 return; ☎877-2222 or 1-800/563-6353). To get to the heart of Labrador, Coastal Labrador Marine runs the *Sir Robert Bond* from Lewisporte in Newfoundland to Happy Valley-Goose Bay (mid-June to mid-Sept 2 weekly; 33hr; adults $97 one-way, cars $160, single cabins $37.50 per night, doubles $75; ☎1-800/563-6353). The Viking Trail Association (July to mid-Oct; ☎454-2332 or 1-800/563-6353, *www.vikingtrail.org*) in conjunction with the provincial government, operates a foot-passenger steamship, the *Northern Ranger*, from St Anthony to numerous coastal settlements in Labrador. Sailing on ten designated days, it takes twelve days to complete a return journey from St Anthony to Nain, and it's possible to travel just a segment of the journey; rates are 25¢ per nautical mile plus the cost of a bunk in a cabin, which starts at $27.50 per night; for your own double cabin, reckon on $77 per night.

The 416-kilometre **rail** line that links Sept-Îles in Québec with Labrador City and Schefferville is primarily an industrial link, but there is limited space for passengers and the journey is an exhilarating ride over high bridges, through dense forest and stunted tundra, past seventy-metre-high waterfalls, deep gorges and rocky mountains – a special dome car allows passengers to appreciate the awesome views. Trains for Labrador City leave Sept-Îles every Tuesday at 7pm and Thursday at 9am, and take around eight hours ($115 return); trains run to Schefferville from Sept-Îles on Thursday at 9am (11hr; $156 return). Contact the Québec North Shore and Labrador Railway (☎709/944-8205 or 418/968-7805) for reservations.

It's possible to **drive** to Labrador from Québec via the 580-kilometre Route 389 from Baie-Comeau to Labrador City and Wabush; the road is partly paved and partly gravel and has fuel, food and accommodation services along much of its length. There are rumours of a planned bus service – contact the station in Baie-Comeau for the latest (☎418/296-2593).

Getting around

With the exception of the rail line that terminates at Schefferville, there is no land-based public transport in Labrador, and the unpaved 526-kilometre road linking Happy Valley-Goose Bay to Labrador City via Churchill Falls can only be used with ease in summer and takes, on average, ten hours to traverse. (From mid-May to mid-June, when there's the greatest chance of rain and the road becomes muddy, the Happy Valley-Goose Bay to Churchill Falls section is closed altogether.) The only other road is the 81-kilometre Route 510, which runs north from Blanc-Sablon in Québec to Red Bay. For nondrivers, or for those who want to reach the far-off outposts, there are **internal flights** run by Air Labrador in Happy Valley-Goose Bay (☎896-3387); the flight to Nain (daily except Sat) costs $437 return. Alternatively, but more expensive, is the coastal service of the *Northern Ranger* steamship (see above).

Blanc-Sablon to Red Bay

The car ferry from St Barbe in Newfoundland across the Strait of Belle Isle to Blanc-Sablon makes it possible to explore the coastal settlements along an 81-kilometre road

(Route 510) to Red Bay, then return to Newfoundland on the second boat of the day – a possibility that more tourists exploit every year. The trip over is an experience in itself, with the vessel dwarfed by icebergs floating down the strait from Greenland, and minke and humpback whales a constant sight.

This coast has been inhabited for over nine thousand years, first by caribou-hunters and then by Basque whalers, but permanent settlements did not evolve until the turn of the eighteenth century, when fishermen from Newfoundland began summer migrations to these well-stocked waters. Those who chose to live here all year were known in Newfoundland as "livyers" and led terribly harsh lives under the control of the English merchants' corrupt truck system and the supplies of alcohol that kept them in a constant state of debt. Their standard of living was greatly improved by Wilfred Grenfell, the superintendent of the Mission to Deep Sea Fishermen from 1892, who established hospitals, orphanages and nursing stations all along the coast, and succeeded in bringing the truck system to an end (see p.446). The livyers, incidentally, were the first to train **Labrador retrievers** to catch any fish that fell off the hook.

Along Route 510

Villages such as L'Anse-au-Loup, Capstan Island and West St Modeste are the descendants of the fishing camps that huddled against eastern Labrador's cliffs. The only sights that might detain you are the 7500-year-old **burial mound** of a 12-year-old Indian boy at L'Anse-Amour, which is the oldest-known funeral monument in North America; a 33-metre mid-nineteenth-century **lighthouse** at Point Amour, one of the tallest lighthouses in Atlantic Canada (June–Oct daily 10am–5.30pm; $2.50); and the **Labrador Straits Museum** (July to mid-Sept daily 10am–6pm; $2) between Forteau and L'Anse-au-Loup, which traces the area's history, with particular emphasis on the important contributions made by Labrador women. Every year in mid-August Forteau plays host to the annual Bakeapple Folk Festival. Contact the Gateway to the Straits Visitor Centre (☎931-2013) for more information on the festival and an update on accommodations in the area.

There are also several **places to stay** along this stretch of the 510: the *Beachside Hospitality Home* (☎931-2662, 931-2053 or 1-877/663-8999; ②) and the *Northern Light Inn* (☎931-2332 or toll-free in Atlantic provinces 1-800/563-3188, *www.labradorstraits.nf.ca/nli.html*; ③/④) are both in L'Anse-au-Clair, only 8km from the ferry terminal; *Grenfell Louie A Hall B&B* (☎931-2916, *www3.nf.sympatico.ca/peggy.hancock*; ②) and the *Seaview Motel and Cabins* (☎931-2840, fax 931-2842; ③) are in Forteau, the next settlement northeast; the *Lighthouse Cove B&B* (☎927-5690; ①) is in nearby L'Anse Amour; *Barney's Bed & Breakfast* (☎927-5634, fax 927-5609; ②) is in L'Anse-au-Loup, 3km northeast of Forteau; and the *Oceanview Resort* (☎927-5288, fax 927-5894, *www.seascape.com/labrador*; ③), is in West St Modeste, a few kilometers north of L'Anse-au-Loup.

Red Bay

RED BAY, 80km from Blanc-Sablon and at the end of Route 510, was the largest **whaling port** in the world in the late sixteenth century and is the most worthwhile place to visit on Labrador's east coast. At its peak, over a thousand men lived here during the whaling season, producing half a million gallons of whale oil to be shipped back on a month-long voyage to Europe. Whale oil was used for light, lubrication and as an additive to drugs, soap and pitch, and one 55-gallon barrel could fetch a price equal to $10,000 today – so for the **Basques** the discovery of Labrador's right-whale stocks was equivalent to striking oil. However, as well as the treacherous journey from Spain to what they knew as Terranova, the Basques withstood terrible hardships to claim their rich booty. Once in Labrador, they rowed fragile wooden craft called *chalupas* into these rough seas and then attached drogues to the whales to slow them down. It was then a matter of following their prey for hours until the whale surfaced and could be lanced to death. Three factors brought the whale boom to an end: first, the Basques were so successful that within thirty years they had killed off more than 15,000 whales; second, the industry became more hazardous with early freeze-ups in the 1570s; and finally, the Basque ships and men were absorbed into the ill-fated Spanish Armada of 1588.

Serious study of this fascinating area began in 1977, when marine archeologists discovered the remains of three Basque galleons and several *chalupas*. Most notable of these vessels was the *San Juan* galleon, which was split in half by an iceberg in 1565, with the loss of one black rat – its bones were found in a wicker basket with a scattering of codfish bones, which showed that the heading and splitting techniques were identical to those used by the Labrador fishermen today. On land, excavations uncovered try-works (where the whale blubber was boiled down into oil), personal artefacts and, in 1982, a cemetery on Saddle Island where the remains of 160 young men were found. Many were lying in groups, indicating that they died as crew members when chasing the whales, but some had not been buried – which suggests that the community had died of starvation when an early freeze dashed their chances of getting home.

New objects are constantly being discovered and a **Visitor Centre** (mid-June to Sept Mon–Sun 9am–8pm; $5; ☎920-2197) at the **Red Bay National Historic Site** allows you to explore the archeological sites. An excellent half-hour documentary at the centre shows footage of the discovery that revealed so much about Canada's early history. If you're feeling adventurous you can also take a boat trip to Saddle Island (Mon–Sat 3 daily 9am–4pm; $2), where you can roam around the whaler's cemetery. On Saddle Island you can enjoy a self-guided tour of the archeological sites. If you are lucky you may also spot a few whales in the distance.

Red Bay's *Whaling Station Cabins*, 61 East Harbour Drive (☎ & fax 920-2156; ③), offers en-suite rooms with cable TV, and has the best **restaurant** in the area, while more basic **accommodation** is available at the *Basinview Bed & Breakfast*, 145 Main Hwy (☎920-2002; ①/②), run by friendly owners with a knowledge of the town's Basque whaling history.

SPECIALIST TOUR COMPANIES

BreakAway Adventures, c/o Larry Bradley, 4 Cook St, Happy Valley-Goose Bay, Labrador A0P 1E0 (☎896-9343). Guided or unguided wilderness river trips in a kayak at $40–60 per day. April–Oct.

Labrador Adventure Treks, c/o Jim Learning, PO Box 163, Happy Valley-Goose Bay, Labrador A0P 1E0 (☎896-5720). Camping, canoeing, tours, white-water canoeing and kayak trips in central Labrador. One day to two weeks. July–Sept.

Labrador Scenic Limited, PO Box 233, North West River, Labrador A0P 1M0 (☎ & fax 497-8326). Wilderness tours lasting up to two weeks and costing from around $180 per day. Also canoe and kayak rentals. March–Oct. Winter snowmobile tours (half-day $90; full day $180).

Nunatsuak Limited (Atsanik Lodge), c/o Tom Goodwin, PO Box 10, Nain, Labrador A0P 1L0 (☎922-2910, or 922-2812 off-season). Weekly scheduled boat tour offering excursions to sights north of Nain, including the Torngat Mountains and Saglek fjord. $600 per day. April–Oct.

T&R Marina, 1 Hamilton River Rd, Happy Valley-Goose Bay, Labrador A0P 1E0 (☎896-2766). Boat tours on the Churchill River to Muskrat Falls or Mud Lake. Half-day (4hr; $40), full day (12hr; $60) or evening (3hr; $25). May–Oct.

Wilderness Excursions, c/o Mr Lindo Watkins, 322 Curtis Crescent, Labrador City, Labrador A2V 2B9 (☎944-5341). Day and overnight dogsled excursions in Labrador West. Mid-Feb to early April.

Northern Labrador

So far, the north is the most untouched area of Labrador, a region where the nomadic Inuit and Naskapi have managed to escape the clutches of modern Canadian society – though the production of souvenirs such as the soapstone carvings available all over Canada is now an intrinsic part of their economy. Few visitors venture this far: once you've reached Happy Valley-Goose Bay from Lewisporte on the Sir Robert Bond, it takes a further four or five days for the coastal boats to reach their northerly limit of Nain – and a sudden storm can leave you stranded for days in one of the tiny settlements.

Most of the coastal villages beyond Happy Valley-Goose Bay began as fur-trading posts in the nineteenth century, though some date back to the eighteenth-century establishment of missions by the **Moravian Brethren**, a small German missionary sect. Their old mission – consisting of a church, residence, store, storehouse and small huts to house visiting native peoples – still stands at **Hopedale**, 150km south of Nain (July–Sept by appointment; $5; ☎933-3777 or 623-2601), and at **NAIN** the mission has been converted into a museum called **Piulimatsivik** – Inuit for "place where we keep the old things" (July–Sept by appointment; donation; ☎922-2327 or 922-2158). From Nain you can travel onwards to the flat-topped **Torngat Mountains**, the highest range east of the Rockies; contact Nunatsuak Limited at the *Atsanik Lodge* (☎922-2910; ④), whose owners charter boats for up to five people at $600 per day. They will take you wherever you want to go and pick you up when you've finished exploring, but you need all your own equipment. An astounding trip is to the **Nachvak Fjord**, near Labrador's northernmost extremity, where the razorback mountains soar out of the sea at an angle of nearly eighty degrees to a height of 915m. En route you're likely to spot grey seals, whales, peregrine falcons and golden eagles.

Happy Valley-Goose Bay and around

GOOSE BAY, located on the broad Churchill River as it opens into Hamilton Inlet, along with the adjacent former trapping community of **HAPPY VALLEY**, is Labrador's principal air-transport hub. Goose Bay itself had been, since World War II, primarily a **military base** for American, Canadian and NATO forces. Privatized in 1997, it's now a training ground for NATO troops to fly low-level sorties. Happy Valley, by contrast, is where most of the shops and restaurants are located.

The Town
The town is a fairly quiet laid-back place, with sandy paths instead of sidewalks, which peter out into dirt and gravel at the edges of town. However, the roar of **low-flying military aircraft**, the thunderous noise swelling up when you least expect it, and lasting for about ten seconds at a time, frequently punctuates the stillness. There are few sights to occupy your visit here, but if you're here in late July or early August the **Labrador Canoe Regatta** is the area's most important festival; the hectic, carnival-like event is held on a weekend and features canoe races, musical performances and pavilions serving traditional food. There are also two museums: the **Northern Lights Military Museum**, 170 Hamilton River Rd (Mon–Wed & Sat 9am–5.30pm, Thurs & Fri 9am–9pm; free), an eclectic collection of military memorabilia, stuffed wildlife displays and model trains; and the **Labrador Military Museum**, in a large hangar on C Street on the base (June–Aug Mon–Fri 10am–5pm, Sat & Sun 2–4pm; Sept–May by appointment; ☎896-6900 ext 2177), where the history of the British, American, Dutch and

German – as well as Canadian – military presence is documented through displays such as flags, insignia and radar apparatus. Particularly poignant are the references to the all-too-frequent fatal **air crashes** that have occurred here in the past forty years.

Practicalities

The tiny **airport** is located on the base, just a few kilometres north of town. As there's no shuttle bus or public transport, you'll have to rely on renting a car. Tilden and Budget have booths at the airport and both charge about $40 per day, with the first 100km per day free. To get to town, take C Street and Loring Drive and turn right at the traffic lights (the only ones in town) onto Hamilton River Road. On the way into Goose Bay, notice the metal **chain-link fence** indicating that you've left the base and entered civilian territory. **Taxis** cost about $7.50 to Goose Bay, $10 to Happy Valley.

The helpful staff at the **Visitor Centre**, 365 Hamilton River Rd (June–Aug daily 9am–9pm; Sept–May Mon–Fri 9am–5pm; ☎896-8787) will provide you with brochures and help you plan your trips out of town to places such as North West River (see below). Some of the staff will even act as your tour guides. Happy Valley-Goose Bay, as befits its status as a transport hub, has a reasonable range of **accommodation**. The three best choices – all fairly standard motel-type lodgings with the usual facilities – are the large, prefabricated *Aurora Hotel*, 382 Hamilton River Rd (☎896-3398 or 1-800/563-3066, *www.aurorahotel.com*; ④/⑤), or the impersonal *Labrador Inn* next door (☎896-3351 or 1-800/563-2763; ④), both in Goose Bay; and the *Royal Inn*, 3 Royal St (☎896-2456, *royal.inn@sympatico.ca;* ③/④), in Happy Valley. The best places to **eat** are *Tricia Dee's*, 96 Hamilton River Rd, specializing in steaks and ribs, and the *Midway Gardens Restaurant*, 350 Hamilton River Rd. At *Trappers Cabin Bar and Grill*, 1 Aspen Rd, you cook your steak yourself on their grill. Happy Valley-Goose Bay is a hard-drinking town, so there are plenty of places to quench your thirst: liveliest are *Mulligan's Pub*, 368 Hamilton River Rd, and *Maxwell's II/Bentley's*, 97 Hamilton River Rd, the town's main nightspot.

Around Happy Valley-Goose Bay

Although Happy Valley-Goose Bay is an isolated town, there are still some excursions to be made beyond its boundaries. The furthest you can go on paved road is about 40km to Sheshatsheits and North West River, passing the turn-off for the Lewisporte ferry and then a large ski hill. Be sure and stop to see **Simeon Falls**, a forest waterfall in the middle of a dense, moss-covered thicket. It's easy to miss: watch for a sign on the road that says "Waterfall 600ft" and then walk along a short winding trail over a tangle of tree roots.

NORTH WEST RIVER itself is a small former fur-trading community picturesquely sited on a broad isthmus between two vast bodies of water: Grand Lake, a deep fresh-water lake to the west, and Lake Melville, an inland sea with tides and long sandy beaches to the east. For a panoramic **view**, drive the 2km up to **Sunday Hill** on a rather rough, potholed road; you'll be rewarded with sweeping vistas of both lakes and the Mealy and Mokami ranges in the distance. In the village the main attraction is the home and **studio of John Goudie**, on River Road (Mon–Fri 8am–5pm, Sat & Sun 10am–5pm), a local artist who makes furniture and jewellery out of Labradorite, a lustrous crystallized stone. He'll show you his studio where he and his assistants craft the stone and then take you into his house to see the furniture he's made, as well as a huge Labradorite-studded fireplace.

The **Labrador Interpretive Centre**, located on Hillview Drive above the town (daily: 1–4pm; free), has displays of Innu and Inuit crafts, quilts and sculpture, as well as ancient artefacts found in nearby graves. There's also a display relating to the tragic **Hubbard expedition** in 1903, when three ill-equipped men set out from the town by canoe to explore the interior, resulting in one death. Directions to the centre are poor:

take the road sharp left immediately after crossing the bridge and continue driving up the hill to the end of the road.

The Innu village of **SHESHATSHEITS** (pronounced "shesh-ah-shee"), across the small harbour is worth a stroll as long as you don't linger too long; it's a traditional village and doesn't really encourage tourists.

To experience the Labrador countryside at its most awe-inspiring, make a trip to **Muskrat Falls**, a thunderous falls on the Churchill River, which is as close to a safari trek as you'll get in Labrador without going too far from civilization. To get there, drive out of Happy Valley on the Trans-Labrador Route 500. After about 40km, watch for a rather small sign on the left indicating a narrow dirt road, down which you drive about 10km and then park your car. From there it's another twenty-minute hike on a rough unmarked trail down to the bank of the river, where you can view the falls from a spray-covered rocky outcrop. There are no facilities along the way, so be sure to take good walking shoes, plenty of drinking water and insect repellent.

Western Labrador

From Happy Valley-Goose Bay it's also possible in the summer months to drive across to **Labrador City** and adjacent **Wabush** via **Churchill Falls** on the Trans-Labrador Highway (Route 500) – one of the least frequented stretches of road in eastern Canada, so take all necessary supplies, including fuel, with you, as there are no services along the route.

Churchill Falls
Rising from a spring high on the Labrador plateau, the **Churchill River** plunges 75m into the McLean Canyon as the **Churchill Falls**, about 300km west of Happy Valley-Goose Bay, as part of a 335-metre descent within a 26-kilometre stretch. In order to exploit the massive power of this tumult, an area three and a half times the size of Lake Ontario was dammed for the incredible Churchill Falls hydroelectric development, a project conceived by the premier, Joey Smallwood, in 1952 as part of a drive to save Newfoundland's economy, whose only industrial plant at that time was a small copper mine on the northeast coast. Wrangling with possible US backers and then with the Québec government delayed its commencement until 1967, when a workforce of thirty thousand finally began the largest civil engineering project in North America. The town of **CHURCHILL FALLS** is simply an outgrowth of the power plant; if you want to stay here for a long look at the falls – which are half as high again as Niagara – **accommodation** and **food** are available at the *Churchill Falls Inn* (☎925-3211 or 1-800/229-3269; ④). **Tours** of the plant are offered daily (9am, 1pm & 7pm; 2hr–2hr 30min; free; for further information, call the *Churchill Falls Inn*).

Labrador City
A further 260km west it's a shock to come across **LABRADOR CITY** and neighbouring **Wabush**, two planned mining communities of wide streets and a couple of malls in the middle of nowhere; both were established in the 1950s and, with 10,500 people, make up the largest concentration of people in Labrador. Labrador City, as a terminus of the **rail line** from Sept-Îles, is a convenient gateway into Labrador's hinterland, but little else will bring you here. If you want to stay, **accommodation** is available at the *Carol Inn*, 215 Drake Ave (☎944-7736, *carolinn@cancom.net*; ④–⑥), and the *Two Seasons Inn* on Avalon Drive (☎944-2661 or 1-800/670-7667, *www.twoseasonsinn.nf.ca*; ④). The best choices for **eating** are the *Terrace Dining Room* in the *Two Seasons Inn*, and the *Cornelius Restaurant* in Bruno Plaza, 118 Humphrey Rd. **Duley Lake Park**, 10km from town, is a large **camping** area with over one hundred sites (day-use $4,

overnight $9; late June to early Sept; ☎282-3660) and excellent facilities for swimming and boating.

Schefferville

When the IOC mining operation opened the first Labrador iron-ore mine in the 1950s at **SCHEFFERVILLE** – the other rail terminus, 190km beyond Labrador City – they recruited a band of migratory Naskapi as cheap labour, so beginning a particularly woeful episode in the history of Canada's native peoples. In 1978 the natives signed an agreement giving them compensation for their lost land and exclusive hunting and fishing rights, but by that time the majority were so debilitated by alcohol that a return to their former existence was impossible. When the mine closed in the late 1980s, the Naskapi were left to fend for themselves while the white workers moved on to employment in other mines. Schefferville is now a run-down, blackfly-ridden reserve where houses can be bought for less than $10. Lying just over the border in Québec, the town is essentially a dead-end spot and only worth visiting as the terminus of the spectacular rail journey from Sept-Îles (there's no vehicular access); the only **accommodation** is the *Hotel-Motel Royal*, 182 Rue Montagnais (☎585-2605; ③).

travel details

Trains

Labrador City to: Sept-Îles (2 weekly; 8hr).

Schefferville to: Sept-Îles (1 weekly; 11hr).

Buses

St John's to: Channel-Port aux Basques (1 daily; 12hr 35min); Clarenville (1 daily; 3hr); Corner Brook (1 daily; 10hr 25min); Grand Falls (1 daily; 6hr 45min); Lewisporte (1 daily; 5hr 55min).

Ferries

Argentia to: North Sydney, Nova Scotia (mid-June to Aug 3 weekly; early Sept to mid-Sept 2 weekly; 14hr).

Channel-Port aux Basques to: North Sydney, Nova Scotia (early Jan to mid-Jan 1–2 daily except Mon & Tues; mid-Jan to mid-June & mid-Sept to Dec 1–2 daily; mid-June to mid-Sept 1–3 daily; 5–7hr).

Lewisporte to: Happy Valley-Goose Bay (mid-June to mid-Sept 2 weekly; 33hr).

St Anthony to: Nain, via Labrador north shore ports (early July to mid-Oct weekly; 5–6 days).

St Barbe to: Blanc-Sablon (May–Dec 1–3 daily; 1hr 30min).

Flights

Happy Valley-Goose Bay to: Charlottetown (2 daily; 3hr 45min); Churchill Falls (3 weekly; 45min); Deer Lake (4 daily; 1hr 20min); Halifax (4 daily; 3hr 10min); Montréal (4 daily; 4hr); Québec City (4 daily; 3hr 25min); St John's (4 daily; 2hr–2hr 20min); Wabush (1 daily; 1hr 15min).

St John's to: Charlottetown (4–6 daily; 2hr 50min); Churchill Falls (3 weekly; 4hr 20min); Corner Brook (2–4 daily; 1hr 10min); Deer Lake (2–4 daily; 50min); Gander (3–6 daily; 40min); Halifax (4–6 daily; 1hr 10min); Happy Valley-Goose Bay (4 daily; 2hr–2hr 20min); Montréal (3–6 daily; 2hr 55min); Ottawa (4–5 daily; 3hr 35min); Québec City, no direct flights (3–5 daily; 4hr 40min); St Anthony (1–2 daily except Sat; 1hr 15min); St Pierre (3 weekly; 1hr 15min); Toronto (5–7 daily; 3hr 25min); Wabash (1–2 daily; 3hr 15min).

Wabush to: Deer Lake (6 weekly; 1hr 55min–2hr 15min); Happy Valley-Goose Bay (1–2 daily; 1hr 5min); Montréal (1–2 daily; 3hr 10min); Ottawa (1 daily; 3hr 45min); Québec City (1–2 daily; 2hr 20min); St John's (1–2 daily; 3hr 15min); Sept-Îles (6 weekly; 55min).

CHAPTER FIVE

MANITOBA AND SASKATCHEWAN

The provinces of **Manitoba** and **Saskatchewan**, a vast tract bounded by the Ontario border to the east and the Rocky Mountains in Alberta to the west, together comprise a region commonly called "the prairies". In fact, flat treeless plains are confined to the southern part of **central Canada** and even then they are broken up by the occasional river valley and range of low-lying hills, which gradually raise the elevation from sea level at Hudson Bay to nearly 1200m near the Rockies. Furthermore, the plains themselves are divided into two broad geographical areas: the semi-arid short **grasslands** that border the United States in Alberta and Saskatchewan, and the **wheat-growing belt**, a crescent-shaped expanse to the north of the grasslands. In turn, this wheat belt borders the low hills, mixed farms and sporadic forests of the **aspen parkland**, a transitional zone between the plains and the **boreal forest**, whose trees, rocky outcrops, rivers and myriad lakes cover well over half of the entire central region, stretching to the Northwest Territories in Saskatchewan and Alberta and as far as the treeless **tundra** beside Hudson Bay in Manitoba, and in the new territory of Nunavut.

If you're here in the winter, when the temperature can fall to between –30°C and –40°C, and the wind rips down from the Arctic, it's hard to imagine how the European pioneers managed to survive, huddled together in remote log cabins or even sod huts. Yet survive they did, and they went on to cultivate, between about 1895 and 1914, the great swath of land that makes up the wheat belt and the aspen parkland, turning it into one of the most productive wheat-producing areas in the world. By any standards, the development of this farmland was a remarkable achievement, but the price was high: the nomadic culture of the **Plains Indians** was almost entirely destroyed and the disease-ravaged, half-starved survivors were dumped in a string of meagre reservations. Similarly, the **Métis**, descendants of white fur traders and native women who for more than two centuries had acted as intermediaries between the two cultures, found themselves overwhelmed, their desperate attempts to maintain their independence leading to a brace of futile rebellions under the leadership of Louis Riel in 1869–70 and 1885.

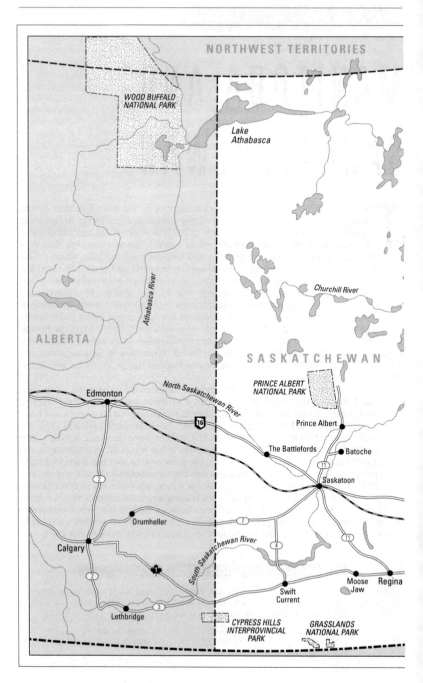

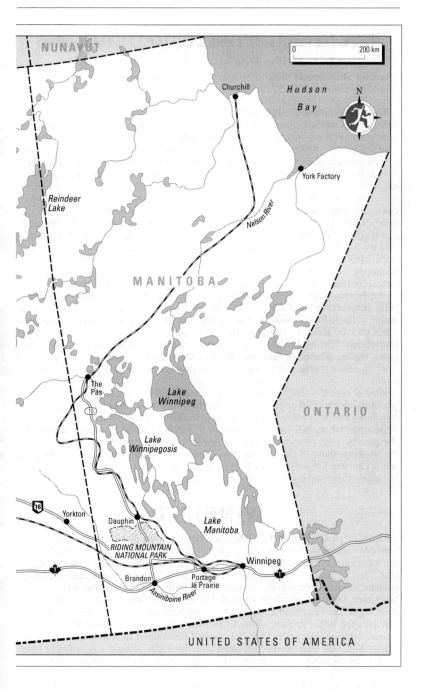

With the Métis and the Indians out of the way, thousands of European immigrants concentrated on their wheat yields, but they were the victims of a one-crop economy, their prosperity dependent on the market price of grain and the freight charges imposed by the railroad. Throughout the twentieth century, the region's farmers experienced alarming changes in their fortunes as bust alternated with boom, a situation that continues to dominate the economies of Saskatchewan and eastern Alberta today.

Central Canada is not the most popular tourist destination in the country, its main cities caricatured as dull and unattractive, its scenery considered monotonous. To some extent, these prejudices stem from the route of the **Trans-Canada Highway**, which contrives to avoid nearly everything of interest on its way from Winnipeg to Calgary, a generally boring and long drive that many Canadians prefer to do at night when, they say, the views are better. However, on the Trans-Canada itself, busy **Winnipeg** – easily the largest city in central Canada – is well worth a visit for its museums, restaurants and nightlife, while, just to the south of the highway on the Saskatchewan–Alberta border, there are the delightful wooded ridges of the **Cypress Hills Interprovincial Park**, which includes the restored Mountie outpost of **Fort Walsh**. It has to be said, though, that the **Yellowhead Route** from Winnipeg – Hwy 16 – makes a far more agreeable journey, with pleasant stops at **Saskatoon** and the **Battlefords**. This road is also within easy reach of central Canada's two outstanding parks, **Riding Mountain National Park** in Manitoba and **Prince Albert National Park** in Saskatchewan, both renowned for their lakes, forest-hiking and canoeing routes.

Most of central Canada's boreal forest is inaccessible except by private float plane, but all the major cities and the region's tourist offices have lists of tour operators and suppliers who run or equip a whole variety of trips into the more remote regions – from white-water rafting and canoeing, through to hunting, fishing and bird-watching. It's also possible to fly or travel by train to **Churchill**, a remote and desolate settlement on the southern shore of Hudson Bay that's one of the world's best places to see polar bears. One word of warning: the boreal forests swarm with voracious insects such as blackflies and mosquitoes, so don't forget your insect repellent.

WINNIPEG

With 667,000 inhabitants, **WINNIPEG** accounts for roughly two-thirds of the population of Manitoba, and lies at the geographic centre of the country, sandwiched between the American frontier to the south and the infertile Canadian Shield to the north and east. The city has been the gateway to the prairies since 1873, and became the transit point for much of the country's transcontinental traffic when the railroad arrived twelve years later. From the very beginning, Winnipeg was described as the city where "the West began", and its polyglot population, drawn from almost every country in Europe, was attracted by the promise of the fertile soils to the west. But this was no classless pioneer town: as early as the 1880s the city had developed a clear pattern of residential segregation, with leafy prosperous suburbs to the south, along the Assiniboine River, while to the north lay "Shanty Town". The long-term effects of this division have proved hard to erase, and today the dispossessed still gather round the cheap dorms just to the north of the business district, a sad rather than dangerous corner near the main intersection at Portage Avenue and Main Street. Winnipeg's skid row is only a tiny part of the downtown area, but its reputation has hampered recent attempts to reinvigorate the city centre as a whole: successive administrations in the last twenty years have refurbished warehouses and built walkways along the Red and Assiniboine rivers, but the new downtown apartment blocks remain hard to sell, and most people stick resolutely to the suburbs.

That apart, Winnipeg makes for an enjoyable stopover, and all of the main attractions are within easy walking distance of each other. The **Manitoba Museum of Man and Nature** has excellent displays on the history of the province and its various geographic areas; the **Exchange District**, recently declared a National Historic Site, features some good examples of Canada's early twentieth-century architecture; the **Winnipeg Art Gallery** has the world's largest collection of Inuit art; and, just across the Red River, the suburb of **St Boniface** has a delightful museum situated in the house and chapel of the Grey Nuns, who arrived here by canoe from Montréal in 1844. Winnipeg is also noted for the excellence and diversity of its **restaurants**, while its flourishing performing-arts scene features everything from ballet and classical music through to C&W and jazz.

Finally, the city makes a useful base for exploring the area's attractions, the most popular of which – chiefly **Lower Fort Garry** – are on the banks of the Red River as it twists its way north to Lake Winnipeg, 60km away. On the lake itself, **Grand Beach Park** has the province's finest stretches of sandy beach, just two-hours' drive from the city centre.

A brief history of Winnipeg

Named after the Cree word for murky water ("win-nipuy"), Winnipeg owes much of its history to the Red and Assiniboine rivers, which meet just south of today's city centre at the confluence called **The Forks**. The first European to reach the area was Pierre Gaultier, Sieur de la Vérendrye, an enterprising explorer who founded **Fort Rouge** near the convergence of the two rivers in 1738. This settlement was part of a chain of fur-trading posts he built to extend French influence into the west. Prospering from good connections north along the Red River to Lake Winnipeg and Hudson Bay, and west along the Assiniboine across the plains, the fort became one of the region's most important outposts within twenty years.

After the defeat of New France in 1763, local trading activity was absorbed by the Montréal-based **North West Company**, which came to dominate the fur trade at the expense of its rival, the **Hudson's Bay Company**. The latter continued to operate from fortified coastal factories staffed by British personnel, expecting their Indian trading partners to bring their pelts to them – unlike their rivals, who were prepared to live and travel among the natives. This inflexible policy looked like the ruination of the company until it was rescued by Thomas Douglas, the Earl of Selkirk, who bought a controlling interest in 1809.

In the three years **Lord Selkirk** took to turn the business round, he resettled many of his own impoverished Scottish crofters around The Forks, buying from his own company a huge tract of farmland, which he named the **Red River Colony**, or Assiniboia. The arrival of these colonists infuriated the Nor'Westers, who saw the Scottish settlement as a direct threat to their trade routes. They encouraged their Métis allies and employees to harry the Scots and for several years there was continuous skirmishing, which reached tragic proportions in 1816, when 21 settlers were killed by the Métis in the **Seven Oaks Massacre**.

Just five years later the two rival fur-trading firms amalgamated under the "Hudson's Bay Company" trade name, bringing peace and a degree of prosperity to the area. Yet the colony remained a rough-and-ready place, as a chaplain called John West lamented: "Almost every inhabitant we passed bore a gun upon his shoulder and all appeared in a wild and hunter-like state". For the next thirty years, the colony sustained an economic structure that suited both the farmers and the Métis hunters, and trade routes were established along the Red River with Minnesota, south of the border. But in the 1860s this balance of interests collapsed with the decline of the buffalo herds, and the Métis faced extreme hardship just at the time when the Hudson's Bay Company had itself lost effective administrative control of its territories.

At this time of internal crisis, the politicians of eastern Canada agreed the federal union of 1867, opening the way for the transfer of the Red River Colony from British to Canadian control. The Métis majority – roughly 6000 compared to some 1000 whites – were fearful of the consequences and their resistance took shape round **Louis Riel**, under whose dexterous leadership they captured the Hudson's Bay Company's Upper Fort Garry and created a provisional government without challenging the sovereignty of the crown. A delegation went to Ottawa to negotiate the terms of their admission into the Dominion, but their efforts were handicapped by the execution by Métis of an English settler from Ontario, **Thomas Scott**. The subsequent furore pushed prime minister John A. Macdonald into dispatching a military force to restore "law and order"; nevertheless, the **Manitoba Act** of 1870, which brought the Red River into the Dominion, did accede to many of the demands of the Métis, at the price of Riel's exile, and guaranteed the preservation of the French culture and language in the new province – although in practice this was not effectively carried out.

The eclipse of the Métis and the security of Winnipeg – as it became in 1870 – were both assured when the **Canadian Pacific Railway** routed its transcontinental line through The Forks in 1885. With the town's commodity markets handling the expanding grain trade and its industries supplying the vast rural hinterland, its population was swelled by thousands of immigrants, particularly from the Ukraine, Germany and Poland; in 1901 it had risen to 42,000. By World War I Winnipeg had become the third largest city in Canada and the largest grain-producing centre in North America, and by 1921 the population had reached 192,000. More recently, the development of other prairie cities, such as Regina and Saskatoon, has undermined something of Winnipeg's pre-eminence, but the city is still the economic focus and transport hub of central Canada.

The Manitoba telephone code is ☎204.

Arrival, information and transport

Winnipeg **airport** is some 7km west of the city centre. There's a **tourist information desk** inside the airport concourse at the north end of the main level (daily 8am–9.45pm; ☎774-0031 or 1-800/665-0204, fax 788-0245), which has a good range of leaflets on the city and its principal attractions, along with accommodation listings. Close by, a display board advertising the city's grander hotels is attached to a free phone for on-the-spot hotel reservations. From outside the terminal building, Winnipeg Transit **bus** #15 (daily: every 20–30min 6.15am–12.45am; flat fare $1.60) runs downtown, dropping passengers at or near most of the larger hotels; tickets are bought from the driver. **Taxis** charge around $10–14 for the same journey, but are cheaper if you're prepared to share; **limos** cost $20–30 per person, $11 shared.

The **Mall Centre bus station** is on the west side of the downtown area at Portage Avenue and Memorial Boulevard (daily 6.30am–midnight). **Union Station**, the city's **train station**, is on Main Street, just south of Portage, and has connecting trains to Churchill, Toronto and Saskatoon for Vancouver. For bus and train enquiries, see "Listings" on p.479.

Information

Tourism Winnipeg has an **information office** at 279 Portage (Mon–Fri 8.30am–4.30pm; ☎943-1970 or 1-800/665-0204, fax 942-4043, *www.tourism.winnipeg.mb.ca*), as well as at the airport (see opposite). A comprehensive range of leaflets on both the city and province is also available at the **Explore Manitoba Centre** adjacent to the Johnston Terminal (Mon–Thurs, Sat & Sun 10am–6pm, Fri 10am–8pm; ☎945-3777 ext AA0 or 1-800/665-0040, *www.travelmanitoba.com*), where travel counsellors can also plan your itinerary. All outlets provide free city maps, a Winnipeg Transit bus plan, accommodation listings, a restaurant guide, an historic and architectural guide to the downtown area and the free *Where* magazine, Winnipeg's bimonthly listings of activities and attractions. You can also call ☎942-2535 (24hr) for recorded information on events and sights in the city.

If you're heading off to one of the provincial parks, you should visit **Manitoba Conservation**, 200 Saulteaux Crescent (Mon–Fri 8am–4.30pm; ☎945-6784 or 1-800/214-6497). It has a wide selection of maps and will provide specialist advice on anything from weather conditions to outfitters and guides. The **Parks Canada Kiosk**, in the Explore Manitoba Centre at The Forks (Mon–Fri 8.30am–4.30pm; ☎1-888/748-2928), offers a similar service for the region's national parks.

Orientation and city transport

Winnipeg's main north–south artery is **Main Street**, which runs roughly parallel to the adjacent Red River. The principal east–west drag is **Portage Avenue**, which begins at its junction with Main. The downtown core falls on either side of Portage, beginning at Main and ending at Memorial Boulevard; it's bounded by Broadway to the south and Logan Avenue to the north. A twenty-minute stroll takes you from end to end, whilst the suburbs and the more outlying attractions are easy to reach by **bus**.

Winnipeg Transit has an excellent range of citywide services (flat fare $1.60 per journey), with tickets and transfers for trips involving more than one bus available from the driver – exact fare only. The **Transit Service Centre**, in the underground concourse at Portage and Main (Mon–Fri 8.15am–4.45pm) – in a hard to find location in the Scotiabank concourse – sells a book of ten tickets for $15.50, a five-day weekday pass ($14) and a seven-day pass, valid Mon–Sun ($15.50). Free route maps are available here, as well as at the tourist offices, and details of services are printed at the back of the Winnipeg telephone directory. There's also a Transit Service Booth (Mon–Thurs 10am–6pm, Fri & Sat 10am–5pm, Sun 1–5pm) in the foyer of the Winnipeg Centennial Library, 251 Donald St. If you want to cover a lot of the downtown attractions in a short space of time, you'll find the #99 Downtown Flyer Service handy. It's a free service whereby you can get on or off at 22 bus stops in an area bounded roughly by Portage Avenue, Memorial Boulevard, Broadway, Pioneer Boulevard (for The Forks) and Main Street (service Mon–Fri 11am–3.30pm, Sat 11am–5pm, Sun noon–5pm). **Bike rental** is available at the youth hostel (see p.468); for details of **car rental** agencies and **taxi** companies, see "Listings", p.468.

Winnipeg also has a transport **information service** (Mon–Sat 6am–10pm, Sun 6.30am–10pm; ☎986-5700) and a **Handi-Transit** door-to-door minibus facility for disabled visitors (Mon–Fri 6.30am–midnight, Sat 7.30am–midnight, Sun 8.30am–10pm; information on ☎986-5722).

TOURS IN AND AROUND WINNIPEG

Bus and **boat tours** of the city leave from the dock beside Provencher Bridge at The Forks (see p.473). There are walking tours of the Exchange District from Old Market Square (May–Aug hourly except Mon 10am–3pm; 1hr 30min; $5; ☎942-6716), guided walks around local art galleries from Winnipeg Art Gallery (July & Aug Wed, Thurs & Sat; $4.95; ☎786-6641) and Selkirk Avenue in the North End (June–Aug Tues–Sat 10am & 2pm; free; 1hr; ☎586-3445 or 586-2720). Horse-drawn wagons are available to take you around St Boniface, the French quarter (June–Aug; ☎235-1406). Wild-Wise Wilderness Adventures (☎788-1070, fax 788-1001) organizes historical canoe excursions for groups of ten people, where you paddle along the Red and Assiniboine rivers in the spirit of the pioneer voyageur guides and fur traders.

Companies operating half-day, day-, overnight and week-long tours out of Winnipeg include Anishinabe Camp and Cultural Tours (May–Sept; ☎925-2030, fax 725-2127) to Riding Mountain National Park, for aboriginal culture, sleeping in tepees and participating in traditional ceremonies and powwow dancing; Aurora Canada Tours (Nov–April; ☎ & fax 942-8140), for one-day to two-week tours observing bird and plant life, and viewing the Northern Lights; The Great Gray Owl Wilderness Adventure Camp (☎237-LAKE or ☎1-800/565-2595) for ecologically sound trips to Atikaki Wilderness Provincial Park; Canadian Trails Adventure Tours (year-round; ☎1-800/668-BIKE) for bicycle tours; B&B Scuba (☎257-3696 or 1-888/257-3696) for week-long scuba diving tours that include snorkelling with beluga whales; Frog in the Pocket (☎885-0344) for eco-tours on the natural and cultural history of Manitoba, with visits to boreal forests and other ecosystems; and Akeesha Dove (May–Oct; ☎339-1154), for a visit to the Spirit Sands "desert".

Accommodation

Most of Winnipeg's **hotels** are within walking distance of the bus and train stations, and there's rarely any difficulty in finding somewhere to stay. The modern hotels are standard-issue skyscrapers that concentrate on the business clientele; most of these start at ⑤, but some of them offer weekend discounts and up to twenty percent reductions if you stay for three or four nights. The smaller and older downtown hotels start at ①, but at this price the rooms are basic and often grimy – a more comfortable place is likely to be in ②–③. (Avoid the "flophouses", the cheap dorms calling themselves "hotels" on Main St, just north of Portage Ave.) Breakfast is extra almost everywhere.

The major approach roads are dotted with **motels** (from ① up to ③/④), of which the largest concentrations are along the Pembina Highway, which runs south from the city centre as Route 42, and along Portage, which runs west forming part of the Trans-Canada Highway (Route 1). Two recommended motels on these routes are the no-frills *Comfort Inn South by Journey's End*, 3109 Pembina Highway (☎269-7390 or 1-800/228-5150, fax 261-7565; ④) with a restaurant and free local calls, and the smaller drive-up hotel, the *Red Lion Inn*, 3252 Portage Ave (☎ & fax 837-5871; ②).

Tourism Winnipeg has the details of some thirty **B&B** addresses (mostly in ②), with breakfasts that vary from frugal continental to a complete meal. Most of these are affiliated to Bed and Breakfast of Manitoba, 434 Roberta Ave (☎661-0300 or ☎1-877/304-0300), an agency that makes reservations upon payment of a deposit equivalent to one night's stay. Unfortunately, most of their B&Bs are far from central, but some of the more convenient locations are given below. The **youth hostel**, within easy walking distance of the bus station, is supplemented in summer by less conveniently located rooms at the University of Manitoba.

The tourist offices will help arrange hotel and B&B accommodation and there's also a free phone number for **reservations** (☎1-800/665-0040). For hostel information, call Hostelling International (☎784-1131). Manitoba Natural Resources has a toll-free reservation service for campsites in 35 provincial parks (Mon–Fri 9am–8pm, Sat 10am–5pm; $6.75 booking fee; ☎948-3333 or 1-888/482-2267).

Hotels

Balmoral Motor Hotel, 621 Balmoral St at Notre Dame Ave (☎943-1544, fax 943-9571). In the northwest corner of downtown, with a laundry room, a coffee shop and the opportunity to get a tan on their sunbeds. ①.

Best Western Carlton Inn, 220 Carlton St (☎942-0881 or 1-800/528-1234, fax 943-9312, *www.bestwestern.com*). One of the more agreeable cheap hotels, centrally located opposite the city's Convention Centre, with motel-style rooms, restaurant and pool. ③.

Charter House, 330 York Ave at Hargrave St (☎942-0101 or 1-800/782-0175, fax 956-0665). A good location and reasonable rates make up for the absence of character. ③.

Crowne Plaza Winnipeg Downtown, 350 St Mary Ave at Hargrave St (☎942-0551 or 1-800/2-CROWNE, fax 943-8702). Stay in tasteful, opulent rooms adjoining the Convention Centre, with restaurants and pools. ④.

Fort Garry, 222 Broadway (☎942-8251 or 1-800/665-8088, fax 942-7036, *www.fortgarryhotel.com*). Built in neo-Gothic style between 1911 and 1914 near the train station and lavishly refurbished, with an elegant, balconied foyer leading to 250 rooms. ⑥.

Gordon Downtowner, 330 Kennedy St at Ellice Ave (☎943-5581, fax 947-3041, *www.downtowner.mb.ca*). Probably Winnipeg's most comfortable cheap hotel with restaurant and bar. ②.

Mariaggi's Theme Suite Hotel, 231 McDermot Ave (☎947-9447, fax 956-4980, *www.mariaggis.com*). Pay through the nose but reap the rewards of Hawaiian-, Mexican-, Moroccan- or African-themed suites or a tropical penthouse. Couples only. ⑦.

Osborne Village Motor Inn, 160 Osborne St (☎452-9824, fax 452-0035). Basic accommodation in the heart of lively Osborne Village. Bands often play downstairs and the rooms are not soundproofed. ①.

Radisson Hotel Winnipeg Downtown, 288 Portage Ave at Smith St (☎956-0410 or 1-800/333-3333, fax 949-1162, *www.radissonhotel.ca*). One of the city's largest and most recently renovated hotels, with fine views from the top floors, as well as a gym, saunas, whirlpool, swimming pool, plus baby-sitting services. Offers big discounts at weekends. ④.

St Regis, 285 Smith St (☎942-0171 or 1-800/663-7344, fax 943-3077). An historic hotel c.1900 in the downtown area. Tastefully furnished with dining room and coffee shop. The honeymoon suites have hot tubs. Under-18s stay free. ②.

Travelodge Hotel Downtown Winnipeg, 360 Colony St at Portage Ave (☎786-7011 or 1-800/578-7878, fax 772-1443). Big comfortable rooms, next to the bus station and within walking distance of most attractions. ③.

Bed and breakfasts

Bob & Margaret's, 950 Palmerston Ave (☎774-0767). A 15min bus ride on #10 from downtown, this riverside B&B has one bedroom suite only, with TV room and private bathroom. Bikes and canoes can be rented. ②.

Butterfly Bed and Breakfast, 226 Walnut St (☎783-6664). Two cosy rooms with shared bathroom in a central location, just off Portage Ave. ②.

Cowan's Castle, 39 Eastgate (☎786-4848). A 1907 four-bed heritage home on the Assiniboine River, 20-minutes' walk to downtown. Serves delicious home-cooked breakfasts. ②.

Gîte de la Cathédrale Bed and Breakfast, 581 rue Langevin, St Boniface (☎233-7792). Run by French Manitobans, this B&B in the heart of St Boniface offers Québécois breakfasts of pancakes and maple syrup, omelettes and French toast, with service in French. Five flowery bedrooms with shared bathroom. ②.

Mary Jane's Place, 144 Yale Ave (☎453-8104). A gracious Georgian-style home with oak panelling and stained-glass windows, 10min by bus #29 from Portage Ave. ②.

West Gate Manor Bed and Breakfast, 71 West Gate (☎772-9788, fax 772-9782). Pleasant rooms with Victorian period furnishings in Armstrong Point, within walking distance of downtown. ②.

Hostel and college rooms

Guest House International, 168 Maryland St (☎772-1272 or 1-800/743-4423, fax 772-4117, *www.ourworld.compuserve.com/homepages/backpackers*). A restored Victorian house with six comfortable dorms, four private bedrooms and walls decorated with art by aboriginal children. Bus #29 from the train station, or nine blocks from the bus station. The area, though residential, can be a bit dodgy at night. Facilities include a laundry, kitchen, game room and Internet access. Reservations recommended in summer. Check-in daily 8am–midnight. ①.

Ivey House International Youth Hostel, 210 Maryland St at Broadway (☎772-3022, fax 784-1133). A forty-room friendly hostel, clean and well run with some private rooms of 2–4 beds. There's also a lounge, a big kitchen, sun deck, lockers and bike rental. Bus #17 from Vaughan St near the bus station, or #29 from the train station. Often full in the summer. Check-in daily 8am–midnight. ①.

University of Manitoba, Fort Garry campus (☎474-9942). Double rooms and dorm beds available from mid-May to mid-August in basic student accommodations. 10km south of the city centre. ①.

Campsites

Conestoga Campground, 1341 St Anne's Rd at Perimeter Hwy (☎257-7363). Thirteen kilometres southeast of town with most sites having electricity and water. Mid-May to Sept. $12–18.

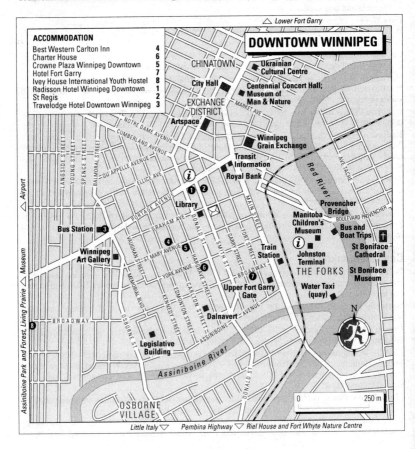

Jones Campground, 588 Trans-Canada Hwy, St François Xavier (☎ & fax 864-2721). In a small town on the Assiniboine River, 15km west of Winnipeg, this campsite has 44 unreserved sites, most with water and electricity as well as toilets, showers and a BBQ area. May–Sept. $10–15.

Traveller's RV Resort, Murdock Rd (☎256-2186, fax 253-9313). The nearest campsite, some 14km southeast of the centre, just off the Trans-Canada, with over fifty unreserved sites and facilities that include showers, toilets and drinking water. May–Sept. $15–25.

The City

The traditional centre of Winnipeg is the intersection of **Portage Avenue and Main Street** just north of **The Forks**, close to the Red River at the start of what was once the main Métis cart track (the Portage Trail) west across the prairies to the Hudson's Bay Company posts, and the principal trail north to Lake Winnipeg linking the riverside farm lots and Lower and Upper Fort Garry. Main Street was, in fact, called the Garry Road until the mid-1870s. Despite its historic associations, in 1979 the city council closed most of the junction to pedestrians in return for the construction of an underground shopping concourse, Winnipeg Square. While you're here, have a look at the grand Neoclassical **Bank of Montréal** on the southeast side of the intersection, its fussily carved capitals in stark contrast to the sharp, clean lines of its skyscraper neighbours. The intersection is also known as the windiest of any city or town in Canada.

The Exchange District

Just to the north of the Portage and Main intersection, the **Exchange District National Historic Site** is a rough rectangle of old warehouses, former commodity exchanges and commercial buildings that are the best-preserved group of any city in Canada. Many of them were converted, from the late 1970s onwards, into art galleries, boutiques, antique shops and restaurants. The effective centre of the district is the **Old Market Square** at King and Albert streets and Bannatyne Avenue, with its weekend produce market, flea markets and buskers. This part of town was built during Winnipeg's boom, a period of frenzied real-estate speculation and construction that peaked in 1882, but only lasted until the outbreak of World War I. The standard architectural design, used for most of the office buildings and nearly all the warehouses, was simple and symmetrical, the plain brick walls topped off by decorative stone cornices. However, one or two companies financed extravagant variations, notably the **Electric Railway Chambers Building** at 213 Notre Dame Ave, an imaginative blend of Italian Renaissance and early twentieth-century motifs, its terracotta facade lined with some six thousand electric lights. The district is also one of the city's principal cultural centres, home to such buildings as the **Manitoba Museum of Man and Nature**, the **Ukrainian Cultural and Educational Centre** and the artist-run **Artspace**.

The Manitoba Museum of Man and Nature

In the heart of the Exchange District, at 190 Rupert Ave, the **Centennial Centre** incorporates the **Manitoba Museum of Man and Nature** (late May to early Sept daily 10am–6pm; early Sept to late May Tues–Fri 10am–4pm, Sat, Sun & holidays 10am–5pm; $4.99, recorded information ☎956-2830, *www.manitobamuseum.mb.ca*), an excellent introduction to the province's geographical regions and the history of its peoples. Highlights of the natural-history galleries include an imposing polar bear diorama, a well-illustrated explanation of the Northern Lights and the evocative **Boreal Forest** gallery, where you'll find a waterfall, a family of moose, and a diorama of Cree gathering food and painting sacred designs on rocks. There's also a disconcerting section

THE HISTORY OF THE RAILWAY IN CANADA

Even before Confederation in 1867, Sir John A. Macdonald, Canada's first prime minister, grasped the need to physically link the disparate provinces of the new nation. Each area needed lines of communication to the east and west to counteract the natural tug of the neighbouring parts of the USA to the south. Both the Maritime Provinces and British Columbia joined the Confederation on the condition that rail links would be built to transport their goods throughout the land. Railway construction of this scale was a huge undertaking for such a young country and outside finance was the only answer.

From 1855, lines were constructed in eastern Ontario and Québec, culminating in the completion in 1876 of the Intercolonial Railway, which linked central Canada with the Maritime Provinces. Progress of the transcontinental line to the Pacific, however, was impeded by the Riel rebellion at the Red River in 1869–70, and in 1871 the Parliamentary Opposition labelled the entire scheme "an act of insane recklessness". Two years later Macdonald's Conservative government fell after implication in scandals involving the use of party funds in railway contracts, and Alexander Mackenzie's subsequent Liberal ministry proceeded so slowly with the railway plans that British Columbia openly spoke of secession if construction was not speeded up. The eventual completion of the Canadian Pacific Railway (CPR) in 1885 finally made Canada "more than a geographical expression", and by the early twentieth century another coast-to-coast line had been completed.

Passage across the hitherto virtually impenetrable Canadian Shield was now feasible and the full agricultural potential of the prairies to the west could be realized. Between 1896 and 1913 more than one million people arrived by train to settle in the prairies, and wheat production rose from 20 million to more than 200 million bushels a year. Additionally, some of the first major mineral finds in northern Ontario were brought to light during the construction of the railway. The years following World War I were a period of economic consolidation, which culminated in the union of various smaller lines into a nationwide system: the Canadian National Railways (CNR), a government-controlled organization.

What has been called "the bizarre project" of the Hudson Bay Railway stemmed from the prairie farmers' desire to create an outlet for trade with the rest of the world that was not dependent on the bankers back east. A first attempt in 1886 foundered when the promoters ran out of money after the first 65km. After many delays this major engineering feat was accomplished in 1929, just in time for the Great Depression.

The impact of the Depression on Canadian railways was particularly severe, leading to stringent economies and pooling of competing lines. World War II saw a rise in profits, but over the subsequent decades the story has been one of gradual decline, with freight increasingly travelling by road and air, and passenger services pruned almost to extinction on some lines. By 1992, passengers could no longer cross Canada on the CPR, and one of the world's great train rides was gone for ever. Grain and minerals are still moved by train, however, and the privately owned CPR is now exclusively a freight line. VIA, the passenger branch of CNR, operates virtually all of Canada's passenger services, including the Hudson Bay line, in roadless northern Manitoba – probably the only rail route in North America to still exist primarily as a passenger service.

devoted to the more malicious insects of Manitoba – starring the "no-see-um", a deer fly that specializes in burrowing into the nostrils of caribou. The **Grasslands Gallery** has a small display of Assiniboine Indian artefacts, along with a reconstruction of a tepee and a copy of a pioneer log cabin. There's also an example of the sod houses that the pioneers were forced to build in many parts of the treeless southern plains, and a replica of the odd-looking Red River cart, the Métis's favourite form of land transportation, with massive wheels that could tackle the prairie mud and mire. The museum's most popular exhibit, moored in a massive display area that reproduces a seventeenth-century River Thames dockside, is an impressive full-scale working replica of the

Nonsuch, the ship whose fur-collecting voyage to Hudson Bay in 1668 led to the creation of the Hudson's Bay Company. The new **Hudson's Bay Company Gallery** comprises more than 10,000 artefacts and documents amassed by the Company and which form a record of its links with Manitoba and its impact on Canada as a whole. A reconstructed trading post showcases goods that were exchanged for furs – everything from beads and guns to canned foods. There's also the last surviving York boat used for river and lake travel from the 1800s to the early 1900s, including relics from the ill-fated Franklin Expedition's search for the Northwest Passage and beautiful artworks and crafts produced by the First Nations, Métis and Inuit, among them carved ivory and immaculate beadwork that can't fail to impress. At the end of the gallery a reconstruction of the Hudson's Bay Company's boardroom in London includes a huge ram's head used, unbelievably, as a snuff holder and passed around at dinner parties. The last section of the museum is the **Urban Gallery**, which re-creates the Winnipeg of the early 1920s, a street complete with pharmacy, barber shop, dentist, promenade and cinema showing period films. An additional section, scheduled to open in 2002, is the **Parklands Gallery**, which will house displays and dioramas on the province's largest region.

Also in the Centennial Centre are the **planetarium** (summer daily 11am–6pm; winter Tues–Fri 3pm, Sat, Sun & holidays 11am–4pm; $3.99 and the "Touch the Universe" **science centre** (same hours as museum; $3.99), where more than sixty interactive exhibits focus on the way the universe is perceived by the five senses. An **Adventure Value Pass** for the museum, planetarium and science centre costs $10.99, and allows 3-day all-inclusive admission.

Next door is the **Centennial Concert Hall** (☎949-3999), where performances of the Manitoba Opera, Winnipeg Symphony Orchestra and Royal Winnipeg Ballet are held. Just across the street from the Concert Hall is the modern **City Hall**.

The Ukrainian Centre, Artspace and Chinatown

Two blocks north of the Centennial Centre, the **Ukrainian Cultural and Educational Centre (Oseredok)**, 184 Alexander Ave East at Main Street (Tues–Sat 10am–4pm, Sun 2–5pm; $2), occupies a 1930s office building on the edge of the Exchange District. The second largest ethnic group in Manitoba, the Ukrainians arrived here around 1900, a peasant people united by language and custom, but divided by religion and politics – Orthodox against Catholic, nationalist against socialist. By 1940, the various factions managed to amalgamate to create the Ukrainian Canadian Committee, a loose coalition committed to the country's institutions and the promotion of Ukrainian interests. Their collection of folk art in the fifth-floor **museum** of the complex is an excellent introduction to their strongly maintained traditions, with delightful examples of embroidery, weaving, woodcarving and the exquisite designs of *pysanky*, Easter egg painting. There's also an art gallery, library and gift shop.

Artspace, in a warehouse building at the corner of Arthur Street and Bannatyne Avenue, is the largest artist-run centre in Canada and houses a cinema (see p.479), several galleries and offices for art groups. To see the best of contemporary local and Canadian **art**, check out the SITE Gallery, 2nd Floor, 55 Arthur St (Tues–Sun 11am–4pm), while the Floating Gallery, 100 Arthur St (Tues–Sun 11am–5pm) focuses on photography. A few blocks away, Plug-In, 286 McDermot Ave (Tues–Wed 11am–6pm, Thurs 11am–7.30pm, Fri 11am–5.30pm, Sat 10.30am–4.30pm) is housed in a former warehouse and promotes new art in all media which entails some wacky multimedia installations.

Possibly the most gracious building in the Exchange District is the former **Winnipeg Grain Exchange**, opposite the *Lombard Hotel* on Lombard Avenue. It was built between 1906 and 1928 and was the largest building of its type in Canada; grain offices still occupy some of the floors. Other imposing buildings are the ten-storey **Confederation Life Building**, 457 Main St, which has a curved facade of white terra-cotta, and the massive **Royal Bank Building** at the corner of Main Street and William Avenue.

Adjacent to the Exchange District, north of Rupert Street and west of Main Street, is **Chinatown**, originally settled in the 1920s by immigrants brought to Manitoba to help build the railway into the west. The area has many good restaurants and groceries, as well as shops selling silk fabrics and exotic herbs and spices – though, other than that, not much in the way of sights.

The Forks

South of Portage Avenue along Main Street (take bus #38 or #99 from Portage Ave) rises the ponderous dome of the Beaux Arts-style **Union Station** designed by the architects who did Grand Central Station in New York; it has an indoor market and the **Winnipeg Railway Museum** upstairs (mid-May to early Sept Thurs–Sun & holidays noon–6pm; early Sept to mid-May Sat, Sun & holidays noon–4pm; donation). Immediately south of the station is the present headquarters of the Hudson's Bay Company. Across the street, in a small park, is the stone gate that's the sole remnant of **Upper Fort Garry**, a Hudson's Bay Company fort from 1837 to 1870 and thereafter the residence of Manitoba's lieutenant governors until 1883, when the fort was dismantled. The pointed dormers and turrets behind it belong to the **Hotel Fort Garry**, a chateau-like structure built for the Grand Trunk Railroad.

Behind the station, the chunk of land bordering the Red River as it curves round to **The Forks** was, until recently, one of the country's largest railway yards – you can still see CNR freight cars and cabooses dotted around the grounds. Subsequent redevelopment has turned The Forks into Winnipeg's most visited sight due to its **Explore Manitoba Centre** (see p.465), half tourist information point, half museum, with six reasonably interesting themed displays covering the province's tourist areas. It's worth a quick visit, if only to pick the brains of the very helpful staff and admire the magnificent stuffed polar bear from Churchill, a persistent and dangerous marauder of the town's dump who came to a sticky end. Just east along the river from here is **The Forks National Historic Site**, bearing plaques to celebrate the role of the fur traders and pioneers who first settled here. An archeological excavation site welcomes volunteer diggers from July to October (advance registration required; for further information, call ☎983-6757 or 1-888/748-2928).

Intended to open adjacent to the site – likely by the time of publication – is a long-awaited project called **Spirit Island**, designed to promote First Nations, Metis and Inuit culture via interactive displays and the performing arts.

Nearby, the 1888–89 rail-maintenance shed houses the **Manitoba Children's Museum** (June–Aug Mon–Sat 10am–8pm, Sun & holidays 10am–6pm; Sept–May Mon–Wed 9.30am–5pm, Thurs & Fri 9.30am–8pm, Sat 10am–8pm, Sun 10am–5pm; $4.50 adults, children $4.95; ☎924-4000, *www.childrensmuseum.com*), a hands-on, state-of-the-art enterprise that appeals equally to adults. Five different sections cover aspects of history, science, nature and technology. A vintage steam-engine with a couple of Pullman carriages and a mail office is equipped with tickets, luggage, uniforms and mail; close by, bear, lynx and raccoon costumes are on hand for kids to don while they explore a huge model of an oak tree and its ecosystem. Visitors to the museum can be filmed and have their activities shown simultaneously on two huge video screens, with added optical effects. For older kids, the highlight is probably the fully functioning TV studio where they can experiment with lights and cameras; at certain times, staff conduct interviews with them on their views of current events, which are relayed by one of the local stations.

A couple of minutes' walk away, **The Forks Market** (daily 9.30am–6.30pm, Fri until 9pm) and the **Johnston Terminal**, both old railway buildings, house shops, food stalls, bars, restaurants and (in the Johnston Terminal) the **Costume Museum** with a small collection of vintage clothing (Mon–Thurs & Sat 10am–6pm, Fri 10am–9pm, Sun noon–5pm; donation). **Canoes** can be rented at the Johnston Terminal for the Red and Assiniboine rivers (daily, weather permitting 11am–10pm; $7.50 an hour; ☎783-6633). Paths from the two buildings lead down to the Assiniboine River via an outdoor amphitheatre, where buskers entertain the gathered crowds with anything from hard rock to bagpipe music. Nearby is **The Wall Through Time**, a curving brick barricade covered with plaques and inscriptions recording the historic events of the area. On the banks of the Red River there's a quay beside Provencher Bridge where you can take **boat trips**, which run parallel to the attractive **riverwalk path**, back along the Assiniboine River as far as the Legislative Building on Broadway and in the opposite direction up the Red River (May–Oct daily 1pm, 2hr, $11.75; sunset dinner and dance cruise daily 7pm, 3hr, $12.75; moonlight dance cruise Fri & Sat 10pm, 3hr, $12.75). The Historic Fort Cruise takes you to Lower Fort Garry (see p.481) and back (July–Aug Wed–Fri 9am–4.30pm; $20). One of the boats is a replica paddlewheel vessel. **Water taxis** also leave every fifteen minutes from a quay closer to the market (daily 11am–sunset; 30min; ☎783-6633, *www.icenter.net/-gordcart;* $6) and run along the same route. Alternatively you can check the river out for an hour aboard a 26-foot replica of a birch-bark canoe paddled by a guide in voyageur garb; tickets cost $30 and are available from the Explore Manitoba Centre or from Wild-Wise Wilderness Adventures on ☎788-1070. **Tours** of the city on a double-decker bus also leave from the dock beside the bridge (June–Sept; 9am; 3hr; basic tour $20). For boat- and bus-tour reservations call ☎942-4500 (*www.excape.ca/-paddlewh*). For information on all programmes and activities at The Forks, call the hotline (☎957-7618).

Downtown

Lined by department stores and offices, downtown **Portage Avenue** is the city's main shopping street, with a web of underground passageways and glass-enclosed overhead walkways linking the various malls and large stores and providing welcome relief from the summer heat and winter cold. The largest complex is the ugly postmodern **Portage Place**, on the north side of the avenue, with its main entrance at Kennedy Street (daily: Mon–Wed & Sat 10am–6pm, Thurs & Fri 10am–9pm, Sun noon–5pm). There are over 160 shops and services here, plus a giant-screen IMAX cinema on the third level (information ☎956-IMAX, tickets ☎780-SEAT). Among the many modern buildings that line Portage are some earlier ones that are architecturally attractive: the **Paris Building** at no. 259, with a splendid piered facade and delicate cornice, and the **Boyd Building** at no. 388, with cream and bronze terracotta decoration.

The uncompromisingly modern **Winnipeg Art Gallery (WAG)**, a wedge-shaped building at 300 Memorial Blvd, at Portage Avenue (Tues & Thurs–Sun 11am–5pm, Wed 11am–9pm; mid-June to Aug opens daily at 10am; $4, free on Wed; ☎786-6641, *www.wag.mb.ca*), is the home of the largest public collection of Inuit art in the world, a decent selection of Gothic and Renaissance paintings and a reasonable assortment of modern European art, including works by Miró, Chagall and Henry Moore. The problem is that little of these collections is on display at any one time – much of the available space is taken up by offices while the main display area, on the third floor, is given over to temporary (and often dire) exhibitions of modern Canadian art. The mezzanine level, and often the third floor galleries, are devoted to the Inuits, each temporary display developing a particular theme – from the symbolic significance of different animals to the role of women sculptors in the isolated communities. The gallery also has an open-air sculpture court and a rooftop restaurant.

The Legislative Building, Osborne Village, Little Italy and Dalnavert

A few minutes' walk south of the Art Gallery, along Memorial Boulevard, is the **Manitoba Legislative Building** (July–Sept hourly tours 9am–6pm; rest of year Mon–Fri by appointment; free; ☎945-5813), built between 1913 and 1919 and surrounded by trim lawns and flower borders. The building, made of local Tyndall stone embedded with fossils, has a central pediment decorated with splendidly pompous sculptures representing the ideals of Canadian nationhood. A half-kneeling figure, symbolizing progress, beckons his lazy neighbour to come to the land of promise, whilst a muscular male figure, with a team of powerful horses, idealizes the pioneer spirit. High above, a central square tower rises to a copper-green dome that's topped by the **Golden Boy**, a four-metre-high gold-plated bronze figure that's supposed to embody the spirit of enterprise and eternal youth. Inside, the marble columns and balconies of the foyer house two magnificent life-size buffalo bronzes by the French sculptor Charles Gardet, framing a staircase of brown-veined Carrara marble. The mural over the entrance to the legislative chamber depicting World War I scenes is by the English artist Frank Brangwyn.

Just behind the Legislative Building, across the Assiniboine, lies **Osborne Village**, the bohemian part of town, whose inexpensive bars, restaurants and music joints – strung along Osborne Street – are favourites with the city's students. West off Osborne Street is Corydon Avenue, whose several blocks and side streets comprise **Little Italy**, known for its cappuccino bars and restaurants.

A couple of blocks east of the Legislative Building, **Dalnavert**, at 61 Carlton St (Jan & Feb Sat & Sun noon–4.30pm; March–May & Sept–Dec Tues–Thurs, Sat & Sun noon–4.30pm; June–Aug Tues–Thurs, Sat & Sun 10am–5.30pm; guided tours every 30min; $4; *www.mhs.mb.ca*), was the home of Hugh John Macdonald, the son of Canada's first prime minister and, briefly, premier of Manitoba. Built in 1895 in Queen Anne Revival style, the house has been painstakingly restored, its simple red-brick exterior engulfed by a fanciful wooden veranda, the interior all heavy, dark-stained woods and strong deep colours. Macdonald's conservatism, reflected in the decor, was mellowed by a philanthropic disposition – he even reserved part of his basement for some of the city's destitute.

St Boniface

The suburb of **St Boniface**, a ten-minute walk east of the downtown area just across the Red River (or by bus #10 or #56 from Portage Ave), was a centre of early French-Canadian and Métis settlement. Founded by two French-Canadian Catholic priests in 1818, it retains something of its distinctive character and even today, 27 years after its incorporation into the city of Winnipeg, roughly 25 percent of its population speaks French as a first language. **Walking tours** of St Boniface run from June to August (Mon–Fri 10am, 1pm & 3pm; 1hr; free; ☎235-1406 or 945-1715).

St Boniface's principal historic sights are situated beside the river, along avenue Taché. Walking south from the Provencher Bridge, the massive white-stone facade on the left is all that remains of **St Boniface Cathedral**, a huge neo-Romanesque structure built in 1908 and largely destroyed by fire in 1968. Its replacement, just behind, was designed with an interior in the style of a giant tepee. The large silver-domed building immediately to the east is the **Collège Universitaire de Saint-Boniface**, formerly a Jesuit college and now the French-speaking campus of the University of Manitoba. Here you'll see a controversial modern statue of **Louis Riel** that portrays him as naked and deformed. Its original location was on the grounds of the Legislative Building, but it caused such a storm of protest that it was removed to here in 1994. In front of the cathedral is the cemetery containing Riel's grave, whose modest tombstone gives little indication of the furore surrounding his execution in Regina on November 16, 1885. Only after three weeks did the authorities feel safe enough to move the body, which was then sent secretly by rail to St Boniface. The casket lay overnight in Riel's family home in the suburb of St Vital (see below) before its transfer to the cathedral, where a Requiem Mass was attended by most of the Métis population. That same evening, across the river, Riel's enemies burnt his effigy on a street corner, a symptom of a bitter divide that was to last well into the twentieth century.

Le Musée de Saint-Boniface (June–Sept Mon–Fri 9am–6pm, Sat 10am–5pm, Sun 10am–8pm; Oct–May Mon–Fri 9am–6pm; $2; guided tours available by reservation on ☎237-4500) is housed in an attractive whitewashed building across from the cathedral. The oldest building in Winnipeg and the largest squared-oak log building in North America, it was built between 1846 and 1851 as a convent for the Grey Nuns, a missionary order whose four-woman advance party had arrived by canoe from Montréal in 1844. Subsequently, the building was adapted for use as a hospital, a school and an orphanage. Inside, a series of cosy rooms are devoted to the Red River Colony, notably an intriguing collection of Métis memorabilia that includes colourful sashes – the most distinctive feature of Métis dress. You can also see the battered wooden casket used to transport Riel's body from Regina to St Boniface. There's also a lovely little chapel, whose papier-mâché Virgin was made from an old newspaper that one of the original Grey Nuns found outside Upper Fort Garry when she walked across the frozen river to buy food.

South of the centre: the Riel House and the Fort Whyte Nature Centre

The **Riel House National Historic Site**, 330 River Rd (mid-May to early Sept daily 10am–6pm; donation; ☎257-1783 or 1-888/748-2928, bus #16 from the Portage Place Mall), in the suburb of St Vital, about 10km south of the city centre, is just about worth the trip. The main feature of the site is a tiny clapboard house that was built by the Riels in 1880–81 and stayed in their possession until 1968. Louis Riel never actually lived here, but this was where his body was brought after his execution in 1885, and the house has been restored to its appearance at that time, complete with black-bordered photographs and a few artefacts left by his wife, Marguerite.

Other period furnishings and fittings give a good idea of the life of a prosperous Métis family in the 1880s. The railway had reached St Boniface in 1877, a time when the simple products of the Red River could be supplemented by manufactured goods from the east with relative ease – the iron stove, the most obvious import, improved the ßquality of the Riels' life immeasurably. Costumed guides provide an enjoyable twenty-minute tour of the house and garden, the sole remnant of the once sizeable Riel landholdings.

Across the Red River from the suburb of St Vital, at the city's southern limits, is the **Fort Whyte Centre**, 1961 McCreary Rd (summer Mon & Tues 9am–5pm, Wed–Fri 9am–9pm, Sat, Sun & holidays 10am–9pm; rest of year Mon–Fri 9am–5pm, Sat, Sun & holidays 10am–5pm; $3.50; *www.fortwhyte.org*), an environmental education centre dealing with the diversity of plants and animals of the prairie ecosystem. It's a real outdoors experience, with a wildlife observation tower, herd of bison, deer enclosure and a maze of self-guiding trails through woodlands and marsh, plus an interpretive centre. There's no public transport to Fort Whyte.

West of the centre: Assiniboine Park and the Living Prairie Museum

Some 8km west of the city centre, to the south of Portage Avenue, a great chunk of land has been set aside as **Assiniboine Park** (daily 9am–sunset; free; bus #66 from Broadway at Smith St), whose wooded lawns, gardens, cycling paths, playing fields and zoo attract hundreds of visitors every summer weekend.

The park's English gardens of daisies, marigolds, roses and begonias bloom beneath columns of spruce trees and blend into the excellent Leo Mol Sculpture Garden, which contains the works of Ukrainian artist Leo Mol, who moved to Winnipeg in 1949. Dozens of his graceful sculptures – deer, bears, nude bathers and other whimsical figures – are featured here reflecting in the pond. More can be seen in the nearby glass-walled gallery (June to late Sept daily noon–8pm; free). Mol's studio, just behind the gallery, is also on view. The park's best-known feature is a large, half-timbered **pavilion** in mock-Tudor style – a favourite meeting place for Winnipeggers at the weekend and home to the **Pavilion Gallery Museum** (Tues–Thurs 10am–8pm, Fri–Sun 10am–5pm; free) with a permanent collection of three local artists – Ivan Eyre, Walter J. Phillips and Clarence Tillenius. By the pavilion, completed in 1999, the similarly Tudoresque bandshell of the **Lyric Theatre** has free performances by the Royal Winnipeg Ballet and the Winnipeg Symphony Orchestra, and hosts jazz, folk and drama festivals (☎885-5466 ext 5). The **zoo** (daily 10am–sunset; $3) has over 1300 animals and a giant tropical **conservatory** with a foyer displaying local artwork, a steamy Palm House, floral displays and a restaurant. A statue of Winnie the Pooh on the zoo grounds is a reminder that the fictitious bear was named after a real bear called Winnipeg. Adjoining the park to the south, the 700-acre nature reserve of **Assiniboine Forest** (sunrise–sunset; free), the largest in Canada, is home to deer, ruffled grouse and waterfowl.

A couple of kilometres further west, the **Living Prairie Museum** at 2795 Ness Ave (April–June Sun 10am–5pm; July & Aug daily 10am–5pm; free; guided tours $2.25; bus #24 along Portage) is worth a brief visit, its thirty acres of land forming the largest area of unploughed tall-grass prairie in Manitoba. A small visitor centre provides a wealth of background information on the indigenous plants, whose deep-root systems enable them to withstand both the extreme climate and prairie fires. There's a daily programme of half-hour guided walks, or you can pick up a brochure and stroll alone. Come prepared with insect repellent; the native bugs that thrive among the grass and wild flowers are particularly vicious.

Eating and drinking

Winnipeg boasts literally dozens of good, inexpensive **places to eat**, though many of them in truth emphasize quality over finesse. The wide variety of ethnic restaurants are the exception, ranging from deluxe establishments serving fine French and Italian delicacies, through to Ukrainian and French-Canadian restaurant-bars that cater mainly for their own communities. In the more expensive places it's possible to pay upwards of $50 per person for a full dinner, but $25 per head is a reasonable average elsewhere. Many of Winnipeg's more staid **restaurants** and **restaurant-bars** are concentrated in and around the **downtown** shopping malls, but there's a cluster of more interesting ones in **Osborne Village** and the **Exchange District**, and several other good places dotted around the edges of the centre, notably the Jewish delis and Ukrainian restaurants in the **North End**, around Selkirk Avenue. For **drinking**, many of the city's bars are cheerless places, so it's best to stick to the restaurant-bars.

Restaurants and restaurant-bars

Alycia's, 559 Cathedral Ave at McGregor St. A long-established Ukrainian restaurant, 4km north of the centre, which also serves as an informal social centre with cheap, filling food, including borscht and *holubchi* (stuffed cabbage rolls); dishes for $5–8. Mon–Sat 8am–8pm.

Amici, 326 Broadway (☎943-4997). Expensive but superb and elegant restaurant with Italian food – the desserts are sensational. Dishes for $15–36.

Baked Expectations, 161 Osborne St. Delicious burgers and salads, but especially known for its cheesecakes. Dishes for $3–8.

Bistro Bohemia, 159 Osborne St. Czech restaurant with great herring. Dishes for $8–14.

Carlos & Murphy's, 129 Osborne St. Huge portions of Mexican food from $5–10, and a raucous and dingy bar.

The Chocolate Shop, 268 Portage Ave (☎942-4855). Winnipeg's oldest restaurant, dating its roots to 1918, where you can have your tea leaves and tarot read from 1–9pm. Diner-style establishment with great desserts. Popular karaoke night on Tues.

Forks Market, The Forks. A converted railway shed incorporating some cheap, pleasant bars selling a variety of fast food from Caribbean to Greek; try *Yudyta's* for Ukrainian and *Tavola Calda* for Italian food, both of which are dirt cheap. For a taste of the prairies, head for *Prairie Oyster Café and Steak House*, (where a meal for two with drinks will set you back about $70) on the second level, a mock cowboy ranch which serves wild-rice pudding and wood-grilled rabbit.

Green Gates, 6495 Robin Blvd (☎897-0990). A converted farmhouse, thirty-minutes' drive from downtown but worth the trip for the delicious salads, posh food like grilled pork with scalloped potatoes and salmon with a fresh fruit salsa. Beautiful surroundings and very expensive, with dishes $10–20.

Kelekis, 1100 Main St between Aberdeen and Redwood aves. Another true Winnipeg institution, dishing out greasy fries, hotdogs and enormous hamburgers to people from all walks of life – including Pierre Trudeau – since 1931. Dishes $3–9. Closes 9.45pm.

Le Beaujolais, 131 Blvd Provencher, St Boniface (☎237-6276). Winnipeg's premier French restaurant, with prices to match; reservations recommended. Dishes for $19–26.

Le Café Jardin, at **Centre Culturel Franco-Manitobain**, 340 Blvd Provencher at rue des Meurons, St Boniface. A large cultural complex housing an attractive open-air restaurant featuring traditional French-Canadian food – try the meat pies (*tourtière*) and the bread pudding. Open Mon–Fri 11.30am–2pm. A full meal costs around $15.

Osborne Cyber Café, 118 Osborne St. Newly opened Internet vegetarian café. Open daily until midnight. Free international Internet calls across North America and to some European countries, including the UK.

Pasquale's, 109 Marion St, St Boniface. Delightful, busy little place with well-prepared Italian dishes from $6.

Pembina Village, 333 Pembina Hwy. A local favourite serving excellent Greek food – big feta salads, gyro sandwiches, great roast potatoes and retsina to wash it all down. It's cheap too – dishes around $5.

Rogue's Gallery, 432 Assiniboine Ave. Hip and trendy coffee house serving light meals like falafels and burgers, and decorated with local art.

Sevala's, 390a Blvd Provencher, St Boniface. A plain, sparse, family-style restaurant serving Ukrainian specialities from $5 – best choices are pierogies with various fillings (cabbage, mashed potato). All-you-can-eat buffet for $7.39 (lunch), $9.99 (dinner).

Sofia's Caffè, 635 Corydon Ave. In the heart of Little Italy, this restaurant, with outdoor patio, serves large portions of veal, pasta and the like from $7.

Tavern in the Park, The Pavilion in Assiniboine Park. Perfectly situated in a glass atrium on the back of the fake Tudor Pavilion, and a favourite with Winnipeggers. Expensive, with a lavish buffet on Sundays. Dishes for $16–24.

Tre Visi, 173 McDermot Ave (☎949-9032). Tiny, extremely popular Italian restaurant with good atmosphere and food. Reservations essential. Dishes for $7.50–18.

Wasabi, 105–121 Osborne St. Buzzing, trendy sushi bar in Osborne Village. Sushi from 95¢, $18.95 for a combo platter.

Nightlife and entertainment

Winnipeg tries hard to be the cultural centre of the prairies, and generous sponsorship arrangements support a good range of **theatre**, **ballet**, **opera** and **orchestral music**. The city also has some lively **nightspots**, featuring the best of local and national **rock** and **jazz** talent. For **listings**, consult the Thursday edition of the *Winnipeg Free Press* newspaper or the free news sheet *Uptown*, available from self-serve kiosks all over the city and issued every Thursday. The free magazine *Where*, available from tourist offices, also has listings, but their reports are never critical.

These venues are supplemented by an ambitious summer programme of open-air concerts, notably the nine-day **Jazz Winnipeg Festival** (tickets range from free to $35; ☎989-4656, *www.jazzwinnipeg.com*) towards the end of June, and the **Winnipeg Folk Festival** ($40 per day, $110 for 4-day pass; ☎780-3333 or 1-888/655-5354, *www.wpgfolkfest.mb.ca*), a three-day extravaganza featuring over a hundred concerts, held in early July at Birds Hill Provincial Park, 25km northeast of the city. Apart from the music festivals, the biggest festival in Manitoba is **Folklorama** ($3; ☎1-800/665-0234, *www.folklorama.ca*), held during the first two weeks in August to celebrate Winnipeg's multiethnic population. The festival has over forty pavilions spread out over town, each devoted to a particular country or region. The **Winnipeg Fringe Festival** (tickets range from free to $8; ☎956-1340, *www.mtc.mb.ca*) is a ten-day event of theatrical productions, held in mid-July in the Exchange District. St Boniface's French-Canadian heritage is honoured annually in the **Festival du Voyageur** (☎237-7692, *www.festivalvoyageur.mb.ca*) – ten days of February fun, whose events lead up to a torchlit procession and the Governor's Ball, where everyone dresses up in period costume.

Music venues and clubs

Centre Culturel Franco-Manitobain, 340 Blvd Provencher, St Boniface (☎233-8972). Hosts weekly concerts by French-Canadian musicians. Free jazz sessions on Tuesday at 9pm.

Club 200, 190 Garry St. A popular gay and lesbian club.

Die Maschine Cabaret, 2nd Floor, 108 Osborne St. Winnipeg's most up-to-the-minute club with techno and other cutting-edge nights. Closed Sun.

Gio's Room, 272 Sherbrooke St. One of Winnipeg's better-known gay and lesbian bars, with pool tournaments on Monday, karaoke on Wednesday, a women's night on the first Saturday of every month and strippers every Friday and Saturday. Closed Sun.

Ice Works, 165 McDermot Ave. A thirty-something spot in the Exchange District featuring live entertainment and chart hits.

Jazz on the Rooftop, Winnipeg Art Gallery, 300 Memorial Blvd (☎786-6641 ext 232). Showcases frequent performances by some of Canada's best-known jazz musicians.

Longhorn's Saloon, 1011 Henderson Hwy. Country place with line-dancing lessons on Tuesday.

Ms Purdy's, 226 Main St. Long-running women-only lesbian bar.

Pyramid Cabaret, 176 Fort St. Best new bands perform rockabilly, Celtic, alternative and reggae music. Closed Sun.

Times Change Blues Bar, 234 Main St. Rough-and-ready jazz and blues place. Live entertainment Thursday to Sunday.

Toad in the Hole, 112 Osborne St. Osborne Village's busy pub with British beer and dance floor upstairs.

U41A, *Canad Inn Windsor Park*, 1054 Elizabeth. Massive club with alternative, dance and techno music.

The Zoo, 160 Osborne St. Alternative/rock bar in *Osborne Village Inn* with live heavy-rock acts.

Classical music, opera and ballet

Major performances by the **Winnipeg Symphony Orchestra** ($13–40; ☎949-3999) as well as the **Manitoba Opera** (Nov–April; ☎780-3333, *www.manitobaopera.mb.ca*) take place at the Centennial Concert Hall, 555 Main St, in the Exchange District (☎956-1360); tickets are $11–25. The **Royal Winnipeg Ballet**, (information ☎956-0183, tickets ☎956-2792 or 1-800/667-4792 from outside Winnipeg) – Canada's finest dance company – also performs at the Concert Hall and has an extensive programme of traditional and contemporary ballets; tickets are $9–45, with student and senior-citizen discounts of up to twenty percent.

Cinema and theatre

Winnipeg's largest mainstream **cinema** is the Cineplex-Odeon, 234 Donald St, while Cinema 3, 585 Ellice Ave at Sherbrook Street, shows foreign and second-run films. Cinémathèque, 100 Arthur St (☎925-3457), in the Artspace building, concentrates on Canadian releases. In summer there's also the Cineplex Odeon Drive-In on Portage Street West (☎837-4979). Winnipeg plays host to the world's only all-Canadian film festival – forty short films and premieres of Canadian films shown during the week-long **Local Heroes Festival** (☎956-7800, *www.nsi-canada.ca/localheroes*) in late February.

The city has several professional **theatre** groups: principally the Popular Theatre Alliance of Manitoba, whose modern and imaginative plays are performed at the Gas Station, 445 River Ave at Osborne Street (☎284-9477); and the Prairie Theatre Exchange, Portage Place (☎942-5483), which performs traditional and avant-garde comedy and drama. The Manitoba Theatre Centre, 174 Market Ave (☎ 942-6537 or 1-877/446-4500 outside Winnipeg, *www.mtc.mb.ca*), and the Warehouse Theatre, 140 Rupert Ave (☎943-4849), feature local talent, though Winnipeg's main theatrical events are performed by international touring companies in the Centennial Concert Hall.

Listings

Airlines British Airways (☎1-800/247-9297); Air Canada, 355 Portage Ave (☎943-9361 or 1-888/247-2262, *www.aircanada.ca*); Calm Air (☎1-800/839-2256); Canada 3000, 1610 Ness Ave (☎784-0500 or 777-3000, *www.canada3000tickets.com*).

Baseball Catch the Winnipeg Goldeyes at their new Can West Global Park adjacent to The Forks (☎982-BASE). Tickets cost $5–13. The season runs from late May to early Sept.

Basketball The Winnipeg Cyclone play seventeen home games a season (Dec–March) at the Wind Tunnel, Winnipeg Convention Centre, 375 York Ave (☎925-HOOP, *www.cyclone.mb.ca*).

Bike rental Corydon Cycle Sports, 753 Corydon Ave at Cockburn St, $17 per day (☎452-6531); Olympia Cycle and Ski, 242 Henderson Hwy, $12–27 per day (☎669-5590); Portage Cycle and Sports, 1841 Portage Ave, $15 per day (☎837-6785).

Bookshops Mary Scorer, 389 Graham St at Edmonton Street, is the city's best bookshop, with an excellent range of titles on the Canadian West. The Global Village, 167 Lilac St, is a map and travel shop with a comprehensive selection of specialized maps. Heaven Art and Book Café, 659 Corydon Ave, has a good selection of titles by Manitoban writers and also hosts readings.

Bus enquiries Beaver, 339 Archibald St (☎989-7007); Greyhound, 487 Portage Ave (☎783-8857); Grey Goose, 487 Portage Ave (☎783-4537).

Camping equipment United Army Surplus Sales, 460 Portage Ave at Colony St, sells a wide range of camping and wilderness gear.

Canadian football The Winnipeg Blue Bombers, ten-time winners of the Grey Cup, play at the Winnipeg Stadium, 1465 Maroons Rd, from June to November (information ☎784-2583, tickets ☎780-7328, *www.bluebombers.com*).

Car rental Avis, 155 York (☎989-7521) and at the airport (☎956-2847); Discount, at the airport (☎775-2282); Budget, at the airport (☎989-8510), and downtown at Ellice Ave and Sherbrook St (☎989-8505); Rent-a-wreck, at the airport (☎779-0777 or 1-800/327-0116); and Thrifty, at the airport (☎949-7608), and downtown at 112 Garry St (☎949-7620).

Consulates UK, 229 Athlone Drive (☎896-1380).

Dental emergencies Broadway Dental Centre, 640 Broadway (☎772-3523).

Disabled visitors Disability International, 101–107 Evergreen Place, Winnipeg, Manitoba R3L 2T3 (☎287-8010, fax 453-1367) can help with enquiries.

Emergencies ☎911 for police, fire and ambulance.

Gay and lesbian Winnipeg Rainbow Resource Centre, 1-222 Osborne St (Wed–Fri 1–4.30pm ☎474-0212; recorded information Mon–Sat 7.30–10pm ☎284-5208). Pride Week is held in mid-June.

Hospital and medical centre Grace General Hospital, 300 Booth St (outpatient emergencies on ☎837-0157); Health Sciences Centre, 820 Sherbrook St (☎787-3167).

Ice hockey The Manitoba Moose play International Hockey League games at Winnipeg Stadium, 1465 Maroons Rd (Oct–April, information ☎987-PUCK, tickets 780-7328).

Laundries Shop N Wash Food and Laundromat, 189 Isabel St at Portage Ave; Zip-Kleen, 110 Sherbrook St at Westminster Ave.

Left luggage 24hr coin-operated lockers at the train and bus stations.

Lost property VIA baggage information on ☎949-7481; Winnipeg Transit, at the Portage and Main office (☎986-5054).

Newspapers Dominion News, 263 Portage Ave, has a wide variety of international papers.

Pharmacies Shoppers Drug Mart, 471 River Ave and Osborne St; open 24hr.

Post office The main office is at 266 Graham Ave at Smith St (☎1-800/267-1177); Mon–Fri 8am–5.30pm.

Sexual Assault Crisis Line ☎786-8631.

Swimming Elmwood/Kildonan Park Swimming Pool, 909 Concordia Ave (☎986-6650); Pan-Am Swimming Pool, 25 Poseidon Bay (☎986-5890).

Taxis Duffy's, 871 Notre Dame Ave (☎775-0101); Unicity, 340 Hargrave Place (☎925-3131).

Train enquiries VIA Rail ticket office, 123 Main St (arrival and departure information ☎1-800/835-3037, fares and reservations ☎1-800/561-8630.

Travel agents Apollo Travel, 560 Sargent Ave (☎786-8558); Travel CUTS, 499 Portage Ave (☎783-5353).

Weather ☎983-2050.

Women's contacts Women's Resource Centre, 290 Vaughan St (☎989-4140).

Around Winnipeg

As Winnipeg's dreary suburbs fade into the seamless prairie landscape, the only major interruption is provided by the course of the **Red River** to the north. The sixty-kilometre stretch from the city to Lake Winnipeg – the **Red River Corridor** – was once a tiny part of the supply route that connected the Red River Colony to Hudson Bay, and nowadays it harbours the region's most absorbing tourist attractions, notably a couple of elegant nineteenth-century houses and the refurbished **Lower Fort Garry**. Ornithologists might want to make the trip to the **Oak Hammock Marsh Wildlife Area**, 40km north of Winnipeg, home to thousands of migrating birds, particularly snow- and Canada geese between April and September. In the opposite direction, about 60km southeast of the city in **Steinbach**, the **Mennonite Heritage Village** is worth a peek for its pleasant reconstruction of a nineteenth-century pioneer settlement. Finally, a drive through the **area southwest of Winnipeg** towards the North Dakota border will reward you with some of Manitoba's finest and most typical prairie scenery and take you through neat, tidy Mennonite towns such as **Altona** and **Winkler**.

The Red River Corridor

The trip along the **Red River Corridor** is easily the best day out from Winnipeg, a pleasing diversion along the gentle hills that frame the wide and sluggish river. Driving out from the city on Main Street, which becomes Hwy 9, it's about 10km to the turning for the **River Road Heritage Parkway** (Provincial Road 238), a rough, twisting gravel track that leads to some of the Corridor's lesser attractions. Alternatively, you can keep on the main road for **Selkirk** and **Lower Fort Garry**.

The Beaver **bus** company (☎989-7007) runs a regular service from the bus station at 339 Archibald St in Winnipeg to Lower Fort Garry (or you can catch the boat, see p.473) and Selkirk, but there's no public transport along the Parkway and the road's too rough to cycle.

The Heritage Parkway

Turning off the main road, down the **River Road Heritage Parkway**, it's a few minutes' drive to **Twin Oaks**, built in the 1850s as part of a girls' school for the daughters of Hudson's Bay Company employees, before curving round to **St Andrew's Rectory National Historic Site** (mid-May to early Sept daily 10am–6pm; free), where you'll find exhibits on the Anglican Church's role in helping to settle the prairies and on its early occupants – stern-looking Victorians determined to save the Métis from themselves. Just opposite, the tidy mid-Victorian **St Andrew's Church** has a number of benches still partly covered by buffalo hide, and stained-glass windows brought here from England packed in barrels of molasses.

A couple of minutes' drive further north, the pretty **Captain Kennedy Tea House and Museum** (mid-May to Aug Mon–Sat 10.30am–5pm, Sun & holidays 10.30am–6pm; free) was once the home of Captain William Kennedy, an English-speaking Métis who resigned his Hudson's Bay Company commission because of its increasing involvement with the liquor trade. The house's three main-floor rooms are furnished in 1870s style, and the twee little glassed-in tearoom overlooks the delightful gardens whose terraces, planted with a variety of heritage plant species rare in Canadian public gardens, border the Red River.

Lower Fort Garry

A few minutes' drive north of the tea house, on Hwy 9, 32km from Winnipeg near Selkirk (see below), stands **Lower Fort Garry National Historic Site** (mid-May to Sept daily 9am–5pm; grounds open daily until sunset; $5.50), built as the new headquarters of the Hudson's Bay Company between 1830 and 1847. It was the brainchild of **George Simpson**, governor of the company's northern department, an area bounded by the Arctic and Pacific oceans, Hudson Bay and the Missouri River Valley. Nicknamed the "Little Emperor" for his autocratic style, Simpson selected the site because it was downriver from the treacherous waters of the St Andrew's Rapids and was not prone to flooding, as Upper Fort Garry had been. However, the settlers round The Forks were reluctant to cart their produce down to the new camp and when the governors of Assiniboia refused to move here his scheme collapsed.

Sandwiched between Hwy 9 and the Red River, **Lower Fort Garry** begins at the visitor reception centre, where there's a comprehensive account of the development of the fort and its role in the fur trade. A couple of minutes' walk away, the low, thick limestone walls of the fort protect reconstructions of several company buildings, including the retail store, where a small museum is devoted to Inuit and Indian crafts. Several of the exhibits here are exquisite, particularly the decorated skin pouches and an extraordinary necklace fringed by thin strips of metal cut from a sardine can. Next door, the combined sales shop and clerk's quarters has a fur loft packed with pelts, while the middle of the compound is dominated by the Big House with its low sloping roof, built for Governor Simpson in 1832. People in 1850's period costume stroll the grounds, ensuring the right atmosphere. The restaurant sells good *tortière* – a Québécois meat pie – and bannock (freshly baked bread).

Selkirk and Netley Marsh

About 8km north of the fort, along Hwy 9A, the township of **SELKIRK** was originally chosen as the point where the proposed transcontinental railway was to cross the Red River. Realizing the importance of the railway, the business leaders of Winnipeg – Selkirk's great trade rival – launched a campaign to have the route changed. Their efforts were successful, not least because one of the leading lights of the CPR syndicate, Donald Smith, was a key shareholder in the Hudson's Bay Company, which owned five hundred acres of land around The Forks. Bypassed by the trains, Selkirk slipped into relative obscurity, though it did achieve a degree of prosperity through its shipyards, and retains the dubious title of "Catfish Capital of the World".

Selkirk's only real attraction is the **Marine Museum of Manitoba** (May–Oct Mon–Fri 9am–5pm, Sat, Sun & holidays 10am–6pm; $3.50), situated on the edge of

Selkirk Park at Eveline and Queen streets. The museum consists of seven passenger and freight ships, dragged out of the water and parked on a lawn, as well as a lighthouse, plus a mildly interesting video on the history of Lake Winnipeg's shipping and fishing industries. In Selkirk Park there's a bird sanctuary and a 6.5-metre-high **oxcart**, said to be the world's largest.

If you're in Selkirk in early July, you could take in **the Manitoba Highland Gathering**, a Scottish festival honouring the original settlers. Places to **stay** include the *Selkirk Motor Hotel*, 219 Manitoba Ave (☎482-1900, fax 785-1669; ②) and the *Evergreen Gate B&B*, 1138 River Rd (☎482-6248; ②). You can **camp** at the *Willow Springs Campground*, 13km north of Selkirk on Hwy 320 (☎482-5138; $8–10; May–Oct). For **food**, try *Barney Gargles*, 185 Main St, which has delicious main courses from $6, or *Garden on Eaton Tea House*, 205 Eaton Ave (closed Sun) for its fresh home-cooked food.

From the Marine Museum, Provincial Road 320 heads north 16km to the edge of **Netley Marsh**, a huge swampy delta formed by the Red River as it seeps into Lake Winnipeg. At the end of the road, there's a small **recreation park** with a snack bar, an observation tower and a series of plaques that detail the way of life of the area's native peoples. The marsh is an impenetrable maze for the inexperienced, but you can hire a boat and guide at the park for about $105 a day. On the lake side of the delta, the **Bird Refuge** is one of North America's largest waterfowl nesting areas and there are lots of good fishing spots; the pickerel, or wall-eye, are delicious.

The *Tree House Bed and Breakfast* (☎941-0920; ②), on the edge of the marsh, near the village of Matlock, is a relaxing **place to stay** and absorb the tranquil charms of the wetlands area. Go north on Hwy 9 and turn onto the gravel Route 202.

Oak Hammock Marsh

The **Oak Hammock Marsh Wildlife Management Area** (daily: May–Aug 10am–8pm; Sept–Oct 8.30am to dusk; Nov–April 10am–4.30pm; $3.75, family $13; no camping) is all that remains of the wetlands that once stretched from St Andrews, near the Red River, up to the village of Teulon, and to the west of Netley Creek. Most of this wetland was drained and farmed around the beginning of the twentieth century, but in the 1960s some of the area was restored to its original state and protected by a series of retaining dykes. In addition, a number of islands were built to provide marshland birds a safe place to nest.

To get there from Winnipeg take Hwy 7 or Hwy 8 north for 10km, turn east along Hwy 67, and follow the signs to the Main Mound Area, where there's an excellent **interpretive centre** with hands-on displays about the local environment and wildlife, a picnic site and a couple of observation decks, all connected by a system of dykes and boardwalk trails. The best time to come is in spring or autumn, when the grebes, coots and other residents are joined by thousands of migrating birds, including Canada geese. Another part of the Wildlife Area has been returned to tall-grass prairie, carpeted from mid-June to August with the blooms of wild flowers such as the purple Blazing Star and the speckled red Prairie Lily.

The Mennonite Heritage Village

A spruce reconstruction of a pioneer settlement of the late 1800s is to be found just 2km north of the township of **Steinbach**, which is an hour's drive southeast from Winnipeg along hwys 1 and 12 (2 buses daily). In and around the main street of the **Mennonite Heritage Village** (May–June Mon–Sat 10am–5pm, Sun noon–5pm; July & Aug Mon–Sat 10am–6pm, Sun noon–6pm; Sept Mon–Fri 10am–5pm; Oct–April Mon–Fri

10am–4pm; May–Sept $5, Oct–April $3), there's a church, a windmill and a couple of stores and farmhouses, but it's the general flavour of the place that appeals rather than any particular structure. The Mennonites, a Protestant sect, were founded in the Netherlands under the leadership of Menno Symons in the early sixteenth century. Subsequently the movement divided into two broad factions, with one group refusing to have anything to do with the secular state and sustaining a hostile attitude to private property, and the more "liberal" clans being inclined to compromise. Many of the former – the **Ammanites** – moved to the United States and then Ontario, settling in and around Kitchener-Waterloo, while the more liberal **Untere** migrated to Russia and then Manitoba in the 1870s. There are about 100,000 Mennonites in Canada today. Few of the Manitoba Mennonites, who congregated in and around Steinbach, wear the traditional black and white clothes or live on communal farms, but like all Mennonite communities they maintain a strong pacifist tradition. Costumed guides at the Heritage Village provide an intriguing account of their history, augmented by displays in the tiny museum and the interpretive centre.

The best **accommodation** in the area is to be found in Steinbach. Try the *Frantz Motor Inn*, Hwy 52, just east of town (☎326-9831, fax 326-6913; ②). For a Mennonite meal, **eat** at the cafeteria-style *Livery Barn* in the Heritage Village, with borscht, stone-ground bread, smoked sausages and other delights priced from $3.50 to $7.95. The *Dutch Connection*, 88 Brandt St (☎326-2018; ②) is a motel that sprang up around a successful restaurant, one of the province's better places serving Dutch/Indonesian food at reasonable prices. In keeping with the strict Mennonite beliefs, you'll find that virtually none of the restaurants in the area serve alcohol.

Southwest of Winnipeg

A pleasant day's outing from Winnipeg can be had by making a loop through various towns and villages **southwest of the city**. It's here that you'll encounter the quintessential prairie town – squat false-gabled buildings lining a wide main street, parked half-ton trucks filled with bales of hay, sacks of horsefeed, a sleeping dog or two, and quiet side streets bordered by tall Manitoba oaks or trembling aspen. The drive takes you along part of the Red River and across vast golden wheatfields punctuated only by **grain elevators**, huge storage silos situated at the edge of almost every town, usually with the town's name painted high up in large white letters – though most of these will soon disappear to be replaced by massive concrete terminals (see box, overleaf). Grey Goose **bus** lines depart from their terminal at 487 Portage Ave, in Winnipeg, out to a number of these spots.

ROSENORT, 50km south of Winnipeg on Route 205, off Hwy 75, is the first place of any interest. A Mennonite town, its chief attraction – and a good place to stop for lunch – is the *Rose Lane Heritage House and Tea Room*, 31 Rose Lane, where cracked wheat and cornmeal bread are baked on the premises. **MORRIS**, 15km further on Hwy 75, is home to the annual **Manitoba Stampede and Exhibition**, one of Canada's largest, which takes place during the third week of July in and around a huge recreational complex dominating the town. The area where the Morris River joins the Red River is great for catching wall-eye and catfish, and a Catfish Derby is held here in August. **ST JEAN BAPTISTE**, a bit further south, is an attractive French-speaking community known for producing the type of pea that's used in French-Canadian pea soup. **EMERSON**, 30km south, right on the border with Minnesota and North Dakota, has some interesting architectural tidbits, like the log customs house, Fort Dufferin (the original site of the North West Mounted Police), and the 1917–18 **town hall and courthouse**, at the corner of Church Street and Winnipeg Avenue (Mon–Fri 9am–4pm; free) done in the Neoclassical Prairie style. For **lunch** or afternoon tea, the place to visit is *Aunt Maud's*

GRAIN ELEVATORS

Canada hasn't exactly set the world afire with its contributions to the field of architecture; in fact, it's most distinctive form of building may be the ubiquitous grain elevators found throughout the prairies, warehouses built to store wheat before it was shipped off by the railroad. Most are wooden – the more modern ones are made of steel – but both have the same simple, functional lines rising above the flat prairie land that have earned them the nickname 'prairie sentinels'.

The first grain elevators were built in the 1880s and by 1938 there were 5800 dotted across the region emblazoned with the names of the small towns they mark. However, as transportation of grain switched from rail to road their numbers dwindled to the present 700. In 2000, the Canadian Wheat Board decided to build massive central concrete terminals at main transit points, a move that will make the old-style elevator redundant and no doubt dramatically alter the rural prairie-scape. Grain will now travel by trucks from the new terminals, much to the detriment of the region's already abysmal roads.

In **Inglis**, a tiny town on the west side of Riding Mountain National Park, about 20km east of the Saskatchewan border, a row of 1920s elevators beside an abandoned railway line has been declared a National Historic Site. With very little local concern to preserve the grain elevators, these may be the only "castles of the New World" to survive.

Tea Room, 57 4th St (closed Mon–Wed). **GRETNA**, 25km west of Emerson, is another Mennonite community, as is **WINKLER**, to the northwest, which has several arts and crafts shops, a farmer's market (July–Sept Fri eve), and the August Harvest Festival. It's also a great place to sample genuine **Mennonite food**, served in almost all the cafés and restaurants; be sure to try *platz*, a rhubarb dessert.

West of Winkler is the large town of **MORDEN**, site of the annual Corn and Apple Festival in August, and **DARLINGFORD**, 20km farther west, where a large granite boulder marks the route taken by the eighteenth-century French explorer Sieur de la Vérendrye on his way west in search of a reputed vast "western sea". The land to the south and west of Darlingford begins to descend into the **Pembina River Valley**, which offers magnificent, sweeping views of the prairies. **Kaleida**, a tiny village about 15km southwest of Darlingford, has a charming pioneer stone church and an attractive cemetery.

AROUND MANITOBA

Manitoba is distinguished principally by its **parks**, thousands of acres of wilderness, lake, river and forest that boast wonderful scenery, great hikes and hundreds of kilometres of canoe routes. One of the best is **Riding Mountain National Park**, 250km northwest of Winnipeg, which derives its name from the fur trappers who changed from canoe to horseback to travel across its wooded highlands. On the southern edge of the park, the tourist village of **Wasagaming** is a useful base for exploring the surrounding countryside, which incorporates areas of deciduous and boreal forest, lake and grassland. Manitoba's **provincial parks** include the dramatic landscapes and difficult whitewater canoe routes of the remote **Atikaki Wilderness Park**, the lakeside marshes and forests of **Hecla Park**, and yet more canoe routes in **Duck Mountain Park**, which is also noted for its fishing.

Other than the parks and lakeshores, most of Manitoba's significant attractions are concentrated in and around Winnipeg, and many of the province's smaller villages and towns are not really tourist destinations. The notable exceptions are **Brandon** and **Souris**, both in the southwest corner of the province, and remote **Churchill**, a wild outpost right up north on the shores of Hudson Bay that's a great place for seeing beluga

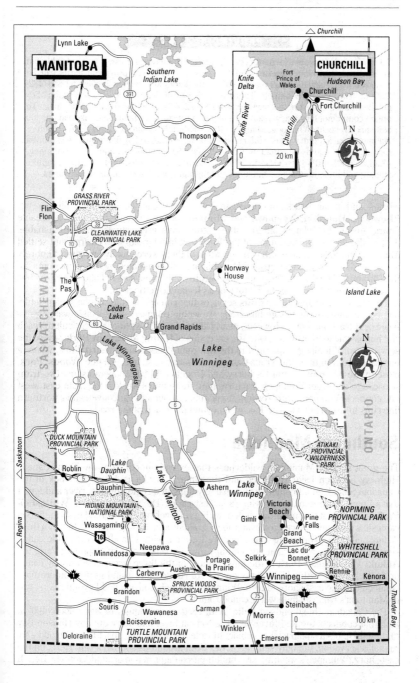

PROVINCIAL PARKS

All of Manitoba's provincial parks cost $5 (good for 3 days) per car; if you enter by foot or bike they're free. Campsites and RV sites in Manitoba's provincial parks can be reserved from April to September by calling the Parks Reservation Service ☎1-888/482-2267 or 948-3333 in Winnipeg. There is a charge of $6.75 for each reservation. For detailed information on the parks call ☎1-800/214-6497 or 945-6784 in Winnipeg. To obtain complimentary maps in advance of your visit contact Manitoba Conservation, 200 Salteaux Crescent, Winnipeg, Manitoba R3J 3W3, *www.gov.mb.ca/natres/parks*. If you're planning a backcountry hike, wilderness canoeing, rafting or kayaking contact Manitoba Conservation, Land Information Centre, Map Sales, 1007 Century St, Winnipeg, Manitoba R3H 0W4 (☎204/945-6666, *www.canadamapsales.com*) for topographic, angling and illustrated maps, and aerial photographs of thirteen major canoe routes.

---

whales and polar bears, but overrun by visitors and documentary film crews. Elsewhere, **Dauphin**, **Neepawa** and **Minnedosa** are three of the more agreeable prairie towns, but almost all the other settlements are virtually indistinguishable, despite the diverse backgrounds of the European immigrants who cleared and settled Manitoba in the late nineteenth century. Most of them were rapidly and almost entirely assimilated, but the villages around Dauphin are still dominated by the onion domes of the Ukrainians' Orthodox churches, and **Gimli**, on the west side of Lake Winnipeg, has a pleasant museum tracing the history of its Icelandic settlement.

There are reasonably regular **bus** services that run between Manitoba's main settlements, and most of the village bus stops are within relatively comfortable walking distance of at least one hotel. However, nearly all of Manitoba's parks are difficult to reach and impossible to tour by bus, with the exception of **Riding Mountain Park**, where the service from Winnipeg stops right in the centre of Wasagaming; **weird Park**, where a bus passes through on the Trans-Canada on its way east; and **Spruce Woods Park**, close to the bus routes from Carberry and Brandon. VIA Rail operates just two **train** services to and from Winnipeg, each running three times weekly: the main east–west line connects Winnipeg with Toronto, Saskatoon, Jasper and Vancouver, and a northern line runs to Churchill, via The Pas, well beyond the reach of the road.

Southeast Manitoba

The great slice of Manitoban wilderness that extends north from the Trans-Canada Highway between Lake Winnipeg and the Ontario border is set on the rock of the Canadian Shield, an inhospitable and sparsely inhabited region of lake, river and forest that's home to three of the province's largest parks. The most southern, **Whiteshell Park** is the oldest and most developed, with a relatively extensive road system, fifteen campsites and one-quarter of Manitoba's holiday and fishing lodges. Just north of Whiteshell Park, **Nopiming Park** is more isolated, with a handful of lakeside campsites that can be reached along two bumpy gravel roads. North of Nopiming Park, the **Atikaki Wilderness Park** is the most remote of the three, accessible only by canoe or float plane. The Atikaki's mile upon mile of rugged forest and granite outcrop are connected to the east shore of Lake Winnipeg by the Bloodvein and Leyond rivers, two of Manitoba's wildest white-water canoe routes.

The Canadian Shield ends at **Lake Winnipeg**, a giant finger of water some 400km long that connects the Red River with the Nelson River and subsequently Hudson Bay to the north. It's a shallow lake, subject to violent squalls, and, apart from the odd aboriginal reservation, the only settlement has been around its southern rim. Here, on the east shore, Winnipeg's wealthy have built their cottages in and around **Victoria Beach** and **Hillside Beach**, but **Grand Beach Provincial Park** still has the lake's finest bathing and long lines of sand dune stretching as far as the eye can see. The beaches of the west shore are poor by comparison, and the old fishing and farming villages that trail up the coast from Winnipeg Beach to Riverton are not of major interest. Immediately to the north of Riverton, **Hecla Provincial Park** is slightly more agreeable, the developed facilities of Gull Harbour Resort supplemented by unspoilt marsh and forest.

Known as the **Interlake**, the marginal farmland that lies between Lake Winnipeg to the east and lakes Manitoba and Winnipegosis to the west is as flat as a pancake and one of the most boring parts of the prairies. The only significant attraction is at the **Narcisse Wildlife Management Area**, 90km north of Winnipeg on Hwy 17, where thousands of red-sided garter snakes gather to mate in April and May, writhing around the bottom of a series of shallow pits in slithering heaps. It's not for the squeamish.

From Winnipeg, there's a twice-weekly Greyhound **bus** service (Tues & Wed) to Rennie and West Hawk Lake in the Whiteshell; one Grey Goose bus a day to Lac du Bonnet, the nearest point to Nopiming Park; a Grey Goose service to Grand Beach on Thursdays and Fridays; and one Grey Goose bus daily, except Saturdays, to **Gimli**, on Hecla Island in Hecla Park.

Whiteshell Provincial Park

Whiteshell Provincial Park takes its name from the small, white seashell, the *megis*, that was sacred to the Ojibwa, who believed the Creator blew through the shell to breathe life into the first human being. These shells, left by the prehistoric lake that covered the entire region, were concentrated along the park's two main rivers, the **Whiteshell** to the south and the **Winnipeg** to the north, the latter an important part of the canoe route followed by the voyageurs of the North West Company on their way from Montréal to the Red River.

Most of the park's visitors head for **FALCON LAKE** and **WEST HAWK LAKE**, two well-developed tourist townships situated on either side of the Trans-Canada Highway, near the Ontario border. Crowded throughout the summer, neither has much to recommend it, though each has a full range of facilities from serviced campsites ($12–17), resort hotels – try the *Penguin Resort* at Falcon Lake (☎ & fax 349-2218; ②–⑤) – petrol stations, grocery stores and miniature golf through to boat and watersports equipment rental. West Hawk Lake, the deepest lake in Manitoba is particularly good for scuba diving. The best places to **eat** in West Hawk Lake are the *Nite Hawk Café*, for home-made burgers, and the *Landing Steak House*, which serves juicy steaks and prime rib. For day-trippers, there's a $5 entrance fee (valid for 3 days) if you're in a car. On the south side of West Hawk Lake, which was formed by a meteorite, the sixteen-kilometre loop of the **Hunt Lake Hiking Trail** passes through cedar and white-pine forests, across sticky aromatic bogs and over rocky outcrops, all in the space of about eight hours. There's a primitive campsite on the trail at Little Indian Bay, but be sure to register at the West Hawk Lake **park office** (May–Sept daily 8.30am–4.30pm; Oct–April Mon–Fri same hours; ☎349-2245) if you're planning to stay overnight, canoe down the Whiteshell River or hike the Mantario Trail (see below).

From West Hawk Lake, Route 44 cuts north towards **CADDY LAKE** (campsites and two holiday lodges), the starting point for one of the area's most beautiful **canoe routes**, the 160-kilometre journey along the Whiteshell River to Lone Island Lake, in the centre of the park. Experienced walkers could tackle the sixty-kilometre loop of the **Mantario Hiking Trail** just to the east of Caddy Lake, along Provincial Road 312; for beginners, there are the **Bear Lake** (8km) and **McGillivray trails** (4km), clearly signposted walks from Hwy 44 to the west of Caddy Lake; they reveal a good sample of the topography of the park – dry ridges dominated by jack pine, bogs crammed with black spruce, and two shallow lakes brown from algae and humic acid. Opposite the start of the Bear Lake Trail, the **Frances Lake** canoe route makes for a pleasant overnight excursion, a twenty-kilometre trip south to the Frances Lake campsite, with three portages past the rapids, and twelve hauls round beaver dams.

Further west, 32km from West Hawk, the village of **RENNIE** is home to the **park headquarters** (Mon–Fri 8.30am–4.30pm; July & Aug also Sat & Sun 9am–4.30pm; ☎369-5426), which has a comprehensive range of information on local trails and canoe routes. The nearby **Alf Hole Goose Sanctuary** (late May to mid–Oct Mon–Fri 10am–5pm, also Sat & Sun until early Sept 10.30am–6pm; free) is best visited in spring or autumn, when the Canada geese pass through on their migration. If you need to **stay** in Rennie as a base for excursions into the park, your choices are the rather primitive *Rennie Hotel* (☎369-5536, fax 369-5261; ②) or the *Rocky Ridge Campground* (☎369-5507; $12–15; May–Sept). From Rennie, the eighty-kilometre stretch of Route 307 passes most of the park's other campsites, lodges, trails and canoe routes.

Nopiming Provincial Park

Separated from the Whiteshell by the Winnipeg River, **Nopiming Provincial Park** is a remote rocky area whose granite shoreline cliffs spread out above black-spruce bogs and tiny sandy beaches – the name is Ojibwa for "entrance to the wilderness". The park's four campsites (all open May–Sept; ☎1-888/482-2267 or 948-3333 in Winnipeg for camping reservations; ☎1-800/214-6497 for park information; $7–10) lie close to its two gravel roads: Route 314, which meanders across the 80km of its western edge, and the far shorter Route 315, a thirty-kilometre track that cuts east below Bird Lake to the Ontario border. Nopiming Park is crossed by the **Oiseau** and **Manigotagan** water-ways, whose creeks and rivers trickle or rush from lake to lake, forming no less than 1200km of possible canoe route. Towards the south of the park, **BIRD LAKE** makes for a useful base, with a main settlement on the south shore that's equipped with a campsite ($7), a grocery store and the cabins of the *Nopiming Lodge* (☎884-2281, fax 884-2402; ③/④; year-round). There's also motorboat rental, as well as canoe and guide rental for excursions to Snowshoe Lake, around falls and over rapids (55km). Near **BISSETT**, in the north of the park, there are several abandoned **gold-mining shafts** from the 1930s.

Atikaki Provincial Wilderness Park

Accessible by float plane from Winnipeg and Lac du Bonnet, the **Atikaki Provincial Wilderness Park** has half a dozen holiday cottages and fishing lodges dotted across some of the finest Canadian Shield scenery in the province. There are no campsites or roads through the park, but the rough gravel track that makes up most of Route 304 does reach Wallace Lake, at the park's southern tip, via the east shore of Lake Winnipeg or Nopiming Park's Route 314. The Atikaki is crisscrossed by canoe routes

---

WILDERNESS TRIPS

The **Manitoba Naturalists Society** runs an excellent programme of Whiteshell Wilderness Adventures during July and August. The trips last for five days, cost $395, and are based at a cabin – recently rebuilt after a fire – on secluded Lake Mantario. All the equipment is provided, as are the services of fully experienced guides, who organize classes in canoeing and survival skills. Reservations are essential: write or call the Mantario Summer Programme, 401-63 Albert St, Winnipeg, Manitoba R3B 1G4 (☎ & fax 943-9029).

that give glimpses of the region's ancient pictograph sites, but they all include difficult white-water stretches that should only be attempted by experienced canoeists.

The park's more popular canoe routes include the dramatic journey down the **Bloodvein River** to Lake Winnipeg, its rapids, falls and wild twistings balanced by peaceful drifts past quiet lakes and wild-rice marshes, and the **Kautunigan Route**, a 500-kilometre excursion that starts at Wallace Lake and threads its way to the mouth of the Berens River on Lake Winnipeg, well to the north of the park. Both routes pass stands of white birch, black spruce, jack pine, elm, oak and maple, and you may catch sight of moose, timber wolves, coyotes and black bears.

Maps are available from Manitoba Conservation, Land Information Centre, Map Sales, 1007 Century St, Winnipeg, Manitoba R3H OW4 (☎945-6666 or 1-877/627-7226); file trip plans with the Lac du Bonnet Natural Resource Office, Box 850, Lac du Bonnet (☎345-1454). Alternatively, several of the outfitters in Winnipeg and Lac du Bonnet organize guided excursions; details are available from the Manitoba Natural Resources Office, 200 Saulteaux Crescent, Winnipeg, Manitoba R3J 3W3 (☎945-6784 or 1-800/214-6497). To obtain information on canoe routes, call the Manitoba Recreational Canoeing Association (☎925-5078). Three-, five- and ten-day **canoeing** and **white-water rafting** excursions in the park are offered by Wilderness Odysseys (☎703/922-0823 or 1-800/443-6199). An invaluable walking guide is Ruth Marr's *The Manitoba Walking and Hiking Guide*, which details more than two hundred routes of varying degrees of difficulty.

Lake Winnipeg

Approached along Hwy 59, the southeast shore of **Lake Winnipeg** has one major attraction, **Grand Beach Provincial Park**, whose long stretch of powdery white sand, high grass-crowned dunes and shallow bathing water make it the region's most popular day-trip. The beach, a favourite swimming spot with Winnipeggers since the 1920s, is divided into two distinct parts, separated by a narrow channel that drains out of a knobbly lagoon, set just behind the lakeshore. The channel is spanned by a tiny footbridge: on the beach to the west are privately owned cottages, sports facilities, motor- and rowboat rental, grocery stores and a restaurant; the eastern section of the beach is less developed, although it does have a large **campsite** (☎1-888/482-2267; $12–14; May–Sept) tucked away amongst the dunes. Both parts of the beach get very crowded on summer weekends. By the campsite office, the **Ancient Beach Trail** follows the line of the prehistoric lake that dominated southern Manitoba in the last Ice Age; allow about an hour for the walk. At **GRAND MARAIS**, just outside the park, you'll find an array of motels, beachside cottages and cabins (②–④; most May–Sept).

Roughly 20km north of Grand Beach Provincial Park, the twin townships of **HILL-SIDE BEACH** and prettier **VICTORIA BEACH** have good sandy beaches, but their well-heeled inhabitants avoid catering for outsiders. There are no campsites and the only **motel** is the *Birchwood* (☎754-2596, fax 756-8898; ②) on the highway, 6km south of Victoria Beach at Traverse Bay; the motel's star facility is the huge patio overlooking the bay.

Gimli and Hecla Provincial Park

In 1875, some two hundred Icelanders moved to the southwestern shore of Lake Winnipeg, where they had secured exclusive rights to a block of land that stretched from today's Winnipeg Beach to Hecla Island, named after a volcano in their homeland. The next year the colonists were struck by a smallpox epidemic, yet they managed to survive and founded the **Republic of New Iceland**, a large self-governing and self-sufficient settlement with its own Icelandic-language school, churches and newspaper. Their independence lasted just twenty years, for in 1897 they acquiesced in the federal government's decision to open their new homeland to other ethnic groups. An identifiable Icelandic community had ceased to exist by the 1920s, but this part of Manitoba still has the largest number of people of Icelandic descent outside Iceland. The residents celebrate their heritage during the Islendingadagurinn (Icelanders' Day) festival, on the first weekend in August, when they dress up in Viking helmets and organize beauty pageants, concerts and firework displays. This rather commercial festival – not to everyone's taste – is held in the largest township, **GIMLI** (literally "paradise"). There's little else to attract visitors to this part of the lake, though Gimli's harbourside, with a fibreglass Viking statue and a massive wharf, is modestly attractive. The **Heritage Museum**, at 62 2nd Ave (May, June & Sept Sat & Sun 10am–5pm; July & Aug daily 10am–6pm; donation), chronicles the history of New Iceland. The **tourist office** is located downtown on 7th Avenue (May–Aug daily 10am–8pm; ☎642-7974).

Gimli doesn't have a lot of **places to stay**, but the best of the lot is the *Lakeview Resort*, 10 Centre St (☎642-8565, fax 642-4400; ④/⑤), which has homely, comfortable suites and rooms, each of which has a balcony overlooking either Gimli or the lake. More affordable is the **B&B** accommodation at *Sunny Side Up B&B*, which has an indoor pool (☎642-8191, *www.sunnysideup.mb.ca*; ②). There's also a **campsite** near the beach, 8km south of town, *Idle-Wheels Tent & Trailer Park* (☎642-5676; $14–17; mid-May to Oct). *Seagull's*, 10 Centre St (☎642-4145), serves Icelandic **food** like gyro and deep-fried fish, which you can wash down with potent schnapps – eat in the large dining room or on the beachside patio.

Roughly 100km to the north, **Hecla Provincial Park** consists of several islands and a slender peninsula that jut out into Lake Winnipeg, almost touching the eastern shore. The park is approached along Hwy 8, which runs across a narrow causeway to the largest of the islands, **Hecla**, where the tourist township of **GULL HARBOUR** has a comprehensive range of facilities. Nearby, on the east side of the island, the original **Hecla Village** (☎279-2056 or 378-2945 for hours) has a number of old houses, a church and a school dating from the early years of Icelandic settlement; a short heritage trail covers the highlights (guided tours available in summer), or you can strike out on one of the island's hiking trails through forest and marsh.

For **accommodation**, there's the luxurious *Gull Harbour Resort* at Riverton (☎279-2041 or 1-800/267-6700, fax 279-2000; ⑤), the bed-and-breakfast *Solmundson Gesta Hus*, in Hecla Village (☎279-2088, *www.heclatourism.mb.ca*; ③), with home-cooked dinners, and a medium-size **campsite** (☎378-2945; $12–14; May–Sept) on the neck of land between Gull Harbour and the lake.

Southwest Manitoba

West of Winnipeg, the Trans-Canada Highway slices across the prairies, past brilliant yellow canola (rapeseed) fields, on its way to Regina, 600km away in Saskatchewan. Dotted with campsites and fast-food joints, the Trans-Canada follows the route of the original transcontinental railroad, passing a series of charmless towns that are at the heart of the province's most fertile farming region. **Brandon**, the province's second largest city, has a handful of Victorian mansions and a lively arts centre, and lies not too far from **Spruce Woods Provincial Park**, a mixed area of forest and desert. Before you get to Brandon, however, immediately to the west of **Portage la Prairie**, the **Yellowhead Highway** cuts northwest from the Trans-Canada to form a more attractive route across the prairies, passing through the pretty little villages of **Neepawa** and **Minnedosa** before running south of **Riding Mountain National Park**.

West along the Trans-Canada and points south

The first major settlement west of Winnipeg is the food-processing centre of **PORTAGE LA PRAIRIE**, Manitoba's third largest city, located in the richest agricultural land in the province. You'll find the **tourist bureau** in the Glesby Centre at 11 2nd St NE (Mon–Fri 8.30am–5pm; ☎857-7778), which has a good range of free literature on the area.

The large **Island Park**, in the city centre is worth a stroll. It's almost completely surrounded by Crescent Lake – not actually a lake but an **oxbow** of the Assiniboine River, formed when a river cuts across the narrow end of a loop in its course and creates an isolated body of water. The limestone **city hall**, on Saskatchewan Avenue, is the most attractive building in town; it was built in the 1890s by the same architect who designed the Parliament Buildings in Ottawa. On the same street is the **Portage Arts Centre and Gallery** (Tues–Sat 11am–5pm; free), featuring frequent exhibitions.

In Portage Mall on Hwy 1A, just west of town next to the Wal-Mart, is a strangely enthralling museum – the **Manitoba Museum of the Titanic** (April–Oct Tues–Fri noon–9pm, Sat noon–6pm, Sun noon–5pm, rest of year by appointment ☎857-SHIP; $7). Just one of the *Titanic*'s 1500 victims came from Portage but four Canadian ships were sent out from the Maritimes after the disaster to pick up bodies. Many of the artefacts in the museum were bought back by the sailors who undertook this gruesome task. Concise displays tell the story of the doomed ship, from background on the White Star Line (the *Titanic*'s owners), through the disaster and *Carpathia*'s rescue of 705 survivors and up to the present day, including the making of the blockbuster movie, *Titanic* (in fact, many of the artefacts were used by the film's art director to make historically accurate props). Among the displays are a deckchair, a life-ring, various clothing and a piece from the ship's elaborately carved oak staircase, as well as crockery and other items that were destined for, but never made it onto, the ship. There's also a mass of correspondence, including *Titanic*'s distress call, a telegram sent to Cape Race in Newfoundland, and sympathy letters sent to survivors as well as newspaper cuttings, photos and stories about some of the passengers – most disturbingly, a photo of two of the deceased in a makeshift morgue. If you feel like you need to take some of this history home with you, hit the museum store, where you can buy a plastic submersible *Titanic* that splits in half as it goes down!

A less interesting attraction, the **Fort la Reine Museum and Pioneer Village** (mid-May to mid-Sept daily 9am–6pm; $2), located on the outskirts of town at the junction of Hwys 1A and 26, remembers an original fort which served as the headquarters of Pierre Gaultier, Sieur de la Vérendrye, during his explorations in the 1740s; the present complex re-creates nineteenth-century life through a trading post, a log homestead, a trapper's cabin, a schoolhouse and a railway caboose.

For **accommodation**, your best bet is the 61-room *Westward Village Inn*, 2401 Saskatchewan Ave W (☎857-9745 or 1-800/817-7855, fax 239-6245; ③/④), with a pool and hot tub, or the cheaper and recently renovated *Westgate Inn Motel*, 1010 Saskatchewan Ave E (☎239-5200, fax 239-0588; ②/③). There's a well-equipped **campsite** 16km east of the city on the Trans-Canada (☎267-2191; $15–20; mid-April to Sept), with a playground, store and hiking trails. The range of good **restaurants** in Portage is limited; try *Bill's Sticky Fingers* a local rib joint at 210 Saskatchewan Ave E; or *Essence Tea House*, 818 Saskatchewan Ave E, for great cheesecake.

Delta Marsh, 25km north of the city on Provincial Road 240, is a wetland extending for some 40km along the southern shore of Lake Manitoba, and is one of the largest waterfowl marshes in North America. From May to September, Delta Marsh Canoe Trips (☎243-2009) arranges guided **tours** of the marsh.

Further west, near **AUSTIN**, 3km south of the Trans-Canada on Hwy 34, the **Manitoba Agricultural Museum** (mid-May to Sept daily 9am–5pm; $5.50) has an exhaustive collection of early twentieth-century farm machinery, from gigantic steam tractors through to threshing machines and balers. The site also includes a **homesteaders' village**, which simulates village life of the late nineteenth century and has the province's largest collection of pioneer household articles. The immensely popular **Manitoba Threshermen's Reunion and Stampede** is held here every year in mid-July, featuring all things "western" – four days of rodeo riding, threshing displays, ploughing competitions, square dancing, jigging and Central Canada's Fiddle Festival. You can camp in the grounds of the museum (☎637-2354, *www.ag-museum.mb.ca*; $10–12; mid-May to Oct); otherwise, B&B **accommodation** is available at *The Oak Tree* (☎637-2029, *www.bedandbreakfast.mb.ca*; ②), next door to the museum.

Spruce Woods Provincial Park

Between Austin and Brandon, about 15km south of the Trans-Canada along Hwy 5, **Spruce Woods Provincial Park** (☎1-800/214-6497) falls on either side of the Assiniboine River, whose confused loops twist slowly south and west. The park has a number of walking trails that begin beside or near the road. To the north, the **Epinette Creek Trails** run through woodland and marsh, the longest being the 25-kilometre Newfoundland Trail. There are a number of unserviced campsites along the various paths.

Roughly 5km south of the Epinette Creek Trails, the **Spirit Sands Trails** cross an area of mixed-grass prairie before entering the shifting sand dunes and pots of quicksand that constitute Manitoba's only **desert**. These "Spirit Sands" were of great religious significance to the Ojibwa who, according to one of the earliest fur traders, Alexander Henry, told "of the strange noises heard in its bowels, and its nightly apparitions". Hire a guide or, if it's too hot to walk, try one of the horse-drawn wagon tours that leave from the start of the trail throughout the summer (May–Sept Mon–Fri by appointment, Sat & Sun noon; July & Aug daily 10am, noon & 2pm; 1hr 30min; $8; ☎827-2800 or 379-2007 off-season). The park is filled with strange, bluish-green ponds formed by the action of underground streams, and has some rare animals, notably the hognose snake and the prairie skink (a lizard); there's also a lot of poison ivy about, so take precautions.

A kilometre or so south of the start of the Spirit Sands, there's a full range of tourist facilities at **Kiche Manitou Lake**, including a large campsite (☎827-2458; May–Sept $14–16), a caravan park, grocery stores, restaurants, a beach, canoe rental and a visitor-services centre (mid-May to early Sept daily; summer ☎827-8850, rest of year ☎834-8800).

CARBERRY is the nearest community of any size to Spruce Woods, and you can use it as a base to explore the park. Other than the **Seton Centre**, 116 Main St (June to early Sept Tues–Sat 1–5pm; donation), displaying the artwork and memorabilia of the naturalist Ernest Thompson Seton, and the local history **Carberry Plains Museum** (July & Aug daily 1–6pm; donation), there's not much to see. You can **stay** at the no-frills *4-Way Motel* (☎834-2878; ①/②) or the more comfortable *Carberry Motor Inn* (☎834-2197, fax 834-2224; ②).

Brandon and around

In 1881, when the CPR decided to route the transcontinental railroad through Winnipeg, it was clear that they would need a refuelling depot in the western part of the province. The ideal location was on the east bank of the Assiniboine River, opposite today's **BRANDON**, 160km from Winnipeg, but a certain Dugald McVicar was already established here. The sudden arrival of all sorts of speculators encouraged McVicar to overreach himself, and he attempted to sell his farm and sod hut to the CPR for around $60,000, prompting a railway negotiator to exclaim, "I'll be damned if a town of any kind is built here". It wasn't, and Brandon was founded 4km to the west. Nowadays, the city is a major agricultural centre, home to several research institutions, Manitoba's largest livestock show – the Royal Manitoba Winter Fair – in late March, the huge First Nations Winter Celebration in January, rodeo finals in November and the Brandon Film Festival in February.

If you want to know what's going on in Brandon and the surrounding region, visit the brand new **Brandon Tourism Centre** on the Trans-Canada Highway (May–Sept Mon–Fri 8.30am–8.30pm, Sat & Sun 10.30am–8.30pm; Oct–April Mon–Fri 8.30am–5pm; ☎729-2133 or 1-888/799-1111, *www.bedb.brandon.mb.ca*). The bureau is part of the Riverbank Discovery Centre and the starting point of several newly laid out trails along the Assiniboine River. Construction of a botanical garden has been started nearby. The centre can provide leaflets on self-guided tours, including the one downtown that highlights the historic buildings for which the city is known, some of which are on the south side of Rosser Avenue. Here, a terrace in the Romanesque Revival style includes the former Mutter Brothers Grocery Store, whose interior has been removed to the **Daly House Museum**, 122 18th St (Wed–Sun 10am–noon & 1–5pm; $2), the restored home of Brandon's first mayor. The highlight of the house, however, is an illuminated, four-storey doll's house, in one of the upstairs bedrooms – complete with minuscule mice and mousetraps.

Other imposing late nineteenth-century residences are located on the stretch of **Louise Avenue** as you walk west to **Brandon University** – note especially the yellow-brick house with the corner turret at no. 1036, and the **Paterson-Matheson House** directly across the street at no. 1039, with a spindle-and-spool carved wooden porch painted bright yellow and green. **Moreland Manor**, the low-slung, red-brick and brown-shingled house, on the corner of Louise Avenue and 14th Street, is as close to a Frank Lloyd Wright design as you'll get in Manitoba. The university itself has a small campus dotted with a mix of old and new buildings, most impressive of which is the original college building, with its ragged silhouette facing you to the right as you approach from Louise Avenue. The university also houses the **B.J. Hales Museum of Natural History** in McMaster Hall (Sept–March Mon, Wed & Fri 10am–noon & 1–4pm, Tues & Thurs 1–4pm; April–Aug closed Tues & Thurs; free), consisting of a large botanical and geological collection and interactive exhibits. The former **courthouse** topped by an octagonal cupola, at 11th Street and Princess Avenue, is Brandon's grandest building.

The **Art Gallery of Southwestern Manitoba**, 638 Princess Ave (July & Aug Mon & Thurs 10am–9pm, Tues, Wed & Fri 10am–5pm; rest of year also open Sat 10am–5pm; free), has changing exhibitions concentrating on the work of Manitoba artists and craftspeople. The gallery, with plans for a splendid roof garden, is due to move to a new location on Rosser Avenue – check at the information centre for details.

The city's **bus terminal**, located at 141 6th St (☎727-0643 or 1-800/661-8747), handles Greyhound buses running to Winnipeg, Regina and Saskatoon, as well as smaller places in southwest Manitoba, and also Grey Goose Lines, which runs buses south on Hwy 10. VIA **trains** on the thrice-weekly Winnipeg to Vancouver run stop north of Brandon along Hwy 10 – it's a twenty-minute taxi ride into town ($15).

Brandon has lots of good places to **stay** in all price ranges. The *Super 8 Motel*, 1570 Highland Ave, just off the Trans-Canada (☎729-8024 or 1-800/800-8000, fax 728-3024; ②/③), is perhaps the best value; a free continental breakfast is provided, and facilities include a pool and a hot tub. Other recommended places are the *Royal Oak Inn*, 3130 Victoria Ave (☎728-5775, fax 726-5828; ④), the city's most reputable accommodation, with a 1930s-theme restaurant, and the *Victoria Inn*, 3550 Victoria Ave W (☎725-1532 or 1-800/852-2710, fax 727-8282; ③), which has comfortable rooms, saunas, a hot tub and swimming pool. For a personalized touch, check out *Casa Maley*, 1605 Victoria Ave (☎728-0812 or 1-877/729-2900, fax 728-6287; ②), a **B&B** in a 1912 Tudor-style home; the

Mounties

Aboriginal dancer

Moraine Lake, Alberta

Lake Louise, Alberta

Prairies

Mount Rundle, Alberta

The Columbia Icefield, Alberta

Dinosaur Provincial Park, Alberta

The Yellowhead Highway and North

Highway 16, one of central Canada's most appealing long-distance drives, is better known as the **Yellowhead Route** – taking its name from a light-haired Iroquois explorer and guide who was called *Tête Jaune* by the voyageurs, the French-speaking boatmen who plied the waterways transporting people, furs and supplies. About 90km along the road from Portage la Prairie lies one of Manitoba's more pleasant townships, tiny **NEEP-AWA**, whose streets are lined with elms and cottonwoods. The town's oldest buildings are spread along and around the principal drag, Mountain Avenue – notably the cosy neo-Romanesque **Knox Presbyterian Church** at Mill Street and 1st Avenue, with an unusual thick, turreted bell tower, and the tidy, late-Victorian County Court House, close to Mountain Avenue and Hamilton Street. Also in the centre, in the old CNR station at the west end of Hamilton Street, the **Beautiful Plains Museum** (mid-May to Aug Mon–Fri 9am–5pm; July & Aug also Sat & Sun 1–5pm; otherwise by appointment; $1; ☎476-3896 or 476-5292 off-season) has fairly diverting displays on the life of the district's pioneers. Margaret Laurence (1926–87), one of Canada's best-known writers, lived in Neepawa in her early years and used the town, called Manawaka in her books, as a setting for many of her novels, which portray strong women struggling against small town life, beginning with the highly acclaimed *The Stone Angel* (1964) and ending with *The Diviners* (1974). You can visit her home, now a **museum**, at 312 1st Ave N (May–Aug Mon–Fri 10am–6pm, Sat & Sun noon–6pm; early Sept & early Oct daily 1–5pm; early Oct to May by appointment ☎476-3612; $2). Laurence is buried in the Riverside Cemetery, in the north of town.

More varieties of **lilies** grow in the area around Neepawa than any other part of the world. If you want to see the flowers in bloom – July to mid-August – you can visit the **Lily Nook**, 4km south of town on Hwy 5 (July to mid-Aug daily 9am–6pm; donation; ☎476-3225). There's also a Lily Festival in Neepawa in the third week of July.

The Yellowhead Highway doubles as Neepawa's Main Street, marking the southern perimeter of the town centre. The **tourist office** (June–Aug Mon & Thurs–Sun 11am–7pm, Tues & Wed 11am–5pm; ☎476-5292) is on the Yellowhead just east of town, beside the Whitemud River. The **bus station** is attached to the Petro Canada petrol station at 52 Main St. For **accommodation**, there's a central riverside **campsite** on Hamilton Street, the *Lions Riverbend Park* (☎476-7607; $9–12; May–Sept) with fishing, a playground and a pool, and two convenient **hotels**, the down-at-heel *Hamilton* at Mountain Avenue and Mill Street (☎476-2368, fax 476-3598; ①), and the equally rudimentary *Vivian*, 236 Hamilton St at 1st Avenue (☎476-5089; ①/②) – both have bars beneath. You'd do better at the three **motels**, all west of town on Hwy 16: the *Neepawa* (☎476-2331, fax 476-3816; ②/③), the large, spotlessly clean *Westway Inn* (☎476-2355, fax 476-3845; ②, breakfast included) or the new *Super 8* (☎476-8888 or 1-800/800-8000; ②/③, breakfast included) with an indoor pool. Or try the *Garden Path B&B*, 536 2nd Ave at Main Street (☎476-3184; ②), in a beautiful 1903 former lumber merchant's home. The **restaurants** downtown are unappealing but the best of the bad bunch on Hwy 16 (Main Street) is the busy *Mr Ribs*, which offers dinners from $6. Better perhaps to head out to the *Prairie Orchard Tea House* (☎368-2486), 13.6km east on Hwy 16, which serves locally grown organic food.

The approach to **MINNEDOSA**, 28km further west of Neepawa is stunning, as the attractive town sits on the flat of a long valley that slowly rises up at each end. The relaxing small-town atmosphere of the place is most appealing and, as it's about halfway between Winnipeg and the Saskatchewan border, it can make for a convenient stop-off. It's also only thirty minutes from Riding Mountain National Park (see overleaf). There's not much to see here except for a bison compound near the Little Saskatchewan River (March–Oct; free), reached by crossing the swinging bridge over the river or turn off Main Street onto 2nd Avenue SE, and then drive five minutes along Beach Road – you can view the bison from a platform in a public car park. A **tourist information centre** (daily 11am–7pm; ☎867-2741), in a 1920s CPR caboose and diesel engine, is located at 26 Main St South beside the boulder-strewn river. The centre is a museum of its own, filled with old railway memorabilia. From here a newly established Heritage Village Walk takes you on a pretty amble along the riverbank, past a salmon ladder to a small collection of heritage buildings, none of which are particularly inspiring.

Minnedosa has a handful of acceptable **motels**, the best being the *Minnedosa Inn*, 138 Main St (☎867-2777; ②). The *Castle*, 149 2nd Ave SW (☎867-2830; ②/③), a Queen Anne-style house on the banks of the Little Saskatchewan River, is one of the more attractive B&Bs in western Manitoba. Delicious German and French **food** is available at *Brede's*, 121 Main St South (Wed–Sun dinner), otherwise the choice is limited to non-descript places along Main Street.

Riding Mountain National Park and Wasagaming

Bisected by Hwy 10 on its way from Brandon to Dauphin, **Riding Mountain National Park** (park entry fee $3.25 per person, $7.50 per group; 4-day pass $7.50 per person, $16 per group) is a vast expanse of wilderness, roughly 50km long and 100km wide, providing some of Manitoba's finest hiking and biking trails and most beautiful scenery. Its eastern perimeter is formed by a 400-metre-high ridge studded with a dense ever-green forest of spruce, pine, balsam fir and tamarack. This soon gives way to a high-land plateau whose mixed forests and lakes form the central, and most scenic, part of the park, bordered to the west by an area of aspen woodland, meadow and open grass-land – the habitat of moose, elk and a carefully tended herd of buffalo, best viewed in the morning or evening, near Lake Audy (45min drive northwest of Wasagaming on a gravel road; no public transport; open year-round; free).

The only settlement of any significance is the tacky tourist centre of **WASAGAM-ING**, beside the main highway on the southern edge of the park, adjoining Clear Lake. The village has a campsite, motels and restaurants, grocery stores, petrol stations, a 1930s log theatre, and boat and canoe rental, but the narrow, scrawny beach is desper-ately overcrowded in July and August, while the lake, though spring-fed, is infested with a parasitic flatworm that can cause the painful skin irritation called "Swimmer's Itch".

Beside the beach, the park's **visitors' information centre** (mid-May to mid-June Mon–Thurs 9.30am–5.30pm, Fri–Sun 10am–8pm; mid-June to early Sept daily 10am–8pm; early Sept to mid-Oct daily 10am–5pm; ☎848-PARK or 1-800/707-8480) has a collection of stuffed animals and environmental displays, and publishes the *Bugle*, a free broadsheet guide to the park's amenities. The staff organize a programme of sum-mer events, featuring free day-long **walks** and **hikes**. The centre also issues **fishing permits** and **backcountry permits** ($4), which are compulsory for overnight stays in the bush. From mid-October to mid-May, when the centre is closed, the **administra-tion office** opposite (Mon–Fri 8am–noon & 1–4.30pm; ☎848-7208) provides a similar service. Most of the trails that begin in or near Wasagaming are short and easy – the longest being the newly completed Clear Lake Trail around Clear Lake's shore (24km). The best of the park's trails is the eight-kilometre **Grey Owl Trail** to Beaver Lodge Lake from Hwy 19, where Grey Owl (see p.284) lived for six months in 1931. This trail connects with the nearest of the overnight routes, the **Cowan Lake Trail**, which branches off to pass through a region of dense forest, small lakes and meadows. All the overnight trails have primitive **campsites**. To really experience the rugged beauty of the park, contact Riding Mountain Nature Tours (☎636-2968, fax 636-2557, *www .golink.com/naturetours/*), which offers a variety of longer **tours**, including horseback riding, hiking, bird-watching and wildlife safaris. To learn more about the history of the park – including Grey Owl's stay here – visit the **Pinewood Museum** at 154 Wasagaming Drive (July & Aug daily 2–4pm; free).

Served by daily buses from Winnipeg, Brandon and Dauphin, Wasagaming's main **bus stop** is on the corner of Wasagaming Drive and Mooswa Drive. For **accommodation**, the *Mooswa Motel & Bungalow*, Mooswa Drive (☎848-2533, fax 848-3569; ②), has delightfully designed modern chalets, motel rooms and bungalows; basic bungalows and log cabins at *Johnson Cabins*, 109 Ta-Wa-Pit Drive (☎848-2524 or 1-888/843-2524, fax 848-2718; ②), are a bit cheaper. *Clear Lake Lodge*, at Ta-Wa-Pit Drive and Columbine Street (☎848-2345; ③), is a comfortable, nonsmoking hotel, but if you want to save money head for the *Manigaming Resort*, 137 Ta-Wa-Pit Drive (☎848-2459; ②), or the *Southgate Motor Hotel* in Onanole, 5km south of Wasagaming (☎848-2158, fax 848-2927; ①). All accommodation in the park is open from May to September or October only, with the exception of the year-round *New Chalet*, 116 Wasagaming Drive (☎848-2892, fax 848-4515; ③). There's only one **campsite**, *Wasagaming Campground*, in the village just beyond the main park gate (☎1-800/707-8480, *www.-parkscanada.pch.gc.ca/riding*; $12–20; May to mid-Oct; reservations advised).

Wasagaming's **restaurants** are poor, with the notable exception of *TR McKoys* in the same log building as the Park Theatre on Wasagaming Drive – it has lunch and dinner menus with pasta dishes from $10 and delicious sandwiches from $7. You can also try the *Mooswa*, where a delicious fresh fish meal will set you back about $20. The best of the cheaper establishments is the *Whitehouse,* also on Wasagaming Drive with burgers, sandwiches and other fast-food grub. The Tempo petrol station opposite rents out **bikes** (☎1-800/816-2524; $7 an hour), while **canoe** and **powerboat** rentals ($17 an hour) are available from the jetty on Clear Lake. **Horseback riding** is available at the riding stables at Triangle Ranch (hourly rides $17; ☎848-4583).

Dauphin

DAUPHIN was founded as a fur-trading post by the French in 1739 and is now a pleasant town that straggles across the flat prairie landscape just to the east of the Vermilion River. Its long **Main Street** features some good examples of early twentieth-century Canadian architecture, but there's only one real attraction, the **Fort Dauphin Museum** (May, June & Sept Mon–Fri 9am–5pm; July & Aug daily 9am–5pm; Oct–April by appointment ☎638-6630; $3). This tidy wooden replica of a North West Company trading outpost, located by the river at the end of 4th Avenue SW, fifteen-minutes' walk from Main Street, holds the stockade where there are reconstructions of several sorts of pioneer building, including a trapper's cabin. If you have time to kill, there's a huge, chateau-like CNR **railway station** on 1st Avenue NW and a modest **arts centre** and gallery at 104 1st Ave NW (Mon–Fri noon–5pm; free) in a striking Romanesque Revival building. At the corner of 1st Street SW and 11th Avenue SW is the Ukrainian **Church of the Resurrection**, with its distinctive clustered domes (by appointment only ☎638-4659, 638-5511 or 638-4618).

The fertile river valley that runs west of Dauphin towards Roblin was a centre of **Ukrainian** settlement between 1896 and 1925, and its village skylines are still dominated by the onion-domed spires of their Orthodox and Catholic churches. There's a modest collection of Ukrainian pioneer artefacts and traditional handicrafts in Dauphin at the **Selo Ukraina Office**, 119 Main St S (Tues–Sat 10am–5pm), but their main task is to organize the **National Ukrainian Festival**, which takes place on the first weekend of August at a purpose-built complex 12km south of Dauphin, just off Hwy 10 on the edge of Riding Mountain Park. The complex has a tiny heritage village dedicated to the early Ukrainian settlers (by appointment only ☎638-9401; free) and a splendid amphitheatre built into a hillside, ideal for the festival's music and dance performances.

Dauphin's **bus station** is at 4th Avenue NE and Main Street, a couple of minutes' walk from the town centre. The **Chamber of Commerce**, 21 3rd Ave NE (Mon–Fri 8.30am–4.30pm; ☎638-4838), provides tourist information. There's also a **tourist**

bureau (mid-May to Aug Mon–Thurs 10am–6pm, Fri–Sun 9am–7pm; ☎638-5295), 2km away on the southern edge of town on Hwy 10, beside the airport.

For **accommodation**, the *Boulevard Motor Hotel*, 28 Memorial Blvd (☎638-4410, fax 638-7642; ②/③), the *Dauphin Inn Motel*, 35 Memorial Blvd (☎638-4430, fax 638-7466; ①/②) and the *Dauphin Community Inn*, 104 Main St N (☎638-4311, fax 638-6469; ①/②), are all (fairly seedy) downtown **hotels**; you may opt instead for either the *Canway Inn Motel and Suites* (☎638-5102 or 1-888/325-3335, fax 638-7475; ②–⑨), roughly 4km south of town near the junction of hwys 5 and 10, with a pool, a sauna and more appealing rooms – four of them have jacuzzis en suite, or the *Touch of Africa Bed & Breakfast* (☎638-0085 or 638-7936, fax 638-8174; ②), on Hwy 10, south of Dauphin opposite the tourist information centre, which keeps ostrichs on its grounds. The *Vermilion Trailer Park & Campground* (☎638-3740 or 622-3109, fax 622-3199; $12–16; May–Oct) is ten-minutes' walk north of Main Street at 21 2nd Ave NW. You can **eat** at *Irving's Steak House & Lounge*, 26 1st Ave NW, which has a real honky-tonk feel, or *Zamrykut's Ukrainian Family Restaurant*, 119 Main St N, a plain establishment that serves delicious home-made food, from borscht through to *pierogies* and *kielbossa* (sausage).

If you want to absorb still more Ukrainian ambience, visit the **Wasyl Negrych Pioneer Farmstead**, near the village of Gilbert Plains, 30km west of Dauphin. Here you'll find Canada's best-preserved and most complete Ukrainian homestead (June–Aug daily 1–5pm; rest of year by appointment; $2; ☎548-2477 or 548-2689). Wasyl and Anna Negrych arrived here in 1897 with their seven children from the Carpathian Mountains. Over the next few years they built the farmstead, which now has ten buildings – an 1899 home that replaced their first log house after it burnt down, three granaries, barns, a chicken coop, pigsty, garages and a bunkhouse with a fully preserved, working peech – the log and clay cookstove that was once the heart of every Ukrainian household. Amazingly, two of Wasyl and Anna's children ran the farmstead according to traditional practises until their deaths in the 1980s, never introducing electricity, sewers or telephone lines. The farmstead is now run by Parks Canada.

Duck Mountain Provincial Park

Duck Mountain Provincial Park, some 100km northwest of Dauphin, is a large slice of the Manitoba Escarpment, comprising several thousand acres of thickly wooded rolling hills punctuated by meadows, bogs, streams and hundreds of tiny lakes. Most of the park is **boreal forest**, a mixture of white spruce, jack pine, balsam fir, aspen and birch, but many of its eastern slopes are covered by maple, burr oak and elm, which are usually found further south. Black bears, moose, white-tailed deer and lynx inhabit the park and it's not unusual to hear the cries of coyotes and wolves at night or the unmistakeable bugling of a bull elk amongst the dense woodland. The park is noted for its fishing, with pickerel, pike and trout in most of its lakes, and the delicious arctic char to the north.

Access to Duck Mountain Park is along two partly paved roads – the east–west Route 367, which branches off Hwy 10 just north of Garland and cuts across the middle of the park to Hwy 83, a distance of 80km; and the south–north Route 366, connecting the town of Grandview, on Hwy 5 just 45km west of Dauphin, with the village of Minitonas, 130km away. Approached along Route 366, the best part of the park is its southeast corner, where **Baldy Mountain** (831m) is the highest point in Manitoba, complete with an observation tower which provides views over the forest. A few kilometres to the north, the twin **West** and **East Blue Lakes** are among the park's finest – curving strips of clear water fed by underground springs. Between the lakes is the **Blue Lakes Campground** (☎1-888/482-2267; May to mid-Sept), close to both the Blue Lakes Trail, a six-kilometre cross-country hike, and the Shining Stone Trail, a short path along the peninsula that juts out into West Blue Lake. The campsite has a beach, a grocery store and petrol station; the camp office advises on boat rental and fishing. There are only unserviced sites here ($10). For serviced sites, try *Childs Lake Campground* (☎546-2463; $12–14; May to mid-Sept), with similar facilities; it's on Route 367 on the west edge of the park.

Great West Trails (☎734-2321) organizes **horseback riding** excursions through the park that include camping and fishing. High Mountain Outfitters (☎967-2077), based in Kelwood, on the east edge of the park, can also arrange a variety of one- to seven-day camping trips.

Northern Manitoba

Running east from the northern end of Lake Winnipegosis and across through the isolated community of Grand Rapids, the 53rd parallel was Manitoba's boundary until 1912, when it was moved up to the 60th parallel on Hudson Bay. This tripled the size of the province and provided its inhabitants with new resources of timber, minerals and hydroelectricity as well as a direct sea route to the Atlantic Ocean. Today's **northern Manitoba** is a vast and sparsely populated tract mostly set on the Canadian Shield, whose shallow soils support a gigantic coniferous forest broken up by a complex pattern of lakes and rivers. It's a hostile environment, the deep, cold winter alternating with a brief, bright summer, when the first few centimetres of topsoil thaw out above the permafrost to create millions of stagnant pools of water, ideal conditions for mosquitoes and blackflies. There are compensations: out in the bush or along the shores of Hudson Bay you'll find a sense of desolate wilderness that's hard to find elsewhere, and a native wildlife that includes caribou, polar bear and all sorts of migratory birds.

Most of the region is inaccessible and its limited **highway system** was built to service the resource towns just to the north of lakes Winnipeg and Winnipegosis. One of these, the paper-and-pulp complex at **The Pas**, is served by buses from Dauphin and Winnipeg, and provides a convenient base for the region's two main parks, **Clearwater Lake** and **Grass River**. Northern Manitoba's key tourist centre, however, is **Churchill**, a remote and windswept township on the southern shore of Hudson Bay where the main attractions are the **polar bears** that congregate along the Bay shore from late June to early November.

Churchill is well beyond the reach of Manitoba's highways, but it is connected to Winnipeg and The Pas by **train** along one of the longest railway lines in the world. The trip from Winnipeg takes about 34 hours, but if you haven't the time there are regular excursion flights from Winnipeg (see "Travel details", p.548).

The Pas and around

Situated 400km north of Dauphin on Hwy 10, on the southern bank of the Saskatchewan River, **THE PAS** – a former fur-trading and missionary centre founded in 1750 – is a town with no specific sights. However, it does host the annual **Northern Manitoba Trappers' Festival** in the third week of February – four days of revelling that include competitions in a number of traditional pioneer skills, like tree-felling, trapsetting, ice-fishing and muskrat-skinning, with the highlight being the World Championship Sled Dog Races and its 50km mushes. If you're in town in mid-August, you can join in the aboriginal celebrations honouring the Cree people **during Opasquiak Indian Days**.

The town's **bus** and **train stations** are right in the centre, a few minutes' walk from the **Municipal Offices** (Mon–Fri 9am–1pm; ☎623-7256), at 324 Ross Ave, which will provide basic tourist information. There's also a **tourist booth** (June–Aug daily 9am–5pm) at the foot of Edwards Avenue, beside the tiny *Devon Park and*

Kinsmen Kampground (☎623-2233; $11–18; May–Sept) and close to two **motels** on Gordon Avenue: the *Golden Arrow* at no. 1313 (☎623-5451, fax 623-5457; ①) and the *La Vérendrye* at no. 1326 (☎623-3431; ②/③); there's also the *Rupert House Hotel* (☎623-3201, fax 623-1651; ①/②) and the three-star *Kikiwak Inn* (☎623-1800 or 1-888/545-4925, fax 623-1812; ③/④). Back in the centre, near the train station, the comfortable *Wescana Inn*, at 439 Fischer Ave (☎623-5446, fax 623-3383; ③), is also a good **place to eat**.

Clearwater Lake Provincial Park

Just 19km north of The Pas, the square-shaped lake and adjoining strip of coniferous forest that constitute **Clearwater Lake Park** are a favourite haunt of the region's anglers, who come here to catch northern pike, whitefish and highly prized lake trout. The park's amenities are concentrated along Route 287, a turning off Hwy 10, which runs along the lake's southern shore past The Pas airport. Beside the road there are four summer **campsites** ($12–14), and a couple of **hunting lodges** (④/⑤) that can be booked at the tourist booth in The Pas. If you're after a **wilderness excursion**, Clearwater Canoe Outfitters (☎624-5606 or 624-5467, fax 624-5467, *www.mts.net-linda/CLEAR.HTM*) rents out a full range of equipment and organizes canoe trips from $25 per day.

Grass River

A further thirty-minutes' drive north up Hwy 10 brings you to the channels and lakes of the **Grass River** water system, which were first charted in the 1770s by **Samuel Hearne**, an intrepid employee of the Hudson's Bay Company who became the first European to reach the Arctic Ocean by land. Hearne witnessed both the development of the Grass River's fur trade and the cataclysmic effects of the smallpox epidemic that followed. He estimated that about ninety percent of the local Chipewyan population were wiped out in the space of a decade, an indication of the scale of a tragedy whose results were compounded by other European diseases, particularly whooping cough and measles. On this and other matters, Hearne was an acute observer of Indian culture and customs. His *Journey to the Northern Ocean* records, for example, the comments of his Chipewyan guide concerning the importance of women:

" 'Women,' added he, 'were made for labour; one of them can carry, or haul, as much as two men can do. They also pitch our tents, make and mend our clothing, keep us warm at night; and, in fact, there is no such thing as travelling any considerable distance in this country without their assistance. Women,' he said again, 'though they do everything, are maintained at trifling expense; for as they always stand to cook, the very licking of their fingers, in scarce times, is sufficient for their subsistence.' "

Grass River Provincial Park

Grass River Provincial Park is made up of several thousand square kilometres of evergreen forest, lake and river interspersed by the granite outcrops of the Canadian Shield. It's noted for its **canoe routes**, the most popular of which runs 180km from the Cranberry Lakes, on the park's western perimeter, to its eastern boundary, where the southern tip of Tramping Lake is located near Hwy 39. It's an excursion of about ten days – all of the route's portages are short and fairly easy and there are lots of basic campsites on the way.

At the start of the canoe route, the first of the three Cranberry Lakes is situated close to **CRANBERRY PORTAGE**, a straggling township on Hwy 10, which runs along the western edge of the park. The settlement has its own park **information kiosk**; a small **campsite** ($10) 1km west of Hwy 10 (☎472-3219, fax 472-3115; $18; mid-May to Sept) with its own beach; a couple of **hotels**, including the *Northern Inn* (☎472-3231; ①), 112 Portage Rd; and a handful of holiday **lodges** (May–Oct only) along its lakeshore, such as the *Viking Lodge* (☎ & fax 472-3337; ④) and the *Caribou Lodge* (☎472-3351, fax 472-3556; ④). Most of the lodges have boat and canoe rentals, and can arrange guided trips and flights to the remoter lakes.

There are other access points to Grass River Park along Hwy 39, which runs along its southern boundary. This hundred-kilometre stretch of road passes three small summer **campsites** (all $10) – *Gyles* (24km east of Hwy 10), *Iskwasum* (40km) and *Reed Lake* (56km) – where park entry points lead to circular canoe trips that can be accomplished within one day.

A worthwhile side-trip can be made from the park to **Wekusko Falls**, about 35km beyond the east boundary of the park along Hwy 39 and then south along a short stretch of gravel road (Hwy 596). Here the Mitishto River drops dramatically in a series of falls and rapids. You can view the spectacle from two suspension footbridges or along the walking trails below.

Flin Flon

At the northern end of Hwy 10, about 60km from Cranberry Portage, the mining township of **FLIN FLON**, on the Saskatchewan border, gouges copper, gold, lead and zinc from a massive seam that was discovered in 1914. A stark, rough-looking town, full of precipitously steep streets, where the houses are built on sheer rock in a barren landscape, Flin Flon takes its unusual name from the hero of an obscure dime-novel entitled *The Sunless City*, which one of the first prospectors was reading at the time of the discovery. In the book, Josiah Flintabbatey Flonatin builds a submarine and enters the bowels of the earth, where he discovers that everything is made of gold. The nearest you'll come to his trip is on the free guided tours of the town's **Hudson Bay Mining and Smelting Plant** (June–Aug Mon, Wed & Fri 8.30am; 2hr; reservations ☎687-2050; over-16s only). Surprisingly, you'll see greenhouses in the depths of the mine, the warm and humid conditions being perfect for growing flowers such as orchids. The mine was due to shut down in 2004, a move that would have meant the end of Flin Flon, but in the summer of 2000 the biggest industrial investment in Manitoba, some $400 million from mining companies, ensured the mine's and the town's future.

Aside from the mine, there's not much to see in Flin Flon, except in July, the town's liveliest month, when it hosts the Trout Festival, with a parade, a Queen Mermaid Pageant, the Great Northern Duck Race – and the tantalizing smell of frying fish.

The town's **bus station** is right in the centre at 63 3rd Ave. About 1km to the east, along Hwy 10A, the **tourist office** (May to end of Sept daily 8am–8pm; ☎687-9758) adjoins the main **campsite** (☎687-9758; $13–15; May–Sept) with a large statue of the intrepid Flintabbatey Flonatin opposite. If you do end up in these parts, you can stay at the cheap and central hotel *Royal*, at 93 Main St (☎687-3437, fax 687-5354; ①/②). If you're feeling the pinch of the north's high prices, try the *Flin Flon Friendship Centre Hostel*, 57 Church St (☎687-3900, fax 687-5328; ①), which offers basic dorm accommodation. For a similarly basic **meal**, try *Mugsy's*, on Main St, or the *Victoria Inn*'s restaurant, 160 Hwy 10.

Churchill

Sitting on the east bank of the Churchill River where it empties into Hudson Bay, **CHURCHILL** has the neglected appearance of many of the settlements of the far north, its unkempt open spaces dotted with the houses of its mixed Inuit, Cree and white population. These grim buildings are heavily fortified against the biting cold of winter and the insects of the summer – ample justification for a local T-shirt featuring a giant mosquito above the inscription "I gave blood in Churchill". That said, the town has long attracted a rough-edged assortment of people with a taste for the wilderness, and nowadays tourists flock here for the wildlife, particularly the polar bears – a lifeline, now that Churchill's grain-handling facilities are underused.

In 1682, the Hudson's Bay Company established a fur-trading post at **York Factory**, a marshy peninsula some 240km southeast of today's Churchill (see p.505). The move was dictated by the fact that the direct sea route here from England was roughly 1500km shorter than the old route via the St Lawrence River, while the Hayes and Nelson rivers gave access to the region's greatest waterways. Within a few years, a regular cycle of trade had been established, with the company's Cree and Assiniboine go-betweens heading south in the autumn to **hunt and trade** for skins, and returning in the spring laden with pelts they could exchange for the company's manufactured goods. Throughout the eighteenth century, before the English assumed control of all facets of the trade and laid off their native intermediaries, both sides seem to have benefited economically, and the reports of the company's traders are sprinkled with bursts of irritation at the bargains forced on them by the natives. The company was always keen to increase its trade, and it soon expanded its operations to Churchill, building the first of a series of forts here in 1717.

In the nineteenth century the development of faster trade routes through Minneapolis brought decline, and by the 1870s both York Factory and Churchill had become remote and unimportant. Then the development of agriculture on the prairies brought a reprieve. Many of the politicians and grain farmers of this new west were determined to break the trading monopoly of Sault Ste Marie in northern Ontario and campaigned for the construction of a new port facility on Hudson Bay, connected by rail to the south through Winnipeg. In the 1920s the Canadian National Railway agreed to build the line, and it finally reached Churchill in April 1929. Unfortunately, despite all the efforts of the railway workers in the teeth of the ferocious climate, the port has never been very successful, largely because the bay is ice-free for only about three months a year.

The town centre

On the northern side of town, the unprepossessing Bayport Plaza is a good place to start a visit, as it incorporates the **Parks Canada Visitor Reception Centre** (June–Nov daily 1–5pm & 6–9pm; Dec–May Mon–Fri 8am–4.30pm; ☎675-8863; free), where displays on the history of the fur trade and the Hudson's Bay Company are jazzed up by films dealing with arctic wildlife, **Prince of Wales' Fort** and the construction of the railway. Opposite the plaza, the **Town Centre Complex** offers a good view over Hudson Bay and has recreational facilities, including a curling rink, hockey rink, swimming pool, bowling alley and a cinema.

Just down the road, the **Eskimo Museum**, 242 La Vérendrye Ave (June–Aug Mon 1–5pm, Tues–Sat 9am–noon & 1–5pm; Sept–May Mon & Sat 1–4.30pm, Tues–Fri 10.30am–noon & 1–4.30pm; donation), houses the Inuit collection of the Oblate Fathers of Mary Immaculate, whose missionary work began around here around 1900. The museum's one large room is dominated by two animal-hide canoes and several stuffed Arctic animals, with Inuit art arranged in cases round the walls. It's a fine range of material, from caribou-antler pictographs and highly stylized soapstone figurines through to walrus-tooth scrimshaws and detailed ivory and stone carvings. The sculptures fall into two distinct periods. Up until the 1940s, the artistic work of the local Inuit was essentially limited to the carving of figurines in walrus ivory, modelled on traditional designs. However, in 1949 a Canadian painter, James Houston, travelled the east coast of Hudson Bay in Québec, encouraging the Inuit to vary their designs and experiment with different materials – which led, in particular, to the development of larger and more naturalistic sculptures carved in soapstone.

One corner of the museum functions as a **gift shop** selling a wide range of prints and carvings, plus a good collection of books on the north. Northern Images, a five-minute

CHURCHILL'S FAUNA AND FLORA

Churchill occupies a transitional zone where the stunted trees of the taiga (subarctic coniferous forest) meet the mosses of the tundra. Blanketed with snow in the winter and covered by thousands of bogs and lakes in the summer, this terrain is completely flat until it reaches the sloping banks of the Churchill River and the ridge around Hudson Bay, whose grey-quartzite boulders have been rubbed smooth by the action of the ice, wind and water.

This environment harbours splendid **wildlife**, including Churchill's premier attraction, the **polar bears**, who start to come ashore when the ice melts on the bay in late June. They must then wait for the ice to form again to support their weight before they can start their seal hunt; a polar bear can detect scent from 32km away and can pick up the presence of seals under a metre of snow and ice. The best months to spot bears are September, October and early November, just before the ice re-forms completely.

In mid-June, as the ice breaks on the Churchill River, the spreading patch of open water attracts schools of white **beluga whales**. As many as 3000 of these intelligent, inquisitive and vocal mammals spend July and August around the mouth of the river, joining the **seals**, who arrive in late March for five months. The area around the town is also on one of the major migration routes for **birds** heading north from April to June and returning south in August or early September. Nesting and hatching take place from early June until early July. A couple of hundred species are involved, including gulls, terns, loons, Lapland longspurs, ducks and geese. The star visitor is the rare Ross's Gull, a native of Siberia, which has nested in Churchill for the past decade. The *Birder's Guide to Churchill* ($7) by Bonnie Chartier lists them all and is available in the town and at the Eskimo Museum.

Churchill is also a great place to see the **aurora borealis** (Northern Lights), whose swirling curtains of blue, green and white are common in the skies between late August and April; occasionally it's seen all year round, and is at its best from January to March. Finally, in spring and autumn the tundra is a colourful sheet of moss, lichens, flowers and miniature shrubs and trees that include dwarf birch, spruce and cranberry.

LOCAL TOUR OPERATORS

Local wildlife tour operators have proliferated over the past few years, offering everything from diving with the whales to viewing the polar bears from helicopters.

One of the best-value is Churchill Wilderness Encounters (☎675-2248 or 1-800/265-9458), whose bus meets the train at the station in Churchill. They offer beluga-whale boat trips (July & Aug; $45), a six-day bird-watching adventure ($1895); afternoon nature tours (July–Sept; $45), involving a drive through the taiga, a walk in the Akudlik Marsh and a trip into the boreal forest region; and bird-watching tours (late May to July; $95).

Based in the Bayport Plaza, North Star Tours (☎675-2629 or 1-800/665-0690) organizes excursions, like snorkelling with whales and iceberg-viewing trips in the middle of June from around $70. Sea North Tours, 39 Franklin St (☎675-2195 or 1-888/348-7591), visits the Prince of Wales Fort and listens in on whales using stereo (tours 3hr; $65). Kayaks & Belugas (May to mid-Sept ☎675-2534) guides paddlers to the whales and icebergs (3hr; $55); no experience necessary. Tundra Buggy Tours (June–Nov ☎675-2121 or 1-800/544-5049, Dec–May; ☎813/894-2852, *www.tundrabuggytours.com*) has a range of excursions in vehicles specially designed to avoid damaging the tundra (starting from $162) – some trips offer overnight lodge accommodation in the heart of the wilderness wildlife area. Midwest Helicopters (☎675-2576) operates helicopter sightseeing tours ($470 for 30min for up to 4 people) with guaranteed polar-bear sightings. Northern Expedition Tours (same phone and Web site as Tundra Buggy Tours) is a specialist aurora borealis operator that offers a chance to see the Northern Lights away from the bright lights of Churchill, while B&B Scuba (☎257-3696) will take you diving amongst the whales for up to a week at a time if you're part of a group (July & Aug only).

walk south on Kelsey Boulevard, sells similar work at higher prices – but its profits go back to the producers.

Cape Merry and Prince of Wales' Fort

A couple of minutes' walk from the town centre, Churchill's grain elevators and silos stand at the base of a narrow peninsula that sticks out into the mouth of the Churchill River. At the tip, approached along a gravel track, **Cape Merry National Historic Site** (guided tours June Tues, Thurs & Sat 10am–2pm; July & Aug Sat 10am–2pm; free) has the remains of an eighteenth-century gun emplacement and a cairn commemorating the Danish explorer Jens Munck, who led an expedition that was forced to winter here in 1619; most of the crew died from cold and hunger.

On the other side of the estuary, **Prince of Wales' Fort National Historic Site** (free tours daily July & Aug, times dependent on tides and weather conditions – ask at the visitors centre or phone the Canadian Parks Service; ☎675-8863) is a partly restored eighteenth-century stone fortress that was built to protect the trading interests of the Hudson's Bay Company from the French. Finished in 1771, this massive structure took forty years to complete, but even then it proved far from impregnable. When a squadron of the French fleet appeared in the bay in 1782 the fort's governor, Samuel Hearne, was forced to surrender without firing a shot because he didn't have enough men to form a garrison. The French spiked the cannon and undermined the walls, and after this fiasco the Company never bothered to repair the damage. The Fort is only accessible as part of a guided tour of the Churchill River organized by Sea North Tours (see box, overleaf).

East of the centre: the Bay Shore Road

East of town, a road runs behind the shoreline past a series of rather eccentric attractions. Near the airport, the **polar bear "prison"** is a large hangar-like compound where dangerous bears are kept until they can be released safely. The problem is that some of the beasts wander into town in search of food and, although most can be scared off quite easily, a handful return. These more persistent specimens are shot with tranquillizers and transported to the compound. It's a necessary precaution, as polar bears can run and swim faster than humans and there are occasional horror stories, such as the owner of a fire-damaged house returning to empty his freezer, only to be trapped and killed by a bear. Repeat bear offenders are given three chances, after which they are humanely destroyed.

Practicalities

Churchill can only be reached by **plane** or **train**. VIA Rail (☎1-800/561-8630, *www.via.ca*) runs a summer service five times a week from Winnipeg (rest of the year thrice weekly; from $274 return, if booked seven days in advance). Calm Air (☎956-6196 or 1-800/839-2256) has daily flights from Winnipeg ($1213 return, $673 with two-weeks' advance booking) and Canadian Airlines (☎632-1250 or 1-800/665-1177) operates a daily service in conjunction with Calm Air ($1229 return, $689 with two-weeks' advance booking). The town's **airport** is 7km from the centre, and each flight attracts the minibuses of the main tour operators, who will provide onward transport for about $10. Alternatively, Churchill Taxi, 31 Thompson St (☎675-2345), charges about $12 for the same service. The **train station** is right in the town centre, a few metres from the **Visitor Information Bureau** on Kelsey Boulevard (July & Aug Tues–Fri 8am–1.30pm, Sat 8am–3.30pm; ☎675-2022 or 1-888/389-2327) and a five-minute walk from the Bayport Plaza, where there's a **Parks Canada Visitor Reception Centre** (see p.502 for details).

There are no campsites or hostels in Churchill, so visitors are dependent on the town's **hotels**, which are so uniformly drab it's hard to see why they vary in price. All are within easy walking distance of the train station, and all should be booked in advance no matter what the time of year. The best of the bunch are the *Northern Nights Travel Lodge*, 101 Kelsey Blvd (☎675-2403, fax 675-2011; ③; June–Nov), with an adjacent restaurant, and the recently renovated *Polar Inn*, 15 Franklin St (☎675-8878, fax 675-2647; ③) with TVs and telephones in the rooms, a souvenir shop and mountain bikes for rent. The hotels can get booked up quite rapidly by tour groups so you may prefer to stay at the friendly **B&Bs** run by Vera Gould and her family: Vera's is at 87 Hearne St (☎675-2544; ③), her daughter, Anne, has *La Peruse*, 100 Button St (☎675-2254, fax 675-2140; ③) and her son, Donald, runs the *Polar Bear Bed & Breakfast,* 26 Hearne St (☎675-2819; ③).

Churchill's handful of **restaurants** leaves a lot to be desired, with the exception of the expensive *Trader's Table*, 141 Kelsey Blvd, where you can sample caribou burgers, or try the local speciality, arctic char, for around $18. The best snack bar is in the Town Centre Complex, which has burgers from $5; all the hotels also have their own restaurants.

York Factory

The remote **York Factory National Historic Site** (June to mid-Sept daily 8am–5pm, depending on river conditions) lies 240km southeast of Churchill, at the mouth of the Hayes and Nelson rivers. This was the central storehouse of the northwestern fur trade throughout the eighteenth century, its wooden palisades the temporary home of soldiers and explorers, travellers and traders, and settlers bound for the Red River Colony at present-day Winnipeg. With the amalgamation of the North West and Hudson's Bay companies in 1821, it was here that the new governor **George Simpson** set about the delicate task of reconciling the feuds stirred by a generation of inter-company rivalry. In October he arranged his first formal joint banquet, 73 traders facing each other across two long and narrow tables. It was, according to a contemporary, "dollars to doughnuts [whether it would be] a feed or fight", but Simpson's diplomatic skills triumphed, leading to a successful reorganization of trading operations. In its heyday, there were some fifty buildings within the stockade, including a guesthouse, fur stores, trading rooms, living quarters and shops, but they were all destroyed in the 1930s, with the exception of the **main warehouse** (1832), a sturdy wooden building that serves as a reminder of the fort's earlier significance. Wandering around the desolate site today, it's hard to imagine that it was once the largest community in western Canada. Guided tours of the site are available (contact the Parks Canada Visitor Reception Centre in Churchill; $5).

This remote spot can only be reached by **charter flight** – weather permitting – from Thompson, Churchill or Gillam, a hydroelectric centre on the rail line between Winnipeg and Churchill. Or you can get there by **canoe** along the Hayes River from Norway House on the north shore of Lake Winnipeg – an arduous journey of 600km, which should not be undertaken without advice from the Manitoba Parks Department in Winnipeg (☎945-6784 or 1-800/214-6497, *www.gov.mb.ca/natres/parks*). Because of the disturbance to polar bears in the area, camping is not allowed at York Factory. The only place to stay is the *Silver Goose Lodge*, and this must be arranged in advance with the owners (☎652-2776; ④). There are no services, and all supplies must be brought in.

The Seal River

The wild rivers that drain into Hudson Bay constitute some of the most challenging **canoe routes** in Canada, their long stretches of white water demanding considerable planning, experience and skill. One of the more popular is the **Seal River**, whose principal canoe route begins at the tiny Chipewyan village of Tadoule, and then passes through regions of boreal forest and tundra before emptying into Hudson Bay, just 45km west of Churchill. In the summer the estuary is a gathering place for several thousand beluga whales, an amazing sight to witness. There's float-plane transportation to the start of the canoe route and from the mouth of the river at the end, which can take between two and four weeks to reach. For details, contact Dymond Air Services, 23 Selkirk St, Churchill (☎675-8875). For something a bit shorter, you can stay at the *Seal River Heritage Lodge* (☎675-8875 or 1-888/326-7325) on a three-day ($1450) or six-day package ($2300) including all meals, services of a guide, whale-watching expeditions, canoeing trips and wildlife tours.

SASKATCHEWAN

"You'd marry anyone to get out of Moose Jaw, Saskatchewan", Susan Sarandon tells Burt Lancaster in Louis Malle's film *Atlantic City*, and the whole province is regarded with similar disdain by many Canadians. It's certainly not one of the country's glamour regions, remaining as dependent on agriculture as it was when the province was established in 1905, and today producing 42 percent of Canada's wheat, 39 percent of its canola, 35 percent of its rye and 20 percent of its barley. Saskatchewan's farmers often struggle to make ends meet when international prices fall, and consequently they have formed various **Wheat Pools**, which attempt to control freight charges and sell the grain at the best possible time. The political spin-off has been the evolution of a strong socialist tradition, built on the farmers' mistrust of the market. For many years Saskatchewan was a stronghold of the **Cooperative Commonwealth Federation (CCF)**, the forerunner of the New Democratic Party (NDP), and in 1944 the CCF formed the country's first leftist provincial government, pushing through bills to set up state-run medical and social security schemes.

The Saskatchewan telephone code is ☎306.

However underprivileged Saskatchewan might have been in the past, its image as a featureless zone is grossly unfair. Even the dreariest part of the province, to the south of the Yellowhead Highway, has some splendid diversions, notably **Regina**'s intriguing Royal Canadian Mounted Police Museum, and the coulees and buttes of the **Grasslands National Park**. On the Yellowhead itself, **Saskatoon**, Saskatchewan's largest city, has an attractive riverside setting and boasts good restaurants, plus a complex devoted to the culture of the Northern Plains Indians. Further west, **Battleford** has a splendidly restored Mountie stockade, while to the north **Batoche National Historic Park**, occupying a fine location beside the South Saskatchewan River, commemorates the Métis rebellion of 1885. Not far away from Batoche, **Prince Albert National Park** marks the geographical centre of the province, where the aspen parkland of the south meets the boreal forests and lakes of the north. There are some wonderful walks and canoe routes here, even though the park's tourist village, **Waskesiu Lake**, is rather commercialized.

North of Prince Albert Park, the desolate wilderness of the Canadian Shield is mostly inaccessible except by float plane; the main exception is the town of **La Ronge**, which is on the edge of the canoe routes and good fishing waters of **Lac La Ronge Provincial Park** and the **Churchill River**. By comparison, the area bordering eastern Alberta has less to offer, though the desultory prairie landscape that makes up its south and centre does incorporate some of the hills, forests and ravines of the **Cypress Hills Interprovincial Park**.

PROVINCIAL PARKS

Saskatchewan's **provincial parks** (*www.serm.gov.sk.ca*) have a toll-free number ☎1-800/667-2757 or 787-2700 in Regina that will put you through to the park of your choice. All the parks have the same **entrance fees**: daily $7, three-day entry $17, weekly $25, annual $42. Camping fees are $11–24 depending on services provided. Between late June and mid-August you can **reserve** a site in advance at seven of the parks for a $5 fee: **Candle Lake** (☎929-8409); **Cypress Hills** (☎662-4459); **Duck Mountain** (☎542-5513); **Greenwater Lake** (☎278-3532); **Lac La Ronge** (☎425-4234 or 1-800/772-4064); **Meadow Lake** (☎236-7690 or 236-7680); and **Moose Mountain** (☎577-2611).

The region's **public transport** system is limited, but there are regular scheduled **bus** services between most of the major towns, and a useful, once-daily summertime bus from the town of Prince Albert to Waskesiu Lake, in Prince Albert Park, and La Ronge.

Regina

The capital city of Saskatchewan **REGINA** is the commercial and administrative centre of one of the more densely populated parts of central Canada, its services anchoring a vast network of agricultural villages and towns. Yet despite its capital status, brash shopping malls and population of 204,000, Regina acts and feels like a small prairie town. It's a comfortable if unremarkable place to spend a couple of days, with the off-beat attraction of the Royal Canadian Mounted Police Training Academy and Museum, and the opportunity to explore some of southern Saskatchewan's less familiar destinations – such as the Big Muddy Badlands and the Grasslands National Park. If you want to improve your suntan, incidentally, you've also come to the right place – Regina gets more hours of **sunshine** than any other major city in Canada.

In 1881 the Indian Commissioner **Edward Dewdney** became lieutenant-governor of the Northwest Territories, a vast tract of land that spread west from Ontario as far as the Arctic and Pacific oceans. Almost immediately, he decided to move his capital south from the established community of Battleford to **Pile O'Bones**, an inconsequential dot on the map that took its name from the heaps of bleached buffalo bones left along its creek by generations of native hunters. The reason for Dewdney's decision was the routing of the Canadian Pacific transcontinental railroad across the southern plains: the capital city was renamed Regina after Queen Victoria, and Dewdney petitioned for it to be expanded on land to the north of the creek, a plot coincidentally owned by him. The site was terrible: the sluggish creek provided a poor water supply, the clay soil was muddy in wet weather and intolerably dusty in the summer, and there was no timber for building. Accordingly, the railway board refused to oblige, and the end result was farcical: Government House and the Mounted Police barracks were built where Dewdney wanted them, but the train station was a three-kilometre trek to the south.

In 1905 Regina became the capital of the newly created province of **Saskatchewan**, and settlers flocked here from the United States and central Europe. At the heart of an expanding wheat-growing district, the city tripled its population during its first fifteen years. It also overcame its natural disadvantages with an ambitious programme of

INFORMATION NUMBERS

Tourism Saskatchewan ☎787-2300 or 1-877/237-2273, *www.sasktourism.com*

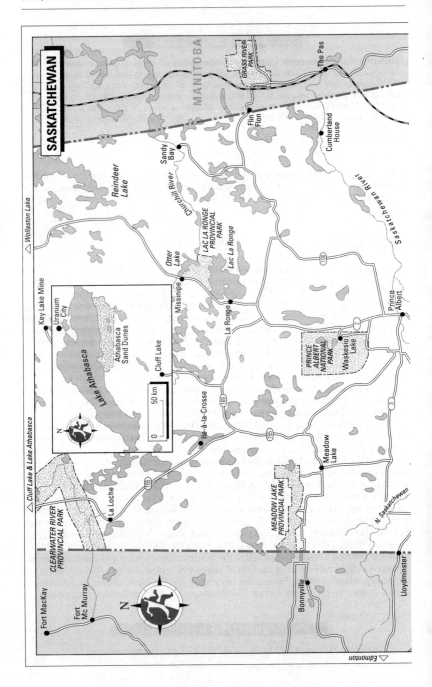

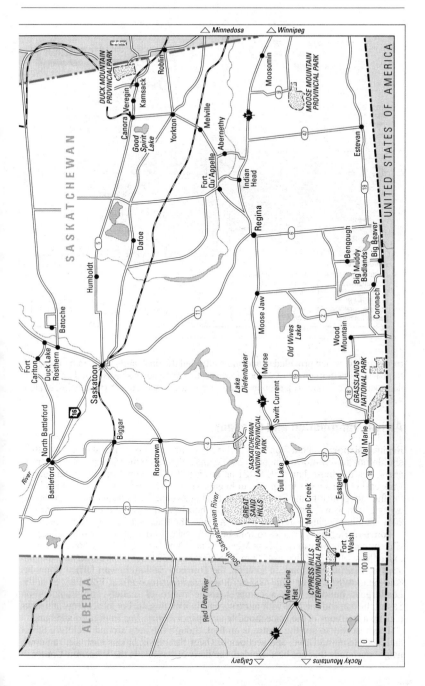

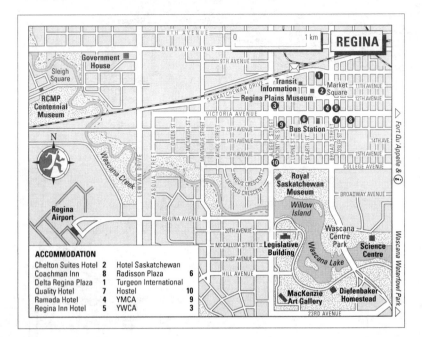

tree-planting, which provided shade and controlled the dust, and by damming the creek to provide a better source of water. However, the city's success was based on the fragile prosperity of a one-crop economy, and throughout the twentieth century boom alternated with bust.

Arrival, information and transport

Regina's **airport** is about 5km west of the city centre; the taxi trip costs roughly $10. A shuttle bus to downtown hotels meets Regina's flights (4pm–midnight; $7). There is also a bus to Moose Jaw (☎949-2121 or 1-877/828-4626; Mon–Fri; $20). A ten-minute walk east of the airport brings you to Regina Transit's **buses** #11 and #13 which leave for the city centre from the junction of Regina Avenue and Pasqua Street (Mon–Sat every 25min 6am–12.30am; Sun 11am–6pm hourly). The **bus station** is downtown at 2041 Hamilton St, just south of Victoria Avenue; the train station is now a casino.

Tourism Regina operates a **tourist bureau** east of town on Hwy 1, really only accessible by car (late May to early Sept Mon–Fri 8am–7pm, Sat & Sun 10am–6pm; early Sept to late May Mon–Fri 8.30am–4.30pm; ☎789-5099 or 1-800/661-5099, *www.tourismregina .com* or *www.inregina.com*). In addition, the **Tourism Saskatchewan Office** (Mon–Fri 8am–5pm; ☎787-2300 or 1-877/237-2273, *www.sasktourism.com*), at 1922 Park St in the Leaderpost building, has a comprehensive range of leaflets and booklets on Saskatchewan and can help with more specific info on Regina. For local events and news pick up a free copy of the twice monthly newspaper *Prairie Dog* from cafés and bars.

The best way to see the centre is on **foot**, though the area around McIntyre Street and Saskatchewan Drive, and sections of Osler Street, six blocks east, are run-down neighbourhoods that are best avoided. Similarly accessible is the **Wascana Centre**, a large multipurpose park and recreational area, whose northern boundary is a few minutes' stroll south of the centre. For longer journeys within the city, **Regina Transit** runs bus services with a standard single fare of $1.50 (exact fare payable to driver), $4.50 for a day-pass or $14 for a book of ten tickets, available at the Tourism Saskatchewan Office or the transit information centre, located at 2124 11th Ave (Mon–Fri 7am–9pm, Sat 9am–4pm; ☎777-7433).

Accommodation

Central Regina has a reasonable range of moderately priced and convenient **hotels**, as well as an excellent **youth hostel**. There's rarely any difficulty in finding a room, but most of the very cheapest places listed by the Tourism Saskatchewan office are effectively grim and cheerless establishments. There's a cluster of reasonably priced, standard **motels** east of the town centre along Hwy 1, which doubles as Victoria Avenue East, and another group of motels south of the centre, along Albert Street. The remaining budget accommodation is provided by a few tiny **B&B** places and three **campsites**.

Hotels and motels

Chelton Suites Hotel, 1907 11th Ave (☎569-4600 or 1-800/667-9922, fax 569-3531). In a plain building in the heart of downtown, this has pleasant, large double rooms with bar, fridge and microwave. ③–⑥.

Coachman Inn, 835 Victoria Ave (☎522-8525, fax 757-5984). An excellent budget choice which is close to Wascana Centre Park and major shopping and sights. ②.

Delta Regina Hotel, 1919 Saskatchewan Drive at Hamilton St (☎525-5255 or 1-800/268-1133, reservations 1-800/209-3555, fax 781-7188). One of Regina's most luxurious hotels, but located in a slightly dodgy part of town. Facilities include cable and satellite TV, and a pool with a three-storey waterslide. ④–⑤.

Quality Hotel, 1717 Victoria Ave at Broad St (☎569-4656 or 1-800/228-5151, fax 569-0010). A good downtown bargain, with comfortable rooms. Ask about the occasional weekend discounts. ②–④.

Ramada Hotel & Convention Centre, 1818 Victoria Ave at Broad St (☎569-1666 or 1-800/667-6500, fax 525-3550). One of the most attractive and well-equipped of Regina's hotels, including comfortable, spacious singles, doubles and en suites, and a large recreation complex. ③.

Regina Inn Hotel, 1975 Broad St (☎525-6767 or 1-800/667-8162, fax 525-3630). Top-quality high-rise hotel in the centre of downtown. Majority of rooms are nonsmoking and there are one-bedroom and jacuzzi suites available. ③.

Regina Travelodge Hotel, 4177 Albert St S (☎586-3443 or 1-800/578-7878, fax 586-9311). A large hotel offering a wide range of facilities, including free coffee in rooms and free local calls. There's also a restaurant, pub and gift shop on the premises. ③/④.

Hotel Saskatchewan Radisson Plaza, 2125 Victoria Ave at Scarth St (☎522-7691 or 1-800/667-5828, fax 522-8988). This large hotel, overlooking Victoria Park, was sensitively restored in 1992 to a luxurious standard and provides a full range of facilities, including a fitness centre with whirlpool. Complimentary pick-up at airport. ④–⑧.

West Harvest Inn, 4025 Albert St (☎586-6755 or 1-800/853-1181, fax 584-1345). One of the best bargains in the Regina area. Newly refurbished singles, doubles and en suites, all come with free in-room coffee and local calls. The inn also has a health spa and gym. ③–⑤.

Bed and breakfasts

B and J's, 2066 Ottawa St (☎522-4575). Situated just south of the city centre and near the General Hospital. Free coffee and pastries in the evening, and free parking. ②.

Daybreak B&B, 316 Habkirk Drive (☎586-0211). In the south of the city, east of Albert St, near the Trans-Canada. Two rooms with a nice old-fashioned feel and the owners offer free pick-up and delivery to airport or bus station. ①.

Morning Glory Manor, corner of Broad St and College Ave (☎525-2945). A charming 1920s home, minutes from downtown and Wascana Centre Park. Off-street parking. ②.

Hostels

Turgeon International Hostel, 2310 McIntyre St (☎791-8165 or 1-800/467-8357, fax 721-2667). HI hostel in a restored heritage house, immediately south of the downtown core, with cooking and laundry facilities. In conjunction with local bus companies, it runs a bus fare system whereby HI members can travel anywhere within Saskatchewan on Saskatchewan Transportation Company buses for just $24 return or receive a twenty percent discount on Greyhound buses. Reservations 7am–11pm. Members $13, nonmembers $18.

YMCA, 2400 13th Ave (☎757-9622). Small budget rooms with weekly rates available. Facilities include a pool and cafeteria. Men only. Singles $24.

YWCA, 1940 McIntyre St (☎525-2141). Budget rooms available, including weekly rates, but about twice as much as at the *YMCA*. Women only. Singles $36.

Campsites

Buffalo Lookout Campground, south of Hwy 1, 5km east of town (☎525-1448). Campsite includes a store, shower house, phones and indoor recreation facilities, as well as a 24hr on-site manager. Open May to mid-Sept. $15.

Kings' Acres Campground, 1km east of town on Hwy 1, behind the Tourism Regina Bureau (☎522-1619). A full range of serviced and unserviced sites on a spacious property, with store, phone, pool, and TV and games room. $19–21. Open March–Oct.

The City

Fifteen-minutes' walk from end to end, Regina's downtown business and shopping core is known as the **Market Square**, a simple gridiron bounded by Saskatchewan Drive and 13th Avenue to the north and south, Osler and Albert streets to the east and west. The rather mundane **Regina Plains Museum** (April–Sept daily 10am–4pm; Oct–March Mon–Fri 10am–4pm; $2), is within Market Square, on the fourth floor of the mall at 1801 Scarth St and 11th Avenue – its modest displays on the city's history are less diverting than the stories of the elderly volunteers who staff the museum. Exhibitions of innovative, and often controversial, contemporary art can be seen at the **Dunlop Art Gallery**, in the Public Library, west of the museum at 2311 12th Ave (Mon–Thurs 9.30am–9pm, Fri 9.30am–6pm, Sat 9.30am–5pm, Sun 1.30–5pm; free). If the museum and gallery has whetted your appetite you should visit the **Antique Mall**, the largest in western Canada, located beyond the railway tracks north of Market Square, at 1175 Rose St (Mon, Tues, Fri & Sat 10am–6pm, Wed & Thurs 10am–9.30pm, Sun 1.30–5pm; free).

Immediately to the west of the Market Square district, across Albert Street, is **Cathedral Village**, with 13th Avenue as its heart. It's an old area with an eclectic mix of boutiques, coffee shops, craft shops and classy restaurants.

Wascana Centre Park

Roughly eight times the size of the Market Square, Regina's most distinctive feature is **Wascana Centre Park**, which begins three blocks south of 13th Avenue and extends southeast to the city limits, following the curves of **Wascana Lake**, which was created as part of a work project for the unemployed in the 1930s. The city's main recreation area, the park is equipped with a bandstand (performances Sun 2–4pm), barbecue pits, snack bars, boating facilities and waterfowl ponds, but for the most part it's a cheerless combination of reed-filled water and bare lawn.

In the northwest corner of the park, near College Avenue and Albert Street, the **Royal Saskatchewan Museum** (daily: May–Aug 9am–5.30pm; Sept–April 9am–4.30pm; free) is devoted to the province's geology and wildlife, starring a giant animated dinosaur called Megamunch. Informative dioramas portray aspects of aboriginal life in the First Nations Gallery, including storytelling, shown in the scene of a grizzled grandfather recounting stories to a couple of rapt youths. In the new Life Sciences Gallery the relationships between habitat, plants and animals are explored with a multitude of skilfully stuffed animals and plastic flora set against backdrops that evoke the diverse eco-regions of Saskatchewan. A couple of minutes' walk to the east is the swimming pool (June–Aug daily 11am–8pm), and close by there's a ferry boat to **Willow Island** (mid-May to Aug Mon–Fri noon–4pm; $2), a favourite picnic spot. Boat tours are available, departing from the observation deck, near the swimming pool (mid-June to Aug Sun & holidays 1–5pm; 20min; $2; ☎522-3661).

Further east, reached by the winding Wascana Drive, is perhaps Regina's main tourist attraction, the **Saskatchewan Science Centre** (late May to early Sept Mon–Fri 9am–6pm, Sat & Sun 11am–6pm; early Sept to late May Tues–Fri 9am–5pm, Sat & Sun noon–6pm; $6.50; hours and admission subject to change, call ☎522-4629 or 1-800/667-6300 for confirmation). The open, airy building houses more than one hundred interactive scientific exhibits, live stage shows and demonstrations; of particular interest is a display on uranium mining and a room which has a direct video link to NASA headquarters in Houston, enabling you to watch the live proceedings when a mission is under way. Another gallery is devoted to the soils and weather of Saskatchewan, and here you can learn about what's involved in running a farm. Also on the premises is an IMAX cinema ($7). A ticket admitting you to both the centre and the cinema costs $12.

On the other side of the lake, accessible from Albert Street, is the grand **Legislative Building** (daily: late May to Sept 8am–9pm; Sept to late May 8am–5pm; free tours every 30min; 2hr), a self-confident cross-shaped structure of Manitoba limestone with an impressive domed tower at its centre. Guided tours take in the oak-and-marble-panelled Legislative Chamber and six small art galleries, the best of which houses Edmund Morris's portraits of local Indian leaders, presented to the province in 1911. A neighbouring corridor is occupied by the paintings of the **Native Heritage Foundation**, some thirty canvases featuring the work of contemporary Métis and native artists, notably Allen Sapp from North Battleford, who has won some international acclaim for his softly coloured studies of life on Saskatchewan's Indian reserves as he remembers them from the 1930s.

A few minutes' walk south of the Legislative Building, just off Albert Street at 23rd Avenue, the **MacKenzie Art Gallery** (daily: 11am–6pm, Wed & Thurs to 10pm; free) has several spacious modern galleries devoted to temporary exhibitions by modern Canadian artists, plus a good permanent collection. It's also the stage for the city's principal theatrical event, **The Trial of Louis Riel** (mid-July to Aug Wed–Fri 8pm; $10; for reservations, call ☎584-8890 or 525-1185), whose text is based on the transcripts of the trial in Regina in September 1885. No other single event in Canada's past has aroused such controversy: at the time, most of English-speaking Canada was determined he should hang as a rebel, whereas his French-Canadian defenders saw him as a patriot and champion of a just cause. Though Riel was subject to visions and delusions, the court rejected the defence of insanity on the grounds that he knew what he was doing. As he exclaimed – "No one can say that the North-West was not suffering last year . . . but what I have done, and risked, rested certainly on the conviction [that I was] called upon to do something for my country". The jury found him guilty, but the execution was delayed while prime minister John A. Macdonald weighed the consequences; in the end, he decided against clemency.

The **Diefenbaker Homestead** (mid-May to Aug daily 10am–8pm; free), about 1km east of the gallery but still within the park, was the boyhood home of John Diefenbaker, Conservative prime minister of Canada from 1957 to 1963. Moved from the township of Borden, Saskatchewan, in 1967, the tiny wooden house has been decked out with original and contemporary furnishings and memorabilia reflecting both Diefenbaker's homespun philosophies and the immense self-confidence that earned him the nickname "Dief the Chief".

In the extreme southeast corner of the park, reached by buses #10 or #12 or by car along Arcola Avenue East and Prince of Wales Drive from the city centre, is the **Wascana Waterfowl Park** (May–Nov daily 9am–9pm; free; bookings and info ☎522-3661), a group of ponds that's a habitat for ducks, pelicans and Canada geese. Birds are identified by a number of display panels on boardwalks, and guided tours are given Monday to Friday between 9am and 4pm.

The Royal Canadian Mounted Police Training Academy

All Mounties do their basic training at the **Royal Canadian Mounted Police Training Academy**, 4km west of the city centre at Dewdney Avenue West, accessible by bus #8 from 11th Avenue at Cornwall Street. Beside the main parade ground of Sleigh Square – site of the closely choreographed Sergeant Major's parade (late May to Aug Mon–Fri 12.45pm) and Sunset Retreat Ceremony (July to mid-Aug Tues 6.45pm) – the RCMP **Centennial Museum** (daily: June to mid-Sept 8am–6.45pm, July & Aug also Tues till 8.45pm; mid-Sept to May 10am–4.45pm; tours Mon–Fri 9am (summer only), 10am, 11am, 1.30pm, 2.30pm & 3.30pm; free) traces the history of the force from early contacts with the Plains Indians and Métis, through to its present role as an intelligence-gathering organization.

Inside the museum, a series of contemporary quotations illustrates the **Long March** that first brought the Mounties to the west from Ontario in 1874. Their destination was Fort Whoop-up, near present-day Lethbridge, Alberta, where they intended to expel the American whiskey traders. However, by the time they arrived they were in a state of complete exhaustion, and it was fortunate that the Americans had already decamped. Another small section deals with **Sitting Bull**, who crossed into Canada after his victory at the Battle of the Little Bighorn in 1876. Fearing reprisals from the furious American army, Sitting Bull spent four years in and around the Cypress Hills, where he developed a friendship with Police Inspector James Walsh. A picture of the chief and his braves, taken at Fort Walsh in 1877, shows an audience of curious Mounties in their pith helmets.

Throughout the museum you'll note the large collection of Mounties' **uniforms**, which show how the style of dress constantly changed throughout the force's history – from the early days of the North West Mounted Police with their jaunty little pillbox hats, through to the first women's uniforms of 1974 (the year women were admitted to the force). Their immediately identifiable scarlet-red tunics, accompanied by royal-blue jodhpurs with a vertical gold stripe down each leg, are worn – surprisingly – only on ceremonial occasions. The more mundane workaday uniform is a brown serge jacket with straight trousers. But to reinforce the romantic Hollywood image of the Mounties, a free cinema, decorated with old movie posters, has continuous runnings of such glorified interpretations as *Rose Marie* (1936), starring Nelson Eddy and Jeanette MacDonald.

On the **tour** of the grounds you're shown the various buildings, including mock-ups of houses where recruits practise family arrests, search warrants and surveillance techniques; the drill hall where new recruits are put through their paces; and the 1883 chapel – Regina's oldest building – a splendid structure furnished in dark, polished oak where you can escape the intense training activity outside.

Government House

Government House, a couple of kilometres west of the city centre at 4607 Dewdney Ave and Lewvan Drive (May–Sept guided tours every 30min Tues–Sun 10am–4pm; free; bus #1, #11 or #13), was the residence of the lieutenant-governors of the Northwest Territories and subsequently Saskatchewan from 1891 to 1945. A stolid yellow-brick building, it has been delightfully restored to its appearance at the end of the nineteenth century, with offices and reception areas downstairs and a splendid, balconied staircase leading up to the second-floor bedrooms. The men's billiards room is decorated with an

THE MOUNTIES

The heroes of a hundred adventure stories, from *Boys' Own* yarns to more eccentric epics such as the movie *Canadian Mounties versus the Atomic Invaders*, the **Mounties** have been the continent's most charismatic good guys ever since Inspector James Morrow Walsh rode into Chief Sitting Bull's Canadian encampment to lay down the law. Coming straight after the Sioux's victory at the battle of the Little Bighorn in 1876, this was an act of extraordinary daring, and it secured the future of the Mounties. The **North West Mounted Police**, as the Mounties were originally called, had been created in Ottawa during the autumn of 1873, simply in order to restore law and order to the "Whoop-up Country" of southern Saskatchewan and Alberta in the aftermath of the Cypress Hills Massacre (see box on p.529). There was no long-term strategy: the force's areas of responsibility were undecided, and even their uniforms had been slung together from a surplus supply of British army tunics that happened to be handy. However, they did a brilliant job of controlling the whiskey traders who had created pandemonium through the unscrupulous sale of liquor to the Plains Indians, and it was soon clear – after Walsh's dealings with Sitting Bull – that they were to become a permanent institution.

The Mounties came to perform a vital role in administering the west on behalf of the federal government, acting both as law enforcement officers and as justices of the peace. From the 1880s their patrols diligently crisscrossed the territory, their influence reinforced by a knowledge of local conditions that was accumulated in the exercise of a great range of duties – from delivering the mail to providing crop reports. Despite this level of autonomy, the Mounties saw themselves as an integral, if remote, part of the British Empire, their actions and decisions sanctioned by the weight of its authority. In this sense, they despised the individualism of the American sheriff and marshal, for the Mounties expected obedience because of the dignity of their office, not because of their speed with a firearm.

The officer corps, most of whom were recruited from the social elite of the eastern provinces, became respected for an even-handedness that extended, remarkably for the period, to their dealings with the Plains Indians. **Crowfoot**, the Blackfoot leader, was even moved to remark, "If the police had not come to the country, where would we all be now? They have protected us as the feathers of a bird protect it from the frosts of winter". Yet the officers' class prejudices had a less positive influence on their approach to law and order – socially disruptive crimes of violence were their main priority, whereas prostitution and drunkenness were regarded as predictable and inevitable nuisances that were confined to the "lower orders". They had a cohesive view of the society they wanted to create, a Waspish patriarchy where everyone knew their place.

After 1920, when the force lost its exclusively western mandate to become the **Royal Canadian Mounted Police**, this conservative undertow became more problematic. Time and again the RCMP supported reactionary politicians who used them to break strikes – like prime ministers Bennett in Saskatchewan in 1933 and 1934, and Joey Smallwood in Newfoundland during 1959 – and they have often been accused of bias in their dealings with the Québécois. That said, although the Mounties are seen by some as a bastion of reaction at odds with multicultural definitions of Canada, for the most part they remain a potent symbol of nationality. And, for Labatts' brewery, the endorsement of Malcolm the Mountie is a sure-fire way to sell beer.

enormous bison head and a lemon-water stand, where the governor and his cronies would dip their fingers to hide the smell of the cigars. There are also a couple of mementos of one of the more eccentric governors, Amédée Forget, whose specially designed "salesman's chair", beside the entrance, was meant to be uncomfortable, with protruding gargoyles sticking into the visitor's spine, legs shorter at the front than the back and a flesh-pinching crack cut across the middle of the seat. The rocking horse in the office was for Forget's pet monkey. High tea, complete with finger sandwiches and fragile china cups, is served in the ballroom one weekend each month between 1.30pm and 4pm.

Eating, drinking and nightlife

Regina has a clutch of good downtown **restaurants**, lively places whose prices are usually very reasonable. However, many of them close early and don't open at all on Sundays; in emergencies try the big hotels whose standard-issue snack bars are nearly always open daily to 9.30pm. The city's **nightlife** is hardly inspiring, but the university students provide a little stimulation for the couple of downtown clubs, whilst local roustabouts and government workers alike tend to stick to C&W. As a general rule, avoid the downtown **bars**, which are really not very pleasant, and try one of Regina's **brewpubs**, though most are a bit far from the centre: *Brewster's*, 1832 Victoria Ave E, has the largest selection of beers; *Bonzinni's*, 4634 Albert St, in South Regina, also serves good Italian food; *The Bushwakker*, 2206 Dewdney Ave, has twelve types of beer, plus a large selection of single-malt Scotches; *The Barley Mill*, 6155 Rochdale Blvd, is an English-style pub.

For **theatre**, call the Regina Performing Arts Centre, 1077 Angus St (☎779-2279 or 779-2277), to find out what's being put on there by the two principal groups, the Saskatchewan Community Theatre and the Regina Little Theatre. The Regina Symphony Orchestra (☎566-9555) performs at the Saskatchewan Centre of the Arts, 200 Lakeshore Drive (☎525-9999 or 1-800/667-8497).

Restaurants and cafés

Alfredo's Fresh Pasta and Grill, 1801 Scarth St at 11th Av. Specializes in home-made pasta dishes and combines a tasty and imaginative menu with good-value main courses from $8. Closed Sun.

Café Ultimate, 1852 Scarth St. Delicious cakes and refreshments to enjoy while you surf the Web; located in the pedestrianized section of Scarth.

Classic Buffet Co, 100 Albert St. Help yourself to the table laid out with pizza, roast beef and fifteen other hot dishes. Early closing.

The Copper Kettle, 1953 Scarth St at 11th Av. A run-down place, but with a great Greek-Canadian menu, including fabulous spinach and feta pizza. Open daily to midnight.

Grabbajabba, 1881 Scarth St, in the McCallum-Hill Centre. European-style coffee house, with cheap soups, sandwiches, salads and desserts plus an astounding array of coffees. Live jazz Friday 8–11pm.

Heliotrope, 2204 McIntyre St. A wholefood vegetarian restaurant with an emphasis on East Indian and Middle Eastern food. Closed Mon & Sun.

The Keg, 4371 Albert St. Good chicken and seafood dishes from $12.

Magellan's Global Coffee House, 1800 College Ave. This place is a Regina institution and claims to have a resident ghost. A wide range of coffees and desserts served in a trendy setting.

Maria's, 1810 Smith St. Excellent Greek dishes from $7. Closed Sun.

Marquee, 2903 Powerhouse Drive, at the Saskatchewan Science Centre. Inventively presented contemporary cuisine, with an emphasis on game.

Neo Japonica, 2167 Hamilton St. Voted best Japanese restaurant in Canada. Excellent tempura and sushi.

Nicky's Café and Bake Shop, 1005 8th Ave. Good Canadian menu at reasonable prices, especially their breakfasts, Saskatoon berry pie and bread. Fresh turkey served daily. Closed Sun.

Orleans, 1822 Broad St (☎525-3636). Authentic, spicy Cajun food for $10–15; their jambalaya is terrific. Centrally located. Reservations recommended.

Sage, 2330 Albert St (☎569-9726). Dine on wild boar and emu, amongst other exotic delights at Regina's top and expensive restaurant.

Saigon by Night, 1840 Broad St between 11th and 12th sts. Popular cheap place for huge helpings of Thai, Vietnamese or Chinese food.

Tanya's Eclectic Café, 2034 Broad St. Groovy café with a colourful arty interior and serving home-made sandwiches, soups and pastas. Closed Sun & Mon.

The Thirteenth Avenue Coffee House, 3136 13th Ave. This coffee house, in Cathedral Village, offers the best cappuccino and espresso in town. Daily 11am–11pm.

Discos and venues

Bricks and **Oscar's**, 1422 Scarth St. Two lively gay bars, the latter with an Oscar Wilde theme.

Cathedral Village Free House, 3062 Albert St at 13th. Massive, new rocking pub/club – probably Regina's most popular hangout, serving locally brewed beers.

Checkers and **Scotland Yard**, in the *Landmark Inn*, 4150 Albert St. The places to be seen in, catering mainly to the fashionable, twentysomething crowd. $2 cover charge.

Good Time Charlie's, in the *Plains Hotel*, 1965 Albert St. Best blues club in Regina. Jam sessions Thursday, Saturday and Sunday night, plus Saturday afternoons. $3–5 cover charge.

The Manhattan Club, 2300 Dewdney Ave. Disco with a chaotic combo of Top 40 and dance mix. $2.25 cover charge on Saturday. Closed Sun & Mon.

OUTside Bar, 2070 Broad St. Popular gay venue.

The Pump, 641 Victoria Ave E. C&W venue with a huge dance floor. Closed Sun.

The State, 1326a Hamilton St. Alternative rap, pop, 1980s hits – all on a heaving multilevel dance floor. Great live bands most nights. $7 cover charge on Fridays. Closed Sun.

Listings

Airlines Air Canada (☎1-888/247-2262); Air Sask (☎1-800/665-7275); Athabaska Airways (☎1-800/667-9356); Northwest Airlines (☎1-800/225-2525).

Airport enquiries ☎761-7555.

Bike rental Joe's Cycle, 2255 Albert St (☎347-7711); Wascana Centre Authority, 2900 Wascana Drive (☎522-3661); Western Cycle, 1745 Hamilton St (☎522-5678); all charge about $23 per day.

Bookshops Book and Brier Patch, 4065 Albert St, has the biggest selection of books in the province; Canada Book, at 1861 Scarth St, off 11th Av, has a good range of titles.

Buses Regina Transit, at 2124 11th Ave (☎777-7433). The city bus station, 2041 Hamilton St, just south of Victoria Av, has services from Greyhound and the provincial carrier, the Saskatchewan Transportation Company (☎787-0101 or 1-800/663-7181).

Camping equipment Fresh Air Experience, 532 Victoria Ave, for most outdoor supplies; Great Northern Rod & Reel, 1121 11th Ave, for fishing gear; Surplus Plus, 2415 11th Ave, for backpacking, canoeing and camping supplies.

Car rental Avis, 2010 Victoria Ave (☎757-1653), and at the airport (☎352-9596); Budget, at the airport (☎791-6818), and 505 McIntyre St (☎791-6810 or 1-800/267-6810); Discount, 1023 Osler St (☎569-1222); Hertz, 2755 Caribou St (☎791-9130) and at the airport (☎791-9131); Thrifty, 1975 Broad St and at the airport (☎525-1000).

Dental emergencies Cathedral Dental Clinic, 3032 13th Ave (☎352-9966); Prairie Dental Clinic, 2109 Retallack St (☎359-7707).

Emergency ☎911 for fire, police and ambulance.

Festivals Buffalo Days is a week-long festival held at the end of July and the beginning of August: several days of craft and livestock exhibitions and music shows ending with a fireworks display. The Kinsmen Rock in the Valley, held in Craven, a 20min drive north of town, is a four-day classic rock festival in mid-July. The mid-June Folk Festival is held in Victoria Park; and the Mosaic Multicultural Festival, held in early June at various locations throughout the city, is a multiethnic celebration, featuring folk dancing and pavilions serving food and drink. On the first weekend of September, Chinese dragon boats rowed by large teams race each other in Wascana Park.

Gay and lesbian Regina Gay-Lesbian Community, 1422 Scarth St (☎522-7343 or information line 525-6046). Pride Week is held in the middle of June, with events around the city.

Hospital Regina General Hospital, 1440 14th Ave (☎766-4444).

Laundries Cathedral Laundromat, 2911 13th Ave (☎525-2665); Cheap Charlie's Laundry, 515 Broad St (☎545-1070).

Left luggage Coin-operated lockers at the bus station.

Lost property ☎777-7433.

Pharmacy Shopper's Drug Mart, 4602 Albert St, is open 24hr.

Police ☎569-3333.

Post office Main office at 2200 Saskatchewan Drive, opposite the Cornwall Centre.

Sexual assault crisis line ☎352-0434, 24hr.

Shopping Cowtown Western Wear, at Western Feed Mills, 745 Park St, for western clothing, boots, hats and accessories; Gourmet Pantry, upper level, Scotia Centre Galleria, 1783 Hamilton St, for Saskatoon foods, such as Saskatoon berry products; Painted Buffalo, 2741 Dewdney Ave, for aboriginal arts and crafts; The Prairie Peddlar, 2206 Dewdney Ave, and Keepsakes Gallery, 2227 14th Ave, for local handicrafts.

Swimming Maple Leaf Pool, 1101 14th St; Wascana Pool, 2211 College Ave.

Taxis Capital Cab, 1358 Cornwall St (☎791-2225); Co-op Taxi, 2614 6th Ave (☎525-2727); Regina Cabs, 3405 Saskatchewan Drive (☎543-9555).

Tours Great Western Adventure Tours, 41 Wesley Rd (☎584-3555) do tours of the city (4hr 30min; $15), as well as to Moose Jaw (6hr; $22) and the Qu'Appelle Valley (7hr; $32 including lunch). Heritage Regina Tours (☎585-4214) have free guided walking tours of the city on Sundays from July to mid-September. RC Tours (☎545-0555) have minibus tours of the city's highlights including the Legislative Building, Royal Canadian Mounted Police Museum and Government House (10am and 1pm, pick-up from downtown hotels; 3hr 30min; $22). The Saskatchewan History & Folklore Society, 1860 Lorne St (☎780-9204 or 1-800/919-9437), organizes one- to four-day tours of the province's historic sites.

Travel agents Marlin Travel, Cornwall Centre, 2102 11th Ave (☎525-3500); Sinfonia, 1801 Scarth St (☎584-9220 or 1-800/667-9220).

Weather ☎780-5744.

Women's contacts Regina Women's Community Centre, 1919 Rose St (☎522-2777).

Northeast of Regina

The slow-moving **Qu'Appelle River** flows 350km from Lake Diefenbaker – 160km west of Regina – to the border with Manitoba, its lush, deep and wide valley a welcome break from the prairies. Punctuated by a series of narrow lakes, and home to half a dozen modest provincial parks, this is one of the province's more popular holiday areas.

Fort Qu'Appelle and around

The river's most pleasant township is **FORT QU'APPELLE**, which sits beside Hwy 10 an hour's drive northeast of Regina, its centre sandwiched between the road and the grooved escarpments of the neighbouring lakes. Roughly ten-minutes' walk from end to end, its leafy gridiron streets fall on either side of Broadway Street, the main drag, whose attractively restored red-brick **Hudson's Bay Company store**, on the corner of Company Avenue, dates from 1897 – the oldest original Hudson's Bay store in Canada. Nearby, at the top end of Bay Avenue, the **museum** (June–Aug daily 10am–noon & 1–5pm; other times by appointment; ☎332-6443 or 332-4319; $2) has a small display on the area's European pioneers and the North West Mounted Police and is joined to the Hudson's Bay Company trading post of 1864. Three blocks to the south, the stone **obelisk** at Fifth Street and Company Avenue commemorates the signing of Treaty Number 4 between the Ojibwa, Cree and Assiniboine of the southern prairies and Lieutenant-Governor Morris in 1874. It was a fractious process. The Ojibwa insisted that the Hudson's Bay Company had stolen "the earth, trees, grass, stones, all that we see with our eyes", hectoring Morris to the point where he finally snapped. He confined the more militant Indian leaders to their tents, an authoritarian manoeuvre that undermined the unity of the Indians, who then signed the treaty in return for various land grants, pensions and equipment.

Near Fort Qu'Appelle, the river bulges into a chain of eight little lakes known collectively as the **Fishing Lakes**. It's possible to drive alongside all of them, but the pick of the bunch is the nearest, **Echo Lake**, which affords pleasant views over the river valley. Between this lake and Pasqua Lake is the scenic **Echo Valley Provincial Park** (May–Sept; visitor centre and Parks office mid-May to Aug ☎332-3215; $7 entry fee,

THE DOUKHOBORS

The first **Doukhobors** developed their dissenting beliefs within the Russian Orthodox Church during the eighteenth century, rejecting both the concept of a mediatory priesthood and the church's formal hierarchy. Later they established an independent sect, but their pacifist and protocommunist views made them unpopular with the tsars, who subjected them to periodic persecution. In the late 1890s they fled Russia for Saskatchewan under the leadership of **Peter Verigin**, a keen advocate of communal labour and the collective ownership of property. Verigin maintained his authority until 1907, when the Canadian government insisted that all Doukhobor homesteads be registered as private property. The colonists were divided, with over one-third accepting the government's proposals despite the bitter opposition of the collectivists, who showed their contempt for worldly possessions by destroying their belongings; some even burnt their clothes and organized Canada's first nude demonstrations. Irretrievably divided, Verigin and his supporters left for British Columbia, but the rest stayed behind to create a prosperous, pacifist and Russian-speaking community, which remained separate and distinct until the 1940s.

camping $13–20), while **Katepwa Point Provincial Park**, an even tinier park (mid-May to Sept; free), sits at the southernmost point of the chain of lakes.

Buses (Mon–Fri 8.45am, 5.30pm & 6.15pm, Sat & Sun 8.45am & 6.15pm) make the seventy-kilometre journey from Regina to Fort Qu'Appelle, where there are three **motels**. The most central is the modern *Country Squire Inn* (☎332-5603, fax 332-6708; ②/③), beside Hwy 10 at the bottom end of Bay Street. There's also an attractive **B&B** in the town: *Company House*, 172 Company Ave (☎332-6333 or 332-7393; ②), which serves up hearty home-cooked breakfasts and is near beaches and fishing, hiking and canoeing areas. On the north side of town, beside Echo Lake and near the golf course, the *Fort* **campsite** (☎332-4614; mid-May to mid-Sept) has an unimaginative setting and sites from $11–15. There are several **restaurants** on Broadway Street, including the Chinese *Jade Palace* at no. 215, and *Bubba's* next door. For more imaginative food, there's the *Off Broadway Bistro*, 12 Boundary Ave, where you can dine on turkey lasagne or *tourtière*. The **tourist information centre** is in the old CNR station at the junction of Boundary Avenue and Hwy 10 (June–Aug daily 9am–7pm; ☎332-4426).

If all accommodation in the popular Qu'Appelle Valley and lakes region is full, head for the small village of **Qu'Appelle**, 20km south of Fort Qu'Appelle on Hwy 35, where you'll find the charming fieldstone *Bluenose Country Vacation Farm* (☎ & fax 699-7192; ③) just north of town; you can also dine in the lovely tearoom, in an enclosed veranda.

About 35km east of Fort Qu'Appelle is the **Motherwell Homestead National Historic Site**, just off Hwy 22 south of the village of Abernethy (daily: May & June 9am–5pm; July & Aug 10am–6pm; $4.50). The large square house, with its odd assortment of multicoloured fieldstones embedded in the exterior walls, and lacy wrought-iron "widow's walk" on the roof, was built in 1898 for W.R. Motherwell, a local farmer and politician who moved to Saskatchewan from Ontario in 1882. He brought with him his knowledge of domestic architecture, for the six-bedroom building is similar to the gracious stone farmhouses of southern Ontario – and actually looks a bit incongruous in its prairie surroundings. Just behind the house, which is restored to its 1912–14 appearance, there's a large red 1907 barn, with farm equipment and roaming farm animals to complete the rustic setting.

Yorkton

Beyond Fort Qu'Appelle, the only town of any note on Hwy 10 before you hit Dauphin (see p.497) is **YORKTON**, which was founded as an agricultural community in the 1880s by farmers from Ontario, although – as with so many other places – it's the

Ukrainian community that features most strongly in the town and the surrounding area. The silver-painted dome and barrel roof of the nave of the white-brick **St Mary's Ukrainian Catholic Church**, at 155 Catherine St (by appointment only ☎783-4594), is the town's most distinctive feature. Inside, there's a large illusionistic painting of the *Coronation of the Virgin* (1939–41) on the surface of the dome – about as close as you'll get in western Canada to the Baroque painted domes in Italian and German churches. The Ukrainian community features strongly in Yorkton's branch of the **Western Development Museum** (May–Aug daily 9am–6pm; $6), devoted to the various ethnic groups who have settled in the region. You'll also find a replica of the interior of a 1902 Catholic church and a superb collection of early twentieth-century Fords and Buicks. However, the most startling sights are the bright-red, huge-wheeled early fire trucks, looking entirely too fragile for their function. If you want to see farmworkers and their fierce-looking machines in action, you could attend the **Threshermen's Show**, held in the grounds of the museum in early August. Also in the city, at the corner of Smith Street and 3rd Avenue is the **Yorkton Arts Council** in the Godfrey Dean Cultural Centre (Tues–Fri 1–5pm, Sat & Sun 2–5pm; free), which has a small but striking permanent collection of the work of Saskatchewan artists, plus several galleries which display temporary exhibitions; the Sports Hall of Fame, located in the older part of the building (by appointment only ☎783-7849; free), is also part of the centre. After the long winter, the town is ready to host the **Yorkton Short Film and Video Festival** in May, the oldest festival of its kind in North America (1947).

Just south of the city, on the Yellowhead Hwy near Rokeby, is the **Parkland Heritage Centre** (mid-May to Sept Mon–Fri 1–8pm, Sat 1–5pm; $2.50), a modest but interesting group of nineteenth-century pioneer buildings brought here from other parts of Saskatchewan.

The smart **Visitors Information Centre** is located at the junction of hwys 9, 10 and 16 (June–Aug Mon–Fri 8am–6pm, Sat & Sun 9am–5pm; Sept–May Mon–Fri 9am–5pm; ☎783-8707 or 1-877/250-6454, *www.touryorkton.com*) and can supply a good range of information and maps on attractions in Yorkton and the area. If you'll want to stay in Yorkton there are several reasonably priced central **hotels**, including the *Holiday Inn*, 100 Broadway St E (☎783-9781 or 1-800/667-1585, fax 782-2121; ③–⑤); and the *Imperial 400 Motel*, 207 Broadway St E (☎783-6581 or 1-800/781-2268, fax 786-6399; ③), both of which serve great Ukrainian food; and the basic *City Limits Inn*, off Broadway Street at 8 Betts Ave (☎782-2435; ①). A pleasant **B&B** is the *Lazy Maples*, 111 Darlington St W (☎783-7078; ②); the owner is an excellent cook and can serve you Ukrainian *pierogies* for breakfast.

You can camp in town at the well-shaded *City of Yorkton* **campsite** (☎786-1757 or 786-1750; $11–15; mid-May to mid-Oct), on Hwy 16A near the Western Development Museum. For **food**, the *Gladstone Inn*, corner of Broadway Street and Gladstone Avenue, is the place to go – it has excellent prime rib. Yorkton's **bus station**, served by three buses daily from Saskatoon, is located downtown on 1st Avenue.

Duck Mountain Provincial Park and around

Duck Mountain Provincial Park, on the Manitoba border some 100km northeast of Yorkton on hwys 9 and 5, is a rugged continuation of the Manitoba Escarpment (see p.498). One of the more attractive smaller parks in Saskatchewan, it's a paradise for hikers, with an extensive system of walking trails – including one that's fully disabled-accessible – and is open year-round. In winter, the park has some of the best snowmobiling and cross-country skiing in the province. The **parks office** near the lake (year-round; ☎542-3482) has all the information on dates and times of the various activities. One of the most popular attractions are the various **horseback-riding** excursions organized by Coyote Creek Stables, located on Lakeshore Drive, just inside the park's main entrance ($16 per hour; ☎542-3439).

The park centres on the roughly circular **Madge Lake**, ringed with aspens, where you'll find a beach, several stores, canteens, recreational and picnic areas, and places that rent canoes, paddleboats and ski equipment. The chalet-style *Duck Mountain Lodge*, overlooking the lake (☎ & fax 542-3466; ②–④), is a relaxing **place to stay**; you can sleep in the large lodge, the two-bedroom town-house units with fireplaces, or the woodland cabins nearby. There's also a **campsite** at Pickerel Point, 4km east of the main Saskatchewan entrance (☎542-3479; $9–17; mid-May to Aug).

KAMSACK, a small town about 10km west of Duck Mountain, is the best place to **stay** if you want to explore the park. The *Woodlander Inn*, corner of Railway Avenue and 3rd Street (☎542-2125 or 542-2105; ①/②), and the *Duck Mountain Motel*, 335 Queen Elizabeth Blvd E (☎542-2656; ②), are the only two in town and are fairly basic, or there's the more costly *Vintage Country Vacation Farm,* on a rough gravel road 4km south of Norquay off Hwy 49, 40km northwest of the park (☎ & fax 594-2629; ③), an attractive parkland country property incorporating a farmstead, a rustic wooden cabin and a three-bedroom country cottage furnished with period antiques.

Another attractive area is **Good Spirit Lake Provincial Park**, off the Yellowhead Hwy 48km northwest of Yorkton, noted for its ecologically fragile sand dunes and the warm, shallow lake itself, which has exceptionally clear water. Here you'll find fine sandy beaches on the south shore, a petrol station, miniature golf course, tennis courts, riding stables, dining and snacking facilities, plus a **campsite** (☎792-4750 or 786-1463; $15–20; mid-May to Sept).

Veregin

An hour's drive northeast of Yorkton, the tiny town of **VEREGIN** is named after Peter Veregin, the leader of the pacifist Doukhobor sect whose seven thousand members migrated to Saskatchewan at the end of the nineteenth century (see box p.519). The town is home to the **National Doukhobor Heritage Village** (mid-May to mid-Sept daily 10am–6pm, by appointment the rest of the year ☎542-4441 or 542-4370; $3), where a modest museum traces the history of the sect and a large, square, refurbished two-storey prayer home contains the living quarters of their leader, complete with many original furnishings. The building, with its encircling veranda and wrought-iron adornment on both levels, dominates a large green lawn and faces the other buildings of the village, most of which were moved here from Doukhobor colonies in other parts of the province. Lined up in a neat row are a farmhouse, blacksmith's shop, granary, bakery, and bathhouse equipped with dried oak leaves that were used to cleanse the skin and make it fragrant. Another smaller prayer home features a Russian library and a display on Tolstoy, whose financial support helped the Doukhobor to migrate. On the grounds is an imposing bronze statue of the writer, donated by the Soviet Union.

Southern Saskatchewan

The 600-kilometre drive across **southern Saskatchewan** on the **Trans-Canada Highway** is crushingly boring, and apart from Regina the only town worth a stopover is **Moose Jaw**, once a Prohibition hangout of American gangsters, including Al Capone. Otherwise the rest of southern Saskatchewan is mostly undulating farmland, broken up by a handful of lakes and rivers, stretches of arid semi-desert and the odd range of wooded hills. In the southeast corner of the province, the lakes, hillocks and aspen, birch and poplar forests of **Moose Mountain Provincial Park** come complete with campsites, nature trails and a resort village. Further west, just south of Regina and near the US border, it's possible to drive across the **Big Muddy Badlands**, but these weathered buttes and conical hills are best explored on the tours that leave the tiny town of **Coronach** throughout the summer. Directly west of here, the **Grasslands**

National Park is still being developed and extended, two separate slices of prairie punctuated by coulees and buttes that add a rare touch of drama to the landscape. Some 200km further, straddling the Alberta border, **Cypress Hills Interprovincial Park** is also well worth a visit, its heavily forested hills and ridges harbouring a restored Mountie outpost, **Fort Walsh**. Further west, the area to the northwest of the small city of **Swift Current** is home to the **Great Sand Hills**, a starkly beautiful desert landscape. Directly south of that is **Maple Creek**, a quintessentially cowboy town with **Hutterite colonies** nearby.

Apart from the daily bus services along the Trans-Canada, the region's **public transport** system is abysmal – to see the parks, you'll need a car.

Moose Mountain Provincial Park

Moose Mountain Provincial Park, just 60km south of the Trans-Canada on Route 9, 230km from Regina, is a rough rectangle of wooded hill and lake whose main resort, **KENOSEE LAKE**, is packed with holiday-makers throughout the season. There's a full range of amenities here, including a **parks office** (Mon–Fri 8am–5pm; ☎577-2600), restaurants, bars, sports facilities, waterslides and canoe and paddleboat rental, but it's still easy enough to escape the crowds and wander off into the surrounding poplar and birch groves. For **accommodation**, *Kenosee Condos and Gardens* (☎577-2331 or 584-1028, fax 347-7923), in the resort village, has luxurious two-bedroom units (⑤), and there are also a number of **campsites** spread out around the lake. Hotel rooms and cabin rentals are also available through the *Kenosee Inn* (☎577-2099, fax 577-2465; ③/④), which is near two golf courses, tennis courts and waterslides. The *Fish Creek* and *Lynwood* **campsites** (☎577-2611 or 577-2600; $15–20; mid-May to early Sept) have the advantage of being right on the western edge of the developed area, a good 2km from the busiest part of the park. If you're **hungry**, try the *Moose Head Dining Room*, on the lake, which serves pizza, pasta, steaks and Saskatoon berry pie.

A short-lived experiment in transplanting English social customs to the prairies is the subject of the **Cannington Manor Provincial Historic Park** (mid-May to Aug daily except Tues 10am–5pm; $2), a partly reconstructed Victorian village about 30km east of Kenosee Lake. Founded in 1882 by Edward Pierce, the would-be squire, the village attracted a number of British middle-class families determined to live as "gentlemen farmers", running small agricultural businesses, organizing tea and croquet evenings and even importing a pack of hounds to stage their own hunts. Their efforts failed when the branch rail line was routed well to the south of Cannington Manor, and by 1900 the settlement was abandoned.

Moose Jaw

MOOSE JAW, 70km west of Regina, was founded as a railway depot in 1882 and is now Saskatchewan's fourth largest city, with 35,000 inhabitants – a number that has remained almost static since the 1940s. It achieved some notoriety during Prohibition in the 1920s, when liquor was smuggled south by car or by train along the Soo Line, which ran from Moose Jaw to Chicago. For most locals this period of bootleggers, gangsters, gamblers and "boozoriums" – liquor warehouses – was not a happy one, and for years various schemes to attract tourists by developing the "Roaring Twenties" theme met with considerable opposition from the substantial portion of the population that actually experienced them. Those suffering from aches and pains, however, welcomed the 1995 opening of the wonderful **Temple Gardens Mineral Spa**, 24 Fairford St E (Sun–Thurs 9am–11pm, Fri & Sat 9am–midnight; single swim $6.95, day-pass $10, Tues half-price) where you can soak in pools of mineral-rich hot waters piped from an underground spring 1km away. For a treat, take a dip in the outdoor pool when it's snowing or at sunset. Funded by hundreds of local shareholders – undeterred by the seemingly incongruous idea of a spa in Moose Jaw – Temple Gardens has brought droves of new visitors to the town and allowed Moose Jaw to develop new attractions like the Tunnels of Little Chicago that focus on and somewhat glorify the town's history. Millions of dollars are being spent to revitalize the downtown area in time for the town's centenary in 2003 (the town gained city status in 1903), so expect some changes. As for the town's curious name, it may have come from an Indian word for "warm breezes", or the jaw-like turn the river takes just outside town, or even the repairs made to a cartwheel by an early pioneer with the assistance of a moose's jawbone.

The **downtown** area is bisected by Main Street, running from north to south, and Manitoba Street, the east–west axis, which is adjacent to the railway line and the Moose Jaw river. The central area is for the moment at least, dispiriting, though a string of **murals** of early pioneer days, concentrated along 1st Avenue NW between Manitoba and Hochelaga streets, do their best to cheer things up. That apart, some of the streets look like they haven't changed much since the 1920s, the wide treeless avenues framed by solemn brick warehouses and hotels and porticoed banks. One block north of Manitoba, the best example is **River Street**, whose rough-and-ready *Royal* and *Brunswick* hotels were once favourite haunts of the gangsters – the street is earmarked for redevelopment in the near future as a cobbled, partly pedestrian street with an amphitheatre for shows.

A network of **tunnels** runs underneath River Street from the basements of the old buildings. No-one knows who built the tunnels, or why. What is known is that they were extended and used in the early 1900s by Chinese railway workers and their families hoping to escape the $500 'head-tax', a measure designed to force them to return to famine-stricken China after the completion of their work on the railway. Later, during Prohibition, Chicago gangsters used the tunnels to negotiate their deals for Canada's liquor supplies and to hide out when things got too 'hot' in Chicago. For a taste of early Moose Jaw history, the city has three **Tunnels of Moose Jaw tours** (daily: 10am–8pm, every 20min; 45min; one tour $11, combination ticket $18); the **Chicago Connection**, a light-hearted look at the capers of Al Capone's men in the tunnels, complete with a speakeasy, police bust and an actor playing the particularly slimy Chief of Police; the more serious **Passage to Fortune**, which tells the horrific story of the Chinese immigrants with re-creations of a Chinese laundry, sweatshops, a herbalist and an opium den; and the **Bootleggers Run**, a comic look at the lives of local bootleggers that features the old train station, now, ironically, a massive liquor store. Costumed guides ham it up, helped by state-of-the-art animatronics – moving, talking mannequins – and old movies through the network of narrow tunnels beneath Main Street. Tours begin at Tunnel Central, 16 Main St North, in a reception area with a beautiful copper ceiling and walls adorned with local photos from the early decades of the twentieth century.

A replica of one of Moose Jaw's original electric trams, the **Moose Jaw Trolley** travels the local sights with a guide who dwells on the town's shady past (May–Sept, 3 daily; Oct–Dec Thurs–Sat 2 daily; 1hr 15min; $8); it leaves from opposite Temple Gardens and from the *Heritage Inn* on Main Street. You can also ride the trolley without a guide (May–Dec Thurs–Sat 11am–3pm; $2) to Moose Jaw's branch of the **Western Development Museum** (Jan–March daily except Mon 9am–6pm; April–Dec daily 9am–6pm; $6), about 2km from the centre, beside the Trans-Canada as it loops around the northern edge of town. Divided into sections covering air, land, water and rail transport, the museum exhibits include a replica of a steamship, several Canadian Pacific railway coaches, a number of fragile old planes, and a 1934 Buick car converted to carry the chief superintendent up and down the rail line.

Moose Jaw is also home to the precision-flying team the **Snowbirds** who zoom across the huge prairie skies at the Saskatchewan Airshow in July ($10).

Practicalities

Moose Jaw's **bus station**, 63 High St E (☎692-2345), is a couple of minutes' walk from Main Street and two blocks north of Manitoba Street, and is served by four to six buses daily from Regina; there are no trains. The **Tourism Moose Jaw** bureau (mid-May to mid-Sept daily 9am–8pm; mid-May Mon–Fri 9am–8pm; ☎692-0555, *www.moosejaw.net/tourism*) is next to a giant concrete moose near the Western Development Museum. The tourist office will be getting a new building in 2001 – look out for the model planes on the roof.

The town has several reasonably priced, central **hotels** and **motels**, including the recently renovated and good value *Capone's Hideaway Theme Motel*, 1 Main St N opposite the defunct train station (☎692-6422 or 1-877/443-2929; ②), where the rooms have been given a 1920s feel; alternatively the *Midtown Hideaway Hotel* is also centrally located at 132 Athabasca St E (☎692-0601; ②). Further out there's a *Comfort Inn,* 155 Thatcher Drive W (☎693-6266 or 1-800/228-5150; ④) and nearby the *Super 8 Motel*, 1706 Main St N (☎692-8888 or 1-800/800-8000; ③). The four-star *Temple Gardens Mineral Spa*, 24 Fairford St East (☎694-5055 or 1-800/718-7727, fax 694-8310; ④–⑦), has luxurious rooms (each with its own jacuzzi, using chlorine-free mineral waters) and spa suites, geothermal pools and facilities for massage, facials, reflexology and hydrotherapy treatments – guests receive a free rubber duck, too. Book well in advance: this is Saskatchewan's most popular hotel. The *Redland Cottage* **B&B** in a tree-lined residential area at 1122 Redland Ave (☎694-5563, fax 693-8933; ②/③) has comfortable bedrooms and full breakfasts. The *River Park Campground* (☎692-5474; mid-April to mid-Oct) is 2km southeast of the centre at 300 River Drive, with sites from $13–18 per night.

Moose Jaw's restaurants would never win any culinary awards, but there are a few worthwhile places to fill your stomach. The *Copper Café*, part of the Yvette Moore Gallery in the 1910 Land Titles building at 76 Fairford St W, has wonderful daily specials, and the adjacent gallery features work by Yvette Moore and her prairie contemporaries (Jan–April Mon–Sat 10am–5pm; May–Dec Mon–Sat 10am–5pm, Sun 1–4pm; free). *Houston Pizza and Steak House*, 117 Main St North, has Italian dishes from $6; the *National Café*, 20 Main St, has a good-value daily smorgasbord; the *Prairie Oasis Restaurant*, junction of Hwy 1 East and Thatcher Drive, specializes in freshly baked pies; and the *Hopkins Dining Parlour*, 65 Athabasca St West, located in a pleasant Victorian house, is a more formal affair with a wide-ranging menu and main courses from $18. For something more exotic, try the well-recommended but unappealingly named *Nit's Thai Food*, 124 Main St N, which has main courses from $6. *Suntree*, 23 Main St N, opposite Tunnel Central, is a coffee house with massive cups of coffee, a twee gift shop and Internet access and, on the other side of the street, *Cash Cable Café* still features the complicated cash carrier system used by department stores, before the invention of the till, that carried shoppers' cash by cable to the accountants upstairs. It's one of only two in the world still operating and was kept in Moose Jaw despite Euro-Disney's attempts to purchase it.

The Big Muddy Badlands

At the end of the last Ice Age, torrents of meltwater produced a massive gash in the landscape to the south of the site of Moose Jaw, near the US border. Edged by rounded hills and flat-topped buttes that rise up to 200m above the valley floor, the **Big Muddy Valley** can best be explored with organized tours from dreary **CORONACH**, about 200km from Regina (July–Aug Sat & Sun; at other times from June–Sept, tours by appointment; $25 by minibus, $10 in your own car with a guide; ☎267-3312 or 267-2150). The tours include: visits to Indian burial cairns; the dramatic **Castle Butte**, a sandstone formation rising above the plains that resembles the backdrop for an American

Western movie; and a couple of outlaw caves, the refuge of American rustlers and rob-
bers like Butch Cassidy and Dutch Henry. Cassidy and his gang, the Wild Bunch,
established an outlaw trail that connected the Big Muddy with Mexico via a series of
safe houses; their antics were curtailed by the arrival of a detachment of Mounties in
1904 led by a certain Corporal Bird, known ruefully as the "man who never sleeps". The
tourist information centre on the highway (mid-June to Aug 9am–7pm; ☎267-3312)
can provide information on the history and geography of the area. If you **stay** in
Coronach there's the *Country Boy Motel* at the junction of hwys 18 and 36, opposite the
Pioneer Grain elevator (☎267-3267; ①–③) with complimentary coffee and fridges in
each of its 21 rooms and the very basic but clean and friendly four-room *Coronach Hotel*
on Main Street (☎267-2063; ①).The only places worth **eating** at are the coffee shop in
the small Coronach Mall, 111 Centre St, and the Chinese *Chopsticks* restaurant at 341
Railway Ave E.

Grasslands National Park and the Eastend area

Directly west of the Big Muddy, accessible along Hwy 18, the **Grasslands National Park**
is predominantly mixed-grass prairie, a flat, bare badlands landscape broken up by splendid coulees, buttes and river valleys – notably the wide ravine edging the Frenchman River
in the western block. Far from the moderating influence of the oceans, the area has a savage climate, with an average low in January of -22°C and temperatures that soar to 40°C
in summer. Even so, this terrain is inhabited by many species that are adapted to cope with
the shortage of water, from flora such as prairie grasses, greasewood, rabbit brush, sagebrush and different types of cacti, to fauna like the graceful pronghorn antelope, the rattlesnake and Canada's only colonies of black-tailed prairie dog.

In 1994, one of only thirteen Tyrannosaurus Rex skeletons in the world was discovered 40km south of the 695-strong town of **EASTEND**, 150km west of the park. The T-
Rex was named Scotty, after the bottle of scotch its discoverers consumed in celebration, and there is now a swish $3.4 million **T-Rex Interpretive Centre** on the gravel
Grid Road no.614 1km north of town (May–Sept daily 9am–5pm; Oct–April Mon–Fri
9am–noon & 1–5pm, Sat & Sun 11am–4pm; $3; ☎295-4009) – the place to hit if you're
travelling with children or suffer from dinomania. Well-informed guides take you
around the museum to view Scotty's bones and serrated teeth as each tiny fragment is
identified in order to piece the skeleton together. Other real and replica fossils – including prehistoric poo – and bones from prehistoric mammals are on display whilst fun
hands-on exhibits, beneath murals of T-Rex, allow you to "arm-wrestle" the beast and
examine vertebrae. A life-size replica of Scotty's skeleton is expected to be on view by
2001 If you're keen on the prehistory of the area, you may want to join one of the
Dinocountry tours (☎295-4009), which depart from the centre to visit a **fossil quarry**
where you can watch paleontologists unearthing fossils (July & Aug daily at 9am, noon
& 3pm; 3hr; $20). For a more hands-on experience there's an **archeological site** for
dinosaur bones near Eastend, where you can dig yourself (July & Aug daily 8.30am;
$50). In the town itself a **museum and cultural centre** with a small **information cen-
tre** located in the old theatre on Red Coat Drive (July & Aug daily 10am–8pm, mid-May
to June by appointment ☎295-3375; $2), featuring paleontological exhibits and a pioneer
log house from the early twentieth-century.

If you want to base yourself in Eastend for a more thorough exploration of the park
and the Frenchman River Valley, you could **stay** at the *Riverside Motel*, just west of town
on Hwy 13 (☎295-3630 or 295-3773; ①/②), which also has **camping** on its grounds for
$1, or at the basic but comfortable *Cypress Hotel*, 343 Red Coat Drive (☎295-3505; ①) in
the middle of town. For **food** *Alleykatz*, 115 Fir Ave, offers up coffees and bagels and
has a gift shop that sells pottery made from the local white-clay. For something more
substantial like hamburgers there's *Jack's Café* on Red Coat Drive.

At present, Grasslands National Park consists of east and west sections separated by private ranches and farms, which the federal government eventually intends to buy, creating a single park stretching from Hwy 4 in the west to Hwy 2/18 in the east. The **west** section is both more scenic and accessible, its limited system of gravel tracks and roads cutting off from hwys 18 and 4, south and east of **VAL MARIE**. This tiny township houses the **Grasslands National Park Reception Centre**, at the junction of Hwy 4 and Centre Street (mid-May to Aug daily 8am–5pm; Sept to mid-May Mon–Fri 8am–noon & 1–4.30pm; ☎298-2257), whose rangers provide advice on weather and road conditions, hand out maps, arrange for guided or self-guided eco-tours, issue camping permits and give tips on animal-spotting and hiking. There are no **campsites** within the park, but camping is allowed within 1km of its roads – take a good supply of water, a stout pair of walking shoes, and a stick to sweep in front of you in tall grass or brush as a warning to rattlesnakes. Animal activity is at its height at dawn and dusk and during spring and autumn; whatever the season, you'll need a pair of binoculars. One of the best hikes is the one to the 70 Mile Butte, a massive flat-topped promontory that is the highest point of land in the region, rising 100m above the valley floor with wonderful views of the waving prairie grasslands all around. To get there, drive south of Val Marie on Hwy 4 and turn east at Butte Road and continue to the end of the road. While there is no marked trail, the way becomes obvious as you begin walking over the hills from the end of the road. Even just a couple of hours' walk will take you through exceptional country.

The only places to **stay** in town are the *Val Marie Hotel*, 221 Centre St (☎298-2007 or 298-2003, fax 298-4612; ①), with seven basic rooms, and a centrally located **campsite** (☎298-2022; May–Oct), where sites cost $7–10. It won't take you long to find the town's only **restaurant**, the antiquated *Rusty's Café* at 217 Centre St.

Swift Current, Maple Creek and around

Driving west from Moose Jaw along the Trans-Canada Highway, it's about 180km to **SWIFT CURRENT**, a small industrial city and farm-research centre that's mostly a convenient stopoff on the long journey on the Trans-Canada between Regina and Calgary, in Alberta. It has limited attractions for the visitor, but if you decide to stay here drop into the helpful **tourist office**, at the junction of hwys 1 and 4 (May–Sept daily 9am–7pm; Oct–April Mon–Fri 9am–noon & 1–5pm; ☎773-7268). The **bus** station is at 143 4th Ave NW, serviced by three buses daily from Regina and one from Saskatoon.

Swift Current has a few modest attractions, the best of which are in **Kinetic Park**, at 17th Avenue and South Railway Street East, where you'll find a **Mennonite Heritage Village** (June–Sept Fri–Sun 2–8pm; other times by appointment on ☎773-7685 or 773-6068; free), consisting of a long rectangular house and adjoining barn built in 1911–15 and six buildings comprising **Doc's Town** (July–Sept Fri–Sun 1–9pm; other times by appointment on ☎773-2944; $2), a replica of an early twentieth-century prairie village – highlights are a fully functioning windmill, a one-room prairie schoolhouse, and an old dance hall (now a tearoom), transported here from a rural Saskatchewan town. The only other worthwhile stopoff is the **Art Gallery of Swift Current**, 411 Herbert St E (Mon–Thurs 2–5pm & 7–9pm, Fri–Sun 1–5pm; July & Aug closed Sun; free), where you'll see changing exhibitions of paintings, sculpture and ceramics by artists from Saskatchewan and elsewhere in Canada.

Strung out along the Trans-Canada as it skirts the north of the city, and along Hwy 4 south towards the Montana border, are several comfortable **motels**, the best of which are the deluxe *Best Western Inn*, just off the Trans-Canada on George Street (☎773-4660 or 1-800/528-1234; ③–⑥), the enormous *Imperial 400*, near the Trans-Canada at 1150 Begg St E, which has waterslides (☎773-2033 or 1-800/781-2268; ②/③) or the *Super 8*

THE HUTTERITES

The **Hutterites**, the only prairie community to have maintained a utopian communal ideal, are members of an Anabaptist sect that takes its name from their first leader, Jacob Hutter. Originating in the Tyrol and Moravia in the sixteenth century, they gradually moved east across central Europe, ending up in Russia, which they abandoned for South Dakota in the 1870s. It was fifty years before they felt obliged to move again, their pacifism recoiling from the bellicosity that gripped their American neighbours during World War I. They moved north between 1918 and 1922, and established a series of **colonies** where they were allowed to educate their own children, speak their own language and have no truck with military service. In these largely self-sufficient communities tasks are still divided according to ability and skill, property is owned communally, and social life is organized around a common dining room and dormitories. Economically prosperous, they continue to multiply, a new branch community being founded whenever the old one reaches a secure population of between one hundred and two hundred. Apart from the occasional skirmish with the outside world when they buy new land, the Hutterites have been left in peace and have resisted the pressures of assimilation more staunchly than their kindred spirits, the Mennonites and the Doukhobors (see box p.519).

Motel, 405 North Service Rd E (☎778-6088 or 1-800/800-8000; ②–④, rates include small breakfast), which has a pool. Just north of the Trans-Canada there's a small but convenient **campsite**, *Trail Campground* (☎773-8088; $12–15; May to mid-Oct). For **restaurants**, try *Carol's Diner*, 914 Central Ave N, specializing in Belgian waffles, or *Humpty's*, at the junction of hwys 1 and 4 East, which does a cheap all-day breakfast. Alternatively, head for *Gramma Bep's* on the east side of town on Hwy 1 for berry pies and coffee – a shop inside also sells jams, soups and sauces made to traditional Saskatchewan recipes.

Perhaps the best reason for stopping at Swift Current is its proximity to the **Great Sand Hills**, over 1900 square kilometres of giant active sand dunes, which is home to hordes of hopping kangaroo rats as well as mule deer and antelope. The best place to view the dunes is 1.5km south off Hwy 32, at the village of **SCEPTRE**, to the north of the hills. The small **Great Sandhills Museum** on Hwy 32 (June–Sept Mon–Sat 9am–noon & 1–4pm, Sun 1–5pm; $2) has displays on the ecology of the hills and can provide information about tours.

About 50km further east from the Great Sand Hills, reached by Hwy 32 (or Hwy 4 north from Swift Current), is the pretty little **Saskatchewan Landing Provincial Park**, situated on both banks of the South Saskatchewan River, where it emerges from razorback hills and opens out into the large, finger-like man-made **Lake Diefenbaker**, created in 1967. The park area was once an important river crossing for Native Canadians and early white settlers, and the staff at the **Goodwin House** Visitors' Centre located in the park (June–Sept Mon–Fri 8am–4pm, Sat & Sun 10am–6pm; Oct–May Mon–Fri 8am–4pm; ☎375-5525 or 375-5527), a beautiful circa 1900 stone house built by a retired member of the North West Mounted Police, can organize nature-trail hikes through coulees and explain the significance of the crossing – once one of the most difficult river crossings in western Canada. There are remains of several ancient tepee encampments in the area. You can **camp** in the north of the park at the *Bear Paw Campground* (☎375-5525 or 375-5527; $15–20; mid-May to Oct) and rent kayaks at the small marina ($6 per hour).

From Swift Current it's another 130km to **MAPLE CREEK**, situated just 8km to the south of the highway on the way to the Cypress Hills. Nicknamed "old cow town", Maple Creek lies at the heart of ranching country, and its streets are full of pick-up trucks, cowboy boots and stetsons, reaching wild heights in early September for the **Cowboy Poetry Gathering**, a literary celebration of the wrangler that draws cowboys from across North America. Some of the late nineteenth-century brick storefronts have survived, and the trim and tidy **Old Timers' Museum** at 218 Jasper St (May–Sept Tues–Sat 9am–5.30pm, Sat & Mon 1–5pm; $3) has pleasant displays on pioneer life and the Mounties. The place is also the market town for a number of **Hutterite colonies**, whose women stand out with their floral dresses and headscarves (see box, overleaf).

The Cypress Hills

South of the Trans-Canada Highway, between Maple Creek and Irvine, in Alberta, the wooded ridges of the **Cypress Hills** rise above the plains in a 130-kilometre-long plateau that in places reaches a height of 1400m – the highest point in Canada between Labrador and the Rockies. Because of its elevation, this area was untouched by glaciers as they moved south during the Ice Age, scouring the land bare of vegetation, and the Cypress Hills are an anomaly in the landscape of the prairies, having a wetter and milder climate than the treeless plains that surround them, creating a rich variety of woodland, wetland and grassland. In turn, this comparatively lush vegetation supports a wealth of wildlife, from the relatively rare elk, lynx, bobcat and coyote through to the more common gopher and raccoon, plus about two hundred species of bird, over half of whom breed in the hills. (Watch out for the colonies of long-necked wild turkeys, as well as the sage grouse, whose bizarre courting rituals involve the male swelling out his chest and discharging air with a sound akin to a gunshot.) One surprise – considering the name – is the absence of cypress trees: the early French voyageurs seem to have confused the area's predominant lodgepole pines with the jack pines of Québec, a species they called *cyprès*. Literal-minded translation did the rest.

Cypress Hills Interprovincial Park

In amongst the cattle ranches two separate sections of the Hills have been set aside to form the **Cypress Hills Interprovincial Park** (entry fee $5): Saskatchewan's Centre Block lies to the south of Maple Creek along Hwy 21, and the larger West Block spans the Saskatchewan–Alberta border, accessible from Maple Creek along Hwy 271 in the east and via Alberta's Hwy 41, off the Trans-Canada, in the west. The Saskatchewan part of the West Block is also attached to Fort Walsh National Historic Park, incorporating a partly refurbished Mountie station and a replica of one of the Battle Creek trading posts. The three north–south access highways present no problems, but it's difficult to drive across the park from east to west as the paved road, known as the Gap Road, is interrupted by two long stretches of gravel and clay track that are positively dangerous in wet weather.

Just 30km south of Maple Creek on Hwy 21, a paved side road heads into the park's **Centre Block**, a rough rectangle of hilly land dominated by a forest of lodgepole pines. At the centre, a pleasant tourist resort surrounds tiny **Loch Leven**, complete with canoe- and bike-rental facilities, shops and a petrol station. There's also a modest nature centre adjoining the park's **administration office** (Mon–Thurs 8am–8pm, Fri–Sun 8am–10pm; ☎662-5411), which has useful maps and trail brochures. The resort is a popular holiday destination, but it's easy to escape the crowds along the half-dozen hiking trails. For **accommodation**, there's one **hotel**, the modern *Cypress Park Resort Inn* (☎662-4477), with rooms and cabins (both ②/③) and apartments (③–⑥). Close by, there are several summer **campsites** (all $13–22), which have to be booked at the campsite office on Pine Avenue, to the west of the centre (mid-May to Aug daily 8.30am–10pm; ☎662-4459). Don't **eat** at the resort; instead, head for the *Cypress Park Café*, right on the lake, where tasty home-cooked meals can be had for as little as $6.

The eastern side of the park's **West Block** has alternating areas of thick forest and open grassland broken up by steep hills and deep, sheltered ravines. Hwy 271 enters

THE CYPRESS HILLS MASSACRE

From the mid-eighteenth century, the Cypress Hills lay in a sort of neutral zone between the **Blackfoot** and the **Cree**, whose intermittent skirmishing was small-scale until the 1860s, when the depletion of the Crees' traditional hunting grounds forced them to move west. Some three thousand Cree reached the Cypress Hills in 1865 and the violence began just four years later with the murder of the Cree peacemaker, Maskepetoon. The ensuing war was overshadowed by the Red River rising of 1869–70 in Manitoba, but casualties were high and its effects were compounded by two smallpox epidemics. In 1871 the Cree sued for peace, but both sides were exhausted, their morale, health and social structures further undermined by the whiskey traders who had moved into the region.

These **whiskey traders**, who were mostly American, brought their liquor north in the autumn, returning south in late spring laden with furs and buffalo robes. Though it was illegal to supply the Indians with booze, the traders spread out across the southern plains, aptly nicknamed **Whoop-up Country**, establishing dozens of trading posts whose occupants were protected from their disorderly customers by log stockades. (They needed to be, as the stuff they sold was adulterated with such substances as red ink, gunpowder and strychnine.) In the spring of 1873, there were two such outposts beside **Battle Creek**, deep in the Cypress Hills, owned by a certain Abel Farwell and his rival Moses Solomon. For reasons that remain obscure, though the prevailing drunkenness played a part, this was the scene of a violent confrontation between a group of white wolf-hunters, whiskey traders and a band of Assiniboine. Equipped with the latest fast-action rifles, the hunters riddled an Assiniboine camp with bullets, killing up to seventy (according to some sources) before returning to the trading posts to celebrate. News of the incident, known as the **Cypress Hills Massacre**, filtered back to Ottawa, and this speeded up the recruitment of the newly formed **North West Mounted Police**, who in the autumn received their first posting west as a detachment to Fort MacLeod, near today's Lethbridge, Alberta. They reached it in early 1874, where they set about suppressing the whiskey trade and establishing law and order.

To consolidate their control of the area, the Mounties built **Fort Walsh**, near Battle Creek, the following year. An unpopular posting, the fort was considered "unhealthy, isolated and indefensible", but it could not be abandoned until 1883, when the last of the restless Indian bands were moved to reservations further north. It was during this period that the fort's first inspector, **James Morrow Walsh**, was faced with an extremely delicate situation. In 1876, **Chief Sitting Bull's** Sioux had exterminated General Custer's army at the battle of the Little Bighorn. Fearing reprisals, five thousand Sioux moved north, establishing their camp at Wood Mountain, 350km east of Fort Walsh. Aware of the danger, Walsh rode into the Sioux encampment with just four other constables to insist that they obey Canadian law. This act of bravery established a rough rapport between the two leaders, and by his tactful dealings with the Sioux Walsh enhanced the reputation of the Mounties, whose efficiency ensured there were no more massacres in the Canadian west.

this section from the east and becomes increasingly bumpy as it twists south towards the **Fort Walsh National Historic Park** and **Visitors Information Centre** (mid-May to Aug daily 9am–5.30pm; ☎662-3590 or off-season ☎662-2645), which has excellent displays on the Plains Indians, the history of the fort and the development of the RCMP.

A five-minute walk behind the information centre, **Fort Walsh** (mid-May to Aug daily 9.30am–5.30pm; $8) sits in a wide, low-lying valley, its trim stockade framed by pine forests. Built in 1875, the fort was abandoned in favour of Maple Creek just eight years later; in 1942 the RCMP acquired the land, and most of the present buildings date from that decade. Guides in period costumes enliven a tour of whitewashed log buildings, the whole site having returned to its original appearance. Close to the fort is a cemetery containing the tombstones of several North West Mounted Police officers.

Every 45 minutes a minibus makes the trip from the information centre over the hills to Battle Creek, where Abel Farwell's whiskey **trading post** has been reconstructed to commemorate the 1873 Cypress Hills Massacre (see box, overleaf). Guides will also take you to the actual site of the Massacre.

The main **accommodation** in this part of the park is the *West Block Campground* (☎662-3606; $13; May to mid-Nov), 5km north of Fort Walsh, in a dense stand of spindly lodgepole pines and with a babbling brook running through it. It's in an isolated spot, so take your own food and drink. From the campsite you can make an expedition to the **Conglomerate Cliffs**, a few kilometres to the northeast near Adams Lake. These are strange-looking walls of rock, some 150m high, composed of multicoloured cobblestones.

There are a variety of guided **tours** of both the Centre and West blocks that will help you to better appreciate the rugged beauty of the area and the high-altitude flora and fauna – much of which is found nowhere else in western Canada except the Rocky Mountains. A tour of the Centre Block (2hr; $65) includes trips to Lookout Point and Bald Butte on the edge of the park, where there are panoramic views north down into the valleys and plains. The more rugged West Block can be experienced on longer tours (4hr, $140; 6hr, $180) that take you over the bone-rattling Gap Road to points of interest such as Fort Walsh and the Conglomerate Cliffs. All tours are led by trained local guides; to book, call ☎662-5411 (Mon–Fri 8am–5pm).

The lodgepole forests and deep coulees of the **Alberta section** of the park are centred on the tourist resort of **ELKWATER**, 34km south of the Trans-Canada on Hwy 41. Curving round the southern shore of Elkwater Lake, the village has a comprehensive range of facilities, from boat and bike rental through to a sandy beach and sauna baths. There's also a **park office** (Mon–Fri 8.15am–noon & 1–4.30pm; ☎403/893-3777) and a **visitors centre** (mid-May to early Sept Mon–Fri 10am–6pm; ☎403/893-3833), which has maps and hiking brochures and runs guided walks throughout the summer. For **accommodation**, there's the *Green Tree Motel* (☎ and fax 403/893-3811; ②/③), which also has self-contained cabins, while the *Elkwater Campground* is relatively luxurious, with both simple and hooked-up sites.

Southwest of Elkwater, a paved road leads to Horseshoe Canyon and **Head of the Mountain**, where there are striking views over the hills towards Montana; other roads lead east to Reesor Lake and Spruce Coulee Reservoir. Beside the roads there are twelve other **campsites**, bookable through the visitors centre.

Saskatoon

Set on the wide South Saskatchewan River at the heart of a vast wheat-growing area, **SASKATOON** is a commercial, manufacturing and distribution centre with a population of around 236,000 – making it Saskatchewan's largest city and, in the opinion of many of its inhabitants, a better claimant to the title of provincial capital than Regina. Ontario Methodists founded the town as a temperance colony in 1883 and named it after the purple berry that grows in the region, but in spite of their enthusiasm the new settlement made an extremely slow start, partly because the semi-arid farming conditions were unfamiliar to them and partly because the Northwest Rebellion of 1885 raised fears of Indian hostility. Although the railroad reached Saskatoon in 1890, there were still only 113 inhabitants at the beginning of the twentieth century. In the next decade, however, there was a sudden influx of European and American settlers and, as the agricultural economy of the prairies expanded, so the city came to be dominated by a group of entrepreneurs nicknamed **boomers**, under whose management Saskatoon became the economic focus of the region. This success was underpinned by the development of a particularly sharp form of municipal loyalty – people who dared criticize

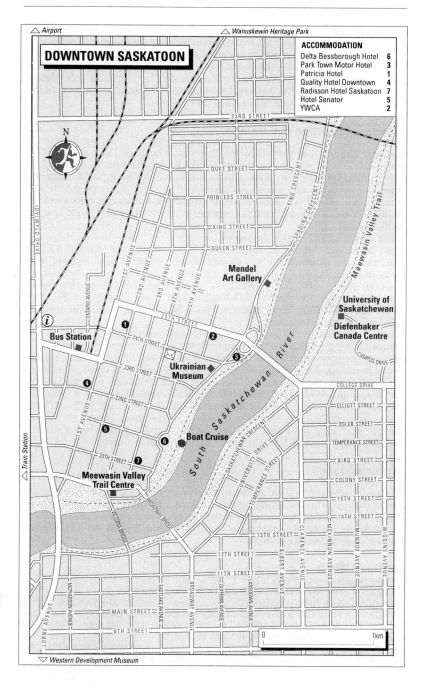

△ Airport   △ Wanuskewin Heritage Park

DOWNTOWN SASKATOON

ACCOMMODATION

Delta Bessborough Hotel	6
Park Town Motor Hotel	3
Patricia Hotel	1
Quality Hotel Downtown	4
Radisson Hotel Saskatoon	7
Hotel Senator	5
YWCA	2

N

33RD STREET

DUKE STREET

PRINCESS STREET

KING STREET

QUEEN STREET

**Mendel
Art Gallery**

**University of
Saskatchewan**

**Diefenbaker
Canada Centre**

CAMPUS DRIVE

IDYLWYLD DRIVE

ONTARIO AVENUE

1ST AVENUE
2ND AVENUE
3RD AVENUE
4TH AVENUE
5TH AVENUE

SPADINA CRESCENT

KING CRESCENT

Meewasin Valley Trail

25TH STREET

ⓘ
Bus Station

❶

❷

24TH STREET

23RD STREET

❸

South Saskatchewan River

COLLEGE DRIVE

ELLIOTT STREET

OSLER STREET

TEMPERANCE STREET

AIRD STREET

COLONY STREET

15TH STREET

14TH STREET

❹

22ND STREET

**Ukrainian
Museum**

❺

❻ **Boat Cruise**

SASKATCHEWAN CRESCENT

UNIVERSITY DRIVE

TEMPERANCE STREET

1ST AVENUE

20TH STREET

❼

**Meewasin Valley
Trail Centre**

△ Train Station

VICTORIA BRIDGE

BROADWAY BRIDGE

13TH STREET

12TH STREET

11TH STREET

CLARENCE AVENUE

ALBERT AVENUE

LANSDOWNE AVENUE

MCKINNON AVENUE

MUNROE AVENUE

WIGGINS AVENUE

MCPHERSON AVENUE

EASTLAKE AVENUE

BROADWAY AVENUE

DUFFERIN AVENUE

MAIN STREET

8TH STREET

LORNE AVENUE

0   1km

▽ Western Development Museum

any aspect of the city, from the poor quality of the water to tyrannical labour practices, were dubbed **knockers**, and their opinions were rubbished by the press. The boomers established a city where community solidarity overwhelmed differences in income and occupation, a set of attitudes that palpably still prevails, making this a pleasant, well-groomed place, albeit one with just a trio of principal tourist attractions – the **Mendel Art Gallery**, a branch of the **Western Development Museum** and, on the outskirts, **Wanuskewin**, a complex dedicated to the Plains Indians.

Arrival, information and transport

Saskatoon **airport**, 7km northwest of the city centre, is connected to downtown by taxi (roughly $15); otherwise, the nearest bus service is #21, which leaves from the junction of Airport Drive and 45th Street, a five-minute walk from the terminal building. The **train station** is 7km west of the town centre, on Chappell Drive, a five-minute walk from the route of bus #3 on Dieppe Street; a taxi to the downtown core costs about $15. Far more convenient is the city's **bus station**, in the centre at 23rd Street East and Pacific Avenue.

The main office of **Tourism Saskatoon** (mid-May to Aug Mon–Fri 8.30am–7pm, Sat & Sun 10am–7pm; Sept to mid-May Mon–Fri 8.30am–5pm; ☎242-1206 or 1-800/567-2444, *www.city.saskatoon.sk.ca*) is in the old CP train station at 6-305 Idylwyld Drive North. In addition to maps and brochures, it has copies of *The Broadway Theatre*, a free bimonthly news sheet that carries details of cultural events. There's also an information centre at the corner of Avenue C North and 47th Street (mid-May to Aug daily 10am–7pm; ☎242-1206). The local newspaper, *The Star Phoenix*, has bland reviews and nightlife listings at the weekend.

Saskatoon's compact city centre is best explored on **foot**, though it takes a little time to work out the street plan, due to the fact that most streets and avenues are given numbers, not names; streets run east–west; avenues, north–south. Edged to the south and east by the river and the adjacent strip of city park, the **downtown core** is bounded by 25th Street East to the north and 1st Avenue to the west. Numbered sequentially, these central **streets** are all "East", with their western extensions starting at either 1st Avenue or Idylwyld Drive. However, the **avenues** change from "South" to "North" right in the centre at 22nd Street East. For the suburbs, **Saskatoon Transit** (☎975-3100) operates an efficient and fairly comprehensive bus-transport system, with a standard adult fare of $1.50 (pay on board; call ☎975-3100 for routes and times).

Accommodation

Saskatoon has a good choice of downtown **hotels** with prices starting at around $40 per double, through to luxury accommodation for about $160. Cheap and convenient alternatives include a YWCA and summer **youth hostel** for women, and a **campsite**. There are also lots of reasonably priced **motels** on Hwy 11 south of town and Hwy 16 going east, with standard facilities (②–④).

Hotels and motels

Colonial Square Motel, 1301 8th St E (☎343-1676 or 1-800/667-3939, fax 956-1313). Eighty simple singles and doubles, all with cable TV. Close to the Broadway Ave area. ③.

Delta Bessborough Hotel, 601 Spadina Crescent and 21st St E (☎683-6910 or 1-888/590-2377, fax 653-2458). Built for the CNR in 1931, the *Bessborough* is an enormous turreted and gabled affair that has been tastefully refurbished in a "French chateau" style that makes it the city's most striking building. Set in Kiwanis Memorial Park, beside the river. ④–⑦.

Park Town Motor Hotel, 924 Spadina Crescent and 25th St E (☎244-5564 or 1-800/667-3999, fax 665-8698). Newly renovated large hotel with river views. Excellent weekend rates. ③.

Patricia Hotel, 345 2nd Ave N at 25th St E (☎242-8861, fax 664-1119). Easily the best of the low-budget hotels – clean, basic dorms, singles and doubles. Free parking. Dorms $12, rooms ①.

Quality Hotel Downtown, 90 22nd St E (☎244-2311 or 1-800/668-4442, fax 664-2234). Conveniently located downtown high-rise hotel. Rooms have complimentary coffee and king-size beds. Undergoing renovations at the time of writing. ④.

Radisson Hotel Saskatoon, 405 20th St E (☎665-3322 or 1-800/333-3333, fax 665-5531). Tower block with luxurious rooms. Fourteen en suites. Good weekend rates. ④–⑥.

Hotel Senator, 243 21st St E at 3rd Ave (☎244-6141). One of the cheapest places in town, but with primitive rooms. ②.

Bed and breakfasts

Brighton House, 1308 5th Ave N (☎664-3278). Nonsmoking clapboard house with a pretty garden and equally flowery bedrooms furnished with antiques. One suite has a private bathroom and sun patio whilst upstairs a family suite is large enough for kids to play in. There's also a hot tub and the use of bikes and a croquet set. ②.

Caswell Bed & Breakfast, 31st St W and Idylwyld Drive (☎933-2249). A down-home, family-style B&B, on a quiet residential street, with three cosy rooms, one en suite with bay window. They also provide pick-up and return to the airport or bus station. ②.

College Drive Lodge, 1020 College Drive (☎665-9111). Budget air-conditioned rooms; laundry, kitchen, complimentary coffee and tea; free parking. Close to University of Saskatchewan. ①.

The Inn, 702 8th Ave N (☎975-3959). Large, comfortable, nonsmoking rooms, with kitchenette and TV room, and free parking. In a pretty residential area close to the Meewasin Valley Trail and the Mendel Art Gallery. ②.

Ninth Street Bed & Breakfast, 227 9th St E (☎224-3754). Three attractive suites with shared bath and great gourmet breakfasts. Bike rental is also provided. In the historic Nutana district and near the Broadway Ave area. ②.

Savelia's Guesthouse, 330 6th Ave N (☎653-4646, fax 653-2017). In a cottage-style, white, wooden house. Old-world atmosphere, with attractively decorated, nonsmoking rooms. Near Mendel Art Gallery and Ukrainian Museum. ①/②.

Hostels and campsites

Gordon Howe Campsite, Ave P S, off 11th St (☎975-3328 or 975-3331). Most comfortable and central of the three city campsites, located near the South Saskatchewan River, 4km south of the centre. Over 130 serviced sites, with barbecue, picnic area, laundry and on-site manager. Open mid-April to Sept. $16–18.

Saskatoon 16 West RV Park, Hwy 16, 1.5km northwest of the city (☎931-8905 or 1-800/478-7833). Twenty-five pull-through sites, plus fifty serviced sites with electric and water hook-ups. Convenience shop on grounds selling Saskatchewan crafts. Open April–Oct. $18–21.50.

University of Saskatchewan, 91 Campus Drive (☎966-8600). Dorm accommodation in student residences. May–Oct. ①.

YWCA Residence, 510 25th St E, at 5th Ave N (☎244-0944, fax 653-2468). Accommodation for single women; long- and short-term stays possible, with good weekly and monthly rates. At the same address, the *YWCA Summer Youth Hostel* offers dormitory beds (①) from June to August for women only. ③.

The City

Most of Saskatoon's principal sights are on or near the **Meewasin Valley Trail**, a circular, nineteen-kilometre walking and cycle route that follows the narrow strip of park along both banks of the river between the Idylwyld Drive and Circle Drive bridges. At the start of the trail, the **Meewasin Valley Centre**, 3rd Avenue South at 19th Street East (Mon–Fri 9am–5pm, Sat & Sun 10.30am–5pm; free; ☎665-6888), provides a useful introduction to the region's history and geography with the aid of maps, old photographs and a video film; a well-stocked gift shop is part of the centre, and there's also a tourist information office (same hours as centre).

A few minutes' walk from the Valley Centre, along the west bank, the **Ukrainian Museum of Canada**, 910 Spadina Crescent E at 24th Street East (May–Sept Mon–Sat 10am–5pm, Sun 1–5pm; Oct–April closed Mon; $2), is the more interesting of the city's two Ukrainian museums, representing the Orthodox as distinct from the Catholic tradition. Displays cover the history of Ukrainian migration, traditional textile design, festivals and Easter-egg painting, the most appealing Ukrainian folk art.

The **Mendel Art Gallery**, overlooking the river from Spadina Crescent, just north of 25th Street East (daily 9am–9pm; free), features temporary shows of modern Canadian and international art. The gallery is named after local magnate Fred Mendel, whose personal collection includes paintings by many of the country's renowned artists – Emily Carr, Lawren Harris and David Milne – and a good selection of Inuit sculpture, a small sample of which is always on display. The building also has a delightful conservatory heaving with plants, a snack bar and an excellent gift shop.

Across the river from the Mendel Art Gallery, over University Bridge, the campus of the **University of Saskatchewan**, with a number of dignified grey-stone buildings in Gothic Revival style, occupies a prime riverbank site just to the north of College Drive. Departmental collections include a **Museum of Antiquities**, in the Murray Building (May to mid-Aug daily 9am–4pm; Sept–April Mon–Fri 9am–noon; closed mid-Dec to mid-Jan; free); and the small **Kenderdine Gallery** (Mon–Fri 11.30am–4.30pm, Sun 12.30–5pm; donation). Neither of these draws as many visitors as the **Diefenbaker Canada Centre**, a museum, archive and research centre at the west end of the campus, beside the river (Mon, Fri & Sat 9.30am–4.30pm, Tues–Thurs 9.30am–8pm, Sun 12.30–5pm; $2). Prime minister from 1957 to 1963, John Diefenbaker was a caricaturist's dream with his large flat face, protruding teeth and wavy white hair, and the museum's high point is its assortment of newspaper cartoons. He was buried just outside the centre in 1979. One of the finest **views** of the city, across the river, is from the grounds of the centre.

Cruises along the South Saskatchewan River, with its weir, sand bars and fast-flowing currents, are organized by Shearwater Boat Cruises on its ship, the *Saskatoon Lady* (May–Aug daily at noon, 1.30pm, 3pm, 4.30pm, 6pm & 7.30pm, additional cruise at 10.30am in July & Aug and at 9pm in May & June; 1hr; $10; ☎549-2452 or 1-888/747-7572); the boat departs from the wharf at the Mendel Art Gallery.

Western Development Museum

On the south side of the river, 8km from the centre, is the Saskatoon branch of the **Western Development Museum**, 2610 Lorne Ave S (Jan–March Tues–Sun 9am–5pm; April–Dec daily same hours; $6), a few minutes' walk from the route of bus #1 from 2nd Avenue in downtown. The principal exhibit here is **Boomtown**, an ambitious reconstruction of a typical Saskatchewan small-town main street circa 1910, complete with boardwalk sidewalks and parked vehicles. More like a film set than a museum, its mixture of replica and original buildings includes a school, a general store, a church, a theatre, a train station and a combined pool hall and barbershop. There's a shop with a range of unusual gifts, and the *Boomtown Café* serves delicious home-cooked meals with a pioneer flavour.

Wanuskewin Heritage Park

Wanuskewin Heritage Park, RR#4 (May to mid-Sept daily 9am–9pm; mid-Sept to April Wed–Sun 9am–5pm; $6.50), twenty-minutes' drive north of the city centre along Warman and Wanuskewin Roads, is designed to be Saskatoon's principal tourist attraction, a lavish tribute to the culture of the Northern Plains Indians – and it's well worth the trip out here, as the commercial aspect is played down in favour of a sensitive interpretation of the Indians' spiritual relationship to the land and to living creatures. Bordering the South Saskatchewan River in the attractive wooded Opamihaw Valley, the park embraces a string of marshy creeks and wooded ridges that have been used by native peoples for more than six thousand years. All along the trails are ecologically fragile plants and flowers that must not be picked. The nineteen sites are connected by trails and walkways to a visitor centre that features reconstructions of tepees, a buffalo pound and a buffalo jump as well as displays on traditional skills as diverse as tool-making and storytelling. For about $49 per person, the park can also arrange for overnight camping in tepees with breakfast, dinner cooked on the fire and interpretive programmes including storytelling and bannock-making (mid-May to Sept), plus longer sessions of two or three nights (book on ☎931-6767). There are also dance demonstrations at the centre (daily 2pm), as well as demonstrations of tepee-raising and simulated buffalo-hunting. The attached **restaurant** specializes in indigenous foodstuffs such as buffalo meat and bannock bread; a gift shop has a full range of authentic arts and crafts by native people. Wanuskewin has been developed with the co-operation of local native peoples, who provide most of the interpretive staff. There is no public transport to Wanuskewin.

Around Saskatoon

Redberry Lake World Biosphere Reserve, about 100km northwest of Saskatoon via hwys 16, 340 and 40 (☎549-2149 or 549-4612), is one of the province's best areas to view over two hundred species of birds. The UNESCO-recognized World Biosphere Reserve (mid-May to mid-Sept daily 10am–6pm; free), on the north shore of the lake, is home to several rare species, including piping plovers and white pelicans. There are trails around the lakeshore, and the Stuart Houston Ecology Centre (mid-May to mid-Sept daily 9am–5pm; ☎549-2400), an interpretive centre with videos and dioramas on the lake's fragile ecosystem. Boat tours (☎1-888/747-7572; 1hr; $25), guided walking tours ($3 per person) and information on a driving tour of the region can also be booked at the centre. Within the reserve, the Redberry Lake Regional Park has **camping** ($8–12).

In the opposite direction, some 120km east of Saskatoon via hwys 16 and 2, is **Little Manitou Lake**. Set in a rather arid landscape, it looks just like any other lake, until you submerge yourself in its murky waters – or rather try to, for it has a saline content three times saltier than ocean water and denser than that of the Dead Sea. You'll find yourself floating on the surface, feet up. The lake has long been known for its healing properties, even by the Indians in the eighteenth and nineteenth centuries, who camped on its shores and called it "lake of the healing waters". You can reach the lake from Saskatoon by bus (Mon, Wed & Fri 6.50pm), which stops in the town of Watrous, 6km south of the lake. From there you can get to tiny **Manitou Beach** on the south shore, where there's the largest and one of the oldest mineral **spas** in Canada, *Manitou Springs Mineral Spa* (daily 9am–10pm; ☎946-2233; ②–④). For $7.40 per swim, or $11.11 for a whole day, you can relax in their mineral pools, reputedly good for rheumatic and arthritic pains. Unfortunately, the spa is dated and not kept very clean and you're better off heading to the spa in Moose Jaw.

Eating, drinking and entertainment

Saskatoon has a useful assortment of **restaurants** clustered in and around the downtown core and along the first couple of blocks of **Broadway Avenue**, which lies just across the river via the bridge at 4th Avenue South and 19th Street East. Broadway is the nearest thing the city has to a "cultural centre", the home of the Broadway Theatre and a handful of vaguely "alternative" shops and cafés. While you're in town, try a bottle of **Great Western Beer** (especially the Brewhouse brand), the product of a local factory whose future was threatened by the merger of two of Canada's giant brewing companies,

Molson and Carling O'Keefe. The workers bought the factory themselves and can barely keep up with demand. It's also customary, while in town, to try a slice of **Saskatoon berry pie**, made with a local berry that has a taste similar to that of a blueberry.

Snack bars and restaurants

Amigos Cantina, 632 10th St E. Mexican specialities, with live background music. Closed Sun.

The Berry Barn, 830 Valley Rd, 11km southwest of town (☎382-7036). It's worth the journey to sample the home-made soups, waffles and pies made on this huge berry farm. Late May to Sept daily 10am–9pm; Oct–Dec Mon–Thurs 10am–5pm, Fri–Sun 10am–9pm.

Café.com, 2698 3rd Ave S. Light lunches and a wide variety of coffees for Internet surfers.

Calories Bakery & Restaurant, 721 Broadway Ave. An atmospheric French-style bistro, with main courses around $8.

Earl's, 610 2nd Ave N and Queen St. Trendy chain with an imaginative menu; vegetarian and other dishes between $5 and $15.

Emily's, 616 10th St E and Broadway Ave. Great home-made meals like broccoli-cheese soup, for under $10.

Grainfields Pancake and Waffle House, 20th St W at Ave P. Huge, mouthwatering selections of pancakes and waffles with a multitude of toppings.

Istanbul Café, 3110 8th St E. Cheap Turkish delights, situated in Bedford Square mall.

John's Prime Rib and Steakhouse, 401 21st St E. Probably the best steaks in town – done any way you want them. Closed Sun.

The Keg, 301 Ontario Ave N. Popular chain serving standard steak and seafood dishes for between $10 and $20.

Lo-Fat Lloyd's, 129 3rd Ave N. A fast-food takeaway where all items have less than thirty percent calories from fat. An oddity, but the food is surprisingly tasty. No dish over $4.

Make Me Well Kitchen, 316 Ave C S. Vegetarian and organic eatery.

Nino's, 801 Broadway Ave. Cosy place with filling pizzas and Greek dishes from as little as $8.

Saigon II, 96 33rd St E. Cheap and filling Vietnamese and Chinese food.

Saskatoon Station Place, corner of Idylwyld Drive and 23rd St. Eat in Pullman cars in a converted train station. Great Sunday brunches.

Taj Mahal, 1013 Broadway Ave (☎978-2227). Fantastic Indian restaurant, reputed to be the best in Canada. The most delicious dishes are those made with coconut (naryal) and the menu has a large vegetarian section. The chutneys are home-made as is the mango ice cream whilst the lassis are made with buttermilk. A meal for two will cost around $40. Closed Mon.

Tarrogans, 119 3rd Ave S (☎664-3599). French cuisine with a twist – try wild mushrooms or pickerel cheeks in *beurre blanc*. One of the city's best eateries and very expensive. Reservations recommended.

Tomas Cook, 5-305 Idylwyld Drive N. Chain serving a wide variety of weekly specials, including filling portions of steaks, ribs (their Greek ribs are best) and chicken from $10.

Bars and clubs

The Artful Dodger, in the Army and Navy Mall, 119 4th Ave S. English pub with occasional live music. Closed Sun.

The Bassment, 245 3rd Ave S. Live jazz Saturday night. Open Sept–June only Sat.

The Black Duck Freehouse, 154 2nd Ave S. Biggest selection of Scotch and beer in Saskatchewan.

Buds, 817 Broadway Ave. Rough-and-ready bar with nightly R&B acts, plus jam sessions Saturday afternoon. $3–5 cover charge.

Champs, 2404 8th St E. Bar with dance floor and sports on loads of TVs – popular with students.

Cheers Brew Pub, 2105 8th St E. Beer brewed on the premises and large portions of ribs and Cajun food for about $10.

The Kooler, 1202 Quebec Ave. Massive nightclub for thirty-somethings.

Long Branch, in the *Sands Hotel*, 806 Idylwyld Drive N. A large, noisy C&W nightspot. Lots of tassels, sequins and stetsons. Thursday to Saturday $1 cover charge.

Film, theatre and classical music

The Broadway Theatre, 715 Broadway Ave (☎652-6556), has the best of foreign and domestic **films**, while the Midtown Plaza Cinema, 1st Avenue South and 21st Street East, has mainstream releases. For **theatre**, the Persephone, 2802 Rusholme Rd (☎384-7727), is the best known of the city's professional companies, with performances featuring mostly modern plays; their season runs from October to May. The Twenty-Fifth Street Theatre, 816 Spadina Crescent E (☎664-2239), performs more occasionally and concentrates on local work. Visiting ballet, theatre and opera stars appear at the Saskatoon Centennial Auditorium, 35 22nd St E (☎665-6414).

Festivals

Saskatoon's biggest and best shindig is the **SaskTel Saskatchewan Jazz Festival** in the last week in June or first week in July; over five hundred musicians perform jazz, gospel and blues across the city, mostly for free (call ☎934-3378 or 1-800/638-1211 for tickets and information). The **Shakespeare on the Saskatchewan Festival**, where the bard's plays are performed in tents on the riverbank by the Mendel Art Gallery, is held on various days from early July to mid-August; call ☎653-2300 for tickets and information. The Twenty-Fifth Street Theatre Company organizes **The Saskatoon International Fringe Festival**, a week of alternative performances held at the end of July and the beginning of August, featuring some fifty theatre groups from all over the world, performing on stages dotted along Broadway Avenue; tickets are all under $8 (☎664-2239). **Folkfest**, a large ethnic festival held in mid-August at various venues around the city, rounds out the summer's activities (☎931-0100 for information; $10 passport to all venues).

Listings

Airlines Air Canada (☎1-888/247-2262 or 652-4181); Air Sask (☎1-800/665-7275); Athabaska Airways (☎1-800/667-9356) serves Saskatchewan and southern Manitoba; Northwest (☎1-800/225-2525); Westjet (☎1-800/538-5696).

Bike rental Bike Doctor, 623 Main St; also from the *Ramada* and *Bessborough* hotels.

Buses Greyhound and the Saskatchewan Transportation Company (both ☎933-8000).

Car rental Avis, airport terminal (☎652-3434 or 1-800/879-2847); Budget, 2215 Ave C N, 234 1st Ave S, 2508 8th St E and the airport (☎664-1692); Discount, 1550 8th St E (☎242-6556); Enterprise, 718D Circle Drive E (652-9119 or 1-800/736-8222) and 215 Idylwyld Drive N (☎244-6900 or 1-800/736-8222); Thrifty, 2130 Airport Drive (☎244-8000).

Gay and lesbian Info ☎665-1224. Pride Week takes place at the end of June.

Hospitals Saskatoon City Hospital, 701 Queen St (☎655-8000); St Paul's, 1702 20th St W (☎665-5000).

Laundries Broadway Laundromat, 835b Broadway Ave at Main St (daily 8am–9pm); Wash 'n' Slosh, 834B Broadway Ave (daily 8am–9pm) – a laundrette-bar.

Left luggage Coin-operated machines at the bus station.

Police 130 4th Ave N (☎975-8300).

Post office Main post office at 202 4th Ave N.

Royal Canadian Mounted Police ☎975-5173.

Taxis Radio Cabs (☎242-1221); United Cabs (☎652-2222).

Train enquiries ☎1-800/835-3037 (arrivals and departures) or 1-800/561-8630 (reservations).

Weather ☎975-4266.

Women Sexual Assault Centre, 24hr (☎244-2224).

Central Saskatchewan

North of Saskatoon you have a choice of two routes. Following the Yellowhead northwest towards Edmonton, you'll come to the **Battlefords**, consisting of grimy and impoverished **North Battleford** and, on the opposite bank of the North Saskatchewan River, the trim riverside streets and refurbished Mountie stockade of **Battleford**. Due north of Saskatoon, the road shadows the South Saskatchewan River on its way to the town of Prince Albert, a distance of 140km, passing the **Batoche National Historic Site**, where the Métis rebellion of 1885 reached its disastrous climax (see box opposite). Further north still, the lakes and wooded hills of **Prince Albert National Park** are among the region's finest, with innumerable canoe and hiking routes into the wilderness. Central Saskatchewan's **public transport** is poor, but there are reasonably regular **buses** between the major towns and a once-daily summertime service to Waskesiu Lake.

Saskatoon to Prince Albert Park

From Saskatoon, Hwy 11 cuts across the narrow slice of prairie that separates the final stretches of the North and South Saskatchewan rivers, before they flow together further to the northeast. There's nothing to see on the road itself, but on the way the briefest of detours will take you to one of the province's more interesting attractions, **Batoche National Historic Site**.

Batoche National Historic Site

The site of the Métis's last stand – and the last place where Canadians fought against Canadians – **Batoche National Historic Site** (May–Sept daily 9am–5pm; $4) occupies a splendid site beside the east bank of the South Saskatchewan River, 90km from Saskatoon just off Provincial Hwy 225. At the entrance to the park, a **visitor reception centre** (☎423-6227) has displays on the culture of the Métis and provides a detailed account of the rebellion, supplemented by a glossy brochure and an excellent 45-minute audiovisual presentation combining slides, spoken narration, music and tableaux of realistic mannequins.

Behind the centre, the main footpath leads to a refurbished Catholic church and adjacent rectory, all that's left of the original village. A few minutes' walk away, in the cemetery perched above the river bank, memorials inscribed with the hoary commendation "a credit to his race" contrast with the rough chunk of rock that commemorates Riel's commander-in-chief **Gabriel Dumont**. A stern and ferocious man, Dumont insisted that he be buried standing up, so that he could enjoy a good view of the river.

The church and cemetery are at the centre of the park's **walking trails**, which extend along the river bank in both directions. Roughly 1km to the south, there's a military graveyard, a Métis farmhouse and the remains of some rifle pits; about the same distance to the north, there's the site of the old ferry crossing, more rifle pits and the foundations of several Métis buildings. With a knowledge of the history, the park becomes an extremely evocative spot.

Duck Lake and Fort Carlton

Back on Hwy 11, on the west side of the South Saskatchewan, the tiny farming community of **DUCK LAKE** – many of whose buildings have outdoor murals depicting local history – is home to a **Regional Interpretive Centre** at 5 Anderson Ave (late May to early Sept daily 10am–5.30pm; $4; ☎467-2057), with displays on Indian, Métis and pioneer society from 1870 to 1905. Prize exhibits include some elaborate Cree costumes; an outfit that belonged to the Sioux chief Little Fox, an adviser to Sitting Bull; and Gabriel Dumont's gold watch, presented to him in New York where he was appearing in Buffalo Bill's Wild West Show.

Continuing 26km west along Hwy 212, you'll reach **Fort Carlton Provincial Historic Park** (mid-May to early Sept daily 10am–6pm; $2.50), a reconstruction of a Hudson's Bay Company trading post circa 1860. Founded in 1810, the riverbank station

THE NORTHWEST REBELLION

The 1869–70 Red River rebellion in Manitoba, led by Louis Riel, won significant conces-sions from the Canadian government but failed to protect the Métis's way of life against the effects of increasing white settlement. Many **Métis** moved west to farm the banks of the **South Saskatchewan**, where the men worked as freighters, traders, horse breeders and translators, acting as intermediaries between the Indians and the Europeans. In itself, the development of these homesteads was a recognition by the Métis that the day of the itinerant buffalo hunter was over. However, when the government surveyors arrived here in 1878, the Métis realized, as they had on the Red River twenty years before, that their claim to the land they farmed was far from secure.

Beginning with the Métis, a general sense of instability spread across the region in the early 1880s, fuelled by Big Bear's and Poundmaker's increasingly restless and hungry **Cree** and by the discontent of the white settlers at the high freight charges levied on their produce. The leaders of the Métis decided to act in June 1884, when they sent a del-egation to Montana, where **Louis Riel** was in exile. Convinced that the Métis were God's chosen instrument to purify the human race, and he their Messiah, Riel was easily per-suaded to return to Canada, where he spent the winter unsuccessfully petitioning the Ottawa government for confirmation of Métis rights.

In March 1885, Riel and his supporters declared a provisional government at Batoche and demanded the surrender of the nearest Mountie outpost, **Fort Carlton**, just 35km to their west on the North Saskatchewan. The police superintendent refused, and the force he dispatched to re-establish order was badly mauled at **Duck Lake**. When news of the uprising reached Big Bear's Cree, some 300km away, they attacked the local Hudson's Bay Company store and killed its nine occupants in the so-called **Frog Lake Massacre**. Within a couple of weeks, no fewer than three columns of militia were con-verging on Big Bear's Cree and the meagre Métis forces at Batoche. The total number of casualties – about fifty altogether – does not indicate the full significance of the engagement, which for the Métis marked the end of their independence and influence. Riel's execution in Regina on November 16, 1885 was bitterly denounced in Québec and remains a potent symbol of the deep divide between English- and French-speaking Canada. In Ontario there was a mood of unrepentant triumphalism, the military success – however paltry – stirring a deep patriotic fervour that excluded Métis and Indian alike.

was fortified in successive decades and became an important centre of the fur and pem-mican trade, until the demise of the buffalo brought an end to its success. Reduced to a warehouse facility in the early 1880s, the fort was garrisoned by the Mounties during the Northwest Rebellion (see box, above), but it was finally burnt down and abandoned in 1885.

The **visitors centre** (☎467-5205) provides an historical introduction to the fort, whose stockade shelters replicas of the clerk's quarters, a sail and harness shop, a fur and provisions store with piles of colourfully striped Hudson's Bay Company blankets and bottles of bright Indian trading beads, and a trading shop, where the merchandise included gunpowder – which meant the clerks were forbidden to light a stove here, no matter what the temperature. Just outside the walls of the stockade are three tepees, neatly aligned along a path. The centre, also offers guided **trail walks**, which allow you to see the remains of rutted wagon trails made by carts carrying supplies to and from the fort. There's also an on-site **campsite** (☎467-5205 or 933-7937; $9; mid-May to early Sept). Take care when hiking or camping, as the wooded gullies of the North Saskatchewan River are home to a large number of **black bears**.

Prince Albert

Founded as a Presbyterian mission in 1866, **PRINCE ALBERT** has a thriving timber industry, is a major transport centre and is the province's oldest and third-largest city, but it's a dull spot, its long main drag, **Central Avenue** (Hwy 2), lined with fast-food joints, petrol stations and shopping malls. Apart from the casino that brings thousands of visitors to town, the only conceivable attractions are the **Historical Museum** at River Street and Central Avenue (mid-May to Aug Mon–Sat 10am–6pm, Sun 10am–8pm; $1.50), given over chiefly to the area's first farmers and loggers, and **Diefenbaker's House** at 246 19th St W (mid-May to Aug Mon–Sat 10am–8pm, Sun 10am–9pm; $3) where John Diefenbaker lived from 1947 until he donated it to the city in 1975. Inside are photos, furnishings, Diefenbaker's campaign posters, fishing rods and a short bed that once belonged to the eccentric John A. Macdonald, former Canadian prime minister – he slept sitting up to prevent demons entering his mouth. You can also see a short video about Diefenbaker's funeral, which involved digging up his wife so they could be buried together. The **Museum of Police and Corrections**, 3700 2nd Ave W (mid-May to Aug daily 10am–6pm; free), in an old North West Mounted Police guardroom, has rather sobering displays relating to the history of law enforcement in northern Saskatchewan.

The appeal of the place is that it has the only **bus** to Prince Albert National Park and La Ronge, the service leaving from the **station** at 20 14th St E and Central Avenue daily at 5pm (☎953-3701). The **tourist information office** (June–Aug Mon–Fri 8.30am–8pm, Sat & Sun 10am–8pm; Sept–May Mon–Fri 8.30am–6pm; ☎953-4386 or 953-4385), in the south of town beside the police museum, provides free town maps and brochures. You can get to Prince Albert by **bus** direct from Saskatoon three times a day departing at 8.30am, 2pm & 6pm.

There's no real reason to stay here, but the town has several central **hotels**, including the *Avenue Motor Hotel*, 1015 Central Ave (☎763-6411; ①/②), whose rooms are grim and basic; the better *Marlboro Inn*, 67 13th St E (☎763-2643 or 1-800/661-7666; ②–④); and the *Prince Albert Inn*, 3680 2nd Ave W (☎922-5000 or 1-800/922-5855; ②) – although the latter can be noisy, as there's a nightclub on the premises and it connects to the casino by a covered walkway. At the south end of Hwy 2 there's the comfortable *South Hill Inn*, 3245 2nd Ave W (☎922-1333 or 1-800/363-4466, fax 763-6408; ②) which also has some outlandish jacuzzi suites (⑥) and a popular bar downstairs. For **campers**, the *Mary Nisbit Campground* (☎953-4880 or 953-4848; $13–16; mid-May to Sept) is situated about 2km north of town, on the other side of the river, beside Hwy 2.

There's not much choice for good **eating** places, but the most expensive and renowned place is *Amy's on Second*, 2990 2nd Ave W, with three-course lunches from $30, and serving local fish such as pickerel. There's also *Diggers Roadhouse*, 2901 2nd Ave West, with specials from $6 and *WK Kitchen*, 2840 2nd Ave W, which dishes up big Chinese buffets at reasonable prices.

Prince Albert National Park and Waskesiu

Some 230km north of Saskatoon, **Prince Albert National Park** is a great tract of wilderness where the aspen parkland of the south meets the boreal forest of the north, a transitional landscape that incorporates a host of rivers and creeks, dozens of deep lakes, pockets of pasture and areas of spruce bog. The shift in vegetation is mirrored by the wildlife, with prairie species such as coyote and wild bison giving way to black bear, moose, wolf, caribou, osprey and eagle further north. There's an entry fee of $4 to the park, with a variety of reductions and special prices for groups and at weekends.

The tourist village of **WASKESIU**, approached from the south by Hwy 263 and from the east by hwys 2 and 264, is the only settlement in the park. Spread out along the southern shore of Waskesiu Lake, it has all the usual facilities, a narrow sandy beach that gets ridiculously overcrowded in summer, and the park's **nature centre**, on Lakeview Drive (late June to Aug daily 10am–5pm; Sept Sat & Sun noon–4pm), which has a hands-on display on the southern boreal forest and its inhabitants. In the centre of Waskesiu, at the junction of Lakeview Drive and Waskesiu Drive, the park's main

information office (mid-May to Aug daily 8am–10pm; Sept to mid-Oct daily 8am–5pm; mid-Oct to mid-May Mon–Sat 8am–4pm; ☎663-4522) gives advice on wildlife and the condition of the hiking trails, along with weather forecasts – particularly important if you intend to use one of the canoe routes. The information office also runs a programme of **guided walks** in July and August and issues backcountry camping permits ($3), which allow visitors to use the primitive, seasonal **campsites** dotted along most of the more substantial trails. Shearwater Boat Cruises runs **boat** trips on the lake (July to mid-Sept daily 1pm, 3pm, 5pm & 7pm; 1hr; $15; ☎982-4478 or 1-888/747-7572). Whatever you do in the park, remember to take insect repellent.

Several of the park's easier **hiking trails** begin in or near Waskesiu, most notably the thirteen-kilometre Kingfisher Trail, which loops through the forest just to the west of the resort. However, the best trails and **canoe routes** begin roughly 15km further north at the bottom end of Kingsmere Lake, accessible by boat or car from Waskesiu. They include a delightful week-long canoe trip that skirts the west shore of Kingsmere Lake before heading through a series of remote lakes amidst dense boreal forest. There's also a twenty-kilometre hike or canoe paddle to the idyllic spot of **Grey Owl's Cabin** (May–Sept), situated beside tiny Ajawaan Lake, near the northern shore of Kingsmere Lake. Grey Owl (see p.284) lived in this cabin from 1931 until 1937, the year before his death, and it was here that he wrote one of his better books, *Pilgrims of the Wild*, and where he, his wife Anahereo and daughter Shirley Dawn are buried. For further information on the trip to the cabin, and on other canoe routes in the park, call the park information office.

Connected by bus to La Ronge to the north and Prince Albert to the south, Waskesiu's **bus stop** is right in the centre, beside a **tourist kiosk** (mid-May to Aug daily 8am–10pm; Sept–Dec & April to mid-May Mon–Fri 8am–4pm; Jan–March daily 8am–4pm; ☎663-5410), which provides free maps of the town. Waskesiu's main street, Waskesiu Drive, runs roughly parallel to and just south of the lake, its western section curving round behind Lakeview Drive. Almost all the **hotels** and **motels** are on or near these two streets, including the *Lakeview Hotel*, Lakeview Drive (☎663-5311; ③) where all rooms have TVs and in-room coffee; and the more luxurious *All Season Waskesiu Lake Lodge*, Lakeview Drive (☎663-6161, fax 663-6144; ⑤; May to mid-Oct) with one- and two-bedroom apartments that include TVs, lakeside decks and barbecues. **Bungalow** and **cabin** accommodation tends to be block-booked from May to mid-October, but you could try the *Armstrong Hillcrest Cabins*, corner of Lakeview Drive and Willow Street (☎663-5481 or 922-2599; ②–⑤; May to mid-Oct), or *Kapasiwin Bungalows* (☎663-5225 or 975-0627; ④; May to mid-Oct), 2km round the lake to the east of the resort, has cabins which form a quiet mini-resort with its own private beach. Waskesiu has two **campsites**: the centrally situated *Trailer Park* (☎663-4522 or 1-877/255-7267; $20; mid-May to Oct, weather permitting) on the north end of Waskesiu Drive near Waskesiu Lodge, and the nearby *Beaver Glen* (☎663-4522, 663-4513 or 1-877/255-7267; $14–18; mid-May to Sept) near Waskesiu Lake. The basic, unserviced *Kingsmere Lake Campgrounds* (☎663-4522 or 1-877/255-7267; $3 backcountry permit from park office; year-round) is near Grey Owl's Cabin. For reservations at all other Prince Albert campsites, call ☎1-800/333-7267.

There are several cheap **restaurants** and **snack bars** in the centre, including the *Park Center Café* opposite the information office, the neighbouring *Mike's Place* with great breakfasts and *Pizza Pete's* with a terrace at 829 Lakeview Drive, which turns out a variety of pizzas and pasta. On the beachfront, *The Beach House* is good for cappuccinos, wraps, desserts and sunsets. For more expensive dining, try the *Mackenzie's Dining Room* at the *Hawood Inn*, 851 Lakeview Drive, where main courses start at around $15, and include good cuts of local beef.

Waskesiu's stores sell a full range of outback **equipment**, but no one rents out camping gear. **Canoe and kayak rentals** are available at the marina (☎763-1278), a five-minute drive from the village.

The Battlefords and westward

Roughly 150km northwest of Saskatoon, the twin townships of **NORTH BATTLE-FORD** and **BATTLEFORD** face each other across the wide valley of the North Saskatchewan River; the former a rough-and-ready industrial settlement, the latter a more sedate little place. From the middle of the eighteenth century, this stretch of the North Saskatchewan River near today's Battlefords formed a natural boundary between the **Blackfeet** to the south and the **Cree** to the north. These two groups were temporary trading partners, the Cree and their Ojibwa allies controlling the flow of European goods, the Blackfeet providing the horses. However, with the arrival of white traders at the start of the nineteenth century, the Blackfeet developed a flourishing trade direct with the Europeans, and by 1870 the Cree and Blackfeet were waging war across the entire length of their frontier, from the Missouri River to Fort Edmonton.

In the 1870s, apprehensive after the Cypress Hills Massacre and the arrival of Sitting Bull and his warriors (see box on p.529), the government speeded its policy of containment and control, determined to push the Plains Indians into reservations and thereby open the area for European settlers. Their chosen instrument was the North West Mounted Police, who in 1876 established a post at Battleford, which then became the regional capital.

With the virtual extinction of the buffalo herds in the late 1870s, the Plains Indians began to starve and Lieutenant-Governor Dewdney used his control of emergency rations to force recalcitrant Indians onto the reservations. Several bands of Cree resisted the process, fighting a series of skirmishes at the same time as the Métis rebellion in Batoche, but by the mid-1880s their independence was over. Meanwhile, Battleford had lost its pre-eminence when the Canadian Pacific Railway routed its transcontinental line through Regina, which became the new capital in 1883. Twenty years later, its prospects

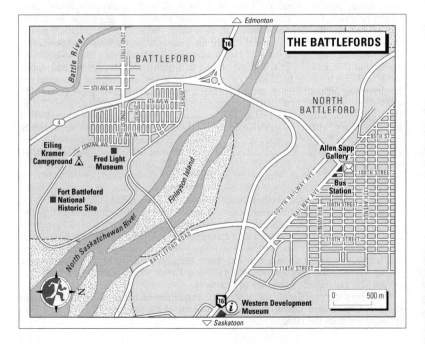

were further damaged by the Canadian Northern Railway, which laid its tracks on the other side of the river, creating the rival town of North Battleford. Since then, Battleford has stagnated and shrunk, while its rival has become a moderately successful industrial and distribution centre, with a population of around fourteen thousand.

The townships

Situated on the east side of the river valley, North Battleford's downtown core is arranged into streets running north–south and avenues running west–east, forming a central gridiron that intersects with Railway Avenue, which runs southeast to north-west. Across the river, some 5km away, Battleford sprawls next to Hwy 4, its streets running from west to east and avenues from north to south.

On the Yellowhead Highway, just east of North Battleford, this town's branch of the **Western Development Museum** (May–Sept daily 9am–5pm, Oct–April Wed–Sun 12.30–4.30pm; $6) deals with the farming history of Saskatchewan. Inside, vintage vehicles and a "Jolly Life of the Farmer's Wife" exhibit of old ranges and laundry equipment recall older, and harder, times, while outside in the Heritage Farm and Village that contains 36 buildings, saved from around the province, including tiny churches and homesteads, banks, a general store, creaky barns and a grain elevator from 1928. The museum is a wonderful way to acquaint yourself with prairie history and realize the harshness and the changes in farming life over the last century. Try to visit on the second weekend in August when the "ghost" village comes alive in the "Those Were the Days" event, which features costumed locals bread-baking and craft-making.

The old municipal library in the centre of **North Battleford**, at 1091 100th St at 11th Avenue, now houses the **Allen Sapp Gallery** (May–Aug daily 1–5pm; Sept–April Wed–Sun same hours; free), showcase for the work of Allen Sapp, a local Cree who is often in attendance dressed in flamboyant cowboy boots, a wide-brimmed stetson and long braids. Perhaps the best known of Canada's contemporary native artists, Sapp trawls his childhood recollections of life on the Red Pheasant reserve in the 1930s for most of his material. His simply drawn figures are characteristically cast in the wide spaces of the prairies, whose delicately blended colours hint at a nostalgic regard for a time when his people had a greater sense of community.

From North Battleford there are two roads over the North Saskatchewan River: a modern flyover that's part of Hwy 16, and the shorter old Route 16A. In Battleford, the **Fred Light Museum**, at 11 20th St E at Central Avenue (mid-May to Aug daily 9am–8pm; free), has a substantial collection of early firearms and military uniforms and a replica of an old general store, but is thoroughly upstaged by **Fort Battleford National Historic Site** (mid-May to mid-Oct daily 9am–5pm; $4), overlooking the river valley from the top of a steep bluff just down the road, accessed from Central Avenue. At the entrance to the park, the visitors information centre (☎937-2621) provides a general introduction to the fort and, next door, the restored barracks contains a display explaining its history, assisted by well-informed, costumed guides.

Within the replica stockade stand four original buildings, including the **Sick Horse Stable**, where the delicate constitutions of the Mounties' horses – most of which came from Ontario – were coaxed into accepting the unfamiliar prairie grasses. Centrepiece of the park is the **Commanding Officer's Residence**, which has been returned to its appearance in the 1880s. Broadly Gothic Revival in style, the hewn-log house contains an enormous carved bed-head and a couple of magnificent black-and-chrome oven ranges, which must have been a nightmare to transport this far west. However, the house was not as comfortable as it seems today, principally because the high ceilings made the rooms almost impossible to heat. As the first commanding officer, James Walker, moaned in 1879, "This morning with the thermometer 37 degrees below, water was frozen on the top of the stove in my bedroom".

Practicalities

All long-distance and local bus services use **North Battleford bus station**, located on the edge of the town centre at 75 E Railway Ave; there's a daily service leaving Saskatoon for North Battleford at 5.15pm (4.30pm on Sat). The **Tourist Information Centre** (June–Aug daily 8am–8pm; ☎445-6226) is on the outskirts 2km away, at the junction of hwys 16 and 40 East, and there's also one in the Fred Light Museum (mid-May to Aug daily 9am–8pm; ☎937-7111) in Battleford, at the junction of hwys 4 and 40. City buses connect the two towns, and there's also one **taxi** firm, Crown Cab (☎445-8155), which charges about $12 for the trip from the bus station to Fort Battleford.

Most of **North Battleford's** central **hotels** are dispiriting, the haunt of the drunk and the dispossessed. Better alternatives include the *Best Canada Motor Inn*, on the corner of 11th Avenue and 100th Street (☎445-8115 or 445-2447; ①), with reasonably comfortable rooms, and the pleasant *Tropical Inn*, on Hwy 16 (☎446-4700 or 1-800/219-5244; ②–④), about 1km east along the Yellowhead from the bus station. North Battleford is short on good **restaurants** – but there are several cheap and central places with filling menus. Try the *Dragon Palace*, 1292 101st St at 13th Avenue, where simple Chinese dishes start at $6.75; or *O'Grady's*, 2491 99th St, serving up standard steak-and-rib fare. Alternatively, *Smitty's Family Restaurant*, just outside the town centre in the *Tropical Inn*, has good, basic dishes from $9, and *Da Vinci's*, also in the *Inn*, features some Saskatchewan specialities on its menu.

Battleford has just one **motel**, the popular *Five Star*, 322 22nd St W (☎937-2651; ①–③), with simple, clean air-conditioned rooms, plus large family units with kitchenettes. The town also has a splendid **campsite** – the *Eiling Kramer Campground* (☎937-6212 or 937-6216; $11–14; early May to Sept) – overlooking the river valley from beside Fort Battleford. For **food**, *Pennydale Junction*, in a converted 1908 CNR train station at 92 22nd St and Main Street, has great seafood, pizzas and steaks from $12. The **Saskatchewan Handcraft Festival**, held in the town each mid-July, is one of the largest and best for crafts in the province.

On from the Battlefords: Lloydminster

Some 140km northwest of the Battlefords you hit the Alberta–Saskatchewan border, and the drab city of **LLOYDMINSTER**, which was founded in 1903 by a group of two thousand British pioneers known as the Barr colonists. A major attraction is the **Barr Colony Heritage Cultural Centre**, located in Weaver Park beside the Yellowhead at 44th Street and 45th Avenue (mid-May to early Sept daily 10am–8pm; early Sept to mid-May Wed–Fri noon–5pm, Sat & Sun 1–5pm; $3.50), and even this is scarcely pulse-racing – a small display on the founders, together with a couple of art galleries and a wildlife exhibition. Perhaps the most interesting aspect of the city is its **geographical location**: the 4th Meridian runs right down 50th Avenue, the main street. Thirty-metre-high metal border markers, shaped like the survey stakes used by the original surveyors when they laid out the border between the two provinces, line Hwy 16 on the north and south sides, and smaller markers line the main street.

Yet Lloydminster is a popular town for a break in the journey, and has lots of **hotels** and **motels** along its two main streets, 44th Street (the Yellowhead) and 50th Avenue (Hwy 17). The pick of these are the *Imperial 400 Motel*, 4320 44th St (☎825-4400 or 1-800/781-2268; ③) with an indoor pool and cable TV; and the *Wayside Inn*, a sprawling complex just west of the city on Hwy 16 on the Alberta side (☎780/875-4404 or 1-800/658-4404; ③). For **camping**, *Weaver Park Campground* (☎825-3726 or 825-6184; mid-April to Oct), next door to the heritage centre, has sites from $12 and a full range of facilities, including showers and a playground. There are limited options if you're **eating** out, but the less mundane establishments are *David's Steak House*, 5501 44th St; *Grainfield's*, in the *West Harvest Inn*, 5620 44th St; or any of the pizza chains around town.

The Lloydminster Tourism and Convention Authority has a **tourist office** at 5001 50th Ave (Mon–Fri 8am–5pm; ☎825-6180 or 1-800/825-6180). Both Tourism Saskatchewan and Alberta Tourism run seasonal **visitor reception centres** on either side of the border. The bus station is on the Alberta side at 50th Street and is served by four buses daily from Saskatoon.

Northern Saskatchewan

Stretching from Prince Albert National Park to the border with the Northwest Territories on the 60th parallel, the inhospitable and largely uninhabited expanse of **northern Saskatchewan** accounts for almost half the province. The region divides into two slightly different areas, the marginally richer flora and fauna of the **Interior Plains** lying south of the more spartan landscapes of the **Canadian Shield**, whose naked rock stretches north of a rough curve drawn between La Loche, La Ronge and Flin Flon, on the Manitoba border.

Northern Saskatchewan's shallow soils are unable to support any form of agriculture, and its native peoples, the **Woodland Cree**, have traditionally survived by hunting, trapping and fishing. In recent times, this precarious and nomadic existence has been replaced by a more settled and restricted life on the reservations which are concentrated around **Lake Athabasca** in the extreme northwest corner of the province. Nearly all the other settlements in the north are **mining towns**, the result of the discovery of uranium in the 1950s. The main exception is the tourist-resort-cum-mining-centre of **La Ronge**, situated on the edge of the lakes and forests of **Lac La Ronge Provincial Park**. La Ronge is also near a section of the **Churchill River**, whose remote waters boast some of the north's longest and most varied canoe routes. Finally, **Clearwater River Provincial Park**, near the Alberta border, provides some of the region's most challenging white-water canoeing.

WILDERNESS CANOEING

Northern Saskatchewan has an abundance of **canoe routes** sprinkled across its thousands of lakes. However, it's important that prospective canoeists come fully prepared both in terms of equipment and knowledge of the proposed route. For independent and experienced wilderness travellers, the **Saskatchewan Environment and Resource Management (SERM)** issues a comprehensive range of free material that includes route descriptions, lists of outfitters, details of campsites and information on climate, wildlife and potential hazards. Some park offices also sell detailed local maps. The department has **offices** in a number of towns, but its **headquarters** are at 3211 Albert St, Regina (Mon–Fri 8am–5pm; ☎787-2700). This office also operates a **toll-free advice line** in summer on ☎1-800/667-2757. You can also get information on canoe routes from Churchill River Canoe Outfitters (☎635-4420) or on-line at *www.lights.com/waterways*, and on canoe outfitters from the Saskatchewan Outfitters Association (☎763-5434).

Saskatchewan has a host of **tour operators** running hunting, fishing and canoe excursions into the north of the province from the middle of May to September. A full list of hunting and fishing outfitters is provided in the *Saskatchewan Fishing and Hunting Guide*, while the *Saskatchewan Vacation Guide* lists operators offering canoeing, birdwatching and wildlife-viewing excursions throughout the province. Both books are available through Tourism Saskatchewan (☎787-2300 or 1-877/237-2273) or at most tourist offices.

For a complete range of topographic maps and canoe-route charts and booklets, plus secondary road maps, contact SaskGeomatics, 2151 Scarth St, Regina S4P 3V7 (☎787-2799).

Although northern Saskatchewan attracts hundreds of hunters, anglers and canoeists throughout the summer, it has an extremely poor public transport system. There's just one really useful **bus**, a daily service connecting Saskatoon, Prince Albert, Waskesiu (mid-May to mid-Sept only) and La Ronge.

La Ronge and around

About 240km north of Prince Albert, readily accessible along Hwy 2/102, the scrawny, straggling resort of **LA RONGE** is sandwiched between the road and the western edge of Lac La Ronge. It was home to an isolated Cree community until the road reached here in 1948. Since then, gold mines and forestry operations have started just to the north of town and the area's lakes and rivers have proved popular with visiting canoeists and anglers.

Falling either side of Boardman Street, the town is fronted by La Ronge Avenue, which runs parallel to the waterfront, the location of the **bus depot**. A few minutes' walk away, in Mistasinihk Place, there's the office of the **Saskatchewan Parks Department** (Mon–Fri 8am–noon & 1–5pm; ☎425-4245 or 1-800/772-4064) and an interpretive centre (same days and hours; ☎425-4350) with exhibits on northern lifestyles, crafts and history. The nearest **visitor reception centre** (mid-May to mid-Sept Mon–Fri 8am–9pm, Sat & Sun 10am–8pm; ☎425-5311) is 2km south of town beside Hwy 2.

A good base for exploring the region, La Ronge has several reasonably priced and central **hotels** and **motels**. These include the *Drifters Motel*, at the entrance to town, beside Hwy 2 (☎425-2224; ③); *La Ronge Motor Hotel*, 1120 La Ronge Ave (☎425-2190 or 1-800/332-6735; ③); and the *Harbour Inn*, overlooking the lake at 1327 La Ronge Ave (☎425-3262 or 1-800/667-4097; ③). There's a series of **campsites** strung along Hwy 102 north of town, the nearest of which is *Nut Point* (☎425-4234 or 1-800/772-4064; $13–18; mid-May to Aug), 1km north via La Ronge Avenue. The only places to **eat** that are not run-of-the-mill are the vaguely Greek *Kostas II*, 707 La Ronge Ave, and *Willow's Café*, 322 Husky Ave, which has fairly tasty home-cooking and pastries.

La Ronge is on the western edge of **Lac La Ronge Provincial Park**, which incorporates all 1300 square kilometres of Lac La Ronge and extends north to encompass a number of smaller lakes and a tiny section of the **Churchill River**, once the main route into the northwest for the voyageurs. The Churchill swerves across the width of the province, from west to east, before heading on into Manitoba, its waterways providing some of the region's longest canoe routes. The parks department in La Ronge (☎425-4245 or 1-800/772-4064) provides a detailed description of the river and its history in their booklet entitled *Saskatchewan's Voyageur Highway: A Canoe Trip*. The park is one of the few areas in the province where you can hike the Canadian Shield. The 15km Nut Point Hiking Trail leaves the campsite and runs along a narrow peninsula that juts into Lac La Ronge, crossing rock ridges through forests and over high, open ridges where you can view the enormous island-studded lake. Less strenuously, these waters are also good for fishing – the walleye, pike and lake trout are delicious.

A number of La Ronge **tour operators** and **outfitters** run and equip fishing and canoeing trips into the park, most of them using its web of lakeside holiday **lodges** and **cabins**; the parks department office has the details. There are also several **campsites** along Hwy 102 including the *Missinipe* (☎425-4234 or 1-800/772-4064; $9–22; mid-May to Aug) on Otter Lake, where the hwy crosses the Churchill River.

North of La Ronge, Hwy 102 deteriorates long before it reaches **MISSINIPE**, 80km away, the home of Horizons Unlimited, Box 1110, La Ronge, Saskatchewan S0J 1L0 (☎635-4420), a highly recommended wilderness-holiday company. Beyond here, the road joins Route 905, a bumpy 300-kilometre track that leads to the uranium mines around Wollaston Lake.

Clearwater River Provincial Park

Apart from Hwy 2/102, the only other paved road running into the heart of northern Saskatchewan is Hwy 155, which extends as far as the tiny town of **LA LOCHE**, near the Alberta border. From here, a rough, gravel track, Route 955 (the Semchuk Trail), passes through **Clearwater River Provincial Park** before continuing on to the uranium mines of Cluff Lake. The park's main feature is the rugged **Clearwater River Valley**, whose turbulent waters are recommended only to the experienced white-water canoeist – you have to navigate 28 sets of rapids. There's a small and simple free **campsite** (☎822-1700; May to mid-Nov) where the river meets the road, but otherwise the nearest accommodation is back in La Loche, 60km to the south. The town has one **motel**, the *Pines Motel* (☎822-2600; ②), located beside the highway, and a parks department office (Mon–Fri 8am–5pm; ☎822-1700). Clearwater Raft Tours, PO Box 2828, Meadow Lake, Saskatchewan SOM 1VO (☎665-7238 or 1-800/661-7275) offers an exciting five-day white-water rafting adventure, including transportation by float plane, services of a guide, tenting accommodation, fishing and all meals. Call for costs.

Lake Athabasca

A particular favourite of the hook-and-bullet brigade – and in recent years, eco-tourists – wild and remote **Lake Athabasca**, close to the 60th parallel, can be reached only by private **float plane**. This is the region's largest lake, and much of its southern shore is protected as the **Athabasca Sand Dunes Provincial Wilderness Park**, the most northerly sand dunes in the world. Several companies organize excursions to the area that include flights, food, accommodation and boat rental; if you can afford $3000–4000 for a six-day trip, try Athabasca Camps, Box 7800, Saskatoon (☎653-5490 or 1-800/667-5490), or TourQuest, Box 26038, Regina (☎731-2377). If you want to take an **eco-tour** of this remote northern region, Athabasca Eco Expeditions, Box 7800, Saskatoon S7K 4R5 (☎653-5490 or 1-800/667-5490) does one- or two-week summer tours led by aboriginal guides who know the area well. Call for costs.

travel details

Trains

Winnipeg to: Brandon North (3 weekly; 2hr 25min); Churchill (5 weekly summer, 3 weekly rest of the year; 33hr 30min); Dauphin (3 weekly; 3hr 55min); Edmonton (3 weekly; 14hr 30min); Jasper (3 weekly; 21hr 15min); Portage La Prairie (3 weekly; 1hr); Saskatoon (3 weekly; 8hr 20min); Sioux Lookout (3 weekly; 6hr 20min); Sudbury (3 weekly; 24hr 40min); The Pas (3 weekly; 11hr 20min); Toronto (3 weekly; 31hr 40min); Vancouver (3 weekly; 38hr 35min).

Buses

Prince Albert to: La Ronge (1 daily; 3hr 15min); Waskesiu (mid-May to mid-Sept 1 daily; 1hr 10min).

Regina to: Calgary (4 daily; 10hr 15min); Coronach (1 daily; 4hr 40min); Medicine Hat (4 daily; 6hr 15min); Moose Jaw (4 daily; 1hr); Prince Albert (1–2 daily; 6hr 50min); Saskatoon (3–5 daily; 3hr 5min); Swift Current (3 daily; 4hr 15min); Yorkton (3 daily; 2hr 35min–4hr 55min).

Saskatoon to: Calgary (2 daily; 8hr 30min); Edmonton (4 daily; 6hr 30min); Lloydminster (3 daily; 3hr 15min); North Battleford (2–4 daily; 1hr 40min); Prince Albert (3 daily; 1hr 50min); Swift Current (1 daily; 3hr 30min); Yorkton (1 daily; 5hr 5min).

Swift Current to: Eastend (1 daily; 2hr).

Winnipeg to: Brandon (1 daily; 4hr 15min); Dauphin (1–3 daily; 4hr 50min); Grand Beach Provincial Park (1 daily; 1hr 40min); Kenora (5 daily; 2hr 30min); Lac du Bonnet (Mon, Wed, Thurs & Sun 3 daily; 2hr); Neepawa (1–3 daily; 2hr 40min); Portage La Prairie (1–3 daily; 1hr 10min); Regina (4 daily; 8hr); Gimli (1 daily; 1hr 45min); Rennie (1 daily; 2hr); Riding Mountain (1–3 daily; 3hr 30min); Saskatoon (1–3 daily; 12hr); Sault Ste

Marie (3 daily; 16hr); Sudbury (3 daily; 25hr); Thunder Bay (3 daily; 10hr 35min); Toronto (3 daily; 31hr); West Hawk Lake (1 daily; 2hr 30min); Yorkton (1–3 daily; 6hr 25min).

Flights

Regina to: Calgary (7 daily; 1hr 20min); Saskatoon (9 daily; 40min); Toronto (5 daily; 3hr); Vancouver (3 daily; 2hr 30min).

Saskatoon to: Calgary (3 daily; 1hr); Regina (8 daily; 40min); Toronto (5 daily; 4hr); Vancouver (4 daily; 2hr 10min).

Winnipeg to: Calgary (3 daily; 2hr 20min); Churchill (Mon–Fri 2 daily; 3hr 40min); Flin Flon (Mon–Fri 1 daily; 2hr 25min); Regina (4 daily; 1hr 10min); Saskatoon (4 daily; 1hr 20min); The Pas (Mon–Fri 2 daily; 1hr 30min); Toronto (8 daily; 2hr 20min); Vancouver (3 daily; 4hr).

CHAPTER SIX

ALBERTA AND THE ROCKIES

Alberta is Canada at its best. For many people the beauty of the **Canadian Rockies**, which rise with overwhelming majesty from the rippling prairies, is one of the main reasons for coming to the country. Most visitors confine themselves to the four contiguous national parks – **Banff**, **Jasper**, **Yoho** and **Kootenay** – enclaves that straddle the southern portion of the range, a vast area whose boundaries spill over into British Columbia. Two smaller parks, **Glacier** and **Mount Revelstoke**, lie firmly in BC and not, technically, in the Rockies, but scenically and logistically they form part of the same region. Managed with remarkable efficiency and integrity, all the parks are easily accessible segments of a much wider wilderness of peaks and forests that extend north from the Canada–US border, before merging into the ranges of the Yukon and Alaska.

If you're approaching the Rockies from the east or the US, you have little choice but to spend time in either Edmonton or Calgary, the transport hubs for northern and southern Alberta respectively. Poles apart in feel and appearance, the two cities are locked in an intense rivalry, in which **Calgary** comes out top in almost every respect. Situated on the **Trans-Canada Highway**, less than ninety minutes from Banff National Park, it is more convenient whether you plan to take in Yoho, Kootenay, Glacier or Revelstoke, or push on to southern British Columbia or the west coast. It also has far more going for it in its own right: the weather is kinder, the Calgary Stampede is one of the country's rowdiest festivals, and the vast revenues from oil and natural gas have been spent to good effect on its downtown skyscrapers and civic infrastructure.

Edmonton is a bleaker city, on the edge of an immense expanse of boreal forest and low hills that stretches to the border of the Northwest Territories and beyond. Bypassed by the Canadian Pacific Railway, which brought Calgary its early boom, Edmonton's main importance to travellers is as a gateway to the Alaska Highway and the Arctic extremities of the Yukon, as well as to the more popular landscapes of northern British Columbia. The **Yellowhead Highway** and Canada's last transcontinental **railway** link Edmonton to the town of Jasper and its national park in about four hours.

ACCOMMODATION PRICE CODES

All the accommodation prices in this book have been coded using the symbols below, corresponding to Canadian dollar rates. Prices are for the least expensive double room in each establishment in high season, excluding special offers. For a full explanation, see p.40 in Basics.

① up to $40	④ $80–100	⑦ $175–240
② $40–60	⑤ $100–125	⑧ $240+
③ $60–80	⑥ $125–175	

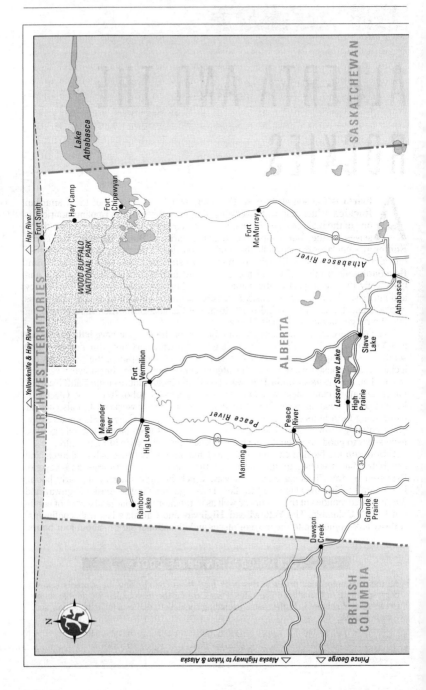

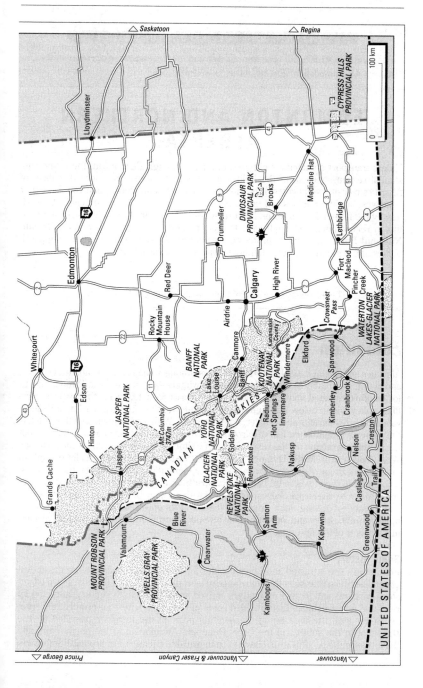

EDMONTON AND NORTHERN ALBERTA

Unless transport connections oblige you to pass through **Edmonton**, there's no substantial reason, apart from the Folk Music Festival, to visit the more downbeat of Alberta's pair of pivotal cities. It is, though, a starting point from which you can either head west into the Rockies and Jasper National Park, or aim for the unimaginable vastness of the far northern interior. **Northern Alberta** contains the only all-weather road link to Yellowknife, capital of the Northwest Territories, but other than **Wood Buffalo National Park** – the largest protected area in Canada – and a surfeit of fishing possibilities, the region has almost nothing to waylay most casual visitors.

The telephone code for Edmonton and Northern Alberta is ☎780.

Edmonton

Alberta's provincial capital, **EDMONTON** is among Canada's most northerly cities, and at times – notably in the teeth of its bitter winters – it can seem a little too far north for comfort. Situated above the waters of the North Saskatchewan River, whose park-filled valley winds below the high-rises of downtown, the city tries hard with its festivals, parks, restaurants and urban-renewal projects. With a downtown area that still has the somewhat unfinished feel of a frontier town, however, it's perhaps appropriate that the premier attraction for the vast majority of visitors is a shopping centre, the infamous **West Edmonton Mall**. This certainly has curiosity value, but not really enough to merit a special journey here. Downtown has a handful of modest sights, though most enjoyment in the city is to be had in **Old Strathcona**, a rejuvenated "historic" district south of the North Saskatchewan River filled with heritage buildings, modest museums and plenty of eating and drinking venues. Edmonton lacks the big set-piece museums of Calgary and Vancouver, but its **Space and Science Centre** is a sight within a whisker of the first rank.

Some history

Edmonton's site attracted aboriginal peoples for thousands of years before the arrival of white settlers, thanks to the abundance of local **quartzite**, used to make sharp-edged stone weapons and tools. **Fur traders** arrived in the eighteenth century, attracted by river and forest habitats that provided some of Canada's richest fur-producing territory. Better still, the area lay at the meeting point of the territory patrolled by the Blackfoot to the south and the Cree, Dene and Assiniboine to the north. Normally these aboriginal peoples would have been implacable enemies, but around Edmonton's future site they were able to coexist when trading with intermediaries like the North West Company, which built built Fort Augustus on Edmonton's present site in 1795. The fort was joined later the same year by **Fort Edmonton**, a redoubtable log stockade built by William Tomison for the Hudson's Bay Company (and named in fine sycophantic fashion after an estate owned by Sir James Winter Lake, the Hudson's Bay Company's deputy governor).

Though the area soon became a major trading district, **settlers** arrived in force only after 1870, when the HBC sold its governing right to the Dominion of Canada. The decline of the fur trade in around 1880 made little impact, as the settlement continued to operate as a staging point for travellers heading north. Worldwide demand for grain also attracted settlers to the region, now able to produce crops despite the poor climate thanks to advances in agricultural technology. Crucially, though, the first trans-Canada railway was pushed through Calgary at Edmonton's expense, and when a spur was built by the Edmonton Railway Company in 1891 it finished south of the town at Strathcona, where a new settlement developed. The city only became firmly established with the Yukon gold rush of 1897, and only then through a scam of tragic duplicity. Prompted by the city's outfitters, newspapers lured prospectors with the promise of an "All Canadian Route" to the gold fields that avoided Alaska and the dreaded Chilkoot Trail (see pp.876–877). In the event, this turned out to be a largely phantom trail across 3000km of intense wilderness. Hundreds of men perished as they pushed north; many of those who survived, or who never set off, ended up settling in Edmonton. World War II saw the city's role reinforced by its strategic position relative to Alaska, while its postwar growth was guaranteed by the **Leduc oil strike** in 1947. By 1956 some 3000 wells were in production within 100km of the city. If Edmonton has achieved any fame since, it has been in the field of **sports**, as the home of Wayne Gretzky, the greatest player in ice-hockey history. Oil money continues to bankroll all sorts of civic improvements, though never quite manages to disguise the city's rather rough-and-ready pioneer roots.

Arrival, transport and orientation

Edmonton is one of the easiest places to reach in western Canada. Its road and rail links are excellent, and the international **airport**, 29km south of downtown off Hwy 2 (Calgary Trail), is served by many national, American and European airlines. There's a small **visitor information desk** (Mon–Fri 7.30am–11.30pm, Sat & Sun 10am–11.30pm; ☎890-8382 or 1-800/268-7134) in the arrivals area: Travelex (daily 5am–11pm; ☎890-2370) **foreign exchange** facilities are upstairs in departures alongside the *Second Cup* coffee concession. The majority of internal flights from the Yukon and Northwest Territories fly here in preference to Calgary; numerous shuttle flights ply between the two cities, and if you phone around, you should be able to pick up some bargain flights. Note that the municipal airport north of downtown, still occasionally mentioned in visitors' blurb, closed to most commercial traffic in 1996; now only very small planes, including one or two shuttle flights from Calgary, use the airport, which is, nevertheless, acquiring a new $300-million international terminal (though until the Air Canada–Canadian Air merger is complete it remains to be seen how exactly that money will be spent). New international connections will certainly be added, including direct flights from Los Angeles and – quite possibly – from the UK.

A shuttle **bus**, the Sky Shuttle (☎465-8515 or 1-888/438-2342, *www.edmontonairports .com*), runs to downtown hotels on three different routes – two serving the university district and the west of the city as well – with services leaving every twenty minutes (every thirty minutes on weekends and holidays) from 4.30am to 12.15am, for $11 one-way, $18 return; there's a dedicated shuttle-info desk almost alongside the visitor-information desk, but you purchase tickets from the driver – the bus leaves from outside arrivals through doors near both desks. Taxis from the airport to the downtown area cost around $35. Note that the airport shuttle's "West End" route will take you directly to the West Edmonton Mall (see p.559): this bus runs every 45 minutes on weekdays and every hour on weekends. The new **Jasper Express** service links Edmonton airport directly with Jasper (information and reservations; ☎1-800/661-4946).

Following the closure to passengers of the famous Rockies railway via Calgary, Edmonton is also where you'll arrive if you take Canada's last remaining transcontinental passenger **train**. The new VIA Rail **station** is now some 3km or ten-minutes' drive northwest of downtown at 12360-121st St (ticket office usually daily 8am–3.30pm, longer hours when trains are due; ticket office ☎422-6032; Via Rail ☎1-800/561-8630, *www.viarail.ca*); the Greyhound **bus terminal** (daily 5.30am–midnight; depot ☎413-8747, Greyhound ☎1-800/661-8747 in Canada, 1-800/231-2222 in the US, *www.greyhound.ca*) is also central at 10324-103rd St and within easy walking distance of central downtown just to the south. It has an *A&W* restaurant, cash machine and lockers ($2). Note that if you're arriving from, or heading to, Calgary on Red Arrow buses (four daily; ☎424-3339 or 1-800/232-1958 in Alberta, *www.redarrow.pwt.ca*), their terminal is at the *Howard Johnson Plaza* hotel at 10010-104th St.

Information centres can be found at the airport in arrivals and dotted around the city, but the most central, on the Pedway Level (one level down from the street and pretty well hidden – follow signs for "Economic Development Edmonton") in the Shaw Conference Centre, 9797 Jasper Ave NW (Mon–Fri 8.30am–4pm; ☎496-8400 or 1-800/463-4667, *www.tourism.ede.org*, *www.infoedmonton.com* or *www.discoveredmonton.com*), have all the usual maps and pamphlets and can also help with accommodation. There's another big information centre south of the city at 2404 Calgary Trail Northbound SW, site of the Imperial Leduc 1 Oil Derrick and Interpretive Centre (June to early Sept daily 8am–9pm; rest of the year Mon–Fri 8.30am–4.30pm, Sat & Sun 9am–5pm).

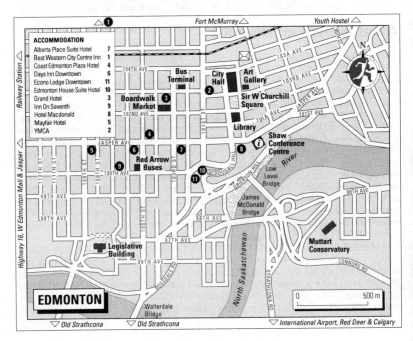

ACCOMMODATION

Alberta Place Suite Hotel	7
Best Western City Centre Inn	1
Coast Edmonton Plaza Hotel	4
Days Inn Downtown	6
Econo Lodge Downtown	11
Edmonton House Suite Hotel	10
Grand Hotel	3
Inn On Seventh	9
Hotel Macdonald	8
Mayfair Hotel	5
YMCA	2

EDMONTON

The downtown area is easily negotiated on foot. Unless you have a car, longer journeys have to be made using **Edmonton Transit**, an integrated bus and light-rail (LRT) system. Interchangeable tickets for bus and LRT cost $1.65; day-passes cost $5. You can buy tickets on buses or from machines in the ten LRT stations. Transfers are available from drivers on boarding for use on other services for ninety minutes. The LRT is free between Grandin and Churchill stations Monday to Friday 9am to 3pm and Saturday 9am to 6pm. Call ☎496-1611 for route and timetable **information** or visit the Customer Services Outlet at Church LRT Station, 99th Street (Mon–Fri 8.30am–4.30pm). For details of taxi companies, see "Listings" on p.563.

Addresses are easy to decipher if you remember that avenues run east–west, with numbers increasing as you travel further north, while streets run north–south, the numbers increasing as you move westwards. Building numbers tend to be tacked onto the end of street numbers, so that 10021-104th Avenue is 21 100th Street, at the intersection with 104th Avenue.

Accommodation

Edmonton has no shortage of **hotels**, due to its importance among business travellers. As the city sees fewer tourists than Calgary, its budget **accommodation** is more available but also less salubrious than that of its southern neighbour. There are plenty of reasonably priced beds in the big middle-ranking hotels – especially out of season. **Motels** can be found in the unlovely outskirts of the city, the main concentrations being along Stony Plain Road (northwest of downtown) and on the Calgary Trail (south). For a free **accommodation reservation service**, contact Alberta Express Reservations (☎464-3515 or 1-800/884-8803, *www.hotelforyou.com*). For details of **B&B** lodgings, contact the visitor centre or Alberta Central Bed & Breakfast Association (☎437-2568, *www.bbcanada.com/albertacentral*), but note that hotel beds in the city are generally not expensive, so you won't necessarily make much of a saving in B&Bs.

Hotels and motels

Alberta Place Suite Hotel, 10049-103rd St (☎423-1565 or 1-800/661-3982, fax 426-6260). Large, well-equipped suites with kitchens and extra facilities; weekly rates available. ④.

Best Western City Centre Inn, 11310-109th St (☎479-2042 or 1-800/666-5026, fax 474-2204, *www.travelweb.com*). Typical property of this reliable mid-priced chain. ④.

Coast Edmonton Plaza Hotel, 10155-105th St (☎423-4811 or 1-800/663-1144, fax 423-3204). Edmonton's top-of-the-pile 299-room hotel is worth considering if you want modern facilities rather than the *Macdonald*'s old-world charm (see below). ⑥.

Days Inn Downtown, 10041-106th St (☎423-1925 or 1-800/267-2191, fax 424-5302). Mid-sized and renovated central motel with parking just off Jasper Ave. ④.

Econo Lodge Downtown, 10209-100th Ave (☎428-6442 or 1-800/613-7043, fax 428-6467). Reliable downtown motel with covered parking, TV, phone and usual facilities. ④.

Edmonton House Suite Hotel, 10205-100th Ave (☎420-4000 or 1-800/661-6562, *www.edmontonhouse.com*). Bigger (300 suites) and more expensive than the *Alberta Place*, but rooms have balconies and views; also an indoor pool and a free shuttle to the West Edmonton Mall. ⑤.

Grand Hotel, 10266-103rd St (☎422-6365, fax 425-9070). Handily located near the bus terminal, this hotel is anything but grand: its 65 rooms, only some with private bath, are used mainly by long-stay residents. ②.

Inn on Seventh, 10001-107th St (☎429-2861 or 1-800/661-7327, fax 426-7225, *www.innon7th.com*). Modern, quiet and civilized high-rise, with variously priced rooms; probably the best of the middle-range hotels and close to two good restaurants – the *Portico* and *Café Select*. ④.

Hotel Macdonald, 10065-100th St (☎424-5181 or 1-800/441-1414, *www.cphotels.ca*). One of the big historic "railway" hotels run by Canadian Pacific, and undoubtedly the first choice if you want to stay in Edmonton in traditional style. Some rooms are a little small for the price, but lots of facilities including pool and health club. ⑦.

Mayfair Hotel, 10815-Jasper Ave (☎423-1650 or 1-800/463-7666, fax 425-6834). This modern city-centre hotel has 100 low-priced rooms, suites and self-catering apartments. ③.

Hostels

Hosteling International Edmonton, 10647-81st Ave (☎988-6836 or 1-877/467-8336, *eihostel@hostellingintl.ca*). This newly converted 104-bed HI hostel in a former convent in the Old Strathcona district is not so convenient for downtown, though the airport shuttle will drop you close by if you ask. Plenty of smart facilities, including laundry, library, bike rental, and roomy kitchen. Check-in after 11am; open 24 hours with no curfew. Dorm beds start at $17. ①.

St Joseph's College, 114th St and 89th Ave (☎492-7681). Small, cheap and popular student rooms; reservations required in summer. Out of the centre but well served by buses, including the #43. ①.

YMCA, 10030-102A Ave (☎421-9622). Men and women are welcome in this clean, refurbished building in an excellent downtown location. Simple three-bunk dorms (2 nights maximum), small private singles and doubles (from $55) are available. ②.

Campsites

Androssan Campground. Located 18km east of downtown on Hwy 16; 24 free sites, but no water or facilities other than fire pits.

Half Moon Lake Resort, 21524 Township Rd 520, Sherwood Park (☎922-3045, *www.halfmoonlakeresort.com*). A large 229-site private campsite with extensive facilities and outdoor activities, 29km east of town on 23rd Ave/Hwy 520 and then 4km down a signposted side road. May to early Oct. $19.

Rainbow Valley Campground, 13204-45th Ave (☎434-5531). The only site within the city limits: 85 sites off the Whitemud Freeway at 119th St and 45th Ave in Whitemud Park. It's full by afternoon in summer, so arrive early or be sure to book. Mid-April to mid-Oct. $15.

Shakers Acres Tent and Trailer Park, 21530-103rd Ave (☎447-3564, fax 447-3924). A rather exposed 170-site ground northwest of the city north of Stony Plain Rd; exit Hwy 16 at Winterburn Rd. April–Oct. $14.

The City

Edmonton feels oddly dispersed, even in the six-block **downtown** area around Sir Winston Churchill Square and along the main east–west drag, **Jasper Avenue** (101st Ave). Bounded to the south by the North Saskatchewan River, this grid holds a few assorted points of interest, though much of the younger and more cosmopolitan Edmonton resides south of the river in **Old Strathcona** (see also "Eating and drinking"). For the **West Edmonton Mall**, the **Space and Science Centre**, and the **Provincial Museum**, you'll need to take transport west from downtown. To stretch your legs, wander up and down the big string of attractive parks that protects the river, or cross the Low Level Bridge to the **Muttart Conservatory**, another worthwhile feat consisting of four space-age glass pyramids filled with flora and natural-history displays.

Downtown

Downtown Edmonton only really comes alive as a place to wander on sunny days when office workers pour out for lunch; otherwise it's really not much of a place to linger unless you're in town for one of the city's many festivals. However, with time to kill the following low-key sites would keep you occupied. The **Edmonton Art Gallery** (Mon–Wed 10.30am–5pm, Thurs & Fri 10.30am–8pm, Sat, Sun & holidays 11am–5pm; $4, free Thurs 4–8pm, ☎422-6223), part of the Civic Centre on 99th Street and 102nd Avenue on the north edge of Sir Winston Churchill Square, deals mainly in modern Canadian artists, though it also hosts many visiting exhibitions. To get here if you're not already downtown, take the #2 bus or LRT to Churchill station. More satisfyingly offbeat is the **Edmonton Police Museum and Archives** on the third floor of the central police station at 9620-103A Avenue (Mon–Sat 9am–3pm, closed public holidays; free; ☎421-2274), which traces the long arm of Albertan law enforcement from the formation of what would become the RCMP (Royal Canadian Mounted Police) in 1873 to the city's current flatfoots. Marvel at handcuffs, old jail cells and a stuffed rat that served time as an RCMP mascot.

Walk across the Low Level Bridge to the distinctive glass pyramids of the **Muttart Conservatory** (Mon–Fri 9am–6pm, Sat & Sun 11am–6pm; $4.75; ☎496-8755), just south of downtown and the river at 9626-96A Street. Three high-tech greenhouses reproduce tropical, temperate and arid climates, complete with the trees and plants (and occasional exotic birds) which flourish in them; a fourth houses a potpourri of experimental botanical projects and temporary exhibitions. If you don't want to walk, take **bus #51** (Capilano) travelling south on 100th Street just south of Jasper Avenue as far as 98th Avenue and 97A Street, then walk one block south.

Finally, you might stop by for a free guided tour of the domed sandstone **Alberta Legislature Building** (March to late May & early Sept to Feb Mon–Fri 9am–4.30pm, Sat & Sun noon–5pm; late May to early Sept Mon–Fri 8.30am–5pm, Sat & Sun 9am–5pm) south of Jasper Avenue on 97th Avenue and 107th Street (the nearest LRT station is Grandin). Set in the manner of a medieval cathedral over an ancient shrine, it was built in 1912 on the original site of Fort Edmonton. Topped by a vaulted dome, it's a big city landmark, its interior reflecting the grandiose self-importance of the province's early rulers, who imported wood for their headquarters from as far afield as Belize: the marble came from Québec, Pennsylvania and Italy, the granite from rival British Columbia. Just to the north, amidst 57 acres of parkland that flanks the building, stands the **Alberta Legislative Assembly Interpretive Centre**, where you can learn more than you probably want to know about Alberta's political history and the building in which much of it took place (same hours as Legislature; ☎427-2826 for general information on the Legislature Building, ☎427-7362 for tour information and booking).

Old Strathcona

The **Strathcona** district south of the North Saskatchewan River grew up at the end of the nineteenth century, thanks to a decision by the Calgary and Edmonton Railway Company (C&E) to avoid the expense of a bridge across the North Saskatchewan River by concluding a rail spur from Calgary south of the river and Edmonton proper. In 1912, when its population had reached about 7500, the new town was incorporated into the city. Today the streets and many of the older buildings have been spruced up in a manner typical of urban-renewal projects – lots of new pavements and fake period street furniture. This said, it's still the city's best-preserved old quarter, and the nicest to wander around on a sunny day. Plenty of buses run here from downtown, or you can walk across the river via the Walterdale or High Level bridges. The best approach is to take the LRT to University station and board buses #8, #43 or #46 to 104th Street and 82nd Avenue.

The area centres on **Whyte Avenue** (82nd Ave) to the south, 109th Street to the west, and 103rd to the east. Most of the cafés, restaurants and shops are on or just off Whyte or 103rd, which makes the **Old Strathcona Foundation** office (summer Mon–Fri 8.30am–4.30pm; rest of the year Tues & Wed 8.30am–4.30pm; ☎433-5866), at 401-10324 Whyte Ave, on the corner of these two thoroughfares, a sensible first port of call. Here you can pick up pamphlets detailing walks and drives that take in the area's historic buildings. Just to the north, on 83rd Avenue, is the **Old Strathcona Farmers' Market** (July & Aug Sat 8am–3pm, Tues & Thurs noon–4pm; rest of the year Sat 8am–3pm; ☎439-1844; free), a happy hunting ground for picnic supplies and craft goods.

If you tire of wandering or sitting in cafés, you can give a little structure to your exploration by heading for one or both of the area's two small museums. Rail buffs should check out the **C&E Railway Museum**, 10447-86th Ave (June to Aug Tues–Sat 10am–4pm, winter by appointment; $2; ☎433-9739), a collection of railway memorabilia, costumes and photos housed in a replica of Strathcona's original 1891 station. Nostalgia buffs might make for the **Telephone Historical Information Centre**, 10437-83rd Ave (Tues–Fri 10am–4pm, Sat noon–4pm; $3; ☎441-2077), a collection of exhibits and displays connected with telecommunications in Edmonton past, present and future housed in Strathcona's original 1912 telephone exchange. It's North America's largest museum of its kind.

The Provincial Museum of Alberta

Housed in a drab building well out in the western suburbs – a ten-minute drive from downtown – at 12845-102nd Ave, the **Provincial Museum of Alberta** (daily 9am–5pm; $6.50; ☎453-9100) makes a reasonable introduction to the history, culture, flora and fauna of western Canada if Edmonton is your first stop in the region. There's no getting round the fact, though, that Calgary, Victoria and Vancouver all have vastly superior museums on similar themes, although much of Edmonton's museum is in the process of being spruced up. To reach it by **bus**, take the #1, #14, #100, #111, #113, #114 or #120 buses heading west to "Jasper Place" on Jasper Avenue.

Natural history exhibits include painted dioramas and stuffed animals, taxidermy being the stock in trade of virtually all western Canada's museums; by far the best section concerns the region's bison herds and their virtual extinction. Other displays include a humdrum collection of domestic appliances, a couple of beautiful chrome stoves and vintage jukeboxes and a rundown of the **native peoples** of the province. The last collection used to be pretty workaday, but has been cheered up considerably by the Syncrude Gallery of Aboriginal Culture, where money from Syncrude, one of the big companies involved in the oil sand business, has produced a series of state-of-the-art multimedia displays that do justice to the history and culture of the Blackfoot and other aboriginal cultures with displays of art, artefacts, and other exhibits. Other more engaging parts of the museum are the Bug, a showcase of live and often exotic insects, and "Earth's Changing Face", a geological display of gems, minerals, rocks and dinosaur exhibits. The museum also comes into its own when hosting temporary and travelling exhibitions from collections and museums around the world – ask at the visitor centre for details of latest exhibitions.

Fort Edmonton Park

Located southwest of the city on a deep-cut bend of the North Saskatchewan River at the southwest end of Quesnell Bridge and Fox Drive, the 158-acre **Fort Edmonton Park** (daily late May to late June Mon–Fri 10am–4pm, Sat & Sun 10am–6pm; late June to early Sept daily 10am–6pm; rest of Sept Mon–Sat 11am–3pm, Sun & holidays 11am–6pm; $7.25 late June to early Sept, ☎5.50 rest of the opening period; ☎496-8787) undertakes to re-create the history of white settlement in Edmonton during the nineteenth century. Everything has been built from scratch and, while you can't fault the attention to detail, the pristine woodwork of the supposedly old buildings hardly evokes period authenticity (though the carpentry methods are apparently those used around 1846). To get here take the LRT to University station and there pick up buses #4, #30, #32 or #106 to Fox Drive, Whitemud Drive and Keillor Road, about ten-minutes' walk from the site, which is off the Whitemud Freeway near the Quesnell Bridge.

The heart of the complex is a facsimile of **Fort Edmonton**, a fur-trading post dominated by the Big House, former home of the Chief Factor, John Rowland, head of the (then) ill-defined Saskatchewan District between 1828 and 1854. Arranged around the house are the quarters of the 130 or so people who called the fort home and who are now represented by appropriately dressed guides pretending to be blacksmiths, shopkeepers and schoolteachers from the era. Edmonton's later, pre-railway age is represented by a rendition of Jasper Avenue as it appeared in 1885, while two other streets simulate 1905 and 1920, complete with working steam engines and trams, which you can ride at no additional cost, to bolster the period effect.

Edmonton Space and Science Centre

The splendid **Edmonton Space and Science Centre** opened in Coronation Park, 11211-142nd St, in 1984, and is now one of the city's principal attractions (Tues–Sun 10am–8.30pm; $6.95, Combo Pack $11.95 includes Zeidler Star Theatre Shows, exhibits and scientific demonstrations or one IMAX film presentation; ☎451-3344 or 452-9100, *www.edmontonscience.com*). The complex has two main attractions: the **Margaret Zeidler Star Theatre** (daily 11am–7pm) houses Canada's largest planetarium dome, several galleries and presents different laser and star shows hourly; and the **IMAX Theatre**, housed with a café and shop in the so-called Lower Gallery, is a large-screen cinema with special-format films and laser shows (prices and times vary according to shows). Elsewhere, the Middle Gallery features a range of temporary exhibitions on scientific and technological themes, while the Upper Gallery contains the **Challenger Centre** and its "Astronaut Missions", designed to allow you to make simulated space missions. There are also assorted displays on advanced communications technology, and a selection of the various science demonstrations you can expect to see around the centre throughout the day. Computers are dealt with in the Dow Computer Lab, while budding astronomers can check in to the centre's **Observatory** (weather allowing Fri 8pm–midnight, Sat & Sun 1–5pm & 8pm–midnight). To **get here** on public transport take a #5 (Westmount) bus travelling west on 102nd Avenue and then north on 124th Street – ask the driver to tell you when you're close.

West Edmonton Mall

"Your Adventure Awaits", announces the brochure to **West Edmonton Mall** (☎444-5200 or 1-800/463-4667, *www.westedmall.com*), preparing you for a place that gets eleven mentions in the *Guinness Book of Records*, including its main claim to fame as the "largest shopping mall in the world." Built at a total cost of $1.1 billion, the complex extends over the equivalent of 115 American football fields (or 48 city blocks) and boasts more than 800 shops – of which some 110 are restaurants – plus 19 cinemas, and 11 department stores. The mall's effect on Edmonton has been double-edged: it employs 15,000 people but has captured thirty percent of the city's retail business, thus crippling the downtown shopping area, though it has also succeeded, to everyone's surprise, in attracting twenty million visitors a year (or 55,000 a day).

Funnily enough, many of the shops are rather downmarket (retail hours are Mon–Fri 10am–9pm, Sat 10am–6pm, Sun noon–6pm), though the sheer size of the place is enough to keep you browsing all day. There's almost a queue of superlatives. Its car park is the world's largest, with room for 20,000 cars; it has the world's largest water park (50 million litres of water); it uses enough power to run a town of 50,000 people; and features the world's only indoor bungee jump (jumps from about $60, to $90 if you want the full video and T-shirt package). The world's largest indoor lake (122m long), part of a cluster of attractions known as **Deep Sea Adventure** (Mon–Thurs 11pm–4.30pm, Fri & Sat 11am–7.30pm, Sun 11am–5.30pm; $13) contains a full-sized replica of Columbus's *Santa Maria*, and four working submarines – more than are owned by the Canadian navy – offering an underwater trip past some 200 different species of marine life. Other distractions here include dolphin shows ($2), canoe rentals, scuba diving and an underwater aquarium ($3 on its own) laced with the inevitable sharks.

Then there's the world's largest indoor **amusement park**, the Galaxyland (Mon–Thurs noon–8pm, Fri & Sat 10am–10pm, Sun 11am–7pm; day-pass $29.95), which features such attractions as the *Drop of Doom*, a thirteen-storey "free-fall experience", and the fourteen-storey *Mindbender* triple-loop roller coaster. The latter, it comes as no surprise to learn, is the world's largest indoor roller coaster. The **World Waterpark**, by contrast, is a superb collection of vast swimming pools, immense water slides and wave pools (Mon–Thurs noon–7pm, Fri & Sat 10am–8pm, Sun 11am–6pm; day-pass $29.95, cheaper after 5pm). If you've still any energy, you can also ice-skate on a National Hockey League-size skating rink ($4.50 a session, skate rental $3). You could round off the day or indulge yourself further in one of the mall's many **cinemas** (including a recently introduced IMAX), the Ice Palace, Dolphin Presentations, Sea Life Caverns, Professor Wem's Golf Adventure, or a variety of clubs. If you want to go the whole hog, then spend the night, in the 354-room **Fantasyland Hotel** (☎444-3000 or 1-800/661-6454; ⑦) where 118 of the rooms are intricately equipped and decorated to fulfil various assorted fantasies: Roman, Hollywood, Arabian, Victorian Coach, African, Igloo, Canadian Rail and, most intriguing of all, Truck. Cheaper rooms are available without jacuzzis and mirrored ceilings. There are over 100 places to **eat** – the best of which are listed below – some lined up on two "theme" streets: Europa Boulevard and a New Orleans-style Bourbon Street.

Bus services to the mall heading west out of downtown include #100, #109, #111 and #113. The monster's location, so far as it has an address (it has five different postal codes and 58 entrances – remember which one you parked by if you've come by car), is 170th Street and 87th Avenue. Maps are available throughout the main building at information booths, where you can also get **information** and any number of facts and figures. If you get tired, scooters can be rented from about $6 an hour. For more information, call ☎444-5200 or 1-800/661-8890.

Eating and drinking

Edmonton has 2000-odd **restaurants**, some of them very good. There's plenty in or near downtown, but if you want a bit of nocturnal zip to go with your meal you'd do best to head out to **Old Strathcona**, a vibrant district of café culture, nightlife and alternative arts located principally along 82nd (Whyte) Avenue between 102nd and 105th streets – any bus marked "University Transit Centre" from 100th Street will get you there. Ethnic options – notably restaurants serving Edmonton's populations of Ukrainian and Eastern European origin – complement the standard Italian-influenced cuisine or steak-and-salmon offerings. Otherwise, the stalls in the downtown mall and streetfront snack bars are lively at lunch time, and all the usual fast-food, snack and breakfast options are available. **Beer** drinkers should be sure to try the local real ale, Big Rock.

Cafés

Café La Gare, 10308a-81st Ave. Small tea-and-coffee joint in Old Strathcona; the sort of place where you can read a book or paper for hours. Occasional evening poetry readings.

Grabbajabba, 82nd Ave and 104th St. Coffee, cake and the works at this very popular nonsmoking café in the heart of Old Strathcona; other outlets around the city.

9th Street Bistro, 9910-109th St. Relaxed and cosy hangout – generous helpings, imaginative soups and good desserts.

Zenari's on First, Manulife Building, 10117-101st St (☎425-6151). This is a great downtown Italian deli/houseware shop with a tremendous lunch counter for soups, salads, sandwiches, pasta, pizza and other Italian staples.

Restaurants

Bistro Praha, 10168-100A St (☎424-4218). A good opportunity to sample Eastern European cuisine, Edmonton style, in the city's oldest European-style restaurant. Slightly highbrow and expensive, though – better for lunch or late at night.

Café Select, 10018-106th St (☎423-0419). An excellent, intimate place, trendy without being intimidating. Serving fine, simple bistro-type food, it's one of downtown's best choices for a late-night treat; book ahead. Moderate.

Da-De-O, 10548A-82nd (Whyte) Ave (☎433-0930). A bright, brash and popular Old Strathcona 1950s-style bistro-diner that claims "loud food and spicy music": this may sound off-putting, but the mostly Cajun food is actually pretty good, the clientele is pleasantly mixed, and things get satisfyingly lively later on. Inexpensive.

De Vine's, 9712-111th St (☎482-6402). Innovative French-Canadian cuisine served in an old residence just outside the city centre with great river-valley views, an excellent place for a romantic or special occasion; book ahead. Moderate.

Earl's, 11830 Jasper Ave (☎448-6582). This invariably excellent chain of relaxed and popular mid-range restaurants has no fewer than eight Edmonton outlets serving modern North American cuisine. This branch, known as the *Tin Palace*, is the most central.

Hardware Grill, 9698 Jasper Ave (☎423-0969). The seasonally inspired Canadian cuisine in the best restaurant in Edmonton is served in a chic modern enivornment with dark hardwood floors, simple lines and elegant linen. Be sure to book. Expensive.

Il Portico, 10012-107th St (☎424-0707). A tasteful and innovative Italian restaurant opposite the *Inn on 7th* hotel with lovely outdoor terrace for dining in good weather. Moderate.

Jack's Grill, 5842-111th St (☎434-1113). Probably a tad too south of the city centre unless you have a car, but this is one of the top-rated places in Edmonton for modern, innovative Pacific Rim cuisine. Moderate.

The King and I, 8208-107th St (☎433-2222). If you want a change from steaks, salmon and the Italian-based cuisine of many Edmonton restaurants, then you can't do better than this superlative Thai restaurant. Moderate.

La Ronde, 10111 Bellamy Hill (☎428-6611). Stunning views of Edmonton from the city's only revolving dining room (atop the *Crowne Plaza Château Lacombe*). The Albertan cooking – steaks, bison, berries – is good too. Dancing nightly, live entertainment Fri–Sun. Expensive.

Mandarin, 11044-82nd Ave (☎433-8494). Edmonton's best Chinese restaurant is located on the western side of the Old Strathcona district. Inexpensive.

Packrat Louie, 10335-83rd Ave (☎433-0123). Bright, young and welcoming bistro in Old Strathcona with generous portions of steaks, salads, chicken and other more sophisticated international dishes. Closed Sun & Mon. Inexpensive to moderate.

Silk Hat, 10251 Jasper Ave (☎425-1920). A fine place to knock back a Molson from the brewery up the road, this local institution's dim interior hasn't altered in forty years. Best known for the 1950s jukeboxes at each booth, but the inexpensive, basic food is as good as the ambience.

Sorrentino's, 10401-82nd Ave (☎439-7700). One of six family-run Italian restaurants with great atmosphere and service serving good affordable food in a pleasant, stylish setting. This the Old Strathcona location: the downtown branch is at 10162-100th St (☎424-7500).

Nightlife and entertainment

Edmonton's enthusiastic self-promotion as Canada's "Festival City" may have something to do with its relative shortage of indigenous **nightlife**. There are any number of small-time nightspots, especially in Old Strathcona, putting on live music, but larger clubs capable of attracting big names are thin on the ground. Such big-name acts as do appear – as well as theatre companies, **Alberta Ballet** (☎428-6839), **Edmonton Opera** (☎429-1000) – tend to use the University of Alberta's Jubilee Auditorium, 87th Avenue and 114th Street (☎427-2760, *www.jubileeauditorium.com*), and the Citadel Theatre, 9828-101A Ave (☎426-4811, 425-1820 or 1-888/425-1820, *www.citadeltheatre.com*): the latter, with five performance spaces, is Canada's largest theatre complex. Some companies, plus the **Edmonton Symphony Orchestra** (☎428-1414, *www.edmontonsymphony.com*), use the excellent new performance space, the Francis Winspear Centre for Music, 4 Sir Winston Churchill Square (☎428-1414, *www.winspearcentre.com*). The season for most of the city's dozen or more theatre companies runs from May to September. For revivals, foreign films and art-house **cinema**, try the old Princess Theatre, 10337-82nd Ave (☎433-0728).

The best **listings** source is the free weekly *Vue* (published Thurs, available from stores, hotels and street kiosks), as well as the entertainment sections of the city's main newspapers, the *Edmonton Journal* and the *Sun*. **Tickets** for most classical music, dance, opera, theatre and other events – including big-name concerts and Edmonton Oilers **ice-hockey** games, which are played in the Skyreach Centre (formerly the Edmonton Coliseum), 118th Avenue and 74th Street – are available from Ticketmaster outlets (☎451-8000) around the city.

Clubs, discos and live music

Blues on Whyte at the *Commercial Hotel*, 10329-82nd Ave (☎439-5058). One of the city's better live music clubs; bands most nights, Saturday jam sessions.

Cook County Saloon, 8010-103rd St (☎432-2665). Deservedly popular, old Strathcona C&W venue, cited as Canada's best country nightclub on a least five occasions by the Canadian Country Music Association. Free dance lessons Thurs 7.30pm to 9pm.

O'Byrne's Irish Pub, 10616-82nd Ave (☎414-67660. Old Strathcona's popular verion of an Irish pub has good food, live music, drink and reasonably authentic atmosphere.

Sidetrack Café, 10333-112th St (☎421-1326). Despite its disconcertingly bombed-out surroundings, this is the city's best live-music venue, where you're most likely to see hugely varied international and local acts of some standing.

Yardbird Suite, 10203-86th Ave (☎432-0428). Live groups nightly (10pm–2am) in the city's top jazz venue; admission is lower for the Tuesday-night jam session. Nonsmoking rule enforced on Friday.

Yuk Yuk's, Bourbon St, Entrance 6, West Edmonton Mall (☎481-9857). Assorted comedy acts every night, featuring well-known US and Canadian names. Wednesday is amateur night; Tuesday, hypnotist night.

Festivals

Hardly any area of entertainment goes uncelebrated by a festival at some time of the year in Edmonton, the self-proclaimed "Festival City". There's almost always something good on. One of the best events – and one of the few to merit a special pilgrimage here – is the **Edmonton Folk Music Festival** (☎429-1899), rated the best in North America by *Rolling Stone*: it's held at Gallagher Park (near the Muttart Conservatory) at the end of the first week in August. Also well regarded are the **International Street Performers Festival** (☎425-5162), which attracts over 1000 street performers in early July; the **International Jazz City Festival** (☎432-7166) at the end of June; and the increasingly popular August **Fringe Festival**, or Fringe Theatre Event (☎448-9000), a ten-day theatrical jamboree that's turned into one of the largest festivals of its kind in North America.

The more contrived and commercial **Klondike Days** (☎471-7210 or 423-2822) is less compelling, a blowout that claims to be the continent's largest "outdoor entertainment" but has rather too obviously been cobbled together to steal some of Calgary's Stampede thunder. Held for ten days during July, this popular outing revolves around a re-creation of the 1890s gold-rush era, with plenty for kids, and a panoply of events: one of the best is "A Taste of Edmonton", where 40-odd local retaurants set up stalls and let you taste tidbits from their menus.

Listings

Airlines Air Canada and Air BC (☎423-1222 or 1-888/247-2262); American (☎1-800/433-7300); Canada 3000 (☎890-4592); Delta (☎426-5990, 890-4410 or 1-800/221-1212); Northwest Airlines (☎1-800/225-2525); NWT Air (☎1-800/267-1247).

Airport information ☎890-8382.

Ambulance ☎911 or 426-3232.

Bike rental River Valley Cycle & Snowboards, 9124-82nd St (☎465-3863).

Bookshops Old Strathcona is renowned for its many stores selling both new and secondhand books: Greenwood's (☎439-2005) on 82nd Ave between 103rd and 104th, is one of the city's best; Athabasca Books (☎431-1776) on 105th St north of 82nd Ave, is a quality secondhand outlet. Or try big modern outlets such as Chapters, 9952-170th St (☎487-6500).

Bus enquiries Greyhound (☎413-8747 or 1-800/661-8747); Jasper Express (☎1-800/661-4946); buses from airport to Jasper. Red Arrow: for Calgary, Red Deer and Fort McMurray (☎424-3339 or 1-800/232-1958). Sky Shuttle/Airporter to and from the airport (☎465-8515).

Car rental Avis (☎890-7596 or 423-2847); Budget (☎448-2000 448-2060, 1-800/661-7027); Discount (☎448-3888 or 1-800/263-2355); Hertz (☎450-9610 or 1-800/263-0600); National (☎1-800/227-7368); Rent-a-Wreck (☎986-3335 or 1-800/223-3033); Thrifty (☎428-8555); Tilden (☎1-800/227-7368).

Dentist Contact the Alberta Dental Association (☎432-1012).

Directory enquiries Telephone information (☎411).

Emergency ☎911.

Exchange Thomas Cook, ManuLife Place, 10165-102nd St (Mon–Fri 9.30am–5.30pm, Sat 11am–4pm; ☎448-3660).

Hospitals Edmonton General, 1111 Jasper Ave (☎482-8111): no emergency service. Emergency departments at Royal Alexandra Hospital, 10240 Kingsway (☎477-4111); Misericordia Community Hospital & Health Centre, 16940-87th Ave (☎930-5611); and University of Alberta Hospital, 8440-112th St (☎407-8822).

Laundry Jasper Place Coin Laundry, 11122-153rd St (daily 7.30am–8pm; ☎454-1907).

Library Centennial Library, 7 Sir Winston Churchill Square (Mon–Fri 9am–9pm, Sat 9am–6pm, Sun 1–5pm; ☎496-7000).

Maps and guides Map Town, 10344-105th St (Mon–Fri 9am–6pm, Sat 10am–2pm; ☎429-2600).

Outdoor equipment Mountain Equipment Co-op, 12328-102nd Ave (☎488-6614); Totem, 7430-99th St (☎432-1223).

Police (☎423-4567, 421-3333 or 945-5330).

Post office 9808-103A Ave (☎944-3271 or 1-800/565-3271).

Public transport ☎496-1611 for all city transport.

Road conditions ☎471-6056.

Taxis Alberta Co-op (☎425-2525); Barrel (☎489-777); Checker Cabs (☎484-8888); Skyline (☎468-4646); Yellow Cabs (☎462-3456).

Tickets For tickets to most sporting and other events, call Ticketmaster ☎451-8000.

Time ☎449-4444.

Tourist information ☎496-8400, 1-800/463-4667 or 1-800/661-8888.

Tours Edmonton Discovery (☎482-5991): nature tours. Nite Tours (☎453-2134): night excursions on London double-decker buses. Out an' About Travel (☎909-8687): general tours.

Train information VIA Rail (☎422-6032 or 1-800/561-8630).

Travel agent Travel Cuts, 10127A-124th St (☎488-8487).

Weather information ☎468-4940.

Northern Alberta

North of Edmonton stretches an all-but-uninhabited landscape of rippling hills, rivers, lakes, lonely farms, open prairie and the unending mantle of the northern forests. Compared to the spectacular mountain scenery to the west, northern Alberta is more akin to the monotony of the central plains of Saskatchewan and Manitoba. Unless you're fishing or boating, or just into sheer untrammelled wilderness, little here is worth detouring for, with the possible exception of the huge **Wood Buffalo National Park** on the border with the Northwest Territories.

The two great north-flowing waterways – the **Peace River** and **Athabasca River** – were the area's traditional arteries, but they have now been superseded by three main roads. The most travelled is **Hwy 16** (the Yellowhead Hwy), which runs due west from Edmonton to Jasper and onwards through the Rockies to Prince George and Prince

Rupert (both in BC); **Hwy 43–Hwy 2** heads to Grande Prairie and Dawson Creek (BC) – Mile Zero of the Alaska Highway; and **Hwy 43–Hwy 35** (the Mackenzie Hwy) bisects northern Alberta and provides its only road link to the Northwest Territories.

Direct long-haul Greyhound **buses** run on all these routes from Edmonton, supplemented by the **VIA Rail** service from Edmonton to Jasper (with connections on to Vancouver or Prince Rupert). Few roads merit travelling for their own sake, particularly for trips to Wood Buffalo National Park or Hay River (NWT). **Flying** can be a valuable time-saving option, but it's going to be very expensive unless you've organized internal flights before coming to Canada (see Basics, p.34).

Highway 16 towards Jasper

Highway 16, or the Yellowhead Highway, is, as Edmonton's Chamber of Commerce likes to call it, "the other Trans-Canada Highway"; the second and less-travelled transcontinental route and – by comparison to the Calgary–Banff route – a longer way of making for the Rocky Mountain national parks. For the first three hours or so it's dull going, but the scenery picks up considerably for the last hour through the eastern margins of the Jasper National Park (see p.643). Jasper town lies 357km west of Edmonton on the highway, an easy journey by car, **bus** (4–5 daily; $49.49) or **train**, whose tracks run parallel to the highway for much of the route (Mon, Thurs & Sat; $125).

Numerous **campsites** and **motels** service the road at regular intervals, the main concentrations being at **Edson**, halfway to Jasper, and **Hinton**. Edson's ten or so motels are all much of a muchness if you're breaking your journey, the cheapest of those you'd want to stay in being the *Summit Motel*, 4818-4th Ave (☎723-6199; ②). Two nearby sites provide camping: the *Lions Club Campground* (☎723-3169; $15; May–Sept) on the east side of town, and the *Willmore Recreation Park* (☎723-4401; $10; May–Oct), 6km south on 63rd Street. The **tourist office** is in RCMP Centennial Park, 5433 3rd Ave (summer daily 8am–6pm; rest of the year Mon–Fri 9am–5pm; ☎723-3339). For **food**, try *Ernie O's*, 4320 2nd Ave (☎723-3600), good for breakfast, or the smarter *Mountain Pizza & Steakhouse*, 5102 4th Ave (☎723-3900).

Highway 43–Highway 2 towards Dawson Creek (BC)

Highway 43 out of Edmonton to Grande Prairie, and **Hwy 2** thereafter, ambles through terminally unexceptional towns, hills and prairie scenery on its way west to Dawson Creek (p.871). It's a mind-numbing day's journey by car or **bus** (2 daily): bus connections run via Grande Prairie (2–4 daily), 463km from Edmonton, where you may wash up if you're forced to break your journey.

Failing dismally to live up to its evocative name, **GRANDE PRAIRIE**'s unfocused sprawl is a legacy of having the luxury of unlimited space in which to build (the centre is a little nicer). The **infocentre** (daily June to early Sept 8.30am–8.30pm; ☎539-7688, *www.city.grand-prairie.ab.ca*) is by Bear Creek Reservoir, off the main highway, which bypasses the main part of town to the west (it's staffed by volunteers, so hours may vary). Most of Grande Prairie's many **motels** are on the strip known as Richmond Avenue (100th Ave), which links the southern part of the highway bypass to downtown. All are vast affairs with bargain prices – the top-of-the-line is the *Golden Inn Hotel*, 11201-100th Ave (☎539-6000 or 1-800/661-7954; ⑤), and one of the cheapest is the *Lodge Motor Inn*, 10909-100th Ave (☎539-4700 or 1-800/661-7874; ③). For **food**, head for the *Trax Dining Room*, 11001-100th Ave (☎532-0776), open early until late for breakfast, lunch and dinner. The bus depot is at 9918-121st St (☎539-1111).

One of Canada's ultimate **cowboy bars**, incidentally, has to be *Kelly's Bar* in the *Sutherland Inn* at **Clairmont**, immediately north of Grande Prairie. Owned by a

Calgary Stampede chuck-wagon champion, it's the sort of place that has saddles for bar stools and serves up shooters in bull-semen collection tubes.

Along Highway 35: Peace River country

Alberta's northern reaches are accessible only from **Hwy 35**, still a route for the adventurous and one which, according to Albertans, shows the real side of the province: a world of redneck homesteads, buffalo burgers, and the sort of genuine C&W bars where strangers on a Friday night meet silent stares but wind up being invited to the hoedown anyway. You'll find such spots more or less everywhere along the route, but very little in the way of motels, garages or campsites, so come prepared. The road itself is well kept and straight, allowing healthier progress than on the more serpentine Alaska Highway to the west. Two Greyhound **buses** run daily from Edmonton to Peace River, and one all the way to Hay River (NWT), where you can make connections for Yellowknife and Fort Smith.

Peace River

If you're travelling under your own steam you'll probably have to stay overnight in **PEACE RIVER**, 486km from Edmonton and the starting point of Hwy 35. The largest town in the region, it has a handful of standard **motels**: the *Peace Valley Inn,* 9609-101st St (☎624-2020 or 1-800/661-5897; ④), alongside a 24-hour *Smitty's Restaurant,* the central *Best Canadian Motor Inn,* 9810-98th St (☎624-2586 or 1-800/461-9782; ②), and – probably the best choice – the large *Traveller's Motor Hotel,* on the northern edge of downtown at 9510-100th St (☎624-3621 or 1-888/700-2264; ③). There's also the 84-site *Peace River Lion's Club* **campsite** with showers (☎624-2120; $13; May–Oct) at Lion's Club Park on the west side of the river. The Greyhound bus depot is downtown at 9801-97th Ave (☎624-1777) – the *Crescent Motor Inn* is two blocks south of here – while the **tourist office** operates out of the old station building at 9309-100th St (summer daily 10am–6pm; ☎624-2044) on the northern edge of the downtown core; the *Peace Valley Inn* and *Traveller's Motor Hotel* are both close by.

Manning

Modern **MANNING**, 50km north of Peace River, is the last sizeable community and services centre for another 200km, making its pair of **motels** vital and often very busy as a result. The sixteen-unit *Garden Court* (☎836-3399; ④) has kitchenettes and is smaller and a shade more expensive than the 42-unit *Manning Motor Inn* (☎836-2801; ③). For the tiny nine-site municipal **campsite** (☎836-3606; $10; May–Sept) on the Notikewin River, turn east at the summer-only **infocentre** (summer daily 9am–5pm; ☎836-3875) on the highway. Camping (25 sites) is also sometimes available on the Condy Meadows golf course (☎836-2176), north of town on Hwy 35 – look for signs ($10).

Only a couple of basic campsites and the odd wind-blown store disturb the peace **north of Manning**, though if you're **camping** it's as well to know you can expect the unwelcome nocturnal attention of bears in these parts. Official tenting spots are *Notikewin Provincial* (☎554-1348; $9; May–Oct), 30km east of Hwy 35 on Hwy 692 – look for the junction 37km north of Manning, and the 49-site *Twin Lakes Provincial Recreation Area* (☎554-1348; $9; May–Sept), a total of 65km north of Manning on Hwy 35.

High Level and beyond

As with all the larger settlements hereabouts, you're only going to stop in **HIGH LEVEL**, 199km north of Manning, if you want a place to bed down. Room rates begin to creep up the further north you go, and most of the town's six **motels** charge around

$60. Book ahead, as rooms are often filled with away from home workers. The ritzi-est are the 75-unit *Four Winds Hotel* (☎926-3736, *www.4windshotel.com*; ②) and the *Our Place Apartment Hotel* (☎926-2556; ③), which has 20 two-bedroom suites with kitchenettes. Then comes the *Stardust Motor Inn* (☎926-4222; ②). The best option for **campers** is to splash out for the private facilities of the 40-site *Aspen Ridge Campground* (☎926-4540; $15; April–Oct), 3km south of the centre on the main road (Hwy 35). The **tourist office** (summer daily 9am–5pm; rest of the year Mon–Fri 9am–5pm; ☎926-4811) is at the southern end of town in the same building as the town's small mus-eum.

Between High Level, the Alberta–NWT Border (191km) and Hay River (NWT), a string of campsites provides the only **accommodation**, and three aboriginal hamlets – Meander River, Steen River and Indian Cabins – offer only food and petrol.

Wood Buffalo National Park

Straddling the border between Alberta and the Northwest Territories, **WOOD BUF-FALO NATIONAL PARK** covers an area larger than Switzerland, making it Canada's largest national park (45,000 square kilometres) and the world's second-largest pro-tected environment (the largest is in Greenland). Though wild and vast in its extent, the park is limited to low hills, lakes, grasslands, boreal forest, salt plains and marsh; these drain into the Peace and Athabasca rivers and then into Lake Claire, forming one of the world's largest freshwater deltas in the process. To the casual visitor the landscape is likely to be a disappointment – there are no real "sights" or scenic set-pieces to com-pare with the Rockies – but for dedicated naturalists or those who are prepared to spend time (and money) allowing the landscapes under their skin, the park holds much of interest, embracing North America's finest karst (limestone) scenery, classic swaths of boreal forest and rare salt-plain habitats in the park's topography.

In addition to the park's 46 species of mammals, including black and grizzly bear and lynx, the Peace–Athabasca river delta in the park's southeast corner boasts 227 species of wildfowl – no fewer than four major migration routes overfly the area. The park is the world's only river rookery of rare white pelicans and the last refuge of the critically endangered **whooping crane** – first discovered in a remote part of the park as late as 1954. Though there were only 21 of the majestic birds when they were first discovered, there are over 130 today – about half the total world population (most of the others being in captivity) – each boasting a 2.4-metre wingspan and nesting far from any human contamination on the park's northern fringes.

The first refuge here was created in 1922 to protect a rather different species – an estimated 1500 **wood buffalo**, the longer-legged, darker and more robust relative of the plains buffalo. At the time they were being hunted to the edge of extinction, much in the manner of the plains bison in the preceding century. Six years later the federal government moved some 6000 plains buffalo to the park from the now nonexistent Buffalo National Park near Wainright, Alberta, when their grazing lands were appro-priated for a firing range. Most of the present herd, now down to some 2500 members, is probably a hybrid strain, and has become the subject of considerable controversy (see box, p.568). At present you'll still see plenty at the roadsides, more often than not wallowing in dust to escape the region's ferocious mosquitoes. The presence of the bisons, not to mention that of the cranes and the various rare and unspoiled habitats, saw the park declared a UNESCO World Heritage Site in 1983.

Access and getting around

Most practicalities and **information** regarding the park are available in Fort Smith (see opposite). **Getting to** the park by road can be a slow business, and is possible only along a 280-kilometre stretch of Hwy 5 from Hay River (NWT) to Fort Smith. Frontier Coachlines, 16-102 Street, Hay River (☎867/874-2566, fax 867/874-2388), runs **buses** from Hay River to Fort Smith (3 weekly on Tues, Thurs & Sat; $48.69 one-way), with services timed to connect with the daily Greyhound from Edmonton. You can also easily **fly** to Fort Smith on scheduled flights with Air Canada from Edmonton, Hay River, Yellowknife and Vancouver, as well as on any number of wing-and-a-prayer charter planes.

Unless you're prepared to backpack or fly into the interior, the only reliable **access** to the park proper is along the 150-kilometre stretch of Hwy 5, which runs through the park's northeastern quadrant and provides its only all-weather road. A 298-kilometre summer-only loop branches off Hwy 5, 8km south of Fort Smith, through the park's southeast corner; some stretches of this are impassable after heavy rain, so check conditions with the park centre in Fort Smith (see below). The west leg of the loop leads to three developed **trails** – Salt River (after 15km), Rainbow Lakes (after 20km) and Pine Lake (after 65km), the last with a nearby **campsite**. Backwoods camping is allowed anywhere as long as it's at least 1500m from Pine Lake or any road or trail. **Canoeing** is wide open: the Athabasca and Peace river system was once the main route for trade from the south, and still offers limitless paddling options.

The park's most-visited backcountry destination is the meadowland and delta habitat at **Sweetgrass Station**, 12km south of the Peace River. Built in 1954 to cull and vaccinate diseased bison (see box, overleaf), the area is a prime spot from which to watch bison and admire the wildlife of the Lake Claire region. You can stay in the cabin (bunks) here free of charge, but must first register with the park visitor centre in Fort Smith (see p.569). Drinking water comes from the river and needs to be boiled and treated. To get here you'll need to canoe or hand over around $370 to Northwestern Air (☎867/872-2216) or other local airline. If this is too much, Northwestern Air runs **flights** over the region for around $70 per person.

Fort Smith

Though it's actually just over Alberta's northern border in the Northwest Territories, **FORT SMITH** (population around 2500) is the only conceivable base for exploring Wood Buffalo National Park. Virtually the last settlement for several hundred kilometres east and north, the town developed along one of the major water routes to the north. Its site was particularly influenced by the need to avoid a violent set of rapids, an interruption to waterborne transport that required a 25-kilometre portage (a stretch of water where canoes had to be carried on land). The Dene natives' name for the area, not surprisingly, was Thebacha, meaning "along the rapids". In 1872 the Hudson's Bay Company built a post, Fort Fitzgerald, at the rapids' southern end. Two years later Fort Smith was established at their northern limit. In time the settlement became the administrative capital of the NWT (despite being only a kilometre from Alberta), a function it fulfilled until as recently as 1967, the year the Canadian federal government promoted Yellowknife to the role.

The disappearance of government jobs has left its mark on the town, as has the opening of the all-weather road between Hay River and Yellowknife, which captured a lot of the freight that used to pass through the region by boat. Nonetheless it's a reasonable enough base, with a handful of things to see around town before visiting the park or pressing on towards Yellowknife. The **Northern Life Museum**, 110 King St (mid-June to early Sept daily 1–5pm), is worth a few minutes to enjoy an excellent collection of traditional artefacts, crafts, fur-trading memorabilia and archive photographs. You might also want to glance at the old **Fort Smith Mission Historic Park**, on the corner of Mercredi Avenue and Breynat Street, former home to the region's bishop, who for years took on many of Fort Smith's bureaucratic responsibilities. For a chance of

BUFFALO KILL

Clean-living Canada rarely causes international environmental outrage, but since 1990 the federal government has been at the heart of a long-simmering row with conservationists. Wood Buffalo's herd of wood buffalo (a unique subspecies of the plains buffalo) is partially infected with tuberculosis and brucellosis, and government scientists on the Environmental Advisory Board claim the only way to prevent the spread of the diseases (which they claim are highly infectious) to Alberta's valuable beef herds is to kill the buffalo herd off. Scientists opposed to the government plan point out that the herd has been infected for years (since they were brought here 75 years ago in fact), has kept the disease to itself, and has survived by internal regulation and natural balance (animals show no outward signs of the diseases or of suffering). Furthermore there has never been an instance of disease transferring itself to humans. Most locals, who are largely opposed to the cull, argue that killing or inoculating every animal would be a daunting task, given the immensity of the animals' range, and that, if even a few were missed, the whole cull would be fruitless as disease would presumably erupt afresh when the herd regenerated. The last partial cull occurred in 1967, following on from a large-scale slaughter in the 1950s.

The restocking issue has opened another can of worms, for at last count there were just eighteen pure-bred, disease-free wood buffalo kept in captivity, and it is from these that the government intends to restart the herd. Most experts argue that the resultant weak, inbred group would compare badly with the large and long-evolved gene pool of the present herd. Other scientists take a completely different line, maintaining that wood buffalo aren't genetically different from their plains cousins and so it wouldn't matter if they were wiped out.

The dispute quickly became extremely messy, reflecting fundamental changes in Canadian attitudes towards the rival claims of business and the environment in a tough financial climate. Some see the hand of Canada's powerful beef lobby guiding the government's actions, while others view it as part of a move to relax the powerful injunctions protecting Canada's national parks and open the way for economic growth in what are, almost by definition, regions of depression and high unemployment. This has already started, with Alberta's government taking plains buffalo off the protected list and putting it onto restaurant menus by promoting buffalo farming to boost its northern economy.

In the saga's most ironic twist, tuberculosis and brucellosis have turned up in farmed game animals (mainly elk), and a huge increase in game farming has led to an explosion in the very diseases a cull of the wild herds would seek to eradicate. Animals bred in captivity are more susceptible to such diseases, and escaping farmed elk are spreading them to areas far beyond the range of Wood Buffalo's supposed culprits. The federal government appointed a committee of interested parties to review the affair. No action was taken, and in 1995 a five-year Research and Containment programme was instigated to review long-term management; as the results are reviewed, the park's buffalo – now around 2500 in all – still nibble contentedly.

seeing the area's famous white pelicans, head for the **Slave River Lookout** on Marine Drive, where there's a telescope trained on their nesting site.

Practicalities and activities

The easiest **access** to Fort Smith and the park is by plane, but isn't cheap: the airport is 5km west of town on McDougal Road, while thrice-weekly Frontier Coachlines (☎867/874-2566, fax 872-4297 in Fort Smith) **buses** run here from Hay River or Yellowknife. If you need a taxi from the airport or around town call Portage Cabs (☎867/872-3333), and for **car rental** contact J & M Enterprises, on Portage Avenue (Mon–Sat 8am–6pm; ☎872-2221, fax 872-5111). Fort Smith's summer-only **infocentre** on Portage Road near the corner with McDougal Road (June–Sept daily 10am–10pm;

☎872-2512) supplies information on the town and Wood Buffalo National Park. The **park visitor centre** and headquarters is a short distance west in the Federal Building at 126 McDougal Rd (summer Mon–Fri 8.30am–5pm, Sat & Sun 10am–5pm; rest of the year Mon–Fri 8.30am–5pm only; ☎867/872-7900 or 872-2349). For advance information, write to Wood Buffalo National Park, Box 750 (EG), Fort Smith, NWT X0E 0P0 (☎872-7961, hotline ☎872-7962, fax 872-3910). Excellent **maps and guides** can be obtained from North of 60 Books (☎867/872-2606, fax 872-4802), just opposite the town infocentre, or by writing to Box 1050, Fort Smith, NWT X0E 0P0.

It's essential to prebook **accommodation** in summer. The cheapest of the town's three hotels is the 24-room *Pinecrest Hotel*, 163 McDougal Rd (☎403/872-2320; ④), but it's worth paying a bit more to stay in the *Pelican Rapids Inn* almost across the road at 152 McDougal Rd (☎867/872-2789; ⑤), a 31-room hotel built in 1997. The *Portage Inn*, 72 Portage Rd (☎867/872-2276, *portageinn@auroranet.nt.ca*; ⑤), has two doubles, five singles and a suite. Lower prices can be found in one of a handful of **B&Bs**: try the three-roomed *Whispering Pines Cottage Tourist Home* (☎872-2628; ④; weekly, monthly and group rates available) or the similarly priced *Thebacha B&B River Trails North* (☎872-2060; ④), which has two doubles and two singles (no smoking and no alcohol). There's a public **campsite** alongside the Slave River on the northern edge of town and the *Queen Elizabeth* site ($12) 4km east towards the airport.

Most of Fort Smith's stores and its few **restaurants** are clustered in a tiny two-block area of downtown. Many locals make for the *Old Skillet Restaurant* in the *Pinecrest Hotel*; for snacks and light meals, try the *J-Bell Bakery* almost opposite the park information office on the corner of McDougal Road and Portage Avenue.

For most people the best way to see the park and its wildlife is to sign up for a **tour**. Fort Smith has plenty of operators: one of the longest-established is Subarctic Wildlife Adventures (☎867/872-2467 or 872-2126, *www.subarcticwildlife.nt.ca*), who offer nine-day subarctic "Wildlife Explorer" tours in the park and Peace–Athabasca delta region, and twelve- or fourteen-day Arctic/subarctic "Wildlife Explorer" tours in Wood Buffalo and the Slave River Rapids area before continuing to the *Bathurst Inlet Lodge* for tundra scenery, musk ox, caribou, birds, wildlife and Inuit culture. They also offer six-hour rafting trips on the Slave River and day bus trips into the park. River Trails North (☎867/872-2060) and Res Delta Tours (☎867/394-3141, fax 394-3413) in Fort Resolution specialize in fishing and two- to seven-day river tours on the Slave River delta, as well as a three-day trip from Fort Resolution to Fort Smith.

> The telephone code for Calgary and Southern Alberta is ☎403.

CALGARY AND SOUTHERN ALBERTA

Perfectly placed where the prairies buckle suddenly into the Rockies, **Calgary** is the obvious focus of **southern Alberta**, and is the best point from which to strike out west into the mountains. Yet, with some of the continent's most magnificent mountains practically on its doorstep, it takes some self-restraint to give the city the couple of days it deserves. Within day-tripping distance lie two unexpected gems: the dinosaur exhibits of the **Royal Tyrrell Museum**, near Drumheller in the strange badlands country to the east; and the **Head-Smashed-In Buffalo Jump**, an aboriginal site in the heart of Alberta's cowboy country to the south. The latter is most easily visited if you're following the southern route of Hwy 3 across the province, as is **Waterton Lakes National Park**, isolated well to the south of the other Canadian Rockies parks.

Calgary

A likeable and booming place, whose downtown skyscrapers soared almost overnight on the back of an oil bonanza in the 1970s, **CALGARY**'s tight high-rise core is good for wandering, and contains the prestigious **Glenbow Museum**. The wooden houses of the far-flung suburbs, meanwhile, recall the city's pioneering frontier origins, which are further celebrated in the annual **Calgary Stampede**, a hugely popular cowboy carnival in which the whole town – and hordes of tourists – revel in a boots-and-stetson image that's still very much a way of life in the surrounding cattle country. Year-round you can dip into the city's lesser museums and historic sites, or take time out in its scattering of attractive city parks.

Some history

Modern Calgary is one of the West's largest and youngest cities, its close to 850,000-strong population having grown from almost nothing in barely 125 years. Long before the coming of outsiders, however, the area was the domain of the **Blackfoot**, who ranged over the site of present-day Calgary for several thousand years. About 300 years ago, they were joined by **Sarcee**, forced south by war from their northern heartlands, and the **Stoney**, who migrated north with Sitting Bull into southern Saskatchewan and then Alberta. Traces of old campsites, buffalo kills and pictographs from all three peoples lie across the region, though these days aboriginal lands locally are confined to a few reserves.

Whites first began to gather around the confluence of the Bow and Elbow rivers at the end of the eighteenth century. Explorer **David Thompson** wintered here during his peregrinations, while the Palliser expedition spent time nearby en route for the Rockies. Settlers started arriving in force around 1860, when hunters moved into the region from the United States, where their prey, the buffalo, had been hunted to the edge of extinction. Herds still roamed the Alberta grasslands, attracting not only hunters but also **whiskey traders**, who plied their dubious wares among whites and aboriginal peoples alike. Trouble inevitably followed, leading to the creation of the West's first North West Mounted Police stockade at Fort Macleod (see p.589). Soon after, in 1875, a second fort was built further north to curb the lawlessness of the whiskey traders. A year later it was christened **Fort Calgary**, taking its name from the Scottish birthplace of its assistant commissioner. The word *calgary* is Gaelic for "clear running water", and it was felt that the ice-clear waters of the Bow and Elbow rivers were reminiscent of the "old country".

By 1883 a station had been built close to the fort, part of the new trans-Canadian **railway**. The township laid out nearby quickly attracted **ranchers** and British gentlemen farmers to its low, hilly bluffs – which are indeed strongly reminiscent of Scottish moors and lowlands – and cemented an enduring Anglo-Saxon cultural bias. Ranchers from the US – where pasture was heavily overgrazed – were further encouraged by an "open grazing" policy across the Alberta grasslands. Despite Calgary's modern-day cowboy life – most notably its famous annual **Stampede** – the Alberta cattle country has been described as more "mild West" than Wild West. Research suggests that there were just three recorded gunfights in the nineteenth century, and poorly executed ones at that.

By 1886 fires had wiped out most of the town's temporary wooded and tented buildings, leading to an edict declaring that all new buildings should be constructed in sandstone (for a while Calgary was known as "Sandstone City"). The fires proved no more than a minor historical hiccup and within just nine years of the railway's arrival Calgary achieved official city status, something it had taken rival Edmonton over 100 years to achieve. Edmonton was to have its revenge in 1910, when it was made Alberta's provincial capital.

CHINOOKS

Winters in Calgary are occasionally moderated by **chinooks**, sudden warming winds that periodically sweep down the eastern flanks of the Rockies. Often heralded by a steely cloud band spreading from the mountains over the city, a chinook can raise the temperature by as much as 10°C in a couple of hours and evaporate a foot of snow in a day. Chinooks are the result of a phenomenon that occurs on leeward slopes of mountains all over the world, but nowhere more dramatically than in the plains of southwestern Alberta. The effect has to do with the way prevailing westerly winds are forced to rise over the Rockies, expanding and cooling on the way up and compressing and warming up again on the way back down. On the way up the cooling air, laden with Pacific moisture, becomes saturated (ie clouds form) and drops rain and snow on the windward (western) side of the mountains. All this condensation releases latent heat, causing the rising air to cool more slowly than usual; but on the leeward descent the air, now relieved of much of its moisture, warms up at the normal rate. By the time it reaches Calgary it's both drier and warmer than it was to start with.

The name comes from the people that traditionally inhabited the area around the mouth of the Columbia River in Washington and Oregon, from where the winds seem to originate; the Chinook people also give us the name of the largest species of Pacific salmon.

Cattle and the coming of the railway generated exceptional growth, though the city's rise was to be nothing compared to the prosperity that followed the discovery of **oil**. The first strike, the famous Dingman's No. 1 Well, took place in 1914 in the nearby Turner Valley. An oil refinery opened in 1923, and since then. Calgary has rarely looked back. In the 25 years after 1950, its population doubled. When oil prices soared during the oil crisis of the 1970s, the city exploded, becoming a world energy and financial centre – headquarters for some four hundred oil and related businesses – with more American inhabitants than any other Canadian city.

Falling commodity prices subsequently punctured the city's ballooning economy, but not before the city centre had been virtually rebuilt and acquired improved and oil-financed cultural, civic and other facilities. Today only Toronto is home to the headquarters of more major Canadian corporations, though the city's optimism is tempered, as elsewhere in Canada, by the notion of **federal disintegration**. Much of the West, which still harbours a sense of a new frontier, is increasingly impatient with the "old East", and happy – if election results are anything to go by – to become increasingly self-sufficient.

Arrival

Approaching Calgary **by air** you're rewarded (in the right weather) with a magnificent view of the Rockies stretching across the western horizon. **Calgary International Airport** (YYC), a modern, often half-deserted strip, is within the city limits about 10km northeast of downtown – a $30 taxi ride. The widely advertised free hotel coaches tend to be elusive, but the reliable **Airporter Bus** (☎531-3909) shuttle into the city departs every thirty minutes and drops at nine downtown hotels: the *Delta Bow, International, Westin, Sheraton Suites, Prince Royal, Ramada, Sandman, Palliser* and *Marriott* (first bus 6.30am, last bus 11.30pm; $8.50 one-way, $15 return). If you're headed for the city bus terminal (see overleaf), the nearest drop-off is the *Sandman*: from here, walk south a block to 9th Avenue and turn right (west) and the terminal's a fifteen-minute walk. Buy Airporter **tickets** from one of a bank of bus-ticket desks lined up in Arrivals (Level 1) by the exit doors: buses depart from Bay 3 immediately outside the terminal.

Over the last few years, **direct services to Banff** and Lake Louise have proliferated, allowing you to jump off the plane, leap into a bus and be in Banff National Park in a couple of hours. Services currently include Laidlaw (1 daily May–Nov, 2 daily Dec–April; $30 to Banff, $38 to Lake Louise; ☎762-9102 or 1-800/661-4946; Calgary Ski Bus to Lake Louise ☎256-8473, *www.laidlawbanff.com*); the Banff Airporter, 8 daily; $36 to Banff; ☎762-3330 or 1-888/449-2901, *www.banffairporter.com*); Brewster Transportation (3 daily to Banff and Lake Louise, 1 daily to Jasper in summer; $36 to Banff, $41 to Lake Louise, $71 to Jasper; ☎403/762-6767 in Banff, ☎403/221-8242 in Calgary, ☎780/852-3332 in Jasper). **Tickets** are available from separate desks adjacent to the Airporter desk in Arrivals. Services leave from Bay 4 or (close by) outside the Arrivals terminal.

There's a small **information centre** disguised as a stagecoach (daily 10am–10pm) in Arrivals and another in Departures (6am–midnight). The Arrivals level also offers courtesy phones to hotels and car-rental agencies, though most of the hotels are well away from the centre.

Calgary's Greyhound **bus terminal** (☎265-9111 or 1-800/661-8747, *www.greyhound.ca*) is comfortable but not terribly convenient. It's located west of downtown at 8th Avenue SW and 850-16th St, a somewhat uninspiring thirty-minute walk to the city centre. Fortunately free tranit buses operate to the C-Train at 7th Avenue SW and 10th Street, the key to the city's central transport system (free from this point through the downtown area). The shuttles leave from Gate 4 within 20 minutes of every bus arrival to the terminal and are announced over the tannoy: keep your ears open. Shuttles return from the same point more or less hourly on the half hour. Alternatively, six-dollar **taxis** for the short run to downtown are plentiful outside the terminal. Left-luggage lockers inside the terminal cost $2 for 24hr, $4 for larger lockers. For airport enquiries and bus and rail travel information, see "Listings" (p.584).

If you're arriving **by car**, the Trans-Canada (Hwy 1) passes through the city to the north of downtown. During its spell in the city limits it becomes 16th Avenue. The major north to south road through the city, Hwy 2, is rechristened the Deerfoot Trail, while the main route south from the US and Waterton Lakes is known as the Macleod Trail, much of which is a fairly grim strip of malls, motels and fast-food joints.

Information and orientation

The main **Visitor Information Services**, part of the Calgary Convention and Visitors Bureau, is on the main floor of the Calgary Tower Centre in the Calgary Tower, 139 Tower Centre, 101-9th Ave SW (mid-May to mid-Sept daily 8am–8pm; mid-Sept to mid-May Mon–Fri 8am–5pm, Sat & Sun 9am–5pm; ☎263-8510 in Calgary, ☎1-800/661-8888 elsewhere in North America; recorded information ☎262-2766). It doles out huge amounts of information and provides a free accommodation-finding service. You can also access Travel Alberta on the Internet (*www.travelalberta.com*). Minor offices operate at the airport (Arrivals level), the Canada Olympic Park and on the westbound side of the Trans-Canada Highway between 58th and 62nd Street NE. The informative monthly *Where Calgary* is free from shops, hotels and the Visitors Bureau.

For all its rapid expansion, Calgary is a well-planned and straightforward city engineered around an inevitable **grid**. The metropolitan area is divided into **quadrants** (NW, NE, SE and SW) with the Bow River separating north from south, Centre Street–Macleod Trail east from west. Downtown – and virtually everything there is to see and do – is in a small area in or close to the SW quadrant. Streets run north–south, avenues east–west, with numbers increasing as you move out from the centre. As with Edmonton, the last digits of the first number refer to the house number – thus 237-8th Ave SE is on 2nd Street at no. 37, close to the intersection with 8th Avenue. It's easy to overlook the quadrant, so check addresses carefully.

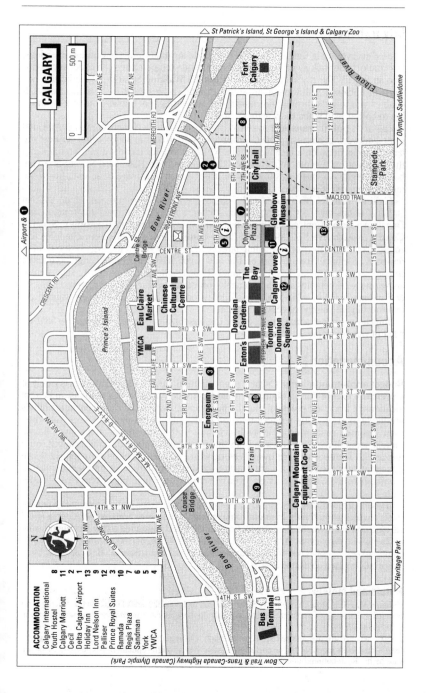

CALGARY

0   500 m

St Patrick's Island, St George's Island & Calgary Zoo

Airport & ❶

Fort Calgary

City Hall ❽

Glenbow Museum

Stampede Park

MACLEOD TRAIL

Olympic Saddledome

Elbow River

Bow River

Prince's Island

Eau Claire Market

Chinese Cultural Centre

YMCA

Devonian Gardens

The Bay

Eaton's

Toronto Dominion Square

Calgary Tower ❶❷

Energeum

Calgary Mountain Equipment Co-op

Bus Terminal

Louise Bridge

Bow River

Heritage Park

Bow Trail & Trans-Canada Highway (Canada Olympic Park)

ACCOMMODATION

Calgary International Youth Hostel	8
Calgary Marriott	11
Cecil	2
Delta Calgary Airport	1
Holiday Inn	13
Lord Nelson Inn	9
Palliser	12
Prince Royal Suites	3
Ramada	10
Regis Plaza	7
Sandman	6
York	5
YWCA	4

City transport

Almost everything in Calgary, barring Stampede locations and a few minor diversions, is a comfortable walk away – except in winter, when temperatures can make any excursion an ordeal. The city's much-vaunted **Plus 15 Walking System**, a labyrinthine network of enclosed walkways 4.5m above ground, is designed to beat the freeze. It enables you to walk through downtown without setting foot outside, but is too confusing to bother with when the weather's fine.

Calgary's **public transport system** is cheap, clean and efficient, comprising an integrated network of buses and the **C-Train** (every 15 to 30min; no late-night service) the latter a cross between a bus and a train, which is free for its downtown stretch along the length of 7th Avenue SW between 10th Street and City Hall at 3rd Street SE. An onboard announcement tells you when the free section is coming to an end. For route information, call ☎276-7801.

Tickets, valid for both buses and C-Train, are available from machines on C-Train stations, shops with a Calgary Transit sticker, and from the main Information and Downtown Sales Centre, also known as the **Calgary Transit Customer Service Centre**, 240-7th Ave SW (Mon–Fri 8.30am–5pm), which also has free schedules and route planners. The one-way adult fare is $1.60 (free for under-6s, $1 for 6–14s), day-pass $5 adults. You can pay on the bus if you have the exact change. Request a transfer from the driver (valid for 90min) if you're changing buses. The sales centre also provides timetables and an invaluable **information line** (Mon–Fri 6am–11pm, Sat & Sun 8am–9.30pm; ☎262-1000): tell them where you are and where you want to go, and they'll give you the necessary details.

You can easily get a **taxi** from outside the bus terminal, or see "Listings" (p.585) for a list of cab companies.

Accommodation

Budget **accommodation** in Calgary is not plentiful, but the little that exists is rarely at a premium except during Stampede (mid-July) when prepaid reservations, in central locations at least, are essential months in advance. Remember that even smart hotels are likely to offer vastly reduced rates on Friday nights and over the weekend, when their business custom drops away. In addition to the recommendations given below, motels abound, mostly well away from the centre along Macleod Trail heading south and on the Trans-Canada Highway heading west. "Motel Village" is a cluster of a dozen or so motels in the $60–70 a night bracket, grouped together at the intersection of 16th Avenue NW and Crowchild Trail; if you're not driving, a taxi ride out here costs about $10.

If you run into difficulties, try Visitor Information Services in the Calgary Tower (see p.577), which should help hunt out rooms at short notice, or consult the Alberta Hotel Association's ubiquitous *Accommodation Guide*. **B&B agencies** to try include the Bed & Breakfast Agency of Alberta (☎543-3901 or 1-800/425-8160, *altabba@home.com*); Canada-West (☎604/990-6730, *www.b-b.com*), or the Alberta Bed & Breakfast Association (*www.bbalberta.com*).

Hotels and motels

Calgary Marriott Hotel, 110-9th Ave SE (☎266-7331 or 1-800/228-9290, fax 262-8442). Not the most expensive of Calgary's smart hotels, but probably the best outside the *Palliser* if you want to stay in some style. ⑦.

Cecil, corner of 4th Ave and 3rd St SE (☎266-2982). Clean and cheap, but a grim place – to say the least – on a busy junction (the airport road); its bar has a rough reputation. No phones, TV or private baths. Rock-bottom budgets and emergencies only. ②.

Delta Calgary Airport Hotel, 2001 Airport Rd (☎291-2600 or 1-800/441-1414, *www.deltahotels .com*). Soundproofed hotel right at the airport if you arrive late or have an early flight out – but it's not cheap. ⑥.

Holiday Inn Calgary Downtown, 119-12th Ave SW (☎266-4611 or 1-800/661-9378, fax 237-0978). An amenity-loaded hotel, but a few blocks off the centre of town. ⑦.

Lord Nelson Inn, 1020-8th Ave SW (☎269-8262 or 1-800/661-6017, fax 269-4868). A ten-storey modern but slightly faded block with 56 rooms close to the more expensive *Sandman*, to which it is inferior; each room with TV and fridge, and just a block from the free C-Train. ④.

Palliser, 133-9th Ave SW (☎262-1234 or 1-800/441-1414, fax 260-1260). This is the hotel royalty chooses when it comes to Calgary, and as smart as you can find in the city if you want traditional style and service (though avoid the back rooms overlooking the rail tracks). Built in 1914, and part of the smart Canadian Pacific chain that owns the *Banff Springs* and *Chateau Lake Louise* hotels. ⑥.

Prince Royal Suites Hotel, 618-5th Ave SW (☎263-0520 or 1-800/661-1592, *www.princeroyal.com*). A mixture of 301 modern studio, one- and two-room suites with full facilities and continental breakfast included. Look out for weekend discounts. ⑥.

Ramada Hotel Downtown, 708-8th Ave SW (☎263-7600 or 1-800/661-8684, *res_dt@telusplanet.net*). A large, comfortable hotel with 200 newly renovated rooms and a swimming pool at the heart of downtown. ⑤.

Regis Plaza Hotel, 124-7th Ave SE (☎262-4641, *regis.plaza@cadvision.com*). An old and unappealing hotel for those who are desperate or almost broke, but just two blocks from the Calgary Tower. Bathroom facilities are shared in ten of the forty rooms: other rooms only have washbasins; beware the rough bar. ③.

Sandman Hotel Downtown Calgary, 888-7th Ave SW (☎237-8626 or 1-800/726-3626, *www.sandman.ca*). An excellent and first-choice mid-range hotel, with 300 totally dependable clean, modern rooms with private bathrooms in high-rise block: extremely handy for the free C-Train. ⑤.

Travelodge, 2750 Sunridge Blvd NE (☎291-1260 or 1-800/578-7878, fax 291-9170), 2304-16th Ave (☎289-0211 or 1-800/578-7878, fax 282-6924), and 9206 Macleod Trail (☎253-7070 or 1-800/578-7878, fax 253-2879). Three chain motels; the least expensive out-of-town choices. The first is convenient to the airport. All ③.

York Hotel, 636 Centre St SE (☎262-5581). Central, with good-sized rooms with TVs and baths and laundry service. ③.

Hostels and student accommodation

Calgary International Youth Hostel, 520-7th Ave SE (☎269-8239, fax 266-6227, *chostel@hostelling-intl.ca*). Close to downtown; two blocks east of City Hall and the free section of the C-Train. Laundry, six- and eight-bed dorms (120 beds in total), four double/family rooms, cooking facilities, bike storage, snack bar. Closed 10am–5pm; midnight curfew. Members $16–18, nonmembers $19–22; family rooms/doubles add $5 per person. ①.

Calgary YWCA, 320-5th Ave SE (☎263-1550). Hotel comfort for women and children only in quiet, safe area; food service, pool, gym, health club and squash courts; book in summer. Singles and dorm beds available from about $35 for singles ($45 double) without bath, $45 ($50) with; sleeping bag space is sometimes provided in summer. ②.

University of Calgary, 3330-24th Ave NW (☎220-3202). Way out in the suburbs, but cheap with a huge number of dorm and private rooms from around $30 in the summer. Take the C-Train or bus #9. The 24hr room-rental office (call first) is in the Kananaskis Building on campus; 33 percent discount for student ID holders. ②.

Campsites

Calaway Park (☎249-7372). About 10km west of the city on the Trans-Canada-Hwy to Banff and the Rockies. It's also within walking distance of the Calaway Park amusement park – Canada's largest. Full facilities, including showers. Mid-May to early Sept. $15.

KOA Calgary West, off the south side of Hwy 1 at the western end of the city, close to Canada Olympic Park (☎288-0411 or 1-800/KOA-0842, fax 286-1612). 224 sites, laundry, store and outdoor pool. Shuttle services to downtown. Mid-April to mid-Oct. $24.

Mountain View Farm Campground (☎293-6640). A 202-site campsite situated on a farm 3km east of the city on the Trans-Canada (Hwy 1). Full services, including showers. $18.

The City

Downtown Calgary lies in a self-evident cluster of mirrored glass and polished granite facades bounded by the Bow River to the north, 9th Avenue to the south, Centre Street to the east and 8th Street to the west. A monument to oil money, the area is about as sleek as an urban centre can be: virtually everything is brand-new, and the modern architecture is easy on the eye. The **city centre**, so far as it has one, is traditionally 8th Avenue between 1st Street SE and 3rd Street SW, a largely pedestrianized area known as **Stephen Avenue Mall**.

Any city tour, though, should start with a trip to the **Glenbow Museum**, while a jaunt up the **Calgary Tower**, across the street, gives a literal overview of the Calgarian hinterland. Thereafter a good deal of the city lends itself to wandering on foot, whether around the mall-laden main streets or to **Prince's Island**, the nearest of many parks, and gentrified **Kensington**, a busy shopping and café district. The appeal of attractions further afield – **Fort Calgary**, **Heritage Park** and the **Calgary Zoo** – will depend on your historical and natural-history inclinations. These sights, together with a crop of special interest **museums**, can be easily reached by bus or C-Train.

The Glenbow Museum

The excellent and eclectic collection of the **Glenbow Museum** is, the Stampede apart, the only sight for which you'd make a special journey to Calgary (May–Oct Mon–Wed, Thurs–Fri 9am–9pm, Sat & Sun 9am–5pm; closed Mon Nov–April; $8; ☎268-4100, *www.glenbow.org*). Although it's opposite the Calgary Tower at 130-9th Ave SE, the main entrance is hidden alongside the Skyline Plaza complex a short way east down the street (there's another entrance from the Stephen Avenue Mall). Built in 1966, the no-expense-spared museum is a testament to sound civic priorities and the cultural benefits of booming oil revenues. Its three floors of displays make a fine introduction to the heritage of the Canadian west.

The permanent collection embraces the eclectic approach, starting with a section devoted to ritual and **sacred art** from around the world and an **art gallery** tracing the development of western Canadian indigenous art. Better still is the European art depicting the culture of aboriginal peoples. Two outlooks prevail – the romantic nineteenth-century image of the Indian as "noble savage", and the more forward-looking analysis of artists from the same period such as Paul Kane, a painter determined to make accurate representations of aboriginal peoples and cultures before their assimilation by white expansion.

The second floor runs the gamut of western Canadian history and heritage, including an outstanding exhibit on First Nations or **aboriginal peoples**. In the treaties section, hidden in a corner almost as if in shame, the museum text skates over the injustices with a glossary of simple facts. On display are the original documents that many chiefs were confused into signing, believing they were peace treaties, when in fact the contracts gave away all land rights to those who drafted them in deliberately incomprehensible legalese. All facets of **native crafts** are explored on this floor, as well, with stunning displays of carving, costumes and jewellery; whilst their emphasis is on the original inhabitants of Alberta – with a special new display on the Blackfoot – the collection also forays into the Inuit and the Métis – the latter being the offspring of native women and white fur traders, and the most marginalized group of all.

Following a historical chronology, the floor moves on to exhibits associated with the fur trade, Northwest Rebellion, the Canadian Pacific, pioneer life, ranching, cowboys, oil and wheat – each era illustrated by interesting and appropriate artefacts of the time – adding up to a glut of period paraphernalia that includes a terrifying exhibit of frontier dentistry, an absurdly comprehensive display of washing machines, and a solitary 1938 bra.

The eccentric top floor kicks off with a pointless display of Calgary Stampede merchandising, before moving on to a huge collection of **military paraphernalia** and a dazzling display of **gems and minerals**, said to be among the world's best. These exhibits are mainly for genre enthusiasts, though the gems are worth a look if only to see some of the extraordinary and beautiful things that come out of the drab mines that fuel so much of western Canada's economy.

Other downtown sights

The **Calgary Tower** (daily: mid-May to mid-Sept 8am–midnight; mid-Sept to mid-May 8am–11pm; $6.15), the city's favourite folly, is a good deal shorter and less imposing than the tourist material would have you believe. An obligatory tourist traipse, the 190-metre-tall salt cellar (762 steps if you don't take the lift) stands in a relatively dingy area at the corner of Centre Street–9th Avenue SW, somewhat overshadowed by downtown's more recent buildings. As a long-term landmark, however, it makes a good starting point for any tour of the city, the Observation Terrace offering outstanding views, especially on clear days, when the snowcapped Rockies fill the western horizon, with the ski-jump towers of the 1988 Canada Olympic Park in the middle distance. Up on the observation platform after your one-minute elevator ride you'll find a snack bar (good value and excellent food), cocktail bar and revolving restaurant (expensive).

Any number of shopping malls lurk behind the soaring high-rises, most notably Toronto Dominion Square (8th Ave SW between 2nd and 3rd streets), the city's main shopping focus and the unlikely site of **Devonian Gardens** (daily 9am–9pm; free; ☎268-3888). Like something out of an idyllic urban Utopia, the three-acre indoor gardens support a lush sanctuary of streams, waterfalls and full-sized trees, no mean feat given that it's located on the fourth floor of a glass-and-concrete glitter palace (access by elevator). Around 20,000 plants round off the picture, comprising some 138 local and tropical species. Benches beside the garden's paths are perfect for picnicking on food bought in the takeaways below, while impromptu concerts are held on the small stages dotted around.

Calgary pays homage to its oil industry in the small but oddly interesting **Energeum** plonked in the main lobby of the Energy Resources Building between 5th Street and 6th Street SW at 640-5th Ave SW (June–Aug Mon–Fri & Sun 10.30am–4.30pm; Sept–May Mon–Fri same hours; free; ☎297-4293). Its audiovisual and presentational tricks take you through the formation, discovery and drilling for coal and oil. Alberta's peculiar and problematic oil sands are explained – granite-hard in winter, mud-soft in summer – and there are dollops of the stuff on hand for some infantile slopping around.

The **Calgary Science Centre** is located one block west of the 10th Street SW C-Train at 701 11th Street and 7th Avenue SW (mid-May to June Tues–Thurs 10am–4pm, Fri–Sun 10am–5pm; call for winter hours; $9 for all exhibits and one Discovery Dome show; ☎221-3700, *www.calgaryscience.ca*). Here you can look through the telescopes of its small observatory, which are trained nightly on the moon, planets and stars (weather permitting). Other daytime highlights here include the interactive exhibits of the Discovery Hall (these change regularly) and the **Discovery Dome**, a multimedia theatre complete with cinema picture images, computer graphics, slide-projected images and a vast speaker system. The on-site **Pleiades Theatre** offers a series of "mystery and murder plays" throughout the year. For details of current shows and exhibitions, call ☎221-3700. To get here, either walk the five blocks west from 6th Street if you're near the Energeum, or take the C-Train along 7th Avenue SW and walk the last block.

Prince's Island, the Bow River and Kensington

Five-minutes' walk north of downtown via a footbridge, **Prince's Island** is a popular but peaceful retreat offering plenty of trees, flowers, an outstanding restaurant, the

THE CALGARY STAMPEDE

An orgy of all things cowboy and cowgirl, the annual **Calgary Stampede** brings around a quarter of a million spectators and participants to the city for ten days during the middle two weeks of July. This is far more than a carefully engineered gift to Calgary's tourist industry, however, for the event is one of the world's biggest rodeos and comes close to living up to its billing as "The Greatest Outdoor Show on Earth". During "The Week", as it's known by all and sundry, the city loses its collective head; just about everyone turns out in white stetsons, bolo ties, blue jeans and hand-tooled boots, addressing one another in a bastardized cowboy C&W slang.

But for all its heavily worked visitor appeal, the competition end of things is taken very seriously. Most of the cowboys are for real, as are the injuries – the rodeo is said to be North America's roughest – and the combined prize money is a very serious $500,000. Even the first show in 1912, masterminded by entrepreneur Guy Weadick, put up $100,000 (raised from four Calgary businessmen) and attracted 60,000 people to the opening parade, a line-up that included 2000 aboriginal people in full ceremonial rig and Pancho Villa's bandits in a show erroneously billed as a swan song for the cowboy of the American West ("The Last and Best Great West Frontier Days"). Around 40,000 daily attended the rodeo events (today's figure is 100,000), not bad considering Calgary's population at the time was only 65,000.

Nowadays the events kick off on Thursday evening at Stampede Park with a show previewing the next ten-days' events. Next day there's the traditional **parade**, timed to begin at 9am, though most spectators are in place along the parade route (which is west along 6th Ave from 2nd St SE, south on 10th St SW and east along 9th Ave) by 6am. The march takes two hours, and involves around 150 entries, 4000 participants and some 700 horses. For the rest of the Stampede the **Olympic Plaza** in downtown (known as Rope Square for the duration) offers free pancake breakfasts daily (8.30–11.30am) and entertainment every morning. Typical events include bands, mock gunfights, square dances, native dancing and country bands. Square dancing also fills parts of Stephen Avenue Mall at 10am every morning. **Nightlife** is a world unto itself, with Stampede locations giving way to music, dancing and mega-cabarets, which involve casts of literally thousands. There's also lots of drinking, gambling, fireworks and general partying into the small hours. Barbecues are the norm, and even breakfast is roped into the free-for-all – outdoor bacon, pancake and flapjack feasts being the traditional way to start the day. "White hatter stew" and baked beans are other inevitable staples.

Stampede's real action, though – the rodeo and allied events – takes place in **Stampede Park**, southeast of downtown and best reached by C-Train (every 10min) to Victoria Park–Stampede Station. This vast open area contains an amusement park,

River Café (see p.583), kids' playground and enough space to escape the incessant stream of joggers pounding the walkways. Between the island and downtown, at the north end of 3rd Street SW (six blocks north of the free C-Train), the wonderful **Eau Claire Market** (food market daily 9am–6pm; shops and restaurants have varying hours; ☎264-6450 or 264-6460 for information, *www.eauclaire.com*) is a bright and deliberately brash warehouse mix of food and craft market, cinemas (including a 300-seat IMAX large-screen complex), buskers, restaurants, walkways and panoramic terraces. All in all it brings some heart to the concrete and glass of downtown – the large communal eating area, in particular, is a good place to people-watch and pick up bargain takeaway Chinese, Japanese, wholefood and burger snacks. The food market is open from 9am to 6pm, but the complex and restaurants are open until late. Note that the tremendous **YMCA** (☎269-6701) opposite the market at 101-3rd St SW has no rooms, though the superb swimming pool, jacuzzi, sauna, squash courts, running track and weights room are open to all (Mon–Fri 5.30am–10.30pm, Sat & Sun 7am–7.30pm; $8; increased admission Mon–Fri 11am–1.30pm and daily 4–6.30pm). Swimmers might be concert and show venues, bars and restaurants and a huge range of stalls and shows that take the best part of a day to see. Entrance is $8, which allows you to see all the **entertainments** except the rodeo and chuck-wagon races. Things to see include the aboriginal village at the far end of the park, where members of the Five Nations peoples (Blackfoot, Blood, Sarcee, Stoney and Piegan) set up a tepee village (tours available); the John Deere Show Ring, scene of the World Blacksmith Competition; the Centennial Fair, which hosts events for children; the Agricultural Building, home to displays of cattle and other livestock; the outdoor Coca-Cola Stage, used for late-night Country shows; and the Nashville North, an indoor Country venue with bar and dancing until 2am.

If you want to see the daily **rodeo** competition – bronco riding, bull riding, native-buffalo riding, branding, calf-roping, steer-wrestling, cow-tackling, wild-cow milking and the rest – you need another ticket ($8 on the day), though unless you've bought these in advance (see below) it's hardly worth it: you'll probably be in poor seats miles from the action and hardly see a thing. Rodeo heats are held each afternoon from 1.30pm for the first eight days, culminating in winner-takes-all finals on Saturday and Sunday (prize money for the top honcho is $50,000). If you want to watch the other big event, the ludicrously dangerous but hugely exciting **chuck-wagon** races (the "World Championship") you need yet another ticket ($8) on the day, though again you need to buy these in advance to secure anything approaching decent seats. The nine contests are held once-nightly at 8pm, the four top drivers going through to the last-night final, where another $50,000 awaits the winner.

It's worth planning ahead if you're coming to Calgary for Stampede. **Accommodation** is greatly stretched – be certain to book ahead – and prices for most things are hiked for the duration. **Tickets** for the rodeo and chuck-wagon races go on sale anything up to a year in advance. They're sold for the Stampede Park grandstand, which is divided into sections. "A" is best and sells out first; "B" and "C" go next. Then comes the smarter Clubhouse Level (D–E are seats; F–G are Clubhouse Restaurant seats, with tickets sold in pairs only). This is enclosed and air-conditioned, but still offers good views and the bonus of bars, lounge area and restaurants. The top of the stand, or Balcony (J–K) is open, and provides a good vantage point for the chuck-wagon races as you follow their progress around the length of the course. Rodeo tickets range from about $17 to $35, chuck-wagon races from $17 to $40; tickets for the finals of both events are a few dollars more in all seats. For ticket order forms, **advance sales** and general information, write to Calgary Exhibition and Stampede, Box 1860, Station M, Calgary, AB T2P 2L8 (☎261-0101, elsewhere in Alberta or North America ☎1-800/661-1260) or call in person at Stampede Headquarters, 1410 Olympic Way SE, or the visitor centre. Tickets are also available from Ticketmaster outlets (☎270-6700).

tempted by the broad, fast-flowing **Bow River** nearby, but it's for passive recreation only – the water is just two hours (were you travelling by car) from its icy source in the Rockies – its dangers underlined by lurid signs on the banks. The river is the focus for Calgary's civilized and excellent 210-kilometre system of recreational **walkways**, asphalt paths (also available to cyclists) that generally parallel the main waterways: maps are available from the visitor centre.

Just east of the market and five blocks north of the C-Train at 197-1st St SW lies the **Calgary Chinese Cultural Centre** (daily: centre 9am–9pm, museum 11am–5pm; $2; ☎262-5071), its big central dome modelled on the Temple of Heaven in Beijing and it claims to be one of the largest Chinese centres in Canada. It forms the focus for Calgary's modest Chinatown and large Chinese-Canadian population, most of whom are descendants of immigrants who came to work on the railways in the 1880s. It contains a small museum and gallery, and a gift shop and restaurant.

A twenty-minute jaunt along the walkway system from Prince's Island in the other direction from the market, **Kensington** is a gentrified café district on 10th St NW and Kensington Road. Shops here sell healing crystals and advertise yoga and personal-growth seminars, though the older cafés, bookshops and wholefood stores are beginning to give way to trinket shops. As an eating area, though, Kensington has been superseded by the increasingly trendy section of 4th Street SW, beyond 17th Avenue.

Fort Calgary

Fort Calgary, the city's historical nexus, stands at 750-9th Ave SE (daily May–Oct 9am–5pm; site free; interpretive centre $5.75; ☎290-1875, *www.fortcalgary.ab.ca*), a manageable eight-block walk east of downtown; you could also take bus #1 to Forest Lawn, bus #14 (East Calgary) from 7th Avenue, or the C-Train free to City Hall and walk the remaining five blocks. Built in under six weeks by the North West Mounted Police in 1875, the fort was the germ of the present city, and remained operative as a police post until 1914, when it was sold – inevitably – to the Canadian Pacific Railway. The whole area remained buried under railway tracks and derelict warehouses until comparatively recently.

Period photographs in the adjoining interpretive centre provide a taste of how wild Calgary still was in 1876. Even more remarkable was the ground that men in the fort were expected to cover: the log stockade was a base for operations between Fort Macleod, 160km to the south, and the similar post at Edmonton, almost 400km to the north. It's not as if they had nothing to do: Crowfoot, most prominent of the great Blackfoot chiefs of the time, commented, "If the Police had not come to the country, where would we all be now? Bad men and whiskey were killing us so fast that very few of us indeed would have been left. The Police have protected us as the feathers of a bird protect it from the winter."

Only a few forlorn stumps of the original building remain, much having been torn down by the developers, and what survives is its site, now a pleasant forty-acre park contained in the angled crook of the Bow and Elbow rivers. Moves have recently been made to begin construction of an exact replica of the original log stockade. The interpretive centre traces Calgary's development with the aid of artefacts, audiovisual displays and "interpretive walks" along the river. Among the more kitsch activities on offer is the opportunity to dress up as a Mountie.

Across the river to the east is **Hunt House**, built in 1876 for a Hudson's Bay official and believed to be Calgary's oldest building on its original site. Close by, at 750-9th Ave SE, on the same side of the Elbow River, is the renovated **Deane House Historic Site and Restaurant** (☎269-7747), built in 1906 by Mountie supremo Superintendent Richard Deane (free tours daily 11am–2pm). It subsequently served time as the home of an artists' co-operative, a boarding house and a stationmaster's house. Today it's a teahouse and restaurant.

St George's Island

St George's Island is home to Calgary's most popular attraction, the **Calgary Zoo, Botanical Gardens and Prehistoric Park**, all at 1300 Zoo Rd (daily 9am–1 hour before dusk; Prehistoric Park open June–Sept only; May–Sept $10; ☎232-9300). It can be reached from downtown and Fort Calgary by riverside path, by C-Train northeast towards Whitehorn, or by car (take Memorial Drive E to just west of Deerfoot Trail). Founded in 1920, this is now Canada's largest zoo (and one of North America's best), with 850,000 annual visitors and some 1200 animals, 400 species and innovative and exciting displays in which the animals are left as far as possible in their "natural" habitats. There are underwater viewing areas for polar bears and sea creatures, darkened rooms for nocturnal animals, a special Australian section, greenhouses for myriad tropical birds, and any number of pens for the big draws like gorillas, tigers, giraffes and African warthogs. Check out the extended North American and Canadian Wilds, Aspen

Woodlands and Rocky Mountains sections for a taste of a variety of fauna. Also worth a look are the Tropical, Arid and Butterfly gardens in the conservatory. There is a fast-food concession, and picnic areas if you want to make a day of it.

The **Botanical Gardens** are dotted throughout the zoo, while the **Prehistoric Park** annexe – a "recreated Mesozoic landscape" – is accessible by suspension bridge across the Bow River (daily June–Sept; free with general admission). Its nineteen life-size dinosaur models, none too convincing in their incongruous settings, are a poor substitute for the superb museum at Drumheller (see p.585), and only the fossils in two adjoining buildings are of more than fleeting interest.

Natural-history enthusiasts might also want to visit the **Inglewood Bird Sanctuary**, on the Bow River's forested flats at 9th Avenue and 20A St SE, 3km downstream of the zoo and east of downtown. Some 230 species are present year-round – more during migratory cycles, around 266 species having been recorded across the sanctuary, a portion of land once owned by Colonel James Walker, one of Calgary's original North West Mounted Police. Some of the birds you might see include bald eagles, Swainson's hawks, ring-necked pheasants, warblers, grey partridges and great horned owls. Numerous duck, geese and other waterfowl are also present, and you may also catch sight of muskrats, beavers, white-tailed and mule deer, foxes and long-tailed weasels. A visitor centre (May–Sept daily 9am–5pm; free; ☎269-6688) offers information, details of the year-round walking trails, and occasional natural history courses to guide nonexperts. To get here, follow 9th Avenue SE to Sanctuary Road and follow signs to the parking area on the river's south bank. On weekdays the #14 bus (East) turns off 9th Avenue at 17th Street SE, leaving you just a short walk from the Sanctuary.

Heritage Park Historical Village

A sixty-acre theme park centred on a reconstructed frontier village 16km southwest of downtown, **Heritage Park** (☎259-1900) replicates life in the Canadian West before 1914 and panders relentlessly to the myth of the "Wild West" (mid-May to early Sept daily 9am–5pm; early Sept to mid-Oct weekends and holidays 9am–5pm; $29 admission with rides, $15 without rides; free pancake breakfast with admission 9–10am). Full of family-oriented presentations and original costumes, this "heritage" offering – the largest of its type in Canada – is thorough enough for you never to feel obliged to see another.

The living, working museum comprises more than 150 **restored buildings**, all transported from other small-town locations. Each has been assigned to one of several communities – fur post, native village, homestead, farm and c.1900 – and most fulfil their original function. Thus you can see a working blacksmith, buy fresh bread, buy a local paper, go to church, even get married. Transport, too, is appropriate to the period, including steam trains, trams, horse-drawn bus and stagecoaches. If you're here for the day you can pick up cakes and snacks from the traditional Alberta Bakery, or sit down to a full meal in the old-style *Wainwright Hotel*.

To get there by car, take either Elbow Drive or Macleod Trail south and turn right on Heritage Drive (the turn-off is marked by a huge, maroon steam engine); **bus** #53 makes the journey from downtown, or you can take the C-Train to Heritage Station and then bus #20 to Northmount.

Eating, drinking and nightlife

Calgary's cuisine can be heavily meat-oriented; Alberta claims, with some justification, to have some of the best **steaks** in the world. With its particular immigration history the city lacks the Ukrainian influences that grace cooking to the north, and often prefers instead to follow the fusion and Pacific Rim trends that have been adopted by most of western Canada's more ambitious restaurants. Most bars and cafés – even the live-music venues – double up as restaurants and invariably serve perfectly good food.

The Toronto Dominion Square and Stephen Avenue malls, on 8th Avenue SW between 1st and 3rd, are riddled with ethnic **takeaways** and café-style restaurants – hugely popular and perfect for lunch or snacks on the hoof. The nicest thing to do is buy food and eat it – with half of Calgary – either in the superb **Eau Claire Market**, which is packed with food stalls and restaurants, or amid the greenery of Devonian Gardens. Elsewhere, the city has an impressive range of middle- to upper-bracket restaurants, where prices are low by most standards.

Calgary is rarely a party town, except during Stampede and a brief fling in summer when the weather allows barbecues and night-time streetlife. Nonetheless, its **bars, cafés and clubs** are all you'd expect of a city of this size, the vast majority of them found in five distinct areas: **Kensington**, with its varied cafés; "**Electric Avenue**", as 11th Avenue SW between 5th and 6th streets is called, which has lost most of its brash and mostly trashy bars, night-time action having moved more to **17th Avenue SW**, a more varied collection of pubs, bars, high-quality restaurants, speciality shops and ethnic eating, and **4th Street SW**, a similarly more refined restaurant area. **Downtown** cafés and pubs are fine during the day but fairly desolate in the evening.

In the specialist clubs the quality of live music is good – especially in jazz, blues and the genre closest to cowtown Calgary's heart, country. The Country Music Association has details of local gigs (☎233-8809). Major **festivals** include an annual Jazz Festival (third week in June) and a folk festival at the end of July on Prince's Island.

Tickets for virtually all events are available on ☎270-6700, and through several Marlin Travel offices around the city. You'll find events listings in the *ffwd* or *Calgary Straight* listings tabloids (both free from stores, hotels, cafés, bars and so on) and Calgary's main dailies, the *Herald* and the *Sun*.

Cafés

Good Earth Café. The original wholefood store and café, known for great and inexpensive home-made food, at 1502-11th St (☎228-9543) was so successful it has spawned five other outlets: the Eau Claire Market (☎237-8684) – with good outside patio – the Central Library and elsewhere.

Nellie's Kitchen, 17th Ave and 7th St SW. Laid-back, popular and informal, and especially busy at breakfast – which they do superbly. Open for breakfast and lunch only.

The Roasterie, 314-10th St NW near Kensington Rd. Nice hangout and café – no meals, but newspapers, notice board and twenty kinds of coffee and snacks.

Restaurants

Bistro Jo Jo, 917-17th Ave SW (☎245-2382). If you want to eat good French food, but balk at the typically high prices, try the exceptional cuisine in this marble-tiled and red-banquette-filled restaurant. Moderate–expensive.

Caesar's Steakhouse, 512 4th Ave SW and 10816 Macleod Trail S (☎264-1222 or 278-3930). Best place for a huge, perfect steak in the sort of wonderfully cheesy steakhouse – think dimly lit "Roman" decor – that's been around for decades.

Chianti Café and Restaurant, 1438-17th Ave SW (☎229-1600). A favourite local spot for years: dark, noisy, well priced and extremely popular (try to book), with no-nonsense pasta basics and the odd fancy dish. Patio for summer dining outdoors. Recommended.

Divino's, 1st St and 9th Ave SW. Café and wine bar opposite the *Palliser* hotel with rather faux mahogany-Tiffany chandelier interior, but good Italian food and particularly noteworthy desserts.

Earl's. This ever-reliable mid-range chain, serving North American food, has six outlets around Calgary, the most popular of which is probably that at 2401-4th St SW (☎228-4141).

Galaxie Diner, 1413-11th St SW (☎228-0001). Very popular place with authentic diner decor, great breakfasts and fine open grill served at moderate prices. Daily 8am–4pm.

Hy's, 316 4th Ave SW (☎263-2222). This deep red-carpeted institution has been serving prime Albertan beef in vast quantities since 1955. Moderate–expensive.

Joey Tomato's, Eau Claire Market (☎263-6336). This inexpensive Mediterranean-style grill is part of a small chain, but no worse for that, and is a lively, informal place for a good meal among the plethora of choices in and around the Eau Claire market.

River Café, Prince Island Park (☎261-7670). With *Teatro* (see below), this is the best of Calgary's restaurants for lunch or dinner: innovative Canadian "Northwestern" cuisine and an informal atmosphere on Prince's Island Park, across the bridge from the Eau Claire Market. Be sure to book.

Silver Dragon, 106-3rd Ave SE (☎264-5326). The first choice in town for an inexpensive Chinese meal: this place has been around for over 30 years and uses a team of 15 Hong Kong-trained chefs to conjure up a menu of some 200 dishes.

Teatro, 200-8th Ave SE (☎290-1012). This is the place to come if you want to dress up a little and drop a little money: the fine Italian-influenced food is on a par with that of the less formal *River Café*. Booking is essential.

Bars

Barley Mill Eatery & Pub, 201 Barclay Parade, Eau Claire Market (☎290-1500). Busy neighbourhood pub that looks and feels the part in Eau Claire Market with an outside patio and 100-year-old bar imported from Scotland inside: 24 draught beers, 40 bottled brews and lots of whiskies.

Ceili's, corner of 5th St and 8th Ave SW (☎508-9999). The larger and generally more lively of Calgary's two main "Irish" pubs.

James Joyce, 114-8th Ave SW (☎262-0708). All the usual clutter, antique bar and drinks associated with faux Irish pubs: popular, and a little calmer and more intimate than its rival, *Ceili's* (see above).

The Ship and Anchor, 17th Ave SW on the corner of 5th St. Long-established neighbourhood pub – friendly and laid-back but jumping, with darts, fine music and excellent pub food. Recommended.

Live-music venues

Crazy Horse, 1311-1st St SW (☎266-3339). Popular dance venue with live music on Thursday nights. Small dance floor.

Desperados, 1088 Olympic Way (☎263-5343). This huge sports and "cowboy" bar supposedly has room for 3500 people; replacing *Dusty's*, a Calgary institution, the jury's still out on whether it will live up to its predecessor.

Kaos Jazz and Blues Bistro, 718-17th Ave (☎228-9997). Best location in the city for jazz, with blues, acoustic and soul also on offer.

The King Edward Hotel, 438-9th Ave SE. Much-loved, down-at-heel location, with consistently good C&W and R&B bands. The Saturday jam session – the blues event of the city – is invariably packed.

Piq Niq Café, 811-1st St SW (☎263-1650). This place isn't bad as a café, but it really comes into its own Thursday to Saturday with good live jazz acts.

Ranchman's Steak House, 9615 Macleod Trail S (☎253-1100). A classic honky-tonk and restaurant, known throughout Canada for the live, happening C&W. Free dance lessons at 7.30pm Monday to Thursday. Free admission before 8pm on Thursday. Closed Sunday.

Senor Frog's, 739-2nd Ave SW (☎264-5100). Three blocks west of the Eau Claire Market. New and popular upbeat restaurant and club, with the club taking precedence Thursday to Saturday from 9pm.

Performing arts, cinema and entertainment

Calgary might come on as a redneck cow town, but it has ten or more professional theatre companies, a ballet company, an opera company and a full-blown symphony orchestra. Much of the city's highbrow cultural life focuses on the **Calgary Centre for the Performing Arts**, a dazzling modern downtown complex with five performance spaces close to the Glenbow Museum, at 205-8th Ave SE (☎294-7455). It's also an occasional venue for the acclaimed Calgary Philharmonic Orchestra (☎571-0270), Theatre Calgary (☎294-7440) and the well-known Alberta Theatre Projects (☎294-7475), which usually produces five fairly avant-garde plays annually. More modest classical concerts include the Music at Noon offerings in the Central Library (Sept–April), and the sessions – planned and impromptu – on the small stages in Devonian Gardens. The long-running and well-known **Lunchbox Theatre**, 2nd Floor, Bow Valley Square, 205-5th Ave SW (☎265-4292 or 265-4293), offers a popular and wildly varied programme aimed at downtown shoppers and passers-by; performances run from September to May and are somewhat irregular, but tend to start daily at noon (except Sun) in the Bow Valley Square on the corner of 6th Avenue and 1st Street SW.

Calgary's **ballet** world is dominated by the young and excellent Alberta Ballet Company (☎245-4222), who perform at various locations around the city. **Opera** is the preserve of Calgary Opera (☎262-7286), whose home base is the Jubilee Auditorium at 1415-14th Ave NW. The season runs from October to April.

For repertory, art-house, classic and foreign **films**, try the newly restored **Uptown Stage & Screen**, 612-8th Ave (☎265-0120) or Plaza Theatre at 1113 Kensington Rd NW; the National Film Board Theatre, 222-1st St SE, puts on free lunch-time shows. The **Museum of Movie Art** at the University of Calgary, 9-3600-21st St NE (Tues–Sat 9.30am–5.30pm), is home to some 4000 cinema posters, some dating back to 1920. For first-run mainstream films, head for the downtown malls – most, including Eau Claire Market, have a cinema complex.

Listings

Airlines Air BC (☎265-9555); Air Canada, 530-8th Ave SW (☎265-9555 or 1-888/247-2262); Alaska Airlines (☎1-800/426-0333); American (☎254-6331 or 1-800/433-7300); British Airways (☎1-800/247-9297); Canada 3000 (☎266-8095); Cathay Pacific (☎1-800/268-6868); Delta (☎1-800/221-1212); Northwest (☎1-800/225-2525); United (☎1-800/241-6522); West Jet (☎250-5839).

Airport enquiries ☎292-8400 or 735-1372.

Ambulance ☎261-4000.

American Express 421-7th Ave SW (☎261-5982 or 1-800/221-7282).

Bookshops Canterbury's Bookshop, 513-8th Ave SW, is the best general bookshop. For maps and travel books, check out Mountain Equipment Co-op, 830-10th Ave SW (☎269-2420), or Map Town, 640-6th Ave SW (☎266-2241).

Bus enquiries Airporter (☎531-3909); Brewster Transportation for airport/Banff/Jasper (☎762-6767, 260-0719 or 1-800/661-1152); Greyhound (☎265-9111 or 1-800/661-8747 in Canada); Laidlaw for airport/Banff/Lake Louise (☎762-9102 or 1-800/661-4946); Red Arrow Express, for Edmonton (☎531-0350 or 1-800/232-1958).

Car rental Avis, 211-6th Ave SW (☎291-1475, 269-6166 or 1-800/879-2847); Budget, 140-6th Ave SE (☎226-1550, 263-0505 or 1-800/268-8900); Hertz (☎221-1300 or 1-800/263-0600 in Canada); Thrifty, 123-5th Ave SE (☎262-4400; airport 221-1806; also 1-800/367-2277).

Consulates Australian (☎1-604/684-1177); German (☎269-5900); Netherlands (☎266-2710); UK (☎1-604/683-4421); US, 1000-615 Macleod Trail SE (☎266-8962).

Emergencies ☎911.

Exchange Currencies International, Calgary Tower, 304-8th Ave SW (☎290-0330).

Hospital Foothills Hospital, 1403-29th Ave (☎670-1110).

Left luggage Facilities at the bus terminal, 850-16th St SW; $2 per 24hr.

Library Central Library, 616-Macleod Trail SE (Mon–Thurs 10am–9pm, Fri–Sat 10am–5pm; ☎260-2600).

Lost property ☎268-1600.

Maps and guides Map Town, 640-6th Ave SW (☎266-2241).

Outdoor gear Mountain Equipment Co-op, 830-10th Ave SW (☎269-2420); Calgary's largest camping and outdoor store: includes excellent books, guides and maps.

Pharmacy ☎253-2605 (24hr).

Police 316-7th Ave SE (☎266-1234); RCMP (☎230-6483).

Post office 220-4th Ave SE (☎292-5434 or Canada Post 1-800/267-1177).

Public transport Calgary Transit (☎262-1000); public-transport information.

Taxis Associated Cabs (☎299-1111); Calgary Cab Co (☎777-2222); Checker (☎299-9999); Yellow Cab (☎974-1111).

Tickets Tickets for events, shows, etc (☎270-6700).

Time ☎263-3333.

Tourist information ☎263-8510 or 1-800/661-8888.

Train information VIA Rail (☎1-800/561-8630 in Canada, 1-800/561-3949 in the US); Rocky Mtn Railtours Calgary–Banff–Vancouver (☎1-800/665-7245).

Travel agent Travel Cuts, 1414 Kensington Rd NW (☎531-2070).

Visitors with disabilities Information on wheelchair-accessible transport services (☎262-1000); Calgary Handi-Bus (☎276-8028).

Weather ☎263-3333.

The Alberta Badlands

Formed by the meltwaters of the last Ice Age, the valley of the Red Deer River cuts a deep gash through the dulcet prairie about 140km east of Calgary, creating a surreal landscape of bare, sunbaked hills and eerie lunar flats dotted with sagebrush and scrubby, tufted grass. On their own, the **Alberta Badlands** – strangely anomalous in the midst of lush grasslands – would repay a visit, but what makes them an essential detour is the presence of the **Royal Tyrrell Museum of Paleontology**, amongst the greatest museums of natural history in North America. The museum is located 8km outside the old coal-mining town of **Drumheller**, a dreary but obvious base if you're unable to fit the museum into a day-trip from Calgary. Drumheller is also the main focus of the **Dinosaur Trail**, a road loop that explores the Red Deer Valley and surrounding badlands; you'll need your own transport for this circuit, and for the trip to the **Dinosaur Provincial Park**, home to the Tyrell Museum Field Station and the source of many of its fossils.

Drumheller

Whatever way you travel, you'll pass through **DRUMHELLER**, a downbeat town in an extraordinary setting roughly ninety-minutes' drive northeast of Calgary. As you approach it from the west, the town is hidden until you come to a virulent-red water tower and the road suddenly drops into a dark, hidden canyon. The otherworldliness of the gloomy, blasted landscape is spookily heightened by its contrast to the vivid colours of the earlier wheat and grasslands.

Drumheller sits at the base of the canyon, surrounded by the detritus and spoil heaps of its mining past – the Red Deer River having exposed not only dinosaur fossils but also (now exhausted) coal seams. The coal attracted the likes of Samuel Drumheller, an early mining pioneer after whom the town is named. The first mine opened in 1911, production reaching a peak after the opening of a rail link to Calgary two years later. In less than fifty years it was all over, coal's declining importance in the face of gas and oil sounding the industry's death knell. These days Drumheller is sustained by agriculture, oil – there are some 3000 wells dotted around the surrounding farmland – and tourism, the **Tyrell Museum of Paleontology** ranking as one of Alberta's biggest draws.

The town is best reached by taking Hwy 2 north towards Edmonton and branching east on Hwy 72 and Hwy 9. It's an easy day-trip with your own transport, and most people make straight for the Tyrell Museum, signposted from Drumheller on Hwy 838 (or "North Dinosaur Trail"). Using one of the two **Greyhound buses** daily from Calgary to Drumheller (figure on around $20 one-way) makes a day-trip more of a squeeze. The depot (☎823-7566) is some way out of the town centre at the Suncity Mall on Hwy 9. It's definitely too far to walk from here or the town centre to the museum, particularly on a hot day, but Badlands Taxis (☎823-6552) or Jack's Taxi (☎823-2220) will run you there from the bus depot for about $10. Failing that you could rent a car: National (☎823-3371 or 1-800/387-4747) is the only agency in town.

There's not much to do in the town itself, despite the best efforts of its **infocentre** at the corner of Riverside Drive and 2nd Street West (June–Aug daily 9am–9pm; Sept–May Mon–Fri 8.30am–4.30pm ; ☎823-1331). For all its half million visitors a year, Drumheller has just 350 or so beds, and, if truth be told, you don't really want to spend a night here. If you have no choice, be sure to book well in advance: virtually everything's gone by mid-afternoon in high season. A limited selection of **accommodation** lies a block from the bus terminal, the best of the downtown hotels being the slightly overpriced *Lodge at Drumheller* (☎823-3322; ③) opposite the hostel at 48 Centre St and Railway Avenue. Other central options include the *Rockhound Motor Inn*, South Railway Drive (☎823-5302; ④); the top-of-the-pile *Inn & Spa at Heartwood Manor*, 320 Railway Drive (☎823-6495 or 1-888/823-6495; ⑤); *Drumheller Inn* (☎823-8400; ⑤), a modern motel on a bluff at 100 S Railway Ave (Hwy 9) off the Hwy 56 approach from the west; and the tasteful log cabins of the pleasanter *Badlands Motel* (☎823-5155; ⑤), 1km out of town on Hwy 838. The **local hostel** is the rather tatty *Alexander International Hostel*, 30 Railway Ave (☎823-6337, ①), and rents bikes and offers beds in eight-person dorms from $20.

Of the town's well-situated **campsites**, the better option is the *Dinosaur Trailer Park* (☎823-3291; $15; April–Oct), across the river north of downtown at the junction of Hwy 56 and Hwy 838. The visitor infocentre has lists of the many other private and provincial campsites (*Little Fish Lake Provincial Park*, 50km southeast of Drumheller on Hwy 573, being the best) up and down the valley.

The tucked-away All West **supermarket** on 1st Street behind the main drag stocks picnic supplies. For cheap eating, the *Diana* on Main Street is half-diner, half-Chinese restaurant, and the *Bridge Greek Restaurant*, 71 Bridge St N, has a relaxed ambience and good food. Better-quality **restaurants** have a reputation of going broke once the tourists have gone home, but currently the two best places to eat are *Jack's Bistro*, 70 Railway Ave (☎823-8422), serving hearty Canadian fare, and the reasonably priced and little-known *Sizzling House*, 160 Centre St (☎823-8098), reckoned to be one of Alberta's best Chinese restaurants. The cafeteria at the museum also makes a reasonable eating option.

The Royal Tyrrell Museum of Paleontology

Packed with high-tech displays, housed in a sleek building and blended skilfully into its desolate surroundings, the **Royal Tyrrell Museum of Paleontology** is an object lesson in museum design (mid-May to early Sept daily 9am–9pm; early Sept to mid-Oct daily 10am–5pm; mid-Oct to mid-May Tues–Sun 10am–5pm; $7.50; ☎823-7707). It attracts half a million-plus visitors a year, and its wide-ranging exhibits are likely to appeal to anyone with even a hint of scientific or natural curiosity. Although it claims the world's largest collection of complete dinosaur skeletons (fifty full-size animals and 80,000 miscellaneous specimens), the museum is far more than a load of old bones, and as well as tracing the earth's history from the year dot to the present day it's also a leading centre of study and academic research. Its name comes from Joseph Tyrrell, who in 1884 discovered the Albertosaurus, first of the dinosaur remains to be pulled from the Albertan badlands.

Laid out on different levels to suggest layers of geological time, the open-plan exhibit guides you effortlessly through a chronological progression, culminating in a huge central hall of over two hundred dinosaur specimens. If there's a fault, it's that the hall is visible early on and tempts you to skip the lower-level displays, which place the dinosaurs in context by skilfully linking geology, fossils, plate tectonics, evolution and the like with Drumheller's own landscape. You also get a chance to peer into the preparation lab and watch scientists working on fossils in one of the world's best-equipped paleontology centres.

By far the most impressive exhibits are the **dinosaurs** themselves. Whole skeletons are immaculately displayed against three-dimensional backgrounds that persuasively depict the swamps of sixty million years ago. Some are paired with full-size plastic dinosaurs, which appear less macabre and menacing than the freestanding skeletons. Sheer size is not the only fascination: Xiphactinus, for example, a four-metre specimen, is striking more for its delicate and beautiful tracery of bones. Elsewhere the emphasis is on the creatures' diversity or on their staggeringly small brains, sometimes no larger than their eyes.

The museum naturally also tackles the problem of the dinosaurs' extinction, pointing out that around ninety percent of all plant and animal species that have ever inhabited the earth have become extinct. Leave a few minutes for the wonderful **paleoconservatory** off the dinosaur hall, a collection of living prehistoric plants, some unchanged in 180 million years, selected from fossil records to give an idea of the vegetation that would have typified Alberta in the dinosaur age.

The Dinosaur Trail

The **Dinosaur Trail** is a catch-all circular road route of 51km from Drumheller embracing some of the viewpoints and lesser historic sights of the badlands and the Red Deer Valley area. The comprehensive *Visitor's Guide to the Drumheller Valley* (free from the Drumheller infocentre) lists thirty separate stopoffs, mostly on the plain above the valley, of which the key ones are: the **Little Church** (6km west of Drumheller), the "Biggest Little Church in the World" (capacity six); **Horsethief Canyon** (17.6km west of the museum) and **Horseshoe Canyon** (19km southwest of the museum on Hwy 9), two spectacular viewpoints of the wildly eroded valley, the latter with good trails to and along the canyon floor; the **Hoodoos**, slender columns of wind-sculpted sandstone, topped with mushroom-like caps (17km southeast of Drumheller on Hwy 10); the still largely undeveloped **Midland Provincial Park**, site of the area's first mines and crisscrossed by badland trails, now home to an interpretive centre (daily 9am–6pm; free); and the **Atlas Coal Mine** (guided tours mid-May to mid-Oct daily 9am–6pm; $4 or $6 for guided tour; ☎822-2220), dominated by the teetering wooden "tipple", once used to sort ore and now a beautiful and rather wistful piece of industrial archeology.

Dinosaur Provincial Park

Drivers can feasibly fit in a trip to **Dinosaur Provincial Park** the same day as the Tyrrell Museum, a 174-kilometre journey from Drumheller to the park, and then head back to Calgary on the Trans-Canada Highway, which runs just south of the park. The nearest town is Brooks, 48km west of the **Royal Tyrrell Museum Field Station**, the park's obvious hub (late May to early Oct daily 8.30am–9pm; early Oct to late May Mon–Fri 9am–4pm; $2; ☎378-4342, reservation line ☎378-4344). The excellent **Dinosaur Provincial Park** campsite in the park beside Little Sandhill Creek is open year-round, but only serviced from May to September ($13) – book on (☎378-3700).

Nestled among some of the baddest of the badlands, the region's landscape is not only one of the most alien in Canada, but also one of the world's richest fossil beds, a superb medley of prairie habitats and ecosystems and (since 1979) a listed UN World Heritage Site. Over 300 complete skeletons have been found and dispatched to museums across the world, representing 35 (or ten percent) of all known dinosaur species. The field station has five self-guided **trails**, the Badlands Trail and Cottonwood Flats Trail being the most worthwhile, and giving a good taste of this extraordinary region. The centre also has a small museum that goes over the same ground as its parent in

Drumheller, leaving the real meat of the visit to the **Badlands Bus Tour**, an excellent ninety-minute guided tour of the otherwise out-of-bounds dinosaur dig near the centre of the park (May–Sept Mon–Fri tours three or more daily, Sat–Sun 7 times daily; $4.50). A few exposed skeletons have been left *in situ*, with panels giving background information. The station also organizes two-hour guided **hikes**, most notably the Centrosaurus Bone Bed Hike (Tues, Thurs, Sat & Sun 9.15am; $4.50), which visits a restricted area where some 300 centrosaurus skeletons have been uncovered. All tours fill up quickly, so it's worth trying to book ahead(☎378-4344).

Highway 3

The most travelled route across southern Alberta is the Trans-Canada Highway, direct to Calgary; **Hwy 3**, branching off at **Medicine Hat**, takes a more southerly course across the plains before finally breaching the Rockies at Crowsnest Pass. This quieter and less spectacular route into the mountains holds a trio of worthwhile diversions: the new **Carriage Centre** near Cardston, the **Head-Smashed-In Buffalo Jump** heritage site, and **Waterton Lakes National Park**, a cross-border park that links with the United States' Glacier National Park.

Medicine Hat

Though **MEDICINE HAT** is barely a hundred years old, the origin of its wonderful name has already been confused. The most likely story has to do with a Cree medicine man who lost his headdress while fleeing a battle with the Blackfoot; his followers lost heart at the omen, surrendered, and were promptly massacred. These days you rarely see the town mentioned without the adage that it "has all hell for a basement", a quotation from Rudyard Kipling coined in response to the huge reserves of natural gas that lurk below the town. Discovered by railway engineers drilling for water in 1883, the gas fields now feed a flourishing petrochemical industry which blots the otherwise park-studded downtown area on the banks of the South Saskatchewan River.

Medicine Hat may claim that its 1440 hours of summer sunshine make it Canada's sunniest city, but its main function is as a major staging post on the Trans-Canada Highway. The world's **tallest tepee** (twenty storeys tall and actually made of metal), on the highway close to the visitor centre, and the nightmare **Riverside Waterslide** at Hwy 1 and Powerhouse Road (mid–May to early Sept daily 10am–8pm; $12.50; ☎529-6218) are the only attractions of note. If you're pulling off the road for a break, the best place for coffee and snacks is *Café Mundo*, 579 3rd St SE (☎528-2808); for lunch try *Caroline's*, 101 4th Ave SE (☎529-5300); and for novelty "Wild West" setting the place to go is the historic *Rustler's*, 901 8th St SW (☎526-8004), one of the town's oldest restaurants. The least expensive of the many **motels** is the *Bel-Aire*, 633 14th St (☎527-4421; ①), conveniently situated at the junction of the Trans-Canada and Hwy 3, though the *Best Western Inn*, on the Trans-Canada at 722 Redcliff Drive (☎527-3700 or 1-800/528-1234; ⑤), is more appealing if around three times the price. The best place around is the smart and comfortable *Medicine Hat Lodge*, 1051 Ross Glen Drive (☎529-2222 or 1-800/661-8095, *www.medhatlodge.com*; ⑤). The main downtown accommodation is the *Medicine Hat Inn Downtown*, 530 4th St SE (☎526-1313 or 1-800/730-3887; ③).

Lethbridge

Alberta's third city, **LETHBRIDGE** is booming on the back of oil, gas and some of the province's most productive agricultural land; none of which is of much consequence to people passing through, whom the city attempts to sidetrack with the **Nikka Yuko**

Centennial Gardens (mid-May to June & Sept daily 9am–5pm; July–Aug daily 9am–9pm; closed Oct to mid-May; $4; ☎328-3511) in its southeastern corner at 7th Avenue and Mayor Macgrath Drive in Henderson Lake Park. Built in 1967 as a symbol of Japanese and Canadian amity, the gardens were a somewhat belated apology for the treatment of Japanese-Canadians during World War II, when 22,000 were interned – 6000 of them in Lethbridge. Four tranquil Japanese horticultural landscapes make up the gardens, along with a pavilion of cypress wood handcrafted in Japan perpetually laid out for a tea ceremony.

Far removed from the gardens' decorum is **Fort Whoop-Up** (June–Aug Mon–Sat 10am–6pm, Sun noon–5pm; Sept–May Tues–Fri 10am–4pm, Sun 1–4pm; $2.50; ☎329-0444) at Indian Battle Park (Scenic Drive at 3rd Ave), a reconstruction of the wild whiskey–trading post set up in 1869 by American desperadoes from Fort Benton, Montana (the first of several in the region). It became the largest and most lucrative of the many similar forts which sprang up illegally all over the Canadian prairies, and led directly to the arrival of the North West Mounted Police in 1874. Aboriginal peoples came from miles around to trade anything – including the clothes off their backs – for the lethal hooch, which was fortified by grain alcohol and supplemented by ingredients such as red peppers, dye and chewing tobacco. The fort was also the scene of the last armed battle in North America between aboriginal peoples (fought between the Cree and Blackfoot nations in 1870).

Lethbridge's third significant sight is the **Sir Alexander Galt Museum** (daily 10am–4.30pm; donation; ☎320-3898) at the western end of 5th Avenue South off Scenic Drive, one of Canada's better small-town museums. It's named after a Canadian high commissioner who in 1882 financed a mine that led to the foundation of Lethbridge. Revamped at vast expense in 1985, the museum offers an overview of the city's history, with displays that cover coal mining, irrigation, immigration and the shameful internment episodes during the 1940s. There are also a couple of galleries devoted to art and other temporary exhibitions.

Practicalities

Four Greyhound **buses** operate daily from Calgary to the Lethbridge bus terminal (☎327-1551) at 411-5th St S. Two buses run daily to Fort Macleod, and two to Medicine Hat and the US border for connections to Great Falls and Helena in Montana. The **tourist office** is at 2805 Scenic Drive at the corner of Hwy 4 and Hwy 5 (summer daily 9am–8pm; winter Mon–Sat 9am–5pm; ☎320-1222 or 1-800/661-1222 from western Canada and northwestern US).

Most of the city's **motels** are on a single strip, Mayor Macgrath Drive; the top-of-the-pile *Sandman Hotel Lethbridge*, at no. 421 (☎328-1111 or 1-800/726-3626; ④), and the less expensive *Chinook Motel*, at no. 1303 (☎328-0555 or 1-800/791-8488; ③), are typical. Downtown the best value is the *Days Inn*, 100 3rd Ave S (☎327-6000 or 1-800/661-8085; ③). The *Henderson Lake Campgrounds* (☎328-5452; $14; May–Oct) are near Henderson Lake on 7th Avenue South alongside the Nikka Yuko Centennial Gardens in Henderson Lake Park. The best downtown **eating** is to be found in the *Lethbridge Lodge Hotel* at 320 Scenic Drive (☎328-1123 or 1-800/661-1232), which boasts *Anton's*, an upmarket restaurant with modern American food, and the cheaper but pleasant and popular *Garden Café*. For downtown coffee and snacks, make for *The Penny Coffee House*, 331 5th St S.

Fort Macleod and around

FORT MACLEOD catches traffic coming up from the States and down from Calgary on Hwy 2, which eases around the town centre via the largely rebuilt wooden palisade of the **Fort Museum** at 219 25th St (May, June & Sept to mid-Oct daily 9am–5pm; July

& Aug daily 9am–8pm; mid-Oct to Dec 23 & March–April Mon–Fri 9am–5pm; $5; ☎553-4703). One for die-hard Mountie fans, this was the first fort established in Canada's Wild West by the North West Mounted Police, who got lost after being dispatched to raid Fort Whoop-Up in Lethbridge, allowing the whiskey traders to flee; finding Whoop-Up empty, they continued west under Colonel James Macleod to establish a permanent barracks here on Oldman Island on the river in 1874. The RCMP "musical ride", a display of precision riding, is performed four times daily in July and August by students in replica dress.

Two daily **buses** serve the town from Lethbridge and between three and five from Calgary, the latter continuing west to Cranbrook, Nelson and eventually to Vancouver in British Columbia. The depot's at 2302 2nd Ave (☎553-3383). The **tourist office** is at the east end of town on 24th Street (mid-May to Aug daily 9am–8pm; ☎553-4955). The town has nine more or less similarly priced **motels**, the most central being the *Fort Motel* on Main Street (☎553-3606; ②). Top choice is the *Sunset Motel* (☎553-4448 or 1-888/554-2784; ④), located on Hwy 3 at the western entrance to town. All motels fill up quickly in summer, so arrive early or call ahead.

Head-Smashed-In Buffalo Jump

The image of Indians trailing a lone buffalo with bow and arrow may be Hollywood's idea of how aboriginal peoples foraged for food, but the truth, while less romantic, was often far more effective and spectacular. Over a period of more than 6000–10,000 years, Blackfoot hunters perfected a technique of luring buffalo herds into a shallow basin and stampeding them to their deaths over a broad cliff, where they were then butchered for meat (dried to make pemmican, a cake of pounded meat, berries and lard), bone (for tools) and hide (for clothes and shelter). Such "jumps" existed all over North America, but the **Head-Smashed-In Buffalo Jump**, in the Porcupine Hills 18km northwest of Fort Macleod on Hwy 785, is the best preserved (daily: mid-May to early Sept 9am–6pm; early Sept to mid-May 10am–5pm; ☎553-2731). Its name, which alone should be enough to whet your appetite, is a literal description of how a nineteenth-century Blackfoot met his end after deciding the best spot to watch the jump was at the base of the cliff, apparently unaware he was about to be visited by some five hundred plummeting buffalo.

The modern **interpretive centre**, a seven-storeyed architectural tour de force, is built into the ten-metre-high and 305-metre-wide cliff near the original jump. Below it, a ten-metre-deep bed of ash and bones accumulated over millennia is protected by the threat of a $50,000 fine for anyone foolish enough to rummage for souvenirs. All manner of artefacts and objects have been discovered amidst the debris, among them knives, scrapers and sharpened stones used to skin the bison. Metal arrowheads in the topmost layers, traded with white settlers, suggest the jump was used until comparatively recently. Nothing can have changed much here over millennia bar the skilfully integrated centre and some modest excavations. The multilevel facility delves deep into the history of the jump and native culture in general, its highlight being a film, *In Search of the Buffalo*, which attempts to re-create the thunderous death plunge using a herd of buffalo, which were slaughtered, frozen and then somehow made to look like live animals hurtling to their deaths (shown half-hourly on Level Four). Around the centre the jump is surrounded by a couple of kilometres of **trails**, the starting point for tours conducted by Blackfoot native guides. No public transport serves the site; taxis from Fort Macleod cost about $20.

Remington-Alberta Carriage Centre

Alberta is hoping that the glittering new **Remington-Alberta Carriage Centre** (daily: mid-May to early Sept 9am–8pm; early Sept to mid-May 10am–5pm; $6.50, carriage rides June–Aug $3; ☎653-1000 or 653-5139) will attract visitors in droves. Although brilliantly executed, its appeal is perhaps more limited, centring on horse-drawn vehicles and evoking the atmosphere of their nineteenth-century heyday. The main hall boasts around sixty working carriages – the core of a private collection begun by Don Remington in the 1950s – and around 140 in passive display, the exhibits cleverly integrated with 25 "stories" that place the carriages in their social and cultural context. Additionally there's the chance to ride the carriages (usually for free), see working stables and admire the magnificent Quarters and Clydesdales that make up the centre's horse herd. Guides are often in period dress, and you can watch craftspeople in the process of building and renovating various carriages. Free guided tours run regularly around the site. The centre lies immediately south of **Cardston** at 623 Main St (across the river from the town centre), just off Hwy 2 about 50km south of Fort Macleod, and is handily placed for Waterton Lakes National Park.

Waterton Lakes National Park

WATERTON LAKES NATIONAL PARK, about 55km south of Fort Macleod, appears at first glance to be simply an addendum to the much larger Glacier National Park, which joins it across the United States border. Despite its modest size, however (just 523 square kilometres), it contains scenery – and trails – as stupendous as any of the bigger Canadian Rockies parks. In particular this is a great place to come for day-hikes, most of which – unlike equivalent walks in Banff and Jasper – can be easily accessed from the park's principal focus, **Waterton Townsite** (or Waterton). Founded in 1895, the park was relaunched in 1932 as an "International Peace Park" to symbolize the understated relationship between Canada and its neighbour. The two parks remain separate national enclaves. Though backpackers can cross the border without formalities, to drive from one to the other you have to exit the park and pass through immigration controls, as stringent as anywhere if you're not a national of either country. In a change to the practice of past years, a **park permit** is required between April and the end of September for all who enter the park: a day-pass is $4 (yearly $28), and group passes (2–10 people) cost $12 daily (see box on p.607 for more details concerning park entry fees).

Some history
These days Waterton is on the road pretty much to nowhere – if you're down this way you're here to see the park or on your way to or from the US. It was a different story in the past, for the region provided a happy hunting ground for **Ktunaxa** (Kootenay) First Peoples, whose home base was across the Continental Divide in the Kootenay region of present-day British Columbia. Around 200 archeological sites betraying their presence have been found in the park. Anything up to 9000 years ago aboriginal peoples crossed the mountains to fish and hunt bison on the prairie grasslands fringing the Waterton region, foodstuffs denied to them in their own aboriginal heartlands. By about 1700 the diffusion of the horse across North America (introduced by the Spanish) allowed rival peoples, namely the Blackfoot, to extend their sphere of influence from central Alberta into the area around Waterton. Their presence and increased mobility made it increasingly difficult for the Ktunaxa to make their habitual incursions, though Blackfoot supremacy in turn was to be cut short by the arrival of pioneer guns and white homesteads. By the mid-nineteenth century the Blackfoot had retreated eastwards, leaving the Waterton area virtually uninhabited. The region was named by Lieutenant Thomas Blakiston, a member of the famous Palliser expedition, in honour of the eighteenth-century British naturalist Charles Waterton.

The area's first permanent white resident, **John George Brown** – or "Kootenai Brown" – was a character straight out of a Wild West fantasy. Born in England and

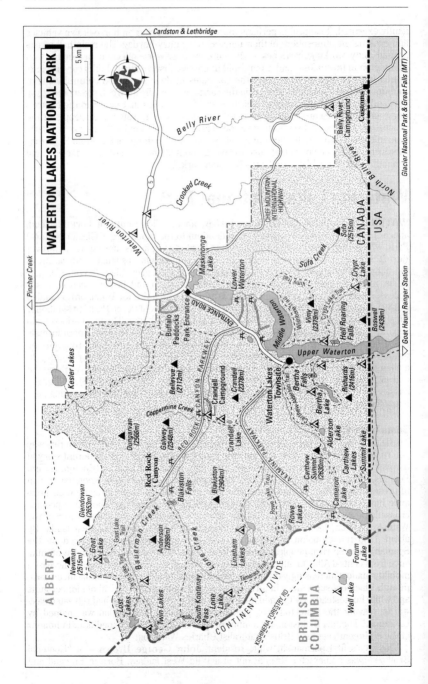

WATERTON LAKES NATIONAL PARK

△ Cardston & Lethbridge

N

0 5 km

ALBERTA

Pincher Creek ▷

Waterton River

Crooked Creek

Belly River

CHIEF MOUNTAIN INTERNATIONAL HIGHWAY

Kesler Lakes

Maskinonge Lake

Lower Waterton

Buffalo Paddocks

Park Entrance

ENTRANCE ROAD

Middle Waterton

Sofa Creek

Sofa (2515m) ▲

Belly River Campground

Customs

CANADA
USA

North Belly River

Glacier National Park & Great Falls (MT) ▷

Goat Haunt Ranger Station ▷

Akamina Trail

Crandell Campground

Bellevue (2112m) ▲

Coppermine Creek

Dungarvan (2566m) ▲

Galwey (2348m) ▲

RED ROCK CANYON PARKWAY

Crandell (2378m) ▲

Crandell Lake

Upper Waterton

Waterton Lakes Townsite

Vimy (2379m) ▲

Crypt Lake

Crypt Lake Trail

Hell Roaring Falls

Boswell (2439m) ▲

Richards (2416m) ▲

Bertha Falls

Bertha Lake

Anderson Lake

AKAMINA PARKWAY

Red Rock Canyon

Blakiston Falls

Blakiston (2904m) ▲

Glendowan (2653m) ▲

Anderson (2698m) ▲

Bauerman Creek

Goat Lake

Goat Lake Trail

Newman (2515m) ▲

Lost Lakes

Twin Lakes

Snowshoe Trail

Lone Creek

Lineham Lakes

South Kootenay Pass

Lone Lake

Rowe Lake Trail

Carthew Summit (2630m) ▲

Carthew Lakes

Summit Lake

Cameron Lake

Rowe Lakes

Forum Lake

Tamarack Trail

CONTINENTAL DIVIDE

KISHINENA FORESTRY RD

Wall Lake

BRITISH COLUMBIA

allegedly educated at Oxford, he spent time with the British Army in India, decamped to San Francisco, chanced his arm in the gold fields of British Columbia and worked for a time as a pony express rider with the US Army. Moving to the Waterton region he was attacked by Blackfoot natives, supposedly wrenching an arrow from his back with his own hands. He was then captured by Chief Sitting Bull and tied naked to a stake, but managed to escape at dead of night to join the rival Ktunaxa natives, with whom he spent years hunting and trapping, until their virtual retreat from the prairies. Marriage in 1869 calmed him down, and encouraged him to build a cabin (the region's first) alongside Waterton Lake. In time he was joined by other settlers, one of whom, Frederick Godsal, a rancher and close personal friend, took up Brown's campaign to turn the region into a **federal reserve**. In 1895 a reserve was duly established, with Brown as its first warden. In 1910 the area was made a "Dominion Park"; a year later it was designated a **national park**, the fourth in Canada's burgeoning park system. Brown, then aged 71, was made its superintendent, but died four years later, still lobbying hard to extend the park's borders. His grave lies alongside the main road into Waterton Townsite.

For all Brown's environmental zeal it was he, ironically, who first noticed globules of **oil** on Cameron Creek, a local river, a discovery that would bring oil and other mineral entrepreneurs to ravage the region. Brown himself actually skimmed oil from the river, bottled it, and sold it in nearby settlements. In 1901 a forest road was ploughed into Cameron Creek Valley. In September of the same year the Rocky Mountain Development Company struck oil, leading to western Canada's first producing oil well (and only the second in the entire country). The oil soon dried up, a monument on the Akamina Parkway (see below) now marking the well's original location. Tourists meanwhile were giving the park a conspicuously wide berth, thanks mainly to the fact that it had no railway (unlike Banff and Jasper), a situation that changed when the Great Northern Railway introduced a bus link here from its Montana to Jasper railway. Visitors began to arrive, the *Prince of Wales* hotel was built, and the park's future was assured. In 1995, some time after the other big parks, UNESCO declared Waterton a World Heritage Site. Today, the park is becoming ever more popular, with the same telltale proliferation of souvenir shops on Waterton Avenue, Waterton Townsite's main street, as you find on Banff town's Banff Avenue.

Waterton Townsite

WATERTON TOWNSITE, the park's only base, accommodation source and services centre, is beautifully set on Upper Waterton Lake, but offers little by way of cultural distraction. Most people are here to walk (see box, pp.600–601), windsurf, horse ride or take boat trips on the lake (see p.595). There are also a handful of town trails, and a trio of cracking hikes – Bertha Lake, Crypt Lake and the Upper Waterton Lakeshore – which start from the townsite (see box on p.600). Having long been a poor relation to the "big four" national parks in the Rockies, Waterton is now so popular that it's essential to book accommodation (see p.597) well in advance for much of July and August.

Two wonderfully scenic access roads from Waterton probe west into the park interior and provide picnic spots, viewpoints and the starting point for most other trails: the **Akamina Parkway** follows the Cameron Creek valley for 20km to Cameron Lake, a large subalpine lake where you can follow easy trails or rent canoes, rowing boats and paddleboats. The **Red Rock Canyon Parkway** weaves up Blakiston Creek for about 15km to the mouth of the water-gouged Red Rock Canyon, so called because of the oxidation of local argillite, a rock with a high iron content that turns rust-red on exposure to the elements. The road's one of the best places to see wildlife in the park without too much effort and, like the Akamina Parkway, has the usual pleasant panoply of picnic sites, trailheads and interpretive notice boards. If you're without transport for these

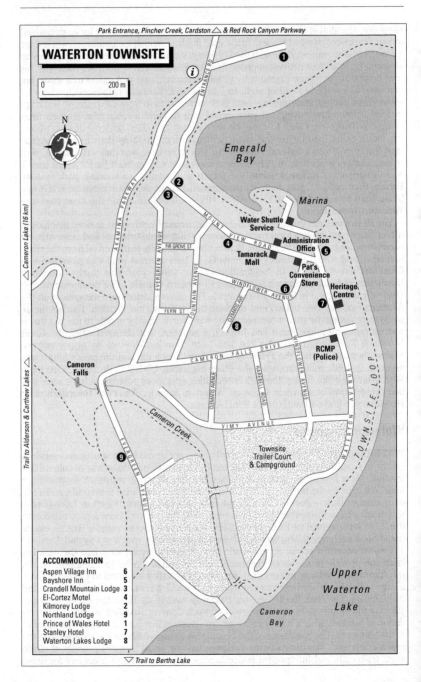

WATERTON TOWNSITE

0 ——— 200 m

N

Park Entrance, Pincher Creek, Cardston △ & Red Rock Canyon Parkway

Emerald Bay

Marina

Water Shuttle Service

Administration Office

Tamarack Mall

Pat's Convenience Store

Heritage Centre

RCMP (Police)

FIR GROVE ST

WINDFLOWER AVENUE

FERN ST

CLEMATIS AVE

CAMERON FALLS DRIVE

Cameron Falls

Cameron Creek

VIMY AVENUE

CLEMATIS AVENUE

HARBELL ROAD

WINDFLOWER AVENUE

WATERTON AVENUE

T O W N S I T E   L O O P

Townsite Trailer Court & Campground

Upper Waterton Lake

Cameron Bay

AKAMINA PARKWAY

EVERGREEN AVENUE

FOUNTAIN AVENUE

MOUNT VIEW ROAD

ENTRANCE RD

EVERGREEN AVENUE

△ Cameron Lake (16 km)

△ Trail to Alderson & Carthew Lakes

▽ Trail to Bertha Lake

ACCOMMODATION

Aspen Village Inn	**6**
Bayshore Inn	**5**
Crandell Mountain Lodge	**3**
El-Cortez Motel	**4**
Kilmorey Lodge	**2**
Northland Lodge	**9**
Prince of Wales Hotel	**1**
Stanley Hotel	**7**
Waterton Lakes Lodge	**8**

roads see "Practicalities" and "Activities" below for details of hiker shuttle services and car and bike rentals.

The third named road in the park, the **Chief Mountain International Highway** (25km) runs east from the park entrance at Maskinonge Lake along the park's eastern border. After 7km it reaches a fine **viewpoint** over the mountain-backed Waterton Valley and then passes the park-run *Belly River Campground* (see p.598) before reaching the US–Canadian **border crossing** (open June to late Sept 7am–10pm). When this crossing's closed, depending on your direction of travel, you have to use the crossings on Alberta's Hwy 2 south of Cardston or Hwy 89 north of St Mary in Montana.

Practicalities

Canadian **access** to Waterton by road is from Fort Macleod via either Hwy 3 west and Hwy 6 south (via Pincher Creek) or on Hwy 2 south to Cardston and then west on Hwy 5. Calgary is 264km and three-hours' drive away; Lethbridge (which has the nearest airport), 130km (75min); and St Mary, Montana, 60km (45min). More than other Rockies' parks this is somewhere you really need your own transport to reach. A small taxi-bus service, the Shuttleton Services (usually three times daily, but ring for services; ☎627-2157) runs between Waterton and the nearest Greyhound depot at Pincher Creek 50km away ($15 one-way, $25 return); a cab from Crystal Taxi (☎627-4262) will cost around $60 for the same run; otherwise there's no public transport to the town or within the park.

Everything you need to explore the park centres on Waterton Townsite. All accommodation is here, bar the campsites, while the national park **visitor centre** is on Entrance Road at the road junction just to the north (daily; May & early Sept 9am–5pm; June–Aug 8am–9pm; ☎859-2445 or 859-2224, *www.watertoninfo.ab.ca*). Further information is available from the Chamber of Commerce (☎859-2303) and at the park's administration office at 215 Mount View Rd outside the visitor centre's summer hours (Mon–Fri 8am–4pm; ☎859-2477, 859-2224 or 859-2275). The free weekly **newspaper**, the *Waterton-Glacier Views* (☎627-2370), also contains visitor information. Be sure to buy the Canadian Parks Service 1:50,000 **map** *Waterton Lakes National Park* ($9.50), if you're going to do any serious walking. It's usually available from the visitor centre and the **Waterton Heritage Centre** in the old firehall at 117 Waterton Ave (May–Oct 1–5pm, longer hours July & Aug; admission to museum by donation; ☎859-2267 or 859-2624). The latter is a combined art gallery, small natural-history museum, bookshop and another useful source of information. For advance information on the park, write to the Superintendent, Waterton Lakes National Park, Waterton Park, AB T0K 2M0.

Pat's Rentals & Convenience Store, a petrol station and camping store on the corner of Mount View Road and Waterton Avenue (☎859-2266), rents out **bikes** and **scooters** by the hour or day and also sells bikes and spares. There's also an ATM here. For **currency exchange**, try the Royal Bank in Tamarack Mall on Waterton Avenue or the Alberta Treasury Branch Agency upstairs at Caribou Clothing on Waterton Avenue (☎859-2604). The Itussististukiopi Coin-Op **laundry** is at 301 Windflower Ave (mid-June to mid-Sept daily 8am–10pm). Waterton Sports and Leisure in Tamarack Mall stocks maps, fishing licences and camping, walking, fishing and mountain-biking equipment and accessories. The **post office** is alongside the fire station on Fountain Avenue. The nearest **hospitals** are in Cardston (☎653-4411) and Pincher Creek (☎627-3333). For the **police**, call ☎859-2244. There's also a 24-hour park emergency number, but it really is for emergencies only (☎859-2636).

Activities

If you want to **cruise the lakes**, the most popular summer activity round these parts, contact Waterton Shoreline Cruises at the marina (☎859-2362). They run scenic two-hour cruises (June–Aug 5 daily; fewer in May & Sept; $21 or $13 one-way) up and down

GEOLOGY, FLORA AND FAUNA

The Waterton area's unique **geological history** becomes clear when you compare its scenery with the strikingly different landscapes of Banff and Jasper national parks to the north (see pp.604–636 and pp.643–658). Rock and mountains in Waterton moved eastward during the formation of the Rockies (see box, p.605), but unlike the ruptured strata elsewhere it travelled as a single vast mass known as the Lewis Thrust. Some 6km thick, this monolith moved over 70km along a 300-kilometre front, the result being that rocks over 1.5 billion years old from the Rockies' "sedimentary basement"– now the oldest surface rocks in the range – finally came to rest undisturbed on *top* of the prairies' far more recent 60-million-year-old shales. Scarcely any zone of transition exists between the two, which is why the park is often known as the place where the "peaks meet the prairies", and its landscapes as "upside-down mountains". The effect was to produce not only slightly lower peaks than to the north, but also mountains whose summits are irregular in shape and whose sedimentary formations are horizontal (very different from the steeply tilted strata and distinctive sawtooth ridges of Banff National Park).

The classic glacial U-shaped Waterton Valley and Upper Waterton Lake (at 150m, the Rockies' deepest lake) are more recent phenomena, gouged out 1.9 million years ago by Ice Age **glaciers** as they carved their way northwards through the present Waterton valley before expiring on the prairies. Upper Waterton Lake and the other two Waterton lakes are residual depressions left after the ice's final retreat 11,000 years ago. Cameron Lake, by contrast, was created when a glacial moraine (debris created by a glacier) dammed the waters of Cameron Creek. The flat townsite area has different origins again, consisting of deposits of silt, mud and gravel washed down from the mountains over the millennia and deposited as an alluvial "fan" across Upper Waterton Lake.

The huge variety of altitude, habitats and climate within the park – a combination of prairie, montane and alpine – mean that plants and wildlife from prairie habitats co-mingle with the species of the purely montane, subalpine and alpine regions found elsewhere. The result is the greatest diversity of **flora and fauna** of any of the western national parks: 1200 plant species – well over half of all that grown in Alberta – and 250 species of birds. The variety is immediately noticeable. As you approach the park on Hwy 5 from the north, a route almost as scenic as the park, you pass through dry prairie **grasslands**. This is home to native grasses such as grama and rough fescue, local

the lake across the US–Canadian border to Goat Haunt in Montana, little more than a quayside and park ranger station, where there is a scheduled thirty-minute stop before the return to Waterton (note that after the ranger station closes in mid-Sept boats no longer stop at Goat Haunt). No immigration procedures are required, but if you wish to camp overnight in the backcountry you need to register with the ranger station. You can take an early boat to Goat Haunt and then return on foot to Waterton on the **Waterton Lakeshore Trail**, an easy four-hour walk (13km one-way). The same company run a ferry to various trails around the lake, most notably a passage ($11 return) to the trailhead of the famed Crypt Lake walk (see box, pp.600–601) and the myriad longer hikes from Goat Haunt in the US. Park Transport in Tamarack Mall on Mount View Road (☎859-2378) organizes two-hour tours round the park ($25), but will also lay on a **taxi** shuttle (from $7.50 to trails on the area's two Parkways: the most popular drop-off is the beginning of the Carthew-Alderson trail (see box, pp.600–601).

Windsurfing is also surprisingly popular locally, thanks to the powerful winds – anything up to 70kph – which often roar across the lakes (Waterton is wetter, windier and snowier than much of Alberta). Winds generally gust south to north, making the beach at Cameron Bay on Upper Waterton Lake a favourite spot for surfers to catch the breeze. The water's cold and deep, though, so you'll need a wet suit. If you want to **swim**, head for the cheap outdoor heated pool on Cameron Falls Drive. **Fishing** is good on the lakes, but species now rapidly disappearing, displaced over the years by cultivated crops. Here, too, you should see the prickly wild rose, Alberta's floral emblem, sagebrush, buckbrush (yellow rose) and pincushion cactus. Entering the park you pass the **wetlands** of Maskinonge Lake on your left, while in the Blakison Valley and around *Belly River Campsite* you are in the realms of **aspen parkland**, a transitional zone between prairie and forest habitats dominated by aspen, willow, white spruce, balsam poplar and flowers such as prairie crocus, snowberry and lily of the valley. Higher up you encounter **montane forest** and subalpine zones, fecund zones rich in plant and animal life easily explored on hikes such as the Bertha Lake and Carthew Lakes trails (see p.600). On the eastern slopes above Cameron Lake are copses of 400-year-old subalpine trees (lodgepole pine, larch, fir, whitebark pine and Engelmann spruce), the oldest forest growth in the park. Here, too, you'll see vast spreads of so-called bear grass, a bright flower-topped grass which can grow up to a metre in height. Trees largely give out in the **alpine zone**, an area of which the park's Crypt Lake is a good example. It is the preserve of heathers, hardy lichens, flower-strewn meadows and rarer high-altitude alpine plants. See Contexts p.934 for more on these various habitats.

If you want to see **fauna**, enquire at the park centre for likely locations and times – autumn days at dawn and dusk are usually best. **Birds** are best seen on Maskinonge and Lower Waterton lakes, Linnet Lake, Cameron Lake and along the easy 45-minute Wishbone Trail off Chief Mountain Highway. The best time to look is during the migratory season between September and November, as the park lies under two major migration routes. Ospreys also nest close to Waterton Townsite. Maskinonge Lake is the place to sit in the hope of seeing mink and muskrats. As for **mammals**, beavers can be seen on the Belly River, and golden-mantled ground squirrels around Cameron Lake and on the Bear's Hump above town; Columbian ground squirrels are ubiquitous. The park has about fifty black bears, but you'll be lucky to see them: your best bet is to scan the slopes of Blakison Valley in July and August as they forage for berries in readiness for hibernation. Grizzlies, moose and cougars are also prevalent, but rarely seen. White-tailed deer nibble up and down the Red Rock Canyon Parkway, while elk and mule deer often wander in and around Waterton town itself. Mountain goats are shy and elusive, but you may glimpse one or two in the rocky high ground above Bertha, Crypt and Goat lakes. Bighorn sheep congregate above the Visitor Centre and the northern flanks of the Blakison Valley.

remember to pick up the compulsory national park permit ($6 a week, $13 annual) from the visitor centre or park administration office. Off the water, **horse riding** is available from the Alpine Stables, PO Box 53, Waterton Park, AB T0K 2M0 (☎859-2462), located just east off the highway about 1km north of the Visitor Centre. On offer are one-hour outings (hourly on the hour; from $17) and two-hour (3 daily; $31), daily and overnight treks. Canadian Wilderness Adventures (☎859-2334, fax 859-2342) offer a range of guided walks and tours long and short. Four kilometres north of town on the main highway is the beautiful eighteen-hole **Waterton Lakes Golf Course** (☎859-2383 or 859-2114): green fees are around $30 (cheaper after 5pm) and club rental from about $8.

Hotels and motels

Aspen Village Inn, Windflower Ave (☎859-2255 or 1-888/859-8669, fax 859-2033). Quiet spot with mountain views opposite the municipal pool; 35 motel rooms and 16 "cottage" rooms, some with kitchenettes. April to mid-Oct. ⑥.

Bayshore Inn, 111 Waterton Ave (☎859-2211 or 1-888/527-9555, fax 859-2291, *www.bayshoreinn.com*). Just south of the marina; very comfortable hotel, with 49 of its seventy units on the lakefront; two-unit and deluxe suites available. Mid-April to mid-Oct. ⑥.

Crandell Mountain Lodge, 102 Mount View Rd, corner of Evergreen Ave (☎859-2288, *www.crandellmountainlodge.com*). Just seventeen nicely finished nonsmoking rooms (two with special wheelchair access) in a pretty lodge; more intimate than some of the town's hotels, with kitchenette and fireplace units available. Easter–Oct. ⑥.

El-Cortez Motel, next to the Tamarack Mall at 208 Mount View Rd (☎859-2366, fax 859-2221). One of the less expensive places in town; 35 rooms including two- and three-room family units; some rooms with kitchenettes. May–Sept. ③.

Kilmorey Lodge, 117 Evergreen Ave (☎859-2334 or 1-888/859-8669, fax 859-2342, *kilmorey@telusplanet.net*). At the northern entrance to town on Emerald Bay; 23 antique-decorated rooms with a lakefront setting and historic old-fashioned feel. Some rooms are small for the price, while others score by virtue of their views (book in advance for these); there's also an excellent restaurant (the *Lamp Post*) and nice *Gazebo Café on the Bay* with outdoor waterfront deck for snacks and light meals. Open all year. ⑤.

The Lodge At Waterton Lakes, Cameron Falls Drive and Windflower Ave (☎859-2151 or 1-888/985-6343, fax 859-2229, *www.watertonresort.com*). Smart 80-room resort hotel; health spa with indoor pool, recreational centre with 18m pool and lots of extra facilities such as kitchenettes in certain deluxe rooms. ⑦.

Northland Lodge, Evergreen Ave (☎ & fax 859-2353, *www.northlandlodge.ab.ca*). Nine nonsmoking and cosy rooms, seven with private bathroom, east of the townsite in the lee of the mountains one block south of Cameron Falls; some with kitchenettes. Mid-May to mid-Oct. ③.

Prince of Wales Hotel, Waterton Lake (☎859-2231, 236-3400 or 602/207-6000, fax 859-2630). Famous and popular old hotel – the best in town – whose 1927 Gothic outline is in almost every picture of Waterton; worth it if you can afford it. Lakeside rooms with views are pricier, but some are rather small, so check what you're getting for your $245. Mid-May to mid-Sept. ⑦.

Stanley Hotel, 112b Waterton Ave (☎859-2345). Old-fashioned and often full nine-roomed hotel. Mid-May to Sept. ③.

Campsites

In addition to the private and three Canadian Parks Service park-run campsites (park campsites are first-come, first-served, and fill quickly in summer), that are detailed below, the national park has provided thirteen designated **backcountry campsites**, where you'll find dry toilets and a surface-water supply; a few of them also have shelters and cooking facilities. To use any, you need a backcountry camping permit, issued on a first-come, first-served basis by the Visitor Centre or Administration Office. A quota system is operated to prevent overcrowding. For information on these and other park campsites, call ☎859-2224, fax 859-2650. Unrestricted camping within the park is usually permitted only at Lineham Lakes, reached by a 4.2-kilometre trail off the north side of the Akamina Parkway 9.5km from Waterton. Note that at park sites you can pay an optional $3 to use the firewood provided.

Belly River Campground, 29km from the townsite, 1km off Chief Mountain Parkway on Hwy 6 (☎859-2224). Smallest (24 sites) and simplest of the park-operated campsites. Self-registration; tap water; kitchen shelters; fireplaces; chemical and pit toilets. Mid-May to Sept. $10.

Crandell Mountain Campground, 8km west of Waterton on the Red Rock Canyon Parkway off Hwy 5 (☎859-2224). Semi-serviced park-run campsite with 129 sites. Tap water; fireplaces; no showers. Mid-May to late Sept. $13.

Crooked Creek, 5.6km east of Waterton Park Gateway on Hwy 5 (☎653-1100). Has 46 sites, seven of which have full service for RVs. Mid-May to early Sept. $11.

Homestead Campground, 3km north of Waterton Park Gateway on Hwy 6 (☎859-2247). Large private 276-site campsite with services, showers, store, video games, laundry, heated outdoor pool, dance floor and many other distractions. May to mid-Sept. $16.

Riverside Campground, 5km east of Waterton Park Gateway (☎653-2888). Private; seventy sites with showers, services, breakfasts and live entertainment and barbecue suppers every Saturday. Mid-May to mid-Sept. $12.

Waterton Townsite Campground, off Vimy Ave (☎859-2224). 238-site serviced park-run campsite in town. First-come, first-served basis, and fills up by mid-afternoon in summer. Showers; no open fires; wheelchair-accessible. Open May to Thanksgiving (second Mon in Oct) but self-registration after Labour Day (in early Sept). $16.

Eating

Lakeside Kootenai Brown Dining Room, Waterton Ave at the *Bayshore Inn* (☎859-2211). One of the better and more elegant spots in town to treat yourself; the dining room overlooks the lake. Open all day for breakfast, lunch and dinner. Moderate.

Lamp Post Dining Room, 117 Evergreen Ave at the *Kilmorey Lodge* (☎859-2334). Old-world appeal and tempting good food without the stuffiness of *Windsor Lounge*; the moderate prices are lower too (7.30am–10pm). The hotel's *Gazebo* café on the waterfront is also good for snacks (10am–10pm).

New Frank's Restaurant, 106 Waterton Ave (☎859-2240). This restaurant serves cheap, odd combinations of breakfasts, burgers, a Chinese buffet plus lunch and six-course buffet specials.

Pearl's, 305 Windflower Ave (☎859-2284). Fresh baking; great first choice for cheap breakfast, lunch, coffee, deli meats, picnic provisions and hikers' takeaway lunches. Indoor and outdoor tables.

Pizza of Waterton, 103 Fountain Ave (☎859-2660). Dough made daily on the premises; good, cheap pizzas to eat in or take away. Open daily 4.30–10pm.

Windsor Lounge, *Prince of Wales Hotel* (☎859-2231). One of several lounges, bars and dining rooms in this posh hotel open for nonpatrons to enjoy afternoon tea, a good breakfast or a refined hour with a drink and great lake views. Dress well, as the place is fairly smart. The *Garden Court* is the most elegant restaurant in the hotel (reservations required).

Crowsnest Pass

The 1382-metre **Crowsnest Pass** is the most southerly of the three major routes into the Rockies and British Columbia from Alberta, and far less attractive than the Calgary and Edmonton approaches. In its early stages as Hwy 3 pushes west out of Fort Macleod across glorious windblown prairie, it augurs well: the settlements are bleaker and more backwoods in appearance, and the vast unbroken views to the mountain-filled horizon appear much as they must have to the first pioneers. As the road climbs towards the pass, however, the grime and dereliction of the area's mining heritage make themselves increasingly felt. Hopes a century ago that Crowsnest's vast coal deposits might make it the "Pittsburgh of Canada" were dashed by disasters, poor-quality coal, complicated seams, cheaper coal from British Columbia and rapid obsolescence. Today much of the area has been declared an Historic District and turned into Alberta's only "ecomuseum", a desperate attempt to bring life and tourist cash back to economically blighted communities (many people commute to work in British Columbia's mines over the Pass or have left altogether). To some extent they've succeeded, though you have to pick your mining-related stopoffs carefully round here. If mines and disaster sites don't appeal, the Crowsnest route west is of most use as a direct route if you're hurrying to Vancouver or aim to explore the Kootenays in southern British Columbia. After breasting the pass, Hwy 3 drops into BC and follows the often spectacular Elk River Valley to join Hwy 95 at Cranbrook (see p.841).

Bellevue and the Frank Slide

Sleepy **BELLEVUE** is the first village worthy of the name after Fort Macleod; an oddball and close-knit spot with an old-world feel unusual in these parts. It's distinguished by a church the size of a dog kennel and a wooden tepee painted lemon yellow, as well as the claim to have "the best drinking water in Alberta". Nonetheless, it supports a small summer-only **infocentre** by the campsite (see p.601) and provides visitors with the opportunity to explore – complete with hard hat and miner's lamp – a wonderfully dark and dank 100m or so of the old **Bellevue Mine** (30min tours every half-hour mid-May to early Sept daily 10am–5.30pm; $6; ☎562-7388). The only mine open to the public locally, it ceased production in 1962, but remains infamous for an explosion in 1910 that destroyed the ventilator fan. Thirty men died in the disaster, though not from the blast, but by breathing so-called "afterdamp", a lethal mixture of carbon dioxide and carbon monoxide left after fire has burnt oxygen from the atmosphere. As if this wasn't

HIKING IN WATERTON LAKES PARK

Waterton Lakes Park's 255km of trails have a reputation as not only the best constructed in the Canadian Rockies (with Yoho's Lake O'Hara), but also among the most easily graded, well marked and scenically routed. Like Moraine Lake in Banff National Park – and unlike Banff and Jasper – you can also access superb walks easily without a car. Bar one or two outlying hikes, three key areas contain trails and trailheads: the **townsite** itself, which has two magnificent short walks; the **Akamina Parkway**; and the **Red Rock Canyon Parkway**. Most walks are day-hikes, climaxing at small alpine lakes cradled in spectacular hanging valleys. Options for backpacking are necessarily limited by the park's size, though the 36-kilometre **Tamarack Trail**, following the crenellations of the Continental Divide between the Akamina Parkway (trailhead as for Rowe Lakes – see opposite) and Red Rock Canyon, is rated as one of the Rockies' greatest high-line treks (maximum elevation 2560m); the twenty-kilometre Carthew–Alderson Trail from Cameron Lake to Waterton (maximum elevation 2311m), a popular day's outing, can be turned into a two-day trip by overnighting at the Alderson Lake campsite. To do it in a day, take advantage of the hiker shuttle service to the trailhead offered by Park Transport (☎859-2378) based in the Tamarack Mall on Mount View Road (see p.596).

In summary, this is a great park in which to base yourself for a few days' hiking: details of hikes are given below, but as a general guide to do the cream of the hikes you'd first stroll the **Bear's Hump** for views of Waterton town and the lakes; then walk all or part of the **Bertha Lake Trail** (day or half-day) from the townsite. Next day take a boat to Goat Haunt and walk back on the **Waterton Lakeshore Trail**. Then try the **Crypt Lake Trail** from the townsite and/or the **Rowe Lake–Lineham Ridge Trail**, both ranked among the best day-walks in the Rockies. Finally gird your loins for the longer **Carthew–Alderson Trail**, possible in a day.

WALKS FROM THE TOWNSITE

In and around the town, there are various short loops: stroll to Cameron Falls, try the Prince of Wales from the Visitor Centre (2km; 45min) or climb the more demanding **Bear's Hump**, also from the centre (1.2km; 200m vertical; 40min one-way); the latter is one of the park's most popular short walks, switchbacking up the slopes to a rocky outcrop with great views of the Waterton Valley. More surprisingly good views can be had from the easily reached viewpoint near the Bison Paddock. Another obvious, and very simple, walk from the town is the Waterton Lakeshore Trail (13km one-way; 100m ascent; 4hr), which follows Upper Waterton Lake's west shore across the US border to Goat Haunt; regular lake ferries sail back to the townsite, completing a lovely round trip (ferry details from the marina or call ☎859-2362; see pp.595–96). Alternatively, catch an early boat and walk back so as not to worry about making a boat connection.

The single most popular half-day or day's walk from the townsite, however, is the classic **Bertha Lake Trail** from Waterton, 5.8km each way with an ascent of 460m (allow 3–4hr for the round trip). It's a short, steep hike beginning on Evergreen Drive to a busy but remarkably unsullied mountain-ringed lake and there's an easy trail that runs right round the lakeshore (adding about another 5km to the trip). If you're not up to this, you can just do the first part of the trail and break off at Lower Bertha Falls (2.9km from the townsite; 150m ascent; 1hr): this deservedly popular section corresponds to the route of the *Bertha Falls Self-Guiding Nature Trail* pamphlet available from the Visitor Centre.

Another excellent, if challenging, walk out of Waterton is the unique **Crypt Lake Trail**, often touted as one of the best in Canada. The 8.7-kilometre hike (one-way; 675m ascent)

enough, Canada's worst mining disaster ever had occurred five years earlier at **HILL-CREST**, a village immediately to the south of Bellevue (signed from Hwy 3), when 189 men were killed by an explosion and the effects of "afterdamp". All were buried together a few centimetres apart in mass graves, now the **Hillcrest Cemetery** on 8th Avenue.

involves a boat trip ($9 round trip) across Upper Waterton Lake to the trailhead on the east side of the lake, a (perfectly safe) climb up a ladder, a crawl through a rock tunnel and a section along a rocky ledge with cable for support. The rewards are the crashing waterfalls and the great glacial amphitheatre containing Crypt Lake (1955m); rock walls tower 600m on three sides, casting a chill shadow that preserves small icebergs on the lake's surface throughout the summer. Allow time to catch the last boat back to Waterton (again, ferry details are on ☎859-2362), and note that it's a good idea to make reservations in summer. Campers should be aware that the site here is one of the most heavily used in the park's backcountry.

TRAILS FROM THE AKAMINA PARKWAY
Most of the trails accessed by the Akamina Parkway leave from the road's end near Cameron Lake. To stretch your legs after the drive up, or if you just want a stroll, try either the Akamina Lake (0.5km; 15min) or Cameron Lakeshore (1.6km; 30min) trails. The best of the longer walks is to Carthew Summit (7.9km one-way; 660m ascent), a superb trail that switchbacks through forest to Summit Lake (4km), a good target in itself, before opening out into subalpine meadow and a final climb to a craggy summit (2310m) and astounding viewpoint. The trail can be continued all the way back to Waterton Townsite (another 12km) – it's then the **Carthew–Alderson Trail** (see opposite), most of whose hard work you've done in getting up to Carthew Summit; from the summit it's largely steeply downhill via Carthew and Alderson lakes (1875m) to Cameron Falls and the townsite (1295m).

Another highly rated trail from the Akamina Parkway is equally appealing – the Rowe Lakes Trail (5.2km one-way; 555m ascent), which is accessed off the Parkway about 5km before Cameron Lake (it is also the first leg of the Tamarack Trail – see opposite). Most people make their way to the Rowe Basin (where there's a backcountry campsite) and then, rather than pushing on towards the Upper Rowe Lakes (1.2km beyond), either camp, turn around or – for stronger walkers – take the trail that branches right from the Upper Rowe path to walk to Lineham Ridge (another 3.4km and 540m ascent). This **Rowe Lake–Lineham Ridge** combination has been cited as some as one of the top five day-hikes in the Rockies. The stiffish walk is rewarded by Lineham Lake, sapphire blue in the valley far below, and a vast sea of mountains stretching to the horizon. Only come up here in good weather, as it's particularly hazardous when visibility's poor and the winds are up.

TRAILS FROM THE RED ROCK CANYON PARKWAY
Most trails on the Red Rock Canyon Parkway, such as the short Red Rock Canyon Trail (700m loop) and Blackiston Falls (1km; 30min), leave from Red Rock Canyon at the end of the road. The most exhilarating option from the head of the road, however, is the Goat Lake Trail (6.7km; 550m ascent), which follows Bauerman Creek on an old fire road (flat and easy, but a little dull) before peeling off right at the 4.3-kilometre mark for the climb to tranquil Goat Lake and ever-improving views (there's a backcountry campsite at the lake). If you ignore the lake turn-off and follow the fire road for another 4km, you come to a junction: one trail leads north to Lost Lake (2km), the other south to the spectacular Twin Lakes area (3.2km). This latter option will bring you to the long-distance Tamarack Trail (see opposite). Walk south on this from Twin Lakes (3.1km) and you can pick up the Blackiston Creek Trail, which will take you back to the head of the Red Rock Canyon Parkway.

Bellevue has a quaint **campsite**, the *Bellecrest Community Association Campground* (☎564-4696; donation), located just off the highway just east of the village: it's open May to October and has 22 "random" sites, toilets, tap water and an on-site ten-seat church with recorded sermons. The site is also handy for the **Leitch Collieries**

Provincial Historic Site, just off the main road to the north before the campsite. This was once the region's largest mining and coking concern; it was also the first to close (in 1915). Today there's little to see in the way of old buildings, but displays and board-walk interpretive trails past "listening posts" fill you in on mining techniques. The over-grown site is also enthusiastically described by interpretive staff (mid-May to mid-Sept daily 10am–4pm; winter site unstaffed; $2; ☎562-7388).

The Crowsnest Pass trail of destruction, death and disaster continues beyond Bellevue. Dominating the skyline behind the village are the crags and vast rock fall of the **Frank Slide**, an enormous landslide that has altered the contours of Turtle Mountain, once riddled with the galleries of local mines. On April 29, 1903 an estimated 100 million tonnes of rock on a front stretching for over 1km and 700m high trundled down the mountain, burying 68 people and their houses in less than two minutes. Amazingly none of the miners working locally were killed – they dug themselves out after fourteen hours of toil. The morbidly interesting **Frank Slide Interpretive Centre**, situated 1.5km off the highway about 1km north of the village, highlights European settlement in the area, the coming of the Canadian Pacific Railway to Alberta and the technology, attitudes and lives of local miners (daily: June to early Sept 9am–8pm; early Sept to May 10am–5pm; $4; ☎562-7388). It's well worth wandering around the site and slide area – there's a 1.5-kilometre trail or you can walk up the ridge above the car park for good views and an idea of the vast scale of the earth movement: no one to this day quite understands the science of how boulders travelled so far from the main slide (several kilometres in many cases). "Air lubrication" is the best theory, a device by which the cascading rock compressed the air in front of it, creating a hov-ercraft-like cushion of trapped air on which it "rode" across the surface.

Blairmore, Coleman and the Pass

BLAIRMORE, 2km beyond the slide, is a scrappy settlement redeemed for the casual visitor only by the walks and four winter and night ski runs on the hill above it (Pass Powder Keg Ski Hill: ☎562-8334 for information). Largest of the Crowsnest towns (pop-ulation around 1800), it has a handful of "historic" buildings, notably the *Cosmopolitan Hotel* – built in 1912 – at 13001-20th Ave (☎562-7321; ②), but neither town or hotel are places to linger. **COLEMAN** is the place to spend the night if you absolutely have to, especially if you've always wanted to be able to say you've seen "the biggest piggy bank in the world", made from an old steam engine once used to pull coal cars in local mines. The town, battered and bruised by mine closures, amounts to little – the small Crowsnest Museum has interesting mining exhibits in the old schoolhouse at 7701-18th Ave (mid-May to Oct daily 9am–6pm; Nov to mid-May Mon–Fri 10am–noon & 1–4pm; $2; ☎563-5434), a single road, a dilapidated strip of houses, three garages and a battered **motel**, the 24-unit *Stop Inn* (☎562-7381; ②). More appealing is the dubiously named ten-unit *Kozy Knest Kabins Triple K Motel* (☎563-5155; ②), open from May to October and more scenically situated 12km west of Coleman on Hwy 3 beside Crowsnest Lake.

Beyond Coleman the road climbs towards **Crowsnest Pass** itself (1382m) and, after a rash of sawmills, the natural scenery finally takes centre stage in a reassuring mix of lakes, mountains and trees protected by **Crowsnest Provincial Park**. A rustic provincial **camp-site** overlooks the lake at Crowsnest Creek, about 15km west of Coleman ($5).

THE CANADIAN ROCKIES

Few North American landscapes come as loaded with expectation as the **Canadian Rockies**, so it's a relief to find that the superlatives are scarcely able to do credit to the region's immensity of forests, lakes, rivers and snowcapped mountains. Although most visitors confine themselves to visiting just a handful of **national parks**, the range spans almost 1500km as far as the Yukon border, forming the vast watershed of the Continental Divide, which separates rivers flowing to the Pacific, Arctic and Atlantic oceans. Landscapes on such a scale make a nonsense of artificial borderlines, and the major parks are national creations that span both Alberta and British Columbia. Four of the parks – Banff, Jasper, Yoho and Kootenay – share common boundaries, and receive the attention of most of the millions of annual visitors to the Rockies.

There's not a great deal to choose between the parks in terms of scenery – they're all fairly sensational – and planning an itinerary that allows you to fit them all in comfortably is just about impossible. Most visitors start with **Banff National Park**, then follow the otherworldly **Icefields Parkway** north to the larger and much less busy **Jasper National Park**. From there it makes sense to continue west to **Mount Robson Provincial Park**, which protects the highest and most dramatic peak in the Canadian Rockies. Thereafter you're committed to leaving the Rockies unless you double back from Jasper to Banff – no hardship, given the scenery – to pick up the Trans-Canada Highway through the smaller **Yoho**, **Glacier** and **Revelstoke** national parks. Finally, **Kootenay National Park** is more easily explored than its neighbours, though you'll have to backtrack towards Banff or loop down from Yoho to pick up the road that provides its only access. The more peripheral, but no less impressive Waterton Lakes National Park, hugging the US border, is covered on pp.591–602.

Though you can get to all the parks by **bus**, travelling by **car** or **bike** is the obvious way to get the most out of the region. Once there, you'd be foolish not to tackle some of the 3000km of trails that crisscross the mountains, the vast majority of which are well worn and well signed. We've highlighted the best short walks and day-hikes in each area, and you can get more details from the excellent **park visitor centres**, which sell 1:50,000 topographical maps and usually offer small reference libraries of trail books; *The Canadian Rockies Trail Guide*, by Brian Patton and Bart Robinson, is invaluable for serious hiking or backpacking. Other activities – fishing, skiing, canoeing, white-water rafting, cycling, horse riding, climbing and so on – are comprehensively dealt with in visitor centres, and you can easily **rent equipment** or sign up for organized tours in the bigger towns.

A word of warning: don't underestimate the Rockies. Despite the impression created by the summer throngs in centres like Banff and Lake Louise, excellent roads and sleek park facilities, the vast proportion of parkland is wilderness and should be respected and treated as such. See Basics, pp.54–57, for more.

Where to go in winter

Six major winter resorts are found in the Rockies – two in Kananaskis Country, two around Banff, and one each near Lake Louise and Jasper. Along with Whistler in British Columbia, these are some of the best, the most popular and the fastest-growing areas in Canada – and not only for downhill and cross-country skiing but also for dog-sledding, ice climbing, skating, snowshoeing, canyon crawling and ice fishing (snowmobiling, note, is not allowed in the parks). At most resorts, the season runs from mid-December until the end of May; conditions are usually at their best in March, when the days are getting warmer and longer, and the snow is deepest. Resort accommodation is hardest to come by during Christmas week, the mid-February school holidays and at Easter.

Nakiska, 25km south of the Trans-Canada Highway in Kananaskis Country, is Canada's newest resort. Developed for the 1988 Winter Olympics, it's one of the most user-friendly on the continent, with state-of-the-art facilities; it has snowmaking on all its varied terrain and plenty of fine cross-country skiing. Fortress Mountain, 15km south of Nakiska on Hwy 40, is a much smaller area, where you're likely to share the slopes with school groups and families.

Banff's resorts are invariably the busiest and most expensive, and heavily patronized by foreigners (especially Japanese). Mount Norquay (see p.624) has long been known as an advanced downhill area – "steep and deep" in local parlance – but has recently expanded its intermediate runs, and also boasts the Canadian Rockies' only night skiing. Higher and more exposed, Sunshine Village (see p.624) has even better scenery but relatively few advanced runs.

Lake Louise's three big hills (see p.635) add up to Canada's most extensive resort, with downhill skiing, plus cross-country trails crisscrossing the valley and the lake area. Jasper's Marmot Basin is a more modest downhill area, but it's quieter and cheaper than those further south, and the park, particularly around Maligne Lake, has almost limitless cross-country skiing possibilities.

Kananaskis Country

Most first-time visitors race straight up to Banff, ignoring the verdant foothill region southwest of Calgary. **Kananaskis Country**, a protected area created out of existing provincial parks to take pressure off Banff, remains almost the exclusive preserve of locals, most of whom come for skiing. Kananaskis embraces a huge tract of the Rockies and has all the mountain scenery and outdoor-pursuit possibilities of the parks, without the people or the commercialism. It is, however, an area without real focus, much of it remote wilderness; nothing in the way of public transport moves out here, and the only fixed accommodation is in expensive, modern lodges – though it's idyllic camping country.

Minor roads from Calgary lead to such smaller foothill areas of the east as Bragg Creek, but the most obvious approach is to take Hwy 40, a major turn off the Trans-Canada Highway, which bisects Kananaskis's high-mountain country from north to south and provides the ribbon to which most of the trails, campsites and scattered service centres cling. About 3km down the highway is the Barrier Lake Information Centre (daily 9am–5pm), where you can get a full breakdown on outdoor activities. Another 40km south of the centre is a short spur off Hwy 40 to Upper Kananaskis Lake, probably the biggest concentration of accessible boating, fishing, camping and hiking possibilities in the region. Popular short hikes include the Expedition Trail (2.4km); it and many others are detailed in the definitive *Kananaskis Country Trail Guide* by Gillean Daffern, which is widely available in Calgary.

The telephone code for Banff and Banff National Park is ☎403.

Banff National Park

BANFF NATIONAL PARK is the most famous of the Canadian Rockies' parks and Canada's leading tourist attraction – so be prepared for the crowds that throng its key centres, **Banff** and **Lake Louise**, as well as the best part of its 1500km of trails, most of which suffer a continual pounding during the summer months. That said, it's worth putting up with every commercial indignity to enjoy the sublime scenery – and if you're camping or are prepared to walk, the worst of the park's excesses are fairly easily left behind. The best plan of attack if you're coming from Calgary or the US is to make straight for Banff, a busy and commercial town where you can pause for a couple of days to soak up the action and handful of sights, or stock up on supplies and make for somewhere quieter as quickly as possible. Then head for nearby Lake Louise, a much smaller but almost equally busy centre with some unmissable landscapes plus good and readily accessible short trails and day-hikes if you just want a quick taste of the scenery. Two popular highways within the park offer magnificent vistas – the **Bow Valley Parkway** from Banff to Lake Louise – a far preferable route to the parallel **Hwy 1** (Trans-Canada) road – and the much longer **Icefields Parkway** from Lake Louise to Jasper. Both are lined with trails long and short, waterfalls, lakes, canyons, viewpoints, pull-offs and a seemingly unending procession of majestic mountain, river, glacier and forest scenery.

THE CREATION OF THE CANADIAN ROCKIES

About 600 million years ago the vast granite mountains of the Canadian Shield covered North America from Greenland to Guatemala (today the Shield's eroded remnants are restricted largely to northeast Canada). For the next 400 million years, eroded debris from the Shield – mud, sand and gravel – was washed westward by streams and rivers and deposited on the offshore "continental slope" (westward because the Shield had a very slight tilt). Heavier elements such as gravel accumulated close to the shore, lighter deposits like sand and mud were swept out to sea or left in lagoons. The enormous weight and pressure of the sediment, which built up to a depth of 20km, converted mud to shale, sand to sandstone and the natural debris of the reefs and sea bed – rich in lime-producing algae – into limestone. Two further stages were necessary before these deposits – now the strata so familar in the profile of the Rockies – could be lifted from the sea bed and left several thousand metres above sea level to produce the mountains we see today.

The mountain-building stage of the Rockies took just 100 million years, with the collision of the North American and Pacific continental plates (gigantic 50-kilometre-thick floating platforms of the earth's crust). About 200 million years ago, two separate strings of volcanic Pacific islands, each half the size of British Columbia, began to move eastward on the Pacific Plate towards the North American coast. When the first string arrived off the coast, the heavier Pacific Plate slid beneath the edge of the North American Plate and into the earth's molten interior. The lighter, more buoyant rock of the islands stayed "afloat", detaching itself from the plate before crashing into the continent with spectacular effect. The thick orderly deposits on the continental slope were crumpled and uplifted, their layers breaking up and riding over each other to produce the coast's present-day interior and Columbia Mountains. Over the next 75 million years the aftershock of the collision moved inland, bulldozing the ancient sedimentary layers still further to create the Rockies' Western Main Ranges (roughly the mountain edge of Yoho and Kootenay national parks), and then moving further east, where some 4km of uplift created the Eastern Main Ranges (the mountains roughly on a line with Lake Louise). Finally the detached islands "bonded" and mingled with the new mainland mountains (their "exotic" rocks can be found in geological tangles as far east as Salmon Arm in BC).

Behind the first string of islands the second archipelago had also now crashed into the continent, striking the debris of the earlier collision. The result was geological chaos, with more folding, rupturing and uplifting of the earlier ranges. About 60 million years ago, the aftershock from this encounter created the Rockies' easternmost Front Ranges (the distinct line of mountains that rears up so dramatically from the prairies), together with the foothills that spill around Kananaskis and Waterton lakes. The third stage of the Rockies' formation, erosion and glaciation, was relatively short-lived, at least three Ice Ages over the last 240,000 years turning the mountains into a region resembling present-day Antarctica. While only mountain summits peeked out from ice many kilometres thick, however, glaciers and the like were applying the final touches, carving sharp profiles and dumping further debris.

Some history

The modern road routes in the park provide transport links that have superseded the railway that first brought the park into being. The arrival of the **Canadian Pacific** at the end of the nineteenth century brought to an end some 10,000 years of exclusive aboriginal presence in the region, an epoch which previously had been disturbed only by trappers and the prodigious exploits of explorers like Mackenzie, Thompson and Fraser, who had sought to breach the Rockies with the help of native guides earlier in the century. Banff itself sprang to life in 1883 after three railway workers stumbled on the present town's Cave and Basin hot springs, its name coined in honour of Banffshire, Scottish birthplace of two of the Canadian Pacific's early financiers and directors. Within two years the government had set aside the Hot Springs Reserve as a protected area, and in 1887 enlarged it to form the **Rocky Mountains Park**, Canada's first national park. However, the purpose was not entirely philanthropic, for the new government-sponsored railway was in desperate need of passengers and profit, and spectacular scenery backed up by luxurious hotels was seen – rightly – as the best way to lure the punters. Cars were actually banned from the park until 1916.

Today the park is not quite at crisis point, but some hard decisions are having to be made. Around four million visitors come to Banff every year and another four million pass through. Together they pump a staggering $750 million or more a year into the local economy. Such figures, despite the best efforts and intentions of the park authorities, inevitably have an effect on the environment. Scientists believe, for example, that the black and grizzly bear populations are dying out (combined numbers of both types of bear here are probably just 100 to 130), while numbers of wolves are declining at only a slightly lower rate than in areas where they have no protection at all (the park has just 35 or 40). Conversely, elk numbers have exploded beyond internally sustainable limits (to about 3200), almost entirely because they've realized the town offers food (tasty surburban grass) and total safety from their natural predators. In the past, there have been some 60 (usually provoked) elk attacks on humans in Banff every year. The sight of elk nibbling on verges in downtown Banff will soon be a thing of the past, however, for around 120 elk have been removed from Banff and its vicinity and relocated elsewhere, and there are plans to remove the remainder. These are just a handful of symptoms of a greater ecological malaise. In response a ceiling of 10,000 has been put on Banff's human population (it's currently around 7600), building is strictly controlled, areas are being closed to the public (even the famous Bow Valley Parkway is closed to traffic for parts of the year). The airport, too, is now all but closed, for it – like much of Banff town and the Bow River Valley – lies right in the path of major wildlife routeways. Many of the big mammals require large areas to survive, larger even than the park's 6641 square kilometres. Experts suggest that Banff's ecosystem is on a knife edge: it may be saved and previous damage restored only if action is taken. Some already has – Banff's elk, for example, are being moved out to reserves – but there's much more work to be done.

Banff

BANFF is the unquestioned capital of the Canadian Rockies, and with its intense summer buzz it can be a fun, bustling and likeable base – but if you've come to commune with nature, you'll want to leave as soon as possible. Although the town is quite small, it handles an immense amount of tourist traffic, much of it of the RV and mega-coach-tour variety. Anything up to 50,000 visitors daily flock here in high season, making this the largest and busiest urban focus of any national park anywhere in the world. Backpackers are abundant in summer, and the Japanese presence is also marked, with a huge number of Japanese signs and menus in shops and restaurants. The Japanese also own around a third of the town's accommodation, including two of the three largest

PARK ENTRY FEES

For more than eighty years motorists and motorcyclists had to buy permits to enter Canada's mountain national parks. Since 1996 a different system has been in operation. Now fees and permits are based on a per-person per-day principle, and **everyone entering any of the Rockies national parks, regardless of mode of entry, must buy a permit**. The revised system is based on the premise that people – not vehicles – use parks, in much the same way as they enter art galleries or museums. Fees are ploughed directly back into the parks, unlike in the past where they were returned to a central revenue pool. The **cost** of a **Day Pass** valid for all four of the Rocky national parks (Banff, Jasper, Yoho and Kootenay) is $5 per day per person. Or you may buy a **Great Western Annual Pass** for $35, valid for unlimited entry to all eleven national parks in western Canada for a year. "Group" day-passes are available for anything between two and ten people at a flat rate: $10 daily, $70 annual. Thus four people in a car, for example, are charged just $10. If you come in by bus you'll not be charged at point of entry – it's up to you to be honest and buy a pass.

Passes can be bought in advance with credit cards by phoning ☎1-800/748-PARK or email *natlparks-ab@pch.gc.ca*. Passes are also sold at some Husky petrol stations or at the Mountain Equipment Co-op shops in Calgary and Vancouver. Permits can bought at the road entrances to all parks (compulsory for people in cars or on bikes), park information centres, some park campsites and (in summer) at automated pass machines within parks. If you buy a couple of day-passes and decide you want to stay on, then you can redeem their cost against a year's pass at park centres on presentation of receipts. Great Western Annual passes are valid for a year from the date of purchase. There's no fee to enter provincial parks.

A separate **backcountry Wilderness Pass** ($6 per person per night to a maximum of $30 per person per trip, vaild in all four national parks – Banff, Jasper, Yoho and Kootenay), available from any park visitor centre or infocentre, is required for all overnight backcountry use. Note that all backcountry areas in all parks have a quota and that it's vital to make bookings well in advance (up to three months) if you wish to walk – and camp on – some of the most popular trails requiring overnight stops. The most popular trails are indicated in the various hiking features throughout the text. Reservations can made by phone or in person at some of the more backcountry campsites, but *not* for the major park-run campsites. There is a $10 nonrefundable booking fee.

hotels, and their investment here is an ongoing bone of contention among some townspeople who would prefer local investment. What's rather odd, given all the people, however, is that there's next to nothing to do or see, save a couple of small museums, a cable-car ride and the chance to gawp at the crowds on **Banff Avenue**, the town's long main street, a thoroughfare lined with probably more souvenir stores and upmarket outdoor-clothing and -equipment shops than anywhere in North America. Whether or not your main aim is to avoid the crowds, however, some contact with the town is inevitable, as it contains essential shops and services almost impossible to come by elsewhere in the park. Many of the more rewarding walks locally are some way from the town – you'll need a car or have to hire a bike to explore properly – but some surprisingly good strolls start just minutes from the main street.

Arrival

Banff is just ninety-minutes' **drive** and 128km west of Calgary on a fast, four-laned stretch of the Trans-Canada. Speed limits outside the park are 110kph, inside 90kph, but watch your speed, as countless animals are killed on the road every year (one reason for the big roadside fences). Lake Louise is 58km away, Jasper 288km and Edmonton 424km. The approach from the west is more winding, the total journey time from Vancouver (952km) being about twelve hours. From the US the quickest access is from Spokane (600km away via Hwy 95) or Kalispell in Montana (Hwy 93).

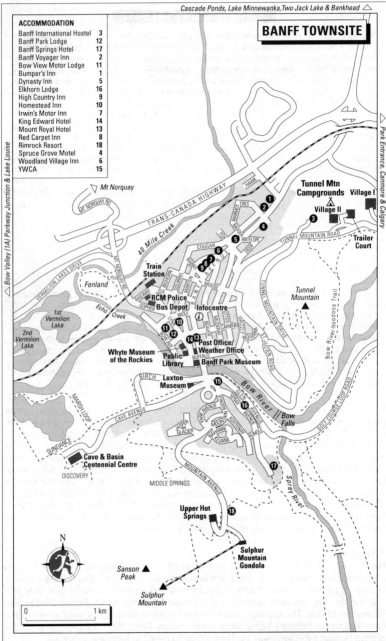

Cascade Ponds, Lake Minnewanka, Two Jack Lake & Bankhead △

BANFF TOWNSITE

ACCOMMODATION

Banff International Hostel	3
Banff Park Lodge	12
Banff Springs Hotel	17
Banff Voyager Inn	2
Bow View Motor Lodge	11
Bumper's Inn	1
Dynasty Inn	5
Elkhorn Lodge	16
High Country Inn	9
Homestead Inn	10
Irwin's Motor Inn	7
King Edward Hotel	14
Mount Royal Hotel	13
Red Carpet Inn	8
Rimrock Resort	18
Spruce Grove Motel	4
Woodland Village Inn	6
YWCA	15

△ Bow Valley (1A) Parkway Junction & Lake Louise

▷ Park Entrance, Canmore & Calgary

△ Mt Norquay

MT. NORQUAY RD

TRANS-CANADA HIGHWAY

40 Mile Creek

VERMILLION LAKES DRIVE

Echo Creek

Fenland

1st Vermilion Lake

2nd Vermilion Lake

MARSH LOOP

SUNDANCE

DISCOVERY

Tunnel Mtn Campgrounds

Village II

Village I

Trailer Court

HAWK

MARMOT CRES

BIGHORN

ANTELOPE

COUGAR

CARIBOU

DEER

TUNNEL MOUNTAIN ROAD

TUNNEL MOUNTAIN DRIVE

Tunnel Mountain

Bow River-hoodoos Trail

Train Station

RCM Police
Bus Depot

RAILWAY

GOPHER

BEAR

RABBIT

MARTEN

SQUIRREL

BANFF AVENUE

MUSKRAT

MOOSE

LYNX

Infocentre
i

WOLF

BEAVER

GRIZZLY

MARSIAL

CARIBOU

ST JULIEN ROAD

WOLVERINE

Whyte Museum
of the Rockies

Public
Library

Post Office/
Weather Office
Banff Park Museum

BIRCH

BUFFALO

Luxton
Museum

Bow River

Bow Falls

GOLF COURSE LOOP ROAD

CAVE AVENUE

Cave & Basin
Centennial Centre

MIDDLE SPRINGS

MOUNTAIN AVENUE

JASPER

GLACIER

PARK AVENUE

MOUNT

NAHANNI

KLUANE

SPRAY AVENUE

MT NORQUAY RD

MOUNT
RUNDLE

COTEAU

Spray River

Upper Hot
Springs

Sulphur
Mountain
Gondola

N

Sanson
Peak

Sulphur
Mountain

0 ——————— 1 km

Six daily Greyhound **buses** from Calgary (1hr 40min; $20 one-way), and five from Vancouver (via either Kamloops or Cranbrook, all via Lake Louise), arrive at the joint Greyhound–Brewster Transportation **bus terminal** at 100 Gopher St (7.30am–10.45pm, otherwise opens 5min before the departure of night buses; ☎762-6767). Increasingly, popular services are provided between Calgary airport and Banff–Lake Louise direct (and vice versa) by Laidlaw (1 daily year-round, 2 daily Dec–April; $30 to Banff, $38 to Lake Louise, $8 Banff to Lake Louise; ☎762-9102 or 1-800/661-4946; Calgary Ski Bus to Lake Louise ☎256-8473, *www.laidlawbanff.com*); the Banff Airporter 8 daily; $36 to Banff; ☎762-3330 or 1-888/449-2901, *www.banffairporter.com*); Brewster Transportation (3 daily to Banff and Lake Louise, 1 daily to Jasper in summer; $36 to Banff, $41 to Lake Louise, $71 to Jasper; ☎762-6767 in Banff, ☎221-8242 in Calgary, ☎780/852-3332 in Jasper). The most useful operator currently – because they have hourly departures between the airport and Banff or Lake Louise (and vice versa) – is Sky Shuttle ($34 to Banff; reservations daily 8am–11pm on ☎762-1010 or 1-888/220-7433, *www.banffskyshuttle.com*). Given the surfeit of operators, some of the services may well go out of business, so check at the airport – the various companies' ticket desks are lined up to the right as you face the main exit door in Arrivals. Note that Brewster run the only service between Calgary, Banff, Lake Louise and Jasper (daily May–Oct 1 or later depending on snow, $51 Banff to Jasper): it's heavily used. There's no VIA Rail passenger service – a private company runs luxury **trains** once a week between Calgary and Vancouver via Banff, but tickets for the two-night trip cost several hundred dollars.

Banff is small enough **to get around** on foot, but to reach the hostel and campsite (some 3km distant) you might need the small town **shuttle bus** operated by Banff Transit ($1 – exact change required; information ☎760-8294). It runs twice-hourly noon to midnight on two routes between mid-May and September, and on one route (the second of those detailed below) from mid-April to mid-May and October to December: the *Banff Springs Hotel*–Spray Avenue–YWCA–Banff Avenue–Trailer RV Parking at the north end of Banff Avenue (leaving the *Banff Springs Hotel* on the hour and half-hour, the RV Parking on the quarter hour) and *Village I* Campground–Tunnel Mountain Road–Otter Street–Banff Avenue–Luxton Museum (leaving *Village I* on the hour and half-hour and the Luxton Museum on the quarter hour). **Taxis** start at $2.60 and then charge around $1.35 a kilometre: from the bus terminal to the hostel or the *Banff Springs Hotel* should cost around $7. For details of taxi firms and **car rentals**, for which bookings should be made well in advance, see "Listings" on p.623.

The telephone code for Banff, Lake Louise and the Banff National Park is ☎403.

Information

Banff's showpiece **Banff Information Centre** is an excellent joint park/Banff and Lake Louise Tourism Bureau venture at 224 Banff Ave (daily: mid-May to mid-June 8am–6pm; mid-June to early Sept 8am–8pm; early Sept to end of Sept 8am–6pm; Oct to mid-May 9am–5pm; Parks Canada information ☎762-1550: town and accommodation information ☎762-8421, recorded message ☎762-4256; National Park information, also at *www.parkscanada.pch.gc.ca/banff*.

The centre has information on almost any park-related or town-related subject you care to name, including bear sightings, trails and the weather, and all manner of commercial tours and outdoor activities. It is also the place to pick up a **park permit** if you haven't already done so (see box on p.607). Among their many free handouts, make a point of asking for the *Banff and Vicinity Drives and Walks* and *The Icefields Parkway* for maps of park facilities, the *Backcountry Visitors' Guide* for an invaluable overview of **backpacking trails** and campsites, and *Trail Bicycling in the National Parks* for conditions and a full list of **mountain-bike trails**.

To the centre's rear there is a selection of maps and guides you can consult free: excellent **topographical maps** can be bought from the "Friends of Banff National Park" shop (☎762-8918) on the left, but note that many of the shorter and more popular trails are well worn and signed, so you won't really need detailed maps unless you're venturing into the backcountry. This is also the place to pick up details or book a place on the various **events** offered by the "Friends", which in past years have included free guided walks daily in the summer to Vermilion Lakes (10am, 2hr 30min), a Discovery Tour of the Cave and Basin Hot Springs (45min) and a Park Museum Wildlife Tour (45min); places on walks are limited, so preregister at the store in the information centre.

The Tourism Bureau will point you in the right direction when it comes to **accommodation** hunting; it maintains a constantly updated vacancies board (though staff aren't allowed to make specific recommendations) and a free courtesy phone. There are also several fee-based alternatives (see box above).

Accommodation

It's almost impossible to turn up after midday in Banff during July and August and find a relatively reasonably priced bed; preplanning is absolutely vital. Anything that can be booked has usually been snapped up – and Banff has over 3500 beds at its disposal nightly – and many visitors are forced to accept top-price places ($150 plus) or backtrack as far as Canmore or even Calgary to find space. The information centre or the **reservation services** (see box, above) may be able to dig something out at short notice.

The Bed & Breakfast and Private Home accommodation list at the infocentre lists forty-plus places with **private rooms** and **B&Bs**, but don't expect too much – they're usually cheapish by Banff standards (typically around $85–120) but among the first places to go each day. Note, too, that "breakfast" usually means continental – just toast, coffee and cereal. The majority are also nonsmoking.

Most of the town's **motels** are on the busy strip-cum-spur from the Trans-Canada into town, and charge uncommonly high rates for basic lodgings – typically around $140 and up for doubles. Bar one or two treats, the list opposite offers accommodation at around the $100 threshold. Off season (Oct–May), rates are usually considerably lower. Note that some of the best-value, least-known and most conveniently located double rooms are offered by the excellent *YWCA* (see under "Hostels", p.612).

Campsites are not quite as bad (the town offers over 1000 pitches), but even these generally fill up by 2pm or 3pm in summer – especially the excellent government campsites, which do not take reservations except for group bookings. In addition to the places listed opposite, remember that there are lovely and less-developed park-run sites available along both the Bow and Icefields parkways to the north. The *Banff International Youth Hostel* (see overleaf) can book you into most of the park's smaller hostels (see box, overleaf).

HOTELS AND MOTELS

Banff Park Lodge Resort, 222 Lynx St (☎762-4433 or 1-800/661-9266, *www.banffparklodge.com*). If you want comfort and stylish, upscale accommodation, but not at *Banff Springs* or *Rimrock Resort* prices, this hotel is the best downtown upmarket choice. ⑧.

Banff Springs Hotel, Spray Ave (☎762-2211 or 1-800/441-1414, *www.cphotels.ca*). One of North America's biggest and most famous hotels, but invariably full in summer, despite having 825 rooms and a current starting rate of $444 – packages can work out cheaper: book ahead and ensure you have a room with a mountain view in the old building. ⑧.

Banff Voyager Inn, 555 Banff Ave (☎762-3301 or 1-800/879-1991, fax 762-4131). Standard 88-unit motel with pool and sauna. ⑤.

Bow View Motor Lodge, 228 Bow Ave (☎762-2261 or 1-800/661-1565, *www.bowview.com*). Good views from some of the rooms. Two-room family units available. ⑥.

Bumper's Inn, Banff Ave and Marmot Crescent (☎762-3386 or 1-800/661-3518, fax 762-8842). Not central, but modern, and relatively well priced; with 37 units (some with kitchenettes), you'll have a reasonable chance of finding space. ⑥.

Dynasty Inn, 501 Banff Ave (☎762-8844 or 1-800/667-1464, fax 762-4418). A 99-unit motel with a range of rooms, some with fireplaces. ⑥.

Elkhorn Lodge, 124 Spray Ave (☎762-2299, fax 762-0646). Eight rooms, four with kitchens and fireplaces, at the southern end of the townsite. ⑤.

High Country Inn, 419 Banff Ave (☎762-2236 or 1-800/661-1244, *www.banffhighcountryinn.com*). Large seventy-unit mid-range motel with some luxury suites. ⑥.

Homestead Inn, 217 Lynx St (☎762-4471 or 1-800/661-1021, fax 762-8877). Mid-priced 27-room motel with standard fittings. ⑥.

Irwin's Motor Inn, 429 Banff Ave (☎762-4566 or 1-800/661-1721, *www.irwinsmotorinn.com*). A variety of rooms with some at the lower end of the price category. ⑥.

King Edward Hotel, 137 Banff Ave, corner of Caribou (☎762-2202 or 1-800/344-4232, *www.banffkingedwardhotel.com*). Twenty-one renovated and relatively well-priced rooms in the heart of town, but most look down on the busy Banff Ave. ⑤.

Mount Royal Hotel, 138 Banff Ave (☎762-3331 or 1-800/267-3035, *www.brewster.ca*). Has a perfect position on Banff Ave at the centre of town and 136 newly renovated, air-conditioned rooms. Most rooms have mountain views. ⑦.

Red Carpet Inn, 425 Banff Ave (☎762-4184 or 1-800/563-4609, fax 762-4894). No-frills 52-unit motel. ⑥.

Rimrock Resort, Mountain Ave (☎762-3356 or 1-800/661-1587, *www.rimrockresort.com*). Superlative, magnificently situated modern 351-room out-of-town hotel – probably the finest in the Rockies. It's high above the town, with great views of the mountains from the smart, modern rooms. ⑧.

Spruce Grove Motel, 545 Banff Ave (☎762-2112, fax 760-5043). The least expensive motel in town; it has 36 units, some with family and kitchenette facilities. ③.

Woodland Village Inn, 449 Banff Ave (☎762-5521, fax 762-0385). The 24 rooms include some with lofts for up to eight people. ⑥.

BED AND BREAKFASTS

Banff Squirrel's Nest, 332 Squirrel St (☎762-4432, fax 762-5167). Two pleasant and well-situated rooms with private bathrooms and sitting room for guests' use. ④.

Beaver Street Suites & Cabins, 222 Beaver St (☎762-5077, fax 762-5071). Five central self-catering cabins and apartments for up to four people. No credit cards. ⑤.

Blue Mountain Lodge, 137 Muskrat St (☎762-5134, fax 762-8086). Ten rooms and two cabins with private or shared bathrooms and a shared kitchen in very central c.1900 Banff landmark building. ④.

Cascade Court, 2 Cascade Court (☎762-2956, fax 762-5653). Two smart nonsmoking rooms across the river from downtown and minutes from the town centre. No credit cards. ④.

Country Cabin, 419 Beaver St (☎762-2789). Quiet cedar cabin (sleeps 3–4) with cooking facilities. Three blocks from downtown. ⑤.

Eleanor's House, 125 Kootenay Ave (☎760-2457, *www.bbeleanor.com*). One of the better but more expensive ($135) B&Bs in town: location-wise it's not perfect – across the river in a quiet side street. Both rooms (twin and double) are en suite and there's a library for idle browsing on rainy days. Open Feb to mid-Oct. ⑥.

A Good Night's Rest, 437 Marten St (☎762-2984). Three rooms in good location; access to fridge and microwaves and a choice of private or shared bathrooms. ⑤.

L'Auberge des Rocheurs, 402 Squirrel St (☎762-9269 or 1-800/266-4413, fax 762-9269). Three quiet central rooms with private bathrooms, nice views with French ownership and hospitality. ⑤.

Rocky Mountain B&B, 223 Otter St (☎ & fax 762-4811). Ten well-priced B&B rooms with kitchenettes and shared or private baths just three blocks from downtown; laundry service also available. ⑤.

Tan-y-Bryn, 118 Otter St (☎762-3696). Eight simple and extremely reasonable B&B rooms (and one cheap "emergency" room) with private or shared bathrooms and in-room continental breakfast. Quiet residential district three blocks from downtown. No credit cards. ②.

HOSTELS

Banff International Youth Hostel HI, Tunnel Mountain Rd (☎762-4122, *banff@hostellingintl.ca*). Modern 216-bed place in great setting, but a 3km slog from downtown – take the Banff Transit bus from Banff Ave. Friendly staff and excellent facilities, which include big kitchen, laundry, lounge area with fireplace and a bike and ski workshop; 24-hour access, no curfew. The infoboard is a good source of advice and ride offers. Good meals available all day in the self-service *Café Alpenglow* (open to the public). Two-, four- or six-bed dorms cost $20 for members, $24 for non-members ($1 dollar less in both cases mid-Oct to April). For family or couple (double) rooms, add $5 per person. Open all day. Reservations a month or more in advance are virtually essential in July and August. ①.

Banff YWCA, 102 Spray Ave (☎762-3560 or 1-800/813-4138, *lodge@ywcabanff.ab.ca*). Much more convenient than the youth hostel. Open to men and women, with plenty of clinically clean rooms, but they're extremely good value and go quickly, so book ahead (at least a week in Aug); 300 dorm bunks ($21 plus refundable $5 key deposit; $20 in winter) available, but bring your own sleeping bag, or rent blankets and pillows ($10 refundable deposit, $5 fee). Also forty private singles and doubles ($55, $83 with private bathroom), rooms with two double beds ($70, $55 with bathroom) and family rooms with three double beds ($95 with private bathroom). Rates drop considerably in winter – doubles are $39 or $45 with private bathroom. The downstairs café has good food and there's a kitchen, laundry and showers ($2.50 for nonresidents) open to all. Dorms ①, private doubles ③.

CAMPSITES

Bow Valley Parkway. There are three park campsites on or just off the Bow Valley Parkway road between Banff and Lake Louise, all within easy reach of Banff if you have transport (less than 30-minutes' drive): Johnston Canyon, Castle Mountain and Protection Mountain. See p.628 for full details.

Tunnel Mountain Village I, 4.3km from town and 1km beyond the hostel on Tunnel Mountain Rd. Huge 622-pitch government-run campsite ($17 plus optional $4 for firewood and fire permit), the nearest to downtown, on the Banff Transit bus from Banff Ave. Arrive early – like all frontcountry

---

HOSTEL RESERVATIONS

Hostel reservations by phone, fax, email and credit card can be made for the following Banff National Park and area hostels by calling ☎403/762-4122, fax 762-3441, *www.hostellingintl.ca/alberta* or writing to *Banff International Youth Hostel*, PO Box 1358, Banff, AB T0L 0C0: *Banff International, Castle Mountain, Hilda Creek, Mosquito Creek, Rampart Creek, Ribbon Creek* and *Whiskey Jack*. For reservations at Lake Louise *International*, contact the hostel directly.

park campsites, it's first-come, first-served. Electricity and hot showers. The nearby 322-site *Tunnel Mountain Trailer Court* ($24) is only for RVs. Early-May to late Sept.

Tunnel Mountain Village II, 2.4km from town and close to *Village I* site. In the summer, available for group camping and commercial tenting only. However, after *Tunnel I* shuts (in late Sept) this government-run 189-pitch site becomes available for general walk-in winter camping ($21 plus optional $4 fire permit). Electricity and hot showers. The two sites are set amid trees, with lovely views, plenty of space and short trails close at hand. Bighorn sheep, elk and even the odd bear may drop in. Year-round.

Two Jack Lakeside, 12km northeast of town on the Lake Minnewanka Rd. Fully serviced eighty-site park-run campsite ($17 plus optional $4 fire permit) with showers. Open mid-May to mid-Sept.

Two Jack Main, 13km northeast of town on Lake Minnewanka Rd. Semi-serviced 381-site park campsite ($13 plus optional $4 fire permit); no showers. Open mid-June to mid-Sept.

The museums

With some of the world's most spectacular mountains on your doorstep, sightseeing in Banff might seem an absurd undertaking, yet it's good to have some rainy-day options. The downtown **Banff Park Museum** at 93 Banff Ave on the right before the Bow River bridge bulges with two floors of stuffed animals, many of which are indigenous to the park (June–Sept daily 10am–6pm; Oct–May Mon–Fri 1–5pm, Sat & Sun 10am–6pm; $2.50 or $7 with the Banff Heritage Passport which also allows admission to the Whyte Museum and the Cave & Basin National Historic Site – see below; ☎762-1558). In many ways the museum chronicles the changes of attitudes to wildlife in the park over the years. Many Victorians wanted to see the park's animals without the tiresome business of having to venture into the backcountry: what better way to satisfy the whim than by killing and stuffing the beasts for permanent display? The hunting of game animals was eventually banned in the park in 1890, but not before populations of moose, elk, sheep, goats and grizzlies had been severely depleted. Game wardens only arrived to enforce the injunction in 1913, and even then they didn't protect the "bad" animals – wolves, coyotes, foxes, cougars, lynx, eagles, owls and hawks – which were hunted until the 1930s as part of the park's "predator-control program". Many of the stuffed victims in the museum date from this period. Sixty years ago a hapless polar bear was even displayed in the park behind the museum, one of sixty species of animals kept in the Banff Zoo and Aviary between 1904 and 1937. Until as recently as about twenty-five years ago, hotels were organizing trips to the town's rubbish dumps to view foraging bears.

Oddly enough, the museum – a fine building whatever your views on what's inside it – might have gone the same way as the animals. In the 1950s, changing attitudes saw the exhibits condemned as dated, and plans were mooted for the museum's demolition. In the event, it survived as a fine piece of frontier Edwardiana, distinguished, in particular, by its preponderance of skylights, essential features at a time when Banff was still without electricity. The lovely wood-panelled **reading room** – a snug retreat, full of magazines and books on nature and wildlife – makes a perfect spot to while away a cold afternoon. In summer, by contrast, the beautiful **riverside park** behind the museum is ideal for a snooze or picnic (people also sleep here unofficially at night – you might get away with a sleeping bag, but certainly not a tent).

Nearby, the excellent **Whyte Museum of the Canadian Rockies** (mid-May to mid-Oct daily 10am–6pm; mid-Oct to mid-May Tues–Sun 1–5pm, Thurs till 9pm; $4 or $7 with the *Banff Heritage Passport* which also allows admission to the Banff Park Museum and the Cave & Basin National Historic Site; ☎762-2291, *www.whyte.org*), next to the library at 111 Bear St, contents itself, among other things, with a look at the Rockies' emergence as a tourist destination through paintings and photographs, and at the early expeditions to explore and conquer the interior peaks. Pictures of bears foraging in Banff rubbish bins and of park rangers grinning over a magnificent lynx they've just shot give some idea of how times have changed. The museum, which opened in 1968, forms part of the Whyte Foundation, created in the 1950s by artists Peter and Catherine Whyte to collate and preserve as great a range of material as possible relating to the Rockies. The gleaming complex is also home to the 2075-volume Alpine Club of Canada library and the 4000-volume Archives of the Canadian Rockies – the largest collection of artistic and historical material relating to the mountains. The museum also hosts temporary exhibitions by local, national and international artists, as well as presenting lectures and walking, nature and gallery tours.

The **Natural History Museum**, upstairs in the Clock Tower Mall at 112 Banff Ave (daily noon–5pm; free; ☎762-4747), is a rather throwaway venture that concentrates on the Rockies' geological history, with a sketchy account of its forests, flowers and minerals.

Across the river, dated displays of native history, birds and animals fill the **Luxton Museum**, an aboriginal peoples-run enterprise attractively housed in a huge wooden stockade, 1 Birch Ave (mid-May to mid-Oct daily 9am–7pm; mid-Oct to mid-May Wed–Sun 1–5pm; $6; ☎762-2388). The museum takes its name from Norman Luxton, a local who ran a trading post here and forged a close relationship with Banff's Stoney native population over the course of sixty years. The exhibits aren't exciting, but the museum shop has some good craft and other items if you're in spending mode.

The Banff Springs Hotel

At around $900 a night for some suites – $1600-plus for the presidential ensemble and its personal glass-sided elevators – plus $20 for any pets, the **Banff Springs Hotel** may be way out of your league, but you can't spend much time in town without coming across at least one mention of the place, and it's hard to miss its landmark Gothic superstructure. Initiated in 1888, it got off to a bad start, when the architect arrived to find the place being built 180 degrees out of kilter: while the kitchens enjoyed magnificent views over the river the guestrooms looked blankly into thick forest. When it finally opened, with 250 rooms and a rotunda to improve the views, it was the world's largest hotel. The thinking behind the project was summed up by William Cornelius Van Horne, the larger-than-life vice-president of the Canadian Pacific Railway, who said of the Rockies, "if we can't export the scenery we'll import the tourists". One of the best ways to make the railway pay, he decided, was to sell people the idea of superb scenery and provide a series of jumbo hotels from which to enjoy it: the *Banff Springs* was the result, soon followed by similar railway-backed accommodation at Lake Louise and Yoho's Emerald Lake. Horne was also the man who, when he discovered the *Banff Springs* was being built back to front, pulled out a piece of paper and quickly sketched a veranda affair, which he decided would put things to rights: he was no architect, but such was his overbearing managerial style that his ad hoc creation was built anyway.

Today the 828-room luxury pile, largely rebuilt between 1911 and 1928, costs around $90,000 a day just to run, but boasts an extraordinary 100 percent occupancy – or over 1700 guests nightly – for half of the year. Busloads of Japanese visitors help make ends meet – the hotel's appearance in a famous Japanese soap having apparently boosted its already rampant popularity. The influx has prompted further rebuilding, including a spa centre being talked of as one of North America's best and a ballroom for 1600 people. The "Building of Banff" trips depart daily at 5pm from the main lobby and cost $5 if you are interested: call ☎762-2211 for further details. Unless you're a fan of kilted hotel staff or Victorian hotel architecture and its allied knick-knacks you can easily give the organized tours a miss. A voyeuristic hour or so can be spent looking around the hotel's three floors on your own (pick up a map in reception, it's almost a mini-village) or taking a coffee, beer or afternoon tea in the second-floor café and Sunroom off the main reception; prices for anything else in most of the sixteen various eating places are ludicrous. It's also worth walking out onto the terrace beyond the Sunroom for some truly spectacular views. You can get out here either by walking along the south bank of the

Bow River (taking in Bow Falls) or picking up the Banff Transit bus from downtown ($1). Walking up or down Spray Avenue is very dull.

The Gondolas

Banff is rightly proud of its two prize **gondolas** (known elsewhere as cable cars). High-price tickets buy you crowds, great views and commercialized summits, but also the chance to do some high-level hiking without the slog of an early-morning climb; they'll also give you a glimpse of the remote high country if you're short of time or unable to walk the trails. The best times to take a ride are early morning or evening, when wildlife sightings are more likely, and when the play of light gives an added dimension to the views.

Sulphur Mountain Gondola

The **Sulphur Mountain Gondola** on Mountain Avenue some 5km south of town trundles 700m skywards at a stomach-churning 51 degrees to immense 360-degree views from two observation terraces and an ugly but surprisingly good-value summit restaurant, Canada's highest (daily: mid-May to late June & mid-Aug to early Sept 8.30am–8pm; late June to mid-Aug 7am–9pm; early Sept to early Oct 8am–6.30pm; early Oct to mid-Dec 8am–4.30pm; $18; ☎762-2523 or 762-5438 for 24-hour recording of opening times, which change slightly from year to year). If you're without transport the only options for getting here are to walk (dull and tiring) or take a taxi from downtown. In summer Brewster Transportation (☎762-6700) run a short **tour shuttle** to the gondola from the town centre (mid-May to mid-Aug daily on the hour 9am–4pm and until 6pm mid-Aug to early Oct): the price ($25) includes the cost of the gondola ticket and return bus shuttle (leaves gondola terminal hourly on the half-hour).

It takes just eight minutes for the glass-enclosed four-passenger cars to reach the 2255-metre high point: eleven million people have come up here on the gondola over the years. From the restaurant a one-kilometre path, the **Summit Ridge Trail**, has been blazed to take you a bit higher, while the short **Vista Trail** leads to the restored weather station and viewpoint on Sanson Peak. Norman Bethune "NB" Sanson was a meteorological buff and first curator of the Banff Park Museum, who between 1903 and 1931 made around 1000 ascents of the mountain – that's before the gondola was built – to take his weather readings. Note that if, like him, you slog the 5.5km up from the car park (see box, pp.620–621) you can ride the gondola down for free. Far too much of the food from the summit restaurant, unfortunately, ends up being eaten by bighorn sheep which, protected within the parks and unafraid of humans, gather here for handouts. Don't encourage them – feeding wildlife is against park regulations and can land you with a stiff fine.

Sunshine Gondola

The newer **Sunshine Gondola**, 18km southwest of town, once whisked you 4km from the Sunshine car park in the Bourgeau Valley to the Sunshine Village Resort at 2215m and some staggering views. At no extra cost, the **Standish Chairlift** led on from the resort to the Continental Divide (2430m) and a post marking the BC–Alberta border, but at the time of writing both have been completely closed for the summer (hours in the past, should it reopen, were July & Aug Mon–Thurs 8.30am–7.30pm, Fri–Sun 8.30am–10.30pm; $12). At present White Mountain Adventures run a shuttle bus (with optional day and half-day guided walks) from Banff to the Sunshine car park in place of the gondola (departs 8.45am, returns 3pm & 5pm; $35 plus $10 for guided walk) and four shuttles from here upwards (9.30am, 10.30am, 11.30am and 1.30pm, returns 1pm, 2pm, 3pm, 4pm & 5pm; $18 including walk): numbers are limited so you should book a place on the bus (☎678-4099 or 1-800/408-005, *www.canadiannatureguides.com*). Two connecting gravel trails can be followed once you're up the mountain through **Sunshine Meadows**, a beautiful and unusually large tract of alpine grassland. The

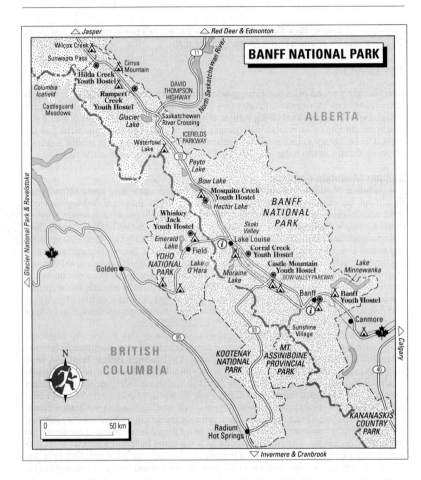

Rock Isle Trail loop starts at the Sunshine Meadows Nature Centre. After 1km, branch right to pass Rock Isle Lake on the left (take the left fork and you'd eventually come to Lake Assiniboine). Around 600m after the branch right you come to a fork: turn left and you loop around the Garden Path Trail (3.8km) past Larix Lake, the Simpson Viewpoint and Grizzly Lake back to the fork. From here it's 500m to a 1.2-kilometre detour to the right to Standish Viewpoint (a dead end). Otherwise head straight on and after 2.8km you come to a junction and the Monarch Viewpoint, where a 1.6-kilometre walk takes you back to the Nature Centre (11.5km total with all loops and detours). Ask for a sketch map of this area from the information centre.

Cave and Basin Hot Springs

Banff also boasts eight **hot springs**, and the next stop after the gondola ride on the standard itinerary is to plunge into the only one of these that's currently commercialized. Today's immersions are usually for pleasure, but in their early days these springs were vital to Banff's rise and popularity, their reputedly therapeutic effects being of great appeal to Canada's ailing Victorian gentry.

Dr R.G. Brett, chief medical officer to the Canadian Pacific Railway, used his position to secure an immensely lucrative virtual monopoly on the best springs. In 1886 he constructed the Grandview Villa, a money-spinning sanitorium promising miracle cures and wonders such as "ice cold temperance drinks". Its handrails were reinforced by crutches abandoned by "cured" patients, though the good doctor reputedly issued crutches to all comers whether they needed them or not.

There may be quieter places in western Canada to take the waters, but hot springs always make for a mildly diverting experience, and even if the crowds are a pain the prices are hardly going to cripple you. On the face of it, the springs at the recently renovated **Cave & Basin National Historic Site** (mid-June to Aug daily 10am–6pm; Sept to mid-June Mon–Thurs 11am–4pm, Fri–Sun 9.30am–5pm; $2.50 or $7 with the Banff Heritage Passport which also allows admission to the Banff Park Museum and Whyte Museum; guided tours free with admission summer daily 11am; ☎762-1566 or 762-1557), southwest of downtown at the end of Cave Avenue, are the best place to indulge. The original cave and spring here are what gave birth to the national park, discovered on November 8, 1883 by three railway navvies prospecting for gold on their day off. Having crossed the Bow River by raft they discovered a warm-watered stream, which they proceeded to follow to a small eddy of sulphurous and undergrowth-clogged water. Close by lay a small hole, the water's apparent source, which on further exploration turned out to be the entrance to an underground cave and warm mineral pool. The government quickly bought the three out, setting about promoting travel to the springs as a means of contributing to the cost of the railway's construction. A 25-square-kilometre reserve was established in 1885, from which the present park eventually evolved.

The first bathhouse was built in 1887, but over the years succumbed to the corrosive effects of chlorine and the pool's natural minerals. The pools finally closed in 1975, were restored (at a cost of $12 million), opened in 1985 and closed again in 1993 (again because of corrosion and falling numbers). Today the pools are still shut to bathers, leaving a popular **interpretive centre**(☎762-1566) to delve into their history and geology. You can walk here in a few minutes from town. From the foyer, where the faint whiff of sulphur is unmistakable, a short tunnel leads to the original cave, where the stench becomes all but overpowering. Smell aside, it's still a rather magical spot, with daylight shining in from a little hole in the roof and the limpid water inviting but tantalizingly out of bounds. Back down the tunnel and up the stairs brings you to a few rooms of interpretive displays, with a film show, some illuminating old photographs and several pertinent quotations, among which is the acid comment of an early travel writer, Douglas Sladen: "though it consists of but a single street", he grumbled about Banff in 1895, "it is horribly overcivilized", an observation not too far off the mark today. Down the stairs from the displays at the rear brings you to the "basin", a small outdoor hot spring that's separate from the cave-spring system, but no less inviting. Alongside is a wooden hut theatre with a half-hour film show.

Immediately outside the centre, the short Discovery Trail (15min) heads up the hill for a view over the site, together with the nearby start of the excellent **Sundance Canyon** surfaced path (see box, p.620). Just below the centre is the **Marsh Loop Trail** (2km; 25min), a treat for naturalists, and **bird-watching** enthusiasts in particular. The area's low-elevation wetlands teem with waterfowl during the winter and spring migrations, with the chance to see – among others – Barrow's goldeneye and all three species of teal: cinnamon, blue-winged and green-winged. The warm microclimate produced here by the springs' warm waters supports mallards over the winter, as well as attracting seasonal rarities such as killdeer, common snipe and rusty blackbird. During the summer you might see belted kingfisher, common yellowthroat, willow flycatcher and red-winged blackbird. Just across the river from here on Vermilion Lakes is the single most important area for bird-watching in the entire park, accessed via trails (see box, pp.620–621) and the Vermilion Lakes Road. Ospreys and bald eagles both nest here, and other highlights include tundra swan, hooded merganser and northern shoveler.

Upper Hot Springs

Unlike the Cave and Basin, there's no problem with swimming in the **Upper Hot Springs**, 4.5km from the town centre on Mountain Avenue, and easily visited after a trip on the Sulphur Mountain Gondola (mid-May to mid-Sept daily 9am–11pm; mid-Sept to mid-May Mon–Thurs & Sun 10am–10pm, Fri & Sat 10am–11pm; $7 mid-May to mid-Oct, $5.50 mid-Oct to mid-May; lockers, towel and swimming costumes – 1920 or 1990 style – rental extra; ☎762-1515 or 762-2500 for spa bookings). First developed in 1901, the springs were laid out in their present form in 1932 and completely renovated in 1996. At 38°C, the water in the outdoor pool provides a steamy temptation, but it receives a lot of traffic from people coming off the Sulphur Mountain Gondola. They also leave a fairly pungent sulphurous aftersmell. You can sign up for relaxing thera-peutic massages ($45) to complement your swim, while adults can make use of the Hot Springs Spa for aromatherapy wrap ($32), steam room, massage, plunge pool and steam and plunge (from $15). Call for details and appointments. If you don't want all this pampering there's a good poolside restaurant with outside terrace, fresh juice bar and hot and cold snacks.

Lake Minnewanka

Lake Minnewanka lies a few kilometres north of the town centre, and is easily accessed by bike or car from the Trans-Canada and the northern end of Banff Avenue on Lake Minnewanka Road. The largest area of water in the national park, its name means "Lake of the Water Spirit", and with the peaks of the Fairholme Range as back-drop it provides a suitably scenic antidote to the bustle of downtown. Various dams aug-mented the lake in 1912, 1922 and 1941 to provide Banff with hydroelectric power, though they've done little to spoil the views, most of which are best enjoyed from the various **boat trips** that depart regularly from the quay in summer (the lake's the only one in the park where public motorboats are allowed). Trips last an hour and a half and travel a fair distance up and down the lake (mid-May to Oct daily at 10.30am, 12.30am, 3pm and 5pm; July & Aug sunset cruise at 7pm; $26; Lake Minnewanka Boat Tours ☎762-3473, *www.minnewankaboattours.com*). Fishing trips can be arranged through the same company. Brewster Transportation offer an inclusive bus tour and cruise from Banff for around $41 (4–5 daily mid-May to early Oct). Confirm current sailing times and arrive a good thirty minutes before sailing to pick up tickets. If you have to kill time waiting for a place there are some easy walking trails along the lake's western side.

Eating and drinking

Banff's 100-plus **restaurants** – more per head of population than anywhere else in Canada – run the gamut from Japanese and other ethnic cuisines to nouvelle-frontier grub. If your funds are limited, the *Banff International Youth Hostel* and the *YWCA* cafe-terias, plus any number of fast-food and take-out options, are probably the best value, while Banff Avenue is lined with good little spots for coffee and snacks, many with pleasant outdoor tables. As for bars and nightlife, given Banff's huge number of sum-mer travellers and large seasonal workforce, there are plenty of people around in summer looking for night-time action.

To stock up if you're camping, use either the big Safeway **supermarket** at 318 Marten St and Elk (daily 9am–10pm), just off Banff Avenue a block down from Wolf Street, or the less frenetic Kellers (daily 7am–midnight), opposite the Whyte Museum at 122 Bear St on the corner of Lynx.

Aurora, 110 Banff Ave (☎762-3343). Very popular bar and nightclub (cheap drinks) attracting a young crowd in the Clock Tower Village Mall; dancing nightly until 2am and live music, usually Friday and Saturday evenings.

Baker Creek Bistro, *Baker Creek Chalets*, Bow Valley Parkway (☎522-2182). As a break from town it's definitely worth driving out here for a meal of innovative and well-cooked staples, like steaks and pastas, in a restaurant frequented by locals as well as tourists. The snug lounge bar is also nice for a drink, especially later in the year when the fire's lit. Moderate.

Balkan Village, 120 Banff Ave (☎762-3454). Greek outlet, known for big portions of reasonable food and belly dancing on Tuesday in the winter to whip things up; in summer the place turns raucous on its own, with frequent impromptu navel displays from well-oiled customers. Service can be a trifle surly. Moderate.

Barbary Coast, upstairs at 119 Banff Ave (☎762-4616). Excellent, if obvious, food – pizza, steaks, burgers and salads – at good prices: the restaurant is full of sporting memorabilia, and the separate popular bar at the front, open till 2am, also does food (with occasional live music).

Bistro, corner of Wolf and Bear next to the Lux Cinema (☎762-8900). A cheaper sister restaurant of *Le Beaujolais*, this is a pleasantly calm place a block or so off Banff Ave where you can enjoy first-rate food in intimate surroundings.

Bumper's, 603 Banff Ave (☎762-2622). A little out of the centre, but this excellent-value steakhouse – one of the town's busiest – still draws in Banff residents and visitors alike. There's a good lounge upstairs, a locals' favourite, for a drink before or after dinner.

Cilantro Mountain Café, *Buffalo Mountain Lodge*, Tunnel Mountain Rd (☎762-2400). A good café-restaurant, with the usual North American fare, that's ideal if you're staying at the hostel or camp-site and want a modest treat; has a nice outside terrace for the summer. Inexpensive.

Earl's, upstairs at the corner of Banff Ave and Wolf St (☎762-4414). You can rarely go wrong at restaurants in this mid-priced Canada-wide chain. Lively, friendly service, plenty of room and con-sistently good food that is extraordinarily eclectic – everything from Thai to Italian influences.

Evelyn's, 201 Banff Ave, corner of Caribou (☎762-0352). One of the best inexpensive places on the strip for breakfast; excellent range of coffees. A second, less busy outlet, *Evelyn's Too*, can be found next to the Lux Cinema at 229 Bear Ave.

Joe Btfspk's [sic] **Diner**, 221 Banff Ave (☎762-5529). Tries too hard to evoke a period feel – red vinyl chairs and black-and-white floors – but does good, if slightly overpriced, food; often busy at peak times.

Le Beaujolais, 212 Banff Ave at Buffalo St (☎762-2712). Known for almost twenty years as one of western Canada's better, smarter and more expensive restaurants. A choice of set-price menus between $40 and $66 help keep tabs on spending. Reservations recommended.

Melissa's, 218 Lynx St (☎762-5511). Probably Banff's most popular daytime destination, set in an old log cabin: big breakfasts, superb mignon steaks, salads and burgers, plus a good upstairs bar, *Mel's*, for a leisurely drink, and a summer patio for food and beer in the sun. Recommended, par-ticularly for lunch. Moderate.

Outa Bounds, 137 Banff Ave (☎762-8434). Though Banff's other major bar and nightclub – along with *Aurora* – is a rather soulless basement bar, with food, pool, dancing and occasional music, it still manages, somehow, to draw in the crowds.

Rose and Crown, upstairs at 202 Banff Ave (☎762-2121). Part of a chain, combining a moderately successful pub atmosphere (darts, mock-Victorian interior) with a family-oriented restaurant. Food is of the pub-lunch variety and later on you can shake a leg in the adjoining nightclub and disco – occasional live music.

St Jame's Gate, 205 Wolf St (☎762-9355). It was only a matter of time before Banff got an Irish pub; hugely popular with locals and visitors alike.

Wild Bill's Legendary Saloon, upstairs at 203 Banff Ave (☎762-0333). Serves good Tex-Mex and vegetarian food (family-oriented until 8pm); doubles as a lively bar with live bands (usually country) Wednesday to Sunday; pool hall and games room. Moderate.

Activities and entertainment

The information centre carries extensive lists and contact information for guides and outfitters for all manner of **outdoor activities**. Among the more passive entertainment are **billiards** upstairs at the *King Edward Hotel*, 137 Banff Ave (☎762-4629; $8 an hour),

WALKS AROUND BANFF

WALKS FROM DOWNTOWN

Banff Townsite is one of two obvious bases for walks in the park (the other is Lake Louise), and trails around the town cater to all levels of fitness. The best short stroll from downtown – at least for flora and fauna – is the **Fenland Trail**, a 1.5-kilometre loop west through the montane wetlands near the First Vermilion Lake (there are three Vermilion lakes, fragments of a huge lake that once probably covered the whole Bow Valley at this point; all can be accessed off Vermilion Lakes Drive). Marsh here is slowly turning to forest, creating habitats whose rushes and grasses provide a haven for wildlife, birds in particular. Ospreys and bald eagles nest around the lake, together with a wide range of other birds and waterfowl, and you may also see beaver, muskrat, perhaps even coyote, elk and other deer. You can walk this and other easy local trails in the company of the "Friends of Banff" – see under "Information" on p.609 for more details.

For a shorter walk, and a burst of spectacular white water, stroll the level and very easy Bow Falls Trail (1km) from beneath the bridge on the south side of the river, which follows the river bank east to a powerful set of waterfalls and rapids just below the *Banff Springs Hotel*. The Hoodoos Trail on the other side of the river (starting at the eastern end of Buffalo St) offers similar views with fewer people, linking eventually to Tunnel Mountain Road if you walk it all the way, which make this a good way to walk into town for the youth hostel and campsites.

The **Marsh Loop Trail** (2km) from Cave Avenue leads along a boardwalk through a marshy habitat renowned for its flora and birds (see p.617): warm waters from the Cave and Basin hot springs immediately above have created a small, anomalous area of lush vegetation. In winter Banff's own wolf pack has been known to hunt within sight of this trail. The **Sundance Canyon Trail** (3.7km), an easy and deservedly popular stroll along a paved path (also popular with cyclists, and rollerbladers – be warned) to the picnic area at the canyon mouth, also starts from close to the springs; you can extend your walk along the 2.1-kilometre loop path up through the canyon, past waterfalls, and back down a peaceful wooded trail. Finally, the most strenuous walk near town is to the summit of Tunnel Mountain. It's approached on a windy track (300m ascent) from the southwest from Tunnel Mountain Drive, culminating in great views over the townsite, Bow River and flanking mountains.

DAY-HIKES NEAR BANFF

Day-hikes from the town centre are limited – you need transport and usually have to head a few kilometres along the Trans-Canada to reach trailheads that leave the flat valley floor for the heart of the mountains. Only a couple of longish ones strike out directly from town: the **Spray River Circuit**, a flat, thirteen-kilometre round trip past the *Banff Springs Hotel* up the Spray River; and the Sulphur Mountain Trail, a 5.5-kilometre switch-

---

ten-pin **bowling** at the *Banff Springs Hotel* (☎762-6892; $3.75 a game, $1.10 shoe rental), and new-release **films** at the Lux Cinema, 229 Bear St (☎762-8595). You can work out or **swim** for a fee in the pools at the *Banff Rocky Mountain Resort* (☎762-5531) or swim at the Sally Borden Recreation Building at the Banff Centre (☎762-6461) and *Douglas Fir Resort* at the corner of Tunnel Mountain Drive and Otter Street (Mon–Fri 4–9.30pm plus 2–9.30pm in summer, Sat–Sun 10am–9.30pm; $7.50; ☎762-5591): the last is especially popular as it also boasts waterslides. Note that the only swimmable lake in the park is Johnson Lake northeast of town off Lake Minnewanka Road: the others are usually glacier-fed and thus immensely cold.

For general bus tours, contact Brewster Transportation (☎762-8400), who've been running trips for decades. For something just a little more demanding there's **golf** at the stunning Banff Springs Golf Course (☎762-6801; from $35 for nine holes, $125 for back that climbs 655m up to the Sulphur Mountain gondola terminal at 2255m (you're better off simply taking the gondola).

Park wardens at the infocentre seem unanimous in rating the **Cory Pass Trail** (5.8km; 915m ascent), combined with the Edith Pass Trail to make a return loop, as the best day-hike close to Banff. The trailhead is signed 6km west of the town off the Bow Valley Parkway, 500m after the junction with the Trans-Canada. The stiff climbing involved, and a couple of scree passages, mean that it's not for the inexperienced or faint-hearted. The rewards are fantastic, with varied walking, a high-mountain environment and spine-tingling views. From the pass itself at 2350m, you can return on the Edith Pass Trail (whose start you'll have passed 1km into the Cory Pass walk), to make a total loop of a demanding 13km.

Another popular local day-hike, the trail to **Cascade Amphitheatre** (2195m), starts at Mount Norquay Ski Area, 6km north of the Trans-Canada Mount Norquay Road. This offers a medley of landscapes, ranging from alpine meadows to deep, ice-scoured valleys and a close view of the knife-edge mountains that loom so tantalizingly above town. Allow about three hours for the 7.7-kilometre (610-metre ascent) walk. For the same amount of effort, you could tackle **Elk Lake** (2165m) from the ski area, though at 13.5km each way it's a long day's hike; some people turn it into an overnight hike by using the campsite 2.5km short of Elk Lake. Shorter, but harder on the lungs, is the third of Banff's popular local walks, **C Level Cirque** (1920m), reached by a four-kilometre trail from the Upper Bankhead Picnic Area on the Lake Minnewanka road east of Banff. Elsewhere, the Sunshine Meadows area has five high trails of between 8km and 20km, all possible as day-hikes and approached either from the Sunshine Gondola (if running) or its parking area, 18km southwest of Banff. There are also some good short trails off the Bow Valley Parkway, most notably the **Johnston Canyon** path (see box, p.627).

The best **backpacking** options lie in the Egypt Lake area west of Banff Townsite, with longer trails radiating from the lake's campsite. Once you're in the backcountry around Banff, however, the combination of trails is virtually limitless. The keenest hikers tend to march the routes that lead from Banff to Lake Louise – the Sawback Trail and Bow Valley Highline, or the tracks in the Upper Spray and Bryant Creek Valley south of the townsite.

If you're planning long walks and overnight trips in backcountry you must have a **Wilderness Pass** ($6 a night from park centres). You should also book backcountry campsites (contact Parks Canada at Lake Louise or Banff visitor centres; ☎762-1556) and walks well in advance ($10 nonrefundable booking fee), as **quotas** operate for all back-country areas – if the quotas fill, you won't be able to walk or camp or may have to make do with a second-choice hike. The most popular of the 50-odd campsites are Marvel Lake, Egypt Lake, Luellen Lake, Aylmer Pass, Mystic Meadow, Fish Lakes, Paradise Valley, Hidden Lake, Baker Lake, Merlin Meadows, Red Deer Lakes and Mount Rundle. Be sure to pick up or send for the Parks Canada *Backcountry Visitors' Guide* pamphlet for further details of the system and of recommended routes.

---

eighteen holes, club rental from $35 for steel, $50 for graphite). You'll need to book well in advance. Free shuttles run to the clubhouse from the *Banff Springs Hotel*. **Bird-watching** with Halfway to Heaven Birdwatching (☎673-2542) costs $30 for a half-day, $65 for a day, with snack or lunch included.

BIKING AND BLADING

Mountain biking is big in the park, with plenty of rental places around town (see "Listings" on p.623). One of the cheapest outlets is Bactrax Bike Rentals, 225 Bear St (daily 8am–8pm; ☎762-8177), where rentals work out at $6–12 an hour or $22–42 a day for mountain bikes, $8 an hour or $30 a day for road bikes: rates include helmet, lock and water bottle. The company also has easy bike tours from one to four hours ($15 per hour, including bike) on paved routes around Sundance Canyon and Vermilion Lakes.

More ambitious rides on the Icefields and Bow Valley parkways or around Moraine Lake can be arranged in Lake Louise at the *Chateau Lake Louise* hotel (see p.634) through Cycling the Rockies (☎522-2211; groups of six or more, $69 per person half-day, $109 full day).

If you're exploring on a bike under your own steam, pick up the *Trail Bicycling Guide* from the infocentre, which outlines some of the dedicated cycling trails: the best known are Sundance (3.7km one-way); Rundle Riverside (8km one-way); Cascade Trail (9km one-way); and the Spray River Loop (4.3km).

Bactrax is also one of four places in town who rent out **rollerblades** (the paved Sundance Canyon Trail near the Cave and Basin centre is a popular run); prices start at $3 an hour. The other outlets are Ski Stop branches at the *Banff Springs Hotel* (☎762-5333) and 203a Bear St (☎760-1650; $6 an hour) and Performance Sports, 220 Bear St (☎762-8222; $20 a day).

BOATING AND FISHING

Boat trips can be taken on Lake Minnewanka (see p.618), as can **fishing** trips, which can be arranged through Lake Minnewanka Boat Tours (☎762-3473). Monod Sports, 129 Banff Ave (☎762-4571), have all-day drift-boat fishing trips on the Bow River and Nakoda Lake for cutthroat and bull trout plus brown and brook trout (both are catch and release, meaning you have to put any caught fish back into the water) at $375 for two people and walk and wade trips ($110 per person): trips include guide, instruction, tackle, wader, drinks and food. Beginner fly-fishers can take an instructional tour with the company. Banff Fishing Unlimited (☎762-4936) have Bow River float trips and walk and wade trips (from $100 per person) and half-day fishing cruises on Lake Minnewanka ($80 per person in a group of six). Similar trips are also offered by Adventures Unlimited (☎762-4554). Tackle can be hired from Performance Ski and Sports, 208 Bear St (☎762-8222). Remember you need a national park licence to fish, available for $6 a week, $13 a year, from tackle shops, most of the above companies or the information centre.

If you want to **rent canoes** for paddling on the Vermilion Lakes or quiet stretches of the Bow River, contact Bow River Canoe Docks ($16 an hour, $40 a day; ☎762-3632); the dock is on the river at Wolf Street. Or learn to **kayak** on the Bow with Alpine Adventures (☎678-8357; six-hour course $99).

HORSE RIDING

Horse riding is easy to organize, with anything from one-hour treks to two-week back-country expeditions available. The leading in-town outfitters are Holiday on Horseback, 132 Banff Ave (☎762-4551). One-, two- and three-hour rides start at about $25, while a six-hour trip up the Spray River Valley costs about $115. You can also take overnight trips to the *Sundance Lodge* from around $300 including all meals. Martin Stables, off Cave Avenue across the river from downtown, have hour to full-day rides ($25–115) and rent horses by the hour from $25. The Corral (☎762-4551) at the *Banff Springs Hotel* lets them out for $29 and offers a three-hour ride from the hotel to Spray River, Sulphur Mountain and Mount Rundle ($64).

WHITE-WATER RAFTING

Best among adrenaline-rush activities is **white-water rafting** on the Kicking Horse River, located a few kilometres up the road in Yoho but accessed by some eight com-panies in Banff and Lake Louise, most of them providing all necessary gear and trans-portation. Other gentler "float" trip options with the same companies are available on the Kananaskis, Kootenay and Bow rivers.

Long-established Hydra River Guides, 209 Bear St (☎762-4554 or 1-800/644-8888, fax 760-3196, *www.raftbanff.com*), has two daily six- and seven-hour trips ($85) in paddle or oar rafts on the Kicking Horse. Wet n' Wild Adventures (☎344-6546 or 1-800/668-9119) has full ($78) and half-day ($55) trips in the Kicking Horse Canyon, a half-day trip ($55) in the wilder lower part of the canyon for more advanced rafters, two-day trips and raft and horse riding combination trips. Wild Water Adventures from Lake Louise (☎522-2211 or 1-888/647-6444) has a half-day trip in the canyon ($69) plus rafting in the canyon for those seeking a gentler look at the Kicking Horse ($59).

Rocky Mountain Raft Tours (☎762-3632) offers more sedate one- and three-hour rides (3 daily; $24) down the Bow River from the canoe docks at Bow Avenue and Wolf Street For half-day trips ($54) on the Kootenay River, contact Kootenay River Runner (☎762-5385 or 1-800/664-4399), which also has three-day ventures and is one of only three companies to offer trips on the wilder, lower section of the Kicking Horse canyon (day-trips at $79 on the Kicking Horse River or $105 in the lower canyon). For gentle float trips on the Bow or Kananaskis rivers, contact Canadian Rockies Rafting (☎678-6535 or 1-877/226-7625): $39 for the Bow, $45 for Kananaskis.

Listings

Ambulance ☎911 or 762-2000.

American Express 130 Banff Ave (☎762-3207).

Bike rental Bactrax, 225 Bear St (☎762-8177); Banff Adventures Unlimited, 211 Bear St (☎762-4554); Inns of Banff, 600 Banff Ave (☎762-4581); Mountain Magic, 224 Bear St (☎762-2591); Performance Ski and Sport, 2nd Floor, 208 Bear St (☎762-8222); Ski Stop outlets at 203a Bear St and *Banff Springs Hotel* (☎760-1650 or 762-5333).

Bookshop Banff Book & Art Den, Clock Tower Mall, 94 Banff Ave (daily: summer 10am–9pm; winter 10am–7pm; ☎762-3919) is excellent for general books and local guides.

Bus information Bus depot, 100 Gopher St (Brewster Transportation ☎762-6767 or 1-800/661-1152; Greyhound ☎762-1092 or 1-800/661-8747); Banff Airporter Banff–Calgary Airport services (☎762-3330 or 1-888/449-2901); Banff Transit town shuttle (☎762-8294); Laidlaw Chateau Lake Louise–Lake Louise–Banff–Calgary Airport (☎762-9102 or 1-800/661-4946); Sky Shuttle Lake Louise–Banff–Calgary Airport (☎762-1010 or 1-888/220-7433).

Camping equipment Tents, outdoor gear and ski equipment to rent from Performance Ski and Sport, 208 Bear St (☎762-8222).

Car rental Avis, Cascade Plaza, Wolf St (☎762-3222 or 1-800/879-2847); Banff Rent-a-Car, 230 Lynx St (☎762-3352), for low-priced used-car rentals; Budget, 208 Caribou St (☎762-4546 or 1-800/268-8900); Hertz, at the *Banff Springs Hotel* (☎762-2027 or 1-800/263-0600); National, corner of Caribou and Lynx (☎762-2688 or 1-800/387-4747); Sears (☎762-4575).

Dentist 210 Bear St (762-3144).

Doctors Dr Ian MacDonald, 216 Banff Ave (☎762-3155); Dr Elizabeth J. Hall-Findlay, 317 Banff Ave (☎762-2055).

Foreign exchange CTM Currency Exchange at 108 Banff Ave, Clock Tower Mall (☎762-4698 or 762-9353), 317 Banff Ave (Cascade Plaza) and the *Banff Springs Hotel*. Visa advances at CIBC, 98 Banff Ave (☎762-4417); MasterCard advances at Bank of Montréal, 107 Banff Ave.

Hospital Mineral Springs Hospital, 301 Lynx St (☎762-2222).

Internet access At the public library (see below).

Laundries Cascade Plaza Coin Laundry, Lower Level, Cascade Plaza, 317 Banff Ave (☎762-2245); also a laundry in Johnny O's Emporium, a small mall at 223 Bear St (Mon–Sat 8am–midnight, Sun 9am–midnight; last wash 10.30pm. If you're at the hostel or campsites, the nearest laundry is the Chalet Coin Laundry on Tunnel Mountain Rd (☎762-5447) at the *Douglas Fir Resort*.

Library 101 Bear St (Mon, Wed, Fri & Sat 11am–6pm, Tues & Thurs 11am–9pm, Sun 1–5pm; ☎762-2661).

Lost property ☎762-1218.

Parks Canada Administration ☎762-1500; campsite info ☎762-1550. Park wardens ☎762-1470. 24hr *emergency* number only ☎762-4506.

Pharmacy Cascade Plaza Drug, Lower Level, Cascade Plaza, 317 Banff Ave; Gourlay's, 229 Bear St (Wolf and Bear Mall); Harmony Drug, 111 Banff Ave.

WINTER IN BANFF

Banff National Park is as enticing in winter as it is the rest of the year. If you're a skier or snowboarder then it's a virtual paradise, for **skiing** here is some of the best and most varied in North America. Yet the park offers the full gamut of winter activities, embracing everything from skating, ice-fishing and toboggan trips to dog-sledding, snowshoeing and sleigh rides. Skiing or snowboarding, though, are the big draws, and of Alberta's six world-class resorts, three are in the park, one in Lake Louise (see p.628) and two close to Banff – **Mount Norquay** and **Sunshine Village**. On top of great snow and pristine runs, you get crisp air, monumental mountains, sky-high forests, and prices and space that make a mockery of Europe's crowded and exorbitant winter playgrounds. You're also pretty certain of snow, sensational views, comfortable hotels and plenty of nightlife. However, what the brochures don't tell you is that here – as in Lake Louise – it can be bitterly cold for virtually all of the skiing season.

MOUNT NORQUAY

Mount Norquay is the closest resort to Banff, just 6km and ten-minutes' drive from downtown. Skiing started on the mountain's steep eastern slopes in the 1920s. In 1948 it gained Canada's first-ever chair lift, immediately gaining a reputation as an experts-only resort – "steep and deep" in local parlance – thanks largely to horrors like the famous double-black diamond Lone Pine run. This reputation has only recently disappeared, the result of a complete revamp and the opening of a new network of lifts on and around Mystic Ridge to provide access to intermediate terrain and 25 runs suitable for all levels of skiers and boarders alike. An express quad chair was installed in 1990, together with two surface lifts, two double chairs and a quad chair.

As a result Norquay is now equally renowned for its uncrowded beginners' slopes as for its expert runs, the terrain breaking down as follows: Novice (11 percent); Intermediate (45 percent); Advanced (28 percent); and Expert (16 percent). The average snowfall is 300cm, and there's snow-making on ninety percent of the terrain. The season runs from early December to mid-April. The highest elevation is 2133m, giving a vertical drop of 497m to the resort's base elevation at 1636m. Amenities include a visitor centre, ski school, rental shop, day-care and – on Wednesdays – the promise of night skiing. Lift tickets are around $35 a day. Accommodation is in Banff, with a free shuttle bus making the tour of local hotels for the short trip to the hill. For more information on the resort write, call or fax Banff Mount Norquay, Box 219, Suite 7000, Banff, AB T0L 0C0 (☎762-4421, fax 762-8133, *www.banffnorquay.com*).

SUNSHINE VILLAGE

Sunshine Village is a stunning resort, situated way up in the mountains at 2160m, 18km southwest of Banff. If anything the scenery's better than at Norquay – you're higher – and you have the plus of the national park's only on-hill accommodation. There's also an incredible 10m of snow a year – so there's no need for snow-making machines – with superb soft, light powder that *Snow Country* magazine has repeatedly voted "The Best Snow in Canada". Skiing started here in 1929 when two locals got lost on Citadel Pass and came back with tales of fantastic open bowls and dream slopes just made for skiing. In 1938 the Canadian National Ski Championships were held here, and by 1942 a portable lift had been installed on site. The biggest change in the area's fortunes came in 1980, when a gondola (cable car) was built to carry skiers (and occasionally summer

Police ☎762-2226.

Post office 204 Buffalo St at the corner of Bear St (Mon–Fri 9am–5.30pm). Stamps and other basic postal services also at Cascade Plaza Drug, Lower Level, Cascade Plaza, 317 Banff Ave; Mailboxes Etc, 226 Bear St; and Goro Canyon Gifts, Banff Park Lodge.

Road conditions ☎762-1450.

walkers) the 6km from the Healy Creek parking area to the self-contained Sunshine Village resort.

Today some 62 uncrowded runs can be accessed on the gondola, three high-speed detachable quads, a triple chair, four double chairs, two T-bars and two beginner rope tows. There's less here for the advanced skier than at Norquay, but plenty for the beginner and competent intermediate. Terrain breaks downs as follows: Novice (20 percent); Intermediate (60 percent) and Expert (20 percent). The top elevation is an incredible 2730m at Lookout Mountain, with a drop to base level of 1070m: all but one or two runs ultimately converge on the village itself. The opening of Goat's Eye Mountain in 1997 has added an express quad and lots of expert-only terrain (with double black runs) but little intermediate skiing and no beginners' runs: it has arguably helped give Sunshine the edge on expert terrain over other resorts. Lift tickets are around $45 a day. Amenities include a day-lodge, day-care, outdoor hot pool, ski school, rental shop and overnight rooms in the Village at the 85-room *Sunshine Inn*, the Rockies' only on-slope accommodation (☎762-4581 or 1-800/661-1272 in Alberta, 1-800/661-1363 in the rest of North America; ⑥). Ski packages are available here for anything between one and seven nights (mid-Nov to late May) beginning at around $90 a night with two-days' skiing: basic overnight charges are between $115 and $170. If you're staying in Banff, shuttle buses run round the hotels and cost around $15 for the round trip. For more information on the resort, write, call or fax Sunshine Village, Box 1510, Banff, AB T0L 0C0 (☎762-6500, *www.skibanff.com*).

WINTER ACTIVITIES

Many of Banff's myriad walking trails are groomed for winter cross-country skiing, details of which can be obtained in the *Nordic Trails in Banff National Park* pamphlet available from the town's visitor centre. Favourite destinations include Sundance Canyon, Spray River, Johnson Lake (above Lake Minnewanka) and around Lake Minnewanka itself. You can hire specialist gear from several outlets around town (see "Listings" on p.623). At a more expensive level, Banff has no heli-skiing of its own, but is the base for the world's largest heli-ski operator, Hans Gmoser's CMH Heli-Skiing, PO Box 1660 (☎762-7100), who offers package tours to various BC destinations. Other operators include RK Heli-Ski (☎762-3771 or 1-800/661-6060), who'll take you out to the Panorama area of the Purcell Mountains in BC, and Mike Wiegele Helicopter Skiing, PO Box 249 (☎762-5548), will take you further afield in BC to the Monashee and Cariboo mountains.

If you want to **ice-skate**, check out the rinks at Banff High School (Banff Ave), on the Bow River (off Bow St) and the *Banff Springs Hotel*; skates can be hired from The Ski Shop, also located in the hotel (☎762-5333). **Snowshoe** or **ice walks** can be arranged through companies based in Canmore, south of Banff, such as Back and Beyond (☎678-6606) or Michele's (☎678-2067): beginners are welcome and pick-ups can be arranged in Banff. Thrill-seeking **dog-sledders** need to contact Howling Dog Tours (☎678-9588) or Snowy Owl Sled Dog Tours (☎678-4369), who for a rather steep fee (reckon on $100 an hour) will take you on a spin. For less adrenaline-filled **sleigh rides** on the frozen Bow River, contact Holiday on Horseback (☎762-4551) for rides to the end of Lake Louise, Brewster Lake Louise sleighrides (☎762-5454) or *Chateau Lake Louise* (☎522-3511 ext 1139). Hotels often provide sledges for **toboggan** runs, of which there are several unofficial examples around town. **Ice-fishing** can be arranged through Banff Fishing Unlimited (☎762-4936, fax 678-8895).

Taxis Alpine (☎762-3727); Banff Limousine (☎762-5466); Banff Taxi (☎762-4444); Legion (☎762-3353); Mountain (☎762-3351); Taxi-Taxi (☎762-3111).

Tourist information ☎762-1550 for park information or 762-8421 for town and accommodation.

Trail conditions ☎762-1550 or 760-1305.

Weather ☎762-4707 or 762-2088 (24hr recording).

Highway 1 and the Bow Valley Parkway

Two roads run parallel through the Bow Valley from Banff to Lake Louise (58km): the faster **Hwy 1** (the Trans-Canada); and the quieter **Bow Valley Parkway**, on the other (north) side of the river, opened in 1989 as a special scenic route. After Banff, there's only one link between the two roads, at Castle Junction, 30km from Lake Louise. Both routes are staggeringly beautiful, as the mountains start to creep closer to the road. For the entire run, the mighty **Bow River**, broad and emerald green, crashes through rocks and forest. Despite the tarmac and heavy summer traffic, the surroundings are pristine and suggest the immensity of the wilderness to come. Sightings of elk and deer are common, particularly around dawn and sundown, and occasionally you'll spot moose. Both roads offer some good **trails**: if you want to tackle one of the most highly rated day-walks in Banff National Park, make for the Bourgeau Lake Trail off Hwy 1 (see box, opposite); for a shorter walk, make for the Johnston Canyon on the Parkway. Note, however, that between 6pm and 9am daily from March 1 to June 25, the 17km of the Bow Valley Parkway between Johnston Canyon and the east entrance off the Trans-Canada (that is, the entrance closest to Banff), is closed to allow the grazing of animals forced by late snow to lower altitudes for food. Access at this time to Johnston Canyon trails and campsite is from Hwy 1.

Highway 1

Most people tend either to cruise Hwy 1's rapid stretch of the Trans-Canada without stopping – knowing that the road north of Lake Louise is more spectacular still – or leap out at every trail and rest stop, overcome with the grandeur of it all. On Greyhound or Brewster **buses** you're whisked through to Lake Louise in about forty minutes; if you're driving, try for the sake of wildlife to stick to the 90kph speed limit. The vast fences that march for kilometre after kilometre along this section of the road are designed to protect animals, not only from traffic but from the brainless visitors who clamber out of their cars to get close to the bears occasionally glimpsed on the road. You won't have to be in the Rockies long during the summer before you're caught in a **bear jam**, when people – contrary to all park laws, never mind common sense – abandon their cars helter-skelter on the road to pursue hapless animals with cameras and camcorders.

The Bow Valley Parkway

If anything, the **Bow Valley Parkway** boasts more scenic grandeur than the Trans-Canada – which is saying something – and offers more distractions if you're taking your time: several trails, campsites, plus plenty of accommodation choices and one excellent eating option. The largest concentration of sightseers is likely to be found at the Merrent turn-off, enjoying fantastic views of the Bow Valley and the railway winding through the mountains.

If you have the time, therefore, the Parkway is the preferable route, and you should budget some time to walk one of the **trails** en route, in particular the easy but impressive **Johnston Canyon Trail** (see box, opposite). En route, some of the various viewpoints and signed pull-offs deserve more attention than others. Around 8km down the highway, look out for the **Backswamp Viewpoint**, where views one-way extend to the mountains and the other across a river swamp area where you might see beaver, muskrat, ospreys and other birds (see opposite), as well as the common butterwort, a purple-flowered carnivorous plant whose diet consists largely of marsh insects. In winter Backswamp Viewpoint is also known locally as one of the most likely areas to spot wolves; at other times of the year you might also see bighorn sheep or mountain goats on the mountain slopes above. Three kilometres further on you come to **Muleshoe Picnic Area**, also noted for its birds and wildfowl (see opposite). Some of the area around shows signs of having been burnt in forest fires, though these areas were deliberately torched by the park authorities to encourage fresh undergrowth and the return of wildlife excluded from more mature forests (for more on this see the "Vermilion Pass" on p.681). Eleven kilometres on, a 400-metre trail takes you to a lovely little lake once known as Lizard Lake after the long-toed salamanders that thrived here. These were eaten when the lake was stocked with trout, and the name's now been changed to Pilot Lake. Three kilometres beyond is the trailhead for the **Johnston Canyon Trail** (see box, below), deservedly the most popular in the area, and three kilometres beyond that **Moose Meadows**, where – name notwithstanding – you'll be mighty lucky to see any moose: habitat changes have forced them out.

If you're a **bird-watcher**, the Parkway is also the route for you. Johnston Canyon is one of only two known breeding sites in Alberta of the black swift – you may see the birds flitting back to their nests at dusk – and is also a breeding place for American dippers, buxom grey birds that have the ability to walk along stream beds underwater and habitually nest below waterfalls. Elsewhere on the Parkway the various pull-offs give you the opportunity to spot species associated with montane forest and meadow zones, notably at the Muleshoe Picnic Area, 21km southeast of Castle Junction, where you might spot western tanagers, pileated woodpeckers and orange-crowned warblers. At various points on the Bow River along the entire run from Banff to Lake Louise you may spot harlequin ducks on the river's islands and gravel bars, as well as spotted sandpipers and common mergansers.

If you want to stay, the road's **accommodation** possibilities make a more rural alternative to Banff and Lake Louise, and are close enough to both to serve as a base if you have transport; as ever, you should book rooms well in advance. Four **lodges** are spaced more or less equally en route and, though expensive, they *may* have room when Lake Louise's hotels are stretched. First is the *Johnston Canyon Resort*, 26km west of Banff and close to the trail that leads to the canyon (☎762-2971, *www.johnstoncanyon.com*; ⑤;

BOW VALLEY TRAILS

Five major trails branch off the Bow Valley Parkway. The best short walk by a long way is the **Johnston Canyon Trail** (2.7km each way), 25km from Banff, an incredibly engineered path to a series of spray-veiled waterfalls. The Lower Falls are 1.1km, the Upper Falls 2.7km from the trailhead on the Parkway. From the upper falls you can continue on to the seven cold-water springs of the Ink Pots, which emerge in pretty open meadows, to make a total distance of 5.8km (215m ascent). Another short possibility is the **Castle Crags Trail** (3.7km each way; 520m ascent) from the signed turn-off 5km west of Castle Junction. Short but steep, and above the tree-line, this walk offers superb views across the Bow Valley and the mountains beyond. Allow ninety minutes one-way to take account of the stiff climb.

The best day-hike is to **Rockbound Lake** (8.4km each way), a steepish climb to 2210m with wild lakeland scenery at the end; allow at least two and a half hours one-way, due to the 760m ascent. Another fifteen-minutes' walk beyond Rockbound and Tower lakes at the end of the trail lies the beautiful Silverton waterfall. The other Parkway trails – **Baker Creek** (20.3km) and **Pulsatilla Pass** (17.1km) – serve to link backpackers with the dense network of paths in the Slate Range northeast of Lake Louise.

The two outstanding trails along Hwy 1 are the trek to **Bourgeau Lake** (7.5km one-way), considered by many among the top five day-hikes in Banff: it starts from a parking area 10km west of Banff – allow two and a half to three hours for the 725-metre ascent – and the long day-hike to **Shadow Lake** (14.3km each way), where the lakeside campsite (at 1840m), in one of the Rockies' more impressive subalpine basins, gives access to assorted onward trails. The main trail starts from the **Redearth Creek** parking area 20km west of Banff (440m ascent; allow 4hr).

mid-May to late Sept), which consists of rustic cabins (some with fireplaces and some with kitchenettes), a shop, garage, tennis court and basic groceries. Next come the chalets, laundry and grocery store of *Castle Mountain Chalets*, 32km west of Banff near Castle Junction (☎762-3868, *www.castlemountain.com*; ⑦; year-round): the log chalets for four with kitchenettes and fireplaces are more expensive, but the best options of all here are the delightful and newly built deluxe cabins for four, five or six people (complete with full kitchens, dishwashers and jacuzzis). Some 5km south of Hwy 1 on Hwy 93 to Radium (27km from Banff) is *Storm Mountain Lodge* (☎762-4155; ⑥; end of May to late Sept) with highly appealing log cabins. Finally there's *Baker Creek Guest Lodge & Bistro*, 12km east of Lake Louise (☎522-3761, *www.bakercreek.com*; ⑤; year-round), with 25 one- and two-room log cabins and lodge rooms for between one and six people: there's also an excellent **restaurant** here that comes with local recommendations and new annexe with eight smart motel-type rooms. By far the least expensive possibility is the Parkway's charming **youth hostel**, *Castle Mountain Hostel*, 1.5km east of Castle Junction (☎762-2367 or 762-4122, *banff@hostellingintl.ca*; members $13, nonmembers $17; ①; year-round but closed Wed). You should call in advance, or better still book ahead through the hostel at Banff (☎762-4122).

Three national park **campsites** provide excellent camping retreats. In order of distance from Banff these are: the very popular 140-pitch *Johnston Canyon* ($17; mid-May to mid-Sept), 25km from Banff is the best equipped, and has full facilities including showers and wheelchair access; after that comes the 40-pitch *Castle Mountain*, 32km from Banff near Castle Junction ($13; late June to early Sept) and with no facilities beyond water and flush toilets; and then the similarly simple 89-pitch *Protection Mountain*, 5km north of Castle Junction (same details). An additional $4 fee is payable at all three if you wish to use firewood.

Lake Louise

The Banff park's other main centre, **Lake Louise**, is very different to Banff – less a town than two distinct artificial resorts. The first is a small mall of shops and hotels just off the Trans-Canada known as **Lake Louise Village**. The second is the lake itself, the self-proclaimed "gem of the Rockies" and – despite its crowds and monster hotel – a sight you have to see. A third area, **Moraine Lake**, 13km south of the village, has almost equally staggering scenery and several magnificent and easily accessed trails. Lake Louise is 4.5km from the village (and 200m higher) on the winding Lake Louise Drive – or, if you're walking, 2.7km on the uphill Louise Creek Trail, 4.5km via the Tramline Trail. You're better off saving the walking for around the lake, however, and taking a taxi (☎522-2020; around $10) from the village (if anything, save the two linking trails for coming down from the lake). All three areas are desperately busy in summer as well as in winter, when people pile in for some of Canada's best powder **skiing** (see box, p.635).

You may find staying near the lakes appealing but very pricey, though if you do want to splash out, the lodge at Moraine Lake makes a dream treat. Nonetheless, the mountains around offer almost unparalleled **hiking country** and the park's most popular day-use area. You'll have to weigh awesome scenery against the sheer numbers, for these are some of the most heavily used trails on the continent – 50,000-plus people in summer – though longer backpacking routes lead quickly away to the quieter spots. If you do intend to hike – and the trails are all a little more accessible and manageable than at Banff – then in an ideal world you'd have two or three days here: one to walk the loop around above Lake Louise (Lake Agnes–Big Beehive–Plain of the Six Glaciers–Lake Louise Shoreline) or the more demanding Saddleback (at a push you could do both in a day if you were fit and keen). Then you'd bike, taxi or drive to Moraine Lake (if you're not staying there), where in a day you could easily walk to

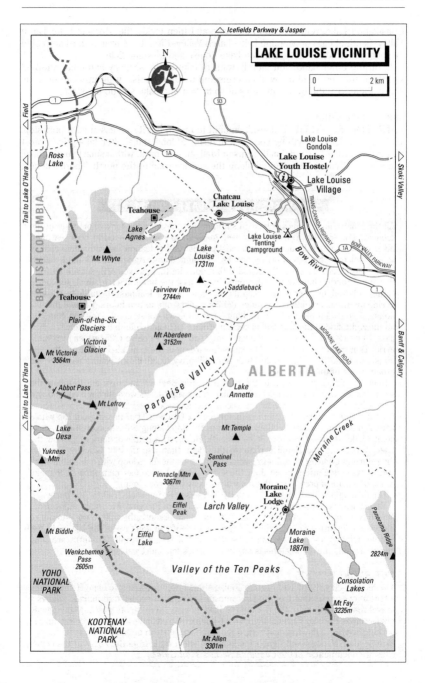

LAKE LOUISE VICINITY

0   2 km

△ Icefields Parkway & Jasper

N

△ Field

△ Trail to Lake O'Hara

BRITISH COLUMBIA

Ross Lake

Teahouse

Lake Agnes

Mt Whyte

Chateau Lake Louise

Lake Louise Gondola

Lake Louise Youth Hostel

Lake Louise Village

△ Shoki Valley

Lake Louise 'Tenting' Campground

Bow River

Lake Louise 1731m

Fairview Mtn 2744m

Saddleback

TRANS-CANADA HIGHWAY

BOW VALLEY PARKWAY

Teahouse

Plain-of-the-Six Glaciers

Victoria Glacier

Mt Aberdeen 3152m

ALBERTA

Mt Victoria 3564m

Abbot Pass

Mt Lefroy

Paradise Valley

Lake Annette

△ Banff & Calgary

MORAINE LAKE ROAD

△ Trail to Lake O'Hara

Lake Oesa

Yukness Mtn

Mt Temple

Moraine Creek

Sentinel Pass

Pinnacle Mtn 3067m

Eiffel Peak

Larch Valley

Moraine Lake Lodge

Mt Biddle

Eiffel Lake

Wenkchemna Pass 2605m

Moraine Lake 1887m

Panorama Ridge

2824m

YOHO NATIONAL PARK

Valley of the Ten Peaks

Consolation Lakes

KOOTENAY NATIONAL PARK

Mt Fay 3235m

Mt Allen 3301m

Consolation Lake, return to Moraine Lake and then tackle the Moraine Lake–Larch Valley–Sentinel Pass or Moraine Lake–Larch Valley–Eiffel Lake trail. A third day could be spent in Paradise Valley between Lake Louise and Moraine Lake.

If, on the other hand, you merely want to take in the scenery and enjoy **modest strolls** in the course of a day, then cruise up to Lake Louise, walk up and down the shore, then drive the twenty minutes or so to Moraine Lake and do the same.

Lake Louise Village

LAKE LOUISE VILLAGE doesn't amount to much, but it's an essential supply stop, with more or less everything you need in terms of food and shelter (at a price). Most of it centres round a single mall, Samson Mall, and car park, with a smart youth hostel and a few outlying motels dotted along the service road to the north. There's almost

---

HIKES AROUND LAKE LOUISE

All the Lake Louise trails are busy in summer, but they're good for a short taste of the scenery. They're also well worn and well marked, so you don't need to be a seasoned hiker or skilled map-reader. The two most popular end at teahouses – mountain chalets selling welcome, but rather pricey, snacks. The signed Lake Agnes Trail (3.4km), said to be the most-walked path in the Rockies (but don't let that put you off), strikes off from the right (north) shore of the lake immediately past the hotel. It's a gradual, 400-metre climb, relieved by ever more magnificent views and a teahouse beautifully situated beside mountain-cradled Lake Agnes (2135m); allow one to two hours. Beyond the teahouse, if you want more of a walk things quieten down considerably. You can continue on the right side of the lake and curve left around its head to climb to an easily reached pass. Here a 200-metre stroll to the left brings you to Big Beehive (2255m), an incredible eyrie, 1km from the teahouse. Almost as rewarding is the trail, also 1km from the teahouse, to Little Beehive, a mite lower, but still privy to full-blown panoramas over the broad sweep of the Bow Valley.

Keener walkers can return to the pass from Big Beehive and turn left to follow the steep trail down to intersect another trail; turning right leads west through rugged and increasingly barren scenery to the second teahouse at the Plain of the Six Glaciers (2100m). Alternatively, the more monotonous Six Glaciers Trail (leaving out the whole Lake Agnes–Big Beehive section) leads from the hotel along the lakeshore to the same point (5.3km to the teahouse; 365m ascent). However, a better option is to follow the Lake Agnes and Big Beehive route to the Plain, then use the Six Glaciers Trail for the return to *Chateau Lake Louise*, which neatly ends the day's loop with a downhill stroll and an easy but glorious finale along the shore of Lake Louise (see map opposite to make sense of what is a pretty straightforward and very well-worn loop).

The main appeal of the last local walk, the less-used Saddleback Trail (3.7km one-way), is that it provides access to the superlative viewpoint of Fairview Mountain. Allow from one to two hours to Saddleback itself (2330m; 595m ascent); the trail to the summit of Fairview (2745m) strikes off right from here. Even if you don't make the last push, the Saddleback views – across to the 1200-metre wall of Mount Temple (3544m) – are staggering. Despite the people, this is one of the park's top short walks.

THE SKOKI VALLEY

The Skoki Valley region east of Lake Louise offers fewer day-hikes; to enjoy it you'll need a tent to overnight at any of the six campsites. The main access trail initially follows a gravel road forking off to the right of the Lake Louise Ski Area, off Hwy 1. Many people hike as far as Boulder Pass (2345m), an 8.6-kilometre trek and 640-metre ascent from the parking area, as a day-trip, and return the same way instead of pushing on to the *Lodge*, 8km beyond. Various well-signposted long and short trails from the *Lodge* or the campsites are documented in the *Canadian Rockies Trail Guide*.

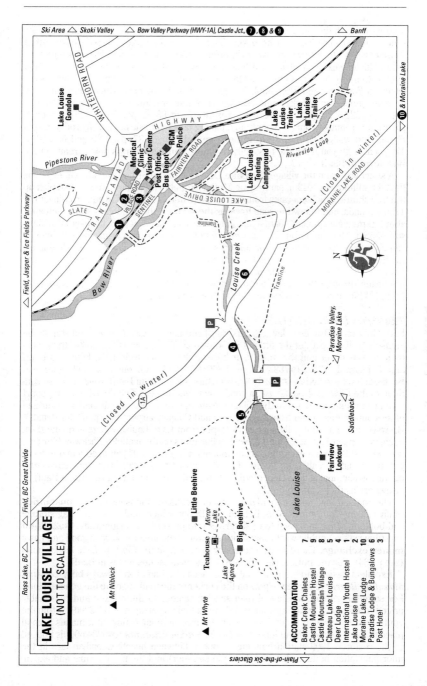

Ski Area △ Skoki Valley △ Bow Valley Parkway (HWY-1A), Castle Jct., **7** **8** & **9** △ Banff

Lake Louise Gondola

WHITEHORN ROAD

HIGHWAY

Pipestone River

Medical Clinic
Visitor Centre
Post Office
Bus Depot
RCM Police

FAIRVIEW ROAD

Lake Louise Trailer
Lake Louise Trailer

Riverside Loop

10 & Moraine Lake

SLATE

VILLAGE ROAD

SENTINEL

2
3
1

TRANS-CANADA

LAKE LOUISE DRIVE

Lake Louise Tenting Campground

MORAINE LAKE ROAD (Closed in winter)

△ Field, Jasper & Ice Fields Parkway

Bow River

Tramline

Louise Creek

6

Tramline

Paradise Valley, Moraine Lake

N

△ Field, BC Great Divide

P

4

P

9

Saddleback

△ Ross Lake, BC

(Closed in winter)

1A

5

Lake Louise

Fairview Lookout

LAKE LOUISE VILLAGE
(NOT TO SCALE)

▲ Mt Niblock

Little Beehive

Mirror Lake

▲ Mt Whyte

Teahouse

Big Beehive

Lake Agnes

△ Plain-of-the-Six Glaciers

ACCOMMODATION
Baker Creek Chalets   7
Castle Mountain Hostel   9
Castle Mountain Village   8
Chateau Lake Louise   5
Deer Lodge   4
International Youth Hostel   1
Lake Louise Inn   2
Moraine Lake Lodge   10
Paradise Lodge & Bungalows   6
Post Hotel   3

nothing to do in the village, and unless you have a vehicle to take you to the lakes (or rent a bike) you're likely to be bored. The impressive **Lake Louise Information Centre**, a few steps from the car park, offers not only information but also high-tech natural-history exhibits (daily: mid-June to early Sept 8am–8pm; early Sept to late Sept & early to mid-June 8am–6pm; Oct–May 9am–4pm; ☎522-3833). Almost as useful is the excellent Woodruff and Blum bookshop (☎522-3842) in the mall, which has a full range of maps, guides and background reading. A couple of doors down, Wilson Mountain Sports (☎522-3636) is good for **bike rental** (from $8–12 per hour, $29–45 a day), rollerblade rentals (from $5–8 per hour), fishing tackle for sale or rent (fly rod $11, spin rod $7 and waders $10) and **equipment rental** (stoves $7, pack $9 and tent $19). They'll also fill you in on the possiblity of **canoe rentals** for trips downstream on the Bow River to Banff.

A short way from the village, the **Lake Louise Gondola** (the "Friendly Giant") runs thirteen minutes to 2042m, partway up Mount Whitehorn (2669m). To reach it, pick up the free shuttle which operates from some village hotels or return to and cross over the Trans-Canada, and follow the road towards the ski area; the gondola is signed left after about 1km (daily: June 8.30am–6pm; July–Aug 8am–6pm; Sept 8.30am–6pm; $13.95; ☎522-3555). Depending on your susceptibility to either vertigo or claustrophobia you can choose between enclosed gondola cars, open chairs, or chairs with bubble domes. At the top (2034m) are the usual sensational views – rated some of the best in the Rockies – a self-service restaurant, sun decks, picnic areas, souvenir shops and several trailheads through the woods and meadows. One track takes you to the summit of Mount Whitehorn, a stiff 600m above the gondola station.

TRANSPORT AND FACILITIES

Four Greyhound **buses** a day ($8) link Banff and Lake Louise (50min) and stop in the Samson Mall car park at the little office known as The Depot (☎522-2080); three continue to Vancouver and the west. Four buses a day return from Lake Louise to Banff and Calgary. Laidlaw (☎762-9102 or 1-800/661-4946) run one bus daily ($8) and Brewster Transportation (☎762-6700) three buses a day from Banff ($11), and also continue to the *Chateau Lake Louise* (a good way to get up here if you're without transport – you can walk back down to the village). Note that there are also direct Brewster and other connections to and from Lake Louise and Calgary airport (see p.572 for details). Brewster also run one daily service to Jasper from Lake Louise village and lake ($44; departs Samson Mall at 4.15pm) as well as bus tours on the Icefields Parkway (8hr oneway; $82, $112 return excluding accommodation in Jasper). If you need a taxi to ferry you to the lakes, call Lake Louise Taxi & Tours (☎522-2020). The only **car-rental agency** is National at The Depot (☎522-3870), but you're better off renting in Banff or elsewhere as their cars go quickly.

The Samson Mall takes care of most practical considerations including a **post office** (daily 6.30am–7pm; ☎522-3870). Behind The Depot, which doubles up as a bag storage and booking office for coach tours and river-rafting trips, are a laundrette (☎522-2143) and (downstairs) public washrooms with showers. The general store is good and has a **money exchange**. There's also a currency exchange at the *Chateau Lake Louise* hotel (see p.634). For the **police**, call ☎522-3811. The nearest hospital is in Banff.

Excellent basic **food** – snacks and coffee – can be had at the always busy *Laggan's Mountain Bakery* (daily 6am–7pm) on the corner of the mall opposite the general store. For something more substantial than snacks, wander to the relaxed and reasonably priced *Bill Peyto's Café* for full and varied meals (daily 7am–9pm; ☎522-2200), within the youth hostel but open to all; in summer the nice outdoor eating area makes a good place to meet people. The unique *Lake Louise Station Restaurant* (☎522-2600) is housed in the restored 1909 station building – choose between hearty Canadian fare in the informal station building (garden dining in summer) and the more formal and expensive restored railway-dining carriages. Some of the best (and pricier) meals can be found in the *Post Hotel* (daily 7am–2pm & 5–9.30pm; ☎522-3989) – reservations are essential for dinner. The best local's hangout is the hotel's *Outpost Pub* (☎522-3989), a snug **bar** that serves light meals from late afternoon. Other good drinking spots include the *Lake Louise Bar and Grill* (☎522-3879) upstairs in the mall, and the lively *Explorers Lounge* (☎522-3791) in the *Lake Louise Inn*, 210 Village Rd.

ACTIVITIES

As for **activities**, most operators – especially rafting companies – are based in Banff or elsewhere (see p.619), though many offer pick-ups in Lake Louise, typically with a $10 add-on to their listed Banff prices; a handful operate trips directly out of Lake Louise itself. Companies actually based in or near the village include Wild Water Adventures (☎678-5058, 522-2211 or 1-888/771-9453) who run half- or full-day white-water rafting trips on the Kicking Horse River in nearby Yoho National Park (half-day trips at 8.30am and 1.30pm, from $69). If you don't want to hike alone, or wish to know more about what you're walking past, the national park and Friends of Banff run **guided walks** three or four times a week in July and August: the Lake Louise Lakeshore Stroll (Mon & Fri 10am; 2hr) and the Plain of the Six Glaciers (Tues, Thurs & Sun 9am; 6hr; $12). Drop by the visitor centre's Friends of Banff store to confirm latest timings and to reserve a place (do so in good time – the walks are popular) or call ☎522-3833. Cyclists can rent bikes from Wilson Mountain Sports in the mall (see opposite), or sign up for **cycling tours** (from $55 for half a day, $85 full day) and transfers that'll take you up to Bow Summit on the Icefields Parkway so you can pedal downhill or freewheel all the way back to Lake Louise. Serious canoeists can rent canoes from Wilson for trips on the Bow River, while more sedate paddlers can **rent canoes** and kayaks (daily in summer 10am–7pm; $30 per hour) at *Chateau Lake Louise* to dabble on Lake Louise itself (☎522-3511).

Good **trout fishing** is possible on the Bow River between Lake Louise and Banff, with support and advice available at the *Castle Mountain Chalets* on the Bow Valley Parkway (see p.626). Rental equipment is again on offer at Wilson Mountain Sports. Compulsory fishing permits ($6 weekly) are available from the visitor centre. If you fancy **horse riding**, contact Brewster Lake Louise Stables at the *Chateau Lake Louise* hotel (☎522-3511 ext 1210, or 762-5454) and enquire about their ninety-minute trips along the shores of Lake Louise ($45), half-day tours ($60) to the Lake Agnes or Plain of the Six Glaciers (see box, p.511) or full-day treks to Paradise Valley and Horseshoe Glacier ($120 including lunch). Timberline Tours (☎522-3743) run similar if slightly cheaper treks from the Lake Louise Corral behind the *Deer Lodge* hotel; all-day trips to the Skoki Valley east of Lake Louise; one- and three-hour trips at Bow Lake on the Icefields Parkway from the *Num-Ti-Jah Lodge* (see p.639).

ACCOMMODATION

Hotel accommodation in or near Lake Louise Village is pricey all year round – reckon on an average of $160 in most places – and almost certain to be full in summer. Bookings are virtually essential everywhere (make them direct or through Banff's **reservation services** (see p.612); at the excellent youth hostel, reservations six months in advance are not unusual. The various options on the Bow Valley Parkway, covered in the preceding section, are all within easy driving or cycling distance.

The lovely 220-site park-run **Lake Louise Campground**, close to the village – follow the signs off Fairview Road up to the lake – gets busy in summer. It's open between mid-May and early October, is partially serviced (it has showers), and sites cost $17; no fires. Sites are close together, though the trees offer some privacy, and with the railway close by, it can be noisy. The nearby *Lake Louise Trailer* site is for RVs (year-round; $21).

Canadian Alpine Centre and International Youth Hostel, on Village Rd just north of the mall across the river (☎522-2200, *llouise@hostellingintl.ca*). A modern 150-bed year-round hostel run jointly with the Canadian Alpine Club. Reservations are virtually essential (up to six months in advance) in summer and winter ski weekends. Check in time is 3pm. ①.

Castle Mountain Youth Hostel, 1.5km east of Castle Junction on Hwy 93 S (☎762-4122, *banff@hostellingintl.ca*). Well-situated for the Bow Valley Parkway and its trails. Sleeps just 36, with bookings possible through the Banff hostel. Dorm beds $13 for members, $17 for nonmembers. ①.

Château Lake Louise (☎522-3511 or 1-800/441-1414, fax 522-3834) has a monopoly on lakeside accommodation; doubles among its 511 rooms and suites cost up to $579, though in low season (Oct–Dec) some are available for around $100, making it one of the least expensive off-season places in the area. If it's beyond your budget, look inside anyway to check out its bizarre appeal. Booking essential. ⑨.

Deer Lodge, on Lake Louise Drive (☎522-3747 or 1-800/661-1595, fax 522-3883). Cheaper of two near-lake alternatives to *Château Lake Louise*, with a good restaurant and within walking distance of the lake. ⑥.

Lake Louise Inn, 210 Village Rd, just north of the village mall to the right (☎522-3791 or 1-800/661-9237, fax 522-2018, *www.lakelouiseinn.com*). The least expensive of the village hotels with a variety of rooms, some with self-catering facilities. ⑥.

Paradise Lodge and Bungalows, on the Lake Louise Drive a short walk from Lake Louise (☎522-3595, fax 522-3987, *www.ParadiseLodge.com*). Pricier of the near-lake options, but with reasonable off-season rates for its 21 self-contained bungalows and 24 one- and two-bedroom suites (some with kitchens). Mid-May to mid-Oct. ⑥.

Post Hotel, Village Rd (☎522-3989 or 1-800/661-1586, fax 522-3966). The top hotel in the village, with a noted restaurant and bar – see overleaf – but expect to pay $300 plus for a room here in summer. ⑧.

The Lake

Before you see **Lake Louise** you see the hotel: *Chateau Lake Louise*, a monstrosity that would surely never get planning permission today. Yet even so intrusive an eyesore fades into insignificance beside the immense beauty of its surroundings. The lake is Kodachrome turquoise, the mountains sheer, the glaciers vast; the whole ensemble is utter natural perfection. Outfitter Tom Wilson, the first white Canadian to see Lake Louise when he was led here by a local native in 1882, wrote, "I never, in all my explorations of these five chains of mountains throughout western Canada, saw such a matchless scene . . . I felt puny in body, but glorified in spirit and soul."

You can't help wishing you could have been Tom Wilson, and seen the spot unsullied by the hotel and before the arrival of the tourists and general clutter. Around 10,000 daily in peak season come here to gawp (car parks often fill by noon), while notice boards on the waterfront seem obsessed with the profoundly dull account of how the lake came by its name – it was named in honour of the fourth daughter of Queen Victoria. The native name translates as the "Lake of the Little Fishes". Wilson, showing precious little wit, originally called it Emerald Lake, for obvious reasons (clearly lacking in any imagination, he coined exactly the same name for the lake he discovered in Yoho; see p.670). More interesting is the account of Hollywood's discovery of the lake in the 1920s, when it was used to suggest "exotic European locations". After Wilson's "discovery" all access was by rail or trail – the station, then known as Laggan, was 6km away. The first hotel appeared in 1890, a simple two-bedroom affair which replaced a tumbledown cabin on the shore. Numerous fires, false starts and additions followed until the present structure made its unwelcome appearance (the final wings were added as recently as 1988). The first road was built in 1926. Be sure to walk here, despite the paths' popularity (see box, p.511). Alternatively, escape the throng – two million people come here each year – by renting an old-style canoe from the office to the left as you face the lake (June–Sept daily 10am–8pm; $30 per hour; maximum of three adults per boat). Don't think about swimming: the water's deep and cold – top temperature in summer is a numbing 4°C.

WINTER IN LAKE LOUISE

In a region already renowned for its **skiing** Lake Louise stands out, regarded by many as among the finest winter resorts in North America. In addition to skiing and snowboarding, there are hundreds of kilometres of cross-country trails, numerous other winter activities, and landscape that's earned the area the title of "North America's Most Scenic Ski Area" from *Snow Country* magazine. It's also Canada's largest ski area, with over forty square kilometres of trails, plenty of mogul fields, lots of challenging chutes, vast open bowls and some of the best "powder" on the continent.

Skiing started here in the 1920s. The first chalet was built in 1930, the first lift in 1954. The resort's real birth can be dated to 1958, when a rich Englishman, Norman Watson – universally known as the "Barmy Baronet" – ploughed a large part of his inheritance into building a gondola on Mount Whitehorn. Further lifts and other developments followed. More would have materialized had it not been for environmental lobbying. Further protests forestalled a bid for the 1968 Winter Olympics and put an end to a plan for a 6500-bed megaresort in 1972. Even so, the resort has grown, and now regularly hosts World Cup skiing events. The only drawback is the phenomenally low temperatures during January and February.

The **ski area** divides into five distinct zones (Front Side, South Face, Larch Area and Ptarmigan-Paradise and Back Bowls), served by three express quad chairs, one quad chair, two triple chairs, three double chairs, a T-bar, a platter lift and a children's rope tow. The huge **terrain** – some of the bowls are the size of entire European resorts – divides as follows: Novice (25 percent), Intermediate (45 percent) and Expert (30 percent). Most of the bowls are above the tree line, but you can also ski on Larch and Ptarmigan, whose varied terrain allows you to follow the sun or duck into the trees when the wind's up. Average seasonal snowfall (early Nov to mid-May) is 360cm, and snow-making is available over much of the area. The top elevation is 2637m, giving a 1000m drop to the base elevation at 1645m. Lift tickets are around $54 a day, but bear in mind that you can invest in the Ski Banff/Lake Louise **Tri-Area Pass**, which you can buy for a minimum of three days ($157) skiing in Lake Louise, Mount Norquay and Sunshine Village (see p.624).

Facilities in the ski area include three day-lodges, each of which has a restaurant and bar, a ski school, ski shop, rental shop, day-care, nursery and lockers. Free shuttles run from Lake Louise, while transfers from Banff cost around $15 return: however, these transfers are included free if you buy the Tri-Area Pass. Free tours of the mountain are also available three times daily. For further **information**, contact Skiing Louise, Suite 505, 1550-8th St SW, Calgary, AB T2R 1K1, or Box 5, Lake Louise, AB T0L 1E0 (☎522-3555, fax 522-2095, *www.skilouise.com*). Reservations can be made by calling ☎2-LOUISE (☎256-8473), or toll-free in North America 1-800/258-7669.

Cross-country skiing in Lake Louise is also phenomenal, with plenty of options around the lake itself, on Moraine Lake Road and in the Skoki Valley area north of the village. For **heli-skiing**, contact RK Heli-Ski (☎342-3889) who have a desk in the *Chateau Lake Louise* hotel (winter daily 4–9pm); one of their shuttle buses leaves from the hotel daily for the two-hour drive to the Purcell Mountains in BC (the region's nearest heli-skiing). The hotel is also the place to hire skates (at Monod Sports) for **ice skating** on the lake, probably one of the most sublime spots imaginable to indulge in the activity (the lake is floodlit after dark to allow night skating). If you want a **sleigh ride** on the lake shore, contact Brewster Lake Louise Sleigh Rides (☎522-3511 or 762-5454). Rides are reasonably priced and last an hour, but reservations are essential: sleighs depart hourly from 11am on weekends, 3pm on weekdays.

Moraine Lake

Not quite so many people as visit Lake Louise make the thirteen-kilometre road journey to **Moraine Lake**, which is smaller than its neighbour although in many ways its scenic superior. If you're without your own transport, you'll have to rely on a bike or taxi ($35) to get here or the new park-run "Vista" bus shuttle (daily every 30min from outside the hostel and Lake Louise campsite; free on production of park pass). The last has been introduced because of the sheer number of visitors in cars and RVs trying to cram into the tiny car park and clogging the approach road. No wonder they come, for this is one of the great landscapes of the region and has some cracking trails into the bargain (see box, p.638). It also holds one of the most enticing and magnificently executed hotels in the entire Rockies: if you're on honeymoon, or just want to push the boat out once, splash out on a night or two in the *Moraine Lake Lodge* (☎522-3733, *www.morainelake.com*; ⑨; May–Oct), a nicely landscaped collection of high-quality cabins plus eight lodge rooms and six other units designed by eminent architect Arthur Erickson (also responsible for Vancouver's UBC Museum of Anthropology and the Canadian Embassy in Washington DC): cabins are probably best, if only for their open fires. It boasts a friendly staff and great privacy, for prices on a par with decidedly more lacklustre hotels in the village and near Lake Louise.

Bar the *Lodge*, with its good little café and top-notch restaurant, nothing disturbs the lake and its matchless surroundings. Until comparatively recently the scene graced the back of Canadian $20 bills, though the illustration did little justice to the shimmering water and the jagged, snow-covered peaks on the eastern shore that inspired the nickname "Valley of the Ten Peaks". The peaks are now officially christened the Wenkchemna, after the Stoney native word for "ten".

The lake itself, half the size of Lake Louise, is the most vivid **turquoise** imaginable. Like Lake Louise and other big Rockies lakes (notably Peyto on the Icefields Parkway), the peacock blue is caused by fine particles of glacial silt, or till, known as rock flour. Meltwater in June and July washes this powdered rock into the lake, the minute but uniform particles of flour absorbing all colours of incoming light except those in the blue–green spectrum. When the lakes have just melted in May and June – and are still empty of silt – their colour is a more normal sky blue. You can admire the lake by walking along the east shore, from above by clambering over the great glacial moraine dam near the lodge (though the lake was probably created by a rock fall rather than glaciation), or from one of the **canoes for rent** on the right just beyond the *Lodge* and car park. For the best overall perspective, tackle the switchback trail through the forest on the east shore (see box, p.638), but check with the visitor centre at Lake Louise for the latest on bear activity – a young grizzly has made the Moraine Lake region its home, and areas are sometimes closed to avoid its coming in contact with humans.

The Icefields Parkway

The splendour of the **Icefields Parkway** (Hwy 93) can hardly be overstated: a 230-kilometre road from Lake Louise to Jasper through the heart of the Rockies, it ranks as one of the world's ultimate drives. Its unending succession of huge peaks, immense glaciers, iridescent lakes, wild-flower meadows, wildlife and forests – capped by the stark grandeur of the Columbia Icefield – is absolutely overwhelming. Fur traders and natives who used the route as far back as 1800 reputedly christened it the "Wonder Trail", though in practice they tended to prefer the Pipestone River Valley to the east, a route that avoided the swamps and other hazards of the Bow Valley. Jim Brewster made the first recorded complete trek along the road's future route in 1904. The present highway was only completed in 1939 and opened in 1940 as part of a Depression-era public-works programme. Although about a million people a year make the journey to experience what the park blurb calls a "window on the wilderness", for the most part you can go your own way in relative serenity.

After 122km, at about its midway point, the Icefields Parkway crosses from Banff into Jasper National Park (about a 2hr drive); you might turn back here, but the divide is almost completely arbitrary, and most people treat the Parkway as a self-contained journey, as we do here. Distances in brackets are from Lake Louise, which is virtually the

PARKWAY HOSTELS

Five **youth hostels** (four open year-round) and twelve excellent park **campsites** (two year-round) are spaced along the Parkway at regular intervals. It's essential to book the hostels, either direct if they have contact details, through the hostel at Banff or on-line at *www.hostellingintl.ca/alberta*. As ever, the frontcountry park campsites are available on a first-come, first-served basis. If you want more comfort, you'll have to overnight at Banff, Lake Louise or Jasper, as the only other accommodation – invariably booked solid – are hotels at Bow Lake, Saskatchewan Crossing, the Columbia Icefield and Sunwapta Falls.

The **Summer Hostel Shuttle** (early June to Sept) runs an extremely useful shuttle service, connecting twelve youth hostels between (and including) Calgary, Banff and Jasper – as well as all the places on the Icefields Parkway and beyond. Shuttles currently depart daily Calgary–Lake Louise–Calgary (leaves Calgary 8.30am, leaves Lake Louise 1pm for Banff, Calgary and Calgary Airport); Sat only Jasper–Lake Louise–Jasper round trip (leaves Jasper 8.30am, leaves Lake Louise 1.30pm); Mon, Wed and Fri at 1pm Lake Louise–Jasper; and Sun, Tues and Thurs Jasper–Lake Louise (8.30am).

Typical fares are $90 for Calgary to Maligne Canyon (Jasper), the longest possible journey, and $25 for the trip between Lake Louise and *Hilda Creek* hostel near the Columbia Icefield. Banff to Lake Louise is $12, Banff to *Jasper International Hostel* $57, and Lake Louise to Jasper $45. Extra fees are payable for bikes (Calgary to Banff costs $10), canoes and other cargo.

For information, call ☎283-5551 or 1-800/248-3837. To make bookings for the shuttle, contact Banff International (☎762-4122), Calgary (☎269-8239), Lake Louise (☎522-2200) or Jasper (☎1-877/852-0781). Current fares and schedules can also be found at *www.hostellingintl.ca/Alberta/transport*. For hostels book no later than 6pm the day before your desired departure with full details of your journey. Once the hostel has confirmed your booking, buy a ticket from any participating Alberta hostel, confirming the shuttle's departure time at the time of purchase. From hostels with phones, use the toll-free number to make enquiries; at those without, reservations can usually be made through the manager. Stand-by tickets may be bought from the van driver at departure, subject to availability. All passengers must have reservations at their destination hostel.

only way to locate places on the road, though everything mentioned is clearly marked off the highway by distinctive brown-green national park signs. Pick up the Parks Canada *In the Shadow of the Great Divide* pamphlet from visitor centres for a detailed map and summary of all the sights and trailheads. You could drive the whole highway in about four hours, but to do so would be to miss out on the panoply of short (and long) trails, viewpoints and the chance just to soak up the incredible scenery.

Access, transport and accommodation

Tourist literature often misleadingly gives the impression that the Icefields Parkway is highly developed. In fact, the wilderness is extreme, with snow often closing the road from October onwards, and there are only two points for **services**, at Saskatchewan Crossing (the one place campers can stock up with groceries, 77km from Lake Louise), where the David Thompson Highway (Hwy 11) branches off for Red Deer, and at the Columbia Icefield (127km).

Brewster Transportation (☎762-6767) runs several tours and a single scheduled bus daily in both directions between Banff or Lake Louise and Jasper from late May to mid-October ($51 one-way from Banff, $44 from Lake Louise), though services at either end of the season are often weather-affected. A word with the driver will usually get you dropped off at hostels and trailheads en route. If you're **cycling** – an increasingly popular way to tackle the journey – note that the grades are far more favourable if you travel from Jasper to Banff (Jasper's 500m higher than Banff).

MORAINE LAKE AND PARADISE VALLEY

MORAINE LAKE

Each of the four basic routes in the **Moraine Lake** area is easily accomplished in a day or less, two with sting-in-the-tail additions if you want added exertion; all start from the lake, which lies at the end of thirteen-kilometre Moraine Lake Road from just outside Lake Louise Village. Before hiking, check with the visitor centre in Lake Louise on the latest restrictions imposed to protect both the bears known to have made the area part of their territory as well as the tourists who hope to catch a glimpse of them. At the time of writing, walks in the Larch Valley and around were restricted. You must walk in groups of at least six people (there are often people waiting to join a group, so you should have no trouble making up the numbers).

The easiest walk is the one-kilometre amble along the lakeshore – hardly a walk at all – followed by the three-kilometre stroll to Consolation Lake, an hour's trip that may be busy but can provide some respite from the frenzy at Moraine Lake itself. This almost level walk ends with lovely views of a small mountain-circled lake, its name coined by an early explorer who thought it a reward and "consolation" for the desolation of the valley which led up to it. If you're tenting, fairly fit, or can arrange a pick-up, the highline Panorama Ridge Trail (2255m) branches off the trail (signed "Taylor Lake") to run 22km to the Banff–Radium highway 7km west of Castle Junction.

The most popular walk (start as early as possible) is the Moraine Lake–Larch Valley–Sentinel Pass Trail, one of the Rockies' premier hikes, which sets off from the lake's north shore 100m beyond the lodge. A stiffish hairpin climb through forest on a broad track, with breathtaking views of the lake through the trees, brings you to a trail junction after 2.4km and some 300m of ascent. Most hikers branch right, where the track levels off to emerge into Larch Valley, broad alpine upland with stands of larch (glorious in late summer and autumn) and majestic views of the encircling peaks. If you have the energy, push on to Sentinel Pass ahead, in all some two-hours' walk and 720m above Moraine Lake. At 2605m, this, along with the Wenkchemna Pass, is the highest point reached by a major trail in the Canadian Rockies. You can see what you're in for from the meadows – but not the airy views down into Paradise Valley from the crest of the pass itself. You could even continue down into Paradise Valley, a tough, scree-filled descent,

Between Lake Louise and the Columbia Icefield

One of the biggest problems in the Rockies is knowing what to see and where to walk among the dozens of possible trails and viewpoints. The Parkway is no exception. The following are the must-sees and must-dos along the 122-kilometre stretch of the Parkway from Lake Louise to the Columbia Icefield: best view – Peyto Lake (unmissable); best lake walk – Bow Lake; best waterfalls – Panther–Bridal Falls; best quick stroll – Mistaya Canyon; best short walk – Parker Ridge; best walk if you do no other – Wilcox Pass. Temptations for longer walks are numerous, and the difficulty, as ever, is knowing which to choose.

The first **youth hostel** north of Lake Louise is *Mosquito Creek* (28km), four log cabins which sleep 38 and have basic food supplies, a kitchen, large common room and a wood-fired sauna (no phone, reservations ☎762-4122; $13 members, $17 nonmembers; year-round, but closure dates may apply; check-in 5–11pm). Slightly beyond is the first park **campsite**, *Mosquito Creek* ($10: mid-June to mid-Sept; 32 sites; water and dry toilets, but no other facilities) and one of the Parkway's two winter campsites (free after mid-Sept; 32 walk-in sites only). You're near the Bow River flats here, and the mosquitoes, as the campsite name suggests, can be a torment. Two hikes start from close to the site: **Molar Pass** (9.8km; 535m ascent; 3hr), a manageable day-trip with good views, and **Upper Fish Lake** (14.8km; 760m ascent; 5hr), which follows the Molar Pass trail for 7km before branching off and crossing the superb alpine meadows of North Molar Pass (2590m).

and complete an exceptional day's walk by picking up the valley loop (see below) back to the Moraine Lake Road. Otherwise return to the 2.4-kilometre junction and, if legs are still willing – you'll have done most of the hard climbing work already – think about tagging on the last part of the third Moraine Lake option.

This third option, the less-walked Moraine Lake–Eiffel Lake–Wenkchemna Pass Trail, follows the climb from the lake as for the Larch Valley path before branching off left instead of right at the 2.4-kilometre junction. It's equally sound, virtually level and if anything has the better scenery (if only because less barren than Sentinel Pass) in the stark, glaciated grandeur to be found at the head of the Valley of the Ten Peaks. It's also much quieter once you're beyond the trail junction. At 2255m, Eiffel Lake is a 5.6-kilometre hike and 370-metre climb in total (allow 2–3hr) from Moraine Lake, and you don't need to go much further than the rock pile and clump of trees beyond the lake to get the best out of the walk. Ahead of you, however, a slightly rougher track continues through bleak terrain to Wenckchemna Pass (2605m), clearly visible 4km beyond. Having got this far, it's tempting to push on; the extra 350-metre climb is just about worth it, if lungs and weather are holding out, for the still broader views back down the Valley of the Ten Peaks. The views beyond the pass itself, however, over the Great Divide into Yoho and Kootenay parks, are relatively disappointing.

PARADISE VALLEY
In 1894, the mountaineer Walter Wilcox deemed **Paradise Valley** an appropriate name for "a valley of surpassing beauty, wide and beautiful, with alternating open meadows and rich forests". North of Moraine Lake, it's accessed via Moraine Lake Road about 3km from its junction with Lake Louise Drive. The walk here is a fairly straightforward hike up one side of the valley and down the other, a loop of 18km with a modest 385m of vertical gain. Most people take in the Lake Annette diversion for its unmatched view of Mount Temple's 1200-metre north face (unclimbed until 1966), and many overnight at the campsite at the head of the valley (9km from the parking area), though this is one of the busiest sites in the park. Others toughen the walk by throwing in the climb up to Sentinel Pass on the ridge south of the valley, which gives the option of continuing down the other side to connect with the Moraine Lake trails (see above).

On the *Num-Ti-Jah Lodge* access road just beyond (37km), a great short trail sets off from beside the lodge to **Bow Lake** and **Bow Glacier Falls** (4.3km; 155m ascent; 1–2hr), taking in the flats around Bow Lake – one of the Rockies' most beautiful – and climbing to some immense cliffs and several huge waterfalls beyond (the trail proper ends at the edge of the moraine after 3.4km, but it's possible to pick your way through the boulders to reach the foot of the falls 900m beyond). If you don't want to walk, take a break instead at the picnic area on the waterfront at the southeast end of the lake. The *Num-Ti-Jah Lodge* itself, just off the road, is one of the most famous old-fashioned lodges in the Rockies, built in 1920 by legendary guide and outfitter Jimmy Simpson (who lived here until 1972). It's the only privately owned freehold in the park – all other land and property is federally owned and leased; be sure to book well in advance to have any chance of securing a room (☎522-2167; ⑥; May–Sept). There's a **coffee shop** here if you need a break, or want to admire the *Lodge*'s strange octagonal structure, forced on Jimmy because he wanted a large building but only had access locally to short timbers. You aren't allowed in the lodge (so guests can enjoy their privacy), but you can take dinner here, or sign up for **horse riding** with Timberline Tours (☎522-3743), available to residents and nonresidents alike: rides include a one-hour trip to Bow Lake; a three-hour ride to Peyto Lake (see below); and a full-day excursion to Helen Lake.

Another 3km up the Parkway comes the pass at Bow Summit, source of the Bow River, the waterway that flows through Banff, Lake Louise and Calgary. (At 2069m, this is the highest point crossed by any Canadian highway.) Just beyond is the unmissable twenty-minute stroll to **Peyto Lake Lookout** (1.4km; elevation loss 100m) one of the finest vistas in the Rockies (signed from the road). The quite beautiful panorama only unfolds in the last few seconds, giving a genuinely breathtaking view of the vivid emerald lake far below; mountains and forest stretch away as far as you can see. Another 3km along the Parkway lies a viewpoint for the Peyto Glacier, part of the much larger Wapta Icefield.

After 57km you reach the *Waterfowl Lakes* **campsite** (116 sites; $13; mid-June to mid-Sept) and the **Chephren Lake Trail** (3.5km; 80m ascent; 1hr), which leads to quietly spectacular scenery with a minimum of effort. The next pause, 14km further on, is the **Mistaya Canyon Trail**, a short but interesting 300-metre breather of a stroll along a river-gouged "slot" canyon: *mistaya*, incidentally, is a Cree word meaning "grizzly bear".

SASKATCHEWAN CROSSING (77km) is the lowest point on the road before the icefields; the 700-metre descent from Bow Summit brings you from the high subalpine ecoregion into a montane environment with its own vegetation and wildlife. Largely free of snow, the area is a favourite winter range for mountain goats, bighorn sheep and members of the deer family. The bleak settlement itself offers expensive food (restaurant and cafeteria), petrol, a spectacularly tacky gift shop and a 66-room **hotel-restaurant**, *Crossing*, that is surprisingly comfy (☎761-7000; ⑤; early March to mid-Nov).

Twelve kilometres north are the *Rampart Creek* thirty-bed **youth hostel**, with two cabins and the "best sauna in the Rockies" (☎439-3139 or through Banff, Lake Louise or Calgary hostels; $13 members, $17 nonmembers; June–Oct open daily all day, check-in 5–11pm; Nov–May Sat & Sun only with reservations), with a basic food store, and a fifty-pitch park-run **campsite** ($10; late June to early Sept). Apparently this area is one of the best black-bear habitats close to the road anywhere in the park. The last of the Banff National Park campsites is the tiny sixteen-pitch *Cirrus Mountain* site at the 103-kilometre mark ($10; late June to early Sept), but its position is precarious, so check it's open before planning a stay (☎762-1550).

Shortly before the spectacular **Panther Falls** (113.5km) the road makes a huge hairpin climb (the so-called "Big Hill"), to open up yet more panoramic angles on the vast mountain spine stretching back towards Lake Louise. The unmarked and often slippery one-kilometre trail to the falls starts from the lower end of the second of two car parks on the right. Beyond it (117km) is the trailhead to **Parker Ridge** (2.4km one-way; elevation gain 210m; allow 1hr one-way, less for the return), which, at 2130m, commands fantastic views from the summit ridge of the Saskatchewan Glacier (at 9km, the Rockies' longest). If you're only going to do one walk after the Peyto Lake Lookout (see above), make it this one: it gets cold and windy up here, so bring extra clothing. Ideally placed for this area and the Columbia Icefield 9km north is the busy *Hilda Creek* **youth hostel** (☎439-3139 or 762-4122; $12 members, $16 nonmembers; check-in 5–11pm) 1km beyond. The setting is stunning, and accommodation (for 21) is in cosy log cabins. Nearby Sunwapta Pass (2023m) marks the border between Banff and Jasper national parks and the watershed of the North Saskatchewan and Sunwapta rivers: the former flows into the Atlantic, the latter into the Arctic Ocean. From here it's another 108km to Jasper.

The Columbia Icefield

Covering an area of 325 square kilometres, the **Columbia Icefield** is the largest collection of ice and snow in the entire Rockies, and the largest glacial area in the northern hemisphere south of the Arctic Circle. It's also the most accessible of some seventeen glacial areas along the Parkway. Meltwater flows from it into the Arctic, Atlantic and Pacific oceans, forming a so-called "hydrological apex" – the only other one in the world is in Siberia. This is fed by six major glaciers, three of which – the Athabasca, Dome and Stutfield – are partially visible from the highway. The ugly and extremely busy **Icefield Centre** (daily: May to early June & Sept to mid-Oct 9am–5pm; early June to Aug 9am–6pm; ☎780/852-6288) provides an eerie viewpoint for the most prominent of these, the Athabasca Glacier, as well as offering the Parks Canada Exhibit Hall and information and slide shows on the glaciers and Canada's most extensive cave system – the Castleguard Caves, which honeycomb the ice but are inaccessible to the public. This is not a place to linger, however, thanks to the legions of people and dozens of tour buses.

You can walk up to the toe of the **Athabasca Glacier** from the parking area at Sunwapta Lake, noting en route the date-markers, which illustrate just how far the glacier has retreated (1.5km in the last 100 years). You can also walk onto the glacier, but shouldn't, as it's riddled with crevasses. Fall in one of these and you probably won't be climbing out. People are killed and injured every year on the glacier: even a slip can rip off great slivers of skin; the effect of sediment frozen into the ice is to turn the glacier surface into a vast and highly abrasive piece of sandpaper. Full-scale expeditions are the preserve of experts but you can join an **organized trip**. Brewster's special "Snocoaches" run ninety-minute, five-kilometre rides over the glacier with a chance to get out and walk safely on the ice (daily: every 15min: early May to Sept 9am–5pm; Oct 10am–4pm depending on weather; $25.95; book tickets at the Centre or call ☎762-6767 or 762-6735 in Banff, 522-3544 in Lake Louise, 870/852-3544 in Jasper, toll-free 1-877/ICE RIDE). They're heavily subscribed, so aim to avoid the peak midday rush by taking a tour before 10.30am or after 3pm. More dedicated types can sign up for the Athabasca Glacier ice walks (3hr walks mid-June to early Sept daily at 11.30pm, $31; 5hr walks Thurs & Sun 11.30am; $37), led by licensed guides. Call ☎780/852-6550, 852-5595 or 1-800/565-6735 for details, or sign up on the spot at the front desk of the Icefields Centre – be sure to bring warm clothes, boots and provisions.

The 32-room *Columbia Icefields Chalet* (☎852-6550; ⑤–⑦) provides excellent but much-sought-after **accommodation** in the Icefields Centre between May and mid-October (note that lower rates apply in May and October). Brewster bus services between Jasper and Banff stop here: it's possible to take a Banff-bound Brewster bus out of Jasper at lunchtime (arrives at the Icefields at 3pm), see the Icefield, and pick up the evening Jasper-bound bus (leaves Icefield at 6.30pm) later the same day.

Two unserviced but very popular **campsites** lie 2km and 3km south of the Icefield Centre respectively: the tent-only 33-site *Columbia Icefield* ($10; mid-May to mid-Oct, or until the first snow), and the 46-site *Wilcox Creek*, which takes tents and RVs ($10; early June to mid-Sept). This latter is also the trailhead for one of the very **finest hikes** in the national park, never mind the highway: the **Wilcox Pass Trail** (4km one-way; 335m ascent; allow 2hr round trip), highly recommended by the park centres and just about every trail guide going. The path takes you steeply through thick spruce and alpine fir forest before emerging suddenly onto a ridge that offers vast views over the Parkway and the high peaks of the icefield (including Mount Athabasca). Beyond, the trail enters a beautiful spread of meadows, tarns and creeks, an area many people choose to halt at or wander all day without bothering to reach the pass itself. You could extend the walk to 11km by dropping from the pass to Tangle Creek further along the parkway.

Beyond the Columbia Icefield

If there's a change **beyond the Columbia Icefield**, it's a barely quantifiable lapse in the scenery's awe-inspiring intensity over the 108-kilometre stretch towards Jasper. As the road begins a gradual descent the peaks retreat slightly, taking on more alpine and less dramatic profiles in the process. Yet the scenery is still magnificent, though by this point you're likely to be in the advanced stages of landscape fatigue. It's worth holding on, though, for two good short trails at Sunwapta and Athabasca falls.

Seventeen kilometres beyond the icefield is the 24-berth, two-cabin *Beauty Creek* **youth hostel** (reservations through *Jasper International Hostel* ☎780/852-3215; $10

BEARS

Two types of **bears** roam the Rockies – black bears and grizzlies – and you don't want to meet either. They're not terribly common in these parts (sightings are all monitored and posted at park centres) and risks are pretty low on heavily tramped trails, but if you're camping or walking it's still essential to be vigilant, obey basic rules, know the difference between a black bear and a grizzly (the latter are bigger and have a humped neck), know how to avoid dangerous encounters, and understand what to do if confronted or attacked. Popular misconceptions about bears abound – that they can't climb trees, for example (they can, and very quickly) – so it's worth picking up the parks service's pamphlet *You are in Bear Country*, which cuts through the confusion and lays out some occasionally eye-opening procedures. Be prepared, and if you don't want to be attacked, follow the cardinal rules: store food and garbage properly, make sure bears know you're there, don't approach or feed them, and, if you find yourself approached by one, don't scream and don't run.

When hiking, walk in a group – bears rarely attack more than four in a group – and make noise, lots of it, as you traverse the wilderness; bears are most threatened if surprised, so warning of your approach will give them time to leave the area. Many people shout, rattle cans with stones in or carry a whistle; be warned, the widely touted hand-held, tinkling bells are not loud enough. Be especially alert and noisy when close to streams, in tall vegetation, crossing avalanche slopes or when travelling into the wind, as your scent won't carry to warn bears of your approach: move straight away from dead animals and berry patches, which are important food sources. Watch for bear signs – get out quick if you see fresh tracks, diggings and droppings – and keep in the open as much as possible.

Camp away from rushing water, paths and animal trails, and keep the site scrupulously clean, leaving nothing hanging around in the open. Lock food and rubbish in a car, or hang it well away from a tent between two trees at least 4m above ground (many campsites have bear poles or steel food boxes). Take all rubbish away – don't bury it (bears'll just dig it up) and certainly don't store it in or near the tent. Avoid smelly foods, all fresh, dried or tinned meat and fish, and never store food, cook or eat in or near the tent – lingering smells may invite unwanted nocturnal visits. Aim to cook at least 50m downwind of the tent: freeze-dried meals and plastic-bag-sealed food is best. Likewise, keep food off clothes and sleeping bags, and sleep in clean clothes at night. Bears have an acute sense of smell, so avoid *anything* strongly scented – cosmetics, deodorant, shampoo, gel, lip balm, insect repellents, toothpaste, sun screen. Bears can be attracted to women during

members, $15 nonmembers; May–Sept; hostel open all day but check-in 5–11pm; partial closure possible Oct–April). Nine kilometres further is the unserviced 25-site *Jonas Creek* **campsite** ($10; mid-May to first snowfall).

A one-kilometre gravel spur leads off the highway to **Sunwapta Falls** (175km from Banff, 55km from Jasper), fifteen-minutes' walk through the woods from the road: they're not terribly dramatic unless in spate, but are interesting for the deep canyon they've cut through the surrounding valley. A short trail along the river bank leads to more rapids and small falls downstream. If you want to put up nearby, the 35-pitch *Honeymoon Lake* **campsite** with kitchen shelter, swimming and dry toilets is 4km further along the Parkway ($10; mid-June to first snowfall).

The last main stop before you're in striking distance of Jasper Townsite, **Athabasca Falls** (30km from Jasper) are impressive enough, but the platforms and paths show the strain caused by thousands of feet, making it hard to feel you're any longer in wilderness. One kilometre away, however, is the excellent *Athabasca Falls* **youth hostel** (☎852-5959, reservations through *Jasper International Hostel* ☎852-3215; $11 members, nonmembers $16; hostel open all day, but check-in 5–11pm), with forty beds in three cabins. Three kilometres back down the road is the 42-site *Mount Kerkeslin* **campsite**, menstruation, so dispose of tampons in an airtight container; they're also attracted by the smell of sex, so watch what you do in your tent if you don't want a rather drastic coitus interruptus.

Bears are unpredictable, and experts simply can't agree on best tactics: there's no guaranteed life-saving way of coping with an aggressive bear. Calm behaviour, however, has proved to be the most successful strategy in preventing an attack after an encounter. Bears don't actually want to attack; they simply want to know you're not a threat. Mothers with cubs are particularly dangerous and prone to suspicion. A bear moving towards you can be considered to have it in for you, other signs being whoofing noises, snapping jaws, and the head down and ears back. A bear raised on its hind legs and sniffing is trying to identify you: if it does it frequently, though, it's getting agitated; ideally, on first encounter you want first to stand stock still, never engage in direct eye contact (perceived as aggressive by the bear) and – absurd as it sounds – start speaking to it in low tones. Whatever you do, don't run, which simply sets off an almost inevitable predator-prey response in the bear (a bear can manage 61kph – that's easily faster than a racehorse or the fastest Olympic sprinter); instead, back away quietly and slowly at the first encounter, speaking gently all the while to the bear. If the backing off seems to be working, then make a wide detour, leave the area or wait for the bear to do so – and always leave it an escape route. If things still look ominous, set your pack gently on the ground as a distraction as you continue to back away.

If you're attacked, things are truly grim, and quack tactics are unlikely to help you. With grizzlies, playing dead – curling up in a ball, protecting face, neck and abdomen – may be effective. Fighting back will only increase the ferocity of a grizzly attack, and there's no way you're going to win. Keep your elbows in to prevent the bear rolling you over, and be prepared to keep the position for a long time until the bear gets bored. You may get one good cuff and a few minutes' attention and that's it – injuries may still be severe but you'll probably live. With a black bear the playing dead routine won't wash, though they're not as aggressive as grizzlies, and a good bop to the nose or sufficient frenzy on your part will sometimes send a black bear running: it's worth a try. Don't play dead with either species if the bear stalks or attacks while you're sleeping: this is more dangerous, as bears are often after food. Instead, try and get away or intimidate – people who have survived such attacks have often had a brave companion who has attacked the bear in return with something big and heavy.

Chemical repellents are available, but of unproven efficacy, and in a breeze you're likely to miss or catch the spray yourself. If this all sounds too scary to make you even contemplate walking or camping, remember that attacks are very rare.

with swimming, kitchen shelter and dry toilets, spread over a tranquil riverside site ($10; mid-June to early Sept).

Highway 93A, the route of the old Parkway, branches off the Icefields Parkway at Athabasca Falls and runs parallel to it for 30km. This alternative route has less dramatic views than the Parkway, as dense trees line the road, but the chances of spotting wildlife are higher.

The telephone code for Jasper and Jasper National Park is ☎780.

Jasper National Park

Although traditionally viewed as the second-ranking of the Rockies' big-four parks after Banff, **JASPER NATIONAL PARK** covers an area greater than Banff, Yoho and Kootenay combined (10,878 square kilometres), and looks and feels far wilder and less

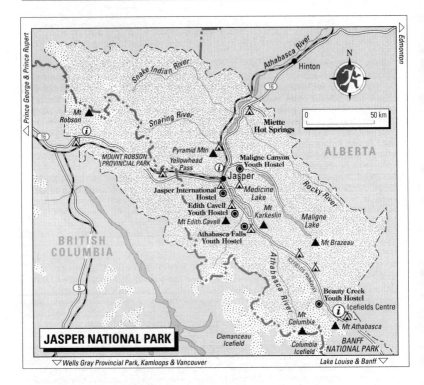

Prince George & Prince Rupert

Edmonton

Snake Indian River

Athabasca River

Hinton

N

16

Mt Robson

Snaring River

16

MOUNT ROBSON PROVINCIAL PARK

Pyramid Mtn

Yellowhead Pass

0   50 km

Miette Hot Springs

Maligne Canyon Youth Hostel

ALBERTA

Jasper

Jasper International Hostel

Edith Cavell Youth Hostel

Mt Edith.Cavell

Athabasca Falls Youth Hostel

Medicine Lake

Mt Karkeslin

Rocky River

Maligne Lake

Mt Brazeau

BRITISH COLUMBIA

5

Athabasca River

ICEFIELDS PARKWAY

Beauty Creek Youth Hostel

Icefields Centre

JASPER NATIONAL PARK

Clemanceau Icefield

Mt Columbia

Columbia Icefield

Mt Athabasca

BANFF NATIONAL PARK

▽ Wells Gray Provincial Park, Kamloops & Vancouver

Lake Louise & Banff ▽

commercialized than its southern counterparts. Its backcountry is more extensive and less travelled, and **Jasper Townsite** (or Jasper), the only settlement, is more relaxed and far less of a resort than Banff and has just half Banff's population. Most pursuits centre on Jasper and the **Maligne Lake** area about 50km southeast of the townsite. Other key zones are **Maligne Canyon**, on the way to the lake; the Icefields Parkway (covered in the previous section); and the **Miette Hot Springs** region, an area well to the east of Jasper and visited for its springs and trails.

The park's **backcountry** is a vast hinterland scattered with countless rough camp-sites and a thousand-kilometre trail system considered among the best in the world for backpackers. Opportunities for day and half-day-hikes are more limited and scattered than in other parks. Most of the shorter strolls from the townsite are just low-level walks to forest-circled lakes; the best of the more exciting day-hikes start from more remote points off the Maligne Lake road, Icefields Parkway (Hwy 93) and Yellowhead Highway (Hwy 16).

Some history

Permanent settlement first came to the Jasper area in the winter of 1810–11. The great explorer and trader David Thomson left **William Henry** at Old Fire Point (just outside the present townsite), while he and his companions pushed on up the valley to blaze a trail over the Athabasca Pass that would be used for more than fifty years by traders crossing the Rockies. In the meantime, Henry established **Henry House**, the first per-manent European habitation in the Rockies (though its exact location has been lost).

Two years later the North West Company established Jasper House at the eastern edge of the park's present boundary. Named after Jasper Hawes, a long-time company clerk there, it moved closer to Jasper Lake in 1829, when the North West and Hudson's Bay companies were amalgamated. By 1880, and the collapse of the fur trade, the post had closed. By 1900, the entire region boasted just seven homesteads.

Like other parks and their townsites, Jasper traces its real origins to the coming of the railway in the late nineteenth century. The Canadian Pacific had brought boom to Banff and Yoho in 1885 when it spurned a route through the Jasper region in favour of a more southerly route. (See "Field", p.661). The **Grand Trunk Pacific Railway** hoped for similar successes in attracting visitors when it started to push its own route west in 1902, and the Jasper Forest Park was duly created in 1908. The government bought up all land locally except for the homestead of Lewis Swift, which remained in stubborn private hands until 1962: the town is now "run" by Parks Canada. By 1911 a tent city known as **Fitzhugh**, named after the company's vice president, had grown up on Jasper's present site, and the name "Jasper" was adopted when the site was officially surveyed. Incredibly, a second railway, the **Canadian Northern** (CNR), was completed almost parallel to the Grand Trunk line in 1913, the tracks at some points running no more than a few metres apart. Within just three years, the line's redundancy became obvious and consolidation took place west of Edmonton, with the most favourably graded portions of the two routes being adopted. The ripped-up rails were then shipped to Europe and used in World War I and Jasper became a centre of operations for the lines in 1924, greatly boosting its importance and population. The first tourist accommodation here was ten tents on the shores of Lac Beauvert, replaced in 1921 by the first *Jasper Lake Lodge*, forerunner of the present hotel. The first road link from Edmonton was completed in 1928. Official national-park designation came in 1930. Today Jasper's still a rail town, with around a third of the population employed by the CNR.

Arrival

Where Banff's strength is its convenience from Calgary, Jasper's is its ease of **access** from Edmonton, with plenty of transport options and approaches, as well as a wide range of onward destinations. **Driving** time from Edmonton (362km) or Banff (287km) is around four hours; from Kamloops (443km) and Calgary (414km) it's about five or six hours. Vancouver is 863km or a 9hr 30min-drive away.

Greyhound (☎852-3926 or 1-800/661-8747) runs four **buses** daily from Edmonton (4hr 45min; $49.49 one-way) along the Yellowhead Highway (Hwy 16), plus onward services to Kamloops ($56.66) and Vancouver ($99.19) via scenic Hwy 5 (4 daily) and Prince George (2 daily; $49.06). Brewster Transportation (☎852-3332 or 1-800/661-1152) operates five-hour services to Banff (1 daily at 1.30pm; $51) via Lake Louise ($44) and continuing to Calgary (1 daily; $71) and Calgary Airport (1 daily; $71; additional connections at Banff), and also runs day-trip tours to Banff, taking in sights on the Icefields Parkway; note, however, that weather can play havoc with Brewster's schedules in October and April (services finish for the year with the first bad snows). Both companies share the same **bus terminal** (daily 6am–8pm; outside regular hours, the terminal opens briefly a few minutes before bus departures), located in the train-station building at 314 Connaught Drive.

There are also left-luggage lockers here and **car rental** offices for Hertz (☎852-3886) and National (☎852-1117). Be sure to have booked cars in advance if you're hoping to pick up vehicles at these outlets – all cars go very quickly, especially on days when trains come in from Vancouver and Edmonton (see below). Other car-rental agencies in town are Avis at the Petro-Canada Service, 300 Connaught Drive (☎852-3970) and Budget, Jasper Shell Service, 638 Connaught Drive (☎852-3222).

VIA Rail **trains** operate to Jasper from Winnipeg and Edmonton and continue to Vancouver (via Kamloops) or Prince Rupert (via Prince George). Coach- (second-)

HIKING IN JASPER NATIONAL PARK

DAY-HIKES

If you haven't travelled to Jasper on the Icefields Parkway, remember that several of the national park's top trails can be accessed from this road: the Wilcox Pass Trail in particular, is one of the finest half-day-hikes anywhere in the Rockies. If you just want a simple stroll closer to town, then think about walking the Old Fort Point Loop (see p.654), the Maligne Canyon (see p.657) and the easy path on the eastern shore of Maligne Lake (see p.657). If you're at Maligne Lake and want a longer walk, one of Jasper's best day-hikes, the Opal Hills Circuit (8.2km round trip, 460m vertical ascent), starts from the picnic area to the left of the uppermost Maligne Lake car park, 48km east of Jasper. After a heart-pumping haul up the first steep slopes, the trail negotiates alpine meadows and offers sweeping views of the lake before reaching an elevation of 2160m; the trip takes about four hours, but you could easily spend all day loafing around the meadows. The Bald Hills Trail (5.2km one-way; 480m ascent) starts with a monotonous plod along a fire road from the same car park, but ends with what Mary Schaffer, one of the area's first white explorers, described as "the finest view any of us had ever beheld in the Rockies"; allow four hours for the round trip, which goes as high as 2170m.

To get to the trailhead for another outstanding day-hike, Cavell Meadows (3.8km one-way; 370m ascent), which is named after a British nurse who was executed for helping the Allies during World War I, drive, cycle or taxi 7.5km south on the Icefields Parkway, then 5km along Hwy 93A and finally 14km up Mount Edith Cavell Road; there's a daily shuttle bus from Jasper and it takes bikes so you can ride back down. Note that if you're driving, an alternating one-way system has been instigated to reduce traffic flow up Mount Edith Cavell Road every day from 10am to 9.30pm between mid-June and mid-October: contact the park information centre for latest timings. The walk's scenery is mixed and magnificent – but the hike is popular, so don't expect solitude. As well as Cavell's alpine meadows, there are views of Angel Glacier and the dizzying north wall of Mount Edith Cavell. Allow two hours for the round trip; the maximum elevation reached is a breathless 2135m.

Further afield – you'll need transport – another superlative short, sharp walk starts from Miette Hot Springs, 58km northeast of Jasper. The Sulphur Skyline (4km one-way; 700m ascent) offers exceptional views of knife-edged ridges, deep gorges, crags and remote valleys. Be sure to take water with you, and allow two hours each way for the steep climb to 2070m. The trailhead is signed from the Miette Hot Springs complex, reached from Jasper by heading 41km east on Hwy 16 and then 17km south; in the past

class tickets currently cost $175 to Vancouver including taxes; Edmonton ($125), Prince Rupert ($146 – excluding the cost of the overnight stay required on this route at Prince George); Prince George ($71); and Kamloops ($110). As this is the only scheduled rail route through the Rockies, summer places are hard to come by, but at other times there's little need to book a seat. Fares are considerably more than those of equivalent buses, and journey times considerably longer. Trains run Edmonton–Jasper (currently Mon, Thurs & Sat; 5hr 30min); Jasper–Edmonton (Mon, Wed & Sat leaving Jasper at 12.25pm); Jasper–Kamloops–Vancouver (Mon, Thurs & Sat at 3.30pm; 15hr 30min); Jasper–Prince George (Wed, Fri & Sun at 12.45pm; 5hr 15min) and Prince George–Prince Rupert (Mon, Thurs & Sat; 12hr 15min). The **ticket office** is open on train days only (☎852-4102 or 1-888/VIA-RAIL, *www.viarail.ca*).

Note that you can experience a taste of the railway on a new arrangement that lets you ride the Jasper–Prince George service for two hours to Mount Robson where the train lets you off before continuing on to Prince George and then Prince Rupert. You can return to Jasper by coach with a guide and stop at some of the sights you've seen from the train. The trip departs at 12.45pm on train days (Wed, Fri & Sun), lasts the shuttles have made the trip in summer – check latest timetables. More soothing, and a good way to round off a day, are the springs themselves, the hottest in the Rockies – so hot in fact they have to be cooled for swimming; there's one pool for soaking, another for swimming, with massages by appointment and not included in pass price (mid-June to early Sept daily 8.30am–10.30pm, $5.50 or $7.75 day-pass; mid-May to mid-June and early Sept to mid-Oct daily 10.30am–9pm, $4.50 or $7 day-pass; ☎866-3939 or 1-800/767-1611, *www.parkscanada.gc.ca/hotsprings/*). You can hire bathing suits, towels and lockers for an extra $3–5. Other trails from the springs make for the Fiddle River (4.3km one-way; 275m ascent) and Mystery Lake (10.5km one-way; 475m ascent).

BACKPACKING TRAILS

Jasper's system of backpacking trails and 111 backcountry campsites makes it one of the leading areas for backcountry hiking in North America. To stay overnight in the backcountry, pick up a Wilderness Permit ($6) within 24 hours of your departure, from the park information centre in Jasper Townsite or at the Columbia Icefield. All trails and campsites operate quota systems; contact the park information office for details and book yourself a backcountry campsite(s) – and thus trail place – as soon as you can. Reservations cost $10 (nonrefundable). Trails remain busy even into September: the busiest are Skyline, Maligne Lake, Brazeau and Tonquin Valley.

The office staff offer invaluable advice, and issue excellent low-price strip maps of several trails. Overnight hikes are beyond the scope of this book – talk to staff or get hold of a copy of *The Canadian Rockies Trail Guide* – but by general consent the finest longdistance trails are the Skyline (44km; 820m ascent) and Jonas Pass (19km; 555m ascent), with the latter often combined with the Nigel and Poboktan passes (total 36km; 750m ascent) to make a truly outstanding walk. Not far behind come two hikes in the Tonquin Valley – Astoria River (19km; 445m ascent) and Maccarib Pass (21km; 730m ascent) and the Fryat Valley (3–4 days). Others to consider are Maligne Pass and the long-distance North and South Boundary trails (the latter both over 160km). To summarize, a quick guide to the best walks in Jasper at a glance:

- Best stroll: Maligne Canyon
- Best short walk: Wilcox Pass (see p.641)
- Best day-hike (easy): Cavell Meadows
- Best day-hike (moderate) Opal Hills
- Best day-hike (strenuous): Sulphur Skyline
- Best backpacking trail: Skyline Trail

four hours in total, and costs $79, including train ticket. For details contact Rocky Mountain Unlimited, 414 Connaught Drive (☎852-4056 or 1-888/SUNDOG1, *www.sundogtours.com*).

Information

The town's superb national park **visitor centre** is at 500 Connaught Drive – 50m east of the station, back from the road on the left in the open grassy area (mid-May to mid-June daily 8am–5pm; mid-June to early Sept daily 8am–7pm; early Sept to mid-May Mon–Fri 9am–5pm, Sat & Sun 8am–5pm; ☎852-6176, *www.parkscanada.pch.gc.ca /jasper*). This is for park-related and campsite information only. For accommodation, contact the Chamber of Commerce office (see overleaf). Apply at the park office for compulsory **national park permits** ($5 daily, $35 annual; see box, p.607) backcountry wilderness permits ($6) and to register for backpacking trails. If you're hiking seriously you might also want to contact the park's Trail Office (May–Oct; ☎852-6177). Out of season, apply to the Park Administration Office located upstairs in the VIA Rail-bus terminal complex (Mon–Fri 8am–4.30pm; ☎852-6162 or 852-6220). The Park Warden Office is 1km away in the Industrial Area off the east side of Hwy 93a as you head towards the junction with Hwy 16 (Mon–Fri 8am–4.30pm; ☎852-6155). For weather reports, call Environment Canada (☎852-3185).

The centre also has a shop (good for **maps**) run by the Friends of Jasper (☎852-4767), who offer a couple of **guided walks**: Jasper – A Walk in the Past (daily from the visitor centre at 7.30pm June–Sept 6, 6.30pm Sept 6–30), which delves into the history of the town, and Pocahontas – A Walk in the Past (daily from car park at the bottom of Miette Hot Springs Rd July–Aug at 2pm), which looks at some of the legends and stories of the region. You should register at the centre for both; payment by donation. Other popular Friends' activities include performances at the Whistler's Campground Theatre (daily: 10pm July to mid-Aug, 9pm mid-Aug to Sept) and wildlife talks at the Wabasso Campground Campfire Circle (July–Sept Sat 9pm).

For information on the town of Jasper, and accommodation in particular, contact the Jasper Chamber of Commerce **infocentre** behind the park office about 100m east on Patricia Street at no. 409 (June to early Sept daily 9am–7pm; rest of the year Mon-Fri 9am–5pm; ☎852-3858).

The local **public library** on Elm Avenue (Mon–Thurs 2–5pm & 7–9pm, Fri 2–5pm, Sat 10am–3pm; ☎852-3652) has a huge number of books on the park, but there's no decent bookshop in town. The **post office** is at 502 Patricia St; the **hospital** at 518 Robson St (☎852-3344). For the **police**, call ☎852-4848. For **Internet access**, use the terminals at the *Soft Rock Internet Café*, 633 Connaught Drive (☎852-5850).

Accommodation

Beds in Jasper are not as expensive or elusive as in Banff, but hotel rooms are still almost unobtainable in late July and August. The Chamber of Commerce will help with accommodation, but do not offer a booking service. If you're desperate, try Jasper Adventure Centre, which offers an accommodation service (☎852-5595 or 1-800/565-7547, *www.JasperAdventureCentre.com*), as does the Jasper Travel Agency, 623 Patricia St (☎852-4400 or 1-800/672-1127, *jtravel@telusplanet.net*), and Rocky Mountain Unlimited, 414 Connaught Drive (☎852-4056, *www.sundogtours.com*).

You could also ask the Chamber of Commerce for the Jasper Home Accommodation Association (JHAA; *www.visit-jasper.com/JHAA.html* or *www.bbcanada.com/jhaa.html*) *Private Home Accommodation List* – Jasper has around sixty **private homes**, which are virtually all priced between $55 and $70 a double (up to a maximum of around $95 for the most expensive), sometimes with a continental breakfast thrown in (note that virtually all are nonsmoking). These rooms also fill up fast.

Most **motels** are spaced out along Connaught Drive on the eastern edge of town – there's relatively little right in the middle of town – and most charge well over $135 for a basic double room, though prices drop sharply off-season. An often cheaper and in many ways more pleasant option is to plump for motels made up of collections of **cabins**; most are within a few kilometres of town. The four park-run **campsites** close to the townsite and the three local hostels (joint reservations on ☎439-3139) all fill up promptly in summer – and it's first-come, first-served – but don't forget the hostels and campsites strung along the Icefields Parkway.

HOTELS, MOTELS AND CHALETS

Alpine Village, 2.5km south of town on Hwy 93A (☎852-3285, fax 852-1955). An assortment of 41 serene one- and two-room cabins, including twelve deluxe cabins and lodge suites, most with great mountain views; big outdoor tub. May to mid-Oct. ⑥.

Amethyst Motor Lodge, 200 Connaught Drive (☎852-3394 or 1-888/852-7737, *www.mtn-park-lodges.com*). Almost 100 newly renovated rooms two blocks from downtown. ⑦.

Astoria Hotel, 404 Connaught Drive (☎852-3351 or 1-800/661-7343, *www.astoriahotel.com*). Adequate central "alpine" hotel, one block from the train station and bus terminal. ⑥.

TAXIS AND SHUTTLE SERVICES

One of the problems you're likely to have in Jasper if you're without transport is getting to some of the more outlying sights, strolls and trailheads. One option is to rent a bike (see "Activities" on p.654). Another is take advantage of a variety of small-scale shuttle services that run to various sights. These tend to come and go year by year, but there's always someone prepared to start up a service. Currently services include the **Tramway Shuttle** (☎852-4056 or 852-8255), which runs nine times daily in summer from outside the Via Rail-bus depot (look out for the white "Sundog" van) to the Jasper Tramway (cable car) at a cost of $24, including Tramway ticket: more importantly, it also takes in the *Jasper International* (or *Whistlers*) *Youth Hostel* for $4. The **Trailhead Shuttle** (☎852-3898 or 852-8389) leaves from Freewheel Cycles, 618 Patricia St, and runs once or twice daily to a variety of trailheads, including the Valley of the Five Lakes, Maligne Canyon and Overlander (all $10) and Marmot Basin Road ($15). Finally, there's the long-established **Maligne Lake Shuttle**, run by Maligne Tours, 627 Patricia St (☎852-3370; 6 departures daily late June to late Sept, 3 daily mid-May to late June and last week of Sept), which will run you all the way to Maligne Lake ($12 or $24 round trip) to coincide with the company's boat cruises on the lake (see p.657), or drop off at Maligne Canyon ($8), *Maligne Canyon Youth Hostel* ($8) and other points on the Maligne Lake Rd such as the Skyline trailheads (north $8, south $12).

For a **taxi**, call Heritage Cab (☎852-5558), Michael Angelo (☎852-7277) or Jasper Taxi (☎852-3600).

Athabasca Hotel, 510 Patricia St (☎852-3386 or 1-800/563-9859, *www.athabascahotel.com*). Central, if rather forbidding hotel, near the station, where the nightly entertainment at *O'Shea's Lounge Bar* may keep you awake. Choice of suite or newly renovated rooms, either en suite or with sinks only and shared facilities. ⑥.

Bear Hill Lodge, 100 Bonhomme St (☎852-3209 or 852-3099, *www.bearhilllodge.com*). Thirty-seven simple-looking but comfortable bungalows, suites, chalet and lodge units, in the townsite but in a pleasant wooded setting. Mid-April to late Oct. ⑤.

Becker's Chalets, 5km south of Jasper on Hwy 93 and Athabasca River (☎852-3779). Ninety-six of the best (and some of the newest) local one-, two-, three- and four-bedroom log cabins, most with wood-burning stoves and kitchenettes. May to mid-Oct. ④.

Jasper Park Lodge, 5km from townsite on Lac Beauvert (☎852-3301 or 1-888/242-3888, *www.jasperparklodge.com*). The town's top upmarket, luxury option, with all the facilities and trimmings of a top-class hotel. ⑨.

Lobstick Lodge, 1200 Geikie at Juniper (☎852-4431 or 1-888/852-7737, *www.mtn-park-lodges.com*). If you're going to pay in-town, east-end motel rates, this big place is among the best all-round choices, but make sure you don't get put in one of the dungeon-like basement rooms. ⑦.

Marmot Lodge, 92 Connaught Drive (☎852-4471 or 1-888/852-7737, *www.mtn-park-lodges.com*). One of the biggest and least expensive of the east-end motels. ⑥.

Patricia Lake Bungalows, 5km northwest of downtown (☎852-3560, *www.patricialakebungalows.com*). Motel or cabin out-of-town base; 35 units on Pyramid Lake Rd, some with fine views over Patricia Lake; fishing and rentals of boats, canoes and paddle boats available. May to mid-Oct. ⑤.

Pine Bungalows, 2km east of Jasper on the Athabasca River (☎852-3491, fax 852-3432). Some 85 good-looking wooden cabins in forest setting, 41 with wood-burning stoves and 72 with kitchenettes. Grocery shop on site. Three-day minimum stay from mid-June to Mid-Sept. May to mid-Oct. ③.

Sawridge Hotel Jasper, 82 Connaught Drive (☎852-5111 or 1-800/661-6427, *www. sawridge.com /Jasper*). Plush and expensive 154-room hotel on the eastern edge of town. ⑧.

Tekarra Lodge (☎852-3058 or 1-888/404-4540, *www.tekarralodge.com*). Forty-two quiet, nicely kitsch wood cabins with wood-burning stoves, located 1km south of town on the Athabasca River off Hwy 93A. Open May–Oct. ⑥.

Whistlers Inn, 105 Miette Ave (☎852-3361 or 1-800/282-9919, *www.whistlersinn.com*). Central but unexciting 41-room motel, opposite the station. ⑥.

BED AND BREAKFASTS

A-1 Tourist Rooms, 804 Connaught Drive (☎852-3325, *lwhitema@telusplanet.net*). Two rooms with shared bathroom on main st close to bus and train. Two-night minimum stay for advance reservations. ②.

Aspen Lodge, 8 Aspen Crescent (☎852-5908, fax 852-5910, *aspnlodg@telusplanet.net*). Two clean, comfortable rooms with private bathrooms on a quiet street 10min walk from downtown. ③.

B & G Accommodation, 204 Colin Crescent (☎852-4345, *wgunrau@telusplanet.net*). Three well-priced rooms with shared bathroom three blocks from downtown. ②.

Creekside Accommodation, 1232 Patricia Crescent (☎852-3530, fax 852-2116, *rushacom@telusplanet.net*). Two bright, clean rooms (shared bath) near Cabin Creek and trails. ②.

Kennedy's Mountain Holiday Rooms, 1115 Patricia Crescent (☎852-3438). Pair of rooms that share bath, patio, living room and great views. ②.

Marchand, Yves and Caroline, 809 Patricia St (☎852-3609, *ymarchand@hotmail.com*). Three good double rooms with shared bathroom in a quiet location 5min from the town centre. A full cooked breakfast is available at an additional charge. ②.

Pooli's Suite, 824 Geikie St (☎852-4379). A one-bedroom suite with two double beds and a pull-out in the living room (sleeps up to six): $65 for two people, $6 for each additional person: private bathroom and use of kitchen for an additional $8. ③.

Rooney's Accommodation, 1114 Patrica St (☎852-4101, *mismaeil@telusplanet.com*). Just out of the town centre comprising two nice rooms with and without private baths. ②.

711 Miette Avenue, 711 Miette Ave (☎852-4029, fax 852-4021). A friendly welcome, nice double room with private entrance and bathroom two blocks from downtown. ③.

TassonInn, 706 Patricia St (☎852-3427, *tassinn@incentre.net*). Two bright and newly renovated rooms with shared bathroom less than a block from the town centre. ②.

Worobec, Wayne and Joan, 1215 Patricia Crescent (☎852-5563, *worobec@telusplanet.net*). A choice of double room with private bathroom or a suite of bedroom, living room and food preparation area for family for two to four people. ④.

HOSTELS

Jasper International Youth Hostel (HI; ☎852-3215; hostel open all day but check-in 8am–midnight). Jasper's principal youth hostel, 7km south of town (500m south of the gondola terminal) on Skytram Rd (Whistlers Mountain Rd), accessed from the Icefields Parkway (Hwy 93). The 4km uphill walk from Hwy 93 is a killer, but shuttles run from downtown, as do taxis (about $14). A modern place with rather overefficient management, its eighty beds fill up quickly in summer, so arrive early or book. Members $16, nonmembers $21. Facilities include laundry, store and bike rentals. ①.

Maligne Canyon Hostel (HI; ☎852-3215). Two cabins in lovely setting with beds for 24 in six-bed rooms 11km east of town near Maligne Canyon; the Maligne Lake Shuttle from downtown or Alberta Hostel Shuttle (see p.637) drop off here daily in summer; members $11, nonmembers $16. Open all day, year-round but check-in 5–11pm and may have closures in winter. ①.

Mount Edith Cavell Hostel, Edith Cavell Rd, 13km off Hwy 93A, 26km south of Jasper (HI; reservations ☎852-3215; check-in 5–11pm). Cosier than the *Jasper International Hostel* (see above), close to trails and with great views of the Angel Glacier. Sleeps 32 in two cabins; outdoor wood-burning sauna. Members $11, nonmembers $16. Mid-June to Oct. Occasionally opens up with key system for skiers in winter. ①.

HOSTEL RESERVATIONS

For reservations at *Jasper International, Maligne Canyon, Edith Cavell, Beauty Creek* and *Athabasca Falls* hostels, call ☎780/852-3215 or 1-877/852-0781, fax 780/852-5560, or email *jihostel@hostellingintl.ca*.

CAMPSITES

Pocahontas, 45km east of Jasper and 1km off Hwy 16 on Miette Rd. One of two to the northeast of Jasper on this road; 130 pitches, hot and cold water and flush toilets but no showers. Mid-May to mid-Oct. $13 plus $4 for use of firewood.

Snaring River, 16km east of Jasper on Hwy 16. Simple 66-site park-run facility. The other simple park campsite east of Jasper; tap water, kitchen shelter, dry toilets only and no showers. Mid-May to early Sept. $10 plus $4 for use of firewood.

Wabasso, 16km south of Jasper on Hwy 93A. A 228-pitch riverside park-run site with flush toilets, hot water but no showers. Wheelchair-accessible. Mid-June to early Sept. $13 plus $4 for use of firewood.

Wapiti, 4km south of the townsite and 1km south of *Whistlers* campsite (see below) on Hwy 93. Big 362-pitch park-run place with flush toilets and coin showers that accepts tents but also caters for up to forty RVs. Wheelchair-accessible. Some ninety sites remain open for winter camping from October – the park's only year-round serviced campsite. Summer $15–18 plus $4 for use of firewood; winter, when there are no showers or other services save water and flush toilets, $13–15 plus $4 for use of firewood.

Whistlers, 3km south of Jasper just west off Hwy 93. Jasper's main 781-site park-run campsite is the largest in the Rockies, with three sections, and prices depending on facilities included. Wheelchair-accessible. If you're coming from Banff, watch for the sign; Brewster buses also usually stop here if you ask the driver. Taxis and shuttles run from Jasper. Early May to early Oct. $15–24, plus $4 for use of firewood.

Jasper Townsite

JASPER's small-town feel comes as a relief after the razzmatazz of Banff: its streets still have the windswept, open look of a frontier town and, though the mountains don't ring it with quite the same majesty as Banff, you'll probably feel the town better suits its wild surroundings. Situated at the confluence of the Miette and Athabasca rivers, its core centres around just two streets: **Connaught Drive**, which contains the bus and train terminal, restaurants, motels and park information centre, and – a block to the west – the parallel **Patricia Street**, lined with more shops, restaurants and the odd hotel. The rest of the central grid consists of homely little houses and the fixtures of small-town life: the post office, library, school and public swimming pool. Apart from the **Yellowhead Museum & Archives** at 400 Pyramid Rd, with its fur trade and railroad displays (mid-May to early Sept daily 10am–9pm; early Sept to Oct daily 10am–5pm; Nov to mid-May Thurs–Sun 10am–5pm; $3 or donation; ☎852-3013) and a cable car (see p.653), nothing here even pretends to be a tourist attraction; this is a place to sleep, eat and stock up. If you're interested in getting to know a little more about the town or park from the locals, contact the Friends of Jasper National Park (☎852-4767), who offer guided walks between July and August, or pick up *Jasper: A Walk in the Past* from local bookshops. If you're still itching for something to do and have a car, a lot of people head 58km northeast of town for a dip in Miette Hot Springs (see hiking box on pp.646–647).

Though Jasper doesn't get as crowded as Banff, it still receives around three million visitors annually, so accommodation, especially in summer, can be extremely tight, though there are numerous B&B options. You are also especially stuck if you don't have a vehicle; trailheads and the best scenery are a long way from downtown. Bikes can be rented at several places and intermittent shuttle services (see box on p.649) and organized tours can run you out of town to **Maligne Lake**, to various trailheads and to some of the more obvious attractions.

Jasper Tramway and the lakes

With little on offer in town you need to use a bike, car or the shuttle services to get anything out of the area. The obvious trip is on Canada's longest and highest tramway, the

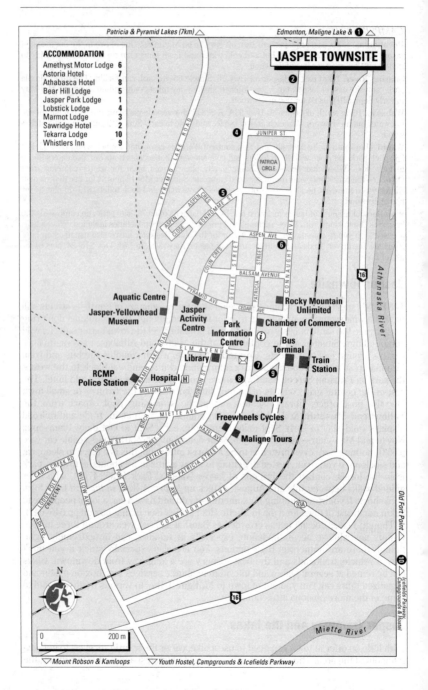

JASPER TOWNSITE

ACCOMMODATION
Amethyst Motor Lodge 6
Astoria Hotel 7
Athabasca Hotel 8
Bear Hill Lodge 5
Jasper Park Lodge 1
Lobstick Lodge 4
Marmot Lodge 3
Sawridge Hotel 2
Tekarra Lodge 10
Whistlers Inn 9

Patricia & Pyramid Lakes (7km)

Edmonton, Maligne Lake &

PYRAMID LAKE ROAD

JUNIPER ST

PATRICIA CIRCLE

ASPEN CRES

BONHOMME ST

ASPEN CLOSE

ASPEN AVE

COLIN CRES

GEIKIE STREET

PATRICIA STREET

CONNAUGHT DRIVE

BALSAM AVENUE

PYRAMID AVE

CEDAR AVE

Aquatic Centre

Rocky Mountain Unlimited

Jasper-Yellowhead Museum

Jasper Activity Centre

Chamber of Commerce

Park Information Centre

ELM AVENUE

Bus Terminal

Library

Train Station

RCMP Police Station

Hospital

MALIGNE AVE

MIETTE AVE

Laundry

BIRCH AVE

ROBSON ST

Freewheels Cycles

HAZEL AVE

Maligne Tours

TONQUIN ST

TURRET ST

GEIKIE STREET

PINE AVE

PATRICIA STREET

CABIN CREEK RD

WILLOW AVE

SPRUCE AVE

LODGE POLE CRESCENT

ASH AVE

CONNAUGHT DRIVE

93A

16

Athabaska River

Old Fort Point

Icefields Parkway, Campgrounds & Hostel

N

0   200 m

Mount Robson & Kamloops

Youth Hostel, Campgrounds & Icefields Parkway

Miette River

Jasper's winter sports tend to be overshadowed by the world-class ski resorts in nearby Banff and Lake Louise. This said, the park has plenty of winter activities and a first-rate ski area in **Marmot Basin** (20min drive from the townsite), a resort with the advantages of cheaper skiing and far less crowded runs than its southern rivals. Skiing in the region began in the 1920s, though the first lift – a 700-metre rope tow – was only introduced in 1961, just a few years after the first road. Today there are a total of seven **lifts**: two T-bars, three double-chair lifts, one triple-chair lift and one high-speed quad-chair lift; few are likely to be crowded in winter. The terrain is a balanced mixture of Novice (35 percent), Intermediate (35 percent) and Expert (30 percent). The drop from the resort's top elevation at 2601m to the base level is 701m: the longest run is 5.6km and there are a total of 52 named trails. Lift passes cost around $35. The season runs from early December to late April. You can rent equipment at the resort or from several outlets in Jasper itself. To get here, jump aboard one of the three daily buses ($5 one-way, $9 return) from downtown hotels, whose rates, incidentally, tumble dramatically during the winter. For more **information** on the resort, contact Marmot Basin Ski-Lifts, PO Box 1300, Jasper, AB T0E 1E0 (☎852-3816, fax 852-3533).

Where Jasper rates as highly, if not more so, than Banff National Park is in the range and quality of its **cross-country skiing**, for its summer backcountry trails lend themselves superbly to winter grooming. Pick up the *Cross-Country Skiing in Jasper National Park* leaflet from the park information centre: the key areas are around the *Whistlers* campsite, Maligne Lake, around Athabasca Falls and along Pyramid Lake Road. For all manner of winter activities such as ice fishing, dog sledding, snowmobiling, heli-skiing, skiing in Banff or Lake Louise and so forth, book through Rocky Mountain Unlimited, 414 Connaught Drive (☎852-4056, *www.sundogtours.com*). Ski and cross-country ski equipment can be **bought or rented** from Totem Ski Rentals, 408 Connaught Drive (☎852-3078), and the Sports Shop, 406 Patricia St (☎852-3654). **Ice skating** takes place on parts of Pyramid Lake and Lac Beauvert, and there are the usual sleigh rides around Jasper and its environs.

Jasper Tramway, 7km south of town on Whistlers Mountain Road, off the Icefields Parkway (daily: April to mid-May and Oct 9.30am–4.30pm; mid-May to early Sept 8.30am–10pm; Sept 9.30am–9pm; $18 return; ☎852-3093). In peak season you may well have a long wait in line for the 2.5-kilometre cable-car ride, whose two thirty-person cars take seven minutes to make the 1000-metre ascent (often with running commentary from the conductor). It leaves you at an interpretive centre, expensive restaurant, and an excellent viewpoint (2285m) where you can take your bearings on much of the park. A steep trail ploughs upwards and onwards to the Whistlers summit (2470m), an hour's walk that requires warm clothes year-round and reveals even more stunning views. A tough but rather redundant ten-kilometre trail follows the route of the tramway from *Jasper International Youth Hostel*; if you walk up, you can ride back down for next to nothing.

Also near the town, a winding road wends north to **Patricia** and **Pyramid lakes**, popular and pretty moraine-dammed lakes about 5km from Jasper and racked full of rental facilities for riding, boating, canoeing, windsurfing and sailing. Food and drink is available locally, but if you're thinking about staying here as a more rural alternative to the townsite the two lakefront lodges are usually heavily booked (the one at Pyramid Lake is open year-round). Short trails, generally accessible from the approach road, include the Patricia Lake Circle, a 4.8-kilometre loop by the Cottonwood slough and creek offering good opportunities for seeing birds and small mammals, like beavers, during early morning and late evening. The island on Pyramid Lake, connected by a bridge to the shore, is an especially popular destination for a day out: continue on the lake road to the end of the lake and you'll find everything a little quieter. Slightly closer to town on

OPERATION HABBAKUK

Behind every triumph of military ingenuity in World War II, there were probably dozens of spectacular and deliberately obfuscated failures. Few have been as bizarre as the one witnessed by Jasper's Patricia Lake. By 1942, Allied shipping losses in the North Atlantic had become so disastrous that almost anything was considered that might staunch the flow. One Geoffrey Pike, institutionalized in a London mental hospital, managed to put forward the idea of a vast aircraft carrier made of ice, a ship that would be naturally impervious to fire when torpedoed, and not melt from under its seamen in the icy waters of the North Atlantic.

Times were so hard that the innovative scheme, despite its odd source, was given serious consideration. Louis Mountbatten, one of the Allied Chiefs of Staff, went so far as to demonstrate the theories with ice cubes in the bath in front of Winston Churchill at 10 Downing St. It was decided to build a thousand-tonne model somewhere very cold – Canada would be ideal – and **Operation Habbakuk** was launched. Pike was released from his hospital on special dispensation and dispatched to the chilly waters of Patricia Lake. Here a substance known as pikewood was invented, a mixture of ice and wood chips (spruce chips were discovered to add more buoyancy than pine). It soon became clear, however, that the 650-metre-long and twenty-storey-high boat stood little chance of ever being seaworthy (never mind what the addition of 2000 crew and 26 aircraft would do for its buoyancy). Pike suggested filling the ice with air to help things along. Further complications arose when the labourers on the project, mostly pacifist Doukhobors (see p.519), became aware of the boat's proposed purpose and refused to carry on working. Spring thaws brought the project to a halt. The following season, with $75 million budgeted for the scheme, it was moved to Newfoundland, where it died a quiet death.

the east side of the Athabasca River, **Lake Edith** and **Lake Annette** are the remains of a larger lake that once extended across the valley floor. Both are similarly busy day-use areas. Their waters are surprisingly warm – in fact they're the warmest in the park, thanks to the lakes' shallow depth. In summer you can lie out on sandy beaches or grassy areas. A clutch of picnic sites are the only development, and the wheelchair-accessible Lee Foundation Trail meanders around Lake Annette (2.4km).

Few other hikes from town are spectacular, but the best of the bunch, the **Old Fort Point Loop** (6.5km round trip), is recommended. Despite being just thirty minutes out of town, it's remarkably scenic, with 360-degree views and lots of quiet corners. To reach the trailhead (1.6km from town) use the Old Fort Exit, following Hwy 93A across the railway and Hwy 16 until you come to the Old Fort Point–Lac Beauvert turn-off; then turn left and follow the road to the car park beyond the bridge. The Valley of the Five Lakes Trail (4.6km) is also good, but the path starts 10km south of town off the Icefields Parkway. For full details of all park walks, ask at the information centre for the free *Day-hiker's Guide to Jasper*.

Activities

The presence of the Athabasca and other rivers around Jasper makes the town a focus of **white-water** and other rafting trips (see box on pp.664–665). If the idea of water appeals, but in much gentler context, the town's **Aquatic Centre** at 401 Pyramid Lake Rd (☎852-3663) is popular, and provides a large **swimming** pool, whirlpool, wading pool, steam room and showers. You can rent towels and costumes if you've come unprepared.

Other tours and activities can be accessed through several operators around town, amongst whom the most wide-ranging is **Rocky Mountain Unlimited**, 414 Connaught Drive (☎852-4056, *www.sundogtours.com*), who run their own tours but also act as a one-stop booking agent for a huge range of tours, including seeing the park by helicopter

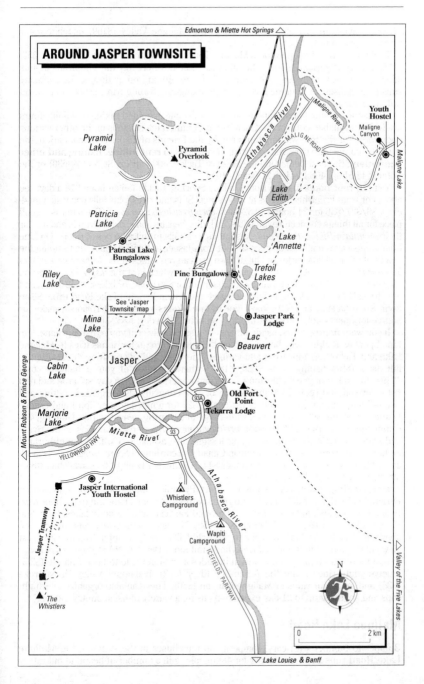

($149), a five-hour bus and hiking tour of the Maligne Valley ($169) or white-water rafting ($79 and up).

The town's other big operator is Maligne Tours at 627 Patricia St (☎852-3370, fax 852-3405, *www.malignelake.com*) – though note that nowhere on the shopfront at this address does it actually say the company's name. Among other things, the company runs boat cruises on Maligne Lake, guided hiking and fishing trips, canoe rentals and rafting excursions.

All manner of short or strenuous and generally cheap guided hiking or wildlife tours are widely available: contact the Chamber of Commerce for details of the other various operators. For the free walking tours run by the Friends of Jasper National Park in the summer, contact the park visitor centre. If you need to **rent hiking, fishing and other equipment**, the best bet is On-Line Sport & Tackle, 600 Patricia St (☎852-3630) or the Totem Ski Shop, 406 Patricia St (☎852-3078).

You can **rent bikes** in town from On-Line Sport & Tackle ($6 an hour, $18 a day; see above) or from Freewheel Cycles at 618 Patricia St (same rates, plus full-suspension models at $9/$27/$36 for 24 hours; ☎852-3898, *www.freewheeljasper.com*). The latter is a good place for all things connected with bikes, including repairs and spares. Drop in and ask for their *Mountain Biking Trail Guide*, a summary of trails to suit all types of riders. On-Line offer a one-way rental with all necessary kit from Jasper to Banff if you're up to riding the length of the Icefields Parkway. Out of town you can rent bikes at the *Jasper International Youth Hostel* (see p.650); at Beauvert Boat & Cycles, which is at the *Jasper Park Lodge* on the shore of Lac Beauvert ($8 an hour, $20 for 4hr or $30 a day for bikes; ☎852-5708); and at Patricia Lake Bungalows, 4.8km northwest of town on Pyramid Lake Road (from $6 an hour, $18 a half-day and $24 a day). For **in-line skates rental** (rollerblades), make for Source for Sports, 406 Patricia St (from $4 an hour, $12 a day; ☎852-3654).

If you want **fishing** tours, tackle for rent or just free advice if you're fishing alone, On-Line Sport & Tackle (see above) is again the operator to go for: it has trips to Maligne Lake and Talbot Lake for trout and various other lake and river-fishing destinations. a full day's (8hr) fishing costs $289, $189 if there are two of you; a half-day costs $249/$149. It'll rent you tackle, too – boots and waders from $30 a day, spin rod and reel ($15), fly-rod and reel ($25) and nets ($5). The company also organizes rafting and horse-riding tours, rents rowboats ($40 daily, $25 for a half-day after 3pm) and canoes (same rates), and sells and hires a wide range of **camping gear**. Currie's Guiding, 414 Connaught Drive (☎852-5650, *www.curriesguiding.com*), offer similar trips on the rivers and over twenty lakes, with fly-fishing lessons also available. **Golf** on a highly rated eighteen-hole course – "Number one in Canada" according to *Score Magazine* – is available at the *Jasper Park Lodge* (green fees $44–95, cheaper twilight fees available; ☎852-6090). You can rent clubs and carts.

Horse-riding enthusiasts should contact Pyramid Stables, 4km from Jasper on Pyramid Lake Road (☎852-3562), who run day-treks and one-, two- and three-hour trips (from $25/$43/$65; full-day rides $125) around Patrician and Pyramid lakes. Ridgeline Riders at Maligne Tours, 627 Patricia St (☎852-3370, *www.malignelake.com*) offer a ride above the tree line at Maligne Lake to the Bald Hills Fire Lookout at 2134m with great views of the lake (3hr 30min; $55). Skyline Trail Rides (☎852-4215) at *Jasper Park Lodge* have a more varied programme which includes a one-hour ride to Lake Annette ($25), ninety-minute rides along the Athabasca River ($33), two-hour "Valley View" treks ($35) and four-hour rides to Maligne Canyon ($70). They can also organize overnight trips and anything up to 21-day expeditions using a variety of backcountry lodges.

Maligne Lake Road

Bumper to bumper with cars, campers and tour buses in the summer, the **Maligne Lake Road** runs east from Jasper for 48km, taking in a number of beautiful but rather busy and overdeveloped sights before reaching the sublime Maligne Lake (pronounced "Ma-leen"), the Rockies' largest glacier-fed lake (and the world's second largest). If you have time to spare, and the transport, you could set aside a day for the trip, white-water raft the Maligne River (see below), or walk one of the trails above Maligne Lake itself. Maligne Tours, 627 Patricia St (☎852-3370, *www.malignelake.com*), books boat tours on the lake (advance booking is highly recommended) and rents out any equipment you may need for canoeing, fishing and so forth (note that rental reservations are also essential in summer). The company also runs a **bus**, the Maligne Lake Shuttle, to the lake eight times daily ($12 one-way), with drop-offs (if booked) at *Maligne Canyon* youth hostel ($8) and the northern ($8) and southern ends ($8/$12) of the Skyline Trail, one of the park's three top backpacking trails (see box, p.646). Joint tickets are offered for the shuttle and other activities organized by the company, notably the cruises, raft trips and horse rides on and around Maligne Lake.

The often rather crowded **Maligne Canyon** is a mere 11km out of Jasper, with an oversized car park and a tacky café/souvenir shop. This heavily sold excursion promises one of the Rockies' most spectacular gorges: in fact the canyon is deep (50m), but almost narrow enough to jump across – many people have tried and most have died in the attempt. In the end the geology is more interesting than the scenery; the violent erosive forces that created the canyon are explained on the main trail loop, an easy twenty-minute amble that can be extended to 45 minutes (few people do this, so the latter part of the trail is often quiet), or even turned into a hike back to Jasper. In winter, licensed guides lead tours (more like crawls) through the frozen canyon – contact Maligne Tours, 626 Connaught Drive, Jasper (details above).

Next stop is picture-perfect **Medicine Lake**, 32km from Jasper, which experiences intriguing fluctuations in level. Its waters have no surface outlet: instead the lake fills and empties through lake-bed sink holes into the world's largest system of limestone caves. They re-emerge some 17km away towards Jasper (and may also feed some of the lakes around Jasper Townsite). When the springs freeze in winter, the lake drains and sometimes disappears altogether, only to be replenished in the spring. The lake's strange behaviour captivated local natives, who believed spirits were responsible, hence the name. Few people spend much time at the lake, preferring to press on to Maligne Lake, so it makes a quietish spot to escape the headlong rush down the road.

At the end of the road, 48km from Jasper, is the stunning **Maligne Lake**, 22km long and 92m deep, and surrounded by snow-covered mountains. The largest lake in the Rockies, its name comes from the French for "wicked", and was coined in 1846 by a Jesuit missionary, Father de Smet, in memory of the difficulty he had crossing the **Maligne River** downstream. The road peters out at a warden station, three car parks and a restaurant flanked by a picnic area and the start of the short, self-explanatory Lake Trail along the lake's east side to the Schäffer Viewpoint (3.2km loop; begin from Car Park 2). A small waterfront area is equipped with berths for glass-enclosed boats that run ninety-minute narrated **cruises** on the lake to Spirit Island: the views are sensational (daily hourly on the hour: mid-May to late June 10am–4pm; late June to early Sept 10am–5pm; early Sept to late Sept 10am–3pm; $32). The boats are small, however, and reservations are vital during peak times, especially as tour companies often block-book entire sailings: again, contact Maligne Tours (see above). Riding, fishing, rafting and guided hiking tours are also available, as are fishing tackle, rowing boat and canoe rentals ($10 a day, $45 per day) and sea kayaks ($60 a day). There are no accommodation or camping facilities here, but two backcountry campsites on the lakeshore can be reached by canoe (details from Jasper's information centre).

Eating

Options for **eating** out are a bit restricted in Jasper – mostly hotel dining rooms – but then the town's rugged ambience doesn't suit fine dining. A reasonable place for a basic budget meal in no-nonsense surroundings is the cheap, friendly *Mountain Foods and Café*, opposite the station at 606 Connaught Drive (☎852-4050), though quality has become variable. Still, the menu is cheap and varied (including vegetarian courses), the staff friendly, and it's a good place to meet people. Also popular is the lively and far more carnivorous *Villa Caruso*, 640 Connaught Drive (☎852-3920), serving giant steaks; if that's too much, they also serve seafood, pasta and pizzas. Best of the mid-range places is the ever-reliable *Earl's* on the second floor at 600 Patricia St on the corner of Miette Avenue. For pizzas cooked in a wood-burning oven, head to the big and bustling *Jasper Pizza Place* (☎852-3225), 402 Connaught Drive, with a rooftop patio for nice days, and for a locals' favourite try *Papa George's*, 406 Connaught Drive (☎852-3351), one of the town's oldest restaurants (opened in 1924). It looks plain and dowdy, but the very varied food is excellent and the portions gargantuan. If you're going for broke, the *Jasper Park Lodge*, Jasper's premier hotel, 5km from town on Lac Beauvert, boasts two outstanding restaurants: *Becker's* is one of the best in Alberta (☎852-3535; May–Oct; dinner only) – reckon on $115 for a gourmet blowout for two – while the *Edith Cavell Room* is only marginally less renowned. Both places have dining rooms with cracking views.

Cafés and nightlife

The best of the **cafés** is the small, nonsmoking *Coco's Café* at 608 Patricia St: inexpensive and vaguely trendy, with newspapers and magazines to pass the time over excellent snacks and coffees. A short distance away, on the upper level of the small "mall" at 610 Patricia St, *Spooner's* (☎852-4046) is also a good place for the usual café drinks and snacks – it has outdoor terrace seating and a bright, airy interior with rooftop and mountain views. Coffee and computer fiends might also head to the *Soft Rock Internet Café* in Connaught Square, a mini "mall" at 633 Connaught Drive. Turn left after the station for the utilitarian but very cheap *Smitty's Restaurant*, where you can drink coffee and write postcards all day.

Most **drinking** goes on in the *Atha-B* lounge at the *Athabasca Hotel*, 510 Patricia St, where the "nightclub" annexe has dancing and live music most nights, though things can get pretty rowdy. For something more relaxed, try *Pete's* bar, upstairs at 614 Patricia St, enter through the nondescript black door – once inside, it's big and bustling, with a laid-back young crowd. Another unpretentious locals' hangout is the *Astoria*'s *De'd Dog Bar* at 404 Connaught Drive, which attracts more of a thirtyish crowd, with big-screen TV, music, darts and food. The bar in *Whistler's Inn* opposite the station has an old-style wooden bar and lots of memorabilia. If you want a more smoochy evening, the *Bonhomme Lounge* at the *Château Jasper*, 96 Geikie St, has a harpist most nights. The Chaba Theatre is a first-run **cinema** directly opposite the station. Nightlife generally is low-key: most of the campsites and motels are too far out of town for people to get in, and the fun is generally of the make-your-own variety out at hostels or campsites. Every second year (even years) the town hosts the **Jasper Heritage Folk Festival** with performers from across North America playing in Centennial Park.

Mount Robson Provincial Park

The extensive **MOUNT ROBSON PROVINCIAL PARK** borders Jasper National Park to the west and protects Mount Robson which, at 3954m, is the highest peak in the Canadian Rockies. Its scenery equals anything anywhere else in the Rockies, and **Mount Robson** itself is one of the most staggering mountains you'll ever encounter. Facilities are thin on the ground, so stock up on food and fuel before entering the park. Around 16km beyond the park's western boundary Hwy 16 comes the Tête Jaune

HIKING IN MOUNT ROBSON PARK

Starting 2km from the park visitor centre, the **Berg Lake Trail** (22km one-way; 795m ascent) is perhaps the most popular short backpacking trip in the Rockies, and the only trail that gets anywhere near Mount Robson. You can do the first third or so as a comfortable and highly rewarding day-walk, passing through forest to lovely glacier-fed Kinney Lake (6.7km; campsite at the lake's northeast corner). Many rank this among the Rockies best day-hikes and it's particularly good for naturalists. Trek the whole thing, however, and you traverse the stupendous Valley of a Thousand Waterfalls – the most notable being sixty-metre Emperor Falls (14.3km; campsites 500m north and 2km south) – and eventually enjoy the phenomenal area around Berg Lake itself (17.4km to its nearest, western shore). Mount Robson rises an almost sheer 2400m from the lakeshore, its huge cliffs cradling two creaking rivers of ice, Mist Glacier and Berg Glacier – the latter, one of the Rockies' few "living" or advancing glaciers, is 1800m long by 800m wide and the source of the great icebergs that give the lake its name. Beyond the lake you can pursue the trail 2km further to Robson Pass (21.9km; 1652m ascent; campsite) and another 1km to Adolphus Lake in Jasper National Park. The most popular campsites are the *Berg Lake* (19.6km) and *Rearguard* (20.1km) campsites on Berg Lake itself; but if you've got a Jasper backcountry permit you could press on to Adolphus where there's a less-frequented site with more in the way of solitude.

Once you're camped at Berg Lake, a popular day-trip is to Toboggan Falls, which starts from the southerly *Berg Lake* campsite and climbs the northeast (left) side of Toboggan Creek past a series of cascades and meadows to eventual views over the lake's entire hinterland. The trail peters out after 2km, but you can easily walk on and upward through open meadows for still better views. The second trail in the immediate vicinity is Robson Glacier (2km), a level walk that peels off south from the main trail 1km west of Robson Pass near the park ranger's cabin. It runs across an outwash plain to culminate in a small lake at the foot of the glacier; a rougher track then follows the lateral moraine on the glacier's east side, branching east after 3km to follow a small stream to the summit of Snowbird Pass (9km total from the ranger's cabin).

Two more hikes start from Yellowhead Lake, at the other (eastern) end of the park. To get to the trailhead for **Yellowhead Mountain** (4.5km one-way; 715m ascent), follow Hwy 16 9km down from the pass and then take a gravel road 1km on an isthmus across the lake. After a steep two-hour climb through forest, the trail levels out in open country at 1830m, offering sweeping views of the Yellowhead Pass area. The **Mount Fitzwilliam Trail** (13km one-way; 945m ascent), which leaves Hwy 16 about 1km east of the Yellowhead Mountain Trail (but on the other side of the highway), is a more demanding walk, especially over its last half, but if you don't want to backpack to the endpoint – a truly spectacular basin of lakes and peaks – you could easily walk through the forest to the campsite at Rockingham Creek (6km).

Cache, where you can pick up one of two immensely scenic roads: the continuation of Hwy 16 north to Prince George (for routes to Prince Rupert, northern BC and the Yukon), or Hwy 5, which heads south past Wells Gray Provincial Park to Kamloops and a whole range of onward destinations: the latter route is dealt with on p.812.

Both road and rail links to the park from Jasper climb through **Yellowhead Pass**, long one of the most important native and fur-trading routes across the Rockies. The pass, 20km west of Jasper Townsite, marks the boundary between Jasper and Mount Robson parks, Alberta and British Columbia, and Mountain and Pacific time zones – set your watch back one hour. This stretch of road is less dramatic than the Icefields Parkway, but then most roads are, given over to mixed woodland – birch interspersed with firs – and mountains that sit back from the road with less scenic effect. The railway meanders alongside the road most of the way, occasionally occupied by epic freight trains hundreds of wagons long – alien intrusions in the usual beguiling wilderness of rocks, river and forest. Just down from the pass, **Yellowhead Lake** is the park's first landmark. Look for moose around dawn and dusk at aptly named **Moose Lake**, another 20km further west.

Mount Robson

Even if the first taste of the park seems relatively tame, the first sight of **Mount Robson** is among the most breathtaking in the Rockies. The preceding ridges creep up in height hiding the massive peak itself from view until the last moment. The British explorer W.B. Cheadle described the mountain in 1863: "On every side the mighty heads of snowy hills crowded round, whilst, immediately behind us, a giant among giants, and immeasurably supreme, rose Robson's peak . . . We saw its upper portion dimmed by a necklace of light, feathery clouds, beyond which its pointed apex of ice, glittering in the morning sun, shot up far into the blue heaven above."

The telephone code for the Mount Robson Provincial Park is ☎250.

The overall impression is of immense size, thanks mainly to the colossal scale of Robson's south face – a sheer rise of 3100m – and to the view from the road, which frames the mountain as a single mass isolated from other peaks. A spectacular glacier system, concealed on the mountain's north side, is visible if you make the popular back-packing hike to the Berg Lake area (see box overleaf). The source of the mountain's name has never been agreed on, but could be a corruption of Robertson, a Hudson's Bay employee who was trapped in the region in the 1820s. Local natives called the peak *Yuh-hai-has-hun* – the "Mountain of the Spiral Road", an allusion to the clearly visible layers of rock that resemble a road winding to the summit. Not surprisingly, this mono-lith was one of the last major peaks in the Rockies to be conquered – it was first climbed in 1913, and is still considered a dangerous challenge.

Practicalities

Trains don't stop anywhere in the park, but if you're travelling by bus you can ask to be let off at Yellowhead Pass or the **Mount Robson Travel Infocentre** (daily June to early Sept 9am–7pm; no phone), located at the Mount Robson viewpoint near the west-ern entrance to the park. Most of the park's few other facilities are found near the infocentre: a **café/garage** (May–Sept) and two fully serviced commercial **campsites** – *Emperor Ridge* (☎566-8438; $13.50; June–Sept), 300m north of Hwy 16 on Kinney Lake Road, and *Mount Robson Lodge & Robson Shadows Campground* (☎566-9190, 566-4821 or 1-888/566-4821; $14.50; mid-May to mid-Oct), 25 nice sites on the Fraser River side of Hwy 16, 5km west of the park boundary. The 144-site *Mount Robson Provincial Park Campground* (☎566-4325; both $17.50; April–Oct) comprises two closely adjacent campsites – *Robson River* and *Robson Meadows* – and is situated further afield on Hwy 16, 22km north of Valemount. It offers hots showers and flush toilets and reservations can be made in advance (see box, p.663). Another park campsite with the same name and the tag "Lucerne" (which has no reservations, dry toilets only and no showers; $12; May–Sept) is situated 10km west of the Alberta border on Hwy 16, just west of the east-ern boundary of the Mount Robson Provincial Park. The only other beds in or near the park are the eighteen log-sided riverfront units (some with kitchens; $5 extra) at the *Mount Robson Lodge* (☎566-4821 or 1-888/566-4821; ④ May–Oct) that owns the *Robson Shadows Campground* (meals, river rafting, helicopter tours and horse riding are avail-able nearby); and the cabins belonging to Mount Robson Adventure Holidays (☎566-4351; ③; June–Sept), 16km east of the infocentre (towards Jasper), though preference for these may go to people signed up for the company's **canoeing** and **hiking** day-trips.

Backcountry camping in the park is only permitted at seven wilderness campsites dotted along the Berg Lake Trail (see box on p.659): to use these you have to register and pay an overnight fee at the infocentre.

Yoho National Park

Wholly in British Columbia on the western side of the Continental Divide, **YOHO NATIONAL PARK**'s name derives from a Cree word meaning "wonder" – a fitting testament to the awesome grandeur of the region's mountains, lakes and waterfalls. At the same time it's a small park, whose intimate scale makes it perhaps the finest of the four parks and the one favoured by Rockies' connoisseurs. The Trans-Canada divides Yoho neatly in half, climbing from Lake Louise over the **Kicking Horse Pass** to share the broad, glaciated valley bottom of the Kicking Horse River with the old Canadian Pacific Railway. The only village, **Field**, has the park centre, services and limited accommodation (the nearest full-service towns are Lake Louise, 28km east, and **Golden**, 54km west). Other expensive accommodation is available at the central hubs, **Lake O'Hara**, the **Yoho Valley** and **Emerald Lake**, from which radiate most of the park's stunning and well-maintained trails – **hiking** in Yoho is magnificent – and a couple of lodges just off the Trans-Canada. Thus these areas – not Field – are the focal points of the park, and get very busy in summer. Side roads lead to Emerald Lake and the Yoho Valley, so if you choose you can drive in, do a hike and then move on at night.

Access to Lake O'Hara is far more difficult, being reserved for those on foot, or those with lodge or campsite reservations, who must book for a special bus (full details are given on pp.664–670). The other five park-run campsites are all much more readily accessible, and there's a single road-accessible youth hostel in the Yoho Valley. The park also operates six backcountry campsites (see p.668). The Trans-Canada also gives direct access to short but scenic trails; as these take only an hour or so, they're the best choice if you only want a quick taste of the park before moving on. If you have time for one day walk, make it the **Iceline–Whaleback–Twin Falls Trail**, rated among the top five day-hikes in the Rockies (see the box on p.666 for details of all hikes in the park). If you're cycling, note that **mountain biking** – very popular in the park – is restricted to several designated trails only: these are Kicking Horse (19.5km); the Amiskwi Trail to the Amiskwi River crossing (24km); the Otterhead Trail to Toche Ridge junction (8km); Ice River to Lower Ice Ridge warden cabin (17.5km); the Talley-Ho Trail (3km); and the Ottertail Trail as far as the warden cabin (14.7km).

> The telephone code for the Yoho National Park is ☎250.

Field

No more than a few wooden houses, and backed by an amphitheatre of sheer-dropped mountains, **FIELD** looks like an old-world pioneer settlement, little changed from its 1884 origins as a railroad-construction camp (named after Cyrus Field, sponsor of the first transatlantic communication cable, who visited Yoho that year). As in other national parks, it was the railway that first spawned tourism in the area: the first hotel in Field was built by Canadian Pacific in 1886, and within a few months sixteen square kilometres at the foot of Mount Stephen (the peak to Field's east) had been set aside as a special reserve. National park status arrived in 1911, making Yoho the second of Canada's national parks.

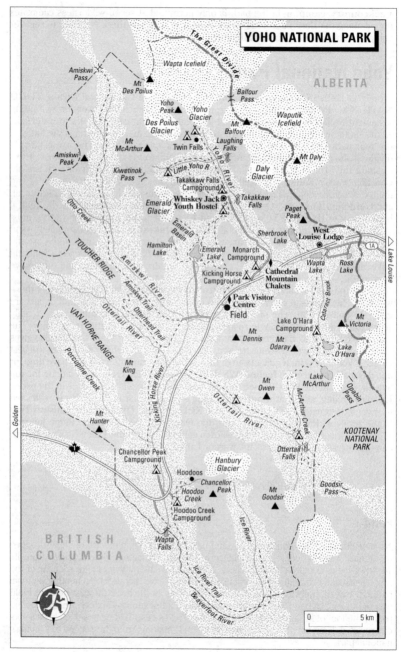

YOHO NATIONAL PARK

ALBERTA

BRITISH COLUMBIA

KOOTENAY NATIONAL PARK

The Great Divide

Wapta Icefield

Amiskwi Pass

Mt Des Poilus

Yoho Peak

Yoho Glacier

Balfour Pass

Waputik Icefield

Des Poilus Glacier

Mt McArthur

Twin Falls

Laughing Falls

Mt Balfour

Mt Daly

Amiskwi Peak

Kiwetinok Pass

Little Yoho R

Daly Glacier

Takakkaw Falls Campground

Yoho River

Otto Creek

Emerald Glacier

Whiskey Jack Youth Hostel

Takakkaw Falls

Paget Peak

West Louise Lodge

Emerald Basin

Sherbrook Lake

Hamilton Lake

Emerald Lake

Monarch Campground

Wapta Lake

Ross Lake

1A

Lake Louise

Toucher Ridge

Amiskwi River

Kicking Horse Campground

Cathedral Mountain Chalets

Cataract Brook

Amiskwi Trail

Otterhead Trail

Park Visitor Centre

Field

Lake O'Hara Campground

Mt Victoria

Van Horne Range

Ottertail River

Kicking Horse River

Mt Dennis

Mt Odaray

Lake O'Hara

Porcupine Creek

Mt King

Mt Owen

Lake McArthur

McArthur Creek

Opabin Pass

Golden

Mt Hunter

Ottertail River

Ottertail Falls

KOOTENAY NATIONAL PARK

Chancellor Peak Campground

Hoodoos

Hanbury Glacier

Mt Goodsir

Goodsir Pass

Hoodoo Creek

Chancellor Peak

Hoodoo Creek Campground

Ice River

Wapta Falls

Ice River Trail

Beaverfoot River

N

0   5 km

Passenger services (other than private excursions) no longer come through Field, but the **railway** is still one of the park "sights", and among the first things you see whether you enter the park from east or west. That it came this way at all was the result of desperate political and economic horse trading. The Canadian Pacific's chief surveyor, Sandford Fleming, wrote of his journey over the proposed Kicking Horse Pass route in 1883: "I do not think I can forget that terrible walk; it was the greatest trial I ever experienced." Like many in the company he was convinced the railway should take the much lower and more amenable Yellowhead route to the north (see "Mount Robson Provincial Park"). The railway was as much a political as a transportational tool, and designed to unite the country and encourage settlement of the prairies. A northerly route would have ignored great tracts of valuable prairie near the US border (around Calgary), and allowed much of the area and its resources (later found to include oil and gas) to slip from the Dominion into the hands of the US. Against all engineering advice, therefore, the railway was cajoled into taking the Kicking Horse route, and thus obliged to negotiate four-percent grades, the greatest of any commercial railway of the time.

The result was the infamous **Spiral Tunnels**, two vast figure-of-eight galleries within the mountains; from a popular viewpoint about 7km east of Field on Hwy 1, you can watch the front of goods trains emerge from the tunnels before the rear wagons have even entered. Still more notorious was the **Big Hill**, where the line drops 330m in just 6km from Wapta Lake to the flats east of Field (the 4.5 percent grade was the steepest in North America). The very first construction train to attempt the descent plunged into the canyon, killing three railway workers. Runaways became so common that four blasts on a whistle became the standard warning for trains careering out of control (the rusted wreck of an engine can still be seen near the main *Kicking Horse Park Campground*). Lady Agnes MacDonald, wife of the Canadian prime minister, rode down the Big Hill on the front cowcatcher (a metal frame in front of the locomotive to scoop off animals) in 1886, remarking that it presented a "delightful opportunity for a new sensation". She'd already travelled around 1000km on her unusual perch: her lily-livered husband, with whom she was meant to be sharing the symbolic trans-Canada journey to commemorate the opening of the railway, managed just 40km on the cowcatcher. Trains climbing the hill required four locomotives to pull a mere fifteen coaches: the ascent took over an hour, and exploding boilers (and resulting deaths) were recurrent.

The Burgess Shales

Yoho today ranks as highly among geologists as it does among hikers and railway buffs, thanks to the world-renowned **Burgess Shales**, an almost unique geological formation situated close to Field village. The shales – layers of sedimentary rock – lie on the upper slopes of Mount Field and consist of the fossils of some 120 types of soft-bodied marine

---

PROVINCIAL CAMPSITES

Tent and RV sites at many public campsites in British Columbia's Provincial Parks can now be reserved in advance through Discover Camping (March to mid-Sept Mon–Fri 7am–7pm, Sat & Sun 9am–5pm Pacific Standard Time; ☎1-800/689-9025 or Vancouver ☎604/689-9025). Reservations can be made up to three months in advance but no later than 48 hours before the first day of arrival. Cancellations can be made after 7pm by following the recorded instructions. A nonrefundable booking fee of $6.42 per night, up to a maximum of three nights ($19.26), is charged. You can stay in any single BC Provincial park for up to fourteen days; advance payment by Visa or MasterCard only, and additional nights once at a campsite are cash only. For general information on the parks, call ☎250/387-4550 or 660-2421 from within Greater Vancouver or ☎1-800/663-7867 from elsewhere in BC, *www.elp.gov.bc.ca/bcparks*.

RAFTING IN THE ROCKIES

If lazing around Maligne Lake in Jasper, or walking the odd trail elsewhere in the Rockies, sounds a bit tame, think about **white-water rafting** – currently all the rage in the national parks, and Jasper in particular. Many operators, notably in Jasper, Golden (near Yoho National Park) and in Banff, cater to an ever-growing demand. Not all trips are white-knuckle affairs. Depending on the river and trip you choose, some rafting tours are just that – gentle rafting down placid stretches of river. Others require that you be fit and a strong swimmer. Trips last anything from a couple of hours to a couple of days. Operators will point to the right trips (see "Activities" sections under national park headings for Banff and Lake Louise operators).

While no previous experience is required for most tours, one or two things are worth knowing; the most important is how rivers are **graded**. White water is ranked in six classes: Class 1 is gentle and Class 6 is basically a waterfall. The **season** generally runs from May to mid-September, with the "biggest" water in June and July, when glacial melt-water is coursing down rivers. Operators are licensed by the park authorities and invariably supply you with everything you need, from the basics of helmet and life jacket to wet suits, wool sweaters and spray jackets depending on the likely severity of the trip. They also provide shuttle services from main centres to the rivers themselves, and many on longer trips include lunch, snack or barbecue in the tour price. Bigger operators may also have on-site shower and changing facilities if you're on a run where you're likely to get seriously wet. On any trip it's probably a good idea to have a change of clothes handy for when you finish, wear training shoes or something you don't mind getting wet, and have a towel and bag for any valuables. Many people sport swimming costumes beneath clothing. Often you can choose between trips – gentle or severe – where you sit back and hang on while others do the work in oared boats, or you join a trip where everyone gets a paddle who wants one.

At Banff the **Bow River** has no major rapids, and gentle one-hour float trips are offered through pretty scenery by several operators. Most companies in Banff or Lake Louise offer trips on one of two rivers to the west of the park. The **Kootenay River** in Kootenay National Park, two hours from Banff, is a Class 2–3 river. The **Kicking Horse River**, a premier destination just an hour from Banff, is a much more serious affair. In and just outside Yoho National Park, it has Class 4 sections (Cable Car, Man Eater Hole, Goat Rapid, Twin Towers and the Roller Coaster) in its upper sections and stretches in the Lower Kicking Horse Canyon which give even seasoned rafters pause for thought.

Jasper has perhaps the most possibilities on its doorstep. The Class 2 **Athabasca River** (from Athabasca Falls, 35km south of the town) is scenic and provides gentle rafting for families or those who just want a quiet river trip from May to October, but it also has one or two harmless white-water sections. The **Sunwapta River** nearby, 55km south

creatures from the Middle Cambrian period (515–530 million years ago), one of only three places in the world where the remains of these unusual creatures are found. Soft-bodied creatures usually proved ill-suited to the fossilization process, but in the Burgess Shales the fossils are so well preserved and detailed that in some cases scientists can identify what the creatures were eating before they died. Plans are in hand to open a major new museum in Field devoted to the Shales, but in the meantime access is restricted to protect the fossils, and fossil-hunting, needless to say, is strictly prohibited. The area can only be seen on two strenuous guided hikes to Walcott's Quarry and the Trilobite beds. The walks are led by qualified guides, limited to fifteen people and run between late June and October. For details and reservations, contact the Yoho Burgess Shale Foundation (☎1-800/343-3006).

Practicalities

Yoho's **park information centre**, marked by a distinctive blue roof about 1km east of Field (daily: mid-May to late June & Sept 9am–5pm; late June to Aug 8.30am–

of Jasper, is a Class 3 river with some thrilling stretches of water, magnificent scenery and good chances to spot wildlife. The **Maligne River**, 45km from town, is Class 2–3+, offering a wide variety of trips between July and September for the many operators who use this river (including a lively 1.6-kilometre stretch of rapids). Yet the most riotous local river is the **Fraser**, accessed an hour west of Jasper in Mount Robson Provincial Park. This is Class 4 in places, but also has some gentle sections where the chance to watch salmon spawning at close quarters from mid-August to September provides an added attraction.

Operators in Jasper include Maligne River Adventures, 627 Patricia St (☎852-3370, fax 852-3405), who run some of the wildest trips in the park: the four-hour "Sunwapta Challenge" ($60) uses six-passenger paddle-assisted rafts to ride parts of the Sunwapta – which means "turbulent river" in the local Stoney language. All equipment is supplied as are changing rooms and hot showers. They also offer two-hour "Mile 5 Run" (3 daily, $40) raft trips on the Athabasca River on small but lively rapids and three-hour "Heritage Run" trips (small paddle raft $55, larger passenger oar raft $40) on the same river suitable for families and children, as well as a three-day wilderness trip to the Kakwa and Smoky rivers. Jasper Raft Tours at Jasper Adventure Centre, 604 Connaught Drive (☎852-2665 or 1-888/553-5628) offer good trips for first-timers: two- to three-hour jaunts twice daily in summer on the Athabasca River in comfortable oar rafts. Tickets cost $41, including shuttle to and from the river, with possible pick-ups from your hotel by prior arrangement; tickets are also available from the Brewster office in the train station. Another long-established company offers similar trips at similar prices to suit all ages and courage levels on several rivers: White Water Rafting (Jasper) Ltd (☎852-7238 or 1-800/557-7328, fax 852-3623, *www.whitewaterjasper.com*), with advance reservations from Freewheel Cycles, 618 Patricia St, and Alpine Petro Canada, 711 Connaught Drive – they claim to run trips in all weathers and make special provisions for visitors with disabilities. A two-hour trip on Grade 2 Athabasca water costs $40, three hours $50 (3 and 2 trips daily respectively); a two-hour Grade 3 trip on the Sunwapta costs $40 (2 daily).

If you want the real **rough stuff** on the Fraser contact Sekani Mountain Tours, Work World Store, 618 Patricia St (☎852-5211), for twenty Class 3 and 4 rapids along the fourteen-kilometre "Rearguard Run" (6hr 30min; $70 including lunch). If you're experienced you can join the 16km of continuous Class 4 and 4+ rapids on the "Canoe River" (8hr; $100) or put these together with the Rearguard in a two-day camping trip for $160. At the other extreme, the same company runs quiet punt-like trips to admire Mount Robson and see the salmon on the Fraser (10km; 5hr 30min; $35), as do Mount Robson Adventure Holidays (2hr; $39; ☎1-800/882-9921), whose twice-daily raft departures are complemented by an evening run during August. They also offer three-hour guided trips by canoe ($45) to Moose Marsh to spot birds and wildlife, with no experience necessary for this or their rafting trips.

7pm; Oct to mid-May 9am–4pm; ☎343-6783 or 343-6433, *www.parkscanada.pch .gc.ca/yoho*), sells park permits, makes backcountry registrations, takes bookings for Lake O'Hara (see p.668), has displays, lectures and slide shows (notably on the famous Burgess Shales), and advises on trail and climbing conditions. It also gives out a useful *Backcountry Guide* with full details of all trails and sells 1:50,000 **maps** of the park. Backcountry camping requires a permit, and if you intend to camp at Lake O'Hara (see p.668) it's essential to make **reservations** at the information centre. The Park Administration Office in Field offers similar help and services in and out of season (Mon–Fri 8am–4.30pm; ☎343-6324). Enquire at the park centre for details of activities arranged by the "Friends of Yoho" (☎343-6393) and the two free guided walks: "Emerald Lakeshore Stroll" (July to late Aug Sat 10am; 2hr 30min/5km; meet at Emerald Lake Trailhead) and "Walk into the Past" (July & Aug Mon & Thurs 7pm; 1hr 30min; meet at the Old Bake oven at *Kicking Horse Campground*). Other park-run activites include Kicking Horse Campground Theatre

HIKES IN YOHO NATIONAL PARK

HIKES FROM LAKE O'HARA

For walking purposes the Lake O'Hara region divides into five basic zones, each of which deserves a full day of exploration: Lake Oesa, the Opabin Plateau (this area and others are often closed to protect their grizzlies), Lake McArthur, the Odaray Plateau and the Duchesnay Basin.

If you have time to do only one day-hike, the classic (if not the most walked) trails are the Wiwaxy Gap (12km; 495m ascent), rated by some among the top five day-walks in the Canadian Rockies, or the Opabin Plateau Trail (3.2km one-way; 250m ascent), from the *Lake O'Hara Lodge* to Opabin Lake. Despite the latter's brevity, you could spend hours wandering the plateau's tiny lakes and alpine meadows on the secondary trails that criss-cross the area. Most people return to O'Hara via the East Circuit Trail, but a still more exhilarating hike – and a good day's outing – is to walk the Yukness Ledge, a section of the Alpine Circuit (see below) that cuts up from the East Circuit just 400m after leaving Opabin Lake. This spectacular high-level route leads to the beautiful Lake Oesa, from where it's just 3.2km down to Lake O'Hara. Oesa is one of many beautiful lakes in the region, and the Lake Oesa Trail (3.2km one-way; 240m ascent) from Lake O'Hara is the single most walked path in the O'Hara area. Close behind comes the Lake McArthur Trail (3.5km one-way; 310m ascent) which leads to the largest and most photographed of the lakes in the Lake O'Hara area. The Odaray Plateau Trail (2.6km one-way; 280m ascent) is another highly rated, but rather overpopular hike.

The longest and least-walked path is the Linda Lake–Cathedral Basin trip, past several lakes to a great viewpoint at Cathedral Platform Prospect (7.4km one-way; 305m ascent). The most challenging hike is the high-level Alpine Circuit (11.8km), taking in Oesa, Opabin and Schaffer lakes. This is straightforward in fine weather, and when all the snow has melted; very fit and experienced walkers should have little trouble, though there's considerable exposure, and some scrambling is required. At other times it's best left to climbers, or left alone completely.

YOHO VALLEY AND EMERALD LAKE HIKES

Most trails in the Yoho Valley area start from the Takakkaw Falls campsite and car park at the end of the Yoho Valley Road. Many of the area's trails connect, and some run over the ridge to the Emerald Lake region, offering numerous permutations. We've tried to highlight the very best. If you want a stroll from the main trailhead at the campsite after a drive or cycle, then walk to Point Lace Falls (1.9km one-way; minimum ascent) or Laughing Falls (3.8km one-way; 60m gain). Another shortish, extremely popular walk from the same car park is the Yoho Pass (10.9km; 310m ascent, 510m height loss), which links to Emerald Lake and its eponymous lodge (though you'll need transport arranged at the lake). A southern branch from this hike will take you over the Burgess Pass and down into Field, another manageable day-trip with fine overviews of the entire area.

If you want to follow the most tramped path in the Yoho Valley, however, take the Twin Falls Trail (8.5km one-way; 290m ascent) from the Takakkaw Falls car park. This easy six-hour return journey passes the Laughing Falls (see above) and has the reward of the Twin Falls cataract at the end, plus fine scenery and other lesser waterfalls en route. Stronger walkers could continue over the highly recommended Whaleback Trail (4.5km one-way; 1hr 30min) to give some quite incredible views of the glaciers at the valley head. A complete circuit returning to Takakkaw Falls with the Whaleback is 20.1km.

(July & Aug Sat, Sun & Tues at 9pm, 8pm last ten days of Aug) and wildlife and other talks at the Hoodoo Creek Campfire Circle (July & Aug Mon & Fri 9pm, 8pm last ten days of Aug).

Whatever other literature may say, there are now no VIA Rail passenger trains to Field. The village is, however, a flag stop for Greyhound **buses** (5 daily in each direc-

If you're allowing yourself just one big walk in Yoho it's going to be a hard choice between the Takakkaw Falls–Twin Falls–Whaleback Trail just described or the Iceline–Little Yoho Valley–(Whaleback)–Twin Falls combination. The latter is often cited as one of the top five day-walks in the Rockies, and on balance might be the one to go for, though both options duplicate parts of one another's route. The Iceline (695m vertical gain), specially built in 1987, also starts close to the Takakkaw Falls car park at the *Whiskey Jack* youth hostel, climbing west through a large avalanche path onto a level bench with jaw-dropping views of the Emerald Glacier above and the Daly Glacier across the valley. It contours above Lake Celeste (a trail drops to this lake, making a shorter 17km circuit in all back to the car park) and then drops to the Little Yoho Valley and back to Takakkaw Falls for a 19.8-kilometre circuit. If you're very fit (or can camp overnight to break the trip), tagging on the Whaleback before returning to Takakkaw Falls makes a sensational 27-kilometre walk with 1000m of ascent.

Most people will want to do this as a backpacking option (there are four backcountry sites up here) – and they don't come much better – though the Iceline–Little Yoho walk coupled with the trek west to the Kiwetinok Pass (30km; 1070m) is also in many people's list of top-five day/backpacking Rocky Mountain walks. Juggling further with the permutations brings the Whaleback into this last combination to make one of the best backpacking routes in the Rockies: Iceline–Little Yoho Valley–Kiwetinok Pass–Whaleback (35.5km, 1375m ascent), a route up there with the Rockwall Trail in Kootenay, Skyline in Jasper and Berg Lake in Mount Robson Provincial Park.

From Emerald Lake, if you just want a stroll, then follow the self-guided and wheelchair-accessible nature trail (4.6km circuit; minimal ascent) around the lake from the parking area to the bridge at the back of the lake. Even shorter is the trail from the entrance to the parking area to Hamilton Falls (1.6km return; minimal ascent). The best day-trip is the comparatively underused but interesting Hamilton Lake Trail (5.5km one-way; 850m vertical; 2–3hr), again leaving from the parking area at the end of Emerald Lake Road. It's demanding and steep in places, and confined to forest for the first hour or so – thereafter it's magnificent, culminating in a classic alpine lake. The more modest climb to Emerald Basin, which you could manage in half a day (4.3km one-way; 300m vertical; 1–2hr), also gives relative peace and quiet, following the lakeshore before climbing through a forest of yew and hemlock, and ending in a small, rocky amphitheatre of hanging glaciers and avalanche paths.

HIKES FROM THE TRANS-CANADA

Five short walks can be accessed off the Trans-Canada Highway as it passes through Yoho. From east to west these are: Ross Lake (1.3km), a stunning little walk given the loveliness of the lake and the ease with which you reach it (accessed 1km south of the Great Divide picnic area); Sherbrooke Lake (3.1km), a peaceful subalpine lake accessible from the Wapta Lake picnic area (5km west of the Great Divide), where stronger walkers can peel off after 1.4km to Paget Lookout for huge views of the Kicking Horse Valley (3.5km; 520m ascent); Mount Stephen Fossil Beds (2.7km), a short but very steep trail, for fossil lovers only, from 1st Street East in Field; Hoodoo Creek (3.1km), on the western edge of the park (22km west of Field), accessed from the 600-metre gravel road from the *Hoodoo Creek* campsite (the steep path leads to the weirdly eroded hoodoos themselves, pillars of glacial debris topped by protective capping stones); and finally Wapta Falls (2.4km), an excellent and almost level forty-minute walk on a good trail to Yoho's largest waterfalls (by volume of water), accessed via a 1.6-kilometre dirt road 25km west of Field.

tion) – wave them down from the Petro-Canada just east of the turn-off from the highway to the village, though most stop anyway to drop packages.

Yoho's popularity and accessibility mean huge pressure on **accommodation** in late July and August: if you're really stuck, you can always make for one of the motels in Golden (see p.671). The only officially listed **rooms** in Field itself, a fine base if you have transport, are at the excellent *Kicking Horse Lodge and Café*, 100 Centre St (café open summer only; ☎343-6303 or 1-800/659-4944; ⑥), though you can also try one of the new so-called B&B "kitchens" – fully furnished suites in private homes – of which there were ten dotted around the village at last count: *Alpenglow Guesthouse* (☎343-6356); *Mount Burgess Bungalow* (☎343-6480); *Bear's Den Guesthouse* (☎343-6439); *Canadian Rockies Guesthouse* (☎343-6046); *Lynx Lair* (☎343-6421); *Mount Stephen Guesthouse* (☎343-6441); *Otterhead Guesthouse* (☎343-6034); *Sunset Guesthouse* (☎343-6333); *Van Horne Guesthouse* (☎343-6380); and *Yoho Accommodation* (☎343-6444 or 343-6445) – all ④. All are similarly and reasonably priced, and all are easily found in the tiny village – call for precise directions – most lying on the central 1st Avenue or parallel Kicking Horse Avenue.

Away from the village, but on or just off the Trans-Canada (Hwy 1), the twenty units of *Cathedral Mountain Chalets* (☎343-6442; off-season from Oct to mid-May ☎ or fax 403/762-0514, *www.cathedralmountain.com*; ⑦; mid-May to mid-Oct), 4km east of Field and fifteen-minutes' drive from Lake Louise (leave the highway at the Takakkaw Falls turn-off), and the bigger and less expensive fifty-room *West Louise Lodge* (☎343-6311; ⑤) just inside the park boundary, 11km west of Lake Louise (with café, restaurant and indoor pool). There's also the **youth hostel** in the Yoho Valley (see p.670), perfectly situated for many superb walks, and an expensive lodge at Emerald Lake.

The most central of the five park-run **campsites**, the 86-site *Kicking Horse* ($18; mid-May to early Oct), lies 5km east of Field just off the Trans-Canada (Hwy 1) near the junction with Yoho Valley Road for Takakkaw Falls. It's fully serviced (coin showers) and pleasingly forested, though it echoes somewhat with goods trains rumbling through day and night. In summer a separate overflow site is often opened (no showers), but even this fills up and you should aim to arrive extremely early. Remember: all park campsites are first-come, first-served. A short distance east up Yoho Valley Road is the second of the park's major campsites, the 46-site *Monarch* ($13; late June to early Sept): the third, the 35-site *Takakkaw Falls* ($13; late June to first snow) lies at the end of the same road by the eponymous falls and is the best-placed for local hikes (see box overleaf). The remaining two sites are both close to the park's western border, lying just north and south of the Trans-Canada: the 106-site *Hoodoo Creek* (no showers; $14; late June to early Sept) and 64-site *Chancellor Peak* (no showers; $13; early May to late Sept). An additional fee of $4 is charged at all campsites for use of firewood.

The six **backcountry campsites** (see maps opposite and p.671) are *McArthur Creek* (ten sites); *Float Creek* (four sites); *Yoho Lake* (eight sites); *Laughing Falls* (eight sites); *Twin Falls* (eight sites); and *Little Yoho* (ten sites): the only facilities are privies (except *Float Creek*) and bear poles. All of these campsites are popular, but unlike the front country campsites (where it's first-come, first-served) between one and three sites at each campsite can be reserved up to 21 days in advance through the park centre at Field. **Random camping** is allowed in the Amiskwi, Otterhead, Lower Ice River and Porcupine valleys, but check current closures: you must be at least 3km from any road, 100m from water, 50m from a trail and purchase the usual $6 backcountry pass.

Lake O'Hara

Backed up against the Continental Divide at the eastern edge of the park, **Lake O'Hara** is one of the Rockies' finest all-round enclaves – staggering scenery, numerous lakes, and an immense diversity of alpine and subalpine terrain. It's a great base for concentrated hiking: you could easily spend a fortnight exploring the well-constructed trails that strike out from the central lodge and campsite. The setting is matchless, the lake framed by two of the peaks that also overlook Lake Louise across the ridge –

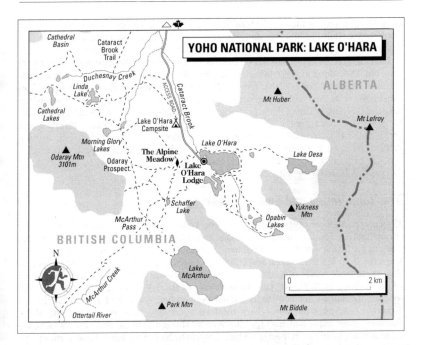

mounts Lefroy (3423m) and Victoria (3464m). The one problem is **access**, which is severely restricted to safeguard the mountain flora and fauna.

To get there, turn off the Trans-Canada onto Hwy 1A (3.2km west of the Continental Divide), cross the railway and turn right onto the gravel road leading to the parking area (1km). This fire road continues all the way up to the lake (13km), but it's not open to general traffic (or bikes – *no* bikes are allowed on the road or anywhere else in the Lake O'Hara region). Getting up here, therefore, is quite a performance, but worth it if you want to hike some of the continent's most stunning scenery. Anybody can walk the 13km up the road, or the more picturesque **Cataract Brook Trail** (12.9km), which runs roughly parallel to the road, but a quota system applies for the bus up here and the campsite at the end; and, after 13km, of course, you'd need to be superfit to get in any meaningful walking in the area where it matters. Aim instead for the special **bus** from the car park up to the lake, but note that priority is given to those with reservations or those with reservations for the lodge, campsite or Alpine Club huts. Reservations for bus and campsite can be made three months in advance by telephone only (March 20–April 18 Mon–Fri 8am–noon; April 19 to mid-June Mon–Fri 8am–4pm; mid-June to Aug daily 8am–4pm; Sept reduced hours; ☎343-6433). If you're going **for the day**, your only feasible buses leave at 8.30am and 10.30am, and the maximum number in a party is six. If you want to use the campsite you have to have dates ready (up to a maximum of four nights), state the number of people, the number of sites required (maximum of two per party, one tent per site) and your preferred bus time (first and second choices from 8.30am, 10.30am, 4.30pm or 7.30pm). The reservation fee for bus (day-use or camp) is $10 and the return bus fare $12, payable by credit card over the phone. Cancellation must be made to an answering machine (☎343-6344); you forfeit your booking fee, and you can't just cancel the first day of several you booked to camp and expect to come later. Cancellations made less than three days in advance mean you lose the booking fee, half the bus fare and, if you're camping, the first night's campsite fee. Cancel after 4pm on the day before your trip and you lose everything.

If all this sounds like Kafka has hit the Rockies, remember the park does merit attention, but if you don't manage to plan in advance there are arrangements for **stand-bys**: six day-use places are available daily and five sites are kept available each night. You must reserve at the Field park-information centre in person the day *before* you wish to take the bus and/or camp: these places are *not* available over the phone, and you'll have to get to the centre early. To stay in one of the 23 rooms at *Lake O'Hara Lodge* (☎250/343-6418, *www.lakeoharalodge.com*; ⑨; mid-June to late Sept & Feb to mid-April), you need to reserve weeks in advance and be prepared to part with a large amount of money. Out of season you can make bookings by post to Box 55, Lake Louise, AB T0L 1E0, or call ☎250/678-4110.

The Yoho Valley and Emerald Lake

Less compact an area than Lake O'Hara, the **Yoho Valley** and nearby **Emerald Lake** are far more accessible for casual visitors, and offer some great sights – the Takakkaw Falls in particular – and a variety of topnotch trails. Both areas were formerly used by the Cree to hide their women and children while the men crossed the mountains into Alberta to trade and hunt buffalo. The eradication of the buffalo herds, and the arrival of the railway in 1884, put paid to such ways. The lake was "discovered" by Tom Wilson, the same Canadian Pacific employee who first saw Lake Louise. He named it Emerald Lake after its colour. Now the lake and valley combine to form one of the Rockies' most important backpacking zones. Though popular and easily reached – access roads head north from the Trans-Canada to both the Emerald and Yoho valleys – the region is not, however, quite as crowded as its counterpart to the south. The scenery is equally mesmerizing, and if fewer of the trails are designed for day-hikes, many of them interlock so that you can tailor walks to suit your schedule or fitness (see box on p.666).

Most trails start from the end of the Yoho Valley Road at the **Takakkaw Falls** parking area; the road leaves the Trans-Canada about 5km east of Field (signed from the *Kicking Horse* campsite), a narrow and switchbacking route unsuitable for trailers and RVs and open in the summer only. It's 14km from the Trans-Canada to the parking area. The cascades' total 254-metre drop make them among the most spectacular road-accessible falls in the mountains: *takakkaw* is a Cree word roughly meaning "it is wonderful". The *Whiskey Jack* **youth hostel**, ideally placed just beyond the end of the Yoho Valley Road, 500m south of Takakkaw Falls, has room for 27 in three dorms (reservations ☎250/762-4122, *www.hostellingintl.ca/alberta*; $15–19; mid-June to mid-Sept). Close by is the park-run *Takakkaw Falls* **campsite** with 35 unserviced sites ($13; mid-June to mid-Sept). Trails to the north (see box, pp.666–667) lead to four further backcountry campsites, while the Alpine Club of Canada operates a members-only trail hut 8.5km north of Takakkaw Falls ($15); reservations are required – write to Box 1026, Banff, AB T0L 0C0, or call ☎250/762-4481.

The Emerald Lake Road leaves the Trans-Canada about 2km west of Field and ends, 8km on, at the *Emerald Lake Lodge* (☎250/343-6321 or 1-800/663-6336, *www.crmr.com*; ⑨), which has a **restaurant** where walking boots are certainly not in order, and a less formal **bar** for drinks and snacks. If you want to stay, advance reservations are essential and prices are steep – between $300 and $400 in high season, less outside summer. Like the Yoho Valley Road, this road offers access to easy strolls and a couple of good day- or half-day hikes (see box, p.666–67).

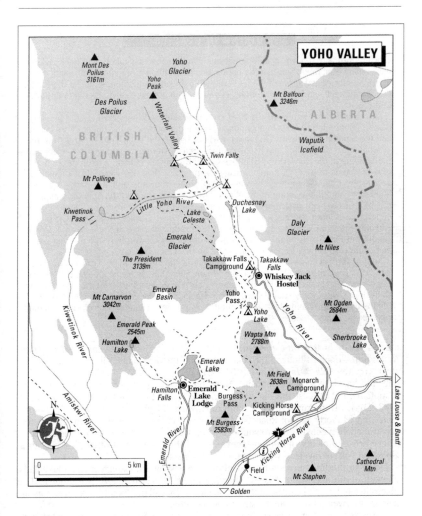

Golden

GOLDEN, 54km west of Field and midway between Yoho and Glacier national parks, is the nearest town to either. Despite its name and mountain backdrop, the part of Golden most people see is little more than an ugly ribbon of motels and garages at the junction of Hwy 1 and Hwy 95. The town proper occupies a semi-scenic site down by the Columbia River, way below the highway strip, but only if you use the municipal campsite or book one of the many rafting and other **tours** based here will you do anything but look down on it from above. The town has a small **museum** at 1302-11th St (July & Aug daily 9am–5pm; $3; ☎250/344-5169). The main **infocentre** is at 500-10th Ave N (year-round; ☎250/344-7125, fax 344-6688), but a small infocentre also sits at the strip's southern end disguised as a plastic and wood tepee (June–Sept). Two hundred

---

HIKING IN GLACIER

Glacier's primary renown is among serious climbers, but day-hikers and backpackers have plenty of options. Some of the park's 21 trails (140km of walking in all) push close to glaciers for casual views of the ice – though only two spots are now safe at the toe of the Illecillewaet – and the backcountry is noticeably less busy than in the Big Four parks to the east.

The easiest short strolls off the road are the Abandoned Rails Trail (1.2km one-way; 30min), along old rail beds to abandoned snowsheds betweeen the Rogers Pass centre and the Summit Monument (suitable for wheelchairs); the Loop Trail (1.6km) from the viewpoint just east of the Loop Brook campsite, full of viewpoints and features relating to the building of the railway; the Hemlock Grove Boardwalk (400m), a stroll through old-growth stands of western hemlock trees, some more than 350 years old (wheelchair-accessible; trailhead midway between *Loop Brook* campsite and the park's western boundary); and the Meeting of the Water Trail (30min) from the *Illecillewaet* campsite, the hub of Glacier's trail network. Six manageable day-hikes from the campsite give superb views onto the glaciers, particularly the Great Glacier, Avalanche Crest and Abbott's Ridge trails. Other hikes, not centred on the campsite, include Bostock Creek (9km) and Flat Creek (9km), a pair of paths on the park's western edge heading north and south respectively from the same point on the Trans-Canada.

Among the backpacking routes, the longest is the Beaver River Trail (30km-plus), which peels off from the highway at the Mount Shaughnessy picnic area on the eastern edge (also a favourite mountain-bike route). The single best long-haul trail, however, is the Copperstain Creek Trail (16km), which leaves the Beaver River path after 3km, and climbs to meadows and bleak alpine tundra from where camping and onward walking options are almost endless.

---

metres north is the **bus terminal**, next to the Chinese-Canadian *Golden Palace Restaurant* – open 24 hours a day, like several of the local joints. All the **motels** on the strip – try the *Selkirk Inn*, Hwy 1 (☎344-6315 or 344-5153; ④) – look over the road or onto the backs of garages opposite. None has anything you could call a view of the mountains, but at least the big *Sportsman*, 1200-12th St N (☎344-2915 or 1-888/477-6783; ③), is off the road. Around 16km northwest of Golden, the *Blaeberry Mountain Lodge*, on Moberly School Road (☎344-5296; ④), is first-rate and beautifully situated: accommodation consists of two simple but comfortable log cabins, a lodge and a tepee. There are also plenty of outdoor activities and the owners will often pick you up in Golden if you're travelling without your own transport.

Down in the town proper, a good place to **eat** standard Canadian fare like salads, chicken, pasta and seafood is the *Turning Point*, 902 11th Ave S. Note that finding places in Golden can be difficult if you don't know that all the "South" streets are on one side of the river, all the "North" streets on the other.

Campsites have prettier settings, particularly the *Whispering Spruce* (☎344-6680; $12–15) at 1430 Golden View Rd on Hwy 1 2km east of the Hwy 95 intersection. The town's own site, the *Golden Municipal Campground* (☎344-5412 or 1-800/622-4653; $13; mid-May to mid-Oct), is on the banks of the river on 10th Avenue, three blocks east of the main street. It has flush toilets, hot showers, wash houses, firewood and is adjacent to a swimming pool and tennis courts.

Glacier National Park

Strictly speaking, **GLACIER NATIONAL PARK** is part of the Selkirk and Columbia Mountains rather than the Rockies, but on the ground little sets it apart from the magnificence of the other national parks, and all the park agencies include it on an equal

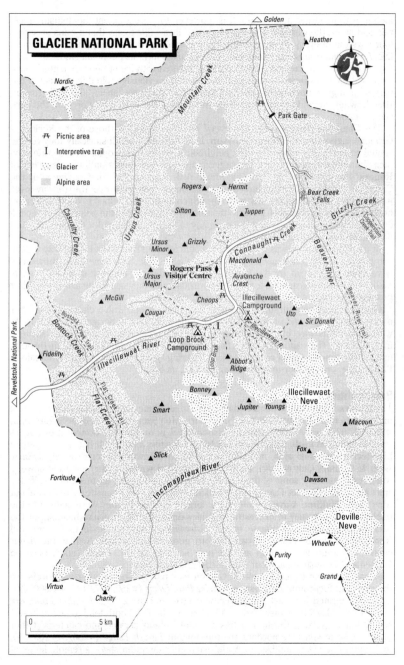

GLACIER NATIONAL PARK

Legend:
- ⅋ Picnic area
- I Interpretive trail
- ∴ Glacier
- ▨ Alpine area

N

△ Golden

▲ Heather

▲ Nordic

Mountain Creek

⅋ Park Gate

Ursus Creek

Casualty Creek

▲ Rogers   ▲ Hermit

▲ Sifton   ▲ Tupper

Bear Creek Falls

Grizzly Creek

Columbian Creek Trail

▲ Ursus Minor   ▲ Grizzly

Connaught Creek ⅋

Rogers Pass Visitor Centre ♦

▲ Macdonald

▲ Ursus Major

▲ Avalanche Crest

Beaver River

Beaver River Trail

△ Revelstoke National Park

Bostock Creek Trail

▲ McGill

⅋ Cheops

I

Illecillewaet Campground ⅋

▲ Uto   ▲ Sir Donald

Bostock Creek

▲ Cougar

Illecillewaet R.

⅋

△ Loop Brook Campground   I

Loop Brook

▲ Fidelity

Illecillewaet River

⅋

Flat Creek Trail

Abbot's Ridge

▲ Bonney

Illecillewaet Neve

▲ Smart

▲ Jupiter   ▲ Youngs

Flat Creek

▲ Macoun

▲ Slick

▲ Fox

▲ Fortitude

Incomappleux River

▲ Dawson

Deville Neve

▲ Wheeler

▲ Purity

▲ Virtue

▲ Charity

▲ Grand

0 _____ 5 km

footing with its larger neighbours. It is, however, to a great extent the domain of ice, rain and snow; the weather is so atrocious that locals like to say that it rains or snows four days out of every three, and in truth you can expect a soaking three days out of five. As the name suggests, **glaciers** – 422 of them – form its dominant landscape, with fourteen percent of the park permanently blanketed with ice or snow. Scientists have identified 68 new glaciers forming on the sites of previously melted ice sheets in the park – a highly uncommon phenomenon. The main ice sheet, the still-growing **Illecillewaet Neve**, is easily seen from the Trans-Canada Highway or from the park visitor centre.

The Columbia range's peaks are every bit as imposing as those of the Rockies – Glacier's highest point, **Mount Dawson**, is 3390m tall – and historically they've presented as much of a barrier as their neighbours. Aboriginal peoples and then railwaymen shunned the icefields and the rugged interior for centuries until the discovery of **Rogers Pass** (1321m) in 1881 by Major A.B. Rogers, the chief engineer of the Canadian Pacific. Suffering incredible hardships, navvies drove the railway over the pass by 1885, paving the way for trains which, until 1916, helped to open the region both to settlers and tourists. Despite the railway's best efforts the pounding of repeated avalanches eventually forced the company to bore a tunnel under the pass, and the flow of visitors fell to almost nothing.

In the 1950s the pass was chosen as the route for the Trans-Canada Highway, whose completion in 1962 once again made the area accessible. This time huge snowsheds were built, backed up by the world's largest **avalanche-control system**. Experts monitor the slopes year-round, and at dangerous times they call in the army, who blast howitzers into the mountains to dislodge potential slips.

Glacier is easy enough to get to, but it doesn't tie in well with a circuit of the other parks; many people end up traversing it at some point simply because the main route west passes this way, but comparatively few stop, preferring to admire the scenery from the road. The visitor centre is a flag stop for Greyhound **buses**, which zip through up to seven times a day in each direction. Entering Glacier you pass from Mountain to Pacific time – remember to set your watch back an hour.

Practicalities

The **Rogers Pass visitor centre** (daily: April to mid-June & mid-Sept to Oct 9am–5pm; mid-June to mid-Sept 8am–8.30pm; Nov Thurs–Mon 9am–5pm; Dec–March 7am–5pm ☎250/837-6274 or 837-7500, *www.parkscanada.pch.gc.ca/glacier*), 1km west of Rogers Pass, is a draw in itself, attracting some 160,000 visitors annually. It houses a variety of high-tech audiovisual aids, including a fun video on avalanche control called *Snow Wars*. In summer (July & Aug), book here for **guided walks** (1–6hr) featuring flowers, wildlife and glaciers, some of them fairly strenuous and lasting up to six hours. Walks start at the Illecillewaet Campground Welcome Station (see opposite). Also ask about trips to the **Nakimu Caves**, some of the largest in Canada: they were opened to the public (in the company of experienced guides only) in 1995. If you're heading for the backcountry, pick up *Footloose in the Columbias*, a hiker's guide to Glacier and Revelstoke national parks; you can also buy good walking **maps**. Next to the visitor centre, a **garage** and a **shop** are the only services on the Trans-Canada between Golden and Revelstoke, an hour's drive east and west respectively.

Accommodation is best sought in Golden (see p.671). The sole in-park **hotels** are the excellent fifty-room *Best Western Glacier Park Lodge* (☎250/837-2126 or 1-800/528-1234; ⑥), located just east of the visitor centre, and the 24-unit *Heather Mountain Lodge* (☎250/344-7490; closed Nov), 20km east of the Pass: both tend to be full in season. If you're passing through, it has a useful 24-hour service and cafeteria. Other places close to Glacier's borders are the ten-unit *Purcell Lodge* (☎250/344-2639; ⑥; mid-June to mid-Oct; mid-Dec to April; two-night minumum stay), a remote lodge at

2180m on the eastern border accessible only by hiking trail, scheduled helicopter flights or winter ski trails; *Canyon Hot Springs Resort Campground*, 35km east of Revelstoke (☎250/837-2420; cabins ⑦, tent sites $19–25; May–Sept), which has mineral hot and warm springs, secluded sites, café, firewood and 12 cabins with B&B deals available; *Hillside Lodge*, 1740 Seward Front Rd (☎250/344-7281; ④) – nine cosy cabins set in sixty acres 13km west of Golden at Blaeberry River with breakfast included; and *Big Lake Resort*, Kinbasket Lake (no phone; rooms ②, tents $12; May–Oct), 25km west of Golden off Hwy 1 at Donald Station.

The park-run **campsites** are the 57-site *Illecillewaet* ($13; mid-June to early Oct; also winter camping), 3.4km west of the visitor centre just off the Trans-Canada (and the trailhead for eight walks), and the twenty-site *Loop Brook*, 2km further west ($13; mid-June to mid-Oct; self-serve check-in), which provides the luxuries of wood, water and flush toilets only on a first-come, first-served basis. If you don't manage to get into these, or want more facilities, there are three commercial campsites west of the park on the Trans-Canada towards Revelstoke. Wilderness camping is allowed anywhere if you register with the visitor centre, pay for a nightly backcountry camping permit ($6) and pitch more than 5km from the road.

Mount Revelstoke National Park

The smallest national park in the region, **MOUNT REVELSTOKE NATIONAL PARK** is a somewhat arbitrary creation, put together at the request of local people in 1914 to protect the Clachnacudainn Range of the Columbia Mountains. The lines on the map mean little, for the thrilling scenery in the 16km of no-man's-land between Glacier and Revelstoke is largely the same as that within the parks. The mountains here are especially steep, their slopes often scythed clear of trees by avalanches. The views from the Trans-Canada, as it peeks out of countless tunnels, are of forests and snowcapped peaks aplenty and, far below, the railway and the Illecillewaet River crashing through a twisting, steep-sided gorge.

The main access to the park interior is the very busy **Summit Road**, or **Summit Parkway** (generally open June–Oct), which strikes north from the Trans-Canada at the town of Revelstoke and winds 26km almost to the top of Mount Revelstoke (1938m) through forest and alpine meadows noted for glorious displays of wild flowers (best during July and Aug). You can also walk this stretch on the **Summit Trail** (10km one-way; 4hr) from the car park at the base of Summit Road. Recent damage to the delicate ecosystem has prompted park authorities to rethink, and often the last 1.5km of the road is closed to cars, leaving the choice of a walk or regular shuttle bus to the summit from a car park at Balsam Lake.

Most of the longer of the park's ten official **trails** start from the top of Summit Road; serious backpackers prefer to head to **Eagle Lake**, off Summit Road, rather than take the more popular **Miller Lake Trail** (6km one-way). The award-winning **Giant Cedars Trail** is a wooded one-kilometre jaunt with ten interpretive exhibits off the road on the park's eastern edge, its boardwalks negotiating a tract of ancient forest crammed with 800-year-old western red cedars and rough-barked western hemlock (the trailhead begins at the Giant Cedars Picnic Area). You could also try the **Skunk Cabbage Boardwalk** (1.2km), an easy trail through temperate forest and wetland inhabited by muskrat, beaver, numerous birds and the eponymous skunk cabbage. **Meadows in the Sky Trail**, by contrast, is a quick one-kilometre paved loop through alpine meadows at the top of Summit Road. Look out for the so-called Icebox, a shaded rock cleft that contains what is reputedly the world's smallest glacier. The *Footloose in the Columbias* booklet, available from Glacier's Rogers Pass visitor centre, has further trail information.

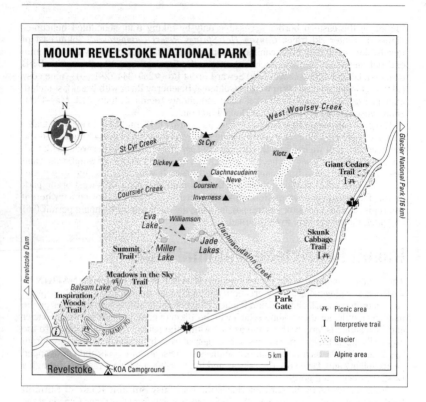

MOUNT REVELSTOKE NATIONAL PARK

West Woolsey Creek

St Cyr Creek   St Cyr

Dickey ▲   Klotz ▲

Clachnacudainn
Neve

Coursier Creek   Coursier ▲   Giant Cedars
Trail
I ⅋

Inverness ▲

Eva   Williamson
Lake   ▲

Summit   Miller   Jade
Trail   Lake   Lakes

Skunk
Cabbage
Trail
I ⅋

Meadows in the Sky
⅋ Trail
I

Balsam Lake
Inspiration
Woods
Trail

SUMMIT RD

Park
Gate

⅋   Picnic area
I   Interpretive trail
⁙   Glacier
▓   Alpine area

0   5 km

Revelstoke   KOA Campground

△ Glacier National Park (16 km)

△ Revelstoke Dam

Clachnacudainn Creek

Revelstoke

REVELSTOKE, the only community within striking range of the park, sits just outside the western boundary, but in its promotional pitch chooses to ignore its scenic appeal in favour of a somewhat unimpressive claim to be "Home of the World's Largest Sculpted Grizzly Bears" (they stand at Mackenzie Ave at the entrance to downtown). Like many mountain towns, it's divided between a motel-and-garage strip along the Trans-Canada and a dispersed, frontier-type collection of houses to the rear. The river and rugged scenery round about redeem it, and the downtown area also has a nice feel, having been spruced up as a placatory measure following the disaster at the dam site (see p.678). If you're without your own vehicle, it's a good twenty-minute walk from the strip. In downtown, you might dip into the small but polished **Revelstoke Railway Museum** (May, June, Sept & Oct Mon–Sat 9am–5pm; July & Aug daily 9am–8pm; $5; ☎250/837-6060), which has a steam engine, snowploughs and assorted memorabilia relating to the building of the stretch of the CPR between Field and Kamloops. If you want to relax close to town, try warm-watered **Williamson Lake**, a favourite swimming spot for locals with mini-golf and campsite 4km south of town east of Airport Way.

Seven daily Greyhound **buses** stop at the town of Revelstoke between Kamloops and Calgary; the terminal is at the west end of the strip, just after the big blue Columbia River bridge (☎250/837-5874). The **infocentre** is 200m beyond on the left at 204 Campbell Ave (daily: May & June 10am–6pm; July & Aug 8am–8pm; ☎250/837-5345, fax 837-4223). Between May and September there's a small additional office where the Trans-Canada and Hwy 23N meet (☎250/837-3522; same hours). Get park information at these offices, or visit the **Park Administration Office** on 3rd Street next door to the **post office** (park office: Mon–Fri 8am–4.30pm; ☎250/837-7500, fax 837-7536) or the Rogers Pass visitor centre. The park office also has a store for the Friends of Mount Revelstoke National Park (☎250/837-2010) which is useful for **maps** and guides.

Accommodation

A far more amenable place to stay than Golden, the town of Revelstoke has plenty of **accommodation** – fifteen-plus motels and half a dozen campsites.

Best Western Wayside Inn, 1901 Laforme Blvd (☎250/837-6161 or 1-800/528-1234, fax 837-5460, *www.bestwestern.com*). The priciest and best of the town's hotels. ⑤.

Columbia Motel, 301 Wright St–2nd St W (☎250/837-2191 or 1-800/663-5303, *www.columbia.revelstoke.com*). With 54 rooms, one of the larger places in town; air-conditioned and heated pool in season as an extra draw. ②.

Daniel's Hostel Guesthouse, 313 1st St (☎250/837-5530). Choice of dorm beds at $15 or private singles and doubles ($30) in a three-storey, 100-year-old house; shared bathrooms and communal kitchen; smoking outside only. ①.

Frontier Motel and Restaurant, 122 N Nakusp Hwy (☎250/837-5119 or 1-800/382-7763, fax 837-6604, *welcome@junction.net*). On the main Trans-Canada away from the town centre; good motel and first-rate food. ②.

Nelles Ranch Bed and Breakfast, Hwy 23 S (☎ & fax 250/837-3800 or 1-888/567-4177). Just six units on a working horse and cattle ranch 2km off the Trans-Canada Hwy. ③.

Peaks Lodge, 5km west of Revelstoke off Hwy 1 (☎250/837-2176 or 1-800/668-0330, fax 837-2133; *peaks@junction.net*). Nice small place (twelve units) in a reasonably rustic setting convenient for hikes, bird-watching and the like. Open mid-May to mid-Oct & mid-Nov to mid-April. ③.

'R' Motel, 1500 1st St (☎250/837-2164, fax 837-6847, *rmotel@junction.net*). One of the cheapest motels in town. ②.

Revelstoke Traveller's Hostel and Guest House, 400 2nd St W (☎250/837-4050, fax 837-5600, *www.hostels.bc.ca*). Cheap private, semi-private and dorm beds convenient for local restaurants and supermarkets. Well-run and offers Internet access, bike rentals and kitchen facilities. ①.

Sandman Inn, 1821 Fraser St (☎250/837-5271 or 1-800/726-3626, *www.sandman.ca*). Part of a usually reliable mid-range hotel chain. Has 83 comfortable, modern rooms, so a good chance of finding space. ④.

CAMPSITES

Revelstoke has no park-run sites. **Backcountry** camping in the park is free, with tent-pads, outhouses and food-storage poles provided at Eva and Jade lakes, but no camping is allowed in the Miller Lake area or anywhere within 5km of the Trans-Canada and Summit Road. Registration at the Park Administration Office is obligatory. The park is so small, however, that you might be better off at some of the area's more developed private **campsites**.

Highway Haven Motel and Campground, Three Valley Lake (☎250/837-2525). 20km west of Revelstoke, near the lake for swimming and boating. Thirty pitches and hot showers. April–Nov. $10.

KOA Revelstoke, 5km east of Revelstoke (☎250/837-2085 or 1-800/562-3905). The best of the area's campsites. Free showers, plus shop and swimming pool. May–Oct. $20–22.50.

Lamplighter Campground, off Hwy 1 before the Columbia River bridge; take Hwy 23 south towards Nakusp and turn into Nixon Rd (first left) (☎250/837-3385, fax 837-5856). A peaceful, fully serviced tent and RV site within walking distance of downtown. Fifty fully serviced sites. Mid-April to mid-Oct. $15.50.

Williamson Lake Campground, 1818 Williamson Lake Rd (☎250/837-5512 or 1-888/676-2267). Nice forty-site lakeside campsite 4km south of the town centre. Free hot showers, canoe and row-boat rentals, flush toilets and beach. Mid-April to Oct. $14.50.

Eating and drinking

Eating possibilities include the *Frontier Restaurant* on the Trans-Canada, part of the eponymous motel near the infocentre, which serves up superior steak-and-salad meals at reasonable prices, with friendly service and a genuine cowpoke atmosphere. In town, the *One-Twelve Restaurant* at 112 Victoria Rd is a favourite, with good food, a lively pub and dance floor.

Revelstoke Dam

A trip to Canada's largest dam may sound dull, but the **Revelstoke Dam** (daily: mid-March to mid-June & early Sept to late Oct 9am–5pm; mid-June to early Sept 8am–8pm; free; ☎250/837-6515) makes an interesting outing. Four kilometres north of the town on Hwy 23, the 175-metre-tall barrier holds back the waters of the Columbia River, around 500km from its source. Its sleek, space-age **visitor centre** offers a two-hour self-guided tour, which omits to tell you that insufficient mapping during the construction caused a landslide that threatened to swamp Revelstoke: millions had to be spent or it would have been curtains for the town. The boring bits of the tour can be skipped in favour of a lift to the top for a great view of the dam and surrounding valley.

> The telephone code for Kootenay National Park is ☎250.

Kootenay National Park

KOOTENAY NATIONAL PARK, lying across the Continental Divide from Banff in British Columbia, is the least known of the four contiguous parks of the Rockies, and the easiest to miss out – many people prefer to follow the Trans-Canada through Yoho rather than commit themselves to the less enthralling westward journey on Hwy 3 imposed by Kootenay. The park's scenery, however, is as impressive as that of its neighbours – it draws three million visitors a year – and if you're not determined to head west you could drive a neat loop from Banff through Kootenay on Hwy 93 to **Radium Hot Springs** (the only town in this area), north on Hwy 95, and back on the Trans-Canada through Yoho to Lake Louise and Banff. You could drive this in a day and still have time for a few short walks and a dip in Radium's hot springs to boot.

In many ways the park's mountains seem closer at hand and more spectacular than on the Icefields Parkway, partly because the road climbs higher over the Continental Divide, and partly because the park's origins guaranteed it an intimate link with the highway. In 1910 Randolph Bruce, a local businessman, persuaded the Canadian government and Canadian Pacific to push a road from Banff through the Rockies to connect the prairies with western seaports (prompted by the hope of promoting a fruit-growing industry in the Columbia Valley). Previously the area had been the reserve of the Kootenai or Ktunaxa natives (*Kootenay* is a native word meaning "people from beyond the hills") and had been explored by David Thompson, but otherwise it was an all but inviolate mountain fastness. The project began in 1911 and produced 22km of road before the money ran out. To wangle more cash British Columbia was forced to cede 8km of land on each side of the highway to the government and, in 1920, 1406 square kilometres of land were established as a national park.

Kootenay lends itself to admiration from a car, bus or bike, mainly because it's little more than a sixteen-kilometre-wide ribbon of land running either side of Hwy 93 for around 100km (the highway here is known as the **Kootenay** or **Banff-Windermere Parkway**). All its numerous easy **short walks** start immediately off the highway, though

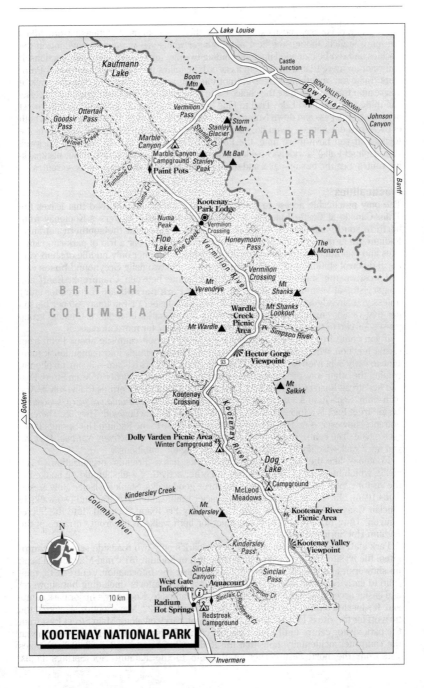

△ Lake Louise

Kaufmann
Lake

Boom
Mtn ▲

Castle
Junction

BOW VALLEY PARKWAY

Bow River

Johnson
Canyon

Vermilion
Pass

Storm
Mtn ▲

Stanley
Glacier

Stanley Cr.

A L B E R T A

Goodsir
Pass

Ottertail
Pass

Helmet Creek

Marble
Canyon

Marble Canyon
Campground

Paint Pots

Stanley
Peak ▲

▲ Mt Ball

△ Banff

Tumbling Cr.

Numa Cr.

Kootenay
Park Lodge ⊙

Vermilion
Crossing

Honeymoon
Pass

Numa
Peak ▲

Floe
Lake

Floe Creek

Vermilion River

Vermilion
Crossing

The
Monarch ▲

B R I T I S H

C O L U M B I A

Mt
Verendrye ▲

Mt
Shanks ▲

Mt Shanks
Lookout

Wardle
Creek
Picnic
Area

Mt Wardle ▲

Simpson River

Hector Gorge
Viewpoint

93

△ Golden

Kootenay
Crossing

Kootenay River

Mt
Selkirk ▲

Dolly Varden Picnic Area
Winter Campground

Dog
Lake

Campground

Kindersley Creek

McLeod
Meadows

95

Columbia River

Mt
Kindersley ▲

Kootenay River
Picnic Area

Kindersley
Pass

Kootenay Valley
Viewpoint

N

Sinclair
Canyon

Aquacourt

Sinclair
Pass

Kimpton Cr.

West Gate
Infocentre

Radium
Hot Springs

Sinclair Cr.

Redstreak Cr.

Redstreak
Campground

0   10 km

KOOTENAY NATIONAL PARK

▽ Invermere

the scenery, of course, doesn't simply stop at the park boundary. Options for **day-hikes** are more limited, though the best of the longer walks are as good as anything in the Rockies and can be extended into outstanding two-day (or more) backpacking options. If you want no more than a stroll from a car or bike follow the **Marble Canyon** and **Paint Pots** trails: for something longer but not too long go for the **Stanley Glacier** walk; if you're after the best day-hike the choice is the **Kindersley Pass Trail**, though it's a close-run thing with the Floe Lake Trail to Floe Lake and its possible continuation northwest over the Numa Pass and down Numa Creek back to the highway. If you have time do both of these two day-hikes – if you do, you'll have done two of the top ten or so walks in the Rockies. If you have more time, the Rockwall Trail (Floe Lake–Numa Pass–Rockwell Pass–Helmet Falls) is widely considered among the Rockies' top three or four backpacking routes. See the box on p.682 and the map opposite to make sense of these routes.

Practicalities

The only practicable access to Kootenay is on Hwy 93, a good road that leaves the Trans-Canada at Castle Junction (in Banff National Park), traverses Kootenay from north to south, and joins Hwy 95 at Radium Hot Springs at the southern entrance. Radium offers the only practical accommodation options, bar a trio of park-run campsites and handful of rooms at Vermilion Crossing, a summer-only huddle of shop, cabins and petrol station midway through the park. The two daily Greyhound **buses** east and west on the southern British Columbia route between Cranbrook, Banff and Calgary stop at Vermilion Crossing and Radium. **Park permits** are required for entry unless you already have a valid permit from Banff, Jasper or Kootenay: $5 per person per day, or $35 for an annual pass valid for eleven parks in western Canada: group passes for two to ten people cost $10 (see box on p.607 for more on passes).

If you come from the east you'll hit the *Marble Canyon* campsite about 15km from Castle Junction, where occasionally in summer there's a simple information kiosk (mid-June to early Sept Mon & Fri–Sun 8.30am–8pm, Tues–Thurs 8.30am–4.30pm; no phone); coming the other way, the main **park visitor centre** is at the corner of Main Street East and Redstreak Road at 7556 Main St in the town of Radium Hot Springs (daily: July & Aug 9am–9pm; Sept–June 9.30am-5.30pm; ☎347-9505, *www.parkscanada.pch.gc.ca/kootenay*). Main Street East is a turn south off Hwy 93 close to its junction with Hwy 95. The park entrance, however, is on Hwy 93 itself farther east close to the Radium Hot Springs Pools (see p.685). The centre provides a free *Backcountry Guide to Kootenay National Park*, all you need walk-wise if you're not planning anything too ambitious.

Kootenay, like the other major Rockies parks, has a "Friends" organization (☎347-6525), which helps run **guided walks** and other activities: walks should be booked at the visitor centre. In Kootenay, there are three good walks: Stanley Glacier (July & Aug Tues 10am; 5hr; 10km; meet at Stanley Glacier trailhead on Hwy 93); and two walks in Sinclair Canyon – "Walk of the Two Lions" (July Fri 10am; 2hr) and "Into the Secret Canyon" (Aug Fri 10am; 1hr 30min; meet for both walks at the front entrance of the Radium Hot Springs Pools).

Park staff are also usually on hand at the park's only two roadside serviced **campsites**: the 98-site *McLeod Meadows*, 25km north of Radium ($13; mid-May to mid-Sept; no showers), and the 61-site *Marble Canyon*, near the Information Centre ($13; mid-June to early Sept; no showers). If you want more comforts (including hot showers) and easier access use the big 242-site *Redstreak* campsite, Kootenay's major park campsite. It's located 3km north of Radium Hot Springs ($17–22; May–Sept; ☎347-9567); the turn-off for the site is Redstreak Road: to reach it, carry on along Main Street East from the park visitor centre until Main Street becomes Redstreak Road. If you're staying at the campsite, incidentally, note that the Redstreak Campground Trail (2.2km) takes you from the northwest corner of the site to the Radium Hot Springs Pools.

The Valleyview Trail (1.4km) takes you from the campsite entrance into Radium village, avoiding Redstreak Road.

A dozen or more **backcountry sites** with pit toilets and firewood are scattered within easy backpacking range of the highway, for which you need a **permit** from the info-centres ($6). The small seven-site *Dolly Varden* park campsite just north of McLeod Meadows opens for **winter camping** (Sept–May; flush toilets only; free).

The only indoor **accommodation** in the heart of the park is ten rustic cottages of the *Kootenay Park Lodge* at Vermilion Crossing (☎762-9196, *www.kootenayparklodge .com*; ④; May–Sept). You'll need to book these well in advance; similarly the twelve cabins at *Mount Assiniboine Lodge* (☎344-2639; ⑤; Feb–April & late June to mid-Oct; reservations obligatory; two-night minimum stay). Located at 2195m within the Assiniboine Provincial Park, this lodge is accessible only by helicopter, skiing or hiking trail. The other listed hotels within the park borders are so close to Radium as to make little difference (see "Radium Hot Springs", p.684).

Vermilion Pass

Vermilion Pass (1637m) marks the northern entrance to the park, the Continental Divide's watershed and the border between Alberta and British Columbia. Little

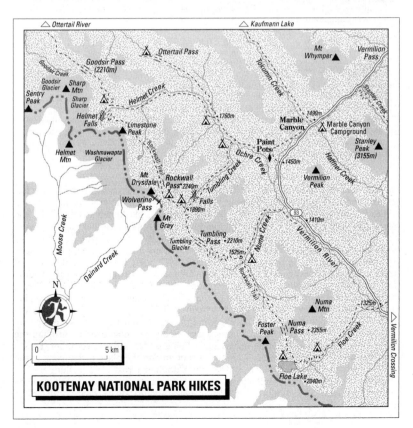

DAY- AND BACKPACKING HIKES IN KOOTENAY

If you have time and energy for only one long walk in Kootenay, make it the Kindersley Pass Trail, a strenuous 9.8-kilometre trail that climbs to **Kindersley Pass** and then cuts northeast for the steep final push to Kindersley Summit (2210m). Here you can enjoy the sublime prospect of an endless succession of peaks fading to the horizon away to the northeast. Rather than double back down through the open tundra, many people push on another 2km (trail vague) and contour around the head of the Sinclair Creek valley before dropping off the ridge (the Kindersley–Sinclair Coll) to follow the well-defined Sinclair Creek Trail (6.4km) down to meet the highway 1km from the starting point (be sure to do the hike this way round – the Sinclair Creek Trail is a long, dull climb).

Most of Kootenay's other longish day-walks are in the park's northern half, accessed on the west side of the highway from the Marble Canyon, Paint Pots, Numa Creek and Floe Lake parking areas. The **Rockwall Trail**, an incredible thirty-kilometre (54km including approach trails; 1450m ascent), backpacking high-level trail, follows the line of the mountains on the west side of the highway, and can be joined using four of the six trails described below. You could walk it in two days, but could easily spend longer, particularly as there are five backcountry campsites en route.

From north to south on the highway, the trails start with the **Kaufmann Lake Trail** (15km one-way; 570m ascent; allow 4–6hr one-way), which climbs to one of the park's loveliest high-mountain lakes (there's also a campsite here). A trail from the Paint Pots runs for 2km before dividing to provide three onward options: the first to the dull Ottertail Pass, the second up **Tumbling Creek** (10.3km; 440m ascent to the intersection with the Rockwall Trail), and the third and best option the **Helmet Creek Trail** (14.3km; 310m ascent), a long day-hike to the amazing 365-metre Helmet Waterfalls (another intersection with the Rockwall Trail). The best of the day-hikes after Kindersley Pass is the easier **Floe Lake Trail** (10.5km; 715m ascent), up to a spellbinding lake edged by a 1000-metre sheer escarpment and a small glacier. There are campsites on the route, and another tie-in to the Rockwall Trail. The **Numa Creek Trail** (6.4km; 115m ascent) to the north is less enthralling – though you could use it as a downhill leg to add to the Floe Lake Trail (see map overleaf) – as are the series of fire-road walks advertised in the park: unless you're mountain biking, therefore, ignore the Simpson River, West Kootenay, Honeymoon Pass and East Kootenay trails.

fanfare, however, accompanies the transition – only the barren legacy of a huge forest fire (started by a single lightning bolt) which ravaged the area for four days in 1968, leaving a 24-square-kilometre blanket of stark, blackened trunks. Take the short **Fireweed Trail** (1km) through the desolation from the car park at the pass to see how nature deals with such disasters, indeed how it seems to invite lightning fires to promote phoenix-like regeneration. The ubiquitous lodgepole pine, for example, specifically requires the heat of a forest fire to crack open its resin-sealed cones and release its seeds. Strange as it seems, forests are intended to burn, at least if a healthy forest is to be preserved: in montane regions the natural "fire return cycles" are a mere 42–46 years; in lower subalpine habitats, 77–130 years; and in upper subalpine areas, 180 years. Forests any older are actually in decline, providing few species and poor wildlife habitats. Ironically, as a result of the national parks' success in preventing forest fires over the last fifty years, many woods are now over-mature and the need for controlled burning is increasingly being addressed. At Vermilion Pass a broad carpet of lodgepole pines have taken root among the blasted remnants of the earlier forest, while young plants and shrubs ("doghair forest") are pushing up into the new clearings. Birds, small mammals and deer, elk and moose are being attracted to new food sources and, more significantly, black and grizzly bears are returning to the area.

Stanley Glacier and Marble Canyon

About 3km south of Vermilion Pass, the small, well-defined **Stanley Glacier Trail** (4.2km; 365m ascent; 1hr 30min) strikes off up Stanley Creek from a parking area on the eastern side of the highway. In its first 2km the trail provides you with a hike through the Vermilion Pass Burn (see opposite), but more to the point pushes into the beautiful hanging valley below Stanley Peak. Here you can enjoy close-up views of the Stanley Glacier and its surrounding recently glaciated landscapes. The area is also known for its fossils, and for the chance to see marmots, pikas and white-tailed ptarmigan.

Marble Canyon, 8km south of Vermilion Pass, the site of a park-run **campsite**, has an easy trail (800m) that's probably the most heavily trafficked of Kootenay's shorter hikes. The track crosses a series of log bridges over Tokumm Creek, which has carved through a fault in the limestone over the last 8000 years, to produce a 600-metre-long and 37-metre-deep gorge. In cold weather this is a fantastic medley of ice and snow, but in summer the climax is the viewpoint from the top of the path onto a thundering waterfall as the creek pounds its way through the narrowest section of the gorge. The rock here was once mistakenly identified as marble – hence the canyon's name; the white marble-like rock is actually dolomite limestone.

One of the park's better longer hikes also starts from the Marble Canyon car park – the **Kaufmann Lake Trail** (15km one-way; 570m ascent; 4–6hr), which follows Tokumm Creek towards the head of the valley at Kaufmann Lake (see box opposite). The first few kilometres of the trail – easy valley and meadow walking – make an appealing hour or so's stroll.

The Paint Pots

You could extend the Marble Canyon walk by picking up the Paint Pots Trail south, which puts another 2.7km onto your walk, or drive 2km south and stroll 1km to reach the same destination. Either way you come first to the Ochre Beds (after 800m) and then (1.5km) to the **Paint Pots**, one of the Rockies' more magical spots: red, orange and mustard-coloured pools prefaced by damp, moss-clung forest and views across the white water of the Vermilion River to the snowcapped mountains beyond. The pools' colours are created by iron-laden water bubbling up from three mineral springs through clay sediments deposited on the bed of an ancient glacial lake.

Aboriginal peoples from all over North America collected the coloured clays from the ponds and ochre beds to make into small cakes, which they baked in embers. The fired clay was then ground into powder – **ochre** – and added to animal fat or fish oil to use in rock, tepee or ceremonial body painting. Ochre has always had spiritual significance for North American natives, in this case the Stoney and Ktunaxa, who saw these oxide-stained pools and their yellow-edged surroundings as inhabited by animal and thunder spirits. Standing in the quiet, rather gloomy glade, particularly on overcast days, it's easy to see why – not that the atmosphere or sanctity of the place stopped European speculators in the 1920s from mining the ochre to manufacture paint in Calgary.

The car park is the trailhead for three longer (day or backpack) trails, all of which kick off along the Ochre Creek Valley: Tumbling Creek Trail, Ottertail Pass Trail and the Helmet Creek–Helmet Waterfalls Trail (see box, opposite).

Vermilion Crossing and Kootenay Crossing

VERMILION CROSSING, 20km south of the Paint Pots Trail, is gone in a flash, but it's the only place, in summer at least, to find lodgings, petrol and food in the park. It also has a new visitor centre, built on the site of a 1920 CPR railway camp. You can also stop to walk the **Verendyre Creek Trail** (2.1km), accessed west off the highway, an easy stroll, but forest-enclosed, and with only limited views of Mount Verendrye as a reward. One of the Rockies' tougher walks heads east from the Crossing, up over Honeymoon Pass and Redearth Pass to Egypt Lake and the Trans-Canada Highway in Banff National Park, while to the south equally demanding trails provide the only westside access into the wilderness of **Mount Assiniboine Provincial Park**. Sandwiched between Kootenay and Banff, this wilderness park was created in honour of Mount Assiniboine (3618m), a sabre-tooth-shaped mountain with one of the most dramatic profiles imaginable, whose native Stoney name means "those who cook by placing hot rocks in water". The **Simpson Road Trail** (8.2km) leads to the park boundary, and then divides into two paths (20km and 32km) to Lake Magog in the heart of Assiniboine. Some 8.5km beyond the Crossing look out for the Animal Lick, a spot where animals come down to lick nutrients from a natural mineral source: with luck you may see elk, mule deer and even moose here. Over the next few kilometres, for similar reasons, you might also see mountain goats by banks at the side of the road.

Kootenay Crossing is no more than a ceremonial spot – it was where the ribbon was cut to open Hwy 93 in 1923 – though a clutch of short trails fan out from its park warden station, and the nearby *Dolly Varden* campsite (see p.681) is the park's only specific site for winter camping. **Wardle Creek** nearby is a good place to unpack a picnic if you're determined to stick to the road.

Around 11km south of the Kootenay Crossing is the **McLeod Meadows** campsite (see p.680), and immediately behind it to the east the easy **Dog Lake Trail** (2.7km), much tramped as an after-dinner leg-stretcher by campers (the trail can also be accessed from the highway at the picnic area 500m south). The path offers glimpses of the Kootenay Valley through the trees, and ends in a marsh-edged lake whose temperate microclimate makes it ideal for nature study. You may see deer, elk and coyotes, and – if you're lucky – bears and moose. Several types of orchid also bloom here in early summer (June & July), including white bog, round-leafed, calypso and sparrow's egg. About 11km further on, the **Kootenay Valley Viewpoint** offers one of the broadest views on the highway, with great vistas of the Mitchell and Vermilion mountain ranges, and with them the inevitable hordes in search of a photo opportunity.

Sinclair Pass

For its final run down out of the park, the highway doglegs west through the **Sinclair Pass**, a red-cliffed gorge filled with the falling waters of Sinclair Creek and the start of the **Kindersley Pass Trail**, possibly the most scenic day-hike in the park (see box on p.682). If this seems too much of a slog, Sinclair Pass offers three far easier short trails, all marked off the highway to the west. The best is the **Juniper Trail** (3.2km), accessed just 300m inside the park's West Gate. The trail drops to Sinclair Creek and over the next couple of kilometres touches dry canyon, arid forest slopes of juniper and Douglas fir, and thick woods of western red cedar, before emerging at the hot springs, or Aquacourt (see opposite), 1.4km up the road from the start. The **Redstreak Creek Trail** (2.7km), 4.5km east of the West Gate, starts off as a good forest walk, but tails off into dullness subsequently, as does the **Kimpton Creek Trail** (4.8km), also on the south side of the road and canyon, accessed 7.5km east of the West Gate.

Radium Hot Springs

RADIUM HOT SPRINGS is far less attractive than its evocative name suggests but, as the service centre for Kootenay, its tacky motels and garages are likely to claim your

Okanagan Valley, British Columbia

Totem pole

The bank at Dawson City, Yukon

Kaskawulsh Glacier, Kluane National Park, Yukon

Hikers in the Canadian Rockies

The Dempster Highway, Northwest Territories

CHAPTER SEVEN

SOUTHERN BRITISH COLUMBIA

The often pristine scenery of **British Columbia** more than lives up to most people's image of the wilds of Canada. What may come as a surprise, however, is the region's sheer natural diversity: between the expected extremes of the mountainous, forested interior and the fjord-cut mountains of the coast lies a jigsaw of landscapes, including genteel farmland, ranching country, immense lakes and even a patch of genuine desert. British Columbia contains both Canada's wettest and its driest climates, and more species of flora and fauna than the rest of the country put together. The range of recreational possibilities is equally impressive: the country's biggest ski area, its warmest lakes and some of its best beaches are all here, not to mention hot springs and hiking, sailing and canoeing galore, as well as some of the best salmon fishing in the world. Interior towns may not always be terribly interesting – **Nelson** is a notable exception – but from almost anywhere in the region you can be sure that secluded and peaceful countryside and myriad outdoor pursuits lie just a few kilometres away.

Culturally and logistically, southern British Columbia stands apart from the northern half of the province, containing most of the roads, towns and accessible sights. Ninety-five percent of the population lives in the south, mainly in **Vancouver**, Canada's third largest city. A cosmopolitan, sophisticated and famously hedonistic place, Vancouver gives the lie to the stereotype of the Canadian west as an introverted, cultural wasteland, its combination of glittering skyline and generous open spaces standing as a model of urban planning. The province's modest capital is **Victoria**, a considerably smaller city on the southern tip of Vancouver Island, which affects a somewhat English ambience to lure more tourists than it probably deserves.

If you're making a circuit of the interior, or even just cutting across it as part of a transcontinental route, you'll want to set aside time for the mountain-hemmed lakes and tidy mining towns of the **Kootenays**, or – if you're into wine tasting or rowdy lakeside resorts – the **Okanagan**. For big wilderness and waterfalls, **Wells Gray Provincial Park** stands out, though exhilarating hikes and camping are possible in dozens of other parks. And if you're looking to ski or snowboard, **Whistler** is one of the world's top resorts. Variety is also the byword for **Vancouver Island**, by far the largest of an archipelago of islets off BC's coast, where in a short time you can move from wild seascapes and rainforest to jagged, glaciated peaks. Vancouver Island can also be used as a springboard for the ferry up the famed **Inside Passage** to Prince Rupert and beyond, or the new Discovery Coast Passage to Bella Coola; inland, roads and rail lines

---

TELEPHONE CODES

The telephone code for British Columbia is ☎250.
The telephone code for Vancouver and vicinity is ☎604.

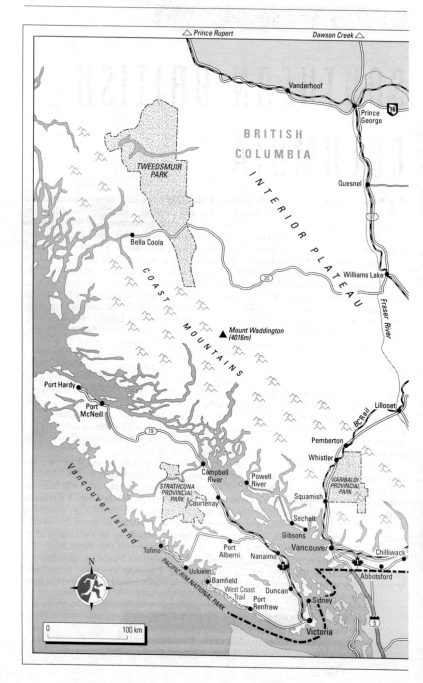

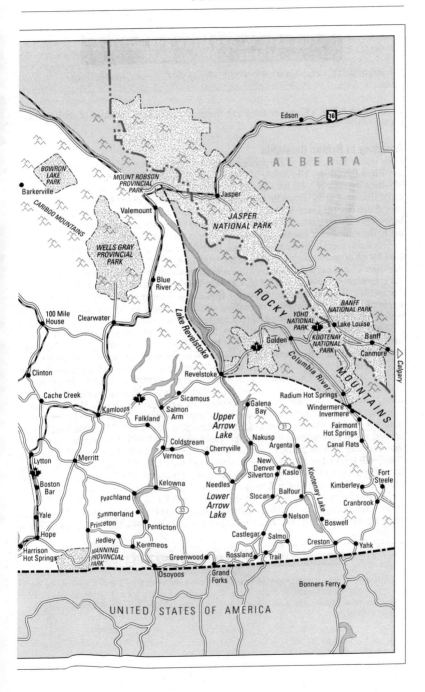

converge to follow a single route north through the endless expanse of the **Cariboo** region of the interior plateau.

A history of British Columbia

Long before the coming of Europeans, British Columbia's coastal region supported five key **First Peoples** – The Kwakiutl, Bella Coola, Nuu-chah-nulth, Haida and Tlingit – all of whom lived largely off the sea and developed a culture in many ways more sophisticated than that of the nomadic and hunting-oriented tribes of the interior. Although it's rare these days to come across aboriginal faces in interior southern BC, aboriginal villages still exist on parts of Vancouver Island, and you can find examples of their totemic art in the excellent museum displays of Victoria and Vancouver.

The British explorer **Francis Drake** probably made the first sighting of the mainland by a European, during his round-the-world voyage of 1579. Spanish explorers sailing from California and Russians from Alaska explored the coast almost two centuries later, though it was another Briton, **Captain Cook**, who made the first recorded landing in 1778. Captain George Vancouver first mapped the area in 1792–94, hard on the heels of the Nuu-chah-nulth Convention of 1790 – a neat piece of colonial bluster in which the British wrested from the Spanish all rights on the mainland as far as Alaska.

Exploration of the interior came about during the search for an easier way to export furs westwards to the Pacific (instead of the arduous haul eastwards across the continent). **Alexander Mackenzie** of the North West Company made the first crossing of North America north of Mexico in 1793, followed by two further adventurers, **Simon Fraser** and **David Thompson**, whose names also resonate as sobriquets for rivers, shops, motels and streets across the region. For the first half of the nineteenth century most of western Canada was ruled as a virtual fiefdom by the **Hudson's Bay Company**, a monopoly that antagonized the Americans, which in turn persuaded the British to formalize its claims to the region to forestall American expansion. The 49th Parallel was agreed as the national boundary, though Vancouver Island, which lies partly south of the line, remained wholly British and was officially designated a crown colony in 1849. The "Bay" still reigned in all but name, however, and took no particular interest in promoting immigration; as late as 1855 the island's white population numbered only 774 and the mainland remained almost unknown except to trappers and the odd prospector.

The discovery of **gold** on the Fraser River in 1858, and in the Cariboo region three years later, changed everything, attracting some 25,000 people to the gold fields and creating a forward base on the mainland that was to become Vancouver. It also led to

---

RESERVING PROVINCIAL CAMPSITES

Tent and RV pitches at certain campsites in British Columbia's provincial parks can be reserved in advance. To make **reservations**, call Discover Camping (☎1-800/689-9025 or 604/689-9025 in greater Vancouver; March to mid-Sept Mon–Fri 7am–7pm, Sat & Sun 9am–5pm) or log-on to their Web site *www.discovercamping.ca*, where reservations can be made and confirmed online. Reservations can be made from up to three months in advance and no later than 48 hours before the first day of arrival. A nonrefundable booking fee of $6.42 per night, to a maximum of $19.26 for three or more nights, is charged (rates include tax). Payment in advance is by Visa or MasterCard only (payment for extra nights once at a campsite is by cash only). You can stay in BC provincial parks up to a maximum of fourteen days in any single park. Information on all aspects of BC's provincial parks is available on the Net at *www.elp.gov.bc.ca/bcparks*.

---

the building of the **Cariboo Road** (the present Hwy 97) and the **Dewdney Trail** (Hwy 3), which opened up the interior and helped attract the so-called **Overlanders** – a huge straggle of pioneers that tramped from Ontario and Québec in the summer of 1862. Britain declared mainland British Columbia a crown colony in 1858 to impose imperial authority on the region and, more importantly, to lay firm claim to the huge mineral wealth that was rightly believed to lie within it. When Canada's eastern colonies formed the Dominion in 1867, though, British Columbia dithered over joining until it received the promise of a railway to link it to the east in 1871 – though the Canadian Pacific didn't actually arrive for another fifteen years.

While British Columbia no longer dithers over its destiny, it still tends to look to itself and the Northwest – and increasingly to the new economic markets of the Pacific Rim – rather than to the rest of Canada. The francophone concerns of the east are virtually nonexistent here – for years, for example, there was just one French school in the entire province. For the most part British Columbians are well off, both financially and in terms of quality of life, and demographically the province is one of the region's youngest. If there are flies in the ointment, they're the environmental pressures thrown up by an economy which relies on primary resources for its dynamism: British Columbia supplies 25 percent of North America's commercial timber and exports significant amounts of hydroelectric power, fish, zinc, silver, oil, coal and gypsum. Few of these can be exploited without exacting a toll on the province's natural beauty; British Columbians may be well off, but they're increasingly aware of the environmental price being paid for their prosperity.

VANCOUVER

Cradled between the ocean and snow-capped mountains, Vancouver's dazzling downtown district fills a narrow peninsula bounded by Burrard Inlet to the north, English Bay to the west and False Creek to the south, with greater Vancouver sprawling south to the Fraser River. Edged around its idyllic waterfront are fine beaches, a dynamic port and a magnificent swath of parkland, not to mention the mirror-fronted ranks of skyscrapers that look across Burrard Inlet and its bustling harbour to the residential districts of North and West Vancouver. Beyond these comfortable suburbs, the Coast Mountains rise in steep, forested slopes to form a dramatic counterpoint to the downtown skyline and the most stunning of the city's many outdoor playgrounds. Small wonder, given Vancouver's surroundings, that Greenpeace was founded in the city.

Vancouver's 1.9 million residents exploit their spectacular natural setting to the hilt, and when they tire of the immediate region can travel a short distance to the

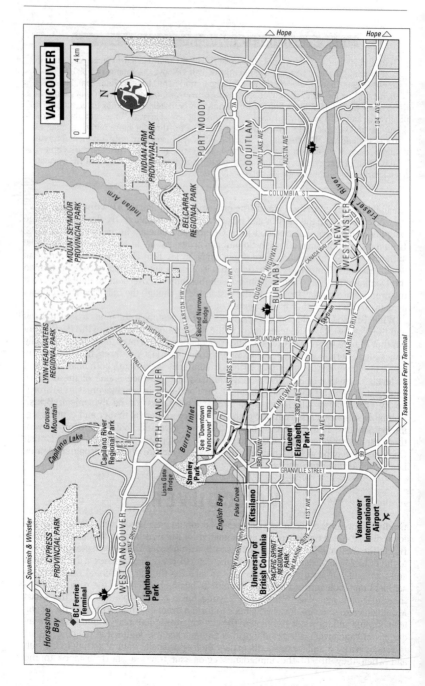

unimaginably vast wilderness of the BC interior. Whether it's sailing, swimming, fishing, hiking, skiing, golf or tennis, locals barely have to move to indulge in a plethora of **recreational** whims. Summer and winter the city oozes hedonism and healthy living – it comes as no surprise to find that you can lounge on beaches downtown – typically West Coast obsessions that spill over into its sophisticated **arts and culture**. Vancouver claims a world-class museum and symphony orchestra, as well as opera, theatre and dance companies at the cutting edge of contemporary arts. Festivals proliferate throughout its mild, if occasionally rain-soaked, summer and numerous music venues provide a hotbed for up-and-coming rock bands and a burgeoning jazz scene.

Vancouver is not all pleasure, however. Business growth continues apace in Canada's third-largest city, much of its prosperity stemming from a **port** so laden with the raw materials of the Canadian interior – lumber, wheat and minerals – that it ranks as one of North America's largest ports, handling more dry tonnage than the West Coast ports of Seattle, Tacoma, Portland, San Francisco and San Diego put together. The port in turn owes its prominence to Vancouver's much-trumpeted position as a **gateway to the Far East**, and its increasingly pivotal role in the new global market of the Pacific Rim. This lucrative realignment is strengthened by a two-way flow in traffic: in the past decade Vancouver has been inundated with Hong Kong Chinese (the so-called "yacht people"), an influx which has pushed up property prices and slightly strained the city's reputation as an ethnically integrated metropolis.

Much of the city's earlier immigration focused on Vancouver's extraordinary **Chinatown**, just one of a number of ethnic enclaves – Italian, Greek, Indian and Japanese in particular – which lend the city a refreshingly gritty quality that belies its sleek, modern reputation. So too do the city's semi-derelict eastern districts, whose worldly lowlife characters, addicts and hustlers are shockingly at odds with the glitzy lifestyles pursued in the lush residential neighbourhoods. Low rents and Vancouver's cosmopolitan young have also nurtured an unexpected **counterculture**, at least for the time being, distinguished by varied restaurants, secondhand shops, avant-garde galleries, clubs and bars – spots where you'll probably have more fun than in many a Canadian city. And at the top of the scale there are restaurants as good – and as varied – as any in North America.

These days Vancouver is more **dynamic** than ever, its growth and energy almost palpable as you walk the streets. In just five years, between 1987 and 1992, the city's population increased by an extraordinary seventeen percent. The downtown population, currently just over half a million, is the fastest-growing on the continent. In response the downtown area is spreading – visibly – to the older and previously run-down districts to the southeast of the old city core. Development over the last decade is symbolized by a superb library and performing-arts complex which constitutes the most expensive capital project ever undertaken in the city. Real estate here is now more expensive than Toronto, and in the 1990s the city became North America's largest film and TV production centre after Los Angeles and New York; *The X Files* is just the most famous of the many movies and programmes that have been, or are being, made here (see p.730 for details of *X Files* tours). Yet, in the peculiar way that seems second nature to Canadians, the changes are being handled in a manner that's enhancing rather than compromising the city's beguiling combination of pleasure, culture, business and natural beauty.

A brief history of Vancouver

Vancouver in the modern sense has existed for a little over 110 years. Over the course of the previous nine thousand years the Fraser Valley was home to the Tsawwassen, Musqueam and another twenty or so native tribes, who made up the Stó:lo Nation, or "people of the river". The fish, particularly salmon, of this river were the Stó:lo lifeblood. Over the millennia these people ventured relatively little into the mountainous interior, something that remains true to this day. One of the things that makes

The telephone code for Vancouver is ☎604.

modern Vancouver so remarkable is how wild and empty British Columbia remains beyond the Fraser's narrow corridor. The Stó:lo inhabited about ten villages on the shores of Vancouver's Burrard Inlet before the coming of the Europeans. A highly developed culture, the Stó:lo were skilled carpenters, canoe-makers and artists, though little in the present city – outside its museums – pays anything but lip service to their existence. Vancouver Island is the nearest best bet if you're in search of latter-day tokens of aboriginal culture.

Europeans appeared on the scene in notable numbers during the eighteenth century, when **Spanish** explorers charted the waters along what is now southwestern British Columbia. In 1778 **Captain James Cook** reached nearby Nootka Sound while searching for the Northwest Passage, sparking off immediate British interest in the area. In 1791 José Maria Narvaez, a Spanish pilot and surveyor, glimpsed the mouth of the Fraser from his ship, the *Santa Saturnia*. This led to wrangles between the British and Spanish, disputes quickly settled in Britain's favour when Spain became domestically embroiled in the aftermath of the French Revolution. **Captain George Vancouver** officially claimed the land for Britain in 1792, but studying the Fraser from a small boat decided that it seemed too shallow to be of practical use. Instead he rounded a headland to the north, sailing into a deep natural port – the future site of Vancouver – which he named Burrard after one of his companions. He then traded briefly with several Squamish tribespeople at X'ay'xi, a village on the inlet's forested headland – the future Stanley Park. Afterwards the Squamish named the spot Whul-whul-Lay-ton, or "place of the white man". Vancouver sailed on, having spent just a day in the region – scant homage to an area that was to be named after him a century later.

Vancouver's error over the Fraser was uncovered in 1808, when Scottish-born Simon Fraser made an epic 1368-kilometre journey down the river from the Rockies to the sea. In 1827 the Hudson's Bay Company set up a fur-trading post at **Fort Langley**, 48km east of the present city, bartering not only furs but also salmon from the Stó:lo, the latter being salted and then packed off to company forts across Canada. The fort was kept free of homesteaders, despite being the area's first major white settlement, their presence deemed detrimental to the fur trade. Major colonization of the area only came after the Fraser River and Cariboo gold rushes in 1858, when **New Westminster** bustled with the arrival of as many as 25,000 hopefuls, many of whom were refugees from the 1849 Californian rush. Many also drifted in from the US, underlining the fragility of the national border and the precarious nature of British claims to the region. These claims were consolidated when British Columbia was declared a crown colony, with New Westminster as its capital. Both were superseded by Fort Victoria in 1868, by which time the gold rush had dwindled almost to nothing.

In 1862, meanwhile, three British prospectors, unable to find gold in the interior, bought a strip of land on the southern shore of Burrard Inlet and – shortsightedly, given the amount of lumber around – started a brickworks. This soon gave way to the Hastings Sawmill and a shantytown of bars which by 1867 had taken the name of **Gastown**, after "Gassy" – as in loquacious – Jack Leighton, proprietor of the site's first saloon. Two years later Gastown became incorporated as the town of **Granville** and prospered on the back of its timber and small coal deposits. The birth of the present city dates to 1884, when the **Canadian Pacific Railway** decided to make it the terminus of its transcontinental railway. In 1886, on a whim of the CPR president, Granville was renamed Vancouver, only to be destroyed on June 13 that year when fire razed all but half a dozen buildings. The setback proved short-lived, and since the arrival of the first train from Montréal in 1887 the city has never looked back.

Arrival and information

Vancouver Airport

Vancouver International Airport is situated on Sea Island, 13km south of the city centre. Its often-used coded abbreviation is YVR. International flights arrive at the majestic new main terminal; domestic flights at the smaller and linked old Main Terminal. If you're an international passenger, you'll find a **tourist information** desk as you exit customs and immigration and before entering the terminal's public spaces (daily 7am–midnight; ☎688-5515). On the right just before this, before you exit to the public spaces, is a desk where you can book taxis, limousines and also buy tickets or obtain information for the bus shuttles to downtown (see below) and direct bus services from the airport to Victoria, Whistler, Bellingham Airport (Seattle) and Sea-Tac Airport in the US. There are also plenty of **foreign exchange** and other facilities, along with freephone lines to several upmarket hotels, in the area. Domestic passengers also have a tourist-information desk just before the terminal exit.

The best way to get into Vancouver is on the private **Airporter bus** (6.45am–1.10am; $10 single, $17 return; ☎946-8866 or 1-800/668-3141), which leaves from a bay to the left immediately outside the main door of the international arrivals; domestic arrivals can walk here if you need visitor information or wait at the domestic arrivals pick-up outside the terminal. You can buy **tickets** from the desk inside international arrivals, from the driver or from the stand set up by the bus stop at the international terminal departure point. Helpful staff and a pamphlet with a useful map help you figure out which drop-offs on the shuttle's three routes are most useful. Note that if you're headed straight for the bus depot (see below) on route #3 you need to transfer to another Airporter service closer to downtown: the driver will tell you all you need to know. Returning to the airport, buses run round the same pick-up points, including the bus depot.

Taxis into town cost about $25, limos around $32 plus tax. **Public transport** is cheaper, but slower and involves a change of bus – take the BC Metro Transit bus #100 to the corner of 70th Street and Granville (it leaves the domestic terminal roughly every 30min), then change to the #20 or #21 which drops off downtown on Granville Street. Tickets cost $2.50 rush hour, $1.75 off-peak, and exact change is required to buy tickets on board: make sure you get a transfer if the driver doesn't automatically give you one (see "City transport", p.697, for more on peak and off-peak times and transfers).

It's also useful to know that you can pick up direct **buses** to Victoria from the airport: ask for details at the bus desk in international arrivals, or go straight to the hotel shuttle bus stop outside the international terminal: Pacific Coach Lines (☎662-8074 or 1-800/661-1725, *www.pacificcoach.com*) run between one and three daily direct services from the airport to Victoria depending on the time of year (1 daily year-round; 2 daily mid-May to late June and early Sept to Oct; 3 daily late June to early Sept; $30.50).

Bus terminal

Vancouver's main **bus terminal**, which is used by Pacific Coach Lines (for Victoria, Vancouver Island), Maverick Coach Lines (Whistler, Sunshine Coast and Nanaimo)

DEPARTURE TAX

All passengers departing from Vancouver International Airport must pay an Airport Improvement Fee – $5 if travelling within BC, $10 within North America (including Mexico and Hawaii) and $15 outside North America. The tax is levied as you pass through the gates and must be paid on the spot with cash or credit.

ONWARDS FROM VANCOUVER

Vancouver is at the hub of transport links to many parts of western Canada. Deciding where to move **onward from the city** – and how to go – presents a wealth of possibilities. We've listed the basic alternatives, together with cross-references to more detailed accounts of the various options.

Alaska and the Yukon You can fly to Whitehorse (see p.879) in the Yukon directly from Vancouver, but there are no nonstop flights to Alaska from the city: all go via Seattle in the US. You can fly to Seattle or take a bus to Sea-Tac Airport in around three hours from Vancouver Airport or various downtown hotels and other locations (see "Arrival and information" overleaf for bus details). You can **drive** to Alaska through southern British Columbia to Dawson Creek, where you can pick up the Alaska Hwy (see p.873) which runs through the Yukon to Fairbanks. Allow at least three days. Alternatively drive to Prince George, head west towards Prince Rupert and then strike north up the more adventurous Cassiar Hwy (see p.867) to connect with the Alaska Hwy in the Yukon. Using **public transport** you could take either a BC Rail train (see opposite) or Greyhound bus to Prince George (one day), connecting with another Greyhound to Dawson Creek and Whitehorse (two days). Alaskon Express buses link Whitehorse with Alaskan destinations.

To travel to Alaska by **boat** from Vancouver you need to go via Bellingham (in the US), Prince Rupert, or Port Hardy on Vancouver Island (see p.787).

British Columbia Two main **road** routes strike east from Vancouver towards Alberta and the Canadian Rockies – the Trans-Canada Highway and Hwy 3, both served by regular Greyhound **buses**. Both give access to the Okanagan (see p.818), known for its warm-watered lakes and summer resorts, and to the beautiful mountain and lakes enclave of the Kootenays (see p.830). VIA **trains** run through the region via Kamloops to Jasper (for the Rockies) and Edmonton three times weekly. Buses and BC Rail trains also serve the **Cariboo** region, the duller central part of the province (see p.803). Several mouthwatering itineraries can be put together by combining car or public transport journeys in the BC interior with BC Ferries' connections from Port Hardy on Vancouver Island (see below) to either Bella Coola or Prince Rupert.

Calgary and the Canadian Rockies It takes between ten and twelve hours to drive to Calgary on the Trans-Canada Hwy, and about ninety minutes less to reach the heart of the Canadian Rockies, Banff. Special express-service Greyhound buses operate over the same route. There is no longer a VIA Rail passenger service to Calgary. Very frequent one-hour flights connect Vancouver and Calgary, and charter operators such as Canada 3000 offer highly competitive rates on this route.

Vancouver Island Numerous **ferries** ply between Vancouver and three points on its eponymous island – Swartz Bay (for Victoria), Nanaimo and Comox. Most leave from Tsawwassen and Horseshoe Bay, terminals about thirty-minutes' drive south and west of downtown respectively. As a foot passenger you can buy inclusive bus and ferry tickets from Vancouver to Victoria or Nanaimo. Car drivers should make reservations well in advance for all summer crossings (see p.734 for full details of getting to Vancouver Island). **Public transport** connects to the Pacific Rim National Park, the island's highlight, and to Port Hardy on the island's northern tip for ferry connections to Prince Rupert and Bella Coola.

and all Greyhound services, is in a slightly dismal area alongside the VIA Rail Pacific Central train station at 1150 Station St; ticket offices for all companies are on the inside on the right as you enter. It's too far to walk to downtown from here, so bear left from the station through a small park, to the Science World–Main St SkyTrain station and it's a couple of stops to downtown (take the train marked "Waterfront"); tickets ($1.75) are available from platform machines. Alternatively, you could take a taxi downtown from the station for about $6–8. There are **left-luggage** facilities here and a useful **hotel board**, whose freephone line connects to some of the city's genuine cheapies (but check locations) – some of whom will deduct the taxi fare from the terminal from your first night's bill.

Trains

The skeletal **VIA Rail** services also operate out of Pacific Central Station (☎640-3741 or 1-800/561-8630, *www.viarail.ca*); they run to and from Jasper ($175), where there are connections (see pp.645–646) for Prince George and Prince Rupert, and on to Edmonton and the east (3 weekly Mon, Thurs & Sat). There is also one daily VIA–Amtrak (☎253/931-8917 or 1-800/872-7245, *www.amtrakcascades.com*) service between Vancouver and Seattle (currently departs 6pm and arrives Seattle at 9.55pm).

A second train station, belonging to the provincial **BC Rail**, at 1311 W 1st St, in North Vancouver (☎984-5246 or 1-800/339-8752 in BC, 1-800/663-8238 from the rest of Canada and US, *www.bcrail.com*), provides passenger services to and from Whistler (1 daily; 2hr 35min), Lillooet (1 daily; 5hr 35min), and Prince George (3 weekly; 13hr 30min) via 100 Mile House, Williams Lake and Quesnel. Note that in the summer they also run very popular **excursion trips** to Squamish aboard the *Royal Hudson* steam train, sometimes combined with a sea cruise. For more on this, see "The Interior" pp.791–805.

Information

The excellent **Vancouver visitor centre** is almost opposite Canada Place (see p.706) at the foot of Burrard Street in the Waterfront Centre, 200 Burrard St at the corner of Canada Place Way (June–Aug daily 8am–6pm; Sept–May Mon–Fri 8.30am–5pm, Sat 9am–5pm; ☎683-2000 or 1-800/663-6000 or 1-800/435-5622, *www.tourismvancouver.com*). It is called by different names depending what you read: the "Tourist InfoCentre" is the most common designation. Besides information on the city and much of southeastern British Columbia, the office provides **foreign exchange** facilities, BC TransLink (transit or public transport) tickets and information, and tickets to sports and entertainment events. It also has one of the most comprehensive **accommodation services** imaginable, backed up by bulging photo albums of hotel rooms and B&Bs: the booking service is free. Smaller kiosks open in the summer (July & Aug) in a variety of locations, usually including Stanley Park and close to the Vancouver Art Gallery on the corner of Georgia and Granville (daily 9.30am–5.30pm, Thurs & Fri till 9pm).

City transport

Vancouver's **public transport** system is an efficient, integrated network of bus, light-rail (SkyTrain), SeaBus and ferry services which are operated by TransLink, formerly – and occasionally still – known as BC Transit (daily 6.30am–11.30pm; ☎521-0400, *www.translink.bc.ca*).

Tickets are valid across the system for bus, SkyTrain and SeaBus. Generally they cost $1.75 for journeys in the large, central Zone 1 and $2.50 or $3.50 for longer two- and three-zone journeys – though you're unlikely to go out of Zone 1. These regular fares apply Monday to Friday from start of service until 6.30pm. After 6.30pm and all day Saturday, Sunday and public holidays, a flat $1.75 fare applies across all three zones.

Tickets are valid for transfers throughout the system for ninety minutes from the time of issue; on buses you should ask for a transfer ticket if the driver doesn't automatically give you one. Otherwise, you can buy tickets individually (or in books of ten for $13.75) at station offices or machines, 7-Eleven, Safeway and London Drugs stores, or any other shop or newsstand displaying a blue TransLink sticker (so-called "FareDealer" outlets). You must carry tickets with you as proof of payment. Probably the simplest and cheapest deal if you're going to be making three or more journeys in a day is to buy a **DayPass** ($7), valid all day across all three zones; Zone 1 monthly passes are $63. If you buy these over the counter at stores or elsewhere (not in machines) they're "Scratch & Ride" – you scratch out the day and month before travel. If you lose anything on the transport system go to the **lost property** office at the SkyTrain Stadium Station (Mon–Fri 8.30am–5pm; ☎682-7887 or 985-7777 for items left on West Van buses). If you don't want to use public transport, **car and bicycle rental** and **taxis** are easy to come by – see "Listings" on p.728 for details.

Buses

The useful *Transit Route Map & Guide* ($1.50) is available from the infocentre and FareDealer shops, while free **bus** timetables can be found at the infocentre, 7-Eleven stores and the central library. The free *Discover Vancouver on the Transit* pamphlet from the infocentre is also extremely useful, though there is talk of discontinuing production of this guide. You can buy tickets on the bus, but make sure you have the right change (they don't carry any) to shovel into the box by the driver; ask specially if you want a transfer ticket. If you have a pass or transfer, simply show the driver. Normal buses stop running around midnight, when a rather patchy "Night Owl" service comes into effect on major routes until about 4am. Note that blue **West Van** buses (☎985-7777) also operate (usually to North and West Vancouver destinations, including the BC Ferries terminal at Horseshoe Bay) in the city and BC Transit tickets are valid on these buses as well. The box below shows some of Vancouver's more useful routes.

BUS ROUTES

Some of the more important Vancouver **bus routes** are:

#1 Gastown–English Bay loop.

#3 and #8 Gastown–Downtown–Marine Drive.

#4 and #10 Granville Street–University of British Columbia–Museum of Anthropology.

#17 and #20 Downtown–Marine Drive; transfer to #100 for the airport at Granville and 70th Street.

#19 Pender Street (Downtown)–Stanley Park (Stanley Park Loop).

#23, #35, #123 and #135 – Downtown (Pender and Burrard)–Stanley Park.

#50 Gastown – False Creek–Broadway.

#51 SeaBus Terminal–Downtown–Granville Island.

#236 Lonsdale Quay terminal (North Vancouver)–Capilano Suspension Bridge–Grouse Mountain.

Some **scenic routes** are worth travelling for their own sakes:

#52 "Around the Park" service takes 30min through Stanley Park (April–Oct Sat, Sun & holidays only); board at Stanley Park Loop (connections from #23, #35 or #135) or Denman Street (connections from #1, #3 or #8).

#210 Pender Street–Phibbs Exchange; change there for the #211 (mountain route) or #212 (ocean views) to Deep Cove.

#250 Georgia Street (Downtown)–North Vancouver–West Vancouver–Horseshoe Bay.

#351 Howe Street–White Rock–Crescent Beach (1hr each way).

SeaBuses

The **SeaBuses** ply between downtown and Lonsdale Quay in North Vancouver, and they're a ride definitely worth taking for its own sake: the views of the mountains across Burrard Inlet, the port and the downtown skyline are superb. The downtown terminal is Waterfront Station in the old Canadian Pacific station buildings at the foot of Granville Street. There is no ticket office, only a ticket machine, but you can get a ticket from the small newsagent immediately on your left as you face the long gallery that takes you to the boats. Two 400-seat catamarans make the thirteen-minute crossing every fifteen to thirty minutes (6.30am–12.30am). Arrival in North Vancouver is at Lonsdale Quay, where immediately to the left is a bus terminal for connections to Grouse Mountain and other North Vancouver destinations. Bicycles can be carried onboard.

Ferries

The city also has a variety of small **ferries** – glorified bathtubs – run over similar routes by two rival companies: Aquabus (☎689-5858) and False Creek Ferries (☎684-7781, *www.granvilleislandferries.bc.ca*). These provide a useful, very frequent and fun service. Aquabus run boats in a continuous circular shuttle from the foot of Hornby Street to the Fish Docks on the seawalk to Vanier Park and the museums, to Granville Island (both \$2), and to the Yaletown dock by the road loop at the east foot of Davie Street (\$3). False Creek Ferries also run to Granville Island (\$2), and also to Vanier Park (\$3 from Granville Island, \$2 from the Aquatic Centre) just below the Maritime Museum – a good way of getting to the park and its museums (see p.712). You buy **tickets** on board with both companies. Both companies also offer what amount to mini-cruises up False Creek, with connections from Granville Island to Science World and the Plaza of Nations. You can pick up the Aquabus boat at the Arts Club Theatre on Granville Island, the foot of Hornby Street downtown or – with False Creek Ferries – below the Aquatic Centre at the foot of Thurlow and northern end of Burrard Bridge, on Granville Island or below the spit and small harbour near the Maritime Museum in Vanier Park.

SkyTrain

Vancouver's single light-rail line – **SkyTrain** – is a model of its type: driverless, completely computerized and magnetically propelled, half underground and half on raised track. It covers 22km (an extension is under construction) between the downtown Waterfront Station (housed in the CPR building with the SeaBus terminal) and the southeastern suburb of New Westminster. Only the first three or four stations – Waterfront, Burrard, Granville and Stadium – are of any practical use to the casual visitor, but the 39-minute trip along the twenty-station line is worth taking if only to see how the Canadians do these things – spotless interiors and Teutonic punctuality.

Accommodation

Vancouver has a surprisingly large number of **inexpensive hotels**, but some – mainly in the area east of downtown – are of a dinginess at odds with the city's highly polished image. Gastown, Chinatown and the area between them hold the cheaper places, often on top of a bar where live bands and late-night drinking will keep you awake till the small hours. These areas are not safe for women at night, and everyone needs to avoid the backstreets. If you really need to stick to the rock-bottom price bracket, you're better off in the hostels, *YWCA* or one of the invariably dodgy hotels north of the Granville Street Bridge, a tame but tacky red-light area. **Mid-range hotels** are still reasonable

($65–100), but Vancouver is a tourist city and things can get tight in summer – book ahead for the best and most popular places such as the *Sylvia* and *Kingston*. A lot of the nicer options (including the *Sylvia*) are in the West End, a quiet residential area bordering Vancouver's wonderful Stanley Park, only five- or ten-minutes' walk from downtown. Out of season, hotels in all categories offer reductions, and you can reckon on thirty percent discounts on the prices below. Remember, too, that the prices below are for doubles, though even the smartest hotels will introduce an extra bed into a double room at very little extra cost if there are three of you.

B&B accommodation can be booked through agencies, but most of them operate as a phone service only and require two-days' notice – it's better to try the infocentre's accommodation service first. Though seldom central or cheap – reckon on $75 plus for a double – B&Bs are likely to be relaxed and friendly, and if you choose well you can have beaches, gardens, barbecues and as little or as much privacy as you want. The following **B&B agencies** have accommodation throughout the city, in Victoria (see p.732), the Gulf Islands and beyond: A B & C B&B of Vancouver (☎298-8815, *www.vancouver-bandb.bc.ca*); All B&B Reservations (☎683-3609, *gorse@interchg.ubc.ca*); Beachside B&B Registry (☎922-7773, *www.beach.bc.ca*); Canada-West Accommodations (☎990-6730, *www.b-b.com*); B&B Town and Country Reservation Service (☎731-5942, *www.tcbb.bc.ca*); and Old English B&B Registry (☎986-5069, *www.oldenglishbandb.bc.ca*).

Vancouver has two good Hostelling International **hostels**, plus a handful of other reasonable privately run hostels. Be warned, though, that there are a rash of dreadful "hotels", "hostels" and "rooming houses" (dirty, badly run and occasionally dangerous), particularly on Hastings Street a few blocks either side of Main Street: don't be tempted into these on any account.

In addition to the hostels, relatively low-price accommodation is available in summer at the **University of British Columbia**, though this is a long way from downtown, and most rooms go to convention visitors (☎822-1000, fax 822-1001, *www.conferences.ubc.ca*). Singles start at $25, with doubles costing a not terribly competitive $93. Vancouver is not a camper's city – the majority of the in-city **campsites** are for RVs only and will turn you away if you've only got a tent. We've listed the few places that won't.

Hotels

Barclay Hotel, 1348 Robson St between Jervis and Broughton sts (☎688-8850, fax 688-2534, *www.barclayhotel.com*). One of the city's better bargains, the *Barclay* is one of the nicer of several hotels at the north end of Robson St, with ninety rooms and a chintzy French rustic ambience. ⑤.

Buchan Hotel, 1906 Haro St between Chilco and Gilford sts (☎685-5354 or 1-800/668-6654, fax 685-5367, *www3.bc.sympatico.ca/buchan/*). Some smallish rooms, past their prime, but still a genuine bargain given the peaceful residential location, only a block from Stanley Park and English Bay Beach. ⑥.

Burrard Motor Inn, 1100 Burrard St near Helmcken St (☎681-2331 or 1-800/663-0366, fax 681-9753). A fairly central and pleasantly dated motel with standard fittings: some rooms look onto a charming garden courtyard, and some have kitchens. ⑤.

Canadian Pacific Hotel Vancouver, 900 W Georgia St at Burrard St (☎684-3131 or 1-800/441-1414, fax 662-1929, *www.cphotels.ca*). This traditional old hotel, given a multimillion-dollar face-lift in 1996, is the city's most famous and prestigious. It's the place to stay if money's no object and you want old-world style and downtown location. Whether you stay here or not, the ground floor *900 West* restaurant and bar is good, as are the various other restaurants, including *Griffins* on the same floor. Doubles among the 550 rooms range from $224 to $589, but low-season rates are available. ⑧.

Canadian Pacific Waterfront Central Hotel, 900 Canada Place Way (☎691-1991 or 1-800/441-1414, *www.cphotels.ca*). Another prestigious *Canadian Pacific* hotel, this time a fabulous multistorey affair on the dazzling downtown waterfront. ⑧.

Hotel Dakota, 654 Nelson St on the corner of Granville (☎605-4333 or 1-888/605-5333, fax 605-4334, *www.hoteldakota.com*). The location is not pleasant, but this is the exception to the rule among the grim hotels at the lower end of Granville St. There are a wide range of clean, cheap and renovated rooms at different prices in a big, bright-looking building. Continental breakfast included. ⑤.

Days Inn Vancouver Downtown, 921 W Pender St at Burrard St (☎681-4335 or 1-877/681-4335, *www.daysinnvancouver.com*). A city institution, this old seventy-room, seven-storey block in the central financial district has more character than most and lots of original Art Deco touches. While it looks tatty from the outside, the interior was renovated in 1999 and the rooms are clean and comfortable; streetfront rooms are likely to be noisy. ⑥.

Dominion Hotel, 210 Abbott St at Water St (☎681-6666, fax 681-5855). A nice, newly decorated old hotel on the edge of Gastown let down by its thunderous live music: it's almost impossible to find a room where you're not kept awake, but at least try to ask for one of the newer rooms with private bathroom as far away as possible from the live bands that play in the bar downstairs. ③.

Granville Island Hotel, 1253 Johnson St (☎683-7373 or 1-800/663-1840, fax 683-3061, *www.granvilleislandhotel.com*). You're away from central downtown, but on the other hand you're in the heart of one of the city's trendiest and most enjoyable little enclaves. You pay a premium for this and for the spectacular waterfront setting. ⑦.

Holiday Inn Hotel & Suites Downtown, 1110 Howe St between Helmcken and Davie sts (☎684-2151 or 1-800/663-9151 in Canada, 1-800/HOLIDAY worldwide, fax 684-4736, *www.atlific.com*). Reasonably central, large and – unlike the dingier hotels nearby – you'll know what to expect, though at this price there's plenty of alternative choice around town. Lots of facilities, including sauna, pool and kids' activity centre, plus rooms with kitchenettes for self-catering. ⑦.

Kingston Hotel, 757 Richards St at Robson St (☎684-9024 or 1-888/713-3304, fax 684-9917, *www.vancouver-bc.com/kingstonhotel*). This popular bargain is handily sited for downtown and its clean and nicely-decorated interior affects the spirit of a "European-style" hotel. Rooms are available with or without private bathroom and there's a modest but free breakfast to start the day. Along with the *Sylvia*, it's by far the best hotel at its price in the city, so book well ahead. Long-stay terms available. ③/④.

Pacific Palisades, 1277 Robson St between Jervis and West Bute sts (☎688-0461 or 1-800/663-1815, fax 891-5130). Not quite up there in the luxury bracket with the *Canadian Pacific* hotels, but still one of the city's best top-price hotels. Many of the rooms have superb views of the sea and mountains, and guests have access to a pool and gym. ⑦.

Patricia Budget Inn Hotel, 403 E Hastings St near Gore St (☎255-4301, fax 254-7154, *www.budgetpathotel.bc.ca*). A well-known and widely advertised budget choice with 92 rooms, but far from downtown in the heart of Chinatown (too far to walk comfortably): an exciting or grim location, depending on your point of view, though some women have reported feeling distinctly unsafe in the area. Clean and renovated, it's the best of the many in this district. ③.

Riviera Hotel, 1431 Robson St between Nicola and Broughton sts (☎685-1301 or 1-888/699-5222, *www.vancouver-bc.com/RivieraHotel*). Reasonably priced central motels such as this place are rare; the one- and two-room suites have kitchenettes. ⑥.

Sandman Hotel Downtown, 180 W Georgia St at Beatty St (☎681-2211 or 1-800/726-3626, fax 681-8009, *www.sandman.ca*). Flagship of a mid-price chain with hotels all over western Canada and well placed at the eastern edge of downtown. Rooms are bland but fine and spacious as far as chain hotels go, which makes this first choice if you want something one up from the *Kingston*. ⑤.

Shato Inn Hotel at Stanley Park, 1825 Comox St between Gilford and Denman sts (☎681-8920). A small, quiet, family-run place two blocks from the park and the beach. Some of the rooms have balconies and/or kitchen units. ⑥.

Sunset Inn Travel Apartments, 1111 Burnaby between Davie and Thurlow sts (☎688-2474 or 1-800/786-1997, fax 669-3340, *www.sunsetinn.com*). One of the best West End "apartment" hotels and a good spot for a longer stay – spacious studio, double or triple rooms (all with kitchens and balconies) with on-site laundry and many nearby shops. Ten-minute walk to downtown. ⑤.

Sylvia Hotel, 1154 Gilford St (☎681-9321, fax 682-3551, *www.sylviahotel.com*). A local landmark located in a "heritage" building, this is a popular place with a high reputation, making reservations essential. It's by the beach two blocks from Stanley Park, and its snug bar, quiet, old-world charm and sea views make it one of Vancouver's best. Rooms are available at different prices depending on size, view and facilities. ③–⑦.

West End Guest House, 1362 Haro St at Jervis St (☎681-2889, fax 688-8812, *www.westendguesthouse.com*). A wonderful small guesthouse with an old-time parlour and bright rooms, each with private bathroom; book well in advance. Full breakfast included. No smoking. ⑥.

Hostels

American Backpackers Hostel, 374 W Pender St between Richards and Homer sts (☎688-0112, fax 685-7989). This is one of the city's newest hostels, and also one of the cheapest. The location is good – just a block or so farther east than the Seymour St *Cambie* hostel (see below) – and various inducements are offered to patrons such as free beer on Saturdays, Internet access, showers, patio, pool table and free pick-ups in a customized '64 Volkswagen Beetle (airport shuttle costs $15). Dorm beds $10, singles $25, doubles $30. No curfew. ②.

Cambie International Hostel, 300 Cambie St at Cordova St (☎684-6466). Private hostel just off Gastown's main streets, so a bolder and more central position than many of the other hostels. Beds are arranged in two- or four-bunk rooms and there are laundry and bike-storage facilities. Downstairs are a bakery, café and bar, so aim for beds away from these if you want a relatively peaceful night's sleep. From $20 per person. No curfew. ②.

Cambie International Hostel, 515 Seymour St at W Pender St (☎684-7757 or 1-888/395-5335, *www.cambiehostels.com*). The newer and more central of the *Cambie*'s stable of hostels (there is a third on Vancouver Island). Like the Gastown hostel (see above), the management has made an effort to ensure that rooms are pleasant, secure and well-kept, and provide laundry, storage and café facilities. From $20 per person. No curfew. ②.

C&N Backpackers Hotel, 927 Main St (☎682-2441 or 1-888/434-6060, *backpackers@sprint.ca*). Well-known backpackers' retreat that has been renamed – previously it was known as *Vincent's* – renovated and is under new management (after reports that its cleanliness and organization had deteriorated). Seedy and inconvenient eastern edge of downtown location but convenient for SkyTrain station; buses #3 or #8 from downtown run along Main St; 150 beds, but you should still book or arrive early (office open 8am–midnight). Beds at $10, $20 and $25 for a bunk, single and double respectively. No curfew. ①.

Global Village Backpackers, 1018 Granville St at Nelson St (☎682-8226 or 1-888/844-7875, fax 682-8240, *www.globalbackpackers.com*). Global Village has followed up the success of a popular hostel in Toronto with a hostel in Vancouver, although their chosen location on Granville – while central and away from the worst of this street's tawdriness – is not the quietest in the city. The hostel has 250 beds in couples' and four-bed rooms, and among its facilities offers a free shuttle from the bus–train station, secure lockers, modern kitchen and common area, games rooms and Internet access. From $24 per person, private doubles from $50. No curfew. ②.

Vancouver Downtown Hostel (HI), 1114 Burnaby St at Thurlow St (☎684-4565 or 1-888/203-4302, fax 684-4540, *www.hihostels.bc.ca*). The newer and more central of the city's two official HI hostels is located in a former nunnery and health-care centre in the city's West End, with 223 beds in shared and private rooms (maximum of four per room). Bike rental and storage as well as laundry, kitchen, Internet kiosk, safe location and storage lockers. Open 24 hours with no curfew. A free shuttle (look for the blue HI logo) operates between the hostel, the *Jericho Beach* hostel (see below) and the Pacific Central railway and bus terminal; if there's no bus, call the hostel to find when the next one is due. Beds cost $19.95 for members ($23.95 for nonmembers), private doubles from $49.95. ①/②.

Vancouver Jericho Beach Hostel (HI), 1515 Discovery St (☎224-3208, fax 224-4852, *www.hihostels.bc.ca*). Canada's biggest youth hostel has a superb and safe position by Jericho Beach south of the city. The hostel fills up quickly, occasionally leading to a three-day limit in summer; open all day, with an excellent cafeteria. There are dorm beds and a few private rooms, with reductions for members and free bunks occasionally offered in return for a couple of hours' work. Facilities include kitchen, licensed café (April–Oct), bike rental and storage, storage lockers and Internet kiosk. Open 24 hours with no curfew, but a "quiet time" is encouraged between 11pm and 7am. To get here from the airport, take the #100 bus to Granville St and 70th Ave and transfer to the #8 Fraser bus; get off at Granville and 6th Ave and cross Granville using the underpass. Then take the #4 UBC bus to NW Marine Drive, turn right on NW Marine Drive and walk 350m downhill to Discovery St. From downtown, take bus #4 from Granville St. ①.

YWCA Hotel/Residence, 733 Beatty St between Georgia and Robson sts (☎895-5830 or 1-800/663-1424, fax 681-2550). An excellent place purpose-built in 1995 in a great east-downtown location close to the central library. The nearest SkyTrain station is Stadium, a five-minute walk. Top-value rooms (especially for small groups) spread over eleven floors with a choice of private, shared or hall bathrooms. TVs in most rooms, plus sports and cooking facilities as well as a cheap cafeteria. Open to men, women and families. Singles ($55–109), doubles ($61, $77 or $99), triples ($96–130), four- ($140) or five-person ($145) rooms available; long-term rates offered in winter. No curfew. ④/⑤.

Camping

Burnaby Cariboo RV Park, 8765 Cariboo Place, Burnaby (☎420-1722, fax 420-4782, *www.bcrv-park.com*). This site has luxurious facilities (indoor pool, jacuzzi, laundry, free showers) and a separate tenting area away from the RVs. Take Gaglardi Way exit (#37) from Hwy 1, turn right at the traffic light, then immediately left. The next right is Cariboo Place. Free shuttle bus to various sights. Open year-round. $21–32.95.

Capilano RV Park, 295 Tomahawk, West Vancouver (☎987-4722, fax 987-2015, *www.capilanorv-park.com*). The most central site for trailers and tents, beneath the north foot of the Lion's Gate Bridge: exit on Capilano Rd S or the Hwy 99 exit off Lion's Gate Bridge. Reservations (with deposit) essential June through August. $20–35.

Mount Seymour Provincial Park, North Vancouver (☎986-2261). Lovely BC provincial park spot, with full facilities, but only a few tent sites alongside car parks 2 and 3. July–Sept. $18.50 per tent.

Richmond RV Park and Campground, Hollybridge and River Rd, Richmond (☎270-7878 or 1-800/755-4905, fax 244-9713). Best of the RV outfits, with the usual facilities; 14km from downtown – take Hwy 99 North to the Westminster Hwy exit (#36) and follow signs. Also space for tents. April 1–Oct 30. $17–26.

The City

Vancouver is not a city which offers or requires lots of relentless sightseeing. Its breathtaking physical beauty makes it a place where often it's enough just to wander and watch the world go by – "the sort of town", wrote Jan Morris, "nearly everyone would want to live in." In summer you'll probably end up doing what the locals do, if not actually sailing, hiking, skiing, fishing or whatever, then certainly going to the beach, lounging in one of the parks or spending time in waterfront cafés.

In addition to the myriad leisure activities, however, there are a handful of sights that make worthwhile viewing by any standards. You'll inevitably spend a good deal of time in the **downtown** area and its Victorian-era equivalent, **Gastown**, now a renovated and less than convincing pastiche of its past. **Chinatown**, too, could easily absorb a morning, and contains more than its share of interesting shops, restaurants and rumbustiously busy streets. For a taste of the city's sensual side, hit **Stanley Park**, a huge area of semi-wild parkland and beaches that crowns the northern tip of the downtown peninsula. Take a walk or a bike ride here and follow it up with a stroll to the **beach**. Be certain to spend a morning on **Granville Island**, by far the city's most tempting spot for wandering and people-watching. If you prefer a cultural slant on things, hit the formidable **Museum of Anthropology** or the museums of the Vanier Park complex, the latter easily accessible from Granville Island.

At a push, you could cram the city's essentials into a couple of days. If you're here for a longer stay, though, you'll want to venture further out from downtown: trips across Burrard Inlet to **North Vancouver**, worth making for the views from the SeaBus ferry alone, lend a different panoramic perspective of the city, and lead into the mountains and forests that give Vancouver its tremendous setting. The most popular trips here are to the Capilano Suspension Bridge, something of a triumph of PR over substance, and to the more worthwhile cable-car trip up **Grouse Mountain** for some staggering views of the city.

Downtown

You soon get the hang of Vancouver's **downtown** district, an arena of streets and shopping malls centred on **Robson Street**. On hot summer evenings it's like a latter-day vision of la dolce vita – a dynamic meeting place crammed with bars, restaurants, late-night stores, and bronzed youths preening in bars or cafés, or ostentatiously cruising in open-topped cars. At other times a more sedate class hangs out on the steps of the Vancouver Art Gallery or glides in and out of the two big department stores, Eaton's

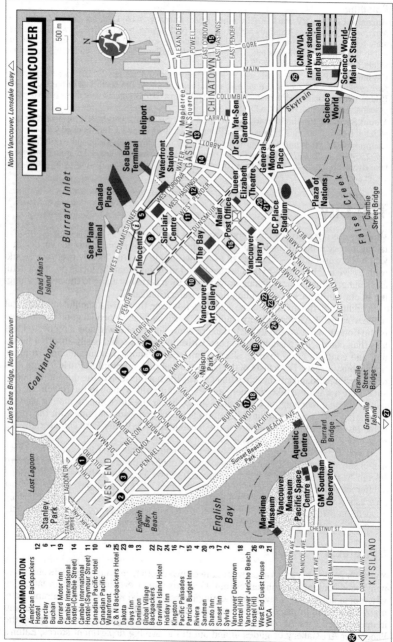

DOWNTOWN VANCOUVER

ACCOMMODATION

American Backpackers Hostel	12
Barclay	6
Buchan	1
Burrard Motor Inn	19
Cambie (International Hostel(Cambie Street)	14
Cambie International Hostel-(Seymour Street)	11
Canadian Pacific Hotel	10
Canadian Pacific Waterfront	5
C & N Backpackers Hotel	25
Dakota	23
Days Inn	8
Dominion	13
Global Village Backpackers	22
Granville Island Hotel	27
Holiday Inn	24
Kingston	16
Pacific Palisades	7
Patricia Budget Inn	15
Riviera	4
Sandman	20
Shato Inn	3
Sunset Inn	17
Sylvia	2
Vancouver Downtown Hostel (HI)	18
Vancouver Jericho Beach Hostel (HI)	26
West End Guest House	9
YWCA	21

VANCOUVER'S BEACHES

Vancouver, it's rather surprising to find, has **beaches**. Perhaps not of Malibu or Bondi standard, but beaches just the same, and ones that look and feel like the real thing, even if much of the sand comes from Japan in container ships. All are clean and well kept: the clarity of the water is remarkable given the size of the city's port – and the majority have lifeguards during the summer months. The best face each other across False Creek and English Bay, starting with Stanley Park's three adjacent beaches: **English Bay Beach**, ranged along Beach Avenue; **Second Beach**, to the north, which also features a shallow onshore swimming pool; and **Third Beach**, further north still, least crowded of the three and the one with the best views of West Vancouver and the mountains. English Bay at the southern end of Denman is the most readily accessible, and easily visited after seeing Stanley Park.

Across the water to the south and west of the Burrard Bridge, **Kitsilano Beach**, or "Kits", is named – like the district behind it – after Chief Khahtsahlano, a Squamish chieftain of a band who once owned the area. Walk here from Vanier Park and the museums (30min) on the coast path or, from downtown, take a #22 **bus** southbound on Burrard Street. Kits is a city favourite and the busiest and most self-conscious of the beaches. It's especially popular with the university, volleyball and rippling torso crowds, and the more well-heeled locals. Families also come here, though, to take advantage of the warm and safe swimming area, while sunbathers can take up a position on the grass to the rear. Vancouver's largest and most popular outdoor heated pool is the **lido** at Yew and Cornwall (daily mid-May to early Sept), while the **shoreline path** is a lovely place for an evening stroll, cycle or time out on a bench to watch the streetlife. Follow the path all the way east and it takes you to Granville Island by way of Vanier Park and the museums. A former hippie and alternative-lifestyle hangout, Kits still betrays shades of its past and, with nearby bars and restaurants to fuel the party spirit, there's always plenty going on (though there's also sometimes a vaguely meat-market sort of atmosphere).

Jericho Beach, west of Kits and handy for the youth hostel, is a touch quieter and serves as a hangout for the windsurfing crowd. Still further west, Jericho blurs into **Locarno Beach** and **Spanish Banks**, progressively less crowded, and the start of a fringe of sand and parkland that continues round to the University of British Columbia (UBC) campus. Locals rate Spanish Banks the most relaxed of the city's beaches, while Locarno is one of its most spectacular, especially at low tide, when the sand seems to stretch for ever. Bikers and walkers use the dirt track at the top of Locarno, beyond which a broad sward of grass with picnic tables and benches runs to the road. You can rent canoes at Jericho from Ecomarine Ocean Kayak, 1688 Duranleau St (☎689-7575).

At low tide the more athletically inclined could walk all the way round to UBC (otherwise take the bus as for the Museum of Anthropology; see p.713), where the famous clothing-optional **Wreck Beach** lies just off the campus area below NW Marine Drive – ask any student to point you towards the half-hidden access paths. It's inevitably aroused a fair bit of prudish criticism in the past, but at the moment attitudes seem more relaxed. The atmosphere is generally laid-back – though women have been known to complain of voyeurs – and nude pedlars are often on hand to sell you anything from pizza and illegal smokeables to (bona fide) massage and hair-braiding. Finally, **Ambleside**, west of the Park Royal Mall along Marine Drive (turn south at 13th St W), is the most accessible beach if you're in North or West Vancouver.

and The Bay. Downtown's other principal thoroughfares are **Burrard Street** – all smart shops, hotels and offices – and **Granville Street**, partly pedestrianized with plenty of shops and cinemas, but curiously seedy in places, especially at its southern end near the Granville Street Bridge. New development, however, is taking downtown's reach further east, and at some point in your stay you should try to catch the public library, opened in 1995, at 350 W Georgia, a focus of this growth and a striking piece of modern architecture to boot.

For the best possible introduction to Vancouver, though, you should walk down to the waterfront and **Canada Place**, the Canadian pavilion for Expo '86, the huge world exhibition held in the city in 1986, and another architectural tour de force that houses a luxury hotel, cruise-ship terminal and two glitzy convention centres. For all its excess, however, it makes a superb viewpoint, with stunning vistas of the port, mountains, sea and buzzing boats, helicopters and float planes. The port activity, especially, is mesmerizing. One of North America's busiest **ports** began by exporting timber in 1864 in the shape of fence pickets to Australia. Today it handles seventy million tonnes of cargo annually, turns over $40 billion in trade and processes 3000 ships a year from almost a hundred countries. Canada Place's design, and the manner in which it juts into the port, is meant to suggest a ship, and you can walk the building's perimeter as if "on deck", stopping to read the boards that describe the immediate cityscape and the appropriate pages of its history. Inside are expensive shops, an unexceptional restaurant and an IMAX cinema ($9.50; ☎682-4629, www.imax.com/vancouver); unfortunately, most of the films shown – often on boats, rock concerts and obscure wildlife – are a waste of a good screen.

An alternative to Canada Place's vantage point, the nearby **Harbour Centre Building** at 555 W Hastings, is one of the city's tallest structures, and is known by locals either as the "urinal" or, more affectionately, the "hamburger", after its bulging upper storeys. On a fine day it's definitely worth paying to ride the stomach-churning, all-glass, SkyLift elevators that run up the side of the tower – 167m in a minute – to the fortieth-storey observation deck, known as "The Lookout!", with its staggering 360-degree views (daily: May–Sept 8.30am–10.30pm; Oct–April 9am–9pm; $9; ☎299-9000 ext 2626, www.harbourcentretower.com). Admission is valid all day so you can return and look out over the bright lights of Vancouver at night.

Much of the **Expo site** here and at other points to the south and east has been levelled or is undergoing rigorous redevelopment, and to see its remaining sights requires a long walk from central downtown (take the SkyTrain or ferries from Granville Island instead). The geodesic dome is the main survivor, and has become a striking city landmark – but the museum it now houses, **Science World** at Québec St–Terminal Avenue near Science World–Main St SkyTrain station – is something of a disappointment (Mon–Fri 10am–5pm, Sat & Sun 10am–6pm; Science World $11.75, OMNIMAX $10; combination tickets $14.75; ☎268-6363 or 443-7440, www.scienceworld.bc.ca). Probably only children, at whom the place seems largely aimed, will be satisfied by the various high-tech, hands-on displays, which include the opportunity to make thunderous amounts of noise on electronic instruments and drum machines. Galleries deal with all manner of science-related themes, but probably the best things here if you're an adult are the building itself and the vast screen of the OMNIMAX Cinema at the top of the dome – though as with the similar screen at Canada Place, only a limited range of quality movies have been produced to suit the format.

Another remnant of the Expo is the 60,000-seat **BC Place Stadium**, 1 Robson St (tours mid-June to early Sept every Tues & Fri at 11am and 1pm; $5; ☎661-7362, www.bcplacestadium.com), the world's largest air-inflated dome; unless you're there for a sporting event such as a BC Lions Canadian football game, the "mushroom" or "marshmallow in bondage", in popular parlance, isn't worth the bother. If you're heading to a game, take the SkyTrain to Stadium station or buses #15 east on Robson or #17 on Burrard. Its thunder has also been slightly stolen by **General Motors Place**, a more recent 20,000-seat stadium (known locally as "The Garage") that's home to the Vancouver Canucks ice-hockey team and Vancouver Grizzlies NBA basketball team. For tickets and details of events call Ticketmaster (☎280-3311).

The Vancouver Art Gallery

Centrally located in the imposing old city courthouse is the rather exorbitant **Vancouver Art Gallery**, located at the corner of Howe and Robson streets (late April to mid-Oct Mon–Wed & Fri–Sun 10am–5.30pm, Thurs 10am–9pm; mid-Oct to late April same hours but closed Mon; $10; ☎662-4700, *www.vanartgallery.bc.ca*). It looks as if it ought to contain a treasure trove of art, but too much space is given to dud works of the sort that give modern art a bad name. What redeems the place are its temporary exhibitions and the powerful and almost surreal works of Emily Carr, who was born on Vancouver Island in 1871 and whose paintings – characterized by deep greens and blues – evoke something of the scale and intensity of the West Coast and its native peoples. A sparse international collection offers Warhol and Lichtenstein, with token rooms of half a dozen Italian, Flemish and British paintings. The **gallery café** is excellent, with a sun-trap of a terrace if you want to sit outside.

Gastown

An easy walk east of downtown – five minutes from Canada Place and concentrated largely on Water Street – **Gastown** is a determined piece of city rejuvenation aimed fair and square at the tourist, distinguished by new cobbles, fake gas lamps, *Ye Olde English Tea Room*-type cafés and a generally over-polished patina. The name derives from "Gassy" Jack Leighton, a retired sailor turned publican and self-proclaimed "mayor", who arrived on site by canoe with his native wife and a mangy yellow dog in 1867, quickly opening a bar to service the nearby lumber mills, whose bosses banned drinking on or near the yards. Leighton's statue stands in **Maple Tree Square**, Gastown's heart, focus of its main streets and reputed site of this first tavern. Trade was brisk, and a second bar opened, soon followed by a village of sorts – "Gassy's Town" – which, though swept away by fire in 1886, formed in effect the birthplace of modern Vancouver. Over the years, the downtown focus moved west and something of Gastown's boozy beginnings returned to haunt it, as its cheap hotels and warehouses turned into a skid row for junkies and alcoholics. By the 1970s the area was declared a historic site – the buildings are the city's oldest – and an enthusiastic beautification programme was set in motion.

The end product never quite became the dynamic, city-integrated spot the planners had hoped, and was slated for years by locals as something of a tourist trap, though recent signs suggest that interesting cafés, clubs and restaurants are slowly beginning to make themselves felt. It's certainly worth a stroll for its buskers, Sunday crowds and occasional points of interest. These do not include the hype-laden two-tonne **steam-powered clock**, the world's first and hopefully last, at the west end of Water Street. It's invariably surrounded by tourists armed with cocked cameras, all awaiting the miniature Big Ben's toots and whistles every fifteen minutes, and bellowing performances on the hour that seem to presage imminent explosion. The steam comes from an underground system that also heats surrounding buildings. Nearby you'll find the **Inuit Gallery**, a large commercial showcase of Inuit art at 345 Water St (Mon–Sat 9.30am–5.30pm).

Probably the most surprising aspect of Gastown, however, is the contrast between its manicured pavements and the down-at-heel streets immediately to the south and east. The bustling hub of **alternative Vancouver**, the area between Gastown and Chinatown is both a skid row and a haven for secondhand clothes shops, bookshops, galleries, new designers and cheap five-and-dimes. In places, however, this area recalls Gastown's bad old days: unpleasantly seedy, pocked with the dingiest of dingy bars and hotels, and inhabited by characters to match.

Chinatown

Vancouver's vibrant **Chinatown** – clustered mainly on Pender Street from Carrall to Gore and on Keefer Street from Main to Gore (buses #22 or #19 east from Pender, or

#22 north from Burrard) – is a city apart. Vancouver's 100,000 or more Chinese make up one one of North America's largest Chinatowns and are the city's oldest and largest ethnic group after the British-descended majority. Many crossed the Pacific in 1858 to join the Fraser Valley gold rush; others followed under contract to help build the Canadian Pacific Railway. Most stayed, only to find themselves being treated appallingly. Denied citizenship and legal rights until as late as 1947, the Chinese community sought safety and familiarity in a ghetto of their own, where clan associations and societies provided for new arrivals and the local poor – and helped build the distinctive houses of recessed balconies and ornamental roofs that have made the area a protected historic site.

Unlike Gastown's gimmickry, Chinatown is all genuine – shops, hotels, markets, tiny restaurants and dim alleys vie for attention amidst an incessant hustle of jammed pavements and the buzz of Chinese conversation. Virtually every building replicates an Eastern model without a trace of self-consciousness, and written Chinese characters feature everywhere in preference to English. Striking and unexpected after downtown's high-rise glitz, the district brings you face to face with Vancouver's oft-touted multiculturalism, and helps explain why Hong Kong immigrants continue to be attracted to the city. It is, however, a district with a distinct edge, and visitors should avoid the area's dingier streets at night and parts of East Hastings near Main Street just about any time.

Apart from the obvious culinary temptations (see "Eating and drinking", beginning on p.718), Chinatown's main points of reference are its **markets**. Some of the best boast fearsome butchery displays and such edibles as live eels, flattened ducks, hundred-year-old eggs and other stuff you'll be happy not to identify. Check out the open-air **night market** at Main and Keefer streets (summer 6pm–midnight), a wonderful medley of sights. Keefer Street is **bakery** row, with lots of tempting stickies on offer like moon cakes and *bao*, steamed buns with a meat or sweet-bean filling. On the corner of Keefer and Main is the Ten Ren Tea and Ginseng Company, with a vast range of teas, many promising cures for a variety of ailments (free tastings). In a similar vein, it's worth dropping into one of the local **herbalists** to browse amongst their panaceas: snakeskins, reindeer antlers, buffalo tongues, dried sea horses and bears' testicles are all available if you're feeling under the weather. Ming Wo, 23 E Pender, is a fantastic cookware shop, with probably every utensil ever devised, while China West, 41 E Pender, is packed with slippers, jackets, pens, cheap toys and the like. Most people also flock dutifully to the 1913 **Sam Kee Building**, at the corner of Carrall and Pender; at just 1.8m across, it's officially the world's narrowest building.

Chinatown's chief cultural attraction is the small **Dr Sun Yat-Sen Garden**, at 578 Carrall St near Pender Street, a 2.5-acre park billed as the first authentic, full-scale classical Chinese garden ever built outside China (May to mid-June 10am–6pm; mid-June to Aug 9.30am–7pm; Sept–April 10am–4.30pm; $6.50, includes free optional tours; ☎689-7133). Named after the founder of the first Chinese Republic, who was a frequent visitor to Vancouver, the park was created for the Expo '86 and cost $5.3 million, $500,000 of which came from the People's Republic accompanied by 52 artisans and 950 crates of materials. The latter included everything from limestone rocks from Taihu – whose jagged shapes are prized in this sort of garden – to the countless tiny pebbles that make up the intricate courtyard pavements. The whole thing is based on classical gardens developed in the city of Suzhou during the Ming dynasty (1368–1644). China's horticultural emissaries, following traditional methods that didn't allow use of a single power tool, spent thirteen months in the city replicating a Suzhou Ming garden to achieve a subtle balance of Yin and Yang: small and large, soft and hard, flowing and immovable, light and dark. Every stone, pine and flower was carefully placed and has symbolic meaning. Hourly free guided tours on the half-hour explain the Taoist philosophy behind the carefully placed elements. At first glance it all seems a touch small and austere, and isn't helped by the preponderance of sponsors' name-plates and glimpses of the road, pub and high-rise outside. After a time, though, the chances are you'll find the garden working its calm and peaceful spell.

Alongside the entrance to the gardens, the **Chinese Cultural Centre Museum & Archives** (Tues–Sun 11am–5pm; $3; ☎687-0282), Chinatown's community focus and a sponsor of New Year festivities, offers classes and hosts changing exhibitions. It also has a museum – the first of its kind dedicated to Chinese-Canadian history – which focuses on early Chinese pioneers and Chinese veterans who served Canada in the two world wars. Next to the gardens and centre is a small and slightly threadbare Dr Sun Yat-Sen Park (free) which, though less worked than the Dr Sun Yat-Sen Garden, is still a pleasant place to take time out from Chinatown. Hours are the same as for the garden, and there's an alternative entrance on Columbia Street and Keefer.

Stanley Park

One of the world's great urban spaces, **Stanley Park** is Vancouver's green heart, helping lend the city its particular character. At nearly 1000 acres, it's the largest urban park in North America – less a tame collection of lawns and elms than a semi-wilderness of dense rainforest, marshland and beaches. Ocean surrounds it on three sides, with a road and parallel cycleway/pedestrian promenade following the sea wall all the way round the peninsula for a total of 10.5km. From here, views of the city and across the water to the mountains are particularly worthwhile. Away from the coastal trail network and main draw – the aquarium – the interior is nearly impenetrable scrub and forest, with few paths and few people. At the same time there are plenty of open, wooded or flower-decorated spaces to picnic, snooze or watch the world go by.

The peninsula was partially logged in the 1860s, when Vancouver was still a twinkle in "Gassy" Jack Leighton's eye, but in 1886 the newly formed city council – showing typical Canadian foresight and an admirable sense of priorities – moved to make what had become a military reserve into a permanent park. Thus its remaining first-growth forest of cedar, hemlock and Douglas fir, and the swamp now known as Lost Lagoon, were saved for posterity in the name of Lord Stanley, Canada's governor general from 1888 to 1893, who dedicated the park "to the use and enjoyment of people of all colours, creeds and customs for all time".

A neat **itinerary** would be to walk or take the bus to the park, stroll or cycle all or part of the sea wall – there's a slew of bike and rollerblade rental places nearby – and then walk back to Denman Street. Here you can grab some food or pause at one of several cafés – the *Bread Garden* midway down Denman on the left at 1040 Denman and Comox is good – and then sit on the grass or sand at English Bay Beach at the foot of the street. The park is a simple though rather dull **walk** from most of downtown, if a fairly lengthy one from the eastern districts. Beach Avenue to the south and Georgia to the north are the best approaches if you're on foot, leading to the southern and northern starts of the sea wall respectively. Walking all the way round the sea-wall path takes about two hours at a brisk lick. Perhaps a better approach is to take a Stanley Park **bus** #23, #35 or #135 from the corner of Burrard and Pender streets downtown, which drop you near the so-called Stanley Park Loop just inside the park by Lost Lagoon and in summer continue deeper into the park to the Upper Zoo Loop (though the zoo's now closed). Other buses which will take you close to the park are the #1 (Beach) to Davie and Beach Avenue and the #3 (Robson) to Denman Street.

If you want to rent a bike, go to the corner of Denman and Georgia streets, where there's a cluster of **bike rental** outlets. Spokes, 1798 W Georgia (☎688-5141), is a big, busy place established in 1938 (from $3.90 an hour for a wide variety of bikes, including children's bikes and tandems with child trailers). You need to leave ID, and a cash or credit-card deposit. Helmets, which are compulsory in BC, and locks are included in the rental. If this place looks too frenetic you might be better advised to walk a few metres up the street, where Bikes 'n' Blades (☎602-9899) is smaller, less busy and rents **rollerblades** as well. Directly opposite at 745 Denman St is Bayshore Bicycle & Rollerblade Rentals (☎688-2453). From Denman it's just a minute's pedalling to the park, but watch the traffic.

If you don't want to walk, cycle or blade, then there's a special TransLink "Stanley Park Shuttle" **bus service**, which runs on a fifteen-minute schedule in summer (daily June–Aug 10am–6.30pm; information ☎257-8400). It makes fourteen stops around the park. You can transfer to the service from the #1 and #3 buses on Denman or the #23, #35 and #135 at Stanley Park Loop: both Denman and the Loop are a few moments' walk from the shuttle's stops at Stanley Park Entrance, Pipeline Road or the Rowing Club. A $2 day-pass for the shuttle (not other TransLink services) is available on board the bus if you want to hop on and off. If you're just using it to see the park, remember you won't need an extra ticket if you've taken a transfer from the driver and make the onward journey round the park within ninety minutes (see "City transport" on p.698). Driving a **car** here is foolish, especially at weekends, when parking is just about impossible.

Taking time in the park, however you do it, especially on a busy Sunday, gives a good taste of what it means to live in Vancouver. The first thing you see is the **Lost Lagoon**, a fair-sized lake that started life as a tidal inlet, and got its name because its water all but disappeared at low tide. Dozens of waterfowl species inhabit its shoreline. Just east are the pretty Rose Garden and Vancouver Rowing Club, before which stands a statue of Scottish poet Robbie Burns. From here you can follow the sea-wall path all the way, or make a more modest loop past the **totem poles** and round Brockton Point.

Moving around the sea wall anticlockwise, odd little sights dot the promenade, all signed and explained, the most famous being the *Girl in a Wetsuit* statue, a rather lascivious update of Copenhagen's *Little Mermaid*. If you want a more focused walk, the **Cathedral Trail**, northwest of the Lost Lagoon, takes you past some big first-growth cedars. **Beaver Lake**, carpeted green with water lilies, is a peaceful spot for a sleep or a stroll. **Lumberman's Arch**, near the aquarium (see below) was raised in 1952 to honour those in the lumber industry, an odd memorial given that the industry in question would probably give its eyeteeth to fell the trees in Stanley Park. Its meadow surroundings are a favourite for families and those looking for a good napping spot. **Prospect Point**, on the park's northern tip, is a busy spot but worth braving for its beautiful view of the city and the mountains rising behind West Vancouver across the water. There's a café-restaurant here, popular for its outdoor deck and sweeping views. West of here lies **Siwash Rock**, an outcrop which has defied the weather for centuries, attracting numerous native legends in the process, and which is distinguished by its solitary tree (not visible from the road, but quickly reached by path). Further around the wall there are various places to eat and drink, the best being the *Teahouse Restaurant* at Ferguson Point, about a kilometre beyond Siwash Rock.

Though people do swim in the sea at beaches around the park's western fringes, most bathers prefer the **swimming pool** next to Second Beach (see box on p.705). Facilities of all sorts – cafés, playgrounds, golf, outdoor dancing – proliferate near the downtown margins. Guided **nature walks** are also occasionally offered around the park; ask at the infocentre for details.

Vancouver Aquarium Marine Science Centre

Stanley Park zoo and its all too obviously distressed animals has now thankfully closed, leaving the **Vancouver Aquarium Marine Science Centre** as the park's most popular destination (daily: July to early Sept 9.30am–7pm; early Sept to June 10am–5.30pm; $13.95; ☎659-3474, *www.vanaqua.org*). At its entrance stands a vast killer whale in bronze, the work of celebrated Haida artist Bill Reid, whose famous *Raven and the Beast* sculpture forms the centrepiece of the Museum of Anthropology (see p.713). The aquarium is ranked among North America's best, and with over a million visitors a year claims to be the most-visited sight in Canada west of Toronto's CN Tower. It contains over 8000 living exhibits representing some 600 different species, though in truth this is a relatively modest summation of the eighty percent of the world's creatures that live in water. Like the zoo before it, the complex has been targeted by animal-rights campaigners for its treatment of performing beluga and killer whales, not to mention cooped-up seals and otters. Given the aquarium's reputation as a tourist attraction, however, as well as its claims as a research centre, the campaigners have a long, uphill battle. The whales in particular are huge draws, but you can't help but feel they should really be in the sea, for all the hoopla surrounding their $14-million marine-mammal area.

The aquarium has several key areas to see. The **Arctic Canada** section concerns itself with the surprisingly fragile world of the Canadian north, with a chance to see whales face to face through glass and hear the sounds of whales, walruses, seals and other creatures in this icy domain. The **Amazon Gallery** displays the vegetation, fishes, iguanas, sloths and other creatures of the rainforest in a climate-controlled environment, while the **Pacific Northwest Habitat** performs a similar role for otters, beavers and other creatures of the waters of BC. The **BC Waters Gallery** and **Ducks Unlimited Wetlands** displays are fairly self-explanatory.

Granville Island

Granville Island, huddled under the Granville Street Bridge south of downtown, is the city's most enticing "people's place" – the title it likes for itself – and pretty much lives up to its claim to be the "heart of Vancouver". Friendly, easy-going and popular, its shops, markets, galleries, marina and open spaces are juxtaposed with a light-industrial setting whose faint whiff of warehouse squalor saves the area from accusations of pretentiousness. The island was reclaimed from swampland in 1917 as an ironworks and shipbuilding centre, but by the 1960s the yards were derelict and the place had become a rat-infested dumping ground for the city's rubbish. In 1972 the federal government agreed to bankroll a programme of residential, commercial and industrial redevelopment that retained the old false-fronted buildings, tin-shack homes, sea wall and rail sidings. The best part of the job had been finished by 1979 – and was immediately successful – but work continues unobtrusively today, the various building projects only adding to the area's sense of change and dynamism. Most people come here during the day, but there are some good restaurants, bars and the Arts Club Theatre, which are all enough to keep the place buzzing at night.

The most direct approach is to take **bus** #50 from Gastown or Granville Street. The walk down Granville Street and across the bridge is deceptively long, not terribly salubrious, and so probably only worthwhile on a fine day when you need the exercise. Alternatively and more fun, private **ferries** ($2, pay on board) ply back and forth almost continuously between the island and little quays at the foot of Hornby Street or the Aquatic Centre at the foot of Thurlow Street (see "Ferries" on p.699). They also connect from Granville Island to Science World (hourly) and, more significantly, to Vanier Park (half-hourly), a much nicer way than bus to get to the park's Vancouver Museum, Maritime Museum and Space Centre (see overleaf). A logical and satisfying day's **itinerary** from downtown, therefore, would take you to Granville Island, to the museums and back by ferry. You might also choose to **walk** from the island along the False Creek sea wall (east) or west to Vanier Park (see overleaf) and Kits Beach.

There's a good **infocentre** at the heart of the island for Island-related information only (☎666-5784), with a **foreign exchange** facility in the same building and ATM machines on the wall outside. Stamps are available from the LottoCentre inside the Public Market Building. Note that many of the island's shops and businesses close on

Mondays, and that if you want a **bus back** to downtown you should *not* take the #51 from the stop opposite the infocentre (it will take you in the wrong direction): walk out of the island complex's only road entrance, and at the junction the #50 stop is immediately on your right.

Virtually the first building you see on the island walking from the bus stop augurs well: the **Granville Island Brewery**, 1441 Cartwright St (tours only June–Sept Mon–Fri on the hour noon–5pm, Sat & Sun on the half-hour 11.30am–5pm; $7; ☎687-2739), a small but interesting concern which offers guided tours that include tastings of its additive-free beers. Dominant amongst the maze of shops, galleries and businesses, the **Granville Island Public Market** (daily 9am–6pm; closed Mon in winter) is the undisputed highlight of the area. On summer weekends it's where people go to see and be seen and it throngs with arts-and-crafts types, and a phalanx of dreadful, but harmless buskers. The quality and variety of **food** is staggering, with dozens of kiosks and cafés selling ready-made titbits and potential picnic ingredients. Parks, patios and walkways nearby provide lively areas to eat and take everything in. Other spots to look out for include Blackberry Books, the Water Park and Kids Only Market (a kids-only playground with hoses to repel intruders) and the bright-yellow *Bridges* pub/restaurant/wine bar, which has a nice outdoor drinking and eating area. You can also rent **canoes** for safe and straightforward paddling in False Creek and English Bay from Ecomarine Ocean Kayak on the island at 1688 Duranleau St (☎689-7575; from $25 for two hours).

The island also has a trio of small, linked **museums** almost opposite the brewery at 1502 Duranleau St (all daily 10am–5.30pm; $6.50; ☎683-1939, *www.modeltrainsmuseum.bc.ca*): these are the self-explanatory Granville Island Model Trains Museum, Model Ships Museum and Sport Fishing museum. These will probably appeal only to children and to model or fishing enthusiasts. The Model Trains Museum claims to contain the largest collection of toy trains in the world on public display.

Vanier Park museum complex

A little to the west of Granville Island, **Vanier Park** conveniently collects most of the city's main museums: the **Vancouver Museum**, the **Maritime Museum** and the **H.R. MacMillan Space Centre** (the last combines the old planetarium and observatory). The complex sits on the waterfront at the west end of the Burrard Bridge, near Kitsilano Beach and the residential-entertainment centres of Kitsilano and West 4th Avenue, and Vanier Park itself is a fine spot to while away a summer afternoon. You could easily incorporate a visit to the museums with a trip to Granville Island using the **ferry** (see overleaf), which docks just below the Maritime Museum. Coming from downtown, take the #22 Macdonald **bus** south from anywhere on Burrard or West Pender – get off at the first stop after the bridge and walk down Chester Street to the park. The park's pleasant but open – there's little shade – and has a few nice patches of sandy beach on its fringes if you don't want to trek all the way to Kits and Jericho beaches (see box, p.705).

The Vancouver Museum

The **Vancouver Museum**, 1100 Chestnut St (Mon–Wed & Fri–Sun 10am–5pm, Thurs 10am–9pm; $8; ☎736-4431, *www.vancouvermuseum.bc.ca*), traces the history of the city and the lower British Columbian mainland, and invokes the area's past in its very form – the flying-saucer shape is a nod to the conical cedar-bark hats of the Northwest Coast natives, former inhabitants of the area. The fountain outside, looking like a crab on a bidet, recalls the animal of native legend that guards the port entrance.

Though it's the main focus of interest at Vanier Park, the museum is not as captivating as you'd expect from a city like Vancouver. It claims 300,000 exhibits, but it's hard to know where they all are, and a visit needn't take more than an hour or so. A patchy collection of baskets, tools, clothes and miscellaneous artefacts of aboriginal peoples – including a huge whaling canoe, the only example in a museum – homes in on the 8000 years before the coming of white settlers. After that, the main collection, weaving in and out of Vancouver's history up to World War I, is full of offbeat and occasionally memorable insights if you have the patience to read the material – notably the accounts of early explorers' often extraordinary exploits, the immigration section (which re-creates what it felt like to travel steerage) and the forestry displays. The twentieth-century section is disappointing, most of the time looking more like an antique shop than a museum.

The H.R. MacMillan Space Centre

The **H.R. MacMillan Space Centre** (July–Aug daily 10am–5pm; Sept–June Tues–Sun 10am–5pm; evening laser shows at varying times Thurs–Sun; $12.50; ☎738-7827, *www.hrmacmillanspacecentre.com*) incorporates the MacMillan Planetarium and a range of space-related displays and shows. Its main draws are its star shows and its rock and laser extravaganzas, the latter for fans of the genre only. The **Gordon Southam Observatory**, nearby, is usually open for public stargazing on clear weekend nights; astronomers are on hand to show you the ropes and help you position your camera for a "Shoot the Moon" photography session of the heavens (call Space Centre for times; free).

The Maritime Museum

The **Maritime Museum**, 1905 Ogden Ave (May–Sept daily 10am–5pm; Oct–April Tues–Sat 10am–5pm, Sun noon–5pm; $7; ☎257-8300), is a short 150-metre walk from the Vancouver Museum and features lovely early photographs evoking c.1900 Vancouver, though the rest of the presentation doesn't quite do justice to the status of the city as one of the world's leading ports. The less arresting displays, however, are redeemed by the renovated *St Roch*, a two-masted schooner that was the first vessel to navigate the famed Northwest Passage in a single season (see box on p.913); it now sits impressively in its own wing of the museum, where it can be viewed by guided tour only. Special summer shows spice things up a little, as do the recent Pirates' Cove and Children's Maritime Discovery Centre, both aimed at making the museum more attractive to children. Outside, just below the museum on **Heritage Harbour** (quay for ferries to and from Granville Island), you can admire, free of charge, more restored old-fashioned vessels.

The Museum of Anthropology

Located well out of downtown on the University of British Columbia campus, the **Museum of Anthropology**, 6393 NW Marine Drive, is far and away Vancouver's most important museum (mid-May to early Sept daily 10am–5pm, until 9pm on Tuesday; early Sept–mid-May Tues 11am–9pm, Wed–Sun 11am–5pm, closed Mon; $7, free Tues 5–9pm; ☎822-3825, *www.moa.ubc.ca*). Emphasizing the art and culture of the natives of the region, and the Haida in particular, its collection of carvings, totem poles and artefacts is unequalled in North America.

To get there by bus, catch the #10 or #4 bus south from Granville Street and stay on until the end of the line. The campus is huge and disorienting – to find the museum, turn right from the bus stop, walk along the tree-lined East Mall to the very bottom (10min), then turn left on NW Marine Drive and walk till you see the museum on the right (another 5min). In the foyer pick up a free mini-guide or the cheap larger booklet – a worthwhile investment, given the exhibits' almost total lack of labelling, but still pretty thin.

Much is made of the museum's award-winning layout, a cool and spacious collection of halls designed by Arthur Erickson, the eminent architect also responsible for converting the Vancouver Art Gallery. Particularly outstanding is the huge **Great Hall**, inspired by native cedar houses, which makes as perfect an artificial setting for its thirty-odd **totem poles** as you could ask for. Huge windows look out to more poles and Haida houses, which you're free to wander around, backed by views of Burrard Inlet and the distant mountains. Most of the poles and monolithic carvings, indoors and out, are taken from the coastal tribes of the Haida, Salish, Tsimshian and Kwakiutl, all of which share cultural elements. The suspicion – though it's never confessed – is that scholars really don't know terribly much of the arcane mythology behind the carvings, but the best guess as to their meaning is that the various animals correspond to different clans or the creatures after which the clans were named. To delve deeper into the complexities, it's worth joining an hour-long, all-year **guided walk**.

One of the museum's great virtues is that none of its displays are hidden away in basements or back rooms; instead they're jammed in overwhelming numbers into drawers and cases in the galleries to the right of the Great Hall. Most of the permanent collection revolves around **Canadian Pacific** cultures, but the **Inuit** and **Far North** exhibits are also outstanding. So, too, are the jewellery, masks and baskets of Northwest native tribes, all markedly delicate after the blunt-nosed carvings of the Great Hall. Look out especially for the argillite sculptures, made from a jet-black slate found only on BC's Haida Gwaii or Queen Charlotte Islands. The **African** and **Asian** collections are also pretty comprehensive, if smaller, but appear as something of an afterthought alongside the indigenous artefacts. A small, technical archeological section rounds off the smaller galleries, along with a new three-gallery wing designed to house the Koerner Collection, an assortment of six hundred European ceramics dating from the fifteenth century onwards.

The museum saves its best for last. Housed in a separate rotunda, **The Raven and the Beast**, a modern sculpture designed by Haida artist Bill Reid, is the museum's pride and joy and has achieved almost iconographic status in the city. Carved from a 4.5-tonne block of cedar and requiring the attention of five people over three years, it describes the Haida legend of human evolution with stunning virtuosity, depicting terrified figures squirming from a half-open clam shell, overseen by an enormous and stern-faced raven. However, beautiful as the work is, its rotunda setting makes it seem oddly out of place – almost like a corporate piece of art.

Around the museum

There are any number of odds and ends dotted around the museum, but they amount to little of real interest. For the exception, turn right out the front entrance and a five-minute walk leads to the **Nitobe Memorial Garden**, a small Japanese garden that might be good for a few minutes of peace and quiet (April–Sept daily 10am–6pm; Oct–March Mon–Fri 10am–2.30pm; $2.50 or $5.75 with the Botanical Garden, free Oct–March; ☎822-6038). It's considered the world's most authentic Japanese garden outside Japan (despite its use of many non-Japanese species), and is full of gently curving paths, trickling streams and waterfalls, as well as numerous rocks, trees and shrubs placed with Oriental precision.

Beyond the garden lies the greater seventy-acre area of the university's **Botanical Garden**, 16th Avenue and SW Marine Drive (same hours as Nitobe Memorial Garden; $4.50 or $5.75 with Nitobe Memorial Garden; ☎822-4208, *www.hedgerows.com*), established in 1916, making it Canada's oldest such garden. Non-gardeners will probably be interested only in the macabre poisonous plants of the Physick Garden, a re-created sixteenth-century monastic herb garden – though most plants here are actually medicinal rather than lethal – and the swaths of shrubs and huge trees in the Asian Garden. If you're more curious or green-fingered, you'll take time to look at all five component parts of the garden. The Asian Garden is cradled amidst a swath of second-growth forest of fir, cedar and hemlock, home to 400 varieties of rhododendrons, roses, flowering vines and floral rarities such as blue Himalayan poppy and giant Himalayan lily. The BC Native Garden shelters some 3500 plants and flowers found across British Columbia in a variety of bog, marsh and other habitats, while the Alpine Garden conjures rare alpine varieties from five continents at around 2000m lower than their preferred altitude. The Food Garden produces a cornucopia of fruit and vegetables from a remarkably restricted area, the entire crop being donated to the Salvation Army.

While you're out at the university, you might also take advantage of the **University Endowment Lands**, on the opposite, west side of the museum. A huge tract of wild parkland – as large as Stanley Park, but used by a fraction of the number of people – the endowment lands boast 48km of trails and abundant wildlife (blacktail deer, otters, foxes and bald eagles). Best of all, there are few human touches – no benches or snack bars, and only the occasional signpost.

North Vancouver

Perhaps the most compelling reason to visit **North Vancouver** (known colloquially as North Van) is the trip itself – preferably by SeaBus – which provides views of not only the downtown skyline but also the teeming port area, a side of the city that's otherwise easily missed. Most of North Van itself is residential, as is neighbouring West Vancouver, whose cosseted citizens boast the highest per capita income in Canada. You'll probably cross to the north shore less for these leafy suburbs than to sample the outstanding areas of natural beauty here: **Lynn Canyon**, **Grouse Mountain**, **Capilano Gorge** (the most popular excursion), **Mount Seymour** and **Lighthouse Park**. All nestle in the mountains that rear up dramatically almost from the West Van waterfront, the proximity of Vancouver's residential areas to genuine wilderness being one of the city's most remarkable aspects. Your best bet if you wish to **hike**, and want the wildest scenery close to downtown, is Mount Seymour (see p.717).

Most of North Vancouver is within a single bus ride of **Lonsdale Quay**, the north shore's SeaBus terminal. **Buses** to all points leave from two parallel bays immediately in front of you as you leave the boat – blue West Van buses are run by an independent company but accept BC Transit tickets. If you've bought a ticket to come over on the SeaBus, remember you have ninety minutes of transfer time to ride buses from the time of purchase, which should be long enough to get you to most of the destinations below.

The **Lonsdale Quay Market**, to the right of the buses, is worth making the crossing for whether or not you intend to explore further. While not as vibrant as Granville Island Market, it's still an appealing place, with great food stalls and takeaways, plus walkways looking out over the port, tugs and moored fishing boats.

Grouse Mountain

The trip to **Grouse Mountain**, named by hikers in 1894 who stumbled across a blue grouse, is a popular one. This is mainly due to the Swiss-built **cable cars** – North America's largest cable cars – which run from the 290-metre base station at 6400 Nancy Greene Way to the mountain's 1250-metre summit (daily 9am–10pm; $17.50; ☎980-9311, *www.grousemountain.com*). A favourite among people learning to **ski** or **snowboard** after work, the mountain's brightly illuminated slopes and dozen or so runs are a North Vancouver landmark on winter evenings. A day-pass coasts $32: for more information call ☎984-0661. In summer, the cable car is an expensive way of getting to the top. It's possible to walk up on the aptly named Grouse Grind Trail from the base station, but it's not a great hike, so settle instead into the inevitable queue for the ticket office (get here early if you can). After two stomach-churning lurches over the cables' twin towers you reach the summit, which, with its restaurants and allied tourist paraphernalia, is anything but wild. The views, though, are stunning, sometimes stretching as far as the San Juan Islands 160km away in Washington State. Have a quick look at the interpretive centre off to the right when you leave the cable car. A 3-D quality film is shown in the theatre downstairs (admission is included in your cable-car ticket) and there are a couple of cafés and a smarter restaurant if you need fortifying after your ascent. The first of the cafés, *Bar 98*, has panoramic views, but it fills up quickly. If you're interested in the *Grouse Nest Restaurant* (☎986-6378 for reservations), note that you can come here in the evening for dinner, accompanied by a fine prospect of the sunset and city lights below. Rides up on the cable car are free with a restaurant booking. Ask at the centre, or small information desk just beyond the centre, about easy **guided walks** (summer daily 11am–5pm): the "Tribute to the Forest" (30min) leaves on the hour, the "Walk in the Woods" every hour on the half-hour (35min).

Walk up the paved paths away from the centre for about five minutes – you can't get lost – and you pass a cabin office offering guided "gravity assisted" (read downhill) **bike tours** from the summit (May–Oct 3 daily; 20km trips cost from around $75, 30km $95 including cable-car fee): behind the office you can sign up for expensive helicopter tours. On the left up the path lies the scene of the "Logging Sports" shows (twice daily; free), involving various crowd-pleasing sawing and wood-chopping displays. Just beyond this is the **Peak Chairlift** (also included in your ticket), which judders upwards for another eight minutes to the mountain's summit: views of the city and Fraser delta are even better, only slightly spoilt by the worn paths and odd buildings immediately below you. Check with the office at the lower cable-car base station for details of long **hikes** – many are down below rather than up at the summit proper. The best easy stroll is to **Blue Grouse Lake** (15min); the Goat Ridge Trail is for experienced hikers. More rugged paths lead into the mountains of the West Coast Range, but for these you'll need maps.

To get directly to the base station of the cable car from Lonsdale Quay, take the special #236 Grouse Mountain **bus** from Bay 8 to the left of the SeaBus terminal. You can also take a #246 Highland bus from Bay 7 and change to the #232 Grouse Mountain at Edgemount Village.

Lynn Canyon Park

Among the easiest targets for a quick taste of backwoods Vancouver is **Lynn Canyon Park** (open all year dawn to dusk), a quiet, forested area with a modest ravine and suspension bridge which, unlike the more popular Capilano Suspension Bridge (see below), you don't have to pay to cross. Several walks of up to ninety minutes take you through fine scenery – cliffs, rapids, waterfalls and, naturally, the eighty-metre-high, bridge over Lynn Creek – all just twenty minutes from Lonsdale Quay. Take bus #228 from the quay to its penultimate stop at Peters Street, from where it's a ten-minute walk to the gorge; alternatively, take the less-frequent #229 Westlynn bus from Lonsdale Quay, which drops you about five minutes closer. Before entering the gorge, it's worth popping into the **Ecology Centre**, 3663 Park Rd, off Peters Road (March–Sept daily 10am–5pm; Oct–Feb Mon–Fri 10am–5pm, Sat & Sun noon–4pm; donation; ☎981-3103 or 987-5922), a friendly and informative place where you can pick up maps and pamphlets on park trails and wildlife.

Capilano River Regional Park

Lying just off the approach road to Grouse Mountain, **Capilano River Park**'s most publicized attraction is the inexplicably popular seventy-metre-high and 137-metre-long **suspension bridge** – the world's longest pedestrian suspension bridge – over the vertiginous Capilano Gorge (daily: May–Sept 8.30am–dusk; Oct–April 9am–5pm; $10.75; ☎985-7474, *www.capbridge.com*). The first bridge here was built in 1889, making this Vancouver's oldest "attraction", though the present structure dates from 1956.

Although part of the park, the footbridge is privately run as a money-making venture. Stick to the paths elsewhere in the park and avoid the pedestrian toll, which buys you miscellaneous tours, forestry exhibits and trails, and a visit to a native carving centre; frankly they don't amount to much, especially when you can have much the same sort of scenery for free up the road. More interesting is the **salmon hatchery** just upstream (usually daily: April–Oct 8am–6pm; Nov–March 8am–4pm, but phone to confirm ☎666-1790; free), a provincial operation dating from 1977 designed to help salmon spawn and thus combat declining stocks: it nurtures some two million fish a year, and was the first of many similar schemes across the province. The building is well designed and the information plaques interesting, but it's a prime stop on city coach tours, so the place can often be packed.

Capilano is probably best visited on the way back from Grouse Mountain – from the cable-car station it's an easy downhill walk (1km) to the north end of the park, below the Cleveland Reservoir, source of Vancouver's often disconcertingly brown drinking water. From there, marked trails – notably the **Capilano Pacific Trail** – follow the eastern side of the gorge to the hatchery (2km). The area below the hatchery is worth exploring, especially the Dog's Leg Pool (1km), which is along a swirling reach of the Capilano River, and if you really want to stretch your legs you could follow the river the full 7km to its mouth on the Burrard Inlet. Alternatively, you could ride the #236 Grouse Mountain bus to the Cleveland Dam or the main park entrance – the hatchery is quickly reached by a side road (or the Pipeline Trail) from the signed main entrance left off Nancy Greene Way. This comes not far after the busy roadside entrance to the Capilano Suspension Bridge (on the bus, ring the bell for the stop after the bridge).

Mount Seymour Provincial Park

Mount Seymour Provincial Park is the biggest (8668 acres) of the North Vancouver parks, the most easterly and the one that comes closest to the flavour of high-mountain scenery. It's 16km north of Vancouver and named after the short-serving BC provincial governor, Frederick Seymour (1864–69). For **information**, call ☎924-2200 or ask at the city infocentre for the blue *BC Parks* pamphlet on the park. To get there by **bus**, take the #239 from Lonsdale Quay to Phibbs Exchange and then the #215 to the Mount Seymour Parkway (1hr) – from there you'll have to walk or cycle up the thirteen-kilometre road to the heart of the park. The road climbs to over 1000m and ends at a car park where boards spell out clearly the trails and mountaineering options available. Views are superb on good days, particularly from the popular **Vancouver Lookout** on the parkway approach road, where a map identifies the city landmarks below. There's also a café, toilets and a small infocentre (summer only). In winter this is the most popular family and learners' **ski area** near Vancouver (call ☎986-2261 for information).

Four major **trails** here are manageable in a day, but be aware that conditions can change rapidly and snow lingers as late as June. The easiest hikes go out to Goldie Lake, a half-hour stroll, and to Dog Mountain, an hour from the parking area (one-way), with great views of the city below. Still better views, requiring more effort, can be had on the trails to First and Second Pump. The wildest and most demanding hike bypasses Mount Seymour's summit and runs by way of an intermittently marked trail to the forest- and mountain-circled Elsay Lake.

Adjacent to the park to the northwest is the **Seymour Demonstration Forest** (☎987-1273), a 14,000-acre area of mostly temperate rainforest, nestled in the lower part of a glacier-carved valley. It's situated at the northern end of Lillooet Road and, if going by public transport, you need to take the #229 Lynn Valley bus to Dempsey Road and Lynn Valley Road. From here it's a ten-minute walk over Lynn Creek via the bridge on Rice Lake Road. You're far better off, however, coming up here on a bike, for the 40km of trails in the area offer some of the best **mountain biking** close to downtown. Forestry education is the area's chief concern, as the area's name suggests, and you can follow various sixty- and ninety-minute marked **hiking trails** that will top up your general knowledge about local trees, soils, fish and wildlife.

Cypress Provincial Park

Cypress Provincial Park, most westerly of the big parks that part-cover the dramatic mountains and forest visible from Vancouver's downtown, is perhaps among BC's most visited day-use parks and probably the most popular of the north shore's protected areas. It takes its name from the huge old red and yellow cedars that proliferate here. Something of a hit with locals who prefer their wilderness just slightly tamed, its trails can be rugged and muddy, but they're always well marked, and even just a few minutes from the parking area you can feel in the depths of the great outdoors. There are several good trails, including the three-kilometre **Yew Lake Trail** – wheelchair-accessible – and the main park trail, which climbs through forest and undergrowth, occasionally opening up to reveal views. The trail also shadows part of Cypress Creek, a torrent that has cut a deep and narrow canyon. For more **information**, ask for the relevant *BC Parks* pamphlet at the infocentre or call ☎926-6007. To get here, take the #253 Caulfield/Park Royal **bus**.

Lighthouse Park

Lighthouse Park, just west of Cypress, offers a seascape semi-wilderness at the extreme western tip of the north shore, 8km from the Lion's Gate Bridge. Smooth granite rocks and low cliffs line the shore, backed by huge Douglas firs up to 1500 years old, some of the best virgin forest in southern BC. The rocks make fine sun beds, though the water out here is colder than around the city beaches. A map at the car park shows the two trails to the 1912 Point Atkinson **lighthouse** itself – you can take one out and the other back, a return trip of about 5km which involves about two-hours' walking. Although the park has its secluded corners (no camping allowed), it can be disconcertingly busy during summer weekends. For more **information** on the park, contact the infocentre or call ☎925-7200 or 925-7000. The West Van #250 **bus** makes the journey all the way from Georgia Street in downtown.

Eating and drinking

Vancouver's restaurants are some of Canada's finest, and span the price spectrum from budget to blowout. If you want to eat well, you'll be spoilt for choice – and you won't have to spend a fortune to do so. As you'd expect, the city also offers a wide range of ethnic cuisines. **Chinese** and **Japanese** cuisines have the highest profile (though the latter tend to be expensive), followed by **Italian**, **Greek** and other European imports. **Vietnamese**, **Cambodian**, **Thai** and **Korean** are more recent arrivals and can often provide the best starting points – cafés and the ubiquitous fast-food chains aside – if you're on a tight budget. Specialist **seafood** restaurants are surprisingly thin on the ground, but those that exist are of high quality and often remarkably cheap. In any case, seafood does crop up on most menus and salmon is heavily featured. **Vegetarians** are well served by a number of specialist places.

   Restaurants are spread around the city – check locations carefully if you don't want to travel too far from downtown – though are naturally thinner on the ground in North and West Vancouver. Places in Gastown are generally tourist-oriented, with some notable exceptions, in marked contrast to Chinatown's bewildering plethora of genuine and reasonably priced options. Downtown also offers plenty of chains and huge choice, particularly with top-dollar places and fast-food fare: the local *White Spot* chain was founded in 1928 and has some thirty locations in Vancouver, and offers good and glorified fast food if time and money are tight – the branch at 1616 W Georgia St between

Seymour and Granville is the most central downtown outlet. Superior chains like *Earl's* and *Milestones* are highly commendable, and a reliable choice for downtown eating right on Robson (see "West Coast" restaurants, p.712).The old warehouse district of **Yaletown**, part of downtown's new southeasterly spread, is also a key – and still developing – eating and nightlife area. Similar places line 4th Avenue in Kitsilano and neighbouring West Broadway, though these require something of a special journey if you're based in or around downtown. Perhaps try them for lunch if you're at the beach (see box, p.705) or visiting the nearby Vanier Park museum complex.

Countless **cafés** are found mainly around the beaches, in parks, along downtown streets, and especially on Granville Island. Many sell light meals as well as the coffee and snack staples. **Little Italy**, the area around Commercial Drive (between Venables and Broadway), is good for cheap, cheerful and downright trendy cafés and restaurants, though as new waves of immigrants fill the area Little Italy is increasingly becoming "Little Vietnam" and "Little Nicaragua". Yaletown and the heavily residential **West End**, notably around Denman and Davie streets – Vancouver's "gay village" – is also booming, the latter having gained a selection of interesting shops and restaurants.

The city also has a commendable assortment of **bars**, many a cut above the functional dives and sham pubs found elsewhere in BC. Note, however, that the definitions of bar, café, restaurant and nightclub can be considerably blurred: food in some form – usually substantial – is available in most places, while daytime cafés and restaurants also operate happily as night-time bars. In this section we've highlighted places whose main emphasis is food and drink; entertainment venues are listed in the next section. Note, too, that Vancouver has a handful of places that stay open all night or until the small hours; a selection of these are listed below.

Cafés and snacks

Bavaria, 203 Carrall St (no phone). A simple, no-frills Gastown place with a couple of tables outside on Maple Tree Square almost in front of Gassy Jack's statue. Particularly recommended for its inexpensive all-day breakfast: if you want something a touch more upmarket, then head for the fine *Pistol Burnes* café on the corner to the right (with lots more outside seating) or *Blake's* (see below) and *The Irish Heather* (see p.723), both just a few doors away.

Blake's, 221 Carrall St near Water St (☎899-3354). One of several cosy and relaxed places on this short Gastown stretch of Carrall St for a coffee, sandwich or snack; a good place to while away an hour writing a postcard or reading the newspaper.

Boulangerie la Parisienne, 1076 Mainland St near Helmcken (☎684-2499). A Yaletown café and bakery with striking and very pretty all-blue interior that – true to its name – opens up French-style on to the pavement in summer.

Bread Garden, 1040 Denman St at Comox (☎685-2996). In Kitsilano at 1880 W 1st at Cypress and 812 Bute, downtown, off Robson. Locals love to moan about the slow service, but food in these hypertrendy deli-cafés is some of the best – and best looking – in the city. Great for people-watching. There are now twelve branches in the Vancouver area. Recommended.

Calabria Coffee Bar, 1745 Commercial Drive (☎253-7017). Very popular café, known to locals as Franks, and tucked away from downtown in "Little Italy". Probably as close as you can get in Vancouver to a genuine Italian bar.

Doll and Penny's, 1167 Davie St between Thurlow and Bute sts (☎685-3417). Fun West End place with big servings, large, gay clientele (but all welcome) and daily drinks specials. Comes alive when the clubs close and stays open to the wee small hours.

Flying Pizza, 3499 Cambie (☎874-8284). If you want pizza this is the place; cheap, thin-crust pizza by the slice (but no alcohol) at five outlets, including Library Square (lunch only), Cornwall Ave (for Kits beach) and just south of the Burrard St Bridge.

Gallery Café, Vancouver Art Gallery, 750 Hornby St (☎688-2233). Relaxed, stylish and pleasantly arty place at the heart of downtown for coffee, good lunches and healthy, high-quality food (especially desserts); also has a popular summer patio. Recommended.

Hamburger Mary's, 1202 Davie St between Bute and Jervis sts (☎687-1293). These may well be the best burgers in the city, though there are plenty of other things on the menu. Lots of people end the evening for a snack at this former West End diner. Outside tables when the weather is fine. Open very late (usually 3am). Recommended.

La Luna Café, 117 Water St between Cambie and Abbot sts (☎687-5862). One of only a couple of places on Gastown's main street that has the character to raise it above the usual tourist-oriented cafés in this part of the city.

The Only Café, 20 E Hastings and Carrall St (☎681-6546). One of Vancouver's most famous institutions, founded in 1912, and worth the trip to the less than salubrious part of town to sample the food and old-world atmosphere. This counter-seating greasy spoon has little more than seafood (perhaps the best in town) and potatoes on its menu; no toilets, no credit cards no licence and no messing with the service. 11am–8pm; closed Sun.

Café S'Il Vous Plaît, 500 Robson St and Richards St. Young, casual and vaguely alternative with good sandwiches, basic home-cooking and local art displays. It is close to the *Kingston Hotel* and central library. Open till 10pm.

Sophie's Cosmic Café, 2095 W 4th Ave at Arbutus St (☎732-6810). This excellent 1950s-style diner is a Kits institution and is packed out for weekend breakfasts and weekday lunch; renowned for its vast, spicy burgers, milkshakes and whopping breakfasts. Recommended.

Chinese

Hon's Wun-Tun House, 108-268 Keefer at Gore St (☎688-0871). Started life as a cheap, basic and popular place known for the house specialities, "potstickers" – fried meat-filled dumplings – and ninety-odd soups (including fish ball and pig's feet). Success has spawned other branches and a slight smartening-up, but the encouraging queues, good food and low prices are mercifully unchanged. No alcohol or credit cards.

Imperial Chinese Seafood Restaurant, 355 Burrard St near Pender St (☎688-8191). A grand and opulent spot in the old Marine Building with good views and busy atmosphere, serving fine, but pricey, food.

Kirin Mandarin, 1166 Alberni near Bute St (☎682-8833). Among the first of the city's smart Chinese arrivals with an elegant decor that's a world away from old-fashioned Chinatown. The superior food is at top-dollar prices but you're repaid with great views of the mountains.

Pink Pearl, 1132 E Hastings near Glen St (☎253-4316). Big, bustling and old-fashioned with highly authentic feel but in a dingy part of town. The moderately priced food has a Cantonese slant, strong on seafood and great for dim sum. It frequently emerges as the city's top Chinese restaurant in dining polls. Recommended.

Shanghai Chinese Bistro, 1128 Alberni St and Thurlow St (☎683-8222). A modern-looking but less ostentatious and more reasonably priced alternative to the *Imperial*, if you want to eat Chinese downtown. The handmade noodles are a must. Open very late (2–3am).

Sun Wong Kee, 4136 Main St (☎879-7231). Some of the city's best and cheapest Chinese food and popular with Chinese families, so get here early. Over 225 items on the menu, yet deep-fried seafood remains a winner.

Italian

CinCin, 1154 Robson St at Bute St (☎688-7338). An excellent downtown option, with stylish, buzzy setting (try to book an outside table in summer), food that merits the highish prices and includes top-grade home-made pastas and desserts. Check the wine list – it's one of the best in the city.

Da Pasta Bar, 1232 Robson St between Jervis and Bute sts (☎688-1288). Deservedly popular mid-priced spot, with varied clientele, in a visually brash place downtown on Robson. You can pick and mix from six pastas and around fourteen inventive sauces and blend to taste. Good for lunch.

Il Giardino di Umberto, 1382 Hornby St at Pacific St (☎669-2422). Sublime and expensive food with a bias towards pasta and game served to a trendy and casually smart thirty-something clientele. Weekend reservations are essential, especially for the nice vine-trailed outside terrace.

The Old Spaghetti Factory, 55 Water St at Abbot St (☎684-1288). Part of an inexpensive chain and hardly *alta cucina*, but a standby if you're in Gastown and better than the tourist trap it appears from the outside, with its spacious 1920s Tiffany interior.

Piccolo Mondo, 850 Thurlow St at Smithe St (☎688-1633). Pricey but excellent food and an award-winning selection of Italian wines. A nicely restrained dining room, just off Robson St, that's not as formal as it first appears. The clientele are expense accounts at lunch and smoochy couples in the evenings. Recommended.

Villa del Lupo, 869 Hamilton St near Smithe St (☎688-7436). Authentic and expensive, high-quality food in a renovated country house – unfussy and elegant – on the eastern edge of downtown midway between the library and Yaletown: there's not a better *osso bucco* in Vancouver.

French

The Hermitage, 115-1025 Robson near Thurlow St (☎689-3237). Warm brick walls, a big fireplace, crisp linen, French-speaking waiters and a courtyard setting give this central and very highly rated restaurant a cosy, almost European feel. The chef here once cooked for King Leopold of Belgium, so he knows his way around food – the onion soup is unbeatable.

Le Crocodile, 100-909 Burrard St, entrance on Smithe St (☎669-4298). Plush, French-Alsace upmarket bistro establishment that pushes *Bishop's* (see below) close for the title of the city's best restaurant and, unlike its rival, it's located downtown. The menu has something for traditionalists and the more adventurous alike. A memorable meal is guaranteed – but check your credit limit first.

Le Gavroche, 1616 Alberni St at Cardero St (☎685-3924). The similarly priced *Le Crocodile* may just take the culinary plaudits, but this other top French restaurant (with a West Coast twist) is not far behind. A formal but amiable place and rated as one of the most romantic places in the city.

Lumière, 2551 W Broadway near Trafalgar St (☎739-8185). Local food critics have named this Vancouver's best restaurant twice in recent years, and it is indeed one of the city's most outstanding places to eat. Cooking here is "contemporary French", and a touch lighter than *Le Crocodile*, though prices are equally elevated. Visitors based in downtown will need to take a cab here: you'll also need to book, for the simple, tasteful dining room accommodates just fifty diners.

Greek

Le Grec, 1447 Commercial Drive (☎253-1253). Popular restaurant with a big range of titbits at reasonable prices, though you'll have to travel out of downtown to enjoy them. Casual and lively later on, especially at weekends.

Orestes, 3116 W Broadway between Trutch and Balaclava sts (☎738-1941). Good, basic food in one of the city's oldest Greek restaurants. Belly dancers shake their stuff Thursday to Saturday and there's live music on Sunday.

Ouzeri, 3189 W Broadway at Trutch St (☎739-9995). A friendly and fairly priced restaurant that is the first port of call if you're at the hostel or beach in Kitsilano.

Stepho's, 1124 Davie St between Thurlow and Bute sts (☎683-2555). This West End restaurant has simple interior, fine food, efficient service and is very popular. Recommended.

Vassilis, 2884 W Broadway near Macdonald St (☎733-3231). Family-run outfit with a high reputation; serves a mean roast chicken. Closed weekends during lunch. Moderate.

West Coast

Bishop's, 2183 W 4th near Yew St (☎738-2025). Consistently ranked one of Vancouver's best restaurants, though it's some way from downtown. Although there's a frequent film-star and VIP presence, the welcome's as warm for everyone. The light and refined "contemporary home cooking" – Italy meets the Pacific Rim – commands high prices but is worth it. First choice for the big, one-off splurge, but booking is essential.

Bridges, 1696 Duranleau, Granville Island (☎687-4400). Unmissable big, yellow restaurant upstairs, pub and informal bistro (the best option) downstairs, with a large outdoor deck. A reliable and very popular choice for a drink or meal on Granville Island.

C Restaurant, 2-1600 Howe St near Pacific Blvd (☎681-1164). The *Fish House at Stanley Park* (see overleaf) is *C*'s only serious rival for the title of best fish and seafood restaurant. The lengthy menu, which contains Southeast Asian influences, might include a choice from the "raw bar" – say a trio of scallop, wasabi salmon and smoked chilli tuna – and unusual fish such as Alaskan arctic char. Views from the dining room are good, too.

Chartwell, *Four Seasons Hotel*, 791 W Georgia St (☎844-6715). Don't let that fact that this is a hotel dining room put you off: the gracious, almost gentleman's club-like ambience is good if you want to dress up or have an indulgent lunch, and fine service, great wine list and progressive Pacific Rim-influenced food makes this one of the top-ten restaurants in Vancouver.

Diva at the Met, *Metropolitan Hotel*, 645 Howe St (☎602-7788). Like the *Chartwell* (see above), *Diva* has carved out a character completely separate from the hotel in which it's lodged. This is among

Vancouver's leading restaurants, thanks to the punchy, imaginative food and the modern, clean-lined dining room. Starters might include smoked salmon with Quebec foie gras, followed by a main course of halibut cheeks with black-olive tapinade. Expensive, but a great pace for a treat or full-on brunch.

Earl's On Top, 1185 Robson St near Bute St (☎669-0020). Come here first if you don't want to mess around scouring downtown for somewhere to eat. The mid-priced, and often innovative, high-quality food is served in a big, open and casual dining area, with outside terrace in the summer. Recommended.

Ferguson Point Teahouse, Ferguson Point, Stanley Park (☎669-3281). A very pretty and romantic spot – ocean view, outside dining – and the best place for a lunch or brunch during a walk or ride round Stanley Park. Be sure to book ahead.

The Fish House at Stanley Park, 2099 Beach Ave and Stanley Park Drive, at the north end of Beach Ave (☎681-7275). The name more or less says it all. The leafy setting in the southwest corner of Stanley Park is almost that of a country estate, and the seafood arguably the city's best. Indulge at the oyster bar, order any available fish baked, broiled, steamed or grilled, and check out the daily specials. Excellent wine list. Expensive but worth it.

Isadora's, 1540 Old Bridge St, Granville Island (☎681-8816). Popular Granville Island choice for a beer or a meal, though *Bridges* is probably a shade better. Fine breakfasts, weekend brunches and light meals with plenty of good veggie/wholefood options. Lots of outdoor seating, but expect queues and slower service at weekends, particularly Sunday brunch. Moderate.

Liliget Feast House, 1724 Davie St at Bidwill St (☎681-7044). This West End aboriginal restaurant – the only one in Vancouver – serves types of food you'll get nowhere else in the city: seaweed, steamed ferns, roast caribou and barbecued juniper duck. However, the cedar tables and benches, designed to resemble a Coast Salish long house, making the dining room a mite austere. Moderate.

Milestone's, 1145 Robson St between Bute and Thurlow sts (☎682-4477) and 1210 Denman St (☎662-3431). Popular mid-market chain restaurants with cheap drinks and food (especially good breakfasts) in very generous portions at the heart of downtown (fast and noisy) and the English Bay Beach end of Denman St (more laid-back). There's also a popular and appealing branch with outdoor terrace in Yaletown at 1109 Hamilton on the corner of Helmcken (☎684-9112).

Tomato Fresh Food Café, 3305 Cambie St (☎874-6020). This high-energy place serves good simple food, with a fresh, health-conscious bias. It's way south of downtown, so it's a good place to stop en route for the airport, Vancouver Island or the ferry terminal at Tsawwassen. Eat in or take away.

Water Street Café, 300 Water St at Cambie St (☎689-2832). The café-restaurant of choice if you wind up in Gastown (located close to the famous steam clock). An airy and casual atmosphere that offers a short but well-chosen menu; consider booking an outside table if you're going to be here for lunch.

Other ethnic restaurants

Chiyoda, 1050 Alberni St at Burrard St (☎688-5050). Everything here, down to the beer glasses, was designed in Japan. A chic but convivial place – the emphasis is on grilled food (*robata*) rather than sushi – that draws in Japanese visitors and businesspeople at lunch and the fashionable in the evenings for moderately-priced dinners.

Ezogiku Noodle Café, 1329 Robson St at Jervis St (☎685-8608). This tiny Japanese noodle house is a perfect place for quick food downtown. The queues are prohibitive, but the turnover's speedy.

Kamei, 1030 W Georgia at Burrard St (☎687-8588). Superlative sushi, but at stratospheric prices. Large and bright, and a menu as long as your arm.

Mescalero's, 1215 Bidwell between Burnaby and Davie sts (☎669-2399). Very popular Mexican-Latin restaurant in the West End with appropriately rustic atmosphere and fit young punters. Moderate.

Phnom-Penh, 244 E Georgia near Gore St (☎682-5777) and 955 W Broadway near Oak St (☎734-8988). Excellent, cheap Vietnamese and Cambodian cuisine, especially seafood, in a friendly, family-oriented restaurant. Recommended.

Pho Hoang, 3610 Main at 20th (☎874-0810) and 238 E Georgia near Gore St (☎682-5666). The first and perhaps friendliest of the many Vietnamese *pho* (beef soup) restaurants now springing up all over the city. Choose from thirty soup varieties with herbs, chillies and lime at plate-side as added seasoning. Open for breakfast, lunch and dinner. The new Chinatown branch is right by the *Phnom-Penh* (see above).

Simply Thai, 1211 Hamilton St, corner of Davie St (☎642-0123). This plain, modern but inviting Yaletown restaurant is packed at lunch (11.30am–3pm) and dinner, thanks to the keen prices and good, authentic food – the chefs are all from Bangkok. Another place, *Thai Urban Bistro*, just up the street at 1119 Hamilton (☎408-7788) is almost as good.

Tojo's, 777 W Broadway at Willow St (☎872-8050). Quite simply the best Japanese food (sushi and more – try the tuna or shrimp dumplings with hot mustard sauce) in the city. Very expensive.

Topanga Café, 2904 W 4th Ave near Macdonald St (☎733-3713). A small but extremely popular and moderate Mexican restaurant; a Vancouver institution.

Vij's, 1480 W 11th Ave near Granville St (☎736-6664). *Vij's* Indian cooking has won just about every award going in Vancouver for Best Ethnic Cuisine. The inexpensive menus change regularly: some excellent vegetarian options.

Vegetarian

The Naam, 2724 W 4th Ave near Stephens St (☎738-7151). The oldest and most popular health-food and vegetarian restaurant in the city. Comfortable and friendly ambience with live folk and other music and outside eating some evenings. Open 24hr. Inexpensive and recommended.

Pubs and Bars

The Arts Club, 1585 Johnston on Granville Island (☎687-1354). *The Arts Club*'s popular *Backstage Lounge*, part of the theatre complex, has a waterfront view, easy-going atmosphere, decent food and puts on blues, jazz and other live music Friday and Saturday evenings. Recommended.

Bar None, 1222 Hamilton St (☎689-7000). Busy, reasonably smart and hip New York-style Yaletown bar and club where you can eat, drink, watch TV, smoke cigars (walk-in humidor), play backgammon or shoot pool and listen to live music.

Blarney Stone, 216 Carrall near Water St (☎687-4322). A lively Irish pub and restaurant, in Gastown, complete with live Irish music and dance floor. Closed Sun.

Darby D. Dawes, 2001 Macdonald St and 4th Ave (☎731-0617). A pub handy for Kits Beach and the youth hostel. People often start the evening here, meals are served 11.30am–7pm, snacks till 10pm, and then move on to the *Fairview* for live blues (see p.725). Live music is only played on Friday and Saturday evenings with jam sessions on Saturday afternoons.

Gerard's, 845 Burrard at Robson St (☎682-5511). The smooth wood-panelled lounge and piano bar with leather chairs and tapestries, all make this very elegant downtown drinking. Also, the place to spot the stars currently filming in town.

The Irish Heather, 217 Carrall St near Water St (☎688-9779). A definite cut above the usual mock-Irish pub, with an intimate bar, live Irish music some nights, excellent food, good Guinness (apparently it sells the seond largest number of pints of the stuff in Canada); and an unexpectedly pretty outdoor area in the back.

La Bodega, 1277 Howe near Davie St (☎684-8815). One of the city's best and most popular places, with tapas and excellent main courses, but chiefly dedicated to lively drinking. It's packed later on, so try to arrive before 8pm. Recommended. Closed Sun.

Rose and Thorne, 757 Richards near Georgia St (☎683-2921). Popular, comfortable place next to the *Kingston Hotel* and very close to the look and feel of an English pub.

Shark Bar & Grill, *The Sandman Hotel*, 180 W Georgia (☎687-4275). The best and busiest of several sports bars in the city. There are 30 screens, a 180-seat oak bar, 22 beers on tap, Italian food from the kitchen, and lots of testosterone.

Sylvia Hotel, 1154 Gilford and Beach (☎688-8865). This nondescript but easy-going hotel bar is popular for quiet drinks and superlative waterfront views, and pleasant after a stroll on English Bay Beach.

Yaletown Brewing Company, 1111 Mainland St (☎681-2739). An extremely large and unmissable bar and restaurant with their own six-beer on-site brewery. Currently very popular, and leading the way in the funky Yaletown revival.

Nightlife and entertainment

Vancouver gives you plenty to do come sunset, laying on a varied and cosmopolitan blend of both **live and dance music**. Clubs are more adventurous than in many a

Canadian city, particularly the fly-by-night alternative dives in the Italian quarter on Commercial Drive and in the backstreets off Gastown and Chinatown. There's also a choice of smarter and more conventional clubs, a handful of discos and a smattering of **gay** and **lesbian** clubs and bars. Summer nightlife often takes to the streets in West Coast fashion, with outdoor bars and (to a certain extent) beaches becoming venues in their own right. Fine weather also allows the city to host a range of **festivals**, from jazz to theatre, and the **performing arts** are as widely available as you'd expect in a city as culturally self-conscious as Vancouver.

The most comprehensive **listings** guide to all the goings-on is *Georgia Straight*, a free weekly published on Thursday; the monthly *Night Moves* concentrates more on live music. These are available in larger stores and street boxes around the city. For detailed information on **gay and lesbian** events, check out *X-xtra*, a free monthly magazine aimed specifically at the gay and lesbian community, which is available at clubs, bookshops and many of the *Georgia Straight* distribution points. Many other free magazines devoted to different musical genres and activities are available at the same points, but they come and go quickly. **Tickets** for many major events are sold through Ticketmaster, based at 1304 Hornby St, which has forty outlets throughout the city (☎280-4444 for concerts, ☎280-4400 for sporting events and ☎280-3311 for the performing arts); they'll sometimes unload discounted tickets for midweek and matinee performances.

Live music and clubs

Vancouver's live-music venues showcase a variety of musical styles, but mainstream **rock** groups are the most common bill of fare; the city is also a fertile breeding ground for **punk** bands, with particularly vocal fans. **Jazz** is generally hot news in Vancouver, with a dozen spots specializing in the genre (ring the Jazz Hot Line at ☎682-0706 for current and upcoming events). And, while Vancouver isn't as cowpoke as, say, Calgary, it does have several clubs dedicated to **country music**, though many are in the outer suburbs.

Many venues also double as clubs and discos, and as in any city with a healthy alternative scene there are also plenty of fun, one-off clubs that have an irritating habit of cropping up and disappearing at speed. Cover charges are usually nominal, and tickets are often available (sometimes free) at record shops. At the other end of the spectrum, the 60,000-seat Pacific Coliseum is on the touring itinerary of most international acts.

Rock

Commodore Ballroom, 870 Granville St at Smithe St (☎681-7838). Still fresh from a $1 million face-lift – which retained its renowned 1929 dance floor – the *Commodore* is the city's best mid-sized venue. There is an adventurous music policy and both local and national DJs frequently spin.

The Rage, 750 Pacific Blvd at Cambie St (☎685-5585). Loud and young, progressive dance and live music club with huge, packed dance floor. It mainly caters for up-and-coming bands: as one critic puts it – "if you've heard it before, you won't hear it here".

Railway Club, 579 Dunsmuir St at Seymour St (☎681-1625). Long-established favourite with excellent bookings, wide range of music (folk, blues, jazz) and a casual atmosphere. Has a separate "conversation" lounge, so it's ideal for a drink (and weekday lunches). Arrive before 10pm at weekends – the place is tiny.

Roxy, 932 Granville St at Nelson St (☎684-7699). Nightly live bands with emphasis on retro 1950s to 1970s music. Casual and fun place for college crowd and people in from the 'burbs.

Sonar, 66 Water St at Abbott St (☎683-6695). Central Vancouver's best-known music venue, with live bands nightly. Convenient mid-Gastown location attracts a varied clientele – it's also known as something of a pick-up spot. Bar food and piano lounge until 9pm, when the band strikes up.

Starfish Room, 1055 Homer St at Nelson St (☎682-4171). Intimate, smoke-filled and loud place known for top local bands, smaller touring bands, occasional bigger names and MOR music at other times.

Jazz and blues

Arts Club Theatre Backstage Lounge, 1585 Johnston, Granville Island (☎687-1354). The lounge is a nice spot to hear R&B, jazz and blues, or watch the boats and sunset on False Creek.

Capone's, 1141 Hamilton St (☎684-7900). This Yaletown spot is primarily a restaurant, but has a stage for live jazz renditions while you eat.

Casbah Jazzbah, 175 W Pender S (☎669-0837). Smooth restaurant-club with live traditional and swing jazz cabaret Thursday to Saturday.

Fairview, 898 W Broadway at the *Ramada Inn* (☎872-1262). Good local blues and 1950s rock in a pub atmosphere with only a small dance floor. Snacks are served during the day and good-value meals in the evening. Open Mon–Sat.

Hot Jazz, 2120 Main St at 5th St (☎873-4131). Oldest and most established jazz club in the city. Mainly traditional swing, Dixieland and New Orleans, played by both local and imported bands. A good dance floor and big bar ensures this place swings past midnight. Wednesday is jam night. Closed Mon & Sun.

Purple Onion, 15 Water St near Abbot St (☎602-9442). Casual club right in the heart of Gastown: top-notch jazz and live Latin music upstairs, dance floor, cigars, oysters and cabaret downstairs. Currently a very popular choice, so expect to wait in line on Friday and Saturday.

Yale, 1300 Granville St at Drake St (☎681-9253). An outstanding venue: *the* place in the city to hear hardcore blues and R&B. Relaxed air, big dance floor and occasional outstanding international names. Often jam sessions with up to 50 players at once, on Saturday (3–8pm) and Sunday (3pm–midnight). Recommended. Closed Mon & Tues.

Country

Boone County Cabaret, 801 Brunette Ave, Coquitlam (☎523-3144). Just off the Trans-Canada (take bus #151) this is suburbia's favourite Country club and it shows – it's typically raucous and crowded. There's no cover Monday to Thursday, and free dance lessons on Monday, Tuesday and Thursday at 8pm. Closed Sun.

JR Country Club, *Sandman Inn*, 180 W Georgia St near Cambie St (☎681-2211). Downtown's main C&W venue highlights top Canadian bands in Old West setting; no cover Monday to Thursday. Closed Sun.

Discos and clubs

Big Bam Boo, 1236 W Broadway near Oak St (☎733-2220). Sports on TV, pool and sushi upstairs; dancing downstairs to safe Top 40 stuff and 1980s throwbacks. Smart place with a strict dress code and generally quotes Thursday to Saturday. Wednesday and Saturday are two of the best "Ladies" nights in the city.

Luv-a-Fair, 1275 Seymour St at Davie St (☎685-3288). This old-timer is probably the city's top club and boasts an excellent dance floor and sound system, along with cutting-edge dance music. The occasional theme nights and live bands have to compete with the everyday madcap, eclectic crowd, ranging from punks to drag queens. Recommended. Closed Sun.

Palladium, 1250 Richards St between Davie and Drake sts (☎688-2648). Bizarre warehouse-sized venue for the art and fashion crowd. Current dance music (different genre most nights) is occasionally enlivened by live shows with the avant-garde art rounding off the experience. Closed Sun.

Richard's on Richards, 1036 Richards St at Nelson St (☎687-6794). A well-known club and disco, but pretentious and aimed at the BMW set. Long waits and dress code. Open Thurs–Sat.

Wett Bar, 1320 Richards St at Drake St (☎662-7707). A hip downtown club where you can expect to hear anything from trip-hop to funky tech-house to hip-hop, depending on which night you show up.

The World, 1369 Richards St (☎688-7806). Currently one of the city's most popular places to retire after clubbing: music, food and nonalcoholic drinks. Open Fri & Sat midnight–5am only.

Comedy club

Yuk Yuk's, Plaza of Nations, 750 Pacific Blvd at Cambie St (☎687-LAFF). Top US and Canadian stand-up acts and the usual scary amateur night on Wednesday. Shows at 9pm, plus Sat & Sun 11.30pm. Closed Mon & Tues.

Gay clubs and venues

Denman Station, 860 Denman St off Robson St (☎669-3488). A friendly basement bar with game shows, karaoke, darts and the like every night for a largely gay and lesbian clientele in an area increasingly becoming a gay "village".

Doll and Penny's, 1167 Davie St between Thurlow and Bute sts (☎685-3417). Fun West End place with big servings and large gay clientele: various theme nights and music nights. Comes alive when other clubs close and stays open to the wee small hours.

Global Beat, 1249 Howe St near Davie St. A gay-owned restaurant and lounge alongside the *Odyssey* (see below).

Heritage House Hotel, 455 Abbott St at Pender St (☎685-7777). The bars here host a number of gay and lesbian nights: currently *Charlie's Bar and Grill* fills up with women only on Sat and *Chuck's Pub* has "Guys in Disguise" on Friday and men-only leather on Saturday; call for latest details.

Numbers, 1042 Davie St at Burrard St (☎685-4077). Good, cruisy multilevel venue and disco, movies and pool tables upstairs, mixed downstairs but with very few women. Theme nights. Open nightly.

Odyssey, 1251 Howe near Davie St (☎689-5256). A young gay and bisexual club with house and techno most nights (expect to queue Fri & Sat). There's a garden in the rear to cool off.

Sublime, 816 Granville (no phone, *sublimenightclub@hotmail.com*). After-hours dance club that runs from 1–6am on Fri and Sat.

Performing arts and cinema

Vancouver serves up enough highbrow culture to suit the whole spectrum of its cosmopolitan population, with plenty of unusual and avant-garde performances to spice up the more mainstream fare you'd expect of a major North American city. The main focus for the city's performing arts is the **Queen Elizabeth Theatre** (☎299-9000) at 600 Hamilton St at Georgia, which plays host to a steady procession of visiting theatre, opera and dance troupes, and even the occasional big rock band. Recently it's been joined by the new **Ford Centre for the Performing Arts** opposite the central library at 777 Homer St (☎280-2222 or 602-0616). For information on the Vancouver arts scene, call the Arts Hotline (☎684-ARTS or 684-2787) or visit their office at 938 Howe St. The refurbished **Orpheum Theatre**, 884 Granville at Smithe (☎665-3050), is Vancouver's oldest theatre and headquarters of the Vancouver Symphony Orchestra. There's also a special line for information relating to dance (☎872-0432). **Tickets** can be obtained from individual box offices or through the Ticketmaster agency (☎280-3311).

The western capital of Canada's film industry, Vancouver is increasingly favoured by Hollywood studios in their pursuit of cheaper locations and production deals. It's therefore no surprise that the spread of **cinemas** is good. Home-produced and Hollywood first-run films play in the downtown cinemas on "Theatre Row" – the two blocks of Granville between Robson and Nelson streets – and other big complexes, and there's no shortage of cinemas for more esoteric productions.

Classical music

Early Music Vancouver (☎732-1610). Early music with original instruments where possible; concerts all over the city, and at the UBC during the Early Music Festival in July and August.

Festival Concert Society (☎736-3737). The society often organizes cheap Sunday morning concerts (jazz, folk or classical) at the Queen Elizabeth Playhouse.

Music-in-the-Morning Concert Society, 1270 Chestnut, Vanier Park (☎873-4612). This began modestly in someone's front room over a decade ago but now organizes innovative and respected concerts of old and new music with local and visiting musicians.

Vancouver Bach Choir (☎921-8012). The city's top nonprofessional choir performs three major concerts yearly at the Orpheum Theatre.

Vancouver Chamber Choir (☎738-6822, *www.vancouverchamberchoir.com*). One of two professional, internationally renowned choirs in the city. They perform at the Orpheum and on some Sunday afternoons at the *Hotel Vancouver.*

Vancouver New Music Society (☎874-6200 or 606-6440). Responsible for several annual concerts of cutting-edge twentieth-century music, usually at the East Cultural Centre (see "Drama" below).

Vancouver Opera (☎682-2871, *www.vanopera.bc.ca*). Four operas are produced annually at the Queen Elizabeth Theatre and productions currently enjoy an excellent reputation.

Vancouver Recital Society (☎736-0363, *www.vanrecital.com*). Hosts two of the best and most popular cycles in the city: the summer Chamber Music Festival (at St George's School) and the main Vancouver Playhouse recitals (Sept–April). Catches up-and-coming performers plus a few major international names each year.

Vancouver Symphony Orchestra (☎684-9100, *www.culturenet.ca/vso*). Presents most concerts at the Orpheum or new Chan Shun Hall on Crescent Rd off NW Marine Drive, but also sometimes gives free recitals in the summer at beaches and parks, culminating in a concert on the summit of Whistler Mountain.

Drama

Arts Club Theatre (☎687-5315, *www.artsclub.com*). A leading light in the city's drama scene, performing at three venues: the main stage, at 1585 Johnston St on Granville Island, offers mainstream drama, comedies and musicals; the next-door bar presents small-scale revues and cabarets; and a third stage, at 1181 Seymour and Davie streets, focuses on avant-garde plays and Canadian dramatists – a launching pad for the likes of Michael J. Fox. The theatre has cult status for its "theatre sports", in which teams of actors compete for applause with improvisation. Beware, as audience participation features highly.

Firehall Arts Centre, 280 E Cordova at Gore St (☎689-0926). The leader of Vancouver's community and avant-garde pack, presenting mime, music, video and visual arts.

Theatre Under the Stars (TUTS), Malkin Bowl, Stanley Park (☎687-0174). Summer productions here are fun and lightweight, but can suffer from being staged in one of Canada's rainiest cities.

Vancouver East Cultural Centre, 1895 Venables St at Victoria St (☎254-9578). Renowned performance space housed in an old church, used by a highly eclectic mix of drama, dance, mime and musical groups.

Vancouver Playhouse Theatre Company, Hamilton St at Dunsmuir St (☎873-3311). One of western Canada's biggest companies. It usually presents six top-quality shows with some of the region's premier performers and designers during its October to May season.

Waterfront Theatre, 1411 Cartwright St, Granville Island (☎685-6217). Home to three resident companies that also hold workshops and readings.

Dance

Anna Wyman Dance Theatre (☎662-8846). Although their repertoire is wide, this group specializes in contemporary dance. As well as standard shows, they occasionally put on free outdoor performances at Granville Island and at Robson Square near the Art Gallery.

Ballet British Columbia (☎732-5003). The province's top company performs – along with major visiting companies – at the Queen Elizabeth Theatre.

EDAM (☎876-9559). Experimental Dance and Music present modern mixes of dance, film, music and art.

Karen Jamieson Dance Company (☎872-5658). Award-winning company and choreographer that often uses Canadian composers and artists, and incorporates native cultural themes.

Cinema

Fifth Avenue Cinemas, 2110 Burrard. Fiveplex cinema run by the founder of the Vancouver Film Festival. It is one of the better in the city for art-house films.

Granville 7, Cinema complex at 855 Granville (☎684-4000). Mainstream first-release films in one of the city centre's main multiscreen complexes.

Pacific Cinémathèque, 1131 Howe St near Helmcken St (☎688-FILM). Best of the art-houses. The programmes are hit-and-miss, but rotate often; over the course of a few nights any film buff should find something playing tempting.

Festivals

Warm summers, outdoor venues and a culture-hungry population combine to make Vancouver an important festival city. Recognized as one of the leading festivals of its kind, Vancouver's annual **International Jazz Festival** (late June to early July) is organized by the Coastal Jazz and Blues Society (☎872-5200, *www.jazzvancouver.com*). Past line-ups have featured such luminaries as Wynton Marsalis, Youssou N'Dour, Ornette Coleman, Carla Bley and John Zorn. Some 800 international musicians congregate annually, many offering workshops and free concerts in addition to paid-admission events.

Other music festivals include the **Vancouver International Folk Music Festival** (☎681-0041, *www.thefestival.bc.ca*), a bevy of international acts centred on Jericho Park and the Centennial Theatre for several days during the third week of July. In July, Vancouver loses its collective head over the **Sea Festival** (☎684-3378) – nautical fun, parades and excellent fireworks around English Bay. Further afield in Whistler (see p.796), there's a **Country & Bluegrass Festival** held in mid-July.

Theatre festivals come thick and fast, particularly in the summer. The chief event is the **Fringe Festival** (☎257-0350, *www.vancouverfringe.com*), modelled on the Edinburgh equivalent. It currently runs to more than 550 shows, staged by some ninety companies at ten venues. There's also an annual **Shakespeare Festival** (June–Aug) in Vanier Park and an **International Comedy Festival** (☎683-0883, *www.comedyfest.com*) in early August on Granville Island. Many of the city's art-house cinemas join forces to host the **Vancouver International Film Festival** (☎685-0260), an annual showcase for more than 150 films running from late September to mid-October.

Listings

Airlines Air BC (☎688-5515 or 1-800/663-3721 in Canada); Air Canada (☎688-5515); American Airlines (☎222-2532 or 1-800/368-1955); British Airways (☎270-8131); Central Mountain Air (☎847-4780 or 1-800/663-3721); Continental (☎1-800/525-0280); Delta (☎1-800/345-3400); Harbour Air Seaplanes: services to Victoria Inner Harbour (☎688-1277 or 1-800/665-0212); Helijet Airways: helicopter service to Victoria (☎273-1414 or 1-800/665-4354); KLM (☎303-3666); North Vancouver (☎604/278-1608); United (☎1-800/241-6522); West Coast Air: seaplane services to Victoria (☎688-9115 or 1-800/347-2222); Whistler Air: direct flights to Whistler from Vancouver Harbour Air Terminal by *Pan Pacific Hotel* (☎932-6615 or 1-888/806-2299).

American Express, Park Place Building, 666 Burrard St, enter at Hornby and Dunsmuir (☎669-2813 or 1-800/772-4473), and is open Mon–Fri 8.30am–5.30pm, Sat 10am–4pm.

Bike rental Bayshore Bicycles & Rollerblade Rentals, 745 Denman St (☎688-2453) and 1610 W Georgia St at Cardero St and the *Westin Bayshore Hotel* (☎689-5071); Harbour Air, Harbour Air Terminal at the waterfront one block west of Canada Place and the foot of Burrard St (☎688-1277) – also rents blades and motorcycles; Spokes, 1798 Georgia at Denman (☎688-5141, *www.vancouverbikerental.com*).

Bookshops Chapters, 788 Robson St (☎682-4066), is a colossal bookshop at the heart of downtown. World Wide Books and Maps, 1247 Granville St, is adequate for maps, guides and travel.

Buses Airporter (☎946-8866 or 1-800/668-3141) for shuttle from Vancouver Airport to bus depot and downtown; Greyhound (☎662-3222 or 1-800/661-8747, *www.greyhound.ca*) for BC, Alberta, Yukon and long-haul destinations including Seattle and the US; Maverick Coach Lines (☎662-8051 or 1-800/972-6300) for the Sunshine Coast, Powell River, Whistler, Pemberton and Nanaimo on

Vancouver Island; Pacific Coach Lines (☎662-8074 or 1-800/661-1725) for Victoria, Vancouver Island; Perimeter (☎266-5386 or 905-0041, *www.perimeterbus.com*) for services between Whistler and Vancouver Airport; Quick Shuttle (☎940-4428 or 1-800/665-2122, *www.quickcoach.com*) for Bellingham Airport, downtown Seattle and SeaTac Airport.

Car rental Budget, airport, 501 W Georgia St and 1705 Burrard St (☎668-7000 or 1-800/268-8900 in Canada, 1-800/527-0700 in US); Exotic Car and Motorcycle Rentals, 1820 Burrard at W 2nd (☎644-9128 or 1-800/566-0343) anything from 355 Ferrari to VW Beetle; Hertz, 1128 Seymour St (☎688-2411 or 1-800/263-0600); National (☎1-800/227-7368), airport (☎207-3730) and 1130 W Georgia at Thurlow (☎609-7150); Rent-a-Wreck, 1083 Hornby St (☎688-0001).

Consulates Australia, 602-999 Canada Place (☎684-1177); Ireland, 1400-100 W Pender St (☎683-8440); New Zealand, 1200-888 Dunsmuir (☎684-7388); UK, 800-1111 Melville (☎683-4421); US, 1095 W Pender (☎685-4311).

Currency Exchange Custom House Currency, 375 Water St, Gastown (☎482-6007); International Securities Exchange, 1169 Robson St near Thurlow (☎683-9666); Thomas Cook, 130-999 Canada Place (☎641-1229); Vancouver Bullion & Currency Exchange, 420 Hornby St (☎685-1008).

Dentists For your nearest dentists, call the College of Dental Surgeons for a referral (☎736-3621). Drop-in dentist, Dentacare (Mon–Fri 8am–5pm only; ☎669-6700), is in the lower level of the Bentall Centre at Dunsmuir and Burrard.

Directory enquiries ☎411.

Doctors The College of Physicians can provide names of three doctors near you (☎733-7758). Drop-in service at Consolidated Care Point Medical Service, 1175 Denman St (☎681-5338) or Medicentre (☎683-8138) in the Bentall Centre (Mon–Fri 8am–5pm; see "Dentists" above).

Emergencies ☎911.

Ferries BC Ferries for services to Vancouver Island (☎1-888/724-5223 in BC); to the Gulf Islands, the Sunshine Coast, Prince Rupert, the Inside Passage and the Queen Charlotte Islands; reservations and information ☎1-888/223-3779 (in BC); Victoria (☎250/386-3431 or recorded information 250/381-5335); Vancouver or from outside BC (☎444-2890), *www.bcferries.com*. Aquabus (☎689-5858) and False Creek Ferries (☎684-7781) for services between downtown, Granville Island and Vanier Park.

Gay and lesbian switchboard Touch-tone guide (☎684-XTRA).

Hospitals St Paul's Hospital is the closest to downtown at 1081 Burrard St near Davie St (☎682-2344). The city hospital is Vancouver General at 855 W 12th near Oak, south of Broadway (☎875-4111).

Laundry Davie Laundromat, 1061 Davie St (☎682-2717); Scotty's One Hour Cleaners, 834 Thurlow near Robson (☎685-7732).

Left luggage At the bus station ($2 per 24hr).

Lost property BC Transit (☎682-7887); West Vancouver Transit (☎985-7777); police (☎665-2232); airport (☎276-6104).

Maps Geological Survey of Canada, 101-605 Robson near Richards (Mon–Fri 8.30am–4.30pm; ☎666-0529). Superb source of official survey maps, including *all* 1:50,000 maps of BC and Yukon.

Optician Same-day service, Granville Mall Optical, 807 Granville and Robson (☎683-4716).

Parking Main downtown garages are at The Bay (entrance on Richards near Dunsmuir), Robson Square (on Smithe and Howe), and the Pacific Centre (on Howe and Dunsmuir) – all are expensive and fill up quickly. A better idea might be to leave your car at the free Park'n'Ride in New Westminster (off Hwy 1).

Pharmacies Shopper's Drug Mart, 1125 Davie and Thurlow (☎669-2424), is open 24hr and has five other outlets open Mon–Sat 9am–midnight, Sun 9am–9pm. Carson Midnite Drug Store, 6517 Main at 49th, is open daily until midnight.

Police RCMP (☎264-3111); Vancouver City Police (☎665-3535).

Post office Main office at 349 W Georgia and Homer (Mon–Fri 8am–5.30pm; ☎662-5722). Post-office information (☎1-800/267-1177).

Taxis Black Top (☎731-1111 or 681-2181); Vancouver Taxi (☎255-5111 or 874-5111); Yellow Cab (☎681-3311 or 681-1111).

Tourist information 200 Burrard St (☎683-2000).

Train enquiries VIA Rail (☎669-3050 or toll-free in Canada only ☎1-800/561-8630, 1-800/561-3949 in the US); BC Rail (reservations and info ☎984-5246 or 1-800/663-8238 in North America; recorded info ☎631-3501); Amtrak (☎1-800/872-7245); Rocky Mountain Railtours (☎606-7200 or 1-800/665-7245) for expensive rail tours through the Rockies.

Weather ☎664-9010.

X Files Tours Contact The X-Tour (☎609-2700, *www.x-tour.com*) for 3–3hr 30min limousine tours of locations connected with *The X Files* series and other film and TV shows shot in Vancouver: from $145.

> The telephone code for Vancouver and vicinity is ☎604. The telephone code for Victoria and Vancouver Island is ☎250.

VANCOUVER ISLAND

VANCOUVER ISLAND's proximity to Vancouver makes it one of western Canada's premier tourist destinations, though its popularity is slightly out of proportion to what is, in most cases, a pale shadow of the scenery on offer on the region's mainland. The largest of North America's west-coast islands, it stretches almost 500km from north to south, but has a population of around only 500,000, mostly concentrated around **Victoria**, whose small-town feel belies its role as British Columbia's second metropolis and provincial capital. It is also the most British of Canadian cities in feel and appearance, something it shamelessly plays up to attract its two million – largely American – visitors annually. While Victoria makes a convenient base for touring the island – and, thanks to a superlative museum, merits a couple of days in its own right – little else here, or (for that matter) in any of the island's other sizeable towns, is enough to justify an overnight stop.

For most visitors Vancouver Island's main attraction is the great outdoors and – increasingly – **whale-watching**, an activity which can be pursued from Victoria, **Tofino**, **Ucluelet** and several other places up and down the island. The scenery is a mosaic of landscapes, principally defined by a central spine of snowcapped mountains which divide it decisively between the rugged and sparsely populated wilderness of the west coast and the more sheltered lowlands of the east. Rippling hills characterize the northern and southern tips, and few areas are free of the lush forest mantle that supports one of BC's most lucrative logging industries. Apart from three minor east–west roads (and some rough logging and gravel roads), all the urban centres are linked by a good highway running along almost the entire length of the east coast.

Once beyond the main towns of **Duncan** and **Nanaimo**, the northern two-thirds of the island is distinctly underpopulated. Locals and tourists alike are lured by the beaches at **Parksville** and **Qualicum**, while the stunning seascapes of the unmissable **Pacific Rim National Park**, protecting the central portion of the island's west coast, and **Strathcona Provincial Park**, which embraces the heart of the island's mountain fastness, are the main destinations for most visitors. Both of these parks offer the usual panoply of outdoor activities, with hikers being particularly well served by the national park's **West Coast Trail**, which is a tough and increasingly popular long-distance path. A newer, but less dramatic (and less busy) trail, the **Juan de Fuca Trail** runs to the south of the park. Shuttle buses and once-daily scheduled bus services from Victoria to points in the park, together with a wonderful approach by **boat** from Port Alberni, offer a choice of beguiling alternative itineraries for exploring the region. Another **boat trip** on a smaller working vessel from the tiny settlements of Tahsis and Gold River to the north is also becoming deservedly popular.

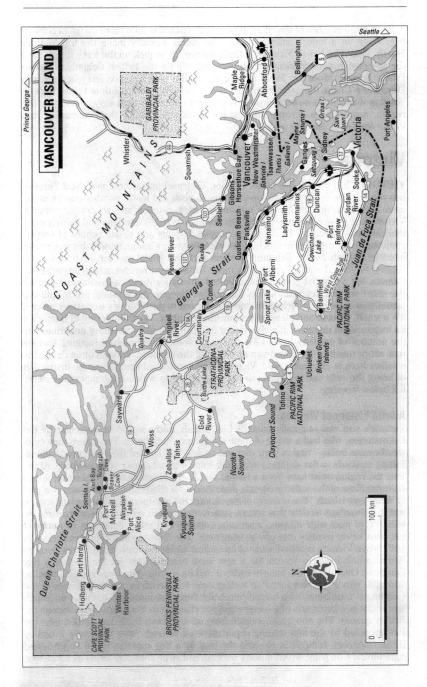

For a large number of travellers, however, the island is little more than a necessary pilgrimage on a longer journey north. Thousands annually make the trip to **Port Hardy**, linked by bus to Victoria, at the northern tip, to pick up the ferry that follows the so-called **Inside Passage**, a breathtaking trip up the British Columbia coast to Prince Rupert. More are likely to pick up on the newer scenic ferry service, the **Discovery Coast Passage**, from Port Hardy to Bella Coola, south of Prince Rupert. You'll probably meet more backpackers plying these routes than anywhere else in the region, many of them en route to the far north, taking the ferries that continue on from Prince Rupert to Skagway and Alaska.

Victoria

VICTORIA has a lot to live up to. Leading US travel magazine *Condé Nast Traveler* has voted it one of the world's top-ten cities to visit, and world number one for ambience and environment. And it's not named after a queen and an era for nothing. Victoria has gone to town in serving up lashings of fake Victoriana and chintzy commercialism – tearooms, Union Jacks, bagpipers, pubs and ersatz echoes of empire confront you at every turn. Much of the waterfront area has an undeniably quaint and likeable English feel – "Brighton Pavilion with the Himalayas for a backdrop", as Kipling remarked – and Victoria has more British-born residents than anywhere in Canada, but its tourist potential is exploited chiefly for American visitors who make the short sea journey from across the border. Despite the seasonal influx, and the sometimes atrociously tacky attractions designed to part tourists from their money, it's a small, relaxed and pleasantly sophisticated place, worth lingering in if only for its inspirational museum. It's also rather genteel in parts, something underlined by the number of gardens around the place and some nine hundred hanging baskets that adorn much of the downtown area during the summer. Though often damp, the weather here is extremely mild: Victoria's meteorological station has the distinction of being the only one in Canada to record a winter in which the temperature never fell below freezing.

A brief history of Victoria

Victoria's site was originally inhabited by **Salish natives**, and in particular by the Lekwammen, who had a string of some ten villages in the area. From here they cultivated camas bulbs – vital to their diet and trade – and applied their advanced salmon-fishing methods to the shoals of migrating salmon in net-strung reefs offshore. At the time the region must have been a virtual paradise. Captain George Vancouver, apparently mindless of the native presence, described his feelings on first glimpsing this part of Vancouver Island: "The serenity of the climate, the innumerable pleasing landscapes, and the abundant fertility that nature puts forth, require only to be enriched by the industry of man with villages, mansions, cottages and other buildings, to render it the most lovely country that can be imagined." The first step in this process began in 1842, when Victoria received some of its earliest **white visitors**, when James Douglas disembarked during a search for a new local headquarters for the Hudson's Bay Company. One look at the natural harbour and its surroundings was enough: this, he declared, was a "perfect Eden", a feeling only reinforced by the friendliness of the indigenous population, who helped him build Fort Camouson, named after an important aboriginal landmark (the name was later changed to Fort Victoria to honour the British queen). The aboriginal peoples from up and down the island settled near the fort, attracted by the new trading opportunities it offered. Soon they were joined by British pioneers, brought in to settle the land by a Bay subsidiary, the Puget Sound Agricultural Company, which quickly built several large company farms as a focus for immigration. In time, the harbour became the busiest west-coast port north of San Francisco and a major base for the British navy's Pacific fleet, a role it still fulfils for the bulk of Canada's present navy.

Boom time came in the 1850s following the mainland gold strikes, when Victoria's port became an essential stopoff and supplies depot for prospectors heading across the water and into the interior. Military and bureaucratic personnel moved in to ensure order, bringing Victorian morals and manners with them. Alongside there grew a rumbustious shantytown of shops, bars and brothels, one bar run by "Gassy" Jack Leighton, soon to become one of Vancouver's unwitting founders.

Though the gold-rush bubble soon burst, Victoria carried on as a military, economic and political centre, becoming capital of the newly created British Columbia in 1866 – years before the foundation of Vancouver. British values were cemented in stone by the Canadian Pacific Railway, which built the *Empress Hotel* in 1908 in place of a proposed railway link that never came. Victoria's planned role as Canada's western rail terminus was surrendered to Vancouver, and with it any chance of realistic growth or industrial development. These days the town survives – but survives well – almost entirely on the backs of tourists (four million a year), the civil-service bureaucracy, and – shades of the home country – retirees in search of a mild-weathered retreat. Its population today is around 330,000, almost exactly double what it was just thirty years ago.

Arrival and information

Victoria International Airport is 20km north of downtown on Hwy 17. The Akal Airporter shuttle bus heads downtown (where it stops at major hotels) every half-hour between about 4.30am and 1am; a single fare for the 45-minute journey is $13 (☎386-2525, 386-2526 or 1-877/386-2525, *www.akalairporter.travel.bc.ca*). Leaving the city for flights, you should call to arrange pick-ups (see "Listings", p.750). Otherwise contact Harbour Air (384-2215 or 1-800/665-0212, *www.harbour-air.com*) or West Coast Air (☎388-4521 or 1-800/347-2222, *www.westcoastair.com*), who operate efficient and quick float planes between Vancouver's port and Victoria's downtown Inner Harbour: both companies share terminals in both cities ($89; planes leave roughly hourly; crossing time is 30 minutes). The **bus terminal** is downtown at 700 Douglas and Belleville, close to the Royal British Columbia Museum; the central VIA **Rail station** is at 450 Pandora St (☎1-800/561-8630), about seven blocks north of the *Empress Hotel*, but you'll only arrive there if you've managed to get a seat on the lone daily train from Courtenay and Nanaimo.

Victoria's busy **infocentre** is at 812 Wharf St, in front of the *Empress Hotel* on the harbour (daily: May–Sept 8.30am–8pm; Oct–April 9am–5pm; ☎953-2033, for accommodation reservations ☎1-800/663-3883, *www.tourismvictoria.com*). It offers help finding accommodation and can book you onto whale-watching and other tours (see box, p.746), while its huge range of information – on both Victoria and Vancouver Island as a whole – makes as good a reason as any for starting a tour of the island from the city. There's also a separate desk for concert, theatre and other tickets. Independent travellers will want to check out the notice board at the **HI youth hostel** (see p.739), which has lots of current practical information.

The best in-town means of transport are the tiny Inner Harbour **ferries**, worth taking just for the ride: try a $10 evening "mini-cruise" around the harbour (tickets on Inner Harbour or book at the infocentre). You're unlikely to need to take a local **bus** anywhere, but if you do, most services run from the corner of Douglas and Yates. The fare within the large central zone is $1.75 – tickets and the DayPass ($5.50) are sold at the infocentre, 7-Eleven stores and other marked outlets, or you can pay on board if you have the exact fare. For 24-hour recorded information on city transport, call the Busline (☎382-6161, *www.bctransit.com*). Other potentially useful private bus lines for **onward travel**

GETTING TO VANCOUVER ISLAND

There are three ways to reach Vancouver Island – by bus and ferry, car and ferry, or air. Most people travelling under their own steam from Vancouver use the first means, which is a simple matter of buying an all-inclusive through-ticket to Victoria. More involved crossings to other points on the island, however, whether from the Canadian or US mainlands, are worth considering if you wish to skip Victoria and head as quickly as possible to Port Hardy for the Inside Passage ferry connections, or to Strathcona or the Pacific Rim parks. You can also reach Victoria directly from Vancouver Airport by inclusive coach and ferry arrangements (see p.695 for details).

FOOT PASSENGERS FROM VANCOUVER

If you're without your own transport, the most painless way to Victoria from Vancouver is to buy a Pacific Coach Lines (PCL; ☎604/662-8074 in Vancouver, 250/385-4411 or 385-3348 in Victoria; toll free ☎1-800/661-1725) ticket at the Vancouver bus terminal at 1150 Station St, which takes you, inclusive of the ferry crossing and journeys to and from ferry terminals at both ends, to Victoria's central bus station at 700 Douglas St. Buses leave hourly in the summer (first bus 5.45am; last bus 8.45pm from July to early Sept, 7.45pm the rest of the year), every two hours in the winter: total journey time is about 3hr 30min and a single ticket costs $26.50 ($51 return). No bookings are necessary or taken: overflow passengers are simply put on another coach. The ferry crossing takes 95 minutes, and offers some stunning views as the boat navigates the narrow channels between the Gulf Islands en route. Be sure to keep your ticket stub for reboarding the bus after the crossing. Coach drivers give you all the practical details en route. It's also worth stocking up on food on board, as subsidized ferry meals are famously cheap (queues form instantly). You can save yourself about $15 by using public transport at each end and buying a ferry ticket separately($9 peak season July to early Sept; $8.50 shoulder mid-March to June, mid-Sept to mid Nov & mid-Dec–Jan 1; $7.50 the rest of the year), but for the extra hassle and time involved it hardly seems worth it. A similar all-inclusive bus/ferry arrangement also operates from Vancouver to Nanaimo on Vancouver Island via the Horseshoe Bay Terminal, about fifteen minutes north of West Vancouver on Hwy 1. You can reach the Horseshoe Bay Terminal by taking bus #250 or #257 from Georgia Street. The ferry charges are the same for foot passengers.

BY CAR FROM BRITISH COLUMBIA

BC Ferries operates four routes to the island across the Georgia Strait from mainland British Columbia (☎1-888/223-3779 from anywhere in BC; otherwise ☎604/444-2890 or ☎250/386-3431 in Vancouver, Victoria or outside BC, *www.bcferries.com*). Reservations on all routes are essential in summer if you want to avoid long waits, and can be made up to 90 minutes prior to sailing. The most direct and heavily used by Victoria–Vancouver passengers is the Tsawwassen–Swartz Bay connection, the route used by Pacific Coach Lines' buses. Tsawwassen is about a forty-minute drive south of downtown Vancouver; Swartz Bay is the same distance north of Victoria. Ferries ply the route almost continuously from 7am to 10pm (sixteen sailings daily in summer, minimum of eight daily in winter). Car tickets cost $32 at weekends (noon Fri to last sailing on Sun) and $30 on weekdays in high season – see above for seasonal breakdown ($28.75/$27 in shoulder season, $24.25/$22.75 in low. A **bike** costs $2.50 year-round. The Mid-Island Express from Tsawwassen to Nanaimo, (Duke Point terminal) midway up the island, has eight or so departures daily on the two-hour crossing. More boats cover the Horseshoe Bay–Nanaimo (Departure Bay terminal) route, a 95-minute journey from a terminal about fifteen-minutes' drive from West

from Victoria include Laidlaw (☎385-4411 or 1-800/318-0818, *www.victoriatours.com*) at the bus terminal, responsible for scheduled services across the island to Duncan ($10 one-way), Chemainus ($12.50), Nanaimo ($17.50), Port Alberni ($30), Tofino ($47.50),

Vancouver. Note that a new ferry terminal, Discovery Point, has been opened at Nanaimo for the first of these crossings. Fares for both these routes are the same as for Tsawwassen to Swartz Bay. The fourth route is Powell River–Comox, Powell River being some 160km northwest of Vancouver on the Sunshine Coast.

FERRIES FROM THE UNITED STATES

Travellers from the United States have several options. Coach and ferry inclusive arrangements are offered by Gray Lines of Seattle, who operate a once-daily service in each direction between Seattle and Victoria (currently leaves 5.30am; $39 one-way, $70 return; ☎250/344-5248, 206/626-5208 or 1-800/544-0739). Washington State Ferries, 2499 Ocean Ave, Sidney (in Victoria ☎250/381-1551 or 250/656-1531 in Sidney, in Seattle ☎206/464-6400 or 1-888/808-7977 in Washington only) runs ferries from Anacortes, ninety minutes north of Seattle, to Sidney, thirty minutes (and 30km) north of Victoria (summer 2 daily in each direction, winter 1 daily; 3hr–3hr 30min), with one of the two summer departures travelling via Orcas and Friday Harbor on the San Juan Islands. Passenger fares are around US$7 (US$2 from the San Juan Islands), a car and driver US$37 (US$15 from the San Juan Islands). Car reservations are required from Orcas and Friday Harbor and can be made by calling at least a day in advance (☎360/378-4777 in Friday Harbor).

Black Ball Transport, 430 Belleville St, Victoria (in BC ☎250/386-2202, in Washington ☎360/457-4491 or 1-800/633-1589) operates a ferry across the Juan de Fuca Strait between Port Angeles on Washington's Olympic Peninsula right to Victoria's Inner Harbour (1–4 daily; 95min). Passenger fares are around US$7 and US$29 for cars. Reservations are not accepted. Car drivers should call ahead in summer to have some idea of how long they'll have to wait.

For foot passengers, and day-trippers in particular, a speedier option is Victoria Express's service from Port Angeles (2 daily late May to late June & Sept to mid-Oct; late June to Aug 3 daily; 55min) to Victoria's Inner Harbour. The fare is US$12.50 one-way, US$25 return. Ferries run only from mid-May to mid-Oct. For information and reservations, call ☎250/361-9144 (Canada), ☎360/452-8088 (Port Angeles) or ☎1-800/633-1589 (Washington). Alternatively, the 300-passenger-only *Victoria Clipper* catamaran travels between Pier 69 in downtown Seattle and Victoria's Inner Harbour in three hours or two hours if you take the more "Turbojet" departures (250 Bellevue St, Victoria; ☎250/382-8100 in Victoria, ☎206/448-5000 in Seattle or 1-800/888-2535 outside Seattle and BC). There is one sailing daily in each direction from January to March and mid-September to December; two sailings daily in the first half of May and second half of September; and four sailings daily from mid-May to mid-September. Tickets prices vary according to season – US$55 single, US$91 return off-season, US$60/99 for three-hour crossings and US$69/115 for the Turbojet in summer.

BY AIR

Several provincial airlines as well as Air Canada fly to Victoria, though it's an expensive way to make the journey if you're only coming from Vancouver. Open return fares from Vancouver typically run to around $140, excursion fares around $100. If you are going to fly, however, it's more fun and more direct to fly from Vancouver harbour to Victoria harbour by helicopter or float plane: Harbour Air and West Coast Air fly from the Tradewinds Marina just west of Canada Place in Vancouver. Helijet Airways (☎604/273-1414) fly from the helipad to the east. Kenmore Air, 6321 NE 175th, Seattle (☎206/486-1257 or 1-800/543-9595, *www.kenmoreair.com*), runs scheduled seaplane services (US$95 one-way; 45min) between downtown Seattle and Victoria's Inner Harbour.

Ucluelet ($47.50), Courtney ($35), Campbell River ($40), Port Hardy ($84.10) and points in between (no reservations are necessary or taken for Laidlaw services). Also useful are Gray Lines of Seattle for a once-daily service to Seattle inclusive of ferry (leaves

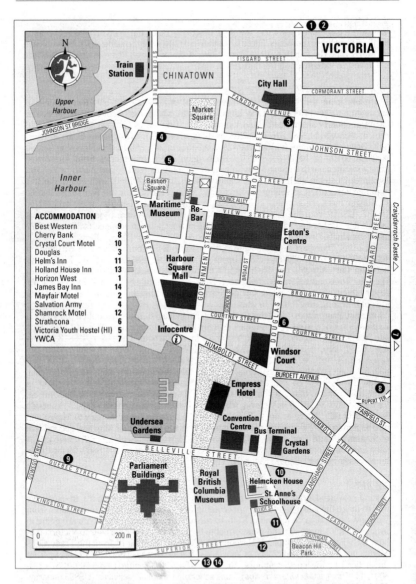

10am; $40; ☎206/626-5208 or 1-800/544-0739). The West Coast Trail Express, 3954 Bow Rd (☎477-8700 or 1-888/999-2288, *www.trailbus.com*), is a high season-only shuttle service (March–Sept) for connections to Port Renfrew and Gordon River (both $30) via French Beach, Jordan River, China Beach and Sooke for the southern trailhead of the West Coast Trail and the newer Juan de Fuca Trail (see p.778 for both trails), as well as links to Bamfield and Pachena Bay (both $50): it also runs between these and other destinations, notably between Bamfield and Port Alberni ($22). Book seats in advance during office hours (March–April Mon–Fri 8am–noon; May–Sept 6.30am–1.30pm & 5.30–8pm).

Accommodation

Victoria fills up quickly in the summer, and most of its budget **accommodation** is well-known and heavily patronized. Top-price hotels cluster around the Inner Harbour area; **hostels** and more downmarket alternatives are scattered all over, though the largest concentration of cheap **hotels** and **motels** is around the Gorge Road and Douglas Street areas northwest of downtown. Reservations are virtually obligatory in all categories, though the infocentre's accommodation service will root out a room if you're stuck (☎1-800/663-3883 in North America, 250/953-2033 from outside North America). They are more than likely to offer you **B&B**, of which the town has a vast selection, though prices for many are surprisingly elevated; many owners of the more far-flung places will pick you up from downtown. Some B&Bs are also real treats – romantic hideaways or housed in lovely old houses. In desperation it's worth consulting one of the specialist B&B agencies such as Canada-West (☎388-4620).

Victoria's commercial **campsites** are full to bursting in summer, with most space given over to RVs. Few of these are convenient for downtown anyway – given that you'll have to travel, you might as well head for one of the more scenic provincial-park sites. Most are on the Trans-Canada Hwy to the north, or on Hwy 14 east of Victoria.

Hotels and motels

Abigail's, 960 McClure St (☎388-5363, fax 388-7787, *www.abigailshotel.com*). A very classy, small hotel in a fine building with log fires, voluminous duvets, jacuzzis and a good breakfast. Situated on the corner of Quadra St, a block east of Blanshard and easy walking distance from the centre. ⑨.

Best Western Inner Harbour, 412 Quebec St between Oswego and Menzies sts (☎384-5122 or 1-888/383-2378, *bestwestern@victoriahotels.com*). Very convenient, central and comfortable, but pricey. ⑦.

Cherry Bank Hotel, 825 Burdett Ave near Blanshard St (☎385-5380 or 1-800/998-6688, fax 383-0949, *www.bctravel.com/cherrybankhotel.html*). Reservations are essential at this deservedly popular and pleasantly eccentric 26-room budget hotel (note rotating mermaid on the roof); excellent rooms and breakfast included. ③.

Crystal Court Motel, 701 Belleville St near Douglas St (☎384-0551, fax 384-5125, *mbscott@vanisle.net*). Large, functional and fairly priced motel well located just one block from the Inner Harbour, though it fronts a fairly busy road. ④.

Douglas Hotel, 1450 Douglas St at Pandora St (☎383-4157 or 1-800/332-9981, fax 383-2279, *www.hoteldouglas.com*). Clean, no-frills and slightly rough-edged big hotel. It is opposite the city hall, close to downtown, and on bus routes #1, #6, #14 and #30. ④.

Helm's Inn, 600 Douglas St near Blanchard and Superior sts (☎385-5767 or 1-800/665-4356, fax 385-2221, *www.helmsinn.com*). Popular if gaudily decorated hotel on the main road just half a block from the Royal BC Museum. One-bedroom and studio suites with kitchens available. Cheaper rates off-season. ⑥.

Holland House Inn, 595 Michigan St near Government St (☎384-6644, fax 384-6117). A comfortable and smart, small hotel located a couple of blocks south of the BC Museum. ⑥/⑦.

Horizon West, 1961 Douglas St at Chatham St (☎382-2111 or 1-800/830-2111, fax 388-5822, *www.bctravel.com*). Reasonably central hotels in this price range are unusual in Victoria, so call ahead to secure one of its eighty rooms. ④.

James Bay Inn, 270 Government St at Toronto St (☎384-7151 or 1-800/836-2649, fax 385-2311, *www.jamesbayinn.bc.ca*). Vying with the *Cherry Bank* as Victoria's best reasonably low-cost option, this Edwardian building was the home of painter Emily Carr. Simple rooms at varying prices, with a restaurant and pub in the basement. Two blocks south of the Government Buildings (buses #5 or #30 to Government and Superior streets). ⑤.

Mayfair Motel, 650 Speed Ave at Douglas St (☎388-7337, fax 388-7398). This small motel 2km north of downtown is ideal if you want to be away from the centre. ③.

Shamrock Motel, 675 Superior St between Government St and Hwy 1 (☎385-8768 or 1-800/294-5544, fax 385-1837). Has just fifteen units, but (with the *Crystal Court*), one of the best-value motels or hotels in the central area. ④.

Strathcona, 919 Douglas St at Courtney St (☎383-7137 or 1-800/663-7476, fax 383-6893). Large, modern hotel where rooms include baths and TVs. There's a "British pub" and restaurant downstairs with booming live and canned music and the nightly dancing may not be to all tastes. ④.

Bed and breakfasts

Ambleside, 1121 Faithful St (☎388-9948 or 1-800/916-9948, fax 383-9317, *www.amblesidebb.com*). Expensive as B&Bs go, but you get a 1919 "craftsman heritage home", a full breakfast and a choice of two tasteful rooms in a pleasant neighbourhood due east of Beacon Hill Park (so a long but pleasant walk to downtown). ⑥.

Andersen House, 301 Kingston St (☎388-4565, fax 388-4563, *andersen@islandnet.com*). Another pricey and tasteful two-room heritage home (built 1891) with private baths and even CD players. ⑥.

Craigmyle B&B Inn, 1037 Craigmyle Rd (☎595-5411, fax 370-5276, *craigmyle@home.com*). By Craigdarroch Castle this friendly antique-furnished home has seventeen rooms, but is 1.5km from downtown. Buses #11 or #14 run from the corner of Fort St and Joan Crescent. ④.

Heathergate House, 122 Simcoe St (☎383-0068 or 1-888/683-0068, fax 383-4320, *www.lvcs.com/heathergate*). Four rooms within walking distance of the Inner Harbour and the sights. ⑤.

Prior House, 620 St Charles St (☎592-8847, fax 592-8223, *www.priorhouse.com*). Pretty swanky for a B&B; once the home of Victoria's lieutenant governor – ask for his suite, complete with bathroom with chandelier. About 2.5km east of downtown in smart Rockland area, so better if you have transport. ⑦.

Ryan's, 224 Superior St (☎389-0012, fax 389-2857). A very pretty 1892 heritage building south of the BC Museum and 5min walk to downtown; all nicely decorated rooms with private bathrooms. ⑥.

Hostels and student accommodation

Backpacker's Hostel, 1608 Quadra St (☎386-4471). This hostel is not too far from downtown – it sits at the corner of Quadra and Pandora sts – and offers dorm beds at $12, singles at $20, a double dorm at $30 and a double room at $35. Weekly rates are also available. Bed linen is included, and there are laundry, kitchen, storage and parking facilities. No curfew. ①.

Beverley Lodge, 1729 Oak Bay Ave (☎598-7323). Hostel with nonsmoking bunk rooms for two, four and six people. A 20min walk from downtown: follow Fort St until it intersects Oak Bay Ave; turn right and the newly renovated four-storey heritage house is four roads down on the right. Or you can catch buses #1 or #2 from opposite *McDonalds* on Douglas St, which drop you virtually outside. Self-serve kitchen and outside deck available. $18 per person. ①.

Ocean Island Backpacker's Inn, 791 Pandora Ave at Blanshard St (☎385-1788 or 1-888/888-4180, *www.oceanisland.com*). A good, reasonably central location in the northeast corner of downtown. The restored 1893 heritage building has dorm beds at $16 (four or six to a room); singles at $19.50 and doubles at $39.50.

Renouf House, 2010 Stanley Ave (☎595-4774, fax 598-1515). A 30min walk east from downtown or catch #10 (Haultain) bus from the corner of Douglas and View and ask to be dropped at Fernwood and Stanley. Then walk a block east on Gladstone to Stanley, turn left at the corner store and the hostel is the white house next door. The owners are great kayaking and sailing experts, so well worth staying here if this is what you want to do on Vancouver Island. Singles/doubles with shared bathroom ($35/50) or singles/doubles with private bathroom ($50/65). ①–④.

Salvation Army Men's Hostel, 525 Johnson St near Store St (☎384-3396). Better than it sounds, being clean and modern, but for men only. Rooms are given on a first-come, first-served basis, with doors open at 4pm. Dorm beds ($19), private rooms and weekly and monthly rates are available. ①.

University of Victoria (☎721-8395 or 721-8396). The nicely situated campus is 20min northeast of downtown near Oak Bay and reached on buses #7 or #14. Ring for the University Housing and

Conference Services, or register on site at the Housing Office, near the campus Coffee Gardens. Offers single and double private rooms with shared bath including breakfast. May–Sept. ①.

Victoria Backpackers' Hostel, 1418 Fernwood Rd (☎386-4471). Battered and laid-back but less convenient than the youth hostel: take bus #1, #10, #11, #14, #27 or #28 towards Fernwood: the #10 to Haultain from the corner of Douglas and Fort is the best bet. Dorm beds, private singles and doubles available with one bunk room reserved for women only. No curfew. Dorm beds $13. ①.

Victoria YM-WCA Women's Residence, 880 Courtney St at Quadra St (☎386-7511). A short stroll from downtown and on the #1 bus route. Mixed cafeteria and sports facilities, including pool, but rooms are for women only. Singles ($38.50) and doubles ($55) available; discounts October to May. ②.

Victoria Youth Hostel (HI), 516 Yates and Wharf (office: Mon–Thurs 7.30am–midnight, Fri–Sun 7am–2am; ☎385-4511, fax 385-3232, *www.hihostels.bc.ca*). A large, modern, and extremely well-run place just a few blocks north of the Inner Harbour. The bunk rooms, though, can be noisy: the reception, rather ominously, sells earplugs. The notice boards are packed with useful information. Members $16.50, nonmembers $20. Just three private doubles are available at $37 for members, $40 for nonmembers. ①/②.

Campsites

Fort Victoria RV and Park Campground, 340 Island Hwy 1A (☎479-8112, fax 479-5806, *www.fortvicrv.com*). Closest site to downtown, located 6km north of Victoria off the Trans-Canada. Take bus #14 (for Craigflower) from the city centre: it stops right by the gate. Large (250-pitch) site mainly for RVs but with a few tent sites; free hot showers. $27–29 per two persons.

Goldstream Provincial Park, 2930 Trans-Canada Hwy (☎387-4363). Although 20km north of the city, this is Victoria's best camping option, with plenty of hiking, swimming and fishing opportunities. Bus #50 from Douglas St will get you here from downtown. $18.50.

McDonald Provincial Park. A government site with limited facilities, 32km from Victoria, but only 3km from the Swartz Bay Ferry Terminal, so useful for boat travellers. $12 in summer, $8 in winter.

Thetis Lake, 1938 Trans-Canada Hwy/West Park Lane (☎478-3845, *petisa@home.com*). Runs a close second to *Goldstream Park* for the pleasantness of its setting, and is only 10km north of downtown. Family-oriented, with 100 sites, laundry and coin-operated showers. $16.

Weir's Beach RV Resort, 5191 Williams Head Rd (☎478-3323, fax 478-1527). Enticing beachfront location 24km east of Victoria on Hwy 14. $35.

The City

The Victoria that's worth bothering with is very small: almost everything worth seeing, as well as the best shops and restaurants, is within walking distance in the **Inner Harbour** area and the Old Town district behind it. On summer evenings this area is alive with strollers and buskers, and a pleasure to wander as the sun drops over the water. Foremost amongst the daytime diversions are the **Royal British Columbia Museum** and the **Empress Hotel**. Most of the other trumpeted attractions are dreadful, and many charge entry fees out of all proportion to what's on show. If you're tempted by the Royal London Wax Museum, the Pacific Undersea Gardens, Miniature World, English Village, Anne Hathaway's Thatched Cottage or any of Victoria's other dubious commercial propositions, details are available from the infocentre. Otherwise you might drop by the modest **Maritime Museum** and think about a trip to the celebrated **Butchart Gardens**, some way out of town, but easily accessed by public transport or regular all-inclusive tours from the bus terminal. If you're around for a couple of days you should also find time to walk around **Beacon Hill Park**, a few minutes' walk from downtown to the south.

The best of the area's beaches are well out of town on Hwy 14 and Hwy 1 (see pp.754–755), but for idling by the sea head down to the pebble shore along the southern edge of Beacon Hill Park. For some local swimming, the best option by far is **Willows Beach** on the Esplanade in Oak Bay, 2km east of Victoria; take bus #1 to Beach and Dalhousie Road. Other good stretches of sand can be found on Dallas Road and at Island View Beach.

The Royal British Columbia Museum

The **Royal British Columbia Museum**, 675 Belleville St (museum: daily 9am–5pm; National Geographic IMAX Theatre daily 10am–8pm; museum $9.65, IMAX Theatre $9.50 (double feature $14.50), combined ticket $15.50; museum ☎356-3701 or 1-888/447-7977, IMAX ☎480-4887, *www.rbcm1.rbcm.gov.bc.ca*), founded in 1886, is one of the best museums in the Northwest, and regularly rated, by visitors and travel magazine polls, as one of North America's top ten. All conceivable aspects of the province are examined, but the **aboriginal peoples** section is probably the definitive collection of a much-covered genre, while the natural-history sections – huge re-creations of natural habitats, complete with sights, sounds and smells – are mind-boggling in scope and imagination. Allow at least two trips to take it all in.

From the word go – a huge stuffed mammoth in the lobby – you can tell that thought, wit and a lot of money have gone into the museum. Much of the cash must have been sunk into its most popular display, the **Open Ocean**, a self-contained, in-depth look at the sea and the deep-level ocean. Groups of ten are admitted into a series of tunnels, dark rooms, lifts and mock-ups of submarines at thirty-minute intervals. You take a time-coded ticket and wait your turn, so either arrive early or reckon on seeing the rest of the museum first. Though rather heavy-handed in its "we're-all-part-of-the-cosmic-soup" message, it's still an object lesson in presentation and state-of-the-art museum dynamics. It's also designed to be dark and enclosed, and signs wisely warn you to stay out if you suffer even a twinge of claustrophobia.

The first floor contains **dioramas**, full-scale reconstructions of some of the many natural habitats found in British Columbia. The idea of re-creating shorelines, coastal rainforests and Fraser Delta landscapes may sound far-fetched, yet all are incredibly realistic, down to dripping water and cool, dank atmospheres. Audiovisual displays and a tumult of information accompany the exhibits (the beaver film is worth hunting down), most of which focus attention on the province's 25,600km of coastline, a side of British Columbia usually overlooked in favour of its interior forests and mountains.

Upstairs on the second floor is the mother of all the tiny museums of bric-a-brac and pioneer memorabilia in BC. Arranged eccentrically from the present day backwards, it explores every aspect of the province's **social history** over two centuries in nit-picking detail. Prominently featured are the best part of an early twentieth-century town, complete with cinema and silent films, plus comprehensive displays on logging, mining, the gold rush, farming, fishing and lesser domestic details, all the artefacts and accompanying information being presented with impeccable finesse.

Up on the mezzanine third floor is a superb collection of **aboriginal peoples' art, culture and history** (see box on p.742). It's presented in gloomy light, against muted wood walls and brown carpet – precautions intended to protect the fragile exhibits, but which also create a solemn atmosphere in keeping with the tragic nature of many of the displays. The collection divides into two epochs – before and after the coming of Europeans – tellingly linked by a single aboriginal carving of a white man, starkly and brilliantly capturing the initial wonder and weirdness of the new arrivals. Alongside are shamanic displays and carvings of previously taboo subjects, subtly illustrating the first breakdown of the old ways. The whole collection reflects this thoughtful and oblique approach, taking you to the point where smallpox virtually wiped out in one year a culture that was eight millennia in the making. A section on land and reservations is left for last – the issues are contentious even today – and even if you're succumbing to museum fatigue, the arrogance and duplicity of the documents on display will shock you. The highlights in this section are many, but try to make a point of seeing the short film footage *In the Land of the War Canoes* (1914), the **Bighouse** and its chants, and the audiovisual display on aboriginal myths and superstition. The **National Geographic Theatre** in the museum plays host to a huge IMAX screen and a changing programme of special format films. Outside the museum, there's also **Thunderbird Park**, a strip of grass with a handful of totem poles.

Helmcken House

Helmcken House (daily 10am–5pm; $4) stands strangely isolated in Thunderbird Park directly adjacent to the museum, a predictable heritage offering that showcases the home, furnishings and embroidery talents of the Helmcken family. Built in 1852, it is the oldest standing home on the island. Dr John Helmcken was Fort Victoria's doctor and local political bigwig, and his house is a typical monument to stolid Victoria values. Upstairs it also contains various attic treasures and some of the good doctor's fearsome-looking medical tools. It's probably only of interest, however, if you've so far managed to avoid any of the Northwest's many hundreds of similar houses. If you do visit, pick up the free guided tapes and listen to "voices from history" (actors and actresses) that give a more personalized slant to the building: listen, for example, to "Aunt Dolly" as she tells why she left the good doctor's room untouched as a shrine after his death. Just behind the house there's another old white-wood building, the **St Anne's Pioneer Schoolhouse** ($2), originally purchased by a Bishop Demers for four sisters of the Order of St Ann, who in 1858 took it upon themselves to leave their Québec home to come and teach in Victoria. Built between 1843 and 1858, it's believed to be one of the oldest, if not the oldest, buildings in Victoria; $2 buys you a peek at the old-fashioned interior and period fittings.

The Parliament Buildings

The huge Victorian pile of the **Parliament Buildings**, at 501 Belleville St (daily: June to early Sept 9am–5pm; early Sept to May 9am–4pm; free; guided tours every 20–30min), is old and imposing in the manner of a large and particularly grand British town hall. Its outline beautifully picked out at night by some three hundred tiny bulbs (though locals grumble about the cost), the domed building is fronted by the sea and well-kept gardens – a pleasant enough ensemble, though it doesn't really warrant the manic enthusiasm visited on it by hordes of summer tourists. You're more likely to find yourself taking time out on the front lawns, distinguished by a perky statue of **Queen Victoria** and a giant sequoia, a gift from California. Designed by the 25-year-old Francis Rattenbury, who was also responsible for the *Empress Hotel* opposite, the building was completed in 1897, at a cost of $923,000, in time for Queen Victoria's jubilee. Figures from Victoria's grey bureaucratic past are duly celebrated, the main door guarded by statues of Sir James Douglas, who chose the site of the city, and Sir Matthew Baillie Begbie (aka the "Hanging Judge"), responsible for law and order during the heady days of gold fever. Sir George Vancouver keeps an eye on proceedings from the top of the dome. Free tours start to the right of the main steps. Guides are chirpy and full of anecdotes. Look out for the dagger which killed Captain Cook, and the gold-plated dome, painted with scenes from Canadian history.

Beacon Hill Park

The best park within walking distance of the town centre is **Beacon Hill Park**, south of the Inner Harbour and a few minutes' walk up the road behind the museum. Victoria is sometimes known as the "City of Gardens", and at the right times of the year this park shows why. Victoria's biggest green space, it has lots of paths, ponds, big trees and quiet corners, and plenty of views over the Juan de Fuca Strait to the distant Olympic Mountains of Washington State (especially on its southern side). These pretty straits, incidentally, are the focus of some rather bad feeling between Victoria and its US neighbour, for the city has a (literally) dark secret: it dumps raw sewage into the strait, excusing itself by claiming it's quickly broken up by the sea's strong currents. Washington State isn't so sure, and there have been plenty of arguments over the matter and, more to the point for city elders, economically damaging convention boycotts by US companies. Either way, it's pretty bad PR for Victoria and totally at odds with its image.

THE NATIVE CULTURES OF THE NORTHWEST COAST

Of all of Canada's aboriginal peoples, the numerous linguistic groups that inhabit the northwest coast of British Columbia have the most sophisticated artistic tradition and the most lavish of ceremonials. Traditionally their social organization stemmed from a belief in a mythical time when humans and animals were essentially the same: each tribe was divided into **kin groups** who were linked by a common supernatural animal ancestor and shared the same names, ritual dances, songs and regalia. Seniority within each kin group was held by a rank of chiefs and nobles, who controlled the resources of private property such as house sites, stands of cedar, and fishing, gathering and hunting territories.

Such privileges, almost unique among Canadian aboriginal groups, led to the accumulation of private wealth, and thus great emphasis was placed on their inheritance. Central to the power structure was the ceremonial **potlatch**, which was held in the winter village, a seasonal resting place for these otherwise nomadic people, located where the supernatural forces were believed to be most accessible. The potlatch marked every significant occasion from the birth of an heir to the raising of a carved pole, and underscored an individual's right to his or her inherited status. Taking its name from the Chinook word for "gift", the potlatch also had the function of **redistributing wealth**. All the guests at the potlatch acted as witnesses to whatever event or object was being validated, and were repaid for their services with gifts from the host chief. Though these gifts often temporarily bankrupted the host, they heightened his prestige and ensured that he would be repaid in kind at a subsequent potlatch.

The most important element of potlatches were the **masked dances** that re-enacted ancestral encounters with supernatural beings, and were the principal means of perpetuating the history and heritage of each kin group. Created by artists whose innovative ideas were eagerly sought by chiefs in order to impress their guests, the dramatic masks were often elaborate mechanisms that could burst open to reveal the wearer or – like the well-known Cannibal Bird – could produce loud and disconcerting noises.

The **Kwakiutl** produced the most developed potlatches, featuring highly ranked dances like the *hamatsa* or **"cannibal dance"**, whose performers had served a long apprenticeship as participants in less-exalted dances. Before the *hamatsa* the initiate was sent to the "Cannibal at the North End of the World", a long period of seclusion and instruction in the snowbound woods. On returning to the village he would seem to be in a complete cannibalistic frenzy and would rush around biting members of the audience. These apparent victims were all paid for their role, which usually involved cutting themselves with

Gardens in the park are alternatively tended and wonderfully wild and unkempt, and were a favoured retreat of celebrated Victorian artist, Emily Carr. They also claim the world's tallest totem pole (at around 40m), Mile Zero of the Trans-Canada Hwy, and – that ultimate emblem of Englishness – a cricket pitch. Some of the trees are massive old-growth timbers that you'd normally only see on the island's west coast. Come here in spring and you'll catch swaths of daffodils and blue camas flowers, the latter a floral monument to Victoria's earliest aboriginal inhabitants, who cultivated the flower for its edible bulb. Some 30,000 other flowers are planted out annually.

Crystal Garden and Butchart Gardens

The heavily advertised **Crystal Gardens**, behind the bus terminal at 713 Douglas St (daily: July & Aug 8.30am–8pm; May–June & Sept–Oct 9am–6pm; Nov–April 10am–4.30pm; $7.50; ☎381-1213, *www.bcpcc.com/crystal*), was designed on the model of London's destroyed Crystal Palace and was billed on opening in 1925 as housing the "Largest Saltwater Swimming Pool in the British Empire". Now much restored, the greenery-, monkey- and bird-filled greenhouse makes for an unaccountably popular tourist spot; only the exterior has any claims to architectural sophistication, and knives to draw a flow of blood – and the *hamatsa* would burst blood-filled bladders in his mouth to add to the carnage, while relatives shook rattles and sang to tame him. A fantastic finale came with the arrival of the loudly clacking "Cannibal Birds", dancers dressed in long strips of cedar bark and huge masks, of which the most fearsome was the "Cannibal Raven", whose long straight beak could crush a human skull. The *hamatsa* would then return in ceremonial finery completely restored to his human state.

As elsewhere in Canada, **European contact** was disastrous for the coastal peoples. The establishment of fur-trading posts in the early nineteenth century led to the abandonment of traditional economic cycles, the loss of their creative skills through reliance on readily available European goods and debilitation from alcohol and internecine wars. Though most of BC remains non-treaty, lands on Vancouver Island were surrendered to become the "Entire property of the White people forever" in return for small payments – the whole Victoria area was obtained for 371 blankets. Infectious disease, the greatest of all threats, reached its peak with the 1862 smallpox epidemic, which spread from Victoria along the entire coast and far into the interior, killing probably a third of BC's aboriginal population.

In this period of decline, potlatches assumed an increased significance as virtually the only medium of cultural continuity, with rival chiefs asserting their status through evermore extravagant displays – even going as far as to burn slaves who had been captured in battle. Excesses such as these and the newly adopted "whiskey feasts" were seen by the **missionaries** as a confirmation that these peoples were enveloped in the "dark mantle of degrading superstition". With BC's entry into confederation the responsibility for the aboriginal peoples fell to the federal government in faraway Ottawa, much of whose knowledge of the aboriginal peoples came from the missionaries – the subsequent **Indian Act**, passed in 1884, prohibited the potlatch ceremony.

For a while the defiant aboriginal groups managed to evade detection by holding potlatches at fishing camps rather than the winter villages, and there were few successful prosecutions until the 1920s. Things came to a head in 1922 with the conviction of 34 Kwakiutl from Alert Bay – all were sentenced to jail terms but a deal was struck whereby all those who surrendered their potlatch regalia were freed. Thirty years later, when potlatching was again legalized, aboriginal pressure began to mount for return of these treasures from the collections into which they had been dispersed, but it took a further twenty years for the federal government to agree to return the goods on condition that they be put on public display. Though the masks totally lose their dramatic emphasis in static exhibitions, many of the more local museums have a dual function as community centres, and as such are vital to the preservation of a dynamic aboriginal culture.

much of its effect is spoilt by the souvenir shops on its ground-floor arcade. Once the meeting place of the town's tea-sipping elite, it still plays host to events such as the Jive and Ballroom Dance Club and the People Meeting People Dance. The daytime draws are the conservatory-type tearoom and tropical gardens. Inhumanely enclosed birds and monkeys, though, are liable to put you off your scones.

If you're into things horticultural you'll want to make a trek out to the heavily over-advertised but celebrated **Butchart Gardens**, 22km north of Victoria at 800 Benvenuto, Brentwood Bay on Hwy 17 towards the Swartz Bay ferry terminal (daily: mid-June to Aug 9am–10.30pm; first half of June & Sept 9am–9pm; rest of the year 9am–sunset; $16.50; ☎652-4422 or 652-5256 for recorded information, *www.butchart-gardens.com*). They're also renowned amongst visitors and locals alike for the stunning **firework displays** that usually take place each Saturday evening in July and August. The gardens are also illuminated during the late-evening opening hours between mid-June and the end of September. To get here by public transport take bus #75 for "Central Sahnich" from downtown. Otherwise there are regular summer **shuttles** (May–Oct daily hourly in the morning, half-hourly in the afternoon; ☎388-5248) from the main bus terminal, where tickets ($24.50) are obtainable not from the main ticket office but from a separate Gray Lines desk: ticket prices include garden entrance and return bus journey. The gardens were started in 1904 by Mrs Butchart wife of a mine-owner and pioneer of Portland Cement in Canada and the US. The initial aim was to landscape one of her husband's quarries – the gardens now cover fifty breathtaking acres, comprising rose, Japanese and Italian gardens and lots of decorative details. About half a million visitors a year tramp through the foliage, which includes over a million plants and seven hundred different species.

The Empress Hotel

A town is usually desperate when one of its key attractions is a hotel, but in the case of Victoria the **Empress Hotel**, 721 Government St (☎384-8111), is so physically overbearing and plays such a part in the town's tourist appeal that it demands some sort of attention. You're unlikely to be staying here – rooms are very expensive – but it's worth wandering through the huge lobbies and palatial dining areas for a glimpse of well-restored colonial splendour. In a couple of lounges there's a fairly limp "Smart Casual" dress code – no dirty jeans, running shoes, short shorts or backpacks – but elsewhere you can wander at will. If you want **take tea**, which is why most casual visitors are here, enter the Tea Lounge by the hotel's side entrance (the right, or south side): there you can enjoy scones, biscuits, cakes and, of course, tea over six courses costing a whopping $42 but you have to abide by the dress code. In other lounges like the Bengal (see below) you can ask for just tea and scones. At the last count the hotel was serving 800 full teas a day in summer and 1.6 million cups of tea a year.

The hotel's **Crystal Lounge** and its lovely Tiffany-glass dome forms the most opulent part of the hotel on view, but the marginally less ornate entrance lounge is *the* place for the charade of afternoon tea, and indulging can be a bit of a laugh. There's also a reasonable bar and restaurant downstairs, **Kipling's**, and the attractive **Bengal Lounge**, compete with tiger-skin over the fireplace, where you can have a curry and all the trimmings for about $15. For a splurge, try the London clubland surroundings – chesterfields and aspidistras – and the champagne-and-chocolate-cake special ($8.50) on offer in the lounge to the left of the entrance lobby. For an even bigger treat, take dinner amidst the Edwardian splendour of the **Empress Dining Room**. As one would expect, meals here are expensive, but the service and food are both top of the line.

The old town

The oldest part of Victoria focuses on **Bastion Square**, original site of Fort Victoria, from which it's a short walk to Market Square, a nice piece of old-town rejuvenation, and the main downtown shopping streets. Bastion Square's former saloons, brothels and warehouses have been spruced up to become offices, cafés and galleries. The modest **Maritime Museum** at 28 Bastion Square (daily 9.30am–4.30pm; $5; ☎385-4222, *www.mmbc.bc.ca*) is of interest mainly for the lovely chocolate-and-vanilla-coloured building in which it's housed, the former provincial courthouse. Displays embrace old charts, uniforms, ships' bells, period photographs, lots of models and a new BC Ferries section on the second floor. On the top floor is the restored vice-admiralty courtroom, once the main seat of justice for the entire province. Note the old open elevator built to reach it, commissioned by Chief Justice Davie in 1901, supposedly because he was too fat to manage the stairs. Just to the north lies the attractive **Market Square**, the old heart of Victoria but now a collection of some 65 speciality shops and cafés around a central courtyard (bounded by Store, Pandora and Johnson sts). This area erupted in 1858 following the gold rush, providing houses, saloons, opium dens, stores and various salacious entertainments for thousands of chancers and would-be immigrants. On the Pandora side of the area was a ravine, marked by the current sunken courtyard, beyond which lay **Chinatown** (now centred slightly further north on Fisgard) the American west coast's oldest. Here, among other things, 23 factories processed 90,000 pounds of opium a year for what was then a legitimate trade and – until the twentieth century – one of BC's biggest industries. As for the downtown **shopping streets**, it's worth looking out for E.A. Morris, a wonderful old cigar and tobacco shop next to *Murchie's* coffee shop at 1110 Government St, and Roger's Chocolates, 913 Government St, whose whopping Victoria creams (among other things) are regularly dispatched to Buckingham Palace for royal consumption.

Other attractions

Outside the Inner Harbour Victoria has a scattering of minor attractions that don't fit into any logical tour of the city – and at any rate are only short-stop diversions. Most have a pioneer slant, though if you want old buildings the best is **Craigdarroch Castle**, nestled on a hilltop in Rockland, one of Victoria's more prestigious easterly neighborhoods, at 1050 Joan Crescent (daily: mid-June to early Sept 9am–7pm; early Sept to mid-June 10am–4.30pm; $8; ☎592-5323, *www.craigdarrochcastle.com*; bus #11 or #14-University from downtown). It was built by Robert Dunsmuir, a caricature Victorian politician, strike-breaker, robber baron and coal tycoon – the sort of man who could change a community's name on a whim (Ladysmith near Nanaimo) – and who was forced to put up this gaunt Gothic pastiche to lure his wife away from Scotland. Only the best was good enough, from the marble, granite and sandstone of the superstructure to the intricately handworked panels of the ceilings over the main hall and staircase. Unfortunately for him the dastardly Dunsmuir never enjoyed his creation – he died before it was finished. There's the usual clutter of Victoriana and period detail, in particular some impressive woodwork and stained and leaded glass.

Much the same goes for the Victorian-Italianate **Point Ellice House & Gardens**, 2616 Pleasant St (mid-May to mid-Sept daily noon–5pm; $4; ☎387-4697; bus #14 from downtown), magnificently re-created but less enticing because of its slightly shabby surroundings. These can be overcome, however, if you make a point of arriving by sea, taking one of the little Harbour Ferry services to the house (10min) from the Inner Harbour. The restored Victorian-style gardens here are a delight on a summer afternoon. The interior – one of the best of its kind in the Northwest – retains its largely Victorian appearance thanks partly to the reduced circumstances of the O'Reilly family, whose genteel slide into relative poverty over several generations (they lived here from 1861 to 1974) meant that many furnishings were simply not replaced. Tea is served on the lawns in the summer: it's a good idea to book ahead ($16.95).

Similar reservations apply to the **Craigflower Manor & Farmhouse** about 9km and fifteen-minutes' drive from downtown on Admiral's Road, or take the #14-Craigflower bus from downtown (May–Oct daily 10am–5pm; $5; ☎387-4697). In its day the latter was among the earliest of Victoria's farming homesteads, marking the town's transition from trading post to permanent community. It was built in a mock-Georgian style in 1856, apparently from timbers salvaged from the first four farmhouses built in the region. Its owner was Kenneth McKenzie, a Hudson's Bay Company bailiff, who recruited fellow Scottish settlers to form a farming community on Portage Inlet. The house was to remind him of the old country (Scotland), and soon became the foremost social centre in the fledgling village – mainly visited by officers because McKenzie's daughters were virtually the only white women on the island.

The **Art Gallery of Greater Victoria**, 1040 Moss St, just off Fort Street (Mon–Sat 10am–5pm, Thurs till 9pm, Sun 1–5pm; $5; bus #10-Haultain, #11 or #14-University from downtown; ☎384-4101, *www.aggv.bc.ca*), is a long way to come and of little interest unless you're partial to contemporary Canadian paintings and Japanese art: the building, housed in the 1890 Spencer Mansion, boasts the only complete Shinto shrine outside Japan. It does, however, have a small permanent collection of Emily Carr's work, and you may catch an interesting temporary exhibition that changes every six weeks.

WHALE-WATCHING TRIPS

The waters around Victoria are not as whale-rich as those around Tofino (see p.768), but there's still a very good chance of spotting the creatures. Three pods of orcas (killer whales) live in the seas around southern Vancouver Island, around a hundred creatures in all, so you may see these, though minke are the most common whale spotted, with occasional greys and humpbacks also present. Bar one or two companies, few outfits offer guaranteed sightings, and many cover themselves by preparing you for the fact that if you don't see whales you stand a good chance of seeing harbour or Dall's porpoises, harbour or elephant seals and California and Steller sea lions.

Day- or half-day trips from the city are becoming massively popular. A couple of years ago there were just two or three companies running trips: now you can hardly move for them. Most offer almost identical trips at identical prices, typically around $55 to $80 for a three-hour outing. Most offer full protective gear, and towels and gloves when required, and all offer life jackets and other safety essentials. Most have a naturalist, or at least a knowledgeable crew member, to fill you in on what you're seeing (or not). The only real variables are the **boats** used, so you need to decide whether you want rigid-hull cruisers (covered or uncovered), which are more comfortable and sedate (and usually most expensive at around $80), a catamaran ($69–80), or the high-speed aluminium-hull inflatables known as "zodiacs" ($55–80), which are infinitely more exhilarating, but can offer a fast and sometimes bumpy ride that makes them unsuitable for pregnant women, young children or people with back problems. They won't have toilets on board either. You might also want to find out whether your chosen company has hydrophone equipment that enables you to listen to the whales' underwater vocalizing.

Note that morning trips can be less choppy than afternoon excursions (bad weather will halt tours), and be sure to take sunglasses, sun block, a tight-fitting hat, good soft-soled footwear, a sound plastic bag for camera and films and a warm sweater. Smoking is invariably not allowed on boats. If you're here just for the day and travelling on zodiacs you might want to bring a change of clothing. Trips often run a little over the scheduled time, so don't make any hard-and-fast plans for catching buses or ferries.

Drop by the **Victoria Infocentre** for details of the tours and options. Its pamphlet racks are stuffed with brochures if you want to compare companies' PR material. Staff can book you a place on any tour, and if you call in early morning they'll probably have the lowdown from the companies on whether whales have been found that day. Companies tend to pool their information, and dash headlong to any sighting. The question of whether the upsurge in boat activity is disturbing the whales or changing their habits seems not to have been addressed. Rules are in place regarding the distance boats must remain from the creatures, but even some of the companies' own photographs seem to suggest boats are getting in extremely close. It can only be a matter of time before the whole issue blows up. All the companies claim to offer top professional services: the two below have been around longer than most.

Seacoast Expeditions are located across the Inner Harbour at the Boardwalk Level, Oceane Pointe Resort, 45 Songhees Rd (☎383-4383 or 1-800/386-1525, *www.seacoastexpeditions.com*). It's ten-minutes' walk across the Johnson Street bridge or take the three-minute harbour ferry crossing to Seacoast: they also have a shuttle-bus pick-up from downtown hotels. Victoria's founding whale-watching company, they've been in the business over a decade and offer four three-hour trips daily in May, June and September, six daily in July and August, and one daily in April and October. They also offer a guaranteed sighting deal (May–Aug only) whereby you carry a pager that tells you to turn up at the office for a tour only when whales have been spotted.

Five Star Charters, located at 706 Douglas St (☎386-3253 or 388-7223, *www.5star-whale.com*), has in the past claimed the highest percentage of whale sightings out of all the tour operators (thanks to spotter boats and a good network of contacts). It runs six daily three-hour trips in the summer as well as an all-day trip on its spotter boat.

Eating and drinking

Although clearly in Vancouver's culinary shadow, Victoria still has a plethora of **restaurants**, some extremely good, offering greater variety – and higher prices – than you'll find in most other BC towns. **Pubs** tend to be plastic mock-ups of their British equivalents, with one or two worthy exceptions, as do the numerous **cafés** that pander to Victoria's self-conscious afternoon-tea ritual. Good snacks and pastry shops abound, while at the other extreme there are budget-busting establishments if you want a one-off treat or a change from the standard Canadian menus that await you on much of the rest of the island. As a quick guide to the best, *Rebecca's* and *Dilettante's* are good for mid-priced lunch or dinners; the *Herald Street Café* or *Water Club* for a pricier but not exorbitant dinner. *Earl's* is part of a reliable mid-price chain, as is *Milestone's*, the latter giving you harbour views from some tables. The slightly wacky *Re-bar* serves what may well be the healthiest food and drinks in North America.

Cafés, tea and snacks

Barb's Fish and Chips, 310 St Lawrence, Fisherman's Wharf off Kingston. Much-loved floating shack that offers classic home-cut chips, fish straight off the boat and oyster burgers and chowder to boot: the small ferries from the Inner Harbour drop you close by.

Bean Around the World, 533 Fisgard St. A nice café with plenty of magazines and games to while away a rainy afternoon.

Blethering Place, 2250 Oak Bay Ave. Along with the *Empress*, known as a place to indulge in the tea-taking custom. Scones, cakes and dainty sandwiches are served up against the background of hundreds of toby jugs and royal-family memorabilia. Perhaps a tad overrated – try the *Windsor House* as an alternative.

Demitasse Coffee Bar, 1320 Blanshard St near Pandora Ave. Popular, elegantly laid-back hole-in-the-wall café with excellent coffee, salads, bagels, lunch-time snacks and an open fire in season. Recommended.

Dutch Bakery & Coffee Shop, 718 Fort St. An institution in Victoria serving pastries and chocolate to take away, or you can eat in the popular if plain coffee shop at the back.

Empress Hotel, 721 Government St. Try tea in the lobby ($29), with tourists and locals alike on their best behaviour amidst the chintz and potted plants. A strict dress code allows no dirty jeans, anoraks or sportswear.

Murchie's Tea and Coffee, 1110 Government St. The best place for basic tea, coffee and cakes in the centre of Victoria's shopping streets.

Re-bar, 50 Bastion Square–Langley St. A great place that serves teas, coffees (charcoal-filtered water) and health food at lunch (usually organically grown), but most remarkable for its extraordinary range of fresh-squeezed juices in strange combinations, smoothies, "power tonics" and frighteningly healthy wheatgrass drinks such as the "Astro Turf" – a carrot, beet, garlic and wheatgrass medley.

Sally's, 714 Cormorant St, near corner of Douglas St. Funky little café and very popular with locals and local office workers despite its location on the northern edge of downtown. Drop by if you're up this way, but don't come specially.

Willie's Bakery, Waddington Alley, off Johnson St. Good little bakery and café with great croissants and lots of outdoor seating in summer.

Windsor House Tea Room, 2450 Windsor Rd. If you're making the effort to come out of town for tea at the famous *Blethering Place*, you could stay on the bus (the #2 Oak Bay) to have your cuppa by the sea here instead.

Restaurants

Da Tandoor, 1010 Fort St (☎384-6333). Tandoori specialist that is, along with the *Taj Mahal*, the best of Victoria's half-dozen or so Indian restaurants offering good, inexpensive food in an over-the-top interior.

Dilettante's Café, 787 Fort St near Blanshard St (☎381-3327). Although a little north of the central core, this vaguely decadent and relaxed single-room restaurant is deservedly popular at lunch. The good food is the usual mixture of Italian, Canadian and Pacific Rim fare.

Earl's, 1703 Blanshard St (☎386-4323). You'll find an *Earl's* in many Northwest towns, but the restaurants are none the worse for being part of a chain: good – not fast – food, with a lively, pleasant interior and friendly service.

Green Cuisine, Courtyard Level, Market Square, 560 Johnson St. Vegetarian restaurant and bakery in pleasant off-street setting with a good hot buffet and salad bar.

Herald Street Café, 546 Herald St (☎381-1441). An excellent and stylish old favourite for Italian food with a Northwest twist. Pricey but still good value with a relaxed, art-filled atmosphere. Well worth the walk from the Inner Harbour.

Il Terrazzo, 555 Johnson St, Waddington Alley (☎361-0028). Smooth, laid-back ambience with lots of red brick and plants and a summer patio that provides the setting for good, moderately expensive North American versions of Italian food.

Le Petit Saigon, 1010 Langley St, off Fort St (☎386-1412). A byword for good low-priced downtown Vietnamese food.

Marina Restaurant, 1327 Beach Drive (☎598-8555). An upscale restaurant with great marine views and a deserved reputation for some of the best fish and seafood in the city.

Milestone's, 812 Wharf St (☎381-2244). Popular mid-priced place slap-bang on the Inner Harbour beneath the infocentre, so lots of bustle, passing trade and good views, but not the place for a quiet meal.

Ming's, 1321 Quadra St (☎385-4405). Regularly voted Victoria's best Chinese restaurant. Inexpensive.

Pagliacci's, 1011 Broad St between Fort and Broughton (☎386-1662). Best restaurant in Victoria if you want a fast, furious atmosphere, live music, good Italian food and excellent desserts. A rowdy throng begins to queue almost from the moment the doors are open.

Periklis, 531 Yates St (☎386-3313). Greek restaurant opposite the youth hostel, often with belly dancers, plate-spinning and good (if predictable), inexpensive Greek food.

Süze, 515 Yates St (☎383-2829). A great place for an early or late-evening drink, thanks to its informal, vaguely exotic feel and wonderfully broad bar; it's also good for an eclectic mix of Mexican, Italian and other dishes, which can be eaten either at tables up on the tiny mezzanine or in the cosy dining room.

Taj Mahal, 679 Herald St (☎383-4662). Housed in a mini Taj Mahal, a bit of a walk from the centre, this inexpensive restaurant serves good Indian food with chicken, lamb and tandoori specialities.

Tomoe, 726 Johnson St (☎381-0223). Victoria's best Japanese restaurant with a comfortable, low-key atmosphere. Fresh produce is flown in daily from Tsukiji, the world's largest fish market. Expensive, but if you like sushi well worth it.

Bars

Big Bad John's, next to the *Strathcona Hotel* at 919 Douglas St. Victoria's most atmospheric bar by far with bare boards, a fug of smoke, and authentic old banknotes and IOUs pasted to the walls. It also hosts occasional live bands and singers, usually of a country-music persuasion.

Charles Dickens Pub, 633 Humboldt St. One of Victoria's hideously mocked-up British pubs but good for a laugh. If this is too much, try the *Garrick's Head* pub, 1140 Government St, which has a cosy fire in winter and lots of outdoor seating in summer.

D'Arcy McGee's, 1127 Wharf St. It was only a matter of time before Victoria acquired an "Irish pub". This one has a prime site on the edge of Bastion Square, offers predictable food and beer, and has excellent occasional live Irish music.

Spinnakers Brew Pub, 308 Catherine St near Esquimalt Rd. Thirty-eight beers, including several home-brewed options, restaurant, live music, occasional tours of the brewery and good harbour views draw a mixed and relaxed clientele. Take bus #23 to Esquimalt Rd.

Swan's Pub, 506 Pandora Ave at Store St. This pretty and highly popular hotel-café-brewery, housed in a 1913 warehouse, is the place to watch Victoria's young professionals at play. Several foreign and six home-brewed beers on tap, with the *Millennium* nightclub (see opposite) in the basement.

Nightlife and entertainment

Nocturnal diversions in Victoria are tame compared to Vancouver's, but there's more to the town than its tearooms and chintzy shops initially suggest. Highbrow tastes are surprisingly well catered for, and there's a smattering of **live music** venues and **discos** to keep you happy for the limited time you're likely to spend in the city. **Jazz** is particularly popular – for information on the city's jazz underground, contact the Victoria Jazz Society, 250-727 Johnson St (☎388-4423).

Listings appear in the main daily newspaper, the *Times-Colonist* and in a variety of free magazines you can pick up in shops, cafés and hotels. **Tickets** for most offerings are available from the city's main performance space, the McPherson Playhouse, 3 Centennial Square, Pandora Avenue and Government Street (☎386-6121).

Clubs, discos and live music

Bartholomew's Bar and Rockefeller Grill, *Executive House Hotel*, 777 Douglas St (☎388-5111). An upbeat pub with a steady diet of local rock and blues bands.

BJ's Lounge, downstairs at 642 Johnson St (☎388-0505). Popular gay dance club playing fairly mainstream Top 40 music.

Esquimalt Inn, 856 Esquimalt Rd (☎382-7161). Long-established venue with country bands most nights and occasional jam sessions. Take the #23 bus.

Evolution, 502 Discovery St (☎388-3000). One of Victoria's more interesting clubs and discos, thanks to plenty of techno and other dance-floor sounds.

Hermann's Jazz Club, 753 View St (☎360-9098). Dimly lit club thick with 1950s atmosphere which specializes in Dixieland but has occasional excursions into fusion and blues. Open Mon–Fri 11.30am–2am, Sat 3pm–2am.

Legends, 919 Douglas St (☎383-7137). Biggest, best and noisiest of the hard-rock venues, this club occupies the garish, neon-lit basement of the *Strathcona Hotel*. Music and dancing nightly.

Millennium, 1605 Store St at Pandora Ave (☎360-9098). You may well have to queue to join the slightly older crew who frequent the basement disco of *Swan's Pub*. Classics from the 1960s and 1970s generally rule along with current Top 40 fodder. Open Tues–Sat.

Pagliacci's, 1011 Broad St (☎386-1662). Live music (jazz, blues, rock and R&B) starting at 9pm Tuesday to Saturday, in a packed and popular restaurant.

Steamers, 570 Yates St (☎381-4340). You'll catch enthusiastic local bands here most nights, playing anything from reggae to Celtic.

Victoria Blues House, 1417 Government St (☎386-1717). Victoria's "House of the Blues" at the *Victoria Plaza Hotel* has disco some nights and local blues and R&B bands most others.

FESTIVALS IN VICTORIA

Summer brings out the buskers and **free entertainment** in Victoria's people-places – James Bay, Market Square and Beacon Hill Park in particular. Annual highlights, arranged chronologically, include:

TerrifVic Jazz Party, April (☎953-2011). A showcase for about a dozen top international bands held in various venues over four days during the second week of the month.

Jazz Fest, June (☎386-6121 for information). More than a hundred assorted lesser bands perform in Market Square and elsewhere over about ten days towards the end of the month.

ICA Folk Fest, June–July (☎388-4728). Extravaganza of folk over eight days at the end of June and beginning of July: the main venues are the Inner Harbour and Market Square.

Victoria International Festival, July and August (☎736-2119). Victoria's largest general arts jamboree. Events take place at a wide variety of locations.

First People's Festival, early August (☎387-2134 or 384-3211). Celebration of the cultures of Canada's aboriginal peoples, usually held in the second week of the month at the Royal BC Museum.

Classic Boat Festival, August 30–September 1 (☎385-7766). Dozens of wooden antique boats on display in the Inner Harbour.

Fringe Festival, late August to mid-September (☎383-2663). Avant-garde performances of all kinds held at seven different venues around central Victoria.

Drama

Belfry Theatre, 1291 Gladstone St and Fernwood Rd (☎385-6815). Foremost of Victoria's companies, with a nationally renowned five-play season. Although it concentrates on contemporary Canadian dramatists, the repertoire runs the gamut of twentieth-century playwrights.

Kaleidoscope Theatre, 556 Herald St (☎383-8124). Theatre troupe known particularly for its work with young audiences.

Victoria Theatre Guild, 805 Langham Court Rd (☎384-2142). A good company performing lightweight musicals, dramas and comedies.

Classical music, opera and dance

Pacific Opera Victoria, 1316b Government St (☎385-0222). Highly acclaimed company which usually produces three operas yearly in February, April and September at the McPherson Playhouse, 3 Centennial Square (box office ☎386-6121).

Victoria Operatic Society, 798 Fairview Rd (☎381-1021). Year-round performances of lightweight operatic fare.

Victoria Symphony Orchestra, 846 Broughton Rd (☎385-9771). Numerous concerts annually, usually performed at the nearby Royal Theatre, 805 Broughton St (☎386-61210).

Listings

Airlines Air BC and Air Canada (☎1-888/247-2262 in North America; *www.aircanada.ca* for offices worldwide); Harbour Air seaplanes to Vancouver (☎384-2215 or 1-800/665-0212); Helijet: helicopter service to Vancouver harbour (☎382-6222 or 1-800/665-4354); Kenmore Air: seaplane service Seattle–Victoria (☎1-800/543-9595 or 206/486-1257); West Coast Air (☎388-4521 or 1-800/347-2222).

American Express 1203 Douglas St (☎385-8731 or 1-800/669-3636); open Mon, Wed & Sat 9.30am–5.30pm, Tues & Fri 9.30am–9pm.

BC Transit City buses (☎382-6161 or 385-2551).

Bike rental Cycle Victoria Rentals, 950 Wharf St (☎885-2453 or 1-877/869-0039, *www.cyclevictoriarentals.com*); Harbour Rentals, 811 Wharf St (☎995-1661 or 1-877/733-6722), rent bikes (from $8 an hour) plus scooters ($16 per hour, $50 daily); kayaks ($15 an hour, $49 daily); rowing boats ($35 for 3 hours); motor boats ($49 an hour); and motor bikes (from $119 a day).

Bookstores Chapters, 1212 Douglas St near corner with View St, is a huge modern bookshop; Munro's Books, 1108 Government St (☎382-2424), is more traditional.

Bus information Airporter shuttle bus from Victoria Airport (☎386-2525). For services to Vancouver, Pacific Coast Lines (☎604/662-8074 in Vancouver or 250/385-4411 at the Victoria bus terminal); for services on the island, Laidlaw (☎385-4411, 388-5248 or 1-800/318-0818). Both operate from the bus terminal at 700 Douglas and Belleville, which also has an office for Greyhound (☎388-5248). Gray Line of Seattle service to Seattle (☎206/626-6090 or 1-800/544-0739). For West Coast Trail Express to Bamfield and Port Renfrew, call ☎477-8700.

Car rental Avis, 62b-1001 Douglas St (☎386-7726 or 1-800/879-2847) and Victoria Airport (☎656-6033); Budget, 757 Douglas St (☎953-5300 or 1-800/668-9833); Island Auto Rentals, 837 Yates St (☎384-4881), guarantee "lowest rates"; National, 767 Douglas St (☎386-1213 or 1-800/387-4747).

Doctors directory ☎383-1193.

Equipment rental Sports Rent, 611 Discovery St, on corner of Government and Discovery sts (☎385-7368), rents bikes, rollerblades, all camping, hiking, climbing and diving gear.

Exchange Currencies International, 724 Douglas St (☎384-6631 or 1-800/706-6656); Custom House Currency, 815 Wharf St (☎389-6001).

Ferries BC Ferries (☎386-3431 or 1-888/223-3779); Black Ball Transport (☎386-2202 or 360/457-4491); Victoria Clipper (☎382-8100, 206/448-5000 or 1-800/888-2535); Washington State Ferries (☎382-1551 or 1-800/542-7052).

Hospitals Fairfield Health Centre, 841 Fairfield Rd (☎389-6300), three blocks from the *Empress Hotel*; Victoria General Hospital, 35 Helmcken Rd (☎727-4212).

Left luggage At bus terminal; $2 per 24hr – but note lockers are stated not to be "secure" at night.

Lost property Contact Victoria police (☎384-4111) or BC Transit's lost-and-found line (☎382-6161).

Maps Crown Publications Inc, 521 Fort St (☎386-4636). Also see "Bookstores" opposite.
Post office 1230 Government and Yates (☎388-3575). Mon–Fri 8.30am–5pm.
Royal Canadian Mounted Police 625 Fisgard and Government (☎384-4111).
Taxis Blue Bird Cabs (☎382-3611); Empire Taxi (☎381-2222); Victoria Taxi (☎383-7111).
Tourist information ☎953-2033. Accommodation reservations ☎1-800/663-3883 in North America.
Train information VIA Rail, 450 Pandora Ave (☎383-4324 or 1-800/561-8630 in Canada and 1-800/561-3949 in USA).
Weather ☎656-3978.

The Southern Gulf Islands

Scattered between Vancouver Island and the mainland lie several hundred tiny islands, most no more than lumps of rock, a few large enough to hold permanent populations and warrant a regular ferry service. Two main clusters are accessible from Victoria: the **Southern Gulf Islands** and the San Juan Islands, both part of the same archipelago, except that the San Juan group is in the United States.

You get a good look at the Southern Gulf Islands on the ferry from Tsawwassen – twisting and threading through their coves and channels, the ride sometimes seems even a bit too close for comfort. The coastline makes for superb **sailing**, and an armada of small boats crisscross between the islands for most of the year. Hikers and campers are also well served, and **fishing**, too, is good, with some of the world's biggest salmon having met their doom in the surrounding waters. The climate is mild, though hardly "Mediterranean" as claimed in the tourist blurbs, and the vegetation is particularly lush. There's also an abundance of marine wildlife (sea lions, orcas, seals, bald eagles, herons, cormorants). All this has made the Gulf Islands the dream idyll of many people from Washington State and BC, whether they're artists, writers, pensioners or dropouts from the mainstream. For full details of what they're all up to, grab a copy of the local listings, the *Gulf Islander*, distributed on the islands and the ferries.

Getting to the islands

BC Ferries (☎250/386-3431 in Victoria) sails to five of the Southern Gulf Islands – **Saltspring**, **Pender**, **Saturna**, **Mayne** and **Galiano** – from Swartz Bay, 33km north of Victoria on Hwy 17 (a few others can be reached from Chemainus and Nanaimo, see p.759 and p.760). Reckon on at least two crossings to each daily, but be prepared for all boats to be jammed solid during the summer. Pick up the company's *Southern Gulf Islands* timetable, widely available on boats and in the mainland infocentres, which is invaluable if you aim to exploit the many inter-island connections. If you just want a quick, cheap cruise, BC Ferries runs a daily four-hour jaunt from Swartz Bay around several of the islands. All the ferries take cars, bikes and motorbikes, though with a car you'll need to make a **reservation** (in Vancouver ☎604/669-1211, in Victoria ☎386-3431 or 1-888/223-3779). Bear in mind that there's next to no public transport on the islands, so what few taxis there are can charge more or less what they wish.

For the San Juans you obviously have to pass through US and Canadian immigration, but you can get good stopover deals on ferries between Sidney on Vancouver Island and Anacortes on the Washington mainland, and foot passengers travel free between the four main San Juan islands.

Aim to have your **accommodation** worked out well in advance in summer. **Campers** should have few problems finding sites, most of which are located in the islands' provincial parks, though at peak times you'll want to arrive before noon to ensure a pitch – there are reservations in some parks (see p.691 for details of booking places). For help with B&Bs, use the *BC Accommodations* guide, or contact the Victoria infocentre or specialist agencies (see p.733).

Saltspring Island

SALTSPRING (pop. 9240), sometimes spelt Salt Spring, is the biggest, most populated and most visited of the islands – its population triples in summer – though if you're without transport think twice about coming here on a day-trip as getting around is pretty tough. It's served by three ferry terminals: **Fulford Harbour**, from Victoria's Swartz Bay (ten sailings daily, more in summer; 35min; foot passengers $6 return, cars $19.25) and **Vesuvius Bay** (from Crofton, near Duncan on Vancouver Island; 13 daily; 20min; same fares) provide links to Vancouver Island; **Long Harbour** connects to points on the BC mainland via other islands. In the past the Saltspring Island Bus service has connected the ferry terminals with **GANGES**, the island's main village, but check with the Victoria infocentre for the latest. For more complicated journeys, call up the Silver Shadow Taxi (☎537-3030) or consider **renting a bike** from the Bike Shop (☎537-1544) on McPhillips Avenue in Ganges or a scooter from Saltspring Marine Rentals (☎537-9100) next to *Moby's Pub* – a popular local hangout – also in Ganges. Locals are a particularly cosmopolitan bunch, the island having been colonized not by whites but by pioneer black settlers seeking refuge from prejudice in the US. If you're here to slum it on a **beach**, the best strips are on the island's more sheltered west side (Beddis Beach in particular, off the Fulford to Ganges road), at Vesuvius Bay and at Drummond Park near Fulford.

Ganges, close to Long Harbour, is armed with a small **infocentre** at 121 Lower Ganges Rd (daily 10am–4pm; ☎537-5252 or 537-4223, *www.saltspring.com*) and a rapidly proliferating assortment of galleries, tourist shops and holiday homes. Community spirits reach a climax during the annual **Artcraft** (late June to mid-Sept), a summer crafts fair that displays the talents of the island's many dab-handed creatives.

Ganges' infocentre is the place to check out the island's relatively plentiful **accommodation**. A lot of independent travellers are lured here by the prospect of the official HI-affiliated **youth hostel**, the lovely *Salt Spring Island Hostel*, set amidst ten peaceful acres on the eastern side of the island at 640 Cusheon Lake Rd (☎537-4149; ①–③). Under your own steam from Victoria, take the #70 Pat Bay Hwy bus ($2.50) to the Swartz Bay ferry terminal. Catch the ferry to Fulford Harbour ($5 return) and ask car drivers disembarking the ferry if they're headed past the hostel on Cusheon Lake Road: if they're locals, most say yes. You can choose between dorm rooms ($15.50–19.50), tepees, tents, tree house and private family room ($40–70) – 22 beds in all. Note, however, that's there's no camping. It's just a short walk to Cusheon Lake or the ocean at Beddis Beach. Otherwise you can choose from the multitudinous (but often exorbitant) B&B options (owners can arrange to pick you up from the ferry) or one of the so-called "resorts" dotted round the island – usually a handful of houses with camping, a few rooms to rent and little else. Each of the ferry terminals also has a range of mid-price motels. Some of the more reasonable include the twelve-unit *Beachcomber Motel* at 770 Vesuvius Bay Rd at Vesuvius Bay 7km from Ganges (☎537-5415, fax 537-1753, *gball@saltspring.com*; ②); the *Harbour House Hotel*, 121 Upper Ganges Rd, Ganges (☎537-5571, *harbourhouse@saltspring.com*; ④), and the 28-unit *Seabreeze Inn* in a park-like setting above Ganges harbour at 101 Bittancourt Rd (☎537-4145, *seabreeze@saltspring.com*; ③).

One of the island's better-known places to **eat** is *The Vesuvius Inn* (☎537-2312) alongside the ferry at Vesuvius Bay, blessed with live music nightly and a great **bar** deck overlooking the harbour where you can eat seafood and the usual range of pastas, chickens and salads. In Ganges, there are numerous cafés and coffee shops: try the popular *Sweet Arts Patisserie Café* at 112 Lower Ganges Rd (opposite the fire station) for high-quality sandwiches.

The island's best hiking and its top **campsite** are to be found in Ruckle Provincial Park. The campsite ($12 in summer, $8 in winter) is at Beaver Point, and is reached by following Beaver Point Road from the Fulford Harbour ferry terminal (9km). There's further walking and good views on and around Mount Maxwell.

Galiano Island

Long and finger-shaped, **Galiano** (pop. 1040) is one of the more promising islands to visit if you want variety and a realistic chance of finding somewhere to stay. There are two ferry terminals: **Sturdies Bay**, which takes boats from the mainland, and **Montague Harbour**, which handles the Vancouver Island crossings (both routes: foot passengers $5, cars $12.75). The **infocentre** is in Sturdies Bay at 2590 Sturdies Bay Rd (May–Sept daily 8am–6pm; ☎539-2233 or 539-2507, *www.galianoisland.com*), which also has bike, boat and canoe rentals, motels, B&B, and an excellent **campsite** at Montague Harbour Provincial Marine Park, 10km from the ferry terminal on the west side of the island (☎250/391-2300; $15 in summer, $8 in winter; 15 reservable tent sites). See box on p.691 for details of provincial park campsite reservations.

The island's main pub, the *Hummingbird Inn* (☎539-5472) is conveniently close to the ferry on Sturdies Road. **Food** is reasonable at the *Hummingbird*, likewise at *La Berengerie*, near Montague Harbour on the corner of Montague and Clanton roads (☎539-5392; ③), a genteel restaurant that also has three B&B rooms upstairs.

For a comfortable stay in peaceful and elegant surroundings (close to Montague Harbour Provincial Marine Park), try the excellent but expensive *Woodstone Country Inn* (☎539-2022 or 1-888/339-2022, *woodstone@gulfislands.com*; ⑥) on Georgeson Bay Road, 4km from the ferry: breakfast and afternoon tea are included in the price. For a special treat book well in advance to secure one of the seven well-priced rooms at the *Sutil Lodge*, Montague Harbour (☎539-2930, *reservations@gulfislands.com*; ④), a restored 1928 fishing lodge on the beach surrounded by twenty acres of forested seclusion with lovely views, great sunsets and general all-round old-style delights. The lodge offers a four-hour nature cruise aboard a catamaran, and there's free ferry and canoe pick-up also. A less exalted but still good choice on the island's quieter northern end are the seven log cabins of the *Bodega Resort*, at 120 Monastee Rd off Porlier Pass Drive and Cook Drive (☎539-2677, *www.cedarplace.com/bodega*; ③), complete with kitchens and wood-burning stoves and set in acres of woods and meadows with sea views.

If you're **canoeing**, stick to the calmer waters, cliffs and coves off the west coast. **Hikers** can walk almost the entire length of the east coast, or climb Mount Sutil (323m) or Mount Galiano (342m) for views of the mainland mountains. The locals' favourite **beach** is at Coon Bay at the island's northern tip.

North and South Pender

The bridge-linked islands of **North** and **South Pender** muster about a thousand people between them, many of whom will try to entice you into their studios to buy local arts and crafts. Ferries come here from Swartz Bay and Tsawwassen (from the latter foot-passenger one-way tickets cost $9, cars $35; $3 and $7 respectively for the former). The **infocentre** is at the ferry terminal in **Otter Bay**, 2332 Otter Bay Rd (daily mid-May to early Sept 9am–6pm; ☎629-6541) on North Pender, home of the Otter Bay Marina, where you can rent **bikes** and buy maps for a tour of the islands' rolling, hilly interior. The best **beaches** are at Hamilton (North Pender) and Mortimer Spit (South Pender).

Accommodation-wise there are plenty of B&Bs, and a small wooded **campsite** at Prior Centennial Provincial Park, 6km south of the Otter Bay ferry terminal (March–Oct; $12). For the only **hotel**-type rooms, as opposed to B&Bs, try the *Inn on Pender Island* prettily situated in 7.5 acres of wooded country near Prior Park at 4709 Canal Rd, North Pender (☎629-3353 or 1-800/550-0172; ③); or the *Bedwell Harbour Island Resort*, 9801 Spalding Rd, South Pender (☎629-3212 or 1-800/663-2899, *bedwell@islandnet.com*; March–Oct; ④), which has a pool, pub, restaurant, store, tennis, harbour views, canoe, boat and bike rentals, and a choice of rooms or cabins; or the three fully equipped self-catering cottages 500m sharp left from the ferry at *Pender Lodge*, 1325 MacKinnon Rd, North Pender (☎629-3221; ⑤/⑥; March–Oct), with tennis court, outdoor pool and private decks.

Mayne and Saturna islands

Mayne is the first island to your left if you're crossing from Tsawwassen to Swartz Bay – which is perhaps as close as you'll get, since it's the quietest and most difficult to reach of the islands served by ferries (one-way tickets in high season cost foot passengers $9, cars cost $35.50) and has few places to stay; fix up accommodation before you arrive. That may be as good a reason as any for heading out here, however, particularly if you have a bike to explore the web of quiet country roads. Best of several **beaches** is Bennett Bay, a sheltered strip with warm water and good sand. It's reached by heading east from Miner's Bay (5min from the ferry terminal at Village Bay) to the end of Fernhill Road and then turning left onto Wilks Road. Village Bay has a summer-only **infocentre** (daily 8am–6pm) which should be able to fill you in on the limited (currently around seven) but expanding number of **B&B** possibilities – though the island is small enough to explore as a day-trip. Try the three-unit *Root Seller B&B*, a kilometre south of the ferry terminal at 478 Village Bay Rd (☎539-2621; ③; March–Oct), or the *Blue Vista Resort*, eight fully-equipped cabins overlooking Bennett Bay on Arbutus Drive 6km from the ferry terminal (☎539-2463; ③), with handy sandy beach, park-like setting and bike rental (no credit cards). The *Tinkerer's B&B* on Miner's Bay at 417 Sunset Place off Georgina Point Road (☎539-2280; ④; mid-April to mid-Oct), 2km from the Village Bay ferry terminal, is offbeat: it rents bikes, provides hammocks and offers "demonstrations of medicinal herb and flower gardens". For a real treat, the best **food** around is to be found at the waterfront *Oceanwood Country Inn*, 630 Dinner Bay Rd (☎539-5074, *www.oceanwood.com*; ⑥), which also has 12 smart rooms.

Saturna, to the south, is another **B&B** hideaway: try the three-room waterfront *Lyall Harbour B&B* (☎539-5577; ④), 500m from the ferry at 121 East Point Rd in Saturna Point, home to a pub, a shop and the **infocentre** (May–Sept daily 8am–6pm; no phone) which will rent you boats and bicycles. Another relatively large place to stay is the *East Point Resort*, East Point Road (☎539-2975; ④), situated in a park-like setting near a gradually sloping sandy beach; the six cabins are fully equipped and you can choose between one- and two-bedroom units – note that in July and August there's a minimum stay of a week. The best local **beach** is at Winter Cove Marine Park (no campsite) and there's walking, wildlife and good views to the mainland from Mount Warburton Pike.

Highway 14: Victoria to Port Renfrew

Highway 14 runs west from **Victoria** to **Port Renfrew** and is lined with numerous beaches and provincial parks, most – especially those close to the city – heavily populated during the summer months. The 107km route is covered in summer by West Coast Trail Express (see p.736), a private bus service intended for hikers walking the West Coast Trail and Juan de Fuca Trail (see p.778), but also popular for the ride alone. Victoria city buses go as far as **SOOKE** (38km; take #50 to Western Exchange and transfer to a #61), best known for its **All Sooke Day** in mid-July, when lumberjacks from all over the island compete in various tests of forestry expertise. The **infocentre** lies across the Sooke River Bridge at 2070 Phillips and Sooke streets (daily 10am–6pm; ☎642-6351, *www.sookemuseum.bc.ca*). This is the last place of any size, so stock up on supplies if you're continuing west. It also has a surfeit of **accommodation**, with a bias towards B&B, if you're caught short. Check out the small **Sooke Region Museum**, (daily: July–Aug 9am–6pm; Sept–June 9am–5pm; donation) in the same place if you want to bone up on the largely logging-dominated local history. Quite a few people make the trip here just for the **food** at *Sooke Harbour House*, 1528 Whiffen Spit (☎642-3421; ⑨), one of the finest restaurants on the West Coast; it's expensive, but has a surprisingly casual atmosphere. It also has a few top-notch **rooms**, but prices range from a prohibitive $270 to $465.

Beaches beyond Sooke are largely grey pebble and driftwood, the first key stop being **French Beach Provincial Park**, 20km onwards from Sooke. An info-board here fills in the natural-history background, and there are maps of trails and the highlights on the road further west. There's good walking on the fairly wild and windswept beach, and a provincial park campsite (summer $12, winter $8) on the grass immediately away from the shore. Sandy, signposted trails lead off the road to beaches over the next 12km to **Jordan River**, a one-shop, one-hamburger-stall town known for its good surf. Just beyond is the best of the beaches on this coast, part of **China Beach Provincial Park** (no camping) reached after a fifteen-minute walk from the road through rainforest. The West Coast Trail Express shuttle bus (see pp.736–737) makes stops at all these parks and beaches on request.

The road is gravel from here on – past Mystic and Sombrio beaches to **PORT RENFREW**, a logging community that's gained from being the western starting point of the **West Coast Trail** (see p.778). A second trail, the **Juan de Fuca Trail**, also starts from Port Renfrew, running east towards Victoria for about 50km. This does not have the complicated booking procedure of the West Coast Trail, but the scenery is also less striking and the going far easier for the less experienced or more safety conscious walker. Car parks and highway access points are also dotted along its length, allowing you to enjoy strolls or day-hikes.

Accommodation in town is still pretty limited: try the four cottages at *Gallaugher's West Coast Fish Camp* off Beach Road (☎647-5535; ④; May–Oct); the five beachfront rooms of the *Arbutus Beach Lodge*, 5 Queesto Drive (☎647-5458, *arbutus@sookenet.com*; ③/④); the *West Coast Trail Motel*, Parkinson Road (☎647-5565, *www.westcoasttrailmotel.com*; ③/④); and the *Trailhead Resort* on Parkinson Road (☎647-5468, *www.trailhead-resort.com*; ③), which has four rooms and nine tent pitches ($4 per person); and the 124-site *Port Renfrew RV Park and Marina* on Gordon River Road (☎647-5430; $12–14; April–Oct), with a separate tenting area across the bridge on the northern side of the village. South of the village on a logging road (6km) is **Botanical Beach**, a sandstone shelf and tidal-pool area that reveals a wealth of marine life at low tide.

If you're driving and don't want to retrace your steps, think about taking the gravel logging roads from the village on the north side of the San Juan River to either Shawnigan Lake or the Cowichan Valley. They're marked on most maps, but it's worth picking up the detailed map of local roads put out by the Sooke Combined Fire Organization (ask at the Victoria infocentre); heed all warnings about logging trucks.

Highway 1: Victoria to Nanaimo

If you leave Victoria with high hopes of Vancouver Island's lauded scenery, **Hwy 1** – the final western leg of the Trans-Canada – will come as a disappointing introduction to what you can expect along most of the island's southeast coast. After a lengthy sprawl of suburbs, blighted by more billboards than you'd see in supposedly less scenic cities, the landscape becomes suddenly wooded and immensely lush; unfortunately the beauty is constantly interrupted by bursts of dismal motels and other highway junk. **Buses** operated by Laidlaw make the trip between Victoria and Nanaimo (6 daily). One **train** a day also covers this route, and beyond to Courtenay, but it's a single-carriage job and gets booked solid in summer; it stops at every stump.

Goldstream Provincial Park

Thetis Lake Regional Park, appearing on the right 11km out of the city, is good for swimming, with forested trails and sandy beaches on two lakes backed by high cliffs; there's a busy beach near the car park, which is quieter round the shore, or beyond at the bottom of the hill at Prior Lake. Prettier still is **Goldstream Provincial Park**, 5km beyond Langford and 20km from the city centre, where you'll find an ancient forest of Douglas fir and western red cedar and a large provincial park **campsite** with good facilities and a visitor centre (summer $18.50, winter $8). There's also a network of marked **trails** to hilltops and waterfalls designed for anything between five minutes and an hour's walking. Try the paths towards Mount Finlayson (three-hour's hard walk if you go all the way to the summit) for views of the ocean – views you also get if you carry on up the highway, which soon meets Saanich Inlet, a bay with a lovely panorama of wooded ridges across the water. Look out for the Malahat Summit (31km from Victoria) and Gulf Islands (33km) viewpoints. To **stay**, the small *Malahat Oceanview Motel* (☎478-9213, *oceanview@coastnet.com*; ③), 35km north of Victoria, is best sited to catch the sea and island vistas.

A scenic diversion off the main road takes you 7km to **Shawnigan Lake**, fringed by a couple of provincial parks: West Shawnigan Park on the lake's northwest side has a safe beach and swimming possibilities. If you're biking or are prepared to tackle pretty rough roads, note the logging road that links the north end of the lake to Port Renfrew on the west coast (check access restrictions at the Victoria infocentre).

Duncan

DUNCAN, 60km north of Victoria, begins inauspiciously, with a particularly scrappy section of highway spoiling what would otherwise be an exquisitely pastoral patch of country. Still, the town's native centre – the Cowichan Native Village – merits a stop, unlike the Glass Castle, a messy affair made from glass bottles off the road to the south, and the even sillier "World's Largest Hockey Stick", arranged as a triumphal arch into the town centre.

Duncan's **infocentre** is at 381A Trans-Canada Hwy opposite the supermarket on the main road (mid-April to mid-Oct Mon–Fri 8.30am–5pm, longer hours July & Aug; ☎746-4636, *duncancc@islandnet.com*), close to the **bus station**, which has six daily connections to and from Victoria (1hr 10min). Duncan is not a place you want even to consider staying in – though there are plenty of motels and campsites if you're stuck – but for **meals** you could try the excellent *Arbutus Café*, 195 Kenneth St, at Jubilee (☎746-5443), which is much-frequented by locals keen for the usual Italian- and Pacific Rim-influenced food. Just east of town, the *Quamichan Inn*, 1478 Maple Bay Rd (☎746-7028), serves up a similar menu and also has its devotees. You could also visit one of several local vineyards: one of the best is the **Vigneti Zenatta Winery**, 5039 Marshall Rd (call for tour details on ☎748-4981 or 748-2338), which has been in business for over forty years; as well as their wine, you can also buy meals here.

Three kilometres south of town on Hwy 1, the *Pioneer House Restaurant* has a rustic log-cabin feel helped by a genuine **saloon bar** transplanted from a period building in Montana. Alternatively, head 10km north of Duncan to the *Red Rooster Diner* (by the Mount Sicker petrol station), reputed to be the greasy spoon immortalized by Jack Nicholson in *Five Easy Pieces*. It's still a classic – good, cheap food, vinyl booths and all the authentic tacky trimmings you'd expect.

Cowichan Native Village

The first real reason to pull over out of Victoria is Duncan's **Cowichan Native Village**, 200 Cowichan Way (daily: 9am–5pm; $6; ☎746-8119), on your left off the highway in the

OLD-GROWTH FORESTS: GOING, GOING, GONE

While Vancouver Island isn't the only place in North America where environmentalists and the forestry industry are at loggerheads, some of the most bitter and high-profile confrontations have taken place here. The island's wet climate is particularly favourable to the growth of thick **temperate rainforest**, part of a belt that once stretched from Alaska to northern California. The most productive ecosystem on the planet, **old-growth** virgin Pacific rainforest contains up to ten times more biomass per acre than its more famous tropical counterpart – and, though it covers a much smaller area, it is being felled at a greater rate and with considerably less media outrage. Environmentalists estimate that British Columbia's portion of the Pacific rainforest has already been reduced by two-thirds; all significant areas will have been felled, they predict, within about ten or fifteen years. The powerful logging industry claims two-thirds survive, but even the Canadian government – largely in thrall to and supportive of the industry – concedes that only a small percentage of the BC rainforest is currently protected.

What is clear is that the government wants a very firm lid kept on the whole affair. In 1990 it commissioned a report into **public opinion** on the issue in the United Kingdom, which takes half of all British Columbia's plywood exports, three-quarters of all its lumber shipments to Europe, and a third of all Canada's paper pulp output. It observed that "UK public opinion appears to be highly uncritical of Canadian forestry, largely because awareness of the subject is low . . . [there is] a reassuringly romantic and simplistic image of Canadian forestry based on a lumberjack in a checked shirt, felling a single tree." The report concluded that "media attention and coverage of Canadian forestry management issues should not be sought". It's hard to see that opinions will have changed much since.

No such apathy exists in British Columbia, however. The controversy over logging often pits neighbour against neighbour, for some 250,000 in the province depend directly or indirectly on the industry, and big multinationals dominate the scene. **Employment** is a major rallying cry here, and the prospect of job losses through industry regulation is usually enough to override objections. The trend towards **automation** only adds fuel to the argument: by volume of wood cut, the BC forestry industry provides only half as many jobs as in the rest of Canada, which means, in effect, that twice as many trees have to be cut down in BC to provide the same number of jobs.

Some **environmental groups** have resorted to such tactics as fixing huge nails in trees at random – these ruin chainsaws and lumber-mill machinery, but also endanger lives. Countless people have been arrested in recent years for obstructing logging operations. The most level-headed and impressive of the conservation groups, the **Western Canada Wilderness Committee** (WCWC), condemns these acts of environmental vandalism, and instead devotes its energies to alerting the public to the landslide damage and destruction of salmon habitats caused by logging, and the dioxin pollution from pulp mills that in the past has closed 220,000 acres of offshore waters to fishing for shellfish. They point out that the battle is over what they call "the last cookies in the jar", for only a handful of the island's 91 watersheds over 12,000 acres have escaped logging; the old-growth bonanza is nearly over, they argue, and the industry might as well wean itself over to sustainable practices now, before it's too late.

In the meantime, however, ninety percent of timber is still lifted from the rainforest instead of from managed stands, clear-cutting of old-growth timber is blithely described by the vast McMillan company as "a form of harvesting", and independent audits suggest that companies are failing to observe either their cutting or replanting quotas. The provincial government has pledged to improve forestry practices, but only a tiny percentage of the province lies within reserves with a degree of environmental protection.

unmissable wooden buildings next to Malaspina College. Duncan has long been the self-proclaimed "City of Totems", reference to a rather paltry collection of poles – arranged mostly alongside the main road – that belong to the local Cowichan tribes, historically British Columbia's largest native group. The tribes, about 3000 strong locally, still preserve certain traditions, and it's been their energy – along with cash from white civic authorities, attuned as ever to potentially lucrative tourist attractions – that have put up the poles and pulled the project together. Much of the heavily worked commercial emphasis is on shifting native crafts, especially the ubiquitous lumpy jumpers for which the area is famous, but you can usually expect to find historical displays and demonstrations of dancing, knitting, carving, weaving and even native cooking.

British Columbia Forestry Museum

Vancouver Island is one of the most heavily logged areas in Canada, and the **BC Forest Discovery Centre**, 1km north of town on Hwy 1 (early May to Sept daily; $8), is run to preserve artefacts from its lumbering heritage; but with industry bigwigs as museum trustees, you can't help feeling it's designed to be something of a palliative in the increasingly ferocious controversy between loggers and environmentalists. Nonetheless, it does a thorough job on trees, and if the forestry displays in Victoria's museum have whetted your appetite, you'll have a good couple of hours rounding off your arboreal education. The entrance is marked by a small black steam engine and a massive piece of yellow logging machinery.

Ranged over a hundred-acre site next to a scenic lake, the well-presented displays tell everything you want to know about trees and how to cut them down. The narrow-gauge steam train round the park is a bit gimmicky (10am–5.30pm only), but a good way of getting around; check out the forest dioramas and the artefacts and archive material in the **Log Museum** in particular. There's also the usual array of working blacksmiths, sawmills, a farmstead, an old logging camp, and a few as-yet-underforested patches where you can take time out.

The complex forms part of the **Cowichan and Chemainus Valleys Ecomuseum**, a vaguely defined park that takes in much of the surrounding area intended to preserve the logging heritage of the area – a curiously ill-defined concept that appears to be largely a PR exercise on the part of the logging companies. Ask for details of tours and maps from the Duncan infocentre, or the Ecomuseum office, 160 Jubilee St (☎748-7620).

The Cowichan Valley

Striking west into the hills from Hwy 1 north of Duncan, Hwy 18 enters the **Cowichan Valley** and fetches up at Cowichan Lake, the largest freshwater lake on the island. Rather than drive, however, the nicest way up the valley is to walk the eighteen-kilometre **Cowichan Valley Footpath**, following the river from Glenora (a hamlet southwest of Duncan at the end of Robertson Rd) to Lake Cowichan Village on the lake's eastern shore. You could do the trip in a day, camp en route, or turn around at Skutz Falls and climb up to the Riverbottom Road to return to Duncan which would be a half-day walk.

A road, rough in parts, circles **Cowichan Lake** (allow 2hr) and offers access to a gamut of outdoor pursuits, most notably fishing – the area is touted, with typical small-town hyperbole, as the "Fly-Fishing Capital of the World". The water gets warm enough for summer swimming, and there's also ample hiking in the wilder country above. At Youbou on the north shore you can visit the **Heritage Mill**, a working sawmill (tours May–Sept): this area boasts some of the most productive forest in Canada, thanks to the lake's mild microclimate, and lumber is the obvious mainstay of the local economy. On the road up to the lake from Duncan you pass the **Valley Demonstration Forest**, another link in the industry's public-relations weaponry, with signs and scenic lookouts explaining the intricacies of forest management.

For details of the area's many tours, trails and outfitters contact the **infocentre** at Lake Cowichan village, 125 South Shore Rd (late May to early Sept daily 9am–8pm; ☎749-3244 or 749-6772). Good, cheap **campsites** line the shore, which despite minimal facilities can be quite busy in summer – don't expect to have the place to yourself. The biggest and best is at Gordon Bay Provincial Park (summer $18.50, winter $8) on the south shore 14km from Lake Cowichan Village, a popular family place but with a quiet atmosphere and a good sandy **beach**. There are also plenty of hotels, motels and the like in all the lakeside settlements.

Chemainus

CHEMAINUS is the "Little Town That Did", as the billboards for miles around never stop telling you. Its mysterious achievement was the creation of its own tourist attraction, realized when the closure of the local sawmill – once amongst the world's largest – threatened the place with almost overnight extinction. In 1983 the town's worthies commissioned an artist to paint a huge **mural** – *Steam Donkey at Work* – recording the area's local history. This proved so successful that some 40 panels quickly followed, drawing some 300,000 visitors annually to admire the artwork and tempting them to spend money in local businesses as they did. As murals go, these are surprisingly good, and if you're driving it's worth the short, well-signed diversion off Hwy 1. You might also want to drop in on the **Chemainus Valley Museum**, 9799 Waterwheel Crescent (March–May & Nov–Dec Wed–Sun 10am–3pm; June–Oct daily 10am–6pm; donation), a community-run museum of local history with displays on logging, mills and pioneer life. Ironically enough, a new sawmill has now opened, though this has done nothing to deter the welcome influx of resident painters and craftspeople attracted by the murals, a knock-on effect that has done much to enliven the village's pleasant community feel.

Buses also detour here on the run up to Nanaimo (☎246-3354 for details), and the train drops you slap-bang next to a mural. You can also pick up a ferry from Chemainus to the small islands of **Kuper** and **Thetis** (both $5 foot passengers, $12.75 for cars). There's a summer-only **infocentre** in town at 9796 Willow St (May to early Sept daily 9am–6pm; ☎246-3251, *www.tourism.chemainus.bc.ca*). If you fancy **staying** – the village's cosy waterside setting is nicer than either Duncan or Nanaimo – it's worth booking ahead, as the village's increasing popularity means the local **hotel** and half a dozen or so B&Bs are in heavy demand in summer. For motel accommodation, try the *Fuller Lake Chemainus Motel*, 9300 Trans-Canada Hwy (☎246-3282 or 1-888/246-3255; ③). The best **B&B** is the pretty *Bird Song Cottage*, 9909 Maple St (☎246-9910, *birdsong@island.net*; ⑤). There's also a tiny **youth hostel** at 3040 Henry Rd (☎246-4407; ①), about 2km north of town off the Ladysmith road (they can pick you up from the village); there's a kitchen and showers, but you're supposed to bring your own sleeping bag. The choice of **campsites** is between the *Chemainus Gardens RV Park*, 3042 River Rd, 1km east of Hwy 1, set in 37 acres of natural forest with separate tenting area, laundry and showers (☎246-3569 or 1-800/341-5060; $15–25), or the larger *Country Maples Campground*, 9010 Trans-Canada Hwy (☎246-2078; $21–29; April–Oct) in sixty acres of open and treed parkland 16km north of Duncan above the Chemainus River with showers, laundry and pool. About 5km south of the village on the river is the quiet *Bald Eagle Campsite*, 8705 Chemainus Rd (☎246-9457; $16–20). All manner of dinky little cafés, shops and tearooms are springing up across the village: for **food**, try the *Upstairs Downstairs Café*, 9745 Willow St, with cheap, varied dishes including several good vegetarian options, or the *Waterford Inn & Restaurant*, five minutes north of the village centre at 9875 Maple St (☎246-1046).

Ladysmith

LADYSMITH's claim to fame is based solely on an accident of geography, as it straddles the 49th Parallel, the latitude that divides mainland Canada and the US. Canada held onto Vancouver Island only after some hard bargaining, even though the boundary's logic ought to put much of it in the States. It was originally named Oyster Bay, but was renamed by Robert Dunsmuir (see below) at the time of the Boer War battle for Ladysmith (many streets bear the name of Boer War generals). There's little to the place other than the usual motels and garages, though a recent attempt to spruce up the older buildings won it a Western Canada Award of Excellence. Ladysmith's scenic profile, it has to be said, would be considerably higher were it not for a huge sawmill and a waterfront hopelessly jammed with lumber. The **infocentre** is a kiosk on the main road at 12615 Trans-Canada Hwy (July–Aug daily 9am–6pm; no phone) and has walking maps of the village's "heritage centre". The **Black Nugget Museum**, 12 Gatacre St (daily noon–4pm; $2), is a restored 1881 hotel stuffed with predictable memorabilia of coal mining and pioneers. If you stop off, check out **Transfer Beach Park** on the harbour, where the water's said to be the warmest in the Pacific north of San Francisco.

For **accommodation**, make for the fourteen-unit *Holiday House Motel*, 540 Esplanade St (☎245-2231, *hhmotel@island.net*; ②), overlooking Ladysmith's waterfront; the *Seaview Marine Resort*, 1111 Chemainus Rd (☎245-3768 or 1-800/891-8832, *www.chemainus.com*; ③), just off the highway 6km south of town (and 8km north of Chemainus) with fully equipped self-catering one- and two-bedroom cottages on the ocean (two-night minimum stay); or the *Inn of the Sea*, 3600 Yellow Point Rd (☎245-2211; ⑥), 13km northeast on the seafront and a popular bolt hole for weekending Victorians. The best **food** option is the oldest "English-style pub" in BC, the *Crow and Gate* off the main road 19km north of the town on Yellow Point Road. For campers, the most central site is the *Sea-RRA RV Park and Campground* in Transfer Beach Park overlooking the port (☎245-5344; $14).

Nanaimo

With a population of about 73,000, **NANAIMO**, 113km from Victoria, is Vancouver Island's second biggest city, the terminal for ferries from Horseshoe Bay and Tsawwassen on the mainland, and a watershed between the island's populated southeastern tip and its wilder, more sparsely peopled countryside to the north and west. In BC, only Vancouver and Kelowna are expanding faster. This said, the town is unexceptional, though the setting, as ever in BC, is eye-catching – particularly around the harbour, which bobs with yachts and rusty fishing boats and, if you've come from Victoria, allows the first views across to the big mountains on the mainland. If you are going to stop here, more than likely it'll be for **Petroglyph Park** or the town's increasingly famous **bungee-jumping** zone. If not, the Nanaimo Parkway provides a 21-kilometre bypass around the town.

Coal first brought white settlers to the region, many of whom made their fortunes here, including the Victorian magnate **Robert Dunsmuir**, who was given £750,000 and almost half the island in return for building the Victoria–Nanaimo railway – an indication of the benefits that could accrue from the British government to those with the pioneering spirit. Five bands of Salish natives originally lived on the site, which they called **Sney-ne-mous**, or "meeting place", from which the present name derives. It was they who innocently showed the local black rock to Hudson's Bay agents in 1852. The old mines are now closed, and the town's pockets are padded today by forestry, deep-sea fishing, tourism and – most notably – by six deep-water docks and a booming port.

The Town

In downtown Nanaimo itself, only two other sights warrant the considerable amount of energy used to promote them. The **Nanaimo District Museum**, just off the main harbour area at 100 Cameron St by the Harbour Park Mall (daily 9am–5pm, closed Jan; $2; ☎753-1821), houses a collection that runs the usual historical gamut of pioneer, logging, mining, native peoples and natural-history displays. The best features are the reconstructed coal mine and the interesting insights into the town's cosmopolitan population – a mix of Polish, Chinese, aboriginal peoples and British citizens – who all see themselves today as some of the island's "friendliest folk". The **Bastion**, close by at the corner of Bastion and Front streets, is a wood-planked tower built by the Hudson's Bay Company in 1853 as a store and a stronghold against native attack, though it was never used for such an attack. It's the oldest (perhaps the only) such building in the west. These days it houses a small **museum** of Hudson's Bay memorabilia (summer only 10am–5pm; donation); its silly tourist stunt, without which no BC town would be complete, is "the only ceremonial cannon firing west of Ontario" (summer only, daily at noon). This is marginally more impressive than the town's claim to have the most retail shopping space per capita in the country.

Nanaimo's outskirts are not pretty, nor, if you keep to the road through town, is the main strip of malls and billboards on and around downtown. Big efforts are being made to spruce the place up, however, not least in the town's 25 or so gardens and small parks. Many of these hug the shore, perfectly aligned for a seafront breath of air. The **Harbourfront Walkway** allows you to stroll 3km along the seafront. Also popular is the Swyalana Lagoon, an artificial tidal lagoon built on a renovated stretch of the downtown harbour in Maffeo Sutton Park. It's become a popular swimming, snoozing and picnic area. Further afield, **Piper's Lagoon Park** offers a windblown, grassy spit, with lots of trails, flowers, rocky bluffs and good sea views; it's off Hammond Bay Road north of the city centre. For **beaches** you could head for **Departure Bay**, again north of the centre off Stewart Avenue. Plenty of local shops rent out a range of marine gear, as well as bikes and boats.

For the wildest of the local parks, head due west of town to **Westwood Lake Park**, good for a couple of hours' lonely hiking and some fine swimming. Tongue-twisting **Petroglyph Provincial Park**, off Hwy 1 3km south of downtown, showcases aboriginal peoples' carvings of the sort found all over BC (particularly along coastal waterways), many of them thousands of years old. Often their meaning is vague, but they appear to record important rituals and events. There are plenty of figures – real and mythological – carved into the local sandstone here, though their potential to inspire wonder is somewhat spoilt by more recent graffiti and the first thin edge of Nanaimo's urban sprawl.

Nanaimo's other major claim to fame is as home of North America's first legal public bungee-jumping site. The **Bungy Zone Adrenalin Centre** is 13km south of the town at 35 Nanaimo River Rd (daily 11.30am–8pm; ☎753-5867 or 1-800/668-7771 and 1-888/668-7874, *www.bungyzone.com*; jumps from around $95): look out for the signed turn off Hwy 1. To date it has played host to around 70,000 safe bungee jumps, including night jumps. It's become so popular three variations have been added to the standard 42-metre plunge off the bridge, all slightly less terrifying than the bungee jump. The "Flying Fox" is a line to which you are fixed extending in a deep arc along the canyon – expect to hit speeds of 100kph; "Rap Jumping" involves a rapid mountaineering rappel straight down from the bridge; while the "Ultimate Swing" lets you jump off the bridge and swing in a big arc at speeds of up to 140kph. The last innovation was described by the safety engineer who inspected it – a man with twenty-years' experience of fairground and other rides – as "the best ride I've ever ridden, and I've ridden them all". There is provision for **camping** here (with showers, laundry and tents for rent), and if you call in advance you should be able to book free shuttles to the site from Victoria and Nanaimo.

Nanaimo, like any self-respecting BC town, also lays on a fair few festivals, best known of which is the annual **Bathtub Race** or **Silly Boat Race**, in which bathtubs are raced (and sunk, mostly) across the 55km to Vancouver. The winner, the first to reach Vancouver, receives the silver Plunger Trophy from the Loyal Nanaimo Bathtub Society. It's all part of the Marine Festival held in the second week of July. More high-brow is the May to June **Nanaimo Festival**, a cultural jamboree that takes place in and around Malaspina College, 900 Fifth St. The town's other minor claim to fame is the **Nanaimo bar**, a glutinous chocolate confection made to varying recipes and on sale everywhere.

Newcastle and Gabriola islands

Barely a stone's throw offshore from Nanaimo lies **Newcastle Island**, and beyond it the larger bulk of **Gabriola Island**, both incongruously graced with palm trees: they're beneficiaries of what is supposedly Canada's mildest climate. Ferries make the crossing every hour on the hour (10am–9pm; foot passengers $5 return, cars $12.75) from Maffeo Sutton Park (the wharf behind the Civic Arena) to **Newcastle Island Provincial Park**, which has a fine stretch of sand, tame wildlife, no cars, and lots of walking and picnic possibilities. It'll take a couple of hours to walk the 7.5-kilometre trail that encircles the island. There are about fifteen daily crossings to Gabriola Island (20min), a much quieter place that's home to about 2000 people, many of them artists and writers. Author Malcolm Lowry, he of *Under the Volcano* fame, immortalized the island in a story entitled *October Ferry to Gabriola Island* (characters in the tale never actually reach the island). Gabriola also offers several **beaches** – the best are Gabriola Sands' Twin Beaches at the island's northwest end and Drumbeg Provincial Park – and lots of scope for scuba diving, bird-watching (eagles and sea birds), beachcombing and easy walking, plus the added curiosity of the **Malaspina Galleries**, a series of caves and bluffs near Gabriola Sands sculpted by wind, frost and surf.

Both islands have numerous **B&Bs** and several **campsites**, though if you're thinking of staying the night it's as well to check first with the Nanaimo infocentre. You can buy snacks on Newcastle from various concessions, notably the newly restored 1931 Pavilion building, but if you're camping take supplies with you.

Information and transport

Nanaimo's **bus terminal** (☎753-4371) is some way from the harbour on the corner of Comox and Terminal, with six daily runs to Victoria, two to Port Hardy and three or four to Port Alberni, for connections to Tofino and Ucluelet. **BC Ferries** (☎386-3431 or 1-888/223-3779) sail to and from Departure Bay, 2km north of downtown (take the Hammond Bay bus #2 to the north end of Stewart Ave), to Tsawwassen (south of Vancouver) and more frequently to Horseshoe Bay on the mainland (summer hourly 7am–9pm; off-season every 2hr; foot passengers $9 one-way, cars $32; cheaper in low season). Another newer terminal, Duke Point, which will take increasing numbers of ferries, operates just to the south of the town. The town lies on the Victoria–Courtenay line and sees two trains daily, northbound around 11am and southbound at 3pm: the station is in the centre of downtown.

You'll find a typically overstocked **infocentre** at Beban House, 2290 Bowen Rd (May–Sept daily 8am–8pm; Oct–April Mon–Fri 9am–5pm; ☎756-0106 or 1-800/663-7337, *www.tourism.nanaimo.bc.ca*). They'll phone around and help with **accommodation** referrals, and shower you with pamphlets on the town and the island as a whole. There are also details of the many boat rides and tours you can make to local sawmills, canneries, nature reserves and fishing research stations.

Accommodation

Nanaimo's cheapest beds are at the central, private **mini-hostel**, the *Nanaimo International Hostel*, 65 Nicol St (☎753-1188, reservations ☎754-9697; ①), located seven blocks south of the bus terminal and one block south of the Harbour Park Shopping Centre off Hwy 1; dorm beds from $15. A handful of camping spots ($8) on the lawn (with ocean views) are also available, plus bike rental. More recent and a touch more expensive is the downtown *Cambie International Hostel*, 63 Victoria Crescent (754-5323; ①), with accommodation for 50 in small dorm rooms; beds cost $25 or $20 with student or HI cards.

Numerous **motels** are clustered on the city limits, the best-known cheapie being the small *Colonial*, 950 Terminal Ave on Hwy 1 (☎754-4415, *colonial@island.net*; ②). For more tasteful lodgings, try the big *Howard Johnson Harbourside Hotel*, 1 Terminal Ave (☎753-2241 or 1-800/663-7322; ③), convenient for the bus terminal, or the *Fairwinds Schooner Cove Resort Hotel and Marina* at 3521 Dolphin Drive (☎468-7691 or 1-800/663-7060, *www.fairwinds.bc.ca*; ⑤), 26km north of town near Nanoose Bay.

If you're **camping**, by far the best choice is Newcastle Island Provincial Park ($12; see opposite), which has the only pitches (18 in all, so arrive early) within walking distance of town. Other sites are spread along the main road to the north and south. The best of these – a rural, watery retreat – is *Brannan Lake Campsites*, 6km north of the ferry terminal off Hwy 19 on a 150-acre working farm at 4228 Biggs Rd (☎756-0404; $16–19). The forestry bigwigs have set up a free site at lovely Nanaimo Lake on Nanaimo Lake Road about ten minutes south of the town.

Where **eating** is concerned, get your obligatory Nanaimo bar, or other cheap edibles, at the food stands in the **Public Market**, which is near the ferry terminal on Stewart Avenue (daily 9am–9pm). The big Overwaitea supermarket is 2km north of town on Hwy 19. For meals try *Gina's*, 47 Skinner St, an unmissable Mexican outfit perched on the edge of a cliff and painted bright pink with an electric blue roof. The town's best **seafood** choice is the *Bluenose Chowder House*, 1340 Stewart Ave (closed Mon), also party to a nice outside terrace. Up the road near the BC Ferry terminal, *The Grotto*, 1511 Stewart Ave, is another reliable choice (closed Sun & Mon). A more recent arrival, and worth a look, is *Missoula's*, on the highway near the Rutherford Mall: both restaurants served the usual range of Canadian and Pacific Rim dishes.

From Nanaimo to Port Alberni

North of Nanaimo Hwy 1 is replaced by **Hwy 19**, a messy stretch of road spotted with billboards and a rash of motels, marinas and clapboard houses. Almost every last centimetre of the coast is privately owned, this being the chosen site of what appears to be every British Columbian's dream holiday home. Don't expect, therefore, to be able to weave through the houses, wooden huts and boat launches to reach the tempting beaches that flash past below the highway. For sea and sand you have to hang on for **Parksville**, 37km north of Nanaimo, and its quieter near-neighbour **Qualicum Beach**.

Parksville marks a major parting of the ways: while Hwy 19 continues up the eastern coast to Port Hardy, **Hwy 4**, the principal trans-island route, pushes west to **Port Alberni** and on through the tremendously scenic Mackenzie Mountains to the Pacific Rim National Park. Laidlaw (☎385-4411 or 388-5248) runs three **buses** daily from Nanaimo to Port Alberni, where there are connecting services for Ucluelet and Tofino in the national park.

Parksville

The approach to **PARKSVILLE** from the south is promising, taking you through lovely wooded dunes, with lanes striking off eastwards to hidden beaches and a half-dozen secluded **campsites**. Four kilometres on is the best of the beaches, stretched along 2km of **Rathtrevor Beach Provincial Park**. In summer this area is madness – there's more beach action here than just about anywhere in the country – and if you want to lay claim to some of the park's **camping** space (summer $18.50, winter $8) expect to start queuing first thing in the morning or take advantage of the provincial park reservations service (see box, p.691). The public sand here stretches for 2km and sports all the usual civilized facilities of Canada's tamed outdoors: cooking shelters, picnic spots and walking trails.

The dross starts beyond the bridge into **Parksville** and its eight blocks of motels and garages. The worst of the development has been kept off the promenade, however, which fronts **Parksville Beach**, whose annual **Sandfest** draws 30,000 visitors a day in July to watch the World Sandcastle Competition. The beach offers lovely views across to the mainland and boasts Canada's warmest sea water – up to 21°C (70°F) in summer. Though busy, it's as immaculately kept as the rest of the town – a tidiness that bears witness to the reactionary civic pride of Parksville's largely retired permanent population. You'll see some of these worthy burghers at play during August, when the town hosts the World Croquet Championships.

For local **information**, Parksville's Chamber of Commerce is clearly signed off the highway in downtown at 1275 E Island Hwy (daily 8am–6pm; ☎248-3613, *www.chamber.parksville.bc.ca*). Ask especially for details of the many **hiking** areas and other nearby refuges from the beaches' summer maelstrom, and **fishing**, which is naturally another of the region's big draws.

If you must **stay**, camping offers the best locations. There are a multitude of cheapish Identikit **motels** in town and "resort complexes" out along the beaches, though summer vacancies are few and far between. South of Rathtrevor Beach Provincial Park, try a pair of cottage resorts that look onto the sea: the big *Tigh-Na-Mara Resort Hotel*, 1095 E Island Hwy (☎248-2072 or 1-800/663-7373, *www.tigh-na-mara.com*; ④–⑦) with log cottages and oceanfront apartments, forest setting, beach, indoor pool and self-catering units; or the smaller and slightly cheaper *Graycrest Seaside Resort*, 1115 E Island Hwy (☎248-6513 or 1-800/663-2636, *www.graycrest.com*; ⑦), which has considerably lower rates off-season. More upmarket still is the *Beach Acres Resort*, 1015 E Island Hwy (☎248-3424 or 1-800/663-7309, *www.beachacresresort.com*; ⑦), set in 57 acres of woodland with its own pool, sandy beach, and forest or ocean-view cabins. Much cheaper is the *Sea Edge Motel*, 209 W Island Hwy (☎248-8377 or 1-800/667-3382, *seaedge@parksville.net*; ⑥), with its own stretch of beach. If you're after one of the cheapest motels, try the *Skylite*, 459 E Island Hwy (☎248-4271 or 1-800/667-1886, *skylitemotel@bctravel.com*; ③).

Qualicum Beach

QUALICUM BEACH, says its Chamber of Commerce, "is to the artist of today what Stratford-on-Avon was to the era of Shakespeare" – a bohemian enclave of West Coast artists and writers that has also been dubbed the "Carmel of the North" after the town in California. Both estimations obviously pitch things ridiculously high, but compared to Parksville the area has more greenery and charm, and it's infinitely less commercialized, though it probably has just as many summer visitors.

More a collection of dispersed houses than a town, Qualicum's seafront is correspondingly wilder and more picturesque – though a big resort development is under construction – skirted by the road and interrupted only by an **infocentre** at 2711 W Island Hwy, the obvious white building midway on the strand (daily 9am–6pm, open longer in summer; ☎752-9532, *www.qualicum.bc.ca*), and a couple of well-sited **hotels**: the *Sand Pebbles Inn* (☎752-6974 or 1-877/556-2326, *www.maxpages.com/pebbles*; ⑤) and the small *Captain's Inn* (☎752-6743; ③). A cluster of **motels** also sit at its northern end, where the road swings inland. There's plenty of other local accommodation and B&Bs

and campsites: contact the infocentre for details. Keep heading north and the road becomes quieter and edged with occasional **campsites**.

Highway 4 to Port Alberni

If you've not yet ventured off the coastal road from Victoria, the short stretch of **Hwy 4 to Port Alberni** offers the first real taste of the island's beauty. The cheapest place to stay along here is the unnamed log-cabin-style **lodgings** (☎248-5694; ②) at 2400 Hwy 4 in Coombs, about 10km west of Parksville – take the third entrance past the school on the south side of the main road. Buses will stop here on request, but there are only a couple of rooms – and no cooking facilities – so call in advance.

The first worthwhile stop is **Englishman River Falls Provincial Park**, 3km west of Parksville and then another 8km south off the highway. Named after an early immigrant who drowned here, the park wraps around the Englishman River, which tumbles over two main sets of waterfalls. A thirty-minute trail takes in both falls, with plenty of swimming and fishing pools en route. The popular year-round provincial park **campsite** (summer $15, winter $8) is on the left off the approach road before the river, nestled amongst cedars, dogwoods – BC's official tree – and lush ferns.

Back on the main highway, a further 8km brings you to the **Little Qualicum Hatchery**, given over to chum, trout and chinook salmon, and just beyond it turn right for the **Little Qualicum Falls Provincial Park**, on the north side of Hwy 4 19km west of Parksville, which is claimed by some to be the island's loveliest small park. A magnificent forest trail follows the river as it drops several hundred metres through a series of gorges and foaming waterfalls. A half-hour stroll gives you views of the main falls, but for a longer **hike** try the five-hour Wesley Ridge Trail. There's a sheltered provincial park **campsite** (summer $15, winter $8) by the river and a recognised **swimming area** on the river at its southern end.

Midway to Port Alberni, the road passes **Cameron Lake** and then an imperious belt of old-growth forest. At the lake's western end, it's well worth walking ten minutes into **McMillan Provincial Park** (no campsite) to reach the famous **Cathedral Grove**, a beautiful group of huge Douglas firs, some of them reaching 70m tall, 2m thick and up to a thousand years old. The park is the gift of the large McMillan timber concern, whose agents have been responsible for felling similar trees with no compunction over the years. Wandering the grove will take only a few minutes, but just to the east, at the Cameron Lake picnic site, is the start of the area's main **hike**. The well-maintained trail was marked out by railway crews in 1908 and climbs to the summit of **Mount Arrowsmith** (1817m), a long, gentle twenty-kilometre pull through alpine meadows that takes between six and nine hours. The mountain is also one of the island's newer and fast-developing ski areas. To stay locally, head for the *Cameron Lake Resort* (☎752-6707; ③; April–Oct), based in a park-like setting on the lake: it has seven cottages and a campsite ($19).

Port Alberni

Self-proclaimed "Gateway to the Pacific" and – along with half of Vancouver Island – "Salmon Capital of the World", **PORT ALBERNI** is a town fairly dominated by the sights and smells of its huge lumber mills. It's also an increasingly popular site for exploring the centre and west coast of the island, and a busy fishing port, situated at the end of the impressive fjord-like Alberni Inlet, Vancouver Island's longest inlet. Various logging and pulp-mill tours are available, but the town's main interest to travellers is as a forward base for the Pacific Rim National Park. If you've ever wanted to hook a salmon, though, this is probably one of the easier places to do so and there are any number of boats and guides ready to help out.

The only conventional sight is the **Alberni Valley Museum**, 4255 Wallace St and 10th Avenue (summer Tues–Sat 10am–5pm, Thurs until 8pm; free; ☎723-2181), home to a predictable but above-average logging and aboriginal peoples collection, a waterwheel and small steam engine. For hot-weather swimming, locals head out to **Sproat Lake Provincial Park**, 8km north of town on Hwy 4. It's a hectic scene in summer, thanks to a fine beach, picnic area and a pair of good campsites ($15; April–Oct), one on the lake, the other north of the highway about 1km away. Of peripheral interest, you can take a guided tour of the world's largest fire-fighting planes or follow the short trails that lead to a few ancient petroglyphs on the park's eastern tip.

Sproat Lake marks the start of the superb scenery that unfolds over the 100km of Hwy 4 west of the town. Only heavily logged areas detract from the grandeur of the Mackenzie Range and the majestic interplay of trees and water. Go prepared, however, as there's no fuel or shops for about two hours of driving.

Practicalities

Laidlaw (☎385-4411 or 1-800/318-0818, *www.victoriatours.com*) runs five **buses** daily to and from Nanaimo, with the terminal on Victoria Quay at 5065 Southgate (though the bus company is based at 4541 Margaret St). Jump off at the 7-Eleven, one stop earlier, to be nearer the centre of town. The same company runs connections from here on to Ucluelet and Tofino in Pacific Rim National Park. Western Bus Lines (☎723-3341) run two services weekly to Bamfield (Mon & Fri; $17 one-way) as does the Pacheenaht First Nation Bus Service (☎647-5521). Several other companies from Victoria (see p.734) make connections to Bamfield for the West Coast Trail (see p.778). For help and information on fishing charters, hiking options, minor summer events, or tours of the two local pulp mills, call in at the **infocentre**, unmissable as you come into town at 2533 Redford St, RR2, Site 215 Comp 10 (daily 9am–6pm; ☎724-6535, *www.alberni.net*), off Hwy 4 east of town – look out for the big yellow mural.

Given the 8am departure of the MV *Lady Rose* (see opposite), there's a good chance you may have to stay overnight in the town. For **accommodation** there are the usual motel choices, though for a good central hotel you might be better off with the *Coast Hospitality Inn*, 3835 Redford St (☎723-8111 or 1-800/663-1144, *www.alberni.net/coasthi/*; ⑥), not cheap, but probably the town's best bet. *The Best Western Barclay*, 4277 Stamp Ave (☎724-7171 or 1-800/563-6590, *www.bestwesternbarclay.com*; ⑤), with outdoor pool and the smaller *Somass Motel & RV*, 5279 River Rd (☎724-3236 or 1-800/927-2217, *www.somass-motel.bc.ca*; ③), are also both reliable choices. Cheaper, and 14km west of town on the lakefront off Hwy 4 at 10695 Lakeshore Rd, is the *Westbay Hotel on Sproat Lake* (☎723-2811 or 1-800/358-2811, *www3.bc.sympatico.ca/westbay*; ③). The infocentre has a list of the constantly changing **B&B** outlets: an excellent first choice is the *Edelweiss B&B*, 2610-12th Ave (☎723-5940; ④), which is not particularly central, but does have very welcoming hosts. For **camping**, best bets are on Sproat Lake (see above), or you can try the small, reasonably central and wooded *Dry Creek Public Campground*, 6230 Beaver Creek Rd at 4th Avenue and Napier Street (☎723-6011; $8–19; May–Sept): ask at the infocentre for directions as it's hard to find. Further afield is the bigger 250-site *China Creek Marina and Campground*, Bamfield Road (☎723-2657; $12–25), 15km south of the town on Alberni Inlet, which has a wooded, waterside location and sandy, log-strewn beach. Camping at Sproat Lake (see above) is excellent, but busy in the summer.

Eating possibilities are numerous. For coffee down by the dock before jumping aboard the MV *Lady Rose*, try the *Blue Door Café*. For lunch, make for the *Swale's Rock*, 5328 Argyle St (☎723-0777), and for **seafood** check out the waterfront *Clockworks*, Harbour Quay (☎723-2333). The *Canal*, 5093 Johnson St, serves good Greek food, and for cheap lunches there's the *Paradise Café*, 4505 Gertrude St, and several deli-bakeries.

The MV Lady Rose

The thing you'll probably most want to do in Port Alberni is to leave it, preferably on the **MV Lady Rose**, a small, fifty-year-old Scottish-built freighter that plies between Kildonan, Bamfield, Ucluelet and the Broken Group Islands (see p.776). Primarily a conduit for freight and mail, it also takes up to a hundred passengers, many of whom use it as a drop-off for canoe trips or the West Coast Trail at Bamfield. You could easily ride it simply for the exceptional scenery – huge cliffs and tree-covered mountains – and for the abundant wildlife (sea lions, whales, eagles, depending on the time of year). Passengers started as something of a sideline for the company that runs the boat, but such has been the boat's popularity that another boat has been added to the "fleet" – the 200-passenger MV *Frances Barkley* – and reservations for trips are now virtually essential. Remember to take a sweater and jacket and wear sensible shoes, for these are still primarily working boats, and creature comforts are few.

The basic year-round **schedule** is as follows: the boat leaves at 8am from the Argyle Pier, 5425 Argyle St at the Alberni Harbour Quay (year-round Tues, Thurs & Sat). It arrives in **Bamfield** ($20 one-way, $40 return) via Kildonan ($12/$24), at 12.30pm and starts its return journey an hour later, reaching Port Alberni again at 5.30pm. From October to May the boat stops on request in advance at the Broken Group Islands ($20/$40). From July 1 to Labour Day only (early Sept) there are additional sailing on this route (same times) on Fridays and Sundays.

From June to late September, there are additional sailings on Monday, Wednesday and Friday to **Ucluelet** and the Broken Group Islands, departing 8am and arriving at Ucluelet at 1pm via the islands, where the boat docks at 11am at Sechart, site of the new *Sechart Whaling Station Lodge* (☎723-8313; ③), the only place to stay if you're not wilderness camping on the archipelago. The return journey starts from Ucluelet at 2pm, calling at Sechart again (3.30pm) before arriving back at Port Alberni (7pm).

Contact Lady Rose Marine Services for information and reservations (☎723-8313 or 1-800/663-7192, *www.ladyrosemarine.com*; April–Sept only). They also offer canoe and kayak rentals and transportation of the same to the Broken Group Islands (canoe and single-kayak rental $30, double kayak $40 daily including lifejackets, paddles, pumps and spray skirts). Note that smaller boats running more irregular services to the same destinations can occasionally be picked up from Tofino and Ucluelet.

Pacific Rim National Park

The **Pacific Rim National Park**, the single best reason to visit Vancouver Island, is a stunning amalgam of mountains, coastal rainforest, wild beaches and unkempt marine landscapes that stretches intermittently for 130km between the towns of Tofino in the north and Port Renfrew to the south. It divides into three distinct areas: **Long Beach**, which is the most popular; the **Broken Group Islands**, hundreds of islets only really accessible to sailors and canoeists; and the **West Coast Trail**, a tough but increasingly popular long-distance footpath. The whole area has also become a magnet for surfing and **whale-watching** enthusiasts, and dozens of small companies run charters out from the main centres to view the migrating mammals. By taking the MV *Lady Rose* from Port Alberni (see above) to Bamfield or Ucluelet or back, and combining this with shuttle buses or Laidlaw buses from Victoria, Port Alberni and Nanaimo, a wonderfully varied combination of itineraries is possible around the region.

Lying at the north end of Long Beach, **Tofino**, once essentially a fishing village, is now changing in the face of tourism, but with its natural charm, scenic position and plentiful accommodation, the town still makes the best base for general exploration. **Ucluelet** to the south is comparatively less attractive, but almost equally geared to providing tours and accommodating the park's 800,000 or so annual visitors. **Bamfield**, a tiny and picturesque community with a limited amount of in-demand accommodation, lies still further south and is known mainly as the northern trailhead of the West Coast Trail and a fishing, marine research and whale-watching centre. Unless you fly in, you enter the park on Hwy 4 from Port Alberni, which means the first part you'll see is **Long Beach** (Hwy 4 follows its length en route for Tofino), so if you're dashing in by car for a day-trip, cut straight to the section dealing with this area on p.772. Long Beach, rather than Tofino, is also the site of the park's main **information centre** and the nearby Wickaninnish Centre, an interpretive centre. Remember that a **park fee** – $8 per vehicle per day – is payable at the park entrance.

Weather in the park is an important consideration, because it has a well-deserved reputation for being appallingly wet, cold and windy – and that's the good days. An average of 300cm of rain falls annually, and in some places it buckets down almost 700cm, well over ten times what falls on Victoria. So don't count on doing much swimming or sunbathing (though **surfing**'s a possibility): think more in terms of spending your time admiring crashing Pacific breakers, hiking the backcountry and maybe doing a spot of beachcombing. Better still, time your visit to coincide with the worst of the weather off-season – **storm-watching** is an increasingly popular park pastime.

Tofino

TOFINO, most travellers' target base in the park, is showing the adverse effects of its ever-increasing tourist influx, but locals are keeping development to a minimum, clearly realizing they have a vested interest in preserving the salty, waterfront charm that brings people here in the first place. Crowning a narrow spit, the village is bounded on three sides by tree-covered islands and water, gracing it with magnificent views and plenty of what the tourist literature refers to as "aquaculture". As a service centre it fulfils most functions, offering food, accommodation and a wide variety of boat and seaplane tours, most of which have a **whale-watching** or fishing angle or provide a means to get out to **islands and hot springs** close by (see opposite). Sleepy in off-season, the place erupts into a commercial frenzy during the summer (hippies, surfer types and easy-going family groups being the most visible visitors), though there's little to do in town other than walk its few streets, enjoy the views and soak up the casual atmosphere.

You might drop into the small **Whale Centre** at 411 Campbell St (March–Oct daily 9am–8pm; free; ☎725-2132), one of many places to book whale-watching tours, but also home to exhibits and artefacts devoted to local seafaring and trading history, whales and aboriginal peoples' culture. Another notable place around town is the **Eagle Aerie Gallery**, 350 Campbell St (☎725-3235), a gallery belonging to noted Tsimshian artist Roy Vickers and housed in a traditional long-house-style building with a beautiful cedar interior. Two fine beaches also lie within walking distance to the southeast of the town: **Mackenzie Beach** and **Chesterman's Beach**, the former one of the warmer spots locally, the latter home to a fair number of out-of-town accommodation possibilities (see p.770). Beyond Chesterman lies Frank Island, a tempting proposition at low tide, but sadly private property. The quietest beach around these parts, though, is **Templar**, a miniature strip of sand: ask at the infocentre for directions.

Tofino's easily reached by Laidlaw **bus** (☎385-4411 or 1-800/318-0818) from Port Alberni (2 daily; 3hr) and Nanaimo (1 daily; 4hr 30min), with a single early-morning connection from Victoria, changing at Nanaimo (6hr 30min; $47.50 one-way). The bus depot is on 1st Street near the junction with Neil Street. For **flights**, the excellent North Vancouver Air (☎604/278-1608 or 1-800/228-6608) operates to here from Vancouver (1hr flight; $175 one-way) and Victoria (45min; $225 one-way). Baxter Aviation (☎250/754-1066, 604/683-6525 in Vancouver or 1-800/661-5599) also run connecting flights to Tofino and Ucluelet (see p.775) from Vancouver harbour, Victoria, Seattle and many other smaller centres. The **infocentre** at 380 Campbell St (March–Sept daily 9am–8pm; ☎725-3414, *tofino@island.net*) can give you the exhaustive lowdown on all the logistics of boat and plane tours.

Trips from Tofino

Once they've wandered Tofino's streets, most people head south to explore Long Beach, or put themselves at the mercy of the boat and plane operators. Their playground is the stretch of ocean and landscapes around Tofino known as **Clayoquot Sound**. The name has gained tremendous resonance over the last few years, largely because it has been the focus for some of the most bitterly fought battles against loggers by environmentalists and aboriginal campaigners. It stretches for some 65km from Kennedy Lake to the south of Tofino to the Hesquiat Peninsula 40km to the north, embracing three major islands – Meares, Vargas and Flores – and numerous smaller islets and coastal inlets. More importantly, it is the largest surviving area of low-altitude temperate **rainforest** in North America. Quite incredibly the BC government gave permission to logging companies in 1993 to fell two-thirds of this irreplaceable and age-old forest. The result was the largest outbreak of **civil disobedience** in Canadian history, resulting in eight hundred arrests, as vast numbers congregated at a peace camp in the area and made daily attempts to stop the logging trucks. The stand-off resulted in partial victory, with the designation of new protected areas and limited recognition of the Nuu-chah-nulth tribes moral and literal rights to the land. The region remains in a precarious position, however, and if it's happened once you can be pretty sure that, where forestry interests are concerned, it'll happen again.

There are five main destinations in this region for boat and float-plane trips. The nearest is **Meares Island**, easily visible to the east of Tofino and just fifteen minutes away by boat. A beautiful island swathed in lush temperate rainforest, this was one of the area's earmarked for the lumberjack's chainsaw, despite its designation as a Nuu-chah-nulth tribal park in 1985. At present its ancient cedars and hemlock are safe, and visible on the Meares Island Big Cedar Trail (3km), which meanders among some of the biggest trees you'll ever see, many of them more than a thousand years old and up to 6m across – big enough to put a tunnel through. **Vargas Island**, the next nearest target, lies just 5km from Tofino to the north, and is visited for its beauty, beaches, kayaking and swimming possibilities. **Flores Island**, 20km to the northwest, is accessed by boat or plane and, like Vargas Island, is partly protected by partial provincial park status. At the aboriginal peoples' community of Ahousat you can pick up the Ahousaht Wild Side Heritage Trail, which runs for 16km through idyllic beach and forest scenery to the Mount Flores viewpoint (886m). This is also a chance to encounter aboriginal culture and people at first hand, with **tours** accompanied by local guides available: see the Tofino infocentre or call ☎725-3309 for details and information on trail conditions.

Perhaps the best, and certainly one of the most popular trips from Tofino, is the 37-kilometre boat or plane ride to **Hot Springs Cove**, site of one of only a handful of hot springs on Vancouver Island (1hr by boat, 15min by float plane). A thirty-minute trek from the landing stage brings you to the springs, which emerge at a piping 43°C and run, as a creek, to the sea via a small waterfall and four pools, becoming progressively cooler. Be prepared for something of a crowd in summer when swimming costumes can be optional. An expensive hotel, the *Hot Springs Lodge* – a way to beat other punters by getting in an early-morning or late-night dip – has opened on the cove near the landing stage (see "Accommodation" overleaf). Finally, a forty-kilometre trip north takes you to **Hesquiat Peninsula**, where you land at or near Refuge Cove, site of a Hesquiat aboriginal village. Locals offer tours here and some lodgings: ask for the latest details at the Tofino infocentre. The infocentre is also the place to pick up information on **tours**: otherwise, contact Seaside Adventures, 300 Main St (☎725-2292 or 1-888/332-4252), Chinook Charters, 450 Campbell St (☎725-3431 or 1-800/665-3646), or

> The telephone code for Victoria and Vancouver Island is ☎250.

the whale-watching companies listed under "Activities" on p.772, most of whom also offer boat tours to the above destinations.

Accommodation

The infocentre may be able to get you into one of the village's ever-expanding roster of **hotels**, **motels** and **B&B**, should you be unwise enough to turn up in Tofino without reservations in high summer. There are two main concentrations of accommodation options: in Tofino itself or a couple of kilometres out of town to the east en route for Long Beach on or near Lynn Road, which overlooks Chesterman Beach. Bed and breakfast options, in particular, tend to be out of town near Chesterman Beach. Note that out of town but across the water (access by water taxi) there's also the desirable but expensive self-contained units at the *Hot Springs Lodge* (☎724-8570; ⑥), the only accommodation at Hot Springs Cove (see overleaf), but book early.

Otherwise you can try one of many **campsites** or the **private hostels** that now seem to spring up overnight here and disappear just as quickly, though local reports suggest some of these places can be pretty unsalubrious, home to a sprinkling of the untrustworthy sort of beach-bum year-round drifters that give travellers a bad name. Current good hostels include the *Tofino Backpackers B&B*, 241 Campbell St (☎725-2288; $10 in winter, $15 in summer), and *Vargas Island Inn & Hostel* (☎725-3309; $30 per person including boat fare), the latter in a good position out on an island north of the town (see overleaf). Best of all is the recent Hostelling International-affiliated *Whalers on the Point Guesthouse*, near the west end of Main Street at 81 West St (☎725-3443, *www.tofinohostel.com*; ①): beds are $22 per person, with a choice of shared or private rooms. Facilities include kitchen, games room, sauna, bike rental and storage, surf and wet-suit lockers, and a shuttle service to Long Beach.

HOTELS AND MOTELS

Cable Cove Inn, 201 Main St (☎725-4236 or 1-800/663-6449, *www.cablecoveinn.com*). Stay in high style in one of six smart rooms at the westernmost edge of town that come complete with jacuzzis, fireplaces and four-poster beds. ⑦.

Dolphin Motel, 1190 Pacific Rim Hwy (☎725-3377, fax 725-3374). Rooms with coffee-maker and fridge or self-catering units 3km south of town; 5min walk to Chesterman Beach. ③.

Duffin Cove and Resort, 215 Campbell St (☎725-3448 or 1-800/222-3588, *www.duffin-cove-resort.com*). Thirteen nice cabins and suites (for one to eight people) with kitchens and seaview balconies just south of the *Cable Cove Inn* at the western edge of town overlooking the Clayoquot Sound. ③.

Maquinna Lodge, 120 1st St (☎725-3261 or 1-800/665-3199, fax 725-3433). Central town location at the corner of Main and 1st St, containing renovated rooms, some overlooking Tofino Harbour and Meares Island. ⑤.

Middle Beach Lodge, 400 Mackenzie Beach (☎725-2900, fax 725-2901, *www.middlebeach.com*). Extremely nice, secluded place south of town and west of Chesterman Beach with big stone fireplace, deep old chairs and the gentle splash of waves on tiny Templar Beach to lull you to sleep. ⑤.

Ocean Village Beach Resort, 555 Hellesen Drive (☎725-3755, *www.travel.bc.ca/o/oceanvillage*). A resort just north of Long Beach, 2km from town on the main road, with good accommodation, ocean views, kitchen units and indoor pool. ⑥.

Schooner Motel, 311 Campbell St (☎725-3478, fax 725-3499). Overlooking Tofino Inlet and Meares Island in the town centre, this motel has some rooms complete with kitchen. ⑥.

Tofino Motel, 542 Campbell St (☎725-2055, fax 725-2455, *www.alberni.net/tofino-motel*). A motel on the eastern edge of town including rooms with balconies offering views of the sea and neighbouring islands. ⑤.

Tofino Swell Lodge, 341 Olsen Rd (☎725-3274). On the eastern edge of town near Crab Dock, this excellent lodge on the waterfront looking out to Meares Island has kitchen or plain sleeping units. ④.

Wickaninnish Inn, Osprey Lane at Chesterman Beach (☎725-3100 or 1-800/333-4604, fax 725-3110, *www.wickinn.com*). If you're feeling like a splurge, shell out for this superb $8.5-million 45-room inn, situated on a rocky promontory at the western end of Chesterman Beach. All rooms are large and have ocean views, fireplaces and baths big enough for two. As well as the obvious local attractions, storm-watching here is a growing wintertime activity. ⑨.

BED AND BREAKFASTS

B&B by the Beach, 1277 Lynn Rd (☎725-2441). Away from the centre of Tofino on Chesterman Beach at its northern end. Rooms have private bathrooms; continental breakfast. ⑤.

Brimar, 1375 Thornberg Crescent (☎725-3410 or 1-800/714-9373). At the south end of Chesterman Beach, off Lynn Rd, these three rooms have good Pacific Ocean views and come with a full breakfast. ⑤.

Crab Dock Guest House, 310 Olsen Rd (☎725-2911, *www.crabdock.com*). Situated a little east of the town at Crab Dock, these three recently built rooms all have private bathroom. A full breakfast is offered but you can also use the guest kitchen, as well as the living room. ⑤.

Gull Cottage, 1254 Lynn Rd (☎725-3177, fax 725-2080, *gullcott@island.net*). A few minutes' walk to the beach, at the west end of Lynn Rd, this Victorian-era home has three rooms (private bathrooms) and a hot tub in the woods. ⑤.

Paddler's Inn, 320 Main St (☎725-4222). A recommended spot on the waterfront right in the middle of town; nonsmoking. ③.

Penny's Place, 565 Campbell St (☎725-3457). A choice of rooms on the east edge of the small downtown with and without private bathrooms offering a full breakfast but nonsmoking. ④/⑤.

The Tide's Inn B&B, 160 Arnet Rd (☎725-3765, fax 725-3325, *tidesinn@island.net*). An easy walk south of town (walk down 1st Ave and turn right) on the waterfront with good views of Clayoquot Sound. ④.

Village Gallery B&B, 321 Main St (☎725-4229, fax 725-3473). Quiet upper room and living room in a heritage building in the centre of town with good ocean view and full breakfast. ④.

West Beach Manor, 1314 Lynn Rd (☎725-2779). Self-contained suites close to Chesterman Beach with kitchens and separate bedrooms with space for up to four people. Minimum two-night stay in high season. ⑥.

Wilp Gybuu (*Wolf House*), 311 Leighton Way (☎725-2330, *wilpgybu@island.net*). Three rooms in a walkable location south of town close to *The Tide's Inn*. Sea views, good breakfast and private en-suite bathroom. ④.

CAMPSITES

Bella Pacifica Campground, Pacific Rim Hwy (☎725-3400, fax 725-2400, *www.bellapacifica.com*). Sites with hot showers, flush toilets and laundry 2km south of town, with wilderness and oceanfront sites, private nature trails to Templar Beach and walk-on access to Mackenzie Beach. Reservations recommended. March–Oct. $24–33.

Crystal Cove Beach Resort, Mackenzie Beach (☎725-4213, fax 725-4219). Sites with flush toilets, laundry and showers and some cabins; 3km south of town in a pretty secluded cove and also 1km from Mackenzie Beach with one- and two-bedroom smart log cabins with kitchens and ocean views. Reservations recommended. $30–50; cabins ⑥.

Mackenzie Beach Resort, 1101 Pacific Rim Hwy (☎725-3439, *www.tofino.bc.com/macbeach*). Located on a fine sandy beach 2km south of Tofino and 10min walk from Long Beach; indoor pool, jacuzzi, hot showers and kayak rentals. Some walk-in beachfront tent sites. $15–30.

Eating and drinking

For **food**, just about everyone in town clusters around the heaving tables of the *Common Loaf Bake Shop* behind the bank at 180 1st St (☎725-3915), deservedly the most popular choice for coffee and snacks. In the evening the home-made dough is turned into pizzas instead of bread and rolls. In a similar vein is the *Alley Way Café*, also behind the bank at Campbell and 1st sts, a friendly locals type of place with newspapers to read and cheap, wholesome food where everything down to the mayonnaise is home-made. Coming into town on the main highway (which becomes Campbell St), the *Café Pamplona* in the Tofino Botanical Gardens is also a good spot for coffee and snacks. The *Crab Bar*, 601 Campbell St, near the corner of Gibson Street (☎725-3733) is some-thing of a local institution, selling little more than crab, seafood, beer, bread and some imaginative salads. One of the best views in town is available at the *Sea Shanty*, 300 Main St (☎725-2902), a restaurant which offers **outdoor dining** overlooking the har-bour and the chance of some tremendous sunsets on fine evenings. Best place for a **beer** and **dancing** is the pub downstairs at the *Maquinna Lodge*, 120 1st St, the place to be on Friday and Saturday nights. For a real treat, head out of town to *The Pointe Restaurant* at the *Wickaninnish Inn* (☎725-3100; see hotel listings overleaf), which for most people's money is the area's best upmarket restaurant, on account of both its food and its views.

Activities

Ucluelet to the south may claim to be "whale-watching capital of the world", but **whales** – the main reason a lot of people are here – are just as easily seen from Tofino. As in Victoria, you have plenty of operators, most costing about the same and offering simi-lar **excursions**: all you have to do is decide what sort of boat you want to go out on – zodiacs (inflatables), which are bouncier, more thrilling and potentially wetter, or rigid-hull cruisers (covered or uncovered), which are more sedate. Remember that if you take tours to Meares Islands, Hot Springs Cove and elsewhere, especially in spring or autumn (best times to see whales), you stand a good chance of seeing whales en route anyway – some operators try to combine whale-watching and excursions. Operators to try include: Cypre Prince Tours midway down the main street at 430 Campbell St (☎725-2202 or 1-800/787-2202); Chinook Charters, 450 Campbell St (☎725-3431 or 1-800/665-3646), who offer trips (2hr 30min) on rigid or zodiac boats; and Jamie's Whaling Station, 606 Campbell St (☎725-3919 or 1-800/667-9913), who also offer a choice of zodiac boats or the twenty-metre *Lady Selkirk*, which comes with heated cabin, no small consideration on cold days, of which Tofino has a few. See "Whales" box, opposite, for more information.

Many of these companies double up as **fishing** charters, though for more specialist operators contact Bruce's Smiley Seas Charters, based at the Methods Marina (May–Sept; ☎725-2557), who're quite happy to have novices aboard; or the Weigh West Marine Resort (☎725-3238 or 1-800/665-8922), who have an inexpensive restaurant as well as lodgings just above the marina at 634 Campbell St. Still on the water, Tofino is quickly becoming the **surfing** capital of Canada, thanks to some enormous Pacific waves, though floating driftwood and big lumps of lumber caught up in the waves can be a hazard. For information, board rental and all other equipment, contact Live to Surf east of the town centre at 1180 Tofino Hwy (☎725-4464). If you want to go out in a **kayak** (no experience required) contact Tofino Sea Kayaking, 320 Main St (☎725-4222 or 1-800/863-4664), who offer day-trips or longer **tours** with lodge accommodation or wilderness camping. Nine holes of **golf** are available at the local course near the airport (☎725-3332), while **guided hikes** and easy nature rambles in the forest and along the seashore are offered by several companies (contact infocentre for details).

Long Beach

The most accessible of the park's components, **LONG BEACH** is just what it says: a long tract of wild, windswept sand and rocky points stretching for about 30km from Tofino to Ucluelet. Around 19km can be hiked unbroken from Schooner Bay in the west to Half Moon Bay in the east. The snow-covered peaks of the Mackenzie Range

WHALES

The Pacific Rim National Park is amongst the world's best areas for **whale-watching**, thanks to its location on the main migration routes, food-rich waters and numerous sheltered bays. People come from all over the world for the spectacle, and it's easy to find a boat going out from Tofino, Ucluelet or Bamfield, most charging around $60–80 a head for the trip depending on duration (usually 2–3hr). Regulations prohibit approaching within 100m of an animal but, though few locals will admit it, there's no doubt that the recent huge upsurge in boat tours has begun to disrupt the **migrations**. The whales' 8000-kilometre journey – the longest known migration of any mammal – takes them from their breeding and calving lagoons in Baja, Mexico, to summer feeding grounds in the Bering and Chukchi seas off Siberia. The northbound migration takes from February to May, with the peak period of passage between March and April. A few dozen animals occasionally abort their trip and stop off the Canadian coast for summer feeding (notably at Maquinna Marine Park, 20min by boat from Tofino). The return journey starts in August, hitting Tofino and Ucluelet in late September and early October. **Mating** takes place in Mexico during December, after which the males turn immediately northwards, to be followed by females and their young in February.

Although killer whales (orcas) are occasionally seen, the most commonly spotted type are **grey whales**, of which some 19,000 are thought to make the journey annually. Averaging 14m in length and weighing 35 to 50 tonnes, they're distinguished by the absence of a dorsal fin, a ridge of lumps on the back, and a mottled blue-grey colour. Females have only one offspring, following a gestation period of thirteen months, and, like the males, cruise at only two to four knots – perfect for viewing and, sadly, for capture.

Even if you don't take a boat trip, you stand a faint chance of seeing whales from the coast as they dive, when you can locate their tails, or during fluking, when the animals surface and "blow" three or four times before making another five-minute dive. There are telescopes at various points along Long Beach, the best known viewpoints being Schooner Cove, Radar Hill, Quistis Point and Combers Beach near Sea Lion Rocks.

rise up over 1200m as a scenic backdrop, and behind the beach grows a thick, lush canopy of coastal rainforest. The white-packed sand itself is the sort of primal seascape that is all but extinct in much of the world, scattered with beautiful, sea-sculpted driftwood, smashed by surf, broken by crags, and dotted with islets and rock pools oozing with marine life. It's worth realizing that Long Beach, while a distinct beach in itself, also rather loosely refers to several other beaches to either side, the relative merits of which are outlined below. If you haven't done so already, driving or biking Hwy 4 along the beach area is the best time to call in at the Pacific Rim National Park **Information Centre** (May to mid-Oct daily 9.30am–5pm; ☎762-4212), located right off Hwy 4 3km northwest of the Ucluelet–Tofino–Port Alberni road junction.

Scenery aside, Long Beach is noted for its **wildlife**, the BC coastline reputedly having more marine species than any other temperate area in the world. As well as the smaller stuff in tidal pools – starfish, anemones, snails, sponges and suchlike – there are large mammals like whales and sea lions, as well as thousands of migrating birds (especially in Oct & Nov), notably pintails, mallards, black brants and Canada geese. Better weather brings out lots of beachcombers (Japanese glass fishing floats are highly coveted), clam diggers, anglers, surfers, canoeists, windsurfers and divers, though the water is usually too cold to venture in without a wet suit, and rip currents and rogue lumps of driftwood crashed around by the waves can make swimming dangerous. Surf guards patrol the Long Beach day-use area in July and August. And finally, try to resist the temptation to pick up shells as souvenirs – it's against park regulations.

LONG BEACH WALKS

With an eye on the weather and tide, you can walk more or less anywhere on and around Long Beach. Various trails and roads drop to the beach from the main Hwy 4 road to Tofino. At the same time there are nine official trails, most of them short and very easy, so you could tackle a few in the course of a leisurely drive or cycle along the road. All the paths are clearly marked from Hwy 4, but it's still worth picking up a *Hiker's Guide* from the infocentre. From east to west you can choose from the following. The linked trails **1** and **2**, the **Willowbrae Trail** (2.8km round trip), are accessed by turning left at the main Hwy 4 junction and driving or biking 2km towards Ucluelet. A level wooded trail then leads from the trailhead towards the beach, following the steps of early pioneers who used this route before the building of roads between Tofino and Ucluelet. Just before the sea it divides, dropping steeply via steps and ramps, to either the tiny Half Moon Bay or the larger, neighbouring Florencia Bay to the north.

All other walks are accessed off Hwy 4 to Tofino, turning right (north) at the main Hwy 4 junction. The gentle **3 Gold Mine Trail** (3km round trip), signed left off the road, leads along Lost Shoe Creek, a former gold-mining area (look out for debris), to Florencia Beach. For walks **4**, **5** and **6**, take the turn left off the highway for the Wickaninnish Centre. The **4 South Beach Trail** (1.5km round trip) leaves from behind the centre, leading above forest-fringed shores and coves before climbing to the headlands for a view of the coast and a chance to climb down to South Beach, famous for its big rock-crashing breakers and the sound of the water ripping noisily through the beach pebbles. The **5 Wickaninnish Trail** (5km) follows the South Beach Trail for a while and then at the top of the first hill is signed left, passing through rainforest – once again this is the route of the old pioneer trail – before ending at the parking area above Florencia Beach to the east. The **6 Shorepine Bog Trail** (800m) is a wheelchair-accessible boardwalk trail (accessed on the left on the access road to the centre) that wends through the fascinating stunted bog vegetation; trees which are just a metre or so tall here can be hundreds of years old.

Moving further west towards Tofino along Hwy 4, the **7 Rain Forest Trails** are two small loops (1km each round trip), one on each side of the road, that follow a boardwalk through virgin temperate rainforest: each has interpretive boards detailing forest life cycle and forest "inhabitants" respectively. Further down the road on the right at the Combers Beach parking area, a road gives access to the gentle **8 Spruce Fringe Trail** (1.5km loop). This graphically illustrates the effects of the elements on spruce forest, following a log-strewn beach fringe-edged with bent and bowed trees before entering more robust forest further from the effects of wind and salt spray. It also crosses willow and crab-apple swamp to a glacial terrace, the site of a former shoreline, past the airport turn-off. The final walk, the **9 Schooner Beach Trail** (1km one-way), leads left off the road through superb tranches of rainforest to an extremely scenic beach at Schooner Cove. This might be the end of the official trails, but don't fail to climb to the viewpoint on **Radar Hill** off to the right as you get closer to Tofino.

The beaches

As this is a national park, some of Long Beach and its flanking stretches of coastline have been very slightly tamed for human consumption, but in a most discreet and tasteful manner. The best way to get a taste of the area is to walk the beaches or forested shorelines themselves – there are plenty of hidden coves – or to follow any of nine very easy and well-maintained **hiking trails** (see box, above). If you're driving or biking along Hwy 4, which backs the beaches all the way, there are distinct areas to look out for. Moving west, the first of these is the five-kilometre **Florencia Beach** (1.5km from the Hwy: access by trails 1, 2, 3 and 5; see box), also known as Wreck Beach and formerly the home of hippie beach dwellers in driftwood shacks before the park's formation. This is something of a local favourite, with relatively few people and good rock pools.

Further along Hwy 4 you come to a turn-off (Long Beach Rd) for the **Wickaninnish Centre** (mid-March to mid-Oct daily 10.30am–6pm; ☎726-4701) on a headland at the start of Long Beach, not to be confused with the similarly named well-known hotel and restaurant closer to Tofino (confusingly, the centre also has a restaurant). Wickaninnish was a noted nineteenth-century aboriginal chief, and arbitrator between Europeans and native fur traders. His name left no doubt as to his number-one status, as it means "having no one in front of him in the canoe". The centre is the departure point for several trails (see box, opposite), has telescopes for whale-spotting and a variety of films, displays and exhibits relating to the park and ocean. Around 8km beyond the Long Beach Road turn-off is the entrance to the Greenpoint park **campsite** and further access to Long Beach, while 4km beyond that lies the turn-off on the right to Tofino's small airstrip. Around here the peninsula narrows, with **Grice Bay** coming close to the road on the right (north side), a shallow inlet known in winter for its countless wildfowl. Beyond the airstrip turn-off comes a trail to Schooner Cove (see box, opposite) and 3.5km beyond that a 1.5-kilometre turn-off to Kap'yong, or **Radar Hill** (96m), the panoramic site of a wartime radar station. By now Tofino is getting close, and 4.5km further on (and a couple of kilometres outside the park boundary) you come to **Cox Bay Beach**, **Chesterman Beach** and **Mackenzie Beach**, all accessed from Hwy 4. Cox and Chesterman are known for their breakers; Mackenzie for its relative warmth if you want to chance a dip.

Practicalities

Long Beach's **Pacific Rim National Park Information Centre** is just off Hwy 4, 3km north of the T-junction for Tofino and Ucluelet. It provides a wealth of material on all aspects of the park, and in summer staff offer guided walks and interpretive programmes (mid-March to early Oct daily 9.30am–5pm; ☎726-4212). For year-round information, call the Park Administration Office (☎726-7721). For more Long Beach information, viewing decks with telescopes and lots of well-presented displays, head for the **Wickaninnish Centre**, Long Beach Road (mid-March to early Oct daily 10.30am–6pm; ☎726-4701).

There is one park **campsite**, the *Greenpoint*, set on a lovely bluff overlooking the beach ($13; drive-in; washrooms but no showers; firewood available; $13). However, it's likely to be full every day in July and August, and it's first-come, first-served, so you may have to turn up for several days before getting a spot. There's usually a waiting-list system, however, whereby you're given a number and instructions as to when you should be able to return. The nearest commercial sites and conventional accommodation are in Tofino and Ucluelet.

Ucluelet

UCLUELET (pop. 1733), 8km south of the main Hwy 4 Port Alberni junction, means "People of the Sheltered Bay", from the native word *ucluth* – "wind blowing in from the bay". It was named by the Nuu-chah-nulth, who lived here for centuries before the arrival of whites who came to exploit some of the world's richest fishing grounds immediately offshore. Today the port is still the third largest in BC by volume of fish landed, a trade that gives the town a slightly dispersed appearance and an industrial fringe – mainly lumber and canning concerns – and makes it a less appealing, if nonetheless popular base for anglers, whale-watchers, water-sports enthusiasts and tourists headed for Long Beach to the north. If you want a breath of air in town, the nearest trails are at **Terrace Beach**, just east of the town off Peninsula Road before the lighthouse.

Buses and **boats** call here from Port Alberni and Tofino – a Laidlaw bus makes the road trip twice a day en route to and from Tofino and Port Alberni, with one connection daily from Port Alberni to Nanaimo and Victoria. Boats from Port Alberni usually dock here three days a week (see p.767). There's plenty of accommodation (though less than Tofino), much of it spread on or just off Peninsula Road, the main approach to and through town from Hwy 4 (see below). A car or bike is useful here, as there's relatively little in the small central area, though location isn't vital unless you want to be near the sea. For full details visit the **infocentre** at the main junction of Hwy 4 (daily June to early Sept daily 9am–6pm; ☎726-4641 or 726-7289, *uco@ucluelet.com*).

Practicalities

The most unusual **hotel** in town is the *Canadian Princess Resort* (☎726-7771 or 1-800/663-7090, *www.obmg.com*; ③–⑥; March–Sept) on Peninsula Road just west of the centre, a hotel with on-shore rooms or one- to six-berth cabins in a 1932 west coast steamer moored in the harbour. You can also book upmarket whale-watching and fishing trips here in big, comfortable cabin cruisers and it has a restaurant open to nonresidents. The two key inexpensive central choices are the *Pacific Rim Motel*, 1755 Peninsula Rd (☎726-7728, *dcorlazz@island.net*; ④), a place between the harbour and small centre near the corner of Bay Street, and the *Peninsula Motor Inn*, a short way east across the road at 1648 Peninsula Rd (☎726-7751; ③). Also convenient is the *Island West Fishing Resort* overlooking the boat basin and marina at 160 Hemlock St (☎726-4624, *www.islandwestresort.com*; ④): it has a pub on site for drinks and food and also organizes fishing charters and tours. Moving east away from the centre to prettier outskirts try *Four Cedar Cottages* (☎726-4284; ⑤), 1183 Eber Rd (take Alder St, off Peninsula Rd), which is very close to the seafront pier, or the *Little Beach Resort*, 1187 Peninsula Rd (☎726-4202; ②–④), with quiet self-contained one- and two-bedroom suites with kitchenettes and just a few steps from Little Beach with great views to the south. Right at the end of Peninsula Road up by the lighthouse are two good **B&B** options: *Spring Cove B&B*, 963 Peninsula Rd (☎726-2955; ④), a quiet oceanfront place with two rooms (shared bathroom), and *Ocean's Edge B&B*, 855 Barkley Crescent (☎726-7099, *www.oceansedge.bc.ca*; ③), a three-room place in old-growth forest with views and private entrance and bathroom.

The **public campsite** (☎726-4355; $22–27; March–Oct) overlooks the harbour at 260 Seaplane Base Rd (first right off Peninsula Rd after the *Canadian Princess*) to the west of the centre and has washroom and shower facilities. The central *Island West Fishing Resort* (see above) also has an RV campsite.

Seafood here is as fresh as it comes, and is best sampled at *Smiley's* just a little west from the *Canadian Princess* at 1992 Peninsula Rd (☎726-4213): a no-frills, no-decor diner popular with locals (eat in or take out), and to work off the meal there's five-pin bowling and billiards here as well. For coffee and snacks head for *Blueberries Café* (☎726-7707) on the strip in town at 1627 Peninsula Rd. It also serves breakfast, lunch and dinner, is licensed, and has an outdoor patio with sea views.

Many companies are on hand to offer whale-watching, fishing and sightseeing **tours**. The longest-established outfit in the region is here, Subtidal Adventures, 1950 Peninsula Rd at the corner of Norah Road (☎726-7336). They run all the usual boat trips in zodiacs or a ten-metre former coastguard rescue vessel, and do a nature tour to the Broken Group Islands with a beach stop.

The Broken Group Islands

The only way for the ordinary traveller to approach these hundred or so islands, speckled across Barkley Sound between Ucluelet and Bamfield, is by sea plane, chartered boat or boat tours from Port Alberni or Ucluelet (see p.776 and above); boats dock at Sechart. Immensely wild and beautiful, the islands have the reputation for tremendous

---

NUU-CHAH-NULTH WHALE HUNTS

All the peoples of the Northwest coast are famed for their skilfully constructed canoes, but only the **Nuu-chah-nulth** – whose name translates roughly as "all along the mountains" – used these fragile cedar crafts to pursue whales, an activity that was accompanied by elaborate ritual. Before embarking on a whaling expedition the whalers had to not only be trained in the art of capturing these mighty animals but also had to be purified through a rigorous programme of fasting, sexual abstinence and bathing. Whalers also visited forest shrines made up of a whale image surrounded by human skulls or corpses and carved wooden representations of deceased whalers – the dead were thought to aid the novice in his task and to bring about the beaching of dead whales near the village.

When the whaler was on the chase, his wife would lie motionless in her bed; it was thought that the whale would become equally docile. His crew propelled the canoe in total silence until the moment of the harpooning, whereupon they frantically back-paddled to escape the animal's violent death throes as it attempted to dive, only to be thwarted by a long line of floats made from inflated sea-lion skins. After exhausting itself, the floating whale was finally killed and boated back to the village, where its meat would be eaten and its blubber processed for its highly prized oil.

---

wildlife (seals, sea lions and whales especially), the best **canoeing** in North America, and some of the continent's finest **scuba diving**. You can hire canoes and gear – contact the *Lady Rose* office in Port Alberni or Sea Kayaking at 320 Main St, Tofino (☎725-4222), and then take them on board the *Lady Rose* to be dropped off en route (check current arrangements). You need to know what you're doing, however, as there's plenty of dangerous water and you should pick up the relevant marine chart (*Canadian Hydrographic Service Chart: Broken Group* 3670), available locally. Divers can choose from among fifty shipwrecks claimed by the reefs, rough waters and heavy fogs that beset the aptly named islands.

The *Sechart Whaling Station Lodge* (book by calling ☎723-8313 or 1-800/663-7192; ⑨) is a potentially magical base for exploring and the only place to **stay** if you're not wilderness camping on the archipelago. Access is via the MV *Lady Rose*, which docks nearby (see p.767 for detailed schedule to the islands). Eight rough **campsites** also serve the group, but water is hard to come by; pick up the park leaflet on camping and freshwater locations. A park warden patrols the region from Nettle Island; otherwise the islands are as pristine as the day they rose from the sea.

Bamfield

BAMFIELD (pop. 256) is a quaint spot, half-raised above the ocean on a wooden boardwalk, accessible by unpaved road from Port Alberni 102km to the north, by boat – the MV *Lady Rose* – or gravel road from Lake Cowichan 113km to the east. Shuttle **buses** run along the Port Alberni road route if you're without transport and don't want to take the boat: for details, see the "West Coast Trail", overleaf. The village is best known as the northern starting point of this trail, but its population jumps to well over 2000 in the summer with the arrival of divers, canoeists, kayakers and fishermen, the last attracted by its suitability as a base for salmon fishing in the waters of Alberni Inlet and Barkley Sound. Plenty of services have sprung up to meet visitors' demands, with lots of tours, fishing charters, stores and galleries, but only relatively limited accommodation (see overleaf).

Despite the influx the village retains its charm, with the boardwalk accessing one side of Bamfield Inlet (the open sea, the other), so that the bay below the boardwalk is a constant hum of activity as boats ply across the water. Trails lead down from the boardwalk to a series of nice small beaches. The village is a good place to join in the activities, bird-watch, walk, beachcomb, sit in cafés or simply relax in a quiet corner with a book. For a short stroll, wander to **Brady's Beach** or the Cape Beale Lighthouse some way beyond. And if you just want to tackle the stage to the trailhead of the West Coast Trail and return to Bamfield in a day, you can walk the 11km (round trip) to the **Pachena Lighthouse**, starting from the Ross Bible Camp on the Ohiaht First Nation campsite at Pachena Beach. After that, the route becomes the real thing.

Accommodation

Bamfield has only limited and mainly expensive **accommodation**. If you think you'll need a bed, definitely make reservations, especially at the small *Seabeam Fishing Resort and Campground* overlooking Grappler Inlet, which runs as a campsite and a small hostel-like hotel with eight rooms (☎728-3286; ①, tent and RV sites $15–20; May–Oct) and phone for directions or for a taxi pick-up. The setting is tranquil, and the resort has a small kitchen, common room with open fire and sixteen beds arranged as one-, two- or three-bed dorms. Price is $20 per person. Otherwise try the *Bamfield Inn*, Customs House Lane, a **lodge** built in 1923 overlooking Bamfield Harbour, Barkley Sound and the islands (☎728-3354; ⑤; Feb–Oct). The modest *McKay Bay Lodge* (☎728-3323; ④; May–Oct) also overlooks the harbour and is good for families and fishing enthusiasts. The biggest place locally is the *Bamfield Trails Motel* overlooking Bamfield Inlet at Frigate Road (☎728-3231 or 728-3215; ④). Another option is the excellent *Woods End Landing Cottages*, 168 Wild Duck Rd, which has six secluded and high-quality self-contained log cottages on a two-acre waterfront site with great opportunities for outdoor activities, bird-watching, scuba diving and kayaking (☎728-3383; ⑦). Similar but more expensive are the central and waterfront *Mills Landing Cottages*, 295 Boardwalk (☎728-2300; ⑦) with one- and two-bed cottages. Less expensive is the five-room *Imperial Eagle Lodge*, 168 Wild Duck Rd (728-3430, *www.imperialeaglelodge.com*; ⑤), which has a spectacular garden setting and fine harbour views plus hiking, fishing and other outdoor activities; breakfast is included in the room price. More **B&B** options are opening each year but try the two-room *Sherry's*, Regent Street (☎728-2323; ③), overlooking Bamfield Harbour, which offers a free pick-up by boat from the dock: showers are shared, but an outdoor hot tub and free canoe use are available. If you're **camping**, try the Ohiaht First Nation campsite at Pachena Beach.

The West Coast Trail

One of North America's classic walks, the **West Coast Trail** starts 5km south of Bamfield (see overleaf) and traverses exceptional coastal scenery for 77km to Port Renfrew. It's no stroll, and though becoming very popular – quotas operate to restrict numbers – it still requires experience of longer walks, proper equipment and a fair degree of fitness. Many people, however, do the first easy stage as a day-trip from Bamfield. Reckon on five to eight days for the full trip; carry all your own food, camp where you can, and be prepared for rain, treacherous stretches, thick soaking forest, and almost utter isolation.

As originally conceived, the trail had nothing to do with promoting the great outdoors. Mariners long ago dubbed this area of coastline the "graveyard of the Pacific", and when the SS *Valencia* went down with all hands here in 1906 the government was persuaded that constructing a trail would at least give stranded sailors a chance to walk to safety along the coast (trying to penetrate the interior's rainforest was out of the question). The path followed a basic telegraph route that linked Victoria with outlying towns and lighthouses, and was kept open by linesmen and lighthouse keepers until the 1960s, when it fell into disrepair. Early backpackers reblazed the old trail; many thousands now make the trip annually, and the numbers, so far as quotas allow, are rising (see below). The trail passes through the land of the Pacheenaht First Nation near Port Renfrew, passing through Ditidaht First Nation country before ending at Bamfield in the traditional territory of the Ohiaht First Nation. Wardens from each of these tribes work in association with Parks Canada to oversee the trail's management and the care of traditional native villages and fishing areas.

Weather is a key factor in planning any trip; the trail is really only passable between June and September (July is the driest month), which is also the only period when it's patrolled by wardens and the only time locals are on hand to ferry you (for a fee) across some of the wider rivers en route. However, you should be prepared for dreadful weather and poor trail conditions at all times. Take cash with you to pay for ferries and nominal fees for camping on native land.

Practicalities

Pre-planning is essential if you wish to walk the trail, as Parks Canada have introduced a **quota system** and reservation-registration procedure to protect the environment. Numbers are limited to around 8000 a year while the path is open (mid-April to end Sept). A total of 52 people are allowed onto the trail each day: 26 starting at Port Renfrew, 26 at Bamfield. **Reservations** can made from March of the year you wish to walk, and the phones start ringing on the first of the month, so move fast. To make bookings, call ☎1-800/663-6000 (Mon–Fri 7am–9pm). Be ready to nominate the location from which you wish to start, the date of departure and the number in your party. July and August are clearly the most popular months. It **costs** $25 to make a reservation (payment by Visa or MasterCard). This is nonrefundable, though you may change your date of departure if spaces are available on another day. Another $75 per person is payable as a user fee, paid in person at the beginning of the trail. Allow another $25 to pay for ferry crossings along the route. You must then register in person at the park centre at Bamfield or Port Renfrew between 9am and 12.30pm on the day you have booked to start your walk. (You may want to arrive the night before – if so, be sure to book accommodation in Bamfield if you're starting there: see below.) If you miss this deadline your place is forfeited and will be given to someone on the **waiting list**.

Of the 52 places available each day, twelve (six at each departure point) are available on a first-come, first-served basis. Unless you're very lucky this still doesn't mean you can just turn up and expect to start walking. You must first register in person at either the Port Renfrew or Bamfield centre. Here you'll be given a waiting-list number and told when to come back, which could be anything between two and ten days.

Further **information** regarding the trail, path conditions and preplanning can be obtained from the Parks Canada offices in Port Renfrew (☎647-5434) and Ucluelet (☎726-7211), or from the infocentres in Tofino, Ucluelet, Long Beach or Port Alberni. An increasing amount of literature and **route guides** are appearing on the trail every year, available directly or by mail order from most BC bookshops (see "Listings" for Vancouver, p.728 and Victoria, p.750). Two of the best are *The West Coast Trail* by Tim Leaden (Douglas and McIntyre, seventh edition; $12.95) and the more irreverent *Blisters and Bliss: A Trekker's Guide to the West Coast Trail* by Foster, Aiteken and Dewey (B&B Publishing Victoria; $10.95). The recommended **trail map** is the 1:50,000 *West Coast Trail, Port Renfrew–Bamfield*, complete with useful hints for walking the trail, available locally or direct from the Ministry of the Environment, 553 Superior St, Victoria (☎387-1441).

Access to and from the trailheads is also an important consideration. Several small shuttle-bus companies have sprung up to run people to the trailheads, mostly from Victoria to Bamfield via Nanaimo, not all of which are likely to survive (consult the Victoria infocentre for latest updates). For the northern trailhead at Bamfield, the most exhilarating and reliable access is via the MV *Lady Rose* or other boats from Port Alberni (see p.767 for full details). Otherwise the West Coast Trail Express, 3954 Bow

Rd, Victoria (May to early Oct; ☎477-8700) runs a daily shuttle bus in each direction between Victoria and Pachena Bay/Bamfield ($50) via Duncan, Nanaimo ($50); to Port Renfrew ($30) and back from Victoria; and between Bamfield and Port Renfrew ($40). Pick-ups are possible from these points, but reservations are essential to secure a seat from any departure point. They also have a daily service to Port Renfrew ($50). Western Bus Lines, 4521 10th Ave, Port Alberni (☎723-3341), also run a service on Monday and Friday along the 100-kilometre gravel road from Port Alberni to the *Tides and Trails Café* in Bamfield; and the Pacheenaht First Nation Service, 4521 10th Ave, Port Alberni (around $35; ☎647-5521), which operates a summer-only bus service along the same route.

North Vancouver Island

It's a moot point where the **north of Vancouver Island** starts, but if you're travelling on Hwy 19 the landscape's sudden lurch into more unspoilt wilderness after Qualicum Beach makes as good a watershed as any. The scenery north of Qualicum Beach is uneventful but restful on the eye, and graced with ever-improving views of the mainland. Along Hwy 19 is the hamlet of Buckley Bay, which consists of a single B&B and the ferry terminal to **Denman** and **Hornby islands** (16 sailings daily; 10min; $4.50 return for foot passengers, $11.25 return for a car).

Few of the towns along Hwy 19 amount to much, and you could bus, drive or hitch the length of Vancouver Island to Port Hardy and take the **Inside Passage** ferry up to Prince Rupert – the obvious and most tantalizing itinerary – without missing a lot. Alternatively, you could follow the main highway only as far as **Courtenay**, and from there catch a ferry across to the mainland. If you have the means, however, try to get into the wild, central interior, much of it contained within **Strathcona Provincial Park**.

Denman and Hornby islands

Denman and **Hornby Islands** are two outposts that have been described, with some justification, as the "undiscovered Gulf Islands". Big-name celebrities have recently bought property here, complementing a population made up of artists, craftspeople and a laid-back (if wary) mishmash of alternative types. Ferries drop you on Denman, with an **infocentre** clearly marked on the road from the terminal (☎335-2293). To get to Hornby you need to head 11km across Denman to another terminal, where a fifteen-minute crossing ($4.50 return for foot passengers, $11.25 return for a car) drops you at Hornby's Shingle Spit dock. Most of what happens on Hornby, however, happens at **Tribune Bay** on the far side of the island, 10km away – try hitching a lift from a car coming off the ferry if you're without transport. There's no public transport on either island, so you'll need a car or bike to explore.

Highlights on Denman, the less retrogressive of the islands, are the beaches of the Sandy Island Marine Park and the trails of Boyle Point Park to the Chrome Island Lighthouse. On Hornby you want to be looking at the **Hellivel Provincial Park** and its trails, the best a six-kilometre (1hr–1hr 30min) loop to Hellivel Bluffs, offering plenty of opportunities to see eagles, herons, spring wild flowers and lots of aquatic wildlife. Whaling Station Bay and Tribune Bay Provincial Park have good beaches (and there's a nudist beach at Little Tribune Bay).

Accommodation and food

Accommodation is in short supply on both islands, and it's virtually essential in summer to have prebooked rooms. On Denman the main options are the *Sea Canary Bed*

& *Breakfast*, 3305 Kirk Rd (☎335-2949; ④), close to the ferry terminal with three **guestrooms**, and the *Hawthorn House Bed and Breakfast*, 3375 Kirk Rd (☎335-0905; ③), a restored 1904 heritage building also with three rooms. There's a small (10-site), rural provincial park **campsite** at Fillongley Provincial Park, close to old-growth forest and pebbly beach 4km across the island from the ferry on the east shore facing the Lambert Channel (summer $15, winter $8). Hornby has more **rooms** and **campsites**: *Sea Breeze Lodge*, Big Tree 3–2, Fowler Road (☎335-2321, *www.seabreezelodge.com*; ⑤), with fifteen waterfront cottages with sea views; *Hornby Island Resort*, Shingle Spit Road (☎335-0136; ③), tents $19), with four waterfront cabins and nine camp sites, tennis court, boat rental, pub, waterfront restaurant and sandy beach; *Days Gone By at Bradsdadsland Campsite*, 1980 Shingle Spit Rd (☎335-0757; tents $20–23; May–Oct), 3.3km from the ferry terminal; *Ford's Cove Marina* at Ford's Cove, 12km from the ferry at Government Wharf (☎335-2169; ③, tents $16–24), with six fully equipped cottages, grocery store and camp and RV sites; and the big *Tribune Bay Campsite*, Shields Road (☎335-2359, *www.tribunebay.com*; $18–24; April–Oct), a treed site close to a sandy beach and with hot showers, restaurant and bike rental.

Eating places on Denman are concentrated near the ferry, the best being the *Denman Island Store and Café*. At the ferry dock on Hornby is *The Thatch*, a tourist-oriented restaurant and deli with great views. Across at Tribune Bay the Co-op (no street address) is the hub of island life, with virtually everything you'll need in the way of food and supplies (☎335-1121). A bike-rental outlet here, the Off-Road Bike Shop, rents bikes in summer.

Courtenay

Back along Hwy 19 beyond Buckley Bay is a short stretch of wild, pebbly beach, and then the Comox Valley, open rural country that's not as captivating as the brochures might lead you to expect. Of three settlements here – Comox, Cumberland and **COURTENAY** – only the last is of real interest for all but the most committed Vancouver Island devotee, and only then as a ferry link to Powell River on the mainland. The terminal is a good twenty-minutes' drive from the town down back roads – hitching is almost impossible, so you have to take a taxi or hold out for the minibus shuttle that leaves the bus depot twice on Tuesday and Friday to connect with sailings. Courtenay is connected to Nanaimo and Victoria by **bus** (4 daily), and is the terminus for **trains** from Victoria (1 daily). If you get stranded in town, there are plenty of **motels** along the strip on the southern approach, close to the black steam engine and **infocentre** at 2040 Cliffe Ave (daily 9am–5pm, longer hours in summer; ☎334-3234). The best **camping** is 20km north of Courtenay at Miracle Beach Provincial Park – a vast, but very popular, tract of sand ($12).

The **Comox Valley** scores higher inland, on the eastern fringes of Strathcona Provincial Park (see p.783) and the new **skiing** areas of Forbidden Plateau and Mount Washington. There's plenty of **hiking** in summer, when the Forbidden Plateau lifts operate at weekends from 11am to 3pm. A great day-hike on Mount Washington is the five-hour walk on well-marked trails from the ski area across Paradise Meadows to Moat Lake or Circlet Lake. For details of tougher walks (Battleship Lake, Lady Lake), ask at the infocentre. Access to the trailheads is by minor road from Courtenay.

Campbell River

Of the hundred or so Canadian towns that claim to be "Salmon Capital of the World", **CAMPBELL RIVER**, 46km north of Courtenay, is probably the one that comes closest to justifying the boast. Fish and fishing dominate the place to a ludicrous degree, and you'll soon be heartily sick of pictures of grinning anglers holding impossibly huge chinook salmon. Massive shoals of these monsters are forced into the three-kilometre channel between the town and the mainland, making the job of catching them little more than a formality. The town grew to accommodate fishermen from the outset, centred on a hotel built in 1904 after word spread of the colossal fish that local Cape Mudge natives were able to pluck from the sea. Today about sixty percent of all visitors come to dangle a line in the water. Others come for the scuba diving, while for the casual visitor the place serves as the main road access to the wilds of Strathcona Provincial Park or an overnight stop en route for the morning departures of the MV *Uchuck III* from Gold River (see p.784).

If you want to **fish**, hundreds of shops and guides are on hand to help out and hire equipment. It'll cost about $20 a day for the full kit, and about $60 for a morning's guidance. Huge numbers of people, however, fish from the 200-metre **Discovery Pier**, Canada's first saltwater fishing pier. **Diving** rentals come more expensive; try Beaver Aquatics near the Quadra ferry dock in Discovery Bay Marina (☎287-7652). If you merely want to know something about salmon before they end up on a plate, drop in on the **Quinsam Salmon Hatchery**, 5km west of town on the road to Gold River (daily 8am–4pm).

Campbell River's well-stocked **infocentre** is at 1235 Shopper's Row (daily 9am–6pm; ☎287-4636). Four Laidlaw **buses** run daily to Victoria, but there's only one, occasionally two, a day north to Port Hardy and towns en route. Airlines big and small also **fly** here, including Air BC, Central Mountain Air and Vancouver Island Air (see Vancouver "Listings" on p.728 for details). The **bus terminal** is on the corner of Cedar and 13th near the Royal Bank (☎287-7151). **Accommodation** is no problem, with numerous motels, Campbell River being a resort first and foremost: try the *Super 8 Motel*, 340 S Island Hwy, on the main road south of town (☎286-6622 or 1-800/800-8000; ④), or the carving-stuffed *Campbell River Lodge and Fishing Resort,* a kilometre north of the town centre at 1760 N Island Hwy (☎287-7446 or 1-800/663-7212, *www .vquest.com/crlodge*; ④). You won't be able to escape the fishing clutter common to all hotels unless you head for a **B&B**. Contact the infocentre for listings, or try *Pier House B&B*, 670 Island Hwy (☎287-2943, *pierhse@island.net*; ④), a three-room 1920s antique-filled heritage home in downtown right by the fishing pier. The place to **camp** locally lies 5km west of town at the *Parkside Campground*, 6301 Gold River Hwy (☎830-1428; $20; May–Oct).

Cheap **places to eat** abound, mainly of the fast-food variety, and in the pricier restaurants there's no prize for spotting the main culinary emphasis. The best burger joint is *Del's Drive-In & Diner*, 1423 Island Hwy, a place with plenty of local colour. For beer and snacks try the *Royal Coachman*, 84 Dogwood St, popular with tourists and locals alike. For a **seafood** treat, head for the *Anchor Inn*, 261 Island Hwy (good views), or the *Gourmet by the Sea* on the main road about 15km south of town at Bennett's Point.

Quadra Island

Quadra Island and its fine beaches and museum are fifteen minutes away from Campbell River and make a nice respite from the fish, though the famous fishing lodge here has been host to such big-name fisherfolk over the years as John Wayne, Kevin Costner and Julie Andrews. Ferries run roughly hourly from the well-signed terminal out of town ($4.50 return for foot passengers, $11.25 return for a car). The main excuse for the crossing is the **Kwagiulth Museum and Cultural Centre**, home to one of the country's most noted collections of aboriginal regalia (June–Sept daily 10am–4.30pm; closed Sun & Mon off-season; $2; ☎285-3733). As elsewhere in Canada, the masks, costumes and ritual objects were confiscated by the government in 1922 in an attempt to stamp out one of the natives' most potent ceremonies, and only came back in the 1980s on condition they would be locked up in a museum. The museum has around three hundred articles, and you should also ask directions to the petroglyphs in the small park across the road.

While on the island you could also laze on its beaches, walk its coastal **trails**, or climb Chinese Mountain for some cracking views. There's swimming in a warm, sheltered bay off a rocky beach at **Rebecca Spit Provincial Park**, a 1.5-kilometre spit near Drew Harbour 8km east of the ferry terminal, but the water's warmer still and a trifle sandier at the more distant **Village Bay Park**. Around ten places offer **accommodation**, including the *Heriot Bay Inn & Marina* on Heriot Bay Road (☎285-3322, *www.heriotbayinn.com*; ⑥, camping from $10–16) which has cottages, camping and RV sites, and the *Whiskey Point Resort Motel*, by the ferry dock at 725 Quathiaski Cove Rd (☎285-2201 or 1-800/622-5311, *www.whiskeypoint.com*; ⑤). The main **campsite** is the *We Wai Kai Campsite*, Rebecca Spit Road (☎285-3111; $15 for sites on the hill, $17 for sites on the beach – book ahead for the latter; mid-May to mid-Sept), 16km northeast of the ferry terminal.

Cortes Island

If you've taken the trouble to see Quadra Island, then you should push on to the still quieter **Cortes Island**, 45 minutes from Quadra on a second ferry (5 daily; foot passenger $5.50 return, car $13.75), an island with a deeply indented coastline at the neck of Desolation Sound, among North America's finest sailing and kayaking areas. Boating aside, it's known for its superlative clams and oysters, exported worldwide, and for one of Canada's leading holistic centres, the Hollyhock Seminar Centre on Highland Road (☎1-800/933-6339), where you can sign up for all manner of body- and soul-refreshing courses and stay in anything from a tent, dorm or private cottage. Other **accommodation** includes *The Blue Heron B&B* (☎935-6584; ③), while you should aim to eat at the *Old Floathouse* (☎935-6631) at the Gorge Marina Resort on Hunt Road, where you can also rent boats and scooters. Places to make for around the island include the small **Smelt Bay Provincial Park**, which has a campsite ($9) and opportunities to swim, fish, canoe and walk, and the **Hague Lake Provincial Park**, signed from Mansons Landing, with several looped trails accessible from different points on the road. If you're in a canoe or boat then you can also make for a couple of marine parks (Von Donop and Mansons Landing) and any number of delightful small bays, lagoons and beaches.

Strathcona Provincial Park

Vancouver Island's largest protected area, and the oldest park in British Columbia, **Strathcona Provincial Park** (established in 1911) is one of the few places on the island where the scenery approaches the grandeur of the mainland mountains. The island's highest point, Golden Hinde (2220m) is here, and it's also a place where there's a good chance of seeing rare indigenous wildlife (the Roosevelt elk, marmot and black-tailed deer are the most notable examples). Only two areas have any sort of facilities for the visitor – **Forbidden Plateau**, approached from Courtenay, and the more popular **Buttle Lake** region, accessible from Campbell River via Hwy 28. The Gold River Minibus will drop you at the head of Buttle Lake, about 40km west of Campbell River (Tues, Thurs & Sun). The rest of the park is unsullied wilderness, but fully open to backpackers and hardier walkers. Be sure to pick up the blue *BC Parks* pamphlet (available from the infocentre at Campbell River and elsewhere): it has a good general map and gives lots of information, such as the comforting fact that there are no grizzly bears in the park.

You'll see numerous pictures of **Della Falls**, around Campbell River, which (at 440m) are Canada's highest (and amongst the world's highest), though unfortunately it'll take a two-day trek and a canoe passage if you're going to see them.

HIKING IN STRATHCONA

Hiking, it hardly needs saying, is superb in Strathcona, with a jaw-dropping scenic combination of jagged mountains – including Golden Hinde (2220m), the island's highest point – lakes, rivers, waterfalls and all the trees you could possibly want. Seven marked **trails** fan out from the Buttle Lake area, together with six shorter nature walks, most less than 2km long, amongst which the Lady Falls and Lupin Falls trails stand out for their waterfall and forest views. All the longer trails can be tramped in a day, though the most popular, the **Elk River Trail** (10km), which starts from Drum Lake on Hwy 28, lends itself to an overnight stop. Popular with backpackers because of its gentle grade, the path ends up at Landslide Lake, an idyllic camping spot. The other highly regarded trail is the **Flower Ridge** walk, which starts at the southern end of Buttle Lake. In the Forbidden Plateau area, named after a native legend that claimed evil spirits lay in wait to devour women and children who entered its precincts, the most popular trip is the **Forbidden Plateau Skyride** to the summit of Wood Mountain where there's a two-kilometre trail to a viewpoint over Boston Canyon. Backcountry camping is allowed throughout the park, and the backpacking is great once you've hauled up onto the summit ridges above the tree line. For serious exploration, buy the relevant topographic maps at MAPS BC, Ministry of Environment and Parks, Parliament Buildings, Victoria.

The approach to the park along Hwy 28 is worth taking for the scenery alone; numerous short trails and nature walks are signposted from rest stops, most no more than twenty-minutes' stroll from the car. **Elk Falls Provincial Park**, noted for its gorge and waterfall, is the first stop, ten minutes out of Campbell River. It also has a large provincial park **campsite**.

Park practicalities

The **Park Visitor Centre** is located at the junction of Hwy 28 and the Buttle Lake road (May–Sept only); fifteen information shelters around the lake also provide some trail and wildlife information. Buttle Lake has two provincial **campsites** with basic facilities – one alongside the park centre at Buttle Lake ($15), the other at Ralph River ($12) on the extreme southern end of Buttle Lake, accessed by the road along the lake's eastern shore. Both have good **swimming** areas nearby. Backcountry camping costs $3, payable at the visitor centre.

The park's only commercial **accommodation** is provided by the *Strathcona Park Lodge* (☎286-3122, *www.strathcona.bc.ca*; ③), just outside the Buttle Lake entrance, a mixture of hotel and outdoor-pursuits centre. You can **rent canoes**, **bikes** and other outdoor equipment, and sign up for any number of organized tours and activities.

Gold River and Tahsis

There's not a lot happening at **GOLD RIVER**, a tiny logging community 89km west of Campbell River – founded in 1965 in the middle of nowhere to service a big pulp mill 12km away at Muchalat Inlet. The place only has a handful of hotels and a couple of shops – but the ride over on Hwy 28 is superb, and there's the chance to explore the sublime coastline by boat, the main reason for the settlement's increasing number of visitors. Year-round, the **MV Uchuck III**, a converted World War II US minesweeper, takes mail, cargo and passengers to logging camps and settlements up and down the surrounding coast on a variety of routes. Like the MV *Lady Rose* out of Port Alberni, what started as a sideline has recently become far more of a commercial enterprise, with glossy pamphlets and extra summer sailings, though it's none the worse for that – you just have to book ahead to make sure of a place. For information and **reservations**, contact Nootka Sound Service Ltd (☎283-2325 or 283-2515).

There are **three basic routes**, all of them offering wonderful windows onto the wilderness and wildlife (whales, bears, bald eagles and more) of the region's inlets, islands and forested mountains. The dock is at the end of Hwy 28, about 15km southwest of Gold River. The **Tahsis Day Trip** ($45) departs at 9am every Tuesday year-round for Tahsis (see below) (arriving at 1pm), returning after a one-hour stopover to Gold River at 6pm. The shorter **Nootka Sound Day Trip** ($40) leaves Gold River every Wednesday at 10am July to mid-September only (returning at 4.30pm), with longer stops at Resolution Sound and Kyuquot (the native word for "Friendly Cove"), the latter involving a $9 landing fee, proceeds from which go to the Mowachaht Band for the redevelopment of the aboriginal site. During the ninety-minute halt you are offered a guided tour by aboriginal guides around their ancestral home. The previous stop, at Friendly Cove, is equally historic, for it was here that Captain Cook made his first-known landing on the west coast in 1778, from which, among other things, was to spring the important sea-otter fur trade. Whites named the area and people here "Nootka", though locals today say *nootka* was merely a word of warning to Cook and his crew, meaning "circle around" to avoid hitting offshore rocks. If you're equipped with provisions and wish to stay over, there are **cabins** and a **campsite** here, but call first to confirm arrangements (☎283-2054). The third trip, the **Kyuquot Adventure** ($195 single, $310 double), is a two-day overnight cruise, departing every Thursday year-round (April–Oct 7am; Nov–March 6am). It takes you much further north up the coast, returning to Gold River at 4 or 5pm on Friday afternoon: accommodation is included, as is breakfast – though you make it yourself from food supplied – and you can buy Thursday's evening meal on board or onshore at Kyuquot. A 25 percent deposit is required for these trips, refundable in full up until two weeks before departure. People on all trips should bring warm and waterproof clothing. There's a coffee shop on board for drinks and hot snacks. **Kayakers** should note that they can be deposited by lift into the sea at most points en route by prior arrangement.

Boat aside, one of the area's two minor attractions is **Quatsino Cave**, the deepest vertical cave in North America, parts of which are open to the public – for details ask at the infocentre; the other is the **Big Drop**, a stretch of Gold River white water known to kayakers worldwide. The local **infocentre** is at the corner of Hwy 28 and Scout Lake Rd (mid-May to mid-Sept; ☎283-2418, *goldriv@island.net*). **Accommodation** is in short supply: the only large place is the *Ridgeview Motel*, located in a panoramic spot above the village at 395 Donner Court (☎283-2277 or 1-800/989-3393, *theridge@oberon.ark.com*; ③) – but the *Peppercorn Trail Motel and Campground* on Mill Road (☎283-2443, *peppercorn @island.net*; ②) also has ten rooms, as well as a **campsite** ($15–18).

Note that there are also two beautiful roads north from Gold River, both rough, but worth the jolts for the scenery. One provides an alternative approach to **TAHSIS**, another logging community 70km northwest of Gold River, which has one **motel** with a restaurant if you need to break your journey: advance summer reservations are needed at the *Tahsis Motel*, Head Bay Road (☎934-6318, *tahsmot@cancom.net*; ③): or try *Fern's Place B&B*, 379 N Maquinna (☎934-7851, *bganyo@cancom.net*; ③). For more background on a lovely part of the coast, with plenty of fishing, boating and hiking opportunities, contact the **infocentre**, a booth on Rugged Mountain Road (late June to early Sept Mon–Sat 10am–4.30pm; ☎934-6667) or the Village Office (Mon–Fri 9am–noon & 1–5pm; ☎934-6622).

North to Port McNeill, Telegraph Cove and Alert Bay

The main highway north of Campbell River cuts inland and climbs through increasingly rugged and deserted country, particularly after Sayward, the one main community en route. Near Sayward is the marvellously oddball **Valley of a Thousand Faces**:

1400 famous faces painted onto cedar logs, the work of a Dutch artist, and more inter-esting than it sounds (May–Aug daily 10am–4pm; donation). Almost alongside, west of Hwy 19 at Sayward Junction, is an RV and tent **campsite**, the *White River Court* (☎282-3265; sites $8). With a car, you could strike off south from here to **Schoen Lake Provincial Park**, located 12km off Hwy 19 on a rough road near of Woss village and featuring a couple of forest trails and a well-kept campsite ($9). Sayward has one **motel**, the *Fisherboy Park*, 400m off Hwy 19 at 1546 Sayward Rd (☎282-3204; ③). **PORT McNEILL**, 180km north of Campbell River and the first real town along Hwy 19, is lit-tle more than a motel and logging centre and not somewhere to spend longer than nec-essary. If you get stuck here, the infocentre's at 351 Shelley Crescent (May to mid-Oct 9am–3pm; ☎956-3131, *www.portmcneillchamber.com*).

Telegraph Cove

By contrast, tiny **TELEGRAPH COVE**, 8km south of Port McNeill and reached by a rough side road, is an immensely likeable place and the best of BC's so-called "board-walk villages": the whole community is raised on wooden stilts over the water, a sight that's becoming ever more popular with tourists. It was built as the terminus of a tree-strung telegraph line from Victoria, and it comes as a surprise to discover that its character is threatened by plans for a massive waterfront development of houses, lodge and restaurant. Some development has already taken place – added moorings, a pub and restaurant – but so far without adversely affecting the village's character. As an added bonus, the village has become one of the island's premier **whale-watch-ing** spots, the main attraction here being the pods of orcas (killer whales) that calve locally. Some nineteen of these families live or visit Robson Bight, 20km down the Johnstone Strait, which was established as an ecological reserve in 1982 (the whales like the gravel beaches, where they come to rub). This is the world's most accessible and predictable spot to see the creatures – around a ninety percent chance in season. The best outfit for a trip to see them is Stubbs Island Charters at the dock at the end of the boardwalk through the old village (☎928-3185, 928-3117 or 1-800/665-3066). The first whale-watching company in BC, they run up to five three- or five-hour trips daily (June–Oct), but they're very popular, so call well in advance to be sure of a place.

In summer you can buy food at a small café, but otherwise the only provision for vis-itors is an incongruous new building with shop, ice-cream counter and coffee bar. The only **accommodation** is the large wooded *Telegraph Cove Resorts* (☎928-3131 or 1-800/200-4665; ⑦, camping $15–23; March–Dec), a short walk from the village and one of the best-located places on Vancouver Island, a reputation that makes reservations essential in summer. It has 19 rooms and 121 RV/tent sites with showers, laundry, restaurant, boat rentals and access to guides, charters and whale-watching tours. The *Hidden Cove Lodge* (☎956-3916, *hidcl@island.net*; ⑤; May–Nov) at Lewis Point, a sec-luded cove on Johnstone Strait 7km from Telegraph Cove, has eight superb lodge units, but they go very quickly. The big *Alder Bay Campsite* 6km off Hwy 19 en route for Telegraph Cove from Port McNeill provides grassy tent sites with ocean views (☎956-4117; reservations recommended; $16–26; May–Sept).

Alert Bay

The breezy fishing village of **ALERT BAY**, on Cormorant Island, is reached by numer-ous daily ferries from Port McNeill just 8km away (foot passenger $5.50 return, car $13.75). The fifty-minute crossing in the migrating season provides a good chance of seeing whales en route. Despite the predominance of the non-native industries (mainly fish processing), half the population of the island are native 'Namgis, and a visit here offers the opportunity to get to grips with something of their history and to meet those who are keeping something of the old traditions alive. Be sure to have prebooked accommodation (see below) before heading out here in high season. The **infocentre** (June–Sept daily; Oct–May Mon–Fri; ☎974-5024, *info@alertbay.com*) is at 116 Fir St to your right as you come off the ferry. Also off to the right from the terminal are the totems of a 'Namgis Burial Ground: you're asked to view from a respectful distance.

Bear left from the terminal out of the main part of the village to reach the excellent **U'Mista Cultural Centre** on Front Street (mid-May to early Sept daily 9am–5pm; Oct to mid-May Mon–Fri 9am–5pm; $5.35; ☎974-5403), a modern building based on old models, which houses a collection of potlatch items and artefacts. It also shows a couple of award-winning films, and you might also come across local kids being taught native languages, songs and dances. More local artefacts are on show in the library and small museum, open most summer afternoons, at 199 Fir St. For years the village also claimed the world's tallest fully carved **totem pole** (other contenders, say knowing villagers, are all pole and no carving), though much to local chagrin Victoria raised a pole in 1994 that *The Guinness Book of Records* has recognized as 2.1m taller. Also worth a look is the wildlife and weird swamp habitat at **Gator Gardens** behind the bay, accessible via several trails and boardwalks.

Most people come over for the day, but **accommodation** options include: the six-room *Orca Inn*, 291 Fir St, ten-minutes' walk from the ferry terminal (☎974-5322 or 1-800/672-2466; ②), with steak and seafood restaurant and café overlooking Broughton Strait and the sea; the *Ocean View Cabins*, 390 Poplar St, 1km from the ferry terminal overlooking Mitchell Bay (☎974-5457; ③); the *Bayside Inn Hotel*, overlooking the harbour, at 81 Fir St (☎974-5857; ②); and the 23-site *Alert Bay Camping and Trailer Park* on Alder Road (☎974-5213, *www.alertbay.com*; $10–15).

Sointula

SOINTULA village is a wonderful aberration. It's located on Malcolm Island, accessible by ferry en route from Port McNeill to Alert Bay (25min; foot passenger $5.50 return car $13.75) and directly from Alert Bay (35min; foot passenger $3.50 one-way, car $5.50). The fishing village would be a good place to wander at any time, thanks to its briney maritime appeal, but what gives added lustre is the fact that it contains a tiny fossil Finnish settlement. An early cult community, it was founded with Finnish pioneers as a model co-operative settlement in 1901 by Matti Kurrika, a curious mixture of guru, dramatist and philosopher. In 1905 the experiment collapsed, but 100 Finns from the original settlement stayed on. Their descendants survive to this day, and you'll still hear Finnish being spoken on the streets. You can wander local beaches, explore the island interior by logging road, or spend a few minutes in the **Sointula Finnish Museum**, which is located on 1st Street just to the left after disembarking the ferry: you'll probably need to call someone (☎973-6353 or 973-6764) to come and open up and show you around.

Port Hardy

Dominated by big-time copper mining, a large fishing fleet and the usual logging concerns, **PORT HARDY**, a total of 485km from Victoria and 230km from Campbell River, is best known among travellers as the departure point for ships plying one of the more spectacular stretches of the famous **Inside Passage** to Prince Rupert (and thence to Alaska) and the newly introduced **Discovery Coast Passage** (see box, overleaf). If you have time to kill waiting for the boat you could drop into the occasionally open **town museum** at 7110 Market St or visit the **Quatse River Salmon Hatchery** on Hardy Bay Road, just off Hwy 19 across from the *Pioneer Inn*.

If possible, though, time your arrival to coincide with one of the Inside Passage **sailings** (see box, overleaf) which leave every other day in summer and twice-weekly in winter. **Bus** services aren't really scheduled to do this for you, with a Laidlaw bus

THE INSIDE PASSAGE

One of Canada's great trips, the **Inside Passage** aboard BC Ferries' *Queen of the North*, between Port Hardy and Prince Rupert on the British Columbia mainland, is a cheap way of getting what people on the big cruise ships are getting: 274 nautical miles of mountains, islands, waterfalls, glaciers, sea lions, whales, eagles and some of the grandest coastal scenery on the continent. By linking up with the Greyhound bus network or the VIA Rail terminal at Prince Rupert, it also makes a good leg in any number of convenient itineraries around British Columbia. Some travellers will have come from Washington State, others will want to press on from Prince Rupert to Skagway by boat and then head north into Alaska and the Yukon (see p.857 for details on the Alaska Marine ferries). A lot of people simply treat it as a cruise, and sail north one day and return south to Port Hardy the next. If nothing else, the trip's a good way of meeting fellow travellers and taking a break from the interminable trees of the BC interior.

The boat carries 750 passengers and 160 cars and runs every two days, departing at 7.30am on **even-numbered days** in August, **odd-numbered days** in June, July, September and the first half of October. The journey takes around fifteen hours, arriving in Prince Rupert about 10.30pm, sometimes with a stop at Bella Bella. Be aware that from about October 15 to May 25 the sailings are less frequent in both directions and are predominantly at night (they leave Port Hardy in the late afternoon), which rather defeats the sightseeing object of the trip. On board there are cafeterias, restaurants and a shop (among other services): at the last, pick up the cheap and interesting *BC Ferries Guide to the Inside Passage* for more on the trip.

The cost from mid-June to mid-September (peak) is $106 single for a foot passenger (May & Oct $85/75; Nov–April $56), $218 for a car (May & Oct $154; Nov–April $114); reservations are **essential** throughout the summer season if you're taking a car or want a cabin. Bookings can be made by phone (☎1-888/223-3779 anywhere in BC, ☎250/386-3431 in Victoria, ☎604/669-1211 in Vancouver, *www.bcferries.com*), fax (☎381-5452 in Victoria) or by post to BC Ferry Corporation, 1112 Fort St, Victoria, BC V8V 4V2. Include name and address; number in party; length, height and type of car; choice of dayroom or cabin; and preferred date of departure and alternatives. Full payment is required up front. **Day cabins** can be reserved by foot passengers, and range from around $24 for two berths with basin, to $45 on the Promenade with two berths, basin and toilet. If you are making the return trip only you can rent **cabins overnight**, saving the hassle of finding accommodation in Port Hardy, but if you do you are obliged to take the cabin for the following day's return trip as well: cabins are not available as an alternative to rooms in town, so don't think you can rent a cabin overnight and then disappear next morning at Prince Rupert. Two-berth overnight cabins range from about $51 with basin only, to $120 for shower, basin and toilet. Reports suggest BC Ferries are not happy for passengers to roll out sleeping bags in the lounge area. If you're making a return trip and want to leave your car behind, there are several supervised lock-ups in Port Hardy: try Daze Parking (☎949-7792) or the *Sunny Sanctuary RV Park* (☎949-8111) just five minutes from the terminal (the town shuttle bus will pick you up from here). You can leave vehicles at the ferry terminal, but there have been incidents of vandalism in recent years: neither BC Ferries nor the Port Hardy infocentre seem to recommend the practice. Note, again, that

meeting each *incoming* sailing from Prince Rupert. A Laidlaw bus (☎949-7532 in Port Hardy, ☎385-4411 or 388-5248 in Victoria) also leaves Victoria daily (currently 11.45am), sometimes with a change in Nanaimo, arriving at the Port Hardy ferry terminal in the evening (currently 9.50pm) to connect with the ferry next morning; in summer an extra service departs from Victoria on the morning before ferry sailings. Maverick Coach Lines (☎250/753-4371 in Nanaimo, ☎604/662-8051 in Vancouver) runs an early-morning bus from Vancouver to Nanaimo (inclusive of ferry), connecting with the daily Laidlaw bus to Port Hardy. You can **fly** from Vancouver International Airport it is vital to book accommodation at your final destination before starting your trip; both Port Hardy and Prince Rupert hotels get very busy on days when the boat arrives.

THE DISCOVERY COAST PASSAGE

The huge success of the Inside Passage sailing amongst visitors led BC Ferries to introduce the **Discovery Coast Passage**, a trip they candidly admit will only pay as a result of tourists. The route offers many of the scenic rewards of the Inside Passage, but over a shorter and more circuitous route between Port Hardy and **Bella Coola**, where you pick up the occasionally steep and tortuous road (Hwy 20) through the Coast Mountains to Williams Lake (see p.803) – it goes nowhere else. En route, the boat, the *Queen of Chilliwack*, stops at Namu, McLoughlin Bay, Shearwater, Klemtu and Ocean Falls (Namu is a request stop and must be booked in advance). If the route takes off as BC Ferries hope, you can expect visitor facilities to mushroom at these places – you can disembark at all of them – but at present the only places to stay overnight are campsites at McLoughlin Bay and a resort, hotels, cabins and B&B at Shearwater. Bella Coola is better-equipped, and will probably become more so as the route becomes better known. BC Ferries is offering inclusive ferry and accommodation **packages** – even renting fishing tackle so you can fish over the side – and these too may mature as the service finds its feet.

Currently there are **departures** roughly every couple of days between late May and the end of September, currently leaving at 9.30am on Tues and Thurs and 9.30pm on Sat, Sun and Mon. There's a slight catch, however, for while the early morning departures offer you plenty of scenery, some arrive at McLoughlin Bay at 7.30pm and Bella Coola at 6.30am in the morning, meaning that the very best bit of the trip – along the inlet to Bella Coola – is in the middle of the night. The 9.30am departures are quicker (they only stop once, at Ocean Falls) and make Bella Coola the same day, arriving at 11pm, so the problem is lessened. Alternatively take the 9.30pm departures and wake at McLoughlin Bay at 7.30am with a further daylight trip towards Bella Coola, arriving at 7.30am the next morning – read the timetables carefully. Making the trip southbound from Bella Coola gets round the problem, though there are similar staggered departure and arrival times (services currently leave Mon, Wed and Fri at 7.30 or 8am, arriving Port Hardy 9.30pm on the Mon departure, 7.45am on Wed sailing and 9am on the Fri boat), with overnight and same-day journeys and a variety of stopping points depending on the day you travel. Unlike the Inside Passage, there are **no cabins**: you sleep in aircraft-style reclining seats and – for the time being – sleeping bags seem OK on the floor: check for the latest on freestanding tents on the decks.

Reservations can be made through BC Ferries (see Inside Passage, opposite, for details). **Prices** for a foot passenger are $110 one-way to Bella Coola, $55 to Namu and $70 to all other destinations. If you want to camp or stop over and hop on and off, the boat fares between any two of McLoughlin Bay, Ocean Falls, Klemtu and Namu are $22 and $40 from any of these to Bella Coola. Cars cost $220 from Port Hardy to Bella Coola, $140 to all other destinations ($45 and $80 respectively for the single-leg options). To take a **canoe** or **kayak** costs $40.75 stowage from Port Hardy to Bella Coola, $30.75 to points en route.

---

to Port Hardy or with Air BC (☎1-800/663-3721 in BC, 1-800/776-3000 in the States, 604/688-5515 in Vancouver, 250/360-9074 in Victoria).

The Port Hardy **ferry terminal** is visible from town but is actually 8km away at Bear Cove, where buses stop before carrying on to terminate opposite the **infocentre**, 7250 Market St (year-round Mon–Fri 9am–5pm; to early June to late Sept 8am–8pm; ☎949-7622, *chamber@capescott.bc.ca*). The infocentre can give you all the details about Port Hardy's tiny but free **museum**, and the immense wilderness of **Cape Scott Provincial Park**, whose interior is accessible only by foot and which is supposed to have some of the most consistently bad weather in the world. As a short taster you could follow the forty-minute hike from the small campsite and trailhead at San Josef River to some sandy beaches. Increasingly popular, but demanding (allow eight hours plus), is the historic **Cape Scott Trail**, part of a complex web of trails hacked from the forest by early Danish pioneers. Around 28km has been reclaimed from the forest, opening a trail to the cape itself.

If you stay in town overnight, leave plenty of time to reach the ferry terminal – sailings in summer are usually around 7.30am. North Island Transportation provides a shuttle-bus service between the ferry and the town's airport, main hotels and the **bus station** at Market Street, whence it departs ninety minutes before each sailing (☎949-6300 for information or to arrange a pick-up from hotel or campsite); otherwise call a **taxi** (☎949-8000).

Many travellers to Port Hardy are in RVs, but there's still a huge amount of pressure on hotel **accommodation** in summer, and it's absolutely vital to call ahead if you're not camping or haven't worked your arrival to coincide with one of the ferry sailings. Note that the ferry from Prince Rupert docks around 10.30pm, so you don't want to be hunting out rooms late at night with dozens of others. There are **rooms** out of town at the *Airport Inn*, 4030 Byng Rd (☎949-9424, *www.airportinn-porthardy.com*; ⑤), but you'd be better off in one of the slightly more upmarket central choices like the *North Shore Inn*, 7370 Market St (☎949-8500; ④), at the end of Hwy 19, where all units have ocean views, or the *Thunderbird Inn*, 7050 Rupert St and Granville (☎949-7767, *tbirdinn@island.net*; ④). The former has nice views of the harbour but sometimes has noisy live music. Five minutes south of town at 4965 Byng Rd, in a park-like setting near the river, is the *Pioneer Inn* (☎949-7271 or 1-800/663-8744, *pioneer@island.net*; ⑤), which has rooms, RV sites and a campsite ($20). Other hotels are the *Glen Lyon Inn* by the marina at 6435 Hardy Bay Rd (☎949-7115, *www.glenlyoninn.com*; ④), and the large 40-room *Quarterdeck Inn*, 6555 Hardy Bay Rd (☎902-0455, *quarterdk@capescott.net*; ⑥), the town's newest hotel – it opened in late 1999: otherwise contact the infocentre for details of the town's five or so B&B options. The *Wildwoods* **campsite** (☎949-6753; $5–15; May–Oct) is a good option, being within walking distance (3km) of the ferry, though it's not too comfy for tenting – or try the *Quatse River Campground* at 5050 Hardy Rd (☎949-2395, *quatse@island.net*; $14–18), with 62 spruce-shaded sites opposite the *Pioneer Inn*, 5km from the ferry dock. Or go for the larger 80-site *Sunny Sanctuary Campground* 1km north of Ferry Junction and Hwy 19 at 8080 Goodspeed Rd (☎949-8111, *sunnycam@capescott.net*; $15–20).

Food here is nothing special, but there's a bevy of budget outlets, so you should be able to fill up for well under $10. Granville and Market streets have the main restaurant concentrations: try *Snuggles*, next to the *Pioneer Inn*, which aims at a cosy English pub atmosphere with live music, theatre (Friday nights) and steaks, salads and salmon grilled over an open fire. The cafeteria-coffee shop in the *Pioneer* does filling breakfasts and other snacks.

THE INTERIOR

It says something about the magnificence of British Columbia's **interior** that you can enter it from Vancouver or the Rockies and find a clutch of landscapes every bit as spectacular as those you've just left. Some people will travel inland from Vancouver, others across country from the Rockies or the US. Unfortunately, whatever your approach, both major routes through the region confine you to some of its least interesting areas. The most obvious and quickest line east or west, the **Trans-Canada Hwy**, isn't worth considering in its entirety unless you're keen to cross the region in a hurry – little west of Revelstoke compares to what you might find further north or south. Nor does **Hwy**

3, rumbling along just north of the US border, offer a convincing reason for sticking to it religiously.

The best option would be to take a meandering course towards the outstanding **Kootenay** region in the province's southeastern corner – an idyllic assortment of mountains and lakes and several towns that are fun to stay in – perhaps by way of the **Okanagan**, an almost Californian enclave of orchards, vineyards, warm lakes and resort towns, whose beaches and scorching summers suck in hordes of holiday-makers from all over Canada and the western United States. From here you could push north to **Kamloops**, a far from exciting town, but the transport hub of the region and a jumping-off point for the magnificent **Wells Gray Provincial Park** or the Yukon. The other major option would be to head south to take in the better parts of Hwy 3 west of Osoyoos, also reasonably easily reached directly from Vancouver, and which includes a corner of **desert** and the spectacular ridges of the **Cascades** and **Coast Mountains**.

The Sunshine Coast

A mild-weathered stretch of sandy beaches, rugged headlands and quiet lagoons running northwest of Vancouver, the **Sunshine Coast** receives heavy promotion – and heavy tourist traffic as a result – though in truth its reputation is overstated and the scenic rewards are slim compared to the grandeur of the BC interior. In summer, however, this area offers some of Canada's best diving, boating and fishing opportunities, all of which stoke a string of busy villages eager to provide accommodation, run tours and rent anything from bikes to full-sized cruisers.

Highway 101 runs the length of the coast, but it's interrupted at two points by sizeable inlets that entail lengthy ferry crossings. Motorists face enormous queues to get on the boats in summer, but the crossings present no problems for bus or foot passengers – indeed, they're the best bits of the trip. Given that the area is hardly worth full-scale exploration by car anyway, you might as well go by **bus**; it's perfectly feasible to get to **Powell River** and back in a day, though it's probably not the first day-trip you'd want to make from Vancouver. Malaspina Coachlines (☎485-5030) runs two buses daily to Powell River (5hr) and a third only as far as **Sechelt** (2hr).

Along Highway 101

Soon reached and well signposted from North Vancouver, **HORSESHOE BAY** is the departure point for the first of the Hwy 101 **ferry** crossings, a half-hour passage through the islands of fjord-like Howe Sound (regular sailings year-round). Ferries also ply from here to Nanaimo on Vancouver Island, with hourly sailings in summer and every other hour off-season. For information on either of these services, contact BC Ferries in Vancouver (☎604/669-1211), or pick up a timetable from the Vancouver infocentre.

GIBSONS, the terminal on the other side of Howe Sound, is a scrappy place spread widely over a wooded hillside – the nicest area is around the busy marina, where you'll find the **infocentre** at 668 Sunny Crest Rd (daily 9am–6pm; ☎604/886-2325). Motels abound, but for decent camping hold out for **Roberts Creek Provincial Park**, 8km northwest of the terminal on Hwy 101 ($12). Beyond, the service and supplies centre of **SECHELT** panders to tourists less than Gibsons, and ongoing development lends the town a messy air which isn't helped by its drab, flat location. Just 4km north, however, **Porpoise Bay Provincial Park** has a campsite (reservations possible, see p.691; $17.50), a sandy beach, good swimming and a few short woodland trails. The main road beyond Sechelt is very pretty, and offers occasional views to the sea when it's not trapped in the trees.

Further west on Hwy 101 is Pender Harbour, a string of small coastal communities of which **MADEIRA PARK** is the most substantial; whales occasionally pass this section of coast – which, sadly, is the source of many of the whales in the world's aquariums – but the main draws are fishing and boating. **Earl's Cove** is nothing but the departure ramp of the second **ferry** en route, a longer crossing (45min), which again offers fantastic views of sheer mountains plunging into the sea. A short trail (4km) from the adjacent car park leads to a viewpoint over the **Skookumchuck Narrows**, where the Sechelt Inlet constricts to produce boiling rapids at the turn of each tide. On board the ferry, look north beyond the low wooded hills to the immense waterfall that drops off a "Lost World"-type plateau into the sea.

From Jervis Bay, the opposite landing stage, the country is comparatively less travelled. A couple of kilometres up the road is the best of all the provincial parks in this region, **Saltery Bay Provincial Park**. Everything here is discreetly hidden in the trees between the road and the coast, and the campsite ($12) – beautifully sited – is connected by short trails to a couple of swimming beaches. The main road beyond is largely enclosed by trees, so there's little to see of the coast, though various **campsites** give onto the sea, notably the big *Oceanside Resort and Cabins* site, 7km short of Powell River, which sits on a superb piece of shoreline (☎604/485-2435 or 1-888/889-2435; ④). Although it's given over mainly to RVs, there are a few sites for tents ($12–14) and cheap cabins (①).

Powell River and beyond

Given its seafront location, **POWELL RIVER** has its scenic side, but like many a BC town its unfocused sprawl and nearby sawmill slightly dampen the overall appeal. The main road cruises past almost 4km of box-like retirement bungalows before reaching the town centre, which at first glance makes it a not terribly captivating resort. If you're catching the **ferry** to Courtenay on Vancouver Island (4 daily; 75min), you might not even see the town site, as the terminal is 2km to the east at Westview, and some of the **buses** from Vancouver are timed to coincide with the boats; if your bus doesn't connect, you can either walk from the town centre or bus terminal or call a taxi (☎604/483-3666). The local **infocentre** (daily 9am–5pm; ☎604/485-4701), which is immediately at the end of the wooden ferry pier at 4690 Marine Ave, can supply a visitors' map with detailed coverage of the many trails leading inland from the coast hereabouts; they can also advise on boat trips on Powell Lake, immediately inland, and tours to Desolation Sound further up the coast.

In the event of having to stay overnight, you can choose from a dozen or so **motels** in town and a couple near the terminal itself. The most central of several **campsites** is the 81-site *Willingdon Beach Municipal Campground* on the seafront off Marine Avenue at 6910 Duncan St (☎604/485-2242; $13–20).

The northern end point of Hwy 101 – which, incidentally, starts in Mexico City, making it one of North America's longest continuous routes – is the hamlet of **LUND**, 28km up the coast from Powell River. **Desolation Sound Marine Provincial Park**, about 10km north of Lund, offers some of Canada's best boating and scuba diving, plus fishing, canoeing and kayaking. There's no road access to the park, but a number of outfitters in Powell River run tours to it and can hire all the equipment you could possibly need – try Westview Live Bait Ltd, 4527 Marine Ave, for **canoes**; Coulter's Diving, 4557 Willingdon Ave, for **scuba gear**; and Spokes, 4710 Marine Drive, for **bicycles**. The more modest **Okeover Provincial Park**, immediately north of Lund, has an unserviced campsite ($12).

The Sea to Sky Highway

A fancy name for Hwy 99 between North Vancouver and Whistler, the **Sea to Sky Highway** has a slightly better reputation than it deserves, mainly because Vancouver's weekend hordes need to reassure themselves of the grandeur of the scenery at their doorstep. It undoubtedly scores in its early coastal stretch, where the road clings perilously to an almost sheer cliff and mountains come dramatically into view on both sides of Howe Sound. Views here are better than along the Sunshine Coast, though plenty of campsites, motels and minor roadside distractions fill the route until the mountains of the Coast Range rear up beyond **Squamish** for the rest of the way to Whistler.

If you've a **car** you're better off driving the highway only as far as **Garibaldi Provincial Park** – the section between Pemberton and Lillooet, the Duffy Lake Road, is very slow-going and often impassable in winter, though the drive is a stunner with wonderful views of lakes and glaciers. Regular buses (see Perimeter details on p.796) connect Vancouver and Whistler (some continue to Pemberton), which you can easily manage as a day-trip (it's 2hr 30min one-way to Whistler from Vancouver by bus), though a far more interesting and popular way of covering this ground is by **train**. BC Rail (☎984-5246 or 1-800/663-8238, *www.bcrail.com*) operates a daily passenger service, the Cariboo Prospector, between North Vancouver and Lillooet ($67 one-way), calling at Whistler ($33 one-way) and other minor stations; the train arrives in Lillooet at 12.35pm and sets off back for Vancouver at 3.30pm, making for an excellent day-trip. The train continues on to Prince George ($196 one-way) on Sunday, Wednesday and Friday; this is a much better way to make the journey than by bus via Hope and Cache Creek. BC Rail's *Royal Hudson* is a fantastic steam engine that travels for two hours from North Vancouver to Squamish (May–Sept Wed–Sun). It leaves Vancouver at 10am, and then leaves from Squamish for the trip back to Vancouver at 2pm. The one-way trip costs $24 or $40 if you want to travel in the dome car and get a real eyeful of the awesome scenery.

Britannia Beach

Road and rail lines meet with some squalor at tiny **BRITANNIA BEACH**, 53km from Vancouver, whose **BC Museum of Mining** is the first reason to take time out from admiring the views (mid-May to June, Sept & Oct Wed–Sun 10am–4.30pm; July & Aug daily 10am–4.30pm; $8.50; ☎604/896-2233, *www.bcmuseumofmining.org*). Centring around what was, in the 1930s, the largest producer of copper in the British Empire, the museum is housed in a huge, derelict-looking building on the hillside and is chock-full of hands-on displays, original working machinery and archive photographs. You can also take guided underground tours around the mine galleries on small electric trains.

Beyond Britannia Beach a huge, chimney-surrounded pulp mill comes into view across Howe Sound to spoil the scenic wonder along this stretch, though **Browning Lake** in **Murrin Provincial Park** makes a nice picnic spot. This is but one of several small coastal reserves, the most striking of which is **Shannon Falls Provincial Park**, 7km beyond Britannia Beach, signed right off the road and worth a stop for its spectacular 335-metre **waterfall**. Six times the height of Niagara, you can see it from the road, but it's only five-minutes' walk to the viewing area at the base, where the proximity of the road, plus a campsite and diner, detract a touch.

Squamish

The sea views and coastal drama end 11km beyond Britannia Beach at **SQUAMISH**, not a pretty place, whose houses spread out over a flat plain amidst warehouses, logging waste and old machinery. However, if you want to climb, windsurf or mountain bike, there's nowhere better in Canada to do so. At a glance, all the town has by way of fame is the vast white granite rock literally overshadowing it, "The Stawamus Chief", which looms into view to the east just beyond Shannon Falls and is claimed to be the world's "second-biggest freestanding granite outcropping" (after Gibraltar, apparently). Over the last few years, the rock has caused the town's stock to rise considerably, for it now rates as one of Canada's top – if not *the* top – spot for **rock climbing**, and the area recently earned provincial-park status. If all you want to do is watch this activity from below, the pull-off beyond the falls is a good spot. Around 200,000 climbers from around the world come here annually, swarming over more than 400 routes over the 625-metre monolith: the University Wall and its culmination, the Dance Platform, is rated Canada's toughest climb. Other simpler but highly rated climbs include Banana Peel, Sugarloaf and Cat Crack, as well as other more varied routes on the adjacent Smoke Bluffs and outcrops in Murrin Provincial Park.

The rock is sacred to the local Squamish, whose ancient tribal name – which means "place where the wind blows" – gives a clue as to the town's second big activity. **Windsurfing** here is now renowned across North America, thanks to some truly extraordinary winds, most drummed up by the vast rock walls around the town and its inlet – which are then funnelled along the inlet's narrow corridor to Squamish at its head. There are strong, consistent winds here to suit all standards, from beginner to worldclass, but the water is cold, so a wet suit's a good idea (there are rental outlets around town). Most people head for the artificial Squamish Spit, a dyke separating the waters of the Howe Sound from the Squamish River, a park area run by the Squamish Windsurfing Society (☎604/926-WIND or 892-2235). It's around 3km from town (ask at the infocentre for directions) and a small fee is payable to the Society to cover rescue boats, insurance and washroom facilities.

Rounding out Squamish's outdoor activities is the tremendous **mountain biking** terrain – there are no less than 63 trails in the area ranging from gnarly single-track trails to readily accessible deactivated forestry roads – and the growing trend of **bouldering**, which involves clambering (very slowly and without ropes) over large boulders.

The town has one more unexpected treat, for the Squamish River, and the tiny hamlet of Brackendale in particular (10km to the north on Hwy 99), is – literally – the world's **bald-eagle** capital. In winter around 2000 eagles regularly congregate here, attracted by the chance to pick off the migrating salmon. The best place to see them is the so-called Eagle Run just south of the centre of Brackendale, and on the river in the Brackendale Eagles Provincial Park with a small shelter and volunteer interpreters on weekends during the eagle season. The birds largely winter on the river's west bank, with the viewing area on the east – eagles will stop feeding if approached within about 150m, so the river provides an invaluable buffer zone. For **accommodation** and **rafting trips** contact the Sunwolf Outdoor Center (☎604/898-1537, *www.mountaininter.net/sunwolf*). It is signposted off Hwy 1 – take a left onto the Squamish Valley Road at the Alice Lake junction 2km past Brackendale, continue for 4km and the centre is on the right. They have three-person cabins on the shore of Cheakamus River (③), some have kitchens (④). To see the eagles from a raft costs $70 per person, including light lunch; a raft trip plus cabin accommodation costs $139 per person, $198 per couple. The centre will also provide transportation to and from Vancouver or Whistler for $138 per person including a raft trip and light lunch. For more information and details on guided walks in the area, contact the Brackendale Art Gallery on Government Road (Jan daily noon–5pm; rest of year Sat & Sun noon–10pm or by appointment on weekdays; ☎604/898-3333), which also exhibits paintings and sculptures by local artists and has a pleasant restaurant.

If Squamish's outdoor activities leave you cold, you might want to look in on the new **West Coast Railway Heritage Park**, Centennial Way (daily 10am–5pm; $6; ☎1-800/722-1233, *www.wcra.org*), signed off Hwy 99 about 3km north of town. The twelve-acre park contains 58 fine old railway carriages and locomotives in a pretty, natural setting.

Practicalities

Most of the relevant parts of the town are concentrated on Cleveland Avenue, including the **infocentre** (May–Sept daily 9am–5pm; Oct–April Mon–Fri 9am–5pm, Sat & Sun 10am–2pm; ☎604/892-9244, *www.squamishchamber.bc.ca*), the big IGA Plus supermarket and the most central **accommodation** if you're not at the hostel, the *August Jack Motor Inn* opposite the infocentre (☎604/892-3504; ③). If you want inside knowledge on the climbing or wildlife, be certain to stay at the superlative *Squamish Hostel* on Buckley Avenue (☎604/892-9240 or 1-800/449-8614; ①). The hostel is a clean and friendly place that offers a kitchen, common room and private rooms as well as shared accommodation. For home-made Mexican **food** the *Coyote Cantina,* on Cleveland Avenue, is great for snacks and meals or there's vegetarian fare at the *Rainforest Grill*, just off 2nd Avenue. Sporty types hang out at the *Brew Pub*, also on Cleveland, which serves pub food and home-brewed beer.

If you're looking into **renting equipment**, Vertical Reality Sports Centre on Cleveland Road (☎604/892-8248) rents out climbing shoes ($10 a day) and mountain bikes ($15–40 a day), whilst Slipstream Rock & Ice (☎604/898-4891 or 1-800/616-1325, *www.slipstreamadventures.com*) offers rock- and ice-climbing guiding and instruction. Most of their tours are for two days and range from $148 to $248 and they teach all abilities. If you are here to climb, there is one key **guide**, available from bookstores in Vancouver (see "Listings" on p.728) as well as the climbing shops in Squamish: *The Climbers Guide to Squamish* by Kevin McLane (Elaho, $34.95). If the new craze of bouldering is your thing then *Squamish Boulder Problems* by Peter Michael (Highball; $19.90) has all the information you need.

Incidentally, if you're in town in August, Squamish proves it hasn't forgotten its lumbering roots by holding what it deems to be the World Lumberjack Competition, and in July the place goes nuts with a ten-day Adventure Festival (☎1-888/684-8828) that kicks off with a chariot race – garbage cans mounted on wheels and pulled by mountain bikes – and includes a mountain bike race with over 800 riders, street hockey, rock-climbing clinics and white-water competitions.

Garibaldi Provincial Park

After about 5km, the road north of Squamish enters the classic river, mountain and forest country of the BC interior. The journey thereafter up to Whistler is a joy, with only the march of electricity pylons to take the edge off an idyllic drive.

Unless you're skiing, **Garibaldi Provincial Park** is the main incentive for heading this way. As you'd expect, it's a huge and unspoilt area which combines all the usual breathtaking ingredients of lakes, rivers, forests, glaciers and the peaks of the Coast Mountains (Wedge Mountain, at 2891m, is the park's highest point). Four rough roads access the park from points along the highway between Squamish and Whistler, but you'll need transport to reach the trailheads at the end of them. Pick up the excellent BC Parks pamphlet for Garibaldi from the Vancouver tourist office for a comprehensive rundown on all trails, campsites and the like. Unless you're camping, the only accommodation close to the park is at Whistler, though with an early start from Vancouver you could feasibly enjoy a good walk and return the same day.

There are five main areas with trails, of which the **Black Tusk/Garibaldi Lake** region is the most popular and probably most beautiful. Try the trail from the parking area at Rubble Creek to Garibaldi Lake (9km; 3hr one-way) or to Taylor Meadows (7km; 2hr 30min one-way). Further trails then fan out from Garibaldi Lake, including one to the huge basalt outcrop of **Black Tusk** (2316m), a rare opportunity to reach an alpine summit without any rock climbing. The other hiking areas from south to north are **Diamond Head**, **Cheakamus Lake**, **Singing Pass** and **Wedgemount Lake**. Access to each is clearly signed from the highway, and all have wilderness campsites and are explored by several trails of varying lengths. Outside these small defined areas, however, the park is untrammelled wilderness. Bear in mind there are also hiking possibilities outside the park from Whistler (see box, p.801), where in summer you can get a head start on hikes by riding up the ski lifts.

Whistler

WHISTLER, 56km beyond Squamish, is Canada's finest four-season resort, and frequently ranks among most people's world top-five winter ski resorts. In 1996, for the first time ever, *Ski*, *Snow Country* and *Skiing* magazines were unanimous in voting it North America's top skiing destination. Skiing and snowboarding are clearly the main activities, but all manner of other winter sports are possible and in summer the lifts keep running to provide supreme highline hiking and other outdoor activities (not to mention North America's finest summer skiing). Standards are high, and for those raised on the queues and waits at European resorts, the ease with which you can get onto the slopes here will come as a pleasant surprise.

The resort consists of two adjacent but separate mountains – **Whistler** (2182m) and **Blackcomb** (2284m) – each with their own extensive lift and chair systems, and each covered in a multitude of runs. Both lift systems are accessed from the resort's heart, the purpose-built and largely pedestrianized **Whistler Village**, the tight-clustered focus of many hotels, shops, restaurants and après-ski activity. Around this core are two other "village" complexes, Upper Village and the recently completed Village North. Around 6km to the south of Whistler Village is **Whistler Creek** (also with a gondola and lift base), which has typically been a cheaper alternative but is now undergoing a $50 million redevelopment that will see its accommodation and local services duplicating those of its famous neighbour. In truth the whole ribbon of land on and just off the main Hwy 99 from Whistler Creek to Whistler Village is gradually being developed – Whistler is the single fastest-growing municipality in BC.

Arrival, information and accommodation

There are several ways of **getting to** Whistler. If you're flying to Vancouver on a skiing package (or otherwise) and want to get straight to the resort, then Perimeter (☎604/266-5386, *www.perimeterbus.com*) run a **bus shuttle** from the airport and various Vancouver hotels to Whistler, with drop-offs at Whistler Creek and several major hotels in and around Whistler Village. Reservations are required for the service, with prepayment by credit card and cancellations allowed up to 24 hours in advance (May–Nov 7 daily, 2 of which are express and do not stop at Vancouver hotels; $46 one-way; Dec–April Mon–Fri 8 daily, including 5 express, Sat & Sun 11 daily, including 9 express $49; 2hr 30min–3hr). Greyhound Buses (☎604/482-8747 in Vancouver, ☎604/932-5031 in Whistler or 1-800/661-TRIP from anywhere in North America, *www.greyhound.ca*) run six daily **bus** services from Vancouver bus depot (see p.695) to the Village (2hr 30min; $20 one-way) via Britannia Beach, Whistler Creek and other stops en route. In winter (Dec–April) Greyhound's ski express leaves Vancouver at 6.30am and goes nonstop to Whistler arriving at 8.30am. You can also travel by BC Rail **train** (☎604/984-5246 or 1-800/663-8238, *www.bcrail.com/bcrpass*) from the station in North Vancouver to Whistler's station near Whistler Creek (1 daily; $33; 2hr 35min). Local buses, WAVE (☎604/932-4040) run a free shuttle service around Whistler Village, Village North and Upper Village as well as buses to Whistler Creek and other destinations ($1.50 flat fare, 5-day pass $5). If you need taxis to get around locally, try Sea to Sky Taxi (☎604/932-3333).

Many people in winter are likely to be on a package. If not, or if you're here in summer, all local **accommodation** can be booked through **Whistler Central Reservations** (☎604/664-5625 or 1-800/WHISTLER, *www.tourismwhistler.com*), who can help find a room or an apartment for you in an appropriate price bracket. If you're booking for winter, note that reservations should be made well in advance. Such is demand that many hotels have a thirty-day cancellation window and may insist on a minimum of three-days' stay. Accommodation is most expensive from February to the end of March and cheapest from May to mid-June and mid-September to mid-November.

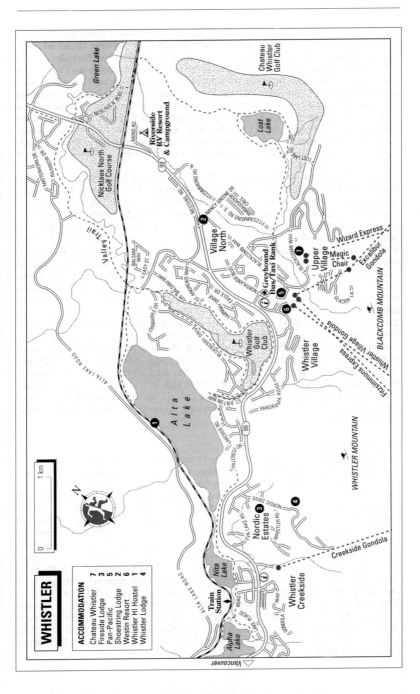

WHISTLER

ACCOMMODATION

Chateau Whistler	7
Fireside Lodge	3
Pan-Pacific	5
Shoestring Lodge	2
Westin Resort	6
Whistler HI Hostel	1
Whistler Lodge	4

For recorded **information** on Whistler-Blackcomb call ☎1-800/766-0449 (☎604/664-5614 from Vancouver or ☎604/932-3434 from Whistler, *www.whistler-blackcomb.com*). Tourism Whistler (☎604/932-3298) is another source of information; they also run the Whistler Activity and Information Centre, in the green-roofed Conference Centre near the Village Square (daily 9am–5pm; ☎604/932-2394). Though they can help with masses of comfortable hotel, chalet and lodge accommodation (remember that chalets can put extra beds in double rooms at nominal rates), and book activities and tickets for local events, they do cater towards the top-end of the market. Whistler Creek is home to the more down-to-earth and friendly **Chamber of Commerce**, 2097 Lake Placid Rd (daily 9am–5pm, longer hours in summer; ☎604/932-5528). Pick up a copy of *Pique*, the free local newspaper available in bars and at the information centres – it'll keep you abreast of happening events.

If you're going to do Whistler in style, the top resort **hotel** is the $75 million *Chateau Whistler* on Blackcomb Way (☎604/938-8000; ⑦). In the same league is the spanking new all-suite *Westin Resort and Spa* (☎1-888/634-5577, *www.westinwhistler.com*; ⑦) with ski-in, ski-out facilities and the *Pan-Pacific* (☎1-888/905-9995, *www.pan-pac.com*; ⑥). At the other end of the scale is the **youth hostel** right on the shores of Alta Lake at 5678 Alta Lake Rd, one of the nicest hostels in BC (☎604/932-5492, *www.hihostels.bc.ca*; ①), a signposted forty-minute walk from Whistler Creek or ten-minute drive to the village centre; local buses (☎604/932-4020) leave the gondola base in the Village four times a day for the hostel and the journey takes fifteen minutes ($1.50; note that BC Rail trains may sometimes stop alongside the hostel if you ask the conductor). As its popular year-round, reserve ahead. The *Shoestring Lodge*, with an adjacent pub, is a good and equally popular alternative. It has private rooms with small bathrooms (②) as well as dorms (①) and is a ten-minute walk north of Whistler Village on Nancy Greene Drive (☎604/932-3338). Another reasonable choice is the *Fireside Lodge*, 2117 Nordic Drive (☎604/932-4545; ②) at Nordic Estates, 3km south of the village. Finally, you could try the *Whistler Lodge* (☎604/932-6604 or 604/228-5851; ①), also on Nordic Drive, which is owned by the University of British Columbia but lets nonstudents stay; check-in time is from 4pm to 10pm. Best of the **campsites** is the *Riverside RV Resort and Campground* (☎1-877/905-5533, *www.whistlercamping.com*), 2km north of Whistler Village, which now has brand-new five-person log cabins for $79–99 and sites for $20.

Whistler Village

WHISTLER VILLAGE is the key to the resort, a newish and rather characterless and pastel-shaded conglomeration of hotels, restaurants, mountain-gear shops and more loud people in fluorescent clothes than are healthy in one place at the same time. Its name is said to derive from the piercing whistle of the marmot, a small and rather chubby mammal, which emits a distinctive shriek as a warning call. Others say the name comes from the sound of the wind whistling through Singing Pass up in the mountains. Whatever its origins, the village has all the facilities of any normal village, with the difference that they all charge more than what you'd pay anywhere else. At the same time it's a somewhat soulless place, very much a resort complex rather than an organic village, though for most people who are here to indulge on the slopes, character is a secondary consideration. Huge amounts of money have been invested in the area since the resort opened in 1980, and the investments have paid off well; the resort's services, lifts and general overall polish are almost faultless, and those of its nearby satellites are not far behind. The resort area averages more than two million visitors a year, and Whistler's challenge is now turning towards being able to rein in development before it spoils the scenery, killing the goose laying the golden egg.

HITTING THE SLOPES

The **skiing and snowboarding season** for Whistler and Blackcomb begins in late November, although sometimes earlier if nature permits. While the amount of snow varies from year-to-year, the yearly average is a whopping thirty-feet of snowfall. Blackcomb closes at the end of April, while Whistler stays open until early June. Then the mountains switch places, as Whistler closes and Blackcomb reopens in early June for glacier skiing and snowboarding, staying open until late July. The lifts are open daily 8.30am–3pm, and until 4pm after January.

Lift tickets give you full use of both Whistler and Blackcomb mountains, and it will take days for even the most advanced skiier or snowboarder to cover all the terrain. Tickets are available from the lift base in Whistler Village, but the queues can be horrendous. Instead, plan ahead and purchase your tickets online from *www.whistler.net*, or in Vancouver from Sport Mart at either 495 8th Ave W (☎604/873-6737) or 735 Thurlow St (☎604/683-2433). Your hotel can often set you up with tickets if you prebook far enough in advance. Call ☎1-877/932-0606 from North America or ☎604/932-0606 from Europe for more information.

Prices increase in peak season – over Christmas and New Year and from mid-February to mid-March – and lift tickets are subject to a seven-percent tax. You can save money by purchasing your lift pass before the end of September or, if you plan to ski regularly at Whistler, by purchasing an **Express Card**. These cost $79 for adults, $67 for youths and $39 for seniors, and are valid all season – scan it each time you ski and it automatically charges your credit card. Your first day skiing is free and then you pay a discounted rate of $35–53 depending on the season; call ☎1-800/766-0449 for more details.

	Adults		Youth (13–18)		Child and Senior (65 plus)	
	Regular	Peak	Regular	Peak	Regular	Peak
One-day	$59	$61	$50	$52	$30	$31
Seven-day	$378	$392	$321	$333	$189	$196
Sightseeing	$21	$21	$18	$18	$14	$14
Afternoon	$44	$46	$37	$39	$21	$23

Intermediate and expert skiers can join the **free tours** of the mountains that leave at 10.30am and 1pm daily. The Whistler All-Mountain tour departs from the Guest Satisfaction Centre at the top of the Whistler Village gondola. The Blackcomb All-Mountain tour meets at the Mountain Tour Centre, top of the Solar Coaster Express, or at the *Glacier Creek Lodge*. To explore Blackcomb's glaciers join the tour at the *Glacier Creek Lodge*, weather permitting.

For **snow conditions** call ☎604/932-4211 in Whistler or ☎604/687-7507 from Vancouver.

Skiing and snowboarding on Whistler and Blackcomb

Winter-sports enthusiasts can argue long and late over the relative merits of **Whistler Mountain** and its rival, Blackcomb Mountain, both accessed from Whistler Village's lifts. Together they have more than two-hundred runs, thirty-three lifts, twelve vast, high-alpine bowls, and three major glaciers. Both are great mountains, and both offer top-notch skiing and boarding, as evidenced by world-class events like the Snowboard FIS World Cup each December and North America's largest annual sports event the World Ski and Snowboard Festival in April – both take place on Whistler. Each mountain has a distinctive character, however, at least for the time being, for major injections of money are on the way to upgrade Whistler Mountain's already impressive facilities. Traditionally Whistler has been seen as the more intimate and homely of the two mountains, somewhere you can ski or board for days on end and never have to retrace your steps. **Highlight runs** for intermediates or confident novices are Hwy 86, Burnt Stew Basin and Franz's Run, a high-velocity cruiser that drops virtually from the tree line right down to Whistler Creek. Real thrill-seekers should head to three steep above-tree-line swaths of snow: Harmony Bowl, Symphony Bowl and Glacier Bowl. Of the 3600 odd acres of terrain, 20 percent is beginner, 55 percent intermediate and 25 percent expert. There are over a hundred marked **trails** and seven major bowls. **Lifts** include two high-speed gondolas, six high-speed quads, two triple and one double chair lift, and five surface lifts. Snowboarders are blessed with a half-pipe and park. Total vertical drop is 1530m and the longest run is 11km.

Blackcomb Mountain, the "Mile-High Mountain", is a ski area laden with superlatives: the most modern resort in Canada, North America's finest summer skiing (on Horstman Glacier), the continent's longest unbroken fall-line skiing and the longest *and* second longest lift-serviced vertical falls in North America (1609m and 1530m). In shape, its trail and run-system resembles an inverted triangle, with ever more skiing and boarding possibilities branching off the higher you go. The most famous run is the double-black diamond Couloir Extreme, the first such run in Canada and one of several precipitous chutes in the Rendezvous Bowl. Three other **runs** are also particularly renowned: the Zig-Zag, a long, winding cruise; Blackcomb Glacier, one of North America's longest above-tree-line runs; and Xhiggy's Meadow on the Seventh Heaven Express. If you're here to board or ski in summer, two T-bars take you up to the wide open cruising terrain on Horstman Glacier.

Blackcomb is slightly smaller than Whistler, at 3341 acres, but has a similar breakdown of **terrain** (15 percent beginner, 55 percent intermediate and 30 percent expert). **Lifts** are one high-speed gondola, six express quads, three triple chair lifts, and seven surface lifts. There are over a hundred marked trails, two glaciers and five bowls along with two half-pipes and a park for snowboarders. Even if you're not skiing, come up here (summer or winter) on the ski lifts to walk, enjoy the **view** from the top of the mountain, or to eat in the restaurants like *Rendezvous* or *Glacier Creek*. If you want some **cross-country skiing** locally, the best spots are 22km of groomed trails around Lost Lake and the *Chateau Whistler* golf course, all easily accessible from Whistler Village.

Eating, drinking and nightlife

When it comes to **food and drink**, Whistler Village and its satellites are loaded with cafés and some ninety restaurants, though none really have an "address" as such. These can come and go at an alarming rate, but one top-rated restaurant of long standing is *Araxi's Restaurant and Antipasto Bar* in Village Square (☎604/932-4540), which serves up West Coast-style fare and inventive pasta dishes – try the amazing mussels in chilli, vermouth and lemon grass followed by a perfect crème brulee for dessert. Equally fine, the *Rim Rock Café & Oyster Bar* in the *Highland Lodge* (☎604/932-5565) is excellent for seafood. For an utter splurge the *Bearfoot Bistro* on Village Green (☎604/932-3433) is an ostentatious place with the likes of black and white truffle salad and yellowfin tuna parfait with beluga caviar on the menu. For a less pricey outing try the Italian *Quattro at Pinnacle* on Main Street (☎604/905-4844), with a menu of Roman and North Italian dishes that includes a lovely rack of lamb with chestnut polenta. In winter and busy summer evenings you'll need to book at all of these. Other more down-to-earth places to try are *Trattoria di Umberto* (☎604/932-5858) in the *Mountainside Lodge*, beside the *Pan-Pacific Hotel*, for a cosy Italian meal, *Thai One On* (☎604/932-4822) for spicy Thai in the Upper Village, and *Zeuski's* (☎604/932-6009), a reasonably priced Greek place in the Town Plaza. For cheap eats, you are pretty much limited to

ACTIVITIES

Outdoor activities aside, there's not a lot else to do in Whistler save sit in the cafés and watch the world go by. In summer, though, chances are you'll be here to walk or mountain bike. If you're **walking**, remember you can ride the ski lifts up onto both mountains for tremendous views and easy access to high-altitude trails (July to early Sept daily 10am–8pm; early Sept to late Sept daily 10am–5pm; late Sept to mid-Oct Sat & Sun 10am–5pm; adults $21, youth and seniors $18). Free mountain walking tours are offered daily at 12.30pm & 2.30pm; call ☎1-800/766-0449 for more details. **Mountain bikers** can also take bikes up and ride down, for an additional $3 charge for the bike. You must have a helmet and the bike undergoes a safety inspection. If you're going it alone, pick up the duplicated sheet of biking and hiking trails from the infocentres (see p.798), or better yet buy the 1:50,000 *Whistler and Garibaldi Region* **map**. The two most popular shorter walks are the **Rainbow Falls** and the six-hour **Singing Pass** trails. Other good choices are the four-kilometre trail to Cheakamus Lake or any of the high-alpine hikes accessed from the Upper Gondola station (1837m) on Whistler Mountain or the Seventh Heaven lift on Blackcomb: you can, of course, come here simply for the view. Among the walks from Whistler Mountain gondola station, think about the **Glacier Trail** (2.5km round trip; 150m ascent; 1hr) for views of the snow and ice in Glacier Bowl – snowshoe rental and tours are possible to let you cross some of the safer snow fields ($15 a day; for tours call Outdoor Adventures ☎604/932-0647 or Whistler Cross Country Ski & Hike ☎604/932-7711 or 1-888/771-2382, *www.whistlerhikingcentre.com*). Or go for the slightly more challenging **Little Whistler Trail** (3.8km round trip; 265m ascent; 1hr 30min–2hr), which takes you to the summit of Little Whistler Peak (2115m) and grand views of Black Tusk in Garibaldi Provincial Park. Remember to time your hike to get back to the gondola station for the last ride down (times vary according to season).

If the high-level stuff seems too daunting (it shouldn't be – the trails are good) then there are plenty of trails (some surfaced) for bikers, walkers and in-line skating around the Village. There are also numerous operators offering guided walks and bike rides to suit all abilities, as well as numerous **rental outlets** for bikes, blades and other equipment around the Village. **All-Terrain Vehicles (ATVs)** can be rented from Canadian All Terrain Adventures (☎1-877/938-1616, *www.cdn-snowmobile.com*) for guided tours that include splurges through mud-pits. If you want to go **horse riding**, contact Edgewater Outdoor Centre (☎604/932-3389), The Adventure Ranch (☎604/932-5078) or Cougar Mountain (☎604/932-4086). Whistler Jet Boat Adventure Ranch (☎604/932-4078) can set you up with **jet boating**, white-water and float **rafting**, as will Whistler River Adventures (☎604/932-3532, *www.whistler-river-adv.com*) and Whistler Jet Boating (☎604/932-3389). You can play tennis at several public courts, or play squash or **swim** at the Meadow Park Sports Centre (☎604/938-7275). If you're a **golfer** the area has four great courses, including one designed by Jack Nicklaus – *Golf* magazine called Whistler "one of the best golf resorts in the world". Despite a recent upgrade, the Whistler Golf Club course remains the cheapest course at $115 (☎1-800/376-1777 or 604/932-3280), while the others, including Nicklaus North (☎604/938-9898), all cost from about $125 at low season to $185 at peak season in July and August. After all that activity there are umpteen **spas** for massage, mud baths and treatments that soothe all aches and pains – try Whistler Body Wrap (☎604/932-4710), Blue Highways Shiatsu and Massage (☎604/938-0777) or for utter luxury Avello (☎604/935-3444).

fast-food places like *Pita Pit* and *Subway* located in the Royal Bank building on Whistler Way. If you're looking to recharge in a **café** after a day on the mountain, try *Peake's Coffee House,* a block behind Main Street near the Gazebo (with Internet access at 20¢ a minute), or *Vitality 4U,* a great juice place on Main Street.

Winter or summer Whistler enjoys a lot of **nightlife** and aprés-ski activity, with visitors being bolstered by the large seasonal workforce – Whistler needs over four thousand people just to keep the show on the road – among which a vocal antipodean presence figures large. If you want relative peace and quiet, the key spot is the smartish *Mallard Bar* (☎604/938-8000) in the *Chateau Whistler* hotel. If you're just off Whistler Mountain, the aprés-ski haunt is the sports-crazy *Longhorn Saloon* (☎604/932-5999) in the Village at the *Carleton Lodge*, with the lively beer-heavy *Merlin's* (☎604/938-7700) in the *Blackcomb Daylodge* performing the same function for Blackcomb. *The Brew House* is a microbrewery at the far end of Village North with a nice view of the waterfall. For people-watching, *Citta* in the Village Square and *Tapley's Neighbourhood Pub* both have wrapround patios whilst *The Amsterdam Café* is a relaxed hangout in the Village Square. Down in Whistler Creek, *Hoz's* on Lake Placid Road is the place for liquid refreshment. As evening draws on, make for *Buffalo Bill's* (☎604/932-6613) at the *Timberline Lodge*, a thirty-something bar/club with comedy nights, hypnosis shows, 13 video screens, a huge dance floor and live music.

A younger set, snowboarding hipsters among them, make for **clubs** in both the Village and North Village. These include *Tommy Africa's*, aka *Tommy's* (☎604/932-6090), who host a very popular 1980s dance night on Mondays; *Savage Beagle Club* (☎604/938-3337), a small, split-level cocktail bar and danceteria; *Maxx Fish* (☎604/932-1904), home to hip-hop and house DJs; the massive mainstream dance club/restaurant/live-music venue *Alpen Rock* (☎604/938-0082); and the lively *Moe Joe's* (☎604/935-1152), where locals hang out to catch DJs and live music. Located in North Village, *Garkinfels*, aka *Garf's* (☎604/32-2323), is currently Whistler's funkiest nightclub.

North to Lillooet

Hwy 99 funnels down to two slow lanes at **PEMBERTON**, where apartments are now mushrooming in the wake of Whistler's popularity – all the skiing here is via helicopter or hiking. Beyond, you're treated to some wonderfully wild country in which Vancouver and even Whistler seem a long way away. Patches of forest poke through rugged mountainsides and scree slopes, and a succession of glorious lakes culminate in Sefton Lake, whose hydroelectric schemes feed power into the grid as far south as Arizona, accounting for the pylons south of Whistler.

At the lumber town of **LILLOOET** the railway meets the Fraser River, which marks a turning point in the scenery as denuded crags and hillsides increasingly hint at the *High Noon*-type ranching country to come. In July and August, the rocky banks and bars of the sluggish, mud-coloured river immediately north of town are dotted with vivid orange and blue tarpaulins. These belong to aboriginal Canadians who still come to catch and dry salmon as the fish make their way upriver to spawn. It's one of the few places where this tradition is continued and it is well worth a stop to watch. The town boasts four central **motels** if you need to stay: best are the *Mile 0 Motel*, 616 Main St (☎604/256-7511 or 1-888/766-4530; ②), downtown, overlooking the river and mountains (kitchenettes available in some units for self-catering), and the *4 Pines Motel* on the corner of 8th Avenue and Russell Street at 108 8th Ave, also with kitchenettes (☎604/256-4247; ②). The **infocentre/museum** is in the old church at 790 Main St (mid-May to June Mon–Sat noon–3pm; July & Aug daily 9am–5pm; Sept Tues–Sat noon–3pm; Oct Wed–Sat 12.30–2.30pm; ☎604/256-4308), with displays of local life past and present. The nearest **campsite** is the riverside *Cayoosh Creek* on Hwy 99 within walking distance of downtown (☎604/256-4180; $13; mid-April to mid-Oct).

From Lillooet, Hwy 99 heads east for 50km to Hwy 97; you can then either turn south towards Cache Creek (see p.809), or snake your way up north to the gold fields of the Cariboo.

The Cariboo

The Cariboo is the name given to the broad, rolling ranching country and immense forests of British Columbia's interior plateau, which extend north of Lillooet between the Coast Mountains to the west and Cariboo Mountains to the east. The region contains by far the dullest scenery in the province, and what little interest it offers – aside from fishing and boating on thousands of remote lakes – comes from its **gold-mining** heritage. Initially exploited by fur traders to a small degree, the region was fully opened up following the discovery of gold in 1858 in the lower Fraser Valley. The building of the **Cariboo Wagon Road**, a stagecoach route north out of Lillooet, spread gold fever right up the Fraser watershed as men leapfrogged from creek to creek, culminating in the big finds at Williams Creek in 1861 and Barkerville a year later.

Much of the old Wagon Road is today retraced by lonely **Hwy 97** (the Cariboo Hwy) and **VIA Rail**, which run in tandem through hour after hour of straggling pine forests and past the occasional ranch and small, marsh-edged lake – scenery that strikes you as pristine and pastoral for a while but which soon leaves you in a tree-weary stupor. If you're forced to stop over, there are innumerable lodges, ranches and motels on or just off the highway, and you can pick up copious material on the region at the Vancouver tourist office or infocentres en route.

> The telephone code for British Columbia outside of the Vancouver area is ☎250.

Clinton and Williams Lake

A compact little village surrounded by green pastures and tree-covered hills, **CLINTON** – named after a British duke – marks the beginning of the heart of Cariboo country. The town has a couple of **bed and breakfasts**, a new **campsite**, *Clinton Pines Campground,* 1204 Cariboo Ave (☎459-0030; $14–24; May–Sept) and a **motel** – the *Nomad* (☎459-2214 or 1-888/776-6623; ②). The three tiny settlements beyond Clinton at 70, 100 and 150 Mile House are echoes of the old roadhouses built by men who were paid by the mile to blaze the Cariboo Wagon Road – which is doubtless why 100 Mile House is well short of a 100 miles from the start of the road. 100 Mile House has a year-round **infocentre** at 422 Cariboo Hwy 97 S (May–Sept daily 9am–6pm, Oct–April Mon–Fri 9am–4pm; ☎395-5353) for details of the fishing, riding and other local outdoor pursuits. There are also a handful of **motels** in or a few kilometres away from town, the biggest in-town choice being the *Red Coach Inn*, 170 Hwy 97 N (☎395-2266 or 1-800/663-8422; ④). The central *Imperial* is smaller and cheaper (☎395-2471; ③).

WILLIAMS LAKE, 14km north of 150 Mile House and still 238km south of Prince George, is a busy and drab transport centre that huddles in the lee of a vast crag on terraces above the lake of the same name. It has plenty of motels, B&Bs, boat launches and swimming spots south of the town – but it's hardly a place you'd want to spend any time, unless you're dead-beat after driving or around on the first weekend in July for its famous **rodeo**. The year-round **infocentre** is at 1148 Broadway S (May–Sept daily 9am–5pm; Oct–April Mon–Fri 9am–4pm; ☎392-5025).

Bella Coola

Highway 20 branches west from Williams Lake, a part-paved, part-gravel road that runs 455km to **BELLA COOLA**, a village likely to gain an ever-greater tourist profile in the wake of the new visitor-oriented ferry service from Port Hardy on Vancouver Island (see p.789). Most of the road ploughs through the interminable forest of the Cariboo Plateau, but the last 100km or so traverses the high and stunningly spectacular peaks of the Coast Mountains and Tweedsmuir Provincial Park. Just outside the park you encounter the notorious "Hill", a hugely winding and precipitous stretch of highway barely tamed by the various upgradings over the years. Until 1953 there was no road link here at all. Instead there was a sixty-kilometre gap in the mountain stretch, a missing link the state refused to bridge. In response the locals of Bella Coola took it upon themselves to build the road on their own, completing their so-called Freedom Road in three years. Previously the settlement was the domain of the Bella Coola, or Nuxalk, a group visited by George Vancouver as early as 1793. In 1869 the Hudson's Bay Company opened a trading post. One house belonging to a company clerk is now all that remains. Besides a small museum and glorious scenery, Bella Coola is hardly stacked with sights. Norwegian settlers, however, perhaps drawn by the fjord-like scenery nearby, were notable early pioneers, and language, heritage and buildings – notably the square-logged barns – all show a Scandinavian touch. **Hagensborg**, a village 18km east of Bella Coola, preserves a particularly strong Nordic flavour. About 10km from the village, roughly midway to Bella Coola, are the **Thorsen Creek Petroglyphs**, a hundred or so rock drawings: the infocentre (see below) should be able to fix you up with a guide to explore the site.

No buses serve Bella Coola and beyond the village there is no onward road route: unless you fly out, you'll have to either head back the way you came or pick up the new **Discovery Coast Passage** boats to Port Hardy that stop off at the port. Boats leave three times a week at 7.30am or 8.30am, arriving in Port Hardy at around 9.30pm that evening or 7.45am or 9am the following morning depending on the number of stops en route (fares are $110 per person or $220 per car; see box, p.789 for full details of the service). If you want to indulge in a plane in or out of town, contact Wilderness Airlines (☎982-2225 or 1-800/665-9453).

Bella Coola's **infocentre** is on the Mackenzie Hwy near town (Mon–Fri daily 9.30am–4.30pm; ☎799-5638). The new ferry service will probably lead to the opening of more hotels and restaurants: currently **accommodation** is provided by the *Bella Coola Valley Inn* (☎799-5316; ③), closest hotel to the ferry terminal, and the *Bella Coola Motel* (☎799-5323; ③) at the corner of Burke and Clayton – both places are downtown. There's also the *Bay Motor Hotel* on Hwy 20, 14km east of the town and 1km from the airport (☎982-2212 or 1-888/982-2212; ③).

Along Hwy 97: north of Williams Lake

North of Williams Lake on Hwy 97, the **Fraser River** re-enters the scenic picture and, after a dramatic stretch of canyon, reinstates more compelling hills and snatches of river meadows. This also marks the start, however, of some of the most concerted **logging operations** in all British Columbia, presaged by increasing numbers of crude pepper-pot kilns used to burn off waste wood. By **QUESNEL**, home of the "world's largest plywood plant", you're greeted with scenes out of an environmentalist's nightmare: whole mountainsides cleared of trees, hill-sized piles of sawdust, and unbelievably large lumber mills surrounded by stacks of logs and finished timber that stretch literally as far as the eye can see. If you're stuck for accommodation (there are a dozen or so hotels) or tempted by any of the many mill tours, contact the **infocentre** in Le Bourdais Park at 705 Carson Ave (March–Oct Mon–Fri 9am–4pm; ☎992-8716 or 1-800/992-4922).

Barkerville

Most people who take the trouble to drive this route detour from Quesnel to **Barkerville Provincial Historic Park**, 90km to the east in the heart of the Cariboo Mountains, the site of the Cariboo's biggest gold strike and an invigorating spot in its own right, providing a much-needed jolt to the senses after the sleepy scenery to the south (June–Sept daily 8am–8pm; $5.50). In 1862 a Cornishman named Billy Barker idly staked a claim here and after digging down a metre or so was about to pack up and head north. Urged on by his mates, however, he dug another couple of spadefuls and turned up a cluster of nuggets worth $600,000. Within months Barkerville, as it was later dubbed, had become the largest city in the region, and rode the boom for a decade until the gold finally ran out. Today numerous buildings have been restored, and the main administrative building has displays on mining methods and the gold rush, together with propaganda on their importance to the province.

If you want to **stay** under cover up here, there are just three options, all at **WELLS**, 8km west of the park: the *Hubs Motel* (☎994-3313; ②); the *Wells Hotel*, 2341 Pooley St (☎994-3427 or 1-800/860-2299; ④), a newly restored 1933 heritage country inn with licensed café and breakfast included; and the *White Cap Motor Inn* (☎994-3489 or 1-800/377-2028; ③) – the last also has RV and camping spaces for $10. Failing this you can **camp** at the three-way campsite at Barkerville Provincial Park adjacent to the old town (reservations possible, see p.691; $9.50–12; June–Sept). Wells has an **infocentre** on Pooley Street, part of a small museum (summer only; ☎994-3237).

If you're continuing from Quesnel north to Prince George and beyond, turn to Chapter Eight, "The North", beginning on p.848.

Vancouver to Kamloops

Many consider the region northeast of Vancouver up to Kamloops as little more than an area to speedily drive through on the way to more exciting prospects like the Okanagan or the Kootenays. While perhaps not completely false, there are a few relatively unknown reasons along the way to take the foot off the pedal and stop. Two major routes **connect Vancouver and Kamloops**, the latter an unexceptional town but almost unavoidable as the junction of major routes in the region. These days anyone in any sort of hurry takes the **Coquihalla Highway** (Hwy 5). The scenery is unexceptional in the early part, but things look up considerably in the climb to the Coquihalla Pass (1244m), when forests, mountains and crashing rivers make a dramatic reappearance – compromised somewhat by old mines, clear-cuts (hillsides completely cleared of trees) and recent road-building scars. There's only a single exit, at the supremely missable town of Merritt, and literally no services for the entire 182km from **Hope** to Kamloops. Come stocked up with fuel and food, and be prepared to pay a toll ($10) at the top of the pass – a wind- and snow-whipped spot that must offer some of the loneliest employment opportunities in the province.

The older, slower and more scenic route from Vancouver is on the **Trans-Canada Highway** or by VIA Rail, both of which follow a more meandering course along the Thompson River and then the lower reaches of the Fraser River. For the first stretch you can also take the less busy Hwy 7, which follows the north shore of the Fraser River from Vancouver and passes by **Harrison Hot Springs** en route to Hope.

Hwy 7 to Hope

Flanked by dreary malls at first, the 150km drive on Hwy 7 from Vancouver to Hope cheers up considerably as the countryside opens up after the small town of **MISSION**, 30km into the journey. If you have the time, you might want to make a quick stop at **Xá:ytem**, BC's oldest dwelling site (late June to Sept daily 10am–4pm; rest of the year by appointment; ☎604/820-9725), located by the highway just before the east side of Mission. People have lived here for as long as nine thousand years, and an ongoing archeological dig has uncovered numerous lithic (stone) artefacts including arrowheads and stones used for cutting and chopping – some were made from obsidian from Oregon, an indication of early trade routes. A newly built Stó:lo long house serves as the site's interpretation centre, and inside you can learn more about the excavations. Be sure to read up on the large boulder, known as Hatzic Rock, that rests on the grounds; it's a sacred spot to the aboriginal community, believed to be three si:yams (respected leaders) who had defied the wishes of the Creator and were turned to stone.

After Mission, the highway snakes through pretty farmland to **HARRISON HOT SPRINGS**, 129km from Vancouver and located on the southern edge of Harrison Lake. While natives believing in the healing properties of the springs came centuries ago, the springs were not popularized until they were "discovered" by gold prospectors in 1858; soon after the town became BC's first resort. Today, tourism remains Harrison Hot Spring's main industry, as attested by the number of modern apartment buildings and motels lining the lake. Still, thanks to the beautiful mountain views, it remains a scenic spot, mercifully free of too much neon and tat. The lake itself is 60km long – making it one of the province's largest lakes – and its waters are very clean, but also very cold. The only swimming option is in the man-made lagoon on the lake's shore, but if you want to play in the lake, boats, windsurfers and jet-skis can be hired from the deck in front of the upmarket *Harrison Hot Springs Resort*. If you're here the weekend after Labour Day, make a point of seeing the incredible sand sculptures on the beach that are created for the **World Championship Sand Sculpture** competition.

To reach the **springs** themselves, it's a short walk along the shore and past the *Harrison Hot Springs Resort* – but they are a piping hot 73°C at the source. In order to make the spring water suitable for soaking, the waters are cooled to 100 degrees and redirected to the **Harrison Hot Springs Public Pool** (Mon–Thurs 9am–9pm, Fri 9am–10pm, Sat 8am–10pm, Sun 8am–9pm; $9) back in town on the intersection of Hot Springs Road and the Esplanade.

The **infocentre** (☎604/796-3425, *www.harrison.ca*) is located in an old logging-camp bunkhouse on Hot Springs Road. For **accommodation** the cheapest **motel** is the *Bungalow*, 511 Lillooet Ave (☎ & fax 604/796-3536; ②), with self-contained lakeside cabins or the *Spa*, 140 Esplanade (☎604/796-2828 or 1-800/592-8828; ②), also by the lake, with in-house massages. *Harrison Heritage House and Kottage* at 312 Lillooet Ave (☎604/796-9552 or 1-800/331-8099; ④) is a pricey but beautiful **B&B** in one of the village's few heritage buildings. The *Harrison Hot Springs Resort* (☎604/796-2244 or 1-800/663-2266, *www.harrisonresort.com*; ⑥), a favourite of Clark Gable's in the 1950s, is a friendly place with indoor and outside pools piped from the springs. There are also ten cabins which are cheaper than the rooms, but these need to be booked well in advance. For **camping** there are several private campsites around but it's best to head for nearby *Sasquatch Provincial Park,* (reservations possible, see p.691, $9.50). **Eating** options are all along the Esplanade by the lake and you can settle for a variety of cuisines from the *Black Forest Steak and Schnitzel House* at no. 180 (☎604/796-9343) to the *Kitami* Japanese restaurant, 318 Hot Springs (☎604/796-2728). For snacks and coffees head for *Muddy Waters* also on Esplanade.

Hope

Reputedly christened by prospectors with a grounding in Dante, **HOPE** – as in "Abandon all hope . . ." – is a pleasant mountain-ringed town that achieved a certain fame as the place wasted in spectacular fashion by Sylvester Stallone at the end of *First Blood*, the first Rambo movie. Despite the number of roads that converge here – the Trans-Canada, Hwy 3 and the Coquihalla – it remains a remarkably unspoilt stopover.

In the past it was rivers, not roads, that accounted for the town's growth: the Fraser and two of its major tributaries, the Skagit and Coquihalla, meet at the townsite. The aboriginal villages here were forced to move when a Hudson's Bay post was established in 1848, the status quo being further disturbed when the gold rush hit in 1858. The bust that followed boom in neighbouring places was averted in Hope, largely because its situation made it an important station stop on the Canadian Pacific. Today the town's pretty location, which catches visitors slightly unaware, is turning it into something of a sight in its own right.

The **infocentre** (daily: summer 8am–8pm; rest of year 9am–5pm; ☎604/869-2021, *www.hopechamber.bc.ca*) is the building next to the artfully dumped pile of antique farm machinery at 919 Water Ave. The town **museum** (May–Sept daily 9am–5pm; donation) is in the same building, and offers the usual hand-me-downs of Hope's erstwhile old-timers. Across the road, the lovely view over the Fraser as it funnels out of the mountains is one of the town's best moments. Time permitting, drop by **Memorial Park** downtown, where trees ravaged by rot have been given a new lease of life by a local chainsaw sculptor. Nearby, the **Christ Church National Historic Site**, built in 1861, is one of BC's oldest churches still on its original site. Another one-off novelty is the "H" tree at the corner of 5th Street and Hudson's Bay Street, two trees cleverly entwined as saplings to grow together in the form of an "H" for Hope.

Hiking, fishing, canoeing, and even gold-panning are all popular time-wasters around the hundreds of local lakes and rivers, details of which are available from the infocentre. Of the hikes, the **Rotary Trail** (3km) to the confluence of the Fraser and Coquihalla rivers is popular, as is the more demanding clamber over gravel paths to the top of **Thacker Mountain** (5km). Another walking expedition worth pursuing is the dark jaunt through the **tunnels** of the abandoned Vancouver–Nelson railway, reached by a short trail from the **Coquihalla Canyon Recreation Area**, 6km northeast of town off Coquihalla Hwy. This was one of the backcountry locations used during the filming of *First Blood*, and offers spectacular views over the cliffs and huge sand bars of the Coquihalla Gorge. **Kawkawa Lake Provincial Park**, 3km northeast of Hope off Hwy 3, is another popular mountain retreat, endowed with plenty of hiking, relaxing and swimming opportunities. The latest big thrill hereabouts, though, is **gliding**, or soaring, the prevailing westerly winds funnelling suddenly into the valley above Hope creating perfect thermals for the sport. The Vancouver Soaring Association (☎604/521-5501), at Hope airport, offer thirty-minute unpowered flights (no experience necessary; $90).

Practicalities

Most of what happens in Hope happens on Hwy 1, here known as Water Avenue. The Greyhound **bus terminal** (on Water Ave) is a critical juncture for bus travellers heading west to Vancouver, north to Kamloops or east to Penticton and the Okanagan. Cheap **motels** proliferate along Hwy 3 leaving town heading east, and though they're mostly all alike, the *Flamingo* (☎604/869-9610; ①), last on the strip, has a nice piney setting. Closer in on the same road, the *Best Western Heritage Inn*, 570 Hope-Princeton Way (☎604/869-7166 or 1-800/528-1234; ③), a lovely grey-wood building smothered in flowers, is also excellent. In town, the *Best Continental Motel*, 860 Fraser Ave (☎604/869-9726; ③), lies a block back from the main highway and is handy for the bus depot; or try the *Windsor Motel* overlooking the park at 778 3rd Ave (☎604/869-9944 or 1-888/588-9944; ②). **Campsites**, too, are numerous, but most are some way from downtown. The town site is at *Coquihalla Campground* (☎604/869-7119 or 1-888/869-7118; $16–22; April–Oct), in a park setting off Hwy 3 and reached via 7th Avenue. The top of the pile is the *KOA Kampground*; 5km west of town on Flood Hope Road (☎604/869-9857 or 1-800/KOA-1631; $19; March–Oct).

Food facilities and late-night entertainment are limited in what is, despite Vancouver's proximity, still a small-time Canadian town. For snacks, try the *Hope Deli* or *Sharon's Lunchbox and Deli* on Wallace Street, or the rock-bottom café in the Greyhound station. For more ambitious fare, try the *Hope Hotel* or *Alpenhaus*, also on Wallace Street.

The Fraser Canyon

Veering north from Hope, the Trans-Canada runs up the Fraser River valley, squeezed here by the high ridges of the Cascade and Coast ranges into one of British Columbia's grandest waterways. Though it's now a transport corridor – the Canadian Pacific Railway also passes this way – the **Fraser Canyon** was long regarded as impassable; to negotiate it, the Trans-Canada is forced to push through tunnels, hug the Fraser's banks, and at times cling perilously to rock ledges hundreds of metres above the swirling waters.

The river is named after **Simon Fraser** (1776–1862), one of North America's most remarkable early explorers, who as an employee of the North West Company established western Canada's first white settlements: Fort McCleod (1805), Fort St James (1806), Fort Fraser (1806) and Fort George (1807). Having traced the route taken by fellow explorer Alexander Mackenzie across the continent, he set out in 1808 to establish a route to the Pacific and secure it for Britain against the rival claims of the US. Instead he travelled the entire 1300-kilometre length of a river – the Fraser – under the mistaken impression he was following the Columbia. "We had to pass where no man should venture", he wrote, making most of the journey on foot guided by local natives, pushing forward using ladders, ropes and improvised platforms to bypass rapids too treacherous to breach by boat. Some thirty-five days were needed to traverse the canyon alone. Reaching the river's mouth, where he would have glimpsed the site of present-day Vancouver, he realized his error and deemed the venture a commercial failure, despite the fact he had successfully navigated one of the continent's greatest rivers for the first time. Few people, needless to say, felt the need to follow Fraser's example until the discovery of **gold** near Yale in 1858; prospectors promptly waded in and panned every tributary of the lower Fraser until new strikes tempted them north to the Cariboo.

Yale

YALE, about 15km north of Hope, opens the canyon with a ring of plunging cliffs. Sitting at the river's navigable limit, it was once a significant site for Canada's aboriginal peoples, providing an important point of departure for the canoes of the Stó:lo ("People of the River"). Tribespeople would come from as far afield as Vancouver Island to plunder the rich salmon waters just above the present townsite. A Hudson's Bay Company post, The Falls, appeared here in the 1840s, later renamed in honour of James Murray Yale, commander of the HBC post at Fort Langley, then one of the predominant white outposts on the BC mainland. Within a decade it became the largest city in North America west of Chicago and north of San Francisco: during the 1858 gold rush, when it marked the beginning of the infamous Cariboo Wagon Road, Yale's population mushroomed to over 20,000, a growth only tempered by the end of the boom and the completion of the Canadian Pacific. Today it's a small lumber town of about 170, though a visit to the **Historic Yale Museum** (June–Sept daily 9am–6pm) on Hwy 1, known here as Douglas Street, offers an exhaustive account of the town's golden age. The **infocentre** is also in the museum (May–Sept daily 9am–6pm; ☎604/863-2324). The monument in front of the building is dedicated to the countless Chinese workers who helped build the Canadian Pacific, one of only a handful of such memorials. You might also want to pay homage at **Lady Franklin Rock**, the vast river boulder which blocked the passage of steamers beyond Yale. It takes its name from Lady Franklin, wife of Sir John Franklin, the Arctic explorer who vanished on a voyage to the Arctic in July 1845.

Numerous expeditions set out to find him (with no luck), and it is said that Lady Franklin, on her own personal odyssey, came as far as Yale and its big boulder. Ask locals for directions. If you fancy a longer walk, take Hwy 1 a kilometre south out of the village for the trailhead of the Spirit Cave Trail, a one-hour walk with fine views of the mountains. For **rooms**, you can't do much better than the *Fort Yale Motel* (☎604/863-2216; ②) at the entrance to the Canyon. Some 11km north of Yale on Hwy 1, the *Colonial Inn* (☎604/863-2277; ②) has cabins and pitches ($12). If you're **camping**, though, you might want to push on 10km towards Hope on Hwy 1 to the *Emory Creek Provincial Park*, a large, peaceful wooded site with river walks and camping sites from April to October ($12).

Hell's Gate and Boston Bar

Around 10km north of Yale on Hwy 1 is the famous **HELL'S GATE**, where – in a gorge almost 180m deep – the huge swell of the Fraser is squeezed into a 38-metre channel of foaming water that crashes through the rocks with awe-inspiring ferocity. The water here is up to 60m deep and as fast-flowing as any you're likely to see. For a good view of the canyon, travel 2km north of Yale on Hwy 1 to the **Alexander Bridge Provincial Park**, where an old section of the highway drops to the Alexander Bridge for some startling panoramas. Eight kilometres further there's a certain amount of resort-like commercialism to negotiate to get down to the river and an "Air-Tram" (cable car) to pay for (daily: April & late Sept to Oct 10am–4pm; May to mid-June & Sept 9am–5pm; mid-June to Aug 9am–6pm; closed Nov–March; $10; ☎604/867-9277, *www.hellsgate .bc.ca*). Close by there are also displays on the various provisions made to help migrating **salmon** complete their journeys, which have been interrupted over the years by the coming of the road and railway beside the Fraser. The river is one of the key runs for Pacific salmon, and every summer and autumn they fill the river as they head for tributaries and upstream lakes to spawn (see p.816). The biggest obstacle to their passage came in 1913, when a landslide occurred during the construction of the Canadian Pacific Railway, yet it wasn't until 1945 that ladders were completed to bypass the fall. The numbers of salmon have never fully recovered.

   BOSTON BAR, 20km north of Yale, is also the main centre for **white-water** rafting trips down the Fraser as far as Yale. Various companies run several trips a week from May to August; contact Frontier River Adventure for details (☎604/867-9244). The village's name, apparently, was coined by locals in villages nearby amazed at the number of American prospectors who seemed to hail from Boston. A "bar", by contrast, was the name given to places where miners stopped to make camp en route for the goldfields. To **stay** locally, make for the *Blue Lake Lodge* (☎604/867-9246 or 1-877/867-9246; ②), located a kilometre east on Blue Lake Road off the highway 15km north of Boston Bar. The only local **campsite**, the *Canyon Alpine RV Park & Campground* (☎604/867-9734 or 1-800/644-7275; $18–22), 5km north, also has a restaurant.

Cache Creek

CACHE CREEK has a reputation as a hitchhiker's black hole and indeed is the sort of sleepy place you could get stuck in for days. Locals also say it didn't help that an infamous child murderer, Charles Olsen, was captured nearby in 1985 – since then they've been understandably wary of picking up strangers. The town's name is accounted for by a variety of legends, the most romantic version concerning a couple of prospectors who buried a hoard of gold and never returned to pick it up. Sadly, it's likelier to derive from early trappers' more prosaic habit of leaving a cache of supplies at points on a trail to be used later.

   Cache Creek is known as the "Arizona of Canada" for its baking summer climate, which settles a heat-wasted somnolence on its dusty streets. The parched, windswept mountains roundabout are anomalous volcanic intrusions in the regional geology, producing a legacy of hard rock and semi-precious stones – including jade – that attract climbers and rock hounds. There's not much else to do here; you can watch semi-precious stones being worked at several places, or check out **Hat Creek Ranch** (mid-May to Sept daily 10am–6pm; $5), a collection of original buildings including a log stopping house, the last remaining of its type, and a reconstruction of a Shuswap village. It's located ten minutes north of Cache Creek by the junction of hwys 97 and 99 (the original Cariboo Wagon Rd). For more local insights visit the **infocentre** on the northwest side of town at 1340 Hwy 97 near the main road junction (summer daily 9am–6pm; ☎604/457-5306). If you're stranded, try one of half-a-dozen **motels**, the most interesting of which is the bizarrely built *Castle Inn*, 1153 E Trans-Canada (☎604/457-9547 or 1-800/457-9547; ②). Less eccentric are the *Bonaparte* on Hwy 97 North (☎604/457-9693 or 1-888/922-1333; ③), with large heated pool, and the central *Sage Hills Motel*, 1390 Hwy 97 N (☎ & fax 604/457-6451; ②), also with pool. The nearest **campsite**, complete with laundry, hot showers and heated outdoor pool, is the *Brookside* (☎604/457-6633; $16–20; April–Oct), located 1km east of town on the main highway.

Kamloops

Almost any trip in southern British Columbia brings you sooner or later to **KAMLOOPS**, a town which has been a transport centre from time immemorial – its name derives from the Shuswap word for "meeting of the rivers" – and which today marks the meeting point of the Trans-Canada and Yellowhead (South) highways, the region's principal transcontinental roads, as well as the junction of the Canadian Pacific and Canadian National railways. The largest interior town in southern British Columbia (pop. 82,000), it's fairly unobjectionable, except when the wind blows from the uptown sawmills, bringing in a putrid smell that hangs heavy in the air. If you're on public transport, there's no particular need to spend any time here; if you're camping or driving, however, it makes a convenient provisions stop, especially for those heading north on Hwy 5 or south on the Coquihalla Hwy, neither of which has much in the way of facilities.

Kamloops is determinedly functional and not a place to spend a happy day wandering, but its downtown does have a spanking new **Art Gallery**, the largest in BC's interior – not that it has much competition. Located in the heart of downtown at 465 Victoria St at 5th (May–Sept Mon, Fri & Sat 10am–5pm, Tues–Thurs 10am–9pm, Sun noon–4pm; Oct–April Mon–Wed, Fri & Sat 10am–5pm, Thurs 10am–9pm, Sun 10am–4pm; $5), the gallery showcases Canadian artists, in particular those from the West and British Columbia.

The **Kamloops Museum** on Seymour Street (Tues–Sat 9.30am–4.30pm; free) is one of the more interesting provincial offerings, with illuminating archive photographs (especially the one of the railway running down the centre of the main street), artefacts, period set-pieces and a particularly well-done section on the Shuswap. The stuffed-animal display, without which no BC museum is complete, has a fascinating little piece on the life cycle of the tick presented without any noticeable irony. For a more complete picture of local aboriginal history and traditions, call at the **Secwepemec Museum & Heritage Park**, just over the bridge on Hwy 5 (summer daily 9am–5pm; winter Mon–Fri 8.30am–4.30pm; $5) or attend the **Kamloops Pow Wow**, held every third weekend in August ($7 a day). If you're travelling with kids and driving, the nonprofit **Wildlife Park**, 15km east of town on the Trans-Canada Hwy (daily 8am–4.30pm; $6, children $3.75), may be worth a stop for its range of local and more exotic animals.

Perhaps the most interesting thing about Kamloops is its surroundings, dominated by strange, bare-earthed brown hills that locals like to say represent the northernmost point of the Mojave Desert. There's no doubting the almost surreal touches of near-desert, which are particularly marked in the bare rock and clay outcrops above the bilious waters of the Thompson River and in the bleached scrub and failing stands of pines that spot the barren hills. Most scenic diversions lie a short drive out of town, and the infocentre has full details of every last local bolt hole, with a special bias towards the two hundred or so trout-stuffed lakes that dot the hinterland. The nearest and most popular on a hot summer's day is **Paul Lake Provincial Park**, 17km northeast of town on a good paved road, with swimming and a provincial campsite ($12).

The telephone code for British Columbia outside of the Vancouver area is ☎250.

Practicalities

The **infocentre**, 1290 W Trans-Canada Hwy (mid-May to mid-Oct Mon–Fri 8am–6pm, Sat & Sun 9am–6pm; mid-Oct to mid-May Mon–Fri 9am–5pm; ☎374-3377 or 1-800/662-1994, *www.venturekamloops.com*) is a good 6km west of downtown, close to the Aberdeen Mall. They have full accommodation and recreational details for the town and much of the province, and a particularly useful book of local trails self-published by a local hiker ($13.90). The **Greyhound terminal** (☎374-1212), on Notre Dame Avenue off Hwy 1, across from the infocentre, is a crucial interchange for buses to all parts of the province; to head into town, jump on the #3 bus that leaves from outside the station. Kamloops is also served by three weekly **trains** in each direction from Edmonton, via Jasper (Mon, Thurs & Sat) and Vancouver (Mon, Wed & Sat). The VIA Rail office is at 95 3rd Ave, behind Landsdowne Street, but is open only on days trains are running (☎372-5858 or 1-800/561-8630).

Kamloops's huge volume of accommodation is aimed fair and square at the motorist and consists of thick clusters of **motels**, most of which blanket the town's eastern margins on Hwy 1 or out on Columbia Street West. The *Thrift Inn*, 2459 Trans-Canada (☎374-2488 or 1-800/661-7769; ①), is probably the cheapest of all, but it's about the last building on eastbound Hwy 1 out of town. You pay a slight premium for central beds, most of which are on Columbia Street: here the *Casa Marquis Motor Inn*, 530 Columbia St (☎372-7761 or 1-800/533-9233; ②) is reasonably priced, or you can try the reliable and recently renovated *Sandman*, 550 Columbia St (☎374-1218 or 1-800/726-3626, *www.sandman.ca*; ②), part of a chain. If you want top-of-the-range comfort after a long journey, make for the central *Stockmen's Hotel & Casino*, 540 Victoria St (☎372-2281 or 1-800/663-2837; ④). A **youth hostel**, *Kamloops Old Courthouse Hostel,* is housed downtown in a restored courthouse building at 7 W Seymour St (☎828-7991; ①): it has dorm beds and a few private rooms. There's also a clutch of motels around the bus terminal, in case you arrive late and have no need to drop into town. The nearest **campsite** is the *Silver Sage Tent and Trailer Park* at 771 Athabasca St E (☎828-2077; $15–18), but if you've got a car aim for the far more scenic facilities at Paul Lake Provincial Park (see above). Snack **food** is cheap and served in generous portions at the popular *Swiss Pastries & Café*, 359 Victoria St, which really is run by Swiss people and does good muesli, cappuccino, sticky buns and excellent bread. The *Grassroots Tea House* (summer only), in Riverside Park at 262 Lorne St, is a nice spot for lunch or dinner washed down with ginseng tea – a local product. If you're splashing out on a proper meal, on the other hand, the best restaurant is the upmarket *Deja Vu*, 172 Battle St (☎374-3227; closed Sun & Mon), where Thai meets France and Japan, though locals also rate the much cheaper, but less exotic, *Ric's Grill* at 227 Victoria St. *Kelly O'Bryans*, 244 Victoria St, is good for a pint, and for supermarket stock-ups there's a Safeway on the corner of Seymour and 5th Avenue.

Highway 5: Clearwater and Wells Gray Park

Northbound **Hwy 5** (here known as the Yellowhead S Hwy) heads upstream along the broad North Thompson River as it courses through high hills and rolling pasture between Kamloops and **Clearwater** and beyond. It is one of the most scenically astounding road routes in this part of the world, and follows the river as it carves through the Monashee Mountains from its source near **Valemount**, to the final meeting with the main Yellowhead Hwy (Hwy 16) at Tête Jaune Cache, a total distance of 338km. The entire latter half of the journey is spent sidestepping the immense **Wells Gray Provincial Park**, one of the finest protected areas in British Columbia.

Greyhound **buses** cover the route on their run between Kamloops and Prince George via Clearwater (3 daily in each direction), as do VIA **trains**, which connect Kamloops with Jasper via Clearwater (3 weekly). To get into Wells Gray without your own transport, however, you'd have to hitch from Clearwater up the 63-kilometre main access road – a feasible proposition at the height of summer, but highly unlikely at any other time. This access road will be enough for most casual visitors to get a taste of the park – you could run up and down it and see the sights in a day – but note that there are some less-travelled gravel roads into other sectors of the park from **Blue River**, 112km north of Clearwater on Hwy 5, and from the village of **100 Mile House**, on Hwy 97 west of the park.

Clearwater

CLEARWATER is a dispersed farming community that's invisible from Hwy 5, and unless you need a place to stay or arrive by rail there's no need to drop down to it at all. Everything you need apart from the odd shop is on or just off the junction between the highway and the slip road to the village, including the **bus stop** and the excellent **info-centre** (daily: June–Aug 8am–8pm; Sept–May 9am–5pm; ☎674-2646), a model of the genre that has immensely useful information on all aspects of Wells Gray Provincial Park. If you're planning on staying locally or doing any walking or canoeing, take time to flick through its reference books devoted to accommodation, trails and paddling routes.

Camping aside, Clearwater is the most realistic place **to stay** along Hwy 5 if you're planning on doing Wells Gray. By far the best prospect, thanks to its lovely views over Dutch Lake, is the *Jasper Way Inn Motel*, 57 E Old North Thompson Hwy, two blocks off Hwy 5 (☎674-3345; ③), 1km off the highway to the west and well signed from the infocentre; some rooms have cooking facilities. If it's full, try the big *Wells Gray Inn* (☎674-2214 or 1-800/567-4088; ①), close by on the main road; the doubles here are more comfortable, but lack the view. The latter is virtually the only place to **eat** locally. As the park becomes more popular, so more places are opening on its fringes: the big new *Clearwater Adventures Resort*, 373 Clearwater Valley Rd (☎674-3909) on the corner of the Yellowhead Hwy and the Wells Grey Park Road, is one such, a combination of cabins (②), chalets (④) and camping and RV sites ($18–32; March–Oct). If you've come for wilderness you probably won't want to be in such a place, but it does also have three restaurants, endless facilities and a whole host of equipment-rental possibilities and organized tours.

Three other **campsites** lie more or less within walking distance of the infocentre: the best – again, on the lake – is the *Dutch Lake Resort and RV Park* (☎674-3351 or 1-888/884-4424; cabins ③, pitch $18; mid-April to mid-Oct;). Don't forget, though, that there are four simple provincial park campsites within the park (see p.814). If you want to be slightly away from Clearwater, stop at the *Birch Island Campground* (☎674-3991 or 674-4054; $14–19; mid-April to Oct), a treed seventy-acre area with tent sites and B&B units (②) overlooking the Thompson River 8km north of the village on Hwy 5.

Blue River and Valemount

Clearwater is by far the best base locally, but you may find the **accommodation** options at Blue River and Valemount (a whopping 225km north of Clearwater on Hwy 5) useful. **BLUE RIVER**, a slip of a place 100km north of Clearwater, has far fewer possibilities, with its cheapest option being the *Blue River Motel* with one- and two-bedroom units two blocks off the highway on Spruce Street (☎673-8387; ②). For a few dollars more you could try the *Mountain View Motel* on 3rd Avenue and Spruce Street (☎673-8366; ②) and, top-of-the-pile, but on the highway, is the fine *Venture Lodge* (☎673-8384; ②). The only **campsites** for miles are the *Eleanor Lake Campsite and Trailer Park* on Herb Bilton Way (☎673-8316; $12–20; May to mid-Oct), with free showers, store and canoe rentals, and the *Blue River Campground and RV Park*, Myrtle Lake Road and Cedar Street (☎673-8203; $12–18; May to mid-Oct), with showers, canoe rentals and a variety of fishing, canoeing and horse-riding tours.

In **VALEMOUNT** there's a seasonal infocentre at 98 Gorse St on Hwy 5 (mid-May to mid-Sept daily 9am–5pm; ☎566-4846) and around ten motels and two campsites. One block off the highway on 5th Avenue are a bunch of **motels**, of which the cheapest is the *Yellowhead* (☎566-4411; May–Oct; ③); the rest have more facilities, but all are pretty soulless, including the *Best Western Canadian Lodge* (☎566-8222; ⑤) with a jacuzzi and kitchenettes; the *Canoe Moutain Lodge* (☎566-9171; ⑤) with duvets on the beds; and the *Chalet Continental*, 1450 5th Ave (☎566-9787; ④) with an indoor pool. On Loseth Road, 1km north of Valemount, is the modern *Irvins Park and Campground* (☎566-4781; $23–32; April–Oct) with activities including horse riding and ATV tours. Another campsite, the wooded *Valemount Campground*, is off the highway in the north side of town (☎566-4141; $19; mid-April to mid-Oct).

Wells Gray Provincial Park

WELLS GRAY PROVINCIAL PARK is the equal of any of the Rocky Mountain national parks to the east: if anything, its wilderness is probably more extreme – so untamed, in fact, that many of its peaks remain unclimbed and unnamed. Wildlife sightings are common – especially if you tramp some of the wilder trails, where encounters with black bears, grizzlies and mountain goats are a possibility, not to mention glimpses of smaller mammals such as timber wolves, coyotes, weasels, martens, minks, wolverines and beavers. Seeing the park is straightforward, at least if you have transport and only want a superficial – but still rewarding – glimpse of the interior. A 63-kilometre **access road** strikes into the park from Hwy 5 at Clearwater, culminating in Clearwater Lake – there's no further wheeled access. Various trails long and short, together with campsites, viewpoints and easily seen waterfalls, are dotted along the road, allowing you to see just about all the obvious scenic landmarks with a car in a day.

With some 250km of maintained trails and dozens of other lesser routes, the park is magnificent for **hiking**. Short walks and day-hikes from the park's access road are described below, but serious backpackers can easily spend a week or more tramping the backcountry hikes, most of which are in the southern third of the park and link together for days of wild hiking and wilderness camping. The longest one-way trail links Clearwater Lake to Kostal Lake trail (26km) and begins on the main Wells Gray park road, just across from *Clearwater Lake* campsite. Steep switchbacks, muddy conditions, thick brush and large deadfall as well as tramping across sharp lava flow and loose rock make the going slow on many of the park's remoter trails. For all the backcountry hikes you need a map and a compass, your own food and water supplies and plenty of insect repellent. Make sure you pick up a free *BC Parks* map-pamphlet at the Clearwater infocentre, and if you're thinking of doing any backcountry exploration you'll want to invest in their more detailed maps and guides. **Cross-country skiing** is also possible, but there are only a few groomed routes in the park: again, details are available at the infocentre.

Another of the park's big attractions is **canoeing** on Clearwater and Azure lakes, the former at the end of the access road, which can be linked with a short portage to make a 100-plus-kilometre dream trip for paddlers; you can rent canoes for long- or short-haul trips from *Clearwater Lake Tours* situated on the south end of Clearwater Lake, 71km from Hwy 5 in Clearwater (☎674-2121 or 674-2971 off-season/evening). **White-water rafting** down the Clearwater River is also extremely popular and recommended, and half-day to full-week tours can be arranged through the Clearwater infocentre or at the two accommodation options below. Several local operators run shorter commercial boat trips around Clearwater Lake, as well as full-scale **tours** featuring horse riding, camping, trekking, fishing, boating and even float-plane excursions around the park – the Clearwater infocentre has the inside story on all of these.

The only indoor **accommodation** in or near the park is in the log cabins at *Wells Gray Ranch* (☎674-2792; ④; mid-May to mid-Oct) just before the park entrance (26km from Hwy 5) on Wells Gray Park Road, or the slightly larger, but equally lonely *Helmcken Falls Lodge* (☎674-3657; ⑤; Jan–March & May–Oct) at the entrance itself (35km from Hwy 5), which offers similar facilities at slightly higher prices. You'll be lucky to find vacancies in summer, so book months in advance if coming in June, July or August. Both of these also have tent pitches, but there's far better roadside **camping** along the park access road at the park's four provincial campsites: *Spahats Campground* a small, forested site only 10km from Hwy 5 at Clearwater Lake on Clearwater Valley Road; the *Dawson Falls*, 5km from the park entrance; *Falls Creek*, 30km from the entrance; and *Clearwater Lake*, 31km from the entrance (all $12; May–Sept). All fill up promptly on summer weekends, but can be reserved through Discover Camping (see p.691). Many backpackers' campsites ($5) dot the shores of the park's major lakes and with no services offered it's not necessary to book; Clearwater Lake Tours operates a water-taxi service, which can drop you off at any site on Clearwater Lake and pick you up at a prearranged time.

Sights and hikes along the access road

Even if you're not geared up for the backcountry, the access road to the park from Clearwater opens up a medley of waterfalls, walks and viewpoints that make a detour extremely worthwhile. The road's paved for the first 30km to the park boundary, but the remaining 33km to Clearwater Lake is gravel. Most of the sights are well signed.

About 8km north of Clearwater, a short walk from the car park at **Spahats Campground** brings you to the 61-metre Spahats Falls, the first of several mighty cascades along this route. You can watch the waters crashing down through layers of pinky-red volcanic rock from a pair of observation platforms, which also provide an impressive and unexpected view of the Clearwater Valley way down below. A few hundred metres further up the road, a fifteen-kilometre gravel lane peels off into the **Wells Gray Recreation Area**; a single trail from the end of the road strikes off into alpine meadows, feeding four shorter day-trails into an area particularly known for its bears. This is also the site of a juvenile correction centre, which must rank as possibly the most beautiful but godforsaken spot to do time in North America. About 15km further up the main access road, a second four-wheel-drive track branches east to reach the trailhead for **Battle Mountain** (19km), with the option of several shorter hikes like the Mount Philip Trail (5km) en route.

Green Mountain Lookout, reached by a rough, winding road to the left just after the park entrance, offers one of the most enormous roadside panoramas in British Columbia, and it's a sight that will help you grasp the sheer extent of the Canadian wilderness: as far as you can see, there's nothing but an almighty emptiness of primal forest and mountains. Various landscape features are picked out on plaques, and the immediate area is a likely place to spot moose.

The next essential stop is **Dawson Falls**, a broad, powerful cascade (91m wide and 18m high) just five-minutes' walk from the road – signed "Viewpoint". Beyond, the road crosses an ugly iron bridge and shortly after meets the start of the **Murtle River Trail** (14km one-way), a particularly good walk if you want more spectacular waterfalls.

Immediately afterwards, a dead-end side road is signed to **Helmcken Falls**, the park's undisputed highlight. The site is heavily visited, and it's not unknown for wedding parties to come up here to get dramatic matrimonial photos backed by the luminous arc of water plunging into a black, carved bowl fringed with vivid carpets of lichen and splintered trees, the whole ensemble framed by huge plumes of spray wafting up on all sides. At 137m, the falls are two and a half times the height of Niagara – or, in the infoboard's incongruous comparison, approximately the same height as the Vancouver skyline.

Continuing north, the park access road rejoins the jade-green Clearwater River, passing tastefully engineered picnic spots and short trails that wend down to the bank for close-up views of one of the province's best white-water-rafting stretches. The last sight before the end of the road is **Ray Farm**, home to John Bunyon Ray, who in 1912 was the first man to homestead this area. Though it's not much to look at, the farm offers a sobering insight into the pioneer mentality – Ray's struggle to scrape a living and raise a family in this harsh environment beggars belief – and the picturesquely ruined, wooden shacks are scattered in a lovely, lush clearing. The park road ends at **Clearwater Lake**, where there are a couple of boat launches, a provincial campsite and a series of short trails clearly marked from the trailhead.

Salmon Arm and the Shuswap

Given the variety of routes across southern BC there's no knowing when you might find yourself in **SALMON ARM**, 108km east of Kamloops, though that's not something that need concern you in planning an itinerary, because the town – the largest of the somewhat bland resorts spread along **Shuswap Lake**'s 1000km of navigable waterways – has relatively little to recommend it. This said, if you fancy fishing, swimming, water-skiing or houseboating, you could do worse than relax for a couple of days in one of the 32 provincial parks or small lakeside villages – Chase, Sorrento, Eagle Bay and others. Depending on the season, you can also watch one of Canada's most famous **salmon-spawning runs**, or indulge in a little **bird-watching**, for the bay at Salmon Arm is one of the world's last nesting areas of the western grebe. As ever in Canada, Salmon Arm and its satellites are much smaller places than their bold label on most maps would suggest. Many of the settlements are oddly dispersed and a touch scrappy and haphazard in appearance, but if you're driving they make a natural break along one of the Trans-Canada's more monotonous stretches. To get anything out of Salmon Arm proper, you'll have to pull off the main drag, which is formed by the Trans-Canada itself, and head to the village a little to the south.

The lake and the surrounding region take their name from the Shuswap natives, the northernmost of the great Salishan family and the largest single tribe in British Columbia. The name of the town harks back to a time when it was possible to spear salmon straight from the lake, and fish were so plentiful that they were shovelled onto the land as fertilizer. Shuswap Lake still provides an important sanctuary for hatched salmon fry before they make their long journey down the Thompson and Fraser rivers to the sea – the abundance of such lakes, together with ideal water temperatures, free-flowing, well-oxygenated and silt-free tributaries, and plenty of sand and gravel beds for egg-laying, make the Fraser River system the continent's greatest salmon habitat.

SPAWN TO BE WILD

At times it seems impossible to escape the **salmon** in British Columbia. Whether it's on restaurant menus, in rivers or in the photographs of grinning fishermen clutching their catch, the fish is almost as much a symbol of the region as its mountains and forests. Five different species inhabit the rivers and lakes of western Canada: **pink, coho, chum, chinook** and, most important of all, the **sockeye**.

Though they start and finish their lives in fresh water, salmon spend about four years in the open sea between times. Mature fish make their epic migrations from the Pacific to **spawn** in the BC rivers of their birth between June and November, swimming about 30km a day; some chinook travel more than 1400km up the Fraser beyond Prince George, which means almost fifty-days' continuous swimming upstream. Though the female lays as many as four thousand eggs, only about six percent of the offspring survive: on the Adams River near Salmon Arm, for example, it's estimated that of four billion sockeye eggs laid in a typical year, one billion survive to become fry (hatched fish about 2cm long), of which 75 percent are eaten by predators before becoming smolts (year-old fish), and only five percent of these then make it to the ocean. In effect each pair of spawners produces about ten mature fish: of these, eight are caught by commercial fisheries and only two return to reproduce.

These are returns that clearly put the salmon's survival and British Columbia's lucrative **fishing industry** on a knife edge. Caught, canned and exported, salmon accounts for two-thirds of BC's $1 billion annual revenues from fishing – the largest of any Canadian province, and its third-ranking money-earner after forestry and energy products. Commercial fishing suffered its first setback in British Columbia as long ago as 1913, when large rock slides at Hell's Gate in the Fraser Canyon disrupted many of the spawning runs. Although fish runs were painstakingly constructed to bypass the slides, new pressures have subsequently been heaped on the salmon by mining, logging, urban and agricultural development, and the dumping of industrial and municipal wastes. An increasingly important line of defence, **hatcheries** have been built on rivers on the mainland and Vancouver Island to increase the percentage of eggs and fry that successfully mature. Meanwhile, overfishing, as the above figures suggest, remains a major concern, particularly as the **drift nets** of Japanese and Korean fleets, designed for neon squid, have over the past decade taken numerous non-target species, including BC and Yukon salmon. Under intense lobbying from Canada and the US, both nations agreed to a moratorium on large-scale drift nets as from June 1992. Since then, various measures have been implemented by the Canadian and BC governments including the closure of the Fraser and Thompson rivers to all salmon fishing in 1999. However, Greenpeace estimates that 764 stocks of salmon in BC and Yukon are either extinct or at risk of becoming extinct.

Therefore, one of the few reasons you might make a special journey to the Salmon Arm area is to watch the huge migrations of **spawning salmon** that take place around October. Up to two million fish brave the run from the Pacific up to their birthplace in the Adams River – one of the most famous spawning grounds in the province. During the spawning time, humans also make there way here in droves; around 250,000 visitors come during the peak week alone. This short stretch of river is protected by **Roderick Haig-Brown Provincial Park**, reached from Salmon Arm by driving 46km west on the Trans-Canada to Squilax and then 5km north on a side road where the park is signposted. If you're thinking of dangling a line, pick up the *Fishing in Shuswap* leaflet from the infocentre in Salmon Arm, and don't forget to get a licence at the same time.

Practicalities

Greyhound **buses** serve Salmon Arm from Vancouver (7 daily), Calgary (4 daily) and Kelowna, Vernon and Penticton (4 daily). The bus terminal is at the West Village Mall on Hwy 1, and the **infocentre** (Mon–Sat 8.30am–5.30pm; ☎832-2230 or 1-877/725-6667) is at 751 Marine Park Drive. You might also contact Tourism Shuswap (☎832-5200 or 1-800/661-4800, *www.shuswap.bc.ca*) for information on the whole region.

One of the most convenient of Salmon Arm's many **motels** is the *Village Motel* (☎832-3955; ②) at 620 Trans-Canada Hwy. More upmarket, and still close to the highway, is the *Best Western Villager West Motor Inn*, 61 10th St SW (☎832-9793 or 1-800/528-1234; ④). There is also a HI-affiliated **youth hostel**, the *Squilax General Store and Caboose Hostel* (☎675-2977; ①) in Chase on the waterfront just off the Trans-Canada. Of several **campsites**, the obvious first choice is the *Salmon Arm KOA*, 3km east of town in a big wooded site, whose excellent facilities include a heated swimming pool (☎832-6489 or 1-800/562-9389; $26; May–Oct). For beds or tent space, the *Salmon River Motel and Campground*, 1km west of downtown at 910 40th St SW (☎832-3065; motel ②, campsite $15.50–19.50), is also good.

For a decidedly alternative form of accommodation, head east along the Trans-Canada to **SICAMOUS**, a pleasant but very busy waterfront village which, though crammed with motels and campsites, is better known for its many upmarket **houseboats**. A few rent by the night, but most tend to be let weekly by about half-a-dozen local agencies scattered around the village. Agencies you might try include *Bluewater Houseboats* (☎836-2255 or 1-800/663-4024; $1485–5295 a week; April–Sept), *Sicamous Creek Marina* (☎836-4611; $1015–2910 a week; April–Oct) or the *Twin Anchors Houseboat Association* (☎836-2450; $745–4495 a week; April–Oct). The village is also the place to pick up a boat for a sightseeing **cruise** on the lake, one of the best ways of enjoying a scenic slice of the region: contact the Shuswap Ferry Lake Service for details of daily summer sailings (☎836-2200). For **information** there's an infocentre at 110 Finlayson St by the Government Dock (Mon–Fri 10am–5pm; June Sat also 10am–3pm; July daily 9am–6pm; ☎836-3313). To **eat** locally, head for the *Mara Lake Inn* (☎836-2126) on the lakeshore 3km south of the village and the Trans-Canada on Hwy 97 which has a gourmet restaurant and newly renovated motel units that look out over Mara Lake (③) and cabins with kitchenettes (②). If you're looking to have a **drink** try *Brothers Pub*, 420 Main St.

Highway 97 to the Okanagan

Passing through landscapes of Eden-like clarity and beauty, **Hwy 97** is a far better entrance to (or exit from) the Okanagan than the dreary road to Salmon Arm (see p.815). The grass-green meadows, grazing cattle and low wooded hills here are the sort of scenery pioneers must have dreamed of: most of the little hamlets en route make charming spots to stay, and if you have time and transport any number of minor roads lead off to small lakes, each with modest recreational facilities.

The highway peels off the Trans-Canada 26km east of Kamloops, its first good stops being **MONTE LAKE**, served by the excellent *Heritage Campsite and RV Park* (☎375-2434; $13.50–16.50; April–Nov) and the equally well-tended and unspoilt public campsite at **Monte Lake Provincial Park**. Both places make good spots to overnight. **WESTWOLD**, 5km beyond, is a dispersed ranching community of clean, old wooden houses and large pastures that present a picture of almost idyllic rural life. **FALKLAND**, 13km beyond, is an unassuming place whose **motel** blends easily into its rustic village atmosphere. The central *Big Highland Motel* (☎379-2249; ①) is on Adelphi Street, but you might also drop into the infant infocentre (summer only) for lists of local B&B. There are also a couple of well-signposted, quiet **campsites** ($12–15). Country lanes lead north and east from here to **Bolean Lake** (10km) at 1437m, served by a lodge and campsite: *Bolean Lake Lodge*, Bolean Lake Road (☎558-9008; rooms ①, tents $14; May–Oct); to **Pillar Lake** (13km) and the *Pillar Lake Resort* (☎379-2623; ①;

May–Oct), which provides cabins and campsite from $12; and to **Pinaus Lake** (10km) and its adjacent cabins and campsite, *Pinaus Lake Camp* (☎542-0624; cabins ②, sites $14; April–Oct).

The O'Keefe Ranch

Twelve kilometres short of Vernon, near the junction with the west-side Okanagan Lake road, stands the **Historic O'Keefe Ranch**, a collection of early pioneer buildings and a tidy little museum that's well worth a half-hour's pause (daily: May, June & Sept to mid-Oct 9am–5pm; July & Aug 9am–7pm; $6). In addition to a proficient summary of nineteenth-century frontier life, the museum contains an interesting section on the role of aboriginal peoples in the two world wars. Some 25 percent of eligible men immediately volunteered for service – a tour of duty that did little to resolve their national dilemma, which the museum sums up pithily with the observation that they belong to that "unhappy group who lost the old but are unable to obtain the new". Outside, a complete period street includes a detailed general store where you can buy oddments from staff in old-time dress – an excessively cute conceit, but one that fails to take the edge off the place's surprisingly successful evocation of an era. You feel the past most strongly in the church and graveyard, where the lovely building and its poignant handful of graves – three generations of O'Keefes, who first settled here in 1867 – capture the isolation and close-knit hardship of pioneer life.

The Okanagan

The vine- and orchard-covered hills and warm-water lakes of the **Okanagan**, located in south-central British Columbia, are in marked contrast to the rugged beauty of the region's more mountainous interior, and have made the region not only one of Canada's most favoured fruit-growing areas but also one of its most popular summer-holiday destinations. However, unless you want (occasionally) rowdy beach life or specifically enjoy mixing with families on their annual holiday, you'll probably want to ignore the area altogether in summer, despite its high word-of-mouth reputation. Three main centres – **Vernon**, **Kelowna** and **Penticton**, ranging from north to south along the 100-kilometre long **Okanagan Lake** – together contain the lion's share of the province's interior population, and all lay on an array of accommodation and mostly tacky attractions for the summer hordes. As ever in BC, however, things improve immeasurably if you can slip away from the towns and head for the hills or quieter stretches of lakeshore.

On the plus side, the almost year-round Californian lushness that makes this "the land of beaches, peaches, sunshine and wine" means that, in the relative peace of **off-season**, you can begin to experience the region's considerable charms: fruit trees in blossom, quiet lakeside villages and free wine tastings in local vineyards. Plus, you can also expect room rates to be up to fifty percent less in the off-season. Kelowna is the biggest and probably best overall base at any time of the year, but local **buses** link all the towns and Greyhounds ply Hwy 97 on their way between Osoyoos and Kamloops or Salmon Arm.

Vernon

The beach scene is less frenetic in **VERNON** than elsewhere in the Okanagan. Located at the junction of Hwys 6 and 97 near the northern edge of Okanagan Lake, the town attracts fewer of the bucket-and-spade brigade, though the emphasis on fruit and the great outdoors is as strong as ever, and the main highway through town is bumper-to-bumper with motels, fast-food joints and ever-more garish neon signs. On the whole it's easier to find a place to stay here than in Kelowna (see overleaf) – but there are also fewer reasons for wanting to do so.

Downtown Vernon centres on 32nd Avenue (Hwy 97) and leaves a far more gracious impression than the town's outskirts by virtue of its elegant tree-lined streets and five hundred listed buildings. The locals are an amenable and cosmopolitan bunch made up of Britons, Germans, Chinese and Salish natives, plus an abnormally large number of Jehovah's Witnesses, whose churches seem to have a virtual monopoly on religious observance in the town. The local **museum**, by the clock tower at 3009 32nd Ave, does the usual job on local history (Mon–Sat 10am–5pm; closed Mon in winter; donation). At the southern entrance to town, **Polson Park** makes a green sanctuary from the crowds, but for beaches you should head 8km south of Vernon to **Kalamalka Provincial Park**, which features a stunning blue-green lake. **Kin Beach** on Okanagan Lake west on Okanagan Landing Road is another good spot. Both have adjoining campsites.

Other outdoor recreation (but not camping) is on hand at **Silver Star Recreation Area**, a steep 22-kilometre drive to the northeast on 48th Avenue off Hwy 97, where in summer a **ski lift** (late June to mid-Oct daily 10am–5pm; $7.50) trundles to the top of Silver Star Mountain (1915m) for wide views and meadow-walking opportunities; the most-used trail wends from the summit back to the base area. This is also a popular mountain-biking route – Monashee Adventure Tours (☎1-888/762-9253) rents out mountain bikes from the hostel (see below) and offers guided tours all over the Okanagan. If you want an eagle's-eye view of the area call Paraglide Canada (☎308-0387, *www.paraglidecanada.com*; $100 per person) for a tandem ride from the top of the mountains.

Practicalities

Vernon's **infocentre** is at 701 Hwy 97 N (June–Aug daily 8am–6pm; Sept–May Mon–Fri 9am–5pm; ☎542-1415 or 1-800/665-0795 for reservations only), along with a seasonal office south of town on the main highway. The **Greyhound station** is on the corner of 30th Street and 31st Avenue (☎545-0527) with connections to Calgary and Vancouver.

A new **hostel**, *Lodged Inn*, 3201 Pleasant Valley Rd (☎549-3742 or 1-888/737-9427, *www.windsrivers.bc.ca*; ①), has dormitory accommodation in a beautiful old house – from the bus station, head to 32nd Avenue, take a right and then the fourth left onto Pleasant Valley Drive. There are also plenty of **motels** in town: a sound if bland choice is the *Sandman Inn* at 4201 32nd St (☎542-4325 or 1-800/726-3626, *www.sandman.ca*; ③). The *Polson Park Motel* (☎549-2231 or 1-800/480-2231; ②), opposite the eponymous park on 24th Avenue, is one of the cheapest options. The *Schell Motel*, 2810 35th St (☎545-1351 or 1-888/772-4355; ②), tempts clients with a pool and sauna. **Campsites** near town all get busy during the high season, and you may have to trek along the lakeshore for some way to strike lucky; try *Dutch's Tent and Trailer Court* (☎545-1023; $17–21; year-round) at 15408 Kalamalka Rd, 3km south of Vernon near Kalamalka Beach. Much more rural is *Ellison Provincial Park*, 16km off to the southwest on Okanagan Lake (reservations possible, see p.691; $15; March–Nov). To the north, 5km south of the O'Keefe Ranch (see opposite), is *Newport Beach Recreational Park* (☎542-7131; $16; mid-May to mid-Oct), situated at Westside Road on Okanagan Lake.

In the **food** department, there are plenty of choices, especially amongst the many cafés and sandwich places. Downtown, try the *Bean to Cup* on 39th Avenue and 27th Street for soups, sandwiches and Internet access, or *The Italian Kitchen*, 3006 30th Ave, serving up food true to its name. At 3127 30th Ave, *KT's* has saltwater aquariums alongside its tables and serves pizza, pasta, sandwiches and burgers. *Sir Winston's*, 2705 32nd St, is the downtown **pub** of choice.

THE LEGEND OF OKANAGAN LAKE

When travelling through the Okanagan Valley, you'll find it hard to avoid **Ogopogo**, the famed lake monster of Okanagan Lake, whose smiling dragon-like face appears on all manner of postcards. billboards and bumper stickers. Its name comes from a 1920s music-hall song – "his mother was an earwig, his father a whale; a little bit of head and hardly any tail; and Ogopogo was his name" – but the myth is much older. The aboriginal Salish peoples believed in such a creature, and referred to it as **N'ha-a-itk**, meaning "Lake Demon" or "Devil of the Lake". Legend has it that the Salish people warned early white settlers of the lake monster, who apparently was a demon-possessed man punished by the gods for murdering a tribal brother. To appease him, the Salish would sacrifice animals whenever crossing near **Rattlesnake Island**, around which the monster supposedly lurked. The early white settlers feared the reptile as well, leaving offerings and even setting up armed patrols along the shores in case of an attack. Nowadays, holidaymakers would be thrilled to spot BC's version of the Loch Ness monster, demon or not, and numerous sightings are claimed every year.

Kelowna

If you're continuing south from Vernon, be sure to take the minor road, known as Okanagan Lake Road, on the western shore of Okanagan Lake – a quiet detour that offers something of the beauty for which the area is frequently praised, but which can be somewhat obscured by the commercialism of towns to the south. From the road, weaving through woods and small bays, the lake looks enchanting. The shore is often steep and there are few places to get down to the water – though at a push you might squeeze a tent between the trees for some unofficial camping.

If you want a summer suntan and cheek-by-jowl nightlife – neither of which you'd readily associate with the British Columbian interior – then **KELOWNA** ("grizzly bear" in the Salish dialect) – is the place to come. People had such a good time here in the summer of 1988 that the annual **Kelowna Regatta** turned into a full-blown and very un-Canadian alcohol-fuelled **riot** in which the police were forced to wade in with truncheons and tear gas.; the main event has since been cancelled in its original format (it's now strictly a family affair), but the beach and downtown bars remain as busy as ever. That this modest city should have fostered such an urban-style melee isn't all that surprising. Compared to other interior towns, Kelowna (pop. 97,000) ranks as a sprawling metropolis, and to the unsuspecting tourist its approaches come as an unpleasant surprise – particularly the appalling conglomeration of motels, garages and fast-food outlets on Hwy 97 at the north end of town.

That said, the lakefront and beaches, though heavily developed, aren't too bad, and off-season Kelowna's undeniably pretty **downtown** can make a good couple of days' respite from mountains and forests. Its attractions are increasingly well-known across BC and remarkable jumps in population have taken place over the last few years: 37,000 people, many of them retirees, have moved here since 1990, creating something of a development nightmare for local planners. Main attractions are the public beach off **City Park**, a lovely green space that fronts downtown, and the strips along Lakeshore Road south of Kelowna's famed pontoon bridge, which tend to attract a younger, trendier crowd – **Rotary Beach** here is a windsurfers' hangout, and **Boyce Gyro Park**, just north, is where the town's teenagers practice their preening. Across the bridge and 2km and 14km respectively up the lake's west bank, **Bear Creek** and **Fintry Provincial Parks** are lovely spots with great beaches and campsites, but they are also horrendously popular (reservations possible at both, see p.691).

Kelowna owes its prosperity primarily to one man, Father Pandosy, a French priest who founded a mission here in 1859 and planted a couple of apple trees two years later.

Much of Canada's **fruit** is now grown in the area – including virtually all the apricots, half the pears and plums, and a third of the country's apples. The infocentre (see below) can point you to dozens of juice, fruit, food and forestry tours, but if you feel like sampling the more hedonistic fruits of Father Pandosy's labours, consider visiting one of the local **vineyards**, all of them known for their open-handed generosity with free samples after a tour of the premises. You can choose from a variety of whites and reds as the valley's microclimates and soil types allow neighbouring vineyards to produce completely different wines. At one time most were crisp, fruity German-style white wines and dessert wines, but now successful red wines and drier whites are emerging. There's even organic champagne at **Summerhill Estate Winery**, 4870 Chute Lake Rd (☎764-8000 or 1-800/667-3538), in a beautiful spot near some hot springs, or try **Calona Wines**, Canada's second-biggest commercial winery and the Okanagan's oldest (founded 1932), just six blocks off Hwy 97 at 1125 Richter Ave (daily: May–Sept 11am–5pm, tours every 2 hours; Oct–April tour at 2pm; ☎762-3332). The infocentre can provide a full rundown of smaller, more far-flung estates. All of the wineries join together in May and late September to lay on the region's annual spring and autumn **wine festivals** (☎861-6654, *www.owfs.com*) when free wine tastings, gourmet dinners, grape stomps and vineyard picnics take place to lure the connoisseur and beginner alike. More context can be found at the **Wine Museum**, 1304 Ellis St (Mon–Sat 10am–5pm, Sun noon–5pm), which is basically a glorified shop with a few exhibits, like a 3000-year-old clay drinking horn from Iran.

Getting away from Kelowna's crowds isn't easy, but the closest you'll come to shaking them off is by climbing **Knox Mountain**, the high knoll that overlooks the city to the north, just five-minutes' drive (or 30min walk) from downtown. It offers lovely views over the lake and town, particularly at sunset, and there's a wooden observation tower to make the most of the panorama. RVs are kept out of the area by a barrier dropped at dusk, but if you take a sleeping bag up – though perhaps not a tent – you might get away with an undisturbed night.

Practicalities

The **bus terminal** is at the east end of town at 2366 Leckie Rd on the corner of Harvey (Hwy 97), and sees off two buses daily to Calgary, Banff, Cache Creek and Kamloops respectively (☎860-3835). The **infocentre** (daily: June–Aug 8am–8pm; Sept–May 8am–5pm; ☎861-1515 or 1-800/663-4345, *www.kelownachamber.org*), five blocks back from the lake at 544 Harvey, has all the information you could possibly need. To **rent a bike**, try Sports Rent at 3000 Pandosy St.

As in Penticton, there's an enormous number of motels and campsites in and around town. However, **accommodation** can still be a major headache in the height of summer unless you can get to one of the **motels** on northbound Hwy 97 early in the morning, but it's a neon- and traffic-infested area well away from downtown and the lake (prices drop the further out you go). The HI-affiliated **youth hostel**, the *SameSun International Motel-Hostel*, is at 245 Harvey St (☎763-9814 or 1-877/562-2783; ①) – from the bus station take bus #10 to Queensway. There's also an unofficial hostel downtown, the *Kelowna International Hostel*, 2343 Pandosy St (☎763-6024; ①): both hostels fill quickly in summer, in which case you may go for the *Okanagan University College*, 3180 College Way (☎762-5445; ②), who let out their campus rooms from May through August. The most affordable central downtown **hotel** is the perfectly placed and very comfortable *Willow Inn* at 235 Queensway (☎762-2122 or 1-800/268-1055; ③) – ring or book very early for summer vacancies, and don't be deterred by the adjoining bar/strip-joint, which appears to be the headquarters of the Kelowna chapter of the Hell's Angels. Another slightly more expensive option is the *Royal-Anne* at 348 Bernard Ave (☎763-2277 or 1-888/811-3400; ④). As ever, the chain hotels also come up trumps: the reasonably central *Sandman Hotel*, 2130 Harvey Ave (☎860-6409 or 1-800/726-3626, *www.sandman.ca*; ③), is a good mid-range bet. More expensive are three highly rated **B&Bs**: the *Casa Rio Lakeside*, 485 Casa Rio Drive, turn off Hwy 97 at Campbell Road (☎769-0076 or 1-800/313-1033; ⑥), which has a private sandy beach and hottub; the *Cedars*, 278 Beach Ave (☎763-1208 or 1-800/822-7100; ⑥), in a beautiful house just outside Kelowna; or the outlying *Grapevine*, 2621 Longhill Rd (☎860-5580; ③; phone for directions).

If you're **camping**, all sites are pretty expensive, and in high season some places may only accept reservations for three days or more: mosquitoes can also be a problem. If you want to stay reasonably close to the action, two campsites conveniently back onto Lakeshore Road: the *Willow Creek Family Campground*, 3316 Lakeshore Rd (☎762-6302; $18–22; year-round), which has free showers and a grassy tenting area flanking a sandy beach; and the *Hiawatha RV Park*, 3787 Lakeshore Rd, with separate tenting area, laundry, heated pool and free hot showers (☎861-4837 or 1-888/784-7275; $29–39; March–Oct). To be sure of camping space, try the *Bear Creek Provincial Park*, 9km west of town on Westside Road off Hwy 97 on the west side of the lake (showers and most facilities; $15.50; March–Nov), or the new *Fintry Provincial Park*, once a working orchard, 34km north of town with similar facilities ($12; April–Oct) – reservations are accepted for both (see box on p.691). Most of the other campsites are on the other side of the lake at Westbank, a left turn off Hwy 97 on Boucherie Road just over the pontoon bridge (but really only accessible by car) – try *West Bay Beach*, 3745 West Bay Rd (☎768-3004; $24–28; March–Oct), with its adjoining alpaca and llama farm.

Most **eating** places are crammed into the small downtown area. The variety is large, and a short walk should offer something to suit most tastes and budgets. Many travellers and young locals head for *Kelly O'Brian's* on Bernard Street, opposite the cinema, which has an "Irish" bar atmosphere and reasonable food. Despite its rather slick cocktail-lounge ambience, *Earl's Hollywood on Top*, 211 Bernard Ave at the corner of Abbott (☎763-2777), is good for ribs, seafood and steaks; go early to get a table on the upstairs patio. For pasta, *Joey Tomato's Kitchen* in the shopping mall at the junction of hwys 97 and 33 is a fun and inexpensive option. At the top of the food tree you could splurge at *De Montreuil*, 368 Bernard Ave (☎860-5508), widely considered the best restaurant in the Okanagan and serving local produce, beef from Alberta and Pacific salmon. A three-course meal costs around $35. Also excellent in the top range is the *Williams Inn*, 526 Laurence Ave (☎763-5136), with an early evening set menu of salads and soups for $12.95 available 5–6.30pm and later an à la carte menu that includes Pacific salmon, weiner schnitzel, venison, quail and sometimes caribou and bison. Dinner for two, with drinks, will set you back about $75.

Penticton

PENTICTON is a corruption of the Salish phrase *pen tak tin* – "a place to stay forever" – but this is not a sobriquet the most southerly of the Okanagan's big towns even remotely deserves. Its summer daily average of ten hours of sunshine ranks it higher than Honolulu, making tourism its biggest industry after fruit (this is "Peach City"). That, along with Penticton's proximity to Vancouver and the US, keeps prices high and ensures that the town and beaches are swarming with water-sports jocks, cross-country travellers, RV skippers and lots of happy families. Off the beaches there's some festival or other playing virtually every day of the year to keep the punters entertained, the key ones being the **Wine Festival** in May and the **Peach Festival** in August.

Most leisure pastimes in Penticton – water-oriented ones in particular – take place on or near Okanagan Lake, just ten blocks from the town centre. **Okanagan Beach** is the closest sand to downtown and is usually covered in oiled bodies for most of its one-kilometre stretch; **Skaha Beach**, 4km south of town on Skaha Lake, is a touch quieter and trendier – both close at midnight, and sleeping on them is out of the question. If the beaches don't appeal, you can take your sun from a cruise on the lake aboard the *Casabella Princess*, which departs from 45 E Lakeshore Drive (call ☎492-4090 for times and prices).

If you're determined to sightsee, the **museum** at 785 Main St has a panoply of predictable Canadiana (Mon–Fri 10am–5pm; donation) and you can take tours around the SS *Sicamous* (May–Sept daily 10am–4pm; Oct–April Mon–Fri 10am–4pm; $3), a beached **paddlesteamer** off Lakeshore Drive on the Kelowna side of town (take in the lovely rose gardens alongside the boat while you're here). Just off Main Street there's the **South Okanagan Art Gallery**, 11 Ellis St, which often carries high-quality shows, and apparently qualifies as the "world's first solar-powered art gallery" (Tues–Fri 10am–5pm, Sat & Sun 1–5pm; donation). More tempting perhaps, and an ideal part of a day's stopover, is a trip to the **Tin Whistle Brewery**, 954 W Eckhardt Ave (drop-in tours and tastings year-round), which offers three English-type ales and a celebrated Peaches and Cream beer (summer only). If your taste is for wine rather than beer, head for the **Hillside Estate Winery**, 1350 Naramata Rd (☎493-4424), **Lake Breeze Vineyard**, Sammet Road (☎496-5659), or **Casobello Wines Vineyard**, 2km south of town off Hwy 97 on Skaha Lake Road, all of which offer tours and tastings. Otherwise, Penticton's main diversions are the curse of many Canadian tourist towns – the water slides.

Practicalities

Arriving by Greyhound, you'll pull into the **bus depot** just off Main Street between Robinson and Ellis streets (☎493-4101); Penticton is a major intersection of routes, with buses bound for Vancouver (6–7 daily), Kamloops (2 daily), Nelson and points east (2 daily). The downtown area is small and easy to negotiate, particularly after a visit to the big **infocentre** at 888 Westminster Ave W (May, June & Sept Mon–Fri 9am–5pm, Sat & Sun 10am–4pm; July & Aug daily 8am–8pm; Oct–April Mon–Fri 9am–5pm, Sat & Sun 11am–4pm; ☎493-4055 or 1-800/663-5052, *www.penticton.org*) on the north side of town – it has an adjacent BC Wine Information Centre, where bottles cost the same as they do at the vineyards. There is also a smaller summer information office south of town on Hwy 97. Both infocentres concentrate on recreational pursuits, and dozens of specialist shops around town rent out equipment for every conceivable activity. For **bikes**, try Riverside Bike Rental at 75 Riverside Drive on the west side of the lakefront (daily May–Sept).

Although Penticton boasts a brimful of **accommodation**, it doesn't make finding a room in summer any easier. In high season it's best to head straight for the infocentre and ask for help, and if this fails there are so many **motels** you can easily walk from one to the next in the hope of striking lucky; most of the cheaper fall-backs line the messy southern approach to the town along Hwy 97. Three of the best and more central choices are the luxurious *Penticton Lakeside Resort & Casino*, 21 Lakeshore Drive W (☎493-8221 or 1-800/663-9400; ⑥); *Tiki Shores Condominium Beach Resort* on the lake at 914 Lakeshore Drive (☎492-8769; ④), and the big *Penticton Inn & Suites*, 333 Martin St (☎492-3600 or 1-800/665-2221; ⑤). Dropping down to mid-range places there's the *Sandman Hotel*, opposite the Convention Centre at 939 Burnaby Ave (☎493-7151 or 1-800/726-3626, *www.sandman.ca*; ③). If you're after somewhere cheap and location doesn't matter too much, try the *Plaza Motel*, 1485 Main St (☎492-8631; ③), halfway between the town's two lakes; the *Waterfront Inn*, 3688 Parkview St (☎ & fax 492-8228 or 1-800/563-6006; ③; May to mid-Oct); or the *Valley Star Motel*, 3455 Skaha Lake Rd (☎492-7205 or 1-888/309-0033; ③), a couple of blocks from Skaha Lake. The HI-affiliated **youth hostel** is at 464 Ellis St (☎492-3992; ①), in an old bunk house.

Most **campsites** have their full-up signs out continuously in summer, and you may well have trouble if you arrive without a reservation. The best and therefore busiest sites are along the lake, and the bulk of the second-rank spots are near the highway on the southern approaches. Recommended are the *South Beach Gardens*, 3815 Skaha Lake Rd (☎492-0628; $18–24; April–Sept), or *Wright's Beach Camp*, south of town on Hwy 97 on Lake Skaha (☎492-7120; $20–30; May–Sept). If you want to camp away from town, make for the *Camp-Along Tent and Trailer Park*, 6km south of the town off Hwy 97 in an apricot orchard overlooking Skaha Lake (☎497-5584 or 1-800/968-5267; $18–27).

Budget **eating** choices don't extend much beyond the fast-food joints and cafés bunched largely around Main Street: try the funky *Green Beanz Cafe*, 218 Martin St, for wraps and organic coffee, or head for the *Elite*, 340 Main St, the best overall for basic burgers, soup and salads. *Theo's* at 687 Main St (☎492-4019) is a friendly, crowded and highly rated Greek place that does big portions. For something different and more upmarket, search out *Salty's Beach House*, 988 Lakeshore Drive (☎493-5001), a restaurant that's eccentric in all departments with a South Seas setting of palm trees and fishing nets and a spicy menu of Caribbean, Thai, Indonesian and Malaysian food.

Highway 3: the border towns

Unless you're crossing the US/Canada border locally, British Columbia's slightly tawdry necklace of border towns between Hope and the Alberta border along **Hwy 3** is as good a reason as any for taking a more northerly route across the the the province. Few of the towns amount to much; if you have to break the journey, aim to do it in **Salmo** or **Castlegar**, towns on which some of the Kootenays' charm has rubbed off. Things are more interesting around **Osoyoos** and **Keremeos**, where the road enters a parched desert landscape after climbing from Hope (see p.806) through the gripping mountain scenery of the Coastal Ranges, passing en route through **Manning Provincial Park**.

If you're crossing over **the border** hereabouts, incidentally, don't be lulled by the remote customs posts into expecting an easy passage: if you don't hold a Canadian or US passport you can expect the sort of grilling you'd get at major entry points.

Manning Provincial Park

One of the few parks in the Coast and Cascade ranges, **Manning Provincial Park** parcels up a typical assortment of mountain, lake and forest scenery about 60km south of Princeton and is conveniently bisected by Hwy 3. Even if you're just passing through it's time well spent walking at least one of the short **trails** off the road, the best of which is the flower-festooned Rhododendron Flats path, located 3km east of the park's west portal. The most popular drive within the park is the fifteen-kilometre side road to **Cascade Lookout**, a viewpoint over the Similkameen Valley and its amphitheatre of mountains; a gravel road carries on another 6km from here to **Blackwall Peak**, the starting point for the **Heather Trail** (10km one-way), renowned for its swaths of summer wild flowers. Other manageable day-hikes leave the south side of the main highway, the majority accessed from a rough road to Lightning Lake just west of the park visitor centre.

The **park visitor centre**, 1km east of the resort (May–Sept daily 9am–8pm), is good for trail leaflets and has history and natural-history exhibitions. **Accommodation** at the *Manning Park Resort* (☎840-8822, *www.manningparkresort.com*; ④), on Hwy 3 almost exactly midway between Princeton and Hope (64km), is made up of cabins and chalets, but all these go quickly in summer. There are also four provincial **campsites** ($9.50–15.50; reservations possible, see p.691) on and off the highway, the best close to the road being *Hampton* and *Mule Deer*, 4km and 8km east of the visitor centre respectively.

Highway 3 from Princeton

Lacklustre low hills ripple around **PRINCETON**'s dispersed collection of drab houses. The **motels** – of which there are plenty – group around a large and grim lumber mill on the east side of town, but you're better off hanging on for Keremeos. However, if circumstances dump you in town overnight, head for the *Riverside Motel* (☎295-6232; ③) at 307 Thomas Ave, three blocks north of the town centre, with fifteen nice individual log cabins. *Global Netrider* on Bridge Street is a laid-back coffee/sandwich place with Internet access. The **bus depot** is at the west end of town by the cheap-and-cheerful eatery *Billie's*, not so far from the virtually redundant **infocentre** (daily 9am–5pm; ☎295-3103), housed in an old Canadian Pacific rail wagon at 195 Bridge St.

HEDLEY, about 20km further on, is an old gold-mining hamlet that today is little more than a single street with great scenery and a couple of motels. Try the *Colonial Inn Bed & Breakfast* (☎292-8131; ④), an historic 1930s house built by the Kelowna Exploration Gold Mining Company to wine and dine potential investors; it has just five rooms, so booking ahead is often necessary. Beyond Hedley, off the highway, lies **Bromley Rock**, a lovely picnic stop looking down on the white water of the Similkameen River. Also west of the village is the *Stemwinder Provincial Park* **campsite** ($12; April–Oct).

West of Keremeos (see below), Hwy 3 retraces the historic **Dewdney Trail**, a 468-kilometre mule track used in the 1860s to link Hope (p.806) with the Kootenay goldfields. Another of British Columbia's extremely picturesque patches of road, for much of the way it follows the ever-narrowing Similkameen Valley, backed by ranks of pines and white-topped mountains. To explore some of the backcountry off the highway, take the 21-kilometre gravel road (signed just west of Keremeos) south into the heart of **Cathedral Provincial Park**, a spectacular upland enclave with an unserviced campsite and 32km of marked trails.

Keremeos

Highway 3 meanders eventually to pretty little **KEREMEOS**, whose aboriginal name supposedly means "where the three winds meet" – a reference to the high breezes that get channelled through the hills hereabouts. The local landscape lurches suddenly into a more rural mode, thanks mainly to a climate that blesses the region with the longest growing season in the country – hence the tag, "Fruit Stand Capital of Canada". Keremeos, whose attractive situation rivals Nelson's (see p.838), spreads over a dried-up lake bed, with hills and mountains rising from the narrow plain on all sides. Lush, irrigated orchards surround the town, offset in spring by huge swaths of flowers across the valley floor, and depending on the season you can pick up fruit and vegetables from stands dotted more or less everywhere: cherries, apricots, peaches, pears, apples, plums and grapes all grow in abundance. If you're not tempted by the food, however, you may be by the **wine tastings** at the organic **St Laszlo Vineyards** (☎499-2856), 1km east of town on Hwy 3.

Keremeos itself is a rustic, two-street affair that's almost unspoilt by neon or urban clutter. A few shopfronts are oldish, and several make a stab at being heritage houses – the wonderful *Pasta Trading Post* on Main Street, for example – and though there's little to see or do (bar the inevitable small-town museum), it's a pleasant spot to spend the night. About 1km east of town on Upper Bench Road is the **Grist Mill** (May–Oct daily 9.30am–5pm; $5.50), a working flour mill dating from 1877 and surrounded by wheat fields and gardens. Restored to its original glory – the lovely general store still flaunts wallpaper from 1894 – it's a pleasant place to while away a half hour and if you're hungry there's a tearoom with soups, sandwiches and goods baked with the mill's flour.

Keremeos' central **infocentre** is at 415 7th Ave near Memorial Park (June–Sept daily 9am–5pm; ☎499-5225). The *Pasta Trading Post* (☎499-2933) is a wonderful place to **eat** locally grown organic produce and home-made pasta sauces; they also have comfortable **rooms** upstairs (③), rates include breakfast and the use of a hot tub. There are a couple of **motels** locally: the cheapest is the *Similkameen* (☎499-5984; ②; April to mid-Oct), 1km west of the centre in open country surrounded by lawns and orchards, with a few tent pitches ($10–15) in summer only, and the nicest is *The Elk* (☎499-2043 or 1-888/499-7773; ②), also with landscaped gardens.

Osoyoos

Beyond Keremeos the road climbs 46km, eventually unfolding a dramatic view, far below, of **OSOYOOS** – meaning "gathered together" – and a sizeable lake surrounded by bare, ochre hills. Descending, you enter one of Canada's strangest landscapes – a bona fide desert of half-bare, scrub-covered hills, sand, lizards, cactus, snakes and Canada's lowest average rainfall (around 25cm per year). Temperatures are regularly 10°C higher than in Nelson, less than a morning's drive away, enabling exotic fruit like bananas and pomegranates to be grown and prompting Osoyoos to declare itself the "Spanish Capital of Canada". The houses are supposed to have been restyled to give the place an Iberian flavour to match its climate, but on the ground it's almost impossible to find any trace of the conversion.

The town is otherwise distinguished by its position beside **Lake Osoyoos** in the Okanagan Valley – Hwy 97, which passes through the town, is the main route into the Okanagan region. In summer the place comes alive with swimmers and boaters, drawn to some of the warmest waters of any lake in Canada, and with streams of American RVs slow-tailing their way northwards to where the real action is.

A visit to the new **Desert Centre** (mid-April to mid-Oct daily 10am–4.30pm, 1hr 30min tours every half-hour; ☎1-877/899-0897; $5), on Hwy 97 just north of town, may be the best way to get oriented here. There are tours over a 1.5km boardwalk through a small area of desert and it's a fascinating ecosystem of some 100 rare plants, including tiny cacti and sage, as well as 300 animals from rattlesnakes to pocket gophers that are now all under serious threat. Once irrigated this land becomes very fertile and only nine percent of the desert survives undisturbed, with a full sixty percent vanished altogether.

The relative lack of crowds and strange scenery might persuade you to do your beach-bumming in Osoyoos, though you may be pushed to find space in any of the town's twenty or so **hotels** and **motels** during high season: cheaper choices include the *Avalon*, 9106 Main St (☎495-6334 or 1-800/264-5999; ③), *Falcon*, 7106 Main St (☎495-7544; ③), and the *Best Western Sunrise Inn,* 5506 Main St (☎495-4000 or 1-877/878-2200; ③), with an indoor pool and restaurant. Most of the motels are across the causeway on the southeastern shore of the lake, alongside the **bus stop**. For more choice and help, contact the **infocentre** at the junction of Hwys 3 and 97 (☎495-7142 or 1-888/676-9667, *www.osoyooschamber.bc.ca*). You're more likely to get a place in one of the half-dozen local **campsites** – try the *Cabana Beach*, 2231 Lakeshore Drive (☎495-7705; $19–29; May–Sept), or the *Inkameep Campground and RV Park* on 45th Street 1km from Hwy 3 East (☎495-7279; $16–25), which also organizes local hikes and night tours of the desert. Local **eateries** are almost entirely of the fast-food variety, but *Beans Desert Bistro*, 8323 Main St (☎495-7742), has good coffee and food, as well as Internet access, or there's *Finny's*, 8311 78th St, for a lengthier menu of salads, steaks and burgers.

Moving on from Osoyoos involves a major decision if you're travelling by car or bike, the choices being to continue east on Hwy 3, or to strike north on Hwy 97 through the Okanagan to the Trans-Canada Hwy. If you're on a Greyhound, the bus heads north and the decision can be deferred until Penticton, the major parting of the ways for services in this part of BC.

Midway, Greenwood and Grand Forks

At **MIDWAY**, some 65km east of Osoyoos on Hwy 3, something of the desert atmosphere lingers, the hills strange, broad whalebacks cut by open valleys and covered in coarse scrub and brown-baked grass. The hamlet's handful of scattered homes are like a windblown and wistful ghost town, making an evocative backdrop for the overgrown train tracks and tiny **railway museum** housed alongside a rusted minuscule steam engine. It's a fascinating little spot. The Kettle River Museum (mid-May to mid-Sept daily 10am–4pm; donation) in the 1900 CPR station 3km out of the village tells the town's story. For more background, contact the **infocentre** on Hwy 3 (June–Sept 9am–6pm; ☎449-2614). To **stay**, check-in to the recently renovated *Mile Zero Motel*, 622 Palmerston St (☎449-2231; ②), or put up a tent at the *Riverfront Municipal Campground* three blocks off Hwy 3 on 6th Avenue which has a washroom but no other services (free).

East out of town, the scenery along Hwy 3 begins to change from a flatter, drier landscape of bleached grass and sagebrush to rather more bland meandering hills. At **GREENWOOD**, however, the pines reappear, heralding a wild, battered brute of a village, which has suffered from the closure of its mines and can't muster much more than a handful of old buildings and some abandoned workings. The **infocentre** is housed on the main road at 214 S Copper St (May–June daily 10am–4pm; ☎445-6355) and has free Internet access. You're pretty sure of a welcome in any of the local **motels**, cheapest of which is the *Evening Star*, 798 N Government St (☎445-6733; ②), at the eastern entrance to town. For **camping** there are a couple of small provincial park sites: *Jewel Lake* ($6; June–Sept), 12km east of Greenwood off Hwy 3; and *Boundary Creek* ($9.50; April–Oct), just west of town off Hwy 3.

GRAND FORKS is not grand at all – it's very small and very dull and little more than a perfunctory transit settlement built on a river flat. Several Greyhound **buses** drop in daily, probably the biggest thing to happen to the place, stopping at *Stanley's*, which is the spot for sustenance unless you shop at the big Overwaitea supermarket alongside. The small **Boundary Museum** (Sept–June Mon–Fri 9am–4.30pm; July–Aug Mon–Fri 9am–4.30pm, Sat & Sun 10am–4pm; $2) by the traffic lights is the standard small-town model and can be seen in about the time it takes for the lights to change. The **infocentre** is next door (Sept–May Mon–Fri 8.30am–4.30pm; June–Aug Mon–Fri 8.30am–4.30pm, Sat & Sun 9am–5pm; ☎442-2833, *www.boundary.bc.ca*). The history of Doukhobor settlers (see box, p.519) is charted at the small **Mountainview Doukhobor Museum** (June–Aug daily 9am–6pm; $2). Just north of town, **Christina Lake** – which claims BC's warmest water – is a modestly unspoilt summer resort with lots of swimming, boating and camping opportunities (two other BC lakes make similar claims for their waters). A dozen or so motels and campsites sprout along its shore, with about the same number in and around the town itself, but it's doubtful that you'd want to use them except in an emergency. For information on the area, contact the Chamber of Commerce on Hwy 3 (☎447-6161).

Trail and Rossland

TRAIL is home to the world's largest lead and zinc smelter, a vast industrial complex whose chimneys cast a dismal shadow over the village's few houses. There's no reason to stop here and you'll probably want to head straight on to **ROSSLAND**, 11km west, which also relies on Trail's smelter for employment and has a mining foundation – gold this time, some $125 million-worth of which was gouged from the surrounding hills around the year 1900 (that's $2 billion-worth at today's prices). If you're into mining heritage, a tour of the **Le Roi Gold Mine** – once one of the world's largest, with 100km of tunnels – and the adjoining **Rossland Historical Museum** will entertain you with fascinating technical and geological background (mid-May to mid-Sept daily 9am–5pm; mine tours May, June & Sept every 1hr 30min, July & Aug every 30min; museum & mine $8, museum only $4).

The **infocentre** (mid-May to Oct daily 9am–5pm; ☎362-7722), in the museum at the junction of the town's two main roads, is most useful for details of the **Nancy Greene Provincial Park** (no showers; $9; May–Sept) northwest of town. Though the park and recreation area is best known for its world-class skiing – the **Red Mountain Ski Area** is a training ground for the Canadian national team – it's also excellent for hiking, an outdoor commodity that isn't easy to come by in these parts. There's a HI-affiliated **youth hostel**, the *Mountain Shadow Hostel* at 2125 Columbia Ave (☎362-7160); a provincial park **campsite** ($7) at the junction of hwys 3 and 3B; and several resort hotels; or try the upmarket twelve-unit *Ram's Head Inn*, 3km west of Rossland on Hwy 3B (☎362-9577 or 1-877/267-4323; ③), with hot tubs and bike rental. Rossland has a few nice places to **eat**: the huge-windowed *Olive Oyl's* (☎362-5322 – reservations recommended), with gourmet pizzas and an incredible banana and date pudding, the cheaper and less formal *Sunshine Café* – both are on Columbia, the main street – or *Mountain Gypsy Café* on Washington Street, good for light lunches and microbrewed beers.

Castlegar

Some 27km north of Trail on Hwy 22, **CASTLEGAR** is a strange diffuse place with no obvious centre, probably because roads and rivers – this is where the Kootenay meets the Columbia – make it more a transport hub than a community. In its time it was famous for its immigrant **Doukhobor** or "Spirit Wrestler" population, members of a Russian sect who fled religious persecution in 1899 from Russia and brought their pacifist-agrarian lifestyle to western Canada. By the 1920s BC had around ninety Doukhobor settlements, each with a co-operative, communal population of around sixty. They arrived in Castlegar in 1908, establishing at least 24 villages in the area, each with Russian names meaning things like "the beautiful", "the blessed" or "consolation". Accomplished farmers, they laboured under the motto "Toil and a Peaceful Life", creating highly successful orchards, farms, sawmills and packing plants. Although their way of life waned after the death of their leader Peter Verigin in 1924, killed by a bomb planted in his railway carriage, the Doukhobors' considerable industry and agricultural expertise transformed the Castlegar area; many locals still practise the old beliefs – Doukhobor numbers are around 5000 across the region – and Russian is still spoken. These days there's also a breakaway radical sect, the Freedomites, or Sons of Freedom, infamous for their eye-catching demonstrations – of which fires and nude parades are just two – against materialism and other morally dubious values.

Much of the community's heritage has been collected in the **Doukhobor Village Museum** (May–Sept daily 9am–5pm; $3.50; ☎365-6622), just off the main road on the right after you cross the big suspension bridge over the Kootenay River. A Doukhobor descendant is on hand to take you through the museum, which houses a winsome display of farm machinery, handmade tools and traditional Russian clothing that's intriguing as much for its alien context as for its content. For a further taste of Doukhobor culture, visit the evocative **Zuckerburg Island Heritage Park** off 7th Avenue, named after a local teacher of Doukhobors who built a log Russian Orthodox Chapel House here: it was bought and restored by the town in 1981, and is reached by a ninety-metre pedestrian suspension bridge.

Castlegar's **infocentre** (Sept–June Mon–Fri 9am–5pm; July & Aug daily 9am–5pm; ☎365-6313, *www.castlegar.com*) is at 1995 6th Ave off the main road as you leave town for Grand Forks. There are some half-dozen motels in and around town: the best **motel** – small, and with a nice view – is the *Cozy Pines* on Hwy 3 on the western edge of town at 2100 Crestview Crescent (☎365-5613; ②). Closer in, the modern and attractive *Best Western Fireside Motor Inn*, 1810 8th Ave at the junction of hwys 3 and 22 (☎365-2128 or 1-800/499-6399; ③), is a touch more expensive. Three kilometres out of town to the west on Hwy 3 is the *Castlegar RV Park and Campground*, 1725 Mannix Rd (☎365-2337; $15–20; April–Oct), with rural setting, separate tenting area, free hot showers, laundry and restaurant. There are also a regional and a provincial park **campsites** in the vicinity: *Pass Creek Regional Park*, which has a nice, sandy beach (☎365-3386; $12; May–Sept), 2km west off Hwy 3A at the Kootenay River Bridge; and the *Syringa Provincial Park* (reservations possible, see p.691; $15; mid-May to mid-Sept), 19km north of Hwy 3 at Castlegar on the east side of Lower Arrow Lake. For cheap **eating**, *Café Friends* back in town at 1102 3rd St has good home-cooked basics.

Salmo

A classic stretch of scenic road, Hwy 3 climbs from Salmo to the fruit-growing plains around Creston via **Kootenay Pass** (1774m) – though the views are less of spectacular mountains than of a pretty tracery of creeks and rivers crashing down through forest on all sides. This is one of the highest main roads in the country – it's frequently closed by bad weather – and it has no services for 70km after Creston, so check your petrol before setting out. If you're cycling, brace yourself for a fifty-kilometre uphill slog, but the reward is an unexpected and stunning lake at the pass, where there's a pull-off picnic area and views of high peaks in the far distance.

Despite the large volume of traffic converging on it along Hwy 3 and Hwy 6, tiny **SALMO** somehow manages to retain a pioneer feel and most of its tidy wooden buildings are fronted by verandas, decked with baskets of flowers in summer. The Chamber of Commerce (Mon–Fri 9am–5pm, plus Sat & Sun same hours July & Aug; ☎365-6313) is at 1995 6th Ave. There's also a **museum** (May–Sept Mon–Fri 10am–4pm; $2) at 4th Street and Railway Avenue that charts the vicissitudes of pioneer life and hosts the odd travelling exhibition. In winter there's **skiing** at the Salmo ski area, 2km east of town.

Buses usually pull in here for a long rest stop at the terminal by the Petro-Canada garage on the north side of the village. If you need to overnight, use either of the two central motels: the *Reno*, 123 Railway Ave (☎357-9937; ②), one block east of the bus terminal, or the *Salcrest*, 110 Motel Ave (☎357-9557; ②), at the junction of Hwys 3 and 6. The nearest **campsite** is the *Selkirk Motel and RV Sites* (☎357-2346; $12–16; units ①; May–Oct), 4km west of town.

For **food**, try *Charlie's Pizza and Spaghetti House*, an old-style diner on 4th Street. Just up the road, the *Silver Dollar Pub* is the town's favourite **bar**, with pool tables, a jukebox and lots of good ol' boys in an atmospheric wooden interior. Salmo Foods, opposite the bar, is the best **supermarket** for stocking up.

Creston

Don't stop in **CRESTON** unless you're a bird-watcher or feel like hunting down such sightseeing frippery as "Canada's best mural" (the original, in McDowell's department store, had spawned another nine pictures around town at last count). The **infocentre** is in a log cabin (one of the town's few buildings of interest) on the east side of town at 711 Canyon St (Mon 9am–5pm, Tues–Sat 9am–6pm; ☎428-4342): use it if by mischance you need **accommodation**, though with twenty or so motels and campsites to choose from you probably won't be fighting for a bed. The cheapest and most central spot is the *Hotel Creston*, 1418 Canyon St (☎428-2225; ②); motels on the town's fringes offer more salubrious, if slightly costlier alternatives. As well as Greyhounds passing through along Hwy 3, Empire Bus Lines runs an early-morning service from here to Spokane, WA (Mon & Thurs–Sun). If you're passing through, you might want to pause for the **Stone House Museum**, 219 Devon St (May–Sept daily 10am–3.30pm, by appointment the rest of the year; ☎428-9262; $2), known for its replica Kuntenai (Ktunaxa) canoe. Similar canoes, with their downpointed ends, are only found elsewhere in the world in parts of eastern Russia, underlining the fact that millennia ago migrations took place across the Bering Straits into North America.

Probably the best reason to spend time locally is the **Creston Valley Wildlife Management Area**, located 10km northwest of town off Hwy 3. Creston overlooks a broad section of valley and lowlands – relatively rare commodities in BC, home to the idly meandering Kootenay River. Over the years the river has repeatedly burst its banks, creating a rich alluvial plain beloved by farmers, and producing the lush medley of orchards and verdant fields that fringe Creston. Much of the flood plain and its wetlands, however – the so-called "Valley of the Swans" – have been preserved in their original state, creating a haven for birds and waterfowl. This area has one of the world's largest nesting osprey populations, while a total of 250 species have been recorded in the confines of the Creston Management Area (not to mention otters, moose and other animals). Birds can be seen from several points, but for full details of the area visit the sanctuary's Wildlife Centre, which provides telescopes and lookouts, a library and theatre, and a wide range of guided walks and canoe trips through the area's forest, marsh and grassland habitats.

The Kootenays

The Kootenays is one of the most attractive and unvisited parts of British Columbia, and one of the most loosely defined. It consists essentially of two major north–south valleys – the Kootenay and the Columbia, which are largely taken up by **Kootenay Lake** and **Upper** and **Lower Arrow Lakes** – and three intervening mountain ranges – the Purcells, Selkirks and Monashees, whose once-rich mineral deposits formed the kernel of the province's early mining industry. **Nelson** is the key town, slightly peripheral to the Kootenays' rugged core, but a lovely place, and one of the few provincial towns that holds out real attractions in its own right. Scattered lakeside hamlets, notably **Kaslo** and **Nakusp**, make excellent bases for excursions into mountain scenery which has a pristine quality rarely found elsewhere. Water-based activities – canoeing and fishing in particular – are excellent, and you can also explore the ramshackle mining heritage of near-ghost towns like **Sandon** and **New Denver**. Many of these towns and villages also have more than their fair share of artists, painters and writers, lending the region considerable cultural lustre.

Getting around the region is tricky without private transport, for there are next to no public services, which is a shame because the roads here are amongst the most scenic in a province noted for its scenery. Even with your own car, there's no way to do the Kootenays justice without retracing your steps at times. You can dip in and out of the region from the Trans-Canada Hwy (to the north) or Hwy 3 (to the south), but any trans-Kootenay route is more attractive than either of these main highways: the most **scenic routes** are Hwy 31A from Kaslo to New Denver, and Hwy 6 from New Denver to Vernon. Given no time constraints, your best strategy would be to enter from Creston and exit via Vernon, which sets you up for the Okanagan.

The telephone code for British Columbia outside of the Vancouver area is ☎250.

Highway 3A to Kootenay Bay

Starting from just north of Creston, **Hwy 3A** picks a slow, twisting course up the eastern shore of **Kootenay Lake** to the free car ferry at Kootenay Bay. Apart from the ample scenic rewards of the lake and the mountains beyond it, the highway is almost completely empty for all of its 79km, and none of the villages marked on maps amount to anything more than scattered houses hidden in the woods. The only noteworthy sight is the **Glass House** (May, June, Sept & Oct daily 9am–5pm; July & Aug 8am–8pm; $6), midway up the lake 7km south of **BOSWELL**, which ranks highly on the list of Canada's more bizarre offerings. Constructed entirely from embalming bottles, the house was built by a Mr David Brown in 1952 after 35 years in the funeral business – "to indulge", so the wonderfully po-faced pamphlet tells you, "a whim of a peculiar nature". The retired mortician travelled widely, visiting friends in the funeral profession until he'd collected 600,000 bottles – that's 250 tonnes' worth – to build his lakeside retirement home. The family continued to live here until curious tourists took the upper hand. Nearby **accommodation** is provided by the four-unit *Heidelburg Inn*, 12866 Hwy 3A (☎223-8263; ②; April–Oct), overlooking the lake, and the lakeside *Mountain Shores Resort and Marina* (☎223-8258; ③; April–Sept), a combination of ten motel-type rooms, cottages and **campsite** ($14–23) with store, hot showers and heated outdoor pool. There's another smaller campsite, *Kootenay Kampsites* (☎223-8488; $16–20; May–Oct), 39km north of Creston with rustic, well-treed sites, laundry and hot showers.

At **GRAY CREEK**, a few kilometres onward, check out the superb **Gray Creek Store**, which boasts the once-in-a-lifetime address of 1979 Chainsaw Avenue and claims, with some justification, to be "The Most Interesting Store You've Ever Seen". The shop basically *is* Gray Creek – it's the sort of place you go to get your chainsaw fixed and where real lumberjacks come for their red-checked shirts. There are two lakeside **campsites** nearby: the *Old Crow* (☎227-9495; $12; May–Oct) and the small *Lockhart Beach* provincial park campsite ($12; May–Sept) with RV and tent sites 13km south of Gray Creek and 20km south of Kootenay Bay (see below). A bit more exotic, *Tipi Camp* (☎227-9555; June–Sept) is situated on Pilot Peninsula, reached by a twice a day 20min boat taxi from Gray Creek. To stay in a tepee you need your own bedding, and it costs $50 a night including water taxi and three meals; day-trips which include transportation, lunch and dinner cost $30. From Gray Greek, the Gray Greek Forest service road (July–Oct) leads 85km east to Kimberley (see p.842), not a short cut by any means, but scenic and adventurous driving nonetheless. Be sure to be stocked up on supplies before setting off.

CRAWFORD BAY and **KOOTENAY BAY** are names on the map that refer in the flesh to the most fleeting of settlements, the latter also being the **ferry terminal** for boats to Balfour on the west shore. Crawford Bay, 3.5km from the terminal, boasts the Kootenay Forge, an old-world forge, where in summer you can often watch blacksmiths working and a number of other artisan shops from traditional broom-makers to weavers. The area has also long been famous for the **Yasodhara Ashram**, 527 Walkes Landing Rd (☎227-9224 or 1-800/661-8711), a spiritual retreat established over thirty years ago. As a place to stay, this side of the crossing is a touch brighter, and there's an **infocentre** (June–Sept daily 9am–5pm; ☎227-9267) just off the road at Crawford Bay, which can help you find some of the nicer accommodation tucked away in the woods nearby. The cheapest **motel** is the *La Chance Swiss* (☎227-9477 or 1-888/366-3385; ③), near the ferry dock, which includes a restaurant (Easter to mid-Oct). The more expensive *Wedgewood Manor Country Inn* (☎227-9233 or 1-800/862-0022; ④; April to mid-Oct), a 1910 heritage building set amidst fifty acres of gardens and estate, is upmarket and extremely pleasant, but you'll have to book well in advance. The better of two **campsites** here is the nicely wooded *Kokanee Chalets, Motel, Campground & RV Park* on Hwy 3A (☎352-3581 or 1-800/448-9292; mid-April to mid-Oct): as well as tent and RV sites ($16–22) it also has motel and chalet rooms around seven-minutes' walk from the beach (③); note, however, that there's also a choice of three reasonable campsites across the water in Balfour.

The nine-kilometre, forty-minute **ferry crossing** – purportedly the longest free ferry crossing in the world – is beautiful. Boats leave every fifty minutes from June to September, and every two hours the rest of the year, but it's a first-come, first-served affair, and in high summer unless you're a pedestrian or bike passenger it may be a couple of sailings before your turn comes round.

Balfour and Ainsworth Hot Springs

Not quite the fishing village it's billed as, **BALFOUR** is a fairly shoddy and dispersed collection of motels, garages and cafés – albeit in verdant surroundings – designed to catch the traffic rolling on and off the Kootenay Lake ferry. RV **campsites** line the road south to Nelson for about 2km, the quietest being those furthest from the terminal, but a much better option is the campsite at Kokanee Creek (reservations possible, see p.691), about 10km beyond Balfour ($17.50; May–Sept) with a sandy beach. The handiest **motel** for the ferry is the *Balfour Beach Inn and Motel*, 8406 Bush (☎ & fax 229-4235; ②), with heated indoor pool but convenient also for the small pebbly beach just north of the terminal.

About 15km north of Balfour on Hwy 31 – look out for the telegraph poles wearing ties – **AINSWORTH HOT SPRINGS** is home to some one hundred residents, making it a town by local standards. The tasteful *Ainsworth Hot Springs Resort* (☎229-4212 or 1-800/668-1171; ⑤) is ideal if you want to stay over while taking in the scalding water of the **mineral springs** (daily 10am–9.30pm; day-pass $10, single visit $6.50), though the chalets are expensive and, despite the lovely views and the health-giving properties of the waters, local opinion rates the Nakusp Hot Springs (see p.837) rather more highly. Note that you don't need to stay in the resort to sample the springs. The nicest local **motel** is the cheaper and smaller eight-room *Mermaid Lodge and Motel* (☎ & fax 229-4969 or 1-888/229-4963; ②) alongside the springs and pools. Cave enthusiasts might want to take a guided tour of **Cody Caves Provincial Park**, 12km up a rough, well-signposted gravel side road off Hwy 3 3km north of town. From the end of the road it's a twenty-minute walk to the caves, whose kilometre or more of galleries can be seen by tour only: contact Hiadventure Corporation (☎353-7425; $12).

A touch further up the increasingly beautiful Hwy 31 comes the self-contained **Woodbury Resort and Marina** (☎353-7177; ②), a collection of motel, cottages, campsite ($16–20), restaurant, pub, store, heated pool, boat rentals and water-sport facilities all pitched on the lakeshore with lovely views and a small beach, it makes an attractive long-term accommodation prospect if you're tenting. Directly opposite is the **Woodbury Mining Museum** (July–Sept daily 9am–6pm; $4; ☎354-4470), a quaint pioneer building crammed with mining regalia and the entrance to a thirty-minute underground tour of the old lead, zinc and silver workings.

Kaslo and around

KASLO must rate as one of British Columbia's most attractive and friendliest little villages. Huddled at the edge of Kootenay Lake and dwarfed by towering mountains, its half-dozen streets are lined with picture-perfect wooden homes and flower-filled gardens. It started life as a sawmill in 1889 and turned into a boom town with the discovery of silver in 1893; diversification, and the steamers that plied the lakes, saved it from the cycle of boom and bust that ripped the heart out of so many similar towns. Today Kaslo remains an urbane and civilized community whose thousand or so citizens work hard at keeping it that way, supporting a cultural centre, art galleries, rummage sales – even a concert society.

The **town hall**, a distinctive green-and-white wooden building dating from 1898, is an architectural gem by any standards, as is the church opposite. Yet Kaslo's main attraction is the SS *Moyie*, the oldest surviving **paddle steamer** in North America (tours May to mid-Sept daily 9am–5pm; $5), which ferried men, ore and supplies along the mining routes from 1898 until the relatively recent advent of reliable roads. Similar steamers were the key to the Kootenays' early prosperity, their shallow draught and featherweight construction allowing them to nose into the lakes' shallowest waters and unload close to the shore. They were, in local parlance, "able to float on dew". Canada claims just six of the 24 paddle steamers left in North America, but in the *Moyie* it has the oldest, launched in 1898 and only mothballed in 1957. Inside is a collection of antiques, artefacts and photographs from the steamer's heyday. Look for the small hut alongside it, the "world's smallest post office" (closed since 1970), and drop in on Kaslo's thriving **arts centre**, the Langham Cultural Society, on A Avenue opposite the post office (☎353-2661), for theatrical performances and art exhibitions. The building, which dates from 1893, began life as a hotel-cum-brothel for miners.

Kaslo makes an ideal base for tackling two of the region's major parks – Kokanee Glacier Provincial Park and the Purcell Wilderness Conservancy – and for pottering around some of the charming lakeshore communities. People at the arts centre can advise on getting to **ARGENTA** (pop. 150), 35km north, a refugee settlement of Quakers who in 1952 came from California, alienated by growing militarism, to start a new life; it's also the western trailhead for the difficult sixty-kilometre **Earl Grey Pass Trail** over the Purcell Mountains to Invermere (p.845). It's a beautiful area, but has no services and only the occasional B&B if you want to stay: ask at the Kaslo infocentre for latest details. This area, incidentally, offers a good chance of seeing **ospreys**: the Kootenays' hundred or so breeding pairs represent the largest concentration of the species in North America.

Practicalities

Finding your way round Kaslo is no problem, nor is getting information – everyone is disarmingly helpful – and there's also a **Chamber of Commerce** (early May to early Oct daily 9am–5pm; ☎ & fax 353-2525, *www.klhs.bc.ca*) at 324 Front St. More or less opposite, Discovery Canada (☎1-888/300-4453) can guide you on local wilderness adventures by foot, mountain bike or kayak.

The best and virtually only central **accommodation** is the *Kaslo Motel*, 330 D Ave (☎353-2431 or 1-877/353-2431; ②). For most other alternatives head towards the marina just north of the centre where en route you'll find, amongst others, the *Sunny Bluffs Cabins & Camp*, 434 N Marine Drive (☎353-2277; ①), offering cabins and camping sites ($10–12) overlooking Kaslo Bay Park. For **B&B** try the *Morningside*, 670 Arena Ave off Hwy 31 at West Kootenay Power Office (☎353-7681; ②; no credit cards). More interesting accommodation possibilities are available further up the lake, many with private lakeside beaches and lovely settings. The most notable are the combined hotel and campsite *Lakewood Inn* (☎353-2395; ③, tent and RV sites $12–20; April–Oct), lakeside log cabins with fully equipped kitchens and camping sites with private beach and boat rentals; it's 6km north of Kaslo on Kohle Road. There are also the *Wing Creek Cabins* (☎353-2475; ③), 7km north at 9114 Hwy 31, and two B&Bs at Argenta – *Earl Grey Pass* (☎366-4472; ①) or *Place Cockaigne* (☎366-4394; ②).

Kaslo has a municipal **campsite** ($13–15) on the flat ground by the lake at the end of Front Street, past the SS *Moyie* on the right. *Mirror Lake Campground* (☎353-7102; $15–18; mid-April to mid-Oct), beautifully situated 2km south of town on the main road to Ainsworth, has more facilities. North of the village on the lake are combined campsite and motel or cabin lodgings (see above), as well as the *Kootenay Lake Provincial*

Park campsite (April–Oct), two small campsites ($7–9.50) 25km north of the village on Hwy 31 with access to sandy beaches.

For **food** and **drink** in Kaslo try the renowned and reasonable *Rosewood Café* (☎353-7673), at the end of Front Street, for glorious salads and steaks. Another option is the town's social hub, the *Treehouse Restaurant*, further down on Front Street, where you can eat superbly and easily strike up conversations. The nearby *Mariner Inn and Hotel* has a beer hall, and is more of a downmarket hangout. For cheap eats, *Meteor Pizza & Cafe* on 4th Street at Front Street serves up home-made pizzas and wraps.

Kokanee Glacier Provincial Park

Kaslo is one of several possible jumping-off points for **Kokanee Glacier Provincial Park**, straddling the Slocan Range of the Selkirk Mountains to the southwest, and the access road from here – signed off Hwy 31A 6km northwest of town – offers the best views and choice of trails. However, the 24-kilometre drive up Keen Creek that follows from the turn-off degenerates in poor weather from compacted gravel to a severely rutted dirt road: this really only makes it suitable for four-wheel-drive vehicles. If you do make it, the road cuts to the heart of the park, reaching the Joker Millsite parking area set amidst spectacular glacier-ringed high country. Of the eleven fine trails in the area, the most obvious **hike** from the car park runs up to Helen Deane and Kaslo lakes (8km round-trip), an easy morning amble. If you're staying overnight you can choose from the usual undeveloped campsites ($5) and three basic **cabins** (summer $15; winter $35) – the main one, *Slocan Chief*, is past Helen Deane Lake alongside a park ranger office.

An easier approach to the park is to drive south of Kaslo on Hwy 3A for around 40km and then follow the road up Kokanee Creek for 16km to park at Lake Gibson. Though further from Kaslo it usually gets you into the park quicker. Other approaches are from Hwy 31 10km north of Ainsworth, driving 13km up Woodbury Creek into the park; from Hwy 6 some 14km north of Slocan, where you drive 13km up Enterprise Creek; and from Hwy 6 14km south of Slocan, where you follow a road up Lemon Creek for 16km. For more **information** on the park, call ☎825-4421 or pick up the blue *BC Parks* pamphlet from local infocentres. To reserve sites, call Discover Camping (see p.691).

Highway 31A and the Slocan Valley

After Kaslo you can either rattle north along a gravel road to link with the Trans-Canada Hwy at Revelstoke, a wild and glorious 150-kilometre drive with a free ferry crossing at **GALENA BAY**, or you can stay in the Kootenays and shuffle west on **Hwy 31A** through the Selkirk Mountains to the **Slocan Valley**. The latter road ascends from Kaslo alongside the Kaslo River, a crashing torrent choked with branches and fallen trees and hemmed in by high mountains and cliffs of dark rock, whose metallic sheen suggests the mineral potential that fired the early growth of so many of the settlements in the region. Near its high point the road passes a series of massively picturesque lakes: **Fish Lake** is deep green and has a nice picnic spot at one end; **Bear Lake** is equally pretty; and **Beaver Pond** is an amazing testament to the beaver's energy and ingenuity.

Sandon

The ghost town of **SANDON**, one of five in the region, is located 13km south of Hwy 31A, up a signed gravel side road that climbs through scenery of the utmost grandeur. Unfortunately, nowadays Sandon is too much ghost and not enough town to suggest how it might have looked in its silver-mining heyday, when it had 24 hotels, 23 saloons, an opera house, thriving red-light district and 5000 inhabitants (it even had electric light, well before Victoria or Vancouver). Its dilapidated, rather than evocative, state is due mainly to a flood, which swept away the earlier boardwalk settlement in 1955, leaving a partly inhabited rump that clutters along Carpenter Creek. Pop into the old City Hall for a walking tour pamphlet from the **infocentre** (May–Oct daily 10am–6pm), then head for the new **museum** (May–Oct Wed–Sun 9.30am–5.30pm; $2) in Sandon's only brick building, the old general store with photos and domestic and commercial artefacts from the town's heyday.

The trip is enhanced, however, if you manage a couple of local **hikes**. Idaho Peak is a must from Sandon, being one of the most accessible and spectacular walks in the area. A reasonable twelve-kilometre gravel access road leads into alpine pastures and a car park: from there it's a five-kilometre round trip to the summit of Mount Idaho and back, with emerging views all the way to the breathtaking panorama at the Forest Service lookout point. Or follow all or part of the **KNS Historic Trail** (6km each way) from the site, which follows the course of the 1895 Kaslo–New Denver–Slocan ore-carrying railway, past old mine works and eventually to fine views of the New Denver Glacier across the Slocan Valley to the west. Coupled with leaflets from the infocentre, the walk vividly documents the area's Wild West mining history, harking back to an era when the district – known as "Silvery Slocan" – produced the lion's share of Canada's silver. "Silver, lead, and hell are raised in the Slocan," wrote one local newspaper in 1891, "and unless you can take a hand in producing these articles, your services are not required." The immense vein of silver-rich galena that started the boom was discovered by accident in 1891 by two colourful prospectors, Eli Carpenter and Jack Seaton, when they got lost on the ridges returning to Ainsworth from Slocan Lake. Back in the bar they fell out over the find, and each raced out with his own team to stake the claim. Seaton won, and was to become a vastly wealthy silver baron who travelled in his own train carriage across Canada, condemning Carpenter to return to his earlier profession as a tightrope walker and to an ultimately penurious death.

New Denver

After the Sandon turn-off Hwy 31A drops into the **Slocan Valley**, a minor but still spectacular lake-bottomed tributary between the main Kootenay and Columbia watersheds, and meets Hwy 6 at **NEW DENVER**. Born of the same silver-mining boom as Kaslo, and with a similarly pretty lakeside setting and genuine pioneer feel, New Denver is, if anything, quieter than its neighbour. The clapboard houses are in peeling, pastel-painted wood, and the tree-lined streets are mercifully free of neon, fast food and most evidence of tourist passage. In town, the **Silvery Slocan Museum**, housed in the old wooden Bank of Montréal building at the corner of 6th Avenue and Bellevue (July & Aug 10.30am–4.30pm; $2; ☎358-2201), is good for twenty minutes on the background and artefacts of the area's mining heritage.

Well-signposted from the highway the moving **Nikkei Internment Memorial Centre** at 306 Josephine St (May–Sept daily 9.30am–5pm, rest of year by appointment; $4; ☎358-7288), is the only museum in Canada dedicated to the 22,000 Nikkei (Canadians of Japanese ancestry) who, in 1942, were forcibly relocated from the coast to remote internment camps in the interior after Pearl Harbour. Beautiful Japanese gardens now surround the wooden shacks and outhouses that the Nikkei were forced to build themselves. Although the majority of Nikkei were Canadian citizens, they were all labelled "enemy aliens" and stripped of their possessions, homes and businesses. It wasn't until 1988 that former prime minister Brian Mulroney finally apologized to Japanese-Canadians and awarded them token monetary compensation. Inside the cultural centre an exhibition tells the story through photos, paintings and artefacts.

There's no official **infocentre** in New Denver, but local bookshops or a business, such as Nuru Designs (summer daily 10am–4pm; ☎358-2733), are the places to contact for specific information on the surrounding valley. As a stopover it's appealing but not quite as enticing as Kaslo; its **accommodation** possibilities include a single beach-hut-type motel, the *Valhalla Inn*, 509 Slocan Ave (☎358-2228; ③); the lakeview *Sweet Dreams Guest House* (☎358-2415; ③), a restored heritage home on Slocan Lake at 720 Eldorado Ave; and the simple *New Denver Municipal Campground* (☎358-2316; $13–16; May–Sept) on the south side of the village. Four kilometres north of town on Hwy 6 is the *Rosebury Provincial Park* campsite ($9.50; April–Oct) on the banks of Wilson Creek, a lightly forested site with lake and mountain views. For **food** in the village try 6th Avenue, where you'll find the relaxed *Apple Tree Sandwich Shop* and the bistro *Panini*. There's more accommodation and a campsite at Silverton, another tiny former mining village just 4.5km south of New Denver on Hwy 6.

Slocan and the Slocan Valley

Southbound out of New Denver, Hwy 6 follows the tight confines of the **Slocan Valley** for another 100km of ineffable mountain and lake landscapes. Be certain to stop at the **Slocan Lake Viewpoint**, 6km out of New Denver, where a short path up a small cliff provides stupendous views. The 125,000-acre **Valhalla Provincial Park** (☎825-3500) wraps up the best of the landscapes on the eastern side of Slocan Lake; a wilderness area with no developed facilities, most of it is out of reach unless you boat across the water, though there are two trails that penetrate it from the hamlet of **SLOCAN**, another former mining village at the south end of the lake. For a taste of the local outdoors, the canter up the old railway bed from Slocan is a popular short hike, and there's more fresh air and good picnicking spots at the nearby Mulvey Basin and Cove Creek **beaches**. Note, too, that gravel roads lead up from Hwy 6 to the more accessible heights of **Kokanee Glacier Provincial Park** to the east (p.834). For more on the area, notably tours into the Valhalla park, contact Slocan's **infocentre**, 903 Slocan St (July–Aug; ☎355-2277).

If you need **accommodation** en route south there are about half-a-dozen options, all in rustic settings with mountain or lake views. Try either *Lemon Creek Lodge* (☎355-2403; cabins ③, campsite $15), 7km south of Slocan on Kennedy Road, or the *Slocan Motel* (☎355-2344; ②), at 801 Harold St in Slocan itself off Hwy 6. In addition to provincial **campsites** at Mulvey Basin and Cove Creek ($9.50; both May–Oct), there's the unserviced *Silverton Municipal Campground* (free; May–Oct), just south of New Denver. More exciting, the *Valhalla Lodge and Tipi Retreat* (☎365-3226; ④; May–Sept) offers an opportunity to stay in the Valhalla Provincial Park either in tepees or waterfront cabins, and use of a hot tub and sauna.

Along Highway 6

Hwy 6 may not be the most direct east–west route through British Columbia, but it's certainly one of the most dramatic, and the one to think about if you're heading towards Revelstoke to the north or the Okanagan to the west. From New Denver it initially strikes north and after 30km passes **Summit Lake**, a perfect jewel of water, mountain and forest that's served by the new *Summit Lake Provincial Park* **campsite** ($15; mid-May to mid-Sept). A rough road ("Take at Your Own Risk") runs south from here into the mountains and a small winter ski area.

Nakusp and onwards

Sixteen kilometres beyond Summit Lake, lakefront **NAKUSP** is, like Kaslo and Nelson, a rare thing in British Columbia: a town with enough charisma to make it worth visiting for its own sake. The setting is par for the course in the Kootenays, with a big lake – **Upper Arrow Lake**, part of the Columbia River system – and the snowcapped Selkirk Mountains to the east providing the majestic backdrop. The nearby hot springs are the main attraction, but you could happily wander around the town for a morning, or boat or swim off the public **beach**. The only actual sight in town is the **Nakusp Museum** in the village hall at 6th Avenue and 1st Street, full of the usual archive material, logging displays and Victorian bric-a-brac (May–Sept Tues–Thurs 12.30–4.30pm, Mon & Fri–Sun 11am–5pm; donation). The helpful **infocentre**, based in the fake paddle-steamer building next door at 92 West St and 6th Avenue just off the main street (summer daily 9am–5pm; winter Mon–Fri 10am–4pm; ☎265-4234 or 1-800/909-8819), can provide details on local fishing, boating and hiking possibilities, and – for those driving onwards – timings for the Galena Bay and Fauquier ferries. Also ask about the possibility of renting houseboats on the lake if you're staying for a few days.

If you're only going to try the hot springs experience once, **Nakusp Hot Springs**, a well-signposted complex 13km northeast of town, is the place to do it (daily: June–Sept 9.30am–10pm; Oct–May 11am–9.30pm; $5, day-pass $7): it's not unusual for late-night informal parties to develop around the two outdoor pools. Unlike many similar enterprises, the natural pools are cleaned each night and are backed up by nice changing facilities, but bear in mind they're very popular in the summer. Note that there are some undeveloped springs within striking distance of here if you have a car. To reach **St Leon Hot Springs**, take Hwy 23 north out of Nakusp for 24km and then turn down the logging road after the second bridge for 10km to the trailhead; the piping-hot springs are 100m away down a steep trail to the river. If you stay on Hwy 23 for about another 10km, you'll reach **Halcyon Hot Springs** (daily 9am–9pm; $6), which was first commercialized in 1888, its waters bottled and sent to England. Today, there are four pools here of varying temperatures, all of which face Upper Arrow Lake and the mountain peaks beyond. Camping is also available for $20.

For a place to **stay** in Nakusp, try the *Selkirk Inn*, 210 6th Ave W (☎265-3666 or 1-800/661-8007; ②), or *Kuskanax/Tenderfoot Lodge*, 515 Broadway (☎265-3618 or 1-800/663-0100; ②), which is equally central but a bit more upmarket and has a recommended Canadian-fare **restaurant**. For cheap, basic hamburgers and pizzas there's *Nick's Place* at 93 5th Ave. Campers would do best to aim for the lovely *Nakusp Hot Springs* **campsite**, near the hot springs at 1701 Canyon Rd (☎265-4528 or 1-800/909-8819; $15; mid-May to mid-Oct); noncampers could try the adjoining *Cedar Chalets* (☎265-4505; ②), but reservations are essential in summer. Another out-of-town campsite is the *McDonald Creek Provincial Park* site ($12; April–Oct), 10km south of Nakusp on Hwy 6, and complete with lakeside beaches.

From Nakusp, you can either continue along Hwy 6 or branch off up Hwy 23, which heads 100km north to Revelstoke (see p.675), a lonely and spectacular journey involving a free ferry crossing halfway at **Galena Bay** (hourly sailings each way).

Fauquier

Highway 6 doglegs south from Nakusp for 57 delightful kilometres to the ferry crossing at **FAUQUIER**. This hamlet consists of a handful of buildings including a garage, a store, the *Mushroom Addition* **café** for coffee and meals, and the only **motel** for kilometres – the *Arrow Lake Motel* (☎269-7622 or 1-888/499-5222; ②), bang on the lakeside near the ferry at 101 Oak St. There's a **campsite** 2km back towards Nakusp, *Plum Hollow Camping*, Needles Road North (☎269-7669; $6–12; March–Nov), marked by two big arrows sticking in the ground. Some 3km beyond that the *Goose Downs* **B&B** (☎265-3139; ②) is signed off Hwy 6.

Onwards from Needles

The free **ferry** across **Lower Arrow Lake** to Needles takes about five minutes, departs half-hourly from 5.15am to 9.45pm, and operates an intermittent shuttle throughout the night. **NEEDLES** amounts to no more than a ramp off the ferry on the other side. There's an unofficial **campsite** at Whatshan Lake, 3km off the highway just after Needles, but otherwise Hwy 6 is a gloriously empty ribbon as it burrows through the staggering Monashee Mountains – though some of the time it's too hemmed in by forest for you to catch anything but trees. After cresting Monashee Pass (1198m), the highway begins the long descent through the **Coldstream Valley** towards the Okanagan. Snow dusts the mountains here almost year-round, crags loom above the meadows that increasingly break the forest cover, and beautiful flower-filled valleys wind down to the highway. The first sign of life in over 100km is the *Gold Panner* **campsite** (☎547-2025; $12–14; April–Oct), a good spot to overnight or to explore the utter wilderness of **Monashee Provincial Park** to the north. The park is reached by rough road from the hamlet of **CHERRYVILLE**, 10km further west, which despite its cartographic prominence is just three houses, a garage and Frank's General Store.

LUMBY, another 20km beyond, is scarcely more substantial, although **rooms** at the *Twin Creeks Motel* (☎547-9221; ②) might be worth considering if it's late, given that the Okanagan lodgings ahead could well be packed. The village also boasts a simple riverside **campsite** run by the local Lions Club (☎547-9504; $7; May–Oct) and there's a seasonal **infocentre** on the highway (July & Aug; ☎547-8844). Beyond the village, the road glides through lovely pastoral country, with orchards, verdant meadows, low, tree-covered hills, and fine wooden barns built to resemble inverted longboats.

The telephone code for British Columbia outside of the Vancouver area is ☎250.

Nelson

NELSON is one of British Columbia's best towns, and one of the few interior settlements you could happily spend two or three days in – longer if you use it as a base for touring the Kootenays by car. The town is home to more than its share of baby-boomers and refugees from the 1960s, a hangover that's nurtured a friendly, civilized and close-knit community, a healthy cultural scene and a liveliness – manifest in alternative cafés, nightlife and secondhand-clothes shops – that you'll be hard pushed to find elsewhere in the province outside Vancouver. There are, apparently, more artists and craftspeople here per head of the nine thousand population than any other town in Canada. At the same time it's a young place permeated with immense civic pride, which was given a further boost by the filming here of *Roxanne*, Steve Martin's spoof version of *Cyrano de Bergerac*. Producers chose the town for its idyllic lakeside setting and 350-plus homes from the late nineteenth to the early twentieth-century, factors which for once live up to the Canadian talent for hyperbole – in this case a claim to be "Queen of the Kootenays" and "Heritage Capital of Western Canada".

Located 34km west of Balfour on Hwy 3A, the town forms a tree-shaded grid of streets laid over the hilly slopes that edge down to the westernmost shores of Kootenay Lake. Most homes are immaculately kept and vividly painted, and even the commercial **buildings** along the parallel main streets – Baker and Vernon – owe more to the vintage architecture of Seattle and San Francisco than to the drab Victoriana of much of eastern Canada. If you want to add purpose to your wanderings, pick up the *Heritage Walking Tour* or the *Heritage Motoring Tour* pamphlets from the **infocentre**, 225 Hall St (June–Aug daily 8am–8pm; Sept–May Mon–Fri 8.30am–5pm; ☎352-3433 or 1-877/663-5706, *www.nelsonchamber.bc.ca*), which takes you around the sort of houses that many Canadians dream of retiring to, and only occasionally oversells a place – notably when it lands you in front of the old jam factory and the electricity substation. Better bets are the courthouse and city hall, both designed by F.M. Rattenbury, also responsible for Victoria's *Empress Hotel* and Parliament Buildings. Free tours with a costumed guide are available from the infocentre in summer. If walking tours aren't your thing, perhaps the town's **shops** may be, particularly those of its artists and crafts-people, who in summer club together to present **Artwalk**, a crawl round many of the town's little galleries. Most of these have regular openings and wine-gorging receptions, making for numerous free-for-all parties. If you don't want to walk, take the restored tram that runs the length of the town's waterfront to the infocentre. Oliver's Books on Baker Street is excellent for maps, guides and general reading, with a bias towards the sort of New Age topics that find a ready market here. Another shop worth a stop is Still Eagle, 557 Ward St, the province's first hemp-store, where even snow-boards are made from hemp.

For the most part the area owes its development to the discovery of copper and silver ore on nearby Toad Mountain at the end of the nineteenth century. Even though the mines declined fairly quickly, Nelson's diversification into gold and lumber, and its roads, railway and waterways, saved it from mining's usual downside. Today mining is back on the agenda as old claims are re-explored, and even if the idea of the town's **Museum of Mines** (daily 10am–4pm; free; ☎352-5242), next to the infocentre, leaves you cold, it's worth meeting the curator, an old prospector who talks at length – and interestingly – on the quest for silver, copper and gold, past and present.

It's probably less worthwhile to trek over to the **Nelson Museum**, about twenty-minutes' walk from the centre, which offers a rather haphazard display that's obviously the work of enthusiastic amateurs (summer daily 1–6pm; winter Mon–Sat 1–4.30pm; $2). There are, however, odd points of interest, notably a chronicle of the original 1886 Silver King Mine that brought the town to life, as well as tantalizingly scant details on the Doukhobor, a Russian religious sect whose members still live in self-contained communities around the Kootenays (see p.827). Better instead to walk to **Lakeside Park** near the Nelson Bridge, where there are surprisingly good sandy **beaches** and picnic areas, boat rentals and waterfront paths. If you're here between May and mid-October, make it a point to stop by the Saturday **Farmers and Artisans Market** in Cottonwood Falls Park (9.30am–3pm). Organic fruits, vegetables, delicious breads and local arts and crafts are all for sale.

Practicalities

Nelson is served by Greyhound **buses** (☎352-3939) that run west to Penticton (for connections to Vancouver, the Okanagan and Kamloops) and east to Cranbrook (connections to Calgary via Banff or Fort Macleod). There are infrequent minibus services to Kaslo (☎353-2492 for details) and Nakusp (☎265-3674), but check with the infocentre before building a trip around these. The depot is on the lakeshore, just below the town proper at Chahko-Mika Mall. If you need a car, Rent-a-Wreck has an outlet here (☎352-5122).

There's a reasonable spread of **accommodation**, but comparatively little in the downtown area: among the central choices are the characterful *Heritage Inn*, 422 Vernon St (☎352-5331, *www.heritageinn.org*; ③) with cosy, old world rooms, and the cheaper and equally central *Dancing Bear Inn*, 171 Baker St (☎352-7573; ①), a nicely renovated HI-affiliated **youth hostel**. For something around twice the price you could try downtown **B&B** options such as the four-room *Emory House*, 811 Vernon St (☎352-7007; ③), or the highly regarded *Inn the Garden*, a restored Victorian home one block south of Baker Street at 408 Victoria St (☎352-3226; ③). Most of the **motels** are on Hwy 31A at the north end of town or over the miniature Forth Road bridge on the north side of the lake. Here you can try the *Villa Motel*, 655 Hwy 3A (☎352-5515 or 1-888/352-5515; ②), with the use of an indoor pool, or the *North Shore Inn*, 687 Hwy 3A (☎352-6606 or 1-800/593-6636; ③), where rates include a coffee and muffin breakfast. The nearest **campsites** are the *City Tourist Park*, on the corner of High Street and Willow (☎352-9031; $13–16; mid-May to early Oct), and *Shannon's RV Park* (☎825-9648; $16–22; mid-May to Sept), 7km from town on the north shore of the lake at 1940 Hwy 3A.

If these are full, head east towards Balfour and the three or more sites near the ferry terminal (see p.832).

The choice of **restaurants** is broad, and you can't go far wrong wandering around and choosing something that looks tempting. *Stanley Baker's*, a locals' place on Baker Street next to the Nelson Shopping Company mall, is good for cappuccino, snacks and big, cheap breakfasts. The *Vienna*, an alternative café and bookshop just off Baker Street opposite the Bank of Montreal, is also worth a try, as is *Orso Negro* on Victoria, a block up from Baker, with bagels and excellent coffee. For lunch or evening meals, downtown residents head to the *Main Street Diner*, 616 Baker St (☎354-4848; closed Sun), or the top-flight *All Seasons Café*, The Alley, 620 Herridge Lane (☎352-0101) which also has a nice patio dining area. Also worth a look is *Max Irma's*, 515a Kootenay St (☎352-2332) while for novelty value you could do worse than spoil your breath at the *Outer Clove*, 353 Stanley St (☎354-1667), where everything from decor to dessert features garlic (it's better than it sounds). At 301 Baker St, *The Rice Bowl* (☎354-4129), a local favourite, uses mainly organic ingredients to serve up fine seafood, sushi and vegan meals in a buzzing environment – note that it closes early, normally by 8pm. For **drinking**, make for *Mike's Bar* round the side of the *Heritage Inn*, 422 Vernon St, which sells the full range of Nelson Brewing Company beers (the brewery was founded in 1893): top tipple is the flagship Old Brewery Ale (OBA). If you're shopping for your own meals, the big **supermarkets** are in or near the mall alongside the bus depot, whilst the excellent Kootenay Co-Op in town at 295 Baker St can satisfy all your organic and wholefood needs – the organic bakery turns out a supreme loaf of bread.

North to Radium Hot Springs

Heading north from Creston and the Kootenays, Hwy 95 travels through scenery as spectacular as anything in the big Rockies parks to the north. The route follows the broad valley bottom of the **Columbia River**, bordered on the east by the Rockies and on the west by the marginally less breathtaking **Purcell Mountains**, though for the most part access to the wilderness here is limited and you'll have to be content with enjoying it from the highway. It's a fast run if you're driving, except where the road hugs the river's dramatic bluffs and sweeping meanders. Hwys 93 and 95 meet near **Cranbrook**, where you can make for either of two US border crossings, double back eastwards on Hwy 3 to Crowsnest Pass and Alberta, or head north for Radium Hot Springs and the entrance to Kootenay National Park (see p.678). Greyhound **buses** ply all these routes, with most connections at Cranbrook.

East from Creston

Some forty kilometres east of Creston, buses drop off at the small Shell garage in unspoilt **YAHK**, no more than a few houses nestled amidst the trees; a good, quiet stopover here is the single **motel**, *Bob's* (☎424-5581; ②), or you can camp at *Yahk Provincial Park* ($12; May to mid-Sept). Hwy 95 branches off from Hwy 3 here and heads south for the US border (11km). Incidentally, the highway crosses a **time zone** between Yahk and Moyie – clocks go forward one hour.

Following Hwy 3 northbound you reach the tiny community of **MOYIE** on the edge of lovely **Moyie Lake**, which provides a welcome visual relief after the unending tree-covered slopes hereabouts. Though there's no motel accommodation, there is a **B&B**, the *Long Shadows House* on Barkley Road just north of the village (☎829-0650; ③). There are also three local **campsites**, including the excellent one at **Moyie Lake Provincial Park** (reservations possible, see p.691; $17.50; May–Sept) – reach it by taking Munro Lake Road west off Hwy 3/95 for a kilometre from the northernmost point of Moyie Lake. Alternatively, you could try the private *Green River Campground,* on the lakeshore, signed about 1km off Hwy 3/95 (☎426-4154; $10–13.50; May–Oct), or the *Moyie River Campground*, 18km south of Cranbrook on Hwy 3/95 (☎489-3047; $9–13.50; April–Nov).

Cranbrook

The regional service and ex-forestry town of **CRANBROOK**, despite a location that marks it out as a transport hub, is one of the most dismal in the province, its dreariness hardly redeemed by the surrounding high mountains. A strip of motels and marshalling yards dominates a downtown area otherwise distinguished only by thrift shops and closing-down sales. Local lifeblood, such as it is, flows from the motels, this being an obvious place to eat, sleep and drive away from the next morning.

The only sight to speak of is the **Canadian Museum of Rail Travel**, a smallish affair that centres on the restored carriages of an old trans-Canada luxury train (July & Aug daily 8am–8pm; rest of the year 10am–6pm; $6.95). The period buildings pushed by the **infocentre**, 2279 Cranbrook St (year-round 9am–5pm; ☎426-5914 or 1-800/222-6174, *www.cranbrookchamber.com*), aren't interesting enough to justify the trawl round the streets. The infocentre was burned down by animal-rights activists in 1999 because of its stuffed-animal display, and not to be outdone they have reopened on the same spot with a new **Wildlife Museum** (same hours) filled with stuffed road-kills from the surrounding area.

You may have to stay in Cranbrook, as there's little in the way of **accommodation** on the roads north and south; there are a dozen or more motels that fit the bill. The top of the range in town is the *Heritage Inn* at 803 Cranbrook (☎489-4301 or 1-800/663-2708; ④), a large, modern motel on the main road. Cheaper and more intimate is the *Heritage Estate Motel* (☎426-3862 or 1-800/670-1001; ②), near the southern edge of town at 362 Van Horne St SW and therefore removed from some of the bleaker corners. The same can be said of a nice **B&B**, the *Singing Pines*, 5180 Kennedy Rd (☎426-5959 or 1-800/863-4969; ④), situated off Hwy 95A 3km north of town in a quiet location with mountain views. The town's *Mount Baker RV Park*, at Baker Park on 14th Avenue and 1st Street (☎1-877/501-2288; $18–24; April–Oct), is the closest **campsite**, though it's a good deal less appealing than the *Jimsmith Provincial Park*, 4km southwest of town, but which has no showers ($12; May–Oct).

The strip offers plenty of cheap **eating** options: for something more welcoming make for the *ABC Family Restaurant* at 1601 Cranbrook St N. The Greyhound **bus terminal** (☎426-3331) is hidden behind *McDonald's* opposite the Mohawk petrol station. Bus services run east to Fernie, Sparwood and southern Alberta (2 daily); west to Nelson, Castlegar and Vancouver (3 daily); north to Kimberley, Radium, Banff and Calgary (1 daily); and south to Spokane in the US (1 daily).

East from Cranbrook

Highway 93 leaves Hwy 95 between Fort Steele (see p.844) and Cranbrook, following Hwy 3 as far as Elko before branching off south for the United States border (91km). An unsullied hamlet of around half a dozen homes, **ELKO** is gone in a flash, but you might want to stop and eat at *Wendy's Place*, a cosy backwoods spot, or to camp at the excellent *Kikomun Creek Provincial Park* **campsite** (reservations possible, see p.691; $17.50; May–Oct), on the eastern shore of the artificial Lake Koocanusa and signed off Hwy 93 3km west of town. The only other local **accommodation** is the *West Crow Motel and Campground* at the entrance to the Elk Valley (☎529-7349; ②, tents and RVs $10–14; year-round), with a secluded tenting area. Hwy 3 offers colossal views of the Rockies and the fast-flowing, ice-clear Elk River, before hitting **FERNIE**, 32km north of Elko, a pleasant place of tree-lined streets, a few motels and small wooden houses, surrounded by a ring of knife-edged mountains. The *Cedar Lodge* (☎423-4622; ③) is the place to stay here or, failing that, the HI-affiliated official **youth hostel**, the *Raging Elk International Hostel*, 892 6th Ave (☎423-6811; ①). The **infocentre** (daily 9am–5pm; ☎423-6868) stands alongside a reconstructed wooden oil derrick 2km north of town on Hwy 3 at Dicken Road. **Mount Fernie Provincial Park** has plenty of hiking trails, picnic areas and a campsite just west of town off Hwy 3 (reservations possible, see p.691; $12; mid-May to mid-Sept). **Fernie Snow Valley**, 5km west of town and 2km off the main highway, boasts what is reputedly the longest ski season in the BC Rockies (Nov–May); it also has few typical resort-type accommodation possibilities.

Hwy 3 leaves the Elk Valley at **SPARWOOD**, 29km beyond Fernie, where signs of the area's coal-mining legacy begin to appear. Close to the town – but barely visible – is Canada's largest open-cast **coal mine**, capable of disgorging up to 18,000 tonnes of coal daily. Tours of the mine (July & Aug Mon–Fri 1.30pm) leave from the local **infocentre** (daily 9am–6pm; ☎425-2423), at the junction of Hwy 3 and Aspen Drive – look for the big miner's statue. The town itself is surprisingly neat and clean, and the obvious *Black Nugget Motor Inn*, Hwy 3 at Red Cedar Drive (☎425-2236 or 1-800/663-2706; ③), makes a convenient place to stay.

Elkford

The remainder of Hwy 3 in British Columbia is despoiled by mining; the road crests the Continental Divide 19km east of Sparwood at **Crowsnest Pass** (see p.599). Far more scenic is the drive north from Sparwood on Hwy 43, which heads upstream beside the Elk River for 35km to **ELKFORD**. Nestled against a wall of mountains to the east and more gentle hills to the west, the village claims to be the "wilderness capital of British Columbia" – a high-pitched punt, but close to the mark if you're prepared to carry on up either of two rough gravel roads to the north. The more easterly road follows the Elk a further 80km to **Elk Lakes Provincial Park** close to the Continental Divide, one of the wildest road-accessible spots in the province (reservations possible, see p.691). The slightly better route to the west heads 55km into the heart of unbeatable scenery below 2792-metre **Mount Armstrong**. Both areas offer excellent chances of spotting wildlife like cougars, deer, moose, elk or members of North America's largest population of bighorn sheep.

Before entering either area, however, it's essential to pick up maps and information at the Elkford **infocentre** (year-round Mon–Fri 8am–5pm; ☎1-877/355-9453), located at the junction of Hwy 43 and Michel Road. It can also give directions to nearby **Josephine Falls**, a few minutes' walk from the parking area on Fording Mine Road. Whether you're staying here or pushing on north, a tent is helpful: the only accommodation options are the *Elkford Motor Inn*, 808 Michel Rd, next to the shopping centre (☎865-2211 or 1-800/203-7723; ②) or the more expensive *Hi Rock Inn*, 2 Chauncey St (☎865-2226; ③). **Camping** can be had at Elkford's municipal campsite (☎865-2650; $12; May–Oct), and at the wilderness campsites around Elk Lakes ($5; June–Sept).

Kimberley

KIMBERLEY, a few kilometres from Cranbrook on Hwy 95A, is Canada's highest city (1117m), and in many ways one of its silliest, thanks to a tourist-tempting ruse to transform itself into a Bavarian village after the imminent closure of the local mine in the 1970s threatened it with economic oblivion. The result is a masterpiece of kitsch that's almost irresistible: buildings have been given a plywood-thin veneer of authenticity, piped Bavarian music dribbles from shops with names like The Yodelling Woodcarver, and even the fire hydrants have been painted to look like miniature replicas of Happy Hans, Kimberley's lederhosened mascot. The ploy might seem absurd, but there's no doubting the energy and enthusiasm that has gone into it, nor the economic rewards that have accrued from the influx of tourists and European immigrants – Germans included – who've provided an authentic range of cafés and restaurants and a variety of family-oriented summer and winter activities.

Most of the Teutonic gloss is around the **Bavarian Platzl** on Spokane Street in the small downtown area, whose fake houses compare poorly with the authentic wooden buildings and more alpine surroundings on the outskirts. If nothing else, you can leave Kimberley safe in the knowledge that you have seen "**Canada's Biggest Cuckoo Clock**", a fraudulent affair which amounts to little more than a large wooden box that twitters inane and incessant music. The dreaded contraption performs on being fed small change, and people oblige often enough so that Happy Hans (rather than a cuckoo) makes his noisy appearance almost continuously; when he doesn't, the council often employs some unfortunate to play the accordion morning, noon and night to keep up the musical interludes.

Apart from the clock, and a small **museum** upstairs in the library down the road, the other main local sight is the **Sullivan Mine**, pre-Bavarian Kimberley's main employer and one of the world's biggest lead and zinc mines. The mine, now closed, is due to be remembered in an **interpretive centre** which will tell the mine's story and include a trip to the original portal – due to high insurance demands the underground mine itself cannot be opened to the public. You can also explore the local history on the **Bavarian City Mining Railway**, a 7-kilometre narrated ride on a train salvaged from a local mine. En route the train travels along steep inclines and switchbacks through the valley, highlighting Kimberley's past mining activities and its future developments now that the lifeblood has run dry. It leaves from the downtown station, a block from the Platz, on Jerry Sorenson Way (June–Sept daily noon–6.30pm; $6). At the station you can also view a mini 1920s mining camp complete with a schoolhouse.

If you're around from early December through April, and feel the need to escape Kimberley's kitsch, head for the Kimberley Alpine **ski resort** (☎427-4881) four kilometres west of town. Owned by Charles Locke, the owner of numerous ski resorts throughout Canada, the resort boasts eight lifts and 67 runs, the longest of which covers more than six kilometres. Passes cost $43 for the day, $35 for the afternoon and $15 for a night-skiing session. Kimberley also boasts one of Canada's most popular **golf** courses, Trickle Creek on Jerry Sorenson Way (☎427-3878; $69 for 18-holes, $28 for a cart), but you'll have to book ahead if you want to play here.

Practicalities

If you need **accommodation**, try the central *Quality Inn of the Rockies*, 300 Wallinger Ave (☎427-2266 or 1-800/661-7559; ③), or the smaller *North Star Motel* (☎427-5633 or 1-800/663-5508; ②) at the northern edge of town: for an extra $5 you can have access to a kitchen. *Same Sun International Travel Hostel* is a new **hostel** on the Platz (☎427-7191; ①) with dormitory accommodation. The nearest **campsite**, the inevitably named *Happy Hans Riverside RV Resort* (☎427-2929; $18–28; May–Oct), is south of the town centre on St Mary's Road and has modern facilities. Drop into the twee but excellent *Chef Bernard* café and **restaurant** opposite the clock, where the owner – heartily sick of Bavaria – often plays Irish fiddle music as a mark of defiance. He's also one of the best local chefs, and people come from miles for his fondue evenings. He has **rooms** upstairs (☎427-2433; ②). A favourite cheap place for lunch and breakfast is *Our Place*, 290 Spokane St, just down from the post office on the main crossroads. For more refined culinary offerings, make for *Pepper's*, 490 Wallinger Ave, a chicken, ribs and pasta place a couple of minutes' walk from the main plaza. Further afield is the *Old Barn House*, about fifteen-minutes' walk or a short drive from the town centre towards the ski area. For full details of Kimberley's many summer events, call in on the **infocentre** (daily: June–Sept 9am–7pm; Oct–May 9am–5pm; ☎427-3666) presently at

350 Ross St, just off the main crossroads past the *Quality Inn* – but it is due to move soon. The key draw is **Julyfest**, which includes a one-week beer festival and – almost inevitably – an international accordion championship.

Fort Steele Heritage Town

If you stick to Hwy 93/95 rather than detouring to Kimberley, you'll come to **FORT STEELE HERITAGE TOWN** (daily: May to early June & mid-Sept to early Oct 9.30am–5.30pm; early June to mid-Sept 9.30am–8pm; $7.50, $3.75 after 5.30pm), an impressively reconstructed c.1900 village of some 55 buildings in a superb mountain-ringed setting. It suffers somewhat by comparison with the similar reconstruction at Barkerville (125 buildings), but that's far further from civilization deep in Cariboo country (see p.804). The Fort Steele settlement started life in the 1860s as a provisions stop and river crossing for gold prospectors heading east to Wildhorse Creek, 6km beyond. By the late 1890s, thanks both to the local discovery of silver, lead and zinc, and the mistaken assumption that the railway would push through here, the population reached four thousand. But by 1910, after the mining frenzy had settled and the Canadian Pacific Railway chose to ride through Cranbrook instead, the population had shrunk to no more than 150.

Though the site was never completely abandoned, there was still much to do when restoration began in 1961. Staffed by volunteers in period dress, the town now consists of numerous buildings, some replicas, some original (1860s), some from the period of Steele's tenure, others brought from elsewhere and rebuilt. Among them are an old-time music hall, a blacksmiths', bakery, printers', general store and many more, with the added novelty of being able to watch people shoe horses, bake bread, make quilts and so forth. More spookily, there's also a restored Masonic Lodge, where a couple of funny-handshakers let you in on various selected "secrets" of masonic life. You can also nab a ride on a steam engine and, if you really must, take a turn on a wagon pulled by the massive Clydesdale horses that are reared in the village. These foibles notwithstanding, proceedings are all under the auspices of the provincial government, so generally lack the commercial frenzy that often characterizes such places. At 8pm most summer evenings the village reopens for an old-time variety show and cabaret.

A couple of ranches and B&Bs aside, there's little accommodation in the immediate vicinity, though there are two **campsites**: the *Fort Steele Resort and RV Park* across from the village (☎489-4268; $15–21), which has all the usual facilities, and the smaller *Original Fort Steele* campsite (☎426-5117; $15–21; June–Sept), on Kelly Road 2km south of the village and with similar facilities. Just east of Fort Steele there's also the *Norbury Lake Provincial Park* campsite ($12; mid-May to mid-Sept) with tent and RV sites. If you can get in, the *Wild Horse Farm* (☎426-6000; ④; May–Oct), with only three **rooms**, is an attractive log-faced "manor house" surrounded by eighty acres of meadows, woods and park-like estate across from the village.

To Fairmont Hot Springs

Back on Hwy 93/95, the Columbia Valley's scenery picks up as the Rockies begin to encroach and the blanket of trees opens up into pastoral river meadows. First stop is **Wasa**, whose lake, protected by the *Wasa Lake Provincial Park*, is warm enough for summer swimming. The lake also has a sizeable provincial park **campsite** (reservations possible, see p.691; $15; May–Sept). **Skookumchuck** ("strong water"), marked as a town on most maps, is in fact little more than a pulp mill whose chimneys belch out unpleasantness that spreads for kilometres downwind.

After a few kilometres the road curves around the **Dutch Creek Hoodoos**, fantastically eroded river bluffs that were created, according to Ktunaxa legend, when a vast wounded fish crawling up the valley expired at this point: as its flesh rotted, the bones fell apart to create the hoodoos. Close by is **Columbia Lake** – not one of the area's most picturesque patches of water, though the *Mountain Village*, a fine wooden **restaurant** crammed with hundreds of old bottles, makes a good meal stop and is just short of a colossal lumber yard that blights **Canal Flats** at the head of the lake. This little area resonates to the history of the wonderful William Adolph Baillie-Grohman, a man whose life was littered with wonderfully eccentric catastrophes. Here, in the 1880s, he planned to build a canal to link the Columbia and Kootenay rivers, also intending to drain virtually all of the Kootenay into the Columbia to prevent flooding (residents up and down the Columbia, not to mention the Canadian Pacific Railway, quickly prevented the latter plan). The canal, however, was completed in 1889, but proved so tortuous and perilous that only two boats ever made it all the way through (in 1894 and 1902). Even then the second boat only made it through by demolishing virtually all of the locks en route. Still, Baille-Grohman had the last laugh, for completing the canal – useless as it was – earned him a provincial land grant of some 30,000 acres. Head to *Canal Flats Provincial Park* (day-use only; April–Oct), 3km north of Canal Flats, if you want to view the remnants of the doomed project.

Just to the south of the Canal Flats mill is the Whiteswan Lake Road turn-off for **Whiteswan Lake Provincial Park**, a handkerchief-sized piece of unbeatable scenery at the end of a twenty-kilometre gravel logging road; the park has five **campsites** ($12; May–Sept) but few trails, as its main emphasis is on boating and trout fishing. Three of the campsites are at Whiteswan Lake itself, the other two at Alces Lake: also keep an eye open for the undeveloped Lussier Hot Springs at the entrance of the park (17.5km from the main road). The same access road, called the Lussier River Road after it passes the park, continues another 30km to **Top of the World Provincial Park**, a far wilder and very beautiful alpine region where you need to be completely self-sufficient – the five walk-in campsites ($5; June–Sept), reached by trail from the parking area at the end of the road, offer water and firewood and spaces for twenty in the Fish Lake cabin ($15; June–Sept). Hiking in the park is good, an obvious jaunt being the trail from the parking area along the Lussier River to Fish Lake (7km one-way; 2hr), where there's an unserviced campsite and a cabin (summer only). Mount Morro (3002m), the peak that looms over the region, is believed to have had great spiritual significance for the Ktunaxa, who came here to mine chert, a hard flinty quartz used to make tools and weapons.

FAIRMONT HOT SPRINGS spills over the Columbia's flat flood plain, less a settlement than an ugly modern upmarket resort that feeds off the appeal of the hot springs themselves. The pools were commandeered from the Ktunaxa (Kootenay) in 1922 for exploitation as a tourist resource; the calcium springs (daily 8am–10pm; $4) were particularly prized by the whites because they lack the sulphurous stench of many BC hot dips. However, the locals have now got their own back by opening some cheaper, makeshift pools above the resort, which are proving very popular with tourists. If you don't fancy coughing up around $159–239 to stay in a room at the swish resort, you could try its big **campsite** (☎345-6311; $15–35), one minute from the pools but only if you're in an RV – they don't want tents – or the *Spruce Grove Resort* (☎345-6561; ④, tents $19; May–Oct), near the river 2km south of Fairmont with rooms and a lovely riverside campsite with outdoor pool.

Invermere

Windermere, 15km north of Fairmont Hot Springs, is little more than a supermarket, petrol station and campsite immediately off the highway, and hardly hints at the presence of **INVERMERE**, about 1km beyond on the western shore of Windermere Lake. White settlement of the region can almost be said to have begun here, for explorer David Thompson passed this way in 1807 as he travelled up the Columbia River. With his abo-

> If you're continuing from Invermere into the **Kootenay National Park** and the Rockies, an account of the park begins on p.678. See p.591 if you're crossing the Crowsnest Pass into southern Alberta for **Waterton Lakes National Park**.

riginal wife, several children and eight companions, he built Kootenay House, the area's first trading post. Its site is marked by a cairn on Westside Road. A feel-good summer resort with the usual range of aquatic temptations, Invermere today makes a nicer accommodation prospect than Radium. However, droves of anglers, boaters and beach bums mean summer vacancies may be in short supply, in which case call the central **infocentre** at 5A Street and 7th Avenue (late July to early Sept daily 8am–8pm; ☎342-6316) for B&B possibilities or head for one of the town's four **motels** – the *Lee-Jay*, 1015 13th St (☎342-9227; ③), is the most reasonable and the *Best Western Invermere Inn* at the heart of downtown at 1310 7th Ave is the smartest (☎342-9246 or 1-800/661-8911; ④). The nearest provincial **campsite**, with vehicle and tent sites, is 7km north at Dry Gulch Provincial Park ($12; May to mid-Sept), but the private *Coldstream Lakeside Campground* (☎342-6793; $25 per vehicle; May–Sept) is on the lake and has a sandy beach. For **food**, try the popular *Myrtle's* on 7th Avenue, *Huckleberry's* on Laurier Street or the *Blue Dog Café* on 7th Avenue, the last being particularly good for vegetarians and wholefood aficionados. For highly regarded local cuisine make for *Strand's Old House*, 818 12th St (☎342-6344). If you want a break from eating, drinking or lazing on beaches, spend a few minutes with the mining, railway and other displays in the **Windermere Valley Museum**, 622 3rd St (June–Sept Tues–Sun 9.30am–4pm; $2; ☎342-9769), housed in a heritage building at the top of the hill and to the right on entering the village.

From Invermere the minor Toby Creek Road climbs west into the mountains to the burgeoning **Panorama Ski Resort** (18km), whose slick facilities include only limited and rather expensive accommodation. At over 1000m, the big 250-room *Panorama Resort* (☎342-6941 or 1-800/663-2929; ⑥) is also open in summer for tennis, riding, white-water rafting and fishing. In summer the chief appeal of the area is hiking, particularly if you continue up the road to the less tainted **Purcell Wilderness Conservancy**, one of the few easily accessible parts of the Purcell Mountains. If you have a tent and robust hiking inclinations, you could tackle the 61-kilometre **trail** through the area to Argenta (see p.833) on the northern end of Kootenay Lake, an excellent cross-country route that largely follows undemanding valleys except when crossing the Purcell watershed at Earl Grey Pass (2256m).

travel details

Trains

Kamloops to: Boston Bar (3 weekly; 4hr); Edmonton (3 weekly; 13hr 15min); Hope (3 weekly; 5hr 15min); Vancouver (3 weekly; 9hr).

North Vancouver to: Lillooet (1 daily; 5hr 35min); Prince George (3 weekly; 13hr 5min); Squamish (1–2 daily; 1hr 20min–2hr); Whistler (1 daily; 2hr 35min).

Vancouver to: Edmonton via Kamloops (3 weekly; 25hr); Jasper (June–Sept daily except Wed; Oct–May 3 weekly; 19hr); Lillooet (mid-June to Oct 1 daily; rest of year 4 weekly; 5hr 30min); Prince George (mid-June to Oct 1 daily; rest of year 3 weekly; 13hr 30min); Whistler (1 daily; 3hr).

Victoria to: Courtenay via Nanaimo (1 round trip daily; 4hr 35min).

Buses

Kamloops to: Kelowna (3 daily; 3hr 40min); Vernon (5 daily; 1hr 50min).

Kelowna to: Castlegar (2 daily; 4hr 45min); Cranbrook (2 daily; 11hr); Nelson (2 daily; 5hr 25min); Penticton (6 daily; 1hr 10min); Vancouver (6 daily; 5hr 30min).

Nanaimo to: Port Alberni (4 daily; 1hr 20min); Port Hardy (1 daily; 6hr 50min); Tofino (1–2 daily; 4hr 30min); Ucluelet (1–2 daily; 3hr 10min); Victoria (7 daily; 2hr 20min).

Port Alberni to: Nanaimo (4 daily; 1hr 20min); Tofino via Ucluelet (1–2 daily; 3hr).

Prince George to: Cache Creek (3 daily; 6hr 30min); Dawson Creek (2 daily; 6hr 30min).

Squamish to: Whistler (7 daily; 1hr 10min).

Vancouver to: Banff (4 daily; 14hr 5min); Bellingham (8–10 daily; 1hr 45min); Cache Creek (2 daily; 5hr 40min); Calgary (4 daily; 16hr); Calgary via Kamloops (6 daily; 13hr); Calgary via Penticton, Nelson and Cranbrook (2 daily; 24hr); Calgary via Princeton and Kelowna (2 daily; 18hr); Chilliwack, for Harrison Hot Springs (10 daily; 1hr 45min); Edmonton via Jasper (3 daily; 16hr 30min); Kamloops (8 daily; 5hr); Kelowna (6 daily; 5hr 30min); Nanaimo (8 daily; 5hr); Pemberton (3 daily; 3hr 10min); Penticton (3 daily; 5hr 20min); Powell River (2 daily; 5hr 10min); Prince George via Cache Creek and Williams Lake (2 daily; 13hr); Salmon Arm (6 daily; 7hr 5min); Seattle, US (8–10 daily; 3hr 15min); Sea-Tac Airport, US (8–10 daily; 4hr 10min); Squamish (6 daily; 1hr 15min); Vernon (6 daily; 6hr); Victoria (8 daily; 5hr); Whistler (6 daily; 2hr 30min).

Victoria to: Bamfield (1–3 daily; 6–8hr); Campbell River (5 daily; 5hr); Nanaimo (7 daily; 2hr 20min); Port Hardy (1 daily; 9hr 45min); Port Renfrew (2 daily; 2hr 30min); Vancouver (8–10 daily; 4hr); Vancouver Airport direct (3 daily; 3hr 30min).

Ferries

Chemainus to: Thetis Island and Kuper Island (minimum of 10 round trips daily; 35min).

Courtenay to: Powell River (4 daily; 1hr 15min).

Nanaimo to: Gabriola Island (17 daily; 20min); Vancouver/Horseshoe Bay Terminal (8 daily; 1hr 35min); Vancouver/Tsawwassen Terminal (8 daily; 2hr).

Northern Gulf Islands: Denman Island to Hornby Island (minimum 12 round trips daily; 10min); Quadra Island to Cortes Island (Mon–Sat 6 daily, Sun 5 daily; 45min); Vancouver Island (Buckley Bay) to Denman Island (18 round trips daily; 10min); Vancouver Island (Campbell River) to Quadra Island (17 round trips daily; 10min).

Port Hardy to: Bella Coola (1 every two days; 15hr 30min–22hr); Prince Rupert (1 every two days; 15hr).

Powell River to: Courtenay-Comox (4 round trips daily; 1hr 15min); Texada Island (10 round trips daily; 35min).

Southern Gulf Islands: Vancouver Island (Crofton) to Saltspring Island/Vesuvius Bay (14 round trips daily; 20min); Vancouver Island (Swartz Bay) to Saltspring Island/Fulford Harbour (10 round trips daily; 35min).

Sunshine Coast: Horseshoe Bay–Snug Cove (15 round trips daily; 20 minutes); Horseshoe Bay–Langdale (8 round trips daily; 40min); Jervis Inlet/Earls Cove–Saltery Bay (8–9 round trips daily; 50min).

Vancouver to: Nanaimo from Horseshoe Bay Terminal (8 daily; 1hr 35min); from Tsawwassen Terminal (8 daily; 2hr); Victoria (Swartz Bay Terminal) from Tsawwassen (hourly summer 7am–9pm; rest of the year minimum 8 daily 7am–9pm; 1hr 35min).

Victoria to: Anacortes and San Juan Islands, US, from Victoria's Inner Harbour (1–2 daily; 2hr 30min); Seattle, US, from Inner Harbour (1–2 daily; 2hr 30min); Vancouver (Tsawwassen) from Swartz Bay (hourly summer 7am–10pm; rest of the year minimum 8 daily; 1hr 35min).

Flights

Vancouver to: Calgary (20 daily; 1hr 15min); Castlegar (1–2 daily; 1hr 20min); Cranbrook (1–2 daily; 2hr 30min); Edmonton (14 daily; 1hr 30min); Kamloops (4–5 daily; 1hr); Kelowna (7–9 daily; 1hr); Montréal (8 daily; 5hr 35min); Ottawa (10 daily; 4hr 40min); Penticton (3–5 daily; 50min); Prince George (5–8 daily; 1hr 10min); Toronto (15 daily; 4hr 55min); Victoria (14 daily; 25min); Winnipeg (8 daily; 2hr 40min).

Victoria to: Calgary (4 daily; 1hr 40min); Vancouver (14 daily; 25min).

CHAPTER EIGHT

THE NORTH

Although much of Canada still has the flavour of the "last frontier", it's only when you embark on the mainland push north to the Yukon that you know for certain you're leaving the mainstream of North American life behind. In the popular imagination, **the north** figures as a perpetually frozen wasteland blasted by ferocious gloomy winters, inhabited – if at all – by hardened characters beyond the reach of civilization. In truth, it's a region where months of summer sunshine offer almost limitless opportunities for outdoor activities and an incredible profusion of flora and fauna; a country within a country, the character of whose settlements has often been forged by the mingling of white settlers and **aboriginal peoples**. The indigenous hunters of the north are as varied as in the south, but two groups predominate: the **Dene**, people of the northern forests who traditionally occupied the Mackenzie River region from the Albertan border to the river's delta at the Beaufort Sea; and the Arctic **Inuit** (literally "the people"), once known as the Eskimos or "fish eaters", a Dene term picked up by early European settlers and now discouraged.

The north is as much a state of mind as a place. People "north of 60" – the 60th Parallel – claim the right to be called **northerners**, and maintain a kinship with Alaskans, but those north of the **Arctic Circle** – the 66th Parallel – look with light-hearted disdain on these "southerners". All mock the inhabitants of the northernmost corners of Alberta and such areas of the so-called Northwest, who, after all, live with the luxury of being able to get around their backcountry by road. To any outsider, however, in terms of landscape and overall spirit the north begins well south of the 60th Parallel. Accordingly, this chapter includes not just the provinces of the "true north" – **Yukon** and parts of the western Arctic and **Northwest Territories** – but also northern **British Columbia**, a region more stark and extreme than BC's southern reaches.

Northern British Columbia

The two roads into the Yukon strike through northern British Columbia: the **Alaska Highway**, connecting **Dawson Creek** to Fairbanks in Alaska, and the adventurous **Cassiar Highway**, from near **Prince Rupert** to **Watson Lake**, on the Yukon border. Though the Cassiar's passage through the Coast Mountains offers perhaps the better landscapes, it's the Alaska Highway – serviced by daily Greyhound **buses** and plentiful motels and campsites – that is more travelled, starting in the rolling wheatlands of the Peace River country before curving into the spruce forests and sawtooth ridges of the northern Rockies. While the scenery is superb, most towns on both roads are battered and perfunctory places built around lumber mills, oil and gas plants and mining camps, though increasingly they are spawning motels and restaurants to serve the surge of summer visitors out to capture the thrill of driving the frontier highways.

The telephone code for British Columbia is ☎250.
The telephone code for the Yukon is ☎867.
The telephone code for the Northwest Territories and Nunavut ☎867.

Equally popular are the **sea journeys** offered along northern British Columbia, among the most breathtaking trips in all Canada. Prince Rupert, linked by ferry to Vancouver Island, is the springboard for boats to the magnificent **Haida Gwaii**, or **Queen Charlotte Islands** – home of the Haida people – and a vital way station for boats plying the Inside Passage up to Alaska.

The Yukon

The Cassiar and Alaska highways converge at **Watson Lake**, a weather-beaten junction that straddles the 60th Parallel and marks the entrance to the **Yukon Territory** (YT), perhaps the most exhilarating and varied destination in this part of the world. Taking its name from a Dene word meaning "great", it boasts the highest mountains in Canada, wild sweeps of forest and tundra, and the fascinating nineteenth-century relic, **Dawson City**. The focus of the Klondike gold rush, Dawson was also the territory's capital until that role shifted south to **Whitehorse**, a town booming on tourism and the ever-increasing exploitation of the Yukon's vast mineral resources.

Road access is easier than you might think. In addition to the Alaska Highway, which runs through the Yukon's southern reaches, the **Klondike Highway** strikes north to link Whitehorse with Dawson City. North of Dawson the **Dempster Highway** is the only road in Canada to cross the Arctic Circle, offering an unparalleled direct approach to the northern tundra and to several remote communities in the Northwest Territories. The Yukon's other major road is the short spur linking the Alaskan port of Skagway to Whitehorse, which shadows the **Chilkoot Trail**, a treacherous track taken by the poorest of the 1898 prospectors that is now a popular long-distance footpath.

Combining coastal ferries with the Chilkoot Trail makes an especially fine itinerary. Following the old gold-rush trail, the route begins at Skagway – reached by ferry from Prince Rupert – then follows the Chilkoot to Whitehorse, before heading north to Dawson City. From there you could continue up the Dempster Highway, or travel on the equally majestic **Top of the World** road into the heart of Alaska. However, many people coming up from Skagway or plying the mainland routes from British Columbia head to Alaska directly on the Alaska Highway, to enjoy views of the extraordinary and largely inaccessible mountain vastness of **Kluane National Park**, which contains Canada's highest peaks and most extensive glacial wilderness.

Nunavut and the Northwest Territories

If the Yukon is the far north at its most accessible, the **Northwest Territories** (NWT) is the region at its most uncompromising. Just three roads nibble at the edges of this almost unimaginably vast area, which occupies a third of Canada's landmass – about the size of India – but contains only 60,000 people, almost half of whom live in or around **Yellowknife**, the territories' peculiarly overblown capital. Unless you're taking the adventurous and rewarding **Dempster Highway** from Dawson City across the tundra to **Inuvik**, Yellowknife will probably feature on any trip to the NWT, as it's the hub of the (rather expensive) flight network servicing the area's widely dispersed communities.

Otherwise most visitors are here to fish or canoe, to hunt or watch wildlife, or to experience the Inuit aboriginal cultures and ethereal landscapes. More for

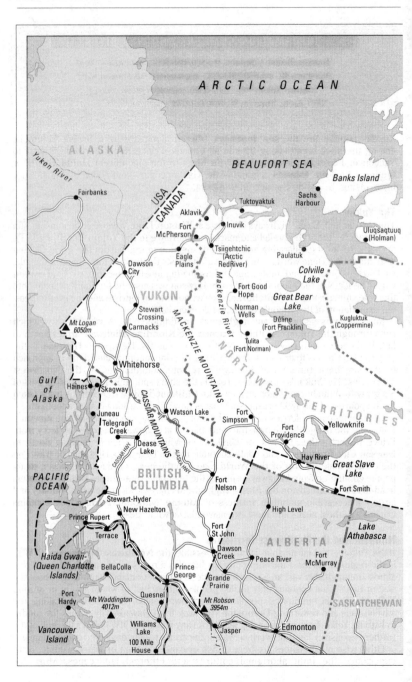

ARCTIC OCEAN

ALASKA

Yukon River

BEAUFORT SEA

Banks Island

Fairbanks

Sachs
Harbour

USA
CANADA

Tuktoyaktuk

Aklavik

Inuvik

Uluqsaqtuuq
(Holman)

Fort
McPherson

Tsiigehtchic
(Arctic
RedRiver)

Paulatuk

Eagle
Plains

Dawson
City

Colville
Lake

YUKON

Fort Good
Hope

Great Bear
Lake

Stewart
Crossing

Norman
Wells

Mt Logan
6050m

Carmacks

Déline
(Fort Franklin)

Kugluktuk
(Coppermine)

MACKENZIE MOUNTAINS

Mackenzie River

Tulita
(Fort Norman)

Whitehorse

NORTHWEST

Gulf
of
Alaska

Haines

Skagway

CASSIAR MOUNTAINS

Watson Lake

Fort
Simpson

TERRITORIES

Juneau
Telegraph
Creek

Fort
Providence

Yellowknife

CASSIAR HWY

Dease
Lake

ALASKA HWY

Hay River

Great Slave
Lake

PACIFIC
OCEAN

BRITISH
COLUMBIA

Fort
Nelson

Fort Smith

Stewart-Hyder

High Level

Lake
Athabasca

Prince Rupert

New Hazelton

Terrace

Fort
St John

ALBERTA

Fort
McMurray

Haida Gwaii-
(Queen Charlotte
Islands)

BellaColla

Dawson
Creek

Peace River

Prince
George

Grande
Prairie

Port
Hardy

Mt Waddington
4012m

Quesnel

Mt Robson
3954m

SASKATCHEWAN

Vancouver
Island

Williams
Lake

Jasper

Edmonton

100 Mile
House

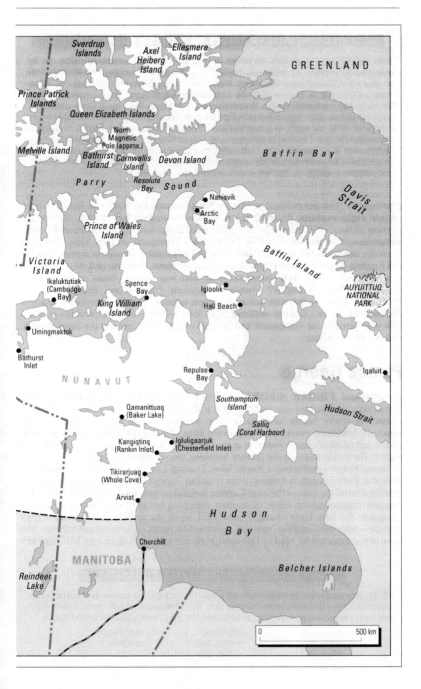

PROVINCIAL CAMPSITES IN BRITISH COLUMBIA

Tent and RV sites at certain campsites in British Columbia's provincial parks can be reserved in advance. To make **reservations**, call Discover Camping (☎1-800/689-9025 or 604/689-9025 in greater Vancouver; March to mid-Sept Mon–Fri 7am–7pm, Sat & Sun 9am–5pm) or log on to their Web site *www.discovercamping.ca*, where reservations can be made and confirmed online. Reservations can be made from up to three months in advance and no later than 48 hours before the first day of arrival. A nonrefundable booking fee of $6.42 per night, to a maximum of $19.26 for three or more nights, is charged (rates include tax). Payment in advance is by Visa or MasterCard only (payment for extra nights once at a campsite is by cash only). You can stay in BC provincial parks up to a maximum of fourteen days in any single park. Information on all aspects of BC's provincial parks is available on the Net at *www.elp.gov.bc.ca/bcparks*.

convenience than any political or geographical reasons, the NWT was formally divided into **eight regions**. From 1999 a new two-way division has applied, the eastern portion of the NWT having been renamed Nunavut (see p.908), a separate entity administered by and on behalf of the region's aboriginal peoples. One effect has been the **renaming** of most settlements with Inuit names, though in many cases the old English-language names appear in much literature. Nunavut and the "old" western NWT issue their own tourist material, and you should obtain a copy of their respective *Arctic Travellers' Nunavut Vacation Planner* and *Explorers' Guide* brochures. These summarize accommodation options, airline connections, many of the available tours – costing anything from $50 to $5000 – and the plethora of outfitters who provide the equipment and backup essential for any but the most superficial trip to the region.

Prince George

Rough-edged **PRINCE GEORGE**, carved from the forest to become British Columbia's sixth largest city (pop. 78,000), is the general area's services and transport centre, so you're highly likely to become acquainted with its dispersed and half-deserted downtown streets. Forestry, in the form of pulp mills, kilns, planers, plywood plants and allied chemical works, is at the core of its industrial landscape – if you ever wanted the inside story on the lumber business, this is where to find it.

Simon Fraser established a North West Trading Company post here in 1805, and named it **Fort George** in honour of the reigning George III. As a commercial nexus it quickly altered the lives of the local **Carrier Sekani** people, who abandoned their semi-nomadic migration from winter to summer villages in favour of a permanent settlement alongside the fort. Little changed until 1914 when the arrival of the Grand Trunk Railway – later the Canadian National – spawned an influx of pioneers and loggers. The town was connected by road to Dawson Creek and the north as late as 1951, and saw

ACCOMMODATION PRICE CODES

All the accommodation prices in this book have been coded using the symbols below, corresponding to Canadian dollar rates. Prices are for the least expensive double room in each establishment in high season, excluding special offers. For a full explanation, see p.40 in Basics.

① up to $40	④ $80–100	⑦ $175–240
② $40–60	⑤ $100–125	⑧ $240+
③ $60–80	⑥ $125–175	

the arrival of the Pacific Great Eastern Railway in 1958 – two developments that give some idea of how recent the opening up of the far north has been.

The town is a disorienting open-plan network of roads and sporadic houses between Hwy 97 and a sprawling downtown area at the junction of the Fraser and Nechako rivers. As far as sightseeing is concerned, you might as well stick to what Prince George does best and take the surprisingly popular free **tours** around some of its big mills and processing plants; to reserve a place, contact Tourism Prince George opposite the bus terminal at 1198 Victoria St and 15th Avenue (Mon–Fri 8.30am–4pm, Sat 9am–4pm, Sun 9am–4pm; longer hours in summer; ☎562-3700 or 1-800/668-7646, *www.tourismpg.bc.ca*). Company buses generally pick up from the Tourism Prince George offices and deliver you to one of several firms, the biggest currently being Northwood Pulp and Timber, where you are shown thousands of seedlings being grown in controlled conditions, the sawmills, and one of the continent's largest pulp mills. Outside, in a graphic illustration of the scale of forestry in the region, logs, planks and piles of sawdust the size of small hills stretch almost as far as the eye can see.

Practicalities

Air BC (☎561-2905 or 1-800/663-3721 in Canada) serves Prince George by air: the airport is 18km east of downtown and linked by regular shuttles. The town is linked by BC Rail to Vancouver (via the Cariboo region), and by VIA Rail to Jasper, Edmonton and beyond eastbound, and Prince Rupert westbound (for the Haida Gwaii/Prince Charlotte Islands and Inside Passage ferries). Only VIA Rail drops you downtown at 1300 1st Ave (☎564-5223 or 1-800/561-8630); if you're heading for motels or the bus terminal use a taxi from either Prince George Taxi (☎564-4444); or Emerald Taxi Ltd (☎563-3333). The **BC Rail** (☎561-4033 or 1-800/663-8238) trains arrive 5km south of downtown on Hwy 97 at the end of Terminal Boulevard, but there's a free connecting bus service to various points, including the motels at the bus terminal and on Hwy 97 for a quick getaway the following day.

The town is also a staging post for **Greyhound** routes to the north, and integral to the main road routes to Dawson Creek (for the Alaska Hwy) and Prince Rupert (for the Cassiar Hwy). The Greyhound **bus terminal**, well south of downtown at 1566 12th Ave (☎564-5454 or 1-800/661-8747), is close to a handful of the town's many hotels and motels.

The best **motel** on the Hwy 97 strip is the big *Spruceland Inn* (☎563-0102 or 1-800/663-3295; ③), at 1391 Central St at the junction of Hwy 97 and 15th Avenue. At the nearby *Esther's Inn* (☎562-4131 or 1-800/663-6844, *www.netbistro.com/esthers*; ③), one block off the highway at 1151 Commercial Drive (10th Ave), the price includes a swimming pool and jacuzzi. Closer to downtown is the comfortable 200-room *Ramada Hotel Downtown Prince George*, 444 George St (☎563-0055 or 1-800/830-8833; ⑤). All the campsites are some way out, the best being the big *Blue Spruce RV & Campground* about 5km west at Kimball Road on Hwy 16 (☎964-7272 or 964-4060; $15.50–21; April to mid-Oct), which includes a heated outdoor pool.

With **food**, don't expect much in the way of culinary sophistication and stick to good chains like *Earl's*, 1440 E Central St, or *White Spot*, 820 Victoria St; otherwise treat yourself to Italian and other mid-priced dishes at *Da Moreno*, 1493 3rd Ave (☎564-7922), probably the best restaurant in town. **Moving on**, three VIA Rail (☎1-800/561-8630) trains run weekly to Prince Rupert and Edmonton via Jasper ($71), a highly scenic journey; BC Rail runs daily trains to Vancouver in summer (3 weekly in winter; $196), but this is a far more tedious trip through almost unending forest until you reach the region around Fraser river well to the south (☎604/984-5246 or 1-800/663-8238). Greyhound runs one bus daily to Whitehorse in the Yukon, two daily to Vancouver, and two daily to Prince Rupert.

THE AURORA BOREALIS

The **aurora borealis**, or "Northern Lights", is a beautiful and ethereal display of light in the upper atmosphere that can be seen over large areas of northern Canada. The night sky appears to shimmer with dancing curtains of colour, ranging from luminescent monotones – most commonly green or a dark red – to fantastic veils that run the full spectrum. The display becomes more animated as it proceeds, twisting and turning in patterns called "rayed bands". As a finale, a corona sometimes appears, in which rays seem to flare in all directions from a central point.

Named after the Roman goddess of dawn, the aurora was long thought to be produced by sunlight reflected from polar snow and ice, or refracted light produced in the manner of a rainbow. Certain Inuit peoples believed the lights were the spirits of animals or ancestors; others thought they represented wicked forces. Old-time gold prospectors thought they might be vapours given off by ore deposits. Research still continues into the phenomenon, but the latest thought is that the aurora is caused by radiation emitted as light from atoms in the upper atmosphere as they are hit by fast-moving electrons and protons. The earth's geomagnetic field certainly plays some part in the creation of the aurora, but its source would appear to lie with the sun – auroras become more distinct and are seen spread over a larger area two days after intense solar activity, the time it takes the "solar wind" to arrive. This wind is composed of fast-moving electrically charged ions. When these hit the earth's atmosphere they respond to the earth's magnetic field and move towards the poles. En route they strike atoms and molecules of gas in the upper atmosphere, causing them to become temporarily charged or ionized. These molecules then release the charge, or energy, usually in the form of light. Different colours are emitted depending on the gases involved: oxygen produces a green colour (or orange at higher altitudes), nitrogen an occasionally violet colour.

You should be able to see the Northern Lights as far south as Prince George in British Columbia, over parts of northern Alberta (where on average they're visible some 160 nights a year) and over much of the Northwest Territories, Nunavut and northern Manitoba. They are at their most dazzling from **December to March**, when nights are longest and the sky darkest, though they are potentially visible all year round. Look out for a faint glow on the northeastern horizon after dusk, and then – if you're lucky – for the full show as the night deepens.

Prince George to Prince Rupert

There are two ways to make the 735-kilometre journey west from **Prince George to Prince Rupert**: using Hwy 16 or the parallel VIA Rail railway, neither of them terribly scenic by BC standards until they reach the glorious river and mountain landscapes of the **Skeena Valley** 150km before Prince Rupert. Most people make this trip as a link in a much longer journey, either to pick up **ferries** north to Alaska or south to Port Hardy on Vancouver Island, or to pick up the start of the Cassiar Hwy, a rough wilderness road that cuts north from the Skeena Valley to meet the Alaska Hwy at Watson Lake over the Yukon border. Unless you fly, it's also the only way to reach the Haida Gwaii/Queen Charlotte Islands, accessible by ferry or plane from Prince Rupert. The best place to pause during the journey is near **Hazelton**, where you can visit a little cluster of **aboriginal villages**.

Vanderhoof to Smithers

Riding out of Prince George you're confronted quickly with the relentless monotony of the Interior Plateau's rolling forests, an arboreal grind broken only by the occasional lake and the grey silhouettes of distant low-hilled horizons. At **VANDERHOOF**, 98km down the highway, gentler patches of pasture begin to poke through the tree cover, but these do little to soften the impact of the town itself. An abrupt grid of garages and motels, it's best known for its July airshow and the more graceful aerial dynamics of thousands of Canadian geese at the nearby **Nechako Bird Sanctuary**. Before pushing on, grab a coffee at the _OK Café_, part of a fine collection of half-timbered heritage houses at the town's western end. If you get stuck, or would prefer to stay in the village rather than Prince George, there are cheap **motels**: the largest of them is the _Grand Trunk Inn_, 2351 Church Ave (☎567-3188 or 1-877/567-3188; ②); or you could try the slightly more expensive _Siesta Motel_ downtown on Hwy 16 (☎567-2365 or 1-800/914-3388, _t_lobelle@yahoo.com_; ③). For **camping**, there's the _Riverside Park Campground_, overlooking the bird sanctuary at 3100 Burrard Ave (☎567-4710; $14; May–Sept). The **infocentre** is at 2353 Burrard Ave (year-round; ☎567-2124 or 1-800/752-4094, _chamber@hwy16.com_).

Beyond here the ride becomes more verdant towards **FORT FRASER**, 50km beyond, a more attractive spot than Vanderhoof itself. If you're **camping**, hold out for the provincial site at Beaumont Provincial Park (☎565-6340; $15), 3.5km to the west, whose meadow site falls away gently to Fraser Lake. The lake has a seasonal **infobooth** on Hwy 16 at Empire Street (late June to early Sept daily 9am–7pm; ☎690-7733, _ffcc@hwy16.com_).

Beyond Burn's Lake the scenery picks up still more, as if preparing for the mountains in the distance, though the run of villages continues to offer little but places to fill either the tank or the stomach. If you're going as far as to **stay** in this region, aim for the _Douglas Motel_ (☎846-5679, _www.monday.com/douglasmotel_; ④), on the banks of the Bulkley River, just 150m out of the unspoilt hamlet of **TELKWA**, 10km east of Smithers. If you do stay, be sure to take a few minutes to stroll up the riverfront street of heritage buildings and its handsome brown-and-white, wood-planked **pioneer museum**.

SMITHERS, the largest place after Prince George (370km to the east), is focused on a single main crossroads on Hwy 16, with an **infocentre** nearby at 1411 Court St (year-round; ☎847-5072 or 1-800/542-6673, _www.bulkley.net/~smichan_) and a big Super-Valu **supermarket** for supplies on the junction itself. If you're overnighting here – and there's plenty of **accommodation** – ignore the brace of motels on the road and settle for the big white-timbered _Hudson Bay Lodge_ (☎847-4581 or 1-800/663-5040, _www.hudsonbaylodge.com_; ④) outside the village as you enter from the east. If this is out of your budget, try the _Florence Motel_ (☎847-2678; ②) on the west side of town – it's half the price – or the _Sandman Inn Smithers_ on Hwy 16, a block from Main Street, part of an invariably trustworthy chain (☎847-2637 or 1-800/726-3626, _www.sandman.ca_; ③).

The Skeena Valley

Hard on the heels of industrial **Terrace**, the **Skeena River** (the "River of the Mists") carves a beautiful valley through the Coast Mountains, an important trade route for aboriginal peoples and stern-wheelers before the coming of the railway in 1912. For a couple of hours the road and railway run past a huge backdrop of snowcapped peaks half-reflected in the mist-wraithed estuary. Out on the water there's a good chance of seeing the ripples of beavers and sea otters, not to mention bald eagles perched on the river's immense log jams. Dark valleys peel off the main river's majestic course, suggestive of a deep, untrodden wilderness, and delicate threads of waterfalls are repeatedly visible though the trees.

Shortly after Hwy 16 meets the river crashing down from the north near Hazelton and New Hazelton, a couple of minor roads strike off to four nearby **Gitxsan aboriginal villages**, places where something of the culture of the area's indigenous Gitxsan peoples has been preserved, along with new examples of totem carving and other crafts. 'Ksan and Kispiox, home to the best totems and long houses, are a few kilometres off Hwy 16 on the minor High Level Road (Hwy 62) out of New Hazelton; just north of 'Ksan a road links west to Gitwangak and Gitanyow (formerly Kitwancool), or they can be reached by continuing west on Hwy 16 a few kilometres and heading north on Hwy 37 (the Cassiar Hwy).

The most easterly of the west coast aboriginal peoples, the Gitxsan – "people of the river of the mists" – traditionally lived off fish and game rather than agriculture, and were consummate artists and carvers. Many of their traditions were eroded by the coming of whites, and by missionaries in particular, but in the 1950s the people's elders made a determined decision to resurrect as much of their dying culture as possible, re-creating an entire 1870 settlement at **'KSAN**. Although there's a good deal of commercialism, this is the village to concentrate on – aboriginal women act as guides around several long houses, giving a commentary on the carvings, clothes, buildings and masks on show, as well as offering accounts of local history (tours mid-April to mid-Oct usually daily 9am–5pm but longer hours July–Aug; $8).

KISPIOX, 13km north of Hazelton, is the ancient Gitxsan home of the Frog, Wolf and Fireweed clans, and was given its name by the old Department for Indian Affairs. It means "place of loud talkers" but locals not surprisingly prefer the traditional name, which is Anspayaxw, meaning "the hidden place". The highlights here are fifteen riverside totems. **GITWANGAK** to the west, just 500m north of the Hwy 16 and Hwy 37 junction, means "the place of rabbits", and was the traditional village home of the Eagle, Wolf and Frog. It, too, has some impressive totems, as does **GITANYOW** – "people of a small village" – 21km north on Hwy 37, whose eighteen poles include the 140-year-old "Hole in the Ice" or "Hole in the Sky" totem. You can sometimes watch poles being repaired at one of two carving sheds around the village.

The nearest **infocentre** for the villages is near New Hazelton at the junction of Hwys 16 and 62 (mid-May to mid-Sept daily 9am–5pm; ☎842-6071 or 842-6571 year-round, *hazletontourist@hotmail.com*), but you should also spend a few minutes looking round the evocative old Victorian streets of old **HAZELTON** 6km to the northwest on Hwy 62. **Accommodation** is limited to a couple of motels in New Hazelton, the cheapest being the *Bulkley Valley Motel*, 4444 Hwy 16 (☎842-6817; ②) Kispiox also has a few rooms and campsite: the *Sportsman's Kispiox Lodge* (☎842-6455 or 1-800/KISPIOX, *www.kispiox.com/lodge*; ④) and the *Kispiox River Resort and Campground* (☎842-6182; ②; camping $12–20; June–Oct).

Prince Rupert

There's a bracing tang of salt and fish on the air in **PRINCE RUPERT**, a distinctive port that comes as an invigorating relief after the run of characterless villages out of Prince George. A good-looking place, similar in appearance to a Scottish fishing town, it looks out over an archipelago of islands and is ringed by mountains that tumble to the sea along a beautiful fjord-cut coastline. A crowd of cars, backpackers and RVs washes daily through its streets off the **Alaska, Queen Charlotte** and **Port Hardy ferries**, complementing the seafront's vibrant activity, and adding to the coffers of a town that's quite clearly on the up and up. There's nothing much to do, but if you're waiting for a boat it's an amiable enough spot and you'll probably bump into more fellow travellers here than almost anywhere else in northern BC.

Arrival

The **Greyhound station** is in the centre of town at 822 3rd Ave and 8th Street (daily 8.30am–8.30pm; ☎624-5090) and handles two buses daily (morning and evening) for the twelve-hour ride to Prince George ($85 one-way). The **VIA Rail train station** is on the waterfront at 1st Avenue and the foot of 2nd Street (open 2hr either side of departures and arrivals; ☎627-7589, 627-7304 or 1-800/561-8630). Trains to Prince George for connections from Prince George to Edmonton via Jasper currently leave on Wednesday,

Friday and Sunday at 8am, arriving in Prince George at 8.10pm. If you're thinking of taking the train right through, note that you have to overnight in Prince George as there are no through-trains to Jasper or Edmonton. The local **airport** is on Digby Island just across the harbour, with ferry connections to the BC and Alaska Marine ferry terminals (see box, below) and shuttle bus connections to downtown. Check-in with your airline in downtown at least two hours before flight departure for the combined shuttle-ferry service to the airport. Air BC (☎624-4554 or 1-800/663-3721) flies to Vancouver and has

---

FERRIES FROM PRINCE RUPERT

Ferry terminals for both BC Ferries (for Port Hardy and the Queen Charlotte Islands) and the Alaska Marine Highway (for Skagway and Alaska Panhandle ports) are at **Fairview Dock**, 2km southwest of town at the end of Hwy 16. Walk-on tickets for foot passengers are rarely a problem at either terminal, but advance reservations are essential if you're taking a car or want a cabin for any summer crossing. A town bus passes the terminal every two or three hours for incoming sailings, but for outbound sailings it's probably best to grab a **taxi** from downtown. You can arrange a pick-up from the ferry by calling Seashore Charters (☎624-5645). Alternatively walk a kilometre to the corner of Pillsbury and Kootenay, where the local #52 bus passes roughly every half an hour (Mon–Sat 7.30am–5.30pm).

BC Ferries operate the MV *Queen of Prince Rupert* **to Skidegate** on the Queen Charlotte Islands daily except Tuesday from July to September at 11am (except Mon 9pm), four times a week the rest of the year (Mon, Tues, Thurs & Fri), a crossing that takes between 6hr 30min and 8hr (depending on weather) and costs $25 ($20 low season: late Sept to early June) one-way for foot passengers (plus $93 low/$76 low season for cars and $6 for bikes). Return ferries from Skidegate operate daily except Sunday, leaving at 11pm and arriving at 7.30am except on some summer Fridays and Saturdays, when the boat docks earlier to provide a connection with the Inside Passage boat to Port Hardy on Vancouver Island (see below). For **reservations** or timetable information, contact Prince Rupert's infocentre or BC Ferries direct on ☎386-3431 (or 1-888/223-3779 anywhere in BC).

Ferries **to Port Hardy** leave every other day in summer at 7.30am (even-numbered days in June, July, Sept and first half of Oct, odd-numbered days in Aug) and once a week in winter for a stunning fifteen-hour cruise that costs $106 one-way for drivers or walk-on passengers (shoulder mid-March to mid-May $75, low season mid-Jan to mid-March $56). Bikes cost $6.50. To take on a car ($218/$154/$116; all excluding driver or passengers) you'll need to have booked at least two months in advance (see also Port Hardy, p.787).

The **Alaska Marine Highway** (☎627-1744 or 1-800/642-0066) ferries run **to Skagway** (via some or all of Ketchikan, Wrangell, Petersburg, Sitka, Hyder, Stewart, Juneau, Haines and Hollis) almost daily in July and August, four times a week for the rest of the summer and in spring and autumn, and twice a week in winter (to Ketchikan, passengers US$38, vehicles US$75; to Juneau, passengers US$104, vehicles US$240; to Haines, passengers US$122, vehicles US$276; to Skagway, passengers US$130, vehicles US$285). Two- or four-berth cabins can also be booked: current prices for a two-berth cabin from Prince Rupert are as follows: Bellingham (US$142), Juneau (US$83), Haines (US$105), Skagway (US$105). Boats stop frequently en route, with the chance to go ashore for a short time, though longer stopovers must be arranged when buying a through-ticket. For all Alaskan sailings turn up at least an hour before departure to go through US customs and immigration procedures if you're a foot passenger, and three hours if you have a car, and note that though the journey takes two days there are various restrictions on the fresh food you can take on board. You may find you can't make telephone or credit-card bookings, and have to pay in person for tickets at the terminal ticket office (May–Sept daily 9am–4pm and 2hr either side of sailings; on days of sailings the rest of the year). Fares are 25 percent lower between October and April.

a base in town at 112 6th St. Local firms Inland Air (☎627-1351 or 1-888/624-2577) and Harbour Air (☎627-1341 or 1-800/689-4234) both run flights to Sandspit on the Queen Charlotte Islands (see p.865).

Many people reach Prince Rupert by **ferry**. For details of how to reach downtown from the **ferry terminal**, which is 2km from town, see the box, overleaf. For **car rentals**, contact National Car Rental (☎624-5318) in the Rupert Mall on 2nd Avenue West.

Accommodation

Finding **accommodation** in Prince Rupert shouldn't present problems outside July and August, when places fill up quickly on days when the ferries come in: book ahead to be on the safe side. If there's nothing in town, you can always backtrack along Hwy 16 to the villages beyond the Skeena Valley. The town's only decent budget option, with basic hostel-type rooms and shared bathrooms, is the quickly filled *Pioneer Rooms*, around the corner from the museum and infocentre at 167 3rd Ave (☎624-2334; ①). The nearest motel to the ferry terminals is the *Totem Lodge Motel*, 1335 Park Ave (☎624-6761 or 1-800/550-0178; ③): Park Avenue is a continuation of 2nd Avenue that runs south to the terminals from downtown. Perhaps the best all-round central choice, especially if you can secure a room with a sea view, is the *Inn on the Harbour*, 720 1st Ave (☎624-9107 or 1-800/663-8155; ③), while most reasonable of the many mid-range establishments is the *Aleeda*, 900 3rd Ave (☎627-1367; ③). *Pacific Inn*, 909 3rd Ave W (☎627-1711 or 1-888/663-1999; ③), is a big and good-value motel, but if you want to go top-of-the-range try the large *Crest Hotel*, 222 1st Ave (☎624-6771 or 1-800/663-8150, *www.cresthotel.bc.ca*; ⑥), or the more reasonable mini-skyscraper *Highliner Inn*, 815 1st Ave W (☎624-9060 or 1-800/668-3115, *www.floriangroup.com*; ④). Further afield, the *Parkside Resort*, 101 11th Ave (☎624-9131 or 1-888/575-2288, *www.marlintravel.com/parkside.htm*; ②), is a smart-looking hotel with good rates about a kilometre out of town and more likely to have room when downtown places are full.

The only big local **campsite** is the *Park Avenue Campground*, 1750 Park Ave (☎624-5861; $13.50; year-round), 1km west of town and 1km from the ferry terminals: it has tent sites but is usually full of RVs. Otherwise the *Parkside Resort* (see above) has some sites ($10–18) that few people know about, and there's also the rural *Prudhomme Lake* provincial campsite (☎798-2277; April–Nov), with forested lakeside sites, 16km east of town on Hwy 16.

The Town

Although you wouldn't know to look at it, the port is one of the world's largest deep-water terminals, and handles a huge volume of trade (grain, coal and fish in particular). In the past the region was the focal point of trade between aboriginal peoples to the north and south, one reason why the Hudson's Bay Company built a post at Fort Simpson, 30km north of the present townsite. It was also the reason why the old Hudson's Bay post was chosen as the terminus of Canada's second **transcontinental rail link**. Work began in 1906, but as time went by it was decided there was a better harbour to the south, a national competition being launched to decide on a name for the new railhead: $250 was paid for "Prince Rupert", named after the company's royal founding member, a label that was duly grafted onto the ramshackle collection of tents that constituted the settlement in 1909. A year later the first town lot was sold for around $500; within twelve months it was worth $17,000. The Grand Trunk Railway chairman, Charles M. Hays, hoped to turn Prince Rupert into a port to rival Vancouver. In 1912 he set off for Britain to raise stock for the venture, but unfortunately booked a return passage on the *Titanic*. Although he went down, the railway was finished two years later – too late, in the event, to steal a march on Vancouver. By 1919 the Grand Trunk was bankrupt, though its restructuring as the Canadian National in 1923 and the magnificence of the port has allowed the town to prosper to this day. For more on the railway and its history, visit the **Kwinitsa Station Railway Museum** just across from the VIA Rail station near the waterfront (early June to early Sept daily 9am–6pm; donation; ☎627-1915 or 627-3207).

Prince Rupert's excellent **Museum of Northern British Columbia** (June–Aug Mon–Sat 9am–8pm, Sun 9am–5pm; Sept–May Mon–Sat 9am–5pm; $5) is alongside the **infocentre** (same hours; ☎624-5637 or 1-800/667-1994 in BC, *prtravel@citytel.net*) on 1st Avenue and McBride Street at the northern end of the town's tight downtown zone. It's housed in an impressive reproduction First Nation cedar long-house and is particularly strong on the culture and history of the local **Tsimshian**. The museum also boasts a clutch of wonderful silent archive films on topics ranging from fishing to the building of the railway – ideal ways to whittle away a wet afternoon, of which storm-lashed Prince Rupert ("City of Rainbows") has plenty. There's also a well-stocked book and gift shop and a carving shed outside where you can sometimes see totems being crafted.

While you're here, check out some of the local **tours** or **boat trips**, many of which are inexpensive and a good way to see the offshore islands and wildlife. The museum runs a tour to sites of archeological interest (mid-June to early Sept daily 1–3.30pm; $22). Otherwise Seashore Charters (☎624-5645) are a good outfit, with two-hour harbour tours, among others, starting at around $50. For an inexpensive (from $3.50) look at the harbour you could jump aboard the Rupert Water Taxi, which leaves for several destinations from the dock at the bottom of McBride Street (check times at the infocentre; departures vary according to school runs). A trip fast becoming famous locally is to **Khuzeymateen Provincial Park** (contact BC Parks on ☎847-7320 for information on two- to ten-day tours), a remote coastal valley 45km to the north of Prince Rupert created in 1994 to protect BC's largest-known coastal population of **grizzly bears**. This is the first park of its kind in the world, but there will certainly be more, especially in BC, where the damage done to declining grizzly habitats by logging, mining, hunting and other concerns – notably the slaughter of the animals for body parts in dubious Oriental remedies – is rapidly becoming one of the keenest environmental issues in the province.

A little out of town, beyond the museum, the gondola ride to **Mount Hays** once gave a bird's-eye view of the harbour and the chance to spot bald eagles. It was also the most popular attraction in town, which makes you wonder why it had to close: check with the infocentre to see if there's news of its reopening. To reach it, or the steep track that currently provides the only route to the top, take the Wantage Road turn-off on Hwy 16 just out of town. It's three hours to the top but you get fairly good views after clambering just a short way up the track. Details of less-energetic **walks** can be obtained from the infocentre.

Eating and drinking

Fresh **fish** is the obvious thing to **eat** locally, preferably at the *Green Apple*, a shack (and town institution) that serves a mean halibut and chips for $6; it's at 301 McBride St (☎627-1666) just before Hwy 16 turns into town. For something a touch more upmarket, locals flock to the *Smile's Seafood Café*, at 113 George Hills Way (☎624-3072), about 300m north of the infocentre, which has been doing a roaring trade on the waterfront since 1934. Also here – just across the road – is *Cowpuccinos*, a good café that's the centre of Prince Rupert's alternative scene. The *Breakers* pub just across the bridge at 117 George Hills Way (☎624-5990) is a popular and inexpensive place to drink and also serves decent food. Also close by, the *Cow Bay Café*, 205 Cow Bay (☎627-1212; closed Mon), pushes *Smile's* close for the best seafood and other meals in town. The **bar** under the *Coast Prince Rupert* high-rise hotel at 118 2nd Ave, between 6th and 7th streets, also does decent if standard Canadian food, and is one of the few places open for breakfast.

Haida Gwaii – The Queen Charlotte Islands

Ranged in an arc some 150km off the Prince Rupert coast, the **Haida Gwaii**, until recently better known as the **Queen Charlotte Islands**, consist of a triangular-shaped archipelago of about two hundred islets that make an enticing diversion from the heavily travelled sea route up through BC. The islands are something of a cult amongst travellers and environmentalists, partly for their scenery, flora and fauna and almost legendary remoteness from the mainstream, but also because they've achieved a high profile in the battle between the forestry industry and ecology activists. At the forefront of the battle are the **Haida**, widely acknowledged as one of the region's most advanced aboriginal groups, who have made the islands their home for over 10,000 years (see box, opposite). Their culture, and in particular the chance to visit their many **deserted villages**, form an increasing part of the islands' attraction, but many people also come here to sample the immensely rich **flora and fauna**, a natural profusion that's earned them the title of the "Canadian Galapagos".

The Haida Gwaii were one of only two areas in western Canada to escape the last Ice Age, which elsewhere altered the evolutionary progress, and which has resulted in the survival of many so-called **relic species**. Species unique to the islands include a fine yellow daisy, the world's largest **black bears**, and subspecies of pine marten, deer mouse, hairy woodpecker, saw-whet owl and Stellar's jay. There are also more **eagles** here than anywhere else in the region, as well as the world's largest population of Peale's peregrine falcons and the elusive **black-footed albatross** – whose wingspan exceeds that of the largest eagles. Fish, too, are immensely plentiful, and there's a good chance of spotting whales, otters, sea lions and other aquatic mammals.

Practicalities

The islands can be accessed either by air or ferry from Prince Rupert. Ferries from Prince Rupert dock at tiny Skidegate near Queen Charlotte City on **Graham Island**, the northern of the group's two main collections of islands (see p.857 for details of ferries from Prince Rupert). Most of the archipelago's six thousand inhabitants live either in Queen Charlotte City or at Masset to the north, leaving the southern cluster of islands across Skidegate Channel – known for convenience as **Moresby Island** – a virtually deserted primal wilderness, but for the small community at Sandspit (see p.865). Regular twenty-minute ferry crossings connect Moresby Island to Skidegate (twelve sailings daily year-round; $4.50, cars $8.50). Or you can **fly** to the islands from Prince Rupert, landing at Sandspit, which has the islands' only airstrip (float planes can land elsewhere). Air BC (☎1-800/663-3721) flies here daily from Vancouver, but you might get better deals out of carriers with offices in Prince Rupert, such as Inland Air (☎627-1351 or 1-888/624-2577) and the larger Harbour Air (☎627-1341 or 1-800/665-0212). Harbour Air, for example, fly to Sandspit twice daily from Prince Rupert and also fly small planes to Masset on the north of Graham Island. It also has other flights around the islands, as do South Moresby Air Charters (☎559-4222 or 1-888/551-4222, *smoresby@qcislands.net*) in Queen Charlotte City, who'll take you out to the deepest of the backwoods.

Noncamping **accommodation** is available only at Sandspit (on Moresby) and Queen Charlotte City, Tl'ell, Masset and Port Clements (on Graham) and should always be prebooked. The only **public transport** at time of writing is a service run by Eagle Cabs (check the current state of the service on ☎559-4461 or 1-877/747-4461) which operates a once-daily shuttle in summer in each direction between Sandspit, across the ferry and then on to Queen Charlotte City, Masset and points in between. Budget (☎637-5688 or 1-800/557-3228) has **car rental** offices in Queen Charlotte City, Masset and Sandspit airport, but in summer you'll need to have booked in advance to secure a

THE HAIDA

The **Haida** are widely considered to have the most highly developed culture and sophisticated art tradition of British Columbia's aboriginal peoples. Extending from the Haida Gwaii (Queen Charlotte Islands) to south Alaska, their lands included major stands of red cedar, the raw material for their huge dugout **canoes**, intricate **carvings** and refined **architecture**. Haida trade links were built on the reputation of their skill – other BC peoples considering the ownership of a Haida canoe, for example, as a major status symbol. Renowned as traders and artists, the Haida were also feared **warriors**, paddling into rival villages and returning with canoes laden with goods, slaves and the severed heads of anyone who had tried to resist. Their skill on the open sea has seen them labelled the "Vikings" of northern America. This success at warfare was due, in part, to their use of wooden slat armour, which included a protective face visor and helmets topped with terrifying images.

Socially the Haida divided themselves into two main groups, the **Eagles** and the **Ravens**, which were further divided into hereditary kin groups named after their original village location. Marriage within each major group – or *moiety* – was considered incestuous, so Eagles would always seek Raven mates and vice versa. Furthermore, descent was traced through the **female line**, which meant that a chief could not pass his property onto his sons because they would belong to a different *moiety* – instead his inheritance passed to his sister's sons. Equally, young men might have to leave their childhood village to claim their inheritance from their maternal uncles.

Haida **villages** were an impressive sight, their vast cedar-plank houses dominated by fifteen-metre totem poles displaying the kin group's unique animal crest or other mythical creatures, all carved in elegantly fluid lines. Entrance to each house was through the gaping mouth of a massive carved figure; inside, supporting posts were carved into the forms of the crest animals and most household objects were similarly decorative. Equal elaboration attended the many Haida ceremonies, one of the most important of which was the **mortuary potlatch**, serving as a memorial service to a dead chief and the validation of the heir's right to succession. The dead individual was laid out at the top of a carved pole near the village entrance, past which the visiting chiefs would walk wearing robes of finely woven and patterned mountain-goat wool and immense headdresses fringed with long sea-lion whiskers and ermine skins. A hollow at the top of each headdress was filled with eagle feathers, which floated down onto the witnesses as the chiefs sedately danced.

After **European contact** the Haida population was devastated by smallpox and other epidemics. In 1787, there were around 8000 Haida scattered across the archipelago. Their numbers were then reduced from around 6000 in 1835 to 588 by 1915. Consequently they were forced to abandon their traditional villages and today gather largely at two sites, Old Masset (pop. 650) and Skidegate (Haida pop. 550). At other locations the homes and totems fell into disrepair, and only at **Sgan Gwaii**, a remote village at the southern tip of the Queen Charlottes, has an attempt been made to preserve an original Haida settlement; it has now been declared a World Heritage Site by UNESCO.

These days the Haida number around 2000, and are highly regarded in the North American art world; Bill Reid, Freda Diesing and Robert Davidson are amongst the best-known figures, and scores of other Haida craftspeople produce a mass of carvings and jewellery for the tourist market. They also play a powerful role in the islands' social, political and cultural life, having been vocal in the formation of sites such as the Gwaii Haanas National Park Reserve (p.866), South Moresby's Haida Heritage Site and Duu Guusd Tribal Park (p.865), the last established to protect old aboriginal villages on Graham Island's northwest coast.

car. Thrifty (☎637-2299) has an office at Sandspit airport and Tilden (☎626-3318) one in Masset. Rates at Rustic Rentals (☎559-4641) out of Charlotte Island Tire in Queen Charlotte City are a touch lower than the main companies. Car rental rates here are expensive, and unless you have a car, bike or canoe it's as well to know that you could be in for a long and expensive trip that shows you very little of what you came for. To see the **Haida villages**, in any case, virtually all of which are on inaccessible parts of Moresby, you'll need to take a boat, and more probably a pricey tour by float plane.

Graham Island

Most casual visitors stick to **Graham Island**, where the bulk of the island's roads and accommodation are concentrated along the eastern side of the island, between **Queen Charlotte City** in the south and **Masset** some 108km to the north. These settlements and the villages in between – Skidegate, Tl'ell and Port Clements – lie along Hwy 16, the principal road, and shelter in the lee of the islands, away from a mountainous and indented rocky west coast that boasts the highest combined seismic, wind and tidal energy of any North American coastline (producing treacherous seas and a tidal range of 8m). Much of the east coast consists of beautiful half-moon, driftwood-strewn beaches and a string of provincial parks where you can appreciate the milder climes produced by the Pacific's Japanese Current, a warming stream that contributes to the island's lush canopy of thousand-year-old spruce and cedar rainforests. On the downside, though, it drenches both sides of the island with endless rainstorms, even in summer. Make sure you pack a raincoat.

Queen Charlotte City

It would be hard to imagine anywhere less like a city than the island's second-largest settlement, **QUEEN CHARLOTTE CITY** (pop. 924), a picturesque fishing village and frontier administrative centre about 5km west of the Skidegate ferry terminal (see p.864). The village takes its name from the ship of Captain George Dixon, the British explorer who sailed to the Haida Gwaii in 1787, thirteen years after first European contact was probably made by the Spaniard Juan Perez. Most of its residents squeeze a living from the McMillan Bloedel timber giant, whose felling exploits have cleared most of the hills around the port, and who control access to many of the island's 2000km of backcountry logging roads. For a fine overview of the place, try the stroll to the top of **Sleeping Beauty Mountain**, which is reached by a rough track from Crown Forest Road near Honna Road. The village **dump** south of the houses rates as another sight for the black bears and bald and golden eagles that often gather there at dusk. Further afield you may be able to watch salmon and other wildlife at the **Skidegate Band Salmon Project** on the Honna Forest Service Road 3km west of town: contact the Band Council for information (☎559-4496). Further away still, you can drive to **Rennell Sound**, a west-coast inlet with shingle beaches accessed by a logging road: take the main logging road north from the town for 22km and then turn left and follow the steep gravel road for 14km, but contact the infocentre before setting out (see below). At the Sound, the **Rennell Sound Recreation Site** offers paths through stands of primal rainforest to isolated sandy beaches and a couple of campsites with a total of ten beachfront wilderness pitches (free).

Otherwise the town is the major place to sign up for any number of outdoor activities; contact the **infocentre**, 3220 Wharf St (daily: mid-May to early Sept 10am–7pm; early May & late Sept 10am–2pm; closed Oct–April; ☎559-8316, *www.qcinfo.com*). The staff are incredibly knowledgeable, and there's a good selection of detailed guides and maps to the area: be sure to pick up the invaluable *Guide to the Queen Charlotte Islands* ($3.95). The centre is also the place to pick up brochures and organize **tours** of the island, with some forty or more fishing, sailing, sightseeing, canoeing and other operators being based in Queen Charlotte City. There's also a **Canadian Parks Service** office for information on Moresby Island's Gwaii Haanas National Park Reserve and Haida Heritage Site (see p.866), west of town along Hwy 33 (Mon–Fri 8am–noon &

1–4.30pm; ☎559-8818). The **Ministry of Forests**, in the obvious blue building on 3rd Avenue (☎559-8447), has information on the free primitive campsites run by the Forest Service on Graham and Moresby islands. If you're planning to drive logging roads, you must call **Weyherhauser** (☎557-6810) – which controls most of these roads on Graham Island – for latest access details. Enquire, too, about their regular forestry tours (they depart Port Clements museum, currently Tues and Thurs at 9am: call the above number to book a place).

ACCOMMODATION AND FOOD

Accommodation is scarce and demand is high in summer, so definitely call ahead to make bookings. The first-choice hotel is probably the *Premier Creek Lodging*, 3101 3rd Ave (☎559-8451 or 1-888/322-3388, *www.qcislands.net/premier*, ④), a splendidly restored 1910 heritage building overlooking the harbour and Bearskin Bay. **Bike rentals** are available here also. Then there's the unique *Gracie's Place*, 3113 3rd Ave (☎559-4262 or 1-888/244-4262, *www.gracies-place.com*; ③), with oceanview rooms, antique furniture and rustic decor; and the *Spruce Point Lodging*, 609 6th Ave (☎559-8234, *www.qcislands.net/sprpoint*; ③), which offers rooms and breakfast overlooking Skidegate Inlet opposite the Chevron garage at the west end of town. Similarly intimate is *Dorothy and Mike's Guest House*, 3125 2nd Ave (☎559-8439; ③), with central rooms and full cooking facilities in a no-smoking environment. A touch closer to the ferry terminal, overlooking Bearskin Bay, is the *Sea Raven Motel*, 3301 3rd Ave (☎559-4423 or 1-800/665-9606, *www.searaven.com*; ③). If you're **camping**, try the unserviced *Haydn Turner Park* (free) in the community park at the western end of town, or the *Kagan Bay Forest Service Campground*, a handful of lovely beachfront pitches on Honna Forest Service Road 5km west of the town.

For **food**, locals make for the *Sea Raven Restaurant* (☎559-8583) located straight up the main road from the dock by the *Sea Raven Motel*. There are also *Margaret's Café*, 3223 Wharf St, on the east side of town, or *Hanging by a Thread* on Wharf close to the infocentre, a fine place whose produce comes from organic farms on the island.

Skidegate

There's not much doing at **SKIDEGATE** (pop. 550), other than the ferries docking at Skidegate Landing 2km away to the south and the chance to browse through the more accessible aspects of Haida culture at the **Haida Gwaii Museum**, located near Second Beach at Qay'llnagaay around 500m east of the ferry terminal (Oct–April Mon & Wed–Fri 10am–noon & 1–5pm, Sat 1–5pm; May & Sept Mon–Fri 9am–5pm, Sat 1–5pm; June–Aug Mon–Fri 9am–5pm, Sat & Sun 1–5pm; $3; ☎559-4643). Among other things, the museum contains the world's largest collection of the Haida's treasured argillite carvings (such carvings are also on display in Vancouver's UBC Museum of Anthropology). Argillite is a form of black slate-like rock found only on the Haida Gwaii, and only in one site whose location is kept a closely guarded secret. Also check out the platform here for viewing grey whales during their migrations (April–May & Sept to early Oct). After doing so, stop by the long-house office alongside the museum to have a chat with the **Haida Gwaii Watchmen**. Bands of Haida "watchmen" were formed in the 1970s to protect aboriginal sites from vandalism and theft, and survive to this day. Ask at the office about seeing the famous *Loo Taas* ("Wave Eater") canoe, which is generally on show here on weekdays. When it's not out on hire to rich tourists – for a mere $1500, or thereabouts – you're very occasionally able to take a six-hour tour in the huge vessel. It was made for the '86 Expo in Vancouver and was the first Haida canoe carved since 1909. You can obtain a permit to visit some of the five hundred or more abandoned aboriginal villages and sites on the southern islands from the long house, or alternatively from the nearby **Skidegate Mission** or Band Council Office close to Skidegate proper – a Haida village 2.5km from the ferry terminal. There's also a carving long house here, where you may be able to watch craftspeople at work. In July and August, the Mission usually hosts a weekly **seafood feast**, open to all-comers for around $25 (check latest details at the Queen Charlotte City infocentre). If you're here to catch the boat across the channel to Moresby Island and Sandspit, the MV *Kuvuna* **ferry** runs twelve times daily year-round (7.30am–10.30pm; 20min; $4.50).

Tl'ell and Port Clements

If you blink you'll miss the ranching community of **TL'ELL** (pop. 138), 36km north of Skidegate, first settled by outsiders in 1904 and home to the Richardson Ranch, the island's oldest working ranch. Stop here and walk down to the sea, where you can stroll for hours on deserted wind-sculpted dunes. It's a community favoured by craftspeople and alternative types – pop into the little café or gallery – and in the past there's been a **hostel** here, the intermittently open *Bellis Lodge* (☎557-4434; ①) – check before turning up. Nearby is the *Tl'ell River House*, off Hwy 16 overlooking Tl'ell River and Hecate Strait, offering ten rooms with kitchenettes and a licensed lounge and **restaurant** (☎557-4211 or 1-800/667-8906); ③). Or try the pleasantly rustic *Cacilia's B&B* just north of Richardson Ranch on the main road (☎557-4664, *www.qcislands.net/ceebysea*; ③; no credit cards), a renovated log house set behind the dunes on Hecate Strait 2km from the Naikoon Park (see below). **Bikes** and **kayaks** are usually available for rent here.

As the road cuts inland for **PORT CLEMENTS** (pop. 577), 21km to the northwest of Tl'ell, it forms the southern border of the **Naikoon Provincial Park**, an enclave that extends over Graham Island's northeast corner and designed to protect fine beach, dune and dwarf-woodland habitats. **Campers** should head for the *Misty Meadows Campground* ($9.50; May–Oct), just south of the Tl'ell River Bridge and 500m north of the **park centre** (☎557-4390) to the north of Tl'ell (backcountry camping is allowed throughout the park). About 8km beyond, look out for the picnic site and trails at the southern tip of **Mayer Lake**, one of the nicer spots to pull over. Port Clements in the past was most famous for the world's only **Golden Spruce** tree, a 300-year-old bleached albino tree – sacred to the Haida – which puzzled foresters by refusing to produce anything but ordinary green-leafed saplings; in 1997 a vandal chopped it down. A rare genetic mutation allowed the tree's needles to be bleached by sunlight and geneticists and foresters are currently trying to produce another tree.

Port Clements' little **infocentre** booth (July to early Sept daily 9am–6pm) is just out of the village, and there's a small **museum** of forestry and pioneer-related offerings at 45 Bayview Drive on the main road into the town (June–Sept Tues–Sun 2–5pm; winter hours according to availability of volunteers; donation). The one official **hotel** is the *Golden Spruce*, 2 Grouse St (☎557-4325 or 1-877/801-4653, *www.qcislands.net/golden*; ②), but it's worth asking around for B&B possibilities. For **food and drink**, the main option is the good *Yakoun River Inn* on Bayview Drive. About 20km north of town on the road for Masset, look out for the signed **Pure Lake Provincial Park**, where on summer days the waters of Pure Lake should be warm enough for swimming.

Masset

MASSET, 40km north of Port Clements, is the biggest place on the islands, a scattered town of some 1490 people, most of whom are employed in fishing and crab-canning. Many visitors are here to bird-watch at the **Delkatla Wildlife Sanctuary**, a saltwater marsh north of the village – contact Delkatla Bay Birding Tours (☎626-5015) for guided visits – that supports 113 bird species, or to walk the trails around Tow Hill 26km to the east (see below). Others come to wander the neighbouring village of **HAIDA**, or "Old Massett" – with an extra "t" – 2km to the west, the administrative centre for the Council of the Haida First Nation and where some six hundred aboriginal people still live and work. Visitors should show respect when visiting totem sites, craft houses and community homes. Many locals are involved in producing crafts for tourists, or organizing wilderness tours, but some are restoring and adding to the few totems still standing locally (it's possible to visit various canoe and carving sheds) and there's a small museum giving some context. For more **information** on where to see carving and on the village in general, visit the Old Massett Council office on Eagle Road (Mon–Fri 9am–5pm; ☎626-3395), where you should also enquire about permission to visit the **Duu Guusd Tribal Park**, established by the Haida to protect villages on the coast to the northwest. Two villages here are still active, and the park is used as a base for the Haida Gwaii Rediscovery Centre, which offers courses to children on Haida culture and history.

The Masset **info booth**, at 1455 Old Beach Rd (July & Aug daily 9am–5pm; ☎626-3982, *www.massetbc.com*), has full details of wildlife and bird-watching possibilities. The Masset Village Office (☎626-3995) on Main Street can also provide invaluable background. Sadly they can't do much about the village's limited **accommodation** prospects, other than point you to the *Harbourview Lodging*, overlooking the harbour at 1608 Delkatla Rd (☎626-5109 or 1-800/661-3314, *lholland@island.net*; ③), *Naden Lodge*, 1496 Delkatla St, corner of Harrison (626-3322 or 1-800/771-TYEE, *www.nadenlodge.bc.ca*; ⑤) or to a handful of intermittently open B&Bs. Outside of town, there's accommodation near South Beach with ocean views at the *Alaska View Lodge*, Tow Hill Rd (☎626-3333, *www.alaskaviewlodge.com*; ③), 10.5km from Masset airport and midway between Masset village and Tow Hill. The only nearby **campsite** is the *Village of Masset RV Site and Campground* ($9–17; no reservations) on Tow Hill Road, 2km north of town alongside the wildlife sanctuary. Further afield there's the *Agate Beach* ($12; May–Sept) in Naikoon Park, a provincial park site near trails and sandy beaches located 26km northeast of Masset off the secondary road towards Tow Hill (see below). To get around, call Vern's Taxi (☎626-3535) or Jerry's Taxi Service in Old Massett (☎626-5017) or **rent a car** from Tilden, 1504 Old Beach Rd (☎626-3318). There are a couple of pizza and takeaway places to **eat** – try the *Café Gallery* on Collision Avenue (☎626-3672) – and a handful of **bars** on Collision Avenue and Main Street, with live music some nights.

Heading away from the village, follow Tow Hill Road to **Tow Hill**, 26km to the east, where you can pick up trails into the Naikoon Park: three begin by the Heillen River at the foot of Tow Hill itself. The easiest is the one-kilometre **Blow Hole Trail**, which drops down to striking rock formations and basalt cliffs by the sea. From here you can follow another path to the top of Tow Hill (109m) for superb views of deserted sandy beaches stretching into the hazy distance. The third track, the **Cape Fife Trail**, is a longer (10km) hike to the east side of the island. Naikoon means "point", a reference to Rose Spit, the twelve-kilometre spit that extends from the park and Graham Island's northeasterly tip. Today it's an ecological and wildlife reserve of beaches, dunes, marsh and stunted forest, but it's also a sacred Haida site, for it was here, according to legend, that the Haida's Raven clan were first tempted from a giant clamshell by a solitary raven.

Moresby Island

Moresby Island is all but free from human contact except for deserted Haida villages, one of which contains the world's largest stand of totems, forestry roads and the small logging community of **Sandspit** (pop. 202). The last lies 15km from the **Alliford Bay** terminal for the inter-island ferry link with Skidegate on Graham Island (12 daily; 20min crossing; $4.50, cars $8.50). Local airlines fly from Prince Rupert to a small airstrip near the village. Budget (☎637-5688 or 1-800/557-3228) and Thrifty (☎637-2299) have **car rental** offices at the airport: for a **taxi** for connections to the ferry, call Bruce's Taxi (☎637-5655).

Most locals here and on Graham Island work in Moresby's forests, and the **forestry issue** has divided the community for years between the Haida and environmentalists – "hippies" in the local parlance – and the lumber workers (the "rednecks" as the environmentalists call them). At stake are the islands' temperate rainforests and the traditional sites of the Haida, themselves politically shrewd media manipulators who've sent representatives to Brazil to advise local aboriginal peoples there on their own rainforest programmes. They've also occasionally provided the muscle to halt logging on the islands, and to prove a point in the past they've blocked access to **Hot Spring Island**, whose thermal pools are a favourite tourist target. On the other hand the forests provide jobs and some of the world's most lucrative timber – a single good sitka trunk can be worth up to $60,000. Currently a compromise has been reached and most of Moresby has National Park Reserve status (established in 1987), though stiff lobbying from the logging companies leaves its position perilous. If you're intending to drive any of the logging roads, however – and most of the handful of roads here *are* logging roads – note that generally they're open to the public at weekends and after 6pm on weekdays: otherwise check for latest details with the local infocentres.

Sandspit's only listed **accommodation**, apart from a couple of intermittently open B&Bs, is the *Moresby Island Guest House*, 385 Alliford Bay Rd overlooking the ocean at Shingle Bay, 1km south of the airport (☎637-5300, *www.bbcanada.com/1651.html*; ③); an airport pick-up is included. Many people choose to sleep on the spit's beaches: Gray Bay, 21km southeast of Sandspit, has primitive and peaceful **campsites** near gravel and sand beaches (for more details, contact the TimberWest forestry offices on Beach Rd; ☎637-5436). For **car rental**, Budget have offices at the airport and in Sandspit at Beach and Blaine Shaw roads (☎637-5688). If you fancy going into the **interior by plane**, contact South Moresby Air Charters (☎559-4222 or 1-888/551-4222) for details of charter flights.

Gwaii Haanas National Park Reserve

If you're determined enough you can canoe, mountain bike or backpack the interior of northern Moresby Island, but you need to know what you're doing – the seas here are especially treacherous for canoeists – and be prepared to lug plenty of supplies. You must, however, join a tour or follow a strict procedure (see below) if you want to visit the **Gwaii Haanas National Park Reserve**, a 90km archipelago that embraces 138 islands, some 500 Haida archeological sites, 5 deserted Haida villages and some 1500km of coastline across the south of the island group. Treaties signed with the federal government in Ottawa in 1990 gave the Haida joint control of this region, and afforded protection to their ancient villages, but many land claims to the region remain unresolved. You need money, time and effort to see the park. There are no roads, and access is by boat or chartered planes only.

The easiest way into the park is with a tour – contact the Queen Charlotte City infocentre (see p.862) for full details. Or make direct contact with companies such as South Moresby Air Charters (☎559-4221 or 1-888/551-4222) or GwaiiEco Tours (☎559-8333, *www.gwaiiecotours.com*); prices start from about $125 for one-day trips. Sandspit's **infocentre** in the airport terminal building (June–Sept daily 9am–6pm; ☎637-5436) also has details of the many tours to the park and the limited facilities on the whole southern half of the archipelago.

Visits to a variety of **Haida sites** and their totems, ruined dwellings and so forth are described here in order of distance (and therefore time and expense) from Sandspit. Closest are **Hlkenul** (Cumshewa) and **K'una** (Skedans) just outside the park, both accessible on day-trips by boat from Moresby Camp on the Cumshewa Inlet, 46km south of Sandspit (access to the Camp is by logging road). Further afield, and in the park proper, are T'aanuu, Hlk'waah – one of the main battlegrounds in the fight to protect the region in the 1980s – and **Gandla K'in** (Hot Spring Island), whose hot springs make it one of the most popular destinations. The finest site of all, of course, is the one that's furthest away: **Sgan Gwaii** (Ninstints) lies close to the southern tip of the archipelago, and was abandoned by the Haida around 1880 in the wake of smallpox epidemics. Today, it contains the most striking of the ruined Haida villages, its long houses and many totems declared a UNESCO World Heritage Site in 1981.

To **visit the reserve** as an independent traveller, you must make an advance reservation or obtain a stand-by space. **Reservations** can be made by calling ☎1-800/HEL-LOBC (within Canada or the United States) or ☎250/387-1642 (outside North America). There is a $15 per person reservation fee (maximum of four people per reservation). If you choose not to make a reservation, then only six places daily are available **stand-by**, available on a first-come, first-served basis starting at the 8am orientation session (see below) at the Queen Charlotte infocentre. There are also **fees** to visit the park: day-trips cost $10 per person plus $10 for each night thereafter, but trips of 6 to 14 nights are payable at a flat fee of $60; stays over 14 nights cost $80.

An **orientation session** is mandatory for all visitors entering Gwaii Haanas, Skedans or T'aanuu. Sessions take around ninety minutes and cover topics such as public safety, no-trace camping, natural and cultural heritage and the Haida Gwaii Watchmen Program. These sessions take place at the Queen Charlotte infocentre or the Gwaii Haanas office on Airport Road, opposite the *Sandspit Inn* (☎559-8818). Before May 15 and after September 15, book sessions through the park office in Queen Charlotte City (see p.862); from mid-May to the end of June, sessions run twice daily – once in the QCC infocentre at 8am and once in the Sandspit Mall office at 11am; from July 1 to mid-September, there are two QCC sessions at 8am and 7.30pm and one in Sandspit at 11am. If you're **travelling with a tour company**, companies check that you've done the orientation and some offer it as part of their package. Apart from some restricted areas, which you are informed of during orientation sessions, you can camp where you wish in the reserve; fees for camping are included in the general fee you pay to enter the park. There are no hotels, hostels or other forms of accommodation.

The Cassiar Highway

The 733km of the **Cassiar Hwy** (Hwy 37) from the Skeena Valley east of Prince Rupert to Watson Lake just inside Yukon Territory are some of the wildest and most beautiful on any British Columbian road. Though less famous than the Alaska Hwy, the road is increasingly travelled by those who want to capture some of the adventure that accompanied the wilder reaches of its better-known neighbour in the 1950s and 1960s.

Some stretches are still gravel, and the petrol and repair facilities, let alone food and lodgings, are extremely patchy: don't contemplate the journey unless your vehicle's in top condition, with two spare tyres and spare fuel containers – fill up wherever possible. The road also provides a shorter route from Prince George to the Yukon than the Alaska Hwy. British Columbia's North by Northwest Tourist Association puts out complete lists of facilities, which are vital accompaniments to any journey and are available from the infocentres in Prince Rupert and Terrace.

If you're ready to drive the distances involved, you'll also probably be prepared to explore the highway's two main side roads to **Stewart** and **Telegraph Creek**, and possibly the rough roads and trails that lead into two wilderness parks midway up the highway – the **Mount Edziza Provincial Park** and the **Spatsizi Plateau Wilderness Park**. If you can't face the highway's entire length, the side-trip to Stewart offers exceptional sea and mountain **scenery**, as well as the chance to cross into Alaska at **Hyder** to indulge in its vaunted alcoholic border initiation (see p.869).

Stewart

The Cassiar Hwy starts near Kitwanga, one of several aboriginal villages off Hwy 16 (see pp.855–856), and a crossroads of the old "grease trail", named after the candlefish oil which was once traded between Coast and Interior peoples. Some hint of the sense of adventure required comes when you hit a section (47km beyond Cranberry Junction), where the road doubles up as an airstrip – planes have right of way. Another 27km on, there's another stretch used as an airstrip in emergencies. Almost immediately after you leave Hwy 16, though, the road pitches into the mesmerizing high scenery of the Coast Ranges, a medley of mountain, lake and forest that reaches a crescendo after about 100km and the side turn to **STEWART**, Canada's most northerly ice-free port. Here a series of immense glaciers culminates in the dramatic appearance of the unmissable **Bear Glacier**, a vast sky-blue mass of ice that comes down virtually to the highway and has the strange ability to glow in the dark. Stewart itself, 37km west of the glacier, is a shrivelled mining centre (pop. 2200) that sits at the end of the Portland Canal, the world's fourth longest fjord, a natural boundary between British Columbia and Alaska that lends the town a superb peak-ringed location (the ferry ride in from Prince Rupert through some of the west coast's wildest scenery is sensational). Dominating its rocky amphitheatre is **Mount Rainey**, whose cliffs represent one of the greatest vertical rises from sea level in the world.

Stewart's **history**, together with that of nearby Hyder (see opposite), might have marked it out as a regional player were it not quite so remote and apparently doomed to ultimate disappointment in every venture ever tried in the town. In the distant past it was an important trading point, marking the meeting point of territories belonging to the Nisga'a and Gitxsan interior aboriginal peoples to the south, the Thaltan to the north, and the Tsesaut and the Tlingit to the east. Captain George Vancouver, searching for the Northwest Passage in 1793, spoke for many who came after him when, having spent an eternity working his way inland up the Portland Canal, he declared himself "mortified with having devoted so much time to so little purpose". Almost exactly a century later the area welcomed its first settlers: in 1896 Captain Gilliard of the US Army Corps built four storehouses here in Hyder – Alaska's first stone buildings – and Stewart itself was named after two of its earliest settlers (Robert and John Stewart). For a time it looked as if the terminus of the trans-Canadian railway might materialize in Stewart, a hope that brought in 10,000 fortune-seeking pioneers. The railway never came, and Stewart's local line was abandoned after a few kilometres. As slump set in, gold was discovered – almost inevitably – and until 1948, when it closed, the Premier Gold and Silver Mine was North America's largest gold mine. Then came a copper mine, its eighteen-kilometre gallery apparently the longest tunnel ever built by boring from just one end. This closed in 1984, but not before 27 men were killed in a mine accident in 1965. All manner of new mining ventures have since been promised. None have materialized, leaving Stewart's scenery its main money-spinner: visitors and B-movie location scouts alike having been lured by the region's cliffs, mountains and glaciers – the *Iceman* and *The Thing* are two of the films to have used the local landscape as a backdrop.

Scenery aside, the main thing to see in town is the **Stewart Historical Museum** housed in the former fire hall at Columbia and 6th Avenue (summer Mon–Fri 1–4pm, Sat & Sun noon–5pm; or by appointment on ☎636-2568). A fine little provincial museum, its exhibits are devoted largely to stuffed wildlife and the town's logging and mining heritage. You might also want to journey out 5km beyond Hyder in Alaska to Fish Creek, where from the special viewing platform above the artificial spawning channel you may be lucky enough to see **black bears** catching some of the world's largest chum salmon. Around town there are also a handful of enticing trails, some along old mining roads: for details, contact the infocentre (see opposite) or visit the British Columbia Forest Service (☎636-2663) office at 8th and Brightwell.

PRACTICALITIES

The town's **infocentre** is housed at 222 5th Ave near Victoria (mid-May to mid-Sept daily; 9am–8pm; ☎636-9224 or 1-888/366-5999, *stewhydcofc@hotmail.com*). If you want to sleep over, there are two **hotels**: the *King Edward Hotel*, 5th and Columbia (☎636-2244 or toll-free in BC 1-800/663-3126; ④), and the *King Edward Motel*, Columbia Avenue (same details): the latter has basic housekeeping units and is $10 more expensive. The *King Edward Hotel* is the town's main **pub**, **restaurant** and **coffee shop** – it's where the locals eat – while visitors prefer the pleasantly polished *Bitter Creek Café* (a block west of the *King Edward*), which offers an eclectic mix of food and an outside deck on warm days. For bread and baked snacks, duck into *Brothers Bakery* next door to the *Bitter Creek*. There's also a late-opening Chinese restaurant, *Fong's Garden*, at 5th and Conway. The nearest **campsite** is the *Rainey Creek Campground* on the edge of town on 8th Avenue (☎636-2537; $14; May–Sept), and the tenting area (as opposed to RVs) is located across Rainey Creek, a pleasant little stream. Ask at the campsite office about the area's nature trails and glacier tours on offer. One of the easiest local trails, the **Rainey Creek Nature Walk**, shadowing the creek for 2.5km to the northern end of town (return to the centre on Railway St), starts here.

In summer Stewart is added to the itinerary of certain sailings of the Alaska Marine Highway ferry service (see box, p.857), albeit infrequently, so with careful planning you could travel overland to Stewart, or ride a boat to Ketchikan and thence to either Skagway or Prince Rupert, to complete a neat circular itinerary.

Hyder

Most people come to **HYDER** (pop. 70), Stewart's oddball twin, simply to drink in one or both of its two bars. It's a ramshackle place – barely a settlement at all – 3km from Stewart across the **border in Alaska** with none of the usual formalities, there being nothing beyond the end of the road but 800km of wilderness. People use Canadian currency, the police are of the Mountie variety and the phone system and code – ☎250 – are also Canadian. At the *Glacier Inn* the tradition is to pin a dollar to the wall in case you return broke and need a drink, and then toss back a shot of hard liquor in one and receive an "I've Been Hyderized" card. The result is many thousands of tacked dollars and the "world's most expensive wallpaper". It sounds a bit of a tourist carry-on, but if you arrive out of season there's a genuine amiability about the place that warrants its claims to be the "The Friendliest Ghost Town in Alaska". The town's two bars are often open 23 hours a day and a couple of **motels** are on hand if you literally can't stand any more: the *Sealaska Inn*, Premier Avenue (☎636-9003; ③), and the preferable *Grand View Inn* (☎636-9174; ③). They're both cheaper than their Stewart equivalents, and as you're in Alaska there's no room tax to pay on top. If you want something to soak up the alcohol, make for the *Sealaska Inn Restaurant* (☎636-2486) for no-nonsense food. The community's little **infocentre**, if you need it, is on the right as you come into town (June to early Sept daily except Wed 9am–1pm).

Dease Lake and Iskut

For several hundred kilometres beyond the Stewart junction there's nothing along the Cassiar other than the odd garage, rest area, campsite, trailhead and patches of burnt or clear-cut forest etched into the Cassiar and Skeena mountains. In places, though, you can still see traces of the incredible 3060km Dominion Telegraph line that used to link the Dawson City gold fields with Vancouver, and glimpses of a proposed railway extension out of Prince George that was abandoned as late as 1977.

DEASE LAKE, the first place of any size, has two **motels**, the *Northway Motor Inn* on Boulder Avenue (☎771-5341; ③) and *Arctic Divide Inn* on the highway (☎771-3119; ③), still 246km from the junction with the Alaska Hwy to the north. Close by lies

ISKUT, an aboriginal village offering tours into the adjacent wilderness parks, which are also accessible by float plane from Dease Lake itself. For **information**, contact the Iskut Band Office (☎234-3331) or local stores and garages. The village **accommodation** amounts to the *Red Goat Lodge* (☎234-3261 or 1-888/733-4628; ④, tents $13; late May to mid-Sept).

The road from Dease Lake is wild and beautiful, the 240km up to the Yukon border from here passing through some of the most miraculous scenery of what is already a superb journey. Some 84km north of Dease Lake is the *Moose Meadows Resort* (radio phone only; ①, tents $10; May to mid-Oct) which has cabins, tent and RV sites, a convenience store and canoe rentals. Much of this area was swamped with gold-hungry pioneers during the **Cassiar Gold Rush** of 1872–80, when the region got its name – possibly from a white prospector's corruption of *kaskamet*, the dried beaver meat eaten by local Kaska. In 1877 Alfred Freedman plucked one of the world's largest pure gold nuggets – a 72-ounce monster – from a creek east of present-day **CASSIAR** (133km from the junction with the Alaska Hwy to the north), though these days the mining has a less romantic allure, being concentrated in an open-pit **asbestos mine** 5km from the village. Most of the world's high-grade asbestos once came from here, and poisonous-looking piles of green chrysotile asbestos tailings are scattered for kilometres around. The mine closed in 1992, transforming the community into a virtual ghost town at a stroke. Equipment has been sold and sites cleared, and the area is off-limits to the public until reclamation is complete.

Telegraph Creek

For a taste of what is possibly a more remarkable landscape than you see on the Cassiar, it's worth driving the potentially treacherous 113-kilometre side road from Dease Lake to **TELEGRAPH CREEK** (allow 2hr in good conditions). It's a delightful river-bank town whose look and feel can scarcely have changed since the beginning of the twentieth century, when it was a major telegraph station and trading post for the gold-rush towns to the north. The road from the Cassiar navigates some incredible gradients and bends, twisting past canyons, old lava beds and touching on several **aboriginal villages**, notably at Tahltan River, where salmon are caught and cured in traditional smokehouses and sold to passing tourists. If you're lucky you might see a Tahltan bear dog, a species now virtually extinct. Only ankle high, and weighing less than fifteen pounds, these tiny animals were able to keep a bear cornered by barking and darting around until a hunter came to finish it off. Telegraph Creek itself is an object lesson in how latter-day pioneers live on the north's last frontiers: it's home to a friendly mixture of city exiles, hunters, trappers and ranchers, but also a cloistered bunch of **religious fundamentalists** who have eschewed the decadent mainstream for wilderness purity. Such groups are growing in outback British Columbia, an as-yet undocumented phenomenon that's creating friction with the easy-going types who first settled the backwoods. Gold has recently been discovered locally, attracting mining companies, so ways of life may be about to change here for all concerned.

Much of the village and village life revolves around the General Delivery – a combined café (the *Riversong*), grocery and garage – and small adjoining **motel**, the *Stikine River Song Lodge* (☎235-3196, *www.stikineriversong.com*; ③), whose rooms include kitchenettes. No one here, except perhaps the Bible brigade, minds if you pitch a tent – but ask around first. Also enquire at the café for details of rafting and other local trips into the backcountry.

If you're continuing up the Cassiar Hwy to Watson Lake and the Alaska Hwy junction, turn to "Watson Lake to Whitehorse", p.875.

Prince George to Dawson Creek

Dawson Creek is the launching pad for the Alaska Hwy. While it may not be somewhere you'd otherwise stop, it's almost impossible to avoid a night here whether you're approaching from Edmonton and the east or **from Prince George** on the scenically more uplifting **John Hart Hwy** (Hwy 97). Named after a former BC premier, this seemingly innocuous road is one of the north's most vital highways. Completed in 1952, it linked at a stroke the road network of the Pacific Coast with that of the northern interior, cutting 800km off the journey from Seattle to Alaska, for example, a trip that previously had to take in a vast inland loop to Calgary. The route leads you out of British Columbia's upland interior to the so-called Peace River country, a region of slightly ridged land that belongs in look and spirit to the Albertan prairies. There's some 409km of driving, and two daily Greyhound **buses** make the journey.

Out of Prince George the road bends through mildly dipping hills and mixed woodland, passing small lakes and offering views to the Rockies, whose distant jagged skyline keeps up the spirits as you drive through an otherwise unbroken tunnel of conifers. About 70km on, **Bear Lake** and the **Crooked River Provincial Park** are just off the road, and it's well worth taking the small lane west of the park entrance to reach an idyllic patch of water fringed on its far shore by a fine sickle of sand. There's a provincial park **campsite** ($15) at the park.

Both Mackenzie Junction, 152km from Prince George, and Mackenzie, 29km off the highway, are scrappy, unpleasant places, easily avoided and soon forgotten as the road climbs to **Pine Pass** (933m), one of the lower road routes over the Rockies, but spectacular all the same. The **Bijoux Falls Provincial Park**, just before it, is good for a picnic near the eponymous falls, and if you want to **camp** plump for the *Pine Valley Park Lodge* ($11; May–Oct), an immensely scenic lakeside spot that looks up to crags of massively stratified and contorted rock just below the pass. Thereafter the road drops steeply through Chetwynd (three motels and a campsite) to the increasingly flatter country that heralds Dawson Creek.

Dawson Creek

Arrive in **DAWSON CREEK** (pop. 11,500) late and leave early: except for a small museum next to the town's eye-catching red grain hopper, and the obligatory photograph of the cairn marking **Mile Zero** of the Alaska Hwy, there's almost nothing to do here for most casual visitors except eat and sleep. Contact the **infocentre** at the museum, 900 Alaska Ave (daily 9am–6pm, longer hours in summer; ☎782-9595, *dctourin@pris.bc.ca*), for details of the **motels** – there are several, mostly concentrated on the Alaska Hwy northeast of town. One of the nicer places is the *Trail Inn*, 1748 Alaska Ave (☎782-8595 or 1-800/663-2749, *www.trailinn.com*; ③), with views of countryside rather than tarmac. None of the local **campsites** and RV parks are places you'd want to linger, but the most attractive is the *Mile 0 RV Park and Campground* (☎782-2590; $10–15; May to mid-Sept), about a kilometre west of the town centre at the junction of Hwy 97 North and Hwy 97 South opposite 20th Street on the Alaska Hwy.

For something to **eat**, call at the excellent *Alaska Café* on 10th Street, an attractive old wooden building completely at odds with the rest of the town. The food and ambience are good – though prices aren't the cheapest – and the bar's not bad either.

Dawson Creek to Whitehorse

The best part of the **Alaska Hwy** – a distance of about 1500km – winds through northern British Columbia from Dawson Creek to Whitehorse, the capital of the Yukon (only

320km of the Alaska Hwy is actually in Alaska). Don't be fooled by the string of villages emblazoned across the area's maps, for there are only two towns worthy of the name en route, **Fort St John** and **Fort Nelson** – the rest are no more than a garage, a store and perhaps a motel. **Watson Lake**, on the Yukon border, is the largest of these lesser spots, and also marks the junction of the Alaska and Cassiar highways. All the way down the road, though, it's vital to book accommodation during July and August.

Driving the Alaska Hwy is no longer the adventure of days past – that's now provided by the Cassiar and Dempster highways. Food, fuel and lodgings are found at between forty- and eighty-kilometre intervals, though cars still need to be in good shape. You should drive with headlights on at all times, and take care when passing or being passed by heavy trucks. It also goes without saying that wilderness – anything up to 800km of it each side – begins at the edge of the highway and unless you're very experienced you shouldn't contemplate any off-road exploration. Any number of guides and pamphlets are available to take you through to Fairbanks, but *The Milepost*, the road's bible is, for all its mind-numbing detail, the only one you need buy.

From mid-May to mid-October daily (except Sun) a **Greyhound bus** leaves Dawson Creek in the morning and plies the road all the way to Whitehorse; it runs on Tuesday, Thursday and Saturday the rest of the year. The twenty-hour trip finishes at around 5am, with only occasional half-hour meal stops, but covers the road's best scenery in daylight.

Dawson Creek to Fort Nelson

You need to adapt to a different notion of distance on a 2500-kilometre drive: on the Alaska Hwy points of interest are a long way apart, and pleasure comes in broad changes in scenery, in the sighting of a solitary moose, or in the passing excitement of a lonely bar. Thus it's forty minutes before the benign ridged prairies around Dawson Creek prompt attention by dropping suddenly into the broad, flat-bottomed valley of the Peace River, a canyon whose walls are scalloped with creeks, gulches and deep muddy scars. Just across the river **FORT ST JOHN**, which, until the coming of the highway (when it was the field headquarters of the road's eastern construction gangs), was a trading post for local Sikanni and Beaver peoples, which had remained little changed since its predecessor sank into the mud of the Peace River (there have been a total of six "Fort St Johns" in various incarnations in the area). The shantytown received a boost when the province's largest oil field was discovered nearby in 1955, and it's now a functional settlement with all the services you need – though at just 75km into the highway it's unlikely you'll be ready to stop. If you are, there's a small museum at 93rd and 100th Street and a handful of **motels**: solid choices are the big *Ramada*, 10103 98 Ave (☎787-0779 or 1-888/346-7711; ④), and the cheaper *Cedar Lodge Motor Inn*, 9824 99 Ave (☎785-8107 or 1-800/661-2210; ②). The **infocentre** is at 9323 100th St (☎785-6037 or 785-3033).

The next stop is the tiny hamlet of **WONOWON** (pop. 84), a military checkpoint in World War II, and at 161km from Dawson typical of the bleak settlements all the way up the road. **PINK MOUNTAIN** (pop. 19), 226km on from Dawson, is much the same, with *Mae's Kitchen* (☎772-3215; ②) the only listed accommodation (other places open and close here regularly). There's also a single **restaurant** favoured by truckers with a reasonable **campsite** across the road (☎772-3226; $8–20; May–Oct). Thereafter the road offers immense **views** of utter wilderness in all directions, the trees as dense as ever, but noticeably more stunted than further south and nearing the limit of commercial viability. Look out for the bright "New Forest Planted" signs, a token riposte from the loggers to the ecology lobby, as they are invariably backed by a graveyard of sickly looking trees. If you're **camping**, look out for two provincial sanctuaries over the remaining 236km to Fort Nelson. Around 60km north of Pink Mountain is the Buckinghorse River Provincial

THE ALASKA HIGHWAY

The **Alaska Hwy** runs northeast from Mile Zero at Dawson Creek through the Yukon Territory to Mile 1520 in Fairbanks, Alaska. Built as a military road, it's now an all-weather highway travelled by daily bus services and thousands of tourists out to recapture the thrill of the days when it was known as the "junkyard of the American automobile". It's no longer a driver's Calvary, but the scenery and the sense of pushing through wilderness on one of the continent's last frontiers remain as alluring as ever and around 360,000 people a year make the journey.

As recently as 1940 there was no direct land route to the Yukon or Alaska other than trails passable only by experienced trappers. When the Japanese invaded the Aleutian Islands during World War II, however, they both threatened the traditional sea routes to the north and seemed ready for an attack on mainland Alaska – the signal for the building of the joint US–Canadian road to the north. A proposed coastal route from Hazelton in British Columbia was deemed too susceptible to enemy attack (it's since been built as the Cassiar Hwy), while an inland route bypassing Whitehorse and following the Rockies would have taken five years to build. This left the so-called **Prairie Route**, which had the advantage of following a line of air bases through Canada into Alaska – a chain known as the **Northwest Staging Route**. In the course of the war, some 8000 planes were ferried from Montana to Edmonton and then to Fairbanks along this route, where they were picked up by Soviet pilots and flown into action on the Siberian front.

Construction of the highway began on **March 9, 1942**, the start of months of misery for the 20,000 mainly US soldiers shanghaied to ram a road through mountains, mud, mosquito-ridden bogs, icy rivers and forest during some of the harshest extremes of weather. Incredibly, crews working on the eastern and western sections met at Contact Creek, British Columbia, in September 1942, and completed the last leg to Fairbanks in October – an engineering triumph that had taken less than a year but cost around $140 million. The first full convoy of trucks to make Fairbanks managed an average 25kph during one of the worst winters in memory.

By 1943 the highway already needed virtual rebuilding, and for seven years workers widened the road, raised bridges, reduced gradients, bypassed swampy ground and started to remove some of the vast bends that are still being ironed out – the reason why it's now only 1488 miles (2394km) to the old Mile 1520 post in Fairbanks. All sorts of ideas have been put forward to explain the numerous curves – that they were to stop Japanese planes using the road as a landing strip, that they simply went where bulldozers could go at the time, or even at one point that they followed the trail of a rutting moose. Probably the chief reason is that the surveying often amounted to no more than a pointed finger aimed at the next horizon. Canada took over control of the road in 1946, but civilian traffic was barred until 1948. Within months of its opening so much traffic had broken down and failed to make the trip that it was closed for a year.

Although the road is now widely celebrated, there are sides to the story that are still glossed over. Many of its toughest sections, for example, were given to black GIs, few of whom have received credit for their part in building the highway – you'll look in vain for black faces amongst the white officers in the archive photos of ribbon-cutting ceremonies. Another often overlooked fact is the road's effect on aboriginal peoples on the route, scores of whom died from epidemics brought in by the workers. Yet another was the building of the controversial "Canadian Oil" or **Canol pipeline** in conjunction with the road, together with huge dumps of poisonous waste and construction junk. Wildlife en route was also devastated by trigger-happy GIs taking recreational pot shots as they worked: the virtual eradication of several species was part of the reason for the creation of the Kluane Game Sanctuary, the forerunner of the Yukon's Kluane National Park (see p.885).

Park campsite ($9); another 69km further is the Prophet River Provincial Recreation Area, with a campsite ($9) overlooking the river: this is good bird-watching country, but it's also good bear country, so be careful (see box on p.642).

Fort Nelson

One of the highway's key stopoffs, **FORT NELSON** greets you with a large poster proclaiming "Jail is only the beginning – don't drink and drive", a sobering sign that hints at the sort of extremes to which people hereabouts might go to relieve the tedium of winter's long semi-twilight. Everything in town, except a small **museum** devoted to the highway's construction, speaks of a frontier supplies depot, the latest in a long line of trading posts attracted to a site that is fed by four major rivers and stands in the lee of the Rockies. Dour buildings stand in a battered sprawl around a windswept grid, only a single notch up civilization's ladder from the time in the late 1950s when this was still a community without power, phones, running water or doctors. Life's clearly too tough here to be geared to anything but pragmatic survival and exploitation of its huge natural-gas deposits – the town has the world's second-largest gas-processing plant and the huge storage tanks to prove it. Aboriginal and white trappers live as they have for centuries, hunting beaver, wolf, wolverine, fox, lynx and mink, as well as the ubiquitous moose, which is still an important food source for many aboriginal people.

The town does, however, have an extraordinary claim to fame, namely that it's home to the **world's largest chopstick factory**, located south of the town off the highway behind the weigh scales at Industrial Park Chopstick Road (☎774-4448 for details of tours). This has nothing to do with gargantuan demand for Chinese food in Fort Nelson – at last count there were only three Chinese restaurants in town – but more to do with the region's high-quality aspen, a wood apparently perfectly suited to producing the dream chopstick. The Canadian Chopstick Manufacturing Company produces an incredible 7.5 million pairs of chopsticks a *day*, or 1.95 billion a year.

The town's **motels** are all much the same and you'll be paying the inflated rates – about $70 for doubles worth half that – which characterize the north. On the town's southern approaches the *Bluebell Inn*, 3907 50th Ave S (☎774-6961 or 1-800/663-5267, *www.pris.bc.ca/bluebell*; ④), is better looking than many of the run-of-the-mill places. The **infocentre** is at Mile 300.5 of the Alaska Hwy (☎774-6868; rest of the year for information, call 774-2541; mid-May to Aug Mon–Sat 9am–5pm).

Fort Nelson to Liard Hot Springs

This stretch is the Alaska Hwy at its best. Landscapes divide markedly around **Fort Nelson**, where the highway arches west from the flatter hills of the Peace River country to meet the **northern Rockies** above the plains and plateau of the Liard River. Within a short time – once the road has picked up the river's headwaters – you're in some of the most grandiose scenery in British Columbia. The area either side of the road is some of the world's wildest – twenty million acres of nothing – and experts say that only parts of Africa surpass the region for the variety of mammals present and the pristine state of its ecosystems. Services and motels become scarcer, but those that exist – though often beaten-up looking places – make atmospheric and often unforgettable stops. The first worthwhile stopoff, a kilometre off the highway on a gravel road, is **Tetsa River Provincial Park**, about 77km west of Fort Nelson, which has a nice and secluded **campsite** ($12; May–Oct) and appealing short hikes through the trees and along the river. Next up is **Stone Mountain Provincial Park**, 139km west of Fort Nelson, with a campsite ($12; May–Oct) which gives access to a short trail (10min) to two hoodoos (rock columns) claimed by myth to be the heads of two devils; a longer trail, the Flower Springs Lake Trail (6km), leads to a delightful upland mountain lake. Other **accommodation** and services include the *Rocky Mountain Lodge* (☎232-5000; ②), 165km on from Fort Nelson with lovely views of the mountains and an adjacent **campsite** ($10).

Toad River, 195km from Fort Nelson, has perhaps the best motel of all on this lonely stretch, the *Toad River Lodge* (☎232-5401; ②), with rooms and cabins (for $10 more) giving superlative views of thickly forested and deeply cleft mountains on all sides. Note that it also has a grocery, petrol station and sites for tents and RVs ($12 for tenting). About 3km to its north is the *Poplars Campground & Café*, with log cabins and fully serviced tent and RV sites (☎232-5465; ②, tent sites $12; May to late Sept); it's an equally attractive spot despite its disconcerting claim to be "Home of the Foot-Long Hot Dog".

Muncho Lake, the next big natural feature, sits at the heart of a large provincial park whose ranks of bare mountains are a foretaste of the barren tundra of the far north. There's a small **motel** and **campsite** at the lake's southern end, but it's worth hanging on for the popular *Flats Provincial Campground* ($12, free Oct; May–Oct), midway up the lake on its eastern side, or the fine *Northern Rockies Lodge-Highland Glen Lodge and Campground* (☎776-3481 or 1-800/663-5269, *www.northern-rockies-lodge.com*; ③) for a choice of log cabins or camping sites ($17–27). Two kilometres north of the Muncho Lake settlement there is the small *McDonald Provincial Campground* ($12).

About 70km beyond the lake is the excellent *Lower Liard River Lodge* (☎776-7341; ②; April–Oct), a wonderfully cosy and friendly spot for food and rooms. (*Liard* comes from the French for "poplar" or "cottonwood tree", a ubiquitous presence in these parts.) It also has RV and tent sites ($8–10) and lies close to one of the most popular spots on the entire Alaska Hwy, the very obvious **Liard Hot Springs**, whose **two thermal pools** (Alpha and Beta) are amongst the best and hottest in BC. Road crews loved these during the construction of the highway, or rather the men did: women in the teams were allowed a soak just once a week. They're reached by a short wooden boardwalk across steaming marsh, and are otherwise unspoilt apart from a wooden changing room and the big high-season crowds (aim to be here early in the day for a dip ahead of the rush). As the marsh never freezes, it attracts moose and grizzlies down to drink and graze, and some 250 plant species grow in the mild microhabitat nearby, including fourteen species of orchid, as well as lobelias, ostrich ferns and other rare boreal forest plants. The nearby *Liard River Hotsprings Provincial Park* **campsite** is one of the region's most popular, and fills up early in July and August: bookings are possible through the provincial park central reservation line (May–Aug $15; Sept–April $9); see box on p.852.

The telephone code for the Yukon is ☎867.

Watson Lake to Whitehorse

Beyond the hot springs the road follows the Liard River, settling into about 135km of unexceptional scenery before **WATSON LAKE**, just over the Yukon border (though the road trips back and forth across the border seven times before hitting the town). Created by the coming of the highway and air base, it's neither attractive nor terribly big, but shops, motels and garages have sprung up here to service the traffic congregating off the Cassiar and Campbell highways to the north and south. In the past the region was the preserve of the Kaska, a people whose centuries-old way of life was altered in the 1870s by the Cassiar gold rush. Another gold rush, the Klondike, gave the settlement its present name, when Frank Watson, an English prospector gave up on his attempts to reach the northern gold fields and stopped here instead. Even if you're just passing through it's well worth pulling off to look at the **Alaska Highway Interpretive Centre** (May–Sept daily 8am–8pm; ☎536-7469), which as well as providing information on the Yukon also describes the highway's construction through

THE CHILKOOT TRAIL

No single image better conjures the human drama of the 1898 gold rush than the lines of prospectors struggling over the **Chilkoot Trail**, a 53-kilometre path over the Coast Mountains between **Dyea**, north of Skagway in Alaska, and **Bennett Lake** on the British Columbian border south of Whitehorse. Before the rush, Dyea was a small village of Chilkat Tlingit, who made annual trade runs over the trail to barter fish oil, clamshells and dried fish with the Tutchone, Tagish and other interior Dene peoples in exchange for animal hides, skin clothing and copper. The Chilkat jealously guarded access to the **Chilkoot Pass** (1122m), the key to the trail and one of only three glacier-free routes through the Coast Mountains west of Juneau. Sheer numbers and a show of force from a US gunboat, however, opened the trail to stampeders, who used it as a link between the ferries at the Pacific Coast ports and the Yukon River, which they then rode to the gold fields at Dawson City.

For much of 1897 the pass and border were disputed by the US and Canada until the Canadian NWMP (Northwest Mounted Police) established a storm-battered shack at the summit and enforced the fateful "ton of goods" entry requirement. Introduced because of chronic shortages in the gold fields, this obliged every man entering the Yukon to carry a ton of provisions – and, though it probably saved many lives in the long run, the rule laid enormous hardship on the back of the stampeders. Weather conditions and the trail's fifty-degree slopes proved too severe even for horses or mules, so that men had to carry supplies on their backs over as many as fifty journeys to move their "ton of goods". Many died in avalanches or lost everything during a winter when temperatures dropped to –51°C and 25m of snow fell. Even so, the lure of gold was enough to drag some 22,000 prospectors over the pass.

These days most people off the **ferries from Prince Rupert and the Alaska Panhandle** make the fantastic journey across the mountains by car or Gray Line bus on Hwy 2 from **Skagway to Whitehorse**. This route parallels that taken by the restored White Pass & Yukon Route railway (WP&YR; mid-May to mid-Sept 1 daily; Skagway–White Pass by train then connecting bus to Whitehorse; $95; ☎983-2217 or 1-800/343-7373, *www.whitepassrailroad.com*), originally built to supersede the Chilkoot Trail. Increasing numbers, however, are walking the old trail, which has been laid out and preserved by the Canadian Parks Service as a **long-distance hikers route**. Its great appeal lies not only in the scenery and natural habitats – which embrace coastal rainforest, tundra and subalpine boreal woodland – but also in the numerous artefacts like old huts, rotting boots, mugs and broken bottles still scattered where they were left by the prospectors.

The trail is well marked, regularly patrolled and generally fit to walk between about June and September, though throughout June you can expect snow on the trail. Most people hike the trail in three or four days and if you're moderately fit it shouldn't be a problem, but there are dangers from bears, avalanches, drastic changes of weather and exhaustion – there's one twelve-kilometre stretch, for example, for which you're advised to allow twelve hours. Almost everyone hikes from south to north.

archive photos and audiovisual displays. It's situated on the highway next to the Chevron garage, close to the famous **Sign Post Forest**. This last bit of gimmickry was started by homesick GI Carl K. Lindley in 1942, who erected a sign pointing the way and stating the mileage to his home in Danville, Illinois. Since then the signs have just kept on coming, and at last count numbered around thirty thousand. You might also want to dip briefly into the **Northern Lights Centre** (June–Aug daily 2–10pm; $6–12; ☎536-7827, *www.yukon.net/northernlights*), a planetarium and science centre that explores the myths, folklore and science behind phenomena such as the aurora borealis (see box, p.854).

Although there are three warming huts on the trail, these aren't designed for sleeping in, and you'll be making use of the nine approved **campsites** spaced at intervals along the trail: no rough camping is allowed.

RESERVATIONS AND PERMITS

An advance **information pack** ($5) can be ordered by calling the **reservation system** (☎867/667-3910 or 1-800/661-0486 between 8.30am and 4pm Pacific Standard Time), or by writing to Chilkoot Trail National Historic Site, 205–300 Main St, Whitehorse, YT, Y1A 2B5. Throughout the hiking season, the number of hikers crossing the Chilkoot Pass into Canada is limited to 50 per day, of which 42 places can be booked in advance ($11) by calling the reservation system. The remaining 8 places are offered on a first-come, first-served basis after 1pm on the day before you plan to start the trail from the Skagway **Trail Center**, Broadway at 1st Avenue in (late May to early Sept daily 8am–4pm). The busy season is July and the first two weeks of August: outside this time you probably don't need to make a reservation.

Whichever way you secure a place on the trail, all hikers need to go to the Trail Center to buy a **permit** ($40), sign a register (for customs purposes) and consult the weather forecast. You'll need to carry **identification**, which means a birth certificate for North Americans (a driver's licence is not acceptable) and a passport for everyone else. You may be required to deal with Canadian customs at the Chilkoot Pass ranger station but more likely you'll do it after your hike at the Alaska–Canada border post at Fraser or in Whitehorse.

If you have made an advance reservation, you'll already have the Canadian Parks Service's *Chilkoot Trail* map (otherwise $2 from the Trail Center or the Canadian Parks Service office at the SS *Klondike* in Whitehorse), which is about the best available.

TRANSPORT AND SUPPLIES

Dyea Dave (☎983-2731) runs a shuttle bus ($10) from Skagway to Dyea, the start of the trail some nine miles northwest of Skagway. The trail finishes at Bennett, where you can get Tutshi Charters (☎867/821-4905) to take you across Lake Bennett to Carcross (Can$65) to meet the Whitehorse-bound Gray Line bus. Alternatively you can walk the eight miles to the highway at Log Cabin (there's a short cut off the trail which avoids Bennett) and meet up with Dyea Dave ($25 for a combined drop-off and pick-up); or **return to Skagway** on the WP&YR railroad. In June, July and August there is the Chilkoot Trail Hikers Service (departs 1pm Alaska time; $25 one-way to Fraser, $65 to Skagway) which is either a railcar or one carriage of the Lake Bennett Excursion that's specially designated for smelly hikers. Remember to buy your tickets before you set off on the trail or you'll have a $15 fee added to the ticket price for the convenience of buying your ticket on the train; and note that for customs reasons the train doesn't stop at Log Cabin.

Remember to take wet-weather gear, matches, some method of water treatment, sun screen, sunglasses, a flashlight and **thirty feet of rope** so that you can sling your food, toothpaste and any scented items over the bear poles at each campsite. Early in the season when there's plenty of snow about, consider **gaiters**, which can be rented in Skagway.

It's still 441km from Watson Lake to Whitehorse and, after the long haul on the Alaska Hwy, a lot of people wisely stop overnight here to recuperate. If you're camping there are no problems, for countless small Yukon government-run **campsites** are dotted along the length of the highway beyond the village; the closest is a rustic site 4km west of the Sign Forest ($8; May–Oct). If you decide to **stay in town** the cheapest options are the *Gateway Motor Inn* (☎536-7744; ③), open 24 hours a day, and the *Cedar Lodge Motel* (☎536-7406, *www.cedarlodge.yk.net*; ③). If these are full you may have to plump for one of the smarter hotels, all of which have rooms for around $95 – the best is the *Belvedere Hotel* (☎536-7712; ⑤), followed by the *Watson Lake Hotel*

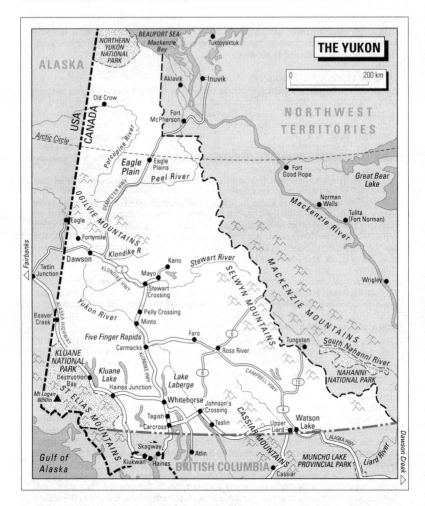

THE YUKON

(☎536-7781; ⑤). Both have dining rooms if you're after food, though the *Watson Lake Hotel* and *Gateway Motor Inn* have some rooms with kitchenettes if you're cooking for yourself.

West of Watson Lake the road picks up more fine mountain scenery, running for hour after hour past apparently identical combinations of snowcapped peaks and thick forest. About 10km before unlovely **TESLIN**, 263km to the west of Watson, look out for the *Dawson Peaks Northern Resort* (☎390-2310; ③), which not only has cabins and a campsite, but also boasts one of the highway's better restaurants; fishing and boat rentals are also available. Teslin itself was founded as a trading post in 1903 and now has one of the region's largest aboriginal populations, many of whom still live by hunting and fishing. The **George Johnston Museum** (mid-May to Sept daily 9am–7pm; $2.50; ☎390-2550) is on the right on the way into the village and has a good collection of local Tlingit artefacts as well as the photos of Johnston, a Tlingit who recorded his culture on film between 1910 and 1940.

Whitehorse

WHITEHORSE is the likeable capital of the Yukon, home to two-thirds of its population (around 24,000 people), the centre of its mining and forestry industries, and a bustling, welcoming stopoff for thousands of summer visitors. Whilst roads bring in today's business, the town owes its existence to the **Yukon River**, a 3000-kilometre artery that rises in BC's Coast Mountains and flows through the heart of the Yukon and Alaska to the Bering Sea. The river's flood plain and strange escarpment above the present town were long a resting point for Dene peoples, but the spot burgeoned into a full-blown city with the arrival of thousands of stampeders in the spring of 1898. Having braved the Chilkoot Pass (see box, p.876) to meet the Yukon's upper reaches, men and supplies then had to pause on the shores of Lineman or Bennett Lake before navigating the **Mile's Canyon** and White Horse rapids southeast of the present town. After the first few boats through had been reduced to matchwood, the Mounties laid down rules allowing only experienced boatmen to take craft through – writer Jack London, one such boatman, made $3000 in the summer of 1898, when more than seven thousand boats left the lakes. After a period the prospectors constructed an eight-kilometre wooden tramway around the rapids, and in time raised a shantytown settlement at the canyon and tramway's northern head to catch their breath before the river journey to Dawson City.

The completion of the White Pass and Yukon Railway (WP&YR) to Whitehorse (newly named after the rapids) put this tentative settlement on a firmer footing – almost at the same time as the gold rush petered out. In the early years of the twentieth century the town's population dwindled quickly from about 10,000 to about 400; for forty years the place slumbered, barely sustained by copper mining and the paddle-wheelers that plied the river carrying freight and the occasional tourist. The town's second boom arrived with the construction of the Alaska Hwy, a kick-start that swelled the town's population from 800 to 40,000 almost overnight, and has stood it in good stead ever since.

> The telephone code for the Yukon is ☎867.

Arrival, information and accommodation

Whitehorse's **airport** is on the bluff above the town, 5km west of downtown; taxis are around $9 to the centre, and the Whitehorse Transit Hillcrest bus ($1.25) runs downtown hourly during the day. If you're taking the bus *to* the airport, pick it up at the Qwanlin Mall at the northern end of 3rd Avenue. The Greyhound **bus terminal** is at 3211 3rd Ave (☎667-2223) at the extreme eastern end of downtown, ten-minutes' walk from Main Street – you turn left out of the terminal for the town centre, something it's as well to know if you stagger off the six-times-weekly Greyhound from Dawson Creek, which arrives around 5am. Alaskon Express buses, or Gray Line of Yukon (☎668-3225) from Fairbanks, Anchorage, Tok and Skagway, also stop here and at the *Westmark Whitehorse* hotel downtown.

Whitehorse's downtown **Yukon Visitor Reception Centre** is on 2nd Avenue and Hanson Street (mid-May to Sept daily 8am–8pm; ☎667-2915). Note that the "reception centre" up on the Alaska Hwy still mentioned in some literature is now the Beringia Centre (see p.883). The Parks Canada information office alongside the SS *Klondike* (May–Sept daily 9am–6pm; ☎667-4511) is the place to pick up information on the Chilkoot Trail. For information on the Yukon's aboriginal cultures, stop by the office of the **Yukon First Nations Tourism Association**, 1109-1st Ave (Mon–Fri 9am–5pm; ☎667-7698, *www.yfnta.org*) and pick up a copy of the *Yukon's First Nations Guide*.

Almost as useful as these is Mac's Fireweed, 203 Main St (Mon–Sat 9am–9pm, Sun 10am–7pm; ☎668-6104), which has a full range of Yukon books, guides and pamphlets you probably won't find elsewhere. For an outstanding selection of **maps** visit Jim's Toy and Gifts, 4137 4th Ave (☎667-2606).

Car rental agencies have desks or courtesy phones at the airport and occasionally a downtown office: Avis, 306 Ray St (☎667-2847); Budget, 4178 4th Ave (☎667-6200 or 1-800/268-8900); and Norcan, 213 Range Rd (☎668-2137) are companies to try, but remember some have restrictions on taking cars on gravel roads if you're thinking of heading north on the Dempster Hwy (see p.895). For **bike rental**, contact Big Bear Adventures (☎633-5642, *www.bear.yk.net*). **Canoes**, paddles and life-jackets plus bikes can be rented from the Kanoe People, Strickland Street and 1st Avenue (☎668-4899, *www.kanoe.yk.net*), who can also set you up with everything you need to paddle to Dawson (700km but lots of people do it): they also organize guided day-trips (from $60) and two-week expeditions on the river.

For **exchange**, plus reservations for ferries and **tickets** for local events, contact Thomas Cook, 2101A 2nd Ave (mid-May to early Sept daily 8am–8pm; rest of the year Mon–Fri 8.30am–5.30pm & Sat 10am–5pm; ☎668-2867).

Accommodation

Whitehorse has a surprising amount of **accommodation** but in summer it gets booked up well in advance. If you arrive cold, contact the visitor centre or try the string of six hotels on Main Street between 1st and 5th avenues. For **B&Bs**, try the information centre's B&B list, or contact the recommendations opposite, but note that places open and close with some regularity. Another option is an **accommodation agency**, Select Reservations, 18 Tagish Rd (☎393-2420 or 1-877/735-3281, *www.yukonalaska/selectrez*), which will help with lodgings of all descriptions across the Yukon, Alaska and northern BC. The *Robert Service* **campsite**, about 2km and twenty-minutes' walk down South Access Road, is set out on the banks of the Yukon River specifically for tents and backpackers (☎668-3721; $12 plus $1 for showers; mid-May to mid-Sept). It gets very busy in summer; if it's full try the woods above the lake down past the dam beyond the campsite or along the bluff above town by the airport.

HOTELS

Airline Inn, 16 Burns Rd (☎668-4400, fax 668-2641). If you arrive late at the airport, or need an early getaway, this is the airstrip's nearest hotel – serviceable enough for its purposes. ③.

Capital Hotel, 103 Main St (☎667-2565, fax 668-4651). This is the place to stay if you want one of the town's more lively, historic and boisterous hotels, complete with fine rooms. ③.

Edgewater Hotel, 101 Main St (☎667-2572, *www.edgewaterhotel.yk.ca*). Good, middle-priced hotel in downtown area. ④.

High Country Inn, 4051 4th Ave, at the far western end, a 10min walk from downtown (☎667-4471, *www.highcountryinn.yk.ca*). An easy-going hotel with a wide variety of excellent room deals and weekly rates. ⑥.

98 Hotel, 110 Wood St (☎667-2641 or 667-2656). Cheap, fairly grim and occasionally with live bands to serenade you through the small hours. ②.

Roadhouse Inn, 2163 2nd Ave (☎667-2594, fax 668-7291). Of a similar standard, but marginally better than the *98 Hotel* and near the bus terminal. ②.

Stratford Motel, 401 Jarvis St (☎667-4243 or 1-800/661-0539, fax 668-7432). Spotlessly clean, newly renovated rooms (some with kitchenettes) and with friendly staff. Three blocks from downtown. Weekly rates available. ④.

Town & Mountain Hotel, 401 Main St (☎668-7644, *www.yukon.com/tm.htm*). Another good and recently renovated middle-priced place. ④.

Westmark Klondike Inn, 2288 2nd Ave (☎668-4747, or 1-800/544-0970, *www.westmarkhotels.com*). One of two top-of-the-range, comfortable hotels belonging to the northern Westmark chain. ⑦.

Westmark Whitehorse Hotel, 201 Wood St (☎668-4700 or 1-800/544-0970, *www.westmarkhotels.com*). If you want to see Whitehorse in style, this is the smartest and most expensive hotel in town. ⑦.

BED AND BREAKFAST

Baker's, 84 11th Ave (☎633-2308). Two rooms (one double, one single) in a quiet area 5km from downtown. Long-established, and patrons are longtime Yukon residents. ③.

Birch Street, 1501 Birch St (☎633-5625, *ditan@netscape.net*). On a bus route to downtown but amidst a quiet setting overlooking the Yukon River Valley close to hiking trails. Full breakfast. Some rooms with private bath. ③.

By the Bluffs, 801 Black St (☎668-4333, *bythebluffs@hotmail.com*). Downtown neighbourhood location and the promise of mountain views, hammock and massage therapist on site. ③.

Casey's, 608 Wood St (☎668-7481, *casey@hypertech.yk.ca*). Downtown location with good breakfasts and evening snacks; kitchen and laundry facilities are available. ③.

Four Seasons, 18 Tagish Rd (☎667-2161, *jeano@yknet.yk.ca*). Centrally located, about 10min walk from downtown and offering full breakfast and snacks. ③.

Hawkins House, 303 Hawkins St (☎668-7638, *www.hawkinshouse.yk.ca*). Old and luxurious Victorian home in downtown; laundry and private bathrooms available. No smoking. ⑥.

International House, 17 14th Ave (☎633-5490, fax 668-4751). A quiet residential location with friendly and relaxed atmosphere created by hosts who have been in the Yukon for nearly forty years. Two blocks off the Alaska Hwy, 10min from downtown, though your hosts will pick you up from the airport or bus depot. ②.

Downtown

Although greater Whitehorse spills along the Alaska Hwy for several kilometres, the old **downtown** core is a forty-block grid centred on Main Street and mostly sandwiched between 2nd and 4th avenues. Though now graced only with a handful of pioneer buildings, the place still retains the dour integrity and appealing energy of a frontier town, and at night the baying of timber wolves and coyotes is a reminder of the wilderness immediately beyond the city limits. Nonetheless, the tourist influx provides a fair amount of action in the bars and cafés, and the streets are more appealing and lively than in many northern towns.

The main thing to see is the **SS Klondike** (May–Sept daily tours every half-hour 9am–6pm; $4; ☎667-4511), one of only two surviving paddle-steamers in the Yukon, now rather sadly beached at the western end of 2nd Avenue at 300 Main St, though it has been beautifully restored to the glory of its 1930s heyday. More than 250 stern-wheelers once plied the river, taking 36 hours to make the 700-kilometre journey to Dawson City, and five days to make the return trip against the current. The SS *Klondike* was built in 1929, sank in 1936, and was rebuilt in 1937 using the original remnants. The largest of all the river's steamers, it then battled against the river until 1955, ferrying 300 tonnes of cargo a trip and making some fifteen round trips a season. Bridges built on the improved road to Dawson increasingly hampered river traffic, though the SS *Klondike*'s end came when an inexperienced pilot ran her aground and condemned her to museum status. Beached at Whitehorse in 1960, the boat is visitable by a 25-minute guided tour only. Before or after a tour, take in the twenty-minute documentary film on the riverboat story in the theatre alongside.

Elsewhere in town you could pop into the **MacBride Museum**, housed in a sod-roofed log cabin at 1st Avenue and Wood Street (May to late Sept daily 10am–6pm; call for winter hours; $4; ☎667-2709), for the usual zoo of stuffed animals, an old WP&YR engine, pioneer and gold-rush memorabilia, as well as hundreds of marvellous **archive photos** and a display on the Asiatic peoples who crossed the Bering Straits to inhabit the Americas. Another in-town sight is the **Old Log Church Museum**, 3rd Avenue and Elliot Street (late May/early June to late Aug/early Sept Mon–Sat 10am–6pm, Sun noon–4pm; $2.50; ☎668-2555, *www.macbridemuseum.com*), a modest museum devoted to the pre-contact life of the region's **aboriginal peoples**, whaling, missionaries, children's toys and music, the gold rush and early exploration. You may find it easy to resist the widely touted Frantic Follies **stage shows** at the *Westmark Whitehorse Hotel* however – expensive (May–Sept; $20) vaudeville acts of the banjo-plucking and frilly-knick-ered-dancing variety that have been playing in town for close to thirty years, but if this sort of thing appeals, call ☎668-2042 for details of "music, mirth and magic, gay Nineties songs, cancan dances and humorous renditions".

The rest of town

Your money's better spent taking one of the **river tours** that shoot the **Miles Canyon** 9km south of the town, otherwise reached off the Alaska Hwy, or from the South Access Road, which hugs the river edge beyond the SS *Klondike*. Whitehorse Transit buses ($1.25) run along the South Access Road from town every hour daily except Sunday. The building of a hydroelectric dam has tamed the rapids' violence and replaced them with **Schwatka Lake**, but the two-hour narrated trip on the MV *Schwatka* (June–Sept daily 2pm & 7pm; $20; ☎668-4716) gives a better view of the river's potential ferocity and the canyon's sheer walls than the viewpoints off the road. Board at the dock above the dam about 3km down Canyon Road. A Taste of '98 Yukon River Tours (☎633-4767) runs similar three-hour sightseeing tours, as well as extended four- to 21-day guided or fully equipped tours to Dawson City and elsewhere. Other **boat trips** include a gentle two-hour raft trip with Miles Canyon Scenic Raft Float (☎633-4386) or a variety of trips with Canadian Yukon Riverboat (☎633-4414): daily trips in summer with breakfast cost $65 (departs 9am), with lunch $70 (1pm), and with dinner $75 (5pm); the basic trip without meals is $55.

If you fancy a **walk**, stroll from the main canyon car park some of the 11km to Canyon City, the all-but-vanished site of the initial stage of the stampeders' tramway at the southern end of the old rapids. You could also walk all the way round Schwatka Lake from Whitehorse, beginning from the bridge by the SS *Klondike*. Pick up details of this and other self-guiding trail booklets from the visitor reception centre (see p.879). If you don't fancy embarking on walks on your own, join the downtown walk offered by the Whitehorse Heritage Buildings Walking Tours, which departs four times daily in high summer at 9am, 11am, 1pm and 3pm from Donnenworth House, 3126 3rd Ave (☎667-4704; $2). Or try the variety of free summer strolls organized by the Yukon Conservation Society, 302 Hawkins St (July & Aug daily; ☎668-5678), two- to six-hour walks that delve into local and natural history, and the Yukon's geology, flora and fauna.

There is another trio of attractions just outside the downtown area, two of the most tempting up on the bluff above the town on the Alaska Hwy close to the airport. One is the excellent **Yukon Transportation Museum** (mid-May to mid-Sept daily 10am–6pm; $4; ☎668-4792), one of the region's best museums. Devoted to the area's transportation history, its displays, murals, superb historical videos, memorabilia and vehicles embrace everything from dog-sledding, early aviation and the construction of the Alaska Hwy to the Canol pipeline, the gold rush and the White Pass and Yukon Railway. Among the things on show are old army jeeps, bicycles, bulldozers, a stagecoach and – suspended from the ceiling – the *Queen of the Yukon*, the territory's first commercial plane. Right next door is the dynamic **Yukon Beringia Interpretive Centre** (mid-May to mid-Sept daily 8.30am–7pm; $6; ☎667-5340, *www.beringia.com*), Beringia being the vast subcontinent that existed some 24,000 years ago when the Yukon and Alaska were joined by a land bridge across the Bering Sea to Arctic Russia. The centre's interactive exhibits, film shows and other displays explore the aboriginal history of the time, the people who crossed this land bridge having ultimately colonized the most distant reaches of present-day North and South America. It also looks at the flora, fauna and geology of the time with the help of paleontological and archeological exhibits, among which the skeletal remains of a 12,000-year-old mammoth figure large.

On a totally different tack, if you fancy total relaxation make for the topnotch **Takhini Hot Springs** (June to early Sept 10am–10pm; rest of the year usually Fri–Sun only – call for precise hours; $4; ☎633-2706), located 31km from Whitehorse off the Klondike Highway to Dawson. The water in the large pool is a piping-hot 36°C, there's no sulphurous aftersmell and the pool is emptied daily. You can camp here ($7) and if you resent paying for the privilege of a hot soak the locals have built a public pool at the outflow point in the stream below.

Eating

Of several friendly laid-back **eating** places, the best overall is the *Talisman Café*, 2112 2nd Ave (Mon–Sat 6am–11pm), which serves a range of full meals, and is also a spot to while away time over a cup of coffee. The *Chocolate Claim* at 305 Strickland (☎667-2202) is a good, welcoming café for coffee, cakes and great chocolate. The *No Pop Sandwich Shop*, 312 Steele St (☎668-3227), is altogether less cosy, but it's popular all the same and the food's fine. Along the avenue, at 411 Alexander St and 4th Avenue, there's the excellent and rather hippie *Alpine Bakery* (☎668-6871; open daily), which is often crammed with campers and whose counter greets you with the Shakespearean sentiment "one feast, one house, one mutual happiness". The centrally located *Sam n' Andy's Tex Mex Bar and Grill*, 506 Main St (☎668-6994), has good food and an outdoor patio, while the popular and lively pub-eatery, the *Yukon Mining Company* at the *High Country Inn* hotel, 4051 4th Ave (☎667-4471), has locally brewed Chilkoot Brewing Company beers and barbecue food on the outdoor deck in summer. If you're feeling flush, two of the town's best restaurants are *Pandas*, 212 Main St (☎667-2632), with Bavarian specialities, or *Antonio's Vineyard*, 202 Strickland St (☎668-6266), which has Greek and Italian dishes (including pizzas) plus Arctic char and other fish and game dishes.

Onward from Whitehorse

Whitehorse provides the main **transport** links not only to most other points in the territory, but also to Alaska and the Northwest Territories. In summer there are regular Canada 3000 (☎604/647-3117 or 1-877/FLYCAN3) **flights** between Vancouver and Whitehorse plus Canadian (☎604/279-6611) **flights** to and from Edmonton and Vancouver: the airline has an office at 4th Avenue and Elliot Street (☎668-3535).

In this part of the world, however, it's also worth knowing the various smaller airline options. Air North (☎668-2228, *www.airnorth.yk.net*) operates sometimes alarmingly old-fashioned looking but totally reliable scheduled planes (usually four weekly) between Whitehorse, Dawson City, Old Crow, Mayo, Juneau and Fairbanks. Alkan Air (☎668-2107, *www.yukonweb.com/tourism/alkanair*) offers flights to and from Dawson City, Faro, Ross River, Old Crow, Watson Lake and a handful of BC destinations – most enable you to make same-day connections to flights from Whitehorse to Vancouver and Edmonton; it also flies to Norman Wells and Inuvik in the NWT. Era Aviation (☎907/266-8393, *www.eraaviation.com*) has a scheduled service between Anchorage and Whitehorse, plus services to Cordova, Kenai, Homer, Kodiak, Iliamna and Valdez. There are also any number of small charter companies who fly into the backcountry (notably Kluane National Park) for sightseeing, wildlife-watching, fishing and photography trips. Contact the visitor centre for details.

Whitehorse is the end of the line for Greyhound **buses** in Canada (☎667-2223). For **Alaska and Yukon stops west of Whitehorse**, the expensive Gray Lines' **Alaskon Express** (☎668-3225) runs from Skagway daily to Whitehorse's bus terminal and *Westmark Whitehorse* hotel (late May to mid-Sept daily; US$45) and then on to Anchorage and Fairbanks (US$170) three times a week (currently Sun, Tues & Thurs, but days of departure vary from year to year so check current times). Note that the bus stops overnight at Beaver Creek at the Yukon–Alaska border (see p.887) en route for Alaska, so you either have to camp or to find the price of accommodation (inform Gray Lines if you wish to stay at the *Westmark* in Beaver Creek as they may be able to obtain a discounted rate). Gray Lines' Whitehorse office is at the *Westmark Whitehorse* hotel, 2nd Avenue and Wood Street (☎668-3225 or 1-800/544-2206 winter only). Currently, a cheaper service based in the US, **Alaska Direct** (☎668-4833 or 1-800/780-6652), operates from Whitehorse to Skagway and vice versa (departs noon; Mon, Tues, Thurs & Sat; US$50; pick-ups arranged from hotels, Main St or bus depot). It runs three times weekly (Sun, Wed, Fri; departs 6am) to Fairbanks (US$140), Anchorage (US$165) and most points north, including Tok, Haines Junction, Burwash Landing and Beaver Creek. Unlike Alaskon, it does not overnight at Beaver Creek en route for Alaska, so you sleep (or otherwise) on the bus.

Dawson City Courier (☎993-6688) operate out of the main bus terminal and run **to Dawson City** at 2am, arriving at Dawson around 9.30pm (daily in July & Aug, times and days vary outside these months, so call for details; $72). It's well worth booking ahead to be sure of seat. If you want to take the **White Pass & Yukon Railway** to Skagway, you can book a bus-train ticket through the railway (☎907/983-2217 or 1-800/343-7373, fax 907/983-2734): buses leave Whitehorse at 1.30pm to connect with the train at Fraser, the line's northern terminus ($95 inclusive one-way; train only $64). If you book in Whitehorse, tickets can be collected at the Gray Lines' desk in the *Westmark Whitehorse Hotel*. If you wish to make a round trip from Whitehorse using the bus-train arrangement you'll need to overnight in Skagway. For more on the railway see also "The Chilkoot Trail" box, p.876.

For **car rental**, try Budget Car and Truck, 4178 4th Ave (☎667-6200), or Norcan, 213 Range Rd (☎668-2137 or 1-800/661-0445, fax 633-7596), which unlike its competitors might rent you a car or truck suitable for gravel roads like the Dempster and Cassiar highways.

Kluane Country

Kluane Country is the pocket of southwest Yukon on and around a scenically stunning 491-kilometre stretch of the Alaska Hwy from Whitehorse to **Beaver Creek** at the border with Alaska. *Kluane* comes from the Southern Tutchone aboriginal word meaning a "place of many fish" after the area's teeming waters, and of **Kluane Lake** in particular, the Yukon's highest and largest stretch of water. These days, though, the name's associated more with the all-but-impenetrable wilderness of Canada's largest mountain park, the **Kluane National Park** – a region that contains the country's highest mountains, the most extensive non-polar ice fields in the world, and the greatest diversity of plant and animal species in the far north. The park's main centre is **Haines Junction** at the intersection of the Alaska Hwy and the Haines Road. Although motels and campsites regularly dot the Alaska Hwy, the only other settlements of any size are **Destruction Bay** and **Burwash Landing** on Kluane Lake. Gray Line's **Alaskon Express** and **Alaska Direct** buses (see above) ply the length of the Alaska Hwy, which is also very popular with hitchhikers.

Haines Junction

A blunt and modern place 160km from Whitehorse, with a fine mountain-circled setting, **HAINES JUNCTION** (pop. 796) mushroomed into life in 1942 during the building of the Alaska Hwy as a base for the US Army Corps of Engineers during construction of the Haines Road – a highway that connects with Skagway's sister port at Haines, 174km to the southeast. Today it's the biggest service centre between Whitehorse and Tok in Alaska, boasting plenty of shops, a handful of accommodation possibilities (contact the visitor centre for B&B details) and lots of **tour and rental companies** for river-rafting, canoeing, fishing, cycling, horse riding and glacier flights in the Kluane National Park. It's the national park's eastern headquarters – the park covers a vast tract west of the Alaska Hwy well to the north and south of the village. The combined Parks Canada and Yukon government **Visitor Reception Centre** is on Logan Street just off the north side of the Alaska Hwy (Yukon Tourism May–Sept daily 8am–8pm; Parks Canada May–Sept daily 9am–7pm, Oct–April Mon–Fri 10am–noon & 1–4pm; ☎634-2345 or 634-7207). The village also has its own information line and Web site (☎634-2519, *www.kluane.com*).

The cheapest of the **motels** is the *Gateway* (open 24hr; ④; ☎634-2371) on the junction of Haines Road and the Alaska Hwy; it has rooms with kitchenettes, laundry and café and a few serviced **sites** to the rear. Or try the *Kluane Park Inn* (☎634-2261; ③; open 24hr) or the nonsmoking *Raven Hotel & Gourmet Dining* (☎634-2500, fax 634-2517, *kluanerv@yknet.yk.ca*; ④), a central place with a decent restaurant that includes breakfast in its room rate. Foodies will love their elegant evening meals, but you're looking at around $80 a head. The *Cozy Corner Motel & Restaurant* (☎634-2511; ③) lies just down the Alaska Hwy on the corner of Bates Road. The simple *Pine Lake* **campsite** ($8; May–Oct) is 7km east of the village signed off the Alaska Hwy, or there's the bigger and more central *Kluane RV Kampground* in town (☎634-2709; $12; May–Sept) which has wooded RV and tent sites, laundry and a grocery store. The best general place **to eat** is the popular *Village Bakery & Deli* (7.30am–9pm daily; ☎634-2867) on Logan Street across from the Visitor Reception Centre.

Kluane National Park

Created in 1972 using land from the earlier Kluane Game Sanctuary, the **KLUANE NATIONAL PARK** contains some of the Yukon's greatest but most inaccessible scenery, and for the most part you must be resigned to seeing and walking its easterly

---

WALKING IN KLUANE NATIONAL PARK

Kluane's **trail system** is still in its infancy, though experienced walkers will enjoy wilderness routes totalling about 250km, most of which follow old mining roads or creek beds and require overnight rough camping. A few more manageable walks start from seven distinct trailheads, each signed from the highways and mapped on pamphlets available from Haines' Reception Centre, where enthusiastic staff also organize popular guided day-walks during the summer.

Three trails start from points along a twenty-kilometre stretch of Haines Road immediately south of Haines Junction. The path nearest to the town, and the most popular walk, is the nineteen-kilometre round trip **Auriol Trail**; nearby, the **Rock Glacier Trail** is a twenty-minute jaunt to St Elias Lake; the third and longest trek is the **Mush Lake Road** route (21.6km one-way). North of Haines Junction, most people walk all or part of two paths that strike out from the Sheep Mountain information kiosk on Kluane Lake – either the **Sheep Mountain Ridge** (11.5km), with good chances of seeing the area's Dall sheep, or the longer **Slim's River West Trail** (28.4km one-way), which offers a relatively easy way to see the edges of the park's ice field interior.

margins from points along the Alaska Hwy (no road runs into the park). Together with the neighbouring Wrangell-St Elias National Park in Alaska the park protects the **St Elias Mountains**, though from the highway the peaks you see rearing up to the south are part of the subsidiary Kluane Range. Beyond them, and largely invisible from the road, are St Elias's monumental **Icefield Ranges**, which contain Mount St Elias (5488m), **Mount Logan** (5950m) – Canada's highest point – and Mount McKinley (6193m) in Alaska, the highest point in North America. These form the world's second highest coastal range (after the Andes). Below them, and covering half the park, is a huge base of mile-deep glaciers and ice fields, the world's largest nonpolar ice field and just one permanent resident, the legendary ice worm. Unless you're prepared for full-scale expeditions, this interior is off-limits, though from as little as $100 you can take plane and helicopter **tours** over the area with companies such as Trans North Helicopters, based on the Alaska Hwy (Mile 1056/Km 1698) between Silver City and the Sheep Mountain Reception Centre (☎668-2177, *www.tntaheli.com/tours.htm*); information on these and other guided tours are available from the Whitehorse Visitor and Haines Junction Reception centres.

On the drier, warmer ranges at the edge of the ice fields a green belt of meadow, marsh, forest and fen provides sanctuary for a huge variety of **wildlife** such as grizzlies, moose, mountain goats and a 4000-strong herd of white **Dall sheep**, the last being the animals the park originally set out to protect. These margins also support the widest spectrum of **birds** in the far north, some 150 species in all, including easily seen raptors such as peregrine falcons, bald eagles and golden eagles, together with smaller birds like arctic terns, mountain bluebirds, tattlers and hawk owls.

Limited **trails** (see box, overleaf) offer the chance to see some of these creatures, but the only **campsite** within the park is at the *Kathleen Lake*, on the Haines Road 16km southeast of Haines Junction ($8) – though there is hotel and camping accommodation along the Alaska Hwy.

Kluane Lake

The Kluane region might keep its greatest mountains out of sight, but it makes amends by laying on the stunning **Kluane Lake** along some 60km of the Alaska Hwy. About 75km northwest of Haines Junction, and hot on the heels of some magnificent views of the St Elias Mountains, the huge lake (some 400 square kilometres in area) is framed on all sides by snow-covered peaks whose sinister glaciers feed its ice-blue waters. It's not part of the national park, but there's still a second park kiosk at its southern tip, the **Sheep Mountain Information Kiosk** (mid-May to early Sept daily 9am–5pm; no phone). About 5km before the kiosk is the *Kluane Bed & Breakfast* (no phone; ③), with four cabins on the lakeshore. A kilometre beyond it lies the *Bayshore Motel and Restaurant* (☎841-4551; ③), open 24 hours a day from May to October; as well as rooms it offers sites for tents and RVs.

If you want to boat or fish there are rental facilities at the two main settlements along the shores, Destruction Bay and Burwash Landing, each of which also has a small selection of **accommodation** to supplement the odd lodges and campsites along the Alaska Hwy. In the smaller **DESTRUCTION BAY** (pop. 44), named when a previous road construction camp was destroyed by a storm in 1942, bed down at the *Talbot Arm Motel* with restaurant, café, store and Chevron garage (☎841-4461; ④). The best overall **campsite** locally is the lovely Yukon government-run *Congdon Creek* ($8) site off the Alaska Hwy, 12km south of Destruction Bay which also offers the start of hiking trails.

At **BURWASH LANDING**, 15km beyond, there's a tiny 1944 Oblate mission church and museum, Our Lady of the Holy Rosary, and the *Burwash Landing Resort* (☎841-4441; ③), with restaurant, store, glacier flights, fishing trips, gold-panning and a big unserviced campsite (free; May–Oct). Five kilometres further south the *Cottonwood*

Park Campground, a private outfit, offers rather more facilities (☎634-2739; $12; mid-May to mid-Oct). Moving on from Burwash, there are just two more major indoor accommodation possibilities before Beaver Creek: 85km east of Burwash is the *Pine Valley Bakery & Lodge* (☎862-7407; ③) and, 36km beyond that, the white *River Motor Inn* (☎862-7408; ③), with café and petrol. Ten kilometres west of the *Pine Valley Bakery & Lodge* are the Yukon government campsites at Lake Creek; additional campsites are situated eleven kilometres further at Pickhandle Lake (both $8).

Beaver Creek

BEAVER CREEK, Canada's westernmost settlement (pop. 145), is the last stop before Alaska. Following concerted lobbying from its inhabitants, however, it no longer hous-es the customs post – this has been moved a couple of kilometres up the road in response to complaints from the locals about the flashing lights and sirens that used to erupt whenever a tourist forgot to stop. Though the border is open 24 hours a day, you may have to stay here, particularly if you're catching the Alaskon **bus** service from Skagway and Whitehorse, which stops overnight at Beaver Creek on trans-Alaskan routes. The bus company can book you into the large and expensive *Westmark Inn* (☎862-7501 or 1-800/544-0970, *www.westmarkhotels.com*; ⑥; May–Sept): if that's too steep you've got the choice of arranging things for yourself at the eccentric twenty-room *Ida's Motel and Restaurant* (☎862-3227; ④; summer 6am–2am, winter 8am–10pm), a distinctive building across the highway or, failing that, at the *1202 Motor Inn* (☎862-7600; ④).

The *Westmark* has a large, serviced **campsite** ($20), though they're happier to see RVs than backpackers (try free camping in the woods). There's a good but small Yukon government-run site located 10km south at the *Snag Junction* ($8; May–Oct). Also be warned that if US Customs take against you or your rucksack, they can insist on seeing at least $400 or so in cash, and won't be swayed by any number of credit cards. For full details on border crossing, and what to expect on the other side, visit the **Yukon Visitor Information Centre** (mid-May to early Sept daily 8am–8pm; ☎862-7321).

Dawson City

Few episodes in Canadian history have captured the imagination like the **Klondike gold rush**, and few places have remained as evocative of their past as **DAWSON CITY**, the stampede's tumultuous capital. For a few months in 1898 this former patch of moose pasture became one of the wealthiest and most famous places on earth, as something like 100,000 people struggled across huge tracts of wilderness to seek their fortunes in the richest gold field of all time.

Most people approach the town on the Klondike Hwy from Whitehorse, a wonderful road running through almost utter wilderness, and knowing the background to the place it's hard not to near the road's end without high expectations. Little at first, how-ever, distinguishes its surroundings. Some 500km from Whitehorse the road wanders through low but steeply sided hills covered in spruce, aspen and dwarf firs, and then picks up a small ice-clear river – the **Klondike**. Gradually the first small spoil heaps appear on the hills to the south, and then suddenly the entire valley bottom turns into a devastated landscape of vast boulders and abandoned workings. The desolate tailings continue for several kilometres until the Klondike flows into the much broader **Yukon** and the town, previously hidden by hills, comes suddenly into view.

An ever-increasing number of tourists and backpackers come up here, many drawn by the boardwalks, rutted dirt streets and dozens of false-fronted wooden houses, oth-ers to canoe the Yukon or travel down the Dempster or Top of the World highways into Alaska and the Northwest Territories. After decades of decline Parks Canada is restoring the town, now deservedly a National Historic Site, a process that is bringing about increased commercialism, increased population (2000 and rising), new hotels and a sense that some of the town's character may be about to be lost. That said, in a spot where permafrost buckles buildings, it snows in August, and temperatures touch –60°C during winters of almost perpetual gloom, there's little real chance of Dawson losing the gritty, weather-battered feel of a true frontier town. More to the point, small-time prospecting still goes on, and there are one or two rough-and-ready bars whose hardened locals take a dim view of sharing their beers, let alone their gold, with coachloads of tourists.

You could easily spend a couple of days here: one exploring the town, the other touring the old Klondike creeks to the east. If at all possible prime yourself beforehand with the background to one of the most colourful chapters in Canada's history: Pierre

THE KLONDIKE GOLD RUSH

Gold rushes in North America during the nineteenth century were nothing new, but none generated quite the delirium of the **Klondike gold rush** in 1898. Over a million people are estimated to have left home for the Yukon gold fields, the largest single one-year mass movement of people in the century. Of these, about 100,000 made it to the Yukon, about 20,000 panned the creeks, 4000 found something and a couple of dozen made – and invariably lost – huge fortunes.

The discovery of gold in 1896 on the Klondike, a tributary of the Yukon River, was the culmination of twenty years of prospecting in the Yukon and Alaska. A Hudson's Bay fur trader first noticed gold in 1842, and the first substantial report was made by an English missionary in 1863, but as the exploitation of gold was deemed bad for trade in both furs and religion neither report was followed up. The first mining on any scale took place in 1883 and gradually small camps sprang up along almost 3200km of river at places like Forty Mile, Sixty Mile and Circle City. All were established before the Klondike strike, but were home to only a few hundred men, hardened types reared on the earlier Californian and British Columbian gold rushes.

The discovery of the gold that started the stampede is inevitably shrouded in myth and countermyth. The first man to prospect near the Klondike River was Robert Henderson, a dour Nova Scotian and the very embodiment of the lone pioneer. In early 1896 he found 8¢ worth of gold in a pan scooped from a creek in the hills above present-day Dawson City. This was considered an excellent return at the time, and a sign to Henderson that the creek would make worthwhile yields. He panned out about $750 with four companions and then returned downriver to pick up supplies.

Henderson then set about finding a route up the Klondike to meet the creek he'd prospected, and at the mouth of the Klondike met George Washington Carmack and a couple of his aboriginal friends, known as Skookum Jim and Tagish Charley. Henderson told Carmack of his hopes for the area, and then – with a glance at the aboriginal pair – uttered the phrase that probably cost him a fortune, "There's a chance for you George, but I don't want any damn Siwashes [aboriginal people] staking on that creek." Henderson wandered off into the hills, leaving Carmack, rankled by the remark, to prospect a different set of creeks – the right ones, as it turned out. On the eve of August 16, Skookum Jim found $4 of gold in a pan on Bonanza Creek, a virtually unprecedented amount at the time. Next day Carmack staked the first claim, and rushed off to register the find leaving Henderson prospecting almost barren ground on the other side of the hills.

By the end of August all of Bonanza had been staked by a hundred or so old-timers from camps up and down the Yukon. Almost all the real fortunes had been secured by the winter of 1896, when the snows and frozen river effectively sealed the region from the outside world. The second phase occurred after the thaw when a thousand or so miners from the West Coast arrived drawn by vague rumours of a big find, emanating from

Berton's widely available bestseller, *Klondike – The Last Great Gold Rush 1896–1899*, is a superbly written introduction both to the period and to the place.

The Town

You should start any wander on **Front Street**, the leading edge of a street grid that runs parallel to the Yukon River and at the junction with King Street is home to the impressive Tourism Yukon **Visitor Reception Centre** (mid-May to mid-Sept daily 8am–8pm; ☎993-5566, *www.dawsoncity.com*). Loaded with a huge amount of material, the place also has a Parks Canada desk and shows good introductory archive and contemporary films throughout the day, as well as letting you leave your bag or pack ($1) while you explore. It also organizes walking tours (June to mid-Sept several daily; $5)

the north. The headlong rush that was to make the Klondike unique, however, followed the docking in July 1897 of the *Excelsior* in San Francisco and the *Portland* in Seattle. Few sights could have been so stirring a proof of the riches up for grabs as the battered Yukon miners who came down the gangplanks dragging bags, boxes and sacks literally bursting with gold. The press were waiting for the *Portland*, which docked with two tons of gold on board, all taken by hand from the Klondike creeks by just a few miners. The rush was now on in earnest.

Whipped up by the media and the outfitters of Seattle and San Francisco, thousands embarked on trips that were to claim hundreds of lives. The most common route – the "poor man's route" – was to take a boat from a West Coast port to Skagway, climb the dreaded **Chilkoot Pass** to pick up the Yukon River at Whitehorse and then boat the last 500 miles to Dawson City. The easiest and most expensive route lay by boat upstream from the mouth of the Yukon in western Alaska. The most dangerous and most bogus were the "All Canadian Route" from Edmonton and the overland trails through the northern wilderness.

The largest single influx came with the melting of the ice on the Yukon in May 1898 – 21 months after the first claim – when a vast makeshift armada drifted down the river. When they docked at Dawson City, the boats nestled six deep along a two-mile stretch of the waterfront. For most it was to have been a fruitless journey – every inch of the creeks having long been staked – yet in most accounts of the stampede it is clear that this was a rite of passage as much as a quest for wealth. Pierre Berton observed that "there were large numbers who spent only a few days in Dawson and did not even bother to visit the hypnotic creeks that had tugged at them all winter long. They turned their faces home again, their adventure over . . . It was as if they had, without quite knowing it, completed the job they had set out to do and had come to understand that it was not the gold they were seeking after all."

As for the gold, it's the smaller details that hint at the scale of the Klondike gold rush: the miner's wife, for example, who could wander the creek by her cabin picking nuggets from the stream bed as she waited for her husband to come home; or the destitutes during the Great Depression who could pan $40 a day from the dirt under Dawson's boardwalks; or the $1000 panned during rebuilding of the Orpheum Theatre in the 1940s, all taken in a morning from under the floorboards where it had drifted from miners' pockets half a century before; or the $200 worth of dust panned nightly from the beer mats of a Dawson saloon during 1897.

By about 1899 the rush was over, not because the gold had run out, but because the most easily accessible gold had been taken from the creeks. It had been the making of Alaska; Tacoma, Portland, Victoria and San Francisco all felt its impact; Edmonton sprang from almost nothing; and Vancouver's population doubled in a year. It was also the first of a string of mineral discoveries in the Yukon and the far north, a region whose vast and untapped natural resources are increasingly the subject of attention from multinationals as rapacious and determined as their grizzled predecessors.

of the town's **heritage buildings** – though these are easily seen on your own, as are the cabins that belonged to two chroniclers of the gold rush, poet **Robert Service** and the better-known **Jack London**. The local **museum** is also good for an hour, and you might want to dabble in the **casino**, though when all's said and done it's the atmospheric streets of Dawson that are most compelling.

The heritage buildings

Fuelled by limitless avarice, Dawson between 1898 and 1900 exploded into a full-blown metropolis of 30,000 people – the largest city in the Canadian West and the equal of places like Seattle and San Francisco in its opportunities for vice, decadence and good living. There were opera houses, theatres, cinemas (at a time when motion-picture houses were just three years old), steam heating, three hospitals, restaurants with French chefs, and bars, brothels and dance halls which generated phenomenal business – one Charlie Kimball took $300,000 in a month from his club, and spent the lot within days. Show girls charged miners $5 – payable in gold – for a minute's dance; slow dances were charged at a higher rate. Cleaners panning the bars' sawdust floors after hours were clearing $50 in gold dust a night. Rules of supply and demand also made Dawson an expensive town, with a single two-metre frontage fetching as much in rent in a month as a four-bedroom apartment in New York cost for two years.

Only a few of the many intact **heritage buildings** around the town date from the earliest days of the rush, dozens having been lost to fire and to permafrost, whose effects are seen in some of the most appealing of the older buildings: higgledy-piggledy collapsing ruins of rotting wood, weeds and rusting corrugated iron. Most of these, thankfully, have been deliberately preserved in their tumbledown state. Elsewhere, almost overzealous restoration projects are in full flow, partly financed by profits from the town casino. Permafrost precluded the construction of brick buildings with deep foundations, so restoration has had to work doubly hard to save what are generally all-wood buildings, most notably the **Palace Grand Theatre** on the corner of 3rd Avenue and King Street (1899). The theatre was originally built from the hulks of two beached paddle steamers, and but for the intervention of the Klondike Visitors Association would have been pulled down for scrap timber in 1960. Tours run daily in summer ($5) and every night in summer except Tuesday. There's a performance of *Gaslight Follies* (mid-May to mid-Sept daily 8pm; $16 on the main floor, $18 on the balcony; ☎993-5575), a predictable medley of cancan, frilly knickers and gold-rush cabaret, though if you're tempted this is among the best of several such shows around the region.

Nearby on the corner of King Street and 3rd Avenue there's the working **1901 Post Office** (June–Aug daily noon–6pm; ☎993-7200); opposite is **Madame Tremblay's Store**; **Harrington's Store** on 3rd Avenue and Princess Street has a "Dawson as They Saw It" exhibition of photos arranged by Parks Canada (June–Aug daily 9am–5pm; free); near the same junction stands **Billy Bigg's Blacksmith Shop**; elsewhere are the cream-and-brown clapboard **Anglican Church**, built in 1902 with money collected from the miners. At 4th Avenue and Queen Street is **Diamond Tooth Gertie's Gambling House**, founded by one of the town's more notorious characters, and still operating as the first legal **casino** in Canada (opened after restoration in 1971) – it's also the world's northernmost casino (mid-May to mid-Sept daily 7pm–2am; $6); you need to be over 19 to gamble and all proceeds from here and several other town sights go to the restoration of Dawson. Also check out the **Firefighters Museum** in City Hall (under restoration at time of writing) where a guide takes you on a tour of old fire tenders, water pumps and other old firefighting equipment. In a town built almost entirely of wood these were once vital to Dawson's survival: the town all but burnt to the ground twice in the space of a year in 1898–99. So far you can't visit one of the town's more obvious old wooden constructions, the **SS Keno** riverboat, moored on the river just down from the visitor centre – it's been under restoration for several years. It was built in

1922 and ran up and down the Stewart River carrying ore from the mines around Mayo. At the Yukon River the ore was unloaded for collection by larger boats and the journey to Whitehorse and the railway. Not all boats were as lucky as the *Keno*, and a good short hike just out of town will take you to a **ships' graveyard**. The improvements to transport links, chiefly the completion of the Klondike Hwy, made many riverboats redundant. Some were beached downstream, where their overgrown carcasses can still be seen with a little effort. Cross the river on the free George Black ferry on Front Street and walk through the campsite and then a further ten minutes along the waterfront to reach the ruins.

The Dawson City Museum

The **Dawson City Museum**, 5th Avenue and Church Street (mid-May or June to Sept daily 10am–6pm; $5; ☎993-5291), has an adequate historical run-through of the gold rush from the first finds, though you get more out of the displays if you have some background to the period. Fascinating old diaries and newspaper cuttings vividly document the minutiae of pioneer life and events such as the big winter freeze of 1897–98 when temperatures reputedly touched –86°C, and of the summer heat wave of 1898 when the sun shone unbroken for almost 23 hours daily, bringing temperatures up to the upper thirties centigrade. The museum also shows some of the hundreds of old films that were discovered under the floorboards of a Dawson building a few years back. Its highlight – in fact, one of Dawson's highlights – is the wistful award-winning black-and-white film, *City of Gold*, a wonderful documentary which first drew the attention of the federal government to Dawson's decline in the 1950s. The museum also holds interesting touring exhibitions in the wood-framed rooms upstairs that once housed the council offices. You might also take a **tour** of the museum building (summer daily 11am, 1pm & 5pm), the former Territorial Administration Building (1901), during which you're shown the old court chambers (still occasionally used), the resource library and archive, the Visible Storage area (with some 6000 of the museum's 30,000 artefacts) and (outside) a view of the Victory Gardens (1910). The obvious **locomotives** outside the museum, incidentally, ran to Dawson from the gold fields between 1906 and 1914.

The Robert Service and Jack London cabins

The cabins of Dawson's two literary lions are only about 100m apart on 8th Avenue, about ten-minutes' walk from Front Street. Most Canadians hold **Robert Service** in high esteem – depite his occasionally execrable verse – and he has a place in the pantheon of Canadian literature. Verses like *The Shooting of Dan McGrew* and *The Cremation of Sam McGee* (see "Contexts", p.949) combine strong narrative and broad comedy to evoke the myth of the North. Born in Preston, England, in 1874, the poet wrote most of his gold-rush verse before he'd even set foot in the Yukon – he was posted by his bank employers to Whitehorse in 1904 and only made Dawson in 1908. He retired a rich man on the proceeds of his writing – he outsold Kipling and was one of the biggest-selling poets of his time – spending his last years mainly in France, where he died in 1958. His **cabin** (June–Sept daily 9am–noon & 1–5pm; $2; ☎993-7200) is probably cosier and better decorated than it was, but it still gives an idea of how most people must have lived once Dawson was reasonably established. During the summer people flock here to hear poetry recitals in front of the cabin from actor Charlie Davies (July & Aug daily 10am & 3pm; $6 for cabin and recital): another actor, Irish-born Tom Byrne, dressed and mannered as the "Bard of the Yukon", performs readings in summer on Front Street (3pm & 8.30pm) between Queen and Princess.

Jack London's Cabin home is an unpersuasive piece of reconstruction, little more than a bleak, blank-walled and incomplete hut (logs from the original were separated and half of them used to build a cabin in Jack London Square in Oakland, California).

London knew far more than Service of the real rigours of northern life, having spent time in 1897 as a ferryman on Whitehorse's Mile's Canyon before moving north to spend about a year holed up on Henderson's Creek above the Klondike River. He returned home to California penniless, but loaded with a fund of material that was to find expression in books like *The Call of the Wild*, *White Fang* and *A Daughter of the Snows*. Alongside the hut there's a good little museum of pictures and memorabilia, presided over by an amiable and knowledgeable curator (hut and museum June to mid-Sept daily 10am–6pm; donation; ☎993-5575). Readings of London's work are given here in summer, currently at noon and 2.30pm.

Practicalities

Dawson City's **airport**, 19km southeast of the town on the Klondike Hwy, is used by scheduled Alkan Air (☎668-2107 or 1-800/661-0432) services to Inuvik (NWT), Old Crow, Mayo and Whitehorse, and by Air North (☎668-2228 or 1-800/661-0407 in Canada, 1-800/764-0407 in the US, *www.airnorth.yk.net*) services to Fairbanks (4 weekly), Whitehorse, Watson Lake and Juneau. Dawson City Courier **buses** (☎993-6688) to and from Whitehorse arrive and depart from behind the visitor centre (daily in summer at 1pm, arrives Whitehorse 9pm; $72). Tickets for all air services, Alaska and BC ferries, sightseeing **tours** of the gold fields (see p.895), and popular four-wheel-drive vehicle tours can be arranged at the excellent Gold City Travel on Front Street opposite the SS *Keno* (☎993-5175 or 993-6424, fax 993-5261). If you need to **rent a car** or 4x4 for the Dempster Hwy (see p.895), contact Budget, 451 Craig St (☎993-5644, *www.yukon.net/budget*).

Another way of exploring the surroundings of Dawson is to take a Gray Line **cruise** on the *Yukon Queen*, which in summer runs daily on the Yukon River, offering a day-long round trip of 105 miles for $209. Stand-by, round trip and one-way tickets are available from Yukon Queen River Cruise on Front Street (☎668-3225, fax 667-4494). Shorter and cheaper ($45) ninety-minute river trips are available on the *Yukon Lou* from the dock behind the Birch Cabin ticket office close to the SS *Keno* (☎993-5482). Trans North Helicopters (☎993-5494) run helicopter trips over the gold fields, the Klondike Valley and Midnight Dome; fixed-wing plane tours are available from Siston Air (☎993-5599) and Bonanza Aviation (☎993-5209). For further details of tours and general information, contact the **Visitor Reception Centre** on Front Street (☎993-5566). Information is also available from the **public library** on 5th and Queen (Tues, Wed & Fri noon–7pm, Thurs noon–8pm, Sat 11am–5pm). For **books and guides** visit Maximilian's (☎993-5486) on the corner of Front and Queen.

Currency exchange and ATM facilities exist at the CIBC bank (☎993-5447) on Queen Street, between Front and 2nd, while **maps** are available from the mining recorder's office alongside the **post office** (Mon–Fri 8.30am–5.30pm; ☎993-5342) on 5th Street between Harper and Princess. For **showers** (there are none at the *Yukon River Campground*), the most central are the tight-fit bathrooms at the laundry behind the Chief Isaac Hale building alongside the visitor centre. There are also showers at the municipal **swimming pool** by the museum.

Accommodation

More and more accommodation is opening in Dawson, but while the increased competition keeps prices steady it isn't bringing them down. In July and August it's pretty much essential to book lodging in advance. The two hostels are likely to be heavily oversubscribed, as are the B&B options, though calls to the latter a couple of days in advance should secure a room. Rates are high in the half-dozen or so mid-range places, most of which look the part of old-fashioned wood- and false-fronted hotels. If you arrive without a room, check with the visitor centre, which keeps an updated record of accommodation availability and will work hard to find you a bed: hotels often offer cheap last-minute deals to fill empty rooms. Note that many places close their doors between September and mid-May.

The main town **campsite** for tents is the government-run *Yukon River Campground* ($8), which is on the west bank of the Yukon on the right about 500m after the fun and free *George Black* seven-minute ferry crossing (see p.895) from the top of Front Street. Black, incidentally, made one of the first journeys to Dawson by car from Whitehorse in 1912 in the (then) record-breaking time of 33 hours. The *Gold Rush Campground* in town at 5th and York is a bleak, fully serviced but busy place designed for RVs (☎993-5247; $20; May–Sept).

Bear Creek B&B, 11km south of Dawson by Bear Creek Historical Site (☎993-5605, *www.yukon.net/bearcreek*). A family-run guesthouse with four rooms in a peaceful natural setting away from town. ③.

Bonanza House B&B, near the museum on 7th Ave and Grant (☎993-5772, fax 993-6509). Offers a two- or three-bedroom suite with shared sitting rooms and TV. ③.

Dawson City B&B, 451 Craig St (☎993-5649, *www.yukon.net/dawsonbb*). Located near the junction of the Yukon and Klondike rivers and arranges pick-ups from the airport or even offers car rentals. ④.

Dawson City Bunkhouse, near the corner of Front and Princess (☎993-6164, fax 993-6051). A good, if noisy, hostel-type place (often known just as "The Bunkhouse") with a choice between rooms with shared bathrooms or private facilities. ④.

Dawson City River Hostel, across the river from downtown; first left after you jump the free ferry (☎993-6823). An HI-affiliated collection of bunks in smart log cabins with a good view of Dawson and the river. There are bunk rooms (two to six people), tent sites, family rooms, a sweat lodge and canoe and bike rentals available. No electricity. Cash only. Open May to mid-Sept. ①.

Downtown Hotel, 2nd and Queen (☎993-5346 or 1-800/764-0514 in BC and the Yukon, *www.downtown.yk.net*). One of the town's plusher wooden-fronted hotels, and – unlike some – open year-round. ⑤.

Eldorado, 3rd and Princess (☎993-5451 or 1-800/661-0518, fax 993-5256). Much the same as the *Downtown*, and also open 24hr year-round. ⑤.

Fifth Ave B&B, on 5th Ave near the museum (☎993-5941, *5thave@dawson.net*). A spacious house with shared kitchen, and optional en suites. ③.

Klondike Kate's Cabins & Rooms, 3rd and King (May–Sept; ☎993-6527, fax 993-6044). Old-fashioned and simple, but clean and warm, offering some of the cheapest rooms in town as well as cabins. ③.

Northern Comfort, 6th and Church (☎993-5271). A centrally located B&B that provides bike rentals. ③.

Trail of '98, 5km out of town at the junction of the Klondike Hwy and Bonanza Creek Rd (☎993-6101). The best budget deal around if you can get four people together for one of the simple $40 cabins. No power or running water, but washrooms are available nearby. ②.

Triple J Hotel, 5th and Queen (☎993-5323 or 1-800/764-3555, *jjj@dawson.net*). Some 47 rooms or cabins with kitchenettes in old-fashioned-style hotel next to *Diamond Tooth Gertie's*. Coin laundry and airport shuttle service. May–Oct. ⑤.

Westmark Inn Dawson, 5th and Harper (☎993-5542 or 1-800/544-0970, *www.westmarkhotels.com*). Part of an upmarket northern chain, and the town's swishest hotel: look out for cut-price promotions to fill empty rooms. ⑥.

Westminster Hotel, 3rd and Queen (☎993-5463, fax 993-6029). Despite the tempting old false-fronted exterior and the clean and cheap rooms, this is a rough-house spot where the miners come in to drink long and noisily into the night. April–Sept. ③.

White Ram B&B, 7th and Harper (☎993-5772, *www.yukon.net/whiteram*). A distinctive pink house that has a hot tub and outside deck. Pick-up from bus on request. ③.

Whitehorse Motel, Front St (☎993-5576). Six cabins with kitchenettes on the waterfront at the northern end of the street beyond the *George Black* ferry. Mid-May to mid-Sept. ③.

Food and nightlife

For **eating** there are several good snack places on Front Street – probably the most popular is *River West Food & Health* (☎993-6339), a healthfood store with café. The excellent *Klondike Kate's* (May–Sept daily 7am–11pm; ☎993-6527), at 3rd and King, is the friendliest and most laid-back place in town for staples like breakfasts and straightforward dinners (and has an outdoor patio). Otherwise, most dining goes on in the restaurants attached to the town's bigger hotels: three of the best are the *Jack London Grill* in the *Downtown Hotel* at 2nd and Queen; the *Bonanza Dining Room* in the Eldorado at 3rd and Princess; and *TJ's* in the *Triple J Hotel* at 5th and Queen. *Madame Zoom's*, at 2nd and King, has good ice cream and frozen yogurts, and for picnic goodies and **self-catering** supplies, there's the Dawson General Store on Front Street at the corner of Queen (☎993-5475) as well as the Farmer's Market on 2nd near Princess.

Nightlife revolves around drinking in the main hotel bars, or an hour or so at *Diamond Tooth Gertie's* at 4th and Queen, Canada's only legal gambling hall (see p.890). You can also catch the almost equally touristy period-costume melodramas and vaudeville acts (see p.890) held at the Palace Grand Theatre (June–Sept nightly at 8pm; $16–18). If you want a taste of a real northern **bar**, try the *Westminster* on 2nd Avenue: it's full of grizzled characters and most certainly not the place for a quiet drink or the faint-hearted: there's live music most nights. Other hotel bars provide more sedate alternatives.

Around Dawson

While in Dawson, make a point of seeing the two creeks where it all started and where most of the gold was mined – **Bonanza and Eldorado**, both over 20km away from the town site along rough roads to the southeast. These days no big working mine survives in the region, though most of the claims are still owned and definitely out of bounds to amateurs. However, it's still possible to see some of the huge dredges that supplanted the individual prospectors, once the easily reached gold had been taken out. Another popular local excursion is to **Midnight Dome**, the gouged-out hill behind the town, while further afield numerous RVs, cyclists and hitchhikers follow the **Top of the World Hwy**, which runs on beyond the Alaskan border to link with the Alaska Hwy at Tetlin Junction.

Bonanza and Eldorado creeks

To reach **Bonanza Creek**, follow the Klondike Hwy – the continuation of Front Street – for 4km to the junction with Bonanza Creek Road. The road threads through scenes of apocalyptic piles of boulders and river gravel for some 12km until it comes to a simple cairn marking **Discovery Claim**, the spot staked by George Carmack after pulling out a nugget the size of his thumb, or so the story goes. Every 150m along the creek in front of you – the width of a claim – was to yield some 3000kg of gold, or about $25 million worth at 1900 prices. Exact amounts of gold taken out are difficult to establish because it was in miners' interests to undervalue their takings to the authorities, but most estimates suggest that around $600-million worth left the creeks between 1897 and 1904. Given a claim's huge value they were often subdivided and sold as "fractions": one miner pulled out over 100kg of gold in eight hours from a fraction – almost $1 million worth.

At Discovery Claim the road forks again, one spur running east up **Eldorado Creek**, if anything richer than Bonanza; the other following Upper Bonanza Road to the summit of **King Solomon's Dome**, where you can look down over smaller scarred rivulets like Hunker and Dominion creeks, before returning in a loop to the Klondike Hwy via Hunker Road.

As time went by and the easily reached gold was exploited, miners increasingly consolidated claims, or sold out to large companies who installed dredges capable of clawing out the bedrock and gravel. Numerous examples of these industrial dinosaurs litter the creeks, but the largest and most famous is the 1912 **No. 4 Dredge** at Claim 17 BD

("Below Discovery") off Bonanza Creek Road, an extraordinary piece of industrial archeology that from the start of operations in 1913 until 1966 dug up as much as 25kg of gold a day. Modern mines are lucky to produce a quarter of that amount in a week.

Without a car you'll have to rent a bike or join up with one of the various **gold-field tours** (from $36 for a 3hr 30min tour) run by Gold City Tours, on Front Street (☎993-5175), either to see the dredges and creeks or to **pan for gold** yourself, at a price. Only three small fractions on Claim 6 can currently be panned free of charge – but enquire at the reception centre for latest locations: for $5 you can pan with a guarantee of finding gold (because it's been put there) on Claim 33.

Midnight Dome and Top of the World Highway

The **Midnight Dome** is the distinctive hill that rears up behind Dawson City, half-covered in stunted pines and half-eaten away by landslips. It's named because from its summit at midnight on June 21 you can watch the sun dip to the horizon before rising again straight away – Dawson being only 300km south of the Arctic Circle. The Midnight Dome Road runs 8km to its summit (884m) from the Klondike Hwy just out of the town proper. Without a car it's an extremely steep haul (ask at the visitor centre for details of the well-worn and partially signed trail), but more than worth the slog for the massive views over Dawson, the gold fields, the Yukon's broad meanders and the ranks of mountains stretching away in all directions. At the summer solstice there's a race to the top and lots of drink-sodden and fancy-dress festivities down in Dawson. Gold City Tours also run regular daytime and evening tours up here.

You can snatch further broad vistas from the **Top of the World Hwy** (Hwy 9), a good summer-only gravel road reached by the *George Black* ferry from Front Street across the Yukon (mid-May to mid-Sept daily 24hr; mid-Sept to mid-May 7am–11pm depending on weather conditions and whether or not the river is frozen; every 45min; free; ☎993-5441). After only 5km the road unfolds a great panorama over the area, and after 14km another **viewpoint** looks out over the Yukon Valley and the **Ogilvie Mountains** straddling the Arctic Circle. Thereafter the road runs above the tree line as a massive belvedere and can be seen switchbacking over barren ridges way into the distance. It hits the **Alaska border** 108km from Dawson, where you can cross only when the customs post is open (May–Sept 9am–9pm). Unlike the Dempster Hwy (see below), there's no **bus** on this route, but you should be able to hitch easily in summer because it's much-travelled as a neat way of linking with the Alaska Hwy at Tok for the roads to Fairbanks and Anchorage or the loop back to Whitehorse. Be prepared to do only about 50kph, and enquire about local difficulties and fuel availability at the Dawson Visitor Reception Centre.

The Dempster Highway

Begun in 1959 to service northern oilfields, and completed over twenty years later – by which time all the accessible oil had been siphoned off – the 741-kilometre **Dempster Highway** between Dawson City and Inuvik in the Northwest Territories is the only road in Canada to cross the **Arctic Circle**, offering a tremendous journey through a superb spectrum of landscapes. An increasingly travelled route – which locals say means four cars an hour – it crosses the **Ogilvie Mountains** just north of Dawson before dropping down to **Eagle Plains** and almost unparalleled access to the subarctic tundra. Shortly before meeting the NWT border after 470km it rises through the **Richardson Mountains** and then drops to the drab low hills and plain of the Peel Plateau and Mackenzie River. For much of its course the road follows the path of the dog patrols operated by the Mounties in the first half of the twentieth century, taking its name from a Corporal W.J.D. Dempster, who in March 1922 was sent to look for a

patrol lost between **Fort McPherson** (NWT) and Dawson. He found their frozen bodies just 26 miles from where they had set off. They were buried on the banks of the Peel
River and there's a monument to their memory at Fort McPherson.

The telephone code for the NWT is ☎867.

Practicalities

The Dempster is a gravel road and the 741-kilometre journey by **car** takes anything
between twelve and fifteen hours in good conditions. It is not, however, a journey to be
undertaken lightly. If you're **cycling** or motorbiking, both increasingly popular ways of
doing the trip, you need to be prepared for rough camping, and should call at the **NWT
Information Centre** on Front Street in Dawson City (May–Sept 9am–7pm; ☎993-6167
or 1-800/661-0788) for invaluable practical as well as anecdotal information from
the staff. If you're without your own transport you might pick up a **lift** here, or take the
twelve-hour **Dempster Highway Bus Service** run by Dawson City Courier (☎993-
6688). Departures currently leave from Dawson to Inuvik on Monday and Friday
between June and mid-September (with returns from Inuvik on Wed and Sun), but
these details are subject to change, so check before planning a trip. **Tickets** cost
$216.45 one-way to Inuvik, less to Eagle Plains and other drop-offs en route. If you're
driving or biking it's also worth checking that the two ferry services (☎1-800/661-0752)
on the route at Peel River and Tsiigehtchic (formerly Arctic Red River) are running
when bad weather threatens, and that you have sufficient fuel in a car to make the long
stretches.

In the Dempster's Yukon section there is **accommodation** only at the 32-room
Eagle Plains Hotel (☎993-2453; ⑨, camping $10; year-round), 363km north of Dawson.
There are also three rudimentary Yukon government **campsites** at Tombstone
Mountain, 72km north of Dawson; at Engineer Creek (194km); and at Rock River
(447km). In July and August there's usually a trailer information kiosk at Tombstone
Mountain with details of good trails from the campsite. Fort McPherson also has a
small summer-only visitor centre in the log building by the monument to Dempster's
"Lost Patrol".

Currently the only other **accommodation** is in the tiny Gwich'in Dene village of
Fort McPherson, 115km south of Inuvik soon after crossing the Peel River. The lodgings amount to the *Bell River Bedrooms* (☎952-2465, fax 952-2212; ④), with showers,
laundry, cable TV and self-serve breakfast; and the *Tetlichi B&B* (☎952-2356; ④), just
one double room with use of kitchen and laundry. There's also the unserviced NWT
government *Nutuiluie Territorial Campground* (547km from Dawson) 10km south of
Fort McPherson ($10; June–Sept). For tours from the village, contact the local
Dempster Patrol (☎952-2053), which runs interesting trips such as visits to the Shildii
Rock, a spot sacred to the Tet'lit Gwich'in, trips to an abandoned Gwich'in camp, and
themed day-tours by boat such as "On the Trail of the Lost Patrol".

The even tinier settlement of **Tsiigehtchic** (formerly Arctic Red River), 80km south
of Inuvik, was founded as a mission in 1868 – a red-roofed mission church from 1931
still stands – acquiring a Hudson's Bay post soon after. Since 1996 it has been known
by its Dene aboriginal name, which means "mouth of the red-coloured river".

Dawson City to the Arctic Circle

Having come this far north it's hard to resist the temptation of crossing the **Arctic
Circle** 403km north of **Dawson City**, a journey that takes you over the most captivating stretch of the highway. At the very least you should take a short ride out of the

mixed deciduous spruce woods of the boreal forests for a look at the tundra which starts beyond the **North Fork Pass** (1370m), just 79km north of Dawson. All distances given below are from Dawson City, almost the only way to locate things on the road.

After the millions of lodgepole pines in this part of the world, it's almost time for a celebration when you pass what are reputedly Canada's most northerly pines (8km). Beyond them you'll see occasional trappers' cabins: the hunting of mink, wolverine and lynx is still lucrative, providing the Yukon's 700 or so full-time trappers with a $1.5-million annual income. At **Hart River** (80km) you may see part of the 1200-strong Hart River Woodland **caribou herd**; unlike the barren-ground herds further north these caribou have sufficient fodder to graze one area instead of making seasonal migrations. **Golden eagles** and **ptarmigan** are also common on willow-lined streams like Blackstone River (93km), as are **tundra birds** like Lapland longspurs, lesser golden plovers, mew gulls and long-tailed jaegers. At Moose Lake (105km), **moose** (needless to say) can often be seen feeding, along with numerous species of waterfowl such as northern shoveller, American widgeon and the **arctic tern**, whose Arctic to Antarctic migration is the longest of any bird.

Chapman Lake (120km) marks the start of the northern Ogilvie Mountains, a region that has never been glaciated and so preserves numerous relic species of plant and insect, as well as providing an important early wintering range for the **Porcupine Caribou Herd**; as many as 40,000 caribou cross the highway in mid-October – they take four days and have right of way. Unique **butterfly** species breed at Butterfly Ridge (155km), close to some obvious caribou trails which cross the region, and it should also be easy to spot Dall sheep, cliff swallows and bald eagles.

The **Arctic Circle** (403km) is marked on the Dempster by a battered roadside cairn, and the occasional summer home of one of the north's premier eccentrics, one Harry Waldron, the self-proclaimed "Keeper of the Arctic Circle". In his late 60s, Harry was wont to sit in a rocking chair in a tuxedo with a glass of champagne and regale all-comers with snippets of Robert Service, facts about the Arctic and some fairly unimpeachable views on the environment. An ex-highway worker, he started his act of his own accord, but proved so popular that he was paid by the Yukon government to sit and do his spiel. After here, the road climbs into the Richardson Mountains to meet the border of the NWT (470km) before the less-arresting flats of the Mackenzie River and the run to Inuvik.

Delta-Beaufort

The **Delta-Beaufort** region centres on the planned government-built town of **Inuvik**, embracing the mighty delta of the **Mackenzie River**, North America's second longest river, and reaching across the Beaufort Sea to Banks Island, the most westerly of Canada's Arctic islands. The delta ranks as one of the continent's great **bird** habitats, with swans, cranes and big raptors amongst the many hundreds of species that either nest or overfly the region during the spring and autumn migration cycles. It also offers the chance of seeing pods of **beluga whales** and other big sea mammals, while local **Inuit** guides on Banks Island should be able to lead you to possible sightings of musk ox, white fox and polar bears.

After Inuvik and the two villages on the short NWT section of the Dempster – Fort McPherson and Tsiigehtchic – the area's other four settlements are **fly-in communities** reached from Inuvik. Two of them, **Aklavik** and **Tuktoyaktuk**, are near – at least, by NWT standards – and are the places to fly out to if you want a comparatively accessible taste of aboriginal northern culture. **Sachs Harbour** (on Banks Island) and **Paulatuk** lie much further afield, and are bases for more arduous tours into the delta and Arctic tundra. Inuvik, along with Yellowknife and Fort Smith, is one of the key centres of the accessible north, and one of the main places from which to make, take or plan tours further afield. Two major – and several minor – **tour companies** run a wide variety of boat and plane tours to all four destinations (see opposite), varying from reasonably priced day-trips to full-on expeditions. Having come this far it's well worth taking one of the shorter tours to the fly-in communities for a taste of Arctic life, and to enjoy the superb bird's-eye view of the delta and surrounding country from the air.

Inuvik

INUVIK – "the place of man" – is the farthest north you can drive on a public highway in North America, unless, that is, you wait for the winter freeze and follow the ice road carved across the frozen sea to the north. Canada's first planned town north of the Arctic Circle, Inuvik was begun in 1954 as an administrative centre to replace Aklavik, a settlement to the west wrongly thought to be doomed to envelopment by the Mackenzie's swirling waters and shifting mud flats. Finished in 1961, it's a strange melting pot of around 3000 people, with Dene, Métis and Inuvialuit living alongside the trappers, pilots, scientists and frontier entrepreneurs drawn here in the 1970s when a boom followed the oil exploration in the delta. Falling oil prices and the rising cost of exploitation, however, soon toppled the delta's vast rigs and it seems the oil is destined to remain largely untapped until well into this century. Today the local economy also relies on government jobs, services and the town's role as a supply and communication centre for much of the western Arctic.

Wandering the town provides an eye-opening introduction to the vagaries of northern life, from the strange stilted buildings designed to prevent their heat melting the permafrost (which would have disastrous effects on foundations, assuming any could be dug), to the strange pipes, or "utilidors", which snake round the streets carrying water, power and sewage lines – again, to prevent problems with permafrost. There are also the all-too-visible signs of the **alcoholism** that affects this and many northern communities – a problem rarely alluded to outside them, partly because the region's aboriginal groups seem to be disproportionately afflicted: suicides here are four times the national average for groups of **aboriginal** people.

On a happier note, the influence of Inuvialuit people in local political and economic life has increased, to the extent that the **Western Claims Settlement Act** of 1984 saw the government cede titles to various lands in the area, returning control that had been lost to the fur trade, the church, oil companies and national government. A potent symbol of the church's local role in particular resides in the town's most-photographed building, the **Igloo Church**, or Our Lady of Victory, a rather incongruous cultural mix. It's on Mackenzie Road, the main street which runs west to east through town, but isn't always open: ask at the rectory for a glimpse inside and for the paintings of local Inuvialuit artist, Mona Thrasher. Much further west on Mackenzie Road you might also want to take a look at the **Ingamo Hall**, a three-storey building built almost entirely from 1000 white-spruce logs brought up the Mackenzie River (local trees, such as there are, don't grow sufficiently to provide the timber required for building).

Practicalities

Canadian North (☎669-4000 or 1-800/661-1505) has daily scheduled **flights** to Inuvik's **Mike Zubko airport** (12km south of town) from Edmonton, usually via Yellowknife, Fort Smith or Hay River. Several regional **airline companies** also run regular services from Yellowknife, Whitehorse, Dawson City and between the numerous smaller destinations in the NWT. The main ones (all area codes ☎867 unless stated) are Air North (☎668-2228, *www.airnorth.yk.net*); Aklak Air (☎777-3555); Alkan Air (☎668-2107); and First Air (☎613/839-3340 or 1-800/267-1247).

A **taxi** (☎777-5050) from the airport should cost around $25–30. As elsewhere in Canada and the NWT, the cheapest way of getting to Inuvik may be to buy an Air Canada pass before arriving in Canada (see Basics, p.34). When talking to airlines about onward flights to the fly-in communities or elsewhere, remember that local tour companies often use their scheduled flights, and may be able to offer better flight-only deals than the airlines (see tour company details below). In summer a **bus** service operates from Dawson (see p.887) – its Inuvik office is at 181 Mackenzie Rd (☎979-4100 or toll-free in northern BC and the Yukon 1-800/661-0721); the **Dempster Hwy** is open year-round except for brief periods during the November freeze and April thaw.

For **information** on Inuvik and the region, contact the **Western Arctic Visitor Centre** (mid-May or June to Sept daily 9am–8/9pm; ☎777-3777), located near the entrance to town at the eastern end of Mackenzie Road at the junction with Loucheux (10min walk from the centre). In town you can dig out more background to the area and access the Internet at the **Inuvik Centennial Library** (Mon & Fri 2–5pm, Tues–Thurs 10am–9pm; ☎777-2749) on Mackenzie Road west of the Igloo church, and pick up **maps**, **guides**, books and charts at the Boreal Bookstore (☎777-3748), located almost opposite the church at the Arctic Tour Company office, 181 Mackenzie Rd. The **post office** is at 187 Mackenzie Rd (☎777-2749), and the **hospital** (☎777-2955) is at the eastern end of town close to the visitor centre. For the **police**, call ☎777-2935.

ACCOMMODATION

There are only three **hotels** in town, and all are almost identically pricey: the big *Eskimo Inn* (☎777-2801 or 1-800/661-0725; ⑤), in central downtown; the *Finto Motor Inn* (☎777-2647 or 1-800/661-0843; ⑥), to the east next door to the Western Arctic Visitor Centre, with a good restaurant; and the central *Mackenzie Hotel* (☎777-2861, *mac@permafrost.com*; ⑥). *Robertson's Bed and Breakfast*, 41 Mackenzie Rd (☎979-3111, *robertbb@permafrost.com*; ④), has nonsmoking rooms, which need to be booked well in advance during summer. So, too, does the central *Polar Bed and Breakfast* (☎777-2554, *islc@permafrost.com*; ④). The *Arctic Chalet Bed and Breakfast* (☎777-3535, *www.yukon-web.com/tourism/arcticchalet*; ④), which is 3km from town, has a log house and cabins. The nearest local **campsite**, the *Happy Valley*, overlooks the delta; the simple and peaceful *Chuk Park* site (☎777-3613; from $15; June–Oct) is 6km out of town on the way to the airport.

EATING

Eating possibilities are largely confined to hotel dining rooms – where at a price you can gorge on char, caribou and musk ox: the best is probably *The Peppermill* at the *Finto Motor Inn*, 288 Mackenzie Rd followed by the *Green Briar Dining Room* (☎777-2414) in the *Mackenzie Hotel*, whose coffee shop is also a good place for breakfast. The *Back Room*, 108 Mackenzie Rd, is famed for its stuffed polar bear, and serves the usual steaks, fish, fries, and won't break the bank. For the best and busiest **bar**, head for the *Zoo* in the *Mackenzie Hotel*, a gathering place for an eclectic mix of locals, backpackers and assorted out-of-towners. The *Trapper Pub* almost opposite the *Eskimo Inn* is a locals' hangout.

CAR AND EQUIPMENT RENTAL, TOUR OPERATORS

Inuvik may be the best place to **rent a car** for the far north, because southern firms tend not to rent vehicles for rough roads, and make hefty charges if you return a car that's obviously been over gravel: Delta Auto Rentals, 25 Carn St (☎777-3535), Marcon Rentals (☎777-4700) and Norcan Leasing (☎777-3044) rent out suitably robust trucks, four-wheel-drives and pick-ups.

Most people who come to Inuvik take a tour of some description. The town's two big **tour operators** are both well worth investigating, as each runs a selection of affordable daily boat and plane tours as well as longer fully blown tours and expeditions: contact the Arctic Tour Company (☎777-4100 or 1-800/661-0721, fax 777-2259), almost opposite the Igloo Church at 181 Mackenzie Rd. Day-trips include tours to the tundra, to Hershel Island, to a traditional bush camp, boat tours on the Mackenzie River, beluga whale-watching and trips to Aklavik by boat or plane; longer tours include three- to five-day trips to Bank's Island and Sachs Harbour to watch wildlife (notably musk ox); whale-watching trips; and a nine-day Mackenzie River trip to Yellowknife. Arctic Nature Tours (☎777-3300, fax 777-3400), with forty-years' experience of the region, run similar trips, but – as their name suggests – have a special bias towards wildlife: trips include tours to view Dall's sheep in the Richardson Mountains, Arctic safaris, Barrenlands photography tours, boat and plane trips to view the Porcupine Caribou Herd, and bird and wildlife visits to Hershel Island. Both these and other companies also run trips to all the fly-in communities below.

The fly-in communities

Accessible only by air except in winter, when incredible snow roads are ploughed across the frozen delta, Delta-Beaufort's four **fly-in communities** are close to some fascinating and relatively accessible Arctic landscapes and cultures. All are served by Inuvik-based Aklak Air, Box 1190, Inuvik (☎777-3555, fax 777-3388) or Arctic Wings, Box 1159, Inuvik (☎777-2220, fax 777-3440). All also have simple stores, though their prices make it wise to take in at least some of your own supplies. Some have hotels, but you should be able to camp close to all four: ask permission first at the village head office. The best way to see them is with a tour company from Inuvik (see overleaf), but even if you're going under your own steam it's still worth checking with the tour companies for discounted flight-only deals.

AKLAVIK (pop. 800), 50km west of Inuvik on the western bank of the Mackenzie delta, means "Place of the Barren Lands Grizzly Bear". A Hudson's Bay post aimed at the trade in muskrat fur was established here in 1918, though for generations before the region had been the home of Inuvialuit families who once traded and frequently clashed with the Gwich'in of Alaska and the Yukon. Today both live together in a town that melds modern and traditional, and whose inhabitants are proud not to have jumped ship when they were invited to leave their sinking town for Inuvik in the 1950s. Most are happy to regale you with stories of the mysterious "Mad Trapper of Rat River", a crazed drifter (supposedly a former Chicago gangster) who reputedly killed trappers for the gold in their teeth. Questions should really have been asked when he arrived in Fort McPherson and purchased – with suspiciously vast amounts of cash – unusually large numbers of guns and ammunition. He then built a cabin-cum-fortress on the delta and shot the constable sent to figure out what was going on. A seven-man posse armed with guns and fistfuls of dynamite were then forced to retreat after a fifteen-hour siege. After fleeing and shooting a Mountie, he grabbed world headlines briefly in 1931 as he managed to elude capture for forty days in the dead of a brutal winter. To this day no one knows who he was, where he came from or why he embarked on his killing spree. He was eventually shot on the Eagle River, surrounded by seventeen men and buzzed by a bomb-carrying light plane: he's buried in town in unconsecrated ground. The Hudson's Bay post is still around, together with a former mission church, now a small museum, but there's no restaurant and only one shop. Arctic Wings and Aklak Air **flights** from Inuvik operate daily except Sunday. A one-day tour with stunning twenty-minute flight and an hour in town from either of Inuvik's big tour companies should cost around $130: for a few dollars more you can fly in and boat out, probably the best way of doing things.

TUKTOYAKTUK, or simply Tuk (pop. around 1000) sits on a sandspit on the Beaufort coast about 137km north of Inuvik, and acts as a springboard for oil workers and tourists, both considered outsiders who have diluted the traditional ways of the whale-hunting Karngmalit (or Mackenzie Inuit), who have lived and hunted in small family groups on this fascinating but inhospitable shore for centuries. Half the families were wiped out in the early twentieth century by an influenza epidemic introduced by outsiders. The Hudson's Bay Company, inevitably, arrived in 1937. Many locals still hunt, fish and trap, but government, tourism and the oil business now pay most wages. This is the most popular tour outing from Inuvik, with trips starting at about $130, a sum worth paying just to enjoy the scenic low-altitude flight up here. Most casual visitors come to see pods of beluga and great bowhead whales, or to look at the world's largest concentration of **pingoes**, 1400 volcano-like hills thrown up by frost heaves across the delta's otherwise treeless flats. This is among the world's largest grouping of these strange features, and includes the world's largest pingo, Ibyuk, a mound 30m high and 1.5km in circumference visible from the village.

Tuk's only **hotels** – booking is essential – are the *Hotel Tuk Inn* (☎977-2381; ⑤), on the main street near the ocean, and the *Pingo Park Lodge* (☎977-2155; ⑥): both have dining rooms open to nonresidents. The Northern supermarket sells groceries. You should be able to **camp** near the beach, but ask first. **Flights** from Inuvik operate daily (upwards of $200 return). Inuvik's main tour companies come out here, but if you want a local operator contact Arctic Tour Company (☎977-2230) for naturalist, fishing, camping, hiking or wildlife-watching tours in the Anderson River area.

PAULATUK (pop. 110), 400km east of Inuvik, is one of NWT's smallest permanent communities. Situated on a spur between the Beaufort and an inland lake, the settlement was started by the Roman Catholic Mission in 1935 as a communal focus for the seminomadic Karngmalit, who despite such paternalism have fought off the adverse effects of missionaries and trader-introduced alcoholism to hang onto some of their old ways. Hunting, fishing and trapping still provide their economic staples, along with handicrafts aimed at the tourists out here mainly for the chance to watch or hunt big game. Key sites for the former activity are the cliffs of the Cape Parry Bird Sanctuary and the **Tuktut National Park** on the Parry Peninsula to the west, a gathering place for the migrating Bluenose caribou herd. Local operators will take you out to both areas, and in spring run trips to look for polar bears on the Amundsen Gulf. The village's name means "place of coal", a reference to the coal seams to the northeast, where the (literally) Smoking Hills take their name from the smouldering coal ignited years ago and still burning. Aklak Air **flights** operate twice weekly from Inuvik.

The only settlement on Bank's Island is **SACHS HARBOUR** (pop. 150–200), situated 520km northeast of Inuvik. It was only permanently settled in the late 1920s, and only then by just three Inuvialuit families. Today it supports a handful of self-sufficient Inuit families who survive largely by outfitting hunters and trapping musk ox for food and underfur (*qiviut*), which is spun and woven into clothes on sale locally. For generations the island has been known as one of the north's finest trapping areas, the abundance of white foxes in particular having long attracted the Inuit and other hunters. Today there's still an abundance of wildlife, including the world's largest grouping of musk ox.

Five double **rooms** are available at *Kuptana's Guest House* (☎690-4151; ⑦ including meals), with shared facilities. Ask first and you should be able to **camp** by the beach. Be warned: there is no restaurant in the town, just a small grocery store. Two Aklak Air **flights** operate from Inuvik weekly (from $350 one-way), though for a little more you can join an all-inclusive Arctic Nature Tours trip from Inuvik.

The Sahtu

The **Sahtu** embraces the Mackenzie River south of its delta as far as Fort Norman and the tranche of land across to and including **Great Bear Lake** to the east, the world's eighth largest lake. There's no year-round road access: you either fly in here, canoe the Mackenzie – no mean feat – or sign up with **fishing** and hunting charters that boat or fly you into the backcountry, home to some of North America's finest fishing lodges and lakes. Great Bear Lake, to name but one, holds world records for most classes of arctic char and for *every* class of lake trout going (top trout overall – weighing in at 30kg – was caught in 1991). In 1994 a road was built to Wrigley, 225km northwest of Fort Simpson, with plans to push it through to Inuvik, but it'll be a long while before this becomes reality. In the meantime, most tours operate out of the area's nominal capital at **Norman Wells**, or its near neighbour **Tulita** (formerly Fort Norman), both on the Mackenzie in the lee of the Franklin Mountains, which separate the river and Great Bear Lake. The area has just three other lonely communities: **Fort Good Hope** on the Mackenzie north of Norman Wells; **Déline** (formerly Fort Franklin) on Great Bear Lake, a self-sufficient Dene community of hunters and trappers; and **Colville Lake**, north of Great Bear Lake, a spot which amounts to little more than a few log cabins in the woods.

Canadian North (☎867/873-6900 or 4484, or 1-800/661-1505 in North America) flies daily to Norman Wells from Inuvik, Yellowknife and Edmonton, and within the area North-Wright Air links all main communities from Norman Wells and fly to Yellowknife and Inuvik (☎587-2333, 587-2288 or 1-800/661-0702, fax 587-2962) as well as offering sightseeing flights.

Norman Wells and Tulita

Ramshackle **NORMAN WELLS** (pop. 550) once owed its economic well-being to **oil** – the local Dene long knew this region as *Le Gohlini* – "where the oil is". The black gold was first noticed by an outsider as a yellow liquid seeping from the rocks by the explorer Alexander Mackenzie as early as 1789, but only rediscovered in 1919 after Dene locals had led geologists to the same spot. Production began in 1932 and was boosted during World War II when the American government sponsored the building of the **Canol Pipeline** to supply the Alaska Hwy – now long abandoned, though for a while the town continued to pump about 30,000 barrels a day through a pipeline to Zama, Alberta. At one time 160 wells pushed out 10 million barrels a year from the field. Economic disaster struck the region in 1996, when it was announced the wells and refinery were to close. The only glimmer of hope is that the works and wells are likely to remain intact for a possible new lease of life sometime in the future. You can follow the oil and Canol story in the **Norman Wells Historical Centre** (summer daily 10am–10pm, but check current opening; ☎587-2415), filled with photographs, modest displays and oddments of memorabilia. Alongside, the settlement's uniquely ecumenical **church** does double duty: Catholics sit on one side, Protestants on the other. These days the Canol's old route is becoming an increasingly popular **long-distance footpath**, a tough three- or four-week 372-kilometre wilderness trail from Norman Wells to the Canol Road above Ross River in the Yukon. Logistics are a problem, but if you want one of the world's tougher treks, this one's up there with the toughest. The mountains east of the town contain some of the NWT's bleaker and more spectacular ranges, but good outdoor skills are a must unless you sign up for a tour.

As for **practicalities**, the airport is a twenty-minute walk from the centre of the village, which runs to a bank, post office, a trio of motels, Northern supermarket and plenty of tumbledown housing. The local **visitor centre** is on the corner of Forestry Road and Mackenzie Drive (☎587-2054). There are three **hotels** in town: the *Mackenzie Valley Hotel* (☎587-2511; ⑤), the *Yamouri Inn* (☎587-2744; ⑥) and the *Rayuka Inn* (☎587-2354; ⑤). A touch cheaper is the intermittently open (call first) *Log Home B&B*, 5km out of town, with a 160-kilometre view from its front porch and weekly and monthly room deals (☎587-2784; ④).

If you want to spend time on the river, Mountain River Outfitters (☎587-2324 or 587-2285) runs day-trips to Fort Good Hope and the Arctic Circle (mid-June to mid-Sept) and also **rents canoes** and other outdoor equipment. For details of the many fishing-charter companies, enquire locally or obtain the *Northwest Territories' Explorers' Guide* from Canadian national tourist offices before you leave home.

TULITA (pop. 300), formerly known as Fort Norman, some 60km to the south, owes its long history to a strategic position at the junction of the Mackenzie and Great Bear rivers (its Dene name means "where the two rivers meet"). Long a Dene aboriginal settlement, it first acquired a trading post in 1810. Today it's an ethnically mixed community that looks to trapping and fishing for its livelihood: many houses have tepees out back for drying and smoking fish. It boasts just a riverfront mid-nineteenth-century church and old Hudson's Bay Company post as "attractions". Most visitors use the settlement to outfit canoe and boat trips downstream to Norman Wells or the Great Bear Lake, the latter lying 128km away on the easily navigable Great Bear River, a popular canoe trip with one simple portage. The *Fort Norman Lodge* (☎588-3320; ⑨) is the only **accommodation** base; reservations are essential and meals can be arranged.

Nahanni-Ram

The **Nahanni-Ram** area in the southwestern corner of the NWT centres on **Fort Simpson**, which is accessible by two long gravel roads: from the west, the **Liard Hwy** follows the Liard Valley from close to Fort Nelson (BC) on the Alaska Hwy; from the east, the **Mackenzie Hwy** follows the Mackenzie Valley from close to Fort Providence and Hay River. Both roads offer drives through a fairly mundane wilderness of boreal forest and muskeg bog, and neither penetrates beyond Fort Simpson to offer ordinary travellers access to the Nahanni National Park, the area's jewel.

With gorges deeper than the Grand Canyon and waterfalls twice the height of Niagara, the 4766 square kilometres of the **NAHANNI NATIONAL PARK** rank as one of the finest national parks in North America and one of the most rugged wilderness areas anywhere in the world. Located close to the Yukon border in the heart of the Mackenzie Mountains, it surrounds the **South Nahanni River**, a renowned 322-kilometre stretch of water whose white-water torrents, pristine mountains and 1200-metre-deep canyons have attracted the world's most eminent explorers and the ultimate thrill-seeking canoeists (the river ranks as one of the best white-water runs in the world). Unless you fit one of these categories, however, or can afford to fork out for guided boat trips or sightseeing by air – well worth the money, even if you're only out in the wilderness for a short time – there's no way of getting close to the best areas, even by backpacking: the park is totally roadless and totally wild. Operators in Fort Simpson cater to all levels of demand, from day-trippers wanting air tours of the big set-pieces to self-contained canoeists and walkers off on month-long expeditions who require no more than a drop-off or pick-up by air. Even self-sufficient explorers should note that it can still save considerable time, hassle and money to take a three- or four-week tour with a licensed outfitter in Fort Simpson. Also note that the popularity of trips means that a reservation and fee system have been instigated for people wishing to use the river: details from the tourist and park offices in Fort Simpson.

Fort Simpson

All means of access and facilities – including tour operators and outfitters – for the park reside in busy **FORT SIMPSON** (pop. 1000), a perfect base 150km to the east at the confluence of the Liard and Mackenzie, two of North America's greatest rivers. This spot has been inhabited for 9000 years by the Slavey peoples and their ancestors, making this the longest continually inhabited region in the NWT. The North West

Company established a fur post here in 1804 at the so-called "Fort of the Forks" (after the river junction). This was renamed Fort Simpson in 1821, but the settlement became as important as much for its role as a staging point for supply boats using the Mackenzie as for its fur-trading potential. Later the inevitable missions arrived – in 1858 and 1894 – so often the bane of indigenous communities. Latterly the area has been an important base for oil exploration projects up and down the Mackenzie, a major regional administrative centre, and a bustling summer base for visitors hiring **camping equipment** or booking onto **tours and charter flights** to the interior.

Most of what you want in town is situated along the main street, **100th Street**, effectively a continuation of the main road through the town. Before this highway was built the main street was the almost parallel Mackenzie Drive on the lake waterfront, at the southern end of which you'll find the site of the old Hudson's Bay Company post and an area known as the "Flat" or the Papal Grounds, the latter an area whose tepee and other development dates from the papal visit here on September 20, 1987 (this area was inhabited until disastrous floods in 1963). A light plane and float-plane airstrip lies just to the northwest of the downtown area, while the bulk of the outfitters' offices are gathered north of the strip at the top of Mackenzie Drive; the main **airport** is 12km south of town.

Practicalities

You can get to Fort Simpson by **bus** using Frontier Coachlines (☎874-2566), which currently runs once weekly between Hay River, Fort Simpson and Yellowknife. By **air** you need to take connecting flights from Yellowknife with Buffalo Airways (☎873-6112, *buffalo@ssmicro.com*). The **visitor centre** (mid-May to early Sept daily 9am–6pm, but 9am–9pm July & Aug; ☎695-3182) lies at the south entrance to town close to the intersection of Antoine Drive and 93rd Avenue (which leads to the Papal Grounds) with 100th Street. For extra information on the Nahanni National Park, contact the **Nahanni National Park Reserve Office**, Box 348 EX, Fort Simpson (☎695-2310 or 695-3151). Note that there is a park day-use fee ($10) and strict quotas on numbers visiting the park, so check latest details whether you intend to visit independently or with a tour. There are also summer **infocentres** at Fort Liard (☎770-4141) and Wrigley (☎581-3321).

If you're hoping to **stay** in town, be sure to book ahead. In town there are three major hotels on or just off 100th Street. The more northerly, on the junction with 101st Avenue, is the *Nahanni Inn* (☎695-2201; ⑥), which also has a coffee shop and dining room; a couple of blocks south is the smaller *Maroda Motel* (☎695-2602; ⑥), half of whose units have fully equipped kitchenettes. Finally, there's the even smaller six-room *Bannockland Inn* (☎695-3337; ⑤). To **eat**, try the dining room of the *Nahanni Inn*, or the *Sub-Arctic* opposite the visitor centre. The local **campsite** is just to the southwest of the Papal Grounds with lots of space, showers and firewood, charging $15 nightly for tent sites, $20 for electrical hook-ups.

As for **tours**, the sky's the limit, and you should be able to organize just about any sort and length of trip into the National Park or elsewhere. For day-trips to the spectacular **Virginia Falls**, one of the most popular day outings in the park (usually with 2 or 3hr on the ground), contact Deh Cho Air (☎770-4103), who also rent canoes, plan fishing charters and organize all manner of other flights and canoe or hiking drop-offs and pick-ups. For trips on the rivers, including day-trips and overnight trips or trips by traditional wooden scows (aboriginal canoes), contact North Nahanni River Tours (☎695-2116 or 1-888/880-6665, *www.nnnlodge.com*). Another outfit that caters to day and half-day visitors wanting to sightsee in the National Park is Nahanni Mountain Lodge (☎695-2505, fax 695-2925). Most of the town's other operators offer full-scale expeditions that run into thousands of dollars: full details are available in Fort Simpson or from the *Northwest Territories Explorers' Guide*, which you can obtain from national tourist offices before you leave.

Big River

BIG RIVER covers the country stretching north from Alberta to the south shore of the Great Slave Lake, and embraces several rivers, including large parts of the Mackenzie and Slave watersheds, and several of the territories' most accessible towns. **Hay River**, near the head of the Mackenzie Hwy from Alberta, is the area's hub and provides a gateway both to the **Great Slave Lake**, the third largest in North America, and to Fort Smith and the upper reaches of the mainly Albertan Wood Buffalo National Park. Unless you're headed for the park, however, or are prepared to drive east to **Fort Resolution** to see one of the most southerly examples of living Dene culture, most of this region and its seemingly limitless ridges of boreal forest is not the most rewarding zone of the north for scenery. However, if you do want to explore, it's relatively easy to get around under your own steam: Greyhound **buses** run daily except Saturday to Hay River – contact the Greyhound office in Hay River on ☎874-6966 or 1-800/661-8747. Here they connect three times weekly with Frontier Coachlines, 16 102nd St (☎874-2566, fax 874-2388), which runs buses to Fort Providence, Yellowknife and connections to Fort Smith.

Hay River

HAY RIVER (pop. 3100) is a typical no-nonsense northern town designed for practicalities rather than sightseeing self-indulgence. Long a strategic site, it's been inhabited for thousands of years by Slavey Dene people attracted by its position on Great Slave Lake at the mouth of the Hay River. White settlers had put it on the map by 1854, but the inevitable Hudson's Bay Company trading post arrived only in 1868, and it wasn't until recently – with the completion of the Mackenzie Hwy, oil and gas exploration, and the arrival of a railway to carry zinc ore from local mines – that the town became an important transport centre. It's now also one of the most important **ports** in the north, shipping freight up the Mackenzie in huge barges to provide a precarious lifeline for High Arctic communities as far away as Inuvik and Tuktoyaktuk. If you're stuck in town, the best way to kill time is to wander the wharves where piles of supplies compete for space with tugs, barges, huge dredges and the town's big fishing fleet.

The town divides into the New Town on the west bank of the Hay River – home to most of the motels, restaurants and key buildings – and the somewhat moribund Vale Island across a bridge to the north: in the latter, which centres on Mackenzie Drive, you'll find the wharves, airport, the remnants of the old town (badly damaged by flooding in 1963), the campsite and a series of passable and popular **beaches** (the last a total of 7km from the centre of New Town). The best sand is near the campsite on the northeast side of the island at the end of 106th Avenue. The **bus depot** is on the right immediately over the bridge: cross back over for the New Town.

The **visitor centre** (mid-May to mid-Sept daily 9am–9pm; ☎874-3180) is on Hwy 2 south of the New Town centre on the corner with McBryan Drive. There's ample **accommodation**, much of it cheaper than elsewhere in the north. Most reasonable is the pretty downbeat *Cedar Rest Motel* (☎874-3732; ②) on the main Hwy 2 south of the New Town downtown area (rooms have kitchenettes). Just north of downtown, on the right between New Town and the Vale Island bridge, is the *Migrator Hotel* (☎874-6792; ④), five-minutes' walk from the town centre. The best if you want comfort after a long haul is the downtown *Ptarmigan Inn*, 10 J. Gagnier St (☎874-6781 or 1-800/661-0842, *randyhi@ssimicro.com*; ⑤): the **restaurant** at the *Ptarmigan*, *The Keys*, is popular. You can **camp** near the beach on Vale Island at the *Hay River Campground* ($13; mid-May to mid-Sept) or to the south of the New Town off Hwy 2 at the private *Paradise Gardens Campground* ($9.50).

The Northern Frontier

The **Northern Frontier** is the broad sweep of lake-spotted barren land between the Great Slave and Great Bear lakes, and is largely the playground of canoeists and naturalists, or of hunters on the trail of the region's 400,000-strong herd of caribou. At its heart lies **Yellowknife**, Canada's most northerly big town and until 1999 the capital of the NWT (see also "Nunavut", p.909). Despite its surreal inappropriateness in a region of virtual wilderness, it's not worth making a special trip to see – though you may find yourself passing through, as it's the main transport hub for movement throughout the territories. **Buses** run here from Edmonton via Hay River, and there are regular Canadian North and NWT Air **flights** from all major Canadian cities, as well as numerous smaller airline connections from most NWT destinations. For **information** and useful brochures on the region, contact NWT Arctic Tourism, Box 610, Yellowknife, NWT X1A 2N5 (☎873-7200 or 1-800/661-0788, fax 873-4059).

Yellowknife

Nothing about **YELLOWKNIFE** – named after the copper knives of Slavey aboriginal people – can hide the fact that it's a city that shouldn't really be here. Its high-rise core of offices and government buildings exists to administer the NWT and support a workforce whose service needs keep a population of some 18,500 occupied in a region whose resources should by rights support only a small town. Even the Hudson's Bay Company closed its trading post here as early as 1823 on the grounds of economics, and except for traces of gold found by prospectors on the way to the Klondike in 1898, the spot was a forgotten backwater until the advent of commercial gold and uranium mining in the 1930s. This prompted the growth of the **Old Town** on an island and rocky peninsula on Great Slave Lake, and then in 1947 the **New Town** on the sandy plain behind it. In 1967, the year a road to the outside world was completed (Edmonton is 1524km away by car), Yellowknife replaced Ottawa as the seat of government for the NWT. Oiled by bureaucratic profligacy and the odd gold mine, the city has blossomed ever since, if that's the word for so dispersed and unprepossessing a place. Today, the chances are you'll only be here en route for somewhere else, for this is the hub of many airline routes across the NWT and parts of Nunavut.

Arrival and information

If you're arriving by **air**, Yellowknife's airport is 5km west of the city on Hwy 3. **Car rental** companies at the airport include Budget (☎873-3366): elsewhere try Yellowknife Motors on the corner of 49th Avenue and 48th Street (☎873-4414). **Taxis** to downtown from the airport cost around $12: call City Cab (☎873-4444) if you need a ride. Three **buses** are run weekly by Frontier Coachlines (☎874-2556) shuttle from Hay River via Fort Smith (around $80 one-way).

The **Northern Frontier Regional Visitors Centre** is on the edge of Frame Lake just north of the Northern Heritage Centre at 4807 49th St (mid-June to late Aug daily 8am–6pm; rest of the year Mon–Fri 9am–5pm & Sat–Sun noon–4pm; ☎873-4262). The **post office** is at 4902 50th St, and the **Stanton Regional Hospital** is off Old Airport Road at Range Lake Road (☎920-4111). For the **police**, call ☎669-1111. To rent camping gear, canoes, snowmobiles, fishing tackle and other **outdoor equipment**, contact Narwhal Northern Adventures, 101 5103-51st Ave (☎873-6443, fax 873-0516), the latter canoe-trip and -rental experts for over 25 years. The visitors centre has **bike rentals** (June–Aug only) at $5 an hour, $12 a half-day or $20 a day (see above).

Accommodation

Hotels in the city have plenty of rooms, but prices are high, and it can be worth looking up one of the dozen or so **B&Bs** if you're on a tight budget: try *Barb's B&B* on Latham Lake at 31 Morrison Drive (☎873-4786, *barbbrom@internorth.com*; ③), where the host will give bird-watching tips (no credit cards) the lakeshore *Captain Ron's B&B* near the *Wildcat Café* in the Old Town at 8 Lessard Drive (☎873-3746; ③); or the *Blue Raven B&B*, 37b Otto Drive (☎873-6328; ④). The *Igloo Inn* (☎873-8511 or 873-5547, *iglooin@internorth.com*; ④) at 4115 Franklin Ave between the Old Town and downtown, is the cheapest of the hotels proper (pay a bit more and you can have a kitchenette), closely followed by the downtown *Northern Lites Motel* (☎873-6023; ④). If you want something more salubrious try the simply appointed *Discovery Inn*, 4701 Franklin Ave (☎873-4151, *discovery2@arcticdata.nt.ca*; ⑤); the facility-laden and smart high-rise *Explorer*, 49th Avenue and 48th Street (☎873-3531 or 1-800/661-0892, *www.explorerhotel.nt.ca*; ⑤); or the swish *Yellowknife Inn*, 50th Street and 49th Street (☎873-2601 or 1-800/661-0580, *reservations@yellowknifeinn.com*; ⑥). The only **campsite** is the fully serviced *Fred Henne Territorial Park* (☎920-2472; $12) by Long Lake off Hwy 3 north of the airport. Trails run to town from here via Frame Lake: allow about an hour – or you can follow the Prospectors' Trail north from the site, a good way to get a taste of the wilderness that encircles Yellowknife.

The City

Visitors are steered carefully down the main street, Franklin Avenue (50th Ave), and the long hill from the New Town to quaint Old Town cabins such as the still-operating **Wildcat Café**, 3904 Wiley Rd (June–Sept daily; ☎873-8850), an atmospheric and endlessly busy little café opened in 1937. Elsewhere the old town is a shakedown of pitted and buckled roads (the result of permafrost) and a few quaintly battered buildings on the aptly named Ragged Ass Road and Willow Road. These are more or less the only remnants of the old times – though if you venture to the outskirts you'll find shanty settlements and scenes of poverty that take the lustre off the high-rises of the city centre. This lends some irony to one of the city's promotional tags – "Where Yesterday Rubs Shoulders with Tomorrow" – coined to underline the city's undeniably striking juxtaposition of the old and new.

Just west of New Town's core lies the **Prince of Wales Northern Heritage Centre** (June to early Sept 10.30am–5.30pm; early Sept to June Tues to Fri 10.30am–5pm & Sat–Sun noon–5pm; free; ☎873-7551), three blocks from downtown on Frame Lake. Yellowknife's key sight, the modern centre peddles a more sanitized view of northern history and aboriginal culture than is on offer in parts of the Old Town, offering extensive displays of northern artefacts, Inuit carvings and persuasive dioramas of local wildlife and habitats. Shops around town also sell a variety of northern aboriginal crafts, still expensive, but cheaper than you'll find in southerly cities; most are beautiful products of a living culture – even if the culture is not at its healthiest in the city itself. The centre's South Gallery deals with displays on aboriginal people, the North Gallery with life in the north after the arrival of Europeans; there's also an Aviation Gallery, devoted to the planes and pilots who for years played (and play) a vital part in keeping the north alive. The centre also houses the NWT Archives, a collection of maps, books, photographs and documents devoted to the region. Just northwest of the centre, also on Frame Lake, stands the $25-million **Northwest Territories Legislative Assembly**, opened in 1993 to house the Territories' 24-strong Legislative Assembly. It's an impressive piece of architecture, much of it open to public view (June–Aug 3 tours daily Mon–Fri at 10.30am, 1.30pm & 3.30pm, Sun 1 tour at 1.30pm; Sept–May 1 tour daily Mon–Fri at 10.30am; free; ☎669-2200).

Otherwise the only things to do close to town are walk the trails around Frame Lake and from the campsite on Long Lake (see above). Or you can drive out on the **Ingraham**

Trail, an 81-kilometre highway that was to be the start of a major NWT "Road to Resources" but which was abandoned in the 1960s. There are plenty of boat launches, picnic sites and campsites en route, as well as short walking trails like the **Cameron River Falls** (48km from Yellowknife) and lakeside beaches where the hardier of the city's population brave the water.

Food, nightlife and festivals

For **food**, join the locals and curious sightseers in the Old Town's *Wildcat Café* (see overleaf) or at the *Prospector Bar and Grill*, 3506 Wiley Rd (☎920-7639). For a more unusual treat, head for *Office*, 4915 50th St (☎873-3750), an excellent place to sample northern specialities such as Arctic char. If you hit a warm summer's day, *Giorgio's*, 5022 47th St (☎873-9640), has an outside terrace. Most of the hotels have good dining rooms and much of the nightlife revolves around their lounges, notably the plush nightclub at the *Explorer* – though you'll meet far more interesting and dubious types at the rough and raucous *Gold Range Hotel*, 5010 50th St (☎873-4441). This is one of *the* great northern **bars**, and claims to sell the second-largest amount of beer per customer of any bar in Canada. For a gentle drink, the *Black Knight Pub* at 4910 49th St is a popular spot.

You'll also have an interesting time if you can contrive to be in town during one of Yellowknife's **festivals**: one of the most intriguing (check it's still running) is the **Caribou Carnival** in March, whose attractions include dog-sled racing, bingo on ice, igloo-building, flour packing and – best of all – "ugliest truck" competitions. Raven Mad Daze, a midsummer celebration taking place each June 21, is celebrated with lots of street events, drinking and high spirits through 24 hours of daylight. More cerebral and fascinating is **Folk on the Rocks** (third weekend of July), when folk singers from across Canada and the US meet Inuit and Dene folk singers, folk dancers and the famous Inuit "throat singers" in an amazing medley of world music.

Yellowknife is, along with Inuvik and Fort Smith, the headquarters of most of the far north's **outfitters and tour operators**. Many outfits run fishing, wildlife, Arctic sightseeing, canoeing, kayaking, boating and other trips, most ranging from one- or two-day outings up to full-blown three-week mini-expeditions to unimaginably wild areas. You'll find a comprehensive listing in the brochure *Northwest Territories Explorers' Guide*, which should be obtainable from national tourist offices before you go. If you decide you want adventure on the spur of the moment, contact the regional visitors centre (see p.906).

Nunavut

Home to only around 26,500 people, the new **Nunavut** territory covers a fifth of Canada's land surface, or 2.1 million square kilometres, an area five times the size of California, stretching west from Hudson Bay then north through the great "Barrenlands" of the interior to the Arctic islands in the north. This is the land of vast caribou migrations, musk oxen, polar bears and endless empty kilometres of fish-filled lakes and rivers. Most of the region's communities are formed of indigenous Inuit people and lie on the arc of Hudson Bay's western coast, from **Arviat** in the south through **Whale Cove** (Tikirarjuaq – "long point"), **Rankin Inlet** (Kangiqtinq – "deep bay") – the area's main transport and administrative centre – to **Chesterfield Inlet** (Igluligaarjuk – "place with a few igloos") and **Coral Harbour** (Salliq – "large flat island") in the north. In all of these you will find an almost unchanged way of life – the local arts and handicrafts are outstanding, and in places you can hear the old drummers and "throat singers" traditionally responsible for handing down the stories and myths of the Inuit. The entire region has just 21km of highway, with the capital at Iqaluit on Baffin Island serving as home to nearly one-fifth of the province's population.

Long an amorphous political entity administered not as a semi-autonomous province but by the federal government, the **Northwest Territories** was formally superseded on April 1, 1999 by a land treaty which divided the old territories in two and created a new central and eastern Arctic territory called **Nunavut** (meaning "Our Land" in the Inuit language). A preliminary division took place as far back as January 1, 1996, and Nunavut is now firmly established as a political and physical entity, with the new region putting out its own heavyweight brochure, the *Arctic Traveller Nunavut Vacation Planner*, full of all the information you are likely to need for casual visits or fully fledged expeditions with tour operators and outfitters (all of whom are listed). The new land deal – the largest in Canadian history – gave their homeland (valued at $1.15-billion) back to the Inuit, who in return renounced their claim to the remainder of the NWT. The deal followed fifteen years of low-profile but effective negotiating and campaigning.

Exploring this region is hugely rewarding – but far from easy. The landscapes are sublime – huge expanses of flower-filled tundra, ice fields, open sea, frozen sea, deep valleys and beautiful vast horizons – but often inhospitable. Access is invariably by plane and therefore expensive, and often the best way to see the region – whatever your chosen interest or activity – is with a tour company, of which there are many. Besides breathtaking landscapes, there's also wildlife, fishing, whale-watching and a plethora of often exotic or high-adventure outdoor activities, not to mention a wide spectrum of cultural interests – anything from Inuit printmakers and carvers to traditional drummers and "throat" singers.

The region's two major centres are covered below, but it's as well to know rough **flight details** and where **accommodation** is available in the smaller communities. Note that hotel prices in the north are invariably per person, not per room, so double all rates if you are two people sharing a double room. Rates sometimes include meals, so are not as steep as they first appear. **CORAL HARBOUR** (pop. 759), the only settlement on Southampton Island is one of the best places to see walrus (on nearby Goats Island), as well as the beautiful Kirchoffer Falls and Thule archeological sites at "Native Point". To stay, it has the small *Leonie's Place* (☎867/925-9751 or 925-8810, fax 925-8606; ⑦ with all meals per person) or the *Esungark Hotel* at the Katudgevik Co-op (☎867/925-9926 or 925-9969, fax 925-8308; ⑦). There are **Calm Air** (☎1-800/839-2256, *www.calmair.com*) flights here three times weekly and one **First Air** (☎1-800/267-1247, *www.firstair.com*) flight weekly from Iqualut via Rankin Inlet.

ARVIAT (pop. 1676), 240km southwest of Rankin Inlet (connected by daily Calm Air flights from Rankin Inlet) means the "place of the bowhead whale" and is particularly known for its crafts and the McConnell River Migratory Bird Sanctuary, home to thousands of nesting waterfowl. For more information on the community call ☎867/857-2841. It offers *Padlei Inns North* (☎867/857-2919, fax 857-2762; ⑥ per person) and *Ralph's B&B* (☎857-2653, 857-2623; ⑥): rates at the latter include three meals a day. At **WHALE COVE** (pop. 331), a traditional hunting, crafts and fishing community 80km south of Rankin Inlet, there's *Tavani Inns North* (☎867/896-9252, fax 896-9087; ⑦ per person with all meals). The similar **CHESTERFIELD INLET** (pop. 364) has daily flights from Rankin Inlet to the south, and one hotel, the *Tangmavik* (☎867/898-9975 or 898-9190, fax 898-9056; ⑦ per person with all meals).

Kangiqtinq (Rankin Inlet)

Although you'll find an old way of life and sublime Arctic scenery in the region, don't expect much in the way of prettiness in the villages: communities are often poor, roads pitted, houses strung out and battered, and the streets festooned with telephone and electric cables. The region currently has just one paved road – from the airport at **KANGIQTINQ** (pop.2189) to the settlement's "downtown". And remember that villages often aren't communities at all in the accepted sense: Rankin Inlet, for example, was only founded in 1955 when the North Rankin Nickel Mine opened. Three years

THE INUIT

"They be like to Tartars, with long blacke haire, broad faces, and flatte noses, and tawnie in colour, wearing Seale skinnes...The women are marked in the faces with blewe streakes downe the cheekes, and round about the eies".

An officer on Frobisher's 1576 search for the Northwest Passage

Distinct from all other Canadian aboriginal peoples by virtue of their culture, language and Asiatic physical features, the **Inuit** are the dominant people of a **territory** that extends all the way from northern Alaska to Greenland. Nowadays increasingly confined to reserves, they once led a **nomadic** existence in one of the most hostile environments on earth, dwelling in domed **igloos** during the winter and **skin tents** in the summer, and moving around using **kayaks** (*umiaks*) or **dog sleds** (*komatik*). The latter were examples of typical Inuit adaptability – the runners were sometimes made from frozen fish wrapped in sealskin and, in the absence of wood, caribou bones were used for crossbars.

Their prey – caribou, musk ox, seals, walruses, narwhals, beluga whales, polar bears, birds and fish – provided oil for heating and cooking, hides for clothing and tents, harpoon lines, ivory and dog harnesses. Using harpoons, bows and arrows and spears, ingenious hunting methods were devised: to catch caribou, for example, huge **inuksuits**, piles of rocks resembling the human form, were used to steer the herd into a line of armed hunters.

The Inuit **diet** was composed totally of flesh, and every part of the animal was eaten, usually raw, from eyeballs to the heart. Delicacies included the plaited and dried intestines of seals and whole sealskins stuffed with small birds and left to putrefy until the contents had turned to the consistency of cheese. All food was **shared** and the successful hunter had to watch his catch being distributed amongst other families in the group, in accordance with specific relationships, before his own kin were allowed the smallest portion. **Starvation** was common – it was not unusual for whole villages to perish in the winter – and consequently **infanticide**, particularly of females, was employed to keep population sizes down. Elderly people who could not keep up with the travelling group were abandoned, a fate that also befell some **offenders** against the social code, though the usual way of resolving conflict was the **song-duel**, whereby the aggrieved would publicly ridicule the behavior of the other, who was expected to accept the insults with good grace.

Making **clothes**, most often of caribou hide, was a task assigned to **women** and was as essential to survival as a man's ability to hunt. Older women also **tattooed** the faces of the younger ones by threading a sinew darkened with soot through the face to make lines that radiated from the nose and mouth. Women were usually betrothed at birth and married at puberty, and both polygamy and polyandry were frequent – though female infanticide made it rare for a man to have more than two spouses.

later the government, shocked at conditions of local Inuit, "moved" people here from their nomadic homes in the wilderness: the resulting settlement, **Itivia** (now all but vanished), a kilometre from Rankin, was a disaster, that was made worse by the closure of the nickel mine in 1962. Only a craft-producing initiative and recent tourism saved the day. Things to see and do include trails, fishing and bird-watching in the Ijiraliq (Meliadine) river valley 5km from the settlement, and a Thule site with stone tent rings, meat caches, kayak racks and underground winter houses.

First Air (see overleaf) has direct **flights** to Rankin Inlet from Iqaluit via Coral Harbour and connecting services from Ottawa and Montréal via Iqualuit on Baffin Island. Calm Air (see overleaf) flies scheduled services from Churchill in Manitoba to Rankin Inlet and most other Keewatin villages. Outfitters and small charter firms here and in all the communities are available to fly or guide you into the interior or out into Hudson Bay for fishing and naturalist trips. Rankin Inlet boasts the small regional **Kivalliq Regional Visitor Centre**, housed – along with the post office – at the

Communion with supernatural spirits was maintained by a **shaman** or *angakok*, who was often a woman, and the deity who features most regularly in Inuit myth is a goddess called **Sedna**, who was mutilated by her father. Her severed fingers became seals and walruses and her hands became whales, while Sedna lived on as the mother and protector of all sea life, capable of withholding her bounty if strict **taboos** were not adhered to. These taboos included keeping land and sea products totally separate – and so seals could never be eaten with caribou and all caribou clothing had to be made before the winter seal hunt.

Although sporadic **European contact** dates back to the Norse settlement of Greenland and some Inuit were visited by early missionaries, it wasn't until the early nineteenth century that the two cultures met in earnest. By 1860 commercial **whalers** had begun wintering around the north of Hudson Bay, employing Inuit as crew members and hunters for their food in return for European goods. Even then, the impact on the Inuit was not really deleterious until the arrival of **American whalers** in Canadian waters in 1890, when the liberal dispensing of alcohol and diseases such as smallpox and VD led to a drastic **decline in population**.

By the early decades of the twentieth century **fur traders** were encouraging the Inuit to stop hunting off the coast and turn inland using firearms and traps. The accompanying **missionaries** brought welcome medical help and schools, but put an end to multiple marriages, shamanism and other traditional practices. More changes came when Inuits were employed to build roads, airfields and other military facilities during World War II and to construct the line of radar installations known as Distant Early Warning during the Cold War era. As well as bringing **new jobs**, this also focused **government attention** on the plight of the Inuit.

The consequent largesse was not wholly beneficial: subsidized housing and welfare payments led many Inuit to abandon their hunting camps and settle in **permanent communities**, usually located in places strategic to Canada's sovereignty in the Arctic. Without knowledge of the English and French languages, these Inuit were left out of all decision-making and often lived in a totally separate part of towns that were administered by outsiders. Old values and beliefs were all but eroded by television and radio, and high levels of depression, alcoholism and violence became the norm. The 1982 ban on European imports of sealskins created mass **unemployment**, and although hunting still provides the basics of subsistence, the high cost of ammunition and fuel makes commercial-scale hunting uneconomical.

All is not gloom, however. Inuit co-operatives are increasingly successful and the production of **soapstone carvings** – admittedly a commercial adulteration of traditional Inuit ivory art – is very profitable. Having organized themselves into politically active groups and secured such **land claims** as Nunavut, the Inuit are slowly rebuilding an ancient culture that was shattered in under half a century.

Siniktarvik Hotel (☎645-5091). As in much of the far north, prices in **hotels** tend to be per person whether you're in a double or single: thus for two people sharing remember you need to *double* our given rate. Rankin Inlet has two accommodation possibilities: the *Siniktarvik Hotel* (☎645-2807 or 645-2949, fax 645-2999; ⑥ per person) and *Ferguson Lake Lodge* (☎867/645-2414, fax 645-2197; ⑥ per person).

Qamanit'uaq (Baker Lake)

Some 260km west of Rankin Inlet at the mouth of the Thelon River lies **Qamanit'uaq** (formerly Baker Lake), population 1453, the Arctic's only inland Inuit community (*Qamanit'uaq* means "far inland" or "huge widening of a river"), which marks both Canada's geographic centre – it has long been a meeting place for members of different Inuit groups – and provides a point of access into the **tundra** that characterizes the vastness of the region. This is a subtle landscape that's worth more than its "Barrenland" label suggests, particularly in summer, when the thaw brings to life thousands of tiny streams and lakes, and some three hundred species of wild flowers amidst the lichens and grasses that provide fodder for huge herds of musk ox and caribou. Millions of wildfowl can also be seen, and the huge skies and flat horizons are also one of the best places in Canada to see the **aurora borealis** (see box p.854). Also be sure to take in the **Traditional Inuit Camp**, a demonstration by Inuit families of the activities, such as hunting, trapping and weaving, that might have taken place in a Caribou Inuit camp.

For **accommodation** there's the *Iglu Hotel* (☎793-2801; ⑥ per person) and the *Baker Lake Lodge* (☎793-2965; ⑤ per person), a group of cabins sleeping a total of twenty. There's also a small community campsite for campers. The summer-only Akumalik **visitors centre** (☎793-2456) occupies a reconstructed 1936 Hudson's Bay Company post in the original building, successor to the 1916 post that originally brought about the settlement's development. There is also an **Inuit Heritage Centre** (July–Aug Mon–Fri 9am–noon & 1–5pm; ☎867/793-2598). Calm Air has daily flights here from Rankin Inlet.

The Arctic Coast

Canada's last frontier, the **Arctic Coast** encompasses the country's northern mainland coast from the Mackenzie to Baffin Island, and – as "coast" is a relative term in a region where the sea is often frozen – numerous islands too, most notably a large part of Victoria Island. It is barren, ice-carved country, comprising a wind-scoured landscape of chill lakes and low hills with not a tree to be seen: it's also nearly completely dark and frozen for nine months of the year, yet still boasts a permanent population of a few hundred. It is home to **Inuit** (see box, overleaf) who as recently as fifty years ago had known little or no contact with the outside world. Few explorers encountered them, and even the most determined of Western agencies – the church and the trading companies – have failed to compromise a people who are still extraordinarily isolated by climate, distance and culture. Today, however, few of the Inuit live according to the ways of popular myth. Except on the odd trapping party, for example, igloos have been replaced by government-built homes, and the bone tools, sledges and kayaks of a generation ago have been superseded by rifles, snow bikes and light aircraft.

You still have to be fairly determined, however, to reach any of the region's **eight communities** (five on the coast, three on islands), let alone explore the hauntingly beautiful ice fields and tundra. People up here are usually looking to spot wildlife, fish, or, more dubiously, to hunt for musk ox, caribou and for polar bears, a practice the government defends by claiming "It's done the Inuit way, using dog teams, on a demanding safari over land and sea ice": it also provides much-needed income for the Inuit, who have the right to sell the limited number of permits. Most visitors base themselves either at **Kugluktuk** (formerly **Coppermine**) or at Victoria Island's **Ikaluktutiak** (formerly **Cambridge Bay**), the transport and service capital. Each main Arctic coast community, remarkably, has **accommodation**, but reservations are vital and prices predictably steep. You need to come prepared: in some cases meals must be booked in advance. Basic groceries are usually available at stores, but there are no banks. As ever, various **tour operators** run trips to and from the main centres: for information, send for the *Arctic Traveller Nunavut Vacation Planner* before you go.

Ikaluktutiak (Cambridge Bay)

IKALUKTUTIAK (pop.1413) – the "fair fishing place" – formerly known as **Cambridge Bay**, lies to the north of the Arctic Circle on the barren southern shore of **Victoria Island**, which at a monster 212,688 square kilometres is Canada's second largest island. As ever in the high Arctic, you need a special reason to come here, for accommodation, food and flights are all hideously expensive. Today it's the regional

THE NORTHWEST PASSAGE

Traversed in its entirety fewer than fifty times, the fabled **Northwest Passage** around the American continent exerts a continuing romantic allure – and, in the wake of oil discoveries in the far north, an increasing economic attraction too. The world's severest maritime challenge, it involves a 1500-kilometre traverse from north of Baffin Island to the Beaufort Sea above Alaska. Some 50,000 icebergs constantly line the eastern approaches and thick pack ice covers the route for nine months of the year, with temperatures rising above freezing only in July and August. Perpetual darkness reigns for four months of the year, and thick fog and blizzards can obscure visibility for the remaining eight months. Even with modern technology navigation is almost impossible: a magnetic compass is useless as the magnetic north lies in the passage, and a gyro compass is unreliable at high latitudes; little is known of Arctic tides and currents; sonar is confused by submerged ice; and the featureless tundra of the Arctic islands provides the only few points of visual or radar reference.

John Cabot can hardly have been happy with his order from Henry VII in 1497 to blaze the northwest trail, the first recorded instance of such an attempt. The elusive passage subsequently excited the imagination of the world's greatest adventurers, men such as Sir Francis Drake, Jacques Cartier, Sir Martin Frobisher, James Cook and **Henry Hudson** – cast adrift by his mutinous crew in 1611 when the Hudson Bay turned out to be an icebound trap rather than the passage.

Details of a possible route were pieced together over the centuries, though many paid with their lives in the process, most famously **Sir John Franklin**, who vanished into the ice with 129 men in 1845. Many rescue parties set out to find Franklin's vessels, HMS *Erebus* and HMS *Terror*, and it was one searcher, **Robert McClure**, who – in the broadest sense – made the first northwest passage in 1854. Entering the passage from the west, he was trapped for two winters, and then sledged to meet a rescue boat coming from the east. The **first sea crossing**, however, was achieved by the Norwegian **Roald Amundsen**, his success in 1906 coming after a three-year voyage. The first single-season traverse was made by a Canadian Mountie, **Henry Larsen**, in 1944 – his schooner, the *St Roch*, is now enshrined in Vancouver's Maritime Museum. More recently huge icebreakers have explored the potential of cracking a commercial route through the ice mainly for the export of oil from the Alaskan and new Beaufort fields and for the exploitation of minerals in Canada's Arctic north.

centre for the Kitikmeot communities and an important staging point for visitors making tours or heading still deeper into the hinterland. Once Nunavut is up and running (see p.908), it will also operate as the administrative focus for the region's western lands, despite a location a full 1300km from Nunavut's capital at Iqaluit. Over the centuries the region was a summer gathering place for the Copper Inuit (so called by the whites because they made many of their tools and weapons from copper), attracted here by the abundance of good hunting, notably seals, caribou and arctic char. The last two are local staples to this day, and still provide work and income, Kitikmeot Meats processing caribou and musk for export, Ikaluktutiak Co-op running a fishery that supplies arctic char nationwide (both concerns are open to the public for direct sales). The Hudson's Bay Company arrived in 1921, late by Canadian standards, and purchased the *Maud*, explorer Roald Amundsen's schooner, for use as a supplies and trading ship. This little piece of Arctic history was used for years before being left to sink into disrepair and ultimately into the harbour, where its hulk can still be seen in the bay.

Practicalities

The region's main **tourist office** is the Arctic Coast Visitors Centre (year-round Mon–Fri 9am–5pm, extended hours in summer and on request at other times; ☎867/983-2842 or 983-2224). It's located in an attractive modern building overlooking the bay, and features displays on the art, history and culture of the Copper and Netsilik Inuit, as well as exhibits of maps and documents that shed light on the age-old search for the Northwest Passage. A library of northern books and videos is also available, and there are pamphlets on self-guided walks around the community. **Scheduled flights** serve Cambridge Bay on Canadian North (☎983-2435 in Cambridge Bay, 1-800/665-1177 in the eastern Arctic, 1-800/426-7000 elsewhere) from Calgary and Edmonton; Aklak Air (☎983-2415) from Inuvik and Delta-Beaufort towns; and First Air (☎1-800/267-1247) from Yellowknife and Baffin Island. Within the Arctic Coast area itself, First Air flies between all the settlements except Bathurst Inlet and Umingmaktok, which can be reached by charter aircraft only.

As regards **accommodation**, there's the *Inns North* or *Ikaluktutiak Co-op Hotel* (☎983-2215, fax 983-2023; ⑤ per person), where meals – which you're almost bound to have to buy – cost around $50–60 a head. There are also one- and two-bedroom apartments, a coffee shop and restaurant. Then there is the smaller and slightly more expensive *Enokhok Inn* (☎983-3810, fax 983-2271; ⑥), which has seven self-contained suites, kitchenettes and provides deals on longer stays. The *Arctic Islands Lodge* (☎983-2345, *ailodge@polarnet.ca*; ⑥) has upscale rooms, a restaurant, coffee shop and laundry, and also offers weekly and monthly rates. You can **camp** at Freshwater Creek, 5km away, and – if you're self-catering – buy supplies at the Northern store. You should also be able to camp on the shoreline of the bay, but ask first, and make sure you are well away from, and out of sight of, any houses.

Kugluktuk (Coppermine)

KUGLUKTUK (pop. 1267) lies to the west of Cambridge Bay in the Canadian "mainland", sitting astride the **Coppermine River** close to the westernmost point of Nunavut (the river lends Kugluktuk its name, which means "place of rapids or moving water"). Yellowknife lies 600km away to the south. A relatively narrow sea passage, the Coronation Gulf, separates the mainland coast from Victoria Island at this point, a vital through-route on the Northwest Passage. The river has long been of primary importance in the region. Copper Inuit, so called because they fashioned tools and weapons from copper, converged at its mouth for a millennium to fish and hunt. In the twentieth century, as the numbers of caribou in the interior have declined, the Inuit have increasingly abandoned their seminomadic ways to settle on the coast. Today hunting and fishing still play a part in generating local income, though latterly tourism and oil and gas exploration have also contributed to local coffers. The river, which rises in the wilderness 360km north of Yellowknife, has also provided a "convenient" way of accessing the far north. It was used by Samuel Hearne, for example, the first white to reach the region, who paddled here on the orders of the Hudson's Bay Company to seek out the source of the copper being traded by the Inuit at company posts to the south. Today the river provides one of the continent's great **canoe trips**, most canoeists (or rafters) joining tours or chartering a plane from Yellowknife to the river's headwaters. The 325-kilometre trip downstream takes around ten days. The trip, among other things, offers sensational opportunities for watching wildlife, but you should also strike lucky with wildlife by walking or taking short tours from Kugluktuk itself. The most popular walk (20km one-way) is to the **Bloody Falls**, so called because a party of Inuit were massacred here following an argument with a group of Dene guides accompanying Hearne (relations between the two aboriginal groups were traditionally poor). If you don't fancy the walk – and it's tough going in places – you can pick up a boat trip up the river to the same point.

Practicalities

Access by **air** is provided through First Air (☎1-800/267-1247) from Yellowknife and other "local" communities. **Information** is available in summer from the Heritage

Visitors Centre (July–Aug daily 8.30am–5pm, on request at other times; ☎867/982-3232). As far as accommodation is concerned there are two options. The central *Coppermine Inn* (☎867/982-3333, fax 982-3340; ⑥ per person) has motel rooms or self-contained units; breakfast, lunch and dinner if you want them should be reserved in advance (you can take meals individually). You could also try the smaller *Enokhok Inn* (☎867/982-3197, fax 982-4291; ⑦ per person inclusive of meals). **Camping** is possible at Kukluktuk Park. As for **eating**, nonresidents can use the *Coppermine Inn*, but you need to book meals a day in advance.

Uluqsaqtuuq (Holman)

One of the region's more northerly communities, **ULUQSAQTUUQ**, or **Holman** (pop. 300), lies across Coronation Gulf on Victoria Island from Cambridge Bay – strictly speaking, just outside Nunavut's borders. Most people are here to fish for trout and arctic char or, remarkably, for the novelty of playing golf on one of the world's most northerly courses. The settlement is situated in a scenic open cove, the half-moon Queen's Bay, backed by massive two-metre bluffs and escarpments. It developed almost by default, when a Hudson's Bay Company post was moved here from Prince Albert Sound in 1939. Inuit had previously summered here in the search for caribou, but the post encouraged some to settle and sell white-fox furs with the Hudson's Bay traders. Today two groups of Inuit – the Copper and Inuvialuit – live here, the region forming part of a designated Inuvialuit settlement area. The community has become particularly well-known for its crafts, notably clothing and traditional tools, but most particularly prints and silk-screened items, a tradition that goes back fifty years, when an Oblate missionary, the Reverend Henri Tardi, came here and taught locals various printing techniques.

You can buy crafts around the settlement, or at the gift shop in the hamlet's only **accommodation**, the *Arctic Char Inn* (☎867/396-3501 or 396-3531, fax 396-3705; ⑦ per person), which has just eight rooms at $180 per person per night. You can **camp** at Okpilik Lake, but should be able to pitch a tent just about anywhere if you ask at the hamlet office. The *Arctic Char Inn* is the only place to **eat**, but there is a Northern groceries store almost opposite for supplies.

Baffin Island

Baffin Island comprises half a million square kilometres of Arctic vastness, whose main attraction is **Auyuittuq National Park Reserve** on the Cumberland Peninsula, Canada's northernmost accessible national park. With a treeless landscape, mountains towering over 1500m, icy glacial streams and 24-hour daylight from May to July, hiking in Auyuittuq offers one of the most majestic experiences in Canada. However, with temperatures rising to a mere 6°C from June to August, it's a brutal environment that will appeal only to the truly adventurous; expensive though they are, package tours are definitely recommended if this is your first venture into such a forbidding place. Be sure to bring all necessary gear with you, as the island supplies arrive just once a year.

The main gateway to Baffin Island – and capital of Nunavut – is the rapidly growing **IQALUIT** (formerly Frobisher Bay), whose name means simply "fish" and whose population of four thousand-plus is dominated by Inuit. The Nunavut Tourism office is here (☎867/979-6551 or 1-800/491-7910, fax 979-1261, *www.nunatour.nt.ca*), as is the **Unikkaarvik Visitor Centre** (July–Aug daily 9am–5pm, other times on request; 867/979-4636, *nunatour@nunanet.com*). So, too, are many of the tour operators who run trips into the interior. Things to see include the St Jude's Anglican church – an igloo-shaped affair like the one in Inuvik (see p.898) – and the collection of Inuit art and artefacts in the **Nunatta Sunakkutaangit Museum** (call for latest times; ☎867/979-5537).

Practicalities

Getting to Baffin Island is only feasible by **air**. First Air (☎1-800/267-1247, or 979-5810 in Iqaluit) and Canadian North (☎1-800/665-1430 in Keewatin, 1-800/665-1177 in Nunavut and the eastern Arctic or 979-5331) make the trip from Montréal (1–2 daily; 3hr) and from Ottawa (4 weekly; 4hr). Ticket **prices** can get as low as $400 return, but are usually nearer $700. First Air also link Yellowknife to Iqaluit (5 weekly; 3hr 50min) for around $700 return. Remember to ask about cheap pass deals and other prebooked flight deals if you're making international flights into Canada: these are often much cheaper bought beforehand in conjunction with the carrier you're using to fly to the country.

Within the island, there is a daily one-hour First Air flight during the summer from Iqaluit to **PANGNIRTUNG**, the gateway to Auyuittuq National Park. There are also scheduled flights to the various small communities and chartered sightseeing flights.

Consult the *Arctic Traveller Vacation Planner* or contact the Iqaluit visitor centre for details of flights and other **information** on outfitters, guides and accommodation. However, hiking maps should be bought in advance from The Canada Map Office, 615 Booth St, Ottawa, ON K1A 0E9. Information on the Auyuittuq park is available from Auyuittuq National Park Reserve, Pangnirtung, NWT XOA 0R0 (☎473-8828).

In summer many of the Inuit families of **Iqaluit** abandon their homes in favour of tents, and your best **accommodation** option is to join them, although there are no fixed campsites. Iqaluit's four main **hotels** charge more or less similar rates – around $140 per person per night – for similar facilities: *The Navigator* (☎979-6201, *navinn@nunanet.com*; ⑥), *Discovery Lodge* (☎979-4433, *disclodge@nunanet.com*; ⑥), *Frobisher Inn* (☎979-2222 or 979-0427, *frobinn@nunanet.com*; ⑥) and *Toonoonik* (☎979-6733; ⑥).

In Pangnirtung there is an established free **campsite**, *Pisuktinee Tungavik*, and a church that will let you sleep on the floor for a donation if you are desperate. The only commercial **accommodation** is the *Auyuittuq Lodge* (☎867/473-8955, fax 473-8611; ⑥). The lodge has good but expensive meals and they usually allow exhausted hikers to use their showers for a few dollars. Each of the following remoter settlements have single and hugely expensive hotels: Arctic Bay, Broughton Island, Cape Dorset, Clyde River, Grise Ford, Hall Beach, Igloolik, Lake Harbour, Pond Inlet, Resolute Bay and Sanilkiluak.

Auyuittuq National Park Reserve

Straddling the Arctic Circle in the northeast of Baffin Island, **Auyuittuq National Park Reserve** is one of the most spectacular destinations in the Canadian north. The heart of the park is the massive **Penney Ice Cap**, a remnant of the ice sheet that extended over most of Canada east of the Rockies about 18,000 years ago, and the major **hiking route** is the 110-kilometre Pangnirtung/Aksayuk Pass, which cuts through the mountains between Cumberland Sound and the Davis Strait. *Auyuittuq* is Inuit for "the land that never melts", but despite the unrelenting cold there is abundant life here: in summer the sparse tundra plants burst into green, the wild flowers are blooming and the amazing array of wildlife includes lemmings, polar bears, caribou, arctic hares and foxes, snow geese, peregrines, narwhals, walruses, bowhead and beluga whales, as well as harp, ringed and bearded seals.

The only transport for the 25km from Pangnirtung to the south entrance of the park is by **freighter canoe**, which the Inuit also charter for fishing, whale-watching and sightseeing trips. The rates on these "canoes" – which are like small fishing boats with outboard motors – are set by the Inuit co-operative, and work out at around $125 for two people one-way, plus $35–60 for each additional person. The boats can only pass through the Pangnirtung Fjord after the ice break-up in July – at other times you have to walk. Arrangements for a canoe pick-up should be possible by radio from the few emergency shelters in the park, but be warned that one summer all the batteries were stolen, so you may have to arrange your pick-up before being dropped off.

Services within the park are extremely limited and the weather is highly unpredictable. Snowstorms, high wind and rain occur frequently, and deaths from hypothermia have been known even in the height of summer. All-weather hiking gear is essential, and a walking stick or ski pole is necessary to assist you with the ice-cold stream crossings which occur every 200–300m and can still be waist-high in July. There is no wood for fuel, as the park is located kilometres north of the tree line, so a camping stove is also essential.

travel details

Trains

Prince George to: Edmonton via Jasper (3 weekly; 8hr 15min); Prince Rupert (3 weekly; 13hr); Vancouver (mid-June to Oct 1 daily; rest of year 3 weekly; 13hr 30min).

Buses

Dawson City to: Inuvik (mid-June to early Sept 2–3 weekly; 12hr); Whitehorse (late June to Sept 3 weekly; Oct & March to early June 2 weekly; rest of year 1 weekly; 7hr 30min).

Dawson Creek to: Edmonton (2 daily; 9hr); Prince George (2 daily; 6hr 30min); Whitehorse (mid-May to mid-Oct 1 daily except Sun; rest of year 3 weekly; 21hr).

Hay River to: Fort Resolution (3 weekly; 6hr); Fort Smith (3 weekly; 7hr); Peace River (daily except Mon; connections for Edmonton and Grande Prairie; 8hr); Yellowknife (3 weekly; 12hr).

Prince George to: Dawson Creek (2 daily; 6hr 30min); Edmonton via Jasper (2 daily; 9hr 45min); Prince Rupert (2 daily; 11hr); Vancouver via Williams Lake and Cache Creek (2 daily; 13hr).

Whitehorse to: Dawson City (June–Sept 3 weekly; Oct & March to early June 2 weekly; rest of year 1 weekly; 7hr 30min); Dawson Creek (mid-May to mid-Oct 1 daily except Sun; rest of year 3 weekly; 21hr); Skagway (mid-May to mid-June 1 daily except Wed & Sun; 4hr).

Flights

Listed below are only the main direct scheduled flights operated by the big carriers; for details on the vast range of small provincial companies operating within the north, see the town entries in the *Guide*.

To Inuvik from: Yellowknife (1 daily; 2hr 35min).

To Iqaluit from: Montréal (1–2 daily; 3hr); Ottawa (4 weekly; 4hr); Yellowknife (5 weekly; 3hr 50min).

To Whitehorse from: Vancouver (3 daily; 2hr 20min).

To Yellowknife from: Cambridge Bay (1 weekly; 1hr 30min); Edmonton (3 daily; 1hr 35min); Fort Smith (1 daily; 1hr 30min); Inuvik (1 daily; 2hr 35min); Norman Wells (1 daily; 1hr 15min); Resolute (2 weekly; 3hr 20min).

PART THREE

THE

CONTEXTS

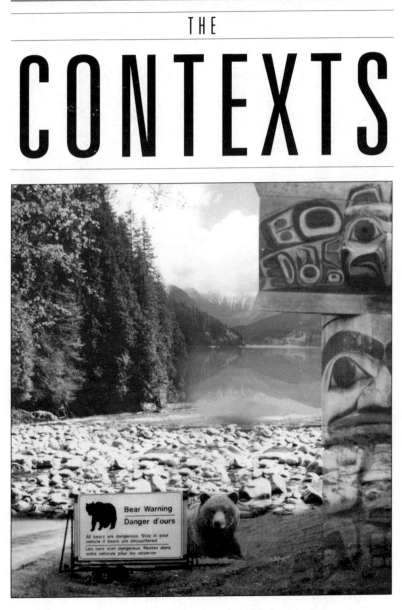

THE HISTORICAL FRAMEWORK

Fully unified only since 1949, and still plagued by the Québec imbroglio, Canada is a country of intertwining histories rather than a single national evolution. Not only does each of its provinces maintain a high degree of autonomy, but each grouping of native peoples can claim a heritage that cannot be fully integrated into the story of white Canada. Such a complex mosaic militates against generalization – although Canadians themselves continue to grapple with the nature of their own identity – but nonetheless what follows attempts to identify key events and themes.

THE BEGINNINGS

The ancestors of the **aboriginal peoples** of North America first entered the continent around 25,000 years ago, when vast glaciers covered most of the northern continents, keeping the sea level far below that of today. It seems likely that North America's first human inhabitants crossed the land bridge linking Asia with present-day Alaska – they were probably Siberian hunter-nomads travelling in pursuit of mammoths, hairy rhinos, bison, wild horses and sloths, the Ice Age animals that made up their diet. These people left very little to mark their passing, apart from some simple graves and the grooved, chipped-stone spear-heads that earned

them the name **Fluted Point People**. In successive waves the Fluted Point People moved down through North America, across the isthmus of Panama, until they reached the southernmost tip of South America. As they settled, so they slowly developed distinctive cultures and languages, whose degree of elaboration depended on the resources of their environment.

About **3000 BC** another wave of migration passed over from Asia to North America. This wave was made up of the first group of **Inuit** migrants who – because the sea level had risen and submerged the land bridge under the waters of today's Bering Strait – made their crossings either in skin-covered boats or on foot over the winter ice. Within the next thousand years the Inuit occupied the entire northern zone of the continent, moving east as far as Greenland and displacing the earlier occupants. These first Inuits – called the **Dorset Culture** after Cape Dorset, on Baffin Island in the Northwest Territories, where archeologists first identified their remains in the 1920s – were assimilated or wiped out by the next wave of Inuit. These crossed into the continent 3000 years ago, creating the **Thule** culture – so called after the Greek word for the world's northernmost extremity. The Thule people were the direct ancestors of today's Inuit.

THE ABORIGINAL PEOPLES

Before the Europeans arrived, the aboriginal peoples – numbering around 300,000 – were divided into three main language groups: Algonkian, Athapascan (principally in the north and west) and Inuktitut (Inuit). Within these groups existed a multitude of cultures. None of these people had a written language, the wheel was unknown to them and their largest draught animal, prior to the introduction of the horse, was the dog. However, over the centuries, each of the tribes developed techniques that enabled them to cope with the problems of survival posed by their environments.

THE NORTHERN PEOPLES

Immediately prior to the arrival of the Europeans, Canada was divided into a number of cultural zones. In the extreme north lived the nomadic **Inuit** (see box, p.910), whose basic unit was the family group, small enough to survive in the precarious conditions. The necessarily small-scale nature of Inuit life meant that they developed no political structures and gathered together in larger groups only if the supply of food required it – when, for example, the arctic char were running upriver from the sea to spawn, or the caribou were migrating.

Immediately to the south of the Inuit, in a zone stretching from the Labrador coast across the Canadian Shield to northern British Columbia, lived the tribes of the **northern forests**. This was a harsh environment, too, and consequently these peoples spent most of their time in small nomadic bands following the game on which they depended. Indeed, variations between the tribes largely resulted from the type of game they pursued: the **Naskapi** fished and hunted seals on the Labrador coast; the **Chipewyan**, occupying the border country between the tundra and forest to the west of Hudson Bay, mainly hunted caribou; the **Wood Cree**, to the south of the Chipewyan, along the Churchill River, hunted deer and moose; and the **Tahltan** of British Columbia combined hunting with seasonal fishing. Like the Inuit, the political structures of these tribes were rudimentary and, although older men enjoyed a certain respect, there were no "chiefs" in any European sense of the term. In fact, decisions were generally made collectively with the opinions of successful hunters – the guarantors of survival – carrying great weight, as did those of their shaman, whose main function was to satisfy the spirits that they believed inhabited every animate and inanimate object around them.

THE IROQUOIS

The southern zone of Canada, stretching from the St Lawrence River along the northern shores of the Great Lakes to southern British Columbia was climatically much kinder, and it's in this region that Canada's native peoples developed their most sophisticated cultures. Here, along the banks of the St Lawrence and the shores of the Great Lakes, lived the **Iroquois-speaking** peoples, divided into three tribal confederacies: the **Five Nations**, the **Huron** (see pp.137–138) and the **Neutrals**.

All three groups cultivated corn (maize), beans and squash in an agricultural system that enabled them to lead a settled life – often in communities of several hundreds. Iroquois society was divided into matriarchal clans, whose

affairs would be governed by a female elder. The clan shared a long house and when a man married (always outside his own clan), he would go to live in the long house of his wife. Tribal chiefs (*sachems*) were male, but they were selected by the female elders of the tribe and they also had to belong to a lineage through which the rank of *sachem* descended. Once selected a *sachem* had to have his rank confirmed by the federal council of the inter-tribal league: in the case of the Five Nations this consisted of *sachems* from the Seneca, Cayuga, Onondaga, Oneida and Mohawk tribes. Iroquoian society had its nastier side, too. An assured winter supply of food enabled the Iroquois to indulge in protracted inter-tribal warfare: in particular, the Five Nations were almost always at war with the Hurons.

THE OJIBWA AND BLACKFOOT PEOPLES

To the west of the Iroquois, between lakes Superior and Winnipeg, lived the **Ojibwa**, forest hunters who learned to cultivate maize from the Iroquois and also harvested the wild rice that grew on the fringes of the region's lakes. Further west still, on the prairies, lived the peoples of the **Blackfoot Confederation**: the **Piegan**, **Blackfoot** and **Blood** tribes. The economy of this grouping was based on the buffalo (or bison): its flesh was eaten; its hide provided clothes and shelter; its bones were made into tools; its sinews were ideal for bow strings; and its hooves were melted down to provide glue. In the late seventeenth century, the hunting techniques of these prairie peoples were transformed by the arrival of the horse, which had made its way – either wild or by trade – from Mexico, where it had been introduced by the Spanish conquistadors. The horse made the bison easy prey and, as with the Iroquois, a ready food supply spawned the development of a militaristic culture centred on the prowess of the tribes' young braves.

THE PACIFIC PEOPLES

On the **Pacific coast**, tribes such as the **Tlingit** and **Salish** were dependent on the ocean, which provided them with a plentiful supply of food. There was little cohesion within tribes and people from different villages – even though of the same tribe – would at times be in conflict with each other. Yet these tribes had a rich ceremonial and cultural life, as exemplified by the excellence of their woodcarvings, whose most conspicuous manifestations were the **totem poles**, which reached colossal sizes in the nineteenth century.

THE COMING OF THE EUROPEANS

The first recorded contact between Europeans and the native peoples of North America occurred in around 1000 AD, when a **Norse** expedition sailing from Greenland landed somewhere on the Atlantic seaboard, probably in Newfoundland (see p.448 for more details). It was a fairly short-lived stay – according to the Icelandic sagas, the Norse were forced to withdraw from the area they called Vinland due to the hostility of the natives.

In 1492 Ferdinand and Isabella of Spain were finally persuaded to underwrite **Christopher Columbus**'s expedition in search of the westward route to Asia. Columbus bumped into the West Indies instead, but his "discovery" of islands that were presumed to lie off India encouraged other European monarchs to sponsor expeditions of their own. In 1497 **John Cabot**, supported by the English king Henry VII, sailed west and sighted Newfoundland and Cape Breton. On his return, Cabot reported seeing multitudes of cod off Newfoundland, and his much-publicized comments effectively started the **Newfoundland** cod fishery. In less than sixty years, up to four hundred **fishing** vessels from Britain, France and Spain were making annual voyages to the Grand Banks fishing grounds around the island. Soon some of the fishermen established shore bases to cure their catch in the sun, and then they started to overwinter here – which was how settlement of the island began.

By the end of the sixteenth century the cod trade was largely controlled by the British and French, and Newfoundland became an early cockpit of English–French rivalries, a colonial conflict that continued until England secured control of the island in the 1713 Treaty of Utrecht.

NEW FRANCE

Meanwhile, in 1535, **Jacques Cartier**, on a voyage paid for by the French crown, made his way down the St Lawrence, also hoping to find Asia. Instead he stumbled upon the Iroquois,

first at Stadacona, on the site of Québec City, and later at Hochelaga, today's Montréal. At both places the Frenchman had a friendly reception, but the Iroquois attitude changed after Cartier seized one of their *sachems* and took him to France. For a time the Iroquois were a barrier to further exploration up the St Lawrence, but subsequently they abandoned their riverside villages (possibly as a result of an epidemic brought about by contact with Europeans and their diseases), enabling French traders to move up the river buying **furs**, an enterprise pioneered by seasonal fishermen.

The development of this trade aroused the interest of the French king, who in 1603 commissioned **Samuel de Champlain** to chart the St Lawrence. Two years later Champlain founded **Port Royal** in today's Nova Scotia, which became the capital of **Acadie** (Acadia), a colony whose agricultural preoccupations were soon far removed from the main thrust of French colonialism along the St Lawrence. It was here, on a subsequent expedition in 1608, that Champlain established the settlement of Québec City at the heart of **New France**, and, to stimulate the fur trade, allied the French with those tribes he identified as likely to be his principal suppliers. In practice this meant siding with the Huron against the Five Nations, a decision that intensified their traditional hostility. Furthermore, the fur trade destroyed the balance of power between the tribes: first one and then another would receive, in return for their pelts, the latest type of musket as well as iron axes and knives, forcing enemies back to the fur trade to redress the military balance. One terrible consequence of such European intervention was the **extermination of the Huron people** in 1648 by the Five Nations, armed by the Dutch merchants of the Hudson River.

As pandemonium reigned among the native peoples, the pattern of life in **New France** was becoming well established. On the farmlands of the St Lawrence a New World feudalism was practised by the land-owning seigneurs and their *habitant* tenants, while the fur territories – entered at Montréal – were extended deep into the interior. Many of the fur traders adopted native dress, learnt aboriginal languages, and took wives from the tribes through which they passed, spawning the mixed-race people known as the **Métis**. The furs they brought back to Montréal were shipped downriver to Québec

City whence they were shipped to France. But the white population in the French colony remained relatively small – there were only 18,000 New French in 1713. In the context of a growing British presence, this represented a dangerous weakness.

THE RISE OF THE BRITISH

In 1670 Charles II of England had established the **Hudson's Bay Company** and given it control of a million and a half square miles adjacent to its namesake bay, a territory named Rupert's Land, after the king's uncle. Four years later the British captured the Dutch possessions of the Hudson River Valley – thereby trapping New France. Slowly the British closed the net: in 1713, they took control of Acadia, renaming it **Nova Scotia** (New Scotland), and in 1755 they deported its French-speaking farmers. When the Seven Years War broke out in 1756, the French attempted to outflank the British by using the Great Lakes route to occupy the area to the west of the British colonies and then, with the help of their native allies, pin them to the coast. In the event the British won the war by exploiting their naval superiority: a large force under the command of **General James Wolfe** sailed up the St Lawrence in 1759 and, against all expectations, successfully scaled the Heights of Abraham to capture Québec City. Montréal fell a few months later – and at that point the French North American empire was effectively finished, though they held onto Louisiana until Napoleon sold it off in 1803.

For the native peoples the ending of the Anglo-French conflict was a mixed blessing. If the war had turned the tribes into sought-after allies, it had also destroyed the traditional inter-tribal balance of power and subordinated native to European interests. A recognition of the change wrought by the end of the war inspired the uprising of the Ottawas in 1763, when **Pontiac**, their chief, led an unsuccessful assault on Detroit, hoping to restore the French position and halt the progress of the English settlers.

Moved largely by a desire for a stable economy, the response of the British Crown was to issue a proclamation which confirmed the legal right of the natives to their lands and set aside the territory to the west of the Appalachian Mountains and the Great Lakes as "**Indian Territory**". Although colonial governors were given instructions to remove trespassers on "Indian Land", in reality the proclamation had little practical effect until the twentieth century, when it became a cornerstone of the native peoples' attempts to seek compensation for the illegal confiscation of their land.

The other great problem the British faced in the 1760s was how to deal with the French-speaking **Canadiens** of the defunct New France – the term *Canadiens* used to distinguish local settlers from those born in France, most of whom left the colony after the British conquest. Initially the British government hoped to anglicize the province, swamping the French-speaking population with English-speaking Protestants. In the event large-scale migration failed to materialize immediately, and the second English governor of Québec, **Sir Guy Carleton**, realized that – as discontent grew in the American colonies – the loyalty of the *Canadiens* was of vital importance.

Carleton's plan to achieve this was embodied in the 1774 **Québec Act**, which made a number of concessions to the region's French speakers: Catholics were permitted to hold civil appointments, the seigneurial system was maintained, and the Roman Catholic Church allowed to collect tithes. Remarkably, all these concessions were made at a time when Catholics in Britain were not politically emancipated.

THE MIGRATIONS

The success of this policy was seen during the **American War of Independence** (1775–83) and the Anglo-American War of 1812. The Canadiens refused to volunteer for the armed forces of the Crown, but equally they failed to respond to the appeals of the Americans – no doubt calculating that their survival as a distinctive cultural group was more likely under the British than in an English-speaking United States.

In the immediate aftermath of the American War of Independence, the population of what was left of British North America expanded rapidly, both in "Canada" – which then covered the present-day provinces of Québec and Ontario – and in the separate colonies of New Brunswick, Nova Scotia, Prince Edward Island and Newfoundland. The first large wave of migration came from the United States as 40,000 **United Empire Loyalists** (see p.382 for more on this group) made their way north to stay within British jurisdiction. Of these, all but 8000 moved to Nova Scotia and New Brunswick, the rest going to the western edge of Québec, where they laid the foundations of the future province of Ontario. Between 1783 and 1812 the population of Canada, as defined at the time, trebled to 330,000, with a large part of the increase being the product of *revanche du berceau* (revenge of the cradle) – an attempt, encouraged by the Catholic clergy, to outbreed the ever-increasing English-speaking population.

However, tensions between Britain and the United States still deterred potential colonists, a problem resolved by the **War of 1812**. Neither side was strong enough to win, but by the Treaty of Ghent in 1814 the Americans recognized the legitimacy of British North America, whose border was established along the **49th parallel** west from Lake of the Woods to the Rockies. Immigration now boomed, especially in the 1840s, when economic crises and shortages in Great Britain, as well as the Irish famine, pushed it up to levels that not even the fertile *Canadiens* could match. Between 1815 and 1850, over 800,000 immigrants poured into British North America. Most headed for "Upper Canada", later called Ontario, which received 66,000 in the year of 1832 alone.

Frenetically the surveyors charted new townships, but could not keep pace with demand. The result was that many native peoples were dispossessed in direct contravention of the 1763 proclamation. By 1806 the region's native peoples had lost 4.5 million acres.

THE DIVISION AND UNION OF CANADA

During this period economic expansion was principally generated by the English-speaking merchants who now controlled the Montréal-based fur trade, organized as the **North West Company**. Seeking political changes that would enhance their economic power, they wanted their own legislative assembly and the universal application of English law, which of course would not have been acceptable to French-speakers.

In 1791, through the **Canada Act**, the British government imposed a compromise, dividing the region into **Upper** and **Lower Canada**, which broadly separated the ethnic groups along the line of the Ottawa River. In Lower Canada, the French-based legal system was retained, as was the right of the Catholic Church to collect tithes, while in Upper Canada, English common law was introduced. Each of the new provinces had an elective assembly, though these shared their limited powers with an appointed assembly, whilst the executive council of each province was responsible to the appointed governor, not the elected assembly. This arrangement allowed the assemblies to become the focal points for vocal opposition, but ultimately condemned them to impotence. At the same time, the plutocrats built up chains of influence and power around the appointed provincial governments: in Upper Canada this grouping was called the **"Family Compact"**, in Lower Canada the **"Château Clique"**.

By the late 1830s considerable opposition had developed to these cliques. In Upper Canada the **Reform Movement** led by **William Lyon Mackenzie** demanded a government accountable to a broad electorate, and the expansion of credit facilities for small farmers. In 1837 both Mackenzie and **Louis-Joseph Papineau**, the reform leader in Lower Canada, were sufficiently frustrated to attempt open rebellion. Neither was successful and both were forced into exile in the United States, but the rebellions did bring home to the British Government the need for effective reform, prompting the **Act of Union** of 1840, which united Lower and Upper Canada with a single assembly.

The rationale for this arrangement was the racist belief that the French-Canadians were incapable of handling elective government without Anglo-Saxon guidance. Nevertheless, the assembly provided equal representation for Canada East and West – in effect the old Lower and Upper Canadas. A few years later, this new assembly achieved **responsible government** almost accidentally. In 1849 the Reform Party, which had a majority of the seats, passed an Act compensating those involved in the 1837 rebellions. The Governor-General, Lord Elgin, disapproved, but he didn't exercise his veto – so, for the first time, a Canadian administration acted on the vote of an elected assembly, rather than imperial sanction.

The Reform Party, which pushed through the compensation scheme, included both French- and English-speakers and mainly represented small farmers and businessmen opposed to the power of the cliques. In the 1850s it became the Canadian **Liberal Party**, but this French–English coalition fell apart with the emergence of "Clear Grit" Liberals in Canada West in the 1860s. This group argued for "Representation by Population" – in other words, instead of equal representation for the two halves of Canada, they wanted constituencies based on the total population. As the English-speakers outnumbered the French, the "Rep by Poppers" rhetoric seemed a direct threat to many of the institutions of French Canada. As a consequence, many French-Canadians transferred their support to the **Conservative Party**, while the radicals of Canada East, the **Rouges**, developed a nationalist creed.

The Conservative Party represented the fusion of a number of elements, including the rump of the business cliques who had been so infuriated by their loss of control that they burnt the Montréal parliament building to the ground in 1849. Some of this group campaigned to break the imperial tie and join the United States, but, when the party fully emerged in 1854, the old "Compact Tories" were much less influential than a younger generation of moderate conservatives. The lynchpin of this younger group was **John A. Macdonald**, who was to form the first federal government in 1868. Such moderates sought, by overcoming the democratic excesses of the "Grits" and the nationalism of the "Rouges", to weld together an economic and political state that would not be absorbed into the increasingly powerful United States.

CONFEDERATION

In the mid-1860s "Canada" had achieved responsible party government, but British North America was still a collection of **self-governing colonies**. In the east, Newfoundland was almost entirely dependent on its cod fishery, Prince Edward Island had a prosperous agricultural economy, and both Nova Scotia and New Brunswick had boomed on the backs of the shipbuilding industry. Far to the west, on the Pacific coast, lay fur-trading British Columbia, which had just beaten off American attempts to annex the region during the Oregon crisis, finally resolved in 1846, when the international frontier was fixed along a westward extension of the original 49th parallel. Not that this was the end of British Columbia's problems: in 1858 gold was discovered beside the Fraser River and, in

response to the influx of American prospectors, British Columbia was hastily designated a Crown Colony – a process that was repeated in 1895 when gold was discovered in the Yukon's Klondike. Between Canada West and British Columbia stretched thousands of miles of prairie and forest, the old Rupert's Land that was still under the extremely loose authority of the Hudson's Bay Company.

The American Civil War raised fears of a US invasion of the incoherently structured British North America, at the same time as "Rep by Poppers" agitation was making problematic the status of the French-speaking minority. These issues prompted a series of conferences to discuss the issue of **Confederation**, and after three years of debate the British Parliament passed the British North America Act of 1867. In effect this was a constitution for the new **Dominion of Canada**, providing for a federal parliament to be established at Ottawa; for Canada East and West to become the provinces of Québec and Ontario respectively; and for each province to retain a regional government and assembly. All of the existing colonies joined the Confederation except British Columbia, which waited until 1871; Prince Edward Island, till 1873; and Newfoundland, which remained independent until 1949.

THE CONSOLIDATION OF THE WEST

Having apparently settled the question of a constitution, the Dominion turned its attention to the west. In 1869, the territory of the Hudson's Bay Company was bought for £300,000 and the **Northwest Territories**, as the area then became known, reverted to the Crown until Canada was ready to administer them. Predictably, the wishes of its population – primarily Plains Indians and 5000 **Métis** – were given no heed. The Métis, whose main settlement was near the site of modern-day Winnipeg, were already alarmed by the arrival of Ontario expansionists and were even more alarmed when government land surveyors arrived to divide the land into lots that cut right across their holdings. Fearful of their land rights, the Métis formed a provisional government under the leadership of **Louis Riel** and prepared to resist the federal authorities (see p.539).

In the course of the rebellion, Riel executed a troublesome Ontario Orangeman by the name of Thomas Scott, an action which created uproar in Ontario. Despite this, the federal government negotiated with a Métis delegation and appeared to meet all their demands, although Riel was obliged to go into exile in the States. As a result of the negotiations, Ottawa created the new province of **Manitoba** to the west of Ontario in 1870, and set aside 140 acres per person for the Métis – though land speculators and lawyers ensured that fewer than twenty percent of those eligible actually got their land.

Dispossession was also the fate of the **Plains Indians**. From 1871 onwards a series of treaties were negotiated, offering native families 160-acre plots and a whole range of goods and services if they signed. By 1877 seven treaties had been agreed (eventually there were eleven), handing over to the government all of the southern prairies. However, the promised aid did not materialize and the native peoples found themselves confined to small, infertile reservations.

The federal government's increased interest in the area – spurred by the **Cypress Hills Massacre** of Assiniboine natives in 1873 (see p.529) – was underlined by the arrival in 1874 of the first 275 members of the newly formed Northwest Mounted Police, the **Mounties** (for more, see p.515). One of their first actions was to expel the American whiskey traders who had earned the region the nickname Whoop-up Country. Once the police had assumed command, Ottawa passed the **Second Indian Act** of 1880, making a Minister of Indian Affairs responsible for the native peoples. The minister and his superintendents exercised a near dictatorial control, so that almost any action that a native person might wish to take, from building a house to making a visit off the reservation, had to be approved by the local official, and often the ministry in Ottawa too. The Act laid down that every aboriginal applicant for "enfranchisement" as an ordinary Canadian citizen had to pass through a three-year probation period and was to be examined to see if he or she had attained a sufficient level of "civilization". If "enfranchised," such people became so-called "non-status Indians", as opposed to the "status Indians" of the reservations.

Meanwhile, during the 1870s, most of the **Métis** had moved west into the territory that would become the province of **Saskatchewan** in 1905. Here they congregated along the Saskatchewan River in the vicinity of Batoche, but once again federal surveyors caught up with them and, in the 1880s, began to divide the land into the familiar gridiron pattern. In 1885, the Métis again rose in **revolt** and, after the return of Riel, formed a provisional government. In March they successfully beat off a detachment of Mounted Police, encouraging the neighbouring Cree people to raid a Hudson's Bay Company Store. It seemed that a general native insurrection might follow, born of the desperation that accompanied the treaty system, the starvation which went with the disappearance of the buffalo, and the ravages of smallpox. The government dispatched a force of 7000 with Gatling guns and an armed steamer, and after two preliminary skirmishes the Métis and the Cree were crushed. Riel, despite his obvious insanity, was found guilty of treason and hanged in November 1885.

The defeat of the Métis opened a new phase in the development of the west. In 1886 the **first train ran from Montréal to Vancouver** and settlers swarmed onto the prairies, pushing the population up from 250,000 in 1890 to 1,300,000 in 1911. Clifford Sifton, Minister of the Interior, encouraged the large-scale immigration from Eastern Europe of what he called "stalwart peasants in sheepskin coats". These Ukrainians, Poles, Czechs and Hungarians ploughed up the grasslands and turned central Canada into a vast granary, leading the Dominion into the "wheat boom" of the early twentieth century.

NATIVE PEOPLES IN THE TWENTIETH CENTURY

For the **native peoples** the opening of the twentieth century ushered in a far from happy time. Herded onto small reservations under the authoritarian paternalism of the ministry, they were subjected to a concerted campaign of Europeanization – ceremonies such as the sun dance and the potlatch were banned, and they were obliged to send their children to boarding schools for ten months of the year. Deprived of their traditions and independence, they lapsed into poverty, alcoholism and apathy. In the late 1940s, the academic Frederick Tisdall estimated that no fewer than 65,000 reservation aboriginals were "chronically sick" from starvation. In addition, the Inuit were drawn into increasing dependence on the Hudson's Bay Company, who encouraged them to concentrate on hunting for furs rather than food, while the twin agencies of the Christian missions and the Royal Canadian Mounted Police worked to incorporate the Inuit into white culture. All over Canada, a major consequence of the disruption of the traditional way of life was the spread of disease, especially TB, which was fifteen to twenty times more prevalent amongst the aboriginal population than amongst whites.

In 1951 a new **Indian Act** increased the autonomy of tribal bands, but despite this and increased federal expenditure, aboriginal people remained well behind the rest of Canadian society. In 1969, the average income of a Canadian family was $8874, whilst 88 percent of aboriginal families earned $3000 or less, with fifty percent earning less than $1000. In recent years, however, native peoples have begun to assert their identity. "Status Indians" are now represented by the **Assembly of First Nations** (AFN), which has, since its foundation in the early 1980s, sponsored a number of legal actions over treaty rights. Many of these cases are based on breaches of the 1763 proclamation, whose terms stated that native land rights could only be taken away by direct negotiation with the Crown. One recent Grand Chief of the AFN, **Ovide Mercredi** – a lawyer and former human-rights commissioner – announced that the objective of the AFN was to secure an equal status with the provincial governments, a stance indicative of the growth in native self-confidence, despite the continuing impoverishment of the reservations. The political weight of the AFN was made clear in the constitutional talks that took place over the establishment of an **Inuit homeland** in the Northwest Territories, a complex negotiation resulting in an agreement to create two self-governing territories in 1999 (see p.908). But not all of Canada's natives see negotiation as their salvation: the action of armed Mohawks to prevent a golf course being built on tribal burial grounds at **Oka** in Québec (p.239) displayed an almost uncontainable anger against the dominant whites, and divided sympathies across the country. Partly as a reaction to the brinksmanship of the Oka militants, a new and more conciliatory leader of the AFN, **Phil Fontaine**, was elected in 1997, but he was replaced in 2000 by Matthew Coon Come, who favours a more aggressive approach.

QUÉBEC AND THE FUTURE OF CANADA

Just as Canada's native peoples drew inspiration from the national liberation movements of the late 1950s and 1960s, so too did the **Québécois**. Ever since the conquest of 1760, francophones had been deeply concerned about *la survivance*, the continuation of their language and culture. Periodically this anxiety had been heightened, notably during both world wars, when the Québécois opposed the introduction of conscription because it seemed to subordinate their interests to those of Britain. Nevertheless, despite these difficulties, the essentially conservative Québécois political–religious establishment usually recommended accommodation with the British and later the federal authorities. This same establishment upheld the traditional values of Catholic rural New France, a consequence of which was that Québec's industry and commerce developed under anglophone control. Thus, in early twentieth-century Montréal, a francophone proletariat worked in the factories of anglophone owners, an anglophone dominance that was compounded by the indifference of Canada's other provinces to French-Canadian interests, spurring the development of a new generation of Québec **separatists**.

Held in Montréal, **Expo '67** was meant to be a confirmation of Canada's arrival as an industrial power of the first rank. However, when France's President de Gaulle used the event as a platform to announce his advocacy of a "free Québec", he ignited a political row that has dominated the country ever since. That same year, **René Lévesque** formed the **Parti Québécois** (PQ), with the ultimate goal of full independence and the slogan *Maîtres chez nous* ("masters in our own house"). In 1968, however, **Pierre Trudeau**, a French-Canadian politician dedicated to the maintenance of the federation, was elected prime minister – and the scene was set for a showdown.

The PQ represented the constitutional wing of a social movement that at its most militant extreme embraced the activities of the short-lived **Front de la Libération du Québec** (FLQ). In 1970 the FLQ kidnapped and murdered Pierre Laporte, the province's Minister of Labour, an action which provoked Trudeau into putting the troops onto the streets of Montréal. This reaction was to benefit the PQ, a modernizing party of the social-democratic left, which came to power in 1976 and set about using state resources to develop economic interests such as the Québec hydroelectric plant on James Bay. It also reformed education – including controversial legislation to make Québec unilingual – and pressed ahead with plans for a referendum on secession. But when the referendum came, in 1980, sixty percent of Québec's electorate voted "*non*" to separation, partly because the 1970s had witnessed a closing of the opportunity gap between the francophone and anglophone communities. This did not, however, end the affair.

In 1985, Québec's PQ government was defeated by **Robert Bourassa**'s Liberals, not so much reflecting a shift in francophone feeling but more Bourassa's espousal of the bulk of the nationalist agenda and what many felt to be the PQ's poor economic track record. The Liberals held power in Québec until 1994, when the PQ bounced back into office, promising to hold another independence referendum. They seemed well set. Polls regularly rated support at around sixty percent, but in 1995 the PQ lost again in a **second referendum** that rejected independence by just 50,000 votes. Despite all the subsequent bluster, this was a political disaster for the PQ, and, with the momentum lost, subsequent polls have seemed to suggest that the separatist bubble may well have burst. If this is the case, one of the key reasons is the PQ's failure to define the precise nature of Québec sovereignty and how future relations with the rest of Canada would be conducted.

THE PRESENT

To say that the rest of Canada has become exasperated by the interminable discussions over the future of Québec would be an understatement – and was never more so than during the **Meech Lake** conference of 1990, which con-spicuously failed to agree on a new decentralized constitution. The conference was convened by the Conservative **Brian Mulroney**, who became the country's premier in 1984. Mulroney had other pressing problems, too, though nothing as fractious as Québec. To begin with, the free trade agreement (NAFTA) between the US and Canada, which Mulroney pushed through parliament, came into effect in 1989, destroying the country's protective tariffs and thereby exposing its industries to undercutting and causing thousands of redundancies. There was also the collapse of the North Atlantic cod fishery, which brought Nova Scotia and Newfoundland to the brink of economic ruin, whilst falls in wheat prices hurt the Prairies. Efforts were made to deal with these issues, but few were satisfied and during Mulroney's second term (1988–93), the premier became a byword for incompetence, his party commonly accused of large-scale corruption. As a result, the **federal elections of November 1993** almost wiped out the Conservatives and, equipped with a huge majority, the new Liberal administration, under **Jean Chrétien**, once Trudeau's Minister of Finance, set about rebuilding federal prestige. A cautious politician, Chrétien has had some success, his pragmatic approach to politics proving sufficiently popular to see him re-elected for a second term in 1997 and a third in 2000, albeit with reduced majorities. However, much of Chrétien's electoral success is down to the balkanization of the Canadian political scene. The Liberals are currently the only party with any claim to a national presence – with the right-wing Canadian Alliance (formerly the Reform Party), for instance, dominating much of the west, but simply failing to show in the east. The long-term consequences of this political reconfiguration are hard to predict, but certainly don't bode well. The future is wide open to the prospect of further political turbulence.

CANADIAN
WILDLIFE

Canada has just about every natural habitat going, from ice-bound polar islands in the far north to sun-drilled pockets of desert along the United States border. Between these extremes the country's mountains, forests and grasslands support an incredible variety and profusion of wildlife – any brief account can only scratch the surface of what it's possible to see.

National and provincial parks offer the best starting places, and we've listed some of the outstanding sites for spotting particular species. However, don't expect to see the big attractions like bears and wolves easily – despite the enthusiasm of guides and tourist offices, these are encountered only rarely.

EASTERN FORESTS

Canada's **eastern forests** divide into two main groups – the Carolinian forest of southwestern Ontario, and the Great Lakes-St Lawrence forest extending from the edge of the Carolinian forest to Lake Superior and the Gulf of St Lawrence.

CAROLINIAN FOREST

The **Carolinian forest** forms a narrow belt of largely deciduous hardwood trees similar to the broad-leaved woodlands found over much of the eastern United States. Trees are often typical of more southerly climes – Kentucky coffee tree,

tulip tree, sassafras, sycamore, chinquapin oak, shagbark hickory and more ordinary staples like beech, sugar maple, basswood and swamp oak. None of these is rare in the US, but in Canada they grow only here, thanks to the region's rich soils and relatively warm, sheltered climate.

A good deal of the Carolinian flora and fauna is coming under increasing threat from southern Ontario's urban and agricultural sprawl. These days much of the original forest has shrunk to a mosaic of fragments protected by national and provincial parks. The forests are most often visited by tourists for the astounding October colours, but if you're looking for **wildlife** you might also catch Canada's only marsupial, the **opossum**; or other southern species like the **fox squirrel** (introduced on Lake Erie's Pelee Island); the **eastern mole**, which occurs only in Essex County on Lake Erie's north shore; and the **eastern vole**, found only in a narrow band around Lake Erie.

Naturalists are equally drawn here for the **birds**, many of which are found nowhere else in Canada, especially during seasonal migrations, when up to one hundred species can easily be seen in a day. Most noteworthy of the more unusual species is the golden swamp warbler, a bird of almost unnaturally colourful plumage. More common visitors are hooded and Kentucky warblers, blue-winged and golden-winged warblers, gnatcatchers and virtually every species of eastern North American hawk. Sharp-shin hawks are common, and during autumn migrations of up to 70,000 broad-winged hawks might be seen in a single day near Port Stanley on Lake Erie's north shore.

In the wetlands bordering the forests, particularly at Long Point on Lake Erie, you can search out **reptiles** found nowhere else in the country. Most impressive is the water-loving fox snake, a harmless animal that often reaches well over a metre in length, but is often killed because of its resemblance to the rattlesnake and venomous copperhead – neither of which is found in the region. Also present, but in marked decline, are several **turtle** species, especially Blanding's, wood, spotted and spiny softshell.

GREAT LAKES-ST LAWRENCE FOREST

Occurring in one of the most densely populated parts of Canada, the mixed conifer forests of the **Great Lakes-St Lawrence** area have been heavily logged and severely affected by urban-

WILDLIFE CHECKLIST

This is by no means an exhaustive list of all Canada's wildlife species and their habitats – it should be treated simply as an indication of the places and the times that you are most likely to see certain species and types of wildlife.

Beluga, fin, humpback, blue and minke whales: near Tadoussac, north of Québec City; summer.

Bison: Wood Buffalo National Park (Alberta).

Black bears: Glacier National Park (BC); Banff and Jasper national parks (BC); Kananaskis Country (Alberta); summer.

Butterfly migrations: Point Pelee and Long Point, Lake Erie (Ontario); spring and autumn.

Caribou: Dempster Hwy north of Dawson City (Yukon); autumn.

Cranes and pelicans: Last Mountain Lake, northwest of Regina (Saskatchewan); late August.

Dall's sheep: Sheep Mountain, Kluane National Park (Yukon); summer.

Desert species: Cacti, sagebrush, rattlesnakes and kangaroo rats around Osoyoos (BC); summer.

Eagles and owls: Boundary Bay, 20km south of Vancouver (BC); winter.

Elk: Banff and Jasper national parks (BC); Kananaskis Country (Alberta); summer.

Grey whales: Pacific Rim National Park, Vancouver Island (BC); spring and summer.

Grizzly bears: Glacier National Park and at Khutzeymateen Estuary, north of Prince Rupert (BC); August.

Killer whales: Robson Bight in Johnstone Strait, Vancouver Island (BC); summer.

Orchids: Bruce Peninsula National Park (Ontario); spring and summer.

Polar bears: near Churchill (Manitoba); autumn.

Prairie species: Hawks, coyotes and rattlesnakes in the Milk River region (Alberta); May and June.

Salmon: Adams River sockeye salmon run near Salmon Arm (BC); October.

Sea birds: Gannets, murres and black kittiwakes around Cape St Mary's (Newfoundland); waterfowl, sea birds and seals in the Queen Charlotte Islands (BC); northern gannets on Bonaventure Island, Gaspé Peninsula (Québec); June and July.

Sea otters and sea lions: off Pacific Rim National Park, Vancouver Island (BC); spring and summer.

Snow geese: Cap-Tourmente, north of Québec City; autumn.

Wild flowers: Numerous woodland species on Vancouver Island and the Gulf Islands, and at Mount Revelstoke National Park (BC); late spring to summer.

---

ization. Most of the trees are southern species – beech and sugar maple, red and white pines – but are mixed with the eastern hemlock, spruce, jack pine, paper birch and balsam fir typical of more northerly forests.

Ironically, widespread human disturbance has, if anything, created a greater diversity of forest types, which makes this region second only to southern British Columbia in the number of bird species it supports. It also provides for large numbers of **white-tailed deer**, a rare beneficiary of logging as it prefers to browse along the edges of clearings. In the evergreen stands on the north shore of the St Lawrence there are also large numbers of Canada's smallest mammal, the **pygmy shrew**. These tiny animals must eat their own weight in food daily and can't rest for more than an hour or so – they'd starve to death if they tried to sleep through the night.

GRASSLAND

Contrary to the popular image of Canada's interior as a huge prairie of waving wheat, true grassland covers only ten percent of the country. Most is concentrated in the southernmost reaches of Alberta and Saskatchewan, with tiny spillovers in Manitoba and British Columbia – areas which lie in the Rockies' rain shadow and are too dry to support forest.

Two grassland belts once thrived in the region, tall-grass prairie in the north and shortgrass in the south. Farming has now not only put large areas of each under crops, but also decimated most of the large mammals that roamed the range – pronghorns, mule deer, white-tailed deer and elk – not to mention their predators, such as wolves, grizzlies, coyotes, foxes, bobcats and cougars.

The most dramatic loss from the grasslands, though, has been **bison** (or buffalo), the continent's largest land mammal. Once numbering an estimated 45 million, bison are now limited to just a few free-roaming herds in Canada. They're extraordinarily impressive animals – the average bull stands six feet at the shoulder and weighs over a ton – and early prairie settlers were so struck with their size that they believed bison, not the climate, had been responsible for clearing the grasslands.

Once almost as prevalent as the bison, but now almost as rare, is the **pronghorn**, a beautiful tawny-gold antelope species. Capable of speeds of over 100kph, it's the continent's swiftest land mammal, so you'll generally see nothing but its distinctive white rump disappearing at speed. Uniquely adapted for speed and stamina, the pronghorn has long legs, a heart twice the size of similar-sized animals, and an astonishingly wide windpipe. It also complements its respiratory machinery by running with its mouth open to gulp maximum amounts of air. Though only the size of a large dog, it has larger eyes than those of a horse, a refinement that spots predators several kilometres away. These days, however, wolves and coyotes are more likely to be after the prairie's new masters – countless small rodents such as gophers, ground squirrels and jackrabbits.

Birds have had to adapt not only to the prairie's dryness but also, of course, to the lack of extensive tree cover, and most species nest on the ground; many are also able to survive on reduced amounts of water and rely on seed-centred diets. Others confine themselves to occasional ponds, lakes and "sloughs", which are important breeding grounds for ducks, grebes, herons, pelicans, rails and many more. Other birds typical of the grassland in its natural state are the marbled godwit, the curlew and raptors such as the **prairie falcon**, a close relation of the peregrine falcon that's capable of diving speeds of up to 290kph.

BOREAL FOREST

The **boreal forest** is Canada's largest single ecosystem, bigger than all the others combined. Stretching in a broad belt from Newfoundland to the Yukon, it fills the area between the eastern forests, grasslands and the northern tundra, occupying a good slice of every province except British Columbia. Only certain **trees** thrive in this zone of long, cold winters, short summers and acidic soils: although the cover is not iden-

tical countrywide, expect to see billions of white and black spruce (plus red spruce in the east), balsam fir, tamarack (larch) and jack pine, as well as such deciduous species as birch, poplar and aspen – all of which are ideal for wood pulp, making the boreal forest the staple resource of the country's **lumber industry**.

If you spend any time in the backcountry you'll also come across **muskeg**: neither land nor water, this porridge-like bog is the breeding ground of choice for pestilent hordes of mosquitoes and blackflies – and Canada has 1.3 million square kilometres of it. It also harbours mosses, scrub willow, pitcher plant, leatherleaf, sundew, cranberry and even the occasional orchid.

The boreal forest supports just about every animal recognized as distinctively Canadian: moose, beaver, black bear, wolf and lynx, plus a broad cross-section of small mammals and creatures such as deer, caribou and coyote from transitional forest-tundra and aspen-parkland habitats to the north and south.

Wolves are still numerous in Canada, but hunting and harassment has pushed them to the northernmost parts of the boreal forest. Their supposed ferocity is more myth than truth; intelligent and elusive creatures, they rarely harm humans, and it's unlikely you'll see any – though you may well hear their howling if you're out in the sticks.

Lynx are even more elusive. One of the northern forest's most elegant animals, this big cat requires a 150- to 200-square-kilometre range, making Canada's northern wilderness one of the world's few regions capable of sustaining a viable population. Nocturnal hunters, lynx feed on deer and moose but favour the hare, a common boreal creature that is to the forest's predators what the lemming is to the carnivores of the tundra.

Beavers, on the other hand, are commonly seen all over Canada. You may catch them at dawn or dusk, heads just above the water as they glide across lakes and rivers. Signs of their legendary activity include log jams across streams and ponds, stumps of felled saplings resembling sharpened pencils, and dens which look like domed piles of mud and sticks.

Lakes, streams and marshy muskeg margins are all favoured by **moose**. A lumbering animal with magnificent spreading antlers, it is the largest member of the deer family and is found over most of Canada, but especially near swampy ground, where it likes to graze on mosses and lichens. It's also a favourite with hunters, and few northern bars are without their moose head – perhaps the only place you'll see this solitary and reclusive species.

Forest wetlands also offer refuge for **ducks and geese**, with loons, grebes and songbirds attracted to their surrounding undergrowth. Canada's three species of ptarmigan – willow, rock and white-tailed – are also common, and you'll see plenty of big **raptors**, including the great grey owl, Canada's largest owl. Many boreal birds migrate, and even those that don't, such as hawks, jays, ravens and grouse, tend to move a little way south, sometimes breaking out into southern Canada in mass movements known as "irruptions". Smaller birds, like chickadees, waxwings and finches, are particularly fond of these sporadic forays.

MOUNTAIN FORESTS

Mountain forests cover much of western Canada and, depending on location and elevation, divide into four types: West Coast, Columbia, montane and subalpine.

WEST COAST FOREST

The **West Coast**'s torrential rainfall, mild maritime climate, deep soils and long growing season produce Canada's most impressive forests and its biggest trees. Swaths of luxuriant temperate **rainforest** cover much of Vancouver Island and the Pacific coast, dominated by Sitka spruce, western red cedar, Pacific silver fir, western hemlock, western yew and, biggest of all, **Douglas fir**, some of which tower 90 metres high and are 1200 years old. However, these conifers make valuable timber, and much of this forest is under severe threat from logging. Some of the best stands – a fraction of the original – have been preserved on the Queen Charlotte Islands and in Vancouver Island's Pacific Rim National Park.

Below the luxuriant, dripping canopy of the big trees lies an **undergrowth** teeming with life. Shrubs and bushes such as salal, huckleberry, bunchberry, salmonberry and twinberry thrive alongside mosses, ferns, lichens, liverworts, skunk cabbage and orchids. All sorts of animals can be found here, most notably the **cougar** and its main prey, the Columbian blacktail **deer**, a subspecies of the mule deer. **Birds** are legion, and include a wealth of woodland

species such as the Townsend's warbler, Wilson's warbler, orange-crowned warbler, junco, Swainson's thrush and golden-crowned kinglet. Rarer birds include the rufous **hummingbird**, which migrates from its wintering grounds in Mexico to feed on the forest's numerous nectar-bearing flowers.

COLUMBIA FOREST

The **Columbia forest** covers the lower slopes (400–1400m) of British Columbia's interior mountains and much of the Rockies. **Trees** here are similar to those of the West Coast's warmer and wetter rainforest – western red cedar, western hemlock and Douglas fir – with Sitka spruce, which rarely thrives away from the coast, the notable exception. The undercover, too, is similar, with lots of devil's club (a particularly vicious thorn), azaleas, black and red twinberry, salmonberry and redberry alder. Mountain lily, columbine, bunchberry and heartleaf arnica are among the common flowers.

Few mammals live exclusively in the forests with the exception of the **red squirrel**, which makes a meal of conifer seeds, and is in turn preyed on by hawks, owls, coyotes and weasels, among others. Bigger predators roam the mountain forest, however, most notably the **brown bear**, a western variant of the ubiquitous **black bear**. Aside from the coyote, the tough, agile black bear is one of the continent's most successful carnivores and the one you're most likely to see around campsites and rubbish dumps. Black bears have adapted to a wide range of habitats and food sources, and their only natural enemies – save wolves, which may attack young cubs – are hunters, who bag some 30,000 annually in North America.

Scarcer but still hunted is the famous **grizzly bear**, a far larger and potentially dangerous creature distinguished by its brownish fur and the ridged hump on its back. Now extinct in many of its original habitats, the grizzly is largely confined to the remoter slopes of the Rockies and West Coast ranges, where it feeds mainly on berries and salmon. Like other bears, grizzlies are unpredictable and readily provoked – see pp.642–643 for tips on avoiding unpleasant encounters.

MONTANE FOREST

Montane forest covers the more southerly and sheltered reaches of the Rockies and the dry plateaux of interior British Columbia, where spindly Douglas fir, western larch, ponderosa pine and the **lodgepole pine** predominate. Like its eastern counterpart, the jack pine, the lodgepole requires intense heat before opening and releasing its seeds, and huge stands of these trees grew in the aftermath of the forest fires which accompanied the building and running of the railways.

Plentiful voles and small rodents attract **coyotes**, whose yapping – an announcement of territorial claims – you'll often hear at night close to small towns. Coyotes are spreading northwards into the Yukon and Northwest Territories and eastwards into Ontario and Québec, a proliferation that continues despite massive extermination campaigns, prompted by the coyotes' taste for livestock.

Few predators have the speed to keep up with coyotes – only the stealthy **cougar**, or wolves hunting in tandem, can successfully bring them down. Cougars are now severely depleted in Canada, and the British Columbia interior and Vancouver Island are the only regions where they survive in significant numbers. Among the biggest and most beautiful of the carnivores, they seem to arouse the greatest bloodlust in hunters.

Ponderosa and lodgepole pines provide fine cover for **birds** like goshawks, Swainson's hawks and lesser species such as ruby-crowned kinglets, warblers, pileated woodpeckers, nuthatches and chickadees. In the forest's lowest reaches the vegetation and birds are those of the southern prairies – semi-arid regions of sagebrush, prickly pear and bunch grasses, dotted with lakes full of common **ducks** such as mallard, shoveler and widgeon. You might also see the cinnamon teal, a red version of the more common green-wing teal, a bird whose limited distribution draws bird-watchers to British Columbia on its own account.

SUBALPINE FOREST

Subalpine forest covers mountain slopes from 1300m to 2200m throughout the Rockies and much of British Columbia, supporting lodgepole, whitebark and limber pines, alpine fir and Engelmann spruce. It also contains a preponderance of **alpine larch**, a deciduous conifer whose vivid autumnal yellows dot the mountainsides to beautiful effect.

One of the more common animals of this zone is the **elk**, or **wapiti**, a powerful member of the deer family which can often be seen summering in large herds above the tree line. Elk court and mate during the autumn, making a thin nasal sound called "bugling". Respect their privacy, as rutting elk have notoriously unpredictable temperaments.

Small herds of **mule deer** migrate between forests and alpine meadows, using small glands between their hooves to leave a scent for other herd members to follow. They're named after their distinctive ears, designed to provide early warning of predators. Other smaller animals which are also attracted to the subalpine forest include the golden-mantled ground squirrel, and birds such as Clark's nutcracker, both tame and curious creatures which often gather around campsites in search of scraps.

ALPINE ZONES

Alpine zones occur in mountains above the tree line, which in Canada means parts of the Rockies, much of British Columbia and large areas of the Yukon. Plant and animal life varies hugely between summer and winter, and according to terrain and exposure to the elements – sometimes it resembles that of the tundra, at others it recalls the profile of lower forest habitats.

In spring, alpine meadows are carpeted with breathtaking displays of **wild flowers**: clumps of Parnassus grass, lilies, anemones, Indian paintbrushes, lupins and a wealth of yellow flowers such as arnica, cinquefoil, glacier lily and wood betony. These meadows make excellent pasture, attracting elk and mule deer in summer, as well as full-time residents such as **Dall's sheep**, the related **bighorn** and the incredible **mountain goat**, perhaps the hardiest of Canada's bigger mammals. Staying close to the roughest terrain possible, mountain goats are equipped with short, stolid legs, flexible toes and nonskid soles, all designed for clambering over near-vertical slopes, grazing well out of reach of their less agile predators.

Marmots, resembling hugely overstuffed squirrels, take things easier and hibernate through the worst of the winter and beyond. In a good year they can sleep for eight months, prey only to grizzly bears, which are strong enough and have the claws to dig down into their dens. In their waking periods they can be tame and friendly, often nibbling contentedly in the sunnier corners of campsites. When threatened, however, they produce a piercing and unearthly whistle. (They can also do a lot of damage: some specialize in chewing the radiator hoses of parked cars.) The strange little **pika**, a relative of the rabbit, is more elusive but keeps itself busy throughout the year, living off a miniature haystack of fodder which it builds up during the summer.

Birds are numerous in summer, and include rosy finches, pipits and blue grouse, but few manage to live in the alpine zone year-round. One which does is the white-tailed **ptarmigan**, a plump, partridge-like bird which, thanks to its heavily feathered feet and legs, is able to snowshoe around deep drifts of snow; its white winter plumage provides camouflage. Unfortunately, ptarmigans can be as slow-moving and stupid as barnyard chickens, making them easy targets for hunters and predators.

COASTLINES

Canada has three coastlines: the Atlantic, the Pacific and the Arctic (dealt with under "Tundra"). Each boasts a profusion of maritime, dunal and intertidal life; the Pacific coast, warmed by the Japanese current, actually has the greatest number of species of any temperate shore. Few people are very interested in the small fry, however – most come for the big mammals, and **whales** in particular.

Grey whales are most common in the Pacific, and are often easily spotted from mainland headlands in the February to May and September to October periods as they migrate between the Arctic and their breeding grounds off Mexico. Once hunted close to the point of extinction, they've now returned in large numbers, and most West Coast harbours have charter companies offering whale-watching tours.

Humpback whales are another favourite, largely because they're curious and follow sightseeing boats, but also because of their surface acrobatics and long, haunting "songs". They too were hunted to near-extinction, and though protected by international agreement since 1966 they still number less than ten percent of their original population.

Vancouver Island's inner coast supports one of the world's most concentrated populations of **killer whales** or **orcas**. These are often seen in family groups or "pods" travelling close to shore, usually on the trail of large fish – which on the West Coast means **salmon**. The orca,

however, is the only whale whose diet also runs to warm-blooded animals – hence the "killer" tag – and it will gorge on walrus, seal and even minke, grey and beluga whales.

Another West Coast inhabitant, the **sea otter**, differs from most marine mammals in that it keeps itself warm with a thick soft coat of fur rather than with blubber. This brought it to the attention of early Russian and British fur traders, and by the beginning of the twentieth century it was virtually extinct. Reintroduced in 1969 to Vancouver Island's northwest coast, they are now breeding successfully at the heart of their original range. With binoculars, it's often easy to spot these charming creatures lolling on their backs, cracking open sea urchins or mussels with a rock and using their stomachs as anvils; they often lie bobbing asleep, entwined in kelp to stop them floating away.

Northern **fur seals** breed on Alaska's Pribilof Islands but are often seen off the British Columbian coast during their migrations. Like their cousin, the northern **sea lion**, a year-round resident, they are "eared seals", who can manage rudimentary shuffling on land thanks to short rear limbs which can be rotated for forward movement. They also swim with strokes from front flippers, as opposed to the slithering, fishlike action of true seals.

The **Atlantic**'s colder waters nurture fewer overall species than the Pacific coast, but many birds and larger mammals – especially **whales** – are common to both. One of the Atlantic region's more distinctive creatures is the **harp seal** (or saddleback), a true seal species that migrates in late winter to breeding grounds off Newfoundland and in the Greenland and White seas. Most pups are born on the pack ice, and for about two weeks sport fluffy white coats that have been highly prized by the fur trade for centuries. Until the late-1960s tens of thousands of young seals died annually in an unsupervised slaughter whose methods – clubbing and skinning alive – brought about outrage on an international scale (see pp.420–421).

TUNDRA

Tundra extends over much of northern Yukon and the Northwest Territories, stretching between the boreal forest and the polar seas. Part grassland and part wasteland, it's a region distinguished by high winds, bitter cold and **permafrost**, a layer of perpetually frozen subsoil which covers over thirty percent of Canada. The tundra is not only the domain of ice and emptiness, however: long hours of summer sunshine and the melting of topsoil nurture a carpet of wild flowers and many species of birds and mammals have adapted to the vagaries of climate and terrain.

Vegetation is uniformly stunted by poor drainage, acidic soils and permafrost, which prevents the formation of deep roots and locks nutrients in the ice. **Trees** like birch and willow can grow, but they spread their branches over a wide area, rarely rising over a metre in height. Over 99 percent of the remaining vegetation consists of perennials like **grasses** and sedges, small flowering annuals, mosses, lichens and shrubs. Most have evolved ingenious ways of protecting themselves against the elements: Arctic cotton grass, for example, grows in large insulated hummocks in which the interior temperature is higher than the air outside; others have large, waxy leaves to conserve moisture or catch as much sunlight as possible. **Wild flowers** during the short, intense spring can be superlative, covering seemingly inert ground in a carpet of purple mountain saxifrage, yellow Arctic poppy, indigo clusters of Arctic forget-me-not and the pink buds of Jacob's ladder.

Tundra grasses provide some of the first links in the food chain, nourishing mammals such as white **Arctic ground squirrels**, also known as parkas, as their fur is used by the Inuit to make parka jackets. Vegetation also provides the staple diet of **lemmings**, amongst the most remarkable of the Arctic fauna. Instead of hibernating these creatures live under the snow, busily tucking away on shoots in order to double their weight daily – the intake they need merely to survive. They also breed almost continuously, which is just as well for they are the mainstay of a long list of predators. Chief of these are **Arctic white foxes**, ermines and weasels, though birds, bears and Arctic wolves may also hunt them in preference to larger prey. Because they provide a staple diet to so many, lemming populations have a marked effect on the life cycles of numerous creatures.

A notable exception is the **caribou**, a member of the reindeer family and the most populous of the big tundra mammals. Caribou are known above all for their epic migrations, frequently involving thousands of animals, which start in March when the herds leave their wintering grounds on the fringes of the boreal forest for calving grounds to the north. The exact purpose of these migrations is still a matter of conjecture. They certainly prevent the overgrazing of the tundra's fragile mosses and lichens, and probably also enable the caribou to shake off some of the wolves that would otherwise shadow the herd (wolves have to find southerly dens at this time to bear their own pups). The timing of treks also means that calving takes place before the arrival of biting insects, which can claim as many calves as predators – an adult caribou can lose as much as a litre of blood a week to insects.

The tundra's other large mammal is the **musk ox**, a vast, shaggy herbivore and close cousin of the bison. The musk ox's Achilles' heel is a tendency to form lines or circles when threatened – a perfect defence against wolves, but not against rifle-toting hunters, who until the introduction of conservation measures threatened to be their undoing. Canada now has some of the world's largest free-roaming herds, although – like the caribou – they're still hunted for food and fur by the Inuit.

Tundra **birds** number about a hundred species and are mostly migratory. Three quarters of these are waterfowl, which arrive first to take advantage of streams, marshes and small lakes created by surface meltwater: Arctic wetlands provide nesting grounds for numerous swans, geese and ducks, as well as the loon, which is immortalized on the back of the Canadian dollar coin. The red-necked **phalarope** is a particularly specialized visitor, able to feed on aquatic insects and plankton, though not as impressive in its abilities as the migratory **Arctic tern**, whose 32,000-kilometre round trip from the Antarctic is the longest annual migration of any creature on the planet. The handful of nonmigratory birds tend to be scavengers like the raven, or predators like the **gyrfalcon**, the world's largest falcon, which preys on Arctic hares and ptarmigan. Jaegers, gulls, hawks and owls largely depend on the lemming: the snowy owl, for example, synchronizes its returns to southern Canada with fouryear dips in the lemming population.

Fauna on the Arctic **coast** has a food chain that starts with plankton and algae, ranging up through tiny crustaceans, clams and mussels, sea cucumbers and sea urchins, cod, ringed and bearded seals, to beluga whales and **polar bears** – perhaps the most evocative of all tundra creatures, but still being killed in their hundreds for "sport" despite almost thirty years of hunting restrictions. Migrating **birds** are espe-cially common here, notably near Nunaluk Spit on the Yukon coast, which is used as a corridor and stopover by millions of loons, swans, geese, plovers, sandpipers, dowitchers, eagles, hawks, guillemots and assorted songbirds.

CANADA'S ABORIGINAL PEOPLES

Nearly a million Canadians can claim at least partial aboriginal ancestry. Aboriginal populations continue to increase, and interest in their cultural heritage, by aborigines and nonaborigines alike, continues to grow. However, the term "aborigine" does not indicate a common or shared culture, only descent from groups of people who arrived on the continent long before Europeans. Canada's constitution specifies three categories of "aboriginal peoples": Indian, Inuit and Métis.

The term "Indian" is now recognized as a misnomer, but other attempts to be more specific, such as "Amerindians" or "Native Canadians", have been no more successful and you're likely to hear several different terms on your travels. The terms "First Nations" and "aboriginals" are in vogue but again there is the possibility of more change. Treated as wards of the federal government since the birth of Canada, the Indians were put in a different legal category from all other Canadians by the Indian Acts in the nineteenth century. Modern legal distinctions divide this group further into those who are recognized as "Indian" by the federal government – a status bestowed on more than 800,000 Canadians – and those who are denied

this recognition, the so-called "non-status Indians". Amongst status Indians there are 633 aboriginal bands (the term "tribe" has also become outmoded) across Canada. Some communities number fewer than 100 inhabitants and others more than 5000. Status enables rights to fishing, hunting and living on a reservation, while nonstatus denies these rights but allows a person to vote, buy property and alcohol. Status can be lost and gained through marriage, an act of parliament or even a band taking a vote on the matter.

Later, as Canada's attention turned to its vast nothern regions, the **Inuit** were also recognized as falling under federal jurisdiction. The Inuit have a separate origin, arriving much later to North America and inhabiting the inhospitable lands of Arctic Canada. The term Inuit totally replaced use of the derogatory term "Eskimo" in the 1970s. Eskimo is an Algonkian word for "eaters of raw meat". The Inuit share a common origin and a single language and at present number around 27,000.

With a current population of 400,000, the **Métis** are the product of the unions between male fur traders, usually French-Canadians, and native women, particularly Cree. For centuries they were not recognized as Canadians or aborigines, and with no rights they wandered the country, unable to settle. After a failed rebellion in 1885, they almost disappeared from social and political life and became "the forgotten people", largely poverty-stricken squatters on Crown land. Finally, in 1982, they were recognized as a First Nation in the Constitution.

ABORIGINAL POPULATION

Population in Canada defining itself as aboriginal: number of individuals and percentage of local population of each region (1996)

		Percentage
Atlantic	37,785	6.1
Québec	71,415	1.0
Ontario	141,525	1.3
Manitoba	128,685	11.7
Saskatchewan	111,245	11.4
Alberta	122,840	4.6
British Columbia	139,655	3.8
Yukon	6,175	20.1
Northwest Territories	39,690	61.9
Total	799,010	2.8

Note: 2001 Census data not available by the time of publication.

Because of the distances separating them, each nation and even each community has its own characteristics. Their personality and culture are fashioned by history, the environment and by their surrounding neighbours. A large part of the aboriginal people live in relatively close contact with nonaboriginal people and interact on a daily basis with cultures that have a determining influence on their way of life.

If there is any thread linking these groups, it is the cultural revival experienced over the last forty years. Under the banner of national political movements, all of these groups have renewed their commitment to organizing their social world, to re-establishing legal relationships to the land, and to maintaining and revitalizing their cultures and languages.

COLONIZATION

When Europeans first arrived in northern North America they saw it as a *terra nullius* – empty land – but in reality it was a complex environment containing many cultures and communities. On the west coast the peoples had built societies of wealth and sophistication with plentiful resources from the sea and forest; in the prairies and northern tundra, the aborigines lived off the vast herds of buffalo and caribou; in central Canada the forests were home to peoples who harvested wild rice from the marshes and grew corn, squash and beans by the rivers, supplementing their harvest with fishing and hunting; on the east coast and in the far north, the sea and land supplied their needs, and with incredible ingenuity enabled the inhabitants to survive harsh conditions.

Encounters between aboriginal and nonaboriginal people began to increase in number and complexity in the 1500s. There was an increased exchange of goods, trade deals, friendships and intermarriage as well as military and trade alliances. For at least two hundred years, the newcomers would not have been able to survive the rigours of the climate, succeed in their businesses (fishing, whaling, fur trading), or dodge each other's bullets, without aboriginal help.

Meanwhile **diseases** (typhoid, influenza, diptheria, plague, measles, tuberculosis, venereal disease and scarlet fever) killed tens of thousands – it is estimated that within a 200-year period aboriginal populations were reduced by as much as 95 percent.

As the fur trade intensified, the animal populations were wiped out in certain areas. This not only removed the traditional hunting practices but sparked off **inter-tribal wars**, all the more bloody now firearms were involved.

During this period, the French and British were few in number, the land seemed inhospitable and they feared attack from the aboriginal nations surrounding them. They were also fighting wars for trade and dominance – they needed alliances with Indian nations, so many **treaties** were consequently negotiated. The treaties seemed to recognize the nationhood of aboriginal peoples and their equality but also demanded the authority of the monarch and, increasingly, the ceding of large tracts of land (particularly to British control for settlement and protection from seizure by the French and Americans). Usually what was agreed orally differed from what actually appeared in the treaties. The aborigines did accept the monarch, but only as a kind of kin figure, a distant "protector" who could be called on to safeguard their interests and enforce treaty agreements. They had no notion of giving up their land, a concept foreign to aboriginal cultures:

In my language, there is no word for "surrender". There is no word. I cannot describe "surrender" to you in my language, so how do you expect my people to [have] put their X on "surrender"?

Chief François Paulette.

In 1763, the **Royal Proclamation** was a defining document in the relationship between the natives and the newcomers. Issued in the name of the king, it summarized the rules and regulations that were to govern British dealings with the aboriginal peoples – especially in relation to the question of land. It stated that aboriginal people were not to be "molested or disturbed" on their lands. Transactions involving aboriginal land were to be negotiated properly between the Crown and "assemblies of Indians". Aboriginal lands were to be acquired only by fair dealing: treaty, or purchase by the Crown. The aboriginal nations were portrayed as autonomous political entities, with their own internal political authority. Allowing for British settlement, it still safeguarded the rights of the aborigines.

By the 1800s, the relationship between aboriginal and nonaboriginal people began to tilt on its foundation of rough equality. Through immigration the number of settlers was swelling, while disease and poverty continued to diminish aboriginal populations – by 1812, whites outnumbered indigenous people in Upper Canada by ten to one. The fur trade, which was established on a solid economic partnership between traders and trappers, was a declining industry. The new economy was based on timber, mining and agriculture and it needed land from the natives, who began to be seen as "impediments to progress". Colonial governments in Upper and Lower Canada no longer needed military allies, the British were victors in Canada, and the USA had won its independence. There was also a new attitude of European superiority over all other peoples and policies of domination and assimilation slowly replaced those of partnership.

Ironically, the transformation from respectful coexistence to **domination** by nonaboriginal laws and institutions began with the main instruments of the partnership: the treaties and the Royal Proclamation of 1763. These documents offered aboriginal people not only peace and friendship, respect and approximate equality, but also "protection". Protection was the leading edge of domination. At first, it meant preservation of aboriginal lands and cultural integrity from encroachment by settlers. Later, it meant "assistance", a code word implying an encouragement to stop being a part of aboriginal society and merge into the settler society.

Protection took the form of compulsory education, economic adjustment programmes, social and political control by federal agents, and much more. These policies, combined with missionary efforts to civilize and convert, tore wide holes in aboriginal cultures, autonomy and identity.

RESERVES

In 1637, with a Jesuit settlement at Sillery in New France, the establishment of "**reserves**" of land for aboriginal peoples (usually of inadequate size and resources) began. Designed to "protect", they instead led to isolation and impoverishment. In 1857 the Province of Canada passed an act to "Encourage the Gradual Civilization of the Indian tribes" – Indians of "good character" could be declared "non-Indian" by a panel of whites. Only one man, a Mohawk, is known to have accepted the invitation.

Confederation in 1867 was negotiated without reference to aboriginal nations. Indeed, newly elected Prime Minister John A. Macdonald announced that it would be his government's goal to "do away with the tribal system, and assimilate the Indian people in all respects with the inhabitants of the Dominion".

The **British North America Act**, young Canada's new constitution, made "Indians, and Lands reserved for the Indians" a subject for government regulation, like mines or roads. Indians became wards of the federal government and Parliament took on the job with vigour – passing laws to replace traditional aboriginal governments with band councils who had insignificant powers, taking control of valuable resources located on reserves, taking charge of reserve finances, imposing an unfamiliar system of land tenure, and applying nonaboriginal concepts of marriage and parenting.

These and other laws were codified in the main **Indian Acts** of 1876, 1880 and 1884. The Department of the Interior (later, Indian Affairs) sent Indian agents to every region to see that the laws were obeyed. In 1884, the **potlatch ceremony**, central to the cultures of west-coast aboriginal nations, was outlawed. A year later the **sun dance**, central to the cultures of prairie aboriginal nations, was outlawed. Participation was a criminal offence.

In 1885, the Department of Indian Affairs instituted a **pass system**. No outsider could come onto a reserve to do business with an aboriginal resident without permission from the Indian agent (a sort of government official with law-enforcement powers). Occasionally all aboriginal persons could not *leave* the reserve without permission from the Indian agent, either. Reserves were beginning to resemble prisons.

In 1849, the first of what would become a network of residential schools for aboriginal children was opened in Alderville, Ontario. Church and government leaders had come to the conclusion that the problem (as they saw it) of aboriginal independence and "savagery" could be solved by taking children from their families at an early age and instilling the ways of the dominant society during eight or nine years of residential schooling far from home. Attendance was compulsory. Aboriginal languages, customs and native skills were suppressed. The bonds between many hundreds of aboriginal children, their families and whole nations were broken.

During this stage Canadian governments moved aboriginal communities from one place to another at will. If aboriginal people were thought to have too little food, they could be relocated where game was more plentiful or jobs might be found. If they were suffering from illness, they could be sent to new communities where health services, sanitary facilities and permanent housing might be provided. If they were in the way of expanding agricultural frontiers, or in possession of land needed for settlement, they could be removed "for their own protection". If their lands contained minerals to be mined, forests to be cut, or rivers to be dammed, they could be displaced "in the national interest".

The result of centuries of mistreatment is that by almost every statistical indicator the aboriginal population is highly **disadvantaged** compared to all other Canadians. The problems affecting aboriginal peoples are grim, as alcoholism, drug use and sexual abuse continue to plague reserves. Infant mortality is twice as high among natives than nonnatives, suicide rates among young people are five times higher among Indians than other Canadians, and life expectancy is seven years less for natives. Native peoples are also vastly overrepresented in jails across the country.

RESURGENCE

The **1940s** were the beginning of a new era. Around 3000 aborigines and unrecorded numbers of Métis and nonstatus Indians had fought for their country in both **World Wars**, and although accepted on the battlefield they were still badly treated at home. Aboriginal leaders emerged, forcefully expressing their people's desire to gain their rightful position of equality with other Canadians and maintain their cultural heritage, and in British Columbia, Alberta, Saskatchewan and Ontario, aboriginals formed provincially based organizations to protect and advance their interests. The Canadian public became more aware of the shocking way native society was being treated and how far their living standards had fallen behind all other groups of citizens. The **1951 Indian Act** rescinded the laws banning the potlatch and other ceremonies and aboriginal members were given the freedom to enter public bars to consume alcohol. But, on the whole, government oppression remained formidable. The **right to vote** in federal elections was granted only in 1960.

The rebirth of Canada's indigenous people can be traced to 1969, when a federal **"white paper"** proposed the elimination of Indian status. The result was a native backlash that forced the Trudeau Government to retreat and led to the creation of the **National Indian Brotherhood**, the forerunner of today's **Assembly of First Nations**.

Also in 1969, all Indian agents were withdrawn from reserves, and aboriginal political organizations started receiving government funding. Increasingly, these organizations focused on the need for full recognition of their aboriginal rights and renegotiation of the treaties. They believed that only in this way could they rise above their disadvantaged position in Canadian society. By 1973, aboriginals had local control of education and today more than half of all aboriginal students who live on reserves attend their own community schools.

RECLAIMING THE LAND

Land reserved for aboriginal people was steadily whittled away after its original allocation. Almost two-thirds of it has "disappeared" by various means since Confederation. In some cases, the government failed to deliver as much land as specified in a treaty. In other cases, it expropriated or sold reserved land, rarely with aboriginals as willing vendors. Once in a while, outright fraud took place. Even when aboriginals were able to keep hold of reserved land, the government sometimes sold its resources to outsiders. Some aboriginal nations have gone to court to force governments to recognize their rights to land and resources, and some have been successful. A series of court decisions in the 1970s confirmed that aboriginal peoples have more than a strong moral case for redress on land and resource issues – they have legal rights.

In recent years, Canada has come to a few new treaty-like **agreements**. The Innu and Cree took Québec to court in 1973, to stop a major hydroelectric project that threatened to decimate their traditional hunting grounds. The consequent **James Bay and Northern Québec Agreement**, signed in 1975, gave Innu and Crees (and later the Naskapi) $225 million over 20 years in return for 981,610 square kilometres of territory. They were also given lands with exclusive hunting and trapping rights, native-controlled education and health authorities. With their funds the Cree have set up successful businesses such as Air Creebec and the Cree Construction Company. The **Cree-Naskapi Act**, passed in 1984, followed and enabled the Cree and Naskapi to establish their own forms of self-government – the first such legislation in Canada.

In 1973, the Supreme Court of Canada's decision on the Haida Indians led the federal government to establish a negotiating process to resolve **land claims** by recognizing two broad classes of claims – comprehensive and specific. Comprehensive claims are based on the recognition that there are continuing aboriginal rights to lands and natural resources and have a wide scope including such things as land title, fishing and trapping rights, financial compensation and other social and economic benefits. Specific claims deal with specific grievances that aborigines may have regarding the fulfilment of treaties.

In 1982, the government's recognition of land claims was renewed by a constitutional change, which touched off further favourable court decisions leading to new treaties with the Inuit of the Northwest Territories (1984 and 1993), the Yukon First Nations (1993) and the Nisga'a in BC (1996).

From the early 1970s until March 1996, the government provided aboriginal groups with approximately $380 million to prepare their claims. This money enabled aboriginal peoples to conduct research into **treaties and rights** and to research, develop and negotiate their claims. But the negotiations have been notoriously long and painstaking, and until 1990 there was a limit of no more than six comprehensive claims at one time.

ENTERPRISE

The ownership of land and control over funding have brought opportunities for economic self-sufficiency and expansion previously unavailable to aboriginal groups. This last decade has seen the rapid growth of a **free-enterprise** economy among Canada's aboriginals, especially in the cities. In 1995 there were an estimated 18,000 aboriginal-owned businesses across Canada. About 66 percent of aboriginal businesses were in the service sector; 13 percent were in construction and related sectors. Another 12 percent were in the primary industries such as mining and forestry, and 9 percent were businesses related to food processing,

clothing, furniture, publishing and other manufacturing. One fast-growing area is aboriginal tourism, where an insight is given into culture and environment. However, employment and subsequent social problems (particularly among the growing young population) are still rampant.

Each year the oil-rich aborigines get $32 million in petroleum revenues. This upsurge in revenue would seem to bode well, but migration from the still impoverished reserves to the city (which began three decades ago) is on the increase, resulting in an unskilled and impoverished underclass of aborigines in Canadian cities and a subsequent increase in social fragmentation, greater unrest and increased crime. Most of the aborigine newcomers to the cities are young, and they are increasingly angry with the federal government and their own leaders. With 60 percent of aboriginal populations now city-based, there has also been the formation of young **street gangs**. Such gangs have made a mark in Winnipeg, which has the nation's biggest aboriginal urban population.

The **anger** that the street gangs epitomize has risen across native communities. Gang members complain about financial and political corruption by their leaders; young people, who make up more than half of the native population, say they are being ignored by an uncaring federal government and ineffectual elders. As a young native activist said recently, "Most of us have nothing to lose, so we will do what we have to to have our voices heard." **Violence** is inevitable, and flared up most notoriously with an armed standoff between Mohawk militants and the Canadian military at Oka in 1990 (see p.239). Five years later there was trouble again at Gustafsne Lake in the British Columbia interior and Ipperwash Provincial Park on the shores of Lake Huron. Meanwhile, the white attitude to militancy has hardened. Tough prison sentences are passed out to native protesters who break the law, yet there is little punishment for police officers who overstep the mark – in 1997, an Ontario Provincial policeman was given two years of community service after he was found guilty of criminal negligence in the fatal shooting of an aborigine demonstrator at Ipperwash Provincial Park.

CHANGE

The showdowns attracted much media attention and after Oka the government funded a $60 million exhaustive **Royal Commission on Aboriginal Peoples**, which was finally published six years later in November 1996 and called for fundamental change and self-government for aboriginals. The document presented a devastating account of the everyday struggle facing Canada's aboriginal peoples, including a catalogue of deprivation, mistreatment and official neglect suffered by native children in the residential schools. The report went on to recommend the creation of an aboriginal parliament to decide on land claims, establish a native university and steer an ambitious twenty-year multimillion dollar programme of economic aid to counter native unemployment and poor housing and health conditions. The majority of the recommendations seem to have been totally ignored by the present Liberal government – they've made it clear that broad structural change, particularly anything connected with the Constitution, is simply not on its agenda.

In 1998, the government did, however, formally apologise to the aboriginal peoples for the way they had been mistreated and offered compensation to those abused in the school system.

On April 1, 1999, after decades of negotiations and planning, the creation of a new province, **Nunavut**, redrew Canada's borders and gave one-fifth of its landmass to Canada's smallest native population, the Inuit. Known as "our land" in Inuktitut, the two million square kilometres of Nunavut is home to a self-governed population of 27,000, 85 percent of which is Inuit.

More recently, in July 2000, the Supreme Court of British Columbia upheld the Nisga'a land treaty as constitutionally valid. This came after Liberals in British Columbia tried to quash the $487 million deal, which gives 2000 square kilometres of land, $170 million fishing and logging rights and a significant degree of self-government to the Nisga'a.

For their part the formerly fractured **Assembly of First Nations**, which represents

"status Indians", enjoyed three years of relative calm under its national chief, Phil Fontaine, who lifted the AFN out of its debt, inherited from his predecessor, Ovide Mercredi, who had taken a much more hardline approach to aboriginal sovereignty. Fontaine also signed a co-operation agreement, in July 1999, with the Washington-based National Congress of American Indians, America's largest Indian organization, to expand trade and cultural exchanges.

For all his achievements, Fontaine was seen as being too cosy with the government in Ottawa and in September 2000, Mathew Coon Come, a tough-talking Cree leader from northern Québec, was elected the new national chief, perhaps signalling a return to more confrontational politics between Canada's natives and the federal government.

CULTURAL REVIVAL

Beyond this volatile scenario there have been dramatic improvements secured since World War II that have led to a revival of interest in their own culture for many aboriginal people. Ceremonies, like the summer powwow celebrations, and art forms that have been almost forgotten, are being revived through research and reconstruction. There are aboriginal theatre groups that reinterpret the legends for modern audiences, aboriginal authors and poets who are publishing works that present unique and indigenous viewpoints; and aboriginal painters and sculptors who are using a mix of traditional and modern techniques to produce vivid and exciting works of art. A public television channel for indigenous people – the **Aboriginal Peoples Television Network** (APTN) – has been on the air since 1999. However, the resultant optimism has been tempered by the threat of possible violence as Canada's First Nations seek redress from cultural oppression – as Coon Come declared, "Behaving like good little Indians never got us anywhere. There is a social time bomb that is ticking away in the many Indian communities throughout Canada."

BOOKS

Most of the following books should be readily available in the UK, US or Canada. We have given publishers for each title in the form UK/US publisher, unless the book is published in one country only; o/p means out of print. Note that virtually all the listed books published in the US will be stocked by major Canadian bookshops; we've indicated those books published only in Canada.

TRAVEL

Hugh Brody *Maps and Dreams* (Faber/ Waveland; both o/p). Brilliantly written account of the lives and lands of the Beaver natives of northwest Canada. For further acute insights into the ways of the far north see also the same author's *Living Arctic* (Faber, o/p/University of Washington Press) and *The People's Land: Eskimos and Whites in the Eastern Arctic* (Douglas & McIntyre, US, o/p).

P. Browning *The Last Wilderness* (Hutchinson/ Great West Books, o/p). An engrossing description of a harsh and lonely canoe journey through the Northwest Territories.

Ranulph Fiennes *The Headless Valley* (Hodder & Stoughton, UK, o/p). Tales of derring-do from noted adventurer, white-water rafting down the South Nahanni and Fraser rivers of British Columbia and the old NWT.

Barry Lopez *Arctic Dreams: Imagination and Desire in a Northern Landscape* (Picador/ Bantam). Extraordinary, award-winning book combining natural history, physics, poetry, earth sciences and philosophy in a dazzling portrait of the far north.

David McFadden *Trip Around Lake Ontario* (Coach House Press, 1988; reprinted in Great Lakes Suite/Talon Books). Part of a trilogy detailing the author's circumnavigation of lakes Ontario, Erie and Huron written in a deceptively simple style.

Gary and Joannie McGuffin *Canoeing Across Canada* (Diadem, UK, o/p). Reflections on a 6000-mile journey through the country's rivers and backwaters.

Susanna Moodie *Roughing It in the Bush: or Forest Life in Canada* (McClelland & Stewart). Wonderful narrative written in 1852, describing an English couple's slow ruin as they attempt to create a new life in southeastern Ontario.

Jan Morris *O Canada: Travels in an Unknown Country* (Robert Hale, o/p/HarperCollins, o/p) Musings from this well-known travel writer after a coast-to-coast Canadian trip.

Duncan Pryde *Nununga: Ten Years of Eskimo Life* (Eland/Hippocrene). Less a travel book than a social document from a Glaswegian who left home at eighteen to spend ten years with the Inuit.

CULTURE AND SOCIETY

John Bently-Mays *Emerald City: Toronto Visited* (Viking, o/p). Thoughtful critical essays about Toronto, its architecture and its inhabitants.

David Cruise & Alison Griffiths *The Great Adventure: How the Mounties conquered the West* (St Martin's Press, US). Contemporary accounts of the Mounties' first major expedition into the West from the strange assortment of men who made up this legendary force.

Beatrice Culleton *April Raintree* (Pemmican, Canada/Peguis, US). Heart-rending account of the enforced fostering of Métis children in Manitoba during the 1950s.

Don Dumond *The Eskimos and Aleuts* (Thames & Hudson). Anthropological and archeological tour de force on the prehistory, history and culture of northern peoples: backed up with fine maps, drawings and photographs.

Christian F. Feest *Native Arts of North America* (Thames & Hudson). This attractively illustrated book covers every aspect of North American native art in revealing detail. Everything you've ever wanted to know – and probably a good bit more.

Paul Fleming *The North American Indians in Early Photographs* (Phaidon/HarperCollins, o/p in

US). Stylized poses don't detract from a plaintive record of a way of life that has all but vanished.

Glenn Gould The Solitude Trilogy (CBC PSCD 2003–3). These CDs comprise three extraordinary sound documentaries made by Gould for CBC (who also recorded his music) concerning life in the extreme parts of Canada. A fascinating insight into harsh lifestyles in the words of the people themselves.

Alan D. McMillan Native Peoples and Cultures of Canada (Orca, US). Comprehensive account of Canada's native groups from prehistory to current issues of self-government and land claims. Well-written, though more an academic textbook than a leisure-time read.

Dennis Reid A Concise History of Canadian Painting (Oxford University Press). Not especially concise, but a thorough trawl through Canada's leading artists, with bags of biographical detail and lots of black-and-white (and a few colour) illustrations of major works.

Mordecai Richler Oh Canada! Oh Québec! (Chatto & Windus/Knopf). A satirical chronicle of the hysteria, zeal and chicanery surrounding Québec's independence movement.

Harold Towne and David P. Silcox Tom Thomson: The Silence in the Storm (McClelland & Stewart, o/p). A study of the career and inspirations of Tom Thomson, one of Canada's best-known artists. Towne, the co-writer, is also a major Canadian artist.

The True North – Canadian Landscape Painting 1896–1939 (Lund Humphries). A fascinating and well-illustrated book exploring how Canadian artists have treated the country's challenging landscapes.

William White (ed) The Complete Toronto Dispatches, 1920–1924 (Charles Scribners Sons). Ernest Hemingway's first professional writing job was with The Toronto Star as both a local reporter and as a European correspondent. This is a collection of his dispatches for the paper.

BIOGRAPHY

Anahareo Grey Owl and I: a New Autobiography (Davies, Canada). The story of Grey Owl's Iroquois wife, their fight to save the beaver from extinction and her shock at discovering that her husband was in fact an Englishman. Good insights into the changing life of Canada's natives in the twentieth century.

Grey Owl The Men of the Last Frontier; Pilgrims of the Wild; The Adventures of Sajo and Her Beaver People; Tales of an Empty Cabin (all o/p). First published in the 1930s, these books romantically describe life in the wilds of Canada at the time when exploitation was changing the land forever. Grey Owl's love of animals and the wilderness are inspiring and his forward-thinking, ecological views are particularly startling.

Richard Gwyn Smallwood: the Unlikely Revolutionary (McClelland & Stewart, Canada). Detailed biography of Joey Smallwood, the Newfoundland premier who pushed his island into Confederation in 1949. Gwyn's exploration of island corruption and incompetence is incisive and intriguing in equal measure.

Paul Kane Wanderings of an Artist among the Indians of North America (Dover). Kane, one of Canada's better-known landscape artists, spent two and a half years travelling from Toronto to the Pacific Coast and back in the 1840s. His witty, racy account of his wanderings makes a delightful read.

James MacKay Robert Service: Vagabond of Verse (Mainstream, UK). Not the first, but certainly the most substantial biography discussing this prominent Canadian poet's life and work.

Peter F. Ostwald Glenn Gould: The Ecstasy and Tragedy of Genius (W. W. Norton & Co). A biography by a psychiatrist (100 percent Freud-free) of Canada's most famous musician. The eccentric pianist comes across as a rather inhuman egotist but with a talent to make this sufferable to many of his followers.

Constance Rooke Writing Home: a PEN Anthology (McClelland & Stewart). A handful of Canada's leading contemporary authors muse on the idea of home. Though more an insight into the inner workings of writers' minds than Canadian culture, this book's "sampler" style makes it a welcome partner on cross-country journeys.

HISTORY

Fred Anderson Crucible of War: The Seven Years' War and the Fate of the British Empire in British North America, 1754–1766 (Faber & Faber). Lucid and extraordinarily well-researched account of this crucial period in the development of North America. At 800-odd pages, it's perhaps a little too detailed for many tastes, but it's a fascinating read. Included is the story of the fall of Fort William Henry, as celebrated in the film, *The Last of the Mohicans*.

Owen Beattie and John Geiger *The Fate of the Franklin Expedition 1845–48* (Bloomsbury/ NAL-Dutton, o/p). An account both of the doomed expedition to find the Northwest Passage and the discovery of artefacts and bodies still frozen in the northern ice; worth buying for the extraordinary photos.

Carl Benn *The Iroquois in the War of 1812* (University of Toronto Press). In 1812 the United States, at war with Canada, invaded and briefly occupied York (Toronto). The role played by the Five Nations and Iroquois peoples in the war was pivotal in Canada's survival, and the ramifications of the War of 1812 affected the aboriginal people of Ontario for years to come.

Pierre Berton *Klondike: the Last Great Goldrush 1896–1899* (McClelland & Stewart, US). Exceptionally readable account from one of Canada's finest writers of the characters and epic episodes of the Yukon gold rush. Other Berton titles include *The Arctic Grail* (Viking, o/p/Penguin), describing the quest for the North Pole and the Northwest Passage from 1818 to 1919; *The Last Spike* (Penguin, US), an account of the history and building of the transcontinental railway; *The Mysterious North: Encounters with the Canadian Frontier 1947–1954* (McClelland & Stewart, Canada); *Flames across the Frontier* (Penguin, US), episodes from the often uneasy relationship between Canada and the US; and *Vimy* (McClelland and Stewart), an account of the World War I battle fought mainly by Canadians which Berton sees as a turning point in the nation's history.

Gerald Friesen *The Canadian Prairies: a History* (University of Toronto Press). Stunningly well-researched and detailed account of the development of Central Canada. A surprisingly entertaining book that's particularly good on the culture of the Métis and Plains Indians.

Harold Innis *The Fur Trade in Canada: An Introduction to Canadian Economic History* (University of Toronto). The words "dramatic, sweeping and engaging" are not usually associated with books on economic history, but in this case they fit the bill. Innis's study is invaluable for the insight it gives to pre-European Canada, and its trading customs with Ontario's native peoples.

Kenneth McNaught *The Penguin History of Canada* (Penguin). Recently revised and concise analysis of the country's economic, social and political history.

Peter Neary and Patrick O'Flaherty *Part of the Main: an Illustrated History of Newfoundland and Labrador* (Breakwater, Canada). Lively text and excellent illustrations make this the best account of the province's history, though it's short of contemporary information.

Peter C. Newman *Caesars of the Wilderness* (Penguin, o/p). Highly acclaimed and readable account of the rise and fall of the Hudson's Bay Company.

George Woodcock *A Social History of Canada* (Penguin, o/p). Erudite and incisive book about the peoples of Canada and the country's development. Woodcock is the most perceptive of Canada's historians and his work has the added advantage of being very readable. Also by the author is *The Canadians* (Harvard University Press, US, o/p), a lavishly illustrated and brilliantly lucid attempt to summarize the Canadian experience.

NATURAL HISTORY

Richard Chandler *The Macmillan Field Guide to North Atlantic Shorebirds* (Macmillan, UK, o/p). Well-illustrated and comprehensive handbook.

The Pocket Guide Series (Dragon's World, UK). Clearly laid-out and well-illustrated, the Pocket Book series are excellent basic handbooks for general locations of species, identification and background. Individual titles are: *The Pocket Guide to Mammals of North America* (John Burton); *The Pocket Guide to Birds of Prey of North America* (Philip Burton); *The Pocket Guide to Wild Flowers of North America* (Pamela Forey); *The Pocket Guide to Trees of North America* (Alan Mitchell); *The Pocket Guide to Birds of Western North America* (Frank Shaw).

Lyall Watson *Whales of the World* (Hutchinson/ NAL-Dutton, both o/p). Encyclopedic and lavishly illustrated guide to the whale.

FICTION

Margaret Atwood *Surfacing* (Virago/Fawcett). Canada's most eminent novelist is not always easy reading, but her analysis, particularly of women and society, is invariably witty and penetrating. In *Surfacing* (Virago/Fawcett), the remote landscape of northern Québec plays an instrumental part in an extreme voyage of self-discovery. Regeneration through exploration of the past is also the theme of *Cat's Eye* (Virago/Doubleday) and *Lady Oracle* (Virago/Doubleday), while the collection of short stories *Wilderness Tips* (Virago/Bantam) sees women ruminating over the bastards in their lives. *Alias Grace* (Virago/Doubleday) is a dark and sensual tale centred around the true story of one of Canada's most notorious female criminals of the 1840's. Atwood's latest offering, *The Blind Assassin* (Bloomsbury/Bantam Doubleday Dell), is a "Canadian dynastic epic" and won the prestigious Booker Prize in the UK in 2000.

Robertson Davies For many years the leading figure of Canada's literary scene, Davies died in 1995 at the age of 82. Amongst his considerable output are big, dark and complicated webs of familial and social history which include wonderful evocations of the semi-rural Canada of his youth. A good place to start is *What's Bred in the Bone*, part of *The Cornish Trilogy*, whose other titles are *The Rebel Angels* and *The Lyre of Orpheus* (all Penguin). Similarly intriguing is *Fifth Business* (Penguin), the first part of *The Deptford Trilogy*.

Lovat Dickson *Wilderness Man* (Abacus, UK, o/p). The fascinating story of Archie Belaney, the Englishman who became famous as his adopted persona, Grey Owl. Written by his English publisher and friend, who was one of many that did not discover the charade until after Grey Owl's death.

William Gibson *Virtual Light* (Penguin/Bantam Spectra) and *Idoru* (Penguin/Berkeley) are the best recent books from the master of cyberdom. The impact of technologies on human experience and the overlapping of artifice and reality are his significant themes.

Hammond Innes *Campbell's Kingdom* (Pan/Addison-Wesley). A melodrama of love and oil-drilling in the Canadian Rockies – though the landscape's less well evoked than in *The Land God Gave to Cain* (Pan/Carroll & Graf, o/p), the story of one man's search for "gold and truth" in Labrador.

Margaret Laurence *A Jest of God; The Stone Angel; The Diviners* (all Virago/University of Chicago Press). Manitoba-born Laurence epitomized the new vigour that swept through the country's literature during the Sixties – though the best of her fiction was written in England. Most of her books are set in the fictional prairie backwater of Manawaka, and explore the loneliness and frustration of women within an environment of stifling small-town conventionality. Always highly revered at home, Laurence's reputation is on the increase abroad.

Stephen Leacock *Sunshine Sketches of a Little Town* (McClelland & Stewart/New Canadian Library). Whimsical tale of Ontario small-town life; the best of a series based on the author's summertime stays in Orillia.

Jack London *The Call of the Wild; White Fang and Other Stories* (Penguin). London spent over a year in the Yukon gold fields during the Klondike gold rush. Many of his experiences found their way into his vivid if sometimes overwrought tales of the northern wilderness, but he left behind a burning evocation of the North.

Malcolm Lowry *Hear Us O Lord from Heaven thy Dwelling Place* (Carroll & Graf). Lowry spent almost half his writing life (1939–54) in log cabins and beach houses he built for himself around Vancouver. *Hear Us O Lord* is a difficult read to say the least: a fragmentary novella which, amongst other things, describes a disturbing sojourn on Canada's wild Pacific coast.

Ann-Marie MacDonald. *Fall on Your Knees* (Vintage/Simon & Schuster). Entertaining, epic-style family saga from this young, Toronto-based writer with an astute eye for characters and a fine storytelling touch. The novel follows the fortunes of four sisters from Halifax, against a backdrop which sweeps from World War II to the New York jazz scene.

Alistair MacLeod *No Great Mischief* (Cape). This forceful, evocative novel tells the tale of a family of Gaelic-speaking Nova Scotians from Cape Breton. Some of the episodes are brilliantly written – others less so – but it is still one of the best Canadian novels of the 1990s.

Anne Michaels *Fugitive Pieces* (Bloomsbury/Knopf). This debut novel from an award-winning poet concerns survivors from the Nazis who emigrate to Canada. Their relationship deepens but memory and the past are never far away. A beautiful work.

W.O. Mitchell *Who Has Seen the Wind* (Canongate/Little, Brown). Canada's equivalent of *Huckleberry Finn* is a folksy story of a young boy coming of age in small-town Saskatchewan, with great offbeat characters and fine evocations of prairie life. Mitchell's *The Vanishing Point* (Macmillan, US), though witty and fun to read, is a moving testimony to the complexities of native assimilation in a country dominated by "immigrants".

L.M. Montgomery *Anne of Green Gables* (Puffin/Pengiun). Growing pains and bucolic bliss in a children's classic from 1908. Bound to appeal to little girls of all ages.

Brian Moore *Black Robe* (Flamingo/NAL-Dutton). Moore emigrated to Canada from Ireland in 1948 and stayed long enough to gain citizenship before moving on to California. *Black Robe* – the story of a missionary's journey into native territory – is typical of the author's preoccupations with Catholicism, repression and redemption.

Alice Munro *Lives of Girls and Women* (Penguin/NAL-Dutton); *The Progress of Love* (Vintage/Penguin); *The Beggar Maid* (Penguin); *Friend of My Youth* (Vintage); *Dance of the Happy Shades* (Penguin/Vintage); *Who Do You Think You Are?* (Penguin); *Something I've Been Meaning to Tell You* (Penguin/Plume); *The Moons of Jupiter* (Penguin). Amongst the world's finest living short-story writers, Munro deals primarily with the lives of women in the semi-rural and Protestant backcountry of southwest Ontario. Unsettling emotions are never far beneath the surface. Among her more recent works, *Open Secrets* (Vintage) focuses on stories set in two small Ontario towns from the days of the early settlers to the present.

New Oxford Book of Canadian Short Stories in English (ed Margaret Atwood and Robert Weaver; OUP). A broad selection which delves beyond the better-known names of Alice Munro and Margaret Atwood, with space being given to diaspora writers. While the intention is to celebrate Canadian writing, some of the works offer a stangely negative view of the country.

Michael Ondaatje *In the Skin of a Lion* (Picador/McKay) Highly charged work with intriguing insights into the essence of Toronto and its people.

Oxford Book of Canadian Ghost Stories (OUP, US, o/p). Over twenty stories, including W.P. Kinsella's *Shoeless Joe Jackson Comes to Iowa* – the inspiration for the fey *Field of Dreams*.

Oxford Companion to Canadian Literature (OUP, o/p). At almost 900 pages, this is the last word on the subject, though it is more useful as a work of reference than as a primer for the country's literature.

E. Annie Proulx *The Shipping News* (Fourth Estate/Simon & Schuster). The 1994 Pulitzer Prize-winner is a rambling, inconclusive narrative of a social misfit who finds love and happiness of sorts in small-town Newfoundland. Superb descriptions of sea, weather and all things fishy (as distinct from some very average characterization) make it an essential primer for any visitor to the province.

Nino Ricci *Where Has She Gone?* (McClelland & Stewart). The third in a trilogy that began with *Lives of the Saints*, this book is about an Italian-Canadian family's sometimes tragic attempts to find its identity.

Mordecai Richler French-Canadian, working-class and Jewish – Yiddishkeit is Richler's bag. He is the laureate of the minority within a minority within a minority. All his novels explore this relation with broad humour and pathos. In *The Apprenticeship of Duddy Kravitz* (Penguin), Richler uses his early experiences of Montréal's working-class Jewish ghetto in many of his novels, especially in this, his best-known work, an acerbic and slick cross-cultural romance built around the ambivalent but tightly drawn figure of Kravitz. Richler's pushy and ironic prose is not to all tastes, but you might also try *Solomon Gursky Was Here* (Vintage/DIANE) or his latest book, *Barney's Version* (Chatto & Windus/Knopf) – a rip-roaring comic portrait of a reckless artist *manqué*.

Carol Shields *Happenstance*; *The Stone Diaries*; *Larry's Party* (all Fourth Estate/Penguin). Winner of the Pulitzer Prize, Shields is much lauded for the detail she finds in the everyday.

There are moments of great beauty and sensitivity in these books which chronicle frankly the experiences of bourgeois North American suburbia.

Elizabeth Smart *By Grand Central Station I Sat Down and Wept* (Flamingo/Vintage). A cult masterpiece which lyrically details the writer's love affair with the English poet George Barker.

Susan Swan *The Wives of Bath* (Alfred J. Knopf). At a Toronto girls' school in the Sixties, the protagonist, Mouse, struggles with notions of feminine beauty as her best friend struggles with gender identity. A wry novel written in a genre the author describes as "sexual gothic".

Audrey Thomas *The Wild Blue Yonder* (Fourth Estate). A collection of witty tales about male–female relationships by a renowned Canadian short-story writer.

Jane Urquhart *The Underpainter* (Bloomsbury/Viking). A painful book concerning the life of a narcissistic painter who uses and leaves his muse but ultimately finds the demands of art destroy his humanity.

John Wyndham *The Chrysalids* (Penguin/Carroll & Graf). A science-fiction classic built around a group of telepathic children and their adventures in post-Holocaust Labrador.

POETRY

Elizabeth Bishop *The Complete Poems* (Chatto & Windus/Farrar, Straus & Giroux). Though American by birth, Bishop spent much of her youth in Nova Scotia. Many of her early poems feed off her Canadian childhood and her fascination with the country's rough landscapes.

Leonard Cohen *Poems: 1956–1968* (Cape/Penguin, o/p). A fine collection from a Sixties survivor who enjoyed high critical acclaim as a poet before emerging as a husky-throated crooner of bedsit ballads. See also his *Beautiful Losers*, one of the most aggressively experimental Canadian novels of the Sixties (Black Spring Press/Vintage).

New Oxford Book of Canadian Verse (ed. Margaret Atwood; OUP). Canadian poets are increasingly finding a distinctive voice, but few except this collection's editor have made much impact outside their native country. Atwood's own sharp, witty examinations of nationality and gender are among the best in

this anthology – more of her verse is published in the UK by Virago.

Robert Service *The Best of Robert Service* (A&C Black/Running Press). Service's Victorian ballads of pioneer and gold-rush life have a certain charm and they capture the essence of the gold-rush period amongst which the *Songs of a Sourdough* collection of 1907 is perhaps the most memorable.

SPECIALIST GUIDES

Don Beers *The Wonder of Yoho* (Rocky Mountain Books, Canada). Good photos and solid text extolling the delights of Yoho National Park in the Rockies.

Darryl Bray *Kluane National Park Hiking Guide* (Travel Vision, Canada). A much-needed guide to long and short walks in a park where the trail network is still in its infancy.

Neil G. Carey *A Guide to the Queen Charlotte Islands* (Northwest Books, US). An authoritative guide to islands which are difficult to explore and ill-served by back-up literature.

Ron Dalby *The Alaska Highway: an Insider's Guide* (Fulcrum). Less detailed but less dry than its main competitor, the better-known and encyclopedic *Milepost* (Northwest Books).

John Dodd and Gail Helgason *The Canadian Rockies Access Guide* (London Pine, US). Descriptions of 115 day-hikes, with degrees of difficulty, time needed, sketch maps of routes, wildlife descriptions and numerous photos.

David Dunbar *The Outdoor Traveller's Guide to Canada* (Stewart, Tabori & Chang). Too bulky to be a useful guide in the field, but a lavishly illustrated introduction to the outdoor pursuits, wildlife and geology of 37 of the country's best national and provincial parks.

Heather Elton *Banff's Best Day Hikes* (Lone Pine, US and Canada). Good selection of walks in and around Banff town and national park with adequate maps and tempting photos.

Ben Gadd *A Handbook of the Canadian Rockies* (Corax). Widely available in western Canada's larger bookshops, this is a lovingly produced and painstakingly detailed account of walks, flora, fauna, geology and anything else remotely connected with the Rockies.

The Lost Moose Catalogue (Lost Moose Publishing, Canada). Highly entertaining and iconoclastic magazine-style guide and commentary on the contemporary mores of the Yukon and far north.

Teri Lydiard *The British Columbia Bicycling Guide* (Gordon Soules, US). Small but extremely detailed pointer to some tempting routes, backed up with good maps.

Janice E. Macdonald *Canoeing Alberta* (Macdonald, Canada). A canoeist's Bible, with many detailed accounts of the province's waterways, and especially good on routes in the Rockies.

Ken Madsen and Graham Wilson *Rivers of the Yukon* (Primrose Publishing, Canada). An invaluable guide to some of the country's best canoeing rivers.

Linda Moyer and Burl Willes *Unexplored Islands of the US and Canadian West Coast* (John Muir). A generous portion of the guide is devoted to an intimate but rather homely run through some of British Columbia's lesser-known islands.

Bruce Obee *The Pacific Rim Explorer* (Whitecap, UK). A good overall summary of the walks, wildlife and social history of the Pacific Rim National Park and its nearby towns. The same writer's *The Gulf Islands Explorer* and, in the same series, Eliane Jones' *The Northern Gulf Islands Explorer*, are also useful.

Brian Patton and Bart Robinson *The Canadian Rockies Trail Guide* (Summerthought, Canada). An absolutely essential guide for anyone wishing to do more than simply scratch the surface of the Rockies' walking possibilities.

Betty Pratt-Johnson (Adventure Publishing, Canada). The author has produced five separate books whose 157 canoeing routes provide the definitive account of how and where to canoe the lakes and rivers of British Columbia.

Archie Shutterfield *The Chilkoot Trail: a Hiker's Historical Guide* (Northwest Books, US). A pithy accompaniment to the Chilkoot Trail that should be read in conjunction with Pierre Berton's *Klondike*.

Sierra Club of West Canada *The West Coast Trail* (Douglas & McIntyre, Canada). Now in its sixth edition, this is probably the best of several guides to Vancouver Island's popular but demanding long-distance footpath.

LANGUAGE

Canada has two official languages – English and French – but there are numerous native tongues as well. Tensions between the two main groups play a prominent part in the politics of Canada, but the native languages are more or less ignored except in the country's most remote areas, particularly in the Northwest Territories and Nunavut, where Inuktitut, the language of the Inuit, is spoken widely. The Inuit are the only native population with their own-language TV channel; the only group afforded comparable attention are the Montagnais – Montagnais-Naskapi translations appear in northern Québec and Labrador official publications.

In a brief glossary such as this there is no space to get to grips with the complexities of aboriginal languages, and very few travellers would have any need of them anyway – most natives (including those in Québec) have a good knowledge of English, especially if they deal with tourists in any capacity. If you plan to be spending much time in French-speaking Canada, consider investing in the **Rough Guide to French** (Penguin), a pocket-guide in a handy A–Z format.

FRENCH IN QUÉBEC

Québec's official language differs from its European source in much the same way North

FRENCH WORDS AND PHRASES

BASICS

Good morning/ afternoon/Hello	*Bonjour*	I live in	*Je demeure à*
		Today	*Aujourd'hui*
Good evening	*Bonsoir*	Tomorrow	*Demain*
Good night	*Bonne nuit*	Day after tomorrow	*Après-demain*
Goodbye	*Au revoir*	Yesterday	*Hier*
Yes	*Oui*	Now	*Maintenant*
No	*Non*	Later	*Plus tard*
Please	*S'il vous/te plaît*	Wait a minute!	*Un instant!*
Thank you	*Merci (beaucoup)*	In the morning	*Le matin*
(very much)		In the afternoon	*L'après-midi*
You're welcome	*Bienvenue/de rien/*	In the evening	*Le soir*
	Je vous en prie	Here/there	*Ici/là*
OK	*D'accord*	Good/bad	*Bon/mauvais*
How are you?	*Comment allez-vous?/Ça va?*	Big/small	*Grand/petit*
Fine, thanks	*Très bien, merci*	Cheap/expensive	*Bon marché/cher*
Do you speak English?	*Parlez-vous anglais?*	Early/late	*Tôt/Tard*
I don't speak French	*Je ne parle pas français*	Hot/cold	*Chaud/froid*
I don't understand	*Je ne comprends pas*	Near/far	*Près (pas loin)/loin*
I don't know	*Je ne sais pas*	Vacant/occupied	*Libre/occupé*
Excuse me	*Je m'excuse*	Quickly/slowly	*Vite/lentement*
Excuse me	*Excusez-moi*	Loudly/quietly	*Bruyant/tranquille*
(in a crowd)		With/without	*Avec/sans*
Sorry	*Pardon/désolé(e)*	More/less	*Plus/moins*
I'm English/	*Je suis anglais(e)/*	Enough/no more	*Assez/ça suffit*
Scottish/Welsh/	*écossais(e)/gallois(e)/*	Mr	*Monsieur*
Irish/American/	*irlandais(e)/américain(e)/*	Mrs	*Madame*
Australian	*australian(e)*	Miss	*Mademoiselle*

continued overleaf

continued from previous page

QUESTIONS AND DIRECTIONS

Where?	*Où?*	Can you give me	*Pouvez-vous me*
When?	*Quand?*	a lift to . . . ?	*conduire jusqu'à . . . ?*
What? (what is it?)	*Quoi? (qu'est-ce que c'est?)*	Can you tell me when to get off?	*Pouvez-vous me dire quand descendre?*
How much/many?	*Combien?*	What time is it?	*Quelle heure est-il?*
Why?	*Pourquoi?*	What time does	*À quelle heure*
It is/there is (is it/ is there . . . ?)	*C'est/Il y a (est-ce que/ Y a-t-il . . . ?)*	it open? How much does	*ça ouvre? Combien cela coûte-t-il?*
How do I get to . . . ?	*Où se trouve...?*	it cost?	
How far is it to. . . ?	*À quelle distance est-il à . . . ?*	How do you say it in French?	*Comment ça se dit en français?*

NUMBERS

1	*un/une*	14	*quatorze*	70	*soixante-dix*
2	*deux*	15	*quinze*	80	*quatre-vingts*
3	*trois*	16	*seize*	90	*quatre-vingt-dix*
4	*quatre*	17	*dix-sept*	100	*cent*
5	*cinq*	18	*dix-huit*	101	*cent-et-un*
6	*six*	19	*dix-neuf*	110	*cent-dix*
7	*sept*	20	*vingt*	200	*deux cents*
8	*huit*	21	*vingt-et-un*	500	*cinq cents*
9	*neuf*	22	*vingt-deux*	1000	*mille*
10	*dix*	30	*trente*	2000	*deux milles*
11	*onze*	40	*quarante*	1,000,000	*un million*
12	*douze*	50	*cinquante*		
13	*treize*	60	*soixante*		

ACCOMMODATION

Is there a campsite nearby?	*Y a-t-il un camping près d'ici?*	How much is it? It's expensive	*C'est combien? C'est cher*
Tent	*Tente*	Is breakfast included?	*Est-ce que le petit*
Cabin	*Chalet*		*déjeuner est compris?*
Youth hostel	*Auberge de jeunesse*	Hotel	*Hôtel*
Do you have anything cheaper?	*Avez-vous quelque chose de meilleur marché?*	I'm looking for a nearby hotel Do you have a room?	*Je cherche un hôtel près d'ici Avez-vous une chambre?*
Full board	*Tout compris*	for one/two/	*pour une/deux/*
Can I see the room?	*Puis-je peux voir la chambre?*	three people for one/two/	*trois personne(s) pour une/deux/*
I'll take this one	*Je vais prendre celle-ci*	three nights	*trois nuit(s)*
I'd like to book a room	*J'aimerais réserver une chambre*	for one/two weeks	*pour une/deux semaine(s)*
I have a booking	*J'ai une réservation*	with a double bed	*avec un lit double*
Can we camp here?	*Pouvons-nous camper ici?*	with a shower/bath hot/cold water	*avec douche/salle de bain eau chaude/froide*

American English differs from British English. Yet while the Québécois French vocabulary, grammar and syntax may not constitute a separate language, the speech of Québec can pose a few problems. Tracing its roots back to seventeenth-century popular French, the Québécois language has preserved features that disappeared long ago in France itself and it has also been affected by its close contact with English. The end result is a dialect that is – frankly – a source of amusement to many French people and bafflement for those educated in the French language back in Europe, not to mention other parts of Canada. Within

TRAVELLING

Aeroplane	*Avion*	One-way/return	*Aller-simple/aller-retour*
Bus	*Autobus*	Can I book a seat?	*Puis-je réserver un siège?*
Train	*Train*	What time does it leave?	*Il part à quelle heure?*
Car	*Voiture*	When is the next	*Quand est le prochain*
Taxi	*Taxi*	bus/train/	*autobus/train/*
Bicycle	*Vélo*	ferry to . . .?	*traversier pour . . .?*
Ferry	*Traversier*	Do I have to change?	*Dois-je transférer?*
Ship	*Bâteau*	Where does it leave from?	*D'où est-ce qu'il part?*
Hitch-hiking	*Faire du pouce*	How many kilometres?	*Combien de kilomètres?*
On foot	*À pied*	How many hours?	*Combien d'heures?*
Bus station	*Terminus d'autobus*	What number	*Quel autobus dois-je*
Railway station	*Gare centrale*	bus do I take to/to	*prendre pour aller*
Ferry terminal	*Le quai du traversier*	get to...?	*à/au . . .?*
Port	*Port*	Where's the road to?	*Où est la route pour . . .?*
A ticket to . . .	*Un billet pour . . .*	Next stop	*Le prochain arrêt*

SOME SIGNS

Entrance/Exit	*Entrée/Sortie*	Platform	*Voie*
Free entrance	*Entrée Libre*	Cash desk	*Caisse*
Gentlemen/Ladies	*Messieurs/Dames*	Go/Walk	*Marchez*
WC	*Toilette*	Stop	*Arrêtez*
Vacant/Engaged	*Libre/Occupé*	Customs	*Douanes*
Open/Closed	*Ouvert/Fermé*	Do not touch	*Défense de toucher*
Arrivals/Departures	*Arrivées/Départs*	Danger	*Danger*
Closed for holidays	*Fermé pour les vacances*	Beware	*Attention*
Pull/Push	*Tirez/Poussez*	First aid	*Premiers soins*
Out of order	*Hors d'usage/Brisé*	Ring the bell	*Sonnez*
To let	*À louer*	No smoking	*Défense de fumer*

DRIVING

Left/right	*Gauche/droite*	No overtaking	*Défenser de dépasser*
Straight ahead	*Tout droit*	Passing lane only	*Voie réservée au*
Turn to the left/right	*Tournez à gauche/droite*		*dépassement*
Car park	*Le terrain de*	Speed	*Vitesse*
	stationnement	Self-service	*Libre-service*
No parking	*Défense de stationner/*	Full service	*Service complet*
	stationnement interdit	Fill the tank with . . .	*Faîtes le plein avec de . . .*
Tow-away zone	*Zone de remorquage*	. . . regular	*. . . l'essence ordinaire*
Cars towed at	*Remorquage à vos frais*	. . . super	*. . . du super*
owner's expense		. . . unleaded	*. . . du sans plomb*
One-way street	*Sens unique*	Check the oil . . .	*Vérifiez l'huile . . .*
No entry	*Défenser d'entrer*	battery . . .	*la batterie . . .*
Slow down	*Ralentir*	radiator . . .	*le radiateur . . .*
Proceed on flashing	*Attendez le feu*	tyre pressure . . .	*pression des pneus . . .*
green light	*vert clignotant*	plugs	*bougies d'allumage*
Turn on headlights	*Allumez vos phares*	Blow up the tyres	*Gonflez les pneus*
No through road	*Cul-de-sac*		

Québec itself there are marked regional differences of pronunciation, so much so that Montréalers find it hard to understand northern Québécois.

The Québécois are extremely sympathetic when visiting English-speakers make the effort to speak French – and most are much more forthcoming with their knowledge of English when talking to a Briton or American than to a Canadian. Similarly easy-going is the attitude towards the formal *vous* (you), which is used less often in Québec – you may even be corrected when saying *S'il vous plaît* with the suggestion that *S'il te plaît* is more appropriate.

Another popular phrase that you are likely to come across is *pas de tout* ("not at all") which in Québec is pronounced *pan toot*, completely different from the French *pa du too*. The same goes for *c'est tout?* ("is that all?" pronounced *say toot*), which you're likely to hear when buying something in a shop.

With **pronunciation** there's little point trying to mimic the local dialect – generally, just stick to the classic French rules. Consonants at the ends of words are usually silent and at other times are much as in English, except that **ch** is always sh, **ç** is s, **h** is silent, **th** is the same as t, **ll** is like the y in yes and **r** is growled.

INDEX

around the world

in twenty years

London Mini Guide ★ London Restaurants ★ Los Angeles ★ Madeira ★ Madrid ★ Malaysia, Singapore & Brunei ★ Mallorca ★ Malta & Gozo ★ Maui ★ Maya World ★ Melbourne ★ Menorca ★ Mexico ★ Miami & the Florida Keys ★ Montréal ★ Morocco ★ Moscow ★ Nepal ★ New England ★ New Orleans ★ New York City ★ New York Mini Guide ★ New York Restaurants ★ New Zealand ★ Norway ★ Pacific Northwest ★ Paris ★ Paris Mini Guide ★ Peru ★ Poland ★ Portugal ★ Prague ★ Provence & the Côte d'Azur ★ Pyrenees ★ The Rocky Mountains ★ Romania ★ Rome ★ San Francisco ★ San Francisco Restaurants ★ Sardinia ★ Scandinavia ★ Scotland ★ Scottish Highlands & Islands ★ Seattle ★ Sicily ★ Singapore ★ South Africa, Lesotho & Swaziland ★ South India ★ Southeast Asia ★ Southwest USA ★ Spain ★ St Lucia ★ St Petersburg ★ Sweden ★ Switzerland ★ Sydney ★ Syria ★ Tanzania ★ Tenerife and La Gomera ★ Thailand ★ Thailand's Beaches & Islands ★ Tokyo ★ Toronto ★ Travel Health ★ Trinidad & Tobago ★ Tunisia ★ Turkey ★ Tuscany & Umbria ★ USA ★ Vancouver ★ Venice & the Veneto ★ Vienna ★ Vietnam ★ Wales ★ Washington DC ★ West Africa ★ Women Travel ★ Yosemite ★ Zanzibar ★ Zimbabwe

also look out for our maps, phrasebooks, music guides and reference books